The Hellenistic philosophers

VOLUME 2

Study of the Stoic, Epicurean and sceptical schools of philosophy has been
hampered by the inaccessibility and difficulty of the surviving evidence. To
help students and scholars, Anthony Long and David Sedley have compiled
a compreh sive sourcebook, which makes the principal texts available to
the widest   ce since classical antiquity. The material is organised by
schools, an   n each school topics are treated thematically, thus
providing   der with immediate access to all the central concepts and
the contro   hey aroused in their historical context.

In volur   authors presented the texts in their own new
translation   npanied by a philosophical and historical commentary
designed fc   , including those with no background in the
classical wc   n its glossary and set of indexes, volume 1 can stand
alone as an   dent tool of study. No knowledge of Greek or Latin is
required.

Volume   ts the collection into a handbook for specialists. It
provides th   and Latin originals of the passages translated in volume
1, sometim   er excerpts, and includes some additional passages. The
texts are ac   ed by critical apparatus, information on context, and
detailed no   is also a large annotated bibliography.

The volu   ld be an excellent scholarly resource for classicists and
specialists ir   philosophy.

The Hellenistic philosophers

VOLUME 2
Greek and Latin texts
with notes and bibliography

A.A.LONG
Irving Stone Professor of Literature, in the Department of Classics,
University of California, Berkeley

D.N.SEDLEY
Professor of Ancient Philosophy, University of Cambridge,
and Fellow of Christ's College

CAMBRIDGE
UNIVERSITY PRESS

PUBLISHED BY THE PRESS SYNDICATE OF THE UNIVERSITY OF CAMBRIDGE
The Pitt Building, Trumpington Street, Cambridge, United Kingdom

CAMBRIDGE UNIVERSITY PRESS
The Edinburgh Building, Cambridge CB2 2RU, UK
40 West 20th Street, New York, NY 10011–4211, USA
10 Stamford Road, Oakleigh, VIC 3166, Australia
Ruiz de Alarcón 13, 28014 Madrid, Spain
Dock House, The Waterfront, Cape Town 8001, South Africa

http://www.cambridge.org

First published 1987
Reprinted 1988
First paperback edition 1989
Reprinted 1992, 1995, 1998, 2000

British Library Cataloguing in Publication data
The Hellenistic philosophers.
Vol 2: Greek and Latin texts with
notes and bibliography
1. Philosophy, Ancient
I. Long, A.A.   II. Sedley, D.N.
180'.938   B171

Library of Congress Cataloguing in Publication
Long, A.A.
The Hellenistic philosophers.
Bibliography
Includes indexes
Contents: v. 2. Greek and Latin texts with
notes and bibliography
1. Philosophy, Ancient
I. Sedley, D.N.
II. Title
B505.L66 1987   186   87-30956

ISBN 0 521 25562 7 hardback
ISBN 0 521 27557 1 hardback

Transferred to digital printing 2003

AN

Contents

Introductory note

This second volume of *The Hellenistic Philosophers* is strictly ancillary to the translations and commentaries which appear in vol. 1. Whereas vol. 1 is designed to be usable on its own, vol. 2 provides the sort of supplementary information required by readers familiar with Greek and Latin. It is not designed to be read in isolation.

The principal object of vol. 2 is to supply the originals of the texts which are translated in vol. 1. These are sometimes presented here in longer excerpts than appear in vol. 1, and in such cases the additional portions are marked by smaller print. Occasionally an entire extra text is added, also in smaller print, and designated with a lower case (instead of the usual upper case) bold letter.

The texts are accompanied by notes. These do not attempt systematic or exhaustive commentary, but offer cross-references, information on context and on further relevant texts, and discussion of obscure or controversial points of interpretation, particularly where this is required in order to justify the translations and interpretations proposed in vol. 1. If our coverage at times seems uneven, that is because we have found that some texts demand extensive elucidation, while others seem able to speak adequately for themselves.

We have not, with one or two special exceptions, attempted to obtain readings of the original manuscripts, but have relied principally on a standard edition of each work. These editions are listed in the Index of sources appended to vol. 1. Although we do not always follow their precise readings or punctuation, we do adopt their systems of sigla in our apparatus criticus, so that readers requiring technical information on the manuscript and editorial traditions can consult them directly. We do not attempt to supply exhaustive information on the textual tradition, but we have tried to give full information at least in all cases where a philosophical interpretation might depend on the reading chosen. Our use of bracketing and other such conventions is standard. However, readers should be warned that some of our texts are papyrological or epigraphic, and that square brackets in such texts enclose editorial *fillings* for lacunae, whereas square brackets in other texts indicate editorial *deletions*, or, if their content opens with '*sc.*', editorial glosses.

References in bold are to our own texts. If the final figure is not in bold, e.g.

70E 2, it refers to the line number in the vol. 2 text. If it is in bold, e.g. **70E** 2, it refers to a subsection of the text, as in vol. 1.

In the notes we have found it hard, for reasons of space, to do justice to all the relevant scholarship. In partial recompense, the bibliography, which is designed for use in company with the notes, often serves as our vehicle for referring to and evaluating the range of existing interpretations. Numbered references in square brackets, e.g. 'Pohlenz [298]', are to entries in the bibliography.

AAL

DNS

Cambridge, June 1986

Early Pyrrhonism

1 Scepticism

A Diogenes Laertius 9.61–2 (Caizzi 1A, 6, 7, 9)

(1) Πύρρων Ἠλεῖος Πλειστάρχου μὲν ἦν υἱός, καθὰ καὶ Διοκλῆς ἱστορεῖ· ὥς φησι δ' Ἀπολλόδωρος ἐν Χρονικοῖς, πρότερον ἦν ζωγράφος, καὶ ἤκουσε Βρύσωνος τοῦ Στίλπωνος, ὡς Ἀλέξανδρος ἐν Διαδοχαῖς, εἶτ' Ἀναξάρχου, ξυνακολουθῶν πανταχοῦ, ὡς καὶ τοῖς γυμνοσοφισταῖς ἐν Ἰνδίᾳ συμμῖξαι καὶ τοῖς Μάγοις. (2) ὅθεν γενναιότατα δοκεῖ φιλοσοφῆσαι, 5
τὸ τῆς ἀκαταληψίας καὶ ἐποχῆς εἶδος εἰσαγαγών, ὡς Ἀσκάνιος ὁ Ἀβ-δηρίτης φησίν. (3) οὐδὲν γὰρ ἔφασκεν οὔτε καλὸν οὔτ αἰσχρὸν οὔτε δίκαιον οὔτ' ἄδικον· καὶ ὁμοίως ἐπὶ πάντων μηδὲν εἶναι τῇ ἀληθείᾳ, νόμῳ δὲ καὶ ἔθει πάντα τοὺς ἀνθρώπους πράττειν· οὐ γὰρ μᾶλλον τόδε ἢ τόδε εἶναι ἕκαστον. (4) ἀκόλουθος δ' ἦν καὶ τῷ βίῳ, μηδὲν ἐκτρεπόμενος μηδὲ 10
φυλαττόμενος, ἅπαντα ὑφιστάμενος, ἁμάξας, εἰ τύχοι, καὶ κρημνοὺς καὶ κύνας καὶ ὅλως μηδὲν ταῖς αἰσθήσεσιν ἐπιτρέπων. σώζεσθαι μέντοι, καθά φασιν οἱ περὶ τὸν Καρύστιον Ἀντίγονον, ὑπὸ τῶν γνωρίμων παρακολου-θούντων. Αἰνεσίδημος δέ φησι φιλοσοφεῖν μὲν αὐτὸν κατὰ τὸν τῆς ἐποχῆς λόγον, μὴ μέντοι γ' ἀπροοράτως ἕκαστα πράττειν. ὁ δὲ πρὸς τὰ 15
ἐνενήκοντα ἔτη κατεβίω.

3 Βρύσωνος Ménage e Suda: δρύσωνος codd.   τοῦ codd.: ἢ Nietzsche, Röper   ὡς–Διαδοχαῖς om.
F   6 Ἀσκάνιος codd.: Ἑκαταῖος Müller   12 ὅλως Cobet: ὅσα codd.: ὅσα ⟨τοιαῦτα⟩ Stephanus
ἐπιτρέπων BP: ἐπιτρέπειν F   14 τῆς om. BP

Context: the opening of Diogenes' life of Pyrrho. The life is a patchwork of various sources and periods, extending from the near-contemporary Antigonus, 13, and Eratosthenes (D.L. 9.66) down to at least the first-century B.C. Aenesidemus, 14.

1   On the sources, Diocles, Apollodorus and Alexander, cf. Mejer [32].

2   **ζωγράφος** This early career, embellished in **B** 1–3 and by Aristocles (Eusebius, *Pr. ev.* 14.18.27), fits Pyrrho's subsequent scepticism suspiciously well; cf. σκηνογραφία, **D** 4.

3   **Βρύσωνος τοῦ Στίλπωνος** A notorious crux, cf. Giannantoni [62], 26–30. Pyrrho cannot have been taught by any son of Stilpo's, since he and Stilpo were of much the same age; and Stilpo is named as Timon's first teacher (D.L. 9.109). The mention of Bryson and Stilpo is an attempt by the 'succession' writers to connect Pyrrho with the Megarians and perhaps thereby to Socrates; cf. Suda s.v. Σωκράτης,

Early Pyrrhonism

an entry which gives Pyrrho a further Socratic pedigree via the local Elean school of Phaedo (note too the connexions drawn between Phaedo, Stilpo and Menedemus at D.L. 2.105). The Socratic succession for Pyrrho was a rival to his Eleatic-Democritean pedigree, as in Eusebius, *Pr. ev.* 14.17.10. Megarian influence on Pyrrho's scepticism has often been posited (cf. Brochard [52], 52 n. 1; von Fritz [71], col. 93; Berti [75], 75), but too uncritically. There are striking similarities between the Megarian Stilpo's Cynic style of moralizing and Timon; cf. Long [69], 71–3. But Timon seems to distance Pyrrho from any interest in Megarian metaphysics; and note his contemptuous dismissal of all Socratics including Megarians, **3D**. On Timon himself, see notes on **3I–m**.

4 Ἀναξάρχου   Material in 72 DK, and cf. von Fritz [71], cols. 94–5. Timon's one reference to him is partly pejorative, fr. 832, but this should not count against his having had decisive influence on Pyrrho.   γυμνοσοφισταῖς Described by Megasthenes and the Cynic Onesicritus at Strabo 15.1.59–65; and cf. Plutarch, *Alex.* 64. Pyrrho's astounding imperturbability (cf. **B–C**) can certainly be compared with the reported anecdotes on Indian asceticism and indifference to conventional values.

5 ὅθεν   The scope of the conjunction probably extends back only to the Indian sages. On γενναιότατα φιλοσοφῆσαι as a characteristically Cynic commendation of Pyrrho's mental and moral pre-eminence, cf. Brancacci [83], 219–30.

6 τὸ . . . εἰσαγαγών   As technical terms, ἐποχή and ἀκαταληψία probably postdate Pyrrho, originating with Zeno and Arcesilaus; see **68** and cf. Couissin [73], 381–6. But **F** and **G** entitle us to attribute concepts of suspension of judgement and non-cognition to early Pyrrhonism, though these should not be assimilated to the use of ἐποχή and ἀκαταληψία in Stoic-Academic debates; cf. Caizzi ad loc.   Ἀσκάνιος   Otherwise unknown, and hence emended by C. Müller, *FHG* II p. 384 n., to 'Hecataeus' of Abdera, a pupil of Pyrrho (D.L. 9.69) and a historian best known for his ethnography. However, the postulated corruption is hard to account for.

7–10   Democritus had contrasted the *conventionality (νόμῳ)* of secondary qualities (γλυκύ, πικρόν etc.) with the *reality* of atoms and void (cf. KRS 549, and vol. 1, 57) and is also credited with saying that 'truth is in the depths', **68A 2**. Pyrrho's claim is that νόμος and ἔθος account for all predications and grounds for action (cf. **I**), since 'nothing exists in truth'. The complete generality of Pyrrho's thesis, as stated here, accords with **F**. But his particular concern with outlawing objective values is evident in the priority given to καλόν, αἰσχρόν, δίκαιον, ἄδικον. For the Democritean background of οὐ μᾶλλον, cf. De Lacy [80]; Graeser [81].

10–15   The picture of Pyrrho's consistent refusal to make conventional discriminations resembles Aristotle's account of how someone (counterfactually) would behave who really rejected the principle of non-contradiction, *Metaph.* Γ.4, 1008b12–26; cf. Long [57], 94–7, and see further note on **F** 12–14. However fanciful, the picture goes back to Antigonus in the 3rd century B.C., in contrast with Aenesidemus' much later claim that Pyrrho's suspension of judgement *qua* philosopher did not make him careless in daily life.

B Diogenes Laertius 9.62–4 (Caizzi 10, part, 28, 11)

Ἀντίγονος δέ φησιν ὁ Καρύστιος ἐν τῷ Περὶ Πύρρωνος τάδε περὶ αὐτοῦ, ὅτι τὴν ἀρχὴν ἄδοξός τε ἦν καὶ πένης καὶ ζωγράφος. σώζεσθαί τε αὐτοῦ ἐν Ἤλιδι ἐν τῷ γυμνασίῳ λαμπαδιστὰς μετρίως ἔχοντας. (1) ἐκπατεῖν τε αὐτὸν καὶ ἐρημάζειν, σπανίως ποτ᾽ ἐπιφαινόμενον τοῖς οἴκοι. τοῦτο δὲ ποιεῖν ἀκούσαντα Ἰνδοῦ τινος ὀνειδίζοντος Ἀναξάρχῳ ὡς οὐκ ἂν ἕτερόν τινα διδάξαι οὗτος ἀγαθόν, 5 αὐτὸς αὐλὰς βασιλικὰς θεραπεύων. ἀεί τ᾽ εἶναι ἐν τῷ αὐτῷ καταστήματι, ὥστ᾽ εἰ καί τις αὐτὸν καταλίποι μεταξὺ λέγοντα, αὐτῷ διαπεραίνειν τὸν λόγον . . . (2) καταληφθεὶς δέ ποτε καὶ αὐτῷ λαλῶν καὶ ἐρωτηθεὶς τὴν αἰτίαν ἔφη μελετᾶν χρηστὸς εἶναι. ἐν τε ταῖς ζητήσεσιν ὑπ᾽ οὐδενὸς κατεφρονεῖτο διὰ τὸ ἐξοδικῶς λέγειν καὶ πρὸς ἐρώτησιν· ὅθεν καὶ 10 Ναυσιφάνην ἤδη νεανίσκον ὄντα θηραθῆναι. ἔφασκε γοῦν γίνεσθαι δεῖν τῆς μὲν διαθέσεως τῆς Πυρρωνείου, τῶν δὲ λόγων τῶν ἑαυτοῦ. ἔλεγέ τε πολλάκις καὶ Ἐπίκουρον θαυμάζοντα τὴν Πύρρωνος ἀναστροφὴν συνεχὲς αὐτοῦ πυνθάνεσθαι περὶ αὐτοῦ. οὕτω δ᾽ αὐτὸν ὑπὸ τῆς πατρίδος τιμηθῆναι ὥστε καὶ ἀρχιερέα καταστῆσαι αὐτὸν καὶ δι᾽ ἐκεῖνον πᾶσι τοῖς φιλοσόφοις ἀτέλειαν ψηφίσασθαι. 15

1 ἐν-Πύρρωνος om. F   10 τὸ ⟨καὶ δι⟩εξοδικῶς Kühn   15 καταστῆσαι BP: τιμηθῆναι F

Context: immediately following **A**.

3 **μετρίως ἔχοντας** 'Well proportioned' (cf. Plato, *Tht.* 191d), not 'indifferent' (Hicks in Loeb ed.).   **ἐκπατεῖν** A characteristic of other philosophers in Diogenes; cf. 1.112, 4.19, 9.3

4–6 The Indian's reproach to Anaxarchus recalls Diogenes the Cynic's contempt for flattery; cf. his frr. 422–5 Giannantoni [36].

6 **ἀεί . . . καταστήματι** Cf. 2B–D.

9 **μελετᾶν** Cf. Epicurus' advice to Menoeceus, **25A** 3 and 23J 1. Pyrrho's pupil Philo was described by Timon as τὸν ἀπ᾽ ἀνθρώπων αὐτόσχολον αὐτολαλητήν (D.L. 9.69).

10 **ἐξοδικῶς . . . ἐρώτησιν** These expressions seem to imply that Pyrrho was equally effective in extended or rhetorical discourse (ἐξοδικῶς) and in dialectic (πρὸς ἐρώτησιν); cf. S.E., *M.* 2.6 (= *SVF* 2.294). On Timon's evidence, however (cf. **2C–D**), Pyrrho's philosophical stance was one of indifference to conventional styles of argument or inquiry.

10–14 The atomist Nausiphanes' interest in Pyrrho is made the more credible by his scepticism about empirical knowledge (Seneca, *Ep.* 88.43–5). On the philosophical significance of Epicurus' admiration for Pyrrho, cf. Sedley [104], 136–7, and Gigante [106], 37–49.

14–15 For discussion, cf. Caizzi [64] ad loc.

C Diogenes Laertius 9.66–7 (Caizzi 15A, 16, 51, 20, part)

(1) καὶ κυνός ποτ᾽ ἐπενεχθέντος διασοβηθέντα εἰπεῖν πρὸς τὸν αἰτιασάμενον, ὡς χαλεπὸν εἴη ὁλοσχερῶς ἐκδῦναι τὸν ἄνθρωπον· διαγωνίζεσθαι δ᾽ ὡς οἷόν τε πρῶτον μὲν τοῖς ἔργοις πρὸς τὰ πράγματα, εἰ δὲ μή, τῷ γε λόγῳ. φασὶ δὲ καὶ σηπτικῶν φαρμάκων καὶ τομῶν καὶ καύσεων ἐπί τινος

3

Early Pyrrhonism

ἕλκους αὐτῷ προσενεχθέντων, ἀλλὰ μηδὲ τὰς ὀφρῦς συναγαγεῖν. καὶ ὁ   5
Τίμων δὲ διασαφεῖ τὴν διάθεσιν αὐτοῦ ἐν οἷς πρὸς Πύθωνα διέξεισιν. (2) ἀλλὰ καὶ
Φίλων ὁ Ἀθηναῖος, γνώριμος αὐτοῦ γεγονώς, ἔλεγεν ὡς ἐμέμνητο
μάλιστα μὲν Δημοκρίτου, εἶτα δὲ καὶ Ὁμήρου, θαυμάζων αὐτὸν καὶ
συνεχὲς λέγων "οἵη περ φύλλων γενεή, τοίη δὲ καὶ ἀνδρῶν" . . . προφέρεσ-
θαι δὲ καὶ . . . ὅσα συντείνει εἰς τὸ ἀβέβαιον καὶ κενόσπουδον ἅμα καὶ   10
παιδαριῶδες τῶν ἀνθρώπων.

2 τὸν om. F

Context: life of Pyrrho.

1–2 The same story, with minor modifications, is cited by Aristocles on
Antigonus of Carystus' authority at Eusebius, Pr. ev. 14.18.26 (Caizzi 15B). ἐκδῦναι Cf. ἔκδυσιν in Timon 2C 3, and the uses of ἀπεκδύνομαι cited by Caizzi [64] in
her note on the latter passage.

3–4 ἔργοις . . . λόγῳ Not flinching at extreme pain, 4–5, presumably
exemplifies διαγωνίζεσθαι . . . ἔργοις, and back-up by λόγος, if one does succumb,
should involve reflection on the complete indifference of everything, A 7–10. Cf. the
involuntary reactions of the Stoic wise man, which do not command his assent, 65Y.

6 Πύθωνα G is quoted from this work, on which see Ferrari [88], 208.

6–11 Aristocles, probably following Antigonus of Carystus, elaborates Pyrrho's
relation to Democritus into 'an encounter with Democritus' books' (Eusebius, Pr. ev.
14.18.27), a characteristic biographical touch (cf. D.L. 7.2 on Zeno of Citium). For
interesting suggestions about what Pyrrho found so attractive in Democritus, cf.
Caizzi [82]. Sextus also records and elaborates Pyrrho's love of Homer, M. 1.272,281.
On the quotation of Homer, Il. 6.146, and the other Homeric lines omitted here, cf.
Conche [72], 26. On the Cynic resonance of the terms ἀβέβαιον . . . παιδαριῶδες,
and on Timon's Silloi as the source of such characterizations of Pyrrho, see Long [69],
69.

D Sextus Empiricus, M. 7.87–8

οὐκ ὀλίγοι δὲ ἦσαν, ὡς προεῖπον, οἱ καὶ τοὺς περὶ Μητρόδωρον καὶ
Ἀνάξαρχον ἔτι δὲ Μόνιμον φήσαντες ἀνῃρηκέναι τὸ κριτήριον, ἀλλὰ
Μητρόδωρον μὲν ὅτι εἶπεν "οὐδὲν ἴσμεν, οὐδ' αὐτὸ τοῦτο ἴσμεν ὅτι οὐδὲν
ἴσμεν", Ἀνάξαρχον δὲ καὶ Μόνιμον ὅτι σκηνογραφίᾳ ἀπείκασαν τὰ ὄντα
τοῖς τε κατὰ ὕπνους ἢ μανίαν προσπίπτουσι ταῦτα ὡμοιῶσθαι ὑπέλαβον.   5

Context: doxography of the criterion of truth.

For Metrodorus of Chios see 70 DK, and for Monimus of Syracuse, frr. 1–5
Giannantoni [36]. Eusebius, Pr. ev. 14.19.8, after citing a version of Metrodorus'
dictum, comments: ἥτις εἰσβολὴ κακὰς ἔδωκεν ἀφορμὰς τῷ μετὰ ταῦτα γενομένῳ
Πύρρωνι. The Cynic Monimus was probably somewhat younger than Pyrrho; his
affinity with early Pyrrhonism is evident in S.E., M. 8.5: τάχα δὲ καὶ Μόνιμος ὁ κύων
[sc. μηθὲν εἶναι φησιν ἀληθές], τῦφον εἰπὼν τὰ πάντα. On τῦφος as a favourite
Cynic term for self-importance and self-deception, and its use by Timon and later
Pyrrhonism, cf. Long [69], 74–5, and the wide-ranging study by Caizzi [84].

4 σκηνογραφίᾳ Cf. Caizzi [64] ad loc.

4

E Diogenes Laertius 9.60

οὗτος [sc. 'Ανάξαρχος] διὰ τὴν ἀπάθειαν καὶ εὐκολίαν τοῦ βίου Εὐδαιμο-
νικὸς ἐκαλεῖτο· καὶ ἦν ἐκ τοῦ ῥᾴστου δυνατὸς σωφρονίζειν.

Context: life of Anaxarchus.

1 ἀπάθειαν   See note on 2F 5-7.

F Aristocles (Eusebius, Pr. ev. 14.18.1-5; Caizzi 53)

(1) ἀναγκαίως δ' ἔχει πρὸ παντὸς διασκέψασθαι περὶ τῆς ἡμῶν αὐτῶν
γνώσεως· εἰ γὰρ αὖ μηδὲν πεφύκαμεν γνωρίζειν, οὐδὲν ἔτι δεῖ περὶ τῶν
ἄλλων σκοπεῖν. ἐγένοντο μὲν οὖν καὶ τῶν πάλαι τινὲς οἱ ἀφέντες τήνδε τὴν
φωνήν, οἷς ἀντείρηκεν 'Αριστοτέλης. (2) ἴσχυσε μὲν τοιαῦτα λέγων καὶ
Πύρρων ὁ 'Ηλεῖος· ἀλλ' αὐτὸς μὲν οὐδὲν ἐν γραφῇ καταλέλοιπεν, ὁ δέ γε   5
μαθητὴς αὐτοῦ Τίμων φησὶ δεῖν τὸν μέλλοντα εὐδαιμονήσειν εἰς τρία
ταῦτα βλέπειν· πρῶτον μέν, ὁποῖα πέφυκε τὰ πράγματα· δεύτερον δέ, τίνα
χρὴ τρόπον ἡμᾶς πρὸς αὐτὰ διακεῖσθαι· τελευταῖον δέ, τί περιέσται τοῖς
οὕτως ἔχουσι. (3) τὰ μὲν οὖν πράγματά φησιν αὐτὸν ἀποφαίνειν ἐπ' ἴσης
ἀδιάφορα καὶ ἀστάθμητα καὶ ἀνεπίκριτα· (4) διὰ τοῦτο μήτε τὰς αἰσθήσεις   10
ἡμῶν μήτε τὰς δόξας ἀληθεύειν ἢ ψεύδεσθαι. διὰ τοῦτο οὖν μηδὲ πιστεύειν
αὐταῖς δεῖν, ἀλλ' ἀδοξάστους καὶ ἀκλινεῖς καὶ ἀκραδάντους εἶναι, περὶ ἑνὸς
ἑκάστου λέγοντας ὅτι οὐ μᾶλλον ἔστιν ἢ οὐκ ἔστιν ἢ καὶ ἔστι καὶ οὐκ ἔστιν
ἢ οὔτε ἔστιν οὔτε οὐκ ἔστιν. (5) τοῖς μέντοι γε διακειμένοις οὕτω
περιέσεσθαι Τίμων φησὶ πρῶτον μὲν ἀφασίαν, ἔπειτα δ' ἀταραξίαν,   15
Αἰνησίδημος δ' ἡδονήν. (6) τὰ μὲν οὖν κεφάλαια τῶν λεγομένων ἐστὶ
ταῦτα.

2 αὖ codd.: αὐτοὶ Diels   4 μὲν τοιαῦτα I^b: μέντοι ταῦτα OD   5 δέ γε I^b: δὲ ON   10 ἀνεπίκριτα
ON: ἀνέγκριτα I^b   διὰ τοῦτο codd.: διὰ τὸ Zeller   12 ἑνὸς ON: om. I^b   14 ἢ οὔτε ἔστιν om. I^b

As the richest single item of evidence for Pyrrho's philosophy, this extract requires
careful scrutiny. We need to determine first its value as historical testimony, and
secondly the nature of the inferences in section 4, which answer the second question in
section 2.

Eusebius' main purpose in Pr. ev. 14 is to contrast Greek philosophers'
disagreements with the consistency of the Hebrews (14.2.7ff.). From 14.16.13 to
14.21.7 he deals with philosophers' discrepant views on epistemology, structuring his
polemical surveys around the trustworthiness or untrustworthiness they ascribe to
sense-perception. Five groups of philosophers are treated: (a) Eleatics (including
Xenophanes) and Megarians, 14.17.1-9; (b) Pyrrhonian Sceptics, 14.18.1-30; (c)
Cyrenaics, 14.18.31-14.19.7; (d) 'Those who say bodily sensations are entirely
trustworthy', including Protagoras and Metrodorus of Chios, 14.19.8-14.20.12; (e)
Epicureans (presented as an offshoot of Cyrenaics), 14.20.13-14.21.7. Nearly all this
material purports to be virtually verbatim quotation from Aristocles of Messene's On
philosophy (probably book 8, so Pr. ev. 14.16.13 in most codd.). Eusebius begins his
extract from Aristocles on Pyrrho by saying one can learn to refute such opinions ἀπὸ
τοῦ δηλωθέντος συγγράμματος ὧδέ πη πρὸς λέξιν ἔχοντος. Many of his quotations

are given this 'verbatim' authorization (e.g. 11.10.16, 11.18.26, 11.23.12), and the independent survival of some of the cited texts (e.g. 11.26.5ff. = Plato, *Alc*.1) justifies the claim.

F, then, should be regarded as an authentic excerpt from Aristocles, a Peripatetic philosopher recently redated by Moraux [14], 83–92, from the late second century A.D. to a period not later than the early first century A.D. Aristocles was bitterly hostile to all the groups of philosophers for whom Eusebius quotes him; in *Pr. ev.*, 14.18.5–7, immediately following F, he refutes the Timon passage (**F** 5–15) at length, and then passes to objections to Pyrrhonism closely based on Aristotle, *Metaph*. *Γ*.5–6, returning to Pyrrho and Timon at 14–19, 26–8. He cites Timon's *Pytho* at 14.18.14 and his *Silloi* at 14.18.16ff., and Antigonus of Carystus' life of Pyrrho at 14.18.26. Aenesidemus is mentioned at F 16, and Aristocles also refers to his Ὑποτύπωσις (14.18.11) and his Μακραὶ στοιχειώσεις (14.18.16). In his conclusion he speaks of Pyrrhonism as 'only recently' revived in Alexandria by Aenesidemus (14.18.29), a remark which speaks strongly in favour of the new chronology of Aristocles' life proposed by Moraux [14], 89.

Aristocles' knowledge of Aenesidemus seems extremely sketchy (cf. Krüger [87], 112–13), and his refutations of Pyrrhonism recall Sextus Empiricus very little (contrast **71D**). He never uses the standard terms ἐποχή and φαινόμενον, and his list of Aenesidemus' nine (*sic*) Modes is defective and garbled (14.18.11). All this tends to suggest that Aristocles' report of Timon is based upon an authentic document of early Pyrrhonism, and is little if at all contaminated by later scepticism. The vocabulary of the text supports this conclusion: Sextus does not use ἀστάθμητος, ἀκλινής or ἀκράδαντος, all of which words are pre-Hellenistic; cf. Caizzi [64] ad loc. (Timon's *Pytho* would be a highly appropriate work in which to report Pyrrho's revelation of the sources of happiness; cf. C 6 and Ferrari [88], 208.)

None of these suggestions implies that Aristocles' report of Timon should be regarded as quotation rather than paraphrase; cf. Stopper [63], 271. but Stopper, 273, is unduly suspicious when he suggests that ἢ καὶ ἔστι καὶ οὐκ ἔστιν ἢ οὔτε ἔστιν οὔτε οὐκ ἔστιν, F 13–14, may be an Aristotelian importation by Aristocles. See below.

5–14   In vol. 1, 16–17, we opt for the metaphysical interpretation of lines 9–11 proposed by Caizzi [64], 225–7, instead of the narrowly epistemological reading fashionable since Zeller [1]. Conceivably Pyrrho argued thus: (a) If the world has a determinate nature, it will be truly or falsely describable by a definite theory. (b) But all existing definite theories about the world conflict with one another in such a way that there is no reason to prefer one such theory to another. (c) Nor is it possible to think of some other definite theory T* which is immune to this absence of preference. (d) Therefore there is no reason to think that the world is truly or falsely describable by a definite theory. (e) But (d) contradicts (a). (f) Therefore the world does not have a determinate nature. (g) And a world which does not have a determinate nature is not something which can be truly or falsely perceived or opined. (h) Therefore our perceptions or opinions are neither true nor false. (Some support for step (b) in this argument may be found in Aenesidemus' report of Pyrrho at **71A** 1.)

12–14   The striking similarity between what the Pyrrhonist should say about each thing and Aristotle's characterization of the ἀφασία of someone who denies the principle of non-contradiction, *Metaph*. *Γ*.4, 1008a30–5, is pointed out by Long [57], 91–3, and Reale [74], 315–21. The triadic structure of 6–14 (cf. Ferrari [78], 362) goes against Stopper's suggestion (see above) that the second and third disjuncts in 13–14 are importations by Aristocles from Aristotle. But Stopper is probably right to object to any formal rejection of the principle of non-contradiction by Timon's Pyrrho. These expansions of the οὐ μᾶλλον formula are best interpreted as indications of the utterly non-committal language that the Pyrrhonist recommends.

16 ἡδονήν   For discussion of this unexpected term, see Caizzi |64| ad loc.

G Diogenes Laertius 9.76 (Caizzi 54, part)

σημαίνει οὖν ἡ φωνή [sc. "οὐ μᾶλλον"], καθά φησι καὶ Τίμων ἐν τῷ Πύθωνι "τὸ μηδὲν ὁρίζειν, ἀλλ' ἀπροσθετεῖν."

For οὐ μᾶλλον in later Pyrrhonism, cf. 71C 6–7. ἀπροσθετεῖν, a hapax, expresses the opposite of προστίθεσθαι in its familar sense, 'vote for', 'assent to'. πρόσθεσις and προστίθεσθαι are found in sceptical texts as synonyms for συγκατάθεσις and συγκατατίθεσθαι, which, by Chrysippus' date, are the standard Stoic expressions for 'assent'. See 69A 7, and, for the combination of both words, S.E., M. 7.225. Timon's use of ἀπροσθετεῖν rather than ἐπέχειν vel sim. probably indicates the absence of any fixed sceptical terminology at this time.

H Diogenes Laertius 9.104–5 (including Caizzi 55, 63A)

πάλιν οἱ δογματικοί φασιν καὶ τὸν βίον αὐτοὺς ἀναιρεῖν, ἐν ᾧ πάντ' ἐκβάλλουσιν ἐξ ὧν ὁ βίος συνέστηκεν. οἱ δὲ ψεύδεσθαί φασιν αὐτούς· οὐ γὰρ τὸ ὁρᾶν ἀναιρεῖν, ἀλλὰ τὸ πῶς ὁρᾶν ἀγνοεῖν. (1) καὶ γὰρ τὸ φαινόμενον τιθέμεθα, οὐχ ὡς καὶ τοιοῦτον ὄν. καὶ ὅτι τὸ πῦρ καίει αἰσθανόμεθα· εἰ δὲ φύσιν ἔχει καυστικὴν ἐπέχομεν. καὶ ὅτι κινεῖταί τις βλέπομεν, καὶ ὅτι φθείρεται· πῶς δὲ ταῦτα γίνεται οὐκ ἴσμεν. μόνον οὖν,   5 φασίν, ἀνθιστάμεθα πρὸς τὰ παρυφιστάμενα τοῖς φαινομένοις ἄδηλα. καὶ γὰρ ὅτε τὴν εἰκόνα ἐξοχὰς λέγομεν ἔχειν, τὸ φαινόμενον διασαφοῦμεν· ὅταν δ' εἴπωμεν μὴ ἔχειν αὐτὴν ἐξοχάς, οὐκέτι ὃ φαίνεται ἕτερον δὲ λέγομεν· (2) ὅθεν καὶ ὁ Τίμων ἐν τῷ Πύθωνί φησι μὴ ἐκβεβηκέναι τὴν συνήθειαν. καὶ ἐν τοῖς Ἰνδαλμοῖς οὕτω λέγει "ἀλλὰ τὸ φαινόμενον πάντη   10 σθένει οὗπερ ἂν ἔλθῃ." (3) καὶ ἐν τοῖς Περὶ αἰσθήσεών φησι, "τὸ μέλι ὅτι ἐστὶ γλυκὺ οὐ τίθημι, τὸ δ' ὅτι φαίνεται ὁμολογῶ."

2 ἀναιρεῖν dgt: ἀναιρεῖ BFP   5 οὖν om. F   10 πάντῃ F, Galenus, De diagnosc. puls. 1.2, 8.781 Kühn: παντὶ BP et S.E., M. 7.30   11 μέλι Cobet: μὲν codd.

Context: Diogenes is reporting later Pyrrhonist replies to the objection by doctrinaire philosophers that scepticism makes life impossible; cf. S.E., PH 1.13, 19–24, 92.

Anecdotes such as A 4 and C 1 imply that such charges were already being advanced against Pyrrho, with Timon answering them as here. Cf. 2D for Pyrrho's case of action. Note that in the gallery of philosophers who make life impossible, Timon's Epicurean contemporary Colotes (cf. note on context of 68H) includes the Academic sceptics but not the Pyrrhonists. Is this due to Epicurean sympathy for Pyrrho (cf. B 2), which may have led them, like Cicero, to emphasize his moral stance rather than his scepticism?

11 σθένει   The verb has an archaic and poetic ring; cf. Aeschylus, Ag. 296;

7

Euripides, *Hec.* 49.　**οὖπερ ἂν ἔλθῃ**　For οὖ = οἷ in later Greek, cf. LSJ s.v. ὅς A b.2. It is odd to write of 'the appearance' as going anywhere; perhaps take an unexpressed τις to be the subject of ἔλθῃ, or suppose a personal subject to have been indicated in the previous line.

11–12　The only surviving reference to this work, which may have dealt with the kind of material found in Aenesidemus' third mode; cf. **72D**. In any case Sextus repeats Timon at *PH* 1. 19–20. At Aristotle, *Metaph.* Γ.4, 1008b20 'sweet or not sweet' exemplifies the kind of opinions that anyone who 'does anything' must have. It is conceivable that the interpretation we give in vol. 1 imputes to Timon too much of later Pyrrhonism. Instead of adumbrating the use of τὸ φαινόμενον as a practical criterion, he might be simply registering the admission that, notwithstanding the complete indeterminacy of nature, things do manifest themselves to human beings in a determinate way; cf. Caizzi [79], 93–5.

I　Sextus Empiricus, *M.* 11.140 (Timon fr. 844, Caizzi 64)

μόνως οὖν ἔσται φυγεῖν ταύτην [*sc.* ἀοχλησίαν], εἰ ὑποδείξαιμεν τῷ ταραττομένῳ κατὰ τὴν τοῦ κακοῦ φυγὴν ἢ κατὰ τὴν τοῦ ἀγαθοῦ δίωξιν, ὅτι **οὔτε ἀγαθόν τι φύσει ἔστι οὔτε κακόν, "ἀλλὰ πρὸς ἀνθρώπων ταῦτα νόμῳ κέκριται", κατὰ τὸν Τίμωνα.**

3 νόμῳ Hirzel: νόῳ codd.

Context: Sextus is concluding an argument that mental disturbance is caused by efforts to pursue the good and avoid the bad. Timon's pentameter line is quoted in support of the non-naturalness of anything good or bad. It probably comes from his *Indalmoi*, the only one of his works known to have been written in elegiacs.

3　Hirzel's emendation is widely accepted, and fits **A 3** very well.

J　Cicero, *Tusc.* 5.85 (Caizzi 69L)

haec [*sc.* Stoicorum, Epicuri, Hieronymi *etc.*] sunt sententiae quae stabilitatis aliquid habeant; nam Aristonis Pyrrhonis Erilli non nullorumque aliorum evanuerunt.

Context: doxography of *bonum*.

For Cicero's grouping of Pyrrho, Aristo and Herillus, see notes on **2G–H**.

K　Seneca, *NQ* 7.32.2 (Caizzi 71)

itaque tot familiae philosophorum sine successore deficiunt: Academici et veteres et minores nullum antistitem reliquerunt; quis est qui tradat praecepta Pyrrhonis?

Context: the decline of philosophy as a sign of general degeneration.

Glucker [42], 340, takes Seneca to know of Aenesidemus' revival of Pyrrhonism at Alexandria, and also to know of it as 'already extinct after the death of Aenesidemus and his pupils'. But this presumes too much. Even if neo-Pyrrhonism was not a formal school, the list of Aenesidemus' successors at D.L. 9.116 speaks against such an extinction, which Glucker posits, it seems, in order to justify his belief in Seneca's knowledge of Alexandrian philosophy. There were many contemporary developments in philosophy of which Seneca makes no mention. Unlike Cicero, however, Seneca does associate Pyrrhonists with scepticism; cf. *Ep.* 88.44.

2 Tranquillity and virtue

A Aristocles (Eusebius, *Pr. ev.* 14.18.17; Timon fr. 782, Caizzi 57, part)

εἰ δ᾽ οὐδὲν ὄφελός ἐστι τῶν λόγων, τί ἡμῖν ἐνοχλοῦσιν; ἢ διὰ τί Τίμων φησίν· "οὐκ ἂν δὴ Πύρρωνί γ᾽ ἐρίσ⟨σ⟩ειεν βροτὸς ἄλλος;"

1 ἡμῖν Stephanus: μὴν codd.

Context: Aristocles confronts the Pyrrhonists with a dilemma: either their λόγοι are intended to improve us, in which case they are not sceptical; or their λόγοι are useless, and it is pointless for Timon to hold up Pyrrho for admiration.

Timon's line is a parody of Homer, *Il.* 3.223: οὐκ ἂν ἔπειτ᾽ 'Οδυσῆί γ᾽ ἐρίσσειεν βροτὸς ἄλλος.

B Aristocles (Eusebius, *Pr. ev.* 14.18.19; Timon fr. 783, Caizzi 58, part)

οὐδὲ γὰρ ἐκεῖνο φαίη τις ἄν, ὅτι τοὺς νόμους δεδοίκασι καὶ τὰς τιμωρίας οἱ τοιοῦτοι· πῶς γὰρ οἵ γε ἀπαθεῖς καὶ ἀτάραχοι, καθάπερ αὐτοί φασιν, ὄντες; ὅ γέ τοι Τίμων ταῦτα καὶ λέγει περὶ τοῦ Πύρρωνος·

> ἀλλ᾽ οἷον τὸν ἄτυφον ἐγὼ ἴδον ἠδ᾽ ἀδάμαστον
> πᾶσιν ὅσοις δάμνανται ὅμως ἄφατοί τε φατοί τε,   5
> λαῶν ἔθνεα κοῦφα, βαρυνόμεν᾽ ἔνθα καὶ ἔνθα
> ἐκ παθέων δόξης τε καὶ εἰκαίης νομοθήκης.

4 ἀλλ᾽ οἷον ON: ἄλλοιον Iᵇ   5 δάμνανται ὅμως Wachsmuth: δάμνανται βροτῶν Iᵇ   6 βαρυνόμεν᾽ Stephanus: βαρύνομεν Iᵇ: βαρυνόμενος ON

Context: continuation (cf. **A**) of Aristocles' criticism of Pyrrhonism.

4 ἀλλ᾽ οἷον and ἴδον indicate the Homeric Nekuia as the model of Timon's parody, as in **3F**; cf. *Od.* 11.519,568 etc. **ἄτυφον** Pyrrho is immune to the τῦφος characteristic of people in general, as too is the Stoic wise man (D.L. 7.117), though not the school's founder in Timon's satire, **3F**; see note on **1D**. **ἀδάμαστον** Of Hades in Homer, *Il.* 9.158.

5 **ἄφατοί τε φατοί τε** So Hesiod, *Erg.* 3.
6 **λαῶν ἔθνεα κοῦφα** Cf. Homer, *Il.* 13.495 and Parmenides, 28 B 6.7 DK.
7 **εἰκαίης νομοθήκης** Epicurus condemns 'legislation' in cosmology, **18C 3**, a passage whose language has much in common with Pyrrhonism. For εἰκαίης, cf. **3G**; the Stoics made ἀνεικαιότης a dialectical virtue, **31B 3**.

C Diogenes Laertius 9.64 (Timon fr. 822, Caizzi 60)

καὶ δὴ καὶ ζηλωτὰς εἶχε πολλοὺς τῆς ἀπραγμοσύνης· ὅθεν καὶ ὁ Τίμων περὶ αὐτοῦ φησιν οὕτως ἐν τῷ Πύθωνι καὶ ἐν τοῖς Σίλλοις·

9

ὦ γέρον, ὦ Πύρρων, πῶς ἢ πόθεν ἔκδυσιν εὗρες
λατρείης δοξῶν [τε] κενεοφροσύνης τε σοφιστῶν,
καὶ πάσης ἀπάτης πειθοῦς τ᾽ ἀπελύσαο δεσμά;   5
οὐδ᾽ ἐμελέν σοι ταῦτα μεταλλῆσαι, τίνες αὖραι
Ἑλλάδ᾽ ἔχουσι, πόθεν τε καὶ εἰς ὅ τι κύρει ἕκαστα.

3 ἔκδυσιν BP: ἔκλυσιν FP(corr.)   4 κενεο- Usener: τε κενο- codd.   6 οὐδ᾽ ἐμελεν P: οὐδε μέλε B: οὐδὲ μέλει F   μεταλλῆσαι Wachsmuth: μεταλλήσειν P(corr): μετάλλησι B: μεταμελήσειν F   τίνες Cobet: τινὸς (τίνος F) codd.

Context: life of Pyrrho.

1 **ἀπραγμοσύνης** Contrast the σοφισταί of **3A**; Pyrrho's indifference to science recalls Plato's and Xenophon's Socrates.

3–4 Cf. Timon's characterization of two of Pyrrho's disciples (D.L. 9.69): he calls Eurylochus πολεμιώτατος τοῖς σοφισταῖς, and Philo indifferent to δόξα and ἔριδες.

6–7 We follow Diels [68], fr. 48 note, in taking these lines to refer to speculation on meteorology and cosmology (for πόθεν . . . ἕκαστα, cf. Simplicius' account of Anaximander, ἐξ ὧν δὲ ἡ γένεσις τοῖς οὖσι, καὶ τὴν φθορὰν εἰς ταῦτα γίνεσθαι, 12 B 1 DK). Lloyd-Jones/Parsons [66] ad loc. favour taking αὖραι to refer to currents of philosophical opinion, and perhaps reading ἑκάστη (Wilamowitz) for ἕκαστα.

D Diogenes Laertius 9.65, Sextus Empiricus, *M.* 11.1, 1.305 (Timon fr. 841, Caizzi 61)

τοῦτό μοι, ὦ Πύρρων, ἱμείρεται ἦτορ ἀκοῦσαι,
πῶς ποτ᾽ ἀνὴρ διάγεις ῥῇστα μεθ᾽ ἡσυχίης
αἰεὶ ἀφροντίστως καὶ ἀκινήτως κατὰ ταὐτὰ
μὴ προσέχων δίνοις ἡδυλόγου σοφίης,
μοῦνος δ᾽ ἀνθρώποισι θεοῦ τρόπον ἡγεμονεύεις,   5
ὃς περὶ πᾶσαν ἐλῶν γαῖαν ἀναστρέφεται,
δεικνὺς εὐτόρνου σφαίρης πυρικαύτορα κύκλον.

2 ἀνὴρ διάγεις Caizzi: ἀνὴρ ὅτ᾽ ἄγεις vel sim. codd.   4 δίνοις Nauck: δειλοῖς codd.   5 δ᾽ Sextus: ἐν Diogenes   ἡγεμονεύεις Sextus: -ων Diogenes   6 ἐλῶν Stephanus: ἐλῶν codd.   7 σφαίρης Diels: σφαίρας codd.

Lines 1, 2, 5 are cited by Diogenes from Timon's *Indalmoi*; line 2, ῥῇστα to end of 4, by Sextus at *M.* 11.1, and 5–7 at *M.* 1.305. For discussion of the language, cf. Caizzi [64] ad loc. Timon's description here of Pyrrho's equipoise, together with other such descriptions (cf. Timon fr. 838), may well be the source of such biographical embellishments as D.L. 9.62–3, 66–8; cf. Long [69], 69.

6–7 With Timon's sun comparison, cf. Lucretius 3.1043–4, on Epicurus. Epicureans and Pyrrho could derive support for their supreme evaluation of tranquillity from such accounts of Democritus as are recorded at D.L. 9.45.

E Sextus Empiricus, *M.* 11.19–20 (Timon fr. 842, Caizzi 62)

περὶ μὲν γὰρ τῆς πρὸς τὴν φύσιν ὑποστάσεως τῶν τε ἀγαθῶν καὶ κακῶν
καὶ οὐδετέρων ἱκανοί πώς εἰσιν ἡμῖν ἀγῶνες πρὸς τοὺς δογματικούς· κατὰ

δὲ τὸ φαινόμενον τούτων ἕκαστον ἔχομεν ἔθος ἀγαθὸν ἢ κακὸν ἢ ἀδιάφορον
προσαγορεύειν, καθάπερ καὶ ὁ Τίμων ἐν τοῖς Ἰνδαλμοῖς ἔοικε δηλοῦν,
ὅταν φῇ·   5

   ἦ γὰρ ἐγὼν ἐρέω, ὥς μοι καταφαίνεται εἶναι,
   μῦθον ἀληθείης ὀρθὸν ἔχων κανόνα,
   ὡς ἡ τοῦ θείου τε φύσις καὶ τἀγαθοῦ αἰεὶ
   ἐξ ὧν ἰσότατος γίνεται ἀνδρὶ βίος.

4 Ἰνδαλμοῖς Fabricius: σινδήμοις vel sim. codd.   6 ἦ Gen.: ἢ N: ᾗ LE   8 ὡς ἡ codd.: ὡς ζῇ
Bury   αἰεί Gen.: ἀεί codd.: ἔχει Natorp: comma post αἰεί del. Burnyeat

6–9   These lines are plausibly taken to be Pyrrho's answer to Timon's question in
D, i.e. they explain the source of his extraordinary equipoise (cf. ἰσότατος, 9).
Traditionally, it was generally supposed that 8 is a complete sentence, meaning 'that
the nature of the divine and the good exists for ever'; but the omission of any verb was
always found difficult. In vol. 1, 21, we accept the radically different interpretation
proposed by Burnyeat [77], whereby the verb to be understood is a predicative ἐστι
and no comma should be placed at the end of the line. On this construal 9 tells us what
the nature of the divine and the good consists in/has as its source, and no claims about
an everlasting nature are made. The great advantage of this interpretation is its ridding
Pyrrho of 'an independent and eternally existing nature' (Burnyeat, 88). Undeniably,
Pyrrho offers a positive rule of life, though qualified by 'how it appears to me', but
one he advances as a truth about himself (cf. the divine equipoise attributed to him in
D) and in such a way that it is also applicable to any man.

   Reale [74], 308–9, has challenged this interpretation. None of his objections to
Burnyeat seem to us decisive. However, Reale's own positive suggestions deserve
consideration, especially his observation of close parallels between Parmenides'
characterization of 'what is' and Pyrrho's equipoise. Reale's thesis in turn is criticized
by Stopper [63], 270–1, who advances the radical suggestion that 9 did not originally
follow directly after 8, so that we have no idea of what Timon's Pyrrho said about the
divine and the good.

   9 ἰσότατος   Note the rarely quoted epitaph of the Pyrrhonist Menecles, dating
from perhaps the 1st. century A.D., and found at Ali-Aga in Phocaea. We cite it from
Peek's *Griechische Vers-Inschriften* 1.603: ὁ τὰς ἀοιδ[ά]ς ἀγεμὼν ἂν Ἑλλάδα | ὁ
παντάπασιν ἐξισώσας τὰν λόγῳ | καὶ τὰν ἀτάραχον ἐν βροτοῖς θεύσας ὁδόν |
Πυρρωνιαστὰς Μενεκλέης ὅδ᾽ εἴμ᾽ ἐγώ.

F Cicero, *Acad.* 2.130 (Caizzi 69A)

hos [*sc.* Eretriacos et Elios] si contemnimus et iam abiectos putamus, illos certe minus despicere
debemus: Aristonem, qui cum Zenonis fuisset auditor re probavit ea quae ille
verbis, nihil esse bonum nisi virtutem nec malum nisi quod virtuti esset
contrarium; in mediis ea momenta quae Zeno voluit nulla esse censuit. huic
summum bonum est in his rebus neutram in partem moveri, quae ἀδιαφορία   5

ab ipso dicitur. Pyrrho autem ea ne sentire quidem sapientem, quae ἀπάθεια nominatur.

6 ἀπάθεια Asconius²: apati codd.

Context: part of Cicero's refutation of Lucullus' defence of Stoic/Antiochean ethics, indicating all the schools' disagreements.

Cicero invariably couples Pyrrho with Aristo (cf. also Caizzi 69D–M), and frequently with the Stoic Herillus. This appears to be due to the Academic tradition, according to which these three philosophers' views on the *summum bonum* failed to fit the *Carneadea divisio* (**64E**) because none of them specified any natural objective for the mind's primary impulse (cf. **G–H**). For Aristo and Herillus, cf. **58F–G**, **I**, with notes.

5–7 ἀδιαφορία is applied to Pyrrho by D.L. 9.66, and ἀπάθεια by Aristocles (ap. Euseb., *Pr. ev.* 14.18.18). Aristotle refers to ἀπάθεια and ἠρεμία as virtues (*EN* II.3, 1104b24); Pohlenz [76], 25, took these to allude to Pyrrho, but this is unconvincing; cf. Democritus ap. D.L. 9.45. ἀπάθεια seems to begin its main ethical life with the Cynics (cf. Polystratus, *De contemptu* 21), thereby entering Stoicism (cf. *SVF* 1.449, 3.144, 448 etc.). By the time of Cicero ἀπάθεια could be used interchangeably with ἀταραξία. Hirzel [30], 15–19, tried to argue that only ἀταραξία expresses Pyrrho's ethical end, while Brochard [52], 58–9, defended ἀπάθεια as well. There is no reason to exclude any of these terms: ἀδιαφορία, as the attitude of acknowledging no differences of value; ἀπάθεια, as the absence of all emotional attachment; and ἀταραξία, as the resulting freedom from disturbance.

G Cicero, *Fin.* 2.43 (Caizzi 69B, part)

quae [*sc.* quae prima natura approbavit] quod Aristoni et Pyrrhoni omnino visa sunt pro nihilo, ut inter optime valere et gravissime aegrotare nihil prorsus dicerent interesse, recte iam pridem contra eos desitum est disputari. dum enim in una virtute sic omnia esse voluerunt, ut eam rerum selectione expoliarent nec ei quicquam, aut unde oriretur, darent, aut ubi niteretur, 5 virtutem ipsam, quam amplexabantur, sustulerunt.

1 quod Madvig: cum codd.

Context: survey of ethical ends.

For the originally Stoic concepts deployed here, see vol. 1, 357–9. If it is not historically accurate to call Pyrrhonian tranquillity *virtus*, the error is understandable in the light of **E**; and cf. **1B** 5, 9.

H Cicero, *Fin.* 4.43 (Caizzi 69C, part)

itaque mihi videntur omnes quidem illi errasse, qui finem bonorum esse dixerunt honeste vivere, sed alius alio magis; Pyrrho scilicet maxime, qui virtute constituta nihil omnino, quod appetendum sit, relinquat; deinde

Aristo, qui nihil relinquere non est ausus, introduxit autem, quibus commotus sapiens
appeteret aliquid, quodcumque in mentem incideret, et quodcumque tamquam occurreret.   5

Context: Cicero's Antiochean criticism of Stoic ethics.

4–5   On Aristo's doctrine, cf. Ioppolo [346], 179–83.

I Athenaeus 337A (Timon fr. 845, Caizzi 65)

παγκάλως δὲ καὶ ὁ Τίμων ἔφη· "πάντων μὲν πρώτιστα κακῶν ἐπιθυμία
ἐστί."

Context: Athenaeus probably found this line in a gnomologium (cf. Caizzi ad loc.);
Timon's Indalmoi (cf. E) would be suitable for its original context, and similarly for
that of the half-line in J. See Burnyeat [77], 89–92, for discussion of the conceptual
connexions between I–J and E.

The harmfulness of ἐπιθυμία is a stock theme both of popular morality (cf. Dover,
Greek popular morality, 208–9) and of Greek philosophical ethics. In particular, early
Pyrrhonism could invoke the support of Democritus (cf. 68 B 70, 223, 236, 284 DK)
and the Cynics (cf. Diogenes frr. 152–246 Giannantoni [36]).

J Sextus Empiricus, M. 11.164 (Timon fr. 846, Caizzi 66, part)

ὑπὸ τυράννῳ ποτὲ γενόμενος καὶ τῶν ἀρρήτων τι ποιεῖν ἀναγκαζόμενος ἢ οὐχ ὑπομενεῖ τὸ
προσταττόμενον, ἀλλ' ἑκούσιον ἑλεῖται θάνατον, ἢ φεύγων τὰς βασάνους ποιήσει τὸ
κελευόμενον, οὕτω τε οὐκέτι "ἄφυγής καὶ ἀναίρετος ἔσται" κατὰ τὸν Τίμωνα, ἀλλὰ
τὸ μὲν ἑλεῖται, τοῦ δ' ἀποστήσεται.

Context: Sextus is stating the objection to Pyrrhonism that suspension of judgement is
inconsistent with the firm choices the victim of a tyrant would make. Cf. 58F 4 for
Aristo's rejoinder to the tyrant case.

3 Timon's polemics

A Diogenes Laertius 9.111 (Timon fr. 775)

τῶν δὲ Σίλλων τρία ἐστίν, ἐν οἷς ὡς ἂν σκεπτικὸς ὢν πάντας λοιδορεῖ καὶ
σιλλαίνει τοὺς δογματικοὺς ἐν παρῳδίας εἴδει. ὧν τὸ μὲν πρῶτον
αὐτοδιήγητον ἔχει τὴν ἑρμηνείαν, τὸ δὲ δεύτερον καὶ τρίτον ἐν διαλόγου
σχήματι. φαίνεται γοῦν ἀνακρίνων Ξενοφάνην τὸν Κολοφώνιον περὶ
ἑκάστων, ὁ δ' αὐτῷ διηγούμενός ἐστι· καὶ ἐν μὲν τῷ δευτέρῳ περὶ τῶν   5
ἀρχαιοτέρων, ἐν δὲ τῷ τρίτῳ περὶ τῶν ὑστέρων· ὅθεν δὴ αὐτῷ τινες καὶ
Ἐπίλογον ἐπέγραψαν. τὸ δὲ πρῶτον ταὐτὰ περιέχει πράγματα, πλὴν ὅτι
μονοπρόσωπός ἐστιν ἡ ποίησις· ἀρχὴ δ' αὐτῷ ἥδε· "ἔσπετε νῦν μοι ὅσοι
πολυπράγμονές ἐστε σοφισταί."

Context: life of Timon.

4   Xenophanes is the subject of Timon frr. 833–4.

8–9   The pejorative invocation of all 'intellectuals' is a parody of Homer, Il.
2.484, and Hesiod, Theog. 114.

9   πολυπράγμονες   Contrast Pyrrho's ἀπραγμοσύνη, 2C 1.

Early Pyrrhonism

B Aristocles (Eusebius, *Pr. ev.* 14.18.28; Timon fr. 785, Caizzi 48A, part)

αὐτὸς [sc. Πύρρων] δ' ὕστερον τοῦτον τὸν τῦφον περιβαλλόμενος καὶ καλῶν ἄτυφον ἑαυτὸν οὐδὲν ἐν γραφῇ κατέλιπεν. ἐγένετο δὲ μαθητὴς αὐτοῦ Τίμων Φλιάσιος, ὃς τὸ μὲν πρῶτον ἐχόρευεν ἐν τοῖς θεάτροις, ἔπειτα δ' ἐντυχὼν αὐτῷ συνέγραψεν ἀργαλέας παρῳδίας καὶ βωμολόχους, ἐν αἷς βεβλασφήμηκε πάντας τοὺς πώποτε φιλοσοφήσαντας. οὗτος γὰρ ἦν ὁ τοὺς Σίλλους γράψας καὶ λέγων· "σχέτλιοι ἄνθρωποι, κάκ' ἐλέγχεα, γαστέρες οἷον, | τοίων   5
ἔκ τ' ἐρίδων ἔκ τε στοναχῶν πέπλασθε" καί· "ἄνθρωποι κενεῆς οἰήσιος ἔμπλεοι
ἀσκοί."

3 παρῳδίας ON: τραγῳδίας I[b]

Context: polemical account of Pyrrho and Timon.

5–6 **σχέτλιοι . . . πέπλασθε** = Timon fr. 784, with the second line a virtual quotation of Empedocles 31 B 124.2 DK.

6 **κενεῆς οἰήσιος** Cf. 1C 10; 2C 4, and for further instances of κενός in Timon, frr. 794–5. **ἀσκοί** Cf. Lloyd-Jones/Parsons [66] ad loc.

C Sextus Empiricus, *M.* 9.57 (Timon fr. 779)

μέμνηται δὲ ταύτης τῆς ἱστορίας καὶ Τίμων ὁ Φλιάσιος ἐν τῷ δευτέρῳ τῶν Σίλλων ταῦτα διεξερχόμενος·

⟨τό⟩τε καὶ μετέπειτα σοφιστῶν
οὔτ' ἀλιγυγλώσσῳ οὔτ' ἀσκόπῳ οὔτ' ἀκυλίστῳ
Πρωταγόρῃ· ἔθελον δὲ τέφρην συγγράμματα θεῖναι,   5
ὅττι θεοὺς κατέγραψ' οὔτ' εἰδέναι οὔτε δύνασθαι
ὁπποῖοί τινές εἰσι καὶ εἴ τινες ἀθρήσασθαι,
πᾶσαν ἔχων φυλακὴν ἐπιεικείης. τὰ μὲν οὖ οἱ
χραίσμησ', ἀλλὰ φυγῆς ἐπεμαίετο, ὄφρα μὴ οὕτως
Σωκρατικὸν πίνων ψυχρὸν πότον Ἀίδα δύη.   10

3 ὥστε LEABR: ὅς τε V: ἔσητε N: ⟨πάντων πρωτίστῳ τό⟩τε Diels   5 συγγράμματα Fabricius: -τι
codd.   7 εἴ Bekker: οἱ codd.   10 Ἀίδα Ménage: -δι codd.   δύη Meineke: δύῃ codd.

For the anecdote and its context, cf. D.L. 9.51–2. In Timon fr. 821 Protagoras is described as ἐριζέμεναι εὖ εἰδώς; cf. **B** 6, **D**, and contrast Pyrrho at **2C–D**.

D Diogenes Laertius 2.107 (Timon fr. 802)

διὰ ταῦτα δὲ καὶ περὶ αὐτοῦ ταῦτά φησι Τίμων, προσπαρατρώγων καὶ τοὺς λοιποὺς Σωκρατικούς·

ἀλλ' οὔ μοι τούτων φλεδόνων μέλει· οὐδὲ γὰρ ἄλλου
οὐδενός, οὐ Φαίδωνος ὅτις γένετ', οὐδ' ἐριδάντεω
Εὐκλείδεω, Μεγαρεῦσιν ὃς ἔμβαλε λύσσαν ἐρισμοῦ.   5

4 ὅτις γένετ' Diels: ὅστις γε τ' vel sim. codd.

Context: Eucleides' logic–chopping.

3 **φλεδόνων** Also applied to Antisthenes, Timon fr. 811. Such consistency in

14

debunking followers of Socrates may be Timon's way of dissociating them from Pyrrho's pedigree (see note on **1A** 3). This line parodies Homer, *Il.* 6.450. Timon had a precedent for his parodic criticism of the Megarians in the Cynic Crates' lines on Stilpo, D.L. 2.118; cf. Long [69], 75, on Crates as a model for the *Silloi*.

E Diogenes Laertius 4.42 (Timon fr. 808)

εἰς δὲ τὸ διαβαλλόμενον αὐτοῦ [sc. ᾿Αρκεσιλάου] φίλοχλον καὶ Τίμων τά τ᾽ ἄλλα φησίν, ἀτὰρ δὴ τοῦτον τὸν τρόπον

ὣς εἰπὼν ὄχλοιο περίστασιν εἰσκατέδυνεν.
οἱ δέ μιν ἠύτε γλαῦκα πέρι σπίζαι τερατοῦντο
ἠλέματον δεικνύντες, ὁθούνεκεν ὀχλοάρεσκος.   5
οὐ μέγα πρῆγμα, τάλας· τί πλατύνεαι ἠλίθιος ὣς;

4 σπίζα codd., corr. H. Iunius   5 ὀχλοάρεσκος dt: ὀχλοαρέσκης P: ὄχλω ἀρέσκεις BF

Timon presumably wanted to contrast Arcesilaus, as a rival sceptic, with Pyrrho. But Diogenes proceeds to indicate how ἄτυφος Arcesilaus really was. Note Timon's description of Heraclitus as ὀχλολοίδορος, fr. 817. For Timon on Arcesilaus, see also **68E 2**.

F Diogenes Laertius 7.15 (Timon fr. 812)

ἦν δὲ [sc. Ζήνων Κιτιεύς] καὶ ζητητικὸς καὶ περὶ πάντων ἀκριβολογούμενος· ὅθεν καὶ ὁ Τίμων ἐν τοῖς Σίλλοις φησὶν οὕτω·

καὶ Φοίνισσαν ἴδον λιχνόγραυν σκιερῷ ἐνὶ τύφῳ
πάντων ἱμείρουσαν· ὁ δ᾽ ἔρρει γυργαθὸς αὐτῇ
σμικρὸς ἐών· νοῦν δ᾽ εἶχεν ἐλάσσονα κινδαψοῖο.   5

3 ἴδον B: ἰδών B(corr.): εἶδον P(corr.)F   4–5 αὐτῇ σμικρὸς Diels: αὐτῆς μικρὸς codd.   5 κινδαψοῖο Diogenes: σκινδαψοῖο Suda

1–2 These lines support Diels' interpretation, [68] ad loc., of 3–5 as a satirical representation of Zeno's attempt to win followers (fish) by means of his logical prowess (the fine mesh of his basket or net). Stoics are extensively covered in the extant fragments of the *Silloi*; cf. Aristo (780, 814), Cleanthes (815), Dionysius of Heraclea (791), and in general (787–8, 813, and possibly 839–40).

5 **κινδαψοῖο** Our vol. 1 translation of this word by 'string of twaddle' is an attempt to do justice both to its earliest usage as a stringed instrument (σκινδαψός LSJ, s.v.), and its philosophical usage, perhaps invented by the Stoics, as a nonsense word like βλίτυρι; cf. **33A** 3.

G Diogenes Laertius 5.11 (Timon fr. 810)

ἀλλὰ καὶ Τίμων αὐτοῦ [sc. ᾿Αριστοτέλους] καθήψατο εἰπών· "οὐδ᾽ ἄρ᾽ ᾿Αριστοτέλους εἰκαιοσύνης ἀλεγεινῆς."

We may understand οὔ μοι μέλει vel sim., as in **D** 3, and cf. fr. 809. With εἰκαιοσύνη, a *hapax*, cf. **2B** 7. Homer, *Il.* 23.701 is the line parodied.

H Diogenes Laertius 9.23 (Timon fr. 818)

Παρμενίδου τε βίην μεγαλόφρονος οὐ πολύδοξον,
ὅς ῥ' ἐκ φαντασίης ἀπάτης ἀνενείκατο νώσεις.

1 μεγαλόφρονος ὁ BP (οὐ dgwco): μεγαλόφρονα τὴν FP(corr.)   2 ὅς BP: ὡς F   ἐκ φαντασίης A.A.
Long: ἀπὸ φαντασίης Wachsmuth: ἐπὶ φαντασίας codd.

Timon's praise of Parmenides recalls his eulogy of Pyrrho in **2C**; cf. Long [69], 86 n. 31.

I Diogenes Laertius 9.25 (Timon fr. 819)

περὶ τούτου καὶ Μελίσσου Τίμων φησὶ ταῦτα·

ἀμφοτερογλώσσου τε μέγα σθένος οὐκ ἀλαπαδνὸν
Ζήνωνος πάντων ἐπιλήπτορος ἠδὲ Μέλισσον
πολλῶν φαντασμῶν ἐπάνω, παύρων γε μὲν ἥσσω.

3 πάντων Plutarch, *Pericl.* 4, 1 ii: πλάτων codd.   Μέλισσον Meineke: -ου codd.

2 **ἀμφοτερογλώσσου** Another neologism, probably a reference to Zeno's dilemmas (cf. Plutarch, *Pericl.* 4) and/or to the tradition that he invented dialectic; so Wachsmuth [67], 98–9. The comment on Melissus may be inspired by 30 B 8 DK.

J Diogenes Laertius 9.40 (Timon fr. 820)

ὅν γε [*sc.* Δημόκριτον] καὶ Τίμων τοῦτον ἐπαινέσας τὸν τρόπον ἔχει

οἷον Δημόκριτόν τε περίφρονα ποιμένα μύθων,
ἀμφίνοον λεσχῆνα μετὰ πρώτοισιν ἀνέγνων.

3 λεσχῆνα Meineke: λέσχην ἅ codd.

2 A close parody of Homer, *Il.* 1.263.

3 **ἀμφίνοον** Probably coined by Timon to express Democritean 'doubt' (cf. ἀμφινοέω, Sophocles, *Ant.* 376) like ἀμφοτερόβλεπτος of Xenophanes, fr. 833, and ἀμφοτερογλώσσου in **I**. Caizzi [82], 16ff., argues for 'ambiguous', suggesting that Timon was also drawing attention to the positive and negative ways in which Democritus' philosophy could be interpreted.

K Diogenes Laertius 10.2 (Timon fr. 825)

καὶ τὸν Τίμωνα φάσκειν περὶ αὐτοῦ [*sc.* Ἐπικούρου]

ὕστατος αὖ φυσικῶν καὶ κύντατος ἐκ Σάμου ἐλθὼν
γραμμοδιδασκαλίδης, ἀναγωγότατος ζωόντων.

3 γραμμο- BF(corr) P: γραμμα- F, Athenaeus 588a

Context: cited by Diogenes as corroboration of Hermippus' claim that Epicurus was a schoolteacher before he encountered Democritus' books and turned to philosophy.
On the hostile biographical tradition concerning Epicurus, see Sedley [104].

1 Sextus Empiricus, *M.* 3.1–2

ἐπεὶ οἱ γεωμέτραι συνορῶντες τὸ πλῆθος τῶν ἐπακολουθούντων αὐτοῖς ἀποριῶν εἰς
ἀκίνδυνον εἶναι δοκοῦν καὶ ἀσφαλὲς πρᾶγμα καταφεύγουσι, τὸ ἐξ ὑποθέσεως αἰτεῖσθαι τὰς
τῆς γεωμετρίας ἀρχάς, καλῶς ἂν ἔχοι καὶ ἡμᾶς τῆς πρὸς αὐτοὺς ἀντιρρήσεως ἀρχὴν
τίθεσθαι τὸν περὶ τῆς ὑποθέσεως λόγον. καὶ γὰρ ὁ Τίμων ἐν τοῖς πρὸς τοὺς φυσικοὺς τοῦτο
ὑπέλαβε δεῖν ἐν πρώτοις ζητεῖν, φημὶ δὲ τὸ εἰ ἐξ ὑποθέσεώς τι ληπτέον. διόπερ καὶ ἡμᾶς   5
οἰκεῖόν ἐστιν ἐκείνῳ στοιχοῦντας τὸ παραπλήσιον ποιεῖν ἐν τῇ πρὸς τοὺς ἀπὸ τῶν
μαθημάτων διεξόδῳ.

ἐξ ὑποθέσεως is one of the five modes of the later Pyrrhonist Agrippa (S.E., *PH* 1.68;
D.L. 9.88), and frequently used by Sextus to attack the doctrinaire philosophers for
beginning their arguments from arbitrary assumptions. The issue was familiar enough
before Timon: Aristotle often criticizes those who demand a proof for everything (cf.
Metaph. Γ.5, 1011a8–10, etc.), a point repeated by Sextus' doctrinaire opponents, *M.*
8.367 ff. Sextus' report of Timon's challenge to the φυσικοί is thus entirely credible,
and the more interesting because of the prominent place given to it in the opening of
his refutation of the geometers. It does not show that Timon was already adumbrating
the modes, but that is not impossible. Much of the material formally incorporated in
them is as old as, or older than, Plato and Aristotle; cf. Long [57] 85–91. For detailed
discussion of 1, cf. Caizzi [79], 96–101.

m Sextus Empiricus, *M.* 10.197; 6.66

[10.197] ἐν ἀμερεῖ γὰρ χρόνῳ οὐδὲν πέφυκε γίνεσθαι μεριστόν, ὥς φησι Τίμων, οἷον τὸ
γίνεσθαι καὶ τὸ φθείρεσθαι καὶ πᾶν ὃ τούτοις ἔοικεν. [6.66] ἐν ἀμερεῖ [*sc.* χρόνῳ] μὲν γὰρ
οὐδὲν δύναται γίνεσθαι μεριστόν, ὥς φησι Τίμων, οἷον τὸ γίνεσθαι, τὸ φθείρεσθαι.

These reports reinforce the impression given by 1 of Timon's interest in contemporary
philosophical debates. Sextus cites Timon in contexts where he is demonstrating that
time is non-existent, whether we make it divisible or indivisible, and Timon's support
is invoked against the latter. The position attributed to Timon recalls Aristotle's
arguments in *Physics* vi.2,232b20–233a12, on the impossibility of time's being
indivisible if magnitude is divisible, or vice versa. Diodorus Cronus' theory of ἀμερῆ
(see 11i) may have influenced Timon; cf. Sedley [11], 84–9; Long [69], 72; Caizzi [79],
101–5.

Epicureanism

PHYSICS

4 The principles of conservation

A Epicurus, *Ep. Hdt.* 38–9

(1) ταῦτα δὲ διαλαβόντας συνορᾶν ἤδη περὶ τῶν ἀδήλων· πρῶτον μὲν ὅτι οὐδὲν γίνεται ἐκ τοῦ μὴ ὄντος. πᾶν γὰρ ἐκ παντὸς ἐγίνετ' ἂν σπερμάτων γε οὐθὲν προσδεόμενον. (2) καὶ εἰ ἐφθείρετο δὲ τὸ ἀφανιζόμενον εἰς τὸ μὴ ὄν, πάντα ἂν ἀπωλώλει τὰ πράγματα, οὐκ ὄντων τῶν εἰς ἃ διελύετο. (3) καὶ μὴν καὶ τὸ πᾶν ἀεὶ τοιοῦτον ἦν οἷον νῦν ἐστι, καὶ ἀεὶ τοιοῦτον ἔσται. (4)   5 οὐθὲν γάρ ἐστιν εἰς ὃ μεταβάλλει. (5) παρὰ γὰρ τὸ πᾶν οὐθέν ἐστιν, ὃ ἂν εἰσελθὸν εἰς αὐτὸ τὴν μεταβολὴν ποιήσαιτο.

1 διαλαβόντας ⟨δεῖ⟩ Arndt   6 μεταβάλλει codd.: μεταβάλῃ φ: μεταβαλεῖ Usener

Context: immediately following the letter's opening methodological pronouncements at **17C**.

1   No need to insert δεῖ, with the majority of editors. It can be understood as carried over from the previous sentence (= **17C** 7–10). See Bollack [122], 173.

4–7   For the doctrine, cf. **e**, **14H** 1, and ps.-Plutarch, *Strom.* 8 (581,17–21 Diels, *Dox.*). Despite a partial Democritean parallel at 68 A 39 DK, Epicurus' most immediate model for the whole passage appears to be Empedocles 31 B 17.30–3 DK.

6   Much light has been shed on this part of the argument by Brunschwig [192]. The two occurrences of γάρ are co-ordinate, introducing two separate arguments for the preceding statement: see Denniston, *The Greek particles*, 64–5, and Brunschwig, 147–8, and cf. **13A**. The interpretation of the first clause suggested in vol. I, 27, 'since there is nothing into which it *passes and thus* changes', might be paralleled by such pregnant uses of the preposition as θεωρεῖν εἰς, 'to go to . . . and watch'. It seems, at any rate, safer than Brunschwig's suggestion that μεταβάλλει should be translated 'transports itself', for which he is able to cite the use of this verb in the sense 'migrate' in Aristotle, *HA* VIII.12: τήν in 7 shows that the 'change' mentioned there is the same as the 'change' already mentioned in 6, and *both* must therefore refer back to the qualitative variation denied in 4–5.

B Lucretius 1.159–73

(1) nam si de nilo fierent, ex omnibu' rebus
    omne genus nasci posset, nil semine egeret.   160

18

(2) e mare primum homines, e terra posset oriri
squamigerum genus et volucres erumpere caelo;
armenta atque aliae pecudes, genus omne ferarum,
incerto partu culta ac deserta tenerent;
nec fructus idem arboribus constare solerent,   165
sed mutarentur, ferre omnes omnia possent.
(3) quippe ubi non essent genitalia corpora cuique,
qui posset mater rebus consistere certa?
(4) at nunc seminibus quia certis quaeque creantur,
inde enascitur atque oras in luminis exit   170
materies ubi inest cuiusque et corpora prima;
(5) atque hac re nequeunt ex omnibus omnia gigni,
quod certis in rebus inest secreta facultas.

Context: see vol. 1, 26.

C Lucretius 1.225–37

(1) praeterea quaecumque vetustate amovet aetas,   225
si penitus peremit consumens materiem omnem,
unde animale genus generatim in lumina vitae
redducit Venus, aut redductum daedala tellus
unde alit atque auget generatim pabula praebens?
unde mare ingenui fontes externaque longe   230
flumina suppeditant? unde aether sidera pascit?
(2) omnia enim debet, mortali corpore quae sunt,
infinita aetas consumpse anteacta diesque.
(3) quod si in eo spatio atque anteacta aetate fuere
e quibus haec rerum consistit summa refecta,   235
immortali sunt natura praedita certe.
(4) haud igitur possunt ad nilum quaeque reverti.

Context: see vol. 1, 26.

D Lucretius 1.665–71

quod si forte alia credunt ratione potesse   665
ignis in coetu stingui mutareque corpus,
scilicet ex nulla facere id si parte reparcent,
occidet ad nilum nimirum funditus ardor
omnis et ⟨e⟩ nilo fient quaecumque creantur.
nam quodcumque suis mutatum finibus exit,   670
continuo hoc mors est illius quod fuit ante.

665 *alia* Lachmann: *mia* OQG: *ulla* Marullus   668 *ardor* O¹Q¹: *amor* O: *arbor* QG

Context: criticism of Heraclitus for the doctrine that fire is the sole element.
670–1   These lines recur at 1.792, 2.753, 3.519.

e Lucretius 2.303–7

> nec rerum summam commutare ulla potest vis;
> nam neque, quo possit genus ullum materiai
> effugere ex omni, quicquam est ⟨extra⟩, neque in omne   305
> unde coorta queat nova vis irrumpere et omnem
> naturam rerum mutare et vertere motus.

305 ⟨*extra*⟩ Munro   *omne* Marullus: *omnes* OQ

Context: after expounding the laws of atomic motion (2.62–293), Lucretius comments that the relative quantities of body and void in the universe do not alter, since no part of them increases or perishes; therefore the patterns of atomic motion are invariable (294–302). He then, in the above lines, adds a further reason for this invariability, that atomic motion cannot be disrupted by anything's departure from, or arrival in, the universe. The denials of generation, annihilation, subtraction and addition correspond closely to **A**, but the lesson drawn from them exceeds the brief of **A**, where atoms and void are as yet unheard of.

5 The basic division

A Epicurus, *Ep. Hdt.* 39–40

(1) ἀλλὰ μὴν καὶ τὸ πᾶν ἐστι ⟨σώματα καὶ κενόν⟩· (2) σώματα μὲν γὰρ ὡς ἔστιν, αὐτὴ ἡ αἴσθησις ἐπὶ πάντων μαρτυρεῖ, καθ' ἣν ἀναγκαῖον τὸ ἄδηλον τῷ λογισμῷ τεκμαίρεσθαι, ὥσπερ προεῖπον. (3) τόπος δὲ εἰ μὴ ἦν, ὃν κενὸν καὶ χώραν καὶ ἀναφῆ φύσιν ὀνομάζομεν, οὐκ ἂν εἶχε τὰ σώματα ὅπου ἦν οὐδὲ δι' οὗ ἐκινεῖτο, καθάπερ φαίνεται κινούμενα. (4) παρὰ δὲ ταῦτα οὐθὲν   5 οὐδ' ἐπινοηθῆναι δύναται οὔτε περιληπτῶς οὔτε ἀναλόγως τοῖς περιληπτοῖς ὡς καθ' ὅλας φύσεις λαμβανόμενα καὶ μὴ ὡς τὰ τούτων συμπτώματα ἢ συμβεβηκότα λεγόμενα.

1 ⟨σώματα καὶ κενόν⟩ Gassendi: ⟨σώματα καὶ τόπος⟩ Usener   3 ὥσπερ προεῖπον. τόπος δὲ εἰ μὴ ἦν, ὃν κενὸν Usener: ὥσπερ προεῖπον τὸ πρόσθεν. εἰ ⟨δὲ⟩ μὴ ἦν ὁ κενὸν alii: ὥσπερ προεῖπον τὸ πρόσθεν. εἰ μὴ ἦν ὃν κενὸν FP: ὥσπερ προεῖπον τὸ πρόσθεν. εἰ μὴ ἦν ὁ κενὸν B(corr.): ὥσπερ προεῖπον τὸ πρόσθε εἰ μὴ ἦν ὃν κενὸν B   5 οὐδὲ Usener: οὔτε codd.

Context: immediately following **4A**.

3 In defence of the readings and supplements adopted, see Sedley [196], 183–4, where the reading of B *ante correctionem* for line 3 is reported in favour of Usener's inspired conjecture.

6–7 For περιληπτός, cf. **11D** 2.

7–8 **συμπτώματα ἢ συμβεβηκότα** Cf. **7**. The expression has helped to foster the impression that these two terms are mutually exclusive, but see vol. 1, 36. Epicurus has no technical term for permanent attributes, and the phrase should be taken to mean 'accidents or attributes in general'. Cf. **15A** 30, with note.

B Lucretius 1.419–44

> (1) omnis, ut est igitur per se, natura duabus

constitit in rebus; nam corpora sunt et inane,   420
haec in quo sita sunt et qua diversa moventur.
(2) corpus enim per se communis dedicat esse
sensus; cui nisi prima fides fundata valebit,
haud erit occultis de rebus quo referentes
confirmare animi quicquam ratione queamus.   425
(3) tum porro locus ac spatium, quod inane vocamus,
si nullum foret, haud usquam sita corpora possent
esse neque omnino quoquam diversa meare;
id quod iam supera tibi paulo ostendimus ante.
(4) praeterea nil est quod possis dicere ab omni   430
corpore seiunctum secretumque esse ab inani,
quod quasi tertia sit numero natura reperta.
(5) nam quodcumque erit, esse aliquid debebit id ipsum
augmine vel grandi vel parvo denique, dum sit.
(6) cui si tactus erit quamvis levis exiguusque,   435
corporis augebit numerum summamque sequetur.
(7) sin intactile erit, nulla de parte quod ullam
rem prohibere queat per se transire meantem,
scilicet hoc id erit, vacuum quod inane vocamus.
(8) praeterea per se quodcumque erit, aut faciet quid   440
aut aliis fungi debebit agentibus ipsum
aut erit ut possint in eo res esse gerique.
(9) at facere et fungi sine corpore nulla potest res
nec praebere locum porro nisi inane vacansque.

433 *aliquid* OQ: *aliquo* Bockemüller   434 post 435 transtulit Lachmann

Context: shortly after **6A**.
    419   *omnis . . . natura*=ἡ τοῦ πάντος φύσις; cf. Plutarch, *Col.* 1112F.
    433–6   Most editors since Lachmann have accepted the transposition of 434 and
435. The sense is then: 'For whatever shall exist, must needs be something in itself; and
if it suffer touch, however small and light, it will swell the sum of body by an increase
great or maybe small, provided it exist at all, and be added to its total' (Bailey). They
hope to find in *esse aliquid . . . id ipsum* a translation of Epicurus' ὡς καθ' ὅλας φύσεις
λαμβανόμενα (**A** 7). We prefer to take *augmen*, probably Lucretius' own coinage, as
'extension' (cf. **14D** 268, and *auctu* at **12C** 482, and 5.1171). The dilemma posed in
435–9 would indeed be invalid without the premise that existence in the proper sense
is spatially extended existence. Otherwise the second horn (437–9) would fail to
exclude alleged incorporeals other than void, e.g. Platonic Forms.

C Aetius 1.20.2 (Usener 271)

Ἐπίκουρος ὀνόμασιν [πᾶσιν] παραλλάττειν κενὸν τόπον χώραν.
1 πᾶσιν del. Usener

Context: comparison of Stoic and Epicurean views on space.

21

Epicurean physics

D Sextus Empiricus, *M.* 10.2 (Usener 271)

διὸ προληπτέον ὅτι κατὰ τὸν Ἐπίκουρον τῆς ἀναφοῦς καλουμένης φύσεως
τὸ μέν τι ὀνομάζεται κενὸν τὸ δὲ τόπος τὸ δὲ χώρα, μεταλαμβανομένων
κατὰ διαφόρους ἐπιβολὰς τῶν ὀνομάτων, ἐπείπερ ἡ αὐτὴ φύσις ἔρημος μὲν
καθεστηκυῖα παντὸς σώματος κενὸν προσαγορεύεται, καταλαμβανομένη
δὲ ὑπὸ σώματος τόπος καλεῖται, χωρούντων δὲ δι' αὐτῆς σωμάτων χώρα   5
γίνεται. κοινῶς μέντοι φύσις ἀναφὴς εἴρηται παρὰ τῷ Ἐπικούρῳ διὰ τὸ
ἐστερῆσθαι τῆς κατὰ ἀντίβασιν ἁφῆς.

Context: introduction of the notion of place.

In the immediately following passage, **49B**, Sextus distinguishes these Epicurean
definitions from a Stoic set of definitions, whose chief difference is that χώρα is
defined as space which is partly empty and partly filled. This is still very close to the
Epicurean account, and indeed another source (Aetius 1.20.1, in the ps.-Plutarch
version) attributes it to the Stoics and Epicurus jointly. But the present text, the only
one to explain ἀναφὴς φύσις, is by far the most helpful in making sense of Epicurus'
own usage.

e Aristotle, *Phys.* IV.6, 213a15–19

οἷον γὰρ τόπον τινὰ καὶ ἀγγεῖον τὸ κενὸν τιθέασιν οἱ λέγοντες, δοκεῖ δὲ πλῆρες μὲν εἶναι,
ὅταν ἔχῃ τὸν ὄγκον οὗ δεκτικόν ἐστιν, ὅταν δὲ στερηθῇ, κενόν, ὡς τὸ αὐτὸ μὲν ὂν κενὸν καὶ
πλῆρες καὶ τόπον, τὸ δ' εἶναι αὐτοῖς οὐ ταὐτὸ ὄν.

Context: introduction of the notion of void for refutation.

f Aristotle, *Phys.* IV.8, 216a26–b16

καὶ καθ' αὑτὸ δὲ σκοποῦσιν φανείη ἂν τὸ λεγόμενον κενὸν ὡς ἀληθῶς κενόν. ὥσπερ γὰρ ἐὰν
ἐν ὕδατι τιθῇ τις κύβον, ἐκστήσεται τοσοῦτον ὕδωρ ὅσος ὁ κύβος, οὕτω καὶ ἐν ἀέρι· ἀλλὰ τῇ
αἰσθήσει ἄδηλον. καὶ αἰεὶ δὴ ἐν παντὶ σώματι ἔχοντι μετάστασιν, ἐφ' ὃ πέφυκε
μεθίστασθαι, ἀνάγκη, ἂν μὴ συμπιλῆται, μεθίστασθαι ἢ κάτω αἰεί, εἰ κάτω ἡ φορὰ ὥσπερ
γῆς, ἢ ἄνω, εἰ πῦρ, ἢ ἐπ' ἄμφω, [ἢ] ὁποῖον ἄν τι ᾖ τὸ ἐντιθέμενον· ἐν δὲ δὴ τῷ κενῷ τοῦτο   5
μὲν ἀδύνατον (οὐδὲν γὰρ σῶμα), διὰ δὲ τοῦ κύβου τὸ ἴσον διάστημα διεληλυθέναι, ὅπερ ἦν
καὶ πρότερον ἐν τῷ κενῷ, ὥσπερ ἂν εἰ τὸ ὕδωρ μὴ μεθίστατο τῷ ξυλίνῳ κύβῳ μηδ' ὁ ἀήρ,
ἀλλὰ πάντῃ διῄεσαν δι' αὐτοῦ. ἀλλὰ μὴν καὶ ὁ κύβος γε ἔχει τοσοῦτον μέγεθος, ὅσον
κατέχει κενόν· ὃ εἰ καὶ θερμὸν ἢ ψυχρόν ἐστιν ἢ βαρὺ ἢ κοῦφον, οὐδὲν ἧττον ἕτερον τῷ εἶναι
πάντων τῶν παθημάτων ἐστί, καὶ εἰ μὴ χωριστόν· λέγω δὲ τὸν ὄγκον τοῦ ξυλίνου κύβου.   10
ὥστ' εἰ καὶ χωρισθείη τῶν ἄλλων πάντων καὶ μήτε βαρὺ μήτε κοῦφον εἴη, καθέξει τὸ ἴσον
κενὸν καὶ ἐν τῷ αὐτῷ ἔσται τῷ τοῦ τόπου καὶ τῷ τοῦ κενοῦ μέρει ἴσῳ ἑαυτῷ. τί οὖν διοίσει
τὸ τοῦ κύβου σῶμα τοῦ ἴσου κενοῦ καὶ τόπου; καὶ εἰ δύο τοιαῦτα, διὰ τί οὐ καὶ ὁποσαοῦν ἐν
τῷ αὐτῷ ἔσται; ἓν μὲν δὴ τοῦτο ἄτοπον καὶ ἀδύνατον. ἔτι δὲ φανερὸν ὅτι τοῦτο ὁ κύβος ἕξει
καὶ μεθιστάμενος, ὃ καὶ τὰ ἄλλα σώματα πάντ' ἔχει. ὥστ' εἰ τοῦ τόπου μηδὲν διαφέρει, τί   15

δεῖ ποιεῖν τόπον τοῖς σώμασιν παρὰ τὸν ἑκάστου ὄγκον, εἰ ἀπαθὲς ὁ ὄγκος; οὐδὲν γὰρ συμβάλλεται, εἰ ἕτερον περὶ αὐτὸν ἴσον διάστημα τοιοῦτον εἴη.

Context: refutation of the notion of void.

8–17   Having shown in 1–8 why void when entered must operate as place, Aristotle resumes his earlier attack (211b14–29) on this idea of place as the interval occupied by a body.

12, 13–14 **ἐν τῷ αὐτῷ**   Since this must mean 'in the same *place*', Aristotle appears to be overlooking his own demonstration (IV.3) that a place cannot itself be in a place.

6 Proof of the existence of void

A Lucretius 1.334–97

(1) quapropter locus est intactus inane vacansque.
quod si non esset, nulla ratione moveri   335
res possent; namque officium quod corporis exstat,
officere atque obstare, id in omni tempore adesset
omnibus; haud igitur quicquam procedere posset,
principium quoniam cedendi nulla daret res.
at nunc per maria ac terras sublimaque caeli   340
multa modis multis varia ratione moveri
cernimus ante oculos, quae, si non esset inane,
non tam sollicito motu privata carerent
quam genita omnino nulla ratione fuissent,
undique materies quoniam stipata quiesset.   345
(2) praeterea quamvis solidae res esse putentur,
hinc tamen esse licet raro cum corpore cernas.
in saxis ac speluncis permanat aquarum
liquidus umor et uberibus flent omnia guttis.
dissipat in corpus sese cibus omne animantum.   350
crescunt arbusta et fetus in tempore fundunt,
quod cibus in totas usque ab radicibus imis
per truncos ac per ramos diffunditur omnis.
inter saepta meant voces et clausa domorum
transvolitant, rigidum permanat frigus ad ossa,   355
quod, nisi inania sint, qua possent corpora quaeque
transire, haud ulla fieri ratione videres.
(3) denique cur alias aliis praestare videmus
pondere res rebus nilo maiore figura?
nam si tantundemst in lanae glomere quantum   360
corporis in plumbo est, tantundem pendere par est,
corporis officiumst quoniam premere omnia deorsum,
contra autem natura manet sine pondere inanis.

23

ergo quod magnumst aeque leviusque videtur,
nimirum plus esse sibi declarat inanis;   365
at contra gravius plus in se corporis esse
dedicat et multo vacui minus intus habere.
est igitur nimirum id quod ratione sagaci
quaerimus admixtum rebus, quod inane vocamus.
(4) illud in his rebus ne te deducere vero   370
possit, quod quidam fingunt, praecurrere cogor.
cedere squamigeris latices nitentibus aiunt
et liquidas aperire vias, quia post loca pisces
linquant, quo possint cedentes confluere undae.
sic alias quoque res inter se posse moveri   375
et mutare locum, quamvis sint omnia plena.
scilicet id falsa totum ratione receptumst.
nam quo squamigeri poterunt procedere tandem,
ni spatium dederint latices? concedere porro
quo poterunt undae, cum pisces ire nequibunt?   380
aut igitur motu privandumst corpora quaeque
aut esse admixtum dicundumst rebus inane
unde initum primum capiat res quaeque movendi.
(5) postremo duo de concursu corpora lata
si cita dissiliant, nempe aer omne necessest,   385
inter corpora quod fiat, possidat inane.
is porro quamvis circum celerantibus auris
confluat, haud poterit tamen uno tempore totum
compleri spatium; nam primum quemque necessest
occupet ille locum, deinde omnia possideantur.   390
quod si forte aliquis, cum corpora dissiluere,
tum putat id fieri quia se condenseat aer,
errat; nam vacuum tum fit quod non fuit ante
et repletur item vacuum quod constitit ante,
nec tali ratione potest denserier aer,   395
nec, si iam posset, sine inani posset, opinor,
ipse in se trahere et partis conducere in unum.

367 *vacui* Pontanus: *vacuum* vel *vacuim* codd.   389 *quemque* Pontanus: *quisque* codd.

Context: shortly after the proof, at 1.265–328, that microscopic bodies exist.

335–45   For the Eleatic counterpart of this argument, see Melissus 30 B 7.7 DK.

370–83   For the ἀντιπερίστασις theory attacked here, cf. Empedocles 31 A 35, B
17.34 DK, and ap. ps.-Ar. *MXG* 976b22–9; Plato, *Tim.* 80c; Aristotle, *Phys.* IV.7,
214a29–32; Strato, fr. 63 Wehrli; and Barnes, *The Presocratic philosophers* (1979),
chapter 19.

384–90   Experiments of this type were widely discussed in the 16th century, and opponents of void held that two perfectly flat contiguous surfaces would be impossible to separate.

391–7 These are difficult lines to interpret in detail, but the general point intended seems to be as follows. It may be alleged that the occupation of the newly created gap by air (*id*, 392) occurs *simultaneously* with the opening of that gap (*tum*, 392), because there is already compressed air between the two bodies, which has merely to expand as they separate. But against this, (a) you cannot compress air in this way [experiments, e.g. with inflated wineskins, would easily suggest this], and (b) if you could, the only explanation would be that prior to compression the air contained void gaps.

7 Secondary attributes

A Lucretius 1.445–82

(1) ergo praeter inane et corpora tertia per se 445
nulla potest rerum in numero natura relinqui,
nec quae sub sensus cadat ullo tempore nostros
nec ratione animi quam quisquam possit apisci.
(2) nam quaecumque cluent, aut his coniuncta duabus
rebus ea invenies aut horum eventa videbis. 450
(3) coniunctum est id quod nusquam sine permitiali
discidio potis est seiungi seque gregari,
pondus uti saxis, calor ignist, liquor aquai,
tactus corporibus cunctis, intactus inani.
(4) servitium contra paupertas divitiaeque, 455
libertas bellum concordia, cetera quorum
adventu manet incolumis natura abituque,
haec soliti sumus, ut par est, eventa vocare.
(5) tempus item per se non est, sed rebus ab ipsis
consequitur sensus, transactum quid sit in aevo, 460
tum quae res instet, quid porro deinde sequatur.
nec per se quemquam tempus sentire fatendumst
semotum ab rerum motu placidaque quiete.
(6) denique Tyndaridem raptam belloque subactas
Troiugenas gentis cum dicunt esse, videndumst 465
ne forte haec per se cogant nos esse fateri,
quando ea saecla hominum, quorum haec eventa fuerunt
irrevocabilis abstulerit iam praeterita aetas.
namque aliud terris, aliud regionibus ipsis
eventum dici poterit quodcumque erit actum. 470
denique materies si rerum nulla fuisset
nec locus ac spatium, res in quo quaeque geruntur,
numquam Tyndaridis forma conflatus amore

ignis Alexandri Phrygio sub pectore gliscens
clara accendisset saevi certamina belli,   475
nec clam durateus Troianis Pergama partu
inflammasset equus nocturno Graiugenarum;
perspicere ut possis res gestas funditus omnis
non ita uti corpus per se constare neque esse,
nec ratione cluere eadem qua constet inane,   480
sed magis ut merito possis eventa vocare
corporis atque loci, res in quo quaeque gerantur.

480 *cluere* Q¹: *fluere* O: *luere* QG

Context: see vol. 1 commentary.

449   *quaecumque cluent* might appear misleadingly to include body and void
themselves, but the phrase is presumably meant to represent ὅσα . . . κατηγορεῖται
σώματος, **B** 2.

coniuncta   These are argued in vol. 1 to be equivalent to Epicurus' τὰ ἀίδιον
συμβεβηκότα (or παρακολουθοῦντα) in **B**. It remains a possibility that, as usually
held, it translates just συμβεβηκότα, and that he takes this to *mean* permanent
attributes. But if so, we have to choose between Lucretius' and (**C**) Demetrius'
interpretations of Epicurus' terminology, and Lucretius' would be less consistent both
with Epicurus' usage in **B** and with the term's regular Greek meaning. Lucretius is
quite capable of coining a precise term where his Greek source lacks one (cf. *animus*,
14B, F), and it is fairer to guess that *coniunctum* is such a case: note that whereas for
eventum (= σύμπτωμα) he tells us that this is the standard term (458), there is no
comparable indication for *coniunctum*. See also note on **5A** 7–8.

464–82   Cf. Furley [168], 13–14. There is no good evidence to connect the
conclusion opposed by Lucretius with any ancient school's doctrine. Furley rightly
rejects a Stoic origin, and his own comparison with the Platonist argument for Forms
reported at Aristotle, *Metaph.* A.9, 990b14–15 provides at best a very tenuous parallel.
Indeed, treated as a doctrine of the continued *per se* existence of historical events like
the Trojan War, it sounds sophistical, and one might wonder why Epicurus did not
simply reply that the Trojan War does *not* exist now. However, treated (as in vol. 1,
37) as claiming continued existence for *facts about* the past, it presents a serious
philosophical point. Its source could be either an adversary or an inquiring mind
within Epicurus' own school. Facts about the past confront Epicurus with a more
serious challenge than other facts, because present facts can easily be analysed as
attributes of existing aggregates, and there are perhaps no facts about the future (see
20H–I).

469   Either the whole world, contrasted with specific locations like Troy and
Mycenae, or perhaps the world *qua* body, contrasted with places *qua* space. Cf.
Wellesley [199].

B Epicurus, *Ep. Hdt.* 68–73

(1) ἀλλὰ μὴν καὶ τὰ σχήματα καὶ τὰ χρώματα καὶ τὰ μεγέθη καὶ τὰ βάρη
καὶ ὅσα ἄλλα κατηγορεῖται σώματος ὡς ἀεὶ συμβεβηκότα – ἢ πᾶσιν ἢ τοῖς

ὁρατοῖς καὶ κατὰ τὴν αἴσθησιν αὐτοῖς γνωστοῖς – οὔθ' ὡς καθ' ἑαυτάς εἰσι
φύσεις δοξαστέον (οὐ γὰρ δυνατὸν ἐπινοῆσαι τοῦτο)· οὔθ' ὅλως ὡς οὐκ
εἰσίν· οὔθ' ὡς ἕτερ' ἄττα προσυπάρχοντα τούτῳ ἀσώματα· οὔθ' ὡς μόρια   5
τούτου, ἀλλ' ὡς τὸ ὅλον σῶμα καθόλου μὲν ⟨ἐκ⟩ τούτων πάντων τὴν
ἑαυτοῦ φύσιν ἔχον ἀίδιον οὐχ οἷόν τε εἶναι, συμπεφορημένων ὥσπερ ὅταν
ἐξ αὐτῶν τῶν ὄγκων μεῖζον ἄθροισμα συστῇ ἤτοι τῶν πρώτων ἢ τῶν τοῦ
ὅλου μεγεθῶν τοῦδέ τινος ἐλαττόνων, ἀλλὰ μόνον ὡς λέγω ἐκ τούτων
ἁπάντων τὴν ἑαυτοῦ φύσιν ἔχον ἀίδιον. (2) καὶ ἐπιβολὰς μὲν ἔχοντα ἰδίας   10
πάντα ταῦτά ἐστι καὶ διαλήψεις, συμπαρακολουθοῦντος δὲ τοῦ ἀθρόου καὶ
οὐθαμῇ ἀποσχιζομένου, ἀλλὰ κατὰ τὴν ἀθρόαν ἔννοιαν τοῦ σώματος
κατηγορίαν εἰληφότος. (3) καὶ μὴν καὶ τοῖς σώμασι συμπίπτει πολλάκις
καὶ οὐκ ἀίδιον παρακολουθεῖ ἃ οὔτ' ἐν τοῖς ἀοράτοις ἔσται οὔτε ἀσώματα.
ὥστε δὴ κατὰ τὴν πλείστην φορὰν τούτῳ τῷ ὀνόματι χρώμενοι φανερὰ   15
ποιοῦμεν τὰ συμπτώματα οὔτε τὴν τοῦ ὅλου φύσιν ἔχειν, ὃ συλλαβόντες
κατὰ τὸ ἀθρόον σῶμα προσαγορεύομεν, οὔτε τὴν τῶν ἀίδιον παρακολου-
θούντων ὧν ἄνευ σῶμα οὐ δύνατον νοεῖσθαι. (4) κατ' ἐπιβολὰς δ' ἄν τινας
παρακολουθοῦντος τοῦ ἀθρόου ἕκαστα προσαγορευθείη, ἀλλ' ὅτε δήποτε
ἕκαστα συμβαίνοντα θεωρεῖται, οὐκ ἀίδιον τῶν συμπτωμάτων παρακο-   20
λουθούντων. (5) καὶ οὐκ ἐξελατέον ἐκ τοῦ ὄντος ταύτην τὴν ἐνάργειαν, ὅτι
οὐκ ἔχει τὴν τοῦ ὅλου φύσιν ᾧ συμβαίνει, ὃ δὴ καὶ σῶμα προσαγορεύομεν,
οὐδὲ τὴν τῶν ἀίδιον παρακολουθούντων. οὐδ' αὖ καθ' αὑτὰ νομιστέον –
οὐδὲ γὰρ τοῦτο διανοητὸν οὔτ' ἐπὶ τούτων οὔτ' ἐπὶ τῶν ἀίδιον συμβεβηκότων. ἀλλ' ὅπερ καὶ φαίνεται συμπτώματα πάντα τὰ σωμάτων   25
νομιστέον, καὶ οὐκ ἀίδιον παρακολουθοῦντα οὐδ' αὖ φύσεως καθ' ἑαυτὰ
τάγμα ἔχοντα. ἀλλ' ὃν τρόπον αὐτὴ ἡ αἴσθησις τὴν ἰδιότητα ποιεῖ
θεωρεῖται. (6) καὶ μὴν καὶ τόδε γε δεῖ προσκατανοῆσαι σφοδρῶς. τὸν γὰρ
δὴ χρόνον οὐ ζητητέον ὥσπερ καὶ τὰ λοιπὰ ὅσα ἐν ὑποκειμένῳ ζητοῦμεν
ἀνάγοντες ἐπὶ τὰς βλεπομένας παρ' ἡμῖν αὐτοῖς προλήψεις, ἀλλ' αὐτὸ τὸ   30
ἐνάργημα καθ' ὃ τὸν πολὺν ἢ ὀλίγον χρόνον ἀναφωνοῦμεν, συγγενικῶς
τοῦτο περιφέροντες, ἀναλογιστέον. καὶ οὔτε διαλέκτους ὡς βελτίους
μεταληπτέον, ἀλλ' αὐταῖς ταῖς ὑπαρχούσαις κατ' αὐτοῦ χρηστέον· οὔτε
ἄλλο τι κατ' αὐτοῦ κατηγορητέον ὡς τὴν αὐτὴν οὐσίαν ἔχον τῷ ἰδιώματι
τούτῳ – καὶ γὰρ τοῦτο ποιοῦσί τινες – ἀλλὰ μόνον ᾧ συμπλέκομεν τὸ   35
ἴδιον τοῦτο καὶ παραμετροῦμεν μάλιστα ἐπιλογιστέον. καὶ γὰρ τοῦτο οὐκ
ἀποδείξεως προσδεῖται ἀλλ' ἐπιλογισμοῦ, ὅτι ταῖς ἡμέραις καὶ ταῖς νυξὶ
συμπλέκομεν καὶ τοῖς τούτων μέρεσιν, ὡσαύτως δὲ καὶ τοῖς πάθεσι καὶ
ταῖς ἀπαθείαις καὶ κινήσεσι καὶ στάσεσιν, ἴδιόν τι σύμπτωμα, περὶ ταῦτα
πάλιν αὐτὸ τοῦτο ἐννοοῦντες, καθ' ὃ χρόνον ὀνομάζομεν.   40

---

2 ὡς ἀεὶ συμβεβηκότα scripsimus: ὡς ἂν εἰς ταῦτα βεβηκότα codd.: ὡσανεὶ συμβεβηκότα Galesius: ὡς
ἂν ἀεὶ συμβεβηκότα Bignone   5 οὔθ' ὡς¹ Gassendi: ὡς οὔθ' codd.   ἕτερ' ἄττα Usener: ἕτερα τὰ
codd.   6 μὲν ⟨ἐκ⟩ Meibom: ἐκ alii   7 τε codd.: δὲ Schneider   συμπεφορημένων BP: -ον
FP(corr.)   14 παρακολουθεῖ ἃ scripsimus: -θει B: -θεῖν FP: -θεῖ, ἃ γ' Bignone   ἔσται Usener: καὶ
codd.   25 σωμάτων Sedley: -τα codd.: -τος Usener   34 ἔχον Usener: ἔχοντος codd.

Epicurean physics

Context: immediately following **14A**.

2 ὡς ἀεὶ συμβεβηκότα Some emendation seems necessary, and the favoured ὡσανεί, 'as if', is scarcely appropriate. Bignone's, which we adopt here (apart from his superfluous ἄν), is greatly superior. Without it, this would be the only point in the passage at which the permanence of permanent attributes was not made explicit. Yet Epicurus can hardly expect the idea of permanence to be already implicit in συμβεβηκότα: not only is this at variance with Greek usage of the term, but he himself uses συμβαίνειν of impermanent attributes at 20 and 22.

3 αὐτοῖς may well be corrupt, but we have let it stand for lack of a plausible emendation.

6–10 ἀλλ' ὡς κτλ. should be read as qualifying οὔθ' ὡς μόρια τούτου by explaining in what sense a body does not (καθόλου μὲν . . .), and in what sense it does (ἀλλὰ μόνον . . .), consist of its permanent attributes. For this use of ἀλλά, cf. 33. Construe οὐχ οἷόν τε εἶναι (7) with ἔχον in 7 and 10, 'it is not able to have': for the construction, a regular one in Epicurus, cf. 10–11.

9 'only in the way I am describing' must principally refer forward to 11–13. Permanent attributes are conceptual parts, not material parts.

11 τοῦ ἀθρόου refers to the complex of permanent attributes (contrast ἄθροισμα, 8, an aggregate of material parts). For this usage, see S.E., *M.* 11.437, and cf. Plato, *Tht.* 157b–c. For Sextus' criticism of the idea, see *M.* 10.240.

36–7 For ἐπιλογισμός, see note on **21V1**.

C Sextus Empiricus, *M.* 10.219–27

(1) Ἐπίκουρος δέ, ὡς αὐτὸν Δημήτριος ὁ Λάκων ἐξηγεῖται, τὸν χρόνον σύμπτωμα συμπτωμάτων εἶναι λέγει, παρεπόμενον ἡμέραις τε καὶ νυξὶ καὶ ὥραις καὶ πάθεσι καὶ ἀπαθείαις καὶ κινήσεσι καὶ μοναῖς. πάντα γὰρ ταῦτα συμπτώματά ἐστι τισὶ συμβεβηκότα, καὶ ὁ χρόνος πᾶσι τούτοις συμπαρεπόμενος εἰκότως ἂν λεχθείη σύμπτωμα συμπτωμάτων. (2)   5 καθόλου γάρ, ἵνα μικρὸν ἄνωθεν προλάβωμεν εἰς τὴν τοῦ λεγομένου παρακολούθησιν, τῶν ὄντων τὰ μέν τινα καθ' ἑαυτὰ ὑφέστηκεν, τὰ δὲ περὶ τοῖς καθ' ἑαυτὰ ὑφεστῶσι θεωρεῖται. καὶ καθ' ἑαυτὰ μὲν ὑφέστηκε πράγματα οἷον αἱ οὐσίαι (ὡς τὸ σῶμα καὶ κενόν), περὶ δὲ τοῖς καθ' ἑαυτὰ ὑφεστῶσι θεωρεῖται τὰ καλούμενα παρ' αὐτοῖς συμβεβηκότα. (3) τούτων   10 δὲ τῶν συμβεβηκότων τὰ μέν ἐστιν ἀχώριστα τῶν οἷς συμβέβηκεν, τὰ δὲ χωρίζεσθαι τούτων πέφυκεν. ἀχώριστα μὲν οὖν ἐστι τῶν οἷς συμβέβηκεν ὥσπερ ἡ ἀντιτυπία μὲν τοῦ σώματος, εἶξις δὲ τοῦ κενοῦ· οὔτε γὰρ σῶμα δυνατόν ἐστί ποτε νοῆσαι χωρὶς τῆς ἀντιτυπίας οὔτε τὸ κενὸν χωρὶς εἴξεως, ἀλλ' ἀίδιον ἑκατέρου συμβεβηκός, τοῦ μὲν τὸ ἀντιτυπεῖν, τοῦ δὲ τὸ   15 εἴκειν. (4) οὐκ ἀχώριστα δέ ἐστι τῶν οἷς συμβέβηκε καθάπερ ἡ κίνησις καὶ ἡ μονή. τὰ γὰρ συγκριτικὰ τῶν σωμάτων οὔτε κινεῖται διὰ παντὸς ἀνηρεμήτως οὔτ' ἀκινητίζει διὰ παντός, ἀλλὰ ποτὲ μὲν συμβεβηκυῖαν ἔχει τὴν κίνησιν, ποτὲ δὲ τὴν μονήν, καίπερ τῆς ἀτόμου, ὅτε καθ' ἑαυτήν ἐστιν, ἀεικινήτου καθεστώσης. ἢ γὰρ κενῷ πελάζειν ὀφείλει ἢ σώματι· εἴτε δὲ   20 κενῷ πελάζοι, διὰ τὴν εἶξιν φέρεται δι' αὐτοῦ, εἴτε σώματι, διὰ τὴν

28

ἀντιτυπίαν ἀποπαλτικῶς ποιεῖται τὴν ἀπ᾽ αὐτοῦ κίνησιν. (5) συμπτώματα
οὖν ταῦτ᾽ ἐστιν οἷς χρόνος παρέπεται, φημὶ δὲ τήν τε ἡμέραν καὶ νύκτα καὶ
ὥραν καὶ τὰ πάθη καὶ τὰς ἀπαθείας, κινήσεις τε καὶ μονάς. ἥ τε γὰρ ἡμέρα
καὶ νὺξ τοῦ περιέχοντος ἀέρος εἰσὶ συμπτώματα, ὧν ἡ μὲν ἡμέρα κατὰ τὸν   25
ἐξ ἡλίου φωτισμὸν συμβαίνει, ἡ δὲ νὺξ κατὰ φωτισμοῦ στέρησιν τοῦ ἐξ
ἡλίου ἐπιγίνεται. ἡ δὲ ὥρα ἤτοι τῆς ἡμέρας ἢ τῆς νυκτὸς μέρος
καθεστηκυῖα πάλιν σύμπτωμα γίνεται τοῦ ἀέρος, ὥσπερ καὶ ἡ ἡμέρα καὶ ἡ
νύξ. ἀντιπαρεκτείνεται δὲ πάσῃ ἡμέρᾳ καὶ πάσῃ νυκτὶ καὶ ὥρᾳ ὁ χρόνος·
παρ᾽ ἣν αἰτίαν μακρά τις ἢ βραχεῖα λέγεται ἡμέρα καὶ νύξ, φερομένων   30
ἡμῶν ἐπὶ τὸν ταύτῃ συμβεβηκότα χρόνον. τά τε πάθη καὶ αἱ ἀπάθειαι ἤτοι
ἀλγηδόνες ἢ ἡδοναὶ ἐτύγχανον, διὰ δὲ τοῦτο οὐκ οὐσίαι τινὲς καθειστήκει-
σαν, ἀλλὰ συμπτώματα τῶν πασχόντων ἤτοι ἡστικῶς ἢ ἀλγεινῶς, καὶ
συμπτώματα οὐκ ἄχρονα. πρὸς τούτοις καὶ ἡ κίνησις, ἔτι δὲ ἡ μονή, ὡς
ἤδη παρεστήσαμεν, τῶν σωμάτων ἐστὶ συμπτώματα καὶ οὐ χωρὶς χρόνου·   35
τὴν γοῦν ὀξύτητα καὶ βραδυτῆτα τῆς κινήσεως, ἔτι δὲ τὴν πλείονα καὶ
ἐλάττονα μονὴν χρόνῳ καταμετροῦμεν. ἀλλὰ γὰρ ἐκ τούτων φανερόν ὅτι ὁ
Ἐπίκουρος ἀσώματον οἴεται τὸν χρόνον ὑπάρχειν, οὐ παραπλησίως δὲ τοῖς Στωικοῖς·
ἐκεῖνοι μὲν γάρ, ὡς λέλεκται, ἀσώματόν τι καθ᾽ αὑτὸ νοούμενον ὑπεστήσαντο τὸν χρόνον,
Ἐπίκουρος δὲ συμβεβηκός τισιν.   40

Context: does time exist? Cf. *PH* 3.137. For Sextus' counterargument, see *M.* 10.238–
47.

1 ἐξηγεῖται All of 1–37 is clearly Demetrius' exegesis of Epicurus. The tentative
language of 5 shows that σύμπτωμα συμπτωμάτων is his proposed interpretation of
Epicurus, not a verbatim quotation, and the rest is in effect an exegesis of **B** in support
of the same interpretation.
37–40 Sextus' own comment, tying this passage up with the preceding one, **27D**.
For the Stoics, see note on **51F** 5–6.

D Polystratus, *De contemptu* 23.26–26.23

(1) ἢ δοκεῖ τ[οί] | τ[ί]ς ἄν σοι ἐκ [τ]ῶν προει|ρημένων λόγων οὐ | κα[κο]πα-
θεῖν ὃ λέγομεν, | ἀλλὰ μᾶλλον π[ε]ιθὼ λα|βεῖν, ὡς ψευδῶς νομί|ζεται τὰ
καλὰ κ[α]ὶ αἰσχρὰ | καὶ ὅσα νομίζε[ταί] | πο|τ᾽ ἄλλα, ἐπειδὴ ο[ὐ]χ
ὥσπερ | χρυσὸς καὶ τὰ το[ι]αῦτα | πανταχοῦ ἐστιν ταῦτά; | (2) ἐμποδὼν
γὰρ ἑκάστωι | δήπου συνορᾶν, ὡς οὐδὲ | μεῖζον καὶ ἐλαττο[ν] τὸ | αὐτὸ   5
πανταχοῦ [κ]αὶ πρὸς | πάντα τὰ μεγέ[θ]η ὁρᾶτα[ι, | οὐδ᾽] ὡσαύ[τως τὸ |
ἡδὺ [καὶ] τὸ ἀηδὲς . . . | ὡσαύτως [δὲ καὶ ἐ]πὶ τῶν | βαρυτέρων καὶ
κουφο|τέρων συμβέβηκεν, | καὶ ἐπὶ τῶν λοι[π]ῶν | δ᾽ ἁπλῶ[ς] δυνά-
με[ν]ων | τὸν αὐτὸν τρόπον ἔ|χει. οὔτε γὰρ ὑγιεινὰ | ταὐτὰ πᾶσιν ὑπάρ-
χει | οὔτε θρεπτικὰ ἢ φθαρ|τικὰ οὔτε τὰ τούτοις | ἐναντία, ἀλλὰ ταῦτὰ   10
τοὺς | μὲν ὑγιάζει καὶ τρέ|φει, τοὺς δ᾽ ἐκ τ[ῶν ἐ]ναν|τίων διατίθησιν. (3)
ὥσ|τε ἢ καὶ ταῦτα πάντα φατέ|ον ψευδῆ εἶναι, ἃ περι|φανῶς ἕκαστος
θεωρεῖ ὃ | ἐργάζεται, ἤ, μὴ βουλό|μενον ἀναισχυντεῖν | καὶ μάχεσθαι τοῖς
φανε|ροῖς, οὐδὲ τὰ καλὰ καὶ τὰ | αἰσχρὰ ἀρτέον ὡς ψευδῶς | νομιζόμενα,

Epicurean physics

ὅτι οὐ πᾶσι ταὐτά ἐστιν ὥσπερ | λίθος ἢ χρυ[σὸ]ς ἢ [ἄλλ]ο | [τι τῶν   1ͻ
τοιούτων ... (4) τ]ὰ πρό[ς τ]ι κατηγ[ορού]||μενα οὐ τ[ὴ]ν αὐτὴν [χ]ώ|ραν
ἔχει τοῖς κατὰ τ[ὴ]ν | ἰδίαν φύσιν λεγ[ο]μένοις | [κ]αὶ μὴ πρό[ς] τι, οὐδὲ
τὰ | μὲν ἀληθῶς ὑπάρχει, | τὰ δ' οὔ. ὥστε τὸ ἀξιοῦν | ταὐτὰ τούτοις
συμβε|βηκένα[[ε]]ι [ε]ὔηθες, ἢ τὰ | μὲν εἶναι, τὰ δὲ μή· καὶ | οὐθὲν
δια[φ]έρει ἀπὸ τῶν|δε τάδε ἀνασκευάζειν | ἢ ἀπὸ τῶνδε τάδε. ἀλ|[λ'   2ͼ
ὁμοίως εὐή]θης ὁ νομί[ζων δεῖν, ἐπειδὴ τὸ μεῖ[ζον καὶ βαρύτερον ἢ
λευ|κότερον καὶ γλυκύτε|ρον τινός ἐστ[ι] μεῖζον, | τινὸς δὲ ἔ[λ]αττον καὶ
βα|ρύτερον, καὶ ἐπὶ τῶν λοι|πῶν ὡσαύτως, καθ' αὑτὸ | δὲ τούτω[ν] οὐθὲν
πέπον|θεν ὅπ[ε]ρ π[ρὸ]ς ἄλλο, οὕτω | καὶ τὸν [λ]ίθο[ν] κα[ὶ] τὸν χρυ|σὸν καὶ
τὰ τ[οι]αῦτα δεῖν, | εἴπ[ερ κατ' ἀλή]θειαν [ἦν, | τῶν αὐτῶν παθῶν]   2
ἐπή[βο]λα γίνεσθαι, ὥστε μὴ πᾶσι] | κ[αὶ πανταχοῦ εἶναι λί]|θο[ν], καὶ
πρ[ὸς μέν τι]|να χρυσόν, πρὸς δ' ἄλλον | τι[ν]ὰ τὴν ἐναντίαν φύ|σιν ἔχειν,
ἐπεὶ δ' οὐκ ἔχει | οὕτως, ψευδῶς ἤδη φάσ|κων ταῦτα νομίζεσθα[ι] | οὐκ
[ὄ]ντα.

(For full apparatus, see Indelli's edition)

Context: an attack on the use of moral relativism to eliminate all ordinary conceptions
of value.

The identity of the opponents is a matter of debate (see introduction to Indelli's
edition), but we favour an exclusively Academic target (see Sedley [142]), which, in
view of Polystratus' mid-third-century date, would mean the circle of Arcesilaus and
Lacydes. For Epicureans on moral relativism, cf. also 22N 6–7. On the present
passage, see especially Striker [640].

1–2 κα[κο]παθεῖν δ λέγομεν I.e. to be upset by the perversity of the doctrine
described, and distrusted by one's fellow men.

8 Atoms

A Epicurus, Ep. Hdt. 40–1

(1) καὶ μὴν καὶ τῶν σωμάτων τὰ μέν ἐστι συγκρίσεις, τὰ δ' ἐξ ὧν αἱ
συγκρίσεις πεποίηνται. (2) ταῦτα δέ ἐστιν ἄτομα καὶ ἀμετάβλητα – εἴπερ
μὴ μέλλει πάντα εἰς τὸ μὴ ὂν φθαρήσεσθαι ἀλλ' ἰσχύοντα ὑπομενεῖν ἐν ταῖς
διαλύσεσι τῶν συγκρίσεων – πλήρη τὴν φύσιν ὄντα καὶ οὐκ ἔχοντα ὅπῃ ἢ
ὅπως διαλυθήσεται. ὥστε τὰς ἀρχὰς ἀτόμους ἀναγκαῖον εἶναι σωμάτων   5
φύσεις.

4 ὄντα καὶ Meibom: ὅταν codd.

Context: immediately following 5A.

1–2 Imitated at Lucretius 1.483–4: corpora sunt porro partim primordia rerum |
partim concilio quae constant principiorum. But Epicurus' own formulation has greater
elegance and strength. He starts with the undeniable existence of compounds,
proceeds to the notion of components, which that of compounds seems to entail, then
sets out the necessary conditions for being a bona fide component. Lucretius, while

superficially echoing Epicurus' words, in fact starts out with an undefended and dogmatic assertion about components.

B Lucretius 1.503–98 (with omissions)

(1) principio quoniam duplex natura duarum
dissimilis rerum longe constare repertast,
corporis atque loci, res in quo quaeque geruntur,   505
esse utramque sibi per se puramque necessest.
nam quacumque vacat spatium, quod inane vocamus,
corpus ea non est; qua porro cumque tenet se
corpus, ea vacuum nequaquam constat inane.
sunt igitur solida ac sine inani corpora prima . . .   510
(2) haec neque dissolui plagis extrinsecus icta
possunt nec porro penitus penetrata retexi
nec ratione queunt alia temptata labare;   530
id quod iam supra tibi paulo ostendimus ante.
nam neque collidi sine inani posse videtur
quicquam nec frangi nec findi in bina secando
nec capere umorem neque item manabile frigus
nec penetralem ignem, quibus omnia conficiuntur.   535
et quo quaeque magis cohibit res intus inane,
tam magis his rebus penitus temptata labascit.
ergo si solida ac sine inani corpora prima
sunt ita uti docui, sint haec aeterna necessest.
(3) praeterea nisi materies aeterna fuisset,   540
antehac ad nilum penitus res quaeque redissent
de niloque renata forent quaecumque videmus.
at quoniam supra docui nil posse creari
de nilo neque quod genitum est ad nil revocari,
esse immortali primordia corpore debent,   545
dissolui quo quaeque supremo tempore possint,
materies ut suppeditet rebus reparandis.
sunt igitur solida primordia simplicitate
nec ratione queunt alia servata per aevum
ex infinito iam tempore res reparare . . .   550
(4) denique iam quoniam generatim reddita finis   585
crescendi rebus constat vitamque tenendi,
et quid quaeque queant per foedera naturai,
quid porro nequeant, sancitum quandoquidem exstat,
nec commutatur quicquam, quin omnia constant
usque adeo, variae volucres ut in ordine cunctae
ostendant maculas generalis corpore inesse,   590

immutabili' materiae quoque corpus habere
debent nimirum. nam si primordia rerum
commutari aliqua possent ratione revicta,
incertum quoque iam constet quid possit oriri,
quid nequeat, finita potestas denique cuique   595
quanam sit ratione atque alte terminus haerens,
nec totiens possent generatim saecla referre
naturam mores victum motusque parentum.

Context: shortly after **7A**.
531 This probably qualifies the whole argument of 528–35, and refers back to
1.221–4.

9 Minimal parts

A Epicurus, *Ep. Hdt.* 56–9

(1) πρὸς δὲ τούτοις οὐ δεῖ νομίζειν ἐν τῷ ὡρισμένῳ σώματι ἀπείρους ὄγκους εἶναι οὐδ᾽ ὁπηλίκους οὖν. (2) ὥστε οὐ μόνον τὴν εἰς ἄπειρον τομὴν ἐπὶ τοὐλαττον ἀναιρετέον, ἵνα μὴ πάντα ἀσθενῆ ποιῶμεν καὶ ταῖς περιλήψεσι τῶν ἀθρόων εἰς τὸ μὴ ὂν ἀναγκαζώμεθα τὰ ὄντα θλίβοντες καταναλίσκειν, (3) ἀλλὰ καὶ τὴν μετάβασιν μὴ νομιστέον γίνεσθαι ἐν τοῖς   5
ὡρισμένοις εἰς ἄπειρον μηδ᾽ ἐ⟨πὶ⟩ τοὐλαττον. (4) οὔτε γὰρ ὅπως, ἐπειδὰν ἅπαξ τις εἴπῃ ὅτι ἄπειροι ὄγκοι ἔν τινι ὑπάρχουσιν ἢ ὁπηλίκοι οὖν, ἔστι νοῆσαι· (5) πῶς τ᾽ ἂν ἔτι τοῦτο πεπερασμένον εἴη τὸ μέγεθος; πηλίκοι γάρ τινες δῆλον ὡς οἱ ἄπειροί εἰσιν ὄγκοι καὶ οὗτοι· ἐξ ὧν, ὁπηλίκοι ἄν ποτε ὦσιν, ἄπειρον ἂν ἦν καὶ τὸ μέγεθος. (6) ἄκρον τε ἔχοντος τοῦ   10
πεπερασμένου διαληπτόν, εἰ μὴ καὶ καθ᾽ ἑαυτὸ θεωρητόν, οὐκ ἔστι μὴ οὐ καὶ τὸ ἑξῆς τούτου τοιοῦτον νοεῖν καὶ οὕτω κατὰ τὸ ἑξῆς εἰς τοὔμπροσθεν βαδίζοντα εἰς τὸ ἄπειρον ὑπάρχειν κατὰ τοσοῦτον ἀφικνεῖσθαι τῇ ἐννοίᾳ. (7) τό τε ἐλάχιστον τὸ ἐν τῇ αἰσθήσει δεῖ κατανοεῖν ὅτι οὔτε τοιοῦτόν ἐστιν οἷον τὸ τὰς μεταβάσεις ἔχον οὔτε πάντῃ πάντως ἀνόμοιον, ἀλλ᾽ ἔχον μέν   15
τινα κοινότητα τῶν μεταβατῶν, διάληψιν δὲ μερῶν οὐκ ἔχον· ἀλλ᾽ ὅταν διὰ τὴν τῆς κοινότητος προσεμφέρειαν οἰηθῶμεν διαλήψεσθαί τι αὐτοῦ, τὸ μὲν ἐπιτάδε, τὸ δὲ ἐπέκεινα, τὸ ἴσον ἡμῖν δεῖ προσπίπτειν. (8) ἑξῆς τε θεωροῦμεν ταῦτα ἀπὸ τοῦ πρώτου καταρχόμενοι καὶ οὐκ ἐν τῷ αὐτῷ, οὐδὲ μέρεσι μερῶν ἁπτόμενα, ἀλλ᾽ ἢ ἐν τῇ ἰδιότητι τῇ ἑαυτῶν τὰ μεγέθη   20
καταμετροῦντα, τὰ πλείω πλεῖον καὶ τὰ ἐλάττω ἔλαττον. (9) ταύτῃ τῇ ἀναλογίᾳ νομιστέον καὶ τὸ ἐν τῇ ἀτόμῳ ἐλάχιστον κεχρῆσθαι· μικρότητι γὰρ ἐκεῖνο δῆλον ὡς διαφέρει τοῦ κατὰ τὴν αἴσθησιν θεωρουμένου, ἀναλογίᾳ δὲ τῇ αὐτῇ κέχρηται. ἐπεί περ καὶ ὅτι μέγεθος ἔχει ἡ ἄτομος, κατὰ τὴν ⟨τῶν⟩ ἐνταῦθα ἀναλογίαν κατηγορήσαμεν, μικρόν τι μόνον   25
μακρὰν ἐκβαλόντες. (10) ἔτι τε τὰ ἐλάχιστα καὶ ἀμιγῆ πέρατα δεῖ νομίζειν τῶν μηκῶν τὸ καταμέτρημα ἐξ αὐτῶν πρώτων τοῖς μείζοσι καὶ ἐλάττοσι

32

παρασκευάζοντα τῇ διὰ λόγου θεωρίᾳ ἐπὶ τῶν ἀοράτων. (11) ἡ γὰρ κοινότης ἡ ὑπάρχουσα αὐτοῖς πρὸς τὰ μετάβολα ἱκανὴ τὸ μέχρι τούτου συντελέσαι, (12) συμφόρησιν δὲ ἐκ τούτων κίνησιν ἐχόντων οὐχ οἷόν τε γίνεσθαι. 30

4 ἀθρόων BP: ἀτόμων F   6 μηδ' ἐ⟨πὶ⟩ Gassendi   9 ἐξ ὧν om. B   10 ἔχοντος Gassendi: -ες codd.   13 κατὰ τοσοῦτον Sedley: κατὰ τοιοῦτον codd.; καὶ τὸ τοιοῦτον Mühll: κατὰ τοῦτον Furley: κατὰ ⟨τὸ⟩ τοιοῦτον Schneider   25 ⟨τῶν⟩ Usener   26 μακρὰν Usener: μακρὸν codd.   ἀμιγῆ codd.: ἀμερῆ Arnim   29 μετάβολα Furley: ἀμετάβολα codd.

Context: immediately after 12A.

2–5   Some scholars see an argument for minima here, perhaps encouraged by the 'conceptual' connotations of ταῖς περιλήψεσι in 3–4 to expect 'theoretical' indivisibility. But this latter expression, although convenient, has no counterpart in the ancient discussions of divisibility. τομή must be that which ἄτομα do not admit, and the argument that follows merely repeats the one for atoms at 8A.

4   τῶν ἀθρόων   See 7B 11, with note.

6   οὔτε   Best taken as co-ordinate with τ' in 8 and with τε in 10, providing three arguments for theoretical indivisibility.   ὅπως   Sc. μετάβασις ἂν γένοιτο, i.e. alluding back to 5–6 rather than forward to ἄπειροι ὄγκοι κτλ. in 7. Only on this reading can 6–7 add anything new – effectively the Zenonian dichotomy argument against motion.

9   B's omission of ἐξ ὧν, endorsed by most editors, was natural once καὶ had been taken to start a new sentence. But the repunctuation adopted here is the easier option, and ἐξ ὧν, 'consisting of which', adds to the clarity of the argument.

13   κατὰ τοσοῦτον   Mühll's καὶ τὸ τοιοῦτον would yield 'arrive in thought at the infinity of even a thing of this kind' (viz. something finite), which would make the argument a mere restatement of 8–10, as well as involving an unfamiliar use of ἀφικνεῖσθαι. 'Reach infinity' must surely be retained, to provide a distinct argument. Schneider's κατὰ ⟨τὸ⟩ τοιοῦτον might mean either 'in such a way', which would merely repeat the sense of οὕτω (12); or 'by means of that which is of this kind', echoing τοιοῦτον at 12, for which one would rather expect κατὰ τὰ τοιαῦτα. Furley's κατὰ τοῦτον, 'according to this opponent', referring back to τις in 7, is more attractive. But the reading adopted above requires even less alteration to the text and introduces a qualification, 'to that extent', which might well be added by way of apology for the extravagant phrase 'reach infinity'.

14–24   The suggestion that Diodorus (fr. 9 Giannantoni) had anticipated Epicurus' use of the sensible minimum in this context (Sedley [11], 86–7, Denyer [209], 36–7) is convincingly opposed by Sorabji [22], 345–7.

18–21   How do minima combine? Konstan [206] has suggested that the question is meant to be an illegitimate one because minima are only conceivable as parts in the first place. So C 1 appears to say, but that cannot be Epicurus' point here because the claim is being explained with regard to sensible minima, which are separable (28–30). The interpretation adopted in vol. 1, that it is ἐξῆς which expresses the way in which minima combine, is in most essentials that of Sorabji [22], 372–5 (although it may be doubted whether he is right that S.E., M. 10.120 shows Diodorus to have anticipated the theory). If Epicurus is conceding that minima do not 'touch' in the technical Aristotelian sense, he should strictly have no place for touch between separate bodies.

Epicurean physics

They could only touch if their extremities touched, and for Epicurus extremities are minima. This would have the advantage of answering a notorious puzzle, why two atoms should not coalesce simply by becoming perfectly adjacent with no intervening void: mere juxtaposition could never cause them to share an extremity in the way in which, say, the two halves of an atom do; an extremity is essentially and inseparably the extremity of some body (C 599ff.; cf. Konstan [206], 407). However, the tangible/ intangible antithesis for body and void (see 5) may suggest that he was not prepared to dispense with the notion of touch in all contexts. (*On touch* is the title of one of his lost works, D.L. 10.28, although it may have dealt with touch as a *sense*.)

24–6   The reference is to **12D** 1. There size is attributed to atoms without explicit argument but implicitly because it is one of the inseparable characteristics of body, as analogy with sensible body might be held to show. Furley [204], 23–4 sees the reference as being to **12B** 1 and **12A**, but these give arguments which only concern the *variety* of atomic shapes and sizes, and which cannot be called analogical.

26 ἀμιγῆ   Those who emend to ἀμερῆ may well be right. τὰ ἐλάχιστα καὶ ἀμερῆ is, for example, Diodorus' standard expression for his minima (cf.11i). On the other hand, ἀμερῆ, while a standard term in the doxographers (cf. **11F, G**), occurs nowhere else in Epicurus' own text. And the transmitted reading is not too inappropriate to retain: minima must, as a matter of fact, be uncompounded as well as partless. πέρατα   This should not, as often, be taken predicatively, 'think of the minima . . . *as* limits'. Whatever point is being made here is established by the analogy with the sensible minimum, as 28–30 reminds us, and sensible minima are *not* necessarily limits. They have nowhere been said to be so, and they differ from real minima precisely in their capacity for independent movement (28–31; see further, vol. 1, 43, and cf. note on **B**).

30–1   Konstan [206], 403–7, suggests that this point is borrowed from Aristotle, *Phys.* VI.1, which he takes to have shown that partless items, although properly regarded as parts of magnitudes, cannot *become* parts. But Aristotle's emphasis there is, we think, rather that partless items, although properly regarded as parts of magnitudes, cannot be *constituent* parts of them; and Epicurus is committed to opposing that contention. The interpretation offered in vol. 1, 43–4, where the thesis is connected instead with *Phys.* VI.10, may raise the objection that Epicurus adopted an alternative account of a minimum's motion from the same chapter, that it 'has moved' but never 'is moving', and that he would hardly need both solutions. But that doctrine is not in evidence in *Ep. Hdt.*, and probably represents a later development in Epicurus' thought under the influence of Diodorus: see vol. 1, 51–2.

B Lucretius 1.746–52

(1) deinde quod omnino finem non esse secandis
corporibus faciunt neque pausam stare fragori
(2) nec prorsum in rebus minimum consistere quicquam;
cum videamus id extremum cuiusque cacumen
esse quod ad sensus nostros minimum esse videtur,   750

34

conicere ut possis ex hoc, quae cernere non quis
extremum quod habent, minimum consistere ⟨in illis⟩.

752 ⟨*in illis*⟩ Munro: ⟨*menti*⟩ Furley

Context: criticism of the four-element theory of Empedocles and his 'inferior'
successors.

746–8 The distinction between physical indivisibles (atoms) and minima is
exactly that made in **A 2–3**.

749–52 This is the one piece of evidence to suggest that the analogy with the
sensible minimum is an independent proof of the actual existence of the 'minimum in
the atom' (cf. vol. 1, 42). Perhaps in Lucretius' Epicurean source the analogy was cited
not as the principal proof but as a confirmatory illustration (cf. **17**), and it will then be
Lucretius' selectivity that has given it this false emphasis. (Cf. his misleading selection
of arguments at 5.546–91, as compared with Epicurus, *Ep. Pyth.* 91, on which see
Sedley [105], 48–52.) What the analogy primarily offers is a clear conception of *how*
minima could perform the function which the Zenonian arguments of **A 4–6** and **C 3**
show they must perform. Lucretius' word *conicere* (751) may even show some grasp of
the point: his only other comparable use of it is at 2.121, where it is used precisely of
conceiving by analogy with the perceptible some independently proven fact about the
microscopic.

The passage also differs from **A** in making the sensible minimum explicitly an
'extremity' or 'limit'. This is not problematic. Normally in dividing a sensible
magnitude into visible minima one will indeed isolate the first of these as an extremity
of it, and that is all that the present passage requires. The difference is just that a
sensible minimum is not, like a real minimum, *essentially* the extremity of something
else: cf. **A 26**, with note.

C Lucretius 1.599–634

(1) tum porro quoniam est extremum quodque cacumen
corporis illius quod nostri cernere sensus   600
iam nequeunt, id nimirum sine partibus exstat
et minima constat natura nec fuit umquam
per se secretum neque posthac esse valebit,
alterius quoniamst ipsum pars primaque et una,
inde aliae atque aliae similes ex ordine partes   605
agmine condenso naturam corporis explent,
quae quoniam per se nequeunt constare, necessest
haerere unde queant nulla ratione revelli.
(2) sunt igitur solida primordia simplicitate
quae minimis stipata cohaerent partibus arte,   610
non ex illorum conventu conciliata,
sed magis aeterna pollentia simplicitate,
unde neque avelli quicquam neque deminui iam
concedit natura reservans semina rebus.
(3) praeterea nisi erit minimum, parvissima quaeque   615

> corpora constabunt ex partibus infinitis,
> quippe ubi dimidiae partis pars semper habebit
> dimidiam partem nec res praefiniet ulla.
> ergo rerum inter summam minimamque quid escit?
> nil erit ut distet; nam quamvis funditus omnis   620
> summa sit infinita, tamen, parvissima quae sunt,
> ex infinitis constabunt partibus aeque.
> quod quoniam ratio reclamat vera negatque
> credere posse animum, victus fateare necessest
> esse ea quae nullis iam praedita partibus exstent   625
> et minima constent natura. quae quoniam sunt,
> illa quoque esse tibi solida atque aeterna fatendum.
> (4) denique si minimas in partis cuncta resolvi
> cogere consuesset rerum natura creatrix,
> iam nil ex illis eadem reparare valeret   630
> propterea quia, quae nullis sunt partibus aucta,
> non possunt ea quae debet genitalis habere
> materies, varios conexus pondera plagas
> concursus motus, per quae res quaeque geruntur.

Context: immediately after **8B**, continuing the arguments for the atomic nature of body.

It may be suspected that Lucretius has himself appended these arguments to the section about atoms rather than devote an entire separate section to so technical a subject as minima. Their relevance to atoms lies in the proper Epicurean principle (**A** 30–1) that minima cannot exist in isolation. However, the correct conclusion from this would be that no process of fragmentation can yield a body smaller than, say, two minima. Lucretius appears to be overstating his case in 609–14 when he maintains that *any* cohesive group of minima will be inseparable.

599–601   Munro, expecting to find here an argument from the sensible minimum to the 'minimum in the atom', indicates a lacuna after 599, to be filled out roughly as follows: ⟨*corporibus, quod iam nobis minimum esse videtur,* | *debet item ratione pari minimum esse cacumen*⟩. But that expectation is questionable (cf. vol. 1, 42, and note on **B** 749–52): in **A** 28–31, the inseparability of minima is distinguished as one point which *cannot* be established by analogy with the sensible. The text as it stands is quite intelligible. All the properties of the minimum listed in 601–4 are deduced from its status as the extremity of a body: if it were not minimal but had parts, one of its parts would have a better claim to be the extremity; and if it were separable it would not be essentially the extremity of something else.

605 **ex ordine**   This translates ἑξῆς, cf. **A** 18.

611   Cf. **A** 30–1.

615–22   Cf. ps.-Aristotle, *Lin. insec.* 968a2ff., and Furley [204], 36–8.

633 **varios**   As Furley shows [204], 38–40, it is the lack of variety among minima that is seen here as ruling out their standing as primary elements (hence *quapropter* at 635, introducing the similar argument against Heraclitus beginning at 645).

d Aristotle, *Phys.* VI.1, 231a21–b10

εἰ δ' ἐστὶ συνεχὲς καὶ ἁπτόμενον καὶ ἐφεξῆς, ὡς διώρισται πρότερον, συνεχῆ μὲν ὧν τὰ
ἔσχατα ἕν, ἁπτόμενα δ' ὧν ἅμα, ἐφεξῆς δ' ὧν μηδὲν μεταξὺ συγγενές, ἀδύνατον ἐξ
ἀδιαιρέτων εἶναί τι συνεχές, οἷον γραμμὴν ἐκ στιγμῶν, εἴπερ ἡ γραμμὴ μὲν συνεχές, ἡ
στιγμὴ δὲ ἀδιαίρετον. οὔτε γὰρ ἐν τὰ ἔσχατα τῶν στιγμῶν (οὐ γάρ ἐστι τὸ μὲν ἔσχατον τὸ δ'
ἄλλο τι μόριον τοῦ ἀδιαιρέτου), οὔθ' ἅμα τὰ ἔσχατα (οὐ γάρ ἐστιν ἔσχατον τοῦ ἀμεροῦς   5
οὐδέν· ἕτερον γὰρ τὸ ἔσχατον καὶ οὗ ἔσχατον). ἔτι δ' ἀνάγκη ἤτοι συνεχεῖς εἶναι τὰς
στιγμὰς ἢ ἁπτομένας ἀλλήλων, ἐξ ὧν ἐστι τὸ συνεχές· ὁ δ' αὐτὸς λόγος καὶ ἐπὶ πάντων τῶν
ἀδιαιρέτων. συνεχεῖς μὲν δὴ οὐκ ἂν εἶεν διὰ τὸν εἰρημένον λόγον· ἅπτεται δ' ἅπαν ἢ ὅλον
ὅλου ἢ μέρος μέρους ἢ ὅλου μέρος. ἐπεὶ δ' ἀμερὲς τὸ ἀδιαίρετον, ἀνάγκη ὅλον ὅλου
ἅπτεσθαι. ὅλον δ' ὅλου ἁπτόμενον οὐκ ἔσται συνεχές. τὸ γὰρ συνεχὲς ἔχει τὸ μὲν ἄλλο τὸ δ'   10
ἄλλο μέρος, καὶ διαιρεῖται εἰς οὕτως ἕτερα καὶ τόπῳ κεχωρισμένα. ἀλλὰ μὴν οὐδὲ ἐφεξῆς
ἔσται στιγμὴ στιγμῇ ἢ τὸ νῦν τῷ νῦν, ὥστ' ἐκ τούτων εἶναι τὸ μῆκος ἢ τὸν χρόνον· ἐφεξῆς
μὲν γάρ ἐστιν ὧν μηθέν ἐστι μεταξὺ συγγενές, στιγμῶν δ' αἰεὶ [τὸ] μεταξὺ γραμμὴ καὶ τῶν
νῦν χρόνος.

Context: analysis of the continuum.

8–10   Cf. **A** 18–20 and **50C 6** for the influence of these lines in Hellenistic debate.

11–14   As Sorabji points out ([22], 367–8), Aristotle's argument against ἀμερῆ 'in
sequence' works only for points and instants, not for partless *magnitudes*, thus leaving
Epicurus with a loophole which his ἑξῆς in **A 8** may be exploiting.

e Aristotle, *Phys.* VI.10, 240b8–241a6

ἀποδεδειγμένων δὲ τούτων λέγομεν ὅτι τὸ ἀμερὲς οὐκ ἐνδέχεται κινεῖσθαι πλὴν κατὰ
συμβεβηκός, οἷον κινουμένου τοῦ σώματος ἢ τοῦ μεγέθους τῷ ἐνυπάρχειν, καθάπερ ἂν εἰ
τὸ ἐν τῷ πλοίῳ κινοῖτο ὑπὸ τῆς τοῦ πλοίου φορᾶς ἢ τὸ μέρος τῇ τοῦ ὅλου κινήσει. (ἀμερὲς δὲ
λέγω τὸ κατὰ ποσὸν ἀδιαίρετον.) καὶ γὰρ αἱ τῶν μερῶν κινήσεις ἕτεραί εἰσι κατ' αὐτά τε τὰ
μέρη καὶ κατὰ τὴν τοῦ ὅλου κίνησιν. ἴδοι δ' ἄν τις ἐπὶ τῆς σφαίρας μάλιστα τὴν διαφοράν·   5
οὐ γὰρ ταὐτὸν τάχος ἐστὶ τῶν τε πρὸς τῷ κέντρῳ καὶ τῶν ἐκτὸς καὶ τῆς ὅλης, ὡς οὐ μιᾶς
οὔσης κινήσεως. καθάπερ οὖν εἴπομεν, οὕτω μὲν ἐνδέχεται κινεῖσθαι τὸ ἀμερὲς ὡς ὁ ἐν τῷ
πλοίῳ καθήμενος τοῦ πλοίου θέοντος, καθ' αὑτὸ δ' οὐκ ἐνδέχεται. μεταβαλλέτω γὰρ ἐκ τοῦ
ΑΒ εἰς τὸ ΒΓ, εἴτ' ἐκ μεγέθους εἰς μέγεθος εἴτ' ἐξ εἴδους εἰς εἶδος εἴτε κατ' ἀντίφασιν· ὁ δὲ
χρόνος ἔστω ἐν ᾧ πρώτῳ μεταβάλλει ἐφ' οὗ Δ. οὐκοῦν ἀνάγκη αὐτὸ καθ' ὃν μεταβάλλει   10
χρόνον ἢ ἐν τῷ ΑΒ εἶναι ἢ ἐν τῷ ΒΓ, ἢ τὸ μέν τι αὐτοῦ ἐν τούτῳ τὸ δ' ἐν θατέρῳ· πᾶν γὰρ τὸ
μεταβάλλον οὕτως εἶχεν. ἐν ἑκατέρῳ μὲν οὖν οὐκ ἔσται τι αὐτοῦ· μεριστὸν γὰρ ἂν εἴη. ἀλλὰ
μὴν οὐδ' ἐν τῷ ΒΓ· μεταβεβληκὸς γὰρ ἔσται, ὑπόκειται δὲ μεταβάλλειν. λείπεται δὴ αὐτὸ
ἐν τῷ ΑΒ εἶναι, καθ' ὃν μεταβάλλει χρόνον. ἠρεμήσει ἄρα· τὸ γὰρ ἐν τῷ αὐτῷ εἶναι χρόνον
τινὰ ἠρεμεῖν ἦν. ὥστ' οὐκ ἐνδέχεται τὸ ἀμερὲς κινεῖσθαι οὐδ' ὅλως μεταβάλλειν· μοναχῶς   15
γὰρ ἂν οὕτως ἦν αὐτοῦ κίνησις, εἰ ὁ χρόνος ἦν ἐκ τῶν νῦν· αἰεὶ γὰρ ἐν τῷ νῦν κεκινημένον ἂν
ἦν καὶ μεταβεβληκός, ὥστε κινεῖσθαι μὲν μηδέποτε, κεκινῆσθαι δ' ἀεί. τοῦτο δ' ὅτι
ἀδύνατον, δέδεικται καὶ πρότερον· οὔτε γὰρ ὁ χρόνος ἐκ τῶν νῦν οὔθ' ἡ γραμμὴ ἐκ στιγμῶν

οὔθ' ἡ κίνησις ἐκ κινημάτων· οὐδὲν γὰρ ἄλλο ποιεῖ ὁ τοῦτο λέγων ἢ τὴν κίνησιν ἐξ ἀμερῶν, καθάπερ ἂν εἰ τὸν χρόνον ἐκ τῶν νῦν ἢ τὸ μῆκος ἐκ στιγμῶν.　20

It is suggested in vol. 1, 43–4 that **A 12**, where minima are denied the power of independent motion, represents Epicurus' acceptance of Aristotle's argument at 1–15. For this, and for Epicurus' response to 15–20, see on **A 30**–1, and vol. 1, 51–2.

f Cicero, *Acad.* 2.106

Polyaenus, qui magnus mathematicus fuisse dicitur, is posteaquam Epicuro adsentiens totam geometriam falsam esse credidit, num illa etiam quae sciebat oblitus est?

Context: Cicero's argument, on behalf of the New Academy, that memory does not depend on κατάληψις.
Cf. **g**.

g Cicero, *Fin.* 1.20

ne illud quidem physici, credere aliquid esse minimum; quod profecto numquam putavisset si a Polyaeno familiari suo geometrica discere maluisset quam illum etiam ipsum dedocere.

Context: general attack by Cicero on Epicurean physics.
At *Fin.* 1.72 the Epicurean spokesman rejects as false *all* the mathematical sciences, but it seems clear that Epicurus' rejection of geometry was the one given most publicity, and was connected with his doctrine of minima: on this and on Epicurus' relation with Polyaenus, cf. Sedley [105]; also Mueller [652].

10 Infinity

A Epicurus, *Ep. Hdt.* 41–2

(1) ἀλλὰ μὴν καὶ τὸ πᾶν ἄπειρόν ἐστι. (2) τὸ γὰρ πεπερασμένον ἄκρον ἔχει· τὸ δὲ ἄκρον παρ' ἕτερόν τι θεωρεῖται· ὥστε οὐκ ἔχον ἄκρον πέρας οὐκ ἔχει· πέρας δὲ οὐκ ἔχον ἄπειρον ἂν εἴη καὶ οὐ πεπερασμένον. (3) καὶ μὴν καὶ τῷ πλήθει τῶν σωμάτων ἄπειρόν ἐστι τὸ πᾶν καὶ τῷ μεγέθει τοῦ κενοῦ. (4) εἴ τε γὰρ ἦν τὸ κενὸν ἄπειρον, τὰ δὲ σώματα ὡρισμένα, οὐθαμοῦ ἂν ἔμενε τὰ 5 σώματα, ἀλλ' ἐφέρετο κατὰ τὸ ἄπειρον κενὸν διεσπαρμένα, οὐκ ἔχοντα τὰ ὑπερείδοντα καὶ στέλλοντα κατὰ τὰς ἀνακοπάς· (5) εἴ τε τὸ κενὸν ἦν ὡρισμένον, οὐκ ἂν εἶχε τὰ ἄπειρα σώματα ὅπου ἐνέστη.

2 δὲ FP: γὰρ B   7 ἀνακοπάς codd.: ἀντικοπάς Meibom

Context: immediately following **8A**. On the historical significance of the theory, see Furley [211].

4 **τὸ πᾶν** This has already been analysed as bodies plus void at **5A**.

7 **ἀνακοπάς** Meibom's emendation to Epicurus' regular term ἀντικοπάς is attractive, but Usener ([133], 56) rightly cites the parallel of Plutarch, *De facie* 931B, οὐ παρέχων ἀνακοπὰς οὐδ' ἀντερείδων.

B Lucretius 1.958–97

(1) omne quod est igitur nulla regione viarum
finitumst; (2) namque extremum debebat habere.
extremum porro nullius posse videtur   960
esse, nisi ultra sit quod finiat; ut videatur
quo non longius haec sensus natura sequatur.
nunc extra summam quoniam nil esse fatendum,
non habet extremum, caret ergo fine modoque.
nec refert quibus adsistas regionibus eius;   965
usque adeo, quem quisque locum possedit, in omnis
tantundem partis infinitum omne relinquit.
(3) praeterea si iam finitum constituatur
omne quod est spatium, siquis procurrat ad oras
ultimus extremas iaciatque volatile telum,   970
id validis utrum contortum viribus ire
quo fuerit missum mavis longeque volare,
an prohibere aliquid censes obstareque posse?
alterutrum fatearis enim sumasque necessest.
quorum utrumque tibi effugium praecludit et omne   975
cogit ut exempta concedas fine patere.
nam sive est aliquid quod probeat efficiatque
quominu' quo missum est veniat finique locet se,
sive foras fertur, non est a fine profectum.
hoc pacto sequar atque, oras ubicumque locaris   980
extremas, quaeram quid telo denique fiat.
fiet uti nusquam possit consistere finis
effugiumque fugae prolatet copia semper.
(4) praeterea spatium summai totius omne
undique si inclusum certis consisteret oris   985
finitumque foret, iam copia materiai
undique ponderibus solidis confluxet ad imum
nec res ulla geri sub caeli tegmine posset
nec foret omnino caelum neque lumina solis,
quippe ubi materies omnis cumulata iaceret   990
ex infinito iam tempore subsidendo.
at nunc nimirum requies data principiorum
corporibus nullast, quia nil est funditus imum
quo quasi confluere et sedis ubi ponere possint.
semper in assiduo motu res quaeque geruntur   995
partibus in cunctis infernaque suppeditantur
ex infinito cita corpora materiai.

971 *id validis* Lambinus: *invalidis* codd.   996 *in* P: *e* M: om. OQG

Epicurean physics

Context: as in **A**, following the proofs of the atomic nature of body (**8B**), although Lucretius has inserted between the two passages a digression refuting rival theories of the elements (1.635–920).

Attempts have been made to establish a correlation between these arguments and those in **A**, but apart from that of **A** 1–2 with **B** 1–2 there seems to be little exact correspondence.

961–2   Bailey's 'so that there is seen to be a spot farther than which the nature of our sense cannot follow it' (|154|, ad loc.), and the similar versions of other editors, seem to give sensation an inappropriate role in the argument. They are right to link *videtur* (960) and *videatur* (961) with Epicurus' θεωρεῖται (**A** 2), but this later term is one used to span the transition between simple seeing (θεωρεῖν) and conceptual viewing (διὰ λόγου θεωρεῖν, cf. **11D** 4, **E** 12), and the same point should be intended here. From directly viewing (*videtur*, 960) the fact that everything with an extremity has something else to flank it, one can proceed to a conceptual view (*videatur*, 961) of the applicability of the same principle even beyond the range of actual vision (literally 'to where this kind of sensation no longer reaches', 962).

968–74   Cf. the similar examples used by Archytas, 47 A 24, DK, and the Stoics, **49F**.

977–8   The translation 'and bring it about that it arrives not whither it was sped, nor plants itself in the goal . . .' (Bailey) takes *fini* (978) as an ablative, meaning 'in the target'. This involves an improbable change in the sense of *finis*, which elsewhere in the immediate context is 'limit', and introduces the utterly inappropriate idea that the exploratory spear was aimed at a target. It therefore seems better to take *finique locet se* (978) as co-ordinate with the subjunctives in 977, and *fini* as a predicative dative, 'and station *itself* as a limit'. If a body blocks the spear from passing the supposed limit of the universe, that body has a better claim to be called the 'limit' than the initially chosen boundary immediately adjacent to it: hence (979) 'what it started from was not the limit'.

983   Our translation is adopted from Gottschalk [212].

996–7   Lucretius has been arguing that the observed ubiquity of motion conflicts with the view that there is an absolute bottom to the universe. So the point added here is probably that this perpetual motion must exist even below us, where matter is likewise in motion (*cita*) 'from infinity' – either 'out of infinite space' (as at 1.1036, 6.666), or 'from infinite time past' (as at 1.1025, 2.255), perhaps more appropriately to the argument (cf. 995).

C Epicurus, *Ep. Hdt.* 60

(1) καὶ μὴν καὶ τοῦ ἀπείρου ὡς μὲν ἀνωτάτω ἢ κατωτάτω οὐ δεῖ κατηγορεῖν τὸ ἄνω ἢ κάτω, ὡς μέντοι τὸ ὑπὲρ κεφαλῆς, ὅθεν ἂν στῶμεν, εἰς ἄπειρον ἄγειν ὂν μηδέ ποτε φανεῖσθαι τοῦτο ἡμῖν, ἢ τὸ ὑποκάτω, τοῦ νοηθέντος εἰς ἄπειρον ἅμα ἄνω τε εἶναι καὶ κάτω πρὸς τὸ αὐτό. τοῦτο γὰρ ἀδύνατον διανοηθῆναι. (2) ὥστε ἔστι μίαν λαβεῖν φορὰν τὴν ἄνω νοουμένην   5
εἰς ἄπειρον καὶ μίαν τὴν κάτω, ἂν καὶ μυριάκις πρὸς τοὺς πόδας τῶν ἐπάνω τὸ παρ' ἡμῶν φερόμενον ⟨εἰς⟩ τοὺς ὑπὲρ κεφαλῆς ἡμῶν τόπους ἀφικνῆται, ἢ ἐπὶ τὴν κεφαλὴν τῶν ὑποκάτω τὸ παρ' ἡμῶν κάτω

φερόμενον· (3) ἡ γὰρ ὅλη φορὰ οὐθὲν ἧττον ἑκατέρα ἑκατέρᾳ ἀντικειμένη
ἐπ᾽ ἄπειρον νοεῖται.   10

1 ἦ P: καὶ BF   2 ὡς μέντοι Sedley: εἰς μέντοι P: ἴσμεν τοι B: μέντοι FP(corr.)   3 μηδέ ποτε Sedley:
μηδέποτε codd.   7 ⟨εἰς⟩ Mühll: ⟨ἐς⟩ Usener

Context: between **9A** and **11E**.
For other readings of the passage, see especially Bailey [117] ad loc., Mau [205],
Konstan [214]. The interpretation adopted here has much in common with the first
two.
  1–2 For μέν . . . μέντοι, cf. *Ep. Men.* 134.
  3 ὄν is here taken as the participial form of ἔστι, 'it is possible', used in an
accusative absolute construction (cf. Demosthenes 50.22).
  3–4 Both instances of τοῦτο are best taken as having the same reference, namely
the existence of an absolute top and bottom.
  τοῦ νοηθέντος Partitive genitive, principally dependent on τὸ ὑποκάτω, 'the
lower part of that which is conceived . . .'
  6–9 Mau takes the reference to those above and below us to be to situations
within our world, e.g. multi-storey buildings; but the implication of the singular τὸ
φερόμενον is that even a single trajectory might arrive ten thousand times at the feet of
those above, which even allowing for some exaggeration, seems plausible only if
multiple worlds are envisaged.

11 Atomic motion

A Epicurus, *Ep. Hdt.* 43–4

(1) κινοῦνταί τε συνεχῶς αἱ ἄτομοι (φησὶ δὲ ἐνδοτέρω καὶ ἰσοταχῶς αὐτὰς κινεῖσθαι
τοῦ κενοῦ τὴν εἶξιν ὁμοίαν παρεχομένου καὶ τῇ κουφοτάτῃ καὶ τῇ βαρυτάτῃ) τὸν αἰῶνα,
καὶ αἱ μὲν εἰς μακρὰν ἀπ᾽ ἀλλήλων διιστάμεναι, αἱ δὲ αὐτοῦ τὸν παλμὸν
ἴσχουσαι, ὅταν τύχωσι τῇ περιπλοκῇ κεκλειμέναι ἢ στεγαζόμεναι παρὰ
τῶν πλεκτικῶν. (2) ἥ τε γὰρ τοῦ κενοῦ φύσις ἡ διορίζουσα ἑκάστην αὐτὴν   5
τοῦτο παρασκευάζει, τὴν ὑπέρεισιν οὐχ οἵα τε οὖσα ποιεῖσθαι· (3) ἥ τε
στερεότης ἡ ὑπάρχουσα αὐταῖς κατὰ τὴν σύγκρουσιν τὸν ἀποπαλμὸν
ποιεῖ, ἐφ᾽ ὁπόσον ἂν ἡ περιπλοκὴ τὴν ἀποκατάστασιν ἐκ τῆς συγκρούσεως
διδῷ. (4) ἀρχὴ δὲ τούτων οὐκ ἔστιν, ἀιδίων τῶν ἀτόμων οὐσῶν καὶ τοῦ
κενοῦ.   10

3 αὐτοῦ Brieger: αὐτὸν codd.   4 ἴσχουσαι Brieger: ἴσχουσιν codd.   τῇ περιπλοκῇ Usener: τὴν
περιπλοκὴν codd.   παρὰ dgt: περὶ cett.   9 ἀιδίων Gassendi: αἰτίων codd.

Context: immediately following **12B**.
  1–2 The interpolated scholion refers to **E**.
  3–4 For the role of this vibration in the production of simulacra, see **15A 8**.
  9–10 Gassendi's simple emendation is eminently plausible, but even if the MSS
reading were retained, with Bailey ([117] ad loc., 'There is no beginning to these
motions, because their cause is the atoms and the void'), the point made would be
more or less the same.

B Lucretius 2.80–124

(1) si cessare putas rerum primordia posse   80
cessandoque novos rerum progignere motus,
avius a vera longe ratione vagaris.
(2) nam quoniam per inane vagantur, cuncta necessest
aut gravitate sua ferri primordia rerum
aut ictu forte alterius. (3) nam ⟨cum⟩ cita saepe   85
obvia conflixere, fit ut diversa repente
dissiliant; neque enim mirum, durissima quae sint
ponderibus solidis neque quicquam a tergo ibus obstet.
(4) et quo iactari magis omnia materiai
corpora pervideas, reminiscere totius imum   90
nil esse in summa, neque habere ubi corpora prima
consistant, quoniam spatium sine fine modoquest,
immensumque patere in cunctas undique partis
pluribus ostendi et certa ratione probatumst.
quod quoniam constat; nimirum nulla quies est   95
reddita corporibus primis per inane profundum.
(5) sed magis assiduo varioque exercita motu
partim intervallis magnis confulta resultant,
pars etiam brevibus spatiis vexantur ab ictu.
(6) et quaecumque magis condenso conciliatu   100
exiguis intervallis convecta resultant,
indupedita suis perplexis ipsa figuris,
haec validas saxi radices et fera ferri
corpora constituunt et cetera ⟨de⟩ genere horum.
paucula quae porro magnum per inane vagantur   105
cetera dissiliunt longe longeque recursant
in magnis intervallis, haec aera rarum
sufficiunt nobis et splendida lumina solis;
multaque praeterea magnum per inane vagantur,
conciliis rerum quae sunt reiecta nec usquam   110
consociare etiam motus potuere recepta.
(7) cuius, uti memoro, rei simulacrum et imago
ante oculos semper nobis versatur et instat.
contemplator enim, cum solis lumina cumque
inserti fundunt radii per opaca domorum: 115
multa minuta modis multis per inane videbis
corpora misceri radiorum lumine in ipso
et velut aeterno certamine proelia pugnas
edere turmatim certantia nec dare pausam,
conciliis et discidiis exercita crebris;   120

conicere ut possis ex hoc, primordia rerum
quale sit in magno iactari semper inani.
dumtaxat rerum magnarum parva potest res
exemplare dare et vestigia notitiai.

85 ⟨cum⟩ Lachmann   88 *tergo ibus* Voss: *tergibus* codd.   105 *paucula* L: *cetera* (ex 106) Merrill   106 *cetera* OQG: *paucula* (ex 105) Merrill

Context: the opening stages of Lucretius' account of atomic motion.

80–1   Lucretius has just been explaining the continuity of natural processes as due to the reciprocal character of all motion and change in the world (2.67–79), and this leads him to note that if, contrary to his view, atoms could come to a halt, it would correspondingly be necessary to suppose that they could restart their motion from scratch.

89–96   Cf. **10B 4**.

105–6   These lines have caused much difficulty (see Bailey [154] ad loc.), but the text is quite intelligible provided *paucula* is understood as 'few and far between', i.e. 'widely scattered', cf. 3.278, 4.71.

112–24   For this traditional atomist simile, cf. Democritus frr. 200–3, 206 Luria.

121–4   The analogy does not prove the perpetual motion of atoms, but offers a model to aid our conception of it; *notitiai* (124) probably translates προλήψεως (on which see **17**).

C   Lucretius 2.142–64

(1) nunc quae mobilitas sit reddita materiai
corporibus paucis licet hinc cognoscere, Memmi.
(2) primum aurora novo cum spargit lumine terras
et variae volucres nemora avia pervolitantes   145
aera per tenerum liquidis loca vocibus opplent,
quam subito soleat sol ortus tempore tali
convestire sua perfundens omnia luce,
omnibus in promptu manifestumque esse videmus.
at vapor is quem sol mittet lumenque serenum   150
non per inane meat vacuum; quo tardius ire
cogitur, aerias quasi dum diverberat undas.
nec singillatim corpuscula quaeque vaporis
sed complexa meant inter se conque globata;
quapropter simul inter se retrahuntur et extra   155
officiuntur, uti cogantur tardius ire.
(3) at quae sunt solida primordia simplicitate,
cum per inane meant vacuum nec res remoratur
ulla foris atque ipsa suis e partibus unum
unum in quem coepere locum conixa feruntur,   160
debent nimirum praecellere mobilitate
et multo citius ferri quam lumina solis

Epicurean physics

multiplexque loci spatium transcurrere eodem
tempore quo solis pervulgant fulgura caelum.

Context: shortly after **B**.

The comparison is, of course, between the speed of individual atoms and the *perceptible* speed of light. The individual atoms composing the light all travel at the uniform atomic speed, but in complex patterns of motion which retard their *linear* progress: cf. **D 2, E 4**.

D Epicurus, *Ep. Hdt.* 46–7 (= **15A 2**)

(1) καὶ μὴν καὶ ἡ διὰ τοῦ κενοῦ φορὰ κατὰ μηδεμίαν ἀπάντησιν τῶν ἀντικοψάντων γινομένη πᾶν μῆκος περιληπτὸν ἐν ἀπερινοήτῳ χρόνῳ συντελεῖ. (2) βράδους γὰρ καὶ τάχους ἀντικοπὴ καὶ οὐκ ἀντικοπὴ ὁμοίωμα λαμβάνει. (3) οὐ μὴν οὐδ' ἅμα κατὰ τοὺς διὰ λόγου θεωρητοὺς χρόνους αὐτὸ τὸ φερόμενον σῶμα ἐπὶ τοὺς πλείους τόπους ἀφικνεῖται – ἀδιανόη-   5
τον γάρ. (4) καὶ τοῦτο συναφικνούμενον ἐν αἰσθητῷ χρόνῳ ὅθεν δήποθεν τοῦ ἀπείρου οὐκ ἐξ οὗ ἂν περιλάβωμεν τὴν φορὰν τόπου ἔσται ἀφιστάμενον· (5) ἀντικοπῇ γὰρ ὅμοιον ἔσται, κἂν μέχρι τοσούτου τὸ τάχος τῆς φορᾶς μὴ ἀντικοπῇ ὂν καταλίπωμεν. (6) χρήσιμον δὴ καὶ τοῦτο κατασχεῖν τὸ στοιχεῖον.   10

5 αὐτὸ Mühll: κατὰ codd.: καὶ Usener   8 τοσούτου FP: τούτου B   9 ἀντικοπῇ ὂν Sedley: ἀντικοπεον BP: ἀντικοπτέον FP(corr.): ἀντικοπτόμενον Meibom: ἀντικόπτον vel ἀντίκοπον Usener: ἀντικοπὲν Mühll

Context: proof of the enormous speed of images (see **15A**). The principle is presented by Epicurus as an entirely general one about atomic motion, although it is here, in the theory of vision, that its chief usefulness lies.

3–4   Cf. **E 4**.

4 **τοὺς διὰ λόγου θεωρητοὺς χρόνους**   See on **E 11–12**.

5–8   These lines are problematic, and have been construed in a number of different ways. We suggest, at all events, that ἀδιάνοητον γὰρ καὶ τοῦτο can hardly be taken together, as in the MSS and many editions, since in what precedes nothing else has been dismissed, even implicitly, as inconceivable. The compound συναφικ-νεῖσθαι, which occurs only here, ought to mean 'arrive jointly (with something else)', not 'arrive simultaneously (with its departure)': so presumably Epicurus is now talking about perceptible arrivals of atoms (cf. ἐν αἰσθητῷ χρόνῳ), and chooses a verb which will allow for the fact that atoms only arouse sense-perception when arriving in aggregations like the images which cause vision.

E Epicurus, *Ep. Hdt.* 61–2

(1) καὶ μὴν καὶ ἰσοταχεῖς ἀναγκαῖον τὰς ἀτόμους εἶναι, ὅταν διὰ τοῦ κενοῦ εἰσφέρωνται μηθενὸς ἀντικόπτοντος. (2) οὔτε γὰρ τὰ βαρέα θᾶττον οἰσθήσεται τῶν μικρῶν καὶ κούφων, ὅταν γε δὴ μηδὲν ἀπαντᾷ αὐτοῖς· οὔτε τὰ μικρὰ τῶν μεγάλων, πάντα πόρον σύμμετρον ἔχοντα, ὅταν μηθὲν μηδὲ

44

11 *Atomic motion*

ἐκείνοις ἀντικόπτῃ· (3) οὔθ᾽ ἡ ἄνω οὔθ᾽ ἡ εἰς τὸ πλάγιον διὰ τῶν κρούσεων 5
φορά, οὔθ᾽ αἱ κάτω διὰ τῶν ἰδίων βαρῶν. ἐφ᾽ ὁπόσον γὰρ ἂν κατίσχῃ
ἑκάτερων, ἐπὶ τοσοῦτον ἅμα νοήματι τὴν φορὰν σχήσει, ἕως ἀντικόψῃ ἢ
ἔξωθεν ἢ ἐκ τοῦ ἰδίου βάρους πρὸς τὴν τοῦ πλήξαντος δύναμιν. (4) ἀλλὰ
μὴν καὶ κατὰ τὰς συγκρίσεις θάττων ἑτέρα ἑτέρας ῥηθήσεται τῶν ἀτόμων
ἰσοταχῶν οὐσῶν, τῷ ἐφ᾽ ἕνα τόπον φέρεσθαι τὰς ἐν τοῖς ἀθροίσμασιν 10
ἀτόμους καὶ κατὰ τὸν ἐλάχιστον συνεχῆ χρόνον, εἰ μὴ ἐφ᾽ ἕνα κατὰ τοὺς
λόγῳ θεωρητοὺς χρόνους· ἀλλὰ πυκνὸν ἀντικόπτουσιν, ἕως ἂν ὑπὸ τὴν
αἴσθησιν τὸ συνεχὲς τῆς φορᾶς γίνηται. τὸ γὰρ προσδοξαζόμενον περὶ τοῦ
ἀοράτου, ὡς ἄρα καὶ οἱ διὰ λόγου θεωρητοὶ χρόνοι τὸ συνεχὲς τῆς φορᾶς ἕξουσιν, οὐκ
ἀληθές ἐστιν ἐπὶ τῶν τοιούτων· ἐπεὶ τό γε θεωρούμενον πᾶν ἢ κατ᾽ ἐπιβολὴν λαμβανόμενον 15
τῇ διανοίᾳ ἀληθές ἐστι.

6 αἱ BP: ἡ P(corr.)F   7 ἑκάτερων codd.: ἑκάτερον Usener

Context: immediately following **10C.**

5–6   Strictly θᾶττον οἰσθήσεται from 2–3 should be understood here, but by
now the predicate to be supplied from the previous sentence can be taken simply as
'will differ in speed'. That explains the plural αἱ of the best MSS: it is important that
the different *types* of motion listed do not differ in speed, but equally important that
even within a single type, among downward motions themselves, one is not faster
than another 'because of their individual weights' (cf. **H** 3).

6–7   ἑκάτερων does not require the usual emendation to -ον, but can be taken as a
partitive genitive with ἐφ᾽ ὁπόσον (for which see *Ep. Pyth* 110), 'to whatever distance
of either ones', i.e. 'however far along either kind of trajectory', the reference of the
plural ἑκάτερων being (a) upwards and sideways motions due to impacts, and (b)
downward motions due to weights. κατίσχῃ (tentatively translated 'gets') is difficult:
the only plausible parallel is at Herodotus 3.28, where κατίσχειν ἐπί . . . is used of a
flash of light 'reaching' something.

11–12   The two kinds of time mentioned here are a subject of controversy, cf.
Mau [205], 41ff. What is fairly clear is that 'times seen by reason' here and at **D** 4 are
periods of time too short to be detected by the senses, as **15D** 794–6 confirms. But
there is no implication in the expression λόγῳ θεωρητός that the times are indivisible,
as is widely held, and the uses to which they are put in these passages do not require
that they be. (For indivisible times, see on **G**; it is suggested in vol. 1 that this element
of the Epicurean theory postdates *Ep. Hdt.*) These imperceptible times most naturally
contrast with perceptible times, as at **D** 4–6 and **15D** 794–6, and the argument itself
seems to require that 'the smallest continuous time' at 11 similarly be perceptible. The
common-sense objection that Epicurus is imagining will be that, *to all appearances*, all
the particles in a moving body move with the body and at the same speed as it. Mau's
suggestion that 'the smallest continuous time' is still imperceptible (although not
partless, as he takes the λόγῳ θεωρητοὶ χρόνοι to be) would rob the objection of any
force; and besides, Epicurus' answer at 13–16 shows that he takes the objection to rest
on a false inference from the visible to the invisible. So the 'smallest continuous time'
ought to be a perceptible time. It is, presumably, not the shortest perceptible time, but
the shortest timespan within which some *continuity* of motion can be detected. The

45

Epicurean physics

shortest perceptible time would be seen as partless, so that no change could be discerned during it (cf. **9A 7**).

13–16   Cf. Furley [241], 614–16; Sedley [126], 24–5. Given the disparity, in this instance, between the macroscopic and the microscopic, the objector's error must lie in his analogical inference from the one to the other, and not in the macroscopic appearances themselves, which on Epicurus' epistemological theory must be true (see **16**).

15 **τὸ θεωρούμενον**   'What is seen'. For κατ' ἐπιβολὴν λαμβανόμενον τῇ διανοίᾳ, see vol. 1, 90, on the 'focusing of thought into an impression'.

F Simplicius, *In. Ar. Phys.* 938,17–22 (Usener 277)

εἰ γὰρ μὴ ἦν πᾶν μέγεθος διαιρετόν, οὐχ οἷόν τε ἦν τὸ βραδύτερον ἀεὶ ἐν τῷ
ἴσῳ χρόνῳ ἔλαττον κινεῖσθαι τοῦ θάττονος· τὸ γὰρ ἄτομον καὶ τὸ ἀμερὲς
ἐν τῷ αὐτῷ χρόνῳ καὶ τὸ θᾶττον διέρχεται καὶ τὸ βραδύτερον· εἰ γὰρ ἐν
πλείονι, ἐν τῷ ἴσῳ ἔλαττόν τι τοῦ ἀμεροῦς διελεύσεται. διὸ καὶ τοῖς περὶ
Ἐπίκουρον ἀρέσκει ἰσοταχῶς πάντα διὰ τῶν ἀμερῶν κινεῖσθαι, ἵνα μὴ τὰ   5
ἄτομα αὐτῶν διαιρούμενα μηκέτι ἄτομα ᾖ.

Context: commentary on *Physics* VI.2,232a23ff.

Simplicius ignores the Epicurean technical distinction between a minimum partless entity and an atom (on which see **8–9**).

G Simplicius, *In Ar. Phys.* 934,18–30 (Usener 278, part)

ἐπάγει δὲ καὶ ἄλλο ἄτοπον ἀκολουθοῦν ταύτῃ τῇ ὑποθέσει, τὸ κεκινῆσθαί τι μὴ πρότερον
κινούμενον, οἷον βεβαδικέναι τι μὴ πρότερον βαδίσαν. κεῖται μὲν γὰρ κινεῖσθαι τὸ Ω τὴν
ΔΕΖ κίνησιν ἐπὶ τοῦ ΑΒΓ μεγέθους· οὔτε δὲ ἐπὶ τοῦ Α κινεῖται, κεκίνηται γὰρ ἐπ' αὐτοῦ,
οὔτε ἐπὶ τοῦ Β, ὁμοίως δὲ οὐδὲ ἐπὶ τοῦ Γ· τὴν ὅλην ἄρα κίνησιν κεκινημένον ἔσται μὴ
κινούμενον αὐτὴν πρότερον. ὅτι δὲ οὐ πάντῃ ἀπίθανον ταύτην τέθεικε τὴν   5
ἔνστασιν, δηλοῖ τὸ καὶ θέντος αὐτὴν καὶ διαλύσαντος τοὺς περὶ Ἐπίκουρον
ὅμως, ὕστερον γενομένους οὕτω λέγειν τὴν κίνησιν γίνεσθαι. ἐξ ἀμερῶν
γὰρ καὶ τὴν κίνησιν καὶ τὸ μέγεθος καὶ τὸν χρόνον εἶναι λέγοντες ἐπὶ μὲν
τοῦ ὅλου μεγέθους τοῦ ἐξ ἀμερῶν συνεστῶτος κινεῖσθαι λέγουσι τὸ
κινούμενον, καθ' ἕκαστον δὲ τῶν ἐν αὐτῷ ἀμερῶν οὐ κινεῖσθαι ἀλλὰ   10
κεκινῆσθαι, διὰ τὸ εἰ τεθείη καὶ ἐπὶ τούτων κινεῖσθαι τὸ ἐπὶ τοῦ ὅλου
κινούμενον, διαιρετὰ αὐτὰ ἔσεσθαι.

5 ἀπίθανον codd.: πιθανόν Furley

Context: commentary on *Physics* VI.1, 232a1–17.

7–8   Indivisible units of time are represented as Epicurean only here, at S.E. *M.* 10.142, and at P. Herc. 698, fr 23 *N* (Scott [149], 290); the evidence for them in the Epicurean Demetrius of Laconia, P. Herc. 1012, 48.1–15 is textually too insecure (see Sorabji [22], 375–6). Anyone adopting the staccato theory of motion might be tempted to include them, both because Diodorus had done so (**i** 17–24) and because Aristotle had argued (*Phys.* VI.1, 231b18–232a22), if less than cogently (see Sorabji [22], 366–7), that either magnitude, time and motion all consist of indivisibles or none do. But if Epicurus did indeed follow these leads, his precise reasoning does not survive. It could have been done by re-applying his arguments at **9A 1–6** against infinitely divisible magnitudes.

H Lucretius 2.216–50

(1) illud in his quoque te rebus cognoscere avemus,
corpora cum deorsum rectum per inane feruntur
ponderibus propriis, incerto tempore ferme
incertisque locis spatio depellere paulum,
tantum quod momen mutatum dicere possis.   220
(2) quod nisi declinare solerent, omnia deorsum,
imbris uti guttae, caderent per inane profundum,
nec foret offensus natus nec plaga creata
principiis: ita nil umquam natura creasset.
(3) quod si forte aliquis credit graviora potesse   225
corpora, quo citius rectum per inane feruntur,
incidere ex supero levioribus atque ita plagas
gignere quae possint genitalis reddere motus,
avius a vera longe ratione recedit.
nam per aquas quaecumque cadunt atque aera rarum,   230
haec pro ponderibus casus celerare necessest
propterea quia corpus aquae naturaque tenvis
aeris haud possunt aeque rem quamque morari,
sed citius cedunt gravioribus exsuperata.
at contra nulli de nulla parte neque ullo   235
tempore inane potest vacuum subsistere rei,
quin, sua quod natura petit, concedere pergat;
omnia quapropter debent per inane quietum
aeque ponderibus non aequis concita ferri.
haud igitur poterunt levioribus incidere umquam   240
ex supero graviora neque ictus gignere per se
qui varient motus per quos natura gerat res.
(4) quare etiam atque etiam paulum inclinare necessest
corpora; nec plus quam minimum, ne fingere motus
obliquos videamur et id res vera refutet.   245
namque hoc in promptu manifestumque esse videmus,
pondera, quantum in sest, non posse obliqua meare,
ex supero cum praecipitant, quod cernere possis.
sed nil omnino ⟨recta⟩ regione viai
declinare quis est qui possit cernere sese?   250

249 *recta* add. L: ⟨*nulla*⟩ Lachmann

Context: the laws of atomic motion.

Epicurean physics

For the same argument, see Cicero, *Fin.* 1.18–20, *Fat* 22.

243 etiam atque etiam This may conceivably qualify *inclinare* – atoms swerve 'again and again' (thus Kleve [257]), but it would be characteristic of Lucretius to mean 'again and again I say', as at 1.295.

244 minimum This translates ἐλάχιστον. That the swerve is by exactly one minimum is also reported at **18G 6**; Cicero, *Fin.* 1.19, *Fat.* 22, 46; Plutarch, *An. procr.* 1051C, *Soll. an.* 964C.

i Sextus Empiricus, M. 10.85–6, 97, 118–20

κομίζεται δὲ καὶ ἄλλη τις ἐμβριθὴς ὑπόμνησις εἰς τὸ μὴ εἶναι κίνησιν ὑπὸ Διοδώρου τοῦ Κρόνου, δι' ἧς παρίστησιν ὅτι κινεῖται μὲν οὐδὲ ἕν, κεκίνηται δέ. καὶ μὴ κινεῖσθαι μέν, τοῦτο ἀκόλουθόν ἐστι ταῖς κατ' αὐτὸν τῶν ἀμερῶν ὑποθέσεσιν. τὸ γὰρ ἀμερὲς σῶμα ὀφείλει ἐν ἀμερεῖ τόπῳ περιέχεσθαι, καὶ διὰ τοῦτο μήτε ἐν αὐτῷ κινεῖσθαι (ἐκπεπλήρωκε γὰρ αὐτόν, δεῖ δὲ τόπον ἔχειν μείζονα τὸ κινησόμενον) μήτε ἐν ᾧ μὴ ἔστιν· οὔπω γὰρ ἔστιν   5
ἐν ἐκείνῳ, ἵνα καὶ ἐν αὐτῷ κινηθῇ. ὥστε οὐδὲ κινεῖται. κεκίνηται δὲ κατὰ λόγον· τὸ γὰρ πρότερον ἐν τῷδε τῷ τόπῳ θεωρούμενον, τοῦτο ἐν ἑτέρῳ νῦν θεωρεῖται τόπῳ· ὅπερ οὐκ ἂν ἐγεγόνει μὴ κινηθέντος αὐτοῦ. οὗτος μὲν οὖν ὁ ἀνὴρ ἐπαρήγειν θελήσας τῷ οἰκείῳ δόγματι ἄτοπόν τι προσήκατο· πῶς γὰρ οὐκ ἄτοπον τὸ μηδενὸς κινουμένου λέγειν τι κεκινῆσθαι;
... τοιαῦται μὲν αἱ πρὸς τὸν λόγον ἐνστάσεις, δοκεῖ δὲ Διόδωρος πρὸς τὴν πρώτην εὐθὺς   I
ὑπηντηκέναι διδάσκων ὅτι ἐνδέχεται τῶν συντελεστικῶν ἀληθῶν ὄντων τὰ τούτων παρατατικὰ ψευδῆ τυγχάνειν. ἔστω γάρ τινα πρὸ ἐνιαυτοῦ γεγαμηκέναι καὶ ἕτερον μετ' ἐνιαυτόν. οὐκοῦν ἐπὶ τούτων τὸ μὲν "οὗτοι ἔγημαν" ἀξίωμα συντελεστικὸν ὂν ἀληθές ἐστιν, τὸ δ' "οὗτοι γαμοῦσι" παρατατικὸν καθεστὼς ψεῦδός ἐστίν· ὅτε γὰρ οὗτος ἐγάμει, οὔπω οὗτος ἐγάμει, καὶ ὅτε οὗτος ἐγάμει, οὐκέτι οὗτος ἐγάμει. τότε δ' ἂν ἦν ἀληθὲς ἐπ' αὐτῶν τὸ   I
οὗτοι γαμοῦσιν, εἰ ὁμόσε ἐγάμουν. δύναται οὖν τοῦ συντελεστικοῦ ἀληθοῦς ὄντος ψεῦδος εἶναι τὸ τούτου παρατατικόν ... ὅθεν τὰς μὲν τοιαύτας ἐπιχειρήσεις παραιτητέον, ἐκείνοις δὲ μάλιστα χρηστέον τοῖς λόγοις. εἰ κινεῖταί τι, νῦν κινεῖται· εἰ νῦν κινεῖται, ἐν τῷ ἐνεστῶτι χρόνῳ κινεῖται· εἰ δὲ ἐν τῷ ἐνεστῶτι χρόνῳ κινεῖται, ἐν ἀμερεῖ χρόνῳ ἄρα κινεῖται. εἰ γὰρ μερίζεται ὁ ἐνεστὼς χρόνος, πάντως εἰς τὸν παρῳχηκότα καὶ μέλλοντα μερισθήσεται, καὶ   2
οὕτως οὐκέτ' ἔσται ἐνεστώς. εἰ δ' ἐν ἀμερεῖ χρόνῳ τι κινεῖται, ἀμερίστους τόπους διέρχεται. εἰ δὲ ἀμερίστους τόπους διέρχεται, οὐ κινεῖται. ὅτε γὰρ ἔστιν ἐν τῷ πρώτῳ ἀμερεῖ τόπῳ, οὐ κινεῖται· ἔτι γὰρ ἔστιν ἐν τῷ πρώτῳ ἀμερεῖ τόπῳ. ὅτε δὲ ἔστιν ἐν τῷ δευτέρῳ ἀμερεῖ τόπῳ, πάλιν οὐ κινεῖται ἀλλὰ κεκίνηται. οὐκ ἄρα κινεῖταί τι.

Context: does motion exist?

8 οἰκείῳ δόγματι The staccato account of motion was, then, Diodorus' own doctrine (albeit with strong Aristotelian antecedents, cf. **9e**), not just a dialectical ploy. It probably served his formally Eleatic stance, redeeming the sensible world by analysing motion as a succession of static positions (see Denyer [209]).

12–16 For further examples in support of Diodorus' logical thesis, see S.E., *M.* 10.98–102.

17–24 The passage contains no attribution to Diodorus, and indeed at S.E., *M.* 10.143 Sextus shows that he himself does not know the thesis of indivisible units of time to be Diodorean. Nevertheless, a powerful case for a Diodorean origin is made by Denyer [209] and Sorabji [22], 19.

21–2   A feature of the (presumed) Diodorean theory, not replicated in Epicurus' version, is the derivation of the existence of partless magnitudes *from* that of partless times (although there is no reason to doubt that Diodorus, like Epicurus in **9A 3–6, C 3**, also used arguments of a Zenonian nature against infinite divisibility). As Denyer [209] has shown, the derivation is valid provided Diodorus is allowed the further premise that an object moving from A to B must pass through all intervening places.

12 Microscopic and macroscopic properties

A Epicurus, *Ep. Hdt.* 55–6

(1) ἀλλὰ μὴν οὐδὲ δεῖ νομίζειν πᾶν μέγεθος ἐν ταῖς ἀτόμοις ὑπάρχειν, ἵνα μὴ τὰ φαινόμενα ἀντιμαρτυρῇ· (2) παραλλαγὰς δέ τινας μεγεθῶν νομιστέον εἶναι. βέλτιον γὰρ καὶ τούτου προσόντος τὰ κατὰ τὰ πάθη καὶ τὰς αἰσθήσεις γινόμενα ἀποδοθήσεται. (3) πᾶν δὲ μέγεθος ὑπάρχον οὔτε χρήσιμόν ἐστι πρὸς τὰς τῶν ποιοτήτων διαφοράς, ἀφῖχθαί τε ἀμέλει ⟨ἔδει⟩ καὶ πρὸς ἡμᾶς ὁρατὰς ἀτόμους· ὃ οὐ θεωρεῖται γινόμενον, οὔθ' ὅπως ἂν γένοιτο ὁρατὴ ἄτομος ἔστιν ἐπινοῆσαι.   5

1 δεῖ Casaubon: ἀεὶ codd.   4 ὑπάρχον codd.: ὑπάρχειν Usener   5–6 ἀμέλει ⟨ἔδει⟩ Sedley: ἀμέλει codd.: ἀμ' ἔδει Usener   6 οὔθ' Usener: οὐδ' codd.

Context: immediately following **D**.

For Epicurus' target, Democritus' supposition of very large atoms, see Democritus fr. 207 Luria. It is widely doubted that Democritus can have held such an outrageous view. But it is a natural outcome of his οὐ μᾶλλον principle, by which any upper limit would be judged arbitrary and indefensible. Our failure to observe large atoms would be easily explained by his thesis (frr. 295, 382–3 Luria, cf. fr. 316) that in the cosmic vortex the largest atoms sink to the bottom—far down beneath us. Enormous atoms would admittedly weaken atomism's resilience to Zeno's divisibility paradoxes; but the idea is reported as an innovation on Democritus' part (fr. 206 Luria), and may date from a period in which the Zenonian threat had receded from prominence and atomist cosmology was being explored in its own right.

B Epicurus, *Ep. Hdt.* 42–3

(1) πρός τε τούτοις τὰ ἄτομα τῶν σωμάτων καὶ μεστά, ἐξ ὧν καὶ αἱ συγκρίσεις γίνονται καὶ εἰς ἃ διαλύονται, ἀπερίληπτά ἐστι ταῖς διαφοραῖς τῶν σχημάτων· οὐ γὰρ δυνατὸν γενέσθαι τὰς τοσαύτας διαφορὰς ἐκ τῶν αὐτῶν σχημάτων περιειλημμένων. (2) καὶ καθ' ἑκάστην δὲ σχημάτισιν ἁπλῶς ἄπειροί εἰσιν αἱ ὅμοιαι, ταῖς δὲ διαφοραῖς οὐχ ἁπλῶς ἄπειροι ἀλλὰ μόνον ἀπερίληπτοι (οὐδὲ γάρ φησιν ἐνδοτέρω εἰς ἄπειρον τὴν τομὴν τυγχάνειν. λήγει δέ, ἐπειδὴ αἱ ποιότητες μεταβάλλονται), εἰ μέλλει τις μὴ καὶ τοῖς μεγέθεσιν ἁπλῶς εἰς ἄπειρον αὐτὰς ἐκβάλλειν.   5

6 λήγει Hermann: λέγει codd.: λήγειν Usener

Context: immediately following **10A**.

6–7　The scholion is rightly ended at μεταβάλλονται by Mühll; most editors include the words which follow, but these appear to be part of Epicurus' argument, cf. **C 2**. The scholion is a rather inefficient reference to **D**'s argument that there must be something, viz. atoms, to survive all qualitative change. The emendation λήγει is irresistible—'it [division] comes to an end'—but there is no need to emend further to produce an infinitive, with Usener, since the scholiast is quite capable of shifting from *oratio obliqua* to *oratio recta* in this way, cf. *Ep. Hdt.* 44 fin.

7–8　The vagueness of this argument no doubt arises from the fact that it precedes, and hence cannot invoke, Epicurus' proofs of an upper limit to atomic size (**A**) and of minimal magnitudes (**9A**). In Lucretius (cf. **C**) the order has been suitably adjusted.

C Lucretius 2.478–531

(1) quod quoniam docui, pergam conectere rem quae
ex hoc apta fidem ducat, primordia rerum
finita variare figurarum ratione. 480
(2) quod si non ita sit, rursum iam semina quaedam
esse infinito debebunt corporis auctu.
namque in eadem una cuiusvis iam brevitate
corporis inter se multum variare figurae
non possunt: fac enim minimis e partibus esse 485
corpora prima tribus, vel paulo pluribus auge;
nempe ubi eas partis unius corporis omnis,
summa atque ima locans, transmutans dextera laevis,
omnimodis expertus eris, quam quisque det ordo
formai speciem totius corporis eius, 490
quod superest, si forte voles variare figuras,
addendum partis alias erit; inde sequetur,
assimili ratione alias ut postulet ordo,
si tu forte voles etiam variare figuras:
ergo formarum novitatem corporis augmen 495
subsequitur. quare non est ut credere possis
esse infinitis distantia semina formis,
ne quaedam cogas immani maximitate
esse, supra quod iam docui non posse probari.
(3) iam tibi barbaricae vestes Meliboeaque fulgens 500
purpura Thessalico concharum tacta colore,
aurea pavonum ridenti imbuta lepore
saecla, novo rerum superata colore iacerent
et contemptus odor smyrnae mellisque sapores,
et cycnea mele Phoebeaque daedala chordis 505
carmina consimili ratione oppressa silerent;
namque aliis aliud praestantius exoreretur.

cedere item retro possent in deteriores
omnia sic partis, ut diximus in meliores.
namque aliis aliud retro quoque taetrius esset   510
naribus auribus atque oculis orisque sapori.
quae quoniam non sunt, ⟨sed⟩ rebus reddita certa
finis utrimque tenet summam, fateare necessest
materiem quoque finitis differre figuris.
(4) denique ab ignibus ad gelidas hiemum usque pruinas   515
finitumst retroque pari ratione remensumst.
omnis enim calor ac frigus mediique tepores
interutrasque iacent explentes ordine summam.
ergo finita distant ratione creata,
ancipiti quoniam mucroni utrimque notantur,   520
hinc flammis illinc rigidis infesta pruinis.
(5) quod quoniam docui, pergam conectere rem quae
ex hoc apta fidem ducat, primordia rerum,
inter se simili quae sunt perfecta figura,
infinita cluere. etenim distantia cum sit   525
formarum finita, necesse est quae similes sint
esse infinitas aut summam materiai
finitam constare, id quod non esse probavi
versibus ostendens corpuscula materiai
ex infinito summam rerum usque tenere,   530
undique protelo plagarum continuato.

Context: following the illustrations at 2.381–477 (including F) of the explanatory
value of atomic shape. But Lucretius intended to insert between the two passages a
proof, corresponding to A, of the limited range of atomic sizes. He refers to such a
proof implicitly at 481–2 and explicitly at 498–9. That it was meant to stand
immediately before C can be inferred from 478–9, where hoc must refer to it, and not
to the theme of 381–477.
485–96   See the helpful comments of Furley [204], 41–3.
528–31   The reference is to 10B.

D   Epicurus, Ep. Hdt. 54–5

(1) καὶ μὴν καὶ τὰς ἀτόμους νομιστέον μηδεμίαν ποιότητα τῶν φαινομένων
προσφέρεσθαι πλὴν σχήματος καὶ βάρους καὶ μεγέθους καὶ ὅσα ἐξ
ἀνάγκης σχήματος συμφυῆ ἐστι. (2) ποιότης γὰρ πᾶσα μεταβάλλει· αἱ δὲ
ἄτομοι οὐδὲν μεταβάλλουσιν, ἐπειδή περ δεῖ τι ὑπομένειν ἐν ταῖς
διαλύσεσι τῶν συγκρίσεων στερεὸν καὶ ἀδιάλυτον, ὃ τὰς μεταβολὰς οὐκ   5
εἰς τὸ μὴ ὂν ποιήσεται οὐδ' ἐκ τοῦ μὴ ὄντος, ἀλλὰ κατὰ μεταθέσεις ἐν
πολλοῖς, τινῶν δὲ καὶ προσόδους καὶ ἀφόδους. (3) ὅθεν ἀναγκαῖον τὰ μὴ
μετατιθέμενα ἄφθαρτα εἶναι καὶ τὴν τοῦ μεταβάλλοντος φύσιν οὐκ
ἔχοντα, ὄγκους δὲ καὶ σχηματισμοὺς ἰδίους (τοῦτο γὰρ καὶ ἀναγκαῖον)

Epicurean physics

ὑπομένειν. (4) καὶ γὰρ ἐν τοῖς παρ᾽ ἡμῖν μετασχηματιζομένοις κατὰ τὴν   10
περιαίρεσιν τὸ σχῆμα ἐνυπάρχον λαμβάνεται, αἱ δὲ ποιότητες οὐκ
ἐνυπάρχουσαι ἐν τῷ μεταβάλλοντι, ὥσπερ ἐκεῖνο καταλείπεται, ἀλλ᾽ ἐξ
ὅλου τοῦ σώματος ἀπολλύμεναι. (5) ἱκανὰ οὖν τὰ ὑπολειπόμενα ταῦτα τὰς
τῶν συγκρίσεων διαφορὰς ποιεῖν, ἐπειδή περ ὑπολείπεσθαί γέ τινα
ἀναγκαῖον καὶ ⟨μὴ⟩ εἰς τὸ μὴ ὂν φθείρεσθαι.   15

7 μὴ del. Weil: δὴ Usener: μὲν Kochalsky   9–10 τοῦτο (κτλ.) codd.: ταῦτα γὰρ καὶ ἀναγκαῖον
ὑπομένειν Meibom   15 ⟨μὴ⟩ Aldobrandinus

Context: immediately following **15A**.

    1–2   In the remainder of the passage ποιότητες are secondary properties only; so
also probably at **A** 5. The implication, here alone, that they include primary
properties like shape may be the result of carelessness of expression.

    7   μή is unjustifiably excised by all editors except Bollack [122]. Since it has been
established (4–7, echoing **8A**) that change can only be by transference of parts, it is a
perfectly proper inference that *those things which do not admit of transference of parts*, the
atoms, cannot change, and, more specifically, cannot change their mass or shape (7–
10).

    10–13   Cf. **E 4**.

    13–15   Epicurus has maintained in 10–13 that in the process of pulverizing a
sensible body a primary property like shape endures even when secondary
properties – odour, for example – have vanished. But how do we know that the
primary properties which are left (τὰ ὑπολειπόμενα ταῦτα) do not also perish as the
process continues? That is, in effect, the question which the ἐπειδή περ . . . clause
answers: *something* must survive the process, if there is not to be destruction into
nothing; and that something can only be the primary properties (which are in
themselves sufficient to account for all macroscopic *explananda*).

E Lucretius 2.730–833 (with omissions)

        (1) nunc age dicta meo dulci quaesita labore   730
        percipe, ne forte haec albis ex alba rearis
        principiis esse, ante oculos quae candida cernis,
        aut ea quae nigrant nigro de semine nata;
        nive alium quemvis quae sunt imbuta colorem,
        propterea gerere hunc credas, quod materiai   735
        corpora consimili sint eius tincta colore.
        nullus enim color est omnino materiai
        corporibus, neque par rebus neque denique dispar.
        (2) in quae corpora si nullus tibi forte videtur
        posse animi iniectus fieri, procul avius erras.   740
        nam cum caecigeni, solis qui lumina numquam
        dispexere, tamen cognoscant corpora tactu
        ex ineunte aevo nullo coniuncta colore,
        scire licet nostrae quoque menti corpora posse

verti in notitiam nullo circumlita fuco.   745
denique nos ipsi caecis quaecumque tenebris
tangimus, haud ullo sentimus tincta colore . . .
(3) praeterea si nulla coloris principiis est
reddita natura et variis sunt praedita formis,
e quibus omne genus gignunt variantque colores,
propterea magni quod refert semina quaeque   760
cum quibus et quali positura contineantur
et quos inter se dent motus accipiantque,
perfacile extemplo rationem reddere possis
cur ea quae nigro fuerint paulo ante colore,
marmoreo fieri possint candore repente;   765
ut mare, cum magni commorunt aequora venti,
vertitur in canos candenti marmore fluctus.
dicere enim possis, nigrum quod saepe videmus,
materies ubi permixta est illius et ordo
principiis mutatus et addita demptaque quaedam,   770
continuo id fieri ut candens videatur et album.
quod si caeruleis constarent aequora ponti
seminibus, nullo possent albescere pacto.
nam quocumque modo perturbes caerula quae sint,
numquam in marmoreum possunt migrare colorem . . .   775
(4) quin etiam quanto in partis res quaeque minutas
distrahitur magis, hoc magis est ut cernere possis
evanescere paulatim stinguique colorem;
ut fit ubi in parvas partis discerpitur austrum:
purpura poeniceusque color clarissimu' multo,   830
filatim cum distractum est, disperditur omnis;
noscere ut hinc possis prius omnem efflare colorem
particulas quam discedant ad semina rerum.

Context: the start of the third main section of book 2, on the absence of secondary
properties from atoms. (For a similar argument, see Philodemus, *Sign.* 18.3–10.)
   740 **animi iniectus** Probably = ἐπιβολὴ τῆς διανοίας (see **17**).
   745 **notitiam** Probably = πρόληψιν (see **17**).

F Lucretius 2.381–407

(1) perfacile est animi ratione exsolvere nobis
quare fulmineus multo penetralior ignis
quam noster fluat e taedis terrestribus ortus.
dicere enim possis caelestem fulminis ignem
subtilem magis e parvis constare figuris   385
atque ideo transire foramina quae nequit ignis

noster hic e lignis ortus taedaque creatus.
(2) praeterea lumen per cornum transit, at imber
respuitur. quare? nisi luminis illa minora
corpora sunt quam de quibus est liquor almus aquarum.   390
(3) et quamvis subito per colum vina videmus
perfluere, at contra tardum cunctatur olivum,
aut quia nimirum maioribus est elementis
aut magis hamatis inter se perque plicatis,
atque ideo fit uti non tam diducta repente   395
inter se possint primordia singula quaeque
singula per cuiusque foramina permanare.
(4) huc accedit uti mellis lactisque liquores
iucundo sensu linguae tractentur in ore;
at contra taetra absinthi natura ferique   400
centauri foedo pertorquent ora sapore;
ut facile agnoscas e levibus atque rutundis
esse ea quae sensus iucunde tangere possunt,
at contra quae amara atque aspera cumque videntur,
haec magis hamatis inter se nexa teneri   405
proptereaque solere vias rescindere nostris
sensibus introituque suo perrumpere corpus.

Context: in the section (2.333–477) on the wide variety of atomic shapes and sizes,
which immediately precedes C.

13 Cosmology without teleology

A Epicurus, *Ep. Hdt.* 45

ἀλλὰ μὴν καὶ κόσμοι ἄπειροί εἰσιν, οἵ θ᾽ ὅμοιοι τούτῳ καὶ οἱ ἀνόμοιοι. αἵ τε
γὰρ ἄτομοι ἄπειροι οὖσαι, ὡς ἄρτι ἀπεδείχθη, φέρονται καὶ πορρωτάτω.
οὐ γὰρ κατανήλωνται αἱ τοιαῦται ἄτομοι, ἐξ ὧν ἂν γένοιτο κόσμος ἢ ὑφ᾽
ὧν ἂν ποιηθείη, οὔτ᾽ εἰς ἕνα οὔτ᾽ εἰς πεπερασμένους, οὔθ᾽ ὅσοι τοιοῦτοι
οὔθ᾽ ὅσοι διάφοροι τούτοις. ὥστε οὐδὲν τὸ ἐμποδοστατῆσόν ἐστι πρὸς τὴν   5
ἀπειρίαν τῶν κόσμων.

1 καὶ οἱ P: καὶ BF

Context: shortly after **11A**.

B Epicurus, *Ep. Pyth.* 88

κόσμος ἐστὶ περιοχή τις οὐρανοῦ, ἄστρα τε καὶ γῆν καὶ πάντα τὰ
φαινόμενα περιέχουσα, ἀποτομὴν ἔχουσα ἀπὸ τοῦ ἀπείρου καὶ καταλή-
γουσα ἐν πέρατι ἢ ἀραιῷ ἢ πυκνῷ καὶ οὐ λυομένου πάντα τὰ ἐν αὐτῷ
σύγχυσιν λήψεται – καὶ λήγουσα ἢ ἐν περιαγομένῳ ἢ ἐν στάσιν ἔχοντι καὶ

στρογγύλην ἢ τρίγωνον ἢ οἵαν δήποτε περιγραφήν· πανταχῶς γὰρ   5
ἐνδέχεται· τῶν γὰρ φαινομένων οὐδὲν ἀντιμαρτυρεῖ ⟨ἐν⟩ τῷδε τῷ κόσμῳ,
ἐν ᾧ λῆγον οὐκ ἔστι καταλαβεῖν.

2–3 κατα- secl. Mühll   4 καὶ λήγουσα Gassendi: καὶ λήγουσαν codd.: secl. Mühll   6 ⟨ἐν⟩ Usener

Context: immediately following the Letter to Pythocles' methodological introduction at
18C.

2   'The infinite' is probably the infinite void (cf. 23m with note), and being 'cut
off' from it may be no more than having firm boundaries, in a way that e.g. a free-
falling shower of atoms (as in 11H) does not. Cf. the account of world formation
attributed to Leucippus at D.L. 9.31 (=67 A 1 DK, KRS 563): φέρεσθαι κατὰ
ἀποτομὴν ἐκ τῆς ἀπείρου πολλὴ σώματα . . . εἰς μέγα κενόν.
4   Cf. 18D and Ep. Pyth. 92: in our world we cannot tell whether what revolves is
the heaven itself or just the heavenly bodies.
5–7   The multiple possibilities are all those mentioned in 2–5. All concern the
outermost layer of a world—which in our own world is quite unavailable to
inspection. For the 'non-contestation' methodology, see 18.

C Epicurus, Ep. Hdt. 73–4

(1) ἐπί τε τοῖς προειρημένοις τοὺς κόσμους δεῖ καὶ πᾶσαν σύγκρισιν
πεπερασμένην τὸ ὁμοειδὲς τοῖς θεωρουμένοις πυκνῶς ἔχουσαν νομίζειν
γεγονέναι ἀπὸ τοῦ ἀπείρου, πάντων τούτων ἐκ συστροφῶν ἰδίων
ἀποκεκριμένων καὶ μειζόνων καὶ ἐλαττόνων· (2) καὶ πάλιν διαλύεσθαι
πάντα, τὰ μὲν θᾶττον, τὰ δὲ βραδύτερον, καὶ τὰ μὲν ὑπὸ τῶν τοιῶνδε, τὰ   5
δὲ ὑπὸ τῶν τοιῶνδε τοῦτο πάσχοντα.

Context: following 7B.
3   γεγονέναι ἀπὸ τοῦ ἀπείρου I.e., as in B 2, by being separated off from the
infinite void.
4–6   For the mortality of worlds, see note on G.

D Lucretius 2.1052–1104 (with omissions)

(1) nullo iam pacto veri simile esse putandumst,
undique cum versum spatium vacet infinitum
seminaque innumero numero summaque profunda
multimodis volitent aeterno percita motu,   1055
hunc unum terrarum orbem caelumque creatum,
nil agere illa foris tot corpora materiai . . .
(2) huc accedit ut in summa res nulla sit una,
unica quae gignatur et unica solaque crescat,
quin alicuiu' siet saecli permultaque eodem
sint genere. in primis animalibus inice mentem;   1080
invenies sic montivagum genus esse ferarum,
sic hominum genitam prolem, sic denique mutas

55

squamigerum pecudes et corpora cuncta volantum.
quapropter caelum simili ratione fatendumst
terramque et solem lunam mare, cetera quae sunt,   1085
non esse unica, sed numero magis innumerali;
quandoquidem vitae depactus terminus alte
tam manet haec et tam nativo corpore constant,
quam genus omne quod hic generatimst rebus abundans.
(3) quae bene cognita si teneas, natura videtur   1090
libera continuo dominis privata superbis
ipsa sua per se sponte omnia dis agere expers.
nam pro sancta deum tranquilla pectora pace
quae placidum degunt aevum vitamque serenam,
quis regere immensi summam, quis habere profundi   1095
indu manu validas potis est moderanter habenas,
quis pariter caelos omnis convertere et omnis
ignibus aetheriis terras suffire feraces,
omnibus inve locis esse omni tempore praesto,
nubibus ut tenebras faciat caelique serena   1100
concutiat sonitu, tum fulmina mittat et aedes
saepe suas disturbet et in deserta recedens
saeviat, exercens telum quod saepe nocentis
praeterit exanimatque indignos inque merentis?

1089 *hic* Bernays *generatimst* Munro: *his generatim* QV   *abundans* O: *abundat* Marullus: *abundant*
QV   1094 *aevom vitamque* Avancius: *aevo multamque* OQV

Context: digression, following the denial of secondary attributes for atoms at 2.730–1022 (including **12E**).

E Lucretius 4.823–57

(1) illud in his rebus vitium vementer avemus   [822]
te fugere, errorem vitareque praemetuenter,   [823]
lumina ne facias oculorum clara creata,   825   [824]
prospicere ut possimus, et ut proferre queamus   [825]
proceros passus, ideo fastigia posse
surarum ac feminum pedibus fundata plicari,
bracchia tum porro validis ex apta lacertis
esse manusque datas utraque ⟨ex⟩ parte ministras,   830
ut facere ad vitam possemus quae foret usus.
cetera de genere hoc inter quaecumque pretantur
omnia perversa praepostera sunt ratione,
(2) nil ideo quoniam natumst in corpore ut uti
possemus, sed quod natumst id procreat usum.   835
nec fuit ante videre oculorum lumina nata

nec dictis orare prius quam lingua creatast,
sed potius longe linguae praecessit origo
sermonem multoque creatae sunt prius aures
quam sonus est auditus, et omnia denique membra   840
ante fuere, ut opinor, eorum quam foret usus.
haud igitur potuere utendi crescere causa.
(3) at contra conferre manu certamina pugnae
et lacerare artus foedareque membra cruore
ante fuit multo quam lucida tela volarent,   845
et vulnus vitare prius natura coegit
quam daret obiectum parmai laeva per artem.
scilicet et fessum corpus mandare quieti
multo antiquius est quam lecti mollia strata,
et sedare sitim prius est quam pocula natum.   850
haec igitur possent utendi cognita causa
credier, ex usu quae sunt vitaque reperta.
(4) illa quidem sorsum sunt omnia quae prius ipsa
nata dedere suae post notitiam utilitatis.
quo genere in primis sensus et membra videmus;   855
quare etiam atque etiam procul est ut credere possis
utilitatis ob officium potuisse creari.

823 *avemus* Bernays: *inhaerens* Marullus: *inesse* OQ   824 *te fugere* Bailey: *effugere* OQ   826 *queamus*
Lachmann: *via* OQ   [826] ante 822 transtulit Q¹   830 ⟨*ex*⟩ Lambinus

Context: digression immediately following **15D**.

F Lucretius 5.156–234

(1) dicere porro hominum causa voluisse parare
praeclaram mundi naturam proptereaque
allaudabile opus divum laudare decere
aeternumque putare atque immortale futurum
nec fas esse, deum quod sit ratione vetusta   160
gentibus humanis fundatum perpetuo aevo,
sollicitare suis ulla vi ex sedibus umquam
nec verbis vexare et ab imo evertere summa,
cetera de genere hoc adfingere et addere, Memmi,
desiperest. (2) quid enim immortalibus atque beatis   165
gratia nostra queat largirier emolumenti,
ut nostra quicquam causa gerere aggrediantur?
quidve novi potuit tanto post ante quietos
inlicere ut cuperent vitam mutare priorem?
nam gaudere novis rebus debere videtur   170
cui veteres obsunt; sed cui nil accidit aegri

tempore in anteacto, cum pulchre degeret aevum,
quid potuit novitatis amorem accendere tali?
(3) quidve mali fuerat nobis non esse creatis?
an, credo, in tenebris vita ac maerore iacebat,   175
donec diluxit rerum genitalis origo?
natus enim debet quicumque est velle manere
in vita, donec retinebit blanda voluptas.
qui numquam vero vitae gustavit amorem
nec fuit in numero, quid obest non esse creatum?   180
(4) exemplum porro gignundis rebus et ipsa
notities hominum divis unde insita primum est,
quid vellent facere ut scirent animoque viderent,
quove modost umquam vis cognita principiorum
quidque inter sese permutato ordine possent,   185
si non ipsa dedit specimen natura creandi?
(5) namque ita multa modis multis primordia rerum
ex infinito iam tempore percita plagis
ponderibusque suis consuerunt concita ferri
omnimodisque coire atque omnia pertemptare,   190
quaecumque inter se possent congressa creare,
ut non sit mirum si in talis disposituras
deciderunt quoque et in talis venere meatus,
qualibus haec rerum geritur nunc summa novando.
(6) quod ⟨si⟩ iam rerum ignorem primordia quae sint,   195
hoc tamen ex ipsis caeli rationibus ausim
confirmare aliisque ex rebus reddere multis,
nequaquam nobis divinitus esse paratam
naturam rerum: tanta stat praedita culpa.
principio quantum caeli tegit impetus ingens,   200
inde avidam partem montes silvaeque ferarum
possedere, tenent rupes vastaeque paludes
et mare quod late terrarum distinet oras.
inde duas porro prope partis fervidus ardor
assiduusque geli casus mortalibus aufert.   205
quod superest arvi, tamen id natura sua vi
sentibus obducat, ni vis humana resistat . . .
praeterea genus horriferum natura ferarum
humanae genti infestum terraque marique
cur alit atque auget? cur anni tempora morbos   220
apportant? quare mors immatura vagatur?
(7) tum porro puer, ut saevis proiectus ab undis
navita, nudus humi iacet, infans, indigus omni
vitali auxilio, cum primum in luminis oras

nixibus ex alvo matris natura profudit,   225
vagituque locum lugubri complet, ut aequumst
cui tantum in vita restet transire malorum.
at variae crescunt pecudes armenta feraeque
nec crepitacillis opus est nec cuiquam adhibendast
almae nutricis blanda atque infracta loquella   230
nec varias quaerunt vestis pro tempore caeli,
denique non armis opus est, non moenibus altis,
qui sua tutentur, quando omnibus omnia large
tellus ipsa parit naturaque daedala rerum.

186 *specimen* Pius: *speciem* OQ   195 ⟨*si*⟩ Marullus

Context: immediately following **23L**, on the gods' detachment.
  156 **hominum causa**   Cf. **G 5**. This is a weakened version of the Stoic thesis
(**54N**) that the world was created for the sake of gods and men. We know of no clear
evidence for such a view among pre-Hellenistic philosophers. This constitutes a
difficulty for Furley's generally plausible thesis [168], contested by Schmidt [169], that
the Stoics are not among Lucretius' targets. But Xen., *Mem.* 4.3 comes close.

G Cicero, *ND* 1.18–24

tum Velleius fidenter sane, ut solent isti, nihil tam verens quam ne dubitare aliqua de re
videretur, tamquam modo ex deorum concilio et ex Epicuri intermundiis descendisset, (1)
"audite" inquit "non futtilis commenticiasque sententias, non opificem
aedificatoremque mundi Platonis de Timaeo deum, nec anum fatidicam
Stoicorum Pronoeam, quam Latine licet Providentiam dicere, neque vero mundum   5
ipsum animo et sensibus praeditum rutundum ardentem volubilem deum,
portenta et miracula non disserentium philosophorum sed somniantium. (2)
quibus enim oculis animi intueri potuit vester Plato fabricam illam tanti
operis, qua construi a deo atque aedificari mundum facit; quae molitio quae
ferramenta qui vectes quae machinae qui ministri tanti muneris fuerunt; quem   10
ad modum autem oboedire et parere voluntati architecti aer ignis aqua terra
potuerunt; unde vero ortae illae quinque formae, ex quibus reliqua formantur, apte cadentes
ad animum afficiendum pariendosque sensus? longum est ad omnia, quae talia sunt ut optata
magis quam inventa videantur; sed illa palmaris, quod, qui non modo natum
mundum introduxerit sed etiam manu paene factum, is eum dixerit fore   15
sempiternum. hunc censes primis ut dicitur labris gustasse physiologiam id est
naturae rationem, qui quicquam quod ortum sit putet aeternum esse posse?
quae est enim coagmentatio non dissolubilis, aut quid est cuius principium
aliquod sit nihil sit extremum? (3) Pronoea vero si vestra est Lucili eadem,
requiro quae paulo ante, ministros machinas omnem totius operis dissignatio-   20
nem atque apparatum; sin alia est, cur mortalem fecerit mundum, non, quem
ad modum Platonicus deus, sempiternum. (4) ab utroque autem sciscitor cur
mundi aedificatores repente exstiterint, innumerabilia saecla dormierint; non

enim si mundus nullus erat saecla non erant (saecla nunc dico non ea quae dierum noctiumque numero annuis cursibus conficiuntur; nam fateor ea sine   2 mundi conversione effici non potuisse; sed fuit quaedam ab infinito tempore aeternitas, quam nulla circumscriptio temporum metiebatur, spatio tamen qualis ea fuerit intellegi potest, quod ne in cogitationem quidem cadit ut fuerit tempus aliquod nullum cum tempus esset) – isto igitur tam inmenso spatio quaero Balbe cur Pronoea vestra cessaverit. laboremne fugiebat? at iste nec attingit deum nec erat ullus,   3 (cum omnes naturae numini divino, caelum ignes terrae maria, parerent. quid autem erat quod concupisceret deus mundum signis et luminibus tamquam aedilis ornare? si ut deus ipse melius habitaret, antea videlicet tempore infinito in tenebris tamquam in gurgustio habitaverat. post autem: varietatene eum delectari putamus, qua caelum et terras exornatas videmus? quae ista potest esse oblectatio deo? quae si esset, non ea tam diu carere potuisset. (5) an haec, ut fere   3 . dicitis, hominum causa a deo constituta sunt? sapientiumne? propter paucos igitur tanta est rerum facta molitio. an stultorum? at primum causa non fuit cur de inprobis bene mereretur; deinde quid est adsecutus, cum omnes stulti sint sine dubio miserrimi, maxime quod stulti sunt (miserius enim stultitia quid possumus dicere), deinde quod ita multa sunt incommoda in vita, ut ea   4 (sapientes commodorum conpensatione leniant, stulti nec vitare venientia possint nec ferre praesentia. qui vero mundum ipsum animantem sapientemque esse dixerunt, nullo modo viderunt animi natura intellegentis in quam figuram cadere posset. de quo dicam equidem paulo post, nunc autem hactenus: admirabor eorum tarditatem qui animantem inmortalem et eundem beatum rutundum esse velint, quod ea forma neget ullam   4 esse pulchriorem Plato: at mihi vel cylindri vel quadrati vel coni vel pyramidis videtur esse formosior. quae vero vita tribuitur isti rutundo deo? nempe ut ea celeritate contorqueatur cui par nulla ne cogitari quidem possit; in qua non video ubinam mens constans et vita beata possit insistere. quodque in nostro corpore si minima ex parte significetur molestum sit, cur hoc idem non habeatur molestum in deo? terra enim profecto, quoniam mundi pars est, pars est etiam dei;   5 (atqui terrae maxumas regiones inhabitabilis atque incultas videmus, quod pars earum adpulsu solis exarserit, pars obriguerit nive pruinaque longinquo solis abscessu; quae, si mundus est deus, quoniam mundi partes sunt, dei membra partim ardentia partim refrigerata ducenda sunt . . ."

Context: the opening of the polemical introduction to Velleius' speech in defence of Epicurean theology.

The emphasis given to Plato and the Stoics here and at *ND* 1.36–41 contrasts with the cursory treatment at ibid. 1.25–35 of *all* the other Greek philosophers, including a brief attack on Aristotle (ibid. 33) based solely on his exoteric *De philosophia*. This supports our contention (vol. 1, 65) that Aristotle is not a major target for the Epicureans on this topic. As for Aristotle's related doctrine of the eternity of the world, it receives no direct Epicurean opposition (for a probable Stoic attack on the Aristotelian thesis, cf. **46J** note). Instead, both Velleius here and Lucretius (5.235–415) treat it as uncontroversial that the world had a beginning, and reserve their criticisms for the allegedly Platonic thesis that it will never perish. (On the evidence of the present passage, the Epicureans must be numbered along with Aristotle among those who took the *Timaeus* as a literal chronological account of the creation.)

13 Cosmology without teleology

12 **quinque formae** At *Tim.* 53c–56c Plato assigns four of the five regular solids to each of the four standard elements listed in 11. The fifth regular solid, the dodecahedron, is said at *Tim.* 55c to have been used 'in the decoration of the whole'. This apparently alludes not to a further set of particles, but to the heaven itself, fitted out with the twelve signs of the zodiac. If so, Velleius' target here could be a deviant interpretation of the Platonic theory (see Pease [329] ad loc.) in which the dodecahedron was assigned to the particles of a fifth element, aether – whose first appearance in the Platonic corpus as a distinct element is at *Epinomis* 981c. On the other hand, that would leave it obscure why this fifth element is not added to Velleius' list at 11. It is perhaps safer to suspect a confusion.

23–9 Velleius is evidently rebutting or anticipating a possible reply based on the *Timaeus*: since time only began with the creation of the heavens (*Tim.* 37c–38b), no chronological questions can be asked about a pre-cosmic era. For the debate, see Sorabji [22], esp. chh. 15 and 17.

30 **Pronoea . . . cessaverit** A somewhat distorted rendition of the Stoic doctrine at 28O 4, 46O.

44 **paulo post** See 23E 6.

H Cicero, *ND* 1.51–6

at quaerere a nobis Balbe soletis quae vita deorum sit quaeque ab is degatur aetas. ea videlicet qua nihil beatius nihil omnibus bonis affluentius cogitari potest. nihil enim agit, nullis occupationibus est inplicatus, nulla opera molitur, sua sapientia et virtute gaudet, habet exploratum fore se semper cum in maximis tum in aeternis voluptatibus. (1) hunc deum rite beatum dixerimus, vestrum vero laboriosissimum. sive enim ipse mundus 5 deus est, quid potest esse minus quietum quam nullo puncto temporis intermisso versari circum axem caeli admirabili celeritate: nisi quietum autem nihil beatum est; sive in ipso mundo deus inest aliquis, qui regat qui gubernet qui cursus astrorum mutationes temporum rerum vicissitudines ordinesque conservet, terras et maria contemplans hominum commoda vitasque tueatur, 10 ne ille est inplicatus molestis negotiis et operosis. nos autem beatam vitam in animi securitate et in omnium vacatione munerum ponimus. (2) docuit enim nos idem qui cetera, natura effectum esse mundum, nihil opus fuisse fabrica, tamque eam rem esse facilem, quam vos effici negetis sine divina posse sollertia, ut innumerabiles natura mundos effectura sit efficiat effecerit. quod 15 quia quem ad modum natura efficere sine aliqua mente possit non videtis, ut tragici poetae cum explicare argumenti exitum non potestis confugitis ad deum. cuius operam profecto non desideraretis, si inmensam et interminatum in omnis partis magnitudinem regionum videretis, in quam se iniciens animus et intendens ita late longeque peregrinatur, ut nullam tamen oram ultimi videat in qua possit insistere. in hac igitur 20 inmensitate latitudinum longitudinum altitudinum infinita vis innumerabilium volitat atomorum, quae interiecto inani cohaerescunt tamen inter se et aliae alias adprehendentes continuantur; ex quo efficiuntur eae rerum formae et figurae, quas vos effici posse sine follibus et incudibus non putatis. itaque inposuistis in cervicibus nostris sempiternum dominum, quem dies et noctes timeremus. quis enim non timeat omnia providentem et cogitantem et 25

Epicurean physics

animadvertentem et omnia ad se pertinere putantem curiosum et plenum negotii deum? hinc vobis extitit primum illa fatalis necessitas, quam εἱμαρμένην dicitis, ut quicquid accidat id ex aeterna veritate causarumque continuatione fluxisse dicatis. quanti autem haec philosophia aestimandast, cui tamquam aniculis, et his quidem indoctis, fato fieri videantur omnia. sequitur μαντική vestra, quae Latine divinatio dicitur, qua tanta inbueremur superstitione si vos audire   30 vellemus, ut haruspices augures harioli vates coniectores nobis essent colendi. his terroribus ab Epicuro soluti et in libertatem vindicati nec metuimus eos quos intellegimus nec sibi fingere ullam molestiam nec alteri quaerere, et pie sancteque colimus naturam excellentem atque praestantem.

Context: immediately following **23E**.
  5–11   For these alternative Stoic views of god, see e.g. **54B**.
  18–20 Cf. Lucretius 1.72ff., and the arguments in **10**.
  26–8   Cf. **55L**.
  29–31 For Stoic approval of divination, see **42C–E**.

I Lucretius 5.837–77

(1) multaque tum tellus etiam portenta creare
conatast mira facie membrisque coorta,
androgynem, interutrasque nec utrum, utrimque remotum,
orba pedum partim, manuum viduata vicissim,   840
multa sine ore etiam, sine vultu caeca reperta,
vinctaque membrorum per totum corpus adhaesu,
nec facere ut possent quicquam nec cedere quoquam
nec vitare malum nec sumere quod foret usus.
cetera de genere hoc monstra ac portenta creabat,   845
nequiquam, quoniam natura absterruit auctum
nec potuere cupitum aetatis tangere florem
nec reperire cibum nec iungi per Veneris res.
multa videmus enim rebus concurrere debere,
ut propagando possint procudere saecla;   850
pabula primum ut sint, genitalia deinde per artus
semina qua possint membris manare remissa;
feminaque ut maribus coniungi possit, habere
mutua qui mutent inter se gaudia uterque.
multaque tum interiisse animantum saecla necessest
nec potuisse propagando procudere prolem.
(2) nam quaecumque vides vesci vitalibus auris,
aut dolus aut virtus aut denique mobilitas est
ex ineunte aevo genus id tutata reservans.
multaque sunt, nobis ex utilitate sua quae   860
commendata manent, tutelae tradita nostrae.
principio genus acre leonum saevaque saecla

62

13 Cosmology without teleology

tutatast virtus, vulpis dolus et fuga cervos.
at levisomna canum fido cum pectore corda
et genus omne quod est veterino semine partum   865
lanigeraeque simul pecudes et bucera saecla
omnia sunt hominum tutelae tradita, Memmi.
nam cupide fugere feras pacemque secuta
sunt et larga suo sine pabula parta labore,
quae damus utilitatis eorum praemia causa.   870
(3) at quis nil horum tribuit natura, nec ipsa
sponte sua possent ut vivere nec dare nobis
utilitatem aliquam quare pateremur eorum
praesidio nostro pasci genus esseque tutum,
scilicet haec aliis praedae lucroque iacebant   875
indupedita suis fatalibus omnia vinclis,
donec ad interitum genus id natura redegit.

841 multa OQ: muta Naugerius   852 remissa Lachmann: remissis codd.

Context: the early history of the world.

This passage has been much admired for its apparent anticipation of some of the principles of Darwinism. Although it misses the crucial roles of heredity and gradual adaptation over centuries, it certainly exploits the notion of the survival of the fittest. For its possible indebtedness to Empedocles, see on J.

837 **tellus** According to Lucretius (2.1150–6, 5.791–825), the first living creatures sprang from the earth: even today the earth is fertile enough to generate plants, worms, insects etc., so in its prime it was quite capable of producing all manner of life forms.

J Simplicius, In Ar. Phys. 371,27–372,14

διὰ τί γὰρ ἄλλα μὲν ἀπόλλυται ὑπὸ τῶν οἰκείων μορίων, ὡς ἀετοὶ τοῦ ῥάμφους
ἐπικαμπτομένου λιμώττοντες, ἄλλα δὲ σώζεται, εἰ μὴ ἐκ ταὐτομάτου ταῦτα οὕτως
συνέτρεχε. καὶ ὅπου μὲν οὕτως πάντα συνέβη συνδραμεῖν, ὥσπερ καὶ εἰ ἕνεκά του ἐγίνετο,
ταῦτα, κἂν ἐκ ταὐτομάτου συνέστη, ἐπειδὴ ἐπιτηδείως συνέστη, διεσώθη· ὅσα δὲ μὴ
οὕτως, ἀπώλετο καὶ ἀπόλλυται. (1) ὥσπερ Ἐμπεδοκλῆς κατὰ τὴν τῆς φιλίας   5
ἀρχήν φησι γενέσθαι ὡς ἔτυχε μέρη πρῶτον τῶν ζώων, οἷον κεφαλὰς καὶ
χεῖρας καὶ πόδας, ἔπειτα συνιέναι ταῦτα "βουγενῆ ἀνδρόπρωρα, τὰ δ᾽
ἔμπαλιν ἐξανατέλλειν", "ἀνδρογενῆ" δηλονότι "βούπρωρα", τουτέστιν ἐκ
βοὸς καὶ ἀνθρώπου. καὶ ὅσα μὲν οὕτω συνέστη ἀλλήλοις ὥστε δύνασθαι
τυχεῖν σωτηρίας, ἐγένετο ζῶα καὶ ἔμεινεν διὰ τὸ ἀλλήλοις ἐκπληροῦν τὴν   10
χρείαν, τοὺς μὲν ὀδόντας τέμνοντάς τε καὶ λεαίνοντας τὴν τροφήν, τὴν δὲ
γαστέρα πέττουσαν, τὸ δὲ ἧπαρ ἐξαιματοῦν. καὶ ἡ μὲν τοῦ ἀνθρώπου
κεφαλὴ τῷ ἀνθρωπίνῳ σώματι συνελθοῦσα σώζεσθαι ποιεῖ τὸ ὅλον, τῷ δὲ
τοῦ βοὸς οὐ συναρμόζει καὶ διόλλυται· ὅσα γὰρ μὴ κατὰ τὸν οἰκεῖον
συνῆλθε λόγον, ἐφθάρη. τὸν αὐτὸν δὲ τρόπον καὶ νῦν πάντα συμβαίνει. (2)   15
ταύτης δοκοῦσι τῆς δόξης τῶν μὲν ἀρχαίων φυσικῶν ὅσοι τὴν ὑλικὴν

63

Epicurean physics

ἀνάγκην αἰτίαν εἶναι τῶν γινομένων φασί, τῶν δὲ ὑστέρων οἱ Ἐπικούρειοι. ἡ δὲ πλάνη γέγονεν αὐτοῖς, ὥς φησιν Ἀλέξανδρος, ἀπὸ τοῦ ἡγεῖσθαι
πάντα τὰ ἕνεκά του γινόμενα κατὰ προαίρεσιν γίνεσθαι καὶ λογισμόν, τὰ
δὲ φύσει μὴ οὕτως ὁρᾶν γινόμενα.   20

Context: commentary on Aristotle, *Phys.* 11.8, 198b16–34.

7–8   From Empedocles 31 B 61 DK = KRS 379.

16–18   That the Epicurean account, as represented in **I**, was indebted to this
theory of Empedocles' need not be doubted. However, it is probably a mistake to
assume that Empedocles' own motivation was the defence of a non-teleological world
view. Aristotle, by whom Simplicius is heavily influenced here, tends to treat the
Empedoclean theory as a paradigm of anti-teleology because it was apparently the
only model he could find in the work of his predecessors of what a non-teleological
explanation of nature would look like. (He never reports any such theory from
Democritus, for example.) This interpretation is consistent with the four-stage
account of zoogony attributed to Empedocles by Aetius (5.19.5 = 31 A 72 DK; see
KRS 375 and commentary), in which the random hybrids described in the present
passage are preceded by a first stage where individual limbs exist in isolation. But it
should be noticed that those solitary limbs were not themselves the product of
accident, but of subtle design. The eye for example was devised by Aphrodite, like a
lantern built by a lantern-maker for a preconceived purpose (31 A 86 + 84 DK, KRS
389). Even when allowance is made for an element of metaphor here, it is clear that
Empedocles' zoogonical theory treated the origin of individual limbs and organs in a
quite teleological way – entirely contrary to an Epicurean text like **E**. He perhaps
introduced the subsequent stage of random combinations principally in order to
explain the immense *diversity* of animal forms.

14 Soul

A Epicurus, *Ep. Hdt.* 63–7

(1) μετὰ δὲ ταῦτα δεῖ συνορᾶν ἀναφέροντα ἐπὶ τὰς αἰσθήσεις καὶ τὰ πάθη –
οὕτω γὰρ ἡ βεβαιοτάτη πίστις ἔσται – ὅτι ἡ ψυχὴ σῶμά ἐστι λεπτομερὲς
παρ' ὅλον τὸ ἄθροισμα παρεσπαρμένον, προσεμφερέστατον δὲ πνεύματι
θερμοῦ τινα κρᾶσιν ἔχοντι καὶ πῆ μὲν τούτῳ προσεμφερές, πῆ δὲ τούτῳ·
ἔστι δὲ τὸ μέρος πολλὴν παραλλαγὴν εἰληφὸς τῇ λεπτομερείᾳ καὶ αὐτῶν   5
τούτων, συμπαθὲς δὲ τούτῳ μᾶλλον καὶ τῷ λοιπῷ ἀθροίσματι· (2) τοῦτο
δὲ πᾶν αἱ δυνάμεις τῆς ψυχῆς δηλοῦσι καὶ τὰ πάθη καὶ αἱ εὐκινησίαι καὶ αἱ
διανοήσεις καὶ ὧν στερόμενοι θνήσκομεν. (3) καὶ μὴν καὶ ὅτι ἔχει ἡ ψυχὴ
τῆς αἰσθήσεως τὴν πλείστην αἰτίαν δεῖ κατέχειν· οὐ μὴν εἰλήφει ἂν
ταύτην, εἰ μὴ ὑπὸ τοῦ λοιποῦ ἀθροίσματος ἐστεγάζετό πως. τὸ δὲ λοιπὸν   10
ἄθροισμα παρασκευάσαν ἐκείνῃ τὴν αἰτίαν ταύτην μετείληφε καὶ αὐτὸ
τοιούτου συμπτώματος παρ' ἐκείνης, οὐ μέντοι πάντων ὧν ἐκείνη
κέκτηται· (4) διὸ ἀπαλλαγείσης τῆς ψυχῆς οὐκ ἔχει τὴν αἴσθησιν. οὐ γὰρ

14 Soul

αὐτὸ ἐν ἑαυτῷ ταύτην ἐκέκτητο τὴν δύναμιν, ἀλλ' ἑτέρῳ ἅμα συγγεγενη-
μένῳ αὐτῷ παρεσκεύαζεν, ὃ διὰ τῆς συντελεσθείσης περὶ αὐτὸ δυνάμεως   15
κατὰ τὴν κίνησιν σύμπτωμα αἰσθητικὸν εὐθὺς ἀποτελοῦν ἑαυτῷ ἀπεδίδου
κατὰ τὴν ὁμούρησιν καὶ συμπάθειαν καὶ ἐκείνῳ, καθάπερ εἶπον. (5) διὸ δὴ
καὶ ἐνυπάρχουσα ἡ ψυχὴ οὐδέποτε ἄλλου τινὸς μέρους ἀπηλλαγμένου
αἰσθητήσει· ἀλλ' ἃ ἂν καὶ ταύτης συναπόληται τοῦ στεγάζοντος λυθέντος
εἴθ' ὅλου εἴτε καὶ μέρους τινός, ἐάν περ διαμένῃ, ἕξει τὴν αἴσθησιν. τὸ   20
δὲ λοιπὸν ἄθροισμα διαμένον καὶ ὅλον καὶ κατὰ μέρος οὐκ ἔχει τὴν
αἴσθησιν ἐκείνου ἀπηλλαγμένου, ὅσον ποτέ ἐστι τὸ συντεῖνον τῶν ἀτόμων
πλῆθος εἰς τὴν τῆς ψυχῆς φύσιν. (6) καὶ μὴν καὶ λυομένου τοῦ ὅλου
ἀθροίσματος ἡ ψυχὴ διασπείρεται καὶ οὐκέτι ἔχει τὰς αὐτὰς δυνάμεις οὐδὲ
κινεῖται, ὥστε οὐδ' αἴσθησιν κέκτηται. οὐ γὰρ οἷόν τε νοεῖν αὐτὸ   25
αἰσθανόμενον μὴ ἐν τούτῳ τῷ συστήματι καὶ ταῖς κινήσεσι ταύταις
χρώμενον, ὅταν τὰ στεγάζοντα καὶ περιέχοντα μὴ τοιαῦτα ᾖ, ἐν οἷς νῦν
οὖσα ἔχει ταύτας τὰς κινήσεις. (7) ἀλλὰ μὴν καὶ τόδε γε δεῖ προσκατα-
νοεῖν, ὅτι τὸ ἀσώματον λέγεται κατὰ τὴν πλείστην ὁμιλίαν τοῦ ὀνόματος
ἐπὶ τοῦ καθ' ἑαυτὸ νοηθέντος ἄν· καθ' ἑαυτὸ δὲ οὐκ ἔστι νοῆσαι τὸ   30
ἀσώματον πλὴν τοῦ κενοῦ. τὸ δὲ κενὸν οὔτε ποιῆσαι οὔτε παθεῖν δύναται,
ἀλλὰ κίνησιν μόνον δι' ἑαυτοῦ τοῖς σώμασι παρέχεται. ὥστ' οἱ λέγοντες
ἀσώματον εἶναι τὴν ψυχὴν ματαιίζουσιν. οὐθὲν γὰρ ἂν ἐδύνατο ποιεῖν οὔτε
πάσχειν, εἰ ἦν τοιαύτη· νῦν δ' ἐναργῶς ἀμφότερα ταῦτα διαλαμβάνεται
περὶ τὴν ψυχὴν τὰ συμπτώματα. ταῦτα οὖν πάντα τὰ διαλογίσματα περὶ ψυχῆς   35
ἀνάγων τις ἐπὶ τὰ πάθη καὶ τὰς αἰσθήσεις, μνημονεύων τῶν ἐν ἀρχῇ ῥηθέντων, ἱκανῶς
κατόψεται τοῖς τύποις ἐμπεριειλημμένα εἰς τὸ κατὰ μέρος ἀπὸ τούτων ἐξακριβοῦσθαι
βεβαίως.

5 τὸ codd.: τι Woltjer   7 δηλοῦσι Gassendi: δῆλον codd.   19 ἀναισθητήσει Kühn: ἀναισθήσει B: ἀναισθησία FP: ἀναισθητεῖ Schneider   ταύτης συν- Sedley: ταύτῃ ξυν- codd.: ταύτης ξυν-Usener   20 ἔξει Usener: ὀξὺ codd.: σώζει Mühll   28 post τόδε scholion (=i)   29 λέγεται Bignone: λέγει γὰρ codd.: λέγομεν Mühll: λέγει–ὀνόματος ut schol. excl. Usener   34 διαλαμβάνεται Bailey: διαλαμβάνει codd.

Context: between **11E** and **7B**.

3 **ἄθροισμα** Epicurus scrupulously avoids contrasting the soul with the 'body' in this context, since soul is also body. Hence the constant circumlocutions.

πνεύματι It is obviously tempting to compare the identical term for the 'breath' which constitutes the soul in Stoicism (**53G**). Note, however, that Stoic πνεῦμα is warm breath, a universal life force, whereas Epicurean πνεῦμα is wind (at least on Lucretius' evidence; see also note on **C** 1–3), singled out for its motive power (**C, D 4**; cf. Lucretius 4.892–902) and kept quite distinct from the warmth-giving element (indeed, it contributes *coldness* at **D 4**). What really deserves comparison with Stoic 'breath' is the *amalgam* of wind and heat described here.

5–6 Kerferd [220] interprets as follows: 'The part (viz. the soul itself) has acquired great mobility as a result of the lightness of parts of just these things

Epicurean physics

(πνεῦμα and heat)'. But there are two reasons for preferring the more favoured interpretation of παραλλαγήν as 'difference', assumed in our translation 'But there is that part which differs greatly also from wind and heat themselves in its fineness of structure'. First, a comparison seems required here if τούτῳ μᾶλλον in 6 is to be intelligible; the genitive of comparison (τούτων) is well attested with παραλλάσσειν, for which Epicurus' παραλλαγὴν εἰληφέναι is merely a periphrasis. Second, by singling out πνεῦμα and heat as responsible for the soul's mobility, Kerferd's interpretation is letting these usurp the role which in Lucretius is fulfilled *par excellence* by the 'nameless' element. This would hardly leave enough common ground between *Ep. Hdt.* and Lucretius to justify speaking of the same theory underlying both. And if we were now, with Heinze [159] and Kerferd, to take τὸ μέρος as referring to the soul itself (cf. Diogenes of Oenoanda 37.3.9–10, τὸ ψυχικὸν ἡμῶν . . . μέρος), Epicurus would be saying that the soul, although resembling wind and heat, differs (ἔστι . . . εἰληφός as periphrastic perfect – Kerferd) from them both in its fineness: the unwelcome implication would be that the atoms characteristic of wind and heat are not present in the soul at all, contrary to all the other evidence. Hence caution and economy bring us back to the majority view that τὸ μέρος refers to the nameless soul-element of the Lucretian account. (This would have been clearer, as Kerferd rightly points out, had Epicurus put a καί before τὸ μέρος; but the καί before αὐτῶν already carries much of the same force, so that an additional καί would have read oddly.) On this account, then, *Ep. Hdt.* already picks out three of the eventual four soul-elements. The talk in 3–4 of soul resembling, rather than containing, wind and heat, does not count against their being in a sense ingredients, but is meant to allow for the fact that soul is a 'blend' in which the individual ingredients so recombine as to lose their separate identity. See further vol. 1, 71, and notes on **B–C** below. Similar language is not required in the case of the nameless element, since it has no known separate identity in the first place. As for 'air', we must take it either that it had not yet at the relatively early date of *Ep. Hdt.* (cf. Sedley [105], n. 73) been added as a distinct element of the soul, or that πνεῦμα was understood as covering both 'wind' and 'air'. In favour of the latter alternative, see note on **C** 1–3.

As for the silence here about the mind–spirit distinction (cf. **B, i**), it need represent no more than Epicurus' choice of emphases, and not doctrinal incompleteness at the date of *Ep. Hdt.* It is, however, uncertain that the distinction was already in the system which he had inherited from Democritus (cf. Democritus frr. 68–9, 452–8 Luria).

13–17   The imperfects, and likewise the pluperfect, may be of the 'dialectical' kind (represented by 'we saw that . . .' in our translation), resuming points held already to have been established at 10–13: hence also καθάπερ εἶπον, 17. The present sentence is not, however, straight repetition, but expands the earlier account of the joint functioning of soul and body by describing its inception during the process of birth itself: this assumption seems to make the best sense of κίνησιν ('process') and εὐθύς in 16. Alternatively, the past tenses may have the same force as that in **j** 357.

17   συμπάθειαν   Cf. 6, and note on **B** 168.

17–23   Diogenes of Oenoanda, 37.1–4, expands on this evidence of the soul's having 'the greater share of the responsibility' (τοῦ τῆς αἰτίας πλεονεκτή[μ]ατος; cf. 8–9): even a body severely reduced by disease or mutilation is often kept alive by the soul; whereas a perfectly intact body cannot retain sensation once the soul has been separated from it.

22–3 **συντεῖνον** . . . **εἰς**   This is rightly taken by Bignone [121] and Bailey [117] as 'contributing to . . .', 'going to make up . . .', citing the parallels of *Ep. Hdt.* 79 and 80; see also *Ep. Pyth.* 84. Editorial importations of 'attunement' or 'tension' seem alien to the Epicurean theory. The point of the elaborate phrase will be to allow for the supposed fact that some soul atoms remain even in the dead body – see Lucretius 3.713ff.

25 **αὐτό**   The use of the neuter to refer to soul must pick up ἐκείνου . . . ὅσον κτλ. at 22–3.

30–2   Cf. **5B 8–9**.

B   Lucretius 3.136–76

> (1) nunc animum atque animam dico coniuncta teneri
> inter se atque unam naturam conficere ex se,
> sed caput esse quasi et dominari in corpore toto
> consilium quod nos animum mentemque vocamus.
> idque situm media regione in pectoris haeret.   140
> hic exsultat enim pavor ac metus, haec loca circum
> laetitiae mulcent; hic ergo mens animusquest.
> cetera pars animae per totum dissita corpus
> paret et ad numen mentis momenque movetur.
> (2) idque sibi solum per se sapit, ⟨id⟩ sibi gaudet,   145
> cum neque res animam neque corpus commovet ulla
> et quasi, cum caput aut oculus temptante dolore
> laeditur in nobis, non omni concruciamur
> corpore, sic animus nonnumquam laeditur ipse
> laetitiaque viget, cum cetera pars animai   150
> per membra atque artus nulla novitate cietur.
> verum ubi vementi magis est commota metu mens,
> consentire animam totam per membra videmus
> sudoresque ita palloremque exsistere toto
> corpore et infringi linguam vocemque aboriri,   155
> caligare oculos, sonere auris, succidere artus,
> denique concidere ex animi terrore videmus
> saepe homines; facile ut quivis hinc noscere possit
> esse animam cum animo coniunctam, quae cum animi vi
> percussast, exim corpus propellit et icit.   160
> (3) haec eadem ratio naturam animi atque animai
> corpoream docet esse. ubi enim propellere membra,
> corripere ex somno corpus mutareque vultum
> atque hominem totum regere ac versare videtur,
> quorum nil fieri sine tactu posse videmus   165
> nec tactum porro sine corpore, nonne fatendumst
> corporea natura animum constare animamque?

Epicurean physics

praeterea pariter fungi cum corpore et una
consentire animum nobis in corpore cernis.
si minus offendit vitam vis horrida teli   170
ossibus ac nervis disclusis intus adacta,
at tamen insequitur languor terraeque petitus
suavis et in terra mentis qui gignitur aestus,
interdumque quasi exsurgendi incerta voluntas.
ergo corpoream naturam animi esse necessest,   175
corporeis quoniam telis ictuque laborat.

145 ⟨id⟩ Wakefield   146 ulla codex Laurentianus 35.31: una OQV

Context: the opening of Lucretius' own account of soul, following rejection of the
theory that soul is an attunement.

139 **animum mentemque**   Lucretius is announcing that these terms will
operate as straight synonyms in his discourse, as indeed they do. We have, therefore,
to avoid confusion, adopted the single translation 'mind' for both.

141   For Stoic defence of the same view, see **34J, 53U, 65H**.

143   Lucretius curiously omits to provide a term for ψυχή, and *anima* often has to
stand in for it (as explicitly from **F** 1 on).

168 **pariter fungi**   = συμπάσχειν, cf. **A** 6, 17. The dominant sense is that of
being affected in a comparable way by the same thing at the same time; but the
alternative translation *mutua fungi* at 3.801 appears to add the idea of interaction
between the two, as in the Stoic account of the συμπάθεια between soul and body
(**45C**).

C Aetius 4.3.11 (Usener 315)

Ἐπίκουρος [*sc.* λέγει τὴν ψυχὴν] κρᾶμα ἐκ τεττάρων, ἐκ ποιοῦ πυρώδους,
ἐκ ποιοῦ ἀερώδους, ἐκ ποιοῦ πνευματικοῦ, ἐκ τετάρτου τινὸς ἀκατονο-
μάστου· τοῦτο δ᾽ ἦν αὐτῷ τὸ αἰσθητικόν. ὧν τὸ μὲν πνεῦμα κίνησιν, τὸν δὲ
ἀέρα ἠρεμίαν, τὸ δὲ θερμὸν τὴν φαινομένην θερμότητα τοῦ σώματος, τὸ δ᾽
ἀκατονόμαστον τὴν ἐν ἡμῖν ἐμποιεῖν αἴσθησιν· ἐν οὐδενὶ γὰρ τῶν   5
ὀνομαζομένων στοιχείων εἶναι αἴσθησιν.

Context: doxography of physicalist theories of soul.

1 **κρᾶμα**   'Blend', the product of a κρᾶσις, or 'blending' (cf. **A** 4). The
importance of this technical concept is well brought out by Kerferd [220], 89–91.
Alexander, *Mixt.* 214, 28–215, 8 (Usener 290) is no doubt right to attribute to Epicurus
this doctrine of true blending as the recombination of the individual atoms of the
original substances into a new substance. But one may, following the lead of Todd
[203], 297, doubt Alexander's belief that in this Epicurus was revising the existing
Democritean position, and also wonder why the theory should, as Kerferd maintains,
imply a doctrine of molecules. There seems to be no good evidence for Epicurean
molecules (cf. Kerferd, 89), and Epicurus, even if he had thought of the possibility,
might well have rejected it on the ground that patterns of atomic motion in a κρᾶμα
might range beyond any supposed molecular grouping, thus depriving 'molecules' of
sufficient permanence.

1–3   These are the four Lucretian elements of the soul, exactly as listed also by Plutarch (*Col.* 1118E = Usener 314), except that Plutarch has the standard θερμοῦ instead of πυρώδους (as does the present text itself at 4; see further on **i** below). It follows that the Greek term translated *ventus* by Lucretius is πνεῦμα (see further, note on **A** 3), which is indeed Epicurus' regular term for 'wind' in *Ep. Pyth.* The adjectival endings, -ώδους and -ικοῦ correspond to Epicurus' talk of resemblance in **A** 3ff., to emphasize that the elements air, etc. are not themselves present in the blend, but only their constituent atoms. The difference between 'wind' and 'air' remains problematic, and Lucretius does little to help at 3.231–6. One expects the two to consist of the same kind of atoms in different arrangements or patterns of motion – thus Lucretius 6.685, *ventus enim fit ubi est agitando percitus aer.* But it is hard to see how this difference could survive, other than perhaps accidentally, in a κρᾶμα, in which the constituent atoms are anyway recombined in new patterns. Presumably, then, there are only three kinds of soul atoms, with the 'airy' ones behaving sometimes like still air and sometimes like wind, thus accounting for rest as well as motion. If so, the four-element scheme is a simplistic overinterpretation by Epicurus' followers, and the threefold scheme of **A** begins to look the more correct of the two.

5–6   Cf. Lucretius 3.238–40.

D   Lucretius 3.258–322

       nunc ea quo pacto inter sese mixta quibusque
       compta modis vigeant rationem reddere aventem
       abstrahit invitum patrii sermonis egestas;   260
       sed tamen, ut potero summatim attingere, tangam.
       (1) inter enim cursant primordia principiorum
       motibus inter se, nil ut secernier unum
       possit nec spatio fieri divisa potestas,
       sed quasi multae vis unius corporis exstant.   265
       quod genus in quovis animantum viscere vulgo
       est odor et quidam calor et sapor, et tamen ex his
       omnibus est unum perfectum corporis augmen;
       sic calor atque aer et venti caeca potestas
       mixta creant unam naturam et mobilis illa   270
       vis, initum motus ab se quae dividit ollis,
       sensifer unde oritur primum per viscera motus.
       (2) nam penitus prorsum latet haec natura subestque,
       nec magis hac infra quicquam est in corpore nostro
       atque anima est animae proporro totius ipsa.   275
       quod genus in nostris membris et corpore toto
       mixta latens animi vis est animaeque potestas,
       corporibus quia de parvis paucisque creatast;
       sic tibi nominis haec expers vis facta minutis
       corporibus latet atque animae quasi totius ipsa   280
       proporrost anima et dominatur corpore toto.

(3) consimili ratione necessest ventus et aer
et calor inter se vigeant commixta per artus
atque aliis aliud subsit magis emineatque
ut quiddam fieri videatur ab omnibus unum,   285
ni calor ac ventus sorsum sorsumque potestas
aeris interemant sensum diductaque solvant.
(4) est etiam calor ille animo, quem sumit, in ira
cum fervescit et ex oculis micat acrius ardor.
est et frigida multa comes formidinis aura   290
quae ciet horrorem membris et concitat artus.
est etiam quoque pacati status aeris ille,
pectore tranquillo qui fit vultuque sereno.
sed calidi plus est illis quibus acria corda
iracundaque mens facile effervescit in ira.   295
quo genere in primis vis est violenta leonum,
pectora qui fremitu rumpunt plerumque gementes
nec capere irarum fluctus in pectore possunt.
at ventosa magis cervorum frigida mens est
et gelidas citius per viscera concitat auras   300
quae tremulum faciunt membris exsistere motum.
at natura boum placido magis aere vivit,
nec nimis irai fax umquam subdita percit
fumida, suffundens caecae caliginis umbram,
nec gelidis torpet telis perfixa pavoris: 305
interutrasque sitast, cervos saevosque leones.
(5) sic hominum genus est. quamvis doctrina politos
constituat pariter quosdam, tamen illa relinquit
naturae cuiusque animi vestigia prima.
nec radicitus evelli mala posse putandumst,   310
quin proclivius hic iras decurrat ad acris,
ille metu citius paulo temptetur, at ille
tertius accipiat quaedam clementius aequo.
inque aliis rebus multis differre necessest
naturas hominum varias moresque sequaces;   315
quorum ego nunc nequeo caecas exponere causas
nec reperire figurarum tot nomina quot sunt
principiis, unde haec oritur variantia rerum.
illud in his rebus video firmare potesse,
usque adeo naturarum vestigia linqui   320
parvula quae nequeat ratio depellere nobis,
ut nil impediat dignam dis degere vitam.

309 *naturae* Marullus: *natura* codd.   321 *nobis* Lachmann: *noctis* O: *noctes* QV

Context: following the enumeration at 231–57 of the soul's four elements.

258 **ea**   The four soul elements.

260 **patrii sermonis egestas**   Kerferd [220], observing that at 1.832 this phrase signals Lucretius' apology for his inability to Latinize a Greek technical term, rightly suggests the same motive here – the lack of a technical vocabulary to convey κρᾶμα at 262–87.

262 **principiorum**   'The elements', i.e. heat, air, etc., cf. **C** 6, στοιχείων. On this, see Kerferd [220], 90–1.

268   For a body as a 'complex' of its permanent properties, see **7B 2–3**.

273–4   The spatial language describes not the location of the fourth element but its relative undetectability, as the analogy at 276–8 explains.

284   Although the three elements of wind, air and heat are thoroughly blended, some will be more prominent than others in the mix. This is presumably to prepare us for the explanation of differences of temperament at 288–322.

317–18   Lucretius' one hint that the account of the soul's composition may be a simplification.

E Lucretius 4.877–91

(1) nunc qui fiat uti passus proferre queamus,
cum volumus, quareque datum sit membra movere,
et quae res tantum hoc oneris protrudere nostri
corporis insuerit, dicam: tu percipe dicta.   880
(2) dico animo nostro primum simulacra meandi
accidere atque animum pulsare, ut diximus ante.
inde voluntas fit; neque enim facere incipit ullam
rem quisquam, quam mens providit quid velit ante.
id quod providet, illius rei constat imago.   885
(3) ergo animus cum sese ita commovet ut velit ire
inque gredi, ferit extemplo quae in corpore toto
per membra atque artus animai dissita vis est.
et facilest factu, quoniam coniuncta tenetur.
(4) inde ea proporro corpus ferit, atque ita tota   890
paulatim moles protruditur atque movetur.

878 *quareque* Merrill: *vareque* OQP: *varieque* ed. Veronensis   890 *ferit* Marullus: *perit* OQ

Context: one in the series of vital functions whose mechanics are explained in book 4.

F Lucretius 3.417–62

(1) nunc age, nativos animantibus et mortalis
esse animos animasque levis ut noscere possis,
conquisita diu dulcique reperta labore
digna tua pergam disponere carmina vita.   420
tu fac utrumque uno sub iungas nomine eorum,

atque animam verbi causa cum dicere pergam,
mortalem esse docens, animum quoque dicere credas,
quatenus est unum inter se coniunctaque res est.
(2) principio quoniam tenuem constare minutis   425
corporibus docui multoque minoribus esse
principiis factam quam liquidus umor aquai
aut nebula aut fumus – nam longe mobilitate
praestat et a tenui causa magis icta movetur;
quippe ubi imaginibus fumi nebulaeque movetur.   430
quod genus in somnis sopiti ubi cernimus alte
exhalare vaporem altaria ferreque fumum;
nam procul haec dubio nobis simulacra geruntur —
nunc igitur quoniam quassatis undique vasis
diffluere umorem et laticem discedere cernis   435
et nebula ac fumus quoniam discedit in auras,
crede animam quoque diffundi multoque perire
ocius et citius dissolvi in corpora prima,
cum semel ex hominis membris ablata recessit.
quippe etenim corpus, quod vas quasi constitit eius,   440
cum cohibere nequit conquassatum ex aliqua re
ac rarefactum detracto sanguine venis,
aere qui credas posse hanc cohiberier ullo,
corpore qui nostro rarus magis incohibensquest?
(3) praeterea gigni pariter cum corpore et una   445
crescere sentimus pariterque senescere mentem.
nam velut infirmo pueri teneroque vagantur
corpore, sic animi sequitur sententia tenvis.
inde ubi robustis adolevit viribus aetas,
consilium quoque maius et auctior est animi vis.   450
post ubi iam validis quassatum est viribus aevi
corpus et obtusis ceciderunt viribus artus,
claudicat ingenium, delirat lingua, ⟨labat⟩ mens,
omnia deficiunt atque uno tempore desunt.
ergo dissolui quoque convenit omnem animai   455
naturam, ceu fumus, in altas aeris auras;
quandoquidem gigni pariter pariterque videmus
crescere et, ut docui, simul aevo fessa fatisci.
(4) huc accedit uti videamus, corpus ut ipsum
suscipere immanis morbos durumque dolorem,   460
sic animum curas acris luctumque metumque;
quare participem leti quoque convenit esse.

444 *incohibensquest* Bergk: *incohibescit* OQV: *incohibens sit* Woltjer   453 ⟨*labat*⟩ Lachmann: ⟨*madet*⟩ Q¹

Context: the opening of Lucretius' long series of arguments for the mortality of the soul.

G Lucretius 3.624–33

praeterea si immortalis natura animaist
et sentire potest secreta a corpore nostro,   625
quinque, ut opinor, eam faciundum est sensibus auctam.
nec ratione alia nosmet proponere nobis
possumus infernas animas Acherunte vagare.
pictores itaque et scriptorum saecla priora
sic animas intro duxerunt sensibus auctas.   630
at neque sorsum oculi neque nares nec manus ipsa
esse potest animae neque sorsum lingua, neque aures;
haud igitur per se possunt sentire neque esse.

632 *animae* Pius: *anima* OQ   633 *haud igitur* Lachmann: *auditum* OQ

Context: argument no. 15 for the mortality of the soul.

H Lucretius 3.806–29

(1) praeterea quaecumque manent aeterna necessest
aut quia sunt solido cum corpore respuere ictus
nec penetrare pati sibi quicquam quod queat artas
dissociare intus partis, ut materiai
corpora sunt quorum naturam ostendimus ante,   810
aut ideo durare aetatem posse per omnem,
plagarum quia sunt expertia, sicut inanest
quod manet intactum neque ab ictu fungitur hilum,
aut etiam quia nulla loci sit copia circum,
quo quasi res possint discedere dissoluique,   815
sicut summarum summast aeterna, neque extra
quis locus est quo diffugiant neque corpora sunt quae
possint incidere et valida dissolvere plaga.
(2) quod si forte ideo magis immortalis habendast,
quod vitalibus ab rebus munita tenetur,   820
aut quia non veniunt omnino aliena salutis
aut quia quae veniunt aliqua ratione recedunt
pulsa prius quam quid noceant sentire queamus,
⟨. . .⟩
praeter enim quam quod morbis cum corporis aegret,
advenit id quod eam de rebus saepe futuris   825
macerat inque metu male habet curisque fatigat
praeteritisque male admissis peccata remordent.

73

Epicurean physics

adde furorem animi proprium atque oblivia rerum,
adde quod in nigras lethargi mergitur undas.

820 *vitalibus* codd.: *letalibus* Lambinus   post 823 lacunam ind. Lambinus

Context: conclusion of the series of arguments for the mortality of the soul.

807–10   See **8**.
811–13   See **5**.
814–18   Cf. **4A 3–5** with notes.

820   *vitalibus* is very tentatively translated 'which affect life', with the understanding that this at least *includes* things which affect it adversely. If this is thought unacceptable, some comparable sense must be found, if necessary by emending, e.g. to Lambinus' *letalibus*. The favoured alternative of translating 'protected by its vital forces' is unbelievable, less because of the slight difficulties of understanding *munita . . . ab* in this way or of seeing what the theory would amount to than because it would make the first of the two alternative explanations of this protection, in 821, utterly inapposite. (Nor is it any help to read the explanatory clauses in 821–3 as giving a second and third reason parallel to that in 820: what then would be the difference between the first and third reason?) **munita tenetur** '. . . it is permanently protected': for the construction, cf. **B** 136, **E** 889.

i Scholion on Epicurus, *Ep. Hdt.* 66 (Usener 311)

λέγει ἐν ἄλλοις καὶ ἐξ ἀτόμων αὐτὴν συγκεῖσθαι λειοτάτων καὶ στρογγυλωτάτων, πολλῷ
τινι διαφερουσῶν τῶν τοῦ πυρός· καὶ τὸ μέν τι ἄλογον αὐτῆς, ὃ τῷ λοιπῷ παρεσπάρθαι
σώματι· τὸ δὲ λογικὸν ἐν τῷ θώρακι, ὡς δῆλον ἔκ τε τῶν φόβων καὶ τῆς χαρᾶς. ὕπνον τε
γίνεσθαι τῶν τῆς ψυχῆς μερῶν τῶν παρ' ὅλην τὴν σύγκρισιν παρεσπαρμένων ἐγκατεχο-
μένων ἢ διαφορουμένων, εἶτα συμπιπτόντων τοῖς πορίμοις. τό τε σπέρμα ἀφ' ὅλων τῶν   5
σωμάτων φέρεσθαι.

5 πορίμοις Apelt: πορυμοῖς codd.

Context: interpolation in **A** 28.

1–2   The 'very smooth and round' atoms could be either all those of the soul, cf. Lucretius 3.187–230, or those of the nameless element, cf. 3.241–4. The latter reading, which seems possible if καί in 1 is given due weight, would make the contrast with fire atoms more intelligible. On the former, we would have to suppose a significant distinction in this context between heat and fire, contrary to the evidence of **C**. In either case, Heinze [159] and Bignone [121] are no doubt right that the remark's original context was a correction of Democritus' view (frr. 443a–451 Luria) that the soul consists entirely of fire atoms, the retort being that sensation is found in none of the named elements like fire (**C**).

2–3   τὸ ἄλογον and τὸ λογικόν (also at Diogenes of Oenoanda 37.1.5–7) may well be Epicurus' standard terminology for what Lucretius calls *anima* and *animus* respectively, although διάνοια might be thought another candidate for *animus*.

3   Cf. **B 1**.

3–6   Cf. Lucretius 4.907–61. For exegesis, see Schrijvers [221].

74

j Lucretius 3.350-69

quod superest, siquis corpus sentire refutat   350
atque animam credit permixtam corpore toto
suscipere hunc motum quem sensum nominitamus,
vel manifestas res contra verasque repugnat.
quid sit enim corpus sentire quis adferet umquam,
si non ipsa palam quod res dedit ac docuit nos?   355
at dimissa anima corpus caret undique sensu;
perdit enim quod non proprium fuit eius in aevo,
multaque praeterea perdit cum expellitur aevo.
dicere porro oculos nullam rem cernere posse,
sed per eos animum ut foribus spectare reclusis,   360
difficilest, contra cum sensus ducat eorum;
sensus enim trahit atque acies detrudit ad ipsas;
fulgida praesertim cum cernere saepe nequimus,
lumina luminibus quia nobis praepediuntur.
quod foribus non fit; neque enim, qua cernimus ipsi,   365
ostia suscipiunt ullum reclusa laborem.
praeterea si pro foribus sunt lumina nostra,
iam magis exemptis oculis debere videtur
cernere res animus sublatis postibus ipsis.

Context: the interdependence of soul and body. Cf. **A 3-4**.

350-8   That the body itself has sensation is a matter of common experience. It is not refuted by the fact that it loses it when the soul departs: that just shows that sensation is not an intrinsic (*proprium*) characteristic of body, but one that depends on the soul – cf. **A 13-17**.

359-69   On the theory here opposed by Lucretius, see Furley [168]. Whoever its author, its significance for Lucretius lies in its dangerous implication that the soul's functions are independent of the body.

15 Sensation, imagination, memory

A Epicurus, *Ep. Hdt.* 46-53

(1) καὶ μὴν καὶ τύποι ὁμοιοσχήμονες τοῖς στερεμνίοις εἰσί, λεπτότησιν ἀπέχοντες μακρὰν τῶν φαινομένων. οὔτε γὰρ ἀποστάσεις ἀδυνατοῦσιν ἐν τῷ περιέχοντι γίνεσθαι τοιαῦται οὔτ' ἐπιτηδειότητες πρὸς κατεργασίας τῶν κοιλωμάτων καὶ λεπτοτήτων γίνεσθαι, οὔτε ἀπόρροιαι τὴν ἑξῆς θέσιν καὶ βάσιν διατηροῦσαι, ἥνπερ καὶ ἐν τοῖς στερεμνίοις εἶχον· τούτους δὲ   5
τοὺς τύπους εἴδωλα προσαγορεύομεν. (2) [= 11D] (3) εἶθ' ὅτι τὰ εἴδωλα ταῖς λεπτότησιν ἀνυπερβλήτοις κέχρηται, οὐθὲν ἀντιμαρτυρεῖ τῶν φαινομένων· ὅθεν καὶ τάχη ἀνυπέρβλητα ἔχει, πάντα πόρον σύμμετρον ἔχοντα πρὸς τῷ ἀπείροις αὐτῶν μηθὲν ἀντικόπτειν ἢ ὀλίγα ἀντικόπτειν,

Epicurean physics

πολλαῖς δὲ καὶ ἀπείροις εὐθὺς ἀντικόπτειν τι. (4) πρός τε τούτοις, ὅτι ἡ   10
γένεσις τῶν εἰδώλων ἅμα νοήματι συμβαίνει. καὶ γὰρ ῥεῦσις ἀπὸ τῶν
σωμάτων τοῦ ἐπιπολῆς συνεχής, οὐκ ἐπίδηλος τῇ μειώσει διὰ τὴν
ἀνταναπλήρωσιν, σῴζουσα τὴν ἐπὶ τοῦ στερεμνίου θέσιν καὶ τάξιν τῶν
ἀτόμων ἐπὶ πολὺν χρόνον, εἰ καὶ ἐνίοτε συγχεομένη, καὶ συστάσεις ἐν τῷ
περιέχοντι ὀξεῖαι διὰ τὸ μὴ δεῖν κατὰ βάθος τὸ συμπλήρωμα γίνεσθαι, καὶ   15
ἄλλοι δὲ τρόποι τινὲς γεννητικοὶ τῶν τοιούτων φύσεών εἰσιν. (5) οὐθὲν γὰρ
τούτων ἀντιμαρτυρεῖ⟨ται⟩ ταῖς αἰσθήσεσιν, ἂν βλέπῃ τις, τίνα τρόπον τὰς
ἐναργείας, ἵνα καὶ τὰς συμπαθείας, ἀπὸ τῶν ἔξωθεν πρὸς ἡμᾶς ἀνοίσει. (6)
δεῖ δὲ καὶ νομίζειν ἐπεισιόντος τινὸς ἀπὸ τῶν ἔξωθεν τὰς μορφὰς ὁρᾶν
ἡμᾶς καὶ διανοεῖσθαι· (7) οὐ γὰρ ἂν ἐναποσφραγίσαιτο τὰ ἔξω τὴν ἑαυτῶν   20
φύσιν τοῦ τε χρώματος καὶ τῆς μορφῆς διὰ τοῦ ἀέρος τοῦ μεταξὺ ἡμῶν τε
κἀκείνων, οὐδὲ διὰ τῶν ἀκτίνων ἢ ὧν δήποτε ῥευμάτων ἀφ᾽ ἡμῶν πρὸς
ἐκεῖνα παραγινομένων, (8) οὕτως ὡς τύπων τινῶν ἐπεισιόντων ἡμῖν ἀπὸ
τῶν πραγμάτων ὁμοχρόων τε καὶ ὁμοιομόρφων κατὰ τὸ ἐναρμόττον
μέγεθος εἰς τὴν ὄψιν ἢ τὴν διάνοιαν, ὠκέως ταῖς φοραῖς χρωμένων, εἶτα   25
διὰ ταύτην τὴν αἰτίαν τοῦ ἑνὸς καὶ συνεχοῦς τὴν φαντασίαν ἀποδιδόντος
καὶ τὴν συμπάθειαν ἀπὸ τοῦ ὑποκειμένου σῴζοντος κατὰ τὸν ἐκεῖθεν
σύμμετρον ἐπερεισμὸν ἐκ τῆς κατὰ βάθος ἐν τῷ στερεμνίῳ τῶν ἀτόμων
πάλσεως. (9) καὶ ἣν ἂν λάβωμεν φαντασίαν ἐπιβλητικῶς τῇ διανοίᾳ ἢ τοῖς
αἰσθητηρίοις εἴτε μορφῆς εἴτε συμβεβηκότων, μορφή ἐστιν αὕτη τοῦ   30
στερεμνίου, γινομένη κατὰ τὸ ἑξῆς πύκνωμα ἢ ἐγκατάλειμμα τοῦ
εἰδώλου· (10) τὸ δὲ ψεῦδος καὶ τὸ διημαρτημένον ἐν τῷ προσδοξαζομένῳ
ἀεί ἐστιν. †(ἐπιμαρτυρηθήσεσθαι ἢ μὴ ἀντιμαρτυρηθήσεσθαι, εἶτ᾽ οὐκ ἐπιμαρτυρουμέ-
νου κατά τινα ἀκίνητον ἐν ἡμῖν αὐτοῖς συνημμένην τῇ φανταστικῇ ἐπιβολῇ, διάληψιν δὲ
ἐχούσῃ, καθ᾽ ἣν τὸ ψεῦδος γίνεται.)† (11) ἥ τε γὰρ ὁμοιότης τῶν φαντασμῶν   35
οἱονεὶ ἐν εἰκόνι λαμβανομένων ἢ καθ᾽ ὕπνους γινομένων ἢ κατ᾽ ἄλλας τινὰς
ἐπιβολὰς τῆς διανοίας ἢ τῶν λοιπῶν κριτηρίων οὐκ ἄν ποτε ὑπῆρχε τοῖς
οὖσί τε καὶ ἀληθέσι προσαγορευομένοις, εἰ μὴ ἦν τινα καὶ ταῦτα πρὸς ἃ
βάλλομεν· (12) τὸ δὲ διημαρτημένον οὐκ ἂν ὑπῆρχεν, εἰ μὴ ἐλαμβάνομεν
καὶ ἄλλην τινὰ κίνησιν ἐν ἡμῖν αὐτοῖς συνημμένην μὲν διάληψιν δὲ   40
ἔχουσαν· κατὰ δὲ ταύτην [τὴν συνημμένην τῇ φανταστικῇ ἐπιβολῇ,
διάληψιν δὲ ἐχούσης], ἐὰν μὲν μὴ ἐπιμαρτυρηθῇ ἢ ἀντιμαρτυρηθῇ, τὸ
ψεῦδος γίνεται· ἐὰν δὲ ἐπιμαρτυρηθῇ ἢ μὴ ἀντιμαρτυρηθῇ, τὸ ἀληθές. (13)
καὶ ταύτην οὖν σφόδρα γε δεῖ τὴν δόξαν κατέχειν, ἵνα μήτε τὰ κριτήρια
ἀναιρῆται τὰ κατὰ τὰς ἐναργείας μήτε τὸ διημαρτημένον ὁμοίως   45
βεβαιούμενον πάντα συνταράττῃ. (14) ἀλλὰ μὴν καὶ τὸ ἀκούειν γίνεται
πνεύματός τινος φερομένου ἀπὸ τοῦ φωνοῦντος ἢ ἠχοῦντος ἢ ψοφοῦντος ἢ
ὅπως δήποτε ἀκουστικὸν πάθος παρασκευάζοντος. τὸ δὲ ῥεῦμα τοῦτο εἰς
ὁμοιομερεῖς ὄγκους διασπείρεται, (15) ἅμα τινὰ διασῴζοντας συμπάθειαν
πρὸς ἀλλήλους καὶ ἑνότητα ἰδιότροπον, διατείνουσαν πρὸς τὸ ἀποστεῖλαν   50
καὶ τὴν ἐπαίσθησιν τὴν ἐπ᾽ ἐκείνου ὡς τὰ πολλὰ ποιοῦσαν, εἰ δὲ μή γε, τὸ
ἔξωθεν μόνον ἔνδηλον παρασκευάζουσαν· (16) ἄνευ γὰρ ἀναφερομένης

76

τινὸς ἐκεῖθεν συμπαθείας οὐκ ἂν γένοιτο ἡ τοιαύτη ἐπαίσθησις. (17) οὐκ
αὐτὸν οὖν δεῖ νομίζειν τὸν ἀέρα ὑπὸ τῆς προιεμένης φωνῆς ἢ καὶ τῶν
ὁμογενῶν σχηματίζεσθαι – πολλὴν γὰρ ἔνδειαν ἕξει τοῦτο πάσχων ὑπ᾽   55
ἐκείνης – ἀλλ᾽ εὐθὺς τὴν γινομένην πληγὴν ἐν ἡμῖν, ὅταν φωνὴν ἀφίωμεν,
τοιαύτην ἔκθλιψιν ὄγκων τινῶν ῥεύματος πνευματώδους ἀποτελεστικῶν
ποιεῖσθαι, ἣ τὸ πάθος τὸ ἀκουστικὸν ἡμῖν παρασκευάζει. (18) καὶ μὴν καὶ
τὴν ὀσμὴν νομιστέον, ὥσπερ καὶ τὴν ἀκοὴν οὐκ ἄν ποτε οὐθὲν πάθος
ἐργάσασθαι, εἰ μὴ ὄγκοι τινὲς ἦσαν ἀπὸ τοῦ πράγματος ἀποφερόμενοι   60
σύμμετροι πρὸς τὸ τοῦτο τὸ αἰσθητήριον κινεῖν, οἱ μὲν τοῖοι τεταραγ-
μένως καὶ ἀλλοτρίως, οἱ δὲ τοῖοι ἀταράχως καὶ οἰκείως ἔχοντες.

3 πρὸς Usener: τοὺς BP: τὰς FP(corr.): τῆς Bailey   9 τῷ ἀπείροις Sedley: τῷ ἀπείρῳ codd.: τῷ ⟨τῷ⟩
ἀπείρῳ Meibom: τὸ ἀπείροις Mühll   12 τῇ μειώσει Usener: ἢ μειώσει F: σημειώσει BP   14 post
συγχεομένη, ὑπάρχει add. F in marg.   17 suppl. Brieger   18 ἐναργείας Gassendi: ἐνεργείας
codd.   20 ἀν ἐναποσφραγίσαιτο Cobet: ἂ μὲν ἀποσφραγίσαιτο codd.   24 ὁμοχρόων Rossi: ἀπὸ
χροῶν codd.   26 ἀποδιδόντος codd.: ἀποδιδόντων Usener   29 πλάσεως dt: πλάσεως cett.   ἦν
ἂν dt: ἦν ἀνα- cett.   31 ἐγκατάλειμμα τοῦ z(corr.)fr: ἐγκαταλείμματος Fz: ἐνκαταλείμματος
B(corr.): ἐγκαταλήμματος P   38 ἃ F: ὃ cett.   40 ⟨τῇ φανταστικῇ ἐπιβολῇ⟩ post μὲν
Usener   41–2 secl. Usener   45 ἐναργείας Gassendi: ἐνεργείας codd.   47 πνεύματος] ῥεύματος
Gassendi   49 διασῴζοντας P(corr.): -οντα BP: -ουσα F   55 πάσχων B(corr.)P: -ον BF   57
ἔκθλιψιν Brieger: ἐκλίθην B: ἐκλήθην P: ἐκ FP(corr.)   τινῶν FP(corr.): τινὸς B   61 πρὸς τὸ F:
πρὸς BP

Context: following **13A**, on the infinite plurality of worlds. The superseded
introduction to Lucretius 4 (45–53) shows that he too originally meant to give the
theory of sensation this position – directly after book 2, which itself concludes with
the infinity of worlds – but later moved it to follow book 3's account of the soul. The
early positioning had the authority of Epicurus' original exposition in *Nat.*, which had
reached this topic by the end of book 2 (=24 Arrighetti [119]).

1–18   The emphasis throughout is on the non-contestation of the theory: for
details of the arguments that this involved see Lucretius 4.54–268, and for the
methodology see **18**.

2 **ἀποστάσεις**   See Usener [133] for parallels. The term is clearly chosen to
distinguish emitted images from συστάσεις (14), self-formed images.

10 **πολλαῖς**   As Mühll notes, the probable explanation of the feminine is that one
is to understand ἀτόμοις. These, however, we take to be not the atoms in the images,
but those in ordinary compounds, whose high collision rate is *contrasted* with the
relatively unobstructed travel of the incomparably diffuse atoms in the images.

12–13   Constant emission of images does not diminish the size of objects, because
the flow is ubiquitous and losses are compensated by new arrivals: cf. Usener 282.

14 **συγχεομένη**   Cf. **16E** 2–4.

18   On the punctuation adopted here (with Bollack [122]), ἀναφέρῃ is to be
supplied in the ἵνα clause, understood from ἀνοίσει. The expression συμπάθειαν
ἀναφέρειν is guaranteed by 52–3, but the phraseology is a little suspect and there is
some temptation to excise ἵνα, with Mühll.

20–3   The 'air' account sounds like Aristotle's. It is often said to be that of
Democritus, but fits him poorly: air has an unclear role in his theory (Theophrastus,
Sens. 50), certainly a minor one (Aristotle, *De an.* II.7, 419a15–17), and in most
respects he comes close to Epicurus' own account. Nor is the 'ray' theory that of

77

Epicurean physics

Empedocles, but rather of Plato in the *Timaeus* and perhaps of Archytas (47 A 25 DK): see D. O'Brien, *JHS* 90 (1970).

24–5 **κατὰ διάνοιαν** See **D 2**.

30 I.e. 'of shape, or of properties in general', cf. **5A** 7–8, with note.

31–2 **κατὰ εἰδώλου** A much debated phrase. The safest reading probably remains to take ἑξῆς πύκνωμα as the succession of images which builds up a single cinematographic impression (cf. Augustine, *Ep.* 118.30; **C**), and the ἐγκατάλειμμα as the continuing mental effect of the single image which (**D 2–4**) can suffice to stir the imagination. But see Avotins [223] and Asmis [225], 126ff. for the theory that images enter the eye piecemeal and are reassembled, which, even if its presence in this passage is open to doubt, is clearly important to the full Epicurean account.

32 **προσδοξαζομένῳ** Cf. **D** 816, Lucretius 4.465, 468.

33–5 This jumble of terminology has been variously emended in the hope of extracting a coherent scholion from it. But although it was no doubt mistakenly copied into the text of *Ep. Hdt.* along with the various scholia (**14i**, etc.), it looks this time more like a reader's marginal jottings, of which neither great erudition nor grammatical coherence should be expected. Thus ἐπιμαρτυρηθήσεσθαι–ἐπιμαρτυρ-ουμένου at 33–4 may just be a misguided gloss on προσδοξαζομένῳ: wrongly taking this rare word to be equivalent to προσδοκωμένῳ, the annotator has speculated that error is being said to lie in that which is expected 'to be attested or uncontested – there then being no attestation', adding at 34–5 a reference to the 'movement' with which error is linked at 39–41 (Usener's emendation τινα κίνησιν for τὴν ἀκίνητον is probably right, but perhaps the remaining irregularities and ellipses should be left).

40–1 Cf. Epicurus, *Nat.* 31.16.5–9, 36.16.2–6. For ἡμῖν αὐτοῖς and διάληψιν, cf. vol. 1, 86. At **20B 5** the self and its non-physical processes differ κατά τινα τρόπον διαληπτικόν from the atomic mechanism: see vol. 1, 109–10.

41–2 A gloss, trying to show how this sentence relates to the previous one. The first five words probably gloss ταύτην, while the last three gloss the ensuing account of attestation and contestation, which the annotator somewhat implausibly takes to expand on διάληψιν at 40.

47 **πνεύματος** Needlessly emended to ῥεύματος by most editors – cf. 57.

49 **ὁμοιομερεῖς ὄγκους** Paraphrased by Aetius (4.19.2) as 'fragments of similar shape'.

51, 53 For ἐπαίσθησις see on **16B** 7.

B Lucretius 4.230–8

praeterea quoniam manibus tractata figura   230
in tenebris quaedam cognoscitur esse eadem quae
cernitur in luce et claro candore, necessest
consimili causa tactum visumque moveri.
nunc igitur si quadratum temptamus et id nos
commovet in tenebris, in luci quae poterit res   235
accidere ad speciem quadrata, nisi eius imago?

esse in imaginibus quapropter causa videtur
cernundi neque posse sine his res ulla videri.

Context: part of the argument at 4.217–68 (the beginning is lost) corresponding to **A**
6.

C Lucretius 4.256–68

(1) illud in his rebus minime mirabile habendumst,
cur, ea quae feriant oculos simulacra videri
singula cum nequeant, res ipsae perspiciantur.
(2) ventus enim quoque paulatim cum verberat et cum
acre fluit frigus, non privam quamque solemus   260 [261]
particulam venti sentire et frigoris eius,   [260]
sed magis unorsum, fierique perinde videmus
corpore tum plagas in nostro tamquam aliquae res
verberet atque sui det sensum corporis extra.
(3) praeterea lapidem digito cum tundimus, ipsum   265
tangimus extremum saxi summumque colorem,
nec sentimus eum tactu, verum magis ipsam
duritiem penitus saxi sentimus in alto

Context: as **B**.
   258 **res ipsae perspiciantur**   Contrary to Bailey's note ad loc., this entirely
proper usage is correct Epicurean doctrine. Cf. Diogenes of Oenoanda, new fr. 5.2.9–
14: τὰ οὖν ἀπὸ τῶν πραγμάτων ῥέοντα εἴδωλα, ἐνπείπτοντα ἡμῶν ταῖς ὄψεσιν, τοῦ
τε ὁρᾶν ἡμᾶς τὰ ὑποκείμενα αἴτια γείνεται . . .

D Lucretius 4.722–822

(1) nunc age quae moveant animum res accipe, et unde
quae veniunt veniant in mentem percipe paucis.
(2) principio hoc dico, rerum simulacra vagari
multa modis multis in cunctas undique partis   725
tenvia, quae facile inter se iunguntur in auris,
obvia cum veniunt, ut aranea bratteaque auri.
quippe etenim multo magis haec sunt tenvia textu
quam quae percipiunt oculos visumque lacessunt,
corporis haec quoniam penetrant per rara cientque   730
tenvem animi naturam intus sensumque lacessunt.
(3) Centauros itaque et Scyllarum membra videmus
Cerbereasque canum facies simulacraque eorum
quorum morte obita tellus amplectitur ossa;
omne genus quoniam passim simulacra feruntur,   735
partim sponte sua quae fiunt aere in ipso,

partim quae variis ab rebus cumque recedunt
et quae confiunt ex horum facta figuris.
nam certe ex vivo Centauri non fit imago,
nulla fuit quoniam talis natura animantis,   740
verum ubi equi atque hominis casu convenit imago,
haerescit facile extemplo, quod diximus ante,
propter subtilem naturam et tenvia texta.
cetera de genere hoc eadem ratione creantur.
(4) quae cum mobiliter summa levitate feruntur,   745
ut prius ostendi, facile uno commovet ictu
quaelibet una animum nobis subtilis imago;
tenvis enim mens est et mire mobilis ipsa.
(5) haec fieri ut memoro, facile hinc cognoscere possis.
quatenus hoc simile est illi, quod mente videmus   750
atque oculis, simili fieri ratione necesse est.
nunc igitur docui quoniam me forte leonem
cernere per simulacra, oculos quaecumque lacessunt,
scire licet mentem simili ratione moveri
per simulacra leonum ⟨et⟩ cetera quae videt aeque   755
nec minus atque oculi, nisi quod mage tenvia cernit.
(6) nec ratione alia, cum somnus membra profudit,
mens animi vigilat, nisi quod simulacra lacessunt
haec eadem nostros animos quae cum vigilamus
usque adeo, certe ut videamur cernere eum quem   760
relicta vita iam mors et terra potitast.
hoc ideo fieri cogit natura, quod omnes
corporis offecti sensus per membra quiescunt
nec possunt falsum veris convincere rebus.
praeterea meminisse iacet languetque sopore   765
nec dissentit eum mortis letique potitum
iam pridem, quem mens vivum se cernere credit.   767
(7) multaque in his rebus quaeruntur multaque nobis   777
clarandumst, plane si res exponere avemus.
quaeritur in primis quare, quod cuique libido
venerit, extemplo mens cogitet eius id ipsum.   780
anne voluntatem nostram simulacra tuentur
et simul ac volumus nobis occurrit imago,
si mare, si terram cordist, si denique caelum?
conventus hominum pompam convivia pugnas,
omnia sub verbone creat natura paratque?   785
cum praesertim aliis eadem in regione locoque
longe dissimilis animus res cogitet omnis.
quid porro, in numerum procedere cum simulacra

cernimus in somnis et mollia membra movere,
mollia mobiliter cum alternis bracchia mittunt   790
et repetunt oculis gestum pede convenienti?
scilicet arte madent simulacra et docta vagantur,
nocturno facere ut possint in tempore ludos.
(8) an magis illud erit verum? quia tempore in uno,
quod sentimus, id est, cum vox emittitur una,   795
tempora multa latent, ratio quae comperit esse,
propterea fit uti quovis in tempore quaeque
praesto sint simulacra locis in quisque parata:
tanta est mobilitas et rerum copia tanta.
[hoc, ubi prima perit alioque est altera nata]   800
[inde statu, prior hic gestum mutasse videtur.]
et quia tenvia sunt, nisi quae contendit, acute
cernere non potis est animus; proinde omnia quae sunt
praeterea pereunt, nisi ⟨si ad⟩ quae se ipse paravit.
ipse parat sese porro speratque futurum   805
ut videat quod consequitur rem quamque; fit ergo.
nonne vides oculos etiam, cum tenvia quae sunt   807
cernere coeperunt, contendere se atque parare,   809
nec sine eo fieri posse ut cernamus acute?   810
et tamen in rebus quoque apertis noscere possis,
si non advertas animum, proinde esse quasi omni
tempore semotum fuerit longeque remotum.
cur igitur mirumst, animus si cetera perdit
praeterquam quibus est in rebus deditus ipse?   815
(9) quod superest, non est mirum simulacra moveri   768
bracchiaque in numerum iactare et cetera membra.
nam fit ut in somnis facere hoc videatur imago;   770
quippe ubi prima perit alioque est altera nata
inde statu, prior hic gestum mutasse videtur.
scilicet id fieri celeri ratione putandumst:
tanta est mobilitas et rerum copia tanta
tantaque sensibili quovis est tempore in uno   775
copia particularum, ut possit suppeditare.   776
deinde adopinamur de signis maxima parvis   816
ac nos in fraudem induimus frustraminis ipsi.
fit quoque ut interdum non suppeditetur imago
eiusdem generis, sed femina quae fuit ante,
in manibus vir uti factus videatur adesse,   820
aut alia ex alia facies aetasque sequatur.
quod ne miremur sopor atque oblivia curant.   [826]

752 *leonem* Lachmann: *leonum* codd.   768–76 post 815 transp. Asmis   800–1 secl. Lachmann, cf.
771–2   804 *si ad quae se* Brieger: *quae ex se* OQL: *quae ex sese* BF   808 = 804 secl. ital.

Epicurean physics

Context: immediately following Lucretius' explanations of sensation.
734 Dreams about the dead are explained only here and at 757–67. Lucretius' remarks in his proems (1.132–5, 4.31–63, 5.54–63, though not, significantly, in the original proem to book 4 which accidentally survives at 4.45–53) show that he meant to work this up into a central theme of book 4, thus complementing book 3's proof of the soul's intrinsic mortality by refuting the main external evidence for its survival. But in the present state of book 4 we are told little, not even the source of the images which cause these dreams. Are they images cast off by the actual person before his death, however long ago? Or are they, more plausibly, images selected by the mind as merely bearing some resemblance to the person?
762–7 Cf. Diogenes of Oenoanda, new fr. 5.4–6.1 (Smith [174]).
768–76 For the transfer of these lines, to follow 815, see the powerful arguments of Asmis [224].
788–93 The second question raised here and answered at the end of the passage is how dream figures can move so rhythmically, if they are not living beings. The language chosen is that appropriate to dancing (e.g. compare 789 with 4.980), but the scientific scope of the question extends to all lifelike movement. Democritus *had* endowed these dream figures with life and the power to affect us for good or evil: cf. **g** 7–8.

E Diogenes of Oenoanda, new fr. 5.3.3–14

] ι ἐνπ[τω]ς . . . .νο. . .τὰ | ὑπὸ τῶν ὄψεων βλεπό|μενα ἡ ψυχὴ παραλαμ-
|βάνει, μετὰ δὲ τὰς τῶν | πρώτων ἐνπτώσεις εἰ|δώλων ποροποιεῖ-
ται | ἡμῶν οὕτως ἡ φύσις | ὥστε, καὶ μὴ παρόντων | ἔτι τῶν πραγμάτων ἃ
τὸ | πρῶτον εἶδεν, τὰ ὅμοι|α τοῖς πρώτοις τῇ δια|νοίᾳ δεχθ[ῆ]ναι καὶ τὰ | [.

For textual information etc., see Smith [174].

Context: Diogenes' physics treatise, section corresponding to Lucretius 4. Dreams are not mentioned until the next column. Hence this column may well be explaining the mechanism of memory in general, not just that of dreaming, even though (cf. Lucretius 4.976–7) what it says is certainly applicable to dreams.

F Diogenes Laertius 10.32 (=**16B 11**)

καὶ γὰρ καὶ ἐπίνοιαι πᾶσαι ἀπὸ τῶν αἰσθήσεων γεγόνασι κατά τε
περίπτωσιν καὶ ἀναλογίαν καὶ ὁμοιότητα καὶ σύνθεσιν, συμβαλλομένου τι
καὶ τοῦ λογισμοῦ.

Context: doxography of Epicurean canonic.

g Diogenes of Oenoanda 7.1.4–2.11 + new fr. 1.2.7–3.14 (with omissions)

(fr. 7) κενὰ μὲν οὖν [σ]κι[α]|γραφήματα τῆς δια|νοίας οὐκ ἔστι τὰ φάσ|ματα, ὡς ἀξιοῦσιν
οἱ | Στωικοί. καὶ γὰρ εἰ μὲν οὖ|τως αὐτὰ λέγουσιν | κενὰ ὡς ἔχοντα μὲν | σωματικὴν φύσιν,
λε|πτὴν δὲ ἄκρως καὶ οὐ|χ ὑπόπτωτον ταῖς αἰσ|θήσεσι, τῇ ἑρμηνείᾳ | [κέχρ]ηνται
κακῇ . . . εἰ δὲ οὕτω κενὰ ὡς οὐ|δ' ὅλως ἔχοντα σωμα|τικὴν φύσιν, ὃ δὴ καὶ | μ[ᾶλ]λον
βούλονται | λέγε[ιν ἢ] τὸ πρῶτον, {λ} , | πῶς οἷόν τε τὸ κενὸν | ἀναζωγραφε[ῖ]σθαι | εἰ οὐδ'   5

ἔστιν; ... (new fr. 1.2.7ff.) οὔ|κουν μὲν κενὰ λέγει | ταῦτα ὡς καὶ δύναμις | τοσαύτη πρόσεσ[τ]ιν. ọὺ | μὴν πάλιν, εἰ μή ἐστιν | κενά, αἴσθησ[ιν] ἔχει | καὶ λογισμὸν καὶ τῷ | ὄντι προσλαλεῖ ἡμε[ῖν], | ὡς ὑπολαμβάνει Δημ[ό]|κριτος. [ἀ]μήχανον γὰρ λε|πτοῖς ὑμέσιν οὕτως καὶ | στερεμνίας φύσεως βά|θος οὐκ ἔχουσ[ι]ν ταῦτα προσ|εῖναι. οὗτοι μὲν οὖν κα|τὰ τὸ ἐναντίον ἐπλανή|θησαν οἵ τε Στωικο[ὶ] κ[αὶ] Δη|μόκριτος. οἱ μὲν γὰρ Στω|ικοὶ καὶ ἦν   10
ἔχουσι δύνα|μιν τῶν φαντασιῶν ἀφαι|ροῦνται· Δημόκριτος δὲ | καὶ ἦν οὐκ ἔχουσι χα[ρί]|ζεται.

For apparatus, see Chilton [170] and [171] and Smith [173] and [176].

Context: Diogenes' physics treatise, cf. E.
For Democritus' view, see also vol. 1, 145, and for the Stoics', **39B** 5–6.
6 λέγει   Sc. Epicurus.

EPISTEMOLOGY

16 The truth of all impressions

A Lucretius 4.469–521

(1) denique nil sciri siquis putat, id quoque nescit
an sciri possit, quoniam nil scire fatetur.   470
hunc igitur contra mittam contendere causam,
qui capite ipse suo in statuit vestigia sese.
(2) et tamen hoc quoque uti concedam scire, at id ipsum
quaeram, cum in rebus veri nil viderit ante,
unde sciat quid sit scire et nescire vicissim,   475
notitiam veri quae res falsique crearit
et dubium certo quae res differre probarit.
(3) invenies primis ab sensibus esse creatam
notitiem veri neque sensus posse refelli.
(4) nam maiore fide debet reperirier illud,   480
sponte sua veris quod possit vincere falsa.
quid maiore fide porro quam sensus haberi
debet? (5) an ab sensu falso ratio orta valebit
dicere eos contra, quae tota ab sensibus orta est?
qui nisi sunt veri, ratio quoque falsa fit omnis.   485
(6) an poterunt oculos aures reprehendere, an auris
tactus? an hunc porro tactum sapor arguet oris,
an confutabunt nares oculive revincent?
non, ut opinor, ita est. nam sorsum cuique potestas
divisast, sua vis cuiquest, ideoque necesse est   490
et quod molle sit et gelidum fervensve seorsum
et sorsum varios rerum sentire colores
et quaecumque coloribu' sint coniuncta videre.
sorsus item sapor oris habet vim, sorsus odores

noscuntur, sorsum sonitus. ideoque necesse est   495
non possint alios alii convincere sensus.
(7) nec porro poterunt ipsi reprehendere sese,
aequa fides quoniam debebit semper haberi.
(8) proinde quod in quoquest his visum tempore, verumst.
(9) etsi non poterit ratio dissolvere causam,   500
cur ea quae fuerint iuxtim quadrata, procul sint
visa rutunda, tamen praestat rationis egentem
reddere mendose causas utriusque figurae,
quam manibus manifesta suis emittere quoquam
et violare fidem primam et convellere tota   505
fundamenta quibus nixatur vita salusque.
(10) non modo enim ratio ruat omnis, vita quoque ipsa
concidat extemplo, nisi credere sensibus ausis
praecipitesque locos vitare et cetera quae sint
in genere hoc fugienda, sequi contraria quae sint.   510
(11) illa tibi est igitur verborum copia cassa
omnis quae contra sensus instructa paratast.
(12) denique ut in fabrica, si pravast regula prima,
normaque si fallax rectis regionibus exit,
et libella aliqua si ex parti claudicat hilum,   515
omnia mendose fieri atque obstipa necesse est
prava cubantia prona supina atque absona tecta,
iam ruere ut quaedam videantur velle, ruantque
prodita iudiciis fallacibus omnia primis,
sic igitur ratio tibi rerum prava necessest   520
falsaque sit, falsis quaecumque ab sensibus ortast.

472 *suo* OQ: *sua* Lachmann   491 *seorsum* Bentley: *videri* codd.: *videre* Martin   493 *videre* Lachmann: *necessest* codd.   495 *noscuntur* Giussani: *nascantur* OQ: *nascuntur* ed. Veronensis   517 *prava* Marullus: *parva* codd.

Context: following Lucretius' accounts of vision and optical illusion. Cf. also vol. 1, 109.

472   See Burnyeat [10], [229] for the recognition of Epicurus' expression περικάτω τρέπεται in this line, and for the dialectical principle involved cf. also **20C** 5. Most editors emend *suo* to *sua*, presumably so that *in* can govern it. The separation of *in . . . vestigia* is no doubt the more irregular usage, but it would be entirely in character for Lucretius to use linguistic disorder to convey the sceptic's confusion (for a nearby example, cf. **13E** 832–3, on the back-to-front nature of teleology).

504–6   Cf. **18A** 29.
513 **regula**   Probably = κανών, for which see **17**.

B Diogenes Laertius 10.31–2

(1) πᾶσα γάρ, φησίν, αἴσθησις ἄλογός ἐστι καὶ μνήμης οὐδεμιᾶς δεκτική·

84

(2) οὔτε γὰρ ὑφ' αὑτῆς κινεῖται οὔτε ὑφ' ἑτέρου κινηθεῖσα δύναταί τι
προσθεῖναι ἢ ἀφελεῖν· (3) οὐδὲ ἔστι τὸ δυνάμενον αὐτὰς διελέγξαι. (4) οὔτε
γὰρ ἡ ὁμογένεια αἴσθησις τὴν ὁμογενῆ διὰ τὴν ἰσοσθένειαν, (5) οὔθ' ἡ
ἀνομογένεια τὴν ἀνομογένειαν, οὐ γὰρ τῶν αὐτῶν εἰσι κριτικαί· (6) οὔτε   5
μὴν λόγος, πᾶς γὰρ λόγος ἀπὸ τῶν αἰσθήσεων ἤρτηται. (7) οὔθ' ἡ ἑτέρα
τὴν ἑτέραν, πάσαις γὰρ προσέχομεν. (8) καὶ τὸ τὰ ἐπαισθήματα δ'
ὑφεστάναι πιστοῦται τὴν τῶν αἰσθήσεων ἀλήθειαν. (9) ὑφέστηκε δὲ τό τε
ὁρᾶν ἡμᾶς καὶ ἀκούειν ὥσπερ τὸ ἀλγεῖν· (10) ὅθεν καὶ περὶ τῶν ἀδήλων
ἀπὸ τῶν φαινομένων χρὴ σημειοῦσθαι. (11) [=15F] (12) τά τε τῶν   10
μαινομένων φαντάσματα καὶ ⟨τὰ⟩ κατ' ὄναρ ἀληθῆ, κινεῖ γάρ· τὸ δὲ μὴ ὂν
οὐ κινεῖ.

2 δύναταί Gassendi: ἀδυνατεῖ codd.   4 αἴσθησις secl. Diano   6 ἤρτηται φ: εἴρηται cett.
7 ἐπαισθήματα BP: ἀνεπαίσθητα FP(corr.)   11 ⟨τὰ⟩ Casaubon

Context: doxography of Epicurean canonic.

6–7 It is unclear how this relates to the arguments of 3–5, which seem in
themselves to cover all possible cases. It apparently caps them with a quite general
consideration, one which differs in not referring to different types of sensation at all.

7 ἐπαισθήματα   The term ἐπαίσθησις seems to be 'sensory recognition' (C 24;
15A 15–16; P. Herc. 19/698, cols. 8–10, in Scott [149] – not a rational judgement as to
an object's identity, but a successfully made sensory apprehension of something,
normally an object or property (34.31.13 Arrighetti [119] is an exception, apparently
a completely untechnical use). ἐπαίσθημα will be explicitly the product, the
accomplished act of recognition, where ἐπαίσθησις can also include the power of
recognition (this accords with Greek usage, and may be the most that can be got out of
the confused Aetius 4.8.2 = Usener 249). But for a different view, see Asmis [225],
162–3. The role of ἐπαισθήματα in the present laconic argument is unclear: perhaps
(cf. 15A 15) the point is that we can be said e.g. to hear external objects, not just their
sounds: the senses successfully put us into contact with external objects in a way the
sceptic would disallow.

10–12   This implicit glossing of ἀληθής as 'real' is made explicit at S.E. M. 8.9
(= Usener 247): for reservations about it as a satisfactory interpretation of Epicurus,
see vol. 1, 85.

11 φαντάσματα   A sign that Epicurus' own words are not being quoted. He uses
this term for impressions in general (cf. 18C 21, 19A 8–9), whereas here it clearly
carries its normal sense 'figments' (cf. its Stoic definition, 39A–B).

C Anonymous Epicurean treatise on the senses (P. Herc. 19/698), cols. 17, 18,
   22, 23, 25, 26, fr. 21

(1) τὴν μὲ[ν] γ[ὰ]ρ [ὄ]|ψιν ὁρατὰ κατα[λ]αμβ[ά]νειν ἡγούμεθ[α], τὴν
δὲ | ἀφὴν ἁπτά, κα[ὶ] τὴν μὲν | χρώματο{ι}ς, τὴν δὲ σώ|ματος, καὶ [τ]ὴν
ἑτέραν | τοῦ τῆς ἑτέρας [κρ]ί|μα[τος] | μηθὲν π[ολ]υπραγμ[ο]|νεῖν·
ἐπειδήπερ εἰ συ[ν]||έβαινε τὴν ὄψιν σώμα|τος μέγεθος καὶ σχῆμα | κ[α]τα-
λαμβάνειν, π[ολὺ] | π[ρ]ότερον ἂν καὶ σῶμα | κ[ατ]ελάμβανεν . . . (2) . . .]   5
τύπον ει[..]ε, καὶ πο[λλά]||κις οὐδὲ αὐ[τὸ] τοῦτο. [εἴ]|περ οὖν οὐθὲν

Epicurean epistemology

ἕτερό[ν] | ἐστι τὸ σχῆμα τὸ ὁρα[τὸν] | ἢ τῶν χρωμάτω[ν] ἡ [ἐξω]||τάτω
θέσις, οὐδὲ τὸ μ[έ]γεθος τὸ ὁρατὸν ἢ τῷ[ν] | πλειόνων χρωμάτω[ν] | ἡ
κατὰ τὸ ἐξ[ω] θέσ[ις,| ἴσ]ω[ς] δύνατον τὴν α[ὐ|τ]ῶν χρωμάτων οὐ|σαν
[ἀ]ντιληπτικὴν [τὴν] | ἐξωτάτω θέσιν τῶ[ν] | χρωμάτων καταλαμ[βά]-   10
|νειν ... (3) ὥστε | κατ' αὐτὴν ἀναλογίαν | κοινὰ κρίματ' εἶναι | τῶν
αἰσθήσεων τού||[των] τὸ σχῆμα καὶ τὸ μέ||[γεθ]ος, ὃν λόγον ἔχει | τ[ὰ το]ῦ
χρώματος π[ρ]ὸς | τὸ χρῶμα, τοῦτον ἐχόν|των [τ]ῶν τοῦ σώματος | πρὸς
τὸ σῶμα, καὶ ὃν | λόγον ἔχει τὸ χρῶμ[α] | πρὸς τὴν διὰ τῆς ὁρά|σεως
[κατ]άληψιν, τοῦ|τον το[ῦ σ]ώματος π[ρ]ὸς | τὴν δ[ιὰ] τῆς ἁφῆς   15
... (4) ... ἀ]|κοῆς, χωρὶς τῶν ἀνω|τάτω καὶ κοινοτάτων | ἃ προδιήλθο-
μεν, κρίμα | κοινὸν οὐκ οἰόμεθα | κατὰ τὸν πρόχειρον | τρόπον εἶναι· κατὰ
δὲ | τὸν οὐ πρόχειρον μέν,|κοινότητα δὲ προσφε|ρόμενον, ὥστ' ἀναλο|γίαν
εὐόδως ἂν ἔχειν | ῥηθῆναι, φήσα[ι]μεν | ἂν κοινὸν αὐτῶν εἶ|ναι κρίμα τὸ
σχῆμα | ... (5) ὥστε | τῶν αἰσ[θ]ήσεων προσ|υπομνήσωμεν ὃ προσ|φέρε-   20
ται ἴδιον ἑκάστη χω|ρὶς τῆς τῶν κρινομέ|νων ἐπ[α]ισθήσεως. ἡ | μὲν
τοίνυν ὅρασις ἰδιώ|τατον ἔ[χ]ει παρὰ τὰς ἄλ|λας, χωρὶς τῆς τῶν
[χ]ρω|μάτων καὶ τῶν πρ[ὸς αὐ]|τὰ κρίσεως, τὸ ἐν ἀποσ|τάσει κα[τ]αλαμ-
βάνειν | τὰς μορφάς, ἐπαισθα|νομένην καὶ τοῦ με|ταξὺ ἑαυ[τ]ῆς τε
κἀκεί||[νων δια]στ[ή]ματ[ος] ... (6) ἡ δὲ ἀφ[ή], κατὰ μὲ[ν] τὸ [ἴ]διον, τὸ   25
μηδεμιᾶς | ἀντιλαμβάνεσθαι ποι|ότητος· κατ[ὰ] δὲ τὸ κοινόν,| ἡ ποιὰ σάρξ
ἐστιν, ὃ πα[ρ]||ακ[ο]λουθεῖ καὶ ταῖς ἄλ|λαις αἰσθήσεσιν, τὸ ἐτε|ρογενῶν
ποιοτήτων | ἀντιλαμβάνεσθαι. [σκ]λη|ρῶν γὰρ καὶ μ[α]λακῶ[ν] | οὖσ[α]
κριτική, καταλαμ|βάνει καὶ θερμὰ καὶ | ψυχρά, τά τε ἐν ἑαυτῆι| καὶ παρ'
ἑαυτῆ[ι ... | (7) τῆς ὁράσεως τοίνυν στερεμνιότητα μὴ κρινούσης, | 30
καταψεύδονταί τ[ι]νες | κρίνειν νομίζοντες·| ὑποβ[ά]λλειν γὰρ αὐτὴν |
καθ' ἁπλῆν προσβο[λ]ὴν | ὅταν π[έ]τρας ὁρῶμ[ε]ν | ...

9 ἴσ]ω[ς Sedley: π]ώ[ς Scott   12 μέ[γεθ]ος: μ[εἰγεθ]ῶν pap. ante corr.   12 τ[ὰ Sedley: τ[ὸ
Scott   28 [σκ]ληρῶν Asmis: [π]ληρῶν Scott
The full text is that of Scott [149], except where otherwise indicated. Fuller papyrological information
will be found there.

Context: a work on the senses by an Epicurean, possibly Philodemus.
26–8   Cf. Plutarch, Col. 1121B–C, τῆς αἰσθήσεως οὐ λεγούσης [corr. Einarson/
De Lacy: λέγουσι codd.] τὸ ἐκτὸς εἶναι θερμὸν ἀλλὰ τὸ ἐν αὐτῇ πάθος γεγονέ⟨ναι⟩
τοιοῦτον ... For 'internal touch' as a common function of the senses, the aspect of
self-awareness in the sensory process, see Cicero, Acad. 2.20 and 76, Aetius 4.8.7
(= SVF 2.852), and note on 53G. Although the only explicit attributions are to the
Cyrenaics and Stoics, Cicero reports it to be a standard philosophical usage. Hence the
suggestion in vol. 1, 84, that the Epicureans are invoking it here. Aetius, loc. cit., may
be right to connect it with Aristotelian κοινὴ αἴσθησις. Before τὸ μηδεμιᾶς (25–6)
and τὸ ἐτε|ρογενῶν (27) understand ἰδιώτατον ἔχει from 22.

D   Epicurus, RS 23

εἰ μαχῇ πάσαις ταῖς αἰσθήσεσιν, οὐχ ἕξεις οὐδ' ἃς ἂν φῇς αὐτῶν

86

διεψεῦσθαι πρὸς τί ποιούμενος τὴν ἀναγωγὴν κρίνῃς.

1 εἰ μάχῃ Bywater: εἰ μὴ codd.

E Sextus Empiricus, M. 7.203–10 (Usener 247)

Ἐπίκουρος δὲ δυοῖν ὄντων τῶν συζυγούντων ἀλλήλοις πραγμάτων, φαντασίας καὶ τῆς δόξης, τούτων τὴν φαντασίαν, ἥν καὶ ἐνάργειαν καλεῖ, διὰ παντὸς ἀληθῆ φησιν ὑπάρχειν. ὡς γὰρ τὰ πρῶτα πάθη, τουτέστιν ἡδονὴ καὶ πόνος, ἀπὸ ποιητικῶν τινων καὶ κατ' αὐτὰ τὰ ποιητικὰ συνίσταται, οἷον ἡ μὲν ἡδονὴ ἀπὸ τῶν ἡδέων, ἡ δὲ ἀλγηδὼν ἀπὸ τῶν ἀλγεινῶν, καὶ οὔτε τὸ τῆς ἡδονῆς ποιητικὸν ἐνδέχεταί ποτε μὴ εἶναι ἡδὺ οὔτε τὸ τῆς ἀλγηδόνος 5 παρεκτικὸν μὴ ὑπάρχειν ἀλγεινόν, ἀλλ' ἀνάγκη καὶ τὸ ἧδον ἡδὺ καὶ τὸ ἀλγῦνον ἀλγεινὸν τὴν φύσιν ὑποκεῖσθαι, οὕτω καὶ ἐπὶ τῶν φαντασιῶν παθῶν περὶ ἡμᾶς οὐσῶν τὸ ποιητικὸν ἑκάστης αὐτῶν πάντῃ τε καὶ πάντως φανταστόν ἐστιν, † ὃ οὐκ ἐνδέχεται ὂν φανταστὸν μὴ ὑπάρχειν κατ' ἀλήθειαν τοιοῦτον οἷον φαίνεται, ποιητικὸν φαντασίας καθεστάναι.† καὶ ἐπὶ τῶν κατὰ μέρος τὸ παραπλήσιον χρὴ λογίζεσθαι. τὸ γὰρ ὁρατὸν οὐ μόνον φαίνεται ὁρατὸν 10 ἀλλὰ καὶ ἔστι τοιοῦτον ὁποῖον φαίνεται· καὶ τὸ ἀκουστὸν οὐ μόνον φαίνεται ἀκουστὸν ἀλλὰ καὶ ταῖς ἀληθείαις τοιοῦτον ὑπῆρχεν, καὶ ἐπὶ τῶν ἄλλων ὡσαύτως. γίνονται οὖν πᾶσαι αἱ φαντασίαι ἀληθεῖς. καὶ κατὰ λόγον· εἰ γὰρ ἀληθὴς φαίνεται φαντασία, φασὶν οἱ Ἐπικούρειοι, ὅταν ἀπὸ ὑπάρχοντός τε καὶ κατ' αὐτὸ τὸ ὑπάρχον γίνηται, πᾶσα δὲ φαντασία ἀπὸ ὑπάρχοντος τοῦ φανταστοῦ καὶ κατ' αὐτὸ τὸ φανταστὸν συνίσταται, πᾶσα 15 κατ' ἀνάγκην φαντασία ἐστὶν ἀληθής. (1) ἐξαπατᾷ δὲ ἐνίους ἡ διαφορὰ τῶν ἀπὸ τοῦ αὐτοῦ αἰσθητοῦ οἷον ὁρατοῦ δοκουσῶν προσπίπτειν φαντασιῶν, καθ' ἥν ἢ ἀλλοιόχρουν ἢ ἀλλοιόσχημον ἢ ἄλλως πως ἐξηλλαγμένον φαίνεται τὸ ὑποκείμενον· ὑπενόησαν γὰρ ὅτι τῶν οὕτω διαφερουσῶν καὶ μαχομένων φαντασιῶν δεῖ τὴν μέν τινα ἀληθῆ εἶναι, τὴν δ' ἐκ τῶν ἐναντίων ψευδῆ 20 τυγχάνειν. ὅ πέρ ἐστιν εὔηθες καὶ ἀνδρῶν μὴ συνορώντων τὴν ἐν τοῖς οὖσι φύσιν. (2) οὐ γὰρ ὅλον ὁρᾶται τὸ στερέμνιον, ἵνα ἐπὶ τῶν ὁρατῶν ποιώμεθα τὸν λόγον, ἀλλὰ τὸ χρῶμα τοῦ στερεμνίου. τοῦ δὲ χρώματος τὸ μέν ἐστιν ἐπ' αὐτοῦ τοῦ στερεμνίου, καθά περ ἐπὶ τῶν σύνεγγυς καὶ ἐκ τοῦ μετρίου διαστήματος βλεπομένων· τὸ δ' ἐκτὸς τοῦ στερεμνίου κἂν τοῖς ἐφεξῆς 25 τόποις ὑποκείμενον, καθά περ ἐπὶ τῶν ἐκ μακροῦ διαστήματος θεωρουμένων· τοῦτο δὲ ἐν τῷ μεταξὺ ἐξαλλαττόμενον καὶ ἴδιον ἀναδεχόμενον σχῆμα τοιαύτην ἀναδίδωσι φαντασίαν, ὁποῖον καὶ αὐτὸ κατ' ἀλήθειαν ὑπόκειται. (3) ὃν περ οὖν τρόπον οὔτε ἡ ἐν τῷ κρουομένῳ χαλκώματι φωνὴ ἐξακούεται οὔτε ἡ ἐν τῷ στόματι τοῦ κεκραγότος ἀλλ' ἡ προσπίπτουσα τῇ 30 ἡμετέρᾳ αἰσθήσει, καὶ ὡς οὐθείς φησι τὸν ἐξ ἀποστήματος μικρᾶς ἀκούοντα φωνῆς ψευδῶς ἀκούειν, ἐπεί περ σύνεγγυς ἐλθὼν ὡς μείζονος ταύτης ἀντιλαμβάνεται, (4) οὕτως οὐκ ἂν εἴποιμι ψεύδεσθαι τὴν ὄψιν, ὅτι ἐκ μακροῦ μὲν διαστήματος μικρὸν ὁρᾷ τὸν πύργον καὶ στρογγύλον, ἐκ δὲ τοῦ σύνεγγυς μείζονα καὶ τετράγωνον, ἀλλὰ μᾶλλον ἀληθεύειν, ὅτι καὶ ὅτε 35 φαίνεται μικρὸν αὐτῇ τὸ αἰσθητὸν καὶ τοιουτόσχημον, ὄντως ἐστὶ μικρὸν καὶ τοιουτόσχημον, τῇ διὰ τοῦ ἀέρος φορᾷ ἀποθραυομένων τῶν κατὰ τὰ εἴδωλα περάτων, καὶ ὅτε μέγα πάλιν καὶ ἀλλοιόσχημον, πάλιν ὁμοίως

Epicurean epistemology

μέγα καὶ ἀλλοιόσχημον, ἤδη μέντοι οὐ τὸ αὐτὸ ἀμφότερα καθεστώς. τοῦτο γὰρ τῆς διαστρόφου λοιπὸν ἔστι δόξης οἴεσθαι, ὅτι τὸ αὐτὸ τό τε ἐκ   40 τοῦ σύνεγγυς καὶ τὸ πόρρωθεν θεωρούμενον φανταστόν. (5) αἰσθήσεως δὲ ἴδιον ὑπῆρχε τοῦ παρόντος μόνον καὶ κινοῦντος αὐτὴν ἀντιλαμβάνεσθαι οἷον χρώματος, οὐχὶ δὲ τὸ διακρίνειν ὅτι ἄλλο μέν ἐστι τὸ ἐνθάδε ἄλλο δὲ τὸ ἐνθάδε ὑποκείμενον. (6) διό περ αἱ μὲν φαντασίαι διὰ ταῦτα πᾶσαί εἰσιν ἀληθεῖς· ⟨αἱ δὲ δόξαι οὐ πᾶσαι ἦσαν ἀληθεῖς⟩, ἀλλ' εἶχόν τινα διαφοράν.   45 τούτων γὰρ αἱ μὲν ἦσαν ἀληθεῖς αἱ δὲ ψευδεῖς, ἐπεί περ κρίσεις καθεστᾶσιν ἡμῶν ἐπὶ ταῖς φαντασίαις, κρίνομεν δὲ τὰ μὲν ὀρθῶς, τὰ δὲ μοχθηρῶς ἤτοι παρὰ τὸ προστιθέναι τι καὶ προσνέμειν ταῖς φαντασίαις ἢ παρὰ τὸ ἀφαιρεῖν τι τούτων καὶ κοινῶς καταψεύδεσθαι τῆς ἀλόγου αἰσθήσεως.

8 ἑκάστης Kayser: ἑκάστου codd.   45 suppl. Usener

Context: the beginning of the section on Epicurus within a brief history of theories of the criterion, almost certainly derived from the *Canonica* of Antiochus (cf. on **18A**, the sequel to this passage; and note the Stoicizing reading of Epicurus at 14–15, for which cf. **40C** 4–5, etc.). The first person singular in 33 shows how little Sextus has adapted his source material.

3–13   This first exegesis of 'all impressions are true' looks too feeble to deserve serious attention, unless the apparent corruption in 8–9 conceals some more subtle ground than that prima facie offered, that every sense-object really is a sense-object.

22–3   Cf. **C 2**.

25–7   The hazy outline of distant objects is attributed to the fact that some of their colour is physically transmitted to the air surrounding them.

27–9   For the same basic interpretation, cf. Plutarch, *Col.* 1121A (Usener 252, part).

36 **τὸ αἰσθητόν**   Not the tower itself, since solid bodies are not the object of vision, but its colour-at-a-distance, an object distinct from its colour-close-up (38–9).

45 **διαφοράν**   This may well be meant to paraphrase Epicurus' διάληψιν at **15A** 40, but if so Antiochus has probably missed the relevant technical sense of the latter term (see vol. 1, 86, 109–10).

F   Sextus Empiricus, *M.* 8.63–4 (Usener 253)

(1) ὁ δὲ Ἐπίκουρος ἔλεγε μὲν πάντα τὰ αἰσθητὰ εἶναι ἀληθῆ καὶ πᾶσαν φαντασίαν ἀπὸ ὑπάρχοντος εἶναι καὶ τοιαύτην ὁποῖόν ἐστι τὸ κινοῦν τὴν αἴσθησιν, (2) πλανᾶσθαι δὲ τοὺς τινὰς μὲν τῶν φαντασιῶν λέγοντας ἀληθεῖς, τινὰς δὲ ψευδεῖς παρὰ τὸ μὴ δύνασθαι χωρίζειν δόξαν ἀπὸ ἐναργείας. (3) ἐπὶ γοῦν τοῦ Ὀρέστου, ὅτε ἐδόκει βλέπειν τὰς Ἐρινύας, ἡ   5 μὲν αἴσθησις ὑπ' εἰδώλων κινουμένη ἀληθὴς ἦν (ὑπέκειτο γὰρ τὰ εἴδωλα), ὁ δὲ νοῦς οἰόμενος ὅτι στερέμνιοί εἰσιν Ἐρινύες ἐψευδοδόξει. καὶ ἄλλως, φησίν, οἱ προειρημένοι τῶν φαντασιῶν διαφορὰν εἰσάγοντες οὐκ ἰσχύουσι πιστώσασθαι τὸ τινὰς μὲν αὐτῶν ἀληθεῖς ὑπάρχειν τινὰς δὲ ψευδεῖς· οὔτε γὰρ φαινομένῳ διδάξουσι τὸ

88

τοιοῦτον (ζητεῖται γὰρ τὰ φαινόμενα) οὔτε ἀδήλῳ (διὰ φαινομένου γὰρ ὀφείλει τὸ ἄδηλον   10
ἀποδείκνυσθαι).

Context: 'Is there anything true?'

5   The text implies that the fantastic images acted on Orestes' eyes, not directly on
his mind. **15D 2–4** may suggest that this is strictly inaccurate. On the other hand, note
the similar but innocuous inaccuracy at **15D 791**.

G   Lucretius 4.353–63

(1) quadratasque procul turris cum cernimus urbis,
propterea fit uti videantur saepe rutundae,
angulus obtusus quia longe cernitur omnis   355
sive etiam potius non cernitur ac perit eius
plaga nec ad nostras acies perlabitur ictus,
aera per multum quia dum simulacra feruntur,
cogit hebescere eum crebris offensibus aer.
hoc ubi suffugit sensum simul angulus omnis,   360
fit quasi ut ad tornum saxorum structa terantur,
(2) non tamen ut coram quae sunt vereque rutunda,
sed quasi adumbratim paulum simulata videntur.

361 *terantur* Munro: *tuantur* OQP: *tuamur* Lachmann

Context: optical illusion.
359   Cf. **E** 37–8.

H   Lucretius 4.364–86

umbra videtur item nobis in sole moveri
et vestigia nostra sequi gestumque imitari;   365
aera si credis privatum lumine posse
indugredi, motus hominum gestumque sequentem.
nam nil esse potest aliud nisi lumine cassus
aer id quod nos umbram perhibere suemus.
nimirum quia terra locis ex ordine certis   370
lumine privatur solis quacumque meantes
officimus, repletur item quod liquimus eius,
propterea fit uti videatur, quae fuit umbra
corporis, e regione eadem nos usque secuta.
semper enim nova se radiorum lumina fundunt   375
primaque dispereunt, quasi in ignem lana trahatur.
propterea facile et spoliatur lumine terra
et repletur item nigrasque sibi abluit umbras.
nec tamen hic oculos falli concedimus hilum.
nam quocumque loco sit lux atque umbra tueri   380

89

illorum est; eadem vero sint lumina necne,
umbraque quae fuit hic eadem nunc transeat illuc,
an potius fiat paulo quod diximus ante,
hoc animi demum ratio discernere debet,
nec possunt oculi naturam noscere rerum.   385
proinde animi vitium hoc oculis adfingere noli.

Context: following G.

I Plutarch, Col. 1109A–E (Usener 250)

ὁ δ' οὖν δόξας τὸ μηδὲν μᾶλλον εἶναι τοῖον ἢ τοῖον 'Επικουρείῳ δόγματι κέχρηται τῷ
πάσας εἶναι τὰς δι' αἰσθήσεως φαντασίας ἀληθεῖς. εἰ γὰρ δυοῖν λεγόντων τοῦ μὲν αὐστηρὸν
εἶναι τὸν οἶνον, τοῦ δὲ γλυκὺν οὐδέτερος ψεύδεται τῇ αἰσθήσει, τί μᾶλλον ὁ οἶνος αὐστηρὸς
ἢ γλυκύς ἐστιν; καὶ μὴν λουτρῷ γε τῷ αὐτῷ τοὺς μὲν ὡς θερμῷ, τοὺς δὲ ὡς ψυχρῷ
χρωμένους ἰδεῖν ἐστιν· οἱ μὲν γὰρ ψυχρόν, οἱ δὲ θερμὸν ἐπεμβάλλειν κελεύουσιν . . . εἴπερ   5
οὖν μὴ μᾶλλόν ἐστιν ἡ ἑτέρα τῆς ἑτέρας ἀληθὴς αἴσθησις, εἰκός ἐστι καὶ τὸ ὕδωρ μὴ μᾶλλον
εἶναι ψυχρὸν ἢ θερμόν . . . εἰ γὰρ αὐτὸ ⟨τὸ⟩ φαινόμενον ἕτερον ἑτέρῳ φάσκει τις,
ἀμφότερα εἶναι λέγων λέληθεν. αἱ δὲ πολυθρύλητοι συμμετρίαι καὶ ἁρμονίαι
τῶν περὶ τὰ αἰσθητήρια πόρων αἵ τε πολυμιξίαι τῶν σπερμάτων, ἃ δὴ
πᾶσι χυμοῖς καὶ ὀσμαῖς καὶ χροιαῖς ἐνδιεσπαρμένα λέγουσιν ἑτέραν ἑτέρῳ   10
ποιότητος κινεῖν αἴσθησιν οὐκ ἄντικρυς εἰς τὸ μὴ μᾶλλον τὰ πράγματα
συνελαύνουσιν αὐτοῖς; τοὺς γὰρ οἰομένους ψεύδεσθαι τὴν αἴσθησιν, ὅτι τὰ
ἐναντία πάθη γινόμενα τοῖς χρωμένοις ἀπὸ τῶν αὐτῶν ὁρῶσι, παραμυθού-
μενοι διδάσκουσιν ὡς ἀναπεφυρμένων καὶ συμμεμιγμένων ὁμοῦ τι
πάντων, ἄλλου δὲ ἄλλῳ πεφυκότος ἐναρμόττειν οὐκ ἔστι τῆς αὐτῆς   15
ποιότητος ἐπαφὴ καὶ ἀντίληψις οὐδὲ πᾶσι τοῖς μέρεσι κινεῖ πάντας
ὡσαύτως τὸ ὑποκείμενον, ἀλλὰ ἐκείνοις ἕκαστοι μόνοις ἐντυγχάνοντες
πρὸς ἃ σύμμετρον ἔχουσι τὴν αἴσθησιν οὐκ ὀρθῶς διαμάχονται περὶ τοῦ
χρηστὸν ἢ πονηρὸν ἢ λευκὸν ἢ μὴ λευκὸν εἶναι τὸ πρᾶγμα, τὰς αὐτῶν
οἰόμενοι βεβαιοῦν αἰσθήσεις τῷ τὰς ἄλλων ἀναιρεῖν. δεῖ δὲ αἰσθήσει μὲν   20
μηδεμιᾷ μάχεσθαι· πᾶσαι γὰρ ἅπτονται τινός, οἷον ἐκ πηγῆς τῆς
πολυμιξίας ἑκάστη λαμβάνουσα τὸ πρόσφορον καὶ οἰκεῖον· ὅλου δὲ μὴ
κατηγορεῖν ἁπτομένους μερῶν· μηδὲ τὸ αὐτὸ οἴεσθαι δεῖν πάσχειν
ἅπαντας, ἄλλους κατ' ἄλλην ποιότητα καὶ δύναμιν αὐτοῦ πάσχοντας. ἆρα
δεῖ σκοπεῖν, τίνες μᾶλλον ἄνθρωποι τὸ μὴ μᾶλλον ἐπάγουσι τοῖς πράγμασιν ἢ οἳ πᾶν μὲν τὸ   25
αἰσθητὸν κρᾶμα παντοδαπῶν ποιοτήτων ἀποφαίνουσι "σύμμικτον ὥστε γλεῦκος ὑλιστή-
ριον" ἕρρειν δὲ ὁμολογοῦσι τοὺς κανόνας αὐτοῖς και παντάπασιν οἴχεσθαι τὸ κριτήριον, ἂν
περ εἰλικρινὲς αἰσθητὸν ὁτιοῦν καὶ μὴ πολλὰ ἕκαστον ἀπολίπωσιν.

7 ⟨τὸ⟩ Einarson/De Lacy   15 αὐτῆς ⟨πᾶσι⟩ Pohlenz   21 μηδεμιᾷ Dübner: μηδὲ δια- codd.

Context: reply to the Epicurean Colotes' attack on Democritus for allegedly holding
that things are 'no more this than that' (a standard sceptic formula, cf. 1F–G, 71C).

8 συμμετρίαι Explained at 15A 23–5, 60–1.

19 **χρηστὸν ἢ πονηρόν** The argument *en passant* defends the objectivity of moral qualities. 'Good' and 'bad' are no doubt included on the ground that they are reducible to the sensible properties 'pleasant' and 'painful'.

17 The criteria of truth

A Diogenes Laertius 10.31

(1) ἐν τοίνυν τῷ Κανόνι λέγων ἐστὶν ὁ Ἐπίκουρος κριτήρια τῆς ἀληθείας εἶναι τὰς αἰσθήσεις καὶ προλήψεις καὶ τὰ πάθη, (2) οἱ δ' Ἐπικούρειοι καὶ τὰς φανταστικὰς ἐπιβολὰς τῆς διανοίας· λέγει δὲ καὶ ἐν τῇ πρὸς Ἡρόδοτον ἐπιτομῇ καὶ ἐν ταῖς Κυρίαις δόξαις.

2-4 οἱ δ' Ἐπικούρειοι-δόξαις secl. Diano   3 καὶ ⟨αὐτὸς⟩ Usener

Context: doxography of Epicurean canonic.

2   The same list appears at Cicero, *Acad.* 2.142.

2-3   For Epicurus' own appeals to φανταστικὴ ἐπιβολὴ τῆς διανοίας, in addition to the texts cited in vol. 1, 90, see **11E** 15-16.

3-4   I.e. at **B**, **C** and **D**.

B Epicurus, RS 24

(1) εἴ τιν' ἐκβαλεῖς ἁπλῶς αἴσθησιν καὶ μὴ διαιρήσεις τὸ δοξαζόμενον κατὰ τὸ προσμενόμενον καὶ τὸ παρὸν ἤδη κατὰ τὴν αἴσθησιν καὶ τὰ πάθη καὶ πᾶσαν φανταστικὴν ἐπιβολὴν τῆς διανοίας, συνταράξεις καὶ τὰς λοιπὰς αἰσθήσεις τῇ ματαίῳ δόξῃ, ὥστε τὸ κριτήριον ἅπαν ἐκβαλεῖς. (2) εἰ δὲ βεβαιώσεις καὶ τὸ προσμενόμενον ἅπαν ἐν ταῖς δοξαστικαῖς ἐννοίαις καὶ   5 τὸ μὴ τὴν ἐπιμαρτύρησιν ⟨. . .⟩ οὐκ ἐκλείψεις τὸ διεψευσμένον· ὥστ' ἐξηρηκὼς ἔσῃ πᾶσαν ἀμφισβήτησιν καὶ πᾶσαν κρίσιν τοῦ ὀρθῶς ἢ μὴ ὀρθῶς.

1-2 κατὰ τὸ προσμενόμενον BP: καὶ τὸ προσμένον F   5 προσμενόμενον BP: προσμένον F   6 lacunam ind. Mühll   6-7 ὥστ' ἐξηρηκὼς Usener: ὡς τετηρηκὼς codd.

2, 5 **προσμενόμενον** 'Evidence yet awaited.' The reading προσμένον has been preferred here, at **C** 9, and at **18B** 3, by all modern editors except Bollack [123]. It is generally glossed as 'that which awaits ἐπιμαρτύρησις'. But the passive form is the reading of the best MSS both here and at **C**, and its shortening by a simple haplography in the inferior MSS is likelier palaeographically than that that same dittography should have occurred independently three times. Even at **18B**, where the active form is found in all MSS, the illustration is 'waiting to get near the tower and find out what it looks like from close to'. This is quite inappropriate to προσμένον on the traditional interpretation, according to which it is the belief, not the observer, that does the waiting. There too, then, the passive form should be adopted.

C Epicurus. Ep. Hdt. 37-8

(1) πρῶτον μὲν οὖν τὰ ὑποτεταγμένα τοῖς φθόγγοις, ὦ Ἡρόδοτε, δεῖ

Epicurean epistemology

εἰληφέναι, ὅπως ἂν τὰ δοξαζόμενα ἢ ζητούμενα ἢ ἀπορούμενα ἔχωμεν εἰς
ταῦτα ἀναγαγόντες ἐπικρίνειν, καὶ μὴ ἄκριτα πάντα ἡμῖν εἰς ἄπειρον
ἀποδεικνύουσιν ἢ κενοὺς φθόγγους ἔχωμεν. ἀνάγκη γὰρ τὸ πρῶτον
ἐννόημα καθ' ἕκαστον φθόγγον βλέπεσθαι καὶ μηθὲν ἀποδείξεως προσ-   5
δεῖσθαι, εἴπερ ἕξομεν τὸ ζητούμενον ἢ ἀπορούμενον καὶ δοξαζόμενον ἐφ' ὃ
ἀνάξομεν. (2) εἶτα κατὰ τὰς αἰσθήσεις δεῖ πάντα τηρεῖν καὶ ἁπλῶς τὰς
παρούσας ἐπιβολὰς εἴτε διανοίας εἴθ' ὅτου δήποτε τῶν κριτηρίων, ὁμοίως
δὲ καὶ τὰ ὑπάρχοντα πάθη, ὅπως ἂν καὶ τὸ προσμενόμενον καὶ τὸ ἄδηλον
ἔχωμεν οἷς σημειωσόμεθα.   10

3 post ἡμῖν, ἢ g: ἢ d: om. cett.   7 εἶτα Gassendi: εἴτε codd.: ἔτι τε Arndt   9 προσμενόμενον BP:
προσμένον FP(corr.)

Context: opening methodological recommendations of the *Letter to Herodotus*.

1–7   For discussion, see especially Striker [9], 68–73. The absence of the actual
word πρόληψις is more economically explained (cf. vol. 1, 89) as due to Epicurus'
avoidance of excessive technical assumptions at the outset than by the suggestion
(Sedley [126], 14) that this part of *Ep. Hdt.* was writen before the term itself had been
introduced.

9 **προσμενόμενον**   See on **B** 2.

D   Epicurus, *Ep. Hdt.* 82

ὅθεν τοῖς πάθεσι προσεκτέον τοῖς παροῦσι καὶ ταῖς αἰσθήσεσι, κατὰ μὲν τὸ
κοινὸν ταῖς κοιναῖς, κατὰ δὲ τὸ ἴδιον ταῖς ἰδίαις, καὶ πάσῃ τῇ παρούσῃ καθ'
ἕκαστον τῶν κριτηρίων ἐναργείᾳ. ἂν γὰρ τούτοις προσέχωμεν, τὸ ὅθεν ὁ τάραχος
καὶ ὁ φόβος ἐγίνετο ἐξαιτιολογήσομεν ὀρθῶς καὶ ἀπολύσομεν, ὑπέρ τε μετεώρων
αἰτιολογοῦντες καὶ τῶν λοιπῶν τῶν ἀεὶ παρεμπιπτόντων, ὅσα φοβεῖ τοὺς λοιποὺς   5
ἐσχάτως.

1 πάθεσι Bonnet: πᾶσι codd.

Context: the need to gear physical research to the goal of tranquillity (cf. **18C**; **25B**).

1–2   For κοιναὶ αἰσθήσεις see Bignone [121] ad loc., and Striker [9], 68, who
helpfully cites Philodemus, *Rhet.* 1.207, 2.41, and Aristotle, *Metaph.* A.1, 981b14.

E   Diogenes Laertius 10.33

(1) τὴν δὲ πρόληψιν λέγουσιν οἱονεὶ κατάληψιν ἢ δόξαν ὀρθὴν ἢ ἔννοιαν ἢ
καθολικὴν νόησιν ἐναποκειμένην, τουτέστι μνήμην, τοῦ πολλάκις ἔξωθεν
φανέντος, οἷον "τὸ τοιοῦτόν ἐστιν ἄνθρωπος". (2) ἅμα γὰρ τῷ ῥηθῆναι
ἄνθρωπος εὐθὺς κατὰ πρόληψιν καὶ ὁ τύπος αὐτοῦ νοεῖται προηγουμένων
τῶν αἰσθήσεων. (3) παντὶ οὖν ὀνόματι τὸ πρώτως ὑποτεταγμένον ἐναργές   5
ἐστι· (4) καὶ οὐκ ἂν ἐζητήσαμεν τὸ ζητούμενον εἰ μὴ πρότερον ἐγνώκειμεν
αὐτό· οἷον "τὸ πόρρω ἑστὼς ἵππος ἐστὶν ἢ βοῦς;" δεῖ γὰρ κατὰ πρόληψιν
ἐγνωκέναι ποτὲ ἵππου καὶ βοὸς μορφήν· (5) οὐδ' ἂν ὠνομάσαμέν τι μὴ
πρότερον αὐτοῦ κατὰ πρόληψιν τὸν τύπον μαθόντες. (6) ἐναργεῖς οὖν εἰσιν

92

αἱ προλήψεις· (7) καὶ τὸ δοξαστὸν ἀπὸ προτέρου τινὸς ἐναργοῦς ἤρτηται,   10
ἐφ' ὃ ἀναφέροντες λέγομεν, οἷον "πόθεν ἴσμεν εἰ τοῦτό ἐστιν ἄνθρωπος;"

5 ὑποτεταγμένον Gassendi (cf. C 1): ἐπι- codd.

Context: doxography of Epicurean canonic (immediately following 16B).
1 For Epicurus as originator of the term πρόληψις, see 23E 3. For the Stoics'
definition and use of it, cf. 40A 3, N, S; and for the Pyrrhonists, 40T.
2 We punctuate after τουτέστι μνήμην, to make this a gloss on the preceding
two words. Other editors take it directly with what follows, but that severs τοῦ
πολλάκις κτλ. from κατάληψιν ἢ δόξαν κτλ., leaving the latter as hopelessly weak
definitions of πρόληψις.
6–9 For the same principle, see 23E 2, 40T 1; S.E., M. 1.57, 11.21; and cf. 39C 4.

18 Scientific methodology

A Sextus Empiricus, M. 7.211–16 (Usener 247, part)

(1) οὐκοῦν τῶν δοξῶν κατὰ τὸν Ἐπίκουρον αἱ μὲν ἀληθεῖς εἰσιν αἱ δὲ
ψευδεῖς, ἀληθεῖς μὲν αἵ τε ἐπιμαρτυρούμεναι καὶ οὐκ ἀντιμαρτυρούμεναι
πρὸς τῆς ἐναργείας, ψευδεῖς δὲ αἵ τε ἀντιμαρτυρούμεναι καὶ οὐκ
ἐπιμαρτυρούμεναι πρὸς τῆς ἐναργείας. (2) ἔστι δὲ ἐπιμαρτύρησις μὲν
κατάληψις δι' ἐναργείας τοῦ τὸ δοξαζόμενον τοιοῦτον εἶναι ὁποῖόν ποτε   5
ἐδοξάζετο, οἷον Πλάτωνος μακρόθεν προσιόντος εἰκάζω μὲν καὶ δοξάζω
παρὰ τὸ διάστημα ὅτι Πλάτων ἐστί, προσπελάσαντος δὲ αὐτοῦ προσεμαρ-
τυρήθη ὅτι ὁ Πλάτων ἐστί, συναιρεθέντος τοῦ διαστήματος, καὶ
ἐπεμαρτυρήθη δι' αὐτῆς τῆς ἐναργείας. (3) οὐκ ἀντιμαρτύρησις δὲ ἐστιν
ἀκολουθία τοῦ ὑποσταθέντος καὶ δοξασθέντος ἀδήλου τῷ φαινομένῳ, οἷον   10
ὁ Ἐπίκουρος λέγων εἶναι κενόν, ὅ πέρ ἐστιν ἄδηλον, πιστοῦται δι'
ἐναργοῦς πράγματος τοῦτο, τῆς κινήσεως· μὴ ὄντος γὰρ κενοῦ οὐδὲ
κίνησις ὤφειλεν εἶναι, τόπον μὴ ἔχοντος τοῦ κινουμένου σώματος εἰς ὃν
περιστήσεται διὰ τὸ πάντα πλήρη εἶναι καὶ ναστά· ὥστε τῷ δοξασθέντι
ἀδήλῳ μὴ ἀντιμαρτυρεῖν τὸ φαινόμενον κινήσεως οὔσης. (4) ἡ μέντοι   15
ἀντιμαρτύρησις μαχόμενόν τί ἐστι τῇ οὐκ ἀντιμαρτυρήσει· ἦν γὰρ
ἀνασκευὴ τοῦ φαινομένου τῷ ὑποσταθέντι ἀδήλῳ, οἷον ὁ Στωικὸς λέγει
μὴ εἶναι κενόν, ἄδηλόν τι ἀξιῶν, τούτῳ δὲ οὕτως ὑποσταθέντι ὀφείλει τὸ
φαινόμενον συνανασκευάζεσθαι, φημὶ δ' ἡ κίνησις· μὴ ὄντος γὰρ κενοῦ
κατ' ἀνάγκην οὐδὲ κίνησις γίγνεται κατὰ τὸν ἤδη προδεδηλωμένον ἡμῖν   20
τρόπον. (5) ὡσαύτως δὲ καὶ ἡ οὐκ ἐπιμαρτύρησις ἀντίξους ἐστὶ τῇ
ἐπιμαρτυρήσει· ἦν γὰρ ὑπόπτωσις δι' ἐναργείας τοῦ τὸ δοξαζόμενον μὴ
εἶναι τοιοῦτον ὁποῖόν περ ἐδοξάζετο, οἷον πόρρωθέν τινος προσιόντος
εἰκάζομεν παρὰ τὸ διάστημα Πλάτωνα εἶναι, ἀλλὰ συναιρεθέντος τοῦ
διαστήματος ἔγνωμεν δι' ἐναργείας ὅτι οὐκ ἔστι Πλάτων. καὶ γέγονε τὸ   25
τοιοῦτον οὐκ ἐπιμαρτύρησις· οὐ γὰρ ἐπεμαρτυρήθη τῷ φαινομένῳ τὸ
δοξαζόμενον. (6) ὅθεν ἡ μὲν ἐπιμαρτύρησις καὶ οὐκ ἀντιμαρτύρησις τοῦ

Epicurean epistemology

ἀληθὲς εἶναί τι ἐστὶ κριτήριον, ἡ δὲ οὐκ ἐπιμαρτύρησις καὶ ἀντιμαρτύρησις τοῦ ψεῦδος εἶναι. πάντων δὲ κρηπὶς καὶ θεμέλιος ἡ ἐνάργεια.

17 ἀνασκευὴ codd.: συνανασκευὴ Gassendi

Context: immediately following **16E**.

Our grounds for naming Antiochus as the source of this text (along with **16E**), and for questioning its evidential value, are fully argued in Sedley [243]. For a more positive assessment, see especially Striker [9].

B Diogenes Laertius 10.34

τὴν δὲ δόξαν καὶ ὑπόληψιν λέγουσιν, ἀληθῆ τέ φασι καὶ ψευδῆ· ἂν μὲν γὰρ ἐπιμαρτυρῆται ἢ μὴ ἀντιμαρτυρῆται, ἀληθῆ εἶναι· ἐὰν δὲ μὴ ἐπιμαρτυρῆται ἢ ἀντιμαρτυρῆται, ψευδῆ τυγχάνειν. ὅθεν ⟨τὸ⟩ προσμενό⟨μενο⟩ν εἰσήχθη· οἷον τὸ προσμεῖναι καὶ ἐγγὺς γενέσθαι τῷ πύργῳ καὶ μαθεῖν ὁποῖος ἐγγὺς φαίνεται.   5

3 ⟨τὸ⟩ Gassendi   προσμενό⟨μενο⟩ν Sedley: προσμένων B: προσμένον B(corr.): πρὸς μὲν ὃν FP

Context: immediately following **17E**.

3 **προσμενό⟨μενο⟩ν** See on **17B**.

4–5 For the tower example, a standard one, see **16E 4, G; 72F 2**.

C Epicurus, *Ep. Pyth.* 85–8

(1) πρῶτον μὲν οὖν μὴ ἄλλο τι τέλος ἐκ τῆς περὶ μετεώρων γνώσεως εἴτε κατὰ συναφὴν λεγομένων εἴτε αὐτοτελῶς νομίζειν ⟨δεῖ⟩ εἶναι ἤπερ ἀταραξίαν καὶ πίστιν βέβαιον, καθάπερ καὶ ἐπὶ τῶν λοιπῶν. (2) μήτε τὸ ἀδύνατον καὶ παραβιάζεσθαι μήτε ὁμοίαν κατὰ πάντα τὴν θεωρίαν ἔχειν ἢ τοῖς περὶ βίων λόγοις ἢ τοῖς κατὰ τὴν τῶν ἄλλων φυσικῶν προβλημάτων   5
κάθαρσιν, οἷον ὅτι τὸ πᾶν σῶμα καὶ ἀναφὴς φύσις ἐστὶν ἢ ὅτι ἄτομα στοιχεῖα, καὶ πάντα τὰ τοιαῦτα δὴ ὅσα μοναχὴν ἔχει τοῖς φαινομένοις συμφωνίαν· ὅπερ ἐπὶ τῶν μετεώρων οὐχ ὑπάρχει, ἀλλὰ ταῦτά γε πλεοναχὴν ἔχει καὶ τῆς γενέσεως αἰτίαν καὶ τῆς οὐσίας ταῖς αἰσθήσεσι σύμφωνον κατηγορίαν. (3) οὐ γὰρ κατὰ ἀξιώματα κενὰ καὶ νομοθεσίας   10
φυσιολογητέον, ἀλλ' ὡς τὰ φαινόμενα ἐκκαλεῖται· οὐ γὰρ ἰδιολογίας καὶ κενῆς δόξης ὁ βίος ἡμῶν ἔχει χρείαν, ἀλλὰ τοῦ ἀθορύβως ἡμᾶς ζῆν. (4) πάντα μὲν οὖν γίνεται ἀσείστως κατὰ πάντων ⟨τῶν⟩ κατὰ πλεοναχὸν τρόπον ἐκκαθαιρομένων συμφώνως τοῖς φαινομένοις, ὅταν τις τὸ πιθανολογούμενον ὑπὲρ αὐτῶν δεόντως καταλίπῃ· ὅταν δέ τις τὸ μὲν ἀπολίπῃ, τὸ   15
δὲ ἐκβάλῃ ὁμοίως σύμφωνον ὂν τῷ φαινομένῳ, δῆλον ὅτι καὶ ἐκ παντὸς ἐκπίπτει φυσιολογήματος, ἐπὶ δὲ τὸν μῦθον καταρρεῖ. (5) σημεῖα δ' ἐπὶ τῶν ἐν τοῖς μετεώροις συντελουμένων φέρει τῶν παρ' ἡμῖν τινα φαινομένων, ἃ θεωρεῖται ἢ ὑπάρχει, καὶ οὐ τὰ ἐν τοῖς μετεώροις φαινόμενα· ταῦτα γὰρ ἐνδέχεται πλεοναχῶς γενέσθαι. (6) τὸ μέντοι   20

94

18 Scientific methodology

φάντασμα ἑκάστου τηρητέον καὶ ἐπὶ τὰ συναπτόμενα τούτῳ διαιρετέον ἃ
οὐκ ἀντιμαρτυρεῖται τοῖς παρ' ἡμῖν γινομένοις πλεοναχῶς συντελεῖσθαι.

2 ⟨δεῖ⟩ Gassendi   6 σῶμα codd.: σῶμα⟨τα⟩ Usener   7 δὴ Bignone: ἦ codd.   8 ὑπάρχει
Gassendi: ὑπάρχειν codd.   11 ἰδιολογίας Stephanus: ἰδιαλογίας BP: ἤδη ἀλογίας FP(corr.)   13
⟨τῶν⟩ Bignone   17 δ' ἐπὶ Usener: δέ τι BP: δέ τινα FP(corr.)   18 φέρει Kühn: φέρειν codd.

Context: methodological introduction to *Letter to Pythocles*.

D Lucretius 5.509–33

(1) motibus astrorum nunc quae sit causa canamus.

(2) principio magnus caeli si vertitur orbis,   510
ex utraque polum parti premere aera nobis
dicendum est extraque tenere et claudere utrimque;
inde alium supra fluere atque intendere eodem
quo volvenda micant aeterni sidera mundi;

(3) aut alium subter, contra qui subvehat orbem,   515
ut fluvios versare rotas atque haustra videmus:

(4) est etiam quoque uti possit caelum omne manere
in statione, tamen cum lucida signa ferantur;

(5) sive quod inclusi rapidi sunt aetheris aestus
quaerentesque viam circum versantur et ignis   520
passim per caeli volvunt summania templa;

(6) sive aliunde fluens alicunde extrinsecus aer
versat agens ignis; (7) sive ipsi serpere possunt
quo cuiusque cibus vocat atque invitat euntis,
flammea per caelum pascentis corpora passim.   525

(8) nam quid in hoc mundo sit eorum ponere certum
difficile est; sed quid possit fiatque per omne
in variis mundis varia ratione creatis,
id doceo plurisque sequor disponere causas,
motibus astrorum quae possint esse per omne;   530
e quibus una tamen sit et hic quoque causa necessest
quae vegeat motum signis; sed quae sit earum
praecipere haudquaquamst pedetemptim progredientis.

531 *sit et hic* Nencini: *sit et haec* Q: *sit in hoc* Munro: *siet hic* Bernays: *siet haec* Lachmann

Context: following Lucretius' account of cosmogony. The corresponding text in
Epicurus is at *Ep. Pyth.* 92.

  The various alternative explanations listed in the *Letter to Pythocles* and Lucretius
5.509–770 and 6.96ff. seem in general to be culled from Presocratic sources. Virtually
any such theory is deemed intrinsically possible, provided only that it is sufficiently
mechanistic in character to exclude divine control (cf. **13**). Those in the present
passage cannot be attributed with certainty: see Bailey [154] ad loc.

95

E Lucretius 6.703–11

sunt aliquot quoque res quarum unam dicere causam
non satis est, verum pluris, unde una tamen sit;
corpus ut exanimum siquod procul ipse iacere   705
conspicias hominis, fit ut omnis dicere causas
conveniat leti, dicatur ut illius una.
nam neque eum ferro nec frigore vincere possis
interiisse neque a morbo neque forte veneno,
verum aliquid genere esse ex hoc quod contigit ei   710
scimus. item in multis hoc rebus dicere habemus.

710 *verum* Marullus: *utrum* OQ

Context: in the middle of a long series of explanations of natural phenomena, paving
the way for four alternative explanations of the Nile's flooding at 712–37.

F Philodemus, *Sign.* 11.32–12.31

(1) τιθεμ[έ]νου γὰρ | τοῦτό τε ἀληθεύ[εσθα]ι, τὸ εἰ τὸ | πρῶτον τὸ
δεύτε[ρο]ν, ὅταν ἀ|ληθὲς ἦι τὸ εἰ μὴ τ[ὸ δ]εύτερον | [οὐ]δὲ τὸ πρῶτον, οὐ
[κα]τὰ τοῦτο | [συν]άγεται τὸ μόνον εἶναι τὸν | [κατὰ τ]ὴν ἀνασκευὴν
τρό||πον ἀναγκαστικόν. (2) τὸ γὰρ εἰ μὴ | τὸ δεύτερον οὐδὲ τὸ πρῶτον
ἀ|ληθὲς [γ]ίνεται ποτὲ μὲν παρό|σον τοῦ δευτέρου καθ᾽ ὑπόθεσιν {σθ} | ἀ-   5
νασκευασθέντος, παρ᾽ αὐτὴν | τὴν ἀνασκευὴν αὐτοῦ καὶ τὸ πρῶ|τον
ἀναιρεῖται, (3) καθάπερ [ἔ]χει | καὶ ἐπὶ τοῦ εἰ ἔστι κίνησ[ις] ἔστιν | κενόν·
ἀναιρεθέντος γὰ[ρ] καθ᾽ ὑ|πόθεσιν τοῦ κενοῦ, παρὰ ψιλὴν | τὴν ἀναίρεσιν
[αὐτ]οῦ καὶ ἡ κίνησις ἀναιρεθή[σεθ᾽], ὥστ᾽ εἰς τὸ | κατ᾽ ἀνασκευὴ[ν γέν]ος
ἐναρμότ|τειν τὸ τοιοῦτο[ο· (4) ποτὲ] δ᾽ οὐχ οὕ|τως ἀλλὰ παρ᾽ [αὐτὸ τὸ μὴ]   10
δύνα||[σ]θαι τὸ μὲν π[ρῶτο]ν ὑπά[ρχ]ον ⟨ν⟩ο|[εῖν] ἢ τοιοῦτον [ὑπάρ]χον τὸ
δὲ | [δ]εύτερ[ον] μὴ [ὑπά]ρχον ἢ μ[ὴ] το[ι]|οῦτον, (5) ο[ἷο]ν ε[ἰ] Π[λά]των
ἐστὶν ἄν|[θρωπος], καὶ Σωκ[ράτ]ης ἐστὶν ἄν|[θρ]ωπ[ος]· τούτου γὰρ
ἀληθοῦς | ὄντ[ος ἀλη]θὲς [γ]ίνεται[ι] καὶ τὸ | εἰ Σωκράτ[ης] οὐκ ἔστιν
ἄνθρωπος, | οὐδὲ Π[λάτ]ων ἐστὶν ἄνθρωπος, | οὐχὶ [τ]ῶι τ[ῆι] Σωκράτους   15
ἀναιρέ|σει συνανασκευά[ζεσθα[ι] τὸν Πλά|τωνα, ἀλλὰ τῶι μὴ δυν[α]τ[-
ὸν] | εἶναι τὸν μὲν Σω[κ]ράτη[ν νοεῖν] | οὐκ ἄνθρω[πον, τ]ὸν δὲ Π[λάτω]|-
να ἄνθρωπον, [ὃ] δὴ τοῦ κ[αθ᾽] ὁμοιότητ[α] ἔχεται τ[ρό]που.

4 τὸ δεύτερον οὐδὲ τὸ πρῶτον Bahnsch: τὸ πρῶτον οὐδὲ τὸ δεύτερον pap.   17 νοεῖν Sedley: εἶναι
Gomperz
For fuller apparatus, see De Lacy [152].

Context: reply to the Stoic Dionysius' first two arguments against the Epicurean
Similarity Method, reported in the lost portion of text preceding **42G**. Philodemus'
source is his Epicurean master Zeno of Sidon (19.4–11).

17 **νοεῖν** This, in preference to Gomperz's εἶναι, is supported by *Sign.* 14.26,
33.1–9. The 'inconceivability' that one of the similar items should lack an essential

18 Scientific methodology

property which the other possesses is presented in the *De signis* as an entirely cogent ground of inference.

G Philodemus, *Sign.* 34.29–36.17

(1) τοῖς δ᾽ ἐπιλαμβα|νομένοις τῆς καθ᾽ ὁμοιότητα | σημειώσεως ἥ τε παραλλαγή | τῶν εἰρημένων ἀνεπισήμαν|τός ἐστι καὶ πῶς τὸ καθὸ λαμ|βάνομεν, οἷον λόγου χάριν ὡς | ὁ ἄνθρωπος καθὸ ἄνθ[ρ]ωπος | θνητός ἐστι· διὸ καί φασιν ἄν ‖ μὲν παριῆται τὸ καθό, τὸν λόγον | ἀπρόβατον ὑπάρξειν, ἄν δὲ πα|ραλαμβάνηται, τῶι κατ᾽ ἀνασκευ|ὴν χρήσασθαι τρόπωι. (2) τὸ γὰρ | τόδε   5
συνηρτῆσθαι τῶιδ᾽ ἐξ ἀ|νάγκης λαμβάνομεν [ἐ]ξ αὐ|τοῦ πᾶσιν οἷς περιεπέσομεν | τεθεωρῆσθαι τοῦτο παρακολου|θοῦν, καὶ ταῦτα ποικίλοις ἐκ ταὐ|τοῦ γένους ἐντετυχηκότων | ζώιοις καὶ παραλλαγὰς κατὰ τἆλ|λα πρὸς ἄλληλ᾽ ἔ|χουσ]ι, τῶν δὲ | το[ιο]ύτων κοιν[οτ]ή[τ]ων πᾶσι | μ[ετ]έχ-
ουσι. (3) τὸν [οὖ]ν φα[με]ν κα[ὶ] | ἄ]νθ[ρ]ωπον [καθὸ κ]αὶ ἦι ἄνθρω[π-   10
ός | ἐσ]τι θνητὸν [εἶν]αι, τῶι π[ε]ρι[πεπ]τ]ωκέναι π[ολλοῖς] καὶ ποικ[ι]λοῖς ἀ]νθρώ[ποις ἐ]ξαλλαγ[έν | δὲ] τ[ο]ιοῦτο σ[ύμπ]τωμα μηδ[έ|ποτ᾽] ἐφευρ-
εῖ[ν, εἴ]ς τοὐναντίον | [τε] μηδὲν ἡμᾶς ἐπισπώμε||[νο]ν, (4) ὥστε κατὰ τὸν τρόπον | [τοῦ]τον εἰλῆφθαι καὶ ἐπὶ τούτων κα[ὶ] ἐπὶ τῶν ἄλλων ἐφ᾽ ὧν τάττομεν τὸ καθὸ καὶ τὸ ἦι, | τ[ὴ]ν ἰδιότητα ἐνδεικνυμέ|νου τοῦ μὴ ἄλλως   15
ἢ σὺν τούτωι | καὶ ἐξ ἀνάγκης παρακολου|θεῖν τοῦτο τούτωι, (5) καὶ οὐκ ἐπὶ | τῶν δι᾽ ἀνασκευαζομένου ση|μείου μόνον λαμβανομέ|νων. καὶ ἐπὶ τούτων δὲ τὸ πᾶ|σιν περιπεσεῖν τοῦτ᾽ ἔχουσιν | παρακολουθοῦν ἐργάζε-ται | τὴν διαβεβαίωσιν. ἐκ γὰρ τοῦ | τὰ παρ᾽ ἡμῖν κινούμενα {ἥ} πάν|τα διαφορὰς μὲν ἄλλας ἔχειν | κοινὸν δὲ τὸ διὰ κενωμάτων, πάν|τως τὸ κἄν   20
τοῖς ἀδήλοις, καὶ ἵνα | μὴ πυρὸς {οὐκ} ὄντος ἢ γεγονότος | ὁ καπνὸς ἀνασκευασθῆι τῶι πάν|τως καὶ ἐπὶ πάντων καπνὸν | ἐκ πυρὸς ἐκκρινόμε-νον τεθε|ωρῆσθαι διατεινόμεθα. (6) διαπί|πτουσιν δὲ καὶ καθόσον οὐ συν|βλέπουσιν τὸ λαμβάνειν ἡμᾶς | ὅτι οὐδὲν ἀντιπίπτει διὰ τῶν | φαινο-μένων. οὐ γὰρ ἱκανὸν εἰς | τὸ προσδέξασθαι τὰς ἐπ᾽ ἐλάχι|στον παρενκλί-   25
σεις τῶν ἀτόμων | διὰ τὸ τυχηρὸν καὶ τὸ παρ᾽ ἡμᾶς, | ἀλλὰ δε[ῖ] προσεπιδεῖξα[ι] καὶ τ[ὸ] | μηδ᾽ ἄλλ[ο] ἔ[ν τούτ]ωι μάχεσθ[αι] | τῶν ἐνα[ρ]γ[ῶν].

8 κατὰ Gomperz: καὶ pap.   11–12 π[ε]ρι[πεπτ]ωκέναι—τ[ο]ιοῦτο Sedley   12 μηδ[έποτ᾽] Sedley
For fuller apparatus, see De Lacy [152].

Context: Philodemus' report of an oral contribution to the same Epicurean–Stoic debate as in **F** by an unidentified Epicurean, replying to the Stoic proposal at **42G 4**. He accepts the suggested rewriting of the inference 'Since all men familiar to us are mortal, men everywhere are mortal' into the essentialist-sounding 'Since the men familiar to us are mortal *in so far as they are men*, men everywhere are mortal', but insists that the 'in so far as' premise is itself established empirically by the Epicurean 'Similarity Method'. However, in being prepared to include 'in so far as they are men' in the premise, this Epicurean goes beyond Zeno of Sidon's rejoinder to the Stoic objection stated in **42G 3**; cf. *Sign.* 16.5–29, 22.28–23.7.

97

Epicurean epistemology

2 τῶν εἰρημένων At 33.33–34.29 Philodemus' Epicurean source has distinguished four uses of καθό. (1) Necessary concomitant, e.g. 'Men in so far as they are men are prone to disease and ageing'; (2) definition and πρόληψις, e.g. 'Man, in so far as he is man, is a rational animal'; (3) attribute . . . (text truncated); (4) necessary concomitant of an attribute, e.g. '⟨A man, in so far as he⟩ is foolish, is utterly unhappy'. However, he adds that all four usages express a necessary connexion, and the thesis in the present passage that 'in so far as' premises are verified empirically seems to be intended as equally applicable to them all.

19–21 On this argument from motion to void, see vol. 1, 32.

25–6 The inference from τὸ παρ' ἡμᾶς to the atomic swerve is well attested, e.g. at **20E 3, F**. A similar inference from the existence of *luck* to that of the swerve is attested only here and at Plutarch, *Soll. an.* 964C (Usener p. 351, 11), and the latter passage is perhaps textually suspect. See further, Long [219], and cf. note on **20A** 7.

26–8 This formal requirement of οὐκ ἀντιμαρτύρησις in confirmation of the atomic swerve is fulfilled at **11H** 249–50.

19 Language

A Epicurus, *Ep. Hdt.* 75–6

(1) ἀλλὰ μὴν ὑποληπτέον καὶ τὴν φύσιν πολλὰ καὶ παντοῖα ὑπὸ αὐτῶν τῶν πραγμάτων διδαχθῆναί τε καὶ ἀναγκασθῆναι, τὸν δὲ λογισμὸν τὰ ὑπὸ ταύτης παρεγγυηθέντα ὕστερον ἐπακριβοῦν καὶ προσεξευρίσκειν, ἐν μέν τισι θᾶττον, ἐν δέ τισι βραδύτερον, καὶ ἐν μέν τισι περιόδοις καὶ χρόνοις ἀπὸ τῶν [ἀπὸ τοῦ ἀπείρου] ⟨ἰδίων χρειῶν κατὰ μείζους ἐπιδόσεις⟩, ἐν δέ   5
τισι κατ' ἐλάττους. (2) ὅθεν καὶ τὰ ὀνόματα ἐξ ἀρχῆς μὴ θέσει γενέσθαι, ἀλλ' αὐτὰς τὰς φύσεις τῶν ἀνθρώπων καθ' ἕκαστα ἔθνη ἴδια πασχούσας πάθη καὶ ἴδια λαμβανούσας φαντάσματα ἰδίως τὸν ἀέρα ἐκπέμπειν στελλόμενον ὑφ' ἑκάστων τῶν παθῶν καὶ τῶν φαντασμάτων, ὡς ἄν ποτε καὶ ἡ παρὰ τοὺς τόπους τῶν ἐθνῶν διαφορὰ ᾖ· (3) ὕστερον δὲ κοινῶς καθ'   10
ἕκαστα ἔθνη τὰ ἴδια τεθῆναι πρὸς τὸ τὰς δηλώσεις ἧττον ἀμφιβόλους γενέσθαι ἀλλήλαις καὶ συντομωτέρως δηλουμένας· (4) τινὰ δὲ καὶ οὐ συνορώμενα πράγματα εἰσφέροντας τοὺς συνειδότας παρεγγυῆσαί τινας φθόγγους· (5) τοὺς ⟨μὲν οὖν⟩ ἀναγκασθέντας ἀναφωνῆσαι, τοὺς δὲ τῷ λογισμῷ ἑλομένους, κατὰ τὴν πλείστην αἰτίαν οὕτως ἑρμηνεῦσαι.   15

5 ἀπὸ τοῦ ἀπείρου secl. Sedley: ἀπὸ τῶν ἀπὸ τοῦ ἀπείρου secl. Mühll   ⟨ἰδίων χρειῶν⟩ Sedley   ⟨κατὰ μείζους ἐπιδόσεις⟩ Leopold   10 ᾖ Usener: εἴη codd.   12 ἀλλήλαις BPF(corr.): -ους F: -οις Meibom   14 τοὺς ⟨μὲν οὖν⟩ Sedley: ⟨καὶ⟩ τοὺς ⟨μὲν⟩ Gassendi: τοὺς del. Usener

Context: following the section on world formation which includes **13C**.

9–10 It is not clear whether these differences are a primary or merely a supplementary factor in the production of different languages and dialects: καί may suggest the latter (see Brunschwig [248]), unless it is an instance of Epicurus' redundant καί (see Usener [133], s.v.), as at **7B** 29. Nor is it made clear how far impressions and reactions result (a) from environmental differences (cf. **22B 1**), and (b) from differing racial physique (cf. **22Q** 5–6).

15 ἑρμηνεῦσαι virtually = 'to use language', just as ἑρμηνεία, 'self-expression', often amounts to 'language' (**G** 6; also Xenophon, *Mem.* 4.3.12, Diodorus Siculus 1.8.3–4). Cf. note on **C** 3.

B Lucretius 5.1028–90

(1) at varios linguae sonitus natura subegit
mittere et utilitas expressit nomina rerum,
(2) non alia longe ratione atque ipsa videtur   1030
protrahere ad gestum pueros infantia linguae,
cum facit ut digito quae sint praesentia monstrent.
sentit enim vis quisque suas quoad possit abuti.
cornua nata prius vitulo quam frontibus exstent,
illis iratus petit atque infestus inurget.   1035
at catuli pantherarum scymnique leonum
unguibus ac pedibus iam tum morsuque repugnant,
vix etiam cum sunt dentes unguesque creati.
alituum porro genus alis omne videmus
fidere et a pinnis tremulum petere auxiliatum.   1040
(3) proinde putare aliquem tum nomina distribuisse
rebus et inde homines didicisse vocabula prima,
desiperest. nam cur hic posset cuncta notare
vocibus et varios sonitus emittere linguae,
tempore eodem alii facere id non quisse putentur?   1045
(4) praeterea si non alii quoque vocibus usi
inter se fuerant, unde insita notities est
utilitatis et unde data est huic prima potestas,
quid vellet facere ut sciret animoque videret?
(5) cogere item pluris unus victosque domare   1050
non poterat, rerum ut perdiscere nomina vellent.
nec ratione docere ulla suadereque surdis,
quid sit opus facto, facilest; neque enim paterentur
nec ratione ulla sibi ferrent amplius auris
vocis inauditos sonitus obtundere frustra.   1055
(6) postremo quid in hac mirabile tantoperest re,
si genus humanum, cui vox et lingua vigeret,
pro vario sensu varia res voce notaret?
cum pecudes mutae, cum denique saecla ferarum
dissimilis soleant voces variasque ciere,   1060
cum metus aut dolor est et cum iam gaudia gliscunt.
quippe etenim licet id rebus cognoscere apertis.
irritata canum cum primum magna Molossum
mollia ricta fremunt duros nudantia dentis,

longe alio sonitu rabie restricta minantur 1065
et cum iam latrant et vocibus omnia complent.
at catulos blande cum lingua lambere temptant
aut ubi eos iactant pedibus morsuque potentes
suspensis teneros imitantur dentibus haustus,
longe alio pacto gannitu vocis adulant 1070
et cum deserti baubantur in aedibus aut cum
plorantes fugiunt summisso corpore plagas.
denique non hinnitus item differre videtur,
inter equas ubi equus florenti aetate iuvencus
pinnigeri saevit calcaribus ictus amoris 1075
et fremitum patulis sub naribus edit ad arma,
et cum sic alias concussis artubus hinnit?
postremo genus alituum variaeque volucres,
accipitres atque ossifragae mergique marinis
fluctibus in salso victum vitamque petentes, 1080
longe alias alio iaciunt in tempore voces
et cum de victu certant praedaeque repugnant.
et partim mutant cum tempestatibus una
raucisonos cantus, cornicum ut saecla vetusta
corvorumque greges ubi aquam dicuntur et imbris 1085
poscere et interdum ventos aurasque vocare.
(7) ergo si varii sensus animalia cogunt,
muta tamen cum sint, varias emittere voces,
quanto mortalis magis aequumst tum potuisse
dissimilis alia atque alia res voce notare! 1090

1033 *quoad* Lambinus: *quod* OQ   1058 *varia* Bentley: *varias* OQ   1064 *fremunt* Marullus: *premunt*
OQ   1068 *iactant* Naugerius: *lactant* OQ   *potentes* OQ: *petentes* l31

Context: immediately following **22K**, which itself describes the use of *pre*-linguistic
gestures in the forming of social compacts.

The argument is: it is natural to human beings both to designate (witness instinctive
pointing by infants), and to utter different sounds in reaction to different stimuli
(witness the instinctive utterances of numerous animal species); to stumble upon a
rudimentary language, they had only to link these two tendencies.

1029   There is no possible ground for seeing any reference here to the later,
artificial stage of language development (**A 3–4**), as Giussani [164], 280, and others
have done.

1030–40   On the potentially un-Epicurean implications of this apparent appeal to
animal instinct, see vol. 1, 64–5. Cf. also the interesting study by Schrijvers [247], who
argues that *sentit* at 1033 represents not instinctive feeling but empirical observation, as
at **21A** 9: he stresses the fact that the young animals are said to start trying to use the
part in question when it has *barely* emerged, but not *before* it has, as the teleologists
normally claimed.

C Diogenes of Oenoanda 10.2.11–5.15

καὶ τῶν | φθόνγων δὲ ἕνεκεν (λέ|γω δὲ τῶν τε ὀνομάτων | καὶ τῶν
ῥημάτων) ὧν | ἐποιήσαντο τὰς πρώτας | ἀναφθένξεις οἱ ἀπὸ | γῆς φύντες
[ἄνθρω]ποι | μήτε τὸν Ἑρμῆν παρα|λαμβάνωμεν εἰς δι|δασκαλίαν, ὧς
φασίν | τινες – περιφανὴς γὰρ | αὕτη γε ἀδολεσχία – | μήτε τῶν φιλο-
σόφων | πιστεύωμεν τοῖς λέ|γουσι κατὰ θέσιν καὶ | διδαχὴν ἐπιτεθῆ-   5
ναι | τὰ ὀνόματα τοῖς πράγ[μα]|σιν, ἵνα αὐτῶν ἔχωσ[ι σημεῖ]|α τῆς πρὸς
[ἀλ]λήλους ἕνε|κα ῥαδίας ἀποδηλώσεως οἱ | ἄνθρωποι. γελοῖον γάρ | ἐστι,
μᾶλλον δὲ παν|τὸς γελοίου γελοιότε|ρον πρὸς τῷ καὶ τὸ ἀ|δύνα[τ]ο[ν] αὐτῷ
προσεῖ|ναι, σ[υνα]γαγεῖν μέν | τινα τὰ [το]σάδε πλήθη | ἕνα τυν[χά]νοντα
(οὐδὲ | γάρ πω τ[ό]τε βασιλέες ἦ|σαν οὐδὲ μὴν γράμμα|τα ὅπου γε μηδὲ οἱ   10
φθόν|γοι – περὶ γὰρ τούτων καὶ [lacuna of a few words] [διὰ] προσταγῆς
τὴν | συ[ν]αγωγὴν αὐτῶν γε|νέσθαι), συναγαγόντα | δὲ καθηγεῖσθαι
γρ[α]μ|ματιστοῦ τρόπον [ῥα]|κεῖδός τινος ἀν[τιλαβό]|μενον, καὶ ἑκάστου
τῷ[ν] | πραγμάτων θινγάνον|τα ἐπιλέγειν ὅτι "του|τε[ὶ] μὲν καλείσθω
λι[θ]ος, τουτεὶ δὲ ξύλον, | [τ]ουτε⟨ὶ⟩ δὲ ἄνθρωπος, | ἢ κύων . . ."   15

10 βασιλέες Chilton [246]
The text is from Chilton [170], which should be consulted for fuller apparatus.

Context: the early history of man – a context in Diogenes' work equivalent to
Epicurus *Nat.* XIII (represented in *Ep. Hdt.* by **A**) and to the second half of Lucretius 5.

3 Ἑρμῆν That Hermes was the inventor of language, ἑρμηνεία, is an
etymological flight of fancy known to Diodorus Siculus (5.75), and possibly
foreshadowed at Plato, *Crat.* 407e–8b.

4–7 It was apparently an unquestioned assumption before Epicurus that language
arose either as a human contrivance or as a gift from the gods: cf. Plato, *Crat.* 439c2,
etc., *Prot.* 322a; Xenophon, *Mem.* 4.3.12; Diodorus Siculus 1.8.3–4, Vitruvius 2.1
(both often held to stem ultimately from Democritus, see Cole [273]).

D Epicurus, Nat. 28, 31.10.2–12

εἰ δὲ | τότε [τα]ὐτό τι διαν[ο]ούμε|νοι ἐλέγομεν κατὰ [τ]ὴν [ἐ]κ|κειμένην
ἑρμηνίαν τῷ | ὅτι πᾶσα ἡ ἁμ[α]ρτία ἐστὶν | τῶν ἀνθρώπων οὐδὲν ἔτε|ρον
ἔχουσα σχῆμα ἢ τὸ ἐπὶ | τῶμ προλήψεων γιγν[ό]|μενον καὶ τῶμ φαιν[ο-
μ]ένων | διὰ τοὺς πολυτρόπους ἐ[θι]|σμοὺς τῶν λέξεων . . .

Readings from Sedley [126]

Context: discussion, in a book written in 296/5 B.C., of Epicurus' own earlier views on
language.

1 εἰ With the apodosis lost, it cannot be judged whether or not the protasis is
counterfactual ('If we had said . . .'). Thus the text maddeningly refuses to tell us
whether Epicurus himself ever entertained the view described here. τότε Not
datable, but no doubt in Epicurus' 'early' works known as the ἀρχαῖα or ἀρχαικά,
which Philodemus mentions as providing Epicurean orthodoxy with a problem

Epicurean epistemology

comparable to the Stoics' embarrassment over Zeno's youthful *Republic* (*De Stoicis* 11.4ff., in Dorandi [334]; cf. notes on **67B, E**).

1-2 **κατὰ [τ]ὴν [ἐ]κ|κειμένην ἑρμηνίαν** Perhaps added because Epicurus is aware that at the time of which he is speaking he had not yet introduced πρόληψις (3; cf. **23E 3**) into his philosophical vocabulary. (ἑρμηνίαν is the papyrus' orthography for -είαν.)

4 The reference is apparently to a time when Epicurus, regarding language as a prime source of error, attempted to reform it for philosophical purposes. See Sedley [126], 22-3. For further speculation on the philosophical significance of this fragment, cf. Long [232], Glidden [250].

E Epicurus, *Nat.* 28.31.13.23–14.12

ἀλλὰ γὰρ ἴσως οὐκ εὔκαιρόν | ἐστ[ι ταῦ]τ[α] προφέροντα μη|κύνει[ν· κ]αὶ μαλ' ὀρθῶς [γε, ὦ]| Μητρόδωρε· πάνυ γὰρ οἶμαί | σε πολλὰ ἂν ἔχειμ προε[ν]έγ|κασθαι ἃ ἐθεώρεις γελοίως [π]|ώ[ς] τι[να]ς ἐγδεξαμένους καὶ π[άν]|τ[α] μᾶλλον ἢ τὸ νοούμενον | κατὰ τὰς λέξεις, οὐκ ἔξω τῶν | ἰθισμένων λέξεων ἡμῶν | χρωμένων οὐδὲ μετατιθέν|των ὀνόματα ἐπὶ τῶμ φανε||[ρ]ῶν.   5

Readings from Sedley [126]

Context: critique of Epicurus' own and his pupil Metrodorus' earlier views on language. Metrodorus had apparently held an extreme conventionalist view of meaning, like that of Hermogenes in Plato's *Cratylus* (Sedley [126], 22).

The scribe's orthography is idiosyncratic: ἐγ- (3) = ἐκ-; ἰθ- (4) = εἰθ-.

3 **τι[να]ς** We suggest in vol. 1, 101, that Epicurus is thinking of Diodorus Cronus' extreme conventionalist theory (**37N–O**). If so, he is perhaps using the absurdity of Diodorus' position as a gentle way of criticizing Metrodorus' former view that no name is better than any other, and defending their current orthodoxy that existing linguistic conventions should be adhered to.

4-6 For Epicurus' avowed respect for current linguistic conventions, cf. **7B** 15; **14A** 28-30; D.L. 10.13; Plutarch, *Col.* 1112F.

F Anon., *In Plat. Theaet.* 22.39–47

Ἐπίκου|[ρ]ος τὰ ὀνόματά φη|σ[ι]ν σαφέστερα εἶναι | τῶν ὅρων, καὶ μέν|τοι καὶ γελοῖον εἶ|ναι, εἴ τις ἀντὶ τοῦ εἰ|πεῖν "χαῖρε Σώκρα|τες" λέγοι "χαῖρε ζῶι|ον λο[γ]ικὸν θνητόν".

Context: comment on the remark at *Tht.* 147b that no one understands a thing's name if he does not know what the thing is.

1 **ὀνόματα** One would expect this to be 'words', rather than '(proper) names'. If so, the example, 'Socrates' is unfortunate.

G Erotianus 34,10–20 (Usener 258)

εἰ γὰρ μέλλοιμεν τὰς πᾶσι γινωσκομένας ἐξαπλοῦν φωνάς, ἤτοι πάσας ὀφειλήσομεν ἐξηγήσασθαι ἤ τινας. ἀλλὰ πάσας μὲν ἀδύνατον, τινὰς δὲ καὶ κενόν. ἢ γὰρ διὰ συνήθων ἐξαπλώσομεν αὐτὰς ῥημάτων ἢ διὰ τῶν μὴ

συνήθων. ἀλλ' αἱ μὲν ἀσυνήθεις εἰς τοῦτο ἀφυεῖς φαίνονται (δεκτὸν γὰρ τὰ
ἧττον γινωσκόμενα διὰ τῶν μᾶλλον γινωσκομένων ἐξαπλοῦν), αἱ δὲ   5
συνήθεις τῷ ἐπ' ἴσης εἶναι φανεραὶ πρὸς τὸ δηλωτικὸν τῆς ἑρμηνείας οὐκ
ἔσονται, ὥς φησιν Ἐπίκουρος. ἀπόλλυται γὰρ ἰδίως τῆς ἑρμηνείας τὸ
φανερόν, ὅθ' ὑπὸ λόγου καθάπερ τινὸς οἰκείου μαγγανεύηται φαρμάκου.

2–3 καὶ κενόν Usener: δίκαιον codd.: ⟨οὐ⟩ δίκαιον Eustachius   4 δεκτὸν codd.: δίκαιον dubitanter
Usener   6 τῷ Stephanus: τὸ codd.: ⟨διὰ⟩ τὸ Turnebus   7 ἔσονται ⟨χρήσιμοι⟩ Usener   ἰδίως
codd.: πως dubitanter Usener

Context: preface to the lexicon, discussing what classes of words should be explained
and by what means.

H Cicero, *Fin.* 1.22 (Usener 243, part)

iam in altera philosophiae parte, quae est quaerendi ac disserendi, quae λογική
dicitur, iste vester plane, ut mihi quidem videtur, inermis ac nudus est. tollit
definitiones, nihil de dividendo ac partiendo docet, non quo modo efficiatur
concludaturque ratio tradit, non qua via captiosa solvantur ambigua
distinguantur ostendit.   5

Context: Cicero's own attack on Epicurus.

I Diogenes Laertius 10.31 (Usener 257)

τὴν διαλεκτικὴν ὡς παρέλκουσαν ἀποδοκιμάζουσιν· ἀρκεῖν γὰρ τοὺς
φυσικοὺς χωρεῖν κατὰ τοὺς τῶν πραγμάτων φθόγγους.

Context: doxography of Epicurean canonic. Followed by **17A**.

  1 **παρέλκουσαν** We translate 'superfluous', but another possibility is 'misleading', 'diversionary'.

J Diogenes Laertius 10.34 (Usener 265)

τῶν τε ζητήσεων εἶναι τὰς μὲν περὶ τῶν πραγμάτων, τὰς δὲ περὶ ψιλὴν τὴν
φωνήν.

Context: as **I**.

K Plutarch, *Col.* 1119F (Usener 259, part)

τίνες μᾶλλον ὑμῶν πλημμελοῦσι περὶ τὴν διάλεκτον, οἳ τὸ τῶν λεκτῶν
γένος, οὐσίαν τῷ λόγῳ παρέχον, ἄρδην ἀναιρεῖτε, τὰς φωνὰς καὶ τὰ
τυγχάνοντα μόνον ἀπολιπόντες, τὰ δὲ μεταξὺ σημαινόμενα πράγματα, δι'
ὧν γίνονται μαθήσεις, διδασκαλίαι, προλήψεις, νοήσεις, ὁρμαί, συγκαταθέσεις, τὸ παράπαν οὐδὲ εἶναι λέγοντες;   5

2 παρέχον Usener: παρέχοντες codd.

Context: attack on Epicurean theology for violating the gods in reality, not just
linguistically. For good measure, he throws in the remark that if linguistic violations

do matter too, none are guiltier of them than the Epicureans – as explained here. For a similar use of Stoic metaphysical doctrine as a weapon against the Epicureans, cf. ibid. 1116в.

ETHICS

20 Free will

A Epicurus, *Ep. Men.* 133–4

(1) ἐπεὶ τίνα νομίζεις εἶναι κρείττονα τοῦ καὶ περὶ θεῶν ὅσια δοξάζοντος καὶ περὶ θανάτου διὰ παντὸς ἀφόβως ἔχοντος καὶ τὸ τῆς φύσεως ἐπιλελογισμένου τέλος, καὶ τὸ μὲν τῶν ἀγαθῶν πέρας ὡς ἔστιν εὐσυμπλήρωτόν τε καὶ εὐπόριστον διαλαμβάνοντος, τὸ δὲ τῶν κακῶν ὡς ἢ χρόνους ἢ πόνους ἔχει βραχεῖς, τὴν δὲ ὑπό τινων δεσπότιν εἰσαγομένην πάντων ἂν γελῶντος ⟨εἱμαρμένην, ἀλλ' ἃ μὲν κατ' ἀνάγκην 5 ὄντα συνορῶντος⟩, ἃ δὲ ἀπὸ τύχης, ἃ δὲ παρ' ἡμᾶς, διὰ τὸ τὴν μὲν ἀνάγκην ἀνυπεύθυνον εἶναι, τὴν δὲ τύχην ἄστατον ὁρᾶν, τὸ δὲ παρ' ἡμᾶς ἀδέσποτον ᾧ καὶ τὸ μεμπτὸν καὶ τὸ ἐναντίον παρακολουθεῖν πέφυκεν; (2) ἐπεὶ κρεῖττον ἦν τῷ περὶ θεῶν μύθῳ κατακολουθεῖν ἢ τῇ τῶν φυσικῶν εἱμαρμένῃ δουλεύειν· ὁ μὲν γὰρ ἐλπίδα παραιτήσεως ὑπογράφει θεῶν διὰ 10 τιμῆς, ἡ δὲ ἀπαραίτητον ἔχει τὴν ἀνάγκην.

5 ἂν γελῶντος Sedley: ἀγγέλοντος BF: ἀγγελῶντος P: ἐγγελῶντος Bailey: ἀγγέλλων Diano   εἱμαρμένην add. Usener   5–6 ἀλλ' ἃ–συνορῶντος add. Sedley: καὶ μᾶλλον ἃ μὲν κατ' ἀνάγκην γίνεσθαι λέγοντος Usener

Context: the beginning of Epicurus' final summing up of his ethical precepts.

5 The proposed reading ἂν γελῶντος would be palaeographically identical with P's ἀγγελῶντος in one of the orthographic systems used in early Epicurean texts: cf. C 9 etc. The point of ἂν is that this idealized sage need not actually have encountered determinism, but would deride it if he did.

5–6 An advantage of the supplement which we print is that it makes the omission readily explicable through homoioteleuton. Cf. also the very similar use of συνορᾶν in C 40.

7 τύχη is said at ibid. 134 not to be an 'unreliable cause'. It seems doubtful whether Epicurus would offer *any* analysis of it at the physical level. Cf. Long [219].

8 Cf. C 2, G.

B Epicurus, *Nat.*, liber incertus, 34.21–2

γί]νεσθαι κατὰ τὸν π[ρ]οειρημένον τρόπον καὶ τῶν [α]ὐτῶν ἀπεργαστικὰ εἶναι· (1) πολλὰ δὲ καὶ τῶνδε καὶ τῶνδ̣[ε φ]ύσιν ἔχοντα ἀπεργαστικὰ [γί]νεσθαι δι' ἑαυτὰ οὐ γίνεται ἀπ[ε]ργαστικά, οὐ διὰ τὴν αὐτὴν αἰτία[ν] τῶν τε ἀτόμων καὶ ἑαυτῶν· (2) οἷς δὴ καὶ μάλιστα μαχόμεθα καὶ ἐπιτιμῶμεν, μ[ι]σοῦντες κατὰ τὴν ἐξ ἀρχῆ[ς] ταραχώδη φύσιν ἔχοντα καθ[ά]περ ἐπὶ τῶν πάντων 5 ζώιων. (3) οὐθὲν γὰρ αὐτοῖς συνήργηκεν εἰς ἔνια ἔργα τε καὶ μεγέθη ἔργων

20 Free will

καὶ διαθέσεων ἡ τῶν ἀτόμων φύσις, ἀλλ' αὐτὰ τὰ ἀπογεγεννημένα τὴν
πᾶσα[ν ἢ] τὴν πλε[ίσ]την κέ[κτ]ητ[αι] αἰτίαν τῶνδέ [τι]νων. (4) ἐκ δ'
ἐκ[ε]ίνης [ἔν]ιαι τῶν [ἀ]τόμων κινήσεις ταραχώδε[ις] κ[ινο]ῦνται, οὐχὶ δὲ
τὰς ἀτ[όμου]ς [.] πάντως [. . . . .]ν[. . . . . . .] πιπτον [. . . . .]έχοντος   10
[(lacuna approx. 45 words)]σεσθαι μαχόμεν[οι πο]λλοῖς ἅμα τῶν ἀν[θρώ]πων καὶ
νουθε[τοῦν]τες, ὃ τῆι τοῦ αὐτο[ῦ τρό]που κατ' ἀνάγκην α[ἰτ]ία[ι] ὑπεναντίον ἐστίν· (5)
οὕτως ἐπειδὰν ἀπογεννηθῇ τι λανβάνον [τι]νὰ [ἐ]τερότη[τα τῶν] ἀτό[μ]ων
κατά τινα τρόπον διαληπτικόν, οὐ τὸν ὡς ἀφ' ἑτέρου δ[ι]αστήματος,
ἰσχάνε[ι] τὴν ἐξ ἑαυ[τοῦ] αἰτίαν, (6) εἶτα [ἀν]αδίδ[ωσι] εὐθὺς μέχρι τῶν   15
[πρ]ώτω[ν] φύσεων καὶ [κ]αν[όνα π]ᾶσαν αὐτὴ[ν] ποιεῖ. (7) ὅθεν δὴ καὶ οἱ
μὴ δυνάμενοι κατὰ τρόπον τὰ τοιαῦτα διαιρεῖν χειμάζουσιν αὐτοὺς περὶ
τὴν τῶν αἰτιῶν ἀπόφασιν· καὶ τού[των ἐ]π' αὐτῶν τοῖς [μ]ὲν μᾶλλο[ν τοῖς δ' ἤ]ττον
μαχ[όμε]θα καὶ ἐ[πιτιμ]ῶμεν κα[. . . . . .]εννο[

5 ἀρχῆ[ς] ⟨σύστασιν⟩ Diano   13 [τ]ι P 697: [. .] P 1056: το O 1056   13–14 [ἐ]τερότη[τα–τινα
697: om. 1056

Note on sigla for **B**, **C** and **j**: P = papyrus Herculanensis (697, 1056, or 1191: these contain parallel texts of
the same book); O = apographum Oxoniense; N = apographum Neapolitanum (O and N are 19th-century
facsimiles of the papyri); αβγ = letters read in P, O, or N of at least one papyrus; ˹αβγ˺ = letters no longer
legible in any P, but given in O or N and altered by editor. Readings of papyri are from Sedley [260], on
which the entire vol. 1 commentary on **20** is based.

Context: from the book's exposition of the αἰτιολογικὸς τρόπος of psychological
explanation (cf. ibid. 34.33.4–7); but the immediate context is lost.

1ff.   The neuter plurals probably have ζῷα as their subject. Cf. **F 1, j** with notes.

4–5   Our translation takes ἔχοντα as the verbal counterpart of ἕξις; but Diano's
supplement has its attractions. For the doctrinal point in these lines, cf. **j**.

9   ἐκ[ε]ίνης   This is taken in the translation to refer back to φύσις in 7. But one
might, slightly less naturally, connect it with αἰτίαν in 8, in which case the point made
would be, as at 15–16, that psychological causation operates on our soul atoms and not
vice versa.

11–12   Although it is unclear just how it stands in relation to 13ff., this phrase
seems to contain an argument very like **C 2**, that moral criticism of others is
inconsistent with determinism. If τρό]που is right, the reference could be to the
'difference of scale' mode mentioned at 14 (cf. also ibid. 34.4.10). That mode would
be, for Epicurus, the principle by which Democritean atomism reduces psychology to
mechanism.

16   [κ]αν[όνα   The reading is very uncertain. If correct, it will mean that the
man who has developed his own principle of conduct goes on to impose it on his own
soul atoms as a pattern regulatory of his behaviour. Even rational principles can
become mechanical habits.

C   Epicurus, *Nat.*, liber incertus, 34.26–30

(1) ἔκ] τε [τῆς πρ]ώτης ἀρχῆς σπέρμ[ατα ἡμῖν ἀ]γωγὰ τὰ μὲν εἰς τάδ[ε] τὰ
δ' εἰς τάδε τὰ δ' εἰς ἄμφω [ταῦ]τά [ἐ]στιν ἀεὶ [κα]ὶ πρά[ξ]εων [καὶ]
διανοήσεων καὶ διαθέ[σε]ων καὶ πλεί[ω] καὶ ἐλάττωι. ὥστε παρ' ἡμᾶς

Epicurean ethics

π[ρῶτον] ἁπλῶς τὸ ἀπογεγεννημένον ἤδη γείνεσθαι, [τ]οῖα ἢ τοῖα, καὶ τὰ
ἐκ τοῦ περιέχοντος κ[α]τ' ἀνάγκην διὰ τοὺς πό[ρους] εἰσρέο[ν]τα παρ'   5
ἡμᾶς π[ο]τε γε[ίνε]σθαι καὶ παρὰ τ[ὰς] ἡμε[τέρα]ς [ἐ]ξ ἡμῶν αὐτ[ῶν]
δόξ[ας …]ει [π]αρὰ τὴν φ[ύ]σι[ν] α[…]υσ[……]υκ[…]θ[……]ει […]
ετησ[………]τα[….]α[.]χε[……]ν[.]υ[…]ωσε[………]νεκε[(lacuna approx.
60 words)]τα τὸμ φυσικὸγ χα[ρα]κτῆρα ὁμοίως καὶ τοῖς τ[….]οις κε[νο]ῖς πόροις
[…τ]ῶν αὐ[τ]ῶν ἰδιοτή[των…]ο[…ἐ]πὶ πάν[τ]ων [………]ντω[………]   10
ἐπειδ[(lacuna approx. 12 words) (2)]εστήκει, ὧν οὐ[… ἀ]πολείπει τὰ πάθη
τοῦ γίνε[σθαι, τὸ] νουθε[τ]εῖν τε ἀλλήλους καὶ μάχε[σ]θαι καὶ μεταρυθμί-
ζειν ὡς ἔχοντας καὶ ἐν ἑαυτοῖς τὴν αἰτίαν καὶ οὐχὶ ἐν τῆι ἐξ ἀρχῆς μόνον
συστάσει καὶ ἐν τῆι τοῦ περιέχοντος καὶ ἐπεισιόντος κατὰ τὸ αὐτόματον
ἀνάγκηι. (3) εἰ γάρ τις καὶ τῶι νουθετεῖν καὶ τῶι νουθετεῖσθαι   15
τὴν κατὰ τὸ αὐ[τό]μα[τ]ον ἀνάγκην προστι[θείη] ἀεὶ τοῦ [τό]θ' ἑαυτῶ[ι]
ὑπάρχο[ντος], μὴ οὐ[χ]ὶ πο[τε] δύν[ηται ταύτ]η [συ]νιέναι [………
………]αλλ[………] ἡμεῖ[ν………]πονε [(lacuna of a few words)
(4) μεμ]φόμενος ἢ ἐπαινῶν· ἀλλ' ε[ἰ] μὲν τοῦτο πράττοι, τὸ [αὐτὸ] ἔργ[ο]ν
ἂν εἴη [κ]ατα[λεί]πων ὃ ἐφ' ἡμῶν αὐτῶν [ποιεῖ] τὴν τῆς αἰτίας πρό[λη]-   20
ψιν, ἐν ὧι οὐ μὲν τὸ δό[γμα …] μετατεθε[ι]μένο[ς …] μὴ πρ[…
………]π[..]τ[……]ο[(lacuna approx. 45 words)] (5) τοι[αύτ]ης πλάνης.
περικά[τω] γὰρ ὁ τοιοῦτος λόγος τρέπεται, καὶ οὐδέποτε δύναται
βεβαιῶσαι ὡς ἐστὶν τοιαῦτα πάντα οἷα τὰ κατ' ἀνάγκην καλούμενα· ἀλλὰ
μάχεταί τινι περὶ αὐτοῦ τούτου ὡς δι' ἑαυτοῦ ἀβελτερευομένωι. (6) κἂν εἰς   25
ἄπειρον φῆι πάλιν κατ' ἀνάγκην τοῦτο πράττειν ἀπὸ λόγων ἀεί, οὐκ
ἐπιλογίζεται ἐν τῶι εἰς ἑαυτὸν τὴν αἰτίαν ἀνά[π]τειν τοῦ κα[τὰ τ]ρόπον
λελογίσθαι εἰς δὲ τὸν ἀμφισβητοῦντα τοῦ μὴ κατὰ τρόπον. (7) εἰ δὲ μὴ ἃ
πο[ιεῖ] ἀπολήγοι [ε]ἰς ἑαυτὸ[ν] ἀλλ' εἰς τὴν [ἀ]νάγ[κην] τ[ι]θείη, [ο]ὐδ' ἂν
ε[..]κα[………]επ[(lacuna approx. 30 words) (8) εἰ τὸ δι' ἡμῶν]   30
αὐτῶγ καλούμενον τῶι τῆς ἀνάγκης ὀνόματι προσαγ[ο]ρεύων [ὄ]νομα
μό[ν]ομ μετατίθετα[ι] ⌈μη⌉δ' ἐπιδίξει ὅτι τοιοῦτό τι ᾧ μοχθηρο[ί εἰσι
τύ]ποι προειλ[η]φότες τὸ δι' ἡμῶ[ν αὐ]τῶν αἴτιογ καλ[οῦμεν], οὔτ'
ἰδ[ι…… (lacuna approx. 25 words)] (9) γενέσθαι, ἀλ[λὰ κε]νὸν [καὶ] τὸ δι'
ἀνάγκην καλ[εῖ]ν πρ[ὸ]⌈ς⌉ ὧν φάτε. ἂν δὲ μ[ή] τις τοῦτο ἀποδείξει, μηδ'   35
ἔχει ἡμῶν [τ]ι συνεργὸν μηδ' ὅρμημα ἀπο[τ]ρέπειν ὧν καλοῦντες δι' ἡμῶν
αὐτῶν τὴν αἰτίαν συντελοῦμεν, ἀλλὰ πάντα ὅσ[α] νῦν δι' ἡμῶν αὐ[τῶ]ν
ὀνομάζοντες τὴν αἰτίαν [εἶναι διαβ]ε[βα]ιούμεθα πράττε[ιν] κατὰ μώραν
ἀνάγκην προσαγορεύων, ὄνομα μόνον ἀμείψει· (10) ἔργον δ' οὐθὲν ἡμῶν
μετακοσμήσει, ὥσπερ ἐπ' ἐνίων ὁ συνορῶν τὰ ποῖα κατ' ἀνάγκην ἐστὶν   40
ἀποτρέπειν εἴωθε τοὺς προθυμουμένους παρὰ βίαν τι π[ρ]άττειν. (11)
ζητήσει δ' ἡ διάνοια εὑρεῖν τὸ ποῖον [ο]ὖν τι δεῖ νομί[ζ]ειν τὸ ἐξ ἡ[μ]ῶν
αὐτῶ[ν π]ως [πρ]αττόμενον [μ]ὴ προθυμ[ουμένων πράτ]τειν. οὐ γὰρ ἔχει
ἄλ[λο τι οὐθὲν εἰ μὴ φά[ναι τὸ] ποῖον [κατ' ἀνάγκην] ἐσ[τὶ… (lacuna
approx. 12 words)]ξ[………………το]ῦ ὀνό[ματος … (lacuna approx. 25 words)]   45
(12) μάλιστα ἀδιανοήτων. ἂν δέ τις τοῦτο μὴ παραβιάζηται, μηδ' αὖ ὃ

ἐξελέγχει τε ἦ ὅ εἰσφέρει πρᾶγμα ἐκτιθεῖ, φωνῇ μόνον ἀμείβεται, καθάπερ
πάλαι θρυλῶ. (13) οἱ δ᾽ αἰτιολογήσαντες ἐξ ἀρχῆς ἱκανῶς, καὶ οὐ μ⌐ό⌐[ν]ον
[τ]ῶν πρὸ αὐτῶν πολὺ διενέγκαντες ἀλλὰ καὶ τῶν ὕστερον πολλαπλ[α]-
σί⌐ως⌐, ἔλαθ⌐ο⌐ν ἑαυτούς, καίπερ ἐν πολλοῖς μεγάλα κουφίσαντες, ε[ἰ]ς   50
τὸ τ[ὴ]ν ἀνάγκην καὶ ταὐτόμ̣α̣τ̣[ο]ν πάντα α[ἰτι]ᾶσθαι. (14) ὁ δὴ λόγος
αὐτὸς ὁ τοῦτο διδάσκων κατεάγνυτο καὶ ἐλάνθανεν τὸν ἄνδρα τοῖς ἔργοις
πρὸς τὴν δόξαν συνκρού[ο]ντα· καὶ εἰ μὴ λήθη τις ἐπὶ τῶν ἔργων τῆς δόξης
ἐνεγείνετο, συνεχῶς ἂν ἑαυτὸν ταράττοντα· ᾗ ι δ᾽ ἐκράτει τὸ τῆς δόξης κἂν
τοῖς ἐσχάτοις π[ε]ριπείπτοντα· ᾗ[ι δὲ] μὴ ἐκράτει στάσεως ἐμπιμπλάμε-   55
νον διὰ τὴν ὑπεναντιότητα τῶν ἔργων καὶ τῆς δόξης· (15) τούτων οὖν
οὕτως ἐχόντων δεῖ κα[ὶ] περὶ οὗ λέγων ἐξ ἀρχῆς εἰς τὸ ταῦτα
παρεκκαθαίρειν ἀφικόμην ἀποδιδόναι, μ[ὴ] κακ[όν τι] τ̣ο̣ι̣ο̣ῦτ̣[ο] ....

13 μόνον 697: om. 1056   16 τόθ᾽ ἑαυτῶ[ι] ὑπά[ρχοντος] μ[ὴ ο]ὐ[χ]ί 697: [ὐ]πάρχο[ν-
τος .]τη[. . . μ]ὴ οὐ[± 23]η 1056 (but τη preserved only in O)   23 ὁ 1191: om. 1056   24 πάντα
οἷα τὰ κατ᾽ἀνάγκην καλοῦμεν 1056: πάν⌐τ⌐ ἀνάγκην καλ[ού]μενα 1191   28–9 ἃ πο[ιεῖ] 1056: om.
697   32 ⌐μὴ⌐: δει O 1191   35 ⌐ς⌐: ε O 1056   50–1 ε[ἰ]ς τὸ Sedley: ἐν· τὸ Gigante   52
ἐλάνθανε 697: [. .]ά[. .]θα[. .]εν P 1056: [ἔ]λαμθα[. .]ν O 1056

For sigla, see on B above. Readings are from Sedley [260]. Note that each of the three scribes had his own
orthographic system, so that the above text, pieced together out of the fragments of the three parallel
papyri, fluctuates between them.   4 γείνεσθαι = γίνεσθαι, cf. 6, 54, 55   9 τὸμ φυσικὸν = τὸν
φυσικόν, cf. 31–3   32 ἐπιδίξει = ἐπιδείξει   47 ἐκτιθεῖ = ἐκτιθῇ.

Context: shortly after **j**, probably concluding Epicurus' discussion of the responsibility
issue.

1 **σπέρματα**   Probably metaphorically, 'potentials'. There is no good evidence in
Epicurus for the equivalent of Lucretius' poetic use of *semina* for 'atoms'.

3 **πλεί[ω] καὶ ἐλάττωι**   It is unclear whether this qualifies the nominatives τὰ
μέν, etc. or the accusatives τάδε, etc.

4–7   On our power to control our intake of εἴδωλα, see **15B**.

16–17   Text *very* uncertain.

19–21   Cf. 30–3. It is precisely our adoption of critical attitudes to others that
creates our preconception of the individual's own self as responsible for his actions.

23 **περικά[τω]** . . . **τρέπεται**   This is the technical Epicurean term for self-
refutation (= περιτρέπεται in later, non-Epicurean texts). Cf. **16A** 1 with note;
Epicurus, *Nat*. 35.11.1–5 (referring to this same argument); Philodemus, *Sign*. 30.14–
15; Burnyeat [10] and [229].

26–7 **οὐκ ἐπιλογίζεται**   See note on **21V** 1.

28–29   The determinist can only halt the regress and eliminate his inconsistency
by ceasing to claim responsibility for being right. Whereupon, Epicurus perhaps went
on to say, he would have no reason left for supposing that he *is* right.

35 **φάτε**   The reading is certain, but puzzling. ὑμεῖς also occurs in the
fragmentary closing sentences of the book (not in Arrighetti [119]), as also in those of
book XXVIII. *On nature* was a lecture course, addressed to Epicurus' pupils, and
sometimes to individuals, like Metrodorus in book XXVIII (see **19E**), with whom he
was engaged in debates. The second person plural at this point in the text may suggest

Epicurean ethics

that a group of Epicurus' own pupils had shown some sympathy for Democritean determinism.

35–6 The colloquial style of *On nature* permits the non-literary Hellenistic construction of ἐάν + indicative, cf. Sedley [126], 69–70.

47 τε The certain reading of P 1191, but probably corrupt. Perhaps an additional verb has fallen out before or after ἐξελέγχει.

47–8 καθάπερ πάλαι θρυλῶ I.e. at 31–2 and 39.

48 For Democritus as an exponent of αἰτιλογία, see his 68 B 118 DK. The plural may have been chosen to pay lip service to Leucippus, although Epicurus is said to have doubted his existence (D.L. 10.13). He lapses into the singular at 52.

48–50 Cf. Lucretius 1.734ff., where Empedocles is contrasted with his 'inferior' successors.

50–1 For the interpretation, see Arrighetti [111].

50 ε[ἱ]ς The facsimile O 1056 gives ἐν. The slight traces remaining in the papyrus today could be compatible with this or with ε[ἱ]ς. The old solution of reading ἐν τῶ as equivalent to ἐν τῷ is orthographically incredible. Gigante's suggestion ([106], 56ff.) of ἕν· τὸ κτλ. is greatly superior. However, our preference for ε[ἱ]ς rests on doubts about the double accusative construction with λανθάνειν (in Plato, *Rep.* 619b and *Leg.* 746b, cited by Gigante, only one accusative appears to serve as object of λανθάνειν, the other as subject; his translations of λανθάνειν ἑαυτόν as 'not pay attention' and of αἰτιᾶσθαι as 'cause' also seem to require justification). With our conjecture, the point made is that the early atomists, in order to maintain their deterministic thesis, had to overlook the contrary evidence available from introspection – 'to escape their own notice'. It is a familiar fact that determinism is more easily believed true of others' behaviour than of one's own immediate decisions and actions.

52 ἐλάνθανεν The certain reading of P 697 (without final ν), and the probable reading of 1056 too. (Earlier editors printed ἐλάμβανεν, on the strength of an insecure reading of O 1056.) It must be accepted in spite of the irregularity of the construction λανθάνειν τινὰ ποιοῦντά τι, 'escape someone's notice that he is doing something'. The verb is appropriate, because Epicurus is at pains throughout to stress that Democritus' error was one of nothing more than oversight. τὸν ἄνδρα 'The great man', i.e. Democritus. For the common Epicurean application of this expression to distinguished predecessors or to the founders of the Epicurean school, cf. Epicurus *Nat.* 26.44.22, 29.26.14; Lucretius 3.371, 5.622; Longo Auricchio [134].

D Epicurus, *SV* 40

ὁ λέγων πάντα κατ' ἀνάγκην γίνεσθαι οὐδὲν ἐγκαλεῖν ἔχει τῷ λέγοντι μὴ πάντα κατ' ἀνάγκην γίνεσθαι· αὐτὸ γὰρ τοῦτό φησι κατ' ἀνάγκην γίνεσθαι.

The saying probably originated as a non-technical summary of C 5.

E Cicero, *Fat.* 21–5

(1) hic primum si mihi libeat adsentiri Epicuro et negare omnem enuntiationem aut veram esse aut falsam, eam plagam potius accipiam, quam fato omnia fieri comprobem: illa enim sententia habet aliquid disputationis, haec vero

non est tolerabilis. itaque contendit omnis nervos Chrysippus, ut persuadeat
omne ἀξίωμα aut verum esse aut falsum. ut enim Epicurus veretur ne, si hoc   5
concesserit, concedendum sit fato fieri quaecumque fiant (si enim alterum
utrum ex aeternitate verum sit, esse id etiam certum, et, si certum, etiam
necessarium: ita et necessitatem et fatum confirmari putat), sic Chrysippus
metuit ne, si non obtinuerit omne quod enuntietur aut verum esse aut falsum,
non teneat omnia fato fieri et ex causis aeternis rerum futurarum. (2) sed   10
Epicurus declinatione atomi vitari necessitatem fati putat. itaque tertius
quidam motus oritur extra pondus et plagam, cum declinat atomus intervallo
minimo (id appellat ἐλάχιστον); quam declinationem sine causa fieri si minus
verbis, re cogitur confiteri. non enim atomus ab atomo pulsa declinat. nam qui
potest pelli alia ab alia, si gravitate feruntur ad perpendiculum corpora   15
individua rectis lineis, ut Epicuro placet? sequitur enim ut [si] alia ab alia
numquam depellatur, ⟨si⟩ ne contingat quidem alia aliam. ex quo efficitur,
etiam si sit atomus eaque declinet, declinare sine causa. (3) hanc Epicurus
rationem induxit ob eam rem, quod veritus est ne, si semper atomus gravitate
ferretur naturali ac necessaria, nihil liberum nobis esset, cum ita moveretur 20
animus ut atomorum motu cogeretur. id Democritus, auctor atomorum,
accipere maluit, necessitate omnia fieri, quam a corporibus individuis naturalis
motus avellere. (4) acutius Carneades, qui docebat posse Epicureos suam
causam sine hac commenticia declinatione defendere. nam cum docerent esse
posse quendam animi motum voluntarium, id fuit defendi melius quam   25
introducere declinationem, cuius praesertim causam reperire non possent: quo
defenso facile Chrysippo possent resistere. (5) cum enim concessissent motum
nullum esse sine causa, non concederent omnia quae fierent fieri causis
antecedentibus: voluntatis enim nostrae non esse causas externas et antecedentis. communi igitur consuetudine sermonis abutimur, cum ita dicimus, velle   30
aliquid quempiam aut nolle sine causa; ita enim dicimus "sine causa", ut
dicamus: sine externa et antecedente causa, non sine aliqua; ut, cum vas inane
dicimus, non ita loquimur ut physici, quibus inane esse nihil placet, sed ita ut
verbi causa sine aqua, sine vino, sine oleo vas esse dicamus, sic, cum sine causa
animum dicimus moveri, sine antecedente et externa causa moveri, non   35
omnino sine causa dicimus. (6) de ipsa atomo dici potest, cum per inane
moveatur gravitate et pondere, sine causa moveri, quia nulla causa accedat
extrinsecus. rursus autem, ne omnes physici inrideamur, si dicamus quicquam
fieri sine causa, distinguendum est et ita dicendum, ipsius individui hanc esse
naturam, ut pondere et gravitate moveatur, eamque ipsam esse causam, cur ita 40
feratur. (7) similiter ad animorum motus voluntarios non est requirenda
externa causa: motus enim voluntarius eam naturam in se ipse continet, ut sit
in nostra potestate nobisque pareat, nec id sine causa; eius rei enim causa ipsa
natura est.

16–17 *si* transp. Madvig

Epicurean ethics

Context: following **38G**, on Chrysippus' argument from bivalence to determinism. 13–18 **sine causa** Here, as at 26 (also ibid. 46–8, Plutarch, *De an. procr.* 1015C; Cicero, *Fin.* 1.19 is the only exception), the swerve's causelessness is the inference of Epicurus' critics, not his express doctrine. The actual position is more complicated. In cosmogony, on which these critics usually concentrate (hence the restriction to perpendicular motion at 14–17), the swerve is indeed causeless. In the mind too it has no physical, or 'natural', cause, as once again the critics stress, cf. ibid. 46–8. But some swerves of mind atoms are engineered by volitions, if the interpretation maintained in vol. 1 is correct. The self and its volitions must be counted as non-physical causes, as the self certainly is at *Nat.* 34.32.21: they are, after all, never listed in the sources on Epicurean physics as causes of atomic motion alongside weight, impact and the swerve (see **11**).

23 Carneades, as often (see vol. 1, 448, 465), was defending a dogmatist position for dialectical purposes, here (cf. 26–7) in order to provide a strong enough counterweight to Chrysippean determinism. (*Fat.* 18–19 probably derives from the same context.) This obliges him to use only authentic Epicurean premises. His evidence is therefore extremely damaging to the widespread view that the swerve plays an integral role in the analysis of volition itself, for Carneades' suggestion to the Epicureans is to abandon the swerve while continuing their defence of the voluntary motion of the mind. His assertion that even without the swerve's assistance volitions are in their nature free from external antecedent causes would be unintelligible if, as is commonly assumed, Epicurean volitions were nothing more than chains of atomic motion. But on the non-reductionist psychology which we attribute to Epicurus in vol. 1 it makes excellent sense. **Epicureos** The point of not naming Epicurus himself is not to differentiate between his views and those of his later followers, but to provide Chrysippus with non-anachronistic opponents.

F Lucretius 2.251–93

(1) denique si semper motus conectitur omnis
et vetere exoritur ⟨motu⟩ novus ordine certo
nec declinando faciunt primordia motus
principium quoddam quod fati foedera rumpat,
ex infinito ne causam causa sequatur,   255
libera per terras unde haec animantibus exstat,
unde est haec, inquam, fatis avulsa voluntas
per quam progredimur quo ducit quemque voluptas,
declinamus item motus nec tempore certo
nec regione loci certa, sed ubi ipsa tulit mens?   260
(2) nam dubio procul his rebus sua cuique voluntas
principium dat et hinc motus per membra rigantur.
nonne vides etiam patefactis tempore puncto
carceribus non posse tamen prorumpere equorum
vim cupidam tam de subito quam mens avet ipsa?   265
omnis enim totum per corpus materiai

copia conciri debet, concita per artus
omnis ut studium mentis conixa sequatur;
ut videas initum motus a corde creari
ex animique voluntate id procedere primum,   270
inde dari porro per totum corpus et artus.
(3) nec similest ut cum impulsi procedimus ictu
viribus alterius magnis magnoque coactu.
nam tum materiem totius corporis omnem
persipicuumst nobis invitis ire rapique,   275
donec eam refrenavit per membra voluntas.
iamne vides igitur, quamquam vis extera multos
pellat et invitos cogat procedere saepe
praecipitesque rapi, tamen esse in pectore nostro
quiddam quod contra pugnare obstareque possit?   280
cuius ad arbitrium quoque copia materiai
cogitur interdum flecti per membra per artus
et proiecta refrenatur retroque residit.
(4) quare in seminibus quoque idem fateare necessest,
esse aliam praeter plagas et pondera causam   285
motibus, unde haec est nobis innata potestas,
de nilo quoniam fieri nil posse videmus.
pondus enim prohibet ne plagis omnia fiant
externa quasi vi. sed ne mens ipsa necessum
intestinum habeat cunctis in rebus agendis   290
et devicta quasi cogatur ferre patique,
id facit exiguum clinamen principiorum
nec regione loci certa nec tempore certo.

252 ⟨*motu*⟩ Bailey: ⟨*motus*⟩ Martin: *semper* L   257 *voluntas* Lambinus: *voluptas* OQUP   258
voluptas ABF: *voluntas* OQU   289 *mens* Lambinus: *res* OQ

Context: the causes of atomic motion (immediately following **11H**).

The reader can be referred to the very extensive critical discussions of this passage,
especially in Bailey [154], Furley [204], Fowler [258], Saunders [259], and Englert
[261].

256 **unde**   Here and at 286 the swerve is that 'from which' free volition arises.
This may be felt to imply a stronger relation between the two than is proposed in the
vol. I commentary. But *no* serious interpretation can make the swerve more than a
necessary condition of free volition, and if that is the relation expressed by *unde* (as
it is at **6A** 383) it may be hard to squeeze any more information out of the
word.   **animantibus**   Cf. **j** below, with note.

259–60 **declinamus–certa**   The expression has a clear echo at 292–3, and may
well be meant to hint at a direct involvement of the swerve in every new autonomous
action.

260 **mens**   This word, here and at 265, is perhaps to be understood as equivalent

to what Lucretius more accurately calls 'the mind's volition' (270) or just 'volition' (261, 276; cf. 268, 281). The slight looseness is natural enough, since the precise significance of 'mind' as the physical organ of thought and emotion will not be established until book 3 (see **14**) and the non-physical character of psychological causation is entirely beyond the scope of his poem.

289 **mens ipsa** Lambinus' widely accepted emendation for *res ipsa* has parallels at 260 and 265. It certainly makes better Latin, and is more consistent with the personalized language of 290–1. Against this, Avotins [255] has rightly stressed that in strict consistency the reference at this point should be to the atom, not to the mind, since the impacts and weight in 288 must still be those named at 285 (cf. also **E 2**) as causes of atomic motion. If on this ground *res* were retained it would have to be translated 'the thing' or 'a thing' and understood as referring to the atom. But it is hard to see why Lucretius should have expressed himself so badly. Probably we should adopt *mens* and guess that he has skated over a move, via the internal necessity imposed on the individual atom by its weight, to the resultant internal necessity imposed on the mind as a whole – the move made explicitly by Cicero at **E 3**, in a text which resembles Lucretius' argument closely enough to be invoked in its interpretation.

G Diogenes of Oenoanda 32.1.14–3.14

[πῶς ἀνῃρημέ]νης οὖν | μαντικῆς σημεῖ]ον εἱμαρμένης ἔστιν | ἄλλο; ἂν
γὰ[ρ] τῷ Δημο|κρίτου τι⟨ς⟩ χ[ρ]ήσηται | λόγῳ, μηδεμίαν μὲν | ἐλευθέραν
[φ]άσκων | ταῖς ἀτόμο[ι]ς κείνη|σιν εἶναι δι[ὰ] τὴν πρὸς | ἀλλήλας σ[ύν]-
κρουσιν | αὐτῶν, ἐν⟨θ⟩[ε]ν δὲ φαί]νεσθαι κατ[η]ναγκασ|μένως π[άντ]α
κεινεῖσ|θαι, φή[σομε]ν πρὸς | αὐτόν· "[οὔκουν] οἶδας, ὅσ|τις ποτὲ εἶ, καὶ   5
ἐλευθέ|ραν τινὰ ἐν ταῖς ἀτό|μοις κείνησιν εἶναι, ἣ[ν] | Δημόκριτος μὲν οὐ|χ
εὗρεν, Ἐπίκουρος δὲ | εἰς φῶ[ς] ἤγαγεν, παρεν|κλιτικὴν ὑπάρχουσαν, ὡς
ἐκ τῶν φαινομέ|νων δείκνυσιν;" τὸ δὲ | μέγιστον· πιστευθεί]σης γὰρ
εἱμαρμένης | αἴρεται πᾶσα νουθεσ[ί]|α καὶ ἐπιτείμησις καὶ | οὐδὲ τοὺς
πονηροὺς [10

For full apparatus, see Chilton [170].

Context: Diogenes' ethical treatise.

7–8 The 'phenomena' cited by Epicurus are presumably those of the type described by Lucretius in **F 2–3**.

8ff. Cf. **A 7–8**, **C 2**.

H Cicero, *Fat*. 37

(1) necesse est enim in rebus contrariis duabus (contraria autem hoc loco ea dico quorum alterum ait quid, alterum negat), ex iis igitur necesse est invito Epicuro alterum verum esse, alterum falsum; ut "sauciabitur Philocteta" omnibus ante saeculis verum fuit, "non sauciabitur" falsum. (2) nisi forte volumus Epicureorum opinionem sequi, qui tales enuntiationes nec veras nec   5
falsas esse dicunt, (3) aut, cum id pudet, illud tamen dicunt quod est

inpudentius, veras esse ex contrariis diiunctiones, sed quae in his enuntiata essent, eorum neutrum esse verum.

Context: defence of the Carneadean distinction between logical and causal determinism (see **70G**).

Hellenistic debate regularly associates this denial of bivalence with Epicurus (cf. also **70G 8**), and seems unaware of the apparent Aristotelian precedent at *Int.* 9. Cf. Sedley [11], 96–9 on the possible role of Diodorus as intermediary.

I Cicero, *Acad.* 2.97 (Usener 376)

etenim cum ab Epicuro, qui totam dialecticam et contemnit et inridet, non inpetrent ut verum esse concedat quod ita effabimur "aut vivet cras Hermarchus aut non vivet", cum dialectici sic statuant omne quod ita disiunctum sit quasi "aut etiam aut non" non modo verum esse sed etiam necessarium, vide quam sit cautus is quem isti tardum putant. "si enim" inquit 5 "alterutrum concessero necessarium esse, necesse erit cras Hermarchum aut vivere aut non vivere; nulla aute/n est in natura rerum talis necessitas."

Context: Cicero's speech for the New Academy, invoking Epicurus against the principle of bivalence maintained by the Stoics. Cf. **34C, 38G**.

j Epicurus, *Nat.*, liber incertus, 34.25.21–34

ἔτι μᾶλλον ἐνίοτ[ε κ]ακίζομεν, ἐν νουθετητ[ικ]ῶι μέντοι μᾶλλον τρόπω[ι], καὶ οὐχ ὥσπερ [τ]ὰ ἄ⌐γ⌐ρια τῶν ζώιων [καθ]αίρομεν μὲν ὁμοίως αὐτὰ τὰ ἀπογεγε[νν]⌐η⌐μένα [κ]αὶ τὴ[ν] σύστασιν εἰς ἕν τι συμπ[λέ]κοντες, οὐ μὴν ο[ὔ]τε τῶι νουθε[τ]ητ[ι]κῶι τρόπωι καὶ ἐπανορθωτικῶι οὔτε τῶι ἁπλῶς ἀ[ντι]ποι[η]τικῶι χρώμεθα |

2 ἄ⌐γ⌐ρια: αερια O 697: α[. . . P 697
Readings of papyri are from Sedley [260]. For sigla, see on **B** above.

Context: comparison of self-determining animals with those which are mere automata.

'We sometimes vilify it [*sc.* a self-determining animal] all the more, but more in an admonitory mode – and not in the way in which we exonerate those animals which are wild by conflating their developments and their make-up alike into a single thing, and indeed do not use either the admonitory and reformatory mode or the simply retaliatory mode.'   Cf. **B 2**. We *hate* wickedness in any animal, but we do not *blame* wild animals, since we regard their eventual development as already built into their congenital nature. *E.g.* we hate, but do not blame, sharks for eating people. For the same issue, cf. Galen, *Quod animi mores* 73,3–74,13, Manilius 4.106–18.

It is unclear how far beyond human beings self-determining animals extend. They include race-horses (**F 2**), and perhaps all animals capable of forming some contractual relation with man or with each other – cf. **22A 2**.

21 Pleasure

A Cicero, *Fin.* 1.29–32, 37–9

(1) quaerimus igitur, quid sit extremum et ultimum bonorum, quod omnium philosophorum sententia tale debet esse, ut ad id omnia referri oporteat, ipsum autem nusquam. hoc Epicurus in voluptate ponit, quod summum bonum esse vult, summumque malum dolorem, idque instituit docere sic: (2) omne animal, simul atque natum sit, voluptatem appetere eaque gaudere ut summo 5 bono, dolorem aspernari ut summum malum et, quantum possit, a se repellere, idque facere nondum depravatum ipsa natura incorrupte atque integre iudicante. itaque negat opus esse ratione neque disputatione, quam ob rem voluptas expetenda, fugiendus dolor sit. sentiri haec putat, ut calere ignem, nivem esse albam, dulce mel, quorum nihil oportere exquisitis 10 rationibus confirmare, tantum satis esse admonere. interesse enim inter argumentum conclusionemque rationis et inter mediocrem animadversionem atque admonitionem; altera occulta quaedam et quasi involuta aperiri, altera prompta et aperta iudicari. (3) etenim quoniam detractis de homine sensibus reliqui nihil est, necesse est quid aut ad naturam aut contra sit a natura ipsa iudicari. ea quid percipit aut quid iudicat, 15 quo aut petat aut fugiat aliquid, praeter voluptatem et dolorem? (4) sunt autem quidam e nostris, qui haec subtilius velint tradere et negent satis esse quid bonum sit aut quid malum sensu iudicari, sed animo etiam ac ratione intellegi posse et voluptatem ipsam per se esse expetendam et dolorem ipsum per se esse fugiendum. itaque aiunt hanc quasi naturalem atque insitam in 20 animis nostris inesse notionem, ut alterum esse appetendum, alterum aspernandum sentiamus. alii autem, quibus ego assentior, cum a philosophis compluribus permulta dicantur, cur nec voluptas in bonis sit numeranda nec in malis dolor, non existimant oportere nimium nos causae confidere, sed et argumentandum et accurate disserendum et rationibus conquisitis de voluptate et dolore disputandum putant. sed ut perspiciatis, unde 25 omnis iste natus error sit voluptatem accusantium doloremque laudantium, totam rem aperiam, eaque ipsa quae ab illo inventore veritatis et quasi architecto beatae vitae dicta sunt, explicabo. (5) nemo enim ipsam voluptatem, quia voluptas sit, aspernatur aut odit aut fugit, sed quia consequuntur magni dolores eos qui ratione voluptatem sequi nesciunt, neque porro quisquam est 30 qui dolorem ipsum, quia dolor sit, amet, consectetur, adipisci velit, sed quia non numquam eius modi tempora incidunt, ut labore et dolore magnam aliquam quaerat voluptatem . . . (6) non enim hanc solam sequimur, quae suavitate aliqua naturam ipsam movet et cum iucunditate quadam percipitur sensibus, sed maximam voluptatem illam habemus, quae percipitur omni 35 dolore detracto. nam quoniam, cum privamur dolore, ipsa liberatione et vacuitate omnis molestiae gaudemus, omne autem id, quo gaudemus, voluptas est, ut omne, quo offendimur, dolor, doloris omnis privatio recte nominata est voluptas. ut enim, cum cibo et potione fames sitisque depulsa est,

ipsa detractio molestiae consecutionem affert voluptatis, sic in omni re doloris 40
amotio successionem efficit voluptatis. (7) itaque non placuit Epicuro medium
esse quiddam inter dolorem et voluptatem; illud enim ipsum, quod
quibusdam medium videretur, cum omni dolore careret, non modo
voluptatem esse, verum etiam summam voluptatem. quisquis enim sentit,
quem ad modum sit affectus, eum necesse est aut in voluptate esse aut in 45
dolore. omnis autem privatione doloris putat Epicurus terminari summam
voluptatem, ut postea variari voluptas distinguique possit, augeri amplificari-
que non possit. (8) at etiam Athenis, ut e patre audiebam facete et urbane Stoicos
irridente, statua est in Ceramico Chrysippi sedentis porrecta manu, quae manus
significet illum in hac esse rogatiuncula delectatum: "numquidnam manus tua 50
sic affecta, quem ad modum affecta nunc est, desiderat?" – nihil sane. – "at, si
voluptas esset bonum, desideraret." – ita credo. – "non est igitur voluptas
bonum." hoc ne statuam quidem dicturam pater aiebat, si loqui posset. conclusum est
enim contra Cyrenaicos satis acute, nihil ad Epicurum.

9 *haec* A: *hoc* NV   11 *tantum* om. BE   13 *indicari* NV   15 post *iudicari* add. V *voluptatem etiam per se expetendam esse et dolorem ipsum per se esse fugiendum*   46 *omnis* Morel: *omni* codd.

Context: opening of Torquatus' exposition of Epicurean ethics. 1–33 treat the grounds
of the hedonism, while 33–54 expound the doctrine that complete absence of pain
constitutes the greatest pleasure. Between sections 5 and 6 we omit *Fin.* 1.32–6, which
amplifies the thesis of section 5 and supports it by historical *exempla*. For Cicero's
criticism of **A**, cf. *Fin.* 2.31ff.

4–8   For similar testimonies, cf. D.L. 10.137; S.E., *PH* 3.194, *M.* 11.96. The
argument from infantile behaviour was almost certainly made more prominent by
later Epicureans, through their competition on this point with the Stoics; cf. **57A 3**. In
Alexander, *Mantissa* 150, even traces of Stoic οἰκείωσις have entered Epicurean
doxography: τοῖς δὲ περὶ Ἐπίκουρον ἡδονὴ τὸ πρῶτον οἰκεῖον [cf. **B** 20–1 and **22C**
4] ἔδοξεν εἶναι ἁπλῶς, προσιόντων δὲ διαρθροῦσθαι ταύτην τὴν ἡδονήν φασιν. Cf.
also Steckel [252], 19–33, who refers to Maximus of Tyre, *Or.* 32 II, where, in an
apparent use of Epicurean doctrine, the primary pursuit of pleasure and avoidance of
pain are presented as the foundation of a creature's self-preservation.

16–25   Such further arguments may be presumed to have been prompted by the
need to defend the doctrine against Stoic and other opponents; cf. Asmis [225], 36–9,
who aptly refers to the similar passage at **23E 6**. *naturalem atque insitam . . . notionem*,
20–1, represents πρόληψις; cf. **23E 2**.

28–33   Cf. **B** 16–25, **D** 1–2.

33–41.   Cf. **R** with notes.

46–7   For *terminari*, cf. ὅρος **C** 1; *variari* translates ποικίλλεσθαι as at **E** 2.

54   The alleged vulnerability of the Cyrenaics to Chrysippus' argument is due to
their admitting only kinetic pleasure; cf. **R**.

B   Epicurus, *Ep. Men.* 127–32

(1) ἀναλογιστέον δὲ ὡς τῶν ἐπιθυμιῶν αἱ μέν εἰσι φυσικαί, αἱ δὲ κεναί. καὶ
τῶν φυσικῶν αἱ μὲν ἀναγκαῖαι, αἱ δὲ φυσικαί μόνον· τῶν δ' ἀναγκαίων αἱ

μὲν πρὸς εὐδαιμονίαν εἰσὶν ἀναγκαῖαι, αἱ δὲ πρὸς τὴν τοῦ σώματος
ἀοχλησίαν, αἱ δὲ πρὸς αὐτὸ τὸ ζῆν. τούτων γὰρ ἀπλανὴς θεωρία πᾶσαν
αἵρεσιν καὶ φυγὴν ἐπανάγειν οἶδεν ἐπὶ τὴν τοῦ σώματος ὑγίειαν καὶ τὴν   5
τῆς ψυχῆς ἀταραξίαν, ἐπεὶ τοῦτο τοῦ μακαρίως ζῆν ἐστι τέλος. τούτου γὰρ
χάριν πάντα πράττομεν, ὅπως μήτε ἀλγῶμεν μήτε ταρβῶμεν· (2) ὅταν δ᾿
ἅπαξ τοῦτο περὶ ἡμᾶς γένηται, λύεται πᾶς ὁ τῆς ψυχῆς χειμών, οὐκ
ἔχοντος τοῦ ζώου βαδίζειν ὡς πρὸς ἐνδέον τι καὶ ζητεῖν ἕτερον ᾧ τὸ τῆς
ψυχῆς καὶ τοῦ σώματος ἀγαθὸν συμπληρώσεται. τότε γὰρ ἡδονῆς χρείαν   10
ἔχομεν ὅταν ἐκ τοῦ μὴ παρεῖναι τὴν ἡδονὴν ἀλγῶμεν· ⟨ὅταν δὲ μὴ
ἀλγῶμεν,⟩ οὐκέτι τῆς ἡδονῆς δεόμεθα. καὶ διὰ τοῦτο τὴν ἡδονὴν ἀρχὴν
καὶ τέλος λέγομεν εἶναι τοῦ μακαρίως ζῆν· ταύτην γὰρ ἀγαθὸν πρῶτον καὶ
συγγενικὸν ἔγνωμεν, καὶ ἀπὸ ταύτης καταρχόμεθα πάσης αἱρέσεως καὶ
φυγῆς καὶ ἐπὶ ταύτην καταντῶμεν ὡς κανόνι τῷ πάθει πᾶν ἀγαθὸν   15
κρίνοντες. (3) καὶ ἐπεὶ πρῶτον ἀγαθὸν τοῦτο καὶ σύμφυτον, διὰ τοῦτο καὶ
οὐ πᾶσαν ἡδονὴν αἱρούμεθα, ἀλλ᾿ ἔστιν ὅτε πολλὰς ἡδονὰς ὑπερβαίνομεν,
ὅταν πλεῖον ἡμῖν τὸ δυσχερὲς ἐκ τούτων ἕπηται· καὶ πολλὰς ἀλγηδόνας
ἡδονῶν κρείττους νομίζομεν, ἐπειδὰν μείζων ἡμῖν ἡδονὴ παρακολουθῇ
πολὺν χρόνον ὑπομείνασι τὰς ἀλγηδόνας. πᾶσα οὖν ἡδονὴ διὰ τὸ φύσιν   20
ἔχειν οἰκείαν ἀγαθόν, οὐ πᾶσα μέντοι αἱρετή· καθάπερ καὶ ἀλγηδὼν πᾶσα
κακόν, οὐ πᾶσα δὲ ἀεὶ φευκτὴ πεφυκυῖα. τῇ μέντοι συμμετρήσει καὶ
συμφερόντων καὶ ἀσυμφόρων βλέψει ταῦτα πάντα κρίνειν καθήκει·
χρώμεθα γὰρ τῷ μὲν ἀγαθῷ κατά τινας χρόνους ὡς κακῷ, τῷ δὲ κακῷ
τοὔμπαλιν ὡς ἀγαθῷ. (4) καὶ τὴν αὐτάρκειαν δὲ ἀγαθὸν μέγα νομίζομεν,   25
οὐχ ἵνα πάντως τοῖς ὀλίγοις χρώμεθα, ἀλλ᾿ ὅπως ἐὰν μὴ ἔχωμεν τὰ πολλά,
τοῖς ὀλίγοις χρώμεθα, πεπεισμένοι γνησίως ὅτι ἥδιστα πολυτελείας
ἀπολαύουσιν οἱ ἥκιστα ταύτης δεόμενοι, καὶ ὅτι τὸ μὲν φυσικὸν πᾶν
εὐπόριστόν ἐστι, τὸ δὲ κενὸν δυσπόριστον. οἵ τε λιτοὶ χυλοὶ ἴσην πολυτελεῖ
διαίτῃ τὴν ἡδονὴν ἐπιφέρουσιν ὅταν ἅπαν τὸ ἀλγοῦν κατ᾿ ἔνδειαν ἐξαιρεθῇ·   30
καὶ μᾶζα καὶ ὕδωρ τὴν ἀκροτάτην ἀποδίδωσιν ἡδονὴν ἐπειδὰν ἐνδέως τις
αὐτὰ προσενέγκηται. τὸ συνεθίζειν οὖν ἐν ταῖς ἁπλαῖς καὶ οὐ πολυτελέσι
διαίταις καὶ ὑγιείας ἐστὶ συμπληρωτικὸν καὶ πρὸς τὰς ἀναγκαίας τοῦ βίου
χρήσεις ἄοκνον ποιεῖ τὸν ἄνθρωπον καὶ τοῖς πολυτελέσιν ἐκ διαλειμμάτων
προσερχομένους κρεῖττον ἡμᾶς διατίθησι καὶ πρὸς τὴν τύχην ἀφόβους   35
παρασκευάζει. (5) ὅταν οὖν λέγωμεν ἡδονὴν τέλος ὑπάρχειν, οὐ τὰς τῶν
ἀσώτων ἡδονὰς καὶ τὰς ἐν ἀπολαύσει κειμένας λέγομεν, ὥς τινες
ἀγνοοῦντες καὶ οὐχ ὁμολογοῦντες ἢ κακῶς ἐκδεχόμενοι νομίζουσιν, ἀλλὰ
τὸ μήτε ἀλγεῖν κατὰ σῶμα μήτε ταράττεσθαι κατὰ ψυχήν. οὐ γὰρ πότοι
καὶ κῶμοι συνείροντες οὐδ᾿ ἀπολαύσεις παίδων καὶ γυναικῶν οὐδ᾿ ἰχθύων   40
καὶ τῶν ἄλλων ὅσα φέρει πολυτελὴς τράπεζα τὸν ἡδὺν γεννᾷ βίον, ἀλλὰ
νήφων λογισμὸς καὶ τὰς αἰτίας ἐξερευνῶν πάσης αἱρέσεως καὶ φυγῆς καὶ
τὰς δόξας ἐξελαύνων ἐξ ὧν πλεῖστος τὰς ψυχὰς καταλαμβάνει θόρυβος. (6)
τούτων δὲ πάντων ἀρχὴ καὶ τὸ μέγιστον ἀγαθὸν φρόνησις· διὸ καὶ
φιλοσοφίας τιμιώτερον ὑπάρχει φρόνησις, ἐξ ἧς αἱ λοιπαὶ πᾶσαι   45

πεφύκασιν ἀρεταί, διδάσκουσα ὡς οὐκ ἔστιν ἡδέως ζῆν ἄνευ τοῦ φρονίμως
καὶ καλῶς καὶ δικαίως, ⟨οὐδὲ φρονίμως καὶ καλῶς καὶ δικαίως⟩ ἄνευ τοῦ
ἡδέως· συμπεφύκασι γὰρ αἱ ἀρεταὶ τῷ ζῆν ἡδέως, καὶ τὸ ζῆν ἡδέως
τούτων ἐστὶν ἀχώριστον.

6 τῆς ψυχῆς B(corr.): om. B ante corr.: τοῦ σώματος cett.   11–12 suppl. Gassendi   16–17 καὶ οὐ
BP(corr.): καὶ FP   22 καὶ secl. Diano   27 χρώμεθα codd.: ἀρκώμεθα Cobet   37 τὰς ἐν φ: τὰς
τῶν ἐν codd.   46 διδάσκουσα Dulac: -σαι codd.   47 suppl. Stephanus

Context: 3 lines after 24A. Having instructed Menoeceus in the right beliefs about
gods and death (the contents of *RS* 1–2), Epicurus turns to the basic principles of his
hedonism.

1–4   This division of desires has a simpler prototype in Plato, *Rep.* 8.558d; cf. also
Aristotle, *EN* III.13, 1118b8. On the term κενός in Epicureanism (standard ethical
jargon at this time, see 1C 10; 2C 4), cf. Konstan [253], 30–3, 49.

9 ζῷου   As in Stoicism (cf. 57A), Epicurus treats man's primary objective as one
that he shares with all animals.

20–1   φύσιν . . . οἰκείαν   Cf. 22C 4, and note on A 4–8.

28–9   φυσικόν and κενόν pick up the division of desires in 1. How could Epicurus
be so confident that everything natural is easy to procure? For a discussion of the
assumptions underlying his claim, cf. Long [280].

36–43   It is generally assumed that Epicurus is distancing himself here from the
Cyrenaics. But there is no reason to read his disclaimers so restrictedly. As the constant
disapproval his own hedonism has encountered over the centuries shows, he could not
be too careful in spelling out its difference from sensual self-indulgence.

45 φρόνησις   What Epicurus seems to envisage is something like the quality of
mind described by Aristotle, *EN* VI.5, 1140a25: τὸ δύνασθαι καλῶς βουλεύσασθαι
περὶ τὰ αὐτῷ ἀγαθὰ καὶ συμφέροντα, οὐ κατὰ μέρος, οἷον ποῖα πρὸς ὑγίειαν, πρὸς
ἰσχύν, ἀλλὰ ποῖα πρὸς τὸ εὖ ζῆν ὅλως. The claim that φρόνησις is even more
precious than philosophy turns out to be a rhetorical exaggeration in the light of such
texts as 25A.

C Epicurus, *RS* 3–4

(1) [3] ὅρος τοῦ μεγέθους τῶν ἡδονῶν ἡ παντὸς τοῦ ἀλγοῦντος ὑπεξαίρεσις.
ὅπου δ᾽ ἂν τὸ ἡδόμενον ἐνῇ, καθ᾽ ὃν ἂν χρόνον ᾖ, οὐκ ἔστι τὸ ἀλγοῦν ἢ
λυπούμενον ἢ τὸ συναμφότερον. (2) [4] οὐ χρονίζει τὸ ἀλγοῦν συνεχῶς ἐν
τῇ σαρκί, ἀλλὰ τὸ μὲν ἄκρον τὸν ἐλάχιστον χρόνον πάρεστι, τὸ δὲ μόνον
ὑπερτεῖνον τὸ ἡδόμενον κατὰ σάρκα οὐ πολλὰς ἡμέρας συμμένει. αἱ δὲ   5
πολυχρόνιοι τῶν ἀρρωστιῶν πλεονάζον ἔχουσι τὸ ἡδόμενον ἐν τῇ σαρκὶ
ἤπερ τὸ ἀλγοῦν.

3 λυπούμενον BP: τὸ λυπ- FP(corr.)   5 συμμένει Bywater: συμβαίνει codd.: ὑπάρχει SV 3

RS 3 fills out the third maxim of the *tetrapharmakos* (25J), and *RS* 4 the fourth.

1   Scholars are probably right in seeing a rejoinder to the Cyrenaics; cf. D.L. 2.89
for their rejection of Epicurus' claim about absence of pain, citing the words τοῦ –
ὑπεξαίρεσις. For a collection of Epicurean texts on limit as an ethical concept, cf.

Epicurean ethics

Krämer [12], 197–8 n. 47, and in general De Lacy [217]. It gives Epicurus a defence against the (probably Platonic) criticism that pleasure, as something indeterminate, cannot be 'the good', which is determinate, Aristotle, *EN* x.2, 1173a15–17.

2–3 Since Bailey [117] ad loc. and Bignone [90], 15–22, it has become customary to explain these lines as a rejection of the Platonic notion of 'mixed pleasures' (e.g. simultaneously experiencing the pain of thirst and the pleasure of quenching it); cf. *Gorg.* 496c–e, *Phileb.* 46b–c. While this historical point is plausible, it has not been noted that 2–3 combined with 1 state the logical equivalence of pleasure and absence of pain. In 1 we learn that absence of pain entails pleasure, and in 2–3 that pleasure entails absence of pain. Epicurus is not of course saying that a person cannot take pleasure in one thing and feel pain at something else at the same time; cf. C 2 and 24D. See further Diano [254], 271–6.

3 λυπούμενον This picks out mental as distinct from bodily pain (ἀλγοῦν).

3–7 Further texts bearing on this passage include Seneca, *Ep.* 78; Diog. Oen. fr. 42; and Usener 447–8. Cf. Bignone [90], 173–89.

D Epicurus, *RS* 8–10

(1) [8] οὐδεμία ἡδονὴ καθ' ἑαυτὴν κακόν· ἀλλὰ τὰ τινῶν ἡδονῶν ποιητικὰ πολλαπλασίους ἐπιφέρει τὰς ὀχλήσεις τῶν ἡδονῶν. (2) [9] εἰ κατεπυκνοῦτο πᾶσα ἡδονή τ⟨όπ⟩ῳ καὶ χρόνῳ καὶ περὶ ὅλον τὸ ἄθροισμα ὑπῆρχεν ἢ τὰ κυριώτατα μέρη τῆς φύσεως, οὐκ ἄν ποτε διέφερον ἀλλήλων αἱ ἡδοναί. (3) [10] εἰ τὰ ποιητικὰ τῶν περὶ τοὺς ἀσώτους ἡδονῶν ἔλυε τοὺς φόβους τῆς 5 διανοίας τούς τε περὶ μετεώρων καὶ θανάτου καὶ ἀλγηδόνων, ἔτι τε τὸ πέρας τῶν ἐπιθυμιῶν ἐδίδασκεν, οὐκ ἄν ποτε εἴχομεν ὅ τι μεμψαίμεθα αὐτοῖς, πανταχόθεν ἐκπληρουμένοις τῶν ἡδονῶν καὶ οὐθαμόθεν οὔτε τὸ ἀλγοῦν οὔτε τὸ λυπούμενον ἔχουσιν, ὅπερ ἐστὶ τὸ κακόν.

1 ἑαυτὸ κακόν BP: ἑαυτὴν κακή FP(corr.)   2 κατεπυκνοῦτο FP(corr.): -νου BP   3 τ⟨όπ⟩ῳ καὶ χρόνῳ Diano: τω ... χρόνῳ B: τῷ καὶ χρόνῳ B(corr.) P: καὶ χρόνῳ FP(corr.): τῷ χρόνῳ Arndt: , καὶ χρόνῳ Mühll: ⟨καὶ τόνῳ⟩ καὶ χρόνῳ Crönert: τ⟨όν⟩ῳ καὶ χρόνῳ Bignone   περὶ ὅλον Rossi: περίοδον BP: περὶ ὁδόν FP(corr.)   7 καὶ τῶν ἀλγηδόνων post ἐπιθυμιῶν add. Diog. Oen. fr. 27   8 ἐκπληρουμένοις Diog. Oen fr. 27: ἐσπλ- codd.

1–2 Cf. A 28–30, B 20–2.

2–4 Our text and translation follow Diano [254], 243–89; see further Rist [95], 114–15, and Gosling/Taylor [19], 378–82. The thought seems to be closely related to C 2, where place and time are similarly related to pleasure and/or absence of pain. We interpret thus: if the bodily location and duration of every pleasure were closely packed (κατεπυκνοῦτο), and if the same condition were applied to all a creature's sentient parts, all pleasures would be identical, in the sense that complete absence of pain and hence maximum pleasure would result, whatever the source of the pleasure. We agree with Gosling/Taylor that Epicurus does not endorse the truth of the protasis, and hence is not claiming that pleasure in fact will ever be utterly homogeneous. For καταπυκνοῦν in connexion with pleasure, see also 54P 9.

5–7 Cf. B 36–43; 25B 1–2. What the sources of dissipated pleasures fail to do, it seems, is to provide the medicaments of the *tetrapharmakos*, 25J.

E Epicurus, *RS* 18, 25, 30

(1) [18] οὐκ ἐπαύξεται ἐν τῇ σαρκὶ ἡ ἡδονή, ἐπειδὰν ἅπαξ τὸ κατ᾽ ἔνδειαν ἀλγοῦν ἐξαιρεθῇ, ἀλλὰ μόνον ποικίλλεται· τῆς δὲ διανοίας τὸ πέρας τὸ κατὰ τὴν ἡδονὴν ἀπεγέννησεν ἥ τε τούτων αὐτῶν ἐκλόγισις καὶ τῶν ὁμογενῶν τούτοις, ὅσα τοὺς μεγίστους φόβους παρεσκεύαζε τῇ διανοίᾳ.
(2) [25] εἰ μὴ παρὰ πάντα καιρὸν ἐπανοίσεις ἕκαστον τῶν πραττομένων ἐπὶ 5
τὸ τέλος τῆς φύσεως, ἀλλὰ προκαταστρέψεις εἴτε φυγὴν εἴτε δίωξιν ποιούμενος εἰς ἄλλο τι, οὐκ ἔσονταί σοι τοῖς λόγοις αἱ πράξεις ἀκόλουθοι.
(3) [30] ἐν αἷς τῶν φυσικῶν ἐπιθυμιῶν, μὴ ἐπ᾽ ἀλγοῦν δὲ ἐπαναγουσῶν ἐὰν μὴ συντελεσθῶσιν, ὑπάρχει ἡ σπουδὴ σύντονος, παρὰ κενὴν δόξαν αὗται γίνονται, καὶ οὐ παρὰ τὴν ἑαυτῶν φύσιν οὐ διαχέονται ἀλλὰ παρὰ τὴν τοῦ 10
ἀνθρώπου κενοδοξίαν.

1–2   Cf. **A** 46–8, **C** 1–3, and Plutarch, *Contra Ep. beat.* 1088C, where ποικίλλεται is expressed by ποικιλμούς τινας οὐκ ἀναγκαίους.

3–4 **τούτων αὐτῶν ... τούτοις**   Not 'these very pleasures and the emotions akin to them' (Bailey [117] ad loc.), but the doctrines concerning the limit of pleasure just stated (with reference to the body) and the related doctrines concerning the irrationality of fearing divine intervention and death. Cf. **25B**, **24C 2**; and for the expression ὁμογενῆ τούτοις, *Ep. Pyth.* 116 and **23J**.

6–7 **τέλος τῆς φύσεως**   = the health of the body and the mind's freedom from disturbance; cf. **B** 4–6. τοῖς λόγοις might mean either Epicurean theories or any theories that someone professes. The second alternative makes a much more interesting point: consistency between thought and action can only be achieved by making the Epicurean τέλος the standard of every choice and avoidance.

8–11 **B** 1 divided desires initially into natural and empty. We now learn that this division does not exclude a combination of natural and empty: a desire (e.g. for sex) can be natural, yet derive its intensity entirely from empty opinion.

F Epicurus, *SV* 17, 21, 25

(1) [17] οὐ νέος μακαριστός, ἀλλὰ γέρων βεβιωκὼς καλῶς· ὁ γὰρ νέος ἀκμὴν πολὺς ὑπὸ τῆς τύχης ἑτεροφρονῶν πλάζεται· ὁ δὲ γέρων καθάπερ ἐν λιμένι τῷ γήρᾳ καθώρμικεν, τὰ πρότερον δυσελπιστούμενα τῶν ἀγαθῶν ἀσφαλεῖ κατακλείσας χάριτι. (2) [21] οὐ βιαστέον τὴν φύσιν ἀλλὰ πειστέον· πείσομεν δὲ τὰς ἀναγκαίας ἐπιθυμίας ἐκπληροῦντες, τάς τε 5
φυσικὰς ἂν μὴ βλάπτωσι, τὰς δὲ βλαβερὰς πικρῶς ἐλέγχοντες. (3) [25] ἡ πενία μετρουμένη τῷ τῆς φύσεως τέλει μέγας ἐστὶ πλοῦτος· πλοῦτος δὲ μὴ ὁριζόμενος μεγάλη ἐστὶ πενία.

2 ἀκμὴν Crönert: ἀκμῇ cod.   7 ἐστὶ vulgo: ἐπὶ cod.

1–4   Old age is not privileged over youth in **25A**, which may cast doubt on Epicurus' authorship of this elaborately phrased but rather trite maxim.

4–5   There is not the least justification for emending πείσομεν to πεισόμεθα with Bailey [117], and for translating, 'we must . . . obey [nature]; and we shall obey her'. Cf. Diano [254] 85–6.

6–8   Adapted by Lucretius in **22L** 1117–19; cf. **B** 31–2.

Epicurean ethics

G Epicurus, *SV* 33, 42, 51, 59

(1) [33] σαρκὸς φωνὴ τὸ μὴ πεινῆν, τὸ μὴ διψῆν, τὸ μὴ ῥιγοῦν· ταῦτα γὰρ ἔχων τις καὶ ἐλπίζων ἕξειν κἂν ⟨Διὶ⟩ ὑπὲρ εὐδαιμονίας μαχέσαιτο. (2) [42] ὁ αὐτὸς χρόνος καὶ γενέσεως τοῦ μεγίστου ἀγαθοῦ καὶ ἀπολαύσεως. (3) [51] πυνθάνομαί σου τὴν κατὰ σάρκα κίνησιν ἀφθονωτέραν διακεῖσθαι πρὸς τὴν ἀφροδισίων ἔντευξιν. σὺ δὲ εἰ μὴ τοὺς νόμους καταλύεις μήτε τὰ καλῶς ἔθη κείμενα κινεῖς μήτε τῶν πλησίον τινὰ λυπεῖς μήτε τὴν σάρκα καταξαίνεις μήτε τὰ ἀναγκαῖα καταναλίσκεις, χρῶ ὡς βούλει τῇ σεαυτοῦ προαιρέσει. ἀμήχανον μέντοι γε τὸ μὴ οὐχ ἑνί γέ τινι τούτων συνέχεσθαι· ἀφροδίσια γὰρ οὐδέποτε ὤνησεν, ἀγαπητὸν δὲ εἰ μὴ ἔβλαψεν. (4) [59] ἄπληστον οὐ γαστήρ, ὥσπερ οἱ πολλοί φασιν, ἀλλὰ δόξα ψευδὴς ὑπὲρ τοῦ ⟨τῆς⟩ γαστρὸς ἀορίστου πληρώματος.

2 κἂν ⟨Διὶ⟩ Hartel; cf. Usener fr. 602: καὶ cod.   3 ἀπολαύσεως Usener: ἀπολύσεως cod.: ἀπολαύσεως ⟨τοῦ κακοῦ⟩ Bignone   4 ἀφ[θονωτέ]ραν P. Berol. 16369: ἀφθονο̅ SV: ἀφθονώτερον Usener   5 εἰ μὴ P. Berol.: ὅτε μήτε SV: ὅταν μήτε Usener   6 ἔθη P. Berol., Hartel: ἔθει SV   πλησίον P. Berol.: πλησίων SV   λυπεῖς P. Berol.: λυπῇς SV   7 εἰ[ς τὰς πόρνας] post ἀναγκαῖα P. Berol. rest. Vogliano: om. SV   ὡς βούλει post προαιρέσει pos. P. Berol.   8 τὸ Usener: τῷ cod.   11 suppl. Usener

1–2   A much quoted and adapted maxim; cf. Arrighetti [119] and Bailey [117] ad loc. For the godlike happiness of the Epicurean philosopher, cf. **23J–K**. The Stoics made the same claim for their wise man: Stobaeus 2.98,19–99,2 (= *SVF* 3.54, part).

3   Adopting Usener's correction, this line would fit Diogenes of Oenoanda's category of pleasures that are synchronous with their sources, fr. 27. It also reads like a version of the Aristotelian thesis that pleasure is complete at any moment, *EN* x.4, 1174b5–6. In that context Aristotle goes on to deny any γένεσις of pleasure, but this anti-Platonic point is hardly his considered view; cf. Gauthier/Jolif comm. ad loc.

4–9   For the text and attribution to Metrodorus, cf. Vogliano [136], 207ff.

10–11   In **24C 2**, on the other hand, the flesh is said to take the limits of pleasure to be infinite.

H Epicurus, *SV* 63, 71, 73, 81

(1) [63] ἔστι καὶ ἐν λεπτότητι καθαριότης, ἧς ὁ ἀνεπιλόγιστος παραπλησίόν τι πάσχει τῷ δι᾽ ἀοριστίαν ἐκπίπτοντι. (2) [71] πρὸς πάσας τὰς ἐπιθυμίας προσακτέον τὸ ἐπερώτημα τοῦτο· τί μοι γενήσεται ἂν τελεσθῇ τὸ κατὰ τὴν ἐπιθυμίαν ἐπιζητούμενον, καὶ τί ἐὰν μὴ τελεσθῇ; (3) [73] καὶ τὸ γενέσθαι τινὰς ἀλγηδόνας περὶ σῶμα λυσιτελεῖ πρὸς φυλακὴν τῶν ὁμοειδῶν. (4) [81] οὐ λύει τὴν τῆς ψυχῆς ταραχὴν οὐδὲ τὴν ἀξιόλογον ἀπογεννᾷ χαρὰν οὔτε πλοῦτος ὑπάρχων ὁ μέγιστος οὔθ᾽ ἡ παρὰ τοῖς πολλοῖς τιμὴ καὶ περίβλεψις οὔτ᾽ ἄλλο τι τῶν παρὰ τὰς ἀδιορίστους αἰτίας.

1 λεπτότητι cod.: λιτότητι Usener   καθαριότης Mühll: καθάριος cod.   8 ἀδιορίστους Usener: ἀζυρισί(έ?)τους cod.

1–2   For λεπτότης = slenderness of means or absence of luxury, cf. λεπτοτάτης, **J** 9. We take the point to be a warning against erring on the side of deficiency as well as excess.

120

2–4 Cf. especially **B** 1–6, **E** 3, **G**, I.
4–6 For the value of learning from experience, cf. **B** 32–6.
6–9 For what does relieve the soul's disturbance, cf. **B** 41–3, **W** 61, **X** 24–8; **25B**.

I Scholion on Epicurus, *RS* 29

φυσικὰς καὶ ἀναγκαίας ἡγεῖται ὁ 'Επίκουρος τὰς ἀλγηδόνος ἀπολυούσας,
ὡς ποτὸν ἐπὶ δίψους· φυσικὰς δὲ οὐκ ἀναγκαίας δὲ τὰς ποικιλλούσας μόνον
τὴν ἡδονήν, μὴ ὑπεξαιρουμένας δὲ τὸ ἄλγημα, ὡς πολυτελῆ σιτία· οὔτε δὲ
φυσικὰς οὔτε ἀναγκαίας, ὡς στεφάνους καὶ ἀνδριάντων ἀναθέσεις.

1 ἀλγηδόνος Weil: -όνας codd.   2 δὲ οὐκ BP: δὲ καὶ οὐκ F

For the classification of ἐπιθυμίαι, cf. **B** 1–4.

2–3   The point must be not that luxurious foods *qua* foods are incapable of
removing the pains of hunger if one is hungry, but that their luxuriousness exemplifies
the object of a desire which, though natural, pertains to variation of existing pleasure
and is unnecessary to the removal of pain. Cf. **J**.

J Porphyry, *Abst.* 1.51.6–52.1 (Usener 464, part)

(1) ὡς τό γε τῆς σαρκοφαγίας οὔτ᾽ ἔλυέν τι ὀχληρὸν τῆς φύσεως οὔθ᾽ ὃ μὴ
συντελούμενον ἐπ᾽ ἀλγηδόνα ἡνύετο, τὴν δὲ χάριν βιαίαν εἶχε καὶ ταχὺ τῷ
ἐναντίῳ μιγνυμένην. οὐ γὰρ πρὸς ζωῆς συμμονήν, πρὸς δὲ ποικιλίαν
ἡδονῶν συνεβάλλετο, ἐοικὸς ἀφροδισίοις ἢ ξενικῶν οἴνων πόσεσιν, ὧν καὶ
χωρὶς διαμένειν δύναται ἡ φύσις. ὧν δὲ χωρὶς οὐκ ἂν ὑπομείνειεν, βραχέα   5
παντάπασίν ἐστι καὶ δυνάμενα ῥᾳδίως καὶ μετὰ δικαιοσύνης καὶ ἐλευθερίας, ἡσυχίας τε καὶ
πολλῆς ῥᾳστώνης πορίζεσθαι. (2) ἔτι δὲ οὐδὲ πρὸς ὑγείαν τὰ κρέα συντελεῖ, ἀλλὰ
μᾶλλον τῇ ὑγείᾳ ἐμποδίζει. δι᾽ ὧν γὰρ ὑγεία ἀνακτᾶται, διὰ τούτων καὶ διαμένει·
ἀνακτᾶται δὲ διὰ τῆς λεπτοτάτης καὶ ἀσάρκου διαίτης, ὥστε καὶ ταύτῃ ἂν συμμείνειεν.

1 οὔτ . . . οὔθ᾽ Usener: οὐδ . . . οὐδ᾽ codd.   2 χάριν βιαίαν Usener: βιαίαν χάριν codd.   9
λεπτοτάτης ed. Bouffartigue: λιτοτάτης silenter Usener

Context: arguments in favour of vegetarianism derived from Epicurus; cf. Porphyry,
Abst. 1.49.1.
1–3   Cf. **B** 36–49, **D** 1.

K Diogenes Laertius 10.121

τὴν εὐδαιμονίαν διχῇ νοεῖσθαι, τήν τε ἀκροτάτην, οἷα ἐστὶ περὶ τὸν θεόν,
ἐπίτασιν οὐκ ἔχουσαν· καὶ τὴν ⟨κατὰ τὴν⟩ προσθήκην καὶ ἀφαίρεσιν
ἡδονῶν.

2 suppl. Usener

Rightly appreciating that divine happiness has its human equivalent (cf. **23J–K**), some
scholars (e.g. Bailey [117] ad loc.) take the second conception to be that of people in
general, and not Epicureans. This is unnecessary. Divine happiness, though the human
ideal, is utterly invariant. But men are subject to unavoidable bodily changes from
which the gods are exempt. Could ἀφαίρεσις also refer to deliberately forgoing

pleasures that result in excess of pain? Support for this might be drawn from ἀφαιρεῖν in **24A 2** and *SV* 18. Cf. also *detrahens* **L** 1–3 (= ἀφαιρῶν).

L Cicero, *Tusc.* 3.41–2 (Usener 67, 69)

(1) "nec equidem habeo, quod intellegam bonum illud, detrahens eas voluptates quae sapore percipiuntur, detrahens eas quae rebus percipiuntur veneriis, detrahens eas quae auditu e cantibus, detrahens eas etiam quae ex formis percipiuntur oculis suaves motiones, sive quae aliae voluptates in toto homine gignuntur quolibet sensu. nec vero ita dici potest, mentis laetitiam   5 solam esse in bonis. laetantem enim mentem ita novi: spe eorum omnium, quae supra dixi, fore ut natura iis potiens dolore careat." atque haec quidem his verbis, quivis ut intellegat quam voluptatem norit Epicurus. (2) deinde paulo infra "saepe quaesivi", inquit, "ex iis qui appellabantur sapientes, quid haberent quod in bonis relinquerent, si illa detraxissent, nisi si vellent voces inanes fundere; nihil 10 ab iis potui cognoscere: qui si virtutes ebullire volent et sapientias, nihil aliud dicent nisi eam viam qua efficiantur eae voluptates quas supra dixi."

2–3 *eas quae rebus percipiuntur veneriis detrahens* V², cf. Athenaeum 278F: om. X   7 *fore* ⟨ *fidentem* ⟩ Giusta

Context: Cicero claims to be quoting from Epicurus' book *qui continet omnem disciplinam tuam* [sc. *Epicuri*]. The Περὶ τέλους is meant; cf. Usener 67.

    1 **nec–intellegam** We take this to mean 'the only way I can conceptualize'; cf. Rist [95], 108–9.

    1–7 These lines strongly support the commonly held view that all the sensory pleasures as mentioned here are 'kinetic'; cf. **Q** 8–9. For doubts, not shared by us, about this view, cf. Gosling/Taylor [19], 375–94. If such sensory pleasures could be counted as 'static' (i.e. pleasant simply *qua* absence of pain), *natura–careat*, 7, loses all point. On *spe*, 6, and its doctrinal importance, cf. Gosling/Taylor [19], 371–2.

    8–12 This passage reads like anti-Stoic polemic, cf. **P**.

M Athenaeus, 546F (Usener 409, 70)

καὶ ὁ Ἐπίκουρος δέ φησιν "ἀρχὴ καὶ ῥίζα παντὸς ἀγαθοῦ ἡ τῆς γαστρὸς ἡδονή· καὶ τὰ σοφὰ ⟨καὶ⟩ τὰ περιττὰ ἐπὶ ταύτην ἔχει τὴν ἀναφοράν." κἂν τῷ Περὶ τέλους δὲ πάλιν φησίν "τιμητέον τὸ καλὸν καὶ τὰς ἀρετὰς καὶ τὰ τοιουτότροπα, ἐὰν ἡδονὴν παρασκευάζῃ· ἐὰν δὲ μὴ παρασκευάζῃ, χαίρειν ἐατέον."   5

2 καὶ legitur ap. Athenaeum 280A

    1–2 For discussion, cf. Gosling/Taylor [19], 352–3, and Sedley [104], 132 and n. 49. Metrodorus amplified the second sentence (Plutarch, *Col.* 1125B); note especially his sardonic expansion of τὰ σοφὰ–περιττὰ into τὰ καλὰ πάντα καὶ σοφὰ καὶ περιττὰ τῆς ἡδονῆς ἐξευρήματα.

    3–4 Cf. **L** 10–12, **P**.

N Plutarch, *Contra Ep. beat.* 1089D (Usener 68, part)

τὸ γὰρ εὐσταθὲς σαρκὸς κατάστημα καὶ τὸ περὶ ταύτης πιστὸν ἔλπισμα

21 *Pleasure*

τὴν ἀκροτάτην χαρὰν καὶ βεβαιοτάτην ἔχειν τοῖς ἐπιλογίζεσθαι δυναμένοις.

Context: polemical comments on the Epicureans' attempts to stabilize their hedonism by taking refuge εἰς τὴν ἀπονίαν καὶ τὴν εὐστάθειαν . . . τῆς σαρκός.
1 Democritus 68 B 191 DK combines εὐσταθής with εὔθυμος; cf. Grilli [269], 101–2. κατάστημα only occurs again in extant Epicurus at fr. 73 Arrighetti [119], a fragmentary letter from Epicurus to Metrodorus which appears to have much in common with N. For ἔλπισμα and for N in general, cf. G 1–2 and L 6.
2 ἐπιλογίζεσθαι Cf. ἐκλόγισις, E 3, and note on V 1.

O Cicero, *Fin.* 2.69

pudebit te, inquam, illius tabulae quam Cleanthes sane commode verbis depingere solebat. iubebat eos qui audiebant secum ipsos cogitare pictam in tabula Voluptatem pulcherrimo vestitu et ornatu regali in solio sedentem, praesto esse Virtutes ut ancillulas, quae nihil aliud agerent, nullum suum officium ducerent, nisi ut Voluptati ministrarent et eam tantum ad aurem   5
admonerent, si modo id pictura intellegi posset, ut caveret ne quid faceret inprudens quod offenderet animos hominum, aut quicquam e quo oriretur aliquis dolor. "nos quidem virtutes sic natae sumus ut tibi serviremus; aliud negotii nihil habemus."

Context: Cicero's refutation of Epicurean hedonism.

P Diogenes of Oenoanda 26.1.2–3.8

ἐγὼ δὲ περὶ μ[ὲν] | τῆς ἀφροσύνης μετὰ μει|κρὸν ἐρῶ, περὶ δὲ τῶν ἀ|ρετῶν καὶ τῆς ἡδονῆς | ἤδη. εἰ μέν, ὦ ἄνδρες, | τὸ μεταξὺ τούτων τε καὶ | ἡμῶν προβεβλημένον | ἐπίσκεψιν εἶχεν "τί τῆς | εὐδαιμονίας ποιητικόν", | ἐβούλοντο δ' οὗτοι τὰς ἀρε|τὰς λέγειν, ὃ δὴ καὶ ἀλη|θὲς ἐτύγχανεν, οὐδὲν | ἀλλ' ἔδει ποιεῖν ἢ τούτοις | [συνο]μογνωμονοῦν|[τας μὴ] ἔχειν   5
πράγμα||[τα. ἐπ]εὶ δ', ὡς λέγω, τὸ πρό|β[λημ]α οὐ τοῦτό ἐστιν | τ⟨ί⟩ [τῆ]ς εὐδαιμονίας ποι|ητ[ι]κόν, τί δὲ τὸ εὐδαι|μον[ε]ῖν ἐστιν καὶ οὐ κα|τὰ τὸ [ἔ]σχατον ἡ φύσις | ἡμῶ[ν] ὀρέγεται, [τ]ὴν | μὲν [ἡ]δονήν [φημ]ι καὶ | νῦν [κ]αὶ ἀεὶ πᾶσιν Ἕλλη|σι κ[αὶ] βαρβάροις μέγα | ἐνβ[ο]ῶν τῆς ἀρίστης | δια[γ]ωγῆς ὑπάρχειν τέ|λος, τὰς δὲ ἀρετὰς τὰς | νῦν ἀκαίρως ὑπὸ τού|των   10
ἐνοχλουμένας | (ἀπὸ γὰρ τῆς τοῦ ποιητικοῦ | χώρας εἰς τὴν τοῦ τέλους | μεταφέρονται) τέλος | μὲν οὐδαμῶς, ποιητι|κὰς δὲ τοῦ τέλους εἶναι.

For full critical apparatus, see Chilton [170].

Q Cicero, *Fin.* 2.9–10

(1) "estne, quaeso", inquam, "sitienti in bibendo voluptas?" "quis istud possit", inquit, "negare?" "eademne, quae restincta siti?" (2) "immo alio genere; restincta enim sitis stabilitatem voluptatis habet", inquit, "illa autem voluptas ipsius restinctionis in motu est." (3) "cur igitur", inquam, "res tam dissimiles eodem

123

Epicurean ethics

nomine appellas?" "quid paulo ante", inquit, "dixerim nonne meministi, cum 5
omnis dolor detractus esset, variari, non augeri voluptatem?" "... ista
varietas quae sit non satis perspicio, quod ais, cum dolore careamus, tum in
summa voluptate nos esse, cum autem vescamur iis rebus quae dulcem motum
afferant sensibus, tum esse in motu voluptatem, quae faciat varietatem
voluptatum, sed non augeri illam non dolendi voluptatem, quam cur voluptatem 10
appelles nescio."

3 *enim* om. RN   *inquit* om. BE   4 *dissimiles] difficiles* A ante corr.   9 *quae* codd.: *qui* Davies; sed cf.
Fin. 2.75

Context: Cicero's refutation of Epicurean hedonism.

As we point out in vol. 1, 123, this passage envisages kinetic pleasure as (a)
coextensive with the process of removing pain, and (b) varying a pre-existing state of
ἀπονία. Rist [95], 106–8, 170–2, following Diano [254], treats (b) alone as the correct
Epicurean position; Gosling/Taylor [19], 374–88, accept (a) as a valid role for kinetic
pleasure, and argue that 'static' pleasures can [also] involve variety. Our view is closer
to theirs, but we do not share their strong doubts about Cicero's reliability. In
particular (see our note on **L**) we think they are too ready to play down the
significance of the distinction between static and kinetic, and to regard sensory
pleasures as instances of the former; see especially **I** and **J**.

R Diogenes Laertius 10.136–7

(1) διαφέρεται δὲ πρὸς τοὺς Κυρηναικοὺς περὶ τῆς ἡδονῆς· οἱ μὲν γὰρ τὴν
καταστηματικὴν οὐκ ἐγκρίνουσι, μόνην δὲ τὴν ἐν κινήσει· ὁ δὲ ἀμφοτέραν
⟨καὶ⟩ ψυχῆς καὶ σώματος, ὥς φησιν ἐν τῷ Περὶ αἱρέσεως καὶ φυγῆς καὶ
ἐν τῷ Περὶ τέλους καὶ ἐν τῷ πρώτῳ Περὶ βίων καὶ ἐν τῇ πρὸς τοὺς ἐν Μυτιλήνῃ
φίλους ἐπιστολῇ. ὁμοίως δὲ καὶ Διογένης ἐν τῇ ἑπτακαιδεκάτῃ τῶν Ἐπιλέκτων καὶ 5
Μητρόδωρος ἐν τῷ Τιμοκράτει λέγουσιν οὕτω· νοουμένης δὲ ἡδονῆς τῆς τε κατὰ κίνησιν
καὶ τῆς καταστηματικῆς. ὁ δ᾽ Ἐπίκουρος ἐν τῷ Περὶ αἱρέσεων οὕτω λέγει· "ἡ
μὲν γὰρ ἀταραξία καὶ ἀπονία καταστηματικαί εἰσιν ἡδοναί· ἡ δὲ χαρὰ καὶ
ἡ εὐφροσύνη κατὰ κίνησιν ἐνέργειαι βλέπονται." (2) ἔτι πρὸς τοὺς
Κυρηναικούς· οἱ μὲν γὰρ χείρους τὰς σωματικὰς ἀλγηδόνας τῶν ψυχικῶν, 10
κολάζεσθαι γοῦν τοὺς ἁμαρτάνοντας σώματι· ὁ δὲ τὰς ψυχικάς. τὴν γοῦν σάρκα τὸ
παρὸν μόνον χειμάζειν, τὴν δὲ ψυχὴν καὶ τὸ παρελθὸν καὶ τὸ παρὸν καὶ τὸ
μέλλον.

1 τῆς om. F   2–3 ἀμφοτέραν F: ἀμφότερα BP: ἀμφοτέρας Gassendi: ἀμφοτέραν ⟨καὶ⟩ A.A. Long; cf.
Merlan [265], 5: ἀμφότερα ⟨τὰ γένη⟩ Bignone   8 γὰρ om. F   9 ἢ om. F   ἐνέργειαι A.A.
Long: ἐνεργείᾳ codd.

Context: Diogenes' summary of Epicurean doctrine.

2–9 In the main we follow the excellent interpretation of Merlan [265], 3–7.
From 8–9 it is clear that Epicurus posited 'static' and 'kinetic' pleasures both of mind
and body. In order to prepare for the mention of these, we must assume the minimal
lacuna of a καί after ἀμφοτέραν in 2; the singular ἀμφοτέραν is defensible as Greek,
though generally rejected in favour of ἀμφότερα. The terms ἀταραξία and ἀπονία

evidently pick out mental and bodily absence of pain respectively, but χαρά and εὐφροσύνη are most naturally interpreted as two terms for kinetic pleasure each of which can apply to mind or body.

9 ἐνέργειαι   Our emendation, which is merely orthographic, is an attempt to restore grammar and sense. The dative has never been satisfactorily explained.

11–13   For the greater magnitude of mental pleasures, see U, V.

S Lucretius 4.622–32

> hoc ubi levia sunt manantis corpora suci,
> suaviter attingunt et suaviter omnia tractant
> umida linguai circum sudantia templa.
> at contra pungunt sensum lacerantque coorta,   625
> quanto quaeque magis sunt asperitate repleta.
> deinde voluptas est e suco fine palati;
> cum vero deorsum per fauces praecipitavit,
> nulla voluptas est, dum in artus diditur omnis.
> nec refert quicquam quo victu corpus alatur,   630
> dummodo quod capias concoctum didere possis
> artubus et stomachi umidulum servare tenorem.

629 *dum–omnis* Marullus: *dum diditur omnis in artus* codd.   632 *umidulum* Lachmann: *umidum* codd.

Context: explanation of taste as direct contact with the atomic structure of the tasted object.

627–9   These lines are crucial to the view defended by Diano [254], 260ff., and elsewhere (see Merlan [265], 11 n. 15 for Diano's other statements of his position) that all kinetic pleasure presupposes static pleasure, and consists only in the variation of the latter. Diano focuses on the fact that the palate, which was previously experiencing no pain (i.e. was already in a condition of static pleasure), is here described as the locus of a kinetic pleasure, but that pleasure is said to cease when the food passes into those regions of the body where the pain of hunger is experienced. In other words, he claims, the actual process of removing pain is not to be regarded as a kinetic pleasure. In our opinion (cf. Merlan [265], 11–13), Diano's influential theory is unconvincing in general, and not even plausible for this passage. The pleasure of taste is obviously not something that is registered by the stomach; but the removal of hunger pain from the stomach would not be something registered by the palate. *nulla voluptas*, 629, should mean no pleasure of *taste*, which is Lucretius' topic here. It implies nothing about the pleasure of actually replenishing one's stomach, to which taste makes no difference, 630–2.

T Cicero, *Tusc.* 5.95 (Usener 439, part)

corpus gaudere tam diu, dum praesentem sentiret voluptatem, animum et praesentem percipere pariter cum corpore et prospicere venientem nec praeteritam praeterfluere sinere: ita perpetuas et contextas voluptates in

sapiente fore semper, cum exspectatio speratarum voluptatum cum percep-
tarum memoria iungeretur.   5

Context: report of Epicureanism.

4–5   For the significance of anticipation and recollection, cf. **L** 6, **N**,with notes, **R**
11–13; **24D**.

U   Cicero, *Fin.* 1.55

(1) nullus in ipsis error est finibus bonorum et malorum, id est in voluptate aut
in dolore, sed in his rebus peccant, cum e quibus haec efficiantur ignorant. (2)
animi autem voluptates et dolores, nasci fatemur e corporis voluptatibus et
doloribus . . . nec ob eam causam non multo maiores esse et voluptates et
dolores animi quam corporis.   5

Context: Torquatus' exposition of Epicurean ethics.

1–2   Cf. **D**1–2.

4–5   Mental pains are also said to be 'worse' than bodily ones, **R** 10–11.

V   Diogenes of Oenoanda 38.1.8–3.14

(1) [δυσε]πιλόγιστος δέ ἐσ|[τι το]ῖς πολλοῖς ἡ τῶν | [ψυχι]κῶν τούτων
ὑπερ||οχὴ] παθῶν. ἐπεὶ γὰρ | [οὐκ] ἔστιν ἐξ ἀντιπα||[ρακρ]ίσεως ὑφ' ἕνα
και||[ρὸν] ἀμφοτέρας παθεῖν | τὰς ἀκρότητας (τῶν | ψυχικῶν λέγω καθὼς | τῶν
τε σωματικῶν), δι|ὰ τὸ σπανίως ποτὲ τοῦ|το συμβαίνειν, καὶ ὅ|ταν δὲ συνβῇ,
⟨τ⟩ὸ [ζ]ῆν ἀ|ναιρεῖσθαι, (2) τού[των] ἑτέρων | τῆς ὑπεροχῆς τὸ κρι|τήριον   5
οὐχ [ε]ὑρί[σ]κεται. | ἀλλ' ὅταν μὲν ἐν ταῖς | σωματικαῖς ἀλγηδόσι | τυν-
χάνῃ τις, φησὶ ταύ|τας τῶν ψυχικῶν εἶναι | μείζονας, ὅταν δ' ἐν | [ταῖς
ψυχικαῖς τυγχάνῃ,] | μ[εί]ζονας εἶναί φησι| | ταύτας. [τῶν γὰρ ἀπόν||των
αἰεὶ τὰ [παρόντα πι||θανώτερα κα[ὶ δῆλος] | ἔκαστός ἐστιν ἢ [δι' ἀνάν||κην
ἢ διὰ ἡδονὴν τ[ῷ] | κατέχοντι αὐτὸν πά|θει τὴν ὑπεροχὴν ἀπ[ο||]δεδωκέναι.   10
(3) σοφὸς | δὲ ἀνὴρ τὸ δυσεπιλό|γιστον τοῦτο τοῖς πο[λ||λοῖς ἐξ ἄλλων τε
ἀν[α]||λογίζεται πολλῶν.

For full apparatus, see Chilton [170].

1   **δυσεπιλόγιστος**   This word, repeated in 11, is not attested elsewhere
according to LSJ. For ἐπιλογισμός in Epicurean ethics, cf. **20A** 2, **C** 27; **24C** 4. On the
interpretation of it as 'empirical reasoning', see Sedley [126], 27–34. Another possible
interpretation is 'direct calculation' by contrast with indirect ἀναλογισμός, as
frequently in the medical tradition: cf. **7B** 36–7.

4–5   Cf. Plutarch, *Contra Ep. beat.* 1103E, who cites as Epicurean the proposition,
ὁ γὰρ πόνος ὁ ὑπερβάλλων συνάψει θανάτῳ.

W   Lucretius 2.1–61

(1) suave, mari magno turbantibus aequora ventis,
e terra magnum alterius spectare laborem;

non quia vexari quemquamst iucunda voluptas,
sed quibus ipse malis careas quia cernere suave est.
suave etiam belli certamina magna tueri   5 [6]
per campos instructa tua sine parte pericli.   [5]
(2) sed nil dulcius est, bene quam munita tenere
edita doctrina sapientum templa serena,
despicere unde queas alios passimque videre
errare, atque viam palantis quaerere vitae,   10
certare ingenio, contendere nobilitate,
noctes atque dies niti praestante labore
ad summas emergere opes rerumque potiri.
(3) o miseras hominum mentis, o pectora caeca!
qualibus in tenebris vitae quantisque periclis   15
degitur hoc aevi quodcumquest! nonne videre
nil aliud sibi naturam latrare, nisi utqui
corpore seiunctus dolor absit, mensque fruatur
iucundo sensu cura semota metuque?
(4) ergo corpoream ad naturam pauca videmus   20
esse opus omnino, quae demant cumque dolorem,
delicias quoque uti multas substernere possint
gratius interdum; neque natura ipsa requirit,
si non aurea sunt iuvenum simulacra per aedes
lampadas igniferas manibus retinentia dextris,   25
lumina nocturnis epulis ut suppeditentur,
nec domus argento fulget auroque renidet
nec citharae reboant laqueata aurataque tecta,
cum tamen inter se prostrati in gramine molli
propter aquae rivum sub ramis arboris altae   30
non magnis opibus iucunde corpora curant,
praesertim cum tempestas arridet et anni
tempora conspergunt viridantis floribus herbas.
nec calidae citius decedunt corpore febres,
textilibus si in picturis ostroque rubenti   35
iacteris, quam si in plebeia veste cubandum est.
(5) quapropter quoniam nil nostro in corpore gazae
proficiunt neque nobilitas nec gloria regni,
quod superest, animo quoque nil prodesse putandum;
si non forte tuas legiones per loca campi   40
fervere cum videas belli simulacra cientis,
ornatas⟨que⟩ armis statuas pariterque animatas,   [43]
subsidiis magnis et ecum vi constabilitas,   [42]
his tibi tum rebus timefactae religiones
effugiunt animo pavidae; mortisque timores   45

tum vacuum pectus linquunt curaque solutum.
(6) quod si ridicula haec ludibriaque esse videmus,
re veraque metus hominum curaeque sequaces
nec metuunt sonitus armorum nec fera tela
audacterque inter reges rerumque potentis   50
versantur neque fulgorem reverentur ab auro
nec clarum vestis splendorem purpureai,
quid dubitas quin omni' sit haec rationi' potestas?
omnis cum in tenebris praesertim vita laboret.
nam veluti pueri trepidant atque omnia caecis   55
in tenebris metuunt, sic nos in luce timemus
interdum, nilo quae sunt metuenda magis quam
quae pueri in tenebris pavitant finguntque futura.
(7) hunc igitur terrorem animi tenebrasque necessest
non radii solis neque lucida tela diei   60
discutiant, sed naturae species ratioque.

5–6 transp. Avancius   18 *mensque* Marullus: *mente* codd.   28 *tecta* Macrobius: *templa* codd.   42–3 transpos. Bailey: om. Q, trium versuum spatio post 41 relicto   43 *ornatas*⟨*que*⟩ Munro: *ornatas* OG   *statuas*] *itastuas* O(corr.)G: *ita statuas* ed. Venet.   *pariter* Lachmann: *tariter* codd.   46 *pectus* Lambinus: *tempus* codd.

    1–13   On these lines, and the whole extract, cf. Konstan [253], 3–16, who aptly compares Democritus 68 B 191 DK for the injunction to compare one's life with those less fortunate. See also Clay [162], 65–6, 219–20.

    22–3   We take *uti* in the sense of *ita ut*, with the subjunctive *possint* dependent on *videmus*. Thus *gratius interdum* makes the important point that the few things needed to satisfy the body's natural and necessary desires remove pain in such a way that they can also often be a source of kinetic pleasure. The phrase *gratius interdum* is normally taken with *requirit*, but word-order and sense are against this. We are grateful to Michael Wigodsky for drawing our attention to this latter point.

X   Lucretius 6.1–28

(1) primae frugiparos fetus mortalibus aegris
dididerunt quondam praeclaro nomine Athenae
et recreaverunt vitam legesque rogarunt,
et primae dederunt solacia dulcia vitae,
cum genuere virum tali cum corde repertum,   5
omnia veridico qui quondam ex ore profudit;
cuius et extincti propter divina reperta
divulgata vetus iam ad caelum gloria fertur.
(2) nam cum vidit hic ad victum quae flagitat usus
omnia iam ferme mortalibus esse parata   10
et, proquam posset vitam consistere tutam,
divitiis homines et honore et laude potentis
adfluere atque bona gnatorum excellere fama,

nec minus esse domi cuiquam tamen anxia corda,
atque animi ingratis vitam vexare ⟨sine ulla⟩   15
pausa atque infestis cogi saevire querellis,
intellegit ibi vitium vas efficere ipsum
omniaque illius vitio corrumpier intus
quae collata foris et commoda cumque venirent;
(3) partim quod fluxum pertusumque esse videbat,   20
ut nulla posset ratione explerier umquam;
partim quod taetro quasi conspurcare sapore
omnia cernebat, quaecumque receperat, intus.
veridicis igitur purgavit pectora dictis
et finem statuit cuppedinis atque timoris   25
exposuitque bonum summum quo tendimus omnes
quid foret, atque viam monstravit, tramite parvo
qua possemus ad id recto contendere cursu.

7 *extincti* Marullus: *extincta* codd.　　11 *posset* Lachmann: *possent* codd.　　14 *corda* Marullus: *cordi*
codd.　　15 suppl. Munro　　16 *cogi* Lambinus: *coget* codd.　　17 *vas* Marullus: *fas* codd.

1–4, 9–13 Notice the positive emphasis on the benefits of high civilization and on
the provision of necessary amenities and security; for discussion of how these bear on
basic assumptions of Epicurean ethics, cf. Long [280].

17–23 Bailey [154] ad loc. refers to Plato, *Protag.* 314a for the comparison of the
mind to a *vas*, but misses the much more telling antecedent in *Gorg.* 493a–494b.

22 Society

A Epicurus, *RS* 31–5

(1) [31] τὸ τῆς φύσεως δίκαιόν ἐστι σύμβολον τοῦ συμφέροντος εἰς τὸ μὴ
βλάπτειν ἀλλήλους μηδὲ βλάπτεσθαι. (2) [32] ὅσα τῶν ζῴων μὴ ἐδύνατο
συνθήκας ποιεῖσθαι τὰς ὑπὲρ τοῦ μὴ βλάπτειν ἄλληλα μηδὲ βλάπτεσθαι,
πρὸς ταῦτα οὐθὲν ἦν δίκαιον οὐδὲ ἄδικον. ὡσαύτως δὲ καὶ τῶν ἐθνῶν ὅσα
μὴ ἐδύνατο ἢ μὴ ἐβούλετο τὰς συνθήκας ποιεῖσθαι τὰς ὑπὲρ τοῦ μὴ   5
βλάπτειν μηδὲ βλάπτεσθαι. (3) [33] οὐκ ἦν τι καθ᾽ ἑαυτὸ δικαιοσύνη, ἀλλ᾽
ἐν ταῖς μετ᾽ ἀλλήλων συστροφαῖς καθ᾽ ὁπηλίκους δή ποτε ἀεὶ τόπους
συνθήκη τις ὑπὲρ τοῦ μὴ βλάπτειν ἢ βλάπτεσθαι. (4) [34] ἡ ἀδικία οὐ καθ᾽
ἑαυτὴν κακόν, ἀλλ᾽ ἐν τῷ κατὰ τὴν ὑποψίαν φόβῳ εἰ μὴ λήσει τοὺς ὑπὲρ
τῶν τοιούτων ἐφεστηκότας κολαστάς. (5) [35] οὐκ ἔστι τὸν λάθρα τι   10
ποιοῦντα ὧν συνέθεντο πρὸς ἀλλήλους εἰς τὸ μὴ βλάπτειν μηδὲ βλάπτεσθαι πιστεύειν ὅτι λήσει, κἂν μυριάκις ἐπὶ τοῦ παρόντος λανθάνῃ. μέχρι γὰρ
καταστροφῆς ἄδηλον εἰ καὶ λήσει.

3 ἄλληλα Gassendi: ἀλλὰ codd.　　4 ἦν Usener: ἢ BP: ἐστιν οὐδὲ F　　12 ἐπὶ *SV* 6: ἀπὸ vel ὑπὸ codd.

1 It is difficult to decide whether σύμβολον is simply equivalent to συνθήκη, or
whether it should be translated 'sign', indicating that the utility of mutual non-

aggression is what the expression 'natural justice' *signifies*; cf. Goldschmidt [276], 27–8.

2 **ζῴων** The Stoics insisted that justice does not apply to human relations with other animals, **57F 5**. Epicurus, unlike Hermarchus (**N 9–10**), does not exclude this in principle; cf. Goldschmidt [276], 43–57.

6 The imperfect ἦν is best interpreted as indicating what always holds good; cf. **B 1** and the Aristotelian expression τὸ τί ἦν εἶναι. It is generally and rightly assumed that Epicurus' denial of justice being καθ' ἑαυτό is most obviously directed against Plato; cf. *Rep.* 2, 358b, 4, 443a–c etc. For antecedents of the contractual conception of justice, cf. Denyer [279]. It should be emphasized that what Epicurus means by 'contract' has nothing to do with the later idea of a *tacit* agreement by our predecessors which provides laws with their current binding force; cf. Long [3], 70–1, and Goldschmidt [276], 73–8.

8–13 The anti-Platonic stance continues; cf. *Gorg.* 509a–c on doing injustice with impunity as the greatest of evils for the wrongdoer. In the Epicurean theory, where injustice is bad solely for its consequences, its badness consists not in the possibility of punishment but in the *certainty* of fearing punishment; cf. *SV* 7, ἀδικοῦντα λαθεῖν μὲν δύσκολον, πίστιν δὲ λαβεῖν ὑπὲρ τοῦ λαθεῖν ἀδύνατον; Lucretius 3.1013–23; and Denyer [279], 147. For further relevant material, see Usener 18, 530.

B Epicurus, *RS* 36–7, 17

(1) [36] κατὰ μὲν ⟨τὸ⟩ κοινὸν πᾶσι τὸ δίκαιον τὸ αὐτό, συμφέρον γάρ τι ἦν ἐν τῇ πρὸς ἀλλήλους κοινωνίᾳ· κατὰ δὲ τὸ ἴδιον χώρας καὶ ὅσων δή ποτε αἰτίων οὐ πᾶσι συνέπεται τὸ αὐτὸ δίκαιον εἶναι. (2) [37] τὸ μὲν ἐπιμαρτυρούμενον ὅτι συμφέρει ἐν ταῖς χρείαις τῆς πρὸς ἀλλήλους κοινωνίας τῶν νομισθέντων εἶναι δικαίων ἔχει τὸ ἐν τοῦ δικαίου χώρᾳ 5 εἶναι, ἐάν τε τὸ αὐτὸ πᾶσι γένηται ἐάν τε μὴ τὸ αὐτό. ἐὰν δὲ νόμον θῆταί τις, μὴ ἀποβαίνῃ δὲ κατὰ τὸ συμφέρον τῆς πρὸς ἀλλήλους κοινωνίας, οὐκέτι τοῦτο τὴν τοῦ δικαίου φύσιν ἔχει. κἂν μεταπίπτῃ τὸ κατὰ τὸ δίκαιον συμφέρον χρόνον δέ τινα εἰς τὴν πρόληψιν ἐναρμόττῃ, οὐδὲν ἧττον ἐκεῖνον τὸν χρόνον ἦν δίκαιον τοῖς μὴ φωναῖς κεναῖς ἑαυτοὺς συνταράττου- 10 σιν ἀλλ' ἁπλῶς εἰς τὰ πράγματα βλέπουσιν. (3) [17] ὁ δίκαιος ⟨βίος⟩ ἀταρακτότατος, ὁ δ' ἄδικος πλείστης ταραχῆς γέμων.

1 add. Gassendi   3 αἰτίων B: αἰτιῶν cett.   5 ἔχει FP: ἔχειν B   5–6 τὸ–εἶναι Mühll: τοῦ δικαίου χώραν εἶναι B: τὸ τοῦ δικαίου χώραν εἶναι F: τὸν τοῦ δικαίου εἶναι P: τὸ τοῦ δικαίου ἐνέχυρον Bailey   6 νόμον Usener: μόνον codd.: ⟨νόμον⟩ μόνον Diano   11 ἀλλ' ἁπλῶς εἰς τὰ Kochalsky: ἀλλὰ πλεῖστα codd.: ἀλλ' εἰς τὰ Usener   11 βίος *SV* 12: om. codd.

1–3 Cf. **N 6–7**.

3–5 Construe τῶν νομισθέντων . . . δικαίων, following Bailey [117] ad loc., as a partitive genitive with τὸ ἐπιμαρτυρούμενον. For ἐπιμαρτύρησις as a method of testing empirical generalizations, see vol. 1, 94–5.

8–11 The requirement of 'fitting the πρόληψις' is repeated in *RS* 38; cf. **17E** and **C 1**, which repeats the point about avoiding 'empty words'. It suits the thought and Epicurean usage to take the πρόληψις to be of utility rather than justice. For a Stoic use of 'fitting' πρόληψις to particular instances, see **40S**.

22 Society

11–12   Clay [268] suggests Solon fr. 11 Diehl³ as Epicurus' model for this maxim: ἐξ ἀνέμων δὲ θάλασσα ταράσσεται· ἦν δέ τις αὐτὴν μὴ κινῇ πάντων ἐστὶ δικαιοτάτη. Certainly the image expressed by γαλήνη was a favourite in Epicureanism; for a wealth of parallels, see Usener [133] s.v.

C Epicurus, RS 7, 40

(1) [7] ἔνδοξοι καὶ περίβλεπτοί τινες ἐβουλήθησαν γενέσθαι, τὴν ἐξ ἀνθρώπων ἀσφάλειαν οὕτω νομίζοντες περιποιήσεσθαι. ὥστ' εἰ μὲν ἀσφαλὴς ὁ τῶν τοιούτων βίος, ἀπέλαβον τὸ τῆς φύσεως ἀγαθόν· εἰ δὲ μὴ ἀσφαλής, οὐκ ἔχουσιν οὗ ἕνεκα ἐξ ἀρχῆς κατὰ τὸ τῆς φύσεως οἰκεῖον ὠρέχθησαν. (2) [40] ὅσοι τὴν δύναμιν ἔσχον τοῦ τὸ θαρρεῖν μάλιστα ἐκ τῶν 5 ὁμορούντων παρασκευάσασθαι, οὕτω καὶ ἐβίωσαν μετ' ἀλλήλων ἥδιστα τὸ βεβαιότατον πίστωμα ἔχοντες, καὶ πληρεστάτην οἰκειότητα ἀπολαβόντες οὐκ ὠδύραντο ὡς πρὸς ἔλεον τὴν τοῦ τελευτήσαντος προκαταστροφήν.

5 τὸ Meibom: τε BP: om. F   6 οὕτω BP: οὗτοι F   ἥδιστα τὸ Usener: ἥδιστον τὸν B: ἥδιστον FP

1–5   Lucretius develops the point at length, L 1120ff., but without entertaining the theoretical possibility that such a life could achieve ἀσφάλεια. What is κατὰ φύσιν ἀγαθόν is anything that does this; cf. RS 6. With τὸ τῆς φύσεως οἰκεῖον, cf. 21B 20–1.

8   The emphasis falls on ἔλεον. Our dead friends are not to be pitied, since death cannot mar their happiness; cf. 24C 2. Likewise, the wise man will be indifferent to his own funeral, Q 10. But if Epicurean sympathy differs from conventional mourning, F 6, the school stressed its rejection of Stoic ἀπάθεια; cf. Q 4, 8, 13, and Usener 120.

D Epicurus, SV 58, 70, 79

(1) [58] ἐκλυτέον ἑαυτοὺς ἐκ τοῦ περὶ τὰ ἐγκύκλια καὶ πολιτικὰ δεσμωτηρίου. (2) [70] μηδέν σοι ἐν βίῳ πραχθείη ὃ φόβον παρέξει σοι, εἰ γνωσθήσεται τῷ πλησίον. (3) [79] ὁ ἀτάραχος ἑαυτῷ καὶ ἑτέρῳ ἀόχλητος.

2 δεσμωτηρίου Usener: -α cod.

1 πολιτικά   Epicurus' injunction to avoid politics is not a recommendation to opt completely out of community life, but to abstain from a public career; cf. Philodemus, Rhet. 2.58, 16 (=Epicurus 10.4 Arrighetti [119]), where Epicurus contrasts 'life's safety' with πολιτικὴ ἀγωνία.

2–3   Cf. A 4–5.

3   The undisturbed man resembles the Epicurean divinity; cf. RS 1 οὔτε αὐτὸ πράγματα ἔχει οὔτε ἄλλῳ παρέχει, and 23J.

E Epicurus, RS 27–8

(1) [27] ὧν ἡ σοφία παρασκευάζεται εἰς τὴν τοῦ ὅλου βίου μακαριότητα, πολὺ μέγιστόν ἐστιν ἡ τῆς φιλίας κτῆσις. (2) [28] ἡ αὐτὴ γνώμη θαρρεῖν τε

131

Epicurean ethics

ἐποίησεν ὑπὲρ τοῦ μηθὲν αἰώνιον εἶναι δεινὸν μηδὲ πολυχρόνιον, καὶ τὴν ἐν
αὐτοῖς τοῖς ὡρισμένοις ἀσφάλειαν φιλίας μάλιστα κατεῖδε συντελουμένην.

2 ἐστιν om. F   4 κατεῖδε Madvig (cf. Cicero, *Fin.* 1.68): κατεῖναι codd.

2–4 We interpret thus: in coming to see that conventionally regarded evils (death
and severe pain, cf. 21C, 25J) are 'limited', we also recognize that these limits are a
safeguard to friendship, since convinced Epicureans will not give up their friends for
fear of death or pain; cf. Cicero, *Fin.* 1.49. Cicero's actual version of the maxim, *Fin.*
1.68, is unconvincing as a translation of line 4, and also fails to connect that line
coherently with what precedes: *eadem sententia confirmavit animum ne quod aut
sempiternum aut diuturnum timeret malum, quae perspexit in hoc ipso uitae spatio amicitiae
praesidium esse firmissimum.*

F Epicurus, *SV* 23, 28, 34, 39, 52, 66, 78

(1) [23] πᾶσα φιλία δι᾽ ἑαυτὴν ἀρετή, ἀρχὴν δὲ εἴληφεν ἀπὸ τῆς ὠφελείας.
(2) [28] οὔτε τοὺς προχείρους εἰς φιλίαν οὔτε τοὺς ὀκνηροὺς δοκιμαστέον·
δεῖ δὲ καὶ παρακινδυνεῦσαι [χάριν] χάριν φιλίας. (3) [34] οὐχ οὕτως χρείαν
ἔχομεν τῆς χρείας παρὰ τῶν φίλων ὡς τῆς πίστεως τῆς περὶ τῆς χρείας. (4)
[39] οὔθ᾽ ὁ τὴν χρείαν ἐπιζητῶν διὰ παντὸς φίλος οὔθ᾽ ὁ μηδέποτε   5
συνάπτων· ὁ μὲν γὰρ καπηλεύει τῇ χάριτι τὴν ἀμοιβήν, ὁ δὲ ἀποκόπτει τὴν
περὶ τοῦ μέλλοντος εὐελπιστίαν. (5) [52] ἡ φιλία περιχορεύει τὴν
οἰκουμένην κηρύττουσα δὴ πᾶσιν ἡμῖν ἐγείρεσθαι ἐπὶ τὸν μακαρισμόν. (6)
[66] συμπαθῶμεν τοῖς φίλοις οὐ θρηνοῦντες ἀλλὰ φροντίζοντες. (7) [78] ὁ
γενναῖος περὶ σοφίαν καὶ φιλίαν μάλιστα γίγνεται· ὧν τὸ μέν ἐστι θνητὸν   10
ἀγαθόν, τὸ δὲ ἀθάνατον.

1 ἀρετή cod.: αἱρετή Usener   3 χάριν¹ secl. Bailey   10 θνητὸν Hartel: νοητὸν cod.

1   We think Usener's emendation has been accepted too readily (cf. Bollack [274],
223–6), especially since on either reading a verb has to be supplied, and the problem of
assigning a *per se* value to something other than pleasure is unaffected. For discussion,
cf. Müller [275], 118ff.; Rist [95], 131–2; and Long [280], 305.
3   Cf. Q 16, 25.
4   With πίστεως, cf. πίστωμα, C 7.
7–8   For discussion, see Bailey [117] ad loc.
9   See note on C 8.
11   Bailey explains ἀθάνατον, 'because it gives a man happiness equivalent to that
of the gods'. But the texts he cites should apply equally to σοφία. It seems better to
regard friendship as a good for the survivor which transcends the death of a friend; cf.
line 9, and Usener 213, ἡδὺ ἡ φίλου μνήμη τεθνηκότος. Also relevant may be the
conception of the Epicurean philosopher/friend as a god; cf. Rist [95], 136; Frischer
[108], 77–86.

G Plutarch, *Contra Ep. beat.* 1097A (Usener 544, part)

αὐτοὶ δὲ δήπου λέγουσιν ὡς τὸ εὖ ποιεῖν ἥδιόν ἐστι τοῦ πάσχειν.

Context: criticism of Epicurean hedonism.

At Plutarch, *Mor.* 778C, Epicurus himself is credited with the claim, τοῦ εὖ πάσχειν τὸ εὖ ποιεῖν οὐ μόνον κάλλιον ἀλλὰ καὶ ἥδιον εἶναι.

H Plutarch, *Col.* 1111B (Usener 546)

καὶ γὰρ τὴν πρόνοιαν ἀναιρῶν εὐσέβειαν ἀπολιπεῖν λέγει, καὶ τῆς ἡδονῆς ἕνεκα τὴν φιλίαν αἱρούμενος ὑπὲρ τῶν φίλων τὰς μεγίστας ἀλγηδόνας ἀναδέχεσθαι.

Context: criticism of Epicurus for alleged inconsistencies.

I Seneca, *Ep.* 19.10 (Usener 542)

"ante" inquit [*sc.* Epicurus] "circumspiciendum est cum quibus edas et bibas quam quid edas et bibas; nam sine amico visceratio leonis ac lupi vita est."

Context: conclusion of a letter recommending Lucilius to take more *otium*.

J Lucretius 5.925–38, 953–61

(1) at genus humanum multo fuit illud in arvis	925
durius, ut decuit, tellus quod dura creasset,	
et maioribus et solidis magis ossibus intus	
fundatum, validis aptum per viscera nervis,	
nec facile ex aestu nec frigore quod caperetur	
nec novitate cibi nec labi corporis ulla.	930
(2) multaque per caelum solis volventia lustra	
vulgivago vitam tractabant more ferarum.	
nec robustus erat curvi moderator aratri	
quisquam, nec scibat ferro molirier arva	
nec nova defodere in terram virgulta neque altis	935
arboribus veteres decidere falcibu' ramos.	
quod sol atque imbres dederant, quod terra crearat	
sponte sua, satis id placabat pectora donum . . .	938
(3) necdum res igni scibant tractare neque uti	953
pellibus et spoliis corpus vestire ferarum,	
sed nemora atque cavos montis silvasque colebant	955
et frutices inter condebant squalida membra	
verbera ventorum vitare imbrisque coacti.	
(4) nec commune bonum poterant spectare neque ullis	
moribus inter se scibant nec legibus uti.	
quod cuique obtulerat praedae fortuna, ferebat	960
sponte sua sibi quisque valere et vivere doctus.	

925 at Lachmann: *et* OQ   934 *molirier* ed. Brix.: *mollirier* (vel *mollerier*) codd.   953 *scibant* AB: *scribant* OQU: *sciebant* Q(corr.)   959 *scibant* AB: *sciebant* OQU

Context: the life of early man, following the generation of vegetation and other living things, including extinct monsters, from the earth.

Lucretius stresses the self-sufficiency and bestiality (note 932) of this life by contrasting it with the technology and social developments of the next stage; see **K**. Contrary to what has often been claimed, he is not an advocate of primitivism; cf. Furley [278], 14–17.

K Lucretius 5.1011–27

(1) inde casas postquam ac pellis ignemque pararunt,
et mulier coniuncta viro concessit in unum
conubium, prolemque ex se videre creatam,
tum genus humanum primum mollescere coepit.
ignis enim curavit ut alsia corpora frigus   1015
non ita iam possent caeli sub tegmine ferre,
et Venus imminuit viris puerique parentum
blanditiis facile ingenium fregere superbum.
(2) tunc et amicitiem coeperunt iungere aventes
finitimi inter se nec laedere nec violari,   1020
et pueros commendarunt muliebreque saeclum,
vocibus et gestu cum balbe significarent
imbecillorum esse aequum misererier omnis.
(3) nec tamen omnimodis poterat concordia gigni,
sed bona magnaque pars servabat foedera caste;   1025
aut genus humanum iam tum foret omne peremptum
nec potuisset adhuc perducere saecla propago.

1013 *conubium* Lachmann: *cognita sunt* codd.: post 1012 lacunam ind. Marullus   1020 *violari* Lachmann: *violare* OQ   1023 *omnis* Marullus: *omni* OQ   1026 *aut* O: *haud* Q

Context: transition to the origins of civilized life, following a contrast between ancient and modern ways of death.

For a study of the features common to Lucretius' and other ancient accounts of the origin of society, cf. Cole [273], 30ff., and see also **67Y** with note.

1019–20   Lucretius makes the Epicurean account of justice (cf. **A**) the motive for forming the first friendships; but this does not imply that his *amicities* is something other than Epicurus' conception of φιλία (as Konstan [253], 43, claims) since we have his own word for the utilitarian origins of friendship; cf. **F** 1, **O** 6–7, and *inimicitiis*, **L** 1146.

L Lucretius 5.1105–57

(1) inque dies magis hi victum vitamque priorem   1105
commutare novis monstrabant rebus et igni
ingenio qui praestabant et corde vigebant.
condere coeperunt urbis arcemque locare
praesidium reges ipsi sibi perfugiumque,
et pecua atque agros divisere atque dedere   1110
pro facie cuiusque et viribus ingenioque;

nam facies multum valuit viresque vigebant.
(2) posterius res inventast aurumque repertum,
quod facile et validis et pulchris dempsit honorem;
divitioris enim sectam plerumque sequuntur   1115
quamlibet et fortes et pulchro corpore creti.
quod siquis vera vitam ratione gubernet,
divitiae grandes homini sunt vivere parce
aequo animo; neque enim est umquam penuria parvi.
(3) at claros homines voluerunt se atque potentis,   1120
ut fundamento stabili fortuna maneret
et placidam possent opulenti degere vitam,
nequiquam, quoniam ad summum succedere honorem
certantes iter infestum fecere viai,
et tamen e summo, quasi fulmen, deicit ictos   1125
invidia interdum contemptim in Tartara taetra;
invidia quoniam, ceu fulmine, summa vaporant   [1131]
plerumque et quae sunt aliis magis edita cumque;   [1132]
ut satius multo iam sit parere quietum   [1127]
quam regere imperio res velle et regna tenere.   1130 [1128]
(4) proinde sine incassum defessi sanguine sudent,   [1129]
angustum per iter luctantes ambitionis;   [1130]
quandoquidem sapiunt alieno ex ore petuntque
res ex auditis potius quam sensibus ipsis,
nec magis id nunc est neque erit mox quam fuit ante.   1135
(5) ergo regibus occisis subversa iacebat
pristina maiestas soliorum et sceptra superba,
et capitis summi praeclarum insigne cruentum
sub pedibus vulgi magnum lugebat honorem;
nam cupide conculcatur nimis ante metutum.   1140
res itaque ad summam faecem turbasque redibat,
imperium sibi cum ac summatum quisque petebat.
(6) inde magistratum partim docuere creare
iuraque constituere, ut vellent legibus uti.
nam genus humanum, defessum vi colere aevum,   1145
ex inimicitiis languebat: quo magis ipsum
sponte sua cecidit sub leges artaque iura.
acrius ex ira quod enim se quisque parabat
ulcisci quam nunc concessumst legibus aequis,
hanc ob rem est homines pertaesum vi colere aevum.   1150
(7) inde metus maculat poenarum praemia vitae.
circumretit enim vis atque iniuria quemque
atque, unde exortast, ad eum plerumque revertit,
nec facilest placidam ac pacatam degere vitam

qui violat factis communia foedera pacis.   1155
etsi fallit enim divum genus humanumque,
perpetuo tamen id fore clam diffidere debet.

1105 *hi victum* Naugerius: *invictum* OQ: *hinc victum* Bockemüller   1110 *pecua* Ernout: *pecudes* OQ: *pecus*
Lachmann   1124 *certantes iter* Marullus: *certantesque inter* O: *certantesque* Q   1131-2 huc transtulit
Munro   1141 *res itaque* l 31: *restaque* OQ   *redibat* l 31: *recidat* Q: *recidit* O   1145 *vi colere* l 31:
vicere O: *vigere* Q: *vi gerere* B

Context: the further development of civilization, following accounts of the origins of
language (=**19B**) and human manipulation of fire.
    1117–19   Cf. **21F 3**.
    1120–30   Cf. **C 1**.
    1151–7   Cf. **A 4–5**.

M Porphyry, *Abst.* 1.7.1–9.4

(1) οἱ δὲ ἀπὸ τοῦ Ἐπικούρου ὥσπερ γενεαλογίαν μακρὰν διεξιόντες φασὶν
ὡς οἱ παλαιοὶ νομοθέται, ἀπιδόντες εἰς τὴν τοῦ βίου κοινωνίαν τῶν
ἀνθρώπων καὶ τὰς πρὸς ἀλλήλους πράξεις, ἀνόσιον ἐπεφήμισαν τὴν
ἀνθρώπου σφαγὴν καὶ ἀτιμίας οὐ τὰς τυχούσας προσῆψαν, τάχα μὲν καὶ
φυσικῆς τινος οἰκειώσεως ὑπαρχούσης τοῖς ἀνθρώποις πρὸς ἀνθρώπους   5
διὰ τὴν ὁμοιότητα τῆς μορφῆς καὶ τῆς ψυχῆς εἰς τὸ μὴ προχείρως φθείρειν
τὸ τοιοῦτον ζῷον ὥσπερ ἕτερόν τι τῶν συγκεχωρημένων· οὐ μὴν ἀλλὰ τὴν
γε πλείστην αἰτίαν τοῦ δυσχερανθῆναι τοῦτο καὶ ἀνόσιον ἐπιφημισθῆναι
τὸ μὴ συμφέρειν εἰς τὴν ὅλην τοῦ βίου σύστασιν ὑπολαβεῖν. (2) ἀπὸ γὰρ τῆς
τοιαύτης ἀρχῆς οἱ μὲν παρακολουθήσαντες τῷ συμφέροντι τοῦ διορίσμα-   10
τος οὐδὲν προσεδεήθησαν ἄλλης αἰτίας τῆς ἀνειργούσης αὐτοὺς ἀπὸ τῆς
πράξεως ταύτης, οἱ δὲ μὴ δυνάμενοι λαβεῖν αἴσθησιν ἱκανὴν τούτου τὸ
μέγεθος τῆς ζημίας δεδιότες ἀπείχοντο τοῦ κτείνειν προχείρως ἀλλήλους.
ὧν ἑκάτερον φαίνεται καὶ νῦν ἔτι συμβαῖνον . . . (3) οὐδὲν γὰρ ἐξ ἀρχῆς
βιαίως κατέστη νόμιμον οὔτε μετὰ γραφῆς οὔτε ἄνευ γραφῆς τῶν   15
διαμενόντων νῦν καὶ διαδίδοσθαι πεφυκότων, ἀλλὰ συγχωρησάντων αὐτῷ
καὶ τῶν χρησαμένων. φρονήσει γὰρ ψυχῆς, οὐ ῥώμῃ σώματος καὶ
δυναστευτικῇ δουλώσει, τῶν ὄχλων διήνεγκαν οἱ τὰ τοιαῦτα τοῖς πολλοῖς
εἰσηγούμενοι, καὶ τοὺς μὲν εἰς ἐπιλογισμὸν τοῦ χρησίμου καταστήσαντες
ἀλόγως αὐτοῦ πρότερον αἰσθανομένους καὶ πολλάκις ἐπιλανθανομένους,   20
τοὺς δὲ τῷ μεγέθει τῶν ἐπιτιμίων καταπλήξαντες. οὐ γὰρ ἦν ἑτέρῳ
χρῆσθαι φαρμάκῳ πρὸς τὴν τοῦ συμφέροντος ἀμαθίαν ἢ τῷ φόβῳ τῆς
ἀφωρισμένης ἀπὸ τοῦ νόμου ζημίας. αὕτη γὰρ κατέχει μόνη καὶ νῦν τοὺς
τυχόντας τῶν ἀνθρώπων καὶ κωλύει τὸ μήτε κοινῇ μήτε ἰδίᾳ τὸ
ἀλυσιτελὲς πράττειν. (4) εἰ δὲ πάντες ἐδύναντο βλέπειν ὁμοίως καὶ   25
μνημονεύειν τὸ συμφέρον, οὐδὲν ἂν προσεδέοντο νόμων, ἀλλ' αὐθαιρέτως
τὰ μὲν εὐλαβοῦντο τῶν ἀπειρημένων, τὰ δὲ ἔπραττον τῶν προστεταγ-
μένων. ἱκανὴ γὰρ ἡ τοῦ χρησίμου καὶ βλαβεροῦ θεωρία τῶν μὲν φυγὴν
παρασκευάσαι, τῶν δὲ αἵρεσιν. ἡ δὲ τῆς ζημίας ἀνάτασις πρὸς τοὺς μὴ

προορωμένους τὸ λυσιτελοῦν. ἀναγκάζει γὰρ δεσπόζειν ἐπικρεμαμένη 30
ταῖς ἀγούσαις ἐπὶ τὰς ἀσυμφόρους πράξεις ὁρμαῖς, καὶ βίᾳ συναναγκάζει
τὸ δέον ποιεῖν. (5) ἐπεὶ καὶ τὸν ἀκούσιον φόνον οὐκ ἔξω πάσης ζημίας
κατέστησαν οἱ νομοθέται, ὅπως μηδεμίαν ἐνδῶσι πρόφασιν τοῖς ἑκουσίως
τὰ τῶν ἀκουσίως δρώντων ἔργα μιμεῖσθαι προαιρουμένοις, ἀλλ' ὅπως μὴ
ἀφύλακτον ᾖ μηδὲ ἠμελημένον τὸ τοιοῦτο, ὥστε πολλὰ πρὸς ἀλήθειαν 35
ἀκούσια συμβαίνειν. οὐ γὰρ συνέφερεν οὐδὲ τοῦτο διὰ τὰς αὐτὰς αἰτίας δι'
ἃς καὶ τὸ καθ' ἑκούσιον τρόπον φθείρειν ἀλλήλους. (6) ὥστε τῶν ἀκουσίων
τῶν μὲν παρὰ τὴν ἀστάθμητον αἰτίαν καὶ ἀφύλακτον γιγνομένων
ἀνθρωπίνῃ φύσει, τῶν δὲ παρὰ τὴν ἡμετέραν ἀμέλειαν καὶ ἀνεπίστατον
τῆς διαφορᾶς, βουληθέντες κωλῦσαι τὴν βλάπτουσαν τοὺς πλησίον 40
ῥαθυμίαν, οὐκ ἀθῷον κατέστησαν ζημίας οὐδὲ τὴν ἀκούσιον πρᾶξιν, ἀλλὰ
τῷ φόβῳ τῶν ἐπιτιμίων ἀφεῖλον τὸ πολὺ τῆς τοιαύτης ἁμαρτίας. (7) οἶμαι
δ' ἔγωγε καὶ τοὺς συγκεχωρημένους ὑπὸ τοῦ νόμου φόνους τὰς
ἀφοσιώσεις λαμβάνειν τὰς εἰθισμένας διὰ τῶν καθαρμῶν παρ' οὐδεμίαν
ἑτέραν αἰτίαν ὑπὸ τῶν πρώτων καλῶς ταῦτα εἰσηγησαμένων ἢ παρὰ τὸ 45
τῆς ἑκουσίου πράξεως ὅτι πλεῖστον βούλεσθαι τοὺς ἀνθρώπους ἀφιστάναι.
πανταχόθεν γὰρ ἐδέοντο τοῦ κωλύσοντος ἑτοίμως πράττειν τὸ μὴ
συμφέρον οἱ τυχόντες. (8) ὅθεν οὐ μόνον ζημίας ἔταξαν οἱ πρῶτοι τοῦτο
συνειδότες, ἀλλὰ καὶ ἕτερον φόβον ἄλογον ἐπήρτησαν, οὐ καθαροὺς
ἐπιφημίσαντες εἶναι τοὺς ὅπως οὖν ἄνθρωπον ἀνελόντας, μὴ χρησαμένους 50
καθαρμοῖς. τὸ γὰρ ἀνόητον τῆς ψυχῆς ποικίλως παιδαγωγηθὲν ἦλθεν εἰς
τὴν καθεστῶσαν ἡμερότητα, προσμηχανωμένων ἐπὶ τῆς ἀλόγου φορᾶς
ἐπιθυμίας τιθασεύματα τῶν ἐξ ἀρχῆς τὰ πλήθη διακοσμησάντων· ὧν ἐστι
καὶ τὸ μὴ κτείνειν ἀλλήλους ἀκρίτως.

9 τὸ Reiske: τῷ codd.   18 δουλώσει Reiske: δουλεύσει codd.   40 τοὺς Fogerolles: αὐτοὺς vel αὖ
τοὺς codd.: αὐτοὺς ⟨τοὺς⟩ Bouffartigue   45 καλῶς Reiske: κακῶς codd.   53 τιθασεύματα τῶν ἐξ
ἀρχῆς Reiske: τιθασσευμάτων ἐξ ἀρχῆς τῶν codd.   διακοσμησάντων Bouffartigue: διακονησάντων
codd.

Context: part of a survey of philosophers hostile to the vegetarianism Porphyry
attributes to Pythagoras and Empedocles. In concluding this survey, Abst. 1.26.4,
Porphyry refers to τοιαῦτα μὲν καὶ τὰ παρὰ . . . Ἑρμάρχῳ [Ἑρμάχῳ codd., corr.
Bernays] . . . τῷ Ἐπικουρείῳ, which is the basis for attributing the gist, if not the
exact wording of M–N, to Hermarchus. Cf. Krohn [137], 6–8; Philippson [272], 315–
19, Cole [273], 71ff.; Goldschmidt [276]; Müller [275], 74ff.

4–7   This additional reason for refraining from homicide, where οἰκείωσις recalls
Stoicism (cf. 57D 2, F, H 1), reads like Porphyry's insertion or embellishment.

19 ἐπιλογισμόν   Cf. N 16, and see note on 21V 1.

48–9   The reference to οἱ συνειδότες recalls the contribution of experts to the
refinement of language, 19A 4. As noted in vol. 1, 135 (and cf. Cole [273], 73), the
evolution of justice from a natural recognition of utility to a codified legal system
precisely parallels the Epicurean account of language development. Cf. also the
distinction between the spontaneous formation of social groups, K 1019–20, and the
subsequent establishment of laws, L 1143–7, which closely resembles M 14–21, 51–3.

Epicurean ethics

Goldschmidt [276], 128–70, seems to conflate justice with the institution of laws, which runs quite counter to **B 2**, and he also understates the continuity between the uncontrived perception of utility (cf. **M** 25–9, **N** 4–23) and the legislators' formal innovations. He was unduly influenced, in our opinion, by the Marxist line of interpretation (cf. Farrington [93], 27; Müller [275], 37ff.) that governmental organization of social life is not deemed to be natural in Epicureanism, but an accidental product of convention. Against this, see Long [280], 287–93, 313–16.

N Porphyry, *Abst.* 1.10.1–12.7

(1) τῶν δὲ λοιπῶν ζώων εἰκότως οὐδὲν διεκώλυσαν φθείρειν οἱ πρῶτοι διορίσαντες ἅ τε δεῖ ποιεῖν ἡμᾶς καὶ ἃ μή· τὸ γὰρ συμφέρον ἐπὶ τούτων ἐκ τῆς ἐναντίας ἀπετελεῖτο πράξεως. οὐ γὰρ δυνατὸν ἦν σῴζεσθαι μὴ πειρωμένους ἀμύνεσθαι αὐτὰ συντρεφομένους μετ' ἀλλήλων. (2) διαμνη-
μονεύοντες δέ τινες τῶν τότε χαριεστάτων ὡς αὐτοί τε ἀπέσχοντο τοῦ 5
κτείνειν διὰ τὸ χρήσιμον πρὸς τὴν σωτηρίαν, τοῖς τε λοιποῖς ἐνεποίουν
μνήμην τοῦ ἀποβαίνοντος ἐν ταῖς μετ' ἀλλήλων συντροφαῖς, ὅπως
ἀπεχόμενοι τοῦ συγγενοῦς διαφυλάττωσι τὴν κοινωνίαν, ἣ συνήργει πρὸς
τὴν ἰδίαν ἑκάστου σωτηρίαν. οὐ μόνον δὲ χρήσιμον ἦν τὸ χωρίζεσθαι μηδὲ
λυμαντικὸν ποιεῖν μηδὲν τῶν ἐπὶ τὸν αὐτὸν τόπον συνειλεγμένων πρὸς τὸ 10
τῶν ἀλλοφύλων ἐξόρισμα ζῴων, ἀλλὰ καὶ πρὸς ἀνθρώπους τοὺς ἐπὶ βλάβῃ
παραγιγνομένους. μέχρι μὲν οὖν τινος διὰ ταύτην ἀπείχοντο τοῦ
συγγενοῦς, ὅσον ἐβάδιζεν εἰς τὴν αὐτὴν κοινωνίαν τῶν ἀναγκαίων ... (3)
ἐλθόντος δὲ ἐπὶ πλέον τοῦ χρόνου καὶ τῆς δι' ἀλλήλων γενέσεως μακρὰν
προηκούσης, ἐξεωσμένων δὲ τῶν ἀλλοφύλων ζῴων †καὶ τῆς παρασπάρ- 1;
σεως†, ἐπιλογισμὸν ἔλαβόν τινες τοῦ συμφέροντος ἐν ταῖς πρὸς ἀλλήλων
τροφαῖς, οὐ μόνον ἄλογον μνήμην. (4) ὅθεν ἐπειράθησαν βεβαιοτέρως
ἀνεῖρξαι τοὺς προχείρως φθείροντας ἀλλήλους καὶ τὴν βοήθειαν ἀσθενεσ-
τέραν κατασκευάζοντας διὰ τὴν τοῦ παρεληλυθότος λήθην. πειρώμενοι δὴ
τοῦτο δρᾶν τὰς ἔτι μενούσας καὶ νῦν κατὰ πόλεις τε καὶ ἔθνη νομοθεσίας 2(
εἰσήνεγκαν, ἐπακολουθήσαντος τοῦ πλήθους αὐτοῖς ἑκουσίως παρὰ τὸ
μᾶλλον ἤδη τοῦ συμφέροντος ἐν τῇ μετ' ἀλλήλων ἀθροίσει λαμβάνειν
αἴσθησιν. ὁμοίως γὰρ εἰς τὴν ἀφοβίαν συνήργει τό τε λυμαντικὸν πᾶν
κτεινόμενον ἀφειδῶς καὶ τὸ χρήσιμον πρὸς τὴν τούτου φθορὰν διατηρούμενον. ὅθεν εἰκότως τὸ μὲν ἀπηγορεύθη, τὸ δὲ οὐκ ἐκωλύθη τῶν 2
εἰρημένων. (5) ἐκεῖνο δὲ λέγειν οὐκ ἔστιν, ὡς ἔνια τῶν ζῴων οὐ φθαρτικὰ
τῆς ἀνθρωπίνης ὄντα φύσεως οὐδὲ καθ' ἕτερον οὐδένα τρόπον λυμαινόμενα
τοὺς βίους συγκεχώρηκεν ὁ νόμος ἀναιρεῖν ἡμῖν. οὐδὲν γάρ, ὡς εἰπεῖν, ἐστὶ
το:οῦτο τῶν ὑπὸ τοῦ νόμου συγκεχωρημένων, ὅπερ οὐκ ἐώμενον
λαμβάνειν τὴν ὑπερβολὴν τῆς ἀφθονίας βλαπτικὸν γίγνοιτ' ἂν ἡμῶν· ἐν δὲ 3(
τῷ νῦν πλήθει διατηρούμενον χρείας παρέχεταί τινας εἰς τὸν βίον ... ὅθεν
τὰ μὲν [sc. λέοντας καὶ λύκους κτλ.] ἄρδην φθείρομεν, τῶν δὲ [sc. προβάτου
καὶ βοῦ κτλ.] τὸ πλεῖον τῆς συμμετρίας ἀφαιροῦμεν. (6) διὰ παραπλησίους
ταῖς εἰρημέναις αἰτίας καὶ τὰ περὶ τὴν ἐδωδὴν διορισθῆναι τῶν ἐμψύχων

138

νομιστέον ὑπὸ τῶν ἐξ ἀρχῆς ταῦτα καταλαβόντων νόμῳ, ἐπὶ δὲ τῶν οὐκ   35
ἐδωδίμων αἴτιον τὸ συμφέρον καὶ ἀσύμφορον. ὥστε τοὺς λέγοντας ὅτι πᾶν
τὸ καλὸν καὶ δίκαιον κατὰ τὰς ἰδίας ὑπολήψεις ἐστὶ περὶ τῶν νενομοθετη-
μένων ἠλιβάτου τινὸς γέμειν εὐηθείας. οὐ γάρ ἐστιν οὕτως ἔχον τοῦτο,
ἀλλ᾽ ὅνπερ τρόπον ἢ ἐπὶ λοιπῶν συμφερόντων, οἷον ὑγιεινῶν τε καὶ ἑτέρων
μυρίων εἰδῶν ⟨ . . . ⟩ (7) ἀλλὰ διαμαρτάνουσιν ἐν πολλοῖς τῶν τε κοινῶν   40
ὁμοίως καὶ τῶν ἰδίων. καὶ γὰρ τὰ παραπλησίως ἐφαρμόττοντα νομοθετή-
ματα πᾶσιν οὐ καθορῶσί τινες, ἀλλ᾽ οἳ μὲν τῶν ἀδιαφόρων δοξάζοντες
εἶναι παραλείπουσιν, οἳ δὲ τὴν ἐναντίαν δόξαν ὑπὲρ αὐτῶν ἔχουσιν, καὶ τὰ
μὴ καθόλου συμφέροντα πανταχοῦ τινες οἴονται συμφέρειν. ὅθεν διὰ τὴν
αἰτίαν ταύτην ἀντέχονται τῶν οὐκ ἐφαρμοττόντων, εἰ καὶ ἐπί τινων   45
ἐξευρίσκουσι τά τε πρὸς αὐτοὺς λυσιτελῆ καὶ τὰ κοινὴν ἔχοντα τὴν
ὠφέλειαν. (8) ὧν ἐστι καὶ τὰ περὶ τὰς ἐδωδὰς τῶν ἐμψύχων καὶ φθορὰς ἐν
τοῖς πλείστοις τῶν ἐθνῶν διατεταγμένα διὰ τὸ τῆς χώρας ἴδιον, οἷς οὐκ
ἀναγκαῖον ἐμμένειν ἡμῖν διὰ τὸ μηδὲ τὸν αὐτὸν οἰκεῖν τόπον. (9) εἰ μὲν οὖν
ἠδύναντο ποιήσασθαί τινα συνθήκην ὥσπερ πρὸς ἀνθρώπους οὕτω καὶ   50
πρὸς τὰ λοιπὰ τῶν ζῴων ὑπὲρ τοῦ μὴ κτείνειν μήτε πρὸς ἡμῶν ἀκρίτως
αὐτὰ κτείνεσθαι, καλῶς εἶχε μέχρι τούτου τὸ δίκαιον ἐξάγειν· ἐπιτεταμέ-
νον γὰρ ἐγίγνετο πρὸς τὴν ἀσφάλειαν. (10) ἐπειδὴ δὲ τῶν ἀμηχάνων ἦν
κοινωνῆσαι νόμου τὰ μὴ δεχόμενα τῶν ζῴων λόγον, διὰ μὲν τοῦ τοιούτου
τρόπου τὸ συμφέρον οὐχ οἷόν τε κατασκευάσασθαι πρὸς τὴν ἀπὸ τῶν   55
ἄλλων ἐμψύχων ἀσφάλειαν μᾶλλόν περ ἢ τῶν ἀψύχων, ἐκ δὲ τοῦ τὴν
ἐξουσίαν λαμβάνειν, ἣν νῦν ἔχομεν, εἰς τὸ κτείνειν αὐτὰ μόνως ἐστὶ τὴν
ἐνδεχομένην ἔχειν ἀσφάλειαν. τοιαῦτα μὲν καὶ τὰ τῶν Ἐπικουρείων.

4 αὐτὰ Fogerolles: τοῦτο codd.   5 αὐτοί Reiske: αὐτοῦ codd.   10–11 τὸ . . . ἐξόρισμα Bouffartigue: τὸ . . . ἐξέρισμα codd.: τὸν . . . ἐξορισμὸν Valentinus   15 προηκούσης Abresch, Reiske:
προσηκούσης codd.   15–16 καὶ τῆς παρασπάρσεως vix sanum: παρασπάσεως ed. pr. et omnes edd.
ante Bouffartigue (quid velit non intellegimus)   22 ἀθροίσει Feliciano: ἀθροισθείση codd.   24
κτεινόμενον Feliciano: ἐκτεινόμενον codd.   26 δὲ Reiske: τε codd.   33 διὰ Reiske: δι' ἃ
codd.   34 αἰτίας Hercher: αἰτίαις codd.   35 νόμῳ Reiske: νόμων codd.   40 lacunam indi-
Bouffartigue   46 αὐτοὺς Hercher: αὐτοὺς codd.

Context: immediately following **M**.
13 ἀναγκαίων   Cf. **S** 4.
16–17   Cf. **M** 19–20.
40–9   These lines apply the lessons of **B** 1–2. For another Epicurean comment on
moral relativism, cf. **7D**.
49–53   See note on **A** 2.

O Cicero, *Fin.* 1.66–70

(1) tribus igitur modis video esse a nostris de amicitia disputatum. alii cum eas
voluptates quae ad amicos pertinerent negarent esse per se ipsas tam
expetendas quam nostras expeteremus, quo loco videtur quibusdam stabilitas
amicitiae vacillare, tuentur tamen eum locum seque facile, ut mihi videtur,

expediunt. (2) ut enim virtutes, de quibus ante dictum est, sic amicitiam   5
negant posse a voluptate discedere. nam cum solitudo et vita sine amicis
insidiarum et metus plena sit, ratio ipsa monet amicitias comparare, quibus
partis confirmatur animus et a spe pariendarum voluptatum seiungi non
potest. (3) atque ut odia, invidiae, despicationes adversantur voluptatibus, sic
amicitiae non modo fautrices fidelissimae, sed etiam effectrices sunt volupta-   10
tum tam amicis quam sibi; quibus non solum praesentibus fruuntur, sed etiam
spe eriguntur consequentis ac posteri temporis. quod quia nullo modo sine
amicitia firmam et perpetuam iucunditatem vitae tenere possumus neque vero
ipsam amicitiam tueri, nisi aeque amicos et nosmet ipsos diligamus, idcirco et
hoc ipsum efficitur in amicitia, et amicitia cum voluptate conectitur. nam et   15
laetamur amicorum laetitia aeque atque nostra et pariter dolemus angoribus.
quocirca eodem modo sapiens erit affectus erga amicum quo in se ipsum,
quosque labores propter suam voluptatem susciperet, eosdem suscipiet
propter amici voluptatem. . . . (4) sunt autem quidam Epicurei timidiores
paulo contra vestra convicia, sed tamen satis acuti, qui verentur ne, si   20
amicitiam propter nostram voluptatem expetendam putemus, tota amicitia
quasi claudicare videatur. itaque primos congressus copulationesque et
consuetudinum instituendarum voluntates fieri propter voluptatem; cum
autem usus progrediens familiaritatem effecerit, tum amorem efflorescere
tantum ut, etiamsi nulla sit utilitas ex amicitia, tamen ipsi amici propter se   25
ipsos amentur. etenim si loca, si fana, si urbes, si gymnasia, si campum, si
canes, si equos, si ludicra exercendi aut venandi consuetudine adamare
solemus, quanto id in hominum consuetudine facilius fieri poterit et iustius!
(5) sunt autem qui dicant foedus esse quoddam sapientium, ut ne minus
amicos quam se ipsos diligant. quod et posse fieri intellegimus et saepe etiam   30
vidimus, et perspicuum est nihil ad iucunde vivendum reperiri posse quod
coniunctione tali sit aptius. (6) quibus ex omnibus iudicari potest non modo
non impediri rationem amicitiae, si summum bonum in voluptate ponatur,
sed sine hoc institutionem omnino amicitiae non posse reperiri.

14 *nisi*] *ipsi* ARV   28 *poterit* edd.: *potuerit* codd.   30 *etiam* Davies: *enim* codd.

Cf. *Fin.* 2.78–85. This passage, and the general issue of friendship and altruism, are
discussed excellently by Mitsis [281]; we have benefited from reading his work in
typescript.

   5–19   This account chimes well with Epicurus' own comments; cf. especially **C 2**,
E 1, F, H.

   19–28   This account, according to Cicero (*Fin.* 2.82), was never stated by
Epicurus himself. It is a response to the Academic (cf. *vestra convicia*, 20), and probably
Stoic, objection that the affectionate element in friendship, 14–19, is not consistent
with its exclusively utilitarian foundation, 5–14; cf. *Fin.* 2.84–5. Hence the revisionary
claim that *amor* can become quite detached from *utilitas*, 24–6.

   29–30   This third account is too condensed to be fully intelligible, nor is it
clarified by Cicero's retort in *Fin.* 2.83. It should be regarded as a second revisionary

answer to the objection set out above. Instead of affection developing by association, as in the second account, the third seems to require 'loving a friend as much as oneself' to be a commitment built into the friendship from its outset.

P Diogenes of Oenoanda 25.2.3–11

καθ᾽ ἐκάστην | μὲν γὰρ ἀποτομὴν | τῆς γῆς ἄλλων ἄλλη | πατρίς ἐστιν, κατὰ δὲ | τὴν ὅλην περιοχὴν | τοῦδε τοῦ κόσμου μί|[α π]άντων πατρίς ἐσ|τιν ἡ πᾶσα γῆ καὶ εἷς | ὁ κόσμος οἶκος.

Context: discussion of what are called 'strangers', but are not really so.

The sentiment is close to that of the Stoic Aristo, **67H**, but no direct influence of Stoicism need be posited. See further on **S**.

Q Diogenes Laertius 10.117–20

(1) βλάβας ἐξ ἀνθρώπων ἢ διὰ μῖσος ἢ διὰ φθόνον ἢ διὰ καταφρόνησιν γίνεσθαι, ὧν τὸν σοφὸν λογισμῷ περιγίνεσθαι. (2) ἀλλὰ καὶ τὸν ἅπαξ γενόμενον σοφὸν μηκέτι τὴν ἐναντίαν λαμβάνειν διάθεσιν μηδὲ πλάττειν ἑκόντα· πάθεσι μᾶλλον συσχεθήσεσθαι, ⟨ὃ⟩ οὐκ ἂν ἐμποδίσαι πρὸς τὴν σοφίαν. οὐδὲ μὴν ἐκ πάσης σώματος ἕξεως σοφὸν γενέσθαι ἂν οὐδ᾽ ἐν παντὶ ⁵ ἔθνει. (3) κἂν στρεβλωθῇ δ᾽ ὁ σοφός, εἶναι αὐτὸν εὐδαίμονα ... ὅτε μέντοι στρεβλοῦται, ἔνθα καὶ μύζει καὶ οἰμώζει. (4) γυναικί τ᾽ οὐ μιγήσεσθαι τὸν σοφὸν ᾗ οἱ νόμοι ἀπαγορεύουσιν ... οὐδὲ κολάσειν οἰκέτας, ἐλεήσειν μέντοι καὶ συγγνώμην τινὶ ἕξειν τῶν σπουδαίων. (5) ἐρασθήσεσθαι τὸν σοφὸν οὐ δοκεῖ αὐτοῖς· οὐδὲ ταφῆς φροντιεῖν ... οὐδὲ ῥητορεύσειν ¹⁰ καλῶς ... καὶ μὴν καὶ γαμήσειν καὶ τεκνοποιήσειν τὸν σοφόν ... οὐδὲ πολιτεύσεσθαι ... οὐδὲ τυραννεύσειν· οὐδὲ κυνιεῖν ... οὐδὲ πτωχεύσειν. ἀλλὰ καὶ πηρωθέντα τὰς ὄψεις μεθέξειν αὐτὸν τοῦ βίου ... καὶ λυπήσεσθαι δὲ τὸν σοφόν ... καὶ δικάσεσθαι· καὶ συγγράμματα καταλείψειν· οὐ πανηγυριεῖν δέ· καὶ κτήσεως προνοήσεσθαι καὶ τοῦ μέλλοντος. φιλαγρή- ¹⁵ σειν τύχῃ τ᾽ ἀντιτάξεσθαι, φίλον τε οὐδένα προήσεσθαι. (6) εὐδοξίας ἐπὶ τοσοῦτον προνοήσεσθαι, ἐφ᾽ ὅσον μὴ καταφρονήσεσθαι. μᾶλλόν τε εὐφρανθήσεσθαι τῶν ἄλλων ἐν ταῖς θεωρίαις. εἰκόνας τε ἀναθήσειν. εἰ ἔχοι, ἀδιαφόρως ἂν σχοίη. μόνον τε τὸν σοφὸν ὀρθῶς ἂν περί τε μουσικῆς καὶ ποιητικῆς διαλέξασθαι· ποιήματα δὲ ἐνεργείᾳ οὐκ ἂν ποιῆσαι. οὐκ ²⁰ εἶναί τε ἕτερον ἑτέρου σοφώτερον. χρηματίσεσθαί τε, ἀλλ᾽ ἀπὸ μόνης σοφίας, ἀπορήσαντα. καὶ μόναρχον ἐν καιρῷ θεραπεύσειν. καὶ ἐπιχαρή- σεσθαί τινι ἐπὶ τῷ διορθώματι· καὶ σχολὴν κατασκευάσειν, ἀλλ᾽ οὐχ ὥστ᾽ ὀχλαγωγῆσαι· καὶ ἀναγνώσεσθαι ἐν πλήθει, ἀλλ᾽ οὐχ ἑκόντα· δογματιεῖν τε καὶ οὐκ ἀπορήσειν· καὶ καθ᾽ ὕπνους δὲ ὅμοιον ἔσεσθαι· καὶ ὑπὲρ φίλου ²⁵ ποτὲ τεθνήξεσθαι.

4 πάθεσι μᾶλλον codd.: πάθεσι μὴν Usener: πάθεσι μ⟨ὴν ὡς⟩ ἄλλον Kochalsky: πάθεσί ⟨τισι⟩ μᾶλλον Bignone   ⟨ὃ⟩ Kochalsky: lacunam ante ἂν ind. Usener   6 ἔθνει FP: ἔθει B   6 δ᾽FP(corr.): om. B   8 οὐδὲ Usener: οὔτε codd.   9 τῶν σπουδαίων F: τὸν σπουδαῖον BP   13 πηρωθέντα Bywater: πηρωθεὶς FP: πυρωθεὶς B   μεθέξειν fr.: μετέξει B: μετάξει FP   16 φίλον BP: φίλων

Epicurean ethics

F   προήσεσθαι Bignone: κτήσεσθαι codd.   18–26 εἰκόνας–τεθνήξεσθαι transtul. huc ex D.L.
10.121 Bignone   19 σχοίη Kühn: σχοίης codd.   20 δὲ Kochalsky: τε codd.   ἐνεργείᾳ Usener:
ἐνεργεῖν codd.

Context: an account of the views of Epicurus and his followers on the wise man.
The similarity to, and difference from, what is attested for Stoicism (cf. D.L. 7.121–
5) are probably deliberate (cf. vol. 1, 138–9) and not simply a doxographical
convenience. Some of what is said here can be assumed to postdate Epicurus.
Most of our omissions in sections 3–5 are of the books to which Diogenes refers for
various doctrines.

   1–2   Cf. L 1120–8, and for Stoics, D.L. 7.123.

   4   As our critical apparatus indicates, several scholars have attempted to get rid of
the assertion that the Epicurean wise man is *more* affected by feelings (sc. than others,
cf. μᾶλλον . . . τῶν ἄλλων, 17–18 below). This does seem a rank falsehood, given the
wise man's freedom from sexual passion, envy, fear of death etc. However, none of
the suggested emendations, except perhaps Usener's, seems at all plausible to us in
sense; and none at all explains the train of thought. The whole of 2–4 concerns the
wise man's διάθεσις. We take πάθεσι συσχεθήσεσθαι to expand and qualify μηδὲ
πλάττειν ἑκόντα: the wise man does not deliberately feign an unwise character; rather
(μᾶλλον, not 'more', as standardly interpreted) 'he will be genuinely moved by
feelings, but this will be no impediment to his wisdom'. Given the very truncated
style of this whole passage, with frequent asyndeton, this reading may even be
adequately supported by the text as it stands, although corruption may be suspected. If
this is on the right lines, the sentiment is anti-Stoic: a permanently wise character is
perfectly compatible with susceptibility to many ordinary human feelings.

   6–7   Likewise the Stoic sage will be happy even in the bull of Phalaris; cf. SVF
3.586. But he does not groan; cf. Epictetus, Diss. 2.13.17.

   7–8   Cf. 21G 3.

   8–9   Both forgiveness and pity are officially alien to the Stoic sage; cf. SVF 3.640–
1.

   9–10   The Stoic sage, by contrast, is allowed to be a lover of the young; cf. note to
66C.

   10–15   Rhetoric, politics, living as a Cynic, and suicide, are all permitted to the
Stoic sage, but grief (13) is not. Cf. 66; 67.

   19–20 μόνον–διαλέξασθαι   For the Stoic sage, cf. SVF 3.294, 654.

   20–1 οὐκ–σοφώτερον   For the same doctrine in Stoicism, cf. 61I 1.

   21–2 χρηματίσεσθαι–θεραπεύσειν   For Stoicism, see 67W.

R Plutarch, Col. 1124D

τελευτῶντος ἤδη τοῦ βιβλίου φησὶν [sc. ὁ Κωλώτης] ὅτι "τὸν βίον οἱ
νόμους διατάξαντες καὶ νόμιμα καὶ τὸ βασιλεύεσθαι τὰς πόλεις καὶ
ἄρχεσθαι καταστήσαντες εἰς πολλὴν ἀσφάλειαν καὶ ἡσυχίαν ἔθεντο καὶ
θορύβων ἀπήλλαξαν· εἰ δέ τις ταῦτα ἀναιρήσει, θηρίων βίον βιωσόμεθα
καὶ ὁ προστυχὼν τὸν ἐντυχόντα μονονοῦ κατέδεται."   5

5 ἐντυχόντα E: ἐντυγχάνοντα B

Context: quotation of Colotes in order to score a point against Epicurean hedonism. Colotes dedicated his book to one of the Ptolemies; cf. 1107D.

3 ἀσφάλειαν   Cf. C.

4–5   Cf. J 958–61.

S Diogenes of Oenoanda, new fr. 21.1.4–14, 2.10–14

τότε ὡς ἀληθῶς ὁ τῶν | θεῶν βίος εἰς ἀνθρώπους | μεταβήσεται. δικαιο-|σύνης γὰρ ἔσται μεστὰ | πάντα καὶ φιλαλληλίας, | καὶ οὐ γενήσεται τειχῶν | ἢ νόμων χρεία καὶ πάν|των ὅσα δι' ἀλλήλους | σκευωρούμεθα. περὶ δὲ | τῶν ἀπὸ γεωργίας ἀναν|καίων . . . καὶ διακόψει [εἰς τὸ] | δέον τὸ συνε[χῶς φι]|λοσοφεῖν τοια[ῦτα· τὰ] | γὰρ γεωργή[ματα ὧν ἡ] | φύσις   5 χρῄζε[ι . . .

For the text with commentary, cf. Smith [178], 21–5.

2 **φιλαλληλίας** On this rare and seemingly late word, Smith comments: 'Even if the *term* φιλαλληλία was borrowed from the Stoics [the adjective but not the noun occurs 4 times in Epictetus], that does not necessarily mean that the *idea* originated with them. It is surely indisputable that . . . φιλαλληλία and φιλανθρωπία were characteristic of the Epicurean community from the beginning.' However, it is less clear that Epicurus himself had hopes of extending the Epicurean community to the entire citizen body (cf. **Q** 5–6). Diogenes' vision of breaking down existing boundaries, here and in **P**, could simply reflect the ideology of the Roman empire. For φιλάλληλος in Stoicism, cf. **67W** 7.

23 God

A Lucretius 5.1161–1225

> (1) nunc quae causa deum per magnas numina gentis
> pervulgarit et ararum compleverit urbis
> suscipiendaque curarit sollemnia sacra,
> quae nunc in magnis florent sacra rebu' locisque,
> unde etiam nunc est mortalibus insitus horror   1165
> qui delubra deum nova toto suscitat orbi
> terrarum et festis cogit celebrare diebus,
> non ita difficilest rationem reddere verbis.
> (2) quippe etenim iam tum divum mortalia saecla
> egregias animo facies vigilante videbant   1170
> et magis in somnis mirando corporis auctu.
> his igitur sensum tribuebant propterea quod
> membra movere videbantur vocesque superbas
> mittere pro facie praeclara et viribus amplis.
> aeternamque dabant vitam, quia semper eorum   1175
> suppeditabatur facies et forma manebat,
> et tamen omnino quod tantis viribus auctos

non temere ulla vi convinci posse putabant.
fortunisque ideo longe praestare putabant,
quod mortis timor haud quemquam vexaret eorum,   1180
et simul in somnis quia multa et mira videbant
efficere et nullum capere ipsos inde laborem.
(3) praeterea caeli rationes ordine certo
et varia annorum cernebant tempora verti
nec poterant quibus id fieret cognoscere causis.   1185
ergo perfugium sibi habebant omnia divis
tradere et illorum nutu facere omnia flecti.
in caeloque deum sedis et templa locarunt,
per caelum volvi quia nox et luna videtur,
luna dies et nox et noctis signa severa   1190
noctivagaeque faces caeli flammaeque volantes,
nubila sol imbres nix venti fulmina grando
et rapidi fremitus et murmura magna minarum.
(4) o genus infelix humanum, talia divis
cum tribuit facta atque iras adiunxit acerbas!   1195
quantos tum gemitus ipsi sibi, quantaque nobis
vulnera, quas lacrimas peperere minoribu' nostris!
nec pietas ullast velatum saepe videri
vertier ad lapidem atque omnis accedere ad aras
nec procumbere humi prostratum et pandere palmas   1200
ante deum delubra nec aras sanguine multo
spargere quadrupedum nec votis nectere vota,
sed mage pacata posse omnia mente tueri.
(5) nam cum suspicimus magni caelestia mundi
templa super stellisque micantibus aethera fixum,   1205
et venit in mentem solis lunaeque viarum,
tunc aliis oppressa malis in pectora cura
illa quoque expergefactum caput erigere infit,
nequae forte deum nobis immensa potestas
sit, vario motu quae candida sidera verset.   1210
temptat enim dubiam mentem rationis egestas,
ecquaenam fuerit mundi genitalis origo,
et simul ecquae sit finis, quoad moenia mundi
solliciti motus hunc possint ferre laborem,
an divinitus aeterna donata salute   1215
perpetuo possint aevi labentia tractu
immensi validas aevi contemnere viris.
(6) praeterea cui non animus formidine divum
contrahitur, cui non correpunt membra pavore,
fulminis horribili cum plaga torrida tellus   1220

contremit et magnum percurrunt murmura caelum?
non populi gentesque tremunt, regesque superbi
corripiunt divum percussi membra timore,
nequid ob admissum foede dictumve superbe
poenarum grave sit solvendi tempus adactum?   1225

1203 *pacata* ed. Jutina: *placata* OQ   1214 *solliciti* Bentley: *et taciti* OQ   1224 *nequid* Lachmann: *ne quod* OQ

Context: the origins of civilization. The passage corresponds to Epicurus, *Nat.* XII, 27.1 (= Usener 84).

1173 **videbantur**   Possibly 'were seen' rather than 'seemed'. But on neither translation would the figures seen have to be actually alive: see **15D 9**.

B Epicurus, *Ep. Men.* 123–4

(1) πρῶτον μὲν τὸν θεὸν ζῷον ἄφθαρτον καὶ μακάριον νομίζων, ὡς ἡ κοινὴ τοῦ θεοῦ νόησις ὑπεγράφη, μηθὲν μήτε τῆς ἀφθαρσίας ἀλλότριον μήτε τῆς μακαριότητος ἀνοίκειον αὐτῷ πρόσαπτε· πᾶν δὲ τὸ φυλάττειν αὐτοῦ δυνάμενον τὴν μετὰ ἀφθαρσίας μακαριότητα περὶ αὐτὸν δόξαζε. (2) θεοὶ μὲν γὰρ εἰσίν· ἐναργὴς γὰρ αὐτῶν ἐστιν ἡ γνῶσις. (3) οἵους δ' αὐτοὺς ⟨οἱ⟩   5
πολλοὶ νομίζουσιν οὐκ εἰσίν· οὐ γὰρ φυλάττουσιν αὐτοὺς οἵους νομίζουσιν. ἀσεβὴς δὲ οὐχ ὁ τοὺς τῶν πολλῶν θεοὺς ἀναιρῶν, ἀλλ' ὁ τὰς τῶν πολλῶν δόξας θεοῖς προσάπτων. οὐ γὰρ προλήψεις εἰσὶν ἀλλ' ὑπολήψεις ψευδεῖς αἱ τῶν πολλῶν ὑπὲρ θεῶν ἀποφάσεις· ἔνθεν αἱ μέγισται βλάβαι αἱ ἐπὶ τοῖς κακοῖς ἐκ θεῶν ἐπάγονται καὶ ὠφέλειαι. (4) ταῖς γὰρ ἰδίαις οἰκειούμενοι   10
διὰ παντὸς ἀρεταῖς τοὺς ὁμοίους ἀποδέχονται, πᾶν τὸ μὴ τοιοῦτον ὡς ἀλλότριον νομίζοντες.

5 ⟨οἱ⟩ Gassendi   9 αἱ ἐπὶ A.A. Long: αἵτιαι codd. (om. co): τε Usener: αἵτιαι τοῖς κακοῖς del. Diano   10 ὠφέλειαι ⟨τοῖς ἀγαθοῖς⟩ Gassendi   12 νομίζοντες codd.: ἐξορίζοντες Schmid

Context: immediately following **25A**, the introduction to the *Letter*.

6 **φυλάττουσιν**   Echoing 3, φυλάττειν. False beliefs that the gods meddle in our affairs fail to ensure their capacity for everlasting bliss (cf. **E 4**). This idea that it is up to men to ensure their gods' imperishability becomes far more readily intelligible on the interpretation which makes Epicurean gods human thought constructs.

10–12   We take the subject to be people in general, the good and the bad alike (cf. *SV* 15), the ἴδιαι ἀρεταί of the latter being such misconceived forms of 'excellence' as power. Although Gassendi's supplement, ⟨τοῖς ἀγαθοῖς⟩ (or perhaps ⟨αἱ ἐπὶ τοῖς ἀγαθοῖς⟩ to fit our emendation in 9) would help clarify this reference, the transmitted reading should stand: Epicurus probably chose not to specify 'for the good' because a correct or relatively correct conception of the divine nature is beneficial not only to those already good, but to anyone at all.

C Epicurus, *Ep. Hdt.* 76–7

(1) καὶ μὴν ἐν τοῖς μετεώροις φορὰν καὶ τροπὴν καὶ ἔκλειψιν καὶ ἀνατολὴν καὶ δύσιν καὶ τὰ σύστοιχα τούτοις μήτε λειτουργοῦντός τινος νομίζειν δεῖ

Epicurean ethics

γίνεσθαι καὶ διατάττοντος ἢ διατάξοντος καὶ ἅμα τὴν πᾶσαν μακαριότητα
ἔχοντος μετὰ ἀφθαρσίας (οὐ γὰρ συμφωνοῦσιν πραγματεῖαι καὶ φροντίδες
καὶ ὀργαὶ καὶ χάριτες μακαριότητι, ἀλλ' ἐν ἀσθενείᾳ καὶ φόβῳ καὶ   5
προσδεήσει τῶν πλησίον ταῦτα γίνεται), (2) μήτε αὖ πῦρ ἅμα ὄντα
συνεστραμμένον τὴν μακαριότητα κεκτημένα κατὰ βούλησιν τὰς κινήσεις
ταύτας λαμβάνειν· (3) ἀλλὰ πᾶν τὸ σέμνωμα τηρεῖν, κατὰ πάντα ὀνόματα
φερόμενα ἐπὶ τὰς τοιαύτας ἐννοίας, ἐὰν μηδὲν ὑπεναντίον ἐξ αὐτῶν τῷ
σεμνώματι δόξῃ· εἰ δὲ μή, τὸν μέγιστον τάραχον ἐν ταῖς ψυχαῖς αὐτὴ ἡ   10
ὑπεναντιότης παρασκευάσει.

3 γίνεσθαι Meibom: γενέσθαι codd.   9 ἐὰν codd.: ἵνα Usener   μηδὲν Meibom: μηδ' codd.
ὑπεναντίον Meibom: ὑπεναντίαις BP: ὑπεναντίαι FP(corr.): ὑπεναντίας z   9–10 δόξῃ Meibom: δόξαι
codd.   ⟨γένωνται⟩ τῷ σεμνώματι δόξαι Gassendi

Context: immediately following **19A** on the origin of language. The juxtaposition is
explicable by the fact that both topics are excerpted from Epicurus' account in *Nat.* XII
of the origins of civilization (see note on **A**, and Sedley [132]). The present passage
may derive from the same section as **A 3**.

1–3   If the interpretation defended in vol. 1 is correct, why does Epicurus not
argue that the gods cannot control celestial events on the ground that they are only
concepts, not living beings? That ground could hardly be established by the present
argument, which merely appeals to the common conception of god as blessed and
imperishable. Hence his argument concerns not his own gods, but a *hypothetical* divine
controller.

6–8   An allusion to the astral gods of Plato and Aristotle.

9 τὰς τοιαύτας ἐννοίας   *Sc.* blessedness and imperishability.

D Lucretius 6.68–79

> quae nisi respuis ex animo longeque remittis
> dis indigna putare alienaque pacis eorum,
> delibata deum per te tibi numina sancta   70
> saepe oberunt; non quo violari summa deum vis
> possit, ut ex ira poenas petere imbibat acris,
> sed quia tute tibi placida cum pace quietos
> constitues magnos irarum volvere fluctus,
> nec delubra deum placido cum pectore adibis,   75
> nec de corpore quae sancto simulacra feruntur
> in mentis hominum divinae nuntia formae,
> suscipere haec animi tranquilla pace valebis.
> inde videre licet qualis iam vita sequatur.

71 oberunt Wakefield: oderunt OQ: aderunt Marullus   73 quietos Marullus: -us OQ   76 feruntur ed.
Brixiensis: fuerunt OQ

Context: the need to exclude the gods from cosmological explanations.

76 **feruntur**   Whether or not this emendation is accepted, there can be little
doubt that Lucretius is here assuming that the divine *simulacra* come to us from the
bodies of the gods. Cf. **L**, with note.

E Cicero, *ND* 1.43–50

(1) ea qui consideret quam inconsulte ac temere dicantur, venerari Epicurum et in eorum ipsorum numero de quibus haec quaestio est habere debeat. (2) solus enim vidit primum esse deos, quod in omnium animis eorum notionem inpressisset ipsa natura. quae est enim gens aut quod genus hominum quod non habeat sine doctrina anticipationem quandam deorum, quam appellat 5 πρόληψιν Epicurus, id est anteceptam animo rei quandam informationem, sine qua nec intellegi quicquam nec quaeri nec disputari potest. quoius rationis vim atque utilitatem ex illo caelesti Epicuri de regula et iudicio volumine accepimus. quod igitur fundamentum huius quaestionis est, id praeclare iactum videtis. cum enim non instituto aliquo aut more aut lege sit opinio 10 constituta maneatque ad unum omnium firma consensio, intellegi necesse est esse deos, quoniam insitas eorum vel potius innatas cognitiones habemus; de quo autem omnium natura consentit, id verum esse necesse est; esse igitur deos confitendum est. (3) quod quoniam fere constat inter omnis non philosophos solum sed etiam indoctos, fatemur constare illud etiam, hanc nos habere sive 15 anticipationem, ut ante dixi, sive praenotionem deorum (sunt enim rebus novis nova ponenda nomina, ut Epicurus ipse πρόληψιν appellavit, quam antea nemo eo verbo nominarat) – hanc igitur habemus, ut deos beatos et inmortales putemus. quae enim nobis natura informationem ipsorum deorum dedit, eadem insculpsit in mentibus ut eos aeternos et beatos haberemus. (4) 20 quod si ita est, vere exposita illa sententia est ab Epicuro, quod beatum aeternumque sit id nec habere ipsum negotii quicquam nec exhibere alteri, itaque neque ira neque gratia teneri, quod quae talia essent inbecilla essent omnia. (5) si nihil aliud quaereremus nisi ut deos pie coleremus et ut superstitione liberaremur, satis erat dictum; nam et praestans deorum natura 25 hominum pietate coleretur, cum et aeterna esset et beatissima (habet enim venerationem iustam quicquid excellit), et metus omnis a vi atque ira deorum pulsus esset; intellegitur enim a beata inmortalique natura et iram et gratiam segregari; quibus remotis nullos a superis inpendere metus. sed ad hanc confirmandam opinionem anquirit animus et formam et vitam et actionem 30 mentis atque agitationem in deo. (6) ac de forma quidem partim natura nos admonet partim ratio docet. nam a natura habemus omnes omnium gentium speciem nullam aliam nisi humanam deorum; quae enim forma alia occurrit umquam aut vigilanti cuiquam aut dormienti? sed ne omnia revocentur ad primas notiones, ratio hoc idem ipsa declarat. nam cum praestantissumam 35 naturam, vel quia beata est vel quia sempiterna, convenire videatur eandem esse pulcherrimam, quae conpositio membrorum, quae conformatio linia-mentorum, quae figura, quae species humana potest esse pulchrior? vos quidem Lucili soletis (nam Cotta meus modo hoc modo illud), cum artificium effingitis fabricamque divinam, quam sint omnia in hominis figura non modo 40 ad usum verum etiam ad venustatem apta describere; quod si omnium

animantium formam vincit hominis figura, deus autem animans est, ea figura profecto est quae pulcherrimast omnium. quoniamque deos beatissimos esse constat, beatus autem esse sine virtute nemo potest nec virtus sine ratione constare nec ratio usquam inesse nisi in hominis figura, hominis esse specie   45 deos confitendum est. (7) nec tamen ea species corpus est sed quasi corpus, nec habet sanguinem sed quasi sanguinem. (haec quamquam et inventa sunt acutius et dicta subtilius ab Epicuro quam ut quivis ea possit agnoscere, tamen fretus intellegentia vestra dissero brevius quam causa desiderat.) Epicurus autem, qui res occultas et penitus abditas non modo videat animo sed etiam sic   50 tractet ut manu, docet eam esse vim et naturam deorum, ut primum non sensu sed mente cernatur, nec soliditate quadam nec ad numerum, ut ea quae ille propter firmitatem στερέμνια appellat, sed imaginibus similitudine et transitione perceptis, cum infinita simillumarum imaginum series ex innu-merabilibus individuis existat et ad deos adfluat, cum maximis voluptatibus in   55 eas imagines mentem intentam infixamque nostram intellegentiam capere quae sit et beata natura et aeterna. summa vero vis infinitatis et magna ac diligenti contemplatione dignissima est. in qua intellegi necesse est eam esse naturam ut omnia omnibus paribus paria respondeant; hanc ἰσονομίαν appellat Epicurus, id est aequabilem tributionem. ex hac igitur illud efficitur, si mortalium tanta multitudo sit, esse inmortalium non minorem, et si   60 quae interimant innumerabilia sint, etiam ea quae conservent vis infinita esse debere.

54 *series* Brieger: *species* codd.   55 *ad deos* codd. (*ad eos* B¹): *ad nos* Lambinus: *a deis* Davies: *a diis ad nos* Heindorf

Context: Velleius' exposition of Epicurean theology, immediately following his critique of rival theories (including **54B**).

6 **informationem**   This (cf. 19) must translate Epicurus' τύπος, cf. **15A**; **17E 2**; **20C 8**.

8 **caelesti**   Translated 'heaven-sent' in vol. 1, despite the un-Epicurean overtones, on the authority of Cicero, *Fin.* 1.63 and Plutarch, *Col.* 1118A. **de regula et iudicio**   This translates περὶ κανόνος καὶ κριτηρίου – a reference to Epicurus' work the *Canon* (see **17A**).

12 **innatas**   The term has raised major problems for the traditional interpretation of Epicurus' theology. If the conception of god is already innate, how can it also result empirically (as it were) from our apprehension in dreams of images coming from him (cf. Kleve [284], ch. 3)? The dilemma does not even arise on the interpretation adopted in vol. 1. What is innate is a predisposition for forming an idealized conception of the happy being we ourselves aim to become.

21–4   For the original Greek of the maxim, see **G** 1–2.

31–46   On the interpretation proposed in vol. 1 it is inevitable that the gods should be anthropomorphic, since they constitute paradigmatic models for our own lives. Still an obligation might arise for the Epicureans to show, in opposition to the Stoic defence of a non-anthropomorphic god (e.g. **54A**), that there is nothing non-ideal about a god in human shape. See also **13G** 42–53, and Kleve [290].

38–41   For this Stoic thesis, see *ND* 2. 133–53.

47–9   The apologetic remarks suggest that Cicero is here simply translating

Epicurus' technical account without understanding it – a fact which virtually guarantees the authenticity of his report.

53–4 **similitudine et transitione** This expression has been widely misunderstood. Many interpreters have followed Philippson [240] in taking it to translate ἡ καθ' ὁμοιότητα μετάβασις, 'inference by similarity' – one of Philodemus' designations of the 'Similarity Method', on which see **18F–G**. On this hypothesis, the text is often read as claiming that we infer the nature of the gods from the similarity of their images to them. What this interpretation misses is that as well as 'inference' μετάβασις can also designate a mode of *concept-formation*. In one Stoic text (**39D 7**) it is itself apparently a species of concept-formation, but Sextus (*M.* 3.40; see Mueller [652], 78), whose usage standardly reflects that current among the dogmatist schools, uses it as the generic name for such processes (the list of which perhaps originated with Epicurus: cf. **15F**). These are all processes by which, starting from perceptually-based impressions, we form such concepts as Centaur, pygmy and giant. They are not processes of inference at all. That this is the sense of *transitio* here is virtually proved by the comparison of **F 2–3**. Thus we must take *similitudine* to constitute a distinct and prior stage. Both Cicero's phraseology and the comparison of **G** make it hard to doubt that the similarity in question is that of the images to each other (cf. **40N 1**), not to the gods. Hence the reference is to the cinematographic effect of a series of similar images. This provides the primary impression of a happy human being, which by *transitio* we intensify into that of an everlasting and supremely blessed being.

54 **series** Brieger's emendation for *species* is hard to resist. As we would expect, and as **G** confirms, what 'flows' is the images, not their appearance. And in Cotta's summary of this passage at 1.105 his phrase *similium accessio* suggests the emended rather than the MS reading. The frequent occurrence of *species* in the preceding paragraphs could easily have influenced the corruption.

55 **ad deos** A merit of the interpretation adopted in vol. 1 is that it renders unnecessary Lambinus' frequently adopted emendation to *ad nos*.

57ff. The return to oratio recta signals that the direct report of Epicurus has finished. The argument now added by Velleius appeals to what may be an authentic Epicurean principle, but puts it to desperately bad use. If accepted, it would wreck the argument for the mortality of the soul at **14H 1**.

F Sextus Empiricus, *M.* 9.42–7

ὁ δὲ Δημόκριτος τὸ ἧττον ἄπορον διὰ τοῦ μείζονος ἀπόρου διδάσκων ἄπιστός ἐστιν. εἰς μὲν γὰρ τὸ πῶς νόησιν θεῶν ἔσχον ἄνθρωποι πολλὰς καὶ ποικίλας ἡ φύσις δίδωσιν ἀφορμάς· τὸ δὲ εἴδωλα εἶναι ἐν τῷ περιέχοντι ὑπερφυῆ καὶ ἀνθρωποειδεῖς ἔχοντα μορφὰς καὶ καθόλου τοιαῦτα ὁποῖα βούλεται αὐτῷ ἀναπλάττειν Δημόκριτος, παντελῶς ἐστι δυσπαράδεκτον.(1) τὰ δὲ αὐτὰ καὶ πρὸς τὸν Ἐπίκουρον ἔνεστι λέγειν, οἰόμενον ὅτι κατὰ   5
τὰς ἐνυπνιδίους φαντασίας τῶν ἀνθρωπομόρφων εἰδώλων ἐνοήθησαν θεοί·
τί γὰρ μᾶλλον ἀπὸ τούτων νόησις ἐγίγνετο θεῶν ἢ ὑπερφυῶν ἀνθρώπων;
καὶ καθόλου καὶ πρὸς πάσας τὰς ἐκκειμένας δόξας ἐνέσται λέγειν, ὅτι οὐ
κατὰ ψιλὸν μέγεθος ἀνθρωποειδοῦς ζῴου νόησιν θεοῦ λαμβάνουσιν
ἄνθρωποι, ἀλλὰ σὺν τῷ μακάριον εἶναι καὶ ἄφθαρτον καὶ πλείστην δύναμιν   10
ἐν τῷ κόσμῳ προφερόμενον. ἅπερ οὐ διδάσκουσιν, ἀπὸ τίνος ἀρχῆς ἢ πῶς

ἐπενοήθη παρὰ τοῖς πρῶτον ἔννοιαν σπάσασι θεοῦ, οἱ τὰς ἐνυπνιδίους
αἰτιώμενοι φαντασίας καὶ τὴν τῶν οὐρανίων εὐταξίαν. (2) οἱ δὲ καὶ πρὸς
τοῦτό φασιν, ὅτι ἡ μὲν ἀρχὴ τῆς νοήσεως τοῦ εἶναι θεὸν γέγονεν ἀπὸ τῶν
κατὰ τοὺς ὕπνους ἰνδαλλομένων ἢ ἀπὸ τῶν κατὰ τὸν κόσμον θεωρου-   1
μένων, τὸ δὲ ἀίδιον εἶναι τὸν θεὸν καὶ ἄφθαρτον καὶ τέλειον ἐν εὐδαιμονίᾳ
παρῆλθε κατὰ τὴν ἀπὸ τῶν ἀνθρώπων μετάβασιν. ὡς γὰρ τὸν κοινὸν
ἄνθρωπον αὐξήσαντες τῇ φαντασίᾳ νόησιν ἔσχομεν Κύκλωπος, ὃς οὐκ ἐῴκει·

> ἀνδρί γε σιτοφάγῳ, ἀλλὰ ῥίῳ ὑλήεντι   20
> ὑψηλῶν ὀρέων, ὅτε φαίνεται οἷον ἀπ' ἄλλων,

οὕτως ἄνθρωπον εὐδαίμονα νοήσαντες καὶ μακάριον καὶ συμπεπληρωμένον πᾶσι τοῖς ἀγαθοῖς, εἶτα ταῦτα ἐπιτείναντες τὸν ἐν αὐτοῖς ἐκείνοις
ἄκρον ἐνοήσαμεν θεόν. καὶ πάλιν πολυχρόνιόν τινα φαντασιωθέντες
ἄνθρωπον οἱ παλαιοὶ ἐπηύξησαν τὸν χρόνον εἰς ἄπειρον, προσσυνάψαντες   2
τῷ ἐνεστῶτι καὶ τὸν παρῳχημένον καὶ τὸν μέλλοντα· εἶτα ἐντεῦθεν εἰς
ἔννοιαν ἀιδίου παραγενόμενοι ἔφασαν καὶ ἀίδιον εἶναι τὸν θεόν. (3) οἱ δὴ
τοιαῦτα λέγοντες πιθανῆς μὲν προΐστανται δόξης, ἠρέμα δὲ εἰς τὸν δι'
ἀλλήλων ἐμπίπτουσι τρόπον, ὅς ἐστιν ἀπορώτατος. ἵνα γὰρ πρῶτον
εὐδαίμονα νοήσωμεν ἄνθρωπον καὶ ἀπὸ τούτου κατὰ μετάβασιν τὸν θεόν,   30
ὀφείλομεν νοῆσαι τί ποτέ ἐστιν εὐδαιμονία, ἧς κατὰ μετοχὴν νοεῖται ὁ
εὐδαίμων. ἀλλ' ἦν γε εὐδαιμονία κατ' αὐτοὺς δαιμονία τις καὶ θεία φύσις,
καὶ εὐδαίμων ἐκαλεῖτο ὁ εὖ τὸν δαίμονα διακείμενον ἔχων. ὥσθ' ἵνα μὲν
λάβωμεν τὴν περὶ ἄνθρωπον εὐδαιμονίαν, πρότερον ἔχειν ὀφείλομεν
νόησιν θεοῦ καὶ δαίμονος, ἵνα δὲ τὸν θεὸν νοήσωμεν, πρότερον ἔχειν   3
ὀφείλομεν ἔννοιαν εὐδαίμονος ἀνθρώπου. τοίνυν ἑκάτερον περιμένον τὴν
ἐκ θατέρου νόησιν ἀνεπινόητον γίνεται ἡμῖν.

Context: critique of theories of the origin of belief in god. The opinions of Democritus
and Epicurus were first summarized at ibid. 19 and 24–5.

4 τοιαῦτα Democritus added that the images were hard to destroy, capable of
speech, endowed with prophetic powers, and beneficent or maleficent (ibid. 19).

8 This criticism now takes in, as well as the Epicurean theory, those of
Democritus and Aristotle (ibid. 19–27). But from 14 onwards the defence offered on
behalf of this group seems exclusively Epicurean. Hence it uses the Hellenistic
μετάβασις theory and the characteristic Epicurean phrase συμπεπληρωμένον ... ἀ-
γαθοῖς (cf. **21B 2**), and while accounting for the ideas of god's happiness and
imperishability it ignores the challenge (10–11) concerning a non-Epicurean attribute
of god, namely power.

32–3 This etymology stems ultimately from Plato, *Tim.* 90c.

G Epicurus, *RS* 1, with scholion

τὸ μακάριον καὶ ἄφθαρτον οὔτε αὐτὸ πράγματα ἔχει οὔτε ἄλλῳ παρέχει, ὥστε οὔτε ὀργαῖς
οὔτε χάρισι συνέχεται· ἐν ἀσθενεῖ γὰρ πᾶν τὸ τοιοῦτον. [ἐν ἄλλοις δέ φησι τοὺς θεοὺς
λόγῳ θεωρητούς, οὓς μὲν κατ' ἀριθμὸν ὑφεστῶτας, οὓς δὲ κατὰ ὁμοείδειαν

ἐκ τῆς συνεχοῦς ἐπιρρύσεως τῶν ὁμοίων εἰδώλων ἐπὶ τὸ αὐτὸ ἀποτετελεσμένων, ἀνθρωποειδεῖς.]   5

3 οὖς . . . οὖς codd.: οὐ . . . ὡς Gassendi: οὐ . . . ⟨οἵ⟩ους Bignone: οὐ . . . ὅσον Diano   4–5 ἀποτετελεσμένων BP: -ους Kühn

3 λόγῳ θεωρητούς   Cf. m below, and 11D 3, E 4. The expression is standardly used by Epicurus for entities not available to the senses but discoverable in thought. If our suggestion in vol. 1 is right, that the first group of gods mentioned here are human sages who have become ethical models for future generations, they will still fit this description because it will be *qua* thought-objects, not *qua* perceptible individuals, that they fulfil this function.   κατ' ἀριθμὸν . . . κατὰ ὁμοείδειαν   For this distinction between numerical identity and formal identity, cf. Galen, *Meth. med.* 10.135, Simplicius, *In Ar. De caelo* 310,5ff.

4–5 ἀποτετελεσμένων   This verb has suffered from overinterpretation (e.g. 'perfected', Bailey). It is one of Epicurus' standard verbs for 'produce' in causal explanations. If the transmitted text is correct, it might be taken with ἐπὶ τὸ αὐτό, '. . . influx of similar images produced (and sent) to the same place . . .'. This is not very convincing, and there is some merit in emending it to -ους with Kühn and understanding that the gods themselves are 'produced from the continuous influx . . .'. Alternatively, one might read -ην and understand that it is the formal unity which is thus produced. Our translation in vol. 1 is designed to hedge our bets between these three possibilities. Not much appears to turn on the choice.

5 ἀνθρωποειδεῖς   Grammatically speaking this awkward afterthought could describe either all the gods or just the second group. Whatever the intention, there can be no doubt that all Epicurus' gods were anthropomorphic.

H Philodemus, *Piet.* 112.1–18 (including Usener 87)

καὶ πᾶσαν μ[ανίαν 'Ε]‖[πίκουρος ἐμ[έμφε]‖το τοῖς τὸ [θεῖον ἐ]‖κ τῶν ὄντων [ἀναι]‖ρούσιν, ὡς κἀ[ν τῷ] | δωδεκάτῳ [Προ]‖δίκῳ καὶ Δια[γόρᾳ] | καὶ ῾Κ῾ριτίᾳ κἄ[λλοις] | μέμφ[εται] φὰς κα[ὶ παρα]‖κόπτ[ει]ν καὶ [μαίνεσ]‖θαι καὶ βακχεύου|σιν αὐτοὺς [εἰ]κά[ζει βουλεύσ[ας] οὐ πράγμ[αθ' ἡ]‖μεῖν παρέχειν οὐ|δ' ἐνοχλεῖν κα[ὐτοὺς] | παραγραμμίζ[ειν] | τὰ τ[ῶ]ν θεῶν [ὀνόμα]‖τα . . .   5

1 καὶ πᾶσαν – [ἀναι]‖ρούσιν Obbink   1–2 ὡς κἀ[ν] – Δια[γόρᾳ] Bücheler   2–3 κἄ[λλοις] – παρα]‖κόπτειν Usener   3 μαίνεσ]‖θαι Gomperz   4 εἰ]κά[ζει Usener   4–5 βου]‖λεύσα[ας] – [ὀνόμα]‖τα Obbink

Context: defence of Epicurus against the charge of impiety.

Book XII of *On nature*, like Lucretius book 5, dealt with the origins of civilization. Epicurus' remark almost certainly occurred in the defence of his own account of the origin of religion against the rival accounts of the three named, who were held to have explained the gods as calculated human fictions. The point of imputing *insanity* to them is not obvious. We owe to D. Obbink the interesting suggestion that it is connected with a strategy for preserving the alleged universality of belief in gods (**E 2**): at *Piet.* 109,17–20 (in Obbink's restoration) Philodemus claims that the gods are worshipped by all men εἰ μὴ παρα]κοποί τινε[ς. This is the earliest extant occurrence of the standard list of atheists, for which cf.

Epicurean ethics

S.E., *M.* 9.51–4. It was widely alleged that Epicurus was really an atheist himself, and his repudiation of atheism just a façade to mollify the public: see the attributions of this view to numerous sources in Cicero, *ND* 1.85, 123, S.E., *M.* 9.58; Eusebius, *Pr. ev.* 14.27.11, 15.5.12. Cf. also D.L. 2.97: Epicurus was said to have drawn heavily on *On the gods* by Theodorus the Atheist. Our interpretation of his theology can, we believe, satisfactorily explain both his vehement repudiation of this charge, and why he tended to attract it.

I P. Oxy. 215, 1.3–24

τ]ὸ τῆς φύσεως, ὡς ἔλεγον, | [οἰ]κεῖον, μηδ' ὅταν γε | [ν]ὴ Δία οὕτωι λέγεται
πά|[λι]ν ὑπὸ τῶν τυχόντων | "[δ]έδο[ι]κα τοὺς θεοὺς πάν|[τας οὓ]ς
σέ[βο]μαι [κ]αὶ τού|[τοι]ς βο[ύ]λ[ο]μαι πάντα κα|[τ]αθύειν καὶ τούτοις
| [ἀν]ατιθέναι." χαριέστε|[ρο]ς μὲν γὰρ ἴσως ποτὲ | [ὁ τ]οιοῦτος ἄλλων
ἰδίω|[τῶ]ν ἐστιν, ὅμως δὲ οὐ|[δὲ] ταύτηι πω τὸ βέβαιον | [εὐ]σεβείας   5
ὑπάρχει. σὺ | [δ', ὦ] ἄνθρωπε, μακαριώ|[τα]τον μέν τι νόμιζε τὸ | [διε]ιλη-
φέναι καλῶς ὃ τὸ | [παν]άριστον ἐν τοῖς οὖσι | [δια]νοηθῆναι δυνάμε|[θα],
κα[ὶ] θαύμαζε ταύτην | [τὴ]ν δ[ι]άληψιν καὶ σέβου | [ἀδ]ε[ί]αι τοῦτο,
ἔπε[ι]τα . . .

2 τυχόντων corr. e πολλῶν P   οὓ]ς Obbink   4 χαριέστε[ρο]ς corr. edd.: χαριεστε[. .]ν P   8
ἀδ]ε[ί]αι Obbink
Restorations other than those noted are by Grenfell and Hunt. For text and discussion, see Obbink [291].

Context: fragmentary Epicurean theological treatise. The papyrus itself probably dates from the first century B.C.

J Epicurus, *Ep. Men.* 135

ταῦτα οὖν καὶ τὰ τούτοις συγγενῆ μελέτα πρὸς σεαυτὸν ἡμέρας, καὶ
νυκτὸς πρὸς τὸν ὅμοιον σεαυτῷ, καὶ οὐδέποτε οὔθ' ὕπαρ οὔτ' ὄναρ
διαταραχθήσῃ, ζήσῃ δὲ ὡς θεὸς ἐν ἀνθρώποις. οὐθὲν γὰρ ἔοικε θνητῷ ζῴῳ
ζῶν ἄνθρωπος ἐν ἀθανάτοις ἀγαθοῖς.

2 πρὸς ⟨τε⟩ Usener

Context: peroration of *Letter*.

K Plutarch, *Contra Ep. beat.* 1091B–C (Usener 419, part)

φεῦ τῆς μεγάλης ἡδονῆς τῶν ἀνδρῶν καὶ μακαριότητος ἦν καρποῦνται
χαίροντες ἐπὶ τῷ μὴ κακοπαθεῖν μηδὲ λυπεῖσθαι μηδὲ ἀλγεῖν. ἆρ' οὐκ
ἄξιόν ἐστιν ἐπὶ τούτοις καὶ φρονεῖν καὶ λέγειν ἃ λέγουσιν, ἀφθάρτους καὶ
ἰσοθέους ἀποκαλοῦντες αὑτοὺς καὶ δι' ὑπερβολὰς καὶ ἀκρότητας ἀγαθῶν
εἰς βρόμους καὶ ὀλολυγμοὺς ἐκβακχεύοντες ὑφ' ἡδονῆς ὅτι τῶν ἄλλων   5
περιφρονοῦντες ἐξευρήκασι μόνοι θεῖον ἀγαθὸν καὶ μέγα, τὸ μηθὲν ἔχειν
κακόν.

Context: criticism of the Epicureans' negative characterization of good.

3 **ἀφθάρτους** For Epicurus' own similar use of this epithet, cf. Usener 141 (to

152

23 God

Colotes), ἄφθαρτός μοι περιπάτει καὶ ἡμᾶς ἀφθάρτους διανοοῦ, and his *Letter to Mother*, 72.1.29–40 Arrighetti [119]. Cf. also J; Metrodorus fr. 37 = SV 10; and SV 36.

L Lucretius 5.146–55

illud item non est ut possis credere, sedis
esse deum sanctas in mundi partibus ullis.
tenvis enim natura deum longeque remota
sensibus ab nostris animi vix mente videtur;
quae quoniam manuum tactum suffugit et ictum,   150
tactile nil nobis quod sit contingere debet.
tangere enim non quit quod tangi non licet ipsum.
quare etiam sedes quoque nostris sedibus esse
dissimiles debent, tenues de corpore eorum;
quae tibi posterius largo sermone probabo.   155

Context: the world is not divine.

Here and at 3.18–24 Lucretius effectively locates the gods in the μετακόσμια or *intermundia*. For a list of references to this doctrine, see the note on Cicero, *ND* 1.18 (**13G** 2) in Pease [329], to which add Philodemus, *De dis* III, 8.31. As Bollack [123] rightly observes, in Epicurus' writings the term occurs only in a non-theological context (*Ep. Pyth.* 88–9).

154 **corpore** Here, as at **D** 76, Lucretius' naive reading of Epicurus' theology immediately puts him in conflict with the latter's technical doctrine that the gods do not have actual bodies (**E** 7). Significantly, the naive reading occurs only in Lucretius' proems, generally acknowledged to be original compositions, whereas the correct Epicurean account is found in **A**, from one of the main expository sections, in which he is certainly following a Greek Epicurean source.

m Aetius 1.7.37 (Usener 355, part)

Ἐπίκουρος ἀνθρωποειδεῖς μὲν τοὺς θεούς, λόγῳ δὲ πάντας θεωρητοὺς διὰ τὴν λεπτομέρ-
ειαν τῆς τῶν εἰδώλων φύσεως. ὁ δ᾽ αὐτὸς ἄλλας τέτταρας φύσεις κατὰ γένος ἀφθάρτους
τάσδε, τὰ ἄτομα τὸ κενὸν τὸ ἄπειρον τὰς ὁμοιότητας· αὗται δὲ λέγονται ὁμοιομέρειαι καὶ
στοιχεῖα.

1 τοὺς EG: πάντας τοὺς (A)BC

1–2 Cf. **G**.

2–3 If we identify τὸ ἄπειρον with τὸ πᾶν, then we have here the three imperishables listed at **14H** 1, plus 'gods' and 'similarities'. On the interpretation adopted in vol. 1 it can be explained why these last two were excluded from the strict list in **14H** but admitted on another occasion. Gods and similarities differ in being not discrete entities but types. Also, their 'imperishability' belongs primarily within the survival time of the human race (although the infinity of the universe could perhaps be held to guarantee the existence of human beings in other worlds and eras). On the theory in **A** 2, **E** 7 and **G**, similarities and gods are not identical: it is the imperishability of the former that grounds that of the latter. The stock of similar images never runs out.

3–4 **ὁμοιομέρειαι καὶ στοιχεῖα** The meaning of ὁμοιομέρεια in Epicureanism is uncertain (cf. *Nat.* 29.27.7; 30.7.5, 12.5, 28.4). Here it might mean similarities of structure (as found among εἴδωλα, cf. **E 7**). The Epicurean στοιχεῖα are atoms (**18C 2**): these likewise offer infinitely many tokens of each type (**12B 2**).

24 Death

A Epicurus, *Ep. Men.* 124–7

(1) συνέθιζε δὲ ἐν τῷ νομίζειν μηδὲν πρὸς ἡμᾶς εἶναι τὸν θάνατον ἐπεὶ πᾶν ἀγαθὸν καὶ κακὸν ἐν αἰσθήσει· στέρησις δέ ἐστιν αἰσθήσεως ὁ θάνατος. (2) ὅθεν γνῶσις ὀρθὴ τοῦ μηθὲν εἶναι πρὸς ἡμᾶς τὸν θάνατον ἀπολαυστὸν ποιεῖ τὸ τῆς ζωῆς θνητόν, οὐκ ἄπειρον προστιθεῖσα χρόνον, ἀλλὰ τὸν τῆς ἀθανασίας ἀφελομένη πόθον. (3) οὐθὲν γάρ ἐστιν ἐν τῷ ζῆν δεινὸν τῷ   5
κατειληφότι γνησίως τὸ μηδὲν ὑπάρχειν ἐν τῷ μὴ ζῆν δεινόν. (4) ὥστε μάταιος ὁ λέγων δεδιέναι τὸν θάνατον οὐχ ὅτι λυπήσει παρών, ἀλλ' ὅτι λυπεῖ μέλλων. ὃ γὰρ παρὸν οὐκ ἐνοχλεῖ, προσδοκώμενον κενῶς λυπεῖ. (5) τὸ φρικωδέστατον οὖν τῶν κακῶν ὁ θάνατος οὐθὲν πρὸς ἡμᾶς, ἐπειδήπερ ὅταν μὲν ἡμεῖς ὦμεν, ὁ θάνατος οὐ πάρεστιν, ὅταν δὲ ὁ θάνατος παρῇ, τόθ'   10
ἡμεῖς οὐκ ἐσμέν. οὔτε οὖν πρὸς τοὺς ζῶντάς ἐστιν οὔτε πρὸς τοὺς τετελευτηκότας, ἐπειδήπερ περὶ οὓς μὲν οὐκ ἔστιν, οἳ δ' οὐκέτι εἰσίν. (6) ἀλλ' οἱ πολλοὶ τὸν θάνατον ὁτὲ μὲν ὡς μέγιστον τῶν κακῶν φεύγουσιν, ὁτὲ δὲ ὡς ἀνάπαυσιν τῶν ἐν τῷ ζῆν ⟨κακῶν αἱροῦνται. ὁ δὲ σοφὸς οὔτε παραιτεῖται τὸ ζῆν⟩ οὔτε φοβεῖται τὸ μὴ ζῆν· οὔτε γὰρ αὐτῷ προσίσταται   15
τὸ ζῆν οὔτε δοξάζεται κακὸν εἶναί τι τὸ μὴ ζῆν. ὥσπερ δὲ τὸ σιτίον οὐ τὸ πλεῖον πάντως ἀλλὰ τὸ ἥδιστον αἱρεῖται, οὕτω καὶ χρόνον οὐ τὸν μήκιστον ἀλλὰ τὸν ἥδιστον καρπίζεται. (7) ὁ δὲ παραγγέλλων τὸν μὲν νέον καλῶς ζῆν, τὸν δὲ γέροντα καλῶς καταστρέφειν, εὐήθης ἐστὶν οὐ μόνον διὰ τὸ τῆς ζωῆς ἀσπαστόν, ἀλλὰ καὶ διὰ τὸ τὴν αὐτὴν εἶναι μελέτην τοῦ καλῶς ζῆν   20
καὶ τοῦ καλῶς ἀποθνήσκειν. (8) πολὺ δὲ χείρων καὶ ὁ λέγων "καλὸν μὲν μὴ φῦναι, | φύντα δ' ὅπως ὤκιστα πύλας 'Αίδαο περῆσαι." εἰ μὲν γὰρ πεποιθὼς τοῦτό φησιν, πῶς οὐκ ἀπέρχεται ἐκ τοῦ ζῆν; ἐν ἑτοίμῳ γὰρ αὐτῷ τοῦτ' ἐστίν, εἴπερ ἦν βεβουλευμένον αὐτῷ βεβαίως· εἰ δὲ μωκώμενος, μάταιος ἐν τοῖς οὐκ ἐπιδεχομένοις.   25

4 ἄπειρον Aldobrandinus: ἄπορον codd.   14–15 suppl. Usener

Context: immediately following **23B**. This sequence of topics, god followed by death, matches to the first part of the *tetrapharmakos* (**25J**) and *RS* 1 and 2: see vol. 1, 156.

21–2 The quotation is from Theognis (425, 427 West).

B Epicurus, *SV* 31

πρὸς μὲν τἆλλα δυνατὸν ἀσφάλειαν πορίσασθαι, χάριν δὲ θανάτου πάντες ἄνθρωποι πόλιν ἀτείχιστον οἰκοῦμεν.

For safety as a dominant goal of human activity, cf. **22C**.

C Epicurus, RS 19–21

(1) [19] ὁ ἄπειρος χρόνος ἴσην ἔχει τὴν ἡδονὴν καὶ ὁ πεπερασμένος, ἐάν τις αὐτῆς τὰ πέρατα καταμετρήσῃ τῷ λογισμῷ. (2) [20] ἡ μὲν σὰρξ ἀπέλαβε τὰ πέρατα τῆς ἡδονῆς ἄπειρα, καὶ ἄπειρος αὐτὴν χρόνος παρεσκεύασεν. ἡ δὲ διάνοια τοῦ τῆς σαρκὸς τέλους καὶ πέρατος λαβοῦσα τὸν ἐπιλογισμὸν καὶ τοὺς ὑπὲρ τοῦ αἰῶνος φόβους ἐκλύσασα τὸν παντελῆ βίον παρεσ- 5
κεύασε, καὶ οὐθὲν ἔτι τοῦ ἀπείρου χρόνου προσεδεήθημεν. ἀλλ᾽ οὔτε ἔφυγε τὴν ἡδονήν, οὐδὲ ἡνίκα τὴν ἐξαγωγὴν ἐκ τοῦ ζῆν τὰ πράγματα παρεσκεύαζεν, ὡς ἐλλείπουσά τι τοῦ ἀρίστου βίου κατέστρεφεν. (3) [21] ὁ τὰ πέρατα τοῦ βίου κατειδὼς οἶδεν ὡς εὐπόριστόν ἐστι τὸ ⟨τὸ⟩ ἀλγοῦν κατ᾽ ἔνδειαν ἐξαιροῦν καὶ τὸ τὸν ὅλον βίον παντελῆ καθιστάν· ὥστε οὐδὲν 10
προσδεῖται πραγμάτων ἀγῶνας κεκτημένων.

3 καὶ codd.: κἂν Diels   6 προσεδεήθημεν F: προσεδέθημεν B(corr.)P: προσεδεήθη· ⟨οὐ⟩ μὴν Usener: προσεδεήθη[μεν] Mühll   9 ⟨τὸ⟩ Casaubon

D Diogenes Laertius 10.22 (Usener 138)

ἤδη δὲ τελευτῶν γράφει πρὸς Ἰδομενέα τήνδε ἐπιστολήν· "τὴν μακαρίαν ἄγοντες καὶ ἅμα τελευτῶντες ἡμέραν τοῦ βίου ἐγράφομεν ὑμῖν ταυτί· στραγγουρικά τε παρηκολουθήκει καὶ δυσεντερικὰ πάθη ὑπερβολὴν οὐκ ἀπολείποντα τοῦ ἐν ἑαυτοῖς μεγέθους· ἀντιπαρετάττετο δὲ πᾶσι τούτοις τὸ κατὰ ψυχὴν χαῖρον ἐπὶ τῇ τῶν γεγονότων ἡμῖν διαλογισμῶν μνήμῃ. σὺ 5
δὲ ἀξίως τῆς ἐκ μειρακίου παραστάσεως πρὸς ἐμὲ καὶ φιλοσοφίαν ἐπιμελοῦ τῶν παίδων Μητροδώρου."

Context: life of Epicurus.

The imperfects (and pluperfect) are of the 'epistolary' variety: the letter is tensed to suit the time of reading, not the time of writing.

E Lucretius 3.830–911

(1) nil igitur mors est ad nos neque pertinet hilum,   830
quandoquidem natura animi mortalis habetur.
(2) et velut anteacto nil tempore sensimus aegri,
ad confligendum venientibus undique Poenis,
omnia cum belli trepido concussa tumultu
horrida contremuere sub altis aetheris oris,   835
in dubioque fuere utrorum ad regna cadendum
omnibus humanis esset terraque marique,
sic, ubi non erimus, cum corporis atque animai
discidium fuerit quibus e sumus uniter apti,
scilicet haud nobis quicquam, qui non erimus tum,   840
accidere omnino poterit sensumque movere,
non si terra mari miscebitur et mare caelo.
(3) etsi iam nostro sentit de corpore postquam

distractast animi natura animaeque potestas,
nil tamen est ad nos qui comptu coniugioque   845
corporis atque animae consistimus uniter apti.
(4) nec, si materiem nostram collegerit aetas
post obitum rursumque redegerit ut sita nunc est
atque iterum nobis fuerint data lumina vitae,
pertineat quicquam tamen ad nos id quoque factum,   850
interrupta semel cum sit repetentia nostri.
et nunc nil ad nos de nobis attinet, ante
qui fuimus, ⟨nil⟩ iam de illis nos adficit angor.
nam cum respicias immensi temporis omne
praeteritum spatium, tum motus materiai   855
multimodis quam sint, facile hoc accredere possis,
semina saepe in eodem, ut nunc sunt, ordine posta
haec eadem, quibus e nunc nos sumus, ante fuisse.   [865]
nec memori tamen id quimus reprehendere mente;   [858]
inter enim iectast vitai pausa vageque   860   [859]
deerrarunt passim motus ab sensibus omnes.   [860]
(5) debet enim, misere si forte aegreque futurumst,   [861]
ipse quoque esse in eo tum tempore, cui male possit   [862]
accidere. id quoniam mors eximit, esseque probet   [863]
illum cui possint incommoda conciliari,   865   [864]
scire licet nobis nil esse in morte timendum
nec miserum fieri qui non est posse neque hilum
differre an nullo fuerit iam tempore natus,
mortalem vitam mors cum immortalis ademit.
(6) proinde ubi se videas hominem indignarier ipsum,   870
post mortem fore ut aut putescat corpore posto
aut flammis interfiat malisve ferarum,
scire licet non sincerum sonere atque subesse
caecum aliquem cordi stimulum, quamvis neget ipse
credere se quemquam sibi sensum in morte futurum.   875
non, ut opinor, enim dat quod promittit et unde,
nec radicitus e vita se tollit et eicit,
sed facit esse sui quiddam super inscius ipse.
vivus enim sibi cum proponit quisque futurum,
corpus uti volucres lacerent in morte feraeque,   880
ipse sui miseret; neque enim se dividit illim
nec removet satis a proiecto corpore et illum
se fingit sensuque suo contaminat adstans.
hinc indignatur se mortalem esse creatum
nec videt in vera nullum fore morte alium se   885
qui possit vivus sibi se lugere peremptum

stansque iacentem se lacerari urive dolere.

nam si in morte malumst malis morsuque ferarum

tractari, non invenio qui non sit acerbum

ignibus impositum calidis torrescere flammis   890

aut in melle situm suffocari atque rigere

frigore, cum summo gelidi cubat aequore saxi,

urgerive superne obtritum pondere terrae.

(7) "iam iam non domus accipiet te laeta neque uxor

optima, nec dulces occurrent oscula nati   895

praeripere et tacita pectus dulcedine tangent.

non poteris factis florentibus esse tuisque

praesidium. misero misere" aiunt "omnia ademit

una dies infesta tibi tot praemia vitae."

illud in his rebus non addunt "nec tibi earum   900

iam desiderium rerum super insidet una."

quod bene si videant animo dictisque sequantur,

dissoluant animi magno se angore metuque.

(8) "tu quidem ut es leto sopitus, sic eris aevi

quod superest cunctis privatu' doloribus aegris.   905

at nos horrifico cinefactum te prope busto

insatiabiliter deflevimus, aeternumque

nulla dies nobis maerorem e pectore demet."

illud ab hoc igitur quaerendum est, quid sit amari

tanto opere, ad somnum si res redit atque quietem,   910

cur quisquam aeterno possit tabescere luctu.

Context: immediately following **14H**, and opening Lucretius' famous diatribe against
the fear of death.
847–61   For a similar argument, cf. ibid. 670–8.

F Lucretius 3.966–1023

(1) nec quisquam in barathrum nec Tartara deditur atra.

materies opus est ut crescant postera saecla;

quae tamen omnia te vita perfuncta sequentur;

nec minus ergo ante haec quam tu cecidere, cadentque.

sic alid ex alio numquam desistet oriri   970

vitaque mancipio nulli datur, omnibus usu.

respice item quam nil ad nos anteacta vetustas

temporis aeterni fuerit, quam nascimur ante.

hoc igitur speculum nobis natura futuri

temporis exponit post mortem denique nostram.   975

numquid ibi horribile apparet, num triste videtur

quicquam, non omni somno securius exstat?

(2) atque ea nimirum quaecumque Acherunte profundo
prodita sunt esse, in vita sunt omnia nobis.
nec miser impendens magnum timet aere saxum   980
Tantalus, ut famast, cassa formidine torpens;
sed magis in vita divum metus urget inanis
mortalis casumque timent quem cuique ferat fors.
(3) nec Tityon volucres ineunt Acherunte iacentem
nec quod sub magno scrutentur pectore quicquam   985
perpetuam aetatem possunt reperire profecto.
quamlibet immani proiectu corporis exstet,
qui non sola novem dispessis iugera membris
obtineat, sed qui terrai totius orbem,
non tamen aeternum poterit perferre dolorem   990
nec praebere cibum proprio de corpore semper.
sed Tityos nobis hic est, in amore iacentem
quem volucres lacerant atque exest anxius angor
aut alia quavis scindunt cuppedine curae.
(4) Sisyphus in vita quoque nobis ante oculos est   995
qui petere a populo fascis saevasque securis
imbibit et semper victus tristisque recedit.
nam petere imperium quod inanest nec datur umquam,
atque in eo semper durum sufferre laborem,
hoc est adverso nixantem trudere monte   1000
saxum quod tamen e summo iam vertice rursum
volvitur et plani raptim petit aequora campi.
(5) deinde animi ingratam naturam pascere semper
atque explere bonis rebus satiareque numquam,
quod faciunt nobis annorum tempora, circum   1005
cum redeunt fetusque ferunt variosque lepores,
nec tamen explemur vitai fructibus umquam,
hoc, ut opinor, id est, aevo florente puellas
quod memorant laticem pertusum congerere in vas,
quod tamen expleri nulla ratione potestur.   1010
(6) Cerberus et Furiae iam vero et lucis egestas,
Tartarus horriferos eructans faucibus aestus,
qui neque sunt usquam nec possunt esse profecto.
sed metus in vita poenarum pro male factis
est insignibus insignis, scelerisque luella,   1015
carcer et horribilis de saxo iactu' deorsum,
verbera carnifices robur pix lammina taedae;
quae tamen etsi absunt, at mens sibi conscia factis
praemetuens adhibit stimulos torretque flagellis,
nec videt interea qui terminus esse malorum   1020

possit nec quae sit poenarum denique finis
atque eadem metuit magis haec ne in morte gravescant.
hic Acherusia fit stultorum denique vita.

Context: shortly after **E**.

G Lucretius 3.1087–94

nec prorsum vitam ducendo demimus hilum
tempore de mortis nec delibare valemus,
quo minus esse diu possimus forte perempti.
proinde licet quot vis vivendo condere saecla;   1090
mors aeterna tamen nilo minus illa manebit,
nec minus ille diu iam non erit, ex hodierno
lumine qui finem vitai fecit, et ille,
mensibus atque annis qui multis occidit ante.

Context: the close of Lucretius' diatribe against the fear of death.

25 Philosophy

A Epicurus, *Ep. Men.* 122

(1) μήτε νέος τις ὢν μελλέτω φιλοσοφεῖν, μήτε γέρων ὑπάρχων κοπιάτω
φιλοσοφῶν. οὔτε γὰρ ἄωρος οὐδείς ἐστιν οὔτε πάρωρος πρὸς τὸ κατὰ
ψυχὴν ὑγιαῖνον. ὁ δὲ λέγων ἢ μήπω τοῦ φιλοσοφεῖν ὑπάρχειν ὥραν ἢ
παρεληλυθέναι τὴν ὥραν ὅμοιός ἐστι τῷ λέγοντι πρὸς εὐδαιμονίαν ἢ μὴ
παρεῖναι τὴν ὥραν ἢ μηκέτι εἶναι. (2) ὥστε φιλοσοφητέον καὶ νέῳ καὶ   5
γέροντι, τῷ μὲν ὅπως γηράσκων νεάζῃ τοῖς ἀγαθοῖς διὰ τὴν χάριν τῶν
γεγονότων, τῷ δὲ ὅπως νέος ἅμα καὶ παλαιὸς ᾖ διὰ τὴν ἀφοβίαν τῶν
μελλόντων· (3) μελετᾶν οὖν χρὴ τὰ ποιοῦντα τὴν εὐδαιμονίαν, εἴπερ
παρούσης μὲν αὐτῆς πάντα ἔχομεν, ἀπούσης δὲ πάντα πράττομεν εἰς τὸ
ταύτην ἔχειν. ἃ δέ σοι συνεχῶς παρήγγελλον, ταῦτα καὶ πρᾶττε καὶ μελέτα, στοιχεῖα   10
τοῦ καλῶς ζῆν ταῦτ᾿ εἶναι διαλαμβάνων.

Context: general protreptic prefaced to the doctrinal main body of the *Letter to Menoeceus*, which continues with **23B**.

B Epicurus, *RS* 11–13

(1) [11] εἰ μηθὲν ἡμᾶς αἱ τῶν μετεώρων ὑποψίαι ἠνώχλουν καὶ αἱ περὶ
θανάτου, μή ποτε πρὸς ἡμᾶς ᾖ τι, ἔτι τε τὸ μὴ κατανοεῖν τοὺς ὅρους τῶν
ἀλγηδόνων καὶ τῶν ἐπιθυμιῶν, οὐκ ἂν προσεδεόμεθα φυσιολογίας. (2) [12]
οὐκ ἦν τὸ φοβούμενον λύειν ὑπὲρ τῶν κυριωτάτων μὴ κατειδότα τίς ἡ τοῦ
σύμπαντος φύσις, ἀλλ᾿ ὑποπτεύοντά τι τῶν κατὰ τοὺς μύθους. ὥστε οὐκ   5
ἦν ἄνευ φυσιολογίας ἀκεραίους τὰς ἡδονὰς ἀπολαμβάνειν. (3) [13] οὐθὲν

Epicurean ethics

ὄφελος ἦν τὴν κατὰ ἀνθρώπους ἀσφάλειαν κατασκευάζεσθαι τῶν ἄνωθεν
ὑπόπτων καθεστώτων καὶ τῶν ὑπὸ γῆς καὶ ἁπλῶς τῶν ἐν τῷ ἀπείρῳ.

2 τε τὸ μὴ κατανοεῖν Lachelier: τετόλμηκα νοεῖν codd.   5 ὑποπτεύοντά τι Usener: ὑποπτευόμενον τι
codd.: ὑποπτεύοντι SV 49

C Porphyry, *Ad Marcellam* 31 (Usener 221)

κενὸς ἐκείνου φιλοσόφου λόγος, ὑφ' οὗ μηδὲν πάθος ἀνθρώπου θεραπεύε-
ται· ὥσπερ γὰρ ἰατρικῆς οὐδὲν ὄφελος ⟨εἰ⟩ μὴ τὰς νόσους τῶν σωμάτων
θεραπεύει, οὕτως οὐδὲ φιλοσοφίας, εἰ μὴ τὸ τῆς ψυχῆς ἐκβάλλει πάθος.

2 ⟨εἰ⟩ Nauck   3 θεραπεύει Mai: -ειν cod.

Context: culmination of a long string of ethical quotations from Epicurus.
For the Epicurean medical metaphor, cf. Gigante [271], Nussbaum [270].

D Epicurus, *SV* 29, 54

(1) [29] παρρησίᾳ γὰρ ἔγωγε χρώμενος φυσιολόγῳ χρησμῳδεῖν τὰ
συμφέροντα πᾶσιν ἀνθρώποις μᾶλλον ἂν βουλοίμην, κἂν μηδεὶς μέλλῃ
συνήσειν, ἢ συγκατατιθέμενος ταῖς δόξαις καρποῦσθαι τὸν πυκνὸν
παραπίπτοντα παρὰ τῶν πολλῶν ἔπαινον. (2) [54] οὐ προσποιεῖσθαι δεῖ
φιλοσοφεῖν, ἀλλ' ὄντως φιλοσοφεῖν· οὐ γὰρ προσδεόμεθα τοῦ δοκεῖν   5
ὑγιαίνειν, ἀλλὰ τοῦ κατ' ἀλήθειαν ὑγιαίνειν.

1 χρησμῳδεῖν Usener: χρησμῳ· δεῖ cod.

E Epicurus, *SV* 45

οὐ κόμπου οὐδὲ φωνῆς ἐργαστικοὺς οὐδὲ τὴν περιμάχητον παρὰ τοῖς
πολλοῖς παιδείαν ἐνδεικνυμένους φυσιολογία παρασκευάζει, ἀλλ' ἀσοβάρους καὶ αὐτάρκεις καὶ ἐπὶ τοῖς ἰδίοις ἀγαθοῖς, οὐκ ἐπὶ τοῖς τῶν πραγμάτων
μέγα φρονοῦντας.

2–3 ἀλλ' ἀσοβάρους Leopold: ἀλλὰ σοβάρους cod.

F Athenaeus 588A (Usener 117)

καὶ πρῶτον μὲν μνησθήσομαι τοῦ φιλαληθεστάτου Ἐπικούρου· ὅστις ἐγκυκλίου παιδείας
ἀμύητος ὢν ἐμακάριζε καὶ τοὺς ὁμοίως αὐτῷ ἐπὶ φιλοσοφίαν παρερχομένους, τοιαύτας
φωνὰς προιέμενος. "μακαρίζω σε, ὦ οὗτος, ὅτι καθαρὸς πάσης παιδείας ἐπὶ
φιλοσοφίαν ὥρμησαι."

3 παιδείας Schweighaüser: αἰτίας codd.

Context: a catalogue of famous courtesans. Epicurus is here being introduced as an
unsophisticated type (the portrait continues directly with the fragment of Timon also
cited at **3K**), in preparation for a scurrilous reference to his courtesan mistress
Leontion.
   3 **οὗτος** 'So and so': Athenaeus has forgotten the name, but we supply it in the
vol. 1 translation, thanks to Plutarch, *Contra Ep. beat.* 1094D, who summarizes the

same letter, with the information that it was addressed to one Apelles. The same summary also confirms the correction παιδείας for αἰτίας.

G Diogenes Laertius 10.6 (Usener 163, part)

ἔν τε τῇ πρὸς Πυθοκλέα ἐπιστολῇ γράφειν· "παιδείαν δὲ πᾶσαν, μακάριε, φεῦγε τἀκάτιον ἀράμενος."

1 παιδείαν FP(corr.): παιδιὰν BF(corr.)P   φεῦγε τἀκάτιον ἀράμενος Gassendi (cf. Plut., *De audiendis poetis* 15D, *Contra Ep. beat.* 1094D): φεύγετε κατιδιαραμεν B: φεύγετε κατιδιεραμεν cett.

H Plutarch, *Contra Ep. beat.* 1095B–C (including Usener 20)

καίτοι τἄλλα μὲν ὡς ἡμῖν ἐπῆλθεν εἴρηται· μουσικὴν δὲ ὅσας ἡδονὰς καὶ χάριτας οἵας φέρουσαν ἀποστρέφονται καὶ φεύγουσιν καὶ βουλόμενος οὐκ ἄν τις ἐκλάθοιτο, δι' ἀτοπίαν ὧν Ἐπίκουρος λέγει, φιλοθέωρον μὲν ἀποφαίνων τὸν σοφὸν ἐν ταῖς Διαπορ-ίαις καὶ χαίροντα παρ' ὀντινοῦν ἕτερον ἀκροάμασι καὶ θεάμασι Διονυσιακ-οῖς, προβλήμασι δὲ μουσικοῖς καὶ κριτικῶν φιλολόγοις ζητήμασιν οὐδὲ   5
παρὰ πότον διδοὺς χώραν, ἀλλὰ καὶ τοῖς φιλομούσοις τῶν βασιλέων παραινῶν στρατηγικὰ διηγήματα καὶ φορτικὰς βωμολοχίας ὑπομένειν μᾶλλον ἐν τοῖς συμποσίοις ἢ λόγους περὶ μουσικῶν καὶ ποιητικῶν προβλημάτων περαινομένους.

Context: attack on the alleged Epicurean preference of sordid to cultural pleasures (including, shortly before, citations of **F** and **G**).

I Epicurus, *SV* 27, 41

(1) [27] ἐπὶ τῶν ἄλλων ἐπιτηδευμάτων μόλις τελειωθεῖσιν ὁ καρπὸς ἔρχεται, ἐπὶ δὲ φιλοσοφίας συντρέχει τῇ γνώσει τὸ τερπνόν· οὐ γὰρ μετὰ μάθησιν ἀπόλαυσις, ἀλλὰ ἅμα μάθησις καὶ ἀπόλαυσις. (2) [41] γελᾶν ἅμα δεῖ καὶ φιλοσοφεῖν καὶ οἰκονομεῖν καὶ τοῖς λοιποῖς οἰκειώμασι χρῆσθαι καὶ μηδαμῇ λήγειν τὰς ἐκ τῆς ὀρθῆς φιλοσοφίας φωνὰς ἀφιέντας.   5

3 μάθησιν Wotke: -σις cod.   4 δεῖ Leopold: δεῖν cod.   5 λήγειν Usener: λέγειν cod.   ὀρθῆς Hartel: ὀργῆς cod.

J Philodemus, *Adversus sophistas* 4.7–14

καὶ δ[ιὰ] π[αντὸς ἔστω | κ]αὶ π[α]νταχῆι παρε⌐π⌐ό|μενο[ν] ἡ τετραφάρμακος· "ἄφοβον ὁ θεός, ἀν[ύ]ποπτον ὁ θάνατος· καὶ | τἀγαθὸν μὲν εὔκτητ[ον], | τὸ δὲ δεινὸν εὐεκκα[ρ]τέρητον."

1 δ[ιὰ] π[αντὸς Comparetti   ἔστω Vogliano   παρε⌐π⌐ό|μενο[ν] Crönert: παρε[2–3]||μενο[P: παρειρο|μενο[O
(For sigla, cf. note on **20B**)

Context: uncertain.
   For text and fuller apparatus, see Gigante [147], 260 n.

Epicurean ethics

K Sextus Empiricus, *M.* 11.168–9 (Usener 219)

ἐπαγγέλλονται γὰρ τέχνην τινὰ περὶ τὸν βίον παραδώσειν, καὶ διὰ τοῦτο Ἐπίκουρος μὲν ἔλεγε τὴν φιλοσοφίαν ἐνέργειαν εἶναι λόγοις καὶ διαλογισμοῖς τὸν εὐδαίμονα βίον περιποιοῦσαν.

Context: 'Is there an art of life?'

1 **ἐπαγγέλλονται** *Sc.* οἱ δογματικοί.
2 **διαλογισμοῖς** For the term, cf. Sedley [126], 13, and **24D** 5.

Stoicism

26 The philosophical curriculum

A Aetius I prooem. 2 (SVF 2.35)

οἱ μὲν οὖν Στωικοὶ ἔφασαν τὴν μὲν σοφίαν εἶναι θείων τε καὶ ἀνθρωπίνων ἐπιστήμην, τὴν δὲ φιλοσοφίαν ἄσκησιν ἐπιτηδείου τέχνης· ἐπιτήδειον δὲ εἶναι μίαν καὶ ἀνωτάτω τὴν ἀρετήν, ἀρετὰς δὲ τὰς γενικωτάτας τρεῖς, φυσικὴν ἠθικὴν λογικήν· δι᾽ ἣν αἰτίαν καὶ τριμερής ἐστιν ἡ φιλοσοφία, ἧς τὸ μὲν φυσικὸν τὸ δὲ ἠθικὸν τὸ δὲ λογικόν· καὶ φυσικὸν μὲν ὅταν περὶ   5
κόσμου ζητῶμεν καὶ τῶν ἐν κόσμῳ, ἠθικὸν δὲ τὸ κατησχολημένον περὶ τὸν ἀνθρώπινον βίον, λογικὸν δὲ τὸ περὶ τὸν λόγον, ὃ καὶ διαλεκτικὸν καλοῦσιν.

2 ἐπιτηδείου τέχνης ABC: inverso ordine vulgo

1–2   For this definition of wisdom, cf. G 5, which adds 'knowledge of causes', with discussion by Kerferd [478], 130–1; Long [429], 308–10; Kidd [381], 275.
2   ἄσκησιν ἐπιτηδείου τέχνης   The expression is awkward. We interpret ἐπιτηδείου as shorthand for περὶ τοῦ ἐπιτηδείου. It is not clear to us why this adjective rather than the familiar συμφέρον or ὠφέλιμον is used. On ἄσκησις, see especially Epictetus, Diss. 3.12.
3   μίαν καὶ ἀνωτάτω   By 'single' and 'highest', as γενικωτάτας shows, the top of a division of virtue is meant (see vol. 1, 193), with physics, ethics, and logic the three most comprehensive species.

B Diogenes Laertius 7.39–41

(1) τριμερῆ φασιν εἶναι τὸν κατὰ φιλοσοφίαν λόγον· εἶναι γὰρ αὐτοῦ τὸ μέν τι φυσικόν, τὸ δὲ ἠθικόν, τὸ δὲ λογικόν. οὕτω δὲ πρῶτος διεῖλε Ζήνων ὁ Κιτιεὺς ἐν τῷ Περὶ λόγου καὶ Χρύσιππος ἐν τῷ α΄ Περὶ λόγου καὶ ἐν τῷ α΄ τῶν Φυσικῶν . . . καὶ Διογένης ὁ Βαβυλώνιος καὶ Ποσειδώνιος. (2) ταῦτα δὲ τὰ μέρη ὁ μὲν Ἀπολλόδωρος τόπους καλεῖ, ὁ δὲ Χρύσιππος καὶ   5
Εὔδρομος εἴδη, ἄλλοι γένη. (3) εἰκάζουσι δὲ ζῴῳ τὴν φιλοσοφίαν, ὀστοῖς μὲν καὶ νεύροις τὸ λογικὸν προσομοιοῦντες, τοῖς δὲ σαρκωδεστέροις τὸ ἠθικόν, τῇ δὲ ψυχῇ τὸ φυσικόν. ἢ πάλιν ᾠῷ· τὰ μὲν γὰρ ἐκτὸς εἶναι τὸ λογικόν, τὰ δὲ μετὰ ταῦτα τὸ ἠθικόν, τὰ δ᾽ ἐσωτάτω τὸ φυσικόν. ἢ ἀγρῷ παμφόρῳ· τὸν μὲν περιβεβλημένον φραγμὸν τὸ λογικόν, τὸν δὲ καρπὸν τὸ   10
ἠθικόν, τὴν δὲ γῆν ἢ τὰ δένδρα τὸ φυσικόν. ἢ πόλει καλῶς τετειχισμένῃ καὶ κατὰ λόγον διοικουμένῃ. (4) καὶ οὐθὲν μέρος τοῦ ἑτέρου προκεκρίσθαι,

Stoicism

καθά τινες αὐτῶν φασιν, ἀλλὰ μεμίχθαι αὐτά. καὶ τὴν παράδοσιν μικτὴν
ἐποίουν. ἄλλοι δὲ πρῶτον μὲν τὸ λόγικον τάττουσι, δεύτερον δὲ τὸ
φυσικόν, καὶ τρίτον τὸ ἠθικόν· ὧν ἐστι Ζήνων ἐν τῷ Περὶ λόγου καὶ   15
Χρύσιππος καὶ Ἀρχέδημος καὶ Εὔδρομος. ὁ μὲν γὰρ Πτολεμαεὺς
Διογένης ἀπὸ τῶν ἠθικῶν ἄρχεται, ὁ δ᾽ Ἀπολλόδωρος δεύτερα τὰ ἠθικά,
Παναίτιος δὲ καὶ Ποσειδώνιος ἀπὸ τῶν φυσικῶν ἄρχονται ... ὁ δὲ
Κλεάνθης ἐξ μέρη φησί, διαλεκτικόν, ῥητορικόν, ἠθικόν, πολιτικόν,
φυσικόν, θεολογικόν. ἄλλοι δ᾽ οὐ τοῦ λόγου ταῦτα μέρη φασίν, ἀλλ᾽ αὐτῆς   20
τῆς φιλοσοφίας, ὡς Ζήνων ὁ Ταρσεύς.

1 φασιν FP: φησίν B   3 τῷ² F: τῇ BP   5 δὲ¹ om. F   8 ἐκτὸς P(corr.): ἔξω F: om. BP   10
⟨οὐ⟩ τὸν μὲν Arnim   12 προκεκρίσθαι codd.: ἀποκεκρίσθαι Cobet   13 ἀλλὰ μεμίχθαι P:
ἀναμεμίχθαι BF   21 τῆς t: om. cett.

Context: the opening of Diogenes' doxography of Stoicism.
6–12   For another account of these similes, cf. S.E., M. 7.17–19.
12 **προκεκρίσθαι**   On the retention of the MSS reading, see Kidd [381], 274–5.

C Plutarch, St. rep. 1035A (SVF 2.42, part)

τὰ ἐν τῷ τετάρτῳ Περὶ βίων ἔχοντα κατὰ λέξιν οὕτως· "πρῶτον μὲν οὖν δοκεῖ μοι
κατὰ τὰ ὀρθῶς ὑπὸ τῶν ἀρχαίων εἰρημένα τρία γένη τῶν τοῦ φιλοσόφου
θεωρημάτων εἶναι, τὰ μὲν λογικὰ τὰ δ᾽ ἠθικὰ τὰ δὲ φυσικά· εἶτα τούτων
δεῖν τάττεσθαι πρῶτα μὲν τὰ λογικὰ δεύτερα δὲ τὰ ἠθικὰ τρίτα δὲ τὰ
φυσικά· τῶν δὲ φυσικῶν ἔσχατος εἶναι ὁ περὶ τῶν θεῶν λόγος· διὸ καὶ   5
τελετὰς ἠγόρευσαν τὰς τούτου παραδόσεις."

4 δεῖν τάττεσθαι XdvzB: δεῖν προτάττεσθαι a: δεῖ προτάττεσθαι ΑβγΕ   6 τούτου Xg: τούτων cett.

Context: Chrysippus' inconsistency in specifying the curriculum of C but regularly
departing from this order in his writings.
2   On the origins of the tripartite division of philosophy, cf. Cherniss [326] ad loc.
6 **τελετάς**   Chrysippus sought to derive τελεταί from τελευταῖος; cf. SVF
2.1008. For discussion of his conception of theology, see Mansfeld [496], 134–6.

D Sextus Empiricus, M. 7.19 (Posidonius fr. 88, part)

ὁ δὲ Ποσειδώνιος, ἐπεὶ τὰ μὲν μέρη τῆς φιλοσοφίας ἀχώριστά ἐστιν
ἀλλήλων, τὰ δὲ φυτὰ τῶν καρπῶν ἕτερα θεωρεῖται καὶ τὰ τείχη τῶν φυτῶν
κεχώρισται, ζώῳ μᾶλλον εἰκάζειν ἠξίου τὴν φιλοσοφίαν, αἵματι μὲν καὶ
σαρξὶ τὸ φυσικόν, ὀστέοις δὲ καὶ νεύροις τὸ λογικόν, ψυχῇ δὲ τὸ ἠθικόν.

Context: discussion of the divisions of philosophy. On Posidonius' preference for the
ζῷον image, cf. Kidd [381], 273–5.

E Ammonius, In Ar. An. pr. 8,20–2; 9,1–2 (SVF 2.49, part)

οἱ μὲν Στωικοὶ τὴν λογικὴν οὐ μόνον ὄργανον οὐκ ἀξιοῦσι καλεῖσθαι

φιλοσοφίας, ἀλλ' οὐδὲ μόριον τὸ τυχὸν ἀλλὰ μέρος . . . φασιν ὅτι αὐτὴ ἡ
φιλοσοφία τὴν λογικὴν ἀπογεννᾷ καὶ ταύτῃ μέρος ἂν εἴη αὐτῆς.

Context: discussion of those 'who do not make logic an ὄργανον.

2 μόριον–μέρος Cf. Ammonius, ibid. 8,34–5 (not in SVF): μέρος δὲ μορίου
διαφέρει, ὅτι τὸ μέρος μέγα μέρος ἐστίν, τὸ δὲ μόριον μέρος ἐστὶν καὶ τοῦ μέρους
μέρος· οἷον μέρος μέν ἐστιν φιλοσοφίας τὸ θεωρητικόν, μόριον δὲ τὸ θεολογικόν.
Philoponus, in his treatment of the same point, In Ar. An. pr. 6,19–7,9 (not in SVF),
says that μόριον refers to 'that which shares the matter and goal of that of which it is a
μόριον', 6,31–2. As reported by him, the Stoics inferred that logic is a μέρος of
philosophy by eliminating the possibilities of its being a μόριον of physics or ethics.

F Seneca, Ep. 88.25–8 (Posidonius fr. 90, part)

(1) multa adiuvant nos nec ideo partes nostri sunt; immo si partes essent, non
adiuvarent. cibus adiutorium corporis nec tamen pars est. aliquod nobis
praestat geometria ministerium: sic philosophiae necessaria est quomodo ipsi
faber, sed nec hic geometriae pars est nec illa philosophiae. (2) praeterea
utraque fines suos habet; sapiens enim causas naturalium et quaerit et novit,   5
quorum numeros mensurasque geometres persequitur et supputat. qua ratione
constent caelestia, quae illis sit vis quaeve natura sapiens scit: cursus et recursus
et quasdam obversationes per quas descendunt et adlevantur ac speciem
interdum stantium praebent, cum caelestibus stare non liceat, colligit mathematicus.
quae causa in speculo imagines exprimat sciet sapiens: illud tibi geometres   10
potest dicere, quantum abesse debeat corpus ab imagine et qualis forma speculi
quales imagines reddat. (3) magnum esse solem philosophus probabit, quantus
sit mathematicus, qui usu quodam et exercitatione procedit. sed ut procedat,
inpetranda illi quaedam principia sunt; non est autem ars sui iuris cui
precarium fundamentum est. philosophia nil ab alio petit, totum opus a solo   15
excitat: mathematice, ut ita dicam, superficiaria est, in alieno aedificat; accipit
prima, quorum beneficio ad ulteriora perveniat.

1 nostri Madvig: nostrae codd.   3 ipsi ς: ipse codd.   8 obversationes Bonnet: observationes codd.   9
stantium P: instantium QVb

Context: the difference between philosophy and liberales artes – geometry, medicine
etc.

Seneca in our extract is answering an anonymous objection that the liberales artes,
because they assist philosophy, should be included as one of its parts. Posidonius has
already been named in section 21 of the same letter, and Kidd [382], 8–10, gives strong
reasons for taking him to be Seneca's source in F.

G Seneca, Ep. 89.4–5

primum itaque, si [ut] videtur tibi, dicam inter sapientiam et philosophiam
quid intersit. sapientia perfectum bonum est mentis humanae; philosophia
sapientiae amor est et adfectatio: haec eo tendit quo illa pervenit . . . sapien-

tiam quidam ita finierunt ut dicerent divinorum et humanorum scientiam;
quidam ita: sapientia est nosse divina et humana et horum causas.   5

1 *ut* om. ψς   3 *eo tendit* Cornelissen: *ostendit* codd.   4 *quidam* B: om. φψ

Context: the scope and division of philosophy.

2 **perfectum**   Cf. **63D**.

4–5   See note on **A** 1–2.

H Stobaeus, 2.67,5–12 (*SVF* 3.294)

φιλομουσίαν δὲ καὶ φιλογραμματίαν καὶ φιλιππίαν καὶ φιλοκυνηγίαν καὶ
καθόλου καὶ κατ᾽ ἐγκυκλίους λεγομένας τέχνας ἐπιτηδεύματα μὲν
καλοῦσιν, ἐπιστήμας δ᾽ οὔ· ἐν ταῖς σπουδαίαις ἕξεσι ταῦτα καταλείπουσι,
καὶ ἀκολούθως μόνον τὸν σοφὸν φιλόμουσον εἶναι λέγουσι καὶ φιλογράμ-
ματον, καὶ ἐπὶ τῶν ἄλλων κατὰ τὸ ἀνάλογον. τό τε ἐπιτήδευμα τοῦτον   5
ὑπογράφουσι τὸν τρόπον· ὁδὸν διὰ τέχνης ἢ μέρους ἄγουσαν ἐπὶ ⟨τὰ⟩ κατ᾽
ἀρετήν.

2 καὶ κατ᾽ codd.: πάσας τὰς Canter: καὶ τὰς Usener   3 ⟨τε⟩ post ἐν Heeren   6 ἢ μέρους Usener:
ἡμέρου codd.   ⟨τὰ⟩ Wachsmuth

Context: doxography of Stoic ethics.

2 **καὶ κατ᾽**   The MSS reading should be retained: φιλομουσία etc. are called
ἐπιτηδεύματα and not ἐπιστῆμαι, whether they are thought of quite generally, or
treated specifically as items of the standard curriculum (ἐγκυκλίους τέχνας). Early
Stoics (cf. **67B** 2; *SVF* 1.349–50) had insisted on the uselessness of the standard
curriculum, at least when detached from philosophy. The later strategy, as set out
here, was to make the wise man the only proper practitioner of this and other
'pursuits'; cf. also *SVF* 3.738–40.

ONTOLOGY

27 Existence and subsistence

A Seneca, *Ep.* 58.13–15 (*SVF* 2.332, part)

Stoici volunt superponere huic etiamnunc aliud genus magis principale
... primum genus Stoicis quibusdam videtur "quid"; quare videatur
subiiciam. in rerum, inquiunt, natura quaedam sunt, quaedam non sunt. et
haec autem quae non sunt rerum natura complectitur, quae animo succurrunt,
tamquam Centauri, Gigantes et quicquid aliud falso cogitatione formatum   5
habere aliquam imaginem coepit, quamvis non habeat substantiam.

Context: a basic lesson in metaphysics, primarily Platonist.

1–2   The apparent disagreement among the Stoics as to whether 'something' or
'existent' (referred to by *huic*, 1) constitutes the highest genus (cf. **30C 4**) is mirrored in
Sextus' vacillation on the point. At *PH* 2.86–7 he makes it 'something' but in the
corresponding argument at *M.* 8.32ff. it is 'existent'.

5   The epistemological status of these mythical creatures is that of figments, φαντάσματα: see **39A–B**.
6 **imaginem . . . substantiam**   The Greek original may be ἔμφασις . . . ὑπόστασις (cf. ps.-Aristotle, *De mundo* 4, 395a28ff., ps.-Plutarch, *Plac.* 894B), the latter standardly being used to designate corporeal existence. If so, Seneca is not here following the restricted Stoic use of ὑφίστασθαι (see vol. 1, 164). Cf. id. *NQ* 1.15.6.

B Alexander, *In Ar. Top.* 301,19–25 (*SVF* 2.329)

οὕτω δεικνύοις ἂν ὅτι μὴ καλῶς τὸ τὶ οἱ ἀπὸ τῆς Στοᾶς γένος τοῦ ὄντος τίθενται· εἰ γὰρ τί, δῆλον ὅτι καὶ ὄν· εἰ δὲ ὄν, τὸν τοῦ ὄντος ἀναδέχοιτο ἂν λόγον. ἀλλ᾽ ἐκεῖνοι νομοθετήσαντες αὐτοῖς τὸ κατὰ σωμάτων μόνων λέγεσθαι διαφεύγοιεν ἂν τὸ ἠπορημένον· διὰ τοῦτο γὰρ τὸ τὶ γενικώτερον αὐτοῦ φασιν εἶναι, κατηγορούμενον οὐ κατὰ σωμάτων μόνον ἀλλὰ καὶ   5
κατὰ ἀσωμάτων.

Context: commentary on *Top.* iv.1, 121a10. With regard to the principle that a species admits the definition of its genus but not vice versa, Alexander observes that there can be no higher genus to which ὄν or ἕν belongs.

C Sextus Empiricus, *M.* 1.17 (*SVF* 2.330)

καὶ μὴν εἰ διδάσκεταί τι, ἤτοι διὰ τῶν οὐτινῶν διδαχθήσεται ἢ διὰ τῶν τινῶν. ἀλλὰ διὰ μὲν τῶν οὐτινῶν οὐχ οἷόν τε διδαχθῆναι· ἀνυπόστατα γάρ ἐστι τῇ διανοίᾳ ταῦτα κατὰ τοὺς ἀπὸ τῆς Στοᾶς.

Context: 'Can anything be taught?'

D Sextus Empiricus, *M.* 10.218 (*SVF* 2.331, part)

ὥσθ᾽ οὗτοι μὲν σῶμα ποιοῦσι τὸν χρόνον, οἱ δὲ ἀπὸ τῆς Στοᾶς φιλόσοφοι ἀσώματον αὐτὸν ᾠήθησαν ὑπάρχειν· τῶν γὰρ τινῶν φασι τὰ μὲν εἶναι σώματα, τὰ δὲ ἀσώματα, τῶν δὲ ἀσωμάτων τέσσαρα εἴδη καταριθμοῦνται ὡς λεκτὸν καὶ κενὸν καὶ τόπον καὶ χρόνον. ἐξ οὗ δῆλον γίνεται, ὅτι πρὸς τῷ ἀσωμάτῳ ὑπολαμβάνειν τὸν χρόνον, ἔτι καὶ καθ᾽ αὑτό τι νοούμενον πρᾶγμα δοξάζουσι τοῦτον.   5

Context: a brief doxography of theories of time. The Stoic theory is presented here and refuted at ibid. 234–7; cf. also **51F** with note.
1 **οὗτοι**   Aenesidemus and Heraclitus.
3–4   For the same list, cf. Plutarch, *Col.* 1116B.

E Sextus Empiricus, *M.* 8.409–10 (*SVF* 2.85, part)

(1) ὥσπερ γάρ, φασίν, ὁ παιδοτρίβης καὶ ὁπλομάχος ἔσθ᾽ ὅτε μὲν λαβόμενος τῶν χειρῶν τοῦ παιδὸς ῥυθμίζει καὶ διδάσκει τινὰς κινεῖσθαι κινήσεις, ἔσθ᾽ ὅτε δὲ ἄπωθεν ἑστὼς καί πως κινούμενος ἐν ῥυθμῷ παρέχει ἑαυτὸν ἐκείνῳ πρὸς μίμησιν, (2) οὕτω καὶ τῶν φανταστῶν ἔνια μὲν οἱονεὶ ψαύοντα καὶ θιγγάνοντα τοῦ ἡγεμονικοῦ ποιεῖται τὴν ἐν τούτῳ τύπωσιν,   5

Stoic ontology

ὁποῖόν ἐστι τὸ λευκὸν καὶ μέλαν καὶ κοινῶς τὸ σῶμα, ἔνια δὲ τοιαύτην ἔχει
φύσιν, τοῦ ἡγεμονικοῦ ἐπ' αὐτοῖς φαντασιουμένου καὶ οὐχ ὑπ' αὐτῶν,
ὁποῖά ἐστι τὰ ἀσώματα λεκτά. οἱ δὲ τοῦτο λέγοντες πιθανῷ μὲν χρῶνται
παραδείγματι, οὐ συνάγουσι δὲ τὸ προκείμενον. ὁ μὲν γὰρ παιδοτρίβης καὶ ὁπλομάχος εἰσὶ
σῶμα, καὶ κατὰ τοῦτο ἐδύναντο φαντασίαν ἐμποιεῖν τῷ παιδί· ἡ δὲ ἀπόδειξις ἀσώματος   10
καθειστήκει, καὶ κατὰ τοῦτο ἐζητεῖτο εἰ δύναται φανταστικῶς τυποῦν τὸ ἡγεμονικόν.

Context: argument against the notion of demonstration (on which see **36B**; **42**), on the
ground that, being an incorporeal λεκτόν, it cannot act upon us (cf. **45**), and hence
cannot produce a cognitive impression (cf. **40**). The portion quoted gives the Stoic
reply (1–8), followed by Sextus' very reasonable rejoinder.

F Simplicius, *In Ar. Cat.* 66,32–67,2 (*SVF* 2.369, part)

οἱ δέ γε Στωικοὶ εἰς ἐλάττονα συστέλλειν ἀξιοῦσιν τὸν τῶν πρώτων γενῶν
ἀριθμὸν καί τινα ἐν τοῖς ἐλάττοσιν ὑπηλλαγμένα παραλαμβάνουσιν.
ποιοῦνται γὰρ τὴν τομὴν εἰς τέσσαρα, εἰς ὑποκείμενα καὶ ποιὰ καὶ πῶς
ἔχοντα καὶ πρός τί πως ἔχοντα.

Context: comparison of the tenfold division of genera in Aristotle's *Categories* with
those of other philosophers. The word γένη is thus dictated by context, and is not
strong evidence for a specifically Stoic usage of the term.
It is also unlikely that the Stoic theory was evolved with Aristotle's *Categories* in
mind. There is no sign that this work was even generally known until the rediscovery
of Aristotle's school treatises in the first century B.C. There then quickly followed a
spate of commentaries and critiques, including one by the Stoic Athenodorus, who
did not treat it as a rival to the Stoic theory, but, interpreting it as an exercise in
linguistic analysis, argued that ten divisions were *too few* for the purpose (Simplicius,
ibid. 18,26ff., 62,24–7, 128,5–8).
Plotinus' long discussion of the four Stoic genera in *Enn.* 6.1.25–30 is excluded
from the testimonies in **27–9**. He certainly knew their names (*SVF* 2.371), but it is
hard to feel that his criticisms relied on much more than intelligent guesswork.

G Galen, *Meth. med.* 10.155,1–8 (*SVF* 2.322, part)

τὴν γὰρ μικρολογίαν τῶν ὀνομάτων, ἣν ἐκομψεύσαντό τινες τῶν
φιλοσόφων . . . παραιτοῦμαι λέγειν τὰ νῦν . . . λέγω δὲ μικρολογίαν, ἐν ᾗ
διαιροῦνται κατὰ γένη τό τε ὂν καὶ τὸ ὑφεστός.

Context: refutation of the suggestion that disease does not really 'exist'. Galen is almost
certainly referring to Stoic doctrine, but his target cannot itself be Stoic: no Stoic
would deny that disease 'exists'. His remark is ostensibly made by way of justification
for a switch on his own part from εἶναι (154,12) to ὑπάρχειν (155,1). This makes it less
certain that he is referring to the Stoic distinction *between* ὄν and ὑφεστός rather than
to distinctions *within* either class.

28 The first and second genera

A Plutarch, *Comm. not.* 1083A–1084A

(1) ὁ τοίνυν περὶ αὐξήσεως λόγος ἐστὶ μὲν ἀρχαῖος· ἠρώτηται γάρ, ὥς φησι
Χρύσιππος, ὑπ' Ἐπιχάρμου· τῶν δ' ἐν Ἀκαδημείᾳ οἰομένων μὴ πάνυ
ῥάδιον μηδ' αὐτόθεν ἕτοιμον εἶναι τὴν ἀπορίαν πολλὰ κατητιᾶσθαι ⟨οὗτοι
καὶ⟩ κατεβόησαν ὡς τὰς προλήψεις ἀναιρούντων καὶ παρὰ τὰς ἐννοίας
⟨φιλοσοφούντων· αὐτοὶ δ' οὐ μόνον οὐδὲ τὰς ἐννοίας⟩ φυλάττουσιν, ἀλλὰ   5
καὶ τὴν αἴσθησιν προσδιαστρέφουσιν. (2) ὁ μὲν γὰρ λόγος ἁπλοῦς ἐστι καὶ
τὰ λήμματα συγχωροῦσιν οὗτοι· τὰς ἐν μέρει πάσας οὐσίας ῥεῖν καὶ
φέρεσθαι, τὰ μὲν ἐξ αὐτῶν μεθιείσας τὰ δέ ποθεν ἐπιόντα προσδεχομένας,
οἷς δὲ πρόσεισι καὶ ἄπεισιν ἀριθμοῖς ἢ πλήθεσι ταῦτα μὴ διαμένειν ἀλλ'
ἕτερα γίνεσθαι, ταῖς εἰρημέναις προσόδοις ⟨καὶ ἀφόδοις⟩ ἐξαλλαγὴν τῆς   10
οὐσίας λαμβανούσης· αὐξήσεις δὲ καὶ φθίσεις οὐ κατὰ δίκην ὑπὸ συνηθείας
ἐκνενικῆσθαι τὰς μεταβολὰς ταύτας λέγεσθαι, γενέσεις [δὲ] καὶ φθορὰς
μᾶλλον αὐτὰς ὀνομάζεσθαι προσῆκον ὅτι τοῦ καθεστῶτος εἰς ἕτερον
ἐκβιβάζουσι τὸ δ' αὔξεσθαι καὶ τὸ μειοῦσθαι πάθη σώματός ἐστιν
ὑποκειμένου καὶ διαμένοντος. (3) οὕτω δέ πως τούτων λεγομένων καὶ   15
τιθεμένων, τί ἀξιοῦσιν οἱ πρόδικοι τῆς ἐναργείας οὗτοι καὶ κανόνες τῶν
ἐννοιῶν; ἕκαστον ἡμῶν δίδυμον εἶναι καὶ διφυῆ καὶ διττόν – οὐχ ὥσπερ οἱ
ποιηταὶ τοὺς Μολιονίδας οἴονται, τοῖς μὲν ἡνωμένους μέρεσι τοῖς δ'
ἀποκρινομένους, ἀλλὰ δύο σώματα ταὐτὸν ἔχοντα χρῶμα, ταὐτὸν δὲ
σχῆμα, ταὐτὸν δὲ βάρος καὶ τόπον ⟨τὸν αὐτὸν ὅμως δὲ διπλᾶ καίπερ⟩ ὑπὸ   20
μηδενὸς ἀνθρώπων ὁρώμενα πρότερον· (4) ἀλλ' οὗτοι μόνοι εἶδον τὴν
σύνθεσιν ταύτην καὶ διπλόην καὶ ἀμφιβολίαν, ὡς δύο ἡμῶν ἕκαστός ἐστιν
ὑποκείμενα, τὸ μὲν οὐσία τὸ δὲ ⟨ἰδίως ποιός⟩, καὶ τὸ μὲν ἀεὶ ῥεῖ καὶ
φέρεται, μήτ' αὐξόμενον μήτε μειούμενον μήθ' ὅλως οἷόν ἐστι διαμένον, τὸ
δὲ διαμένει καὶ αὐξάνεται καὶ μειοῦται καὶ πάντα πάσχει τἀναντία   25
θατέρῳ, συμπεφυκὸς καὶ συνηρμοσμένον καὶ συγκεχυμένον καὶ τῆς
διαφορᾶς τῇ αἰσθήσει μηδαμοῦ παρέχον ἅψασθαι. καίτοι λέγεται μὲν ὁ Λυγκεὺς
ἐκεῖνος διὰ πέτρας καὶ διὰ δρυὸς ὁρᾶν, ἑώρα δέ τις ἀπὸ σκοπῆς ἐν Σικελίᾳ καθεζόμενος τὰς
Καρχηδονίων ἐκ τοῦ λιμένος ναῦς ἐκπλεούσας, ἡμέρας καὶ νυκτὸς ἀπεχούσας δρόμον· οἱ δὲ
περὶ Καλλικράτη καὶ Μυρμηκίδην λέγονται δημιουργεῖν ἅρματα μυίας πτεροῖς καλυπτό-   30
μενα καὶ διατορεύειν ἐν σησάμῳ γράμμασιν ἔπη τῶν Ὁμήρου. (5) ταύτην δὲ τὴν ἐν
ἡμῖν ἑτερότητα καὶ ⟨δια⟩φορὰν οὐδεὶς διεῖλεν οὐδὲ διέστησεν, οὐδ' ἡμεῖς
ᾐσθόμεθα διττοὶ γεγονότες καὶ τῷ μὲν ἀεὶ ῥέοντες μέρει τῷ δ' ἀπὸ
γενέσεως ἄχρι τελευτῆς οἱ αὐτοὶ διαμένοντες. (6) ἁπλούστερον δὲ
ποιοῦμαι τὸν λόγον· ἐπεὶ τέσσαρά γε ποιοῦσιν ὑποκείμενα περὶ ἕκαστον,   35
μᾶλλον δὲ τέσσαρ' ἕκαστον ἡμῶν· ἀρκεῖ δὲ καὶ τὰ δύο πρὸς τὴν ἀτοπίαν.
(7) εἴ γε τοῦ μὲν Πενθέως ἀκούοντες ἐν τῇ τραγῳδίᾳ λέγοντος ὡς "δύο μὲν
ἡλίους ὁρᾷ, διττὰς δὲ Θήβας" οὐχ ὁρᾶν αὐτὸν ἀλλὰ παρορᾶν λέγομεν,
ἐκτρεπόμενον καὶ παρακινοῦντα τοῖς λογισμοῖς· τούτους δ' οὐ μίαν πόλιν,

Stoic ontology

ἀλλὰ πάντας ἀνθρώπους καὶ ζῷα καὶ δένδρα πάντα καὶ σκεύη καὶ ὄργανα   40
καὶ ἱμάτια διττὰ καὶ διφυῆ τιθεμένους οὐ χαίρειν ἐῶμεν, ὡς παρανοεῖν
ἡμᾶς μᾶλλον ἢ νοεῖν ἀναγκάζοντας; (8) ἐνταῦθα μὲν οὖν ἴσως αὐτοῖς
συγγνωστὰ πλάττουσιν ἑτέρας φύσεις ὑποκειμένων· ἄλλη γὰρ οὐδεμία
φαίνεται μηχανὴ φιλοτιμουμένοις σῶσαι καὶ διαφυλάξαι τὰς αὐξήσεις.

3–4 suppl. Pohlenz   5 suppl. Bernardakis   8 τὰ μὲν . . . τὰ δέ Wyttenbach: τὰς μὲν . . . τὰς δέ
codd.   10 suppl. Herwerden   14 ἐκβιβάζουσι Wyttenbach: ἐκβιάζουσι codd.   16 ἐναργείας
Leonicus: ἐνεργείας codd.   18 οἴονται, τοῖς μὲν Pohlenz: οἰόμενοι codd.   20 suppl. Cherniss   23 ⟨ἰδίως ποιός⟩ Sedley (cf. C 2–3): ποιότης Wyttenbach   32 suppl. Wyttenbach

For Epicharmus' version of the Growing Argument (αὐξανόμενος λόγος), see 23 B 2
DK. For its survival into Pyrrhonist scepticism, cf. S.E., *PH* 3.82–4. For more recent
versions, cf. J. Locke, *An essay concerning human understanding* 2.27.3; D. Hume, *A
treatise of human nature* 1.4.6. The title varies in its grammatical form: cf. **A** 1 and **B** 1.
'Growing Argument' is found in Plutarch, *De sera numinis vindicta* 559B, and *Vita
Thesei* 23, and like many puzzle titles (cf. vol. 1, 229) must have a deliberate double
meaning: an argument about a growing man, which itself grows, hydra-like, by
constantly generating new individuals.

21–7   Cherniss ad loc. aptly compares Aristotle, *GC* 1.5, 321b22–4, on which see
Anscombe [403]. Note, however, that Aristotle's 'measure' (ibid. 24–5) is an analogue
for form, not matter as in the Growing Argument (already in Epicharmus, and cf. **A**
2, **D** 5). This discrepancy contributes to the impression that Epicharmus did not
directly influence Aristotle's discussion.

B Anon., *In Plat. Theaet.* 70.5–26

τὸν δὲ | [περ]ὶ τοῦ αὐξομένου | [λ]όγον ἐκείνησεν | [μ]ὲν πρῶτος Πυθα-
[γόρ]ας, ἐκείνησεν | [δὲ] καὶ Πλάτων, ὡς ἐν | [τοῖ]ς εἰς τὸ Συμπόσιον | [ὑ-
π]εμνήσαμεν· ἐπι|[χει]ροῦσι δὲ εἰς αὐτὸ | [καὶ] οἱ ἐξ Ἀκαδημείας, |
μ[α]ρτυρόμενοι μὲν | ὅτι ἀρέσκονται τῶι | εἶναι αὐξήσεις, διὰ δὲ | τὸ τοὺς
Στωικοὺς κα|τασκευάζειν τοῦτο, | οὐ δεόμενον ἀποδεί[ξεω[ς] διδάσκοντες   5
| ὅτι, ἐάν τις τὰ ἐναργῆ | θέληι ἀποδεικνύ|ναι, ἕτερος εἰς τὸ ἐναν|τίον
πιθανωτέρων | εὐπορήσει λόγων.

Context: commentary on Plato, *Tht.* 152d–e, where the flux doctrine is attributed to
nearly all the old thinkers. These include Epicharmus, and in commenting on this
shortly afterwards (71.12ff.) our commentator seems to link the citation of his name
directly to the Growing Argument.

The Academics' purpose in using the argument looks much more weakly sceptical
here than in **A** 2 and 8. Whereas **A** represents the Carneadean Academy, **B** seems to
echo the school's later approach under Philo of Larissa (especially ἐναργῆ, 6: cf.
Cicero, *Acad.* 2.34), whose follower the author may have been (Tarrant [633]).

1–2   Pythagoras is mentioned as the supposed master of Epicharmus. Plato's
detractors alleged that Epicharmus had anticipated his flux doctrine (D.L. 3.12), and in
shifting its origin yet further back to Pythagoras, an acknowledged forerunner of
Plato, our Platonist is no doubt reclaiming it.

28 *The first and second genera*

C P. Oxy. 3008

]σαι δ' εἶναι, τῆς περὶ ἕκαστον | λεγομένης τῶν σωμάτων | δυάδος ἀδιάγνωστον αἰσθή|σει τὴν δ[ι]άφοραν ἐχούσης. | εἰ γὰρ σῶμα μὲν ἰδίως ποι|ὸν οἷον Πλάτων, σῶμά θ' ἡ | οὐσία τοῦ Πλάτωνος, διαφορὰ | δὲ φαινομένη τούτων οὐκ ἔ|στιν οὔτε σχήματος οὔτε | χρώματος οὔτε μεγέθους οὔ⟨τε⟩ | μορφῆς, ἀλλὰ καὶ βάρος ἴσον | καὶ τ[ύ]πος ὁ αὐτὸς   5
ἀμφοτέ|ρων, τίνι διαιροῦντες ὅρῳ | κ[αὶ] χαρακτῆρι νῦν μὲν | φήσομεν αὐτοῦ Πλάτωνος | νῦν δὲ τῆς οὐσίας ἀντιλαμ|βάνεσθαι τῆς Πλάτωνος; | εἰ μὲν γὰρ ἔστιν τις διαφο|ρά, λεγέσθω μετὰ ἀποδεί|[ξεω]ς· εἰ δὲ μηδὲ λέγ-
ειν |

The readings are those of P. Parsons, apart from θ' ἡ in 3, which is based on our own autopsy of the papyrus.

The argument is very close to that of **B**, and a common source may be suspected.

D Stobaeus 1.177,21–179,17 (1–9 = Posidonius fr. 96)

(1) Ποσειδώνιος δὲ φθορὰς καὶ γενέσεις τέτταρας εἶναί φησιν ἐκ τῶν ὄντων εἰς τὸ ὄντα γιγνομένας. (2) τὴν μὲν γὰρ ἐκ τῶν οὐκ ὄντων καὶ τὴν εἰς ⟨τὰ⟩ οὐκ ὄντα, καθάπερ εἴπομεν πρόσθεν, ἐπέγνωσαν ἀνύπαρκτον οὖσαν. (3) τῶν δ' εἰς ⟨τὰ⟩ ὄντα γινομένων μεταβολῶν τὴν μὲν εἶναι κατὰ διαίρεσιν, τὴν δὲ κατ' ἀλλοίωσιν, τὴν δὲ κατὰ σύγχυσιν, τὴν δ' ἐξ ὅλων, λεγομένην δὲ   5
κατ' ἀνάλυσιν. (4) τούτων δὲ τὴν κατ' ἀλλοίωσιν περὶ τὴν οὐσίαν γίγνεσθαι, τὰς δὲ ἄλλας τρεῖς περὶ τοὺς ποιοὺς λεγομένους τοὺς ἐπὶ τῆς οὐσίας γιγνομένους. ἀκολούθως δὲ τούτοις καὶ τὰς γενέσεις συμβαίνειν. (5) τὴν δὲ οὐσίαν οὔτ' αὔξεσθαι οὔτε μειοῦσθαι κατὰ πρόσθεσιν ἢ ἀφαίρεσιν, ἀλλὰ μόνον ἀλλοιοῦσθαι, καθάπερ ἐπ' ἀριθμῶν καὶ μέτρων. (6)   10
καὶ συμβαίνειν ἐπὶ τῶν ἰδίως ποιῶν οἷον Δίωνος καὶ Θέωνος καὶ αὐξήσεις καὶ μειώσεις γίνεσθαι. (7) διὸ καὶ παραμένειν τὴν ἑκάστου ποιότητα [τὰ] ἀπὸ τῆς γενέσεως μέχρι τῆς ἀναιρέσεως, ἐπὶ τῶν ἀναίρεσιν ἐπιδεχομένων ζῴων καὶ φυτῶν καὶ τῶν τούτοις παραπλησίων. (8) ἐπὶ δὲ τῶν ἰδίως ποιῶν φασι δύο εἶναι τὰ δεκτικὰ μόρια, τὸ μέν τι κατὰ τὴν τῆς οὐσίας ὑπόστασιν,   15
τὸ δέ ⟨τι⟩ κατὰ τὴν τοῦ ποιοῦ. τοῦτο γάρ, ὡς πολλάκις ἐλέγομεν, τὴν αὔξησιν καὶ τὴν μείωσιν ἐπιδέχεσθαι· (9) μὴ εἶναι δὲ ταὐτὸν τό τε ποιὸν ἰδίως καὶ τὴν οὐσίαν [ὃ] ἐξ ἧς ἔστι τοῦτο, μὴ μέντοι γε μηδ' ἕτερον, ἀλλὰ μόνον οὐ ταὐτόν, διὰ τὸ καὶ μέρος εἶναι τὴν οὐσίαν καὶ τὸν αὐτὸν ἐπέχειν τόπον, τὰ δ' ἕτερα τινῶν λεγόμενα δεῖν καὶ τόπῳ κεχωρίσθαι καὶ μηδ' ἐν   20
μέρει θεωρεῖσθαι. (10) τὸ δὲ μὴ εἶναι ταὐτὸ τό τε κατὰ τὸ ἰδίως ποιὸν καὶ τὸ κατὰ τὴν οὐσίαν, δῆλον εἶναί φησιν ὁ Μνήσαρχος· ἀναγκαῖον γὰρ τοῖς αὐτοῖς ταὐτὰ συμβεβηκέναι. (11) εἰ γάρ τις πλάσας ἵππον λόγου χάριν συνθλάσειεν, ἔπειτα κύνα ποιήσειεν, εὐλόγως ἂν ἡμᾶς ἰδόντας εἰπεῖν ὅτι τοῦτ' οὐκ ἦν πάλαι, νῦν δ' ἐστίν· ὥσθ' ἕτερον εἶναι τὸ ἐπὶ τοῦ ποιοῦ   25
λεγόμενον. (12) τὸ δὲ καὶ ἐπὶ τῆς οὐσίας καθόλου νομίζειν τοὺς αὐτοὺς εἶναι ταῖς οὐσίαις ἀπίθανον εἶναι φαίνεται· πολλάκις γὰρ συμβαίνει τὴν μὲν οὐσίαν ὑπάρχειν πρὸ τῆς γενέσεως εἰ τύχοι τῆς Σωκράτους, τὸν δὲ

Stoic ontology

Σωκράτην μηδέπω ὑπάρχειν, καὶ μετὰ τὴν τοῦ Σωκράτους ἀναίρεσιν
ὑπομένειν μὲν τὴν οὐσίαν, αὐτὸν δὲ μηκέτ᾽ εἶναι.   30

3 ἐπεγνωσαν codd. 1.155,14ff.: ἀπέσωσαν codd. 1.178,3: ἀπέγνωσαν Diels: ἀπέγνωσεν εἰς Heeren:
ἀπέγνω ὡς ἄν Usener   9 δὲ codd.: γὰρ Heeren   10–11 sic interpunximus: μέτρων [καὶ] συμβαίνει.
ἐπὶ ⟨δὲ⟩ τῶν Heeren   13 ⟨ὡς⟩ ἐπὶ Heeren   16 ποιητοῦ. τὸ γὰρ codd.: corr. Canter   17 δὲ
Diels: τε codd.   19 τὴν οὐσίαν codd.: τῆς οὐσίας corr. Cod. Vat.   26 τὸ δὲ καὶ codd.: τό τε [καὶ]
Heeren

The passage is generally thought to derive from Arius Didymus' *Epitome*. Both Stoics
cited were pupils of Panaetius (died 109 b.c.); the unspecified 'they' are probably the
Stoics of their time.

6–8   It is unclear why qualified individuals should not also be subject to
generation and destruction by ἀλλοίωσις (contrast e.g. Philo, *Aet. mundi* 113), and
indeed Boethus had held that loss of a thing's dominant quality did amount to its
destruction (*SVF* 3 Boethus 7). Perhaps the normal Stoic concentration on living
individuals led Posidonius to suppose that this would only happen in the event of
death (cf. 12–14), which is a form of division (of soul from body, **45D**).

9–10   The reports of Zeno and Chrysippus in **q** also deny growth and diminution
to primary matter, but the resemblance to the doctrine given here is misleading. Their
point is that the *sum* of matter in the world has everlasting fixity, whereas individual
portions of it lose their identity through division and fusion. Here, on the other hand,
it is the portion of matter constituting an individual that is excluded as a proper subject
of growth and diminution, in deference to the Growing Argument.

13   The regular supplement ⟨ὡς⟩ is unnecessary. The qualification, ἐπὶ τῶν κτλ.,
is probably added to allow for the existence of imperishable ἰδίως ποιοί, like Zeus (cf.
O).

19   The weakly attested correction τῆς οὐσίας is usually preferred: but the
substance (=substrate) is part of the qualified individual, and not vice versa.

19–21   Cf. S.E. at M. 9.336 and in **60G 3**; Seneca, *Ep.* 113.4–5 (*SVF* 3.307, part).

E Simplicius, *In Ar. Cat.* 48,11–16

ταύτην δὴ τὴν ἀπορίαν λύων ὁ Πορφύριος (1) "διττόν", φησίν, "ἐστὶν τὸ
ὑποκείμενον, οὐ μόνον κατὰ τοὺς ἀπὸ τῆς Στοᾶς, ἀλλὰ καὶ κατὰ τοὺς
πρεσβυτέρους· (2) ἤ τε γὰρ ἄποιος ὕλη, ἣν δυνάμει καλεῖ ὁ Ἀριστοτέλης,
πρῶτόν ἐστιν τοῦ ὑποκειμένου σημαινόμενον, (3) καὶ δεύτερον, ὃ κοινῶς
ποιὸν ἢ ἰδίως ὑφίσταται· ὑποκείμενον γὰρ καὶ ὁ χαλκός ἐστιν καὶ ὁ   5
Σωκράτης τοῖς ἐπιγινομένοις ἢ κατηγορουμένοις κατ᾽ αὐτῶν."

Context: difficulties concerning Aristotle's distinction between καθ᾽ ὑποκειμένου and
ἐν ὑποκειμένῳ, *Cat.* 2, 1a20ff.

The examples at 5–6 may be Aristotelian and not Stoic, but the reporting seems in
general reliable (cf. **A 4**). Dexippus, *In Ar. Cat.* 23,25ff. (*SVF* 2.374) seems to be
nothing more than a slight expansion of Porphyry's words.

F Iamblichus, *De anima* (Stobaeus 1.367,17–22 = *SVF* 2.826, part)

ἀλλὰ μὴν οἵ γε ἀπὸ Χρυσίππου καὶ Ζήνωνος φιλόσοφοι καὶ πάντες ὅσοι

172

28 *The first and second genera*

σῶμα τὴν ψυχὴν νοοῦσι τὰς μὲν δυνάμεις ὡς ἐν τῷ ὑποκειμένῳ ποιότητας
συμβιβάζουσι, τὴν δὲ ψυχὴν ὡς οὐσίαν προυποκειμένην ταῖς δυνάμεσι
προτιθέασιν, ἐκ δ' ἀμφοτέρων τούτων σύνθετον φύσιν ἀνομοίων συνάγουσιν.   5

G Syrianus, *In Ar. Met.* 28,18–19 (*SVF* 2.398)

καὶ οἱ Στωικοὶ δὲ τοὺς κοινῶς ποιοὺς πρὸ τῶν ἰδίως ποιῶν ἀποτίθενται.

Context: appeal to alleged Peripatetic and Stoic support for a theory of immanent
universals. Needless to say, the Stoic position amounts to very much less than that. For
their treatment of universals, see **30**.

H Simplicius, *In Ar. Cat.* 222,30–3 (*SVF* 2.378, part)

οἱ δὲ Στωικοὶ τὸ κοινὸν τῆς ποιότητος τὸ ἐπὶ τῶν σωμάτων λέγουσιν
διαφορὰν εἶναι οὐσίας οὐκ ἀποδιαληπτὴν καθ' ἑαυτήν, ἀλλ' εἰς ἐννόημα
καὶ ἰδιότητα ἀπολήγουσαν, οὔτε χρόνῳ οὔτε ἰσχύι εἰδοποιουμένην, ἀλλὰ
τῇ ἐξ αὐτῆς τοιουτότητι, καθ' ἣν ποιοῦ ὑφίσταται γένεσις.

2 ἐννόημα Peterson: ἐν νόημα codd.

Context: commentary on *Cat.* 8b26, the meaning of ποιότης.
   Simplicius' subsequent criticisms of this Stoic definition of quality (ibid. 222,33–
223,11) show that it is quoted verbatim from a Stoic source, not in Simplicius' own
words.
   2 ἐννόημα   Certainly the right reading, cf. ibid. 223,6, and **30** below.
   3–4   Cf. **47S 5**.

I Simplicius, *In Ar. De an.* 217,36–218,2 (*SVF* 2.395)

... εἴ γε καὶ ἐπὶ τῶν συνθέτων τὸ ἀτομωθὲν ὑπάρχει εἶδος, καθ' ὃ ἰδίως
παρὰ τοῖς ἐκ τῆς Στοᾶς λέγεται ποιόν, ὃ καὶ ἀθρόως ἐπιγίνεται καὶ αὖ
ἀπογίνεται καὶ τὸ αὐτὸ ἐν παντὶ τῷ τοῦ συνθέτου βίῳ διαμένει, καίτοι τῶν
μορίων ἄλλων ἄλλοτε γινομένων τε καὶ φθειρομένων.

2 ποιόν Hayduck: ποιός codd.

Context: the individuation of souls.
   2   The masculine ποιός, despite the grammatical awkwardness, may be the right
reading, as so often in these texts.

J Dexippus, *In Ar. Cat.* 30,20–6

ἀλλ' εἰ εἶδός ἐστι τὸ κατὰ πλειόνων καὶ διαφερόντων τῷ ἀριθμῷ ἐν τῷ τί
ἐστι κατηγορούμενον, τίνι διαφέρει ὁ ἄτομος καὶ εἰς τοῦ ἀτόμου καὶ ἑνός·
ἐν γὰρ ἀριθμῷ ἐστι καὶ οὗτος κἀκεῖνος. οἱ μὲν οὖν λύοντες τὴν ἀπορίαν
ταύτην κατὰ τὸ ἰδίως ποιόν, τοῦτ' ἐστιν ὅτι ὁ μὲν φέρε γρυπότητι ἢ
ξανθότητι ἢ ἄλλῃ συνδρομῇ ποιοτήτων ἀφώρισται, ἄλλος δὲ σιμότητι ἢ   5

Stoic ontology

φαλακρότητι ἢ γλαυκότητι, καὶ πάλιν ἕτερος ἑτέραις, οὐ καλῶς μοι
δοκοῦσι λύειν.

Context: the meaning of ἄτομον.

1–2   The definition is that given for γένος at Aristotle, *Top.* 1.5, 102a31–2.

5 **συνδρομῇ ποιοτήτων**   This theory is not explicitly assigned to the Stoics, but
note that (a) Simplicius' ἀθρόως (I 2 above; ἄθροισμα is a standard doublet for
συνδρομή) helps to confirm that the Stoics saw a peculiar quality as some sort of
collection or compound; (b) the same theory is used in passing by Porphyry (*In Ar.
Cat.* 129,8–10), who certainly made some use of Stoic metaphysical material (cf.
Simplicius, *In Ar. Cat.* 2,8–9); (c) a version of the συνδρομή theory is perhaps already
detectable in Carneades (**69E** 16, 29), who standardly drew on Stoic doctrine in the
construction of philosophical positions. However, the doctrine as presented here is a
weak one. It is hard to see how any common quality beyond those constituting the
individual's species could be guaranteed to last from birth to death, as on the Stoic
theory it must if it is to be part of the peculiar quality.

4–6   The language is a little sloppy: 'or' must be understood in an inclusive sense
throughout if the idea of a συνδρομή is meant to emerge.

K Simplicius, *In Ar. Cat.* 271,20–2 (*SVF* 2.383)

ἀλλ' οὐδὲ ἡ τῶν Στωικῶν δόξα λεγόντων σώματα εἶναι καὶ τὰ σχήματα,
ὥσπερ καὶ τὰ ἄλλα ποιά, συμφωνεῖ τῇ ᾿Αριστοτέλους δόξῃ περὶ σχημάτων.

Context: comparison of various views on the metaphysical status of shape, derived
from a discussion by Iamblichus.

L Simplicius, *In Ar. Cat.* 217,32–218,1 (*SVF* 2.389, part)

(1) οἱ δὲ Στωικοὶ τῶν μὲν σωμάτων σωματικάς, τῶν δὲ ἀσωμάτων
ἀσωμάτους εἶναι λέγουσι τὰς ποιότητας. (2) σφάλλονται δὲ ἀπὸ τοῦ
ἡγεῖσθαι τὰ αἴτια τοῖς ἀποτελουμένοις ἀφ᾿ ἑαυτῶν ὁμοούσια εἶναι καὶ ἀπὸ
τοῦ κοινὸν λόγον τῆς αἰτίας ἐπί τε τῶν σωμάτων καὶ ἐπὶ τῶν ἀσωμάτων
ὑποτίθεσθαι. (3) πῶς δὲ καὶ πνευματικὴ ἡ οὐσία ἔσται τῶν σωματικῶν   5
ποιοτήτων, αὐτοῦ τοῦ πνεύματος συνθέτου ὄντος . . . ;

Context: shortly after **29g**, among the introductory remarks on *Cat.* 8. Cf. ibid.
209,1ff.

1–2   What are the incorporeal qualities of incorporeals? One might think of, e.g.,
the truth or falsity of a proposition.

2–5   Cf. especially **55A**. If Simplicius' report is to be trusted, we must read into it
a distinction between αἴτιον and αἰτία. The former is, for the Stoics, a cause in the
true sense, a body acting upon a body. So the claim about causes here must be used
solely to justify the claim that the qualities of bodies are corporeal. The further claim
about αἰτία, 'explanation' (cf. the Stoic definition at **55A** 5), which Simplicius
perhaps chooses as a metaphysically less circumscribed notion, will then be added to
extend the point, by parity of reasoning, to incorporeals.

174

28 The first and second genera

3 ἀποτελουμένοις The active verb, 'render', is constructed with double accusative, ἀποτελεῖν τι τοιοῦτο. Since the ἀποτέλεσμα is standardly the 'effect', the ἀποτελούμενον will presumably be the 'thing affected'. It is this, and not the effect, which in Stoic theory is of the same essence as the αἴτιον: see 55A–B.

M Simplicius, *In Ar. Cat.* 214,24–37 (*SVF* 2.391, part)

(1) καὶ οἱ Στωικοὶ δὲ κατὰ τὰς αὐτῶν ὑποθέσεις τὴν αὐτὴν ἂν ἀπορίαν προσαγάγοιεν τῷ λέγοντι λόγῳ κατὰ ποιότητα πάντα τὰ ποιὰ λέγεσθαι. (2) τὰς γὰρ ποιότητας ἐκτὰ λέγοντες οὗτοι ἐπὶ τῶν ἡνωμένων μόνων τὰ ἐκτὰ ἀπολείπουσιν, (3) ἐπὶ δὲ τῶν κατὰ συναφὴν οἷον νεὼς καὶ ἐπὶ τῶν κατὰ διάστασιν οἷον στρατοῦ μηδὲν εἶναι ἐκτὸν μηδὲ εὑρίσκεσθαι 5 πνευματικόν τι ἐν ἐπ' αὐτῶν μηδὲ ἕνα λόγον ἔχον, ὥστε ἐπί τινα ὑπόστασιν ἐλθεῖν μιᾶς ἕξεως. (4) τὸ δὲ ποιὸν καὶ ἐν τοῖς ἐκ συναπτομένων θεωρεῖται καὶ ἐν τοῖς ἐκ διεστώτων· ὡς γὰρ εἷς γραμματικὸς ἐκ ποιᾶς ἀναλήψεως καὶ συγγυμνασίας ἐμμόνως ἔχει κατὰ διαφοράν, οὕτως καὶ ὁ χορὸς ἐκ ποιᾶς μελέτης ἐμμόνως ἔχει κατὰ διαφοράν. διὸ ποιὰ μὲν ὑπάρχει διὰ τὴν 10 κατάταξιν καὶ τὴν πρὸς ἑνὸς ἔργου ⟨συντέλειαν⟩ συνεργίαν, (5) δίχα δὲ ποιότητός ἐστι ποιά· ἕξις γὰρ ἐν τούτοις οὐκ ἔστιν· οὐδὲ γὰρ ὅλως ἐν διεστώσαις οὐσίαις καὶ μηδεμίαν ἐχούσαις συμφυῆ πρὸς ἀλλήλας ἕνωσίν ἐστιν ποιότης ἢ ἕξις.

11 ἑνὸς ἔργου ⟨συντέλειαν⟩ Sedley: ἐν ἔργῳ Arnim

Context: problems that arise from the assumption that quality is prior to the qualified individual. Cf. *SVF* 2.366–8, and **47S**. For a quality as ἐκτόν, 'havable', cf. note on **30A** 6–7.

N Simplicius, *In Ar. Cat.* 212,12–213,1 (*SVF* 2.390, part)

(1) τῶν δὲ Στωικῶν τινες τριχῶς τὸ ποιὸν ἀφοριζόμενοι τὰ μὲν δύο σημαινόμενα ἐπὶ πλέον τῆς ποιότητος λέγουσιν, τὸ δὲ ἓν ἤτοι τοῦ ἑνὸς μέρος συναπαρτίζειν αὐτῇ φασιν. (2) λέγουσιν γὰρ ποιὸν καθ' ἓν μὲν σημαινόμενον πᾶν τὸ κατὰ διαφοράν, εἴτε κινούμενον εἴη εἴτε ἰσχόμενον καὶ εἴτε δυσαναλύτως εἴτε εὐαναλύτως ἔχει· κατὰ τοῦτο δὲ οὐ μόνον ὁ 5 φρόνιμος καὶ ὁ πὺξ προτείνων, ἀλλὰ καὶ ὁ τρέχων ποιοί. (3) καθ' ἕτερον δὲ καθ' ὃ οὐκέτι τὰς κινήσεις περιελάμβανον, ἀλλὰ μόνον τὰς σχέσεις, ὃ δὴ καὶ ὡρίζοντο τὸ ἰσχόμενον κατὰ διαφοράν, οἷός ἐστιν ὁ φρόνιμος καὶ ὁ προβεβλημένος. (4) τρίτον δὲ εἰσῆγον εἰδικώτατον ποιὸν καθ' ὅτι οὐκέτι τοὺς μὴ ἐμμόνως ἰσχομένους περιελάμβανον οὐδὲ ἦσαν ποιοὶ κατ' αὐτούς 10 ὁ πὺξ προτείνων καὶ ὁ προβεβλημένος· (5) καὶ τούτων δὲ τῶν ἐμμόνως ἰσχομένων κατὰ διαφορὰν οἱ μὲν ἀπηρτισμένως κατὰ τὴν ἐκφορὰν αὐτῶν καὶ τὴν ἐπίνοιάν εἰσι τοιοῦτοι, οἱ δὲ οὐκ ἀπηρτισμένως, καὶ τούτους μὲν παρῃτοῦντο, τοὺς δὲ ἀπαρτίζοντας καὶ ἐμμόνους ὄντας κατὰ διαφορὰν ποιοὺς ἐτίθεντο. (6) ἀπαρτίζειν δὲ κατὰ τὴν ἐκφορὰν ἔλεγον τοὺς τῇ 15 ποιότητι συνεξισουμένους, ὡς τὸν γραμματικὸν καὶ τὸν φρόνιμον· οὔτε

175

Stoic ontology

γὰρ πλεονάζει οὔτε ἐλλείπει τούτων ἑκάτερος παρὰ τὴν ποιότητα· ὁμοίως
δὲ καὶ ὁ φίλοψος καὶ ὁ φίλοινος. οἱ μέντοι μετὰ τῆς ἐνεργείας τοιοῦτοι,
ὥσπερ ὁ ὀψοφάγος καὶ ὁ οἰνόφλυξ, ἔχοντες μέρη τοιαῦτα δι᾽ ὧν
ἀπολαύουσιν οὕτως λέγονται. διὸ καὶ εἰ μέν τις ὀψοφάγος, καὶ φίλοψος   2c
πάντως· εἰ δὲ φίλοψος, οὐ πάντως ὀψοφάγος· ἐπιλειπόντων γὰρ τῶν μερῶν
δι᾽ ὧν ὀψοφαγεῖ τῆς μὲν ὀψοφαγίας ἀπολέλυται, τὴν δὲ φίλοψον ἕξιν οὐκ
ἀνῄρηκεν. (7) τριχῶς οὖν τοῦ ποιοῦ λεγομένου ἡ ποιότης κατὰ τὸ
τελευταῖον **ποιὸν συναπαρτίζει** πρὸς τὸ ποιόν. διὸ καὶ ὅταν ὁρίζωνται τὴν
ποιότητα **σχέσιν ποιοῦ**, οὕτως ἀκουστέον τοῦ ὅρου ὡς τοῦ τρίτου ποιοῦ   2⟨
παραλαμβανομένου· μοναχῶς μὲν γὰρ ἡ ποιότης λέγεται κατ᾽ αὐτοὺς τοὺς
Στωικούς, τριχῶς δὲ ὁ ποιός.

Context: introductory comment on *Cat.* 8.

   4 **κατὰ διαφοράν** Distinguished by some intrinsic feature, as opposed to πρός τί
πως ἔχον: 29C; S.E., *M.* 8.161–2, 10.263–5. **κινούμενον, ἰσχόμενον** The
standard Stoic distinction between processes and states; cf. **54T**, etc. For the two senses
of σχέσις, see on **29g** below.

   15–23 The point is that for each type of quality there are two corresponding
ποιοί, definable as (a) possessing the quality, and (b) using it. For example, the quality
φρόνησις is matched by the φρόνιμος (16–17) under (a), and his counterpart under
(b), not specified here, is the φρονῶν (Philo, *Leg. alleg.* 1.67 = *SVF* 3.263). The
technical expression ἀπαρτίζειν κατὰ τὴν ἐκφοράν may point to Antipater as the
Stoic author of the present set of distinctions: cf. **32C 1, E.**

O Plutarch, *Comm. not.* 1077C–E (including *SVF* 2.112)

(1) ἀκοῦσαι τοίνυν ἔστιν αὐτῶν καὶ γράμμασιν ἐντυχεῖν πολλοῖς πρὸς τοὺς
Ἀκαδημαϊκοὺς διαφερομένων καὶ βοώντων ὡς πάντα πράγματα συγ-
χέουσι ταῖς ἀπαραλλαξίαις, ἐπὶ δυεῖν οὐσιῶν ἕνα ποιὸν εἶναι βιαζόμενοι.
(2) καίτοι τοῦτο μὲν οὐκ ἔστιν ὅστις ἀνθρώπων οὐ διανοεῖται, καὶ τοὐναντίον οἴεται θαυμαστὸν εἶναι καὶ παράδοξον, εἰ μήτε φάττα φάττῃ μήτε   5
μελίττῃ μέλιττα μήτε πυρῷ πυρὸς ἢ σύκῳ, τὸ τοῦ λόγου, σῦκον ἐν τῷ
παντὶ χρόνῳ γέγονεν ἀπαράλλακτον. (3) ἐκεῖνα δ᾽ ὄντως παρὰ τὴν ἔννοιάν
ἐστιν, ἃ λέγουσιν οὗτοι καὶ πλάττουσιν, ἐπὶ μιᾶς οὐσίας δύ᾽ ἰδίως γενέσθαι
ποιοὺς καὶ τὴν αὐτὴν οὐσίαν ἕνα ποιὸν ἰδίως ἔχουσαν ἐπιόντος ἑτέρου
δέχεσθαι καὶ διαφυλάττειν ὁμοίως ἀμφοτέρους. εἰ γὰρ δύο, καὶ τρεῖς καὶ   10
τέτταρες ἔσονται καὶ πέντε καὶ ὅσους οὐκ ἄν τις εἴποι περὶ μίαν οὐσίαν·
λέγω δ᾽ οὐκ ἐν μέρεσι διαφόροις, ἀλλὰ πάντας ὁμοίως περὶ ὅλην τοὺς
ἀπείρους. (4) λέγει γοῦν Χρύσιππος ἐοικέναι τῷ μὲν ἀνθρώπῳ τὸν Δία καὶ
τὸν κόσμον τῇ δὲ ψυχῇ πρόνοιαν· ὅταν οὖν ἡ ἐκπύρωσις γένηται, μόνον
ἄφθαρτον ὄντα τὸν Δία τῶν θεῶν ἀναχωρεῖν ἐπὶ τὴν πρόνοιαν, εἶθ᾽ ὁμοῦ   15
γενομένους ἐπὶ μιᾶς τῆς τοῦ αἰθέρος οὐσίας διατελεῖν ἀμφοτέρους.

See Cherniss [326], ad loc., for invaluable commentary.

   3 **ἀπαραλλαξίαις** See note on **52C 6.**
   13–14 For the world as ἰδίως ποιός, cf. **44F 6.**

P Philo, *Aet. mundi* 47–51 (including *SVF* 2.397)

νυνὶ δὲ τοσοῦτον δόξης ἀληθοῦς διήμαρτον, ὥστε λελήθασιν αὐτοὺς καὶ τῇ προνοίᾳ – ψυχὴ δ' ἐστὶ τοῦ κόσμου – φθορὰν ἐπιφέροντες ἐξ ὧν ἀνακόλουθα φιλοσοφοῦσι. (1) Χρύσιππος γοῦν ὁ δοκιμώτατος τῶν παρ' αὐτοῖς ἐν τοῖς Περὶ αὐξανομένου τερατεύεταί τι τοιοῦτον· (2) προκατασκευάσας ὅτι δύο ἰδίως ποιοὺς ἐπὶ τῆς αὐτῆς οὐσίας ἀμήχανον συστῆναι, (3) φησίν· "ἔστω θεωρίας ἕνεκα τὸν 5
μέν τινα ὁλόκληρον, τὸν δὲ χωρὶς ἐπινοεῖσθαι τοῦ ἑτέρου ποδός, καλεῖσθαι δὲ τὸν μὲν ὁλόκληρον Δίωνα, τὸν δὲ ἀτελῆ Θέωνα, κἄπειτα ἀποτέμνεσθαι Δίωνος τὸν ἕτερον τοῖν ποδοῖν." (4) ζητουμένου δή, πότερος ἔφθαρται, τὸν Θέωνα φάσκειν οἰκειότερον εἶναι. (5) τοῦτο δὲ παραδοξολογοῦντος μᾶλλόν ἐστιν ἢ ἀληθεύοντος. πῶς γὰρ ὁ μὲν οὐδὲν ἀκρωτηριασθεὶς μέρος, ὁ Θέων, 10
ἀνήρπασται, ὁ δ' ἀποκοπεὶς τὸν πόδα Δίων οὐχὶ διέφθαρται; (6) "δεόντως" φησίν· "ἀναδεδράμηκε γὰρ ὁ ἐκτμηθεὶς τὸν πόδα Δίων ἐπὶ τὴν ἀτελῆ τοῦ Θέωνος οὐσίαν, καὶ δύο ἰδίως ποιοὶ ἐπὶ τοῦ αὐτοῦ ὑποκειμένου οὐ δύνανται εἶναι. τοιγαροῦν τὸν μὲν Δίωνα μένειν ἀναγκαῖον, τὸν δὲ Θέωνα διεφθάρθαι." "τὰ δ' οὐχ ὑπ' ἄλλων ἀλλὰ τοῖς αὐτῶν πτεροῖς ἁλισκόμενα" 15
φησὶν ὁ τραγικός· ἀπομαξάμενος γάρ τις τὸν τύπον τοῦ λόγου καὶ ἐφαρμόσας τῷ παντὶ κόσμῳ δείξει σαφέστατα καὶ αὐτὴν φθειρομένην τὴν πρόνοιαν. σκόπει δ' ὧδε· ὑποκείσθω ὁ μὲν ὡσανεὶ Δίων ὁ κόσμος – τέλεος γάρ – ὁ δὲ ὡσανεὶ Θέων ἡ τοῦ κόσμου ψυχή, διότι τοῦ ὅλου τὸ μέρος ἔλαττον, καὶ ἀφαιρείσθω, ὥσπερ ἀπὸ τοῦ Δίωνος ὁ πούς, οὕτως καὶ ἀπὸ τοῦ κόσμου ὅσον αὐτοῦ σωματοειδές. οὐκοῦν ἀνάγκη λέγειν ὅτι ὁ μὲν κόσμος οὐκ ἔφθαρται ὁ τὸ 20
σῶμα ἀφαιρεθείς, ὥσπερ οὐδὲ ὁ ἀποκοπεὶς τὸν πόδα Δίων, ἀλλ' ἡ τοῦ κόσμου ψυχή, ὥσπερ Θέων ὁ μηδὲν παθών. ὁ μὲν γὰρ κόσμος ἐπ' ἐλάττονα οὐσίαν ἀνέδραμεν, ἀφαιρεθέντος αὐτῷ τοῦ σωματοειδοῦς, ἐφθάρη δ' ἡ ψυχὴ διὰ τὸ μὴ δύνασθαι δύο ἰδίως ποιοὺς εἶναι περὶ τὸ αὐτὸ ὑποκείμενον. ἔκθεσμον δὲ τὸ λέγειν φθείρεσθαι τὴν πρόνοιαν· ἀφθάρτου δὲ ὑπαρχούσης, ἀνάγκη καὶ τὸν κόσμον ἄφθαρτον εἶναι. 25

4 ἰδίως ποιοὺς Arnim: εἰδοποιοὺς codd.   13 ἰδίως ποιοὶ Arnim: εἰδοποιοὶ codd.   ἐπὶ HP(v): περὶ MU   23 ἰδίως ποιοὺς secundum Arnim scripsimus: εἰδοποιοὺς codd.

Context: attack on the Stoic theory of the conflagration (46).

5ff. **τὸν μέν** Chrysippus had clearly introduced Dion and Theon before the excerpted passage; it is Philo's failure to explain this that has led to confusion about how they are related to each other (see vol. 1, 175).

12 For ἀνατρέχειν ἐπί = 'collapse into', 'become co-extensive with', cf. Plotinus, *Enn.* 6.1.30.

q Stobaeus 1.132,27–133,11; 133,18–23 (*SVF* 1.87 and 2.317, and Posidonius fr. 92)

Ζήνωνος. οὐσίαν δὲ εἶναι τὴν τῶν ὄντων πάντων πρώτην ὕλην, ταύτην δὲ πᾶσαν ἀίδιον καὶ οὔτε πλείω γινομένην οὔτε ἐλάττω· τὰ δὲ μέρη ταύτης οὐκ ἀεὶ ταὐτὰ διαμένειν, ἀλλὰ διαιρεῖσθαι καὶ συγχεῖσθαι. διὰ ταύτης δὲ διαθεῖν τὸν τοῦ παντὸς λόγον, ὃν ἔνιοι εἱμαρμένην καλοῦσιν, οἷόν περ καὶ ἐν τῇ γονῇ τὸ σπέρμα. Χρυσίππου Στωικοῦ. τῶν κατὰ ποιότητα ὑφισταμένων πρώτην ὕλην· ταύτην δὲ ἀίδιον, οὔτε αὔξησιν οὔτε μείωσιν 5

177

ὑπομένουσαν, διαίρεσιν δὲ καὶ σύγχυσιν ἐπιδεχομένην κατὰ μέρη, ὥστε φθορὰς γίνεσθαι ἔκ
τινων μερῶν εἴς τινα, οὐ κατὰ διαίρεσιν, ἀλλὰ κατ᾽ ἀναλογίαν τῇ συγχύσει τινῶν γινομένων
ἐκ τινος. ἔφησε δὲ ὁ Ποσειδώνιος τὴν τῶν ὅλων οὐσίαν καὶ ὕλην ἄποιον καὶ ἄμορφον εἶναι,
καθ᾽ ὅσον οὐδὲν ἀποτεταγμένον ἴδιον ἔχει σχῆμα οὐδὲ ποιότητα καθ᾽ αὑτήν· ἀεὶ δ᾽ ἔν τινι
σχήματι καὶ ποιότητι εἶναι. διαφέρειν δὲ τὴν οὐσίαν τῆς ὕλης, τὴν ⟨αὐτὴν⟩ οὖσαν κατὰ τὴν   10
ὑπόστασιν, ἐπινοίᾳ μόνον.

7 τινων Diels: τῶν codd.   10 ⟨αὐτὴν⟩ Hirzel

Cf. **44D–E**, and **50B** 1. For comment, see note on **D** 9–10.
4 ἐν–σπέρμα   Cf. **46B** 2.

29 The third and fourth genera

A Alexander, *Mantissa* 118,6–8 (*SVF* 2.823)

ὅτι μὴ μία ἡ τῆς ψυχῆς δύναμις, ὡς τὴν αὐτήν πως ἔχουσαν ποτὲ μὲν
διανοεῖσθαι, ποτὲ δὲ ὀργίζεσθαι, ποτὲ δ᾽ ἐπιθυμεῖν παρὰ μέρος δεικ-
τέον . . .

Context: argument for a plurality of powers of the soul.

Alexander characterizes the opposing unitarian view in terminology which sounds
pointedly Stoic. Chrysippus' intellectualist view makes all thoughts and emotions
modifications of a single rational power of the mind; cf. *SVF* 3.257, and **53**. An earlier
mention of the doctrine (*In Ar. De an.* 27,4–8) names Democritus, but in the present
passage the language is more Stoic, and Alexander goes on (ibid. 12–15) to attack the
distinctively Stoic view of the nutritive soul as merely φύσις (see vol. 1, 319–20).

B Seneca, *Ep.* 113.2 (*SVF* 3.307, part)

virtus autem nihil aliud est quam animus quodammodo se habens.

Context: proof of the Stoic paradox that virtues are living beings (cf. **61E**).
Almost the identical analysis is found in a different context at S.E., *M.* 11.23 (*SVF*
3.75, part).

C Simplicius, *In Ar. Cat.* 165,32–166,29 (*SVF* 2.403)

οἱ δὲ Στωικοὶ ἀνθ᾽ ἑνὸς γένους δύο κατὰ τὸν τόπον τοῦτον ἀριθμοῦνται, τὰ μὲν ἐν τοῖς πρός
τι τιθέντες, τὰ δὲ ἐν τοῖς πρός τί πως ἔχουσιν. καὶ τὰ μὲν πρός τι ἀντιδιαιροῦσιν τοῖς καθ᾽
αὑτά, τὰ δὲ πρός τί πως ἔχοντα τοῖς κατὰ διαφοράν, πρός τι μὲν λέγοντες τὸ γλυκὺ καὶ
πικρὸν καὶ τὰ τοιαῦτα, ὅσα τοιῶσδε διατίθησιν, πρός τι δέ πως ἔχοντα οἷον δεξιόν, πατέρα
καὶ τὰ τοιαῦτα· κατὰ διαφορὰν δέ φασιν τὰ κατά τι εἶδος χαρακτηριζόμενα. ὥσπερ οὖν   5
ἄλλη τῶν καθ᾽ αὑτὰ ἔννοια καὶ ἄλλη τῶν κατὰ διαφοράν, οὕτως ἄλλα μὲν τὰ πρός τί ἐστιν,
ἄλλα δὲ τὰ πρός τί πως ἔχοντα. ἀντεστραμμένη δέ ἐστιν τῶν συζυγιῶν ἡ ἀκολουθία. τοῖς
μὲν γὰρ καθ᾽ αὑτὰ συνυπάρχει τὰ κατὰ διαφοράν· καὶ γὰρ τὰ καθ᾽ αὑτὰ ὄντα διαφορὰς ἔχει
τινάς, ὥσπερ τὸ λευκὸν καὶ μέλαν· οὐ μέντοι τοῖς κατὰ διαφορὰν τὰ καθ᾽ αὑτὰ συνυπάρχει·
τὸ γὰρ γλυκὺ καὶ πικρὸν διαφορὰς μὲν ἔχει, καθ᾽ ἃς χαρακτηρίζεται, οὐ μέντοι καθ᾽ αὑτά   10

ἐστιν τοιαῦτα, ἀλλὰ πρός τι. τὰ δὲ πρός τί πως ἔχοντα, ἅπερ ἀντίκειται τοῖς κατὰ
διαφοράν, πάντως καὶ πρός τί ἐστιν· ὁ γὰρ δεξιὸς καὶ πατὴρ μετὰ τοῦ πῶς ἔχειν καὶ πρός τί
εἰσιν. τὸ δὲ γλυκὺ καὶ πικρὸν πρός τι ὄντα κατὰ διαφοράν ἐστιν, τὰ δὲ πρός τί πως ἔχοντα
ἐναντία τοῖς κατὰ διαφορὰν ὑπάρχει. καὶ γὰρ τὰ μὲν πρός τί πως ἔχοντα ἀδύνατον καθ'
αὑτὰ εἶναι ἢ κατὰ διαφοράν· ἐκ γὰρ τῆς πρὸς ἕτερον σχέσεως ἤρτηται μόνης· τὰ μέντοι   15
πρός τι καθ' αὑτὰ μὲν οὐκ ἔστιν, οὐ γάρ ἐστιν ἀπόλυτα, κατὰ διαφορὰν δὲ πάντως ἔσται·
μετὰ γάρ τινος χαρακτῆρος θεωρεῖται. (1) εἰ δὲ δεῖ σαφέστερον μεταλαβεῖν τὰ
λεγόμενα, πρός τι μὲν λέγουσιν, ὅσα κατ' οἰκεῖον χαρακτῆρα διακείμενά
πως ἀπονεύει πρὸς ἕτερον, πρός τι δέ πως ἔχοντα, ὅσα πέφυκεν συμβαίνειν
τινὶ καὶ μὴ συμβαίνειν ἄνευ τῆς περὶ αὐτὰ μεταβολῆς καὶ ἀλλοιώσεως   20
μετὰ τοῦ πρὸς τὸ ἐκτὸς ἀποβλέπειν, ὥστε ὅταν μὲν κατὰ διαφοράν τι
διακείμενον πρὸς ἕτερον νεύσῃ, πρός τι μόνον ἔσται τοῦτο, ὡς ἡ ἕξις καὶ ἡ
ἐπιστήμη καὶ ἡ αἴσθησις· ὅταν δὲ μὴ κατὰ τὴν ἐνοῦσαν διαφοράν, κατὰ
ψιλὴν δὲ τὴν πρὸς ἕτερον σχέσιν θεωρῆται, πρός τί πως ἔχον ἔσται. (2) ὁ
γὰρ υἱὸς καὶ ὁ δεξιὸς ἔξωθέν τινων προσδέονται πρὸς τὴν ὑπόστασιν· διὸ   25
καὶ μηδεμιᾶς γενομένης περὶ αὐτὰ μεταβολῆς γένοιτο ἂν οὐκέτι πατὴρ τοῦ
υἱοῦ ἀποθανόντος οὐδὲ δεξιὸς τοῦ παρακειμένου μεταστάντος· τὸ δὲ γλυκὺ
καὶ πικρὸν οὐκ ἂν ἀλλοῖα γένοιτο, εἰ μὴ συμμεταβάλλοι καὶ ἡ περὶ αὐτὰ
δύναμις. (3) εἰ τοίνυν καὶ μηδὲν αὐτὰ παθόντα μεταβάλλει κατὰ τὴν ἄλλου
πρὸς αὐτὰ σχέσιν, δῆλον ὅτι ἐν τῇ σχέσει μόνῃ τὸ εἶναι ἔχει καὶ οὐ κατά   30
τινα διαφορὰν τὰ πρός τί πως ἔχοντα.

Context: introductory remarks on the category of relation.
    It has been claimed by Graeser [400] that we have here a rival set of four Stoic
'categories': πρός τι, καθ' αὑτό, κατὰ διαφοράν, and πρός τί πως ἔχον. But apart
from the last, which belongs to the standard foursome, these are all terms used in
elucidating and subdividing the second genus, the ποιόν.
    The special use of πρός τί πως ἔχον explained here, perhaps of Academic origin (cf.
Sandbach [304], 42), is arguably also to be found at Aristotle, Cat. 7, 8a28–b3.
    7   The precise force of ἀντεστραμμένη here is unclear to us, although the
terminology is evidently influenced by Aristotle, De int. 13, 22a32–4. If, as one would
expect, it means 'reciprocal', an οὐκ should perhaps be added before it, since the
'sequence of dependences' which follows in 7–14 is in fact non-reciprocal: all καθ'
αὑτά are κατὰ διαφοράν, but not vice versa, and all πρός τί πως ἔχοντα are πρός τι
but not vice versa.

D   Plutarch, St. rep. 1054E–1055A (SVF 2.550, part)

ἀρκεῖ δ' εἰς τοῦτο παραθέσθαι λέξιν ἐκ τοῦ δευτέρου Περὶ κινήσεως. ὑπειπὼν γὰρ ὅτι
τέλεον μὲν ὁ κόσμος σῶμά ἐστιν οὐ τέλεα δὲ τὰ τοῦ κόσμου μέρη τῷ πρὸς
τὸ ὅλον πως ἔχειν καὶ μὴ καθ' αὑτὰ εἶναι καὶ περὶ τῆς κινήσεως αὐτοῦ διελθὼν ὡς
ἐπὶ τὴν συμμονὴν καὶ τὴν συνοχὴν τὴν ἑαυτοῦ κινεῖσθαι διὰ τῶν μερῶν πάντων πεφυκότος,
οὐκ ἐπὶ τὴν διάλυσιν καὶ τὴν θρύψιν, ταῦτ' ἐπείρηκεν· "οὕτω δὲ τοῦ ὅλου τεινομένου εἰς   5
αὐτὸ καὶ κινουμένου καὶ τῶν μορίων ταύτην τὴν κίνησιν ἐχόντων ἐκ τῆς τοῦ σώματος
φύσεως, πιθανὸν πᾶσι τοῖς σώμασιν εἶναι τὴν πρώτην κατὰ φύσιν κίνησιν πρὸς τὸ τοῦ

Stoic ontology

κόσμου μέσον, τῷ μὲν κόσμῳ οὑτωσὶ κινουμένῳ πρὸς αὑτόν, τοῖς δὲ μέρεσιν ὡς ἂν μέρεσιν οὖσιν."

Context: immediately following **49I** (q.v.). An attempt by Plutarch, having interpreted a Chrysippean argument as implying that all body tends towards the centre of space, to show that he elsewhere takes a contradictory view, that body tends towards its *own* centre, i.e. the centre of the corporeal κόσμος. The doctrine quoted in 2–3 is apparently used here to explain why the function of the moving parts of the world is to hold the whole together.

E Galen, *Plac.* 7.1.10–15 (*SVF* 3.259, part)

καίτοι κἀνταῦθα εἴ τις ἐπεξέρχοιτο τῷ λόγῳ τά τε περὶ τῆς διαφορᾶς τῶν ἀρετῶν ἐν τέτταρσι βιβλίοις ὑπὸ Χρυσίππου γεγραμμένα βασανίζων ὅσα τε καθ᾽ ἓν ἄλλο διῆλθεν, ᾧ δείκνυσι ποιὰς εἶναι τὰς ἀρετὰς ἐλέγχων τὸν ᾽Αρίστωνος λόγον, οὐχ ἑνὸς ἢ δυοῖν, ἀλλὰ τριῶν ἢ τεττάρων ἂν δεηθείη βιβλίων. ἔστι μὲν γὰρ κἀνταῦθα λόγος εἰς βραχὺς ἐπιστημονικὸς ἐλέγχων τὸν Χρύσιππον οὔτε τἀληθῆ πρεσβεύοντα καὶ μηκύνοντα   5
περιττῶς. ἀλλὰ οἱ μήτε παιδευθέντες ἐν ἀποδεικτικῇ μεθόδῳ μήθ᾽ ὅλως γνόντες ὁποία τίς ἐστι, μόνῳ δὲ τῷ μεγέθει καὶ πλήθει τῶν ὑπὸ Χρυσίππου γραφέντων βιβλίων προσέχοντες τὸν νοῦν ἀληθῆ νομίζουσι πάνθ᾽ ὑπάρχειν αὐτά. (1) καὶ γὰρ καὶ ὄντως ἐστὶ τὰ πλεῖστα αὐτῶν ἀληθῆ καὶ μάλιστά γε τὰ κατὰ ἐκεῖνο τὸ βιβλίον, ἐν ᾧ δείκνυσι ποιὰς εἶναι τὰς ἀρετάς. ἀλλὰ ὅτι τῷ μίαν ὑποθεμένῳ δύναμιν   10
ὑπάρχειν ἐν τῇ ψυχῇ τὴν λογικήν τε καὶ κριτικὴν ὀνομαζομένην, ἀνελόντι δὲ τὴν ἐπιθυμητικήν τε καὶ θυμοειδῆ, καθάπερ ὁ Χρύσιππος ἀνεῖλε, μάχεται τὰ κατὰ τοῦτο τὸ βιβλίον εἰρημένα ταυτί, μέμψαιτο ἄν τις αὐτῷ· (2) τὸ μέντοι καταβάλλεσθαι τὴν ᾽Αρίστωνος αἵρεσιν ἀληθῶς ὑπὸ τῶν γεγραμμένων οὐκ ἄν τις μέμψαιτο. νομίζει γὰρ ὁ ἀνὴρ ἐκεῖνος μίαν οὖσαν   15
τὴν ἀρετὴν ὀνόμασι πλείοσιν ὀνομάζεσθαι κατὰ τὴν πρός τι σχέσιν. (3) ὁ τοίνυν Χρύσιππος δείκνυσιν οὐκ ἐν τῇ πρός τι σχέσει γινόμενον τὸ πλῆθος τῶν ἀρετῶν τε καὶ κακιῶν, ἀλλὰ ἐν ταῖς οἰκείαις οὐσίαις ὑπαλλαττομέναις κατὰ τὰς ποιότητας, ὡς ὁ τῶν παλαιῶν ἠβούλετο λόγος. ὅπερ καὶ αὐτὸ βραχὺ παρατρέψας ὁ Χρύσιππος ἑτέραις λέξεσι διῆλθεν ἐν τῷ ποιὰς εἶναι τὰς ἀρετὰς τοῖς τε   20
ἐπιχειρήμασιν οὐ πρέπουσι τῷ τὸ λογικὸν εἶναι μόνον τῆς ψυχῆς τεθειμένῳ, τὸ παθητικὸν δὲ ἀνῃρηκότι.

Context: an extended critique of Chrysippus' psychology.
10–13   For Galen's relentless polemic against Chrysippus' psychological monism, cf. **65I, M–P**.

F Seneca, *Ep.* 121.10 (*SVF* 3.184, part)

"constitutio", inquit, "est, ut vos dicitis, principale animi quodammodo se habens erga corpus . . ."

Context: exposition of the Stoic theory of οἰκείωσις at **57B 2**. Even a new-born animal is conscious of its own constitution. But, opponents are represented as saying, how can it be clever enough to grasp something whose definition is so sophisticated?

The Greek original will have been: σύστασίς ἐστιν ἡγεμονικὸν πρὸς τὸ σῶμά πως ἔχον. 'Constitution' belongs neither to the soul nor to the body, but consists in a relationship between the two.

g Simplicius, *In Ar. Cat.* 217,21–5

καὶ οἱ μὲν τοσοῦτον μόνον πλεονάζειν τὸ πῶς ἔχον τοῦ ποιοῦ ὑποτίθενται, καθ' ὅσον τὸ πῶς ἔχον παρεξέτεινεν καὶ ἐπὶ τὰ πρός τί πως ἔχοντα καὶ περιελάμβανεν ταῦτα, τὸ δὲ ποιὸν ἵστατο ἐπὶ μόνων τῶν κατὰ διαφοράν· οἱ δὲ ἄλλην τινὰ τεχνολογίαν ἐπεισῆγον.

Simplicius is discussing certain 'Academics' (identity uncertain – perhaps the school of Eudorus?), whose views seem to be a synthesis of Stoic and Platonist metaphysics (ibid. 217,8–32; cf. 209,10–15). The fact that these heirs to Stoic ontology were left in some perplexity as to the difference between ποιόν and πῶς ἔχον underlines the Stoics' own lack of clarity on the point.

The difficulty may at first seem to be exacerbated by the fact that σχέσις, the cognate noun of πῶς ἔχον, is also one species of the 'qualified' (**28N 3**). But we in fact have here two quite distinct senses of the word. In the former, it is cognate with the active ἔχειν, 'be disposed', and is translated 'disposition'. In the latter, it corresponds to the passive ἴσχεσθαι/ἔχεσθαι, literally 'be held' in such and such a condition (by contrast with κινεῖσθαι, 'be in a changing condition'), and is translated 'state'.

30 Universals

A Stobaeus 1.136,21–137,6 (*SVF* 1.65)

Ζήνωνος· (1) τὰ ἐννοήματά φασι μήτε τινὰ εἶναι μήτε ποιά, ὡσανεὶ δέ τινα καὶ ὡσανεὶ ποιὰ φαντάσματα ψυχῆς· (2) ταῦτα δὲ ὑπὸ τῶν ἀρχαίων ἰδέας προσαγορεύεσθαι. τῶν γὰρ κατὰ τὰ ἐννοήματα ὑποπιπτόντων εἶναι τὰς ἰδέας, οἷον ἀνθρώπων, ἵππων, κοινότερον εἰπεῖν πάντων τῶν ζῴων καὶ τῶν ἄλλων ὁπόσων λέγουσιν ἰδέας εἶναι. (3) ταύτας δὲ οἱ Στωικοὶ   5 φιλόσοφοί φασιν ἀνυπάρκτους εἶναι, καὶ τῶν μὲν ἐννοημάτων μετέχειν ἡμᾶς, τῶν δὲ πτώσεων, ἃς δὴ προσηγορίας καλοῦσι, τυγχάνειν.

1 Ζήνωνος ⟨καὶ τῶν ἀπ' αὐτοῦ⟩ Diels   φασι F: φησι P

1   There is something puzzling about the order μήτε τινὰ ... μήτε ποιά. If concepts are not τινά (on which see **27**), it will go without saying that they are not ποιά either. But although the reverse order would seem more natural, this one is not unparalleled: cf. Plato, *Tht.* 152d2–6. One possibility is to understand 'not somethings, *let alone* qualified things'. A second is to take τινά as *mere* somethings, implying non-corporeal particulars, and ποιά as qualified corporeal entities. On this reading the text would echo the almost certainly correct claim in **D** that Stoic ἐννοήματα are neither bodies nor incorporeals. On the other hand, it is hardly a natural reading, and in any case the important proof in **E** that universals are not τινά is concerned with τινά as particulars, not as incorporeals. A third – the likeliest – interpretation is that by ποιά here are really meant, as so often (cf. **28K, O, P**), not quality-bearing individuals but the qualities themselves. Hence the object of this

Stoic ontology

passage (which compares closely with Aristotle, *Cat.* 5, 3b13–16) will be to eliminate the two metaphysical statuses most likely to be assigned to universals by those who hypostatize them: that of discrete entity (Plato) and that of enmattered quality (very approximately, Aristotle).

2 **φαντάσματα** See **39A–B**, and **j** below.

4 The same examples of Forms are given slightly earlier in the text, in a summary of the Platonic theory (Stobaeus 1.135,23–136,2).

6–7 These notoriously disputed lines become intelligible once three points are appreciated. First, ἡμᾶς picks up ἀνθρώπων (4) and refers to individuals in general *qua* members of species like man. Second, the purpose of the μέν . . . δέ contrast is to distinguish the relationships in which individuals stand to two quite different but easily confused entities, universal concepts and general terms. Cf. Simplicius, *In Ar. Cat.* 209,10–14 (reporting the Academics steeped in Stoic doctrine who also feature in **29g**), where the full list is: ποιότητα ἔχειν, ἐννοήματος μετέχειν, πτώσεως τυγχάνειν, and κατηγόρημα συμβεβηκέναι (τινί); also **E 2**. Third, πτῶσις can serve as a generic term for declinable expressions (see vol. 1, 201), especially nouns and pronouns, of which προσηγορίαι will be mentioned here as one species. As for πτώσεως τυγχάνειν, this is simply to 'bear' such designations; see also note on **33B**.

B Aetius 1.10.5 (*SVF* 1.65)

οἱ ἀπὸ Ζήνωνος Στωικοὶ ἐννοήματα ἡμέτερα τὰς ἰδέας ἔφασαν.

Cf **A 1**.

C Diogenes Laertius 7.60–1

(1) γένος δέ ἐστι πλειόνων καὶ ἀναφαιρέτων ἐννοημάτων σύλληψις, οἷον ζῷον· τοῦτο γὰρ περιείληφε τὰ κατὰ μέρος ζῷα. (2) ἐννόημα δέ ἐστι φάντασμα διανοίας, οὔτε τὶ ὂν οὔτε ποιόν, ὡσανεὶ δέ τι ὂν καὶ ὡσανεὶ ποιόν, οἷον γίνεται ἀνατύπωμα ἵππου καὶ μὴ παρόντος. (3) εἶδος δέ ἐστι τὸ ὑπὸ γένους περιεχόμενον, ὡς ὑπὸ τοῦ ζῴου ὁ ἄνθρωπος περιέχεται. (4) γενικώτατον δέ ἐστιν ὃ γένος ὂν γένος οὐκ ἔχει, οἷον τὸ ὄν. (5) εἰδικώτατον δέ ἐστιν ὃ εἶδος ὂν εἶδος οὐκ ἔχει, ὥσπερ ὁ Σωκράτης. 5

6 οἷον τὸ ὄν F(corr): om. F: οἷον τοῦ BP: οἷον τὸ τί Egli

Context: explanation of Stoic terms relating to definition and classification. Cf. **32**.

4 **ἀνατύπωμα** This word apparently occurs nowhere else. The implication of the -μα termination is that this is not a physical printing (τύπωσις) in the soul, but the product, content, or intentional object of that imprint, a stereotype or pattern created in thought. For a similar opposition between τύπωσις and φάντασμα, see **39A–B**.

6 Cf. note on **27A** 1–2. But the text here is very insecure.

D Alexander, *In Ar. Top.* 359,12–16 (*SVF* 2.329)

οὕτω δειχθήσεται μηδὲ τὸ τὶ γένος ὂν τῶν πάντων· ἔσται γὰρ καὶ τοῦ ἑνὸς γένος ἢ ἐπίσης ὄντος αὐτῷ ἢ καὶ ἐπὶ πλέον· εἴ γε τὸ μὲν ἓν καὶ κατὰ τοῦ ἐννοήματος· τὸ δὲ τὶ κατὰ μόνων σωμάτων καὶ ἀσωμάτων· τὸ δὲ ἐννόημα μηδέτερον τούτων κατὰ τοὺς ταῦτα λέγοντας.

Context: commentary on Aristotle, Top. IV.6, 127a26.
Alexander is probably wrong to suppose that all τινά must be either corporeal or incorporeal: see vol. 1, 165. But he is right both that ἐννοήματα, being mere mental constructs, are neither corporeal nor incorporeal, and that they are not even τινά (cf. A 1, C 2, E).

E Simplicius, In Ar. Cat. 105,7–20 (SVF 2.278)

ἄξιον δὲ ζητεῖν κατὰ τοὺς ὑπόστασιν διδόντας τοῖς εἴδεσιν καὶ γένεσιν εἰ ῥηθήσεται τάδε
εἶναι. (1) καὶ γὰρ καὶ Χρύσιππος ἀπορεῖ περὶ τῆς ἰδέας εἰ τόδε τι ῥηθήσεται.
(2) συμπαραληπτέον δὲ καὶ τὴν συνήθειαν τῶν Στωικῶν περὶ τῶν γενικῶν
ποιῶν, πῶς αἱ πτώσεις κατ᾽ αὐτοὺς προφέρονται καὶ πῶς οὗτινα τὰ κοινὰ
παρ᾽ αὐτοῖς λέγεται καὶ ὅπως παρὰ τὴν ἄγνοιαν τοῦ μὴ πᾶσαν οὐσίαν τόδε   5
τι σημαίνειν καὶ τὸ παρὰ τὸν οὗτιν σόφισμα γίνεται, παρὰ τὸ σχῆμα τῆς
λέξεως, (3) οἷον "εἴ τις ἔστιν ἐν Ἀθήναις, οὐκ ἔστιν ἐν Μεγάροις.
⟨ἄνθρωπος δὲ ἔστιν ἐν Ἀθήναις· οὐκ ἄρα ἔστιν ἄνθρωπος ἐν Μεγάροις.⟩"
(4) ὁ γὰρ ἄνθρωπος οὗ τις ἐστίν· οὐ γάρ ἐστί τις ὁ κοινός· ὡς τινα δὲ αὐτὸν
ἐλάβομεν ἐν τῷ λόγῳ, καὶ παρὰ τοῦτο καὶ τὸ ὄνομα τοῦτο ἔσχεν ὁ λόγος   10
"οὗτις" κληθείς. τὸ αὐτὸ δὲ καὶ ἐπὶ τοῦδε τοῦ σοφίσματός ἐστιν· "ὃ ἐγώ εἰμι, σὺ οὐκ εἶ.
ἄνθρωπος δέ εἰμι ἐγώ. ἄνθρωπος ἄρα σὺ οὐκ εἶ." καὶ γὰρ ἐπὶ τούτου τοῦ σοφίσματος τὸ μὲν
ἐγὼ καὶ σὺ ἐπὶ τῶν ἀτόμων λέγεται· ὁ δὲ ἄνθρωπος ἐπ᾽ οὐδενὶ τῶν ἐν μέρει. γέγονεν οὖν ἡ
παραγωγὴ διότι τῷ οὗτινι ὡς τινὶ ἐχρήσατο.

8 suppl. Kalbfleisch

Context: commentary on Aristotle, Cat. 5, 3b10ff.
For the οὗτις puzzle, cf. 37B 5; D.L. 7.82, 187; Elias, In Ar. Cat. 178; Philoponus, In Ar. Cat. 72, scholium. These last two are no doubt right to see in it an echo of the story at Odyssey 9 – Odysseus' escape from the Cyclops by inducing his victim to announce 'No-One is killing me' – but there is no resemblance in detail.
8   Kalbfleisch's supplement is guaranteed by Elias and the Philoponus scholium, cited above. All three texts share a common source. Cf. also D.L. 7.187.
8–9   ἄνθρωπος could be translated 'a man', but that would not explain Simplicius' ensuing diagnosis of the puzzle and its title in terms of the distinction between κοινός and τις, since 'a man' would designate an individual κοινῶς ποιός, not an ἐννόημα. It must be taken as 'man', as in 'Man has been to the moon', although it may be doubted whether the difference was very apparent to the Greek ear. Elias (loc cit.) has a similar diagnosis. The absurd conclusion is meant to demonstrate the error of treating a universal as a τι, a discrete entity – the error of which Aristotle frequently accuses Plato. Thus treated, it fails to obey basic logical laws. See further, F.
11–14   The sophism which Simplicius adds is attested elsewhere (Gellius, NA 18.13). But it is not an example of the οὗτις, whose major premise must consist of an indefinite and a definite proposition (D.L. 7.82; cf. 37B 5; these terms are explained at 34H), and it is unlikely that the Stoics would regard it as comparable, since 'man' this

Stoic ontology

time occupies the predicate position and signifies a corporeal κοινῶς ποιός, not a universal ἐννόημα.

F Sextus Empiricus 7.246 (*SVF* 2.65, part)

(1) οὔτε δὲ ἀληθεῖς οὔτε ψευδεῖς ἦσαν αἱ γενικαί· (2) ὧν γὰρ τὰ εἴδη τοῖα ἢ τοῖα, τούτων τὰ γένη οὔτε τοῖα οὔτε τοῖα, (3) οἷον τῶν ἀνθρώπων οἱ μέν εἰσιν Ἕλληνες οἱ δὲ βάρβαροι, ἀλλ᾽ ὁ γενικὸς ἄνθρωπος οὔτε Ἕλλην ἐστίν, ἐπεὶ πάντες ἂν οἱ ἐπ᾽ εἴδους ἦσαν Ἕλληνες, οὔτε βάρβαρος διὰ τὴν αὐτὴν αἰτίαν.   5

Context: continuation of **39G**, the Stoic classification of φαντασίαι.

Since the truth value of a φαντασία derives from that of the proposition implicit in it (see vol. 1, 240), it seems to follow from this passage that 'Man is Greek' is neither true nor false, and hence not a well-formed proposition. Cf. **E**. Aristotle in *De int*. 7, by contrast, allows a proposition like 'Man is white', with a universal subject, to be true, so long as 'is white' is true of some individual man or men.

G Syrianus, *In Ar. Met.* 104,17–23 (*SVF* 2.361)

ἀλλὰ μηδὲ τῶν καθ᾽ ἕκαστα [*sc.* ἐπιστήμην εἶναι], εἴτε ῥέοι κατὰ πᾶν, ὡς ὁ Ἡρακλείτου λόγος, εἴτε γίγνοιτο μὲν ἀεὶ καὶ φθείροιτο, διαμένοι δὲ κατὰ τὸ ἑαυτῶν ὅλον διὰ τὴν εἰδητικὴν αἰτίαν, ὡς Πλάτων ἐθέλει, εἴτε καὶ ὄντα τις αὐτὰ καλοίη, ὡς Ἀριστοτέλης εἴωθεν, εἴτε καὶ μόνα εἶναι λέγοι, ὡς οἱ Στωικοί φασιν, ὅμως τό γε ἐπιστήμην εἶναι τῶν ἀτόμων παρὰ πᾶσίν ἐστιν ἀπεγνωσμένον, εἰ μή τις ἐπιστήμην   5
ἐθέλοι καλεῖν τὴν αἴσθησιν.

1 ⟨ᾁ⟩ εἴτε Usener

Context: attempt to deny, contrary to Aristotle, *Metaph*. M.4, 1078b12ff., that Plato's theory of Forms owed any special debt to Heraclitus: on the crucial premises *all* philosophers agree. But lines 4–6 show scant understanding of Stoic epistemology (see especially **41**).

H Syrianus, *In Ar. Met.* 105,21–5 (*SVF* 2.364)

. . . ὡς ἄρα τὰ εἴδη παρὰ τοῖς θείοις τούτοις ἀνδράσιν οὔτε πρὸς τὴν χρῆσιν τῆς τῶν ὀνομάτων συνηθείας παρήγετο, ὡς Χρύσιππος καὶ Ἀρχέδημος καὶ οἱ πλείους τῶν Στωικῶν ὕστερον ᾠήθησαν (πολλαῖς γὰρ διαφοραῖς διέστηκε τὰ καθ᾽ αὑτὰ εἴδη τῶν ἐν τῇ συνηθείᾳ λεγομένων), οὔτε . . .

1 χρῆσιν Petersen: ῥῆσιν codd.

Context: commentary on *Metaph*. A.9, 992b7.

I Sextus Empiricus, *M*. 11.8–11 (*SVF* 2.224)

(1) τὸν γὰρ ὅρον φασὶν οἱ τεχνογράφοι ψιλῇ τῇ συντάξει διαφέρειν τοῦ καθολικοῦ, δυνάμει τὸν αὐτὸν ὄντα. καὶ εἰκότως· ὁ γὰρ εἰπὼν "ἄνθρωπός ἐστι ζῷον λογικὸν θνητόν" τῷ εἰπόντι "εἴ τί ἐστιν ἄνθρωπος, ἐκεῖνο ζῷον

ἐστι λογικὸν θνητόν" τῇ μὲν δυνάμει τὸ αὐτὸ λέγει, τῇ δὲ φωνῇ διάφορον.
(2) καὶ ὅτι τοῦτο, συμφανὲς ἐκ τοῦ μὴ μόνον τὸ καθολικὸν τῶν ἐπὶ μέρους   5
εἶναι περιληπτικόν, ἀλλὰ καὶ τὸν ὅρον ἐπὶ πάντα τὰ εἴδη τοῦ ἀποδιδομένου
πράγματος διήκειν, οἷον τὸν μὲν τοῦ ἀνθρώπου ἐπὶ πάντας τοὺς κατ᾽ εἶδος
ἀνθρώπους, τὸν δὲ τοῦ ἵππου ἐπὶ πάντας τοὺς ἵππους. ἑνός τε ὑποταχθέν-
τος ψεύδους ἑκάτερον γίνεται μοχθηρόν, τό τε καθολικὸν καὶ ὁ ὅρος. (3)
ἀλλὰ γὰρ ὡς ταῦτα φωναῖς ἐξηλλαγμένα κατὰ δύναμίν ἐστι τὰ αὐτά, ὧδε   10
καὶ ἡ τέλειος, φασί, διαίρεσις, δύναμιν ἔχουσα καθολικήν, συντάξει τοῦ
καθολικοῦ διενήνοχεν. ὁ γὰρ τρόπῳ τῷδε διαιρούμενος "τῶν ἀνθρώπων οἱ μέν εἰσιν
Ἕλληνες οἱ δὲ βάρβαροι" ἴσον τι λέγει τῷ "εἴ τινές εἰσιν ἄνθρωποι, ἐκεῖνοι ἢ Ἕλληνές εἰσιν
ἢ βάρβαροι." ἐὰν γάρ τις ἄνθρωπος εὑρίσκηται μήτε Ἕλλην μήτε βάρβαρος, ἀνάγκη
μοχθηρὰν μὲν εἶναι τὴν διαίρεσιν, ψεῦδος δὲ γίνεσθαι τὸ καθολικόν. διόπερ καὶ τὸ   15
οὕτω λεγόμενον "τῶν ὄντων τὰ μέν ἐστιν ἀγαθά, τὰ δὲ κακά, τὰ δὲ τούτων
μεταξύ" δυνάμει κατὰ τὸν Χρύσιππον τοιοῦτόν ἐστι καθολικόν "εἴ τινά
ἐστιν ὄντα, ἐκεῖνα ἤτοι ἀγαθά ἐστιν ἢ κακά ἐστιν ἢ ἀδιάφορα". τὸ μέντοι
γε τοιοῦτον καθολικὸν ψεῦδός ἐστιν ὑποτασσομένου τινὸς αὐτῷ ψεύδους.

Context: logical diagnosis of the ethical division in 16–17, for which see **58A 1**.

1 **τεχνογράφοι** A rare word, perhaps 'writers of technical handbooks'. A τέχνη
is often especially concerned with classification and definition of terminology (e.g.
70B), and that is probably Sextus' point in using the word here. They are not specified
as Stoics, but the identification becomes clear in 17.

3 On the force of εἰ here, see vol. 1, 194.

17 **τινά** This has the technical function (see **27**) of designating particulars, thus
making it clear that the division of types is being rewritten as a conditional ranging
over all token things.

j Aetius 4.11.4–5 (SVF 2.83, part)

ἔστι δ᾽ ἐννόημα φάντασμα διανοίας λογικοῦ ζῴου· τὸ γὰρ φάντασμα ἐπειδὰν λογικῇ
προσπίπτῃ ψυχῇ, τότε ἐννόημα καλεῖται, εἰληφὸς τοὔνομα παρὰ τοῦ νοῦ. διόπερ τοῖς
ἀλόγοις ζῴοις ὅσα προσπίπτει, φαντάσματα μόνον ἐστίν· ὅσα δὲ ἡμῖν καὶ τοῖς θεοῖς, ταῦτα
καὶ φαντάσματα κατὰ γένος καὶ ἐννοήματα κατ᾽ εἶδος· ὥσπερ τὰ δηνάρια καὶ οἱ στατῆρες
αὐτὰ μὲν καθ᾽ αὑτὰ ὑπάρχει δηνάρια ⟨καὶ⟩ στατῆρες· ἐὰν δὲ εἰς πλοίων δοθῇ μίσθωσιν,   5
τηνικαῦτα πρὸς τῷ δηνάρια εἶναι καὶ ναῦλα λέγεται.

Context: continuation of **39E**, on the Stoic theory on the development of conceptions.
This text is completely out of step with all the other evidence on ἐννοήματα. It
represents them as *any* figments of a rational mind, implicitly including fictional
individuals like Pegasus. It is easy to see how the mistake has arisen. The source has
taken a standard *description* of an ἐννόημα as φάντασμα διανοίας λογικοῦ ζῴου (cf. **A
1, C 2**), mistaken it for a complete definition, and tried to explain it accordingly (for
the explanation, with its 'fare' example, cf. *SVF* 1.376, conjecturally attributed to
Aristo), overlooking the fact that the term is restricted to universal concepts.

LOGIC AND SEMANTICS

31 Dialectic and rhetoric

A Diogenes Laertius 7.41–4

(1) τὸ δὲ λογικὸν μέρος φασὶν ἔνιοι εἰς δύο διαιρεῖσθαι ἐπιστήμας, εἰς ῥητορικὴν καὶ εἰς διαλεκτικήν. τινὲς δὲ καὶ εἰς τὸ ὁρικὸν εἶδος τό ⟨τε⟩ περὶ κανόνων καὶ κριτηρίων· ἔνιοι δὲ τὸ ὁρικὸν περιαιροῦσιν. (2) τὸ μὲν οὖν περὶ κανόνων καὶ κριτηρίων παραλαμβάνουσι πρὸς τὸ τὴν ἀλήθειαν εὑρεῖν· ἐν αὐτῷ γὰρ τὰς τῶν φαντασιῶν διαφορὰς ἀπευθύνουσι. (3) καὶ τὸ ὁρικὸν δὲ ⁵ ὁμοίως πρὸς ἐπίγνωσιν τῆς ἀληθείας· διὰ γὰρ τῶν ἐννοιῶν τὰ πράγματα λαμβάνεται. (4) τήν τε ῥητορικὴν ἐπιστήμην οὖσαν τοῦ εὖ λέγειν περὶ τῶν ἐν διεξόδῳ λόγων (5) καὶ τὴν διαλεκτικὴν τοῦ ὀρθῶς διαλέγεσθαι περὶ τῶν ἐν ἐρωτήσει καὶ ἀποκρίσει λόγων· ὅθεν καὶ οὕτως αὐτὴν ὁρίζονται, ἐπιστήμην ἀληθῶν καὶ ψευδῶν καὶ οὐδετέρων. (6) καὶ τὴν μὲν ῥητορικὴν ¹⁰ αὐτὴν εἶναι λέγουσι τριμερῆ· τὸ μὲν γὰρ αὐτῆς εἶναι συμβουλευτικόν, τὸ δὲ δικανικόν, τὸ δὲ ἐγκωμιαστικόν. εἶναι δ' αὐτῆς τὴν διαίρεσιν εἴς τε τὴν εὕρεσιν καὶ εἰς τὴν φράσιν καὶ εἰς τὴν τάξιν καὶ εἰς τὴν ὑπόκρισιν. τὸν δὲ ῥητορικὸν λόγον εἴς τε τὸ προοίμιον καὶ εἰς τὴν διήγησιν καὶ τὰ πρὸς τοὺς ἀντιδίκους καὶ τὸν ἐπίλογον. (7) τὴν δὲ διαλεκτικὴν διαιρεῖσθαι εἴς τε τὸν ¹⁵ περὶ τῶν σημαινομένων καὶ τῆς φωνῆς τόπον· καὶ τὸν μὲν τῶν σημαινομένων εἴς τε τὸν περὶ τῶν φαντασιῶν τόπον καὶ τῶν ἐκ τούτων ὑφισταμένων λεκτῶν, ἀξιωμάτων καὶ αὐτοτελῶν καὶ κατηγορημάτων καὶ τῶν ὁμοίων ὀρθῶν καὶ ὑπτίων καὶ γενῶν καὶ εἰδῶν, ὁμοίως δὲ καὶ λόγων καὶ τρόπων καὶ συλλογισμῶν καὶ τῶν παρὰ τὴν φωνὴν καὶ τὰ πράγματα ²⁰ σοφισμάτων. (8) [=**37C**] (9) εἶναι δὲ τῆς διαλεκτικῆς ἴδιον τόπον καὶ τὸν προειρημένον περὶ αὐτῆς τῆς φωνῆς, ἐν ᾧ δείκνυται ἡ ἐγγράμματος φωνὴ καὶ τίνα τὰ τοῦ λόγου μέρη, καὶ περὶ σολοικισμοῦ καὶ βαρβαρισμοῦ καὶ ποιημάτων καὶ ἀμφιβολιῶν καὶ περὶ ἐμμελοῦς φωνῆς καὶ περὶ μουσικῆς καὶ περὶ ὅρων κατά τινας καὶ διαιρέσεων καὶ λέξεων. ²

2 ⟨τε⟩ Usener   3 περιαιροῦσι FP: περιδιαιροῦσι B   11 εἶναι om. F   15 δὲ F: om. BP   26 καὶ λέξεων om. F.

Context: the beginning of Diogenes' doxography of the logical part of Stoicism.

   2 **τό ⟨τε⟩**   Either Usener's addition of τε, or Apelt's insertion of καί after εἶδος, is necessary, in order to distinguish definitions from criteria; cf. 3–7.

   6 **ἐπίγνωσιν**   Cf. Epictetus, *Diss.* 2.20.21, λαβών τις παρὰ τῆς φύσεως μέτρα καὶ κανόνας εἰς ἐπίγνωσιν τῆς ἀληθείας.

   6–7   For the connexion between definition and ἔννοια, cf. **32D, F, H 8**, and vol. I, 194.

   8–10   On the two definitions of dialectic, see Long [421], 102–6.

   10–15   Cf. Aristotle, *Rhet.* I.3, 1358b7 (the three kinds); I.1, 1354b18 (προοίμιον, διήγησις), III.1, 1403b20 (ὑπόκρισις); III.12, 1414a30 (τάξις); III.19, 1419b10 (ἐπίλογος).

   17–21   See **39A; 33F**.

B Diogenes Laertius 7.46–8 (*SVF* 2.130, part)

(1) αὐτὴν δὲ τὴν διαλεκτικὴν ἀναγκαίαν εἶναι καὶ ἀρετὴν ἐν εἴδει
περιέχουσαν ἀρετάς· (2) τήν τ᾽ ἀπροπτωσίαν ἐπιστήμην τοῦ πότε δεῖ
συγκατατίθεσθαι καὶ μή· (3) τὴν δ᾽ ἀνεικαιότητα ἰσχυρὸν λόγον πρὸς τὸ
εἰκός, ὥστε μὴ ἐνδιδόναι αὐτῷ· (4) τὴν δ᾽ ἀνελεγξίαν ἰσχὺν ἐν λόγῳ, ὥστε
μὴ ἀπάγεσθαι ὑπ᾽ αὐτοῦ εἰς τὸ ἀντικείμενον· (5) τὴν δ᾽ ἀματαιότητα ἕξιν   5
ἀναφέρουσαν τὰς φαντασίας ἐπὶ τὸν ὀρθὸν λόγον. (6) αὐτήν τε τὴν
ἐπιστήμην φασὶν ἢ κατάληψιν ἀσφαλῆ ἢ ἕξιν ἐν φαντασιῶν προσδέξει
ἀμετάπτωτον ὑπὸ λόγου. (7) οὐκ ἄνευ δὲ τῆς διαλεκτικῆς θεωρίας τὸν
σοφὸν ἄπτωτον ἔσεσθαι ἐν λόγῳ· τό τε γὰρ ἀληθὲς καὶ τὸ ψεῦδος
διαγινώσκεσθαι ἀπ᾽ αὐτῆς καὶ τὸ πιθανὸν τό τ᾽ ἀμφιβόλως λεγόμενον   10
διευκρινεῖσθαι· χωρίς τ᾽ αὐτῆς οὐκ εἶναι ὁδῷ ἐρωτᾶν καὶ ἀποκρίνεσθαι. (8)
διατείνειν δὲ τὴν ἐν ταῖς ἀποφάσεσι προπέτειαν καὶ ἐπὶ τὰ γινόμενα, ὥστ᾽
εἰς ἀκοσμίαν καὶ εἰκαιότητα τρέπεσθαι τοὺς ἀγυμνάστους ἔχοντας τὰς
φαντασίας. οὐκ ἄλλως τ᾽ ὀξὺν καὶ ἀγχίνουν καὶ τὸ ὅλον δεινὸν ἐν λόγοις
φανήσεσθαι τὸν σοφόν· τοῦ γὰρ αὐτοῦ εἶναι ὀρθῶς διαλέγεσθαι καὶ   15
διαλογίζεσθαι καὶ τοῦ αὐτοῦ πρός τε τὰ προκείμενα διαλεχθῆναι καὶ πρὸς
τὸ ἐρωτώμενον ἀποκρίνασθαι, ἅπερ ἐμπείρου διαλεκτικῆς ἀνδρὸς εἶναι.

5 ἀπάγεσθαι BP: ὑπάγεσθαι F   10 ἀπ᾽ BFP: ὑπ᾽ dgt   16 προκείμενα P: προσκείμενα B: λεγόμενα
F

Context: immediately following **40C**.

2–8   For these epistemological terms, cf. **41**, especially **C, D, G**; and for discussion
of the dialectical virtues, see Long [421], 107–16.

13–14   For the moral significance of using impressions correctly, cf. **62K**; **63E**.

C Diogenes Laertius 7.83 (*SVF* 2.130)

(1) καὶ τοιοῦτοι μὲν ἐν τοῖς λογικοῖς οἱ Στωικοί, ἵνα μάλιστα κρατύνωσι
διαλεκτικὸν ἀεὶ εἶναι τὸν σοφόν· πάντα γὰρ τὰ πράγματα διὰ τῆς ἐν λόγοις
θεωρίας ὁρᾶσθαι, ὅσα τε τοῦ φυσικοῦ τόπου τυγχάνει καὶ αὖ πάλιν ὅσα τοῦ
ἠθικοῦ (εἰς μὲν γὰρ τὸ λογικὸν τί δεῖ λέγειν;) (2) περί τ᾽ ὀνομάτων
ὀρθότητος, ὅπως διέταξαν οἱ νόμοι ἐπὶ τοῖς ἔργοις, οὐκ ἂν ἔχειν εἰπεῖν. (3)   5
δυοῖν δ᾽ οὐσαιν συνηθείαιν ταῖν ὑποπιπτούσαιν τῇ ἀρετῇ, ἡ μὲν τί ἕκαστόν
ἐστι τῶν ὄντων σκοπεῖ, ἡ δὲ τί καλεῖται.

1 ἵνα–κρατύνωσι FP: τά–κρατύνων B: τά–κρατύνοντες dg: ἵνα–κρατύνουσι Cobet   2 ἀεί P: μόνον B
(corr.): om. BF   3 τε BP: om. F   τόπου dw co: τύπου cett.   4–5 εἰ μὲν γὰρ
τὸν λογικόν τι δεῖ λέγειν περὶ |τε| ὀνομάτων ὀρθότητος, πῶς τὰ κατ᾽ ἀξίαν ὀνόματα ἐπὶ τοῖς ἔργοις οὐκ
ἂν ἔχοι εἰπεῖν; dubitanter Arnim

Context: the conclusion of Diogenes' doxography of Stoic logic.

It seems possible to make sense of this important passage without emendation
(rejecting Long [421], 104). We take τοιοῦτοι, 1, closely with ἵνα, 'the Stoics are like
this, in their logic, in order to . . .'. The development of thought from πάντα γάρ
strongly favours reading ἀεί, not μόνον, in line 2. In 2–4 the wise man's omnipresent
dialectic is justified by its contribution to all three parts of philosophy. Then, at περί τ᾽

187

Stoic logic and semantics

ὀνομάτων–εἰπεῖν, 4–5, Diogenes makes a new point about Stoic dialectic – its lack of concern with historical linguistics. (For the terminology, cf. Plato, *Crat.* 383a, 384d.) As we point out in vol. 1, 195, the early Stoics' interests in etymology were less fanatical than is sometimes supposed, and the subject is notably absent from Diogenes' programme of dialectical studies; cf. **A**. The fact, however, that it was a fashionable Hellenistic subject will account for the explicit reference to its exclusion from the wise man's concerns. As a student of language, he confines his interest to σημαινόμενα and φωνή (**A 7**), which are probably what is meant by the two συνήθειαι, 6. For Chrysippus' use of συνήθεια in the sense 'linguistic practice', cf. **58H**.

D Alexander, *In Ar. Top.* 1,8–14 (*SVF* 2.124)

ἡμᾶς δὲ καλῶς ἔχει προειδέναι ὅτι τὸ τῆς διαλεκτικῆς ὄνομα οὐκ ἐπὶ τὸ
αὐτὸ σημαινόμενον πάντες οἱ φιλόσοφοι φέρουσιν, ἀλλ' οἱ μὲν ἀπὸ τῆς
Στοᾶς ὁριζόμενοι τὴν διαλεκτικὴν ἐπιστήμην τοῦ εὖ λέγειν, τὸ δὲ εὖ λέγειν
ἐν τῷ τὰ ἀληθῆ καὶ τὰ προσήκοντα λέγειν εἶναι τιθέμενοι, τοῦτο δὲ ἴδιον
ἡγούμενοι τοῦ φιλοσόφου κατὰ τῆς τελειοτάτης φιλοσοφίας φέρουσιν   5
αὐτό· καὶ διὰ τοῦτο μόνος ὁ σοφὸς κατ' αὐτοὺς διαλεκτικός.

Context: necessary preliminaries to the study of dialectic. After the Stoics, Alexander refers to Plato.

3 This definition, when compared with **A 7–9**, seems to conflate dialectic with rhetoric; cf. Long [421], 102–3, but note also **G**.

E Sextus Empiricus, *M.* 2.7 (*SVF* 1.75, part)

ἔνθεν γοῦν καὶ Ζήνων ὁ Κιτιεὺς ἐρωτηθεὶς ὅτῳ διαφέρει διαλεκτικὴ
ῥητορικῆς, συστρέψας τὴν χεῖρα καὶ πάλιν ἐξαπλώσας ἔφη "τούτῳ", κατὰ
μὲν τὴν συστροφὴν τὸ στρογγύλον καὶ βραχὺ τῆς διαλεκτικῆς τάττων
ἰδίωμα, διὰ δὲ τῆς ἐξαπλώσεως καὶ ἐκτάσεως τῶν δακτύλων τὸ πλατὺ τῆς
ῥητορικῆς δυνάμεως αἰνιττόμενος.   5

Context: survey of philosophers' accounts of rhetoric.

For Zeno's hand simile illustrating epistemological states, cf. **41A**.

F Cicero, *Top.* 6

(1) cum omnis ratio diligens disserendi duas habeat partis,¹ unam inveniendi alteram iudicandi, utriusque princeps, ut mihi quidem videtur, Aristoteles fuit. (2) Stoici autem in altera elaboraverunt; iudicandi enim vias diligenter persecuti sunt ea scientia quam διαλεκτικήν appellant, inveniendi artem quae τοπική dicitur, quae et ad usum potior erat et ordine naturae certe prior,   5
totam reliquerunt.

1 *partis* vulgo: *artis* Aa²

Context: the beginning of Cicero's treatment of 'topics'.

4–6 Against Cicero's claim, which he repeats at *De or.* 2.159 and *Fin.* 4.10, cf. εὕρεσιν, **A** 13, and vol. 1, 189.

G Cicero, *De or.* 2.157–8

ex tribus istis clarissimis philosophis, quos Romam venisse dixisti, videsne Diogenem eum fuisse, qui diceret artem se tradere bene disserendi et vera ac falsa diiudicandi, quam verbo Graeco διαλεκτικήν appellaret?

Context: the embassy from Athens to Rome in 156/5 B.C., headed by Carneades, Diogenes of Babylon and the Peripatetic Critolaus.
On Carneades' lectures for and against justice on this occasion, cf. **68M**.

H Plutarch, *St. rep.* 1047A–B (*SVF* 2.297–8)

(1) τὴν ῥητορικὴν ὁρίζεται τέχνην περὶ κόσμον καὶ εἰρομένου λόγου τάξιν·
ἔτι δ' ἐν τῷ πρώτῳ καὶ ταῦτα γέγραφεν· "οὐ μόνον δὲ τοῦ ἐλευθερίου καὶ
ἀφελοῦς κόσμου δεῖν οἶμαι ἐπιστρέφεσθαι ⟨ἀλλὰ⟩ κἀπὶ τῷ λόγῳ καὶ τῶν
οἰκείων ὑποκρίσεων κατὰ τὰς ἐπιβαλλούσας τάσεις τῆς φωνῆς καὶ
σχηματισμοὺς τοῦ τε προσώπου καὶ τῶν χειρῶν." (2) οὕτω δέ τις   5
φιλότιμος ἐνταῦθα περὶ τὸν λόγον γενόμενος πάλιν ἐν τῷ αὐτῷ βιβλίῳ,
περὶ τῆς τῶν φωνηέντων συγκρούσεως ὑπειπών, οὐ μόνον φησὶ ταῦτα
παρετέον τοῦ βελτίονος ἐχομένους ἀλλὰ καὶ ποιὰς ἀσαφείας καὶ ἐλλείψεις
καὶ νὴ Δία σολοικισμούς, ἐφ' οἷς ἄλλοι ἂν αἰσχυνθείησαν οὐκ ὀλίγοι.

1 κόσμον Xylander: κόσμου codd.   καὶ εἰρομένου λόγου Meziriac: καὶ εἰρημένου λόγου codd.:
εἰρομένου λόγου καὶ Wyttenbach, Cherniss   2 καὶ¹ Xg: om. cett.   3 ⟨ἀλλὰ⟩ κἀπὶ τῷ λόγῳ
Sandbach: κἀπὶ (κἀπὸ γEn) τῶν λόγων ᾧ codd.   4 τάσεις XgB: στάσεις cett.   6 περὶ τὸν λόγον|
λόγον om. aA: καὶ περιττὸς A(corr.) βγEn   7 ὑπειπών| ἐπειπὼν XgB

Context: example of Chrysippus' flagrant self-contradiction. There is a full discussion of details in Cherniss [326] ad loc.

I Cicero, *Fin.* 4.9 (*SVF* 1.47)

quid? ea quae dialectici nunc tradunt et docent, nonne ab illis instituta aut inventa sunt? de quibus etsi a Chrysippo maxime est elaboratum, tamen a Zenone minus multo quam ab antiquis.

1 aut Schiche: sunt ABER: om. NV: et Orelli   inventa sunt del. Madvig

Context: the Stoics' contributions to logic.
1 **illis**   The early followers of Plato and Aristotle. Cf. Plutarch, *St. rep.* 1045F–
1046A: in his *On dialectic* book 3 Chrysippus defended the subject's importance by appealing to the seriousness with which it was taken by Socrates, Plato, Aristotle, and their later followers down to Polemo and Strato.
2   For a study of Zeno's work in logic, cf. Rist [343].

J Epictetus, *Diss.* 4.8.12 (including *SVF* 1.51)

τίς οὖν ὕλη τοῦ φιλοσόφου; μὴ τρίβων; οὔ, ἀλλὰ ὁ λόγος. τί τέλος; μή τι
φορεῖν τρίβωνα; οὔ, ἀλλὰ τὸ ὀρθὸν ἔχειν τὸν λόγον. ποῖα θεωρήματα; μή τι
τὰ περὶ τοῦ πῶς πώγων μέγας γίνεται ἢ κόμη βαθεῖα; ⟨οὔ,⟩ ἀλλὰ μᾶλλον

Stoic logic and semantics

ἃ Ζήνων λέγει, γνῶναι τὰ τοῦ λόγου στοιχεῖα, ποῖόν τι ἕκαστον αὐτῶν
ἐστι καὶ πῶς ἁρμόττεται πρὸς ἄλληλα καὶ ὅσα τούτοις ἀκόλουθά ἐστιν.   5

3 ⟨οὖ,⟩ ἀλλὰ Upt. cod.

Context: the philosopher's profession.

4–5   While Epictetus may be using Zeno's name loosely, this could be a genuine
reminiscence of the school's founder. What are τὰ τοῦ λόγου στοίχεια? Not 'parts of
speech' in the linguistic sense, as at *SVF* 2.148. Bonhöffer [312], 127 n. 7, renders, 'die
Grundgesetze des Denkens'. On the evidence of **39E 4** and **53V**, we should think
more specifically of ἔννοιαι and προλήψεις. For the general implications of
ἁρμόττεται and ἀκολουθία, cf. Long [426], 95–104.

K Stobaeus 2.22,12–15 (*SVF* 1.49)

Ζήνων τὰς τῶν διαλεκτικῶν τέχνας εἴκαζε τοῖς δικαίοις μέτροις οὐ πυρὸν
οὐδ᾽ ἄλλο τι τῶν σπουδαίων μετροῦσιν, ἀλλ᾽ ἄχυρα καὶ κόπρια.

1 δικαίοις AS: εἰκαίοις B

Context: miscellany of philosophers' remarks on dialectic.

L Plutarch, *St. rep.* 1034E

(1) πρὸς τὸν εἰπόντα "μηδὲ δίκην δικάσῃς, πρὶν ἄμφω μῦθον ἀκούσῃς"
ἀντέλεγεν ὁ Ζήνων τοιούτῳ τινὶ λόγῳ χρώμενος· (2) "εἴτ᾽ ἀπέδειξεν ὁ
πρότερος εἰπών, οὐκ ἀκουστέον τοῦ δευτέρου λέγοντος (πέρας γὰρ ἔχει τὸ
ζητούμενον), εἴτ᾽ οὐκ ἀπέδειξεν (ὅμοιον γὰρ ὡς εἰ μηδ᾽ ὑπήκουσε κληθεὶς
ἢ ὑπακούσας ἐτερέτισεν). (3) ἤτοι δ᾽ ἀπέδειξεν ἢ οὐκ ἀπέδειξεν. (4) οὐκ   5
ἀκουστέον ἄρα τοῦ δευτέρου λέγοντος." (5) τοῦτον δὲ τὸν λόγον ἐρωτήσας
αὐτὸς ἀντέγραφε μὲν πρὸς τὴν Πλάτωνος Πολιτείαν ἔλυε δὲ σοφίσματα,
καὶ τὴν διαλεκτικὴν ὡς τοῦτο ποιεῖν δυναμένην ἐκέλευε παραλαμβάνειν
τοὺς μαθητάς.

1 μηδὲ Basil.: μήτε g: μηδενὶ cett.

Context: Plutarch cites Zeno's argument in order to claim that it made Zeno's
criticisms of Plato superfluous.

1   The fame of this hexameter verse is shown by the complexity of its
transmission; cf. Cherniss [326] ad loc.
7   For Zeno's criticism of Plato's *Republic*, cf. vol. 1, 435. He also wrote a book of
λύσεις and two of ἔλεγχοι, D.L. 7.4.

M Diogenes Laertius 7.25 (*SVF* 1.279)

καὶ πρὸς τὸν δείξαντα δ᾽ αὐτῷ Διαλεκτικὸν ἐν τῷ θερίζοντι λόγῳ ἑπτὰ
διαλεκτικὰς ἰδέας πυθέσθαι, πόσας εἰσπράττεται μισθοῦ· ἀκούσαντα δὲ
ἑκατόν, διακοσίας αὐτῷ δοῦναι. τοσοῦτον ἤσκει φιλομάθειαν.

Context: life of Zeno.
1   For this argument, cf. **37C**.

N Diogenes Laertius 7.160–1 (*SVF* 1.351, part)

τόν τε φυσικὸν τόπον καὶ τὸν λογικὸν ἀνῄρει, λέγων τὸν μὲν εἶναι ὑπὲρ
ἡμᾶς, τὸν δ᾽ οὐδὲν πρὸς ἡμᾶς, μόνον δὲ τὸν ἠθικὸν εἶναι πρὸς ἡμᾶς.
ἐοικέναι δὲ τοὺς διαλεκτικοὺς λόγους τοῖς ἀραχνίοις, ἃ καίτοι δοκοῦντα
τεχνικόν τι ἐμφαίνειν, ἄχρηστά ἐστιν.

2 οὐδὲν BP: οὐδὲ F

Context: life of Aristo.

1–2 See also *SVF* 1.352–7, with discussion by Ioppolo [346], 63–90.
3–4 See also *SVF* 1.391–4.

O Diogenes Laertius 7.182–4 (with omissions; = *SVF* 2.9, 2.1, part)

πρὸς δὲ τὸν κατεξανιστάμενον Κλεάνθους Διαλεκτικὸν καὶ προτείνοντα
αὐτῷ σοφίσματα, "πέπαυσο", εἶπε, "παρέλκων τὸν πρεσβύτερον ἀπὸ τῶν
πραγματικωτέρων, ἡμῖν δὲ τὰ τοιαῦτα πρότεινε τοῖς νέοις" . . . τέλος δ᾽
Ἀρκεσιλάῳ καὶ Λακύδῃ, καθά φησι Σωτίων ἐν τῷ ὀγδόῳ, παραγενόμενος
ἐν Ἀκαδημείᾳ συνεφιλοσόφησε· δι᾽ ἣν αἰτίαν καὶ κατὰ τῆς συνηθείας καὶ   5
ὑπὲρ αὐτῆς ἐπεχείρησε, καὶ περὶ μεγεθῶν καὶ πληθῶν τῇ τῶν Ἀκαδημαικῶν
συστάσει χρησάμενος.

2 παρέλκων FP: περι- BP(corr.)   3 τά–νέοις BP: τοῖς νέοις ταῦτα προτίθει F   7 συστάσει P:
ἐνστάσει B: στάσει F

Context: life of Chrysippus.

5–6. This set of arguments is turned against Chrysippus by Plutarch, *St. rep.*
1036A–E (= **P**, part); for his six books κατὰ τῆς συνηθείας and his seven ὑπὲρ [Cobet,
for MSS περὶ] . . ., cf. D.L. 7.198.
6–7 An intriguing item, which is spoiled by the Loeb mistranslation of σύστασις
by 'method'. In mathematics, σύστασις normally means 'construction' (cf. Proclus,
In Eucl. 1.419, 15–420, 12), and it refers to the composition of geometrical figures in
14 6a DK. Given Arcesilaus' well-attested interest in mathematics (cf. Long [622]),
this testimony rings true, though its precise sense seems impossible to determine.

P Plutarch, *St. rep.* 1035F–1037B (with omissions; = *SVF* 2.127,270,129)

(1) τὸ πρὸς τὰ ἐναντία διαλέγεσθαι καθόλου μὲν οὔ φησιν ἀποδοκιμάζειν,
χρῆσθαι δὲ τούτῳ παραινεῖ μετ᾽ εὐλαβείας, ὥσπερ ἐν τοῖς δικαστηρίοις,
μὴ μετὰ συνηγορίας ἀλλὰ διαλύοντας αὐτῶν τὸ πιθανόν· (2) "τοῖς μὲν γὰρ
ἐποχὴν ἄγουσι περὶ πάντων ἐπιβάλλει" φησί "τοῦτο ποιεῖν καὶ συνεργόν
ἐστι πρὸς ὃ βούλονται· τοῖς δ᾽ ἐπιστήμην ἐνεργαζομένοις καθ᾽ ἣν   5
ὁμολογουμένως βιωσόμεθα, τὰ ἐναντία, στοιχειοῦν καὶ καταστοιχίζειν
τοὺς εἰσαγομένους ἀπ᾽ ἀρχῆς μέχρι τέλους, ἐφ᾽ ὧν καιρός ἐστι μνησθῆναι
καὶ τῶν ἐναντίων λόγων, διαλύοντας αὐτῶν τὸ πιθανόν καθάπερ καὶ ἐν
τοῖς δικαστηρίοις" . . . (3) ἐν τῷ τετάρτῳ Περὶ βίων, ταῦτα γράφων· "οὐχ
ὡς ἔτυχε δ᾽ οὐδὲ τοὺς ἐναντίους ὑποδεικτέον λόγους οὐδὲ πρὸς τὰ ἐναντία   10

Stoic logic and semantics

πιθανὰ ἀλλ' εὐλαβουμένους μὴ καὶ περισπασθέντες ὑπ' αὐτῶν τὰς
κατάληψεις ἀφῶσιν, οὔτε τῶν λύσεων ἱκανῶς ἂν ἀκοῦσαι δυνάμενοι
καταλαμβάνοντές τ' εὐαποσείστως· ἐπεὶ καὶ οἱ κατὰ τὴν συνήθειαν
καταλαμβάνοντες καὶ τὰ αἰσθητὰ καὶ τἆλλα ἐκ τῶν αἰσθήσεων ῥᾳδίως
προίενται ταῦτα, καὶ ὑπὸ τῶν Μεγαρικῶν ἐρωτημάτων περισπώμενοι καὶ   1$
ὑπ' ἄλλων πλειόνων καὶ δυναμικωτέρων ἐρωτημάτων". . . (4) ἐν δὲ τῷ
Περὶ τῆς τοῦ λόγου χρήσεως εἰπών, ὡς οὐ δεῖ τῇ τοῦ λόγου δυνάμει πρὸς
τὰ μὴ ἐπιβάλλοντα χρῆσθαι καθάπερ οὐδ' ὅπλοις, ταῦτ' ἐπείρηκε· "πρὸς
μὲν γὰρ τὴν τῶν ἀληθῶν εὕρεσιν δεῖ χρῆσθαι αὐτῇ καὶ πρὸς τὴν τούτων
συγγένειαν, εἰς τἀναντία δ' οὔ, πολλῶν ποιούντων τοῦτο", πολλοὺς δὴ   2ο
λέγων ἴσως τοὺς ἐπέχοντας.

2 τούτῳ Xg: οὕτω cett.   6 καταστοιχίζειν vel καταστιχίζειν codd: κατατειχίζειν Cherniss   10
οὐδὲ ⟨τὰ⟩ πρὸς Pohlenz, Cherniss   12 οὔτε Reiske: οὐδὲ codd.   20 συγγένειαν codd.:
συγγυμνασίαν Pohlenz, Cherniss   δὴ Emperius: δέ codd.

Context: Chrysippus' inconsistency in propounding the doctrine of **P** when in fact his
own arguments against common sense (see note on **O** 5–6) were stronger than those
for it.

3–4   A certain allusion to the sceptical Academy; cf. vol. 1, 446.
6 **ὁμολογουμένως**   A reference to the ethical end; cf. **63A–B**.
11–13   Cf. **B 2–6**.

Q Diogenes Laertius 7.180 (*SVF* 2.1, part)

οὕτω δ' ἐπίδοξος ἐν τοῖς διαλεκτικοῖς ἐγένετο, ὥστε δοκεῖν τοὺς πλείους
ὅτι εἰ παρὰ θεοῖς ἦν διαλεκτική, οὐκ ἂν ἄλλη ἦν ἢ ἡ Χρυσίππειος.

Context: life of Chrysippus.

R Epictetus, *Diss*. 1.7.2–5, 10 (=**37J** 2)

(1) ζητοῦμεν γὰρ ἐπὶ πάσης ὕλης πῶς ἂν εὕροι ὁ καλὸς καὶ ἀγαθὸς τὴν
διέξοδον καὶ ἀναστροφὴν τὴν ἐν αὐτῇ καθήκουσαν. (2) οὐκοῦν ἢ τοῦτο
λεγέτωσαν, ὅτι οὐ συγκαθήσει εἰς ἐρώτησιν καὶ ἀπόκρισιν ὁ σπουδαῖος ἢ
ὅτι συγκαθεὶς οὐκ ἐπιμελήσεται τοῦ μὴ εἰκῇ μηδ' ὡς ἔτυχεν ἐν ἐρωτήσει
καὶ ἀποκρίσει ἀναστρέφεσθαι, ἢ τούτων μηδέτερον προσδεχομένοις   5
ἀναγκαῖον ὁμολογεῖν, ὅτι ἐπίσκεψίν τινα ποιητέον τῶν τόπων τούτων,
περὶ οὓς μάλιστα στρέφεται ἐρώτησις καὶ ἀπόκρισις. (3) τί γὰρ
ἐπαγγέλλεται ἐν λόγῳ; τἀληθῆ τιθέναι, τὰ ψευδῆ αἴρειν, ⟨πρὸς⟩ τὰ ἄδηλα
ἐπέχειν. ἆρ' οὖν ἀρκεῖ τοῦτο μόνον μαθεῖν; . . . οὐκ ἀρκεῖ.

1 εὕροι Meibom: εὐροοῖ S   5 ἢ Schenkl: μὴ S   8 ⟨πρὸς⟩ Meibom, cf. Epictet., *Diss*. 3.3.2

For discussion of Epictetus' assessment of logic, cf. Long [421], 119–21.

S Epictetus, *Diss*. 1.17.7–8

ἂν δὲ μὴ διαλάβωμεν πρῶτον τί ἐστι μόδιος μηδὲ διαλάβωμεν πρῶτον τί ἐστι
ζυγός, πῶς ἔτι μετρῆσαί τι ἢ στῆσαι δυνησόμεθα; ἐνταῦθα οὖν τὸ τῶν

ἄλλων κριτήριον καὶ δι' οὗ τἆλλα καταμανθάνεται μὴ καταμεμαθηκότες
μηδ' ἠκριβωκότες δυνησόμεθά τι τῶν ἄλλων ἀκριβῶσαι καὶ καταμαθεῖν;

Context: discussion of the proposition that logic is necessary. Epictetus explains here
why the Stoics make it the first subject of study. Cf. Diss. 2.11.13.

T Epictetus, Diss. 2.23.44–6

τί γὰρ κωλύει φράζοντα ὡς Δημοσθένης ἀτυχεῖν; τί δὲ κωλύει συλλογισμοὺς ἀναλύοντα ὡς Χρύσιππος ἄθλιον εἶναι . . . ταῦτα ὅταν λέγω πρός
τινας, οἴονταί με καταβάλλειν τὴν περὶ τὸ λέγειν ἐπιμέλειαν ἢ τὴν περὶ τὰ
θεωρήματα. ἐγὼ δ' οὐ ταύτην καταβάλλω, ἀλλὰ τὸ περὶ ταῦτ' ἀκαταληκτικῶς ἔχειν καὶ ἐνταῦθαι τὰς αὐτῶν ἐλπίδας.   5

4–5 ταῦτ' ἀκαταληκτικῶς Upt. cod.(corr.): ταῦτα καταληκτικῶς S   5 αὐτῶν Koraes: αὑτῶν codd.

Context: the proper use of the faculty of speech.

32 Definition and division

A Diogenes Laertius 8.48

τοῦτον ὁ Φαβωρῖνός φησιν ὅροις χρήσασθαι διὰ τῆς μαθηματικῆς ὕλης,
ἐπὶ πλέον δὲ Σωκράτην καὶ τοὺς ἐκείνῳ πλησιάσαντας, καὶ μετὰ ταῦτ'
Ἀριστοτέλην καὶ τοὺς Στωικούς.

Context: life of Pythagoras.

B Schol. Dion. Thrac. 107,5–7 (SVF 2.226, part)

(1) ὁ δὲ Χρύσιππος λέγει ὅτι ὅρος ἐστὶν ἰδίου ἀπόδοσις, τουτέστιν ὁ τὸ
ἴδιον ἀποδιδούς. (2) ὁ δὲ Ἀντίπατρος ὁ Στωικὸς λέγει "ὅρος ἐστὶ λόγος
κατ' ἀνάγκην ἐκφερόμενος", τουτέστι κατ' ἀντιστροφήν· καὶ γὰρ ὁ ὅρος
ἀντιστρέφειν θέλει.

3 ἀντιστροφήν b: ἀναστροφήν c

Context: prolegomenon to the τέχνη of Dionysius Thrax. Before seeking the
definition of τέχνη, we must seek the definition of 'definition'!
  1 **τουτέστιν ὁ** The masculine is odd, and the entire clause barely amplifies what
precedes. Perhaps read τουτέστιν ὁ ⟨λόγος ὁ⟩?

C Diogenes Laertius 7.60–2

(1) ὅρος δέ ἐστιν, ὥς φησιν Ἀντίπατρος ἐν τῷ πρώτῳ Περὶ ὅρων, λόγος
κατ' ἀνάλυσιν ἀπαρτιζόντως ἐκφερόμενος, (2) ἤ, ὡς Χρύσιππος ἐν τῷ
Περὶ ὅρων, ἰδίου ἀπόδοσις. (3) ὑπογραφὴ δέ ἐστι λόγος τυπωδῶς εἰσάγων
εἰς τὰ πράγματα, ἢ ὅρου ἁπλούστερον τὴν τοῦ ὅρου δύναμιν προσενηνεγ-

Stoic logic and semantics

μένος. (4) [= 30C]) (5) διαίρεσις δέ ἐστι γένους ἡ εἰς τὰ προσεχῆ εἴδη τομή, 5
οἷον "τῶν ζῴων τὰ μέν ἐστι λογικά, τὰ δὲ ἄλογα." (6) ἀντιδιαίρεσις δέ ἐστι
γένους εἰς εἶδος τομὴ κατὰ τοὐναντίον, ὡς ἂν κατ' ἀπόφασιν, οἷον "τῶν
ὄντων τὰ μέν ἐστιν ἀγαθά, τὰ δ' οὐκ ἀγαθά." (7) ὑποδιαίρεσις δέ ἐστι
διαίρεσις ἐπὶ διαιρέσει, οἷον "τῶν ὄντων τὰ μέν ἐστιν ἀγαθά, τὰ δ' οὐκ
ἀγαθά, καὶ τῶν οὐκ ἀγαθῶν τὰ μέν ἐστι κακά, τὰ δὲ ἀδιάφορα." (8) 10
μερισμὸς δέ ἐστι γένους εἰς τόπους κατάταξις, ὡς ὁ Κρῖνις· οἷον "τῶν
ἀγαθῶν τὰ μέν ἐστι περὶ ψυχήν, τὰ δὲ περὶ σῶμα."

3 ἰδίου Arnim: ἡ B (ἡ P): om. F   4 ἡ ὅρου Sedley: ἡ ὅρος codd.

Context: survey of Stoic dialectic (see on 33A).

D Galen, Def. med. 19.348,17–349,4

τινὲς δὲ καὶ οὕτως ὡρίσαντο· "ὅρος ἐστὶ λόγος κατ' ἀνάλυσιν ἀπαρτιζόντως ἐκφερόμενος", ἢ "ὅρος ἐστὶ διὰ βραχείας ὑπομνήσεως εἰς ἔννοιαν
ἡμᾶς ἄγων τῶν ὑποτεταγμένων ταῖς φωναῖς πραγμάτων."

2–3   The same definition is cited at S.E., PH 2.212. There is no firm evidence that
it is Stoic (especially given its somewhat Epicurean ring, cf. 17C 1, E 3), beyond
Galen's coupling of it with the first definition, attested as Stoic in C 1, and the similar
language at F, H 8 and I 1.

E Alexander, In Ar. Top. 42,27–43,2 (SVF 2.228, part)

οἱ δὲ λέγοντες ὅρον εἶναι λόγον κατὰ ἀνάλυσιν ἀπαρτιζόντως ἐκφερόμενον,
ἀνάλυσιν μὲν λέγοντες τὴν ἐξάπλωσιν τοῦ ὁριστοῦ καὶ κεφαλαιωδῶς,
ἀπαρτιζόντως δὲ τὸ μήτε ὑπερβάλλειν μήτε ἐνδεῖν, οὐδὲν ἂν λέγοιεν τὸν
ὅρον διαφέρειν τῆς τοῦ ἰδίου ἀποδόσεως.

2 ὁριστοῦ] ὁριστικοῦ A

Context: commentary on Top 1.5, 101b39, definition of ὅρος as λόγος ὁ τὸ τί ἦν εἶναι
σημαίνων. Alexander has just criticized Antisthenes and 'some of the Stoics' for being
satisfied to regard a definition as conveying just τὸ τί ἦν. His objection is that 'what it
is' may be stated with a formula which fails to convey what the thing's being consists
in. The present remark seems to continue this criticism of the Stoics alluded to, who
must either be, or include, the circle of Antipater, cf. C 1: for the upshot, see vol. 1,
194. Alexander's criticism must be assuming the broad Aristotelian use of ἴδιον for
'peculiar characteristic', a class of which essential, and thus definitional, characteristics
form a sub-class (Top. 1.5, 101b19–23); whereas Stoic usage of the term suggests that
they have this sub-class itself in mind.

3 ἀπαρτιζόντως   For the explanation given here of this term, cf. 28N 6.

F Augustine, Civ. dei 8.7 (SVF 2.106, part)

etiam ipsi Stoici, qui cum uehementer amauerint sollertiam disputandi, quam dialecticam
nominant, a corporis sensibus eam ducendam putarunt, hinc asseuerantes animum

concipere notiones, quas appellant ἐννοίας, earum rerum scilicet quas
definiendo explicant; hinc propagari atque conecti totam discendi docendique
rationem. 5

Context: condemnation of Stoic philosophy for its reliance on the senses, by contrast
with Platonism.

G Galen, *Adv. Lyc.* 3.7 (*SVF* 2.230, part)

ἐν γάρ τοι τῇ γνώσει τῶν διαφορῶν ἑκάστου τῶν ὄντων αἱ τέχναι
συνίστανται. καὶ τοῦτο ἐπὶ πλεῖστον μὲν κἂν τῷ [περὶ] Φιλήβῳ διῆλθεν ὁ
Πλάτων εὐθὺς ἐν ἀρχῇ τοῦ συγγράμματος· ἐφύλαξε δ᾽ αὐτοῦ τὴν γνώμην
Ἀριστοτέλης, Θεόφραστος, Χρύσιππος. καὶ Μνησίθεος, καὶ οὐδεὶς ὅστις οὐ,
διῆλθεν ἐν τῷ περὶ τέχνης γράμματι τὸν αὐτὸν λόγον. 5

Context: attack on Lycus for maintaining that 'one heat does not differ from another'.
2–3 See Plato, *Philebus* 12c–19a.
4 **Μνησίθεος** Distinguished Athenian doctor, fourth century B.C.

H Cicero, *Tusc.* 4.53

(1) dicamus igitur utilem insaniam? tracta definitiones fortitudinis: intelleges
eam stomacho non egere. (2) fortitudo est igitur "adfectio animi legi summae
in perpetiendis rebus obtemperans". (3) vel "conservatio stabilis iudicii in eis
rebus quae formidolosae videntur subeundis et repellendis". (4) vel "scientia
rerum formidolosarum contrariarumque et omnino neglegendarum conser- 5
vans earum rerum stabile iudicium". (5) vel brevius, ut Chrysippus (nam
superiores definitiones erant Sphaeri, hominis in primis bene definientis, ut
putant Stoici; sunt enim omnino omnes fere similes, sed declarant communis
notiones alia magis alia) – (6) quomodo igitur Chrysippus? "fortitudo est"
inquit "scientia rerum perferendarum"; (7) vel "adfectio animi in patiendo ac 10
perferendo summae legi parens sine timore". (8) quamvis licet insectemur
istos, ut Carneades solebat, metuo ne soli philosophi sint. quae enim istarum
definitionum non aperit notionem nostram, quam habemus omnes de
fortitudine tectam atque involutam? qua aperta quis est qui aut bellatori aut
imperatori aut oratori quaerat aliquid neque eos existumet sine rabie 15
quicquam fortiter facere posse?

Context: Cicero's defence of the Stoic treatment of πάθη (see 65).
For further Stoic material on definitions of courage, cf. 61C–D, H.

I Diogenes Laertius 7.199–200

(1) ἠθικοῦ λόγου τοῦ περὶ τὴν διάρθρωσιν τῶν ἠθικῶν ἐννοιῶν σύνταξις
πρώτη· (2) Ὑπογραφὴ τοῦ λόγου πρὸς Θεόπορον α΄, Θέσεις ἠθικαὶ α΄,
Πιθανὰ λήμματα εἰς τὰ δόγματα πρὸς Φιλομαθῆ γ΄, Ὅρων τῶν τοῦ
ἀστείου πρὸς Μητρόδωρον β΄, Ὅρων τῶν τοῦ φαύλου πρὸς Μητρόδωρον

Stoic logic and semantics

β', "Ορων τῶν ἀναμέσων πρὸς Μητρόδωρον β', "Ορων τῶν πρὸς 5
Μητρόδωρον κατὰ γένος ζ', "Ορων τῶν κατὰ τὰς ἄλλας τέχνας πρὸς
Μητρόδωρον α' β'. (3) σύνταξις δευτέρα· Περὶ τῶν ὁμοίων πρὸς
'Αριστοκλέα γ', Περὶ τῶν ὅρων πρὸς Μητρόδωρον ζ'. (4) σύνταξις τρίτη·
Περὶ τῶν οὐκ ὀρθῶς τοῖς ὅροις ἀντιλεγομένων πρὸς Λαοδάμαντα ζ',
Πιθανὰ εἰς τοὺς ὅρους πρὸς Διοσκουρίδην β', Περὶ εἰδῶν καὶ γενῶν πρὸς 10
Γοργιππίδην β', Περὶ τῶν διαιρέσεων α', Περὶ ἐναντίων πρὸς Διονύσιον
β', Πιθανὰ πρὸς τὰς διαιρέσεις καὶ τὰ γένη καὶ τὰ εἴδη, καὶ Περὶ τῶν
ἐναντίων α'. (5) σύνταξις τετάρτη· Περὶ τῶν ἐτυμολογικῶν πρὸς Διοκλέα
ζ', 'Ετυμολογικῶν πρὸς Διοκλέα δ'.

1 διάρθρωσιν B: διόρθωσιν P

1 **διάρθρωσιν** As the following titles show, the idea is that it is definitions that 'articulate' our natural conceptions. This notion of articulation (cf. **F**, **H 5** and **8, 40G 2**; Cicero, *Top.* 31, *Or.* 116) becomes prominent in the work of Epictetus and also in later Academic philosophy, e.g. Anon. *In Plat. Theaet.* 47.33ff., where it is a development of the Platonic theory of recollection. In the absence of clear evidence for it in early Stoicism, we cannot be entirely confident that the heading here dates back to Chrysippus' own time.

J Origen, *Cels.* 1.24 (*SVF* 2.146)

... ἐμπίπτει εἰς τὸ προκείμενον λόγος βαθὺς καὶ ἀπόρρητος, ὁ περὶ
φύσεως ὀνομάτων· πότερον, ὡς οἴεται 'Αριστοτέλης, θέσει εἰσὶ τὰ
ὀνόματα ἤ, ὡς νομίζουσιν οἱ ἀπὸ τῆς Στοᾶς, φύσει, μιμουμένων τῶν
πρώτων φωνῶν τὰ πράγματα, καθ' ὧν τὰ ὀνόματα, καθὸ καὶ στοιχεῖά τινα
τῆς ἐτυμολογίας εἰσάγουσιν. 5

Context: attack on Celsus' view that it makes no difference if God is called 'Zeus', or by any other local name for the supreme deity. In the sequel, Origen adds the Epicurean theory of the origin of language (see **19**) to the list.

2 **'Αριστοτέλης** The reference will be to *De int.* 3, 16a19; 4, 17a1–2.

33 Sayables (*lekta*)

A Diogenes Laertius 7.57 (*SVF* 3 Diogenes 20, part)

διαφέρει δὲ φωνὴ καὶ λέξις, ὅτι φωνὴ μὲν καὶ ὁ ἦχός ἐστι, λέξις δὲ τὸ
ἔναρθρον μόνον. λέξις δὲ λόγου διαφέρει, ὅτι λόγος ἀεὶ σημαντικός ἐστι,
λέξις δὲ καὶ ἀσήμαντος, ὡς ἡ βλίτυρι, λόγος δὲ οὐδαμῶς. διαφέρει δὲ καὶ
τὸ λέγειν τοῦ προφέρεσθαι· προφέρονται μὲν γὰρ αἱ φωναί, λέγεται δὲ τὰ
πράγματα, ἃ δὴ καὶ λεκτὰ τυγχάνει. 5

2 λέξις–ἐστι dg: om. BFP   3 δὲ καί¹ dg: μὲν γάρ BFP   ἀσήμαντος dg: ἄσημος γίνεται BFP

Context: doxography of Stoic dialectic, possibly derived from a handbook by Diocles of Magnesia (D.L. 7.48; cf. **39A**), first century B.C., though the extension of Diogenes'

33 Sayables ('lekta')

excerpt beyond D.L. 7.49 is disputed. The Stoic philosopher chiefly cited by Diogenes in the first part of this survey is Diogenes of Babylon, who wrote a book Περὶ φωνῆς (D.L. 7.55, 57).

1 **λέξις** Defined as φωνὴ ἐγγράμματος, οἷον "ἡμέρα", D.L. 7.56.

2 **λόγος** Defined as φωνὴ σημαντικὴ ἀπὸ διανοίας ἐκπεμπομένη, D.L. 7.56; cf. D. Most editors accept Casaubon's supplement, οἷον "ἡμέρα ἐστί", after ἐκπεμπομένη. This may be right, but there is no reason to think that a λόγος has to be a 'complete sayable', **F 3**.

3 **βλίτυρι** This, together with σκινδαψός (S.E., M. 8.133), was the standard example of a meaningless word. Cf. Galen 8.662 Kühn, where the corresponding verbs are coined, to express his indifference to terminology used to describe the action of the pulse.

5 **λεκτά** The Stoics appear to have invented this usage of the term. Thereafter it became grammarians' jargon for distinguishing the semantic aspect of a word from its sound; cf. Apollonius Dyscolus, *Adv.* 136,32.

B Sextus Empiricus, *M.* 8.11–12 (*SVF* 2.166, part)

(1) ἦν δὲ καὶ ἄλλη τις παρὰ τούτοις διάστασις, καθ' ἣν οἱ μὲν περὶ τῷ σημαινομένῳ τὸ ἀληθές τε καὶ ψεῦδος ὑπεστήσαντο, οἱ δὲ περὶ τῇ φωνῇ, οἱ δὲ περὶ τῇ κινήσει τῆς διανοίας. (2) καὶ δὴ τῆς μὲν πρώτης δόξης προεστήκασιν οἱ ἀπὸ τῆς Στοᾶς τρία φάμενοι συζυγεῖν ἀλλήλοις, τό τε σημαινόμενον καὶ τὸ σημαῖνον καὶ τὸ τυγχάνον, ὧν σημαῖνον μὲν εἶναι τὴν 5 φωνήν, οἷον τὴν Δίων, σημαινόμενον δὲ αὐτὸ τὸ πρᾶγμα τὸ ὑπ' αὐτῆς δηλούμενον καὶ οὗ ἡμεῖς μὲν ἀντιλαμβανόμεθα τῇ ἡμετέρᾳ παρυφισταμένου διανοίᾳ, οἱ δὲ βάρβαροι οὐκ ἐπαΐουσι καίπερ τῆς φωνῆς ἀκούοντες, τυγχάνον δὲ τὸ ἐκτὸς ὑποκείμενον, ὥσπερ αὐτὸς ὁ Δίων. (3) τούτων δὲ δύο μὲν εἶναι σώματα, καθάπερ τὴν φωνὴν καὶ τὸ τυγχάνον, ἓν δὲ ἀσώματον, 10 ὥσπερ τὸ σημαινόμενον πρᾶγμα, καὶ λεκτόν, ὅπερ ἀληθές τε γίνεται ἢ ψεῦδος.

1–2 τῷ σημαινομένῳ Bekker: τὰ σημαινόμενα codd.

Context: doxography of truth.

1–3 Sextus (*M.* 8.13) attributes the second option to Epicurus and Strato; he discusses the third in 137–8, but explicitly doubts its having nameable proponents (13).

5 **τυγχάνον** For the interpretation of this term, see vol. 1, 201. If, as suggested there, something is so called because 'it bears a case' (πτώσεως τυγχάνει), we can understand why πτώσεις were called τευκταί (Simplicius, *In Ar. Cat.* 209,10ff.) by the Stoicizing 'Academics', who feature in **29g**. (Ps.-Ammonius' explanation of τυγχάνοντα, included in *SVF* 2.236, is completely fanciful.) ὀνόματος, or προσηγορίας, τυγχάνειν is commonly used for 'to bear a name' (e.g. **39A 6**; **72N 4**; S.E., *M.* 8.80; Simplicius, *In Ar. Cat.* 32,10; 73,34; 386,29), and πτώσεως τυγχάνειν (which occurs in **O**) is merely the generic counterpart of this.

6 What the bare name 'Dion' signifies is not a λεκτόν or something with a truth value, but 'a peculiar quality' (see **M**). Sextus should have cited an ἀξίωμα in order to make his point properly; cf. **E**, and Long [426], 77 with n. 11.

197

Stoic logic and semantics

7–8 παρυφισταμένου   Cf. C, F 2.
9–11   Cf. E 2, and for the corporeality of φωνή, H.

C   Sextus Empiricus, M. 8.70 (SVF 2.187, part)

ἠξίουν οἱ Στωικοὶ κοινῶς ἐν λεκτῷ τὸ ἀληθὲς εἶναι καὶ τὸ ψεῦδος. λεκτὸν δὲ ὑπάρχειν φασὶ τὸ κατὰ λογικὴν φαντασίαν ὑφιστάμενον, λογικὴν δὲ εἶναι φαντασίαν καθ᾽ ἣν τὸ φαντασθὲν ἔστι λόγῳ παραστῆσαι.

Context: detailed criticism of the views outlined in B.

2–3 λογικὴν φαντασίαν   This comprises the φαντασίαι of rational animals, which are identified with 'thought processes' (νοήσεις), 39A 6.

D   Diogenes Laertius 7.49 (SVF 2.52, part; = 39A 2)

προηγεῖται γὰρ ἡ φαντασία, εἶθ᾽ ἡ διάνοια ἐκλαλητικὴ ὑπάρχουσα, ὃ πάσχει ὑπὸ τῆς φαντασίας, τοῦτο ἐκφέρει λόγῳ.

Context: see 39A 1, which explains the sequence προ- ... εἶθ᾽: φαντασία is the starting-point of any mental act, and therefore prior to assent, cognition etc.

E   Seneca, Ep. 117.13

(1) "sunt" inquit "naturae corporum, tamquam hic homo est, hic equus; has deinde sequuntur motus animorum enuntiativi corporum. (2) hi habent proprium quiddam et a corporibus seductum, tamquam video Catonem ambulantem: hoc sensus ostendit, animus credidit. corpus est quod video, cui et oculos intendi et animum. dico deinde: 'Cato ambulat'. non corpus" inquit   5
"est quod nunc loquor, sed enuntiativum quiddam de corpore, quod alii effatum vocant, alii enuntiatum, alii edictum. (3) sic cum dicimus 'sapientiam', corporale quiddam intellegimus; cum dicimus 'sapit', de corpore loquimur. plurimum autem interest utrum illud dicas an de illo."

7 edictum φψ: dictum B   9 illud ς: illum codd.

Context: exposition of the Stoic distinction between 'goods', which are corporeal (e.g. sapientia), and the incorporeal sayables expressed by the corresponding verbs (e.g. sapere); cf. J 9–11 on φρόνησις/φρονεῖν etc.

2 motus animorum enuntiativi   Cf. διάνοια ἐκλαλητική, D. enuntiatiuus appears to be coined by Seneca to translate ἐκλαλητικός or προφορικός.

7   effatum is Cicero's translation of ἀξίωμα in 37H 34; in 38G 2 and 70G passim he uses enuntiatum and enuntiatio.

9 illud   For the correction to the neuter, cf. corpus, 5–8.

F   Diogenes Laertius 7.63

(1) ἐν δὲ τῷ περὶ τῶν πραγμάτων καὶ τῶν σημαινομένων τόπῳ τέτακται ὁ περὶ λεκτῶν καὶ αὐτοτελῶν καὶ ἀξιωμάτων καὶ συλλογισμῶν λόγος καὶ ὁ περὶ ἐλλιπῶν τε καὶ κατηγορημάτων καὶ ὀρθῶν καὶ ὑπτίων. (2) φασὶ δὲ

198

[τὸ] λεκτὸν εἶναι τὸ κατὰ φαντασίαν λογικὴν ὑφιστάμενον. (3) τῶν δὲ λεκτῶν τὰ μὲν λέγουσιν εἶναι αὐτοτελῆ οἱ Στωικοί, τὰ δ' ἐλλιπῆ. ἐλλιπῆ 5 μὲν οὖν ἐστι τὰ ἀναπάρτιστον ἔχοντα τὴν ἐκφοράν, οἷον "γράφει"· ἐπιζητοῦμεν γάρ, "τίς;" αὐτοτελῆ δ' ἐστὶ τὰ ἀπηρτισμένην ἔχοντα τὴν ἐκφοράν, οἷον "γράφει Σωκράτης". ἐν μὲν οὖν τοῖς ἐλλιπέσι λεκτοῖς τέτακται τὰ κατηγορήματα, ἐν δὲ τοῖς αὐτοτελέσι τὰ ἀξιώματα καὶ οἱ συλλογισμοί καὶ τὰ ἐρωτήματα καὶ τὰ πύσματα. 10

4 τὸ del. Arnim, *SVF* 2.181

Context: see on **A**.

1–3 As is clear from 9–10, propositions and syllogisms are only two of the species of complete sayables; cf. D.L. 7.66–8, which includes imperatives, oaths and addresses. For further species of predicates, cf. D.L. 7.64

6 **γράφει** There is nothing grammatically incomplete about γράφει as an expression. Hence Detel [433], 279, is correct to reject 'writes' as a translation in favour of 'he (she, it) i.e. someone writes'. But what is expressed by γράφει is an incomplete λεκτόν, and not, as Detel suggests, an 'indefinite simple proposition' (**34H 7**).

10 For the difference between ἐρωτήματα and πύσματα, cf. D.L. 7.66.

G Diogenes Laertius 7.64 (*SVF* 2.183, part)

ἔστι δὲ τὸ κατηγόρημα τὸ κατά τινος ἀγορευόμενον ἢ πρᾶγμα συντακτὸν περί τινος ἢ τινῶν, ὡς οἱ περὶ Ἀπολλόδωρόν φασιν, ἢ λεκτὸν ἐλλιπὲς συντακτὸν ὀρθῇ πτώσει πρὸς ἀξιώματος γένεσιν.

3 ὀρθῇ ⟨ἢ πλαγίᾳ⟩ dubitanter Egli

Context: immediately after **F**.

The material difference, if any, between these three accounts of 'predicate' is unclear. (Kneale [405], 144, unaccountably writes of 'two definitions'.) Nor do we know whether περί τινος ἢ τινῶν, 2, simply refers to 'singular or plural subjects' or whether some more subtle point is intended.

H Diogenes Laertius 7.55–6

ζῴου μέν ἐστι φωνὴ ἀὴρ ὑπὸ ὁρμῆς πεπληγμένος, ἀνθρώπου δ' ἔστιν ἔναρθρος καὶ ἀπὸ διανοίας ἐκπεμπομένη, ὡς ὁ Διογένης φησίν, ἥτις ἀπὸ δεκατεσσάρων ἐτῶν τελειοῦται. καὶ σῶμα δ' ἐστὶν ἡ φωνὴ κατὰ τοὺς Στωικούς, ὥς φασιν Ἀρχέδημός τ' ἐν τῇ Περὶ φωνῆς καὶ Διογένης καὶ Ἀντίπατρος καὶ 5 Χρύσιππος ἐν τῇ δευτέρᾳ τῶν Φυσικῶν. πᾶν γὰρ τὸ ποιοῦν σῶμά ἐστι· ποιεῖ δὲ ἡ φωνὴ προσιοῦσα τοῖς ἀκούουσιν ἀπὸ τῶν φωνούντων.

Context: see on **A**.

1–2 For animal and human ὁρμή, cf. **53A, P–R, U**.

3 For the age of rational maturity, see note on **39E** 9–11.

3–6 For similar arguments deducing corporeality, cf. **45C–D; 60S**.

Stoic logic and semantics

I Stobaeus 2.88,2–6 (*SVF* 3.171)

(1) πάσας δὲ τὰς ὁρμὰς συγκαταθέσεις εἶναι, τὰς δὲ πρακτικὰς καὶ τὸ κινητικὸν περιέχειν. (2) ἤδη δὲ ἄλλῳ μὲν εἶναι συγκαταθέσεις, ἐπ᾽ ἄλλο δὲ ὁρμάς· καὶ συγκαταθέσεις μὲν ἀξιώμασί τισιν, ὁρμὰς δὲ ἐπὶ κατηγορή-ματα, τὰ περιεχόμενά πως ἐν τοῖς ἀξιώμασιν †αἱ συγκαταθέσεις.

2 ἄλλῳ Wachsmuth: ἄλλων codd.   4 αἱ συγκαταθέσεις del. Meineke: οἷς συγκατατίθεσθαι Wachsmuth: καὶ συγκαταθέσεσι Usener

Context: account of Stoic doctrine of ὁρμή.

The most thorough discussion of this passage and its implications, which are of crucial importance for understanding the Stoic theory of action, is Inwood [547], 56–66; cf. also Long [434]. Unfortunately, the text is both corrupt and obscure in parts. Perhaps the chief difficulty is to ascertain the force of τὰ περιεχόμενά πως, 4. Interpretation should start from 1: every ὁρμή is a συγκατάθεσις; i.e. every ὁρμή is an act of assent. But plainly not every act of assent is a ὁρμή. Hence, in spite of the identity asserted in 1, there must be something about a ὁρμή (or a hormetic assent) which is not covered simply by its being a συγκατάθεσις. This is explained as 'actually' (ἤδη) a difference between the objects of the two faculties: we assent to certain propositions, but our ὁρμαί are ἐπὶ κατηγορήματα. ἐπί recalls the standard account of ὁρμή as a movement of soul *towards* something, **53Q**. In assenting, we approve the truth of a proposition – e.g. 'I should exercise'. On a Stoic analysis, genuine assent to this proposition will be accompanied by an impulse to exercise. And, from **53R**, the linguistic form that the impulse takes is seen to be imperatival, 'Exercise!'. Hence, it seems, our impulse is not directed to the whole proposition. Having given it our assent, what we are impelled towards is not, 'I should exercise', but exercising, the action to which our assent to the whole proposition impels us. It is perhaps this focus on the predicate of the proposition which accounts for the qualification τὰ περιεχόμενά πως. The predicate expressing the desirable action is *contained* in the proposition; but the proposition itself is not atomic, and thus its predicate can be isolated as the proper object of ὁρμή. For two suggestive parallels for this use of περιέχειν, cf. S.E., *PH* 2.112, 144.

J Stobaeus 2.97,15–98,6 (*SVF* 3.91)

(1) διαφέρειν δὲ λέγουσιν, ὥσπερ αἱρετὸν καὶ αἱρετέον, οὕτω καὶ ὀρεκτὸν καὶ ὀρεκτέον καὶ βουλητὸν καὶ βουλητέον καὶ ἀποδεκτὸν καὶ ἀποδεκτέον. αἱρετὰ μὲν γὰρ εἶναι καὶ βουλητὰ καὶ ὀρεκτὰ ⟨καὶ ἀποδεκτὰ τἀγαθά· τὰ δ᾽ ὠφελήματα αἱρετέα καὶ βουλητέα καὶ ὀρεκτέα⟩ καὶ ἀποδεκτέα, κατη-γορήματα ὄντα, παρακείμενα δ᾽ ἀγαθοῖς. (2) αἱρεῖσθαι μὲν γὰρ ἡμᾶς τὰ   5
αἱρετέα καὶ βούλεσθαι τὰ βουλητέα καὶ ὀρέγεσθαι τὰ ὀρεκτέα. κατηγορη-μάτων γὰρ αἵ τε αἱρέσεις καὶ ὀρέξεις καὶ βουλήσεις γίνονται, ὥσπερ καὶ αἱ ὁρμαί· (3) ἔχειν μέντοι αἱρούμεθα καὶ βουλόμεθα καὶ ὁμοίως ὀρεγόμεθα τἀγαθά, διὸ καὶ αἱρετὰ καὶ βουλητὰ καὶ ὀρεκτὰ τἀγαθά ἐστι. τὴν γὰρ

φρόνησιν αἱρούμεθα ἔχειν καὶ τὴν σωφροσύνην, οὐ μὰ Δία τὸ φρονεῖν καὶ   10
σωφρονεῖν, ἀσώματα ὄντα καὶ κατηγορήματα.

3–4 suppl. Heine   9 τἀγαθά Usener: ἀγαθά codd.

Stobaeus repeats the gist of this material at 2.78,7–12 (= *SVF* 3.89).
3 ὀρεκτά   For the connexion of ὄρεξις with 'goods', cf. note on **56C** 2.
3–4   Heine's supplement draws on Stobaeus, 2.78,13–16: τὰ μὲν ἀγαθὰ πάντα
ἐστὶν ὑπομενετὰ καὶ ἐμμενετά ... τὰ δὲ ὠφελήματα πάντα ὑπομενετέα καὶ
ἐμμενετέα. The distinction between -τός adjectives, which refer to ἀγαθά, and -τέος
adjectives, which refer to ὠφελήματα, is difficult to elucidate, but seems to amount to
the following. The good, as primarily instantiated in virtue, is corporeal (cf. **60S**).
Virtuous actions, such as φρονεῖν, though also describable as 'good' (cf. **60G**), are
incorporeal predicates of someone who 'has' φρόνησις. They, unlike the virtues
themselves, are not 'choiceworthy etc. *things*', but 'what should be chosen etc.' in the
sphere of *action*. The Stoics reported here seem to have authorized ὠφέλημα as the
term to describe the beneficial *result* of virtuous actions, to distinguish this from the
goodness of the virtues themselves, on which it depends. Cf. **60G** 20–2, where a
similar point is made by treating 'good' in reference to virtuous actions as a secondary
and different usage from its application to virtue. For further discussion, cf. Long
[434], 86–90.
6–8 **κατηγορημάτων** ...**ὁρμαί**   For the connexion between these, see **I**.
10–11   Cf. **55A** 3, **B**, for a similar distinction in cause–effect relations.

K Ammonius, *In Ar. De int.* 43,5–15 (FDS 776, part)

λεγόντων δὲ πρὸς αὐτοὺς τῶν Περιπατητικῶν ὡς τὰς μὲν ἄλλας εἰκότως λέγομεν πτώσεις
διὰ τὸ πεπτωκέναι ἀπὸ τῆς εὐθείας, τὴν δὲ εὐθεῖαν κατὰ τίνα λόγον πτῶσιν ὀνομάζειν
δίκαιον ὡς ἀπὸ τίνος πεσοῦσαν; (δῆλον γὰρ ὅτι πᾶσαν πτῶσιν ἀπό τινος ἀνωτέρω
τεταγμένου γίνεσθαι προσήκει), ἀποκρίνονται οἱ ἀπὸ τῆς Στοᾶς ὡς ἀπὸ τοῦ
νοήματος τοῦ ἐν τῇ ψυχῇ καὶ αὕτη πέπτωκεν· ὃ γὰρ ἐν ἑαυτοῖς ἔχομεν τὸ   5
Σωκράτους νόημα δηλῶσαι βουλόμενοι, τὸ Σωκράτης ὄνομα προφερό-
μεθα· καθάπερ οὖν τὸ ἄνωθεν ἀφεθὲν γραφεῖον καὶ ὀρθὸν παγὲν
πεπτωκέναι τε λέγεται καὶ τὴν πτῶσιν ὀρθὴν ἐσχηκέναι, τὸν αὐτὸν τρόπον
καὶ τὴν εὐθεῖαν πεπτωκέναι μὲν ἀξιοῦμεν ἀπὸ τῆς ἐννοίας, ὀρθὴν δὲ εἶναι
διὰ τὸ ἀρχέτυπον τῆς κατὰ τὴν ἐκφώνησιν προφορᾶς.   10

Context: disagreement between Stoics and Peripatetics on whether the nominative
should be called a πτῶσις.

L Schol. Dion. Thrac. 230,24–8 (FDS 781, part)

εἰ ὀρθή, πῶς πτῶσις; ὅτι πέπτωκεν ἐκ τοῦ ἀσωμάτου καὶ γενικοῦ εἰς τὸ
εἰδικόν· ὀρθὴ δέ, ὅτι οὔπω ἐκινήθη εἰς πλάγιον, ἢ ὅτι ἐξ αὐτῆς τὰ
καλούμενα παρὰ τοῖς Στωικοῖς ὀρθὰ ῥήματα, ἅ εἰσιν ἐνεργητικά, οἷον
"Σωκράτης τύπτει".

Context: the nominative case.

Stoic logic and semantics

The first part of this explanation can hardly be Stoic. What is said in 2–4 about the connexion between the nominative and active verbs may illustrate ἀρχέτυπον, K 10; such verbs start from or depend on (ἐξ αὑτῆς) a nominative noun as their subject.

M Diogenes Laertius 7.58 (*SVF* 3 Diogenes 22, part)

ἔστι δὲ προσηγορία μὲν κατὰ τὸν Διογένην μέρος λόγου σημαῖνον κοινὴν ποιότητα, οἷον "ἄνθρωπος", "ἵππος"· ὄνομα δέ ἐστι μέρος λόγου δηλοῦν ἰδίαν ποιότητα, οἷον Διογένης, Σωκράτης· ῥῆμα δέ ἐστι μέρος λόγου σημαῖνον ἀσύνθετον κατηγόρημα, ὡς ὁ Διογένης, ἤ, ὥς τινες, στοιχεῖον λόγου ἄπτωτον, σημαῖνόν τι συντακτὸν περί τινος ἢ τινῶν, οἷον "γράφω",   5 "λέγω".

Context: see on **A**.

1 **λόγου** The Stoics treated what are today called 'parts of speech' as parts of 'language' (λόγος not λέξις, cf. **A**). This is in line with their interest in establishing correspondence between the phonetic aspect of discourse and λεκτά; cf. Frede [418], 59–67, who translates λέξις by 'diction' and λόγος by 'speech'.

2–3 **ποιότητα** Cf. **28G–H**.

4–5 **ἀσύνθετον, ἄπτωτον, συντακτόν** Three ways of indicating what a verb means in abstraction from its subject or syntactical function.

In the text which follows this extract the remaining two 'parts of language' are defined: 'conjunction' (σύνδεσμος) and 'article' (ἄρθρον), to which Antipater added as a sixth part (D.L. 7.57) 'adverb' (μεσότης).

N Ammonius, *In Ar. De int.* 17,24–8 (*FDS* 702, part)

ἡμᾶς ὁ 'Αριστοτέλης διδάσκει διὰ τούτων, τίνα ἐστὶ τὰ προηγουμένως καὶ προσεχῶς ὑπ' αὐτῶν σημαινόμενα, καὶ ὅτι τὰ νοήματα, διὰ δὲ τούτων μέσων τὰ πράγματα, καὶ οὐδὲν ἕτερον δεῖ παρὰ ταῦτα ἐπινοεῖν μέσον τοῦ τε νοήματος καὶ τοῦ πράγματος, ὅπερ οἱ ἀπὸ τῆς Στοᾶς ὑποτιθέμενοι λεκτὸν ἠξίουν ὀνομάζειν.   5

For detailed discussion, cf. Long [426], 79–82. The Aristotelian commentators' inability to view Stoic λεκτά independently of Aristotle's theory of meaning is equally evident in Simplicius, *In Ar. Cat.* 10,3 (cf. 397,8) and Ammonius, *In Ar. An. pr.* 68,4.

O Clement, *Strom.* 8.9.26.5 (*FDS* 763, part)

ἡ πτῶσις δὲ ἀσώματος εἶναι ὁμολογεῖται· διὸ καὶ τὸ σόφισμα ἐκεῖνο οὕτως λύεται· "ὃ λέγεις, διέρχεταί σου διὰ τοῦ στόματος", ὅπερ ἀληθές, "οἰκίαν δὲ λέγεις, οἰκία ἄρα διὰ τοῦ στόματός σου διέρχεται", ὅπερ ψεῦδος· οὐδὲ γὰρ τὴν οἰκίαν λέγομεν σῶμα οὖσαν, ἀλλὰ τὴν πτῶσιν ἀσώματον οὖσαν, ἧς οἰκία τυγχάνει.   5

Context: two lines after **55C**.

Despite the difficulties of reading it as Stoic (see vol. 1, 201), Clement's claim that

33 Sayables ('lekta')

πτῶσις 'is agreed to be incorporeal' cannot, in view of the close proximity of 55C, be dismissed as easily as Frede [418], 31–2 tries to do by reference to Clement's own non-Stoic convictions. Moreover, we find it difficult to make sense of Frede's own claim that 'cases are the qualities that are said by Diogenes Laertius [= M] to be signified by proper names and common . . . nouns' (ibid.). How could cases, which on any analysis are functions of language, be the corporeal qualities of external objects? For an attempt to defend the Stoic tenor of the passage, see Graeser [430], 85–6.

P Sextus Empiricus, *PH* 2.81–3

(1) λέγεται διαφέρειν τῆς ἀληθείας τὸ ἀληθὲς τριχῶς, οὐσίᾳ συστάσει δυνάμει· (2) οὐσίᾳ μέν, ἐπεὶ τὸ μὲν ἀληθὲς ἀσώματόν ἐστιν (ἀξίωμα γάρ ἐστι καὶ λεκτόν), ἡ δὲ ἀλήθεια σῶμα (ἔστι γὰρ ἐπιστήμη πάντων ἀληθῶν ἀποφαντική, ἡ δὲ ἐπιστήμη πῶς ἔχον ἡγεμονικὸν ὥσπερ καὶ ἡ πῶς ἔχουσα χεὶρ πυγμή, τὸ δὲ ἡγεμονικὸν σῶμα· ἔστι γὰρ κατ' αὐτοὺς πνεῦμα)· (3)⁣ 5
συστάσει δέ, ἐπεὶ τὸ μὲν ἀληθὲς ἁπλοῦν τί ἐστιν, οἷον "ἐγὼ διαλέγομαι", ἡ δὲ ἀλήθεια ἀπὸ ⟨τῆς⟩ πολλῶν ἀληθῶν γνώσεως συνίσταται· (4) δυνάμει δέ, ἐπεὶ ἡ μὲν ἀλήθεια ἐπιστήμης ἔχεται, τὸ δὲ ἀληθὲς οὐ πάντως. διόπερ τὴν μὲν ἀλήθειαν ἐν μόνῳ σπουδαίῳ φασὶν εἶναι , τὸ δὲ ἀληθὲς καὶ ἐν φαύλῳ· ἐνδέχεται γὰρ τὸν φαῦλον ἀληθές τι εἰπεῖν.⁣ 10

7 ⟨τῆς⟩ Bekker   γνώσεως codd.: γνώσεων T

Context: refutation of the 'doctrinaire' philosophers' views on ἀλήθεια and ἀληθές. The same doctrine is reported more fully at S.E., *M.* 7.38–45, and attributed there to τινες καὶ μάλιστα οἱ ἀπὸ τῆς Στοᾶς. For detailed discussion, cf. Long [426], 98–102, and [429].

q Porphyry (Ammonius, *In Ar. De int.* 44,19–45,7; *SVF* 2.184)

τὸ κατηγορούμενον ἤτοι ὀνόματος κατηγορεῖται ἢ πτώσεως, καὶ τούτων ἑκάτερον ἤτοι τέλειόν ἐστιν ὡς κατηγορούμενον καὶ μετὰ τοῦ ὑποκειμένου αὔταρκες πρὸς γένεσιν ἀποφάνσεως, ἢ ἐλλιπὲς καὶ προσθήκης τινὸς δεόμενον πρὸς τὸ τέλειον ποιῆσαι κατηγορούμενον. ἂν μὲν οὖν ὀνόματός τι κατηγορηθὲν ἀπόφανσιν ποιῇ, κατηγόρημα καὶ σύμβαμα παρ' αὐτοῖς ὀνομάζεται (σημαίνει γὰρ ἄμφω ταὐτόν), ὡς τὸ περιπατεῖ, οἷον⁣ 5
"Σωκράτης περιπατεῖ"· ἂν δὲ πτώσεως, παρασύμβαμα, ὡσανεὶ παρακείμενον τῷ συμβάματι καὶ ὂν οἷον παρακατηγόρημα, ὡς ἔχει τὸ μεταμέλει, οἷον "Σωκράτει μεταμέλει"· τὸ μὲν γὰρ μεταμελεῖται σύμβαμα εἶναι, τὸ δὲ μεταμέλει παρασύμβαμα οὐ δυνάμενον ὀνόματι συνταχθὲν ἀπόφανσιν ἐργάσασθαι, οἷον "Σωκράτης μεταμέλει" (οὐδεμία γὰρ τοῦτο ἀπόφανσις), ἀλλ' οὔτε κλίσιν ἐπιδέξασθαι δυνάμενον, ὡς τὸ περιπατῶ⁣ 10
περιπατεῖς περιπατεῖ, οὔτε συμμετασχηματισθῆναι τοῖς ἀριθμοῖς· ὥσπερ γὰρ λέγομεν "τούτῳ μεταμέλει", οὕτως καὶ "τούτοις μεταμέλει". καὶ πάλιν ἂν μὲν τὸ τοῦ ὀνόματος κατηγορούμενον δέηται προσθήκης πτώσεως ὀνόματός τινος πρὸς τὸ ποιῆσαι ἀπόφανσιν, ἔλαττον ἢ κατηγόρημα λέγεται, ὡς ἔχει τὸ φιλεῖ καὶ τὸ εὐνοεῖ, οἷον "Πλάτων φιλεῖ" (τούτῳ γὰρ προστεθὲν τὸ τινά, οἷον Δίωνα, ποιεῖ ὡρισμένην ἀπόφανσιν τὴν "Πλάτων⁣ 15
Δίωνα φιλεῖ"), ἂν δὲ τὸ τῆς πτώσεως κατηγορούμενον ᾖ τὸ δεόμενον ἑτέρᾳ συνταχθῆναι

Stoic logic and semantics

πλαγία πτώσει πρὸς τὸ ποιῆσαι ἀπόφανσιν, ἔλαττον ἢ παρασύμβαμα λέγεται, ὡς ἔχει τὸ μέλει, οἷον "Σωκράτει 'Αλκιβιάδου μέλει". ταῦτα δὲ πάντα καλοῦσι ῥήματα. καὶ τοιαύτη μὲν ἡ τῶν Στωικῶν περὶ τούτων παράδοσις.

9 σωκράτης G: Σωκράτει cett.

Context: Ammonius is commenting on Aristotle's distinction between ὄνομα and πτῶσις. At 44,11 he cites Porphyry for the observation that impersonal verbs such as μεταμέλει constitute propositions when combined with a πτῶσις, i.e. an oblique case, but are unsyntactical when combined with an ὄνομα, i.e. a noun in the nominative. At this point he quotes Porphyry's account of the Stoics' treatment of the matter. Porphyry uses these terms in their Aristotelian senses, ignoring the Stoics' extension of πτῶσις to the nominative; cf. **K–L**.

2 **μετὰ τοῦ ὑποκειμένου** A predicate when 'combined with a subject' is complete and has all it needs to constitute a proposition; cf. **F 3, G**.

6–12 **παρασύμβαμα/παρακατηγόρημα** 'Sub-attribute/sub-predicate', describing the relation of impersonal verbs to the dative of the noun.

14 **ἔλαττον ἢ κατηγόρημα** 'An incomplete predicate', for which, in addition to the example given here, cf. **63B 2**.

34 Simple propositions

A Diogenes Laertius 7.65 (*SVF* 2.193, part)

ἀξίωμα δέ ἐστιν ὅ ἐστιν ἀληθὲς ἢ ψεῦδος· ἢ πρᾶγμα αὐτοτελὲς ἀποφαντὸν ὅσον ἐφ' ἑαυτῷ, ὡς ὁ Χρύσιππός φησιν ἐν τοῖς Διαλεκτικοῖς ὅροις, "ἀξίωμά ἐστι τὸ ἀποφαντὸν ἢ καταφαντὸν ὅσον ἐφ' ἑαυτῷ, οἷον ἡμέρα ἐστί, Δίων περιπατεῖ." ὠνόμασται δὲ τὸ ἀξίωμα ἀπὸ τοῦ ἀξιοῦσθαι ἢ ἀθετεῖσθαι.

Context: doxography of Stoic dialectic; see note on **33A**.

1 **ἀξίωμα–ψεῦδος** This is called a 'definition' by Cicero at **37H** 40, and Simplicius, *In Ar. Cat.* 406,21–2, and an 'outline account' (ὑπογράφοντες) by Sextus, *M.* 8.12 (see vol. 1, 193–4 for the difference between these). It certainly marks off ἀξιώματα from other complete λεκτά; cf. **B**. But it lacks the specificity of Chrysippus' definition in 1b–2, since the Stoics did not confine 'true' and 'false' to propositions, but applied them to arguments and impressions as well (**36A–B, 39G**). So ὅ–ψεῦδος should perhaps be interpreted as 'that which is *primarily* true or false'; cf. Frede [407], 40–1.

1–2 **ἢ πρᾶγμα κτλ.** For the same definition (substituting λεκτόν for πρᾶγμα), cf. **35C 2**.

2 **ὅσον ἐφ' ἑαυτῷ** Well explained by Frede [407], 37, as a reference to the intrinsic requirements of an ἀξίωμα as distinct from the extrinsic circumstances which are also necessary for its actual expression.

2–4 **ἀξίωμα–ἀθετεῖσθαι** This passage bristles with problems. First, it is not clear how ἀξίωμα–περιπατεῖ is connected with what precedes. One possibility, suggested to us by Jonathan Barnes and Michael Frede, is to insert ⟨ἤ⟩ either after ἑαυτῷ or after ὅροις. Secondly, as Frede [407], 38–40, has noted, ἢ ἀθετεῖσθαι is utterly

34 Simple propositions

inappropriate to the derivation of ἀξίωμα from ἀξιοῦσθαι. Thirdly, 'being rejected' would only have point if one of the words ἀποφαντόν or καταφαντόν meant 'capable of being denied'. But both words should mean 'capable of being asserted'. The text would be greatly improved by excising ἢ καταφαντόν and ἢ ἀθετεῖσθαι.

B Sextus Empiricus, *M*. 8.74 (*SVF* 2.187, part)

πλὴν ἱκανῆς οὔσης ἐν τοῖς λεκτοῖς διαφορᾶς, ἵνα τι, φασίν, ἀληθὲς ᾖ ἢ ψεῦδος, δεῖ αὐτὸ πρὸ παντὸς λεκτὸν εἶναι, εἶτα καὶ αὐτοτελές, καὶ οὐ κοινῶς ὁποιονδήποτε οὖν ἀλλ' ἀξίωμα· μόνον γὰρ τοῦτο, καθὼς προεῖπον, λέγοντες ἤτοι ἀληθεύομεν ἢ ψευδόμεθα.

Context: survey of the species of αὐτοτελῆ ἀξιώματα.

C Cicero, *Fat*. 38

quod autem uerum non est, qui potest non falsum esse? aut, quod falsum non est, qui potest non uerum esse? tenebitur id, quod a Chrysippo defenditur, omnem enuntiationem aut ueram aut falsam esse; ratio ipsa coget et ex aeternitate quaedam esse uera, et ea non esse nexa causis aeternis, et a fati necessitate esse libera.

2 post *tenebitur* ⟨*igitur*⟩ Christ, ⟨*ergo*⟩ Davies

Context: Cicero supports the Stoic principle of bivalence against the Epicurean denial of it, but resists Chrysippus' claim that it entails determinism. See **37G** and vol. 1, 229, 235, 343.

D Sextus Empiricus, *M*. 8.85-6

(1) φασὶ γὰρ ἀληθὲς μὲν εἶναι ἀξίωμα ὃ ὑπάρχει τε καὶ ἀντίκειταί τινι, ψεῦδος δὲ ὃ οὐχ ὑπάρχει μὲν ἀντίκειται δέ τινι. (2) ἐρωτώμενοι δέ, τί ἐστι τὸ ὑπάρχον, λέγουσι τὸ καταληπτικὴν κινοῦν φαντασίαν· (3) εἶτα περὶ τῆς καταληπτικῆς φαντασίας ἐξεταζόμενοι πάλιν ἐπὶ τὸ ὑπάρχον, ἐπ' ἴσης ὂν ἄγνωστον, ἀνατρέχουσι, λέγοντες "καταληπτική ἐστι φαντασία ἡ ἀπὸ ὑπάρχοντος κατ' αὐτὸ τὸ ὑπάρχον." 5

Context: as **B**.
For a defence of the Stoics against this charge of circular reasoning, and discussion of the term ὑπάρχειν, cf. Long [426], 91-4. On the καταληπτικὴ φαντασία, see **40**.

E Diogenes Laertius 7.65 (*SVF* 2.193, part)

ὁ γὰρ λέγων "ἡμέρα ἐστίν", ἀξιοῦν δοκεῖ τὸ ἡμέραν εἶναι. οὔσης μὲν οὖν ἡμέρας, ἀληθὲς γίνεται τὸ προκείμενον ἀξίωμα· μὴ οὔσης δέ, ψεῦδος.

1 οὖν om. F

Context: immediately following **A**.

Stoic logic and semantics

F Sextus Empiricus, *M.* 8.103

πρὸς τούτοις ὅταν λέγωσι τὸ μὲν "ἡμέρα ἔστιν" ἀξίωμα ἐπὶ τοῦ παρόντος εἶναι ἀληθές, τὸ δὲ "νὺξ ἔστι" ψεῦδος, καὶ τὸ μὲν "οὐχὶ ἡμέρα ἔστι" ψεῦδος, τὸ δὲ "οὐχὶ νὺξ ἔστιν" ἀληθές, ἐπιστήσει ⟨τις⟩, πῶς μία οὖσα καὶ ἡ αὐτὴ ἀπόφασις τοῖς μὲν ἀληθέσι προσελθοῦσα ψευδῆ ταῦτα ποιεῖ, τοῖς δὲ ψευδέσιν ἀληθῆ. 5

2 τὸ δὲ Bekker: ἐπὶ δὲ τοῦ codd.   3 ⟨τις⟩ Bekker

Context: refutation of the doctrine of ἁπλᾶ ἀξιώματα.

2–3 **οὐχί** For the translation, 'Not: it is day', etc., cf. **G**, and Alexander, *In Ar. An. pr.* 402,1–8, where the Stoic negation of 'Socrates is white' is reported as οὐχὶ Σωκράτης ἐστὶ λευκός, not Σωκράτης οὐκ ἔστι λευκός.

G Sextus Empiricus, *M.* 8.88–90 (*SVF* 2.214, part)

(1) οὐ πάνυ δέ γε δύνανται παραστῆσαι τὸ ἀντικείμενον ἡμῖν οἱ Στωικοί· τοίνυν οὐδὲ τὸ ἀληθὲς ἢ ψεῦδος ἔσται γνώριμα. (2) φασὶ γὰρ "ἀντικείμενά ἐστιν ὧν τὸ ἕτερον τοῦ ἑτέρου ἀποφάσει πλεονάζει", οἷον "ἡμέρα ἔστιν – οὐχ ἡμέρα ἔστιν." τοῦ γὰρ "ἡμέρα ἔστιν" ἀξιώματος τὸ "οὐχ ἡμέρα ἔστιν" ἀποφάσει πλεονάζει τῇ οὐχί, καὶ διὰ τοῦτ' ἀντικείμενόν ἐστιν 5 ἐκείνῳ. (3) ἀλλ' εἰ τοῦτ' ἔστι τὸ ἀντικείμενον, ἔσται καὶ τὰ τοιαῦτα ἀντικείμενα, τό τε "ἡμέρα ἔστι ⟨καὶ φῶς ἔστιν" καὶ τὸ "ἡμέρα ἔστιν⟩ καὶ οὐχὶ φῶς ἔστιν"· τοῦ γὰρ "ἡμέρα ἔστιν ⟨καὶ φῶς ἔστιν⟩" ἀξιώματος ἀποφάσει πλεονάζει τὸ "⟨ἡμέρα ἔστιν καὶ⟩ οὐχὶ φῶς ἔστιν". (4) οὐχὶ δέ γε κατ' αὐτοὺς ταῦτα ἀντικείμενά ἐστιν· οὐκ ἄρα ἀντικείμενά ἐστι ⟨ὧν⟩ τὸ 10 ἕτερον τοῦ ἑτέρου ἀποφάσει πλεονάζει. (5) ναί, φασίν, ἀλλὰ σὺν τούτῳ ἀντικείμενά ἐστι, σὺν τῷ τὴν ἀπόφασιν προτετάχθαι τοῦ ἑτέρου· τότε γὰρ καὶ κυριεύει τοῦ ὅλου ἀξιώματος, ἐπὶ δὲ τοῦ "ἡμέρα ἔστιν καὶ οὐχὶ φῶς ἔστιν", μέρος οὖσα τοῦ παντός, οὐ κυριεύει πρὸς τὸ ἀποφατικὸν ποιῆσαι τὸ πᾶν. 15

7–10 suppl. Arnim   11 πλεονάζει Arnim: πλεονάζειν codd.   14 ἀποφατικὸν AB: ἀποφαντικὸν NLEVR

Context: refutation of **D** 1.

12 **προτετάχθαι** Cf. Apuleius, *De int.* 177,26–7: *solum autem abdicativum vocant, cui negativa particula praeponitur.* In the preceding lines Apuleius observes that the Stoics counted 'pleasure is not a good' as an affirmative proposition.

Note too the distinction between 'contradictories', τὰ ἀποφατικῶς ἀντικείμενα (e.g. ἡ ἀρετή and ἡ οὐκ ἀρετή) and 'contraries', τὰ ἐναντία (e.g. ἡ ἀρετή and ἡ κακία), *SVF* 2.175.

H Sextus Empiricus, *M.* 8.93–8 (*SVF* 2.205)

(1) τῶν γὰρ ἀξιωμάτων πρώτην σχεδὸν καὶ κυριωτάτην ἐκφέρουσι διαφορὰν οἱ διαλεκτικοὶ καθ' ἣν τὰ μέν ἐστιν αὐτῶν ἁπλᾶ, τὰ δ' οὐχ ἁπλᾶ. (2) καὶ ἁπλᾶ μὲν ὅσα μήτ' ἐξ ἑνὸς ἀξιώματος δὶς λαμβανομένου

συνέστηκεν, μήτ' ἐξ ἀξιωμάτων διαφερόντων διὰ τινὸς ἢ τινῶν συνδέσμων, οἷον "ἡμέρα ἔστιν, [ἢ] νὺξ ἔστιν, Σωκράτης διαλέγεται", 'πᾶν ὃ 5
τῆς ὁμοίας ἐστὶν ἰδέας . . . (3) τῶν δὲ ἁπλῶν τινὰ μὲν ὡρισμένα ἐστίν, τινὰ
δὲ ἀόριστα, τινὰ δὲ μέσα, (4) ὡρισμένα μὲν τὰ κατὰ δεῖξιν ἐκφερόμενα,
οἷον "οὗτος περιπατεῖ, οὗτος κάθηται" (δείκνυμι γάρ τινα τῶν ἐπὶ μέρους
ἀνθρώπων). (5) ἀόριστα δέ ἐστι κατ' αὐτοὺς ἐν οἷς ἀόριστόν τι κυριεύει
μόριον, οἷον "τὶς κάθηται", (6) μέσα δὲ τὰ οὕτως ἔχοντα "ἄνθρωπος 10
κάθηται" ἢ "Σωκράτης περιπατεῖ." (7) τὸ μὲν οὖν "τὶς περιπατεῖ"
ἀόριστόν ἐστιν, ἐπεὶ οὐκ ἀφώρικέ τινα τῶν ἐπὶ μέρους περιπατούντων·
κοινῶς γὰρ ἐφ' ἑκάστου αὐτῶν ἐκφέρεσθαι δύναται· (8) τὸ δὲ "οὗτος
κάθηται" ὡρισμένον ἐστίν, ἐπείπερ ἀφώρικε τὸ δεικνύμενον πρόσωπον.
(9) τὸ δὲ "Σωκράτης κάθηται" μέσον ὑπῆρχεν, ἐπείπερ οὔτε ἀόριστόν 15
ἐστιν (ἀφώρικε γὰρ τὸ εἶδος), οὔτε ὡρισμένον (οὐ γὰρ μετὰ δείξεως
ἐκφέρεται), ἀλλ' ἔοικε μέσον ἀμφοτέρων ὑπάρχειν, τοῦ τε ἀορίστου καὶ
τοῦ ὡρισμένου. (10) γίνεσθαι δέ φασι τὸ ἀόριστον ἀληθές, τὸ "τὶς
περιπατεῖ" ἢ "τὶς κάθηται", ὅταν τὸ ὡρισμένον ἀληθὲς εὑρίσκηται, τὸ
"οὗτος κάθηται" ἢ "οὗτος περιπατεῖ"· μηδενὸς γὰρ τῶν ἐπὶ μέρους 20
καθημένου οὐ δύναται ἀληθὲς εἶναι τὸ "τὶς κάθηται" ἀόριστον.

4 διαφερόντων ⟨καὶ⟩ Kochalsky   5 ἢ del. Bekker   12 τινα Fabricius: τινας codd.

Context: the dialecticians' account of ἁπλᾶ ἀξιώματα. For the legitimacy of treating
οἱ διαλεκτικοί as including the Stoics, cf. vol. 1, 205 n. 1.

3–5 As an example of δὶς λαμβανομένου, cf. D.L. 7.68 (reading διφορουμένου
for διαφορουμένου, with Frede [407], 50), 'If it is day, it is day'; and for διαφερόντων,
'If it is day, it is light'.

6–7 **ὡρισμένα, ἀόριστα** Theophrastus (cf. Ammonius, *In Ar. De Int.* 90,12–19)
used this terminology to distinguish between 'Socrates is just' and 'Man is just', which
the Stoics classed together as μέσα.

7 **κατὰ δεῖξιν** Frede [407], 54–61, argues that Chrysippus also allowed anaphora
to make a proposition 'definite', e.g. οὗτος in 36B 40–2, taking the δεῖξις there to be
anaphoric, since Zeus cannot literally be pointed to. But the Zeus of the example
could be a statue; and Frede's other arguments for extending the Stoics' use of δεῖξις
beyond demonstrative reference are not compelling; cf. Lloyd [436], and Goulet
[437], 176–8.

9–10 **ἀόριστον̶μόριον** As in G 13, κυριεύει indicates that the relevant term
must 'govern' the proposition, meaning here that e.g. τις must be its subject. The
Stoics also counted the definite article as an 'indefinite term'; cf. Apollonius Dyscolus,
De synt. 1.111, and Frede [407], 63–4.

I Sextus Empiricus, *M.* 8.100 (*SVF* 2.205, part)

καὶ δὴ τὸ ὡρισμένον τοῦτο ἀξίωμα, τὸ "οὗτος κάθηται" ἢ "οὗτος
περιπατεῖ", τότε φασὶν ἀληθὲς ὑπάρχειν, ὅταν τῷ ὑπὸ τὴν δεῖξιν πίπτοντι
συμβεβήκῃ τὸ κατηγόρημα, οἷον τὸ καθῆσθαι ἢ τὸ περιπατεῖν.

3 συμβεβήκῃ N: συμβεβήκοι cett.

Stoic logic and semantics

Context: see on F.

3 συμβεβήκῃ τὸ κατηγόρημα   Cf. 51B 4.

J Galen, Plac. 2.2.9–11 (SVF 2.895, part)

(1) ἃ δ' οὖν ὑπὲρ τῆς "ἐγώ" φωνῆς ἔγραψεν ἐν τῷ πρώτῳ Περὶ ψυχῆς ὁ
Χρύσιππος ὑπὲρ ἡγεμονικοῦ διαλεγόμενος ... (2) "οὕτως δὲ καὶ τὸ ἐγὼ
λέγομεν, κατὰ τοῦτο δεικνύντες ἑαυτοὺς ἐν ᾧ ἀποφαινόμεθα τὴν διάνοιαν
εἶναι, τῆς δείξεως φυσικῶς καὶ οἰκείως ἐνταῦθα φερομένης· (3) καὶ ἄνευ δὲ
τῆς κατὰ τὴν χεῖρα τοιαύτης δείξεως νεύοντες εἰς αὑτοὺς τὸ ἐγὼ λέγομεν,   5
εὐθὺς καὶ τῆς ἐγὼ φωνῆς τοιαύτης οὔσης καὶ κατὰ τὴν ἑξῆς ὑπογεγραμ-
μένην δεῖξιν συνεκφερομένης. (4) τὸ γὰρ ἐγὼ προφερόμεθα κατὰ τὴν
πρώτην συλλαβὴν κατασπῶντες τὸ κάτω χεῖλος εἰς αὑτοὺς δεικτικῶς·
ἀκολούθως δὲ τῇ τοῦ γενείου κινήσει καὶ ἐπὶ τὸ στῆθος νεύσει καὶ τῇ
τοιαύτῃ δείξει ἡ ἑξῆς συλλαβὴ παράκειται οὐδὲν ἀποστηματικὸν παρεμ-   10
φαίνουσα ὅπερ ἐπὶ τοῦ ἐκεῖνος συντέτευχεν."

3 ᾧ ἀποφαινόμεθα scripsimus: τῷ φαίνεσθαι M: ᾧ φαίνεσθαι cett.: ᾧ ἀποφαίνομαι Peterson: τῷ
ἑαυτῶν ἀποφαίνεσθαι Einarson τὴν om. C   5, 8 αὑτοὺς Kühn: αὐτοὺς codd.   10–11
παρεμφαίνουσα Ald.: ἀπῆρεν σημαίνουσα M: παρενσημαίνουσα cett.

Context: criticism of Chrysippus' use of 'inappropriate premises' in his arguments for
proving that the soul's ἡγεμονικόν is in the heart. At Plac. 2.2.7, Galen refers to an
earlier refutation of this same etymology in his lost work On the correctness of names.
   11 ἐκεῖνος The second syllable -κειν- is meant, cf. Galen, Plac. 2.2.16–17. See
also note on K 13–15.

K Diogenes Laertius 7.69–70 (SVF 2.204)

(1) ἐν δὲ τοῖς ἁπλοῖς ἀξιώμασίν ἐστι τὸ ἀποφατικὸν καὶ τὸ ἀρνητικὸν καὶ
τὸ στερητικὸν καὶ τὸ κατηγορικὸν καὶ τὸ καταγορευτικὸν καὶ τὸ
ἀόριστον ... (2) ⟨καὶ τῶν μὲν ἁπλῶν ἀξιωμάτων ἀποφατικὸν μέν ἐστι τὸ
συνεστὸς ἐξ ἀποφατικοῦ μορίου⟩ καὶ ἀξιώματος, οἷον "οὐχὶ ἡμέρα ἐστίν".
εἶδος δὲ τούτου τὸ ὑπεραποφατικόν. ὑπεραποφατικὸν δ' ἐστὶν ἀποφατικὸν   5
ἀποφατικοῦ, οἷον "⟨οὐχὶ⟩ οὐχὶ ἡμέρα ἔστι". τίθησι δὲ τὸ "ἡμέρα ἐστίν".
(3) ἀρνητικὸν δέ ἐστι τὸ συνεστὸς ἐξ ἀρνητικοῦ μορίου καὶ κατηγορήματος, οἷον "οὐδεὶς περιπατεῖ". (4) στερητικὸν δέ ἐστι τὸ συνεστὸς ἐκ
στερητικοῦ μορίου καὶ ἀξιώματος κατὰ δύναμιν, οἷον "ἀφιλάνθρωπός
ἐστιν οὗτος". (5) κατηγορικὸν δέ ἐστι τὸ συνεστὸς ἐκ πτώσεως ὀρθῆς καὶ   10
κατηγορήματος, οἷον "Δίων περιπατεῖ". (6) καταγορευτικὸν δέ ἐστι τὸ
συνεστὸς ἐκ πτώσεως ὀρθῆς δεικτικῆς καὶ κατηγορήματος, οἷον "οὗτος
περιπατεῖ"· (7) ἀόριστον δέ ἐστι τὸ συνεστὸς ἐξ ἀορίστου μορίου ἢ
ἀορίστων μορίων ⟨καὶ κατηγορήματος⟩, οἷον "τὶς περιπατεῖ", "ἐκεῖνος
κινεῖται".   15

3–4 suppl. Egli et Goulet   4 ἀξιώματος BFP: ἀποφατικὸν μὲν dg   6 οὐχὶ[1] add. Goulet   11
Δίων fr.: οὗτος codd.   14 suppl. Hicks

208

Context: see on **33A**.

1–3   On the correctness of counting the three negatives as ἁπλᾶ ἀξιώματα, cf. Frede [407], 69–70. The Stoics appear to have coined the terms ἀρνητικός and καταγορευτικός.

3–4   For the text supplied, cf. Goulet [437], 179–80.

9 **κατὰ δύναμιν**   Probably 'potential', in the sense that φιλάνθρωπός ἐστιν οὗτος could be uttered in a different context; cf. Goulet [437], 181–3.

10 **κατηγορικόν**   The term simply means 'assertoric' or 'affirmative' (contrasted with στερητικός by Aristotle, *An. pr.* 1.4, 26a18), but its definition indicates that it differs from καταγορευτικόν, 11, in lacking a 'deictically' expressed subject. Hence Δίων, not οὗτος, should be read in 11, and κατηγορικόν corresponds to μέσον in the terminology of **H** 10.

13–15   These lines have generated much discussion, the chief problem being the apparent absence of an example to illustrate ἀορίστων μορίων; cf. Frede [407], 59–60. Goulet [437], 194–5 n. 49, ingeniously suggests that ἐκεῖνος may have been regarded as a composite pronoun on the evidence of Apollonius Dyscolus, *Pron.* 58, 3. We find Hicks' supplement, which assumes a haplography from 12, as convincing as any suggestion. Thus τὶς περιπατεῖ and ἐκεῖνος κινεῖται will be two examples of 'indefinite propositions' formed ἐξ ἀορίστου μορίου. The Greek grammarians regarded ἐκεῖνος as exactly similar to οὗτος, taking both pronouns to be capable of referring either deictically or anaphorically; cf. Lloyd [436], 294 n. 7. But J 11 along with this text shows that the Stoics' view was different. Cf. Pachet [435], 242–3.

35 Non-simple propositions

A Diogenes Laertius 7.71–4

(1) τῶν δ' οὐχ ἁπλῶν ἀξιωμάτων συνημμένον μέν ἐστιν, ὡς ὁ Χρύσιππος ἐν ταῖς Διαλεκτικαῖς φησι καὶ Διογένης ἐν τῇ Διαλεκτικῇ τέχνῃ, τὸ συνεστὸς διὰ τοῦ "εἰ" συναπτικοῦ συνδέσμου. ἐπαγγέλλεται δ' ὁ σύνδεσμος οὗτος ἀκολουθεῖν τὸ δεύτερον τῷ πρώτῳ, οἷον "εἰ ἡμέρα ἔστι, φῶς ἔστι". (2) παρασυνημμένον δέ ἐστιν, ὡς ὁ Κρῖνίς φησιν ἐν τῇ 5 Διαλεκτικῇ τέχνῃ, ἀξίωμα ὃ ὑπὸ τοῦ "ἐπεί" συνδέσμου παρασυνῆπται ἀρχόμενον ἀπ' ἀξιώματος καὶ λῆγον εἰς ἀξίωμα, οἷον "ἐπεὶ ἡμέρα ἔστι, φῶς ἔστιν". ἐπαγγέλλεται δ' ὁ σύνδεσμος ἀκολουθεῖν τε τὸ δεύτερον τῷ πρώτῳ καὶ τὸ πρῶτον ὑφεστάναι. (3) συμπεπλεγμένον δέ ἐστιν ἀξίωμα ὃ ὑπό τινων συμπλεκτικῶν συνδέσμων συμπέπλεκται, οἷον "καὶ ἡμέρα ἔστι 10 καὶ φῶς ἔστι". (4) διεζευγμένον δέ ἐστιν ὃ ὑπὸ τοῦ "ἤτοι" διαζευκτικοῦ συνδέσμου διέζευκται, οἷον "ἤτοι ἡμέρα ἔστιν ἢ νὺξ ἔστιν". ἐπαγγέλλεται δ' ὁ σύνδεσμος οὗτος τὸ ἕτερον τῶν ἀξιωμάτων ψεῦδος εἶναι. αἰτιῶδες δέ ἐστιν ἀξίωμα τὸ συντασσόμενον διὰ τοῦ "διότι", οἷον "διότι ἡμέρα ἔστι, φῶς ἔστιν"· οἱονεὶ γὰρ αἴτιόν ἐστι τὸ πρῶτον τοῦ δευτέρου. διασαφοῦν δὲ τὸ μᾶλλον ἀξίωμά ἐστι τὸ 15 συντατ τόμενον ὑπὸ τοῦ διασαφοῦντος τὸ μᾶλλον συνδέσμου καὶ τοῦ ⟨"ἤ"⟩ μέσου τῶν ἀξιωμάτων τασσομένου, οἷον "μᾶλλον ἡμέρα ἔστιν ἢ νὺξ ἐστι". διασαφοῦν δὲ τὸ ἧττον ἀξίωμά ἐστι τὸ ἐναντίον τῷ προκειμένῳ, οἷον "ἧττον νὺξ ἐστιν ἢ ἡμέρα ἔστιν". (5) ἔτι

Stoic logic and semantics

τῶν ἀξιωμάτων κατά τ᾽ ἀλήθειαν καὶ ψεῦδος ἀντικείμενα ἀλλήλοις ἐστίν,
ὧν τὸ ἕτερον τοῦ ἑτέρου ἐστὶν ἀποφατικόν, οἷον τὸ "ἡμέρα ἔστι" καὶ τὸ   2c
"οὐχ ἡμέρα ἔστι". (6) συνημμένον οὖν ἀληθές ἐστιν οὗ τὸ ἀντικείμενον τοῦ
λήγοντος μάχεται τῷ ἡγουμένῳ, οἷον "εἰ ἡμέρα ἔστι, φῶς ἐστι". τοῦτ᾽
ἀληθές ἐστι· τὸ γὰρ "οὐχὶ φῶς", ἀντικείμενον τῷ λήγοντι, μάχεται τῷ
"ἡμέρα ἔστι". συνημμένον δὲ ψεῦδός ἐστιν οὗ τὸ ἀντικείμενον τοῦ
λήγοντος οὐ μάχεται τῷ ἡγουμένῳ, οἷον "εἰ ἡμέρα ἔστι, Δίων περιπατεῖ"·   25
τὸ γὰρ "οὐχὶ Δίων περιπατεῖ" οὐ μάχεται τῷ "ἡμέρα ἔστι". (7)
παρασυνημμένον δ᾽ ἀληθές μέν ἐστιν ὃ ἀρχόμενον ἀπ᾽ ἀληθοῦς εἰς
ἀκόλουθον λήγει, οἷον "ἐπεὶ ἡμέρα ἔστιν, ἥλιός ἐστιν ὑπὲρ γῆς". ψεῦδος δ᾽
ὃ ἢ ἀπὸ ψεύδους ἄρχεται ἢ μὴ εἰς ἀκόλουθον λήγει, οἷον "ἐπεὶ νὺξ ἔστι,
Δίων περιπατεῖ", ἂν ἡμέρας οὔσης λέγηται. αἰτιῶδες δ᾽ ἀληθές μέν ἐστιν ὃ   3c
ἀρχόμενον ἀπ᾽ ἀληθοῦς εἰς ἀκόλουθον λήγει, οὐ μὴν ἔχει τῷ λήγοντι τὸ ἀρχόμενον
ἀκόλουθον, οἷον "διότι ἡμέρα ἔστι, φῶς ἔστι"· τῷ μὲν γὰρ "ἡμέρα ἔστιν" ἀκόλουθεῖ τὸ
"φῶς ἔστι", τῷ δὲ "φῶς ἔστιν" οὐχ ἕπεται τὸ "ἡμέρα ἔστιν". αἰτιῶδες δὲ ψεῦδός ἐστιν ὃ
ἤτοι ἀπὸ ψεύδους ἄρχεται ἢ μὴ εἰς ἀκόλουθον λήγει ἢ ἔχει τῷ λήγοντι τὸ ἀρχόμενον
ἀκόλουθον, οἷον "διότι νὺξ ἔστι, Δίων περιπατεῖ".   3§

16 ⟨ἢ⟩ Arnim   35 ἀκόλουθον Suda: ἀνάκολουθον codd.

Context: immediately following **34K**.

1–5, 21–6 That this criterion of a sound conditional was authorized by
Chrysippus seems probable not only because it appears here in a standard handbook
account but also because the argument at **38E** treats Chrysippus as accepting it and as
taking its consequences to be escapable only by avoiding the conditional formulation
altogether. See Frede [407], 82ff. But there is no reason to attribute its actual
authorship to Chrysippus, and **B 4**'s failure to name him (contrast **B 2–3**, where the
authors of two other criteria are named) counts against any such attribution. The
criterion is often interpreted as equivalent to 'strict implication', which analyses 'If *p*,
q' as 'not possibly both: *p* and not-*q*'. But this latter notoriously carries the paradox
that if *p* is impossible the conditional comes out sound for any value of *q* whatsoever;
and that paradox is in **B 3** rightly seen as an embarrassment for the Diodorean
criterion, not the Chrysippean (see **B 4**). It is better to suppose that the notion of
'conflict' or incompatibility is taken as primitive in Stoicism (see Stopper [63], 285–6):
it is well expressed by the later Stoics represented in Philodemus, *Sign.* (e.g. at **18F**),
with the formula that if you eliminate *q* you *eo ipso* eliminate *p* (see further vol. 1, 96,
264–5). For a 'logical' or 'conceptual' reading of this incompatibility, see Frede [407],
80–93, Sedley [243], 242–56; against, Sorabji [459], 266–70.

5–9, 27–30 For the subconditional see Burnyeat [484], 218–20; Sedley [243],
242–3.

13–15, 30–5 οἱονεί in 14 is superficially explained by the fact that in Stoic theory
propositions, as incorporeals, cannot strictly speaking be causes (**55**). Little else is clear
about these 'causal' propositions. The conditions set out hardly seem appropriate to
cause–effect relations, in which cause is as often inferable from effect as the reverse
(e.g. **51H**).

210

B Sextus Empiricus, *PH* 2.110–13

(1) ἵνα δὲ καὶ ταῦτα παραλίπωμεν, τὸ ὑγιὲς συνημμένον ἀκατάληπτον εὑρεθήσεται. (2) ὁ μὲν γὰρ Φίλων φησὶν ὑγιὲς εἶναι συνημμένον τὸ μὴ ἀρχόμενον ἀπὸ ἀληθοῦς καὶ λῆγον ἐπὶ ψεῦδος, οἷον ἡμέρας οὔσης καὶ ἐμοῦ διαλεγομένου τὸ "εἰ ἡμέρα ἔστιν, ἐγὼ διαλέγομαι", (3) ὁ δὲ Διόδωρος, ὃ μήτε ἐνεδέχετο μήτε ἐνδέχεται ἀρχόμενον ἀπὸ ἀληθοῦς λήγειν ἐπὶ ψεῦδος· 5
καθ' ὃν τὸ μὲν εἰρημένον συνημμένον ψεῦδος εἶναι δοκεῖ, ἐπεὶ ἡμέρας μὲν οὔσης ἐμοῦ δὲ σιωπήσαντος ἀπὸ ἀληθοῦς ἀρξάμενον ἐπὶ ψεῦδος καταλή-ξει, ἐκεῖνο δὲ ἀληθές "εἰ οὐκ ἔστιν ἀμερῆ τῶν ὄντων στοιχεῖα, ἔστιν ἀμερῆ τῶν ὄντων στοιχεῖα"· ἀεὶ γὰρ ἀπὸ ψεύδους ἀρχόμενον τοῦ "οὐκ ἔστιν ἀμερῆ τῶν ὄντων στοιχεῖα" εἰς ἀληθὲς καταλήξει κατ' αὐτὸν τὸ "ἔστιν 10
ἀμερῆ τῶν ὄντων στοιχεῖα". (4) οἱ δὲ τὴν συνάρτησιν εἰσάγοντες ὑγιὲς εἶναί φασι συνημμένον, ὅταν τὸ ἀντικείμενον τῷ ἐν αὐτῷ λήγοντι μάχηται τῷ ἐν αὐτῷ ἡγουμένῳ· καθ' οὓς τὰ μὲν εἰρημένα συνημμένα ἔσται μοχθηρά, ἐκεῖνο δὲ ἀληθές "εἰ ἡμέρα ἔστιν, ἡμέρα ἔστιν". (5) οἱ δὲ τῇ ἐμφάσει κρίνοντές φασιν ὅτι ἀληθές ἐστι συνημμένον οὗ τὸ λῆγον ἐν τῷ 15
ἡγουμένῳ περιέχεται δυνάμει· καθ' οὓς τὸ "εἰ ἡμέρα ἔστιν, ἡμέρα ἐστι" καὶ πᾶν [τὸ] διαφορούμενον ἀξίωμα συνῆμμένον ἴσως ψεῦδος ἔσται· αὐτὸ γάρ τι ἐν ἑαυτῷ περιέχεσθαι ἀμήχανον. (6) ταύτην τοίνυν τὴν διαφωνίαν ἐπικριθῆναι ἀμήχανον ἴσως εἶναι δόξει.

Context: attack on signs; cf. **C**, and **42**.

2 Philo is mentioned as the author of the criterion, but Sextus is quite aware that it had some currency in the Stoa too: **C 3**.

4–5 Modern interpreters standardly apply Diodorus' own definition of 'possible' (**38A–C**) to this criterion, thus reducing it to 'the one which *never* has a true antecedent and a false consequent': and Sextus' ἀεί in 9 may imply the same assumption. But this leaves it unclear why Diodorus in fact chose the more cumbersome phraseology recorded (for which cf. **37A 4**, probably also representing Diodorus' school), and Denyer [463] may well be right to guess that Diodorus deliberately chose a formula which did not presuppose his definition of 'possible' precisely because his Master Argument, which proved that definition, had to use a relatively uncontroversial notion of 'following' in its premises (**38A 4**). The survival here of the unreduced version might thus be evidence that Diodorus' original formulation of his criterion retained favour with logicians who did not accept the conclusion of the Master Argument.

11–14 See on **A 1–5**.

14–16 The definition has a Stoic echo in **36G 4**, but this use of ἔμφασις and ἐμφαίνεσθαι is most commonly found in medical texts (e.g. Galen 10.126,8 Kühn).

16–18 There is no need to take this as anyone's doctrine; it is just part of Sextus' mischievous attempt to make the dogmatists the cause of their own undoing.

C Sextus Empiricus, *PH* 2.104–6

(1) αὐτίκα γοῦν οἱ ἀκριβῶς περὶ αὐτοῦ διειληφέναι δοκοῦντες, οἱ Στωικοί,

Stoic logic and semantics

βουλόμενοι παραστῆσαι τὴν ἔννοιαν τοῦ σημείου, φασὶ σημεῖον εἶναι
ἀξίωμα ἐν ὑγιεῖ συνημμένῳ προκαθηγούμενον, ἐκκαλυπτικὸν τοῦ λήγοντος. (2) καὶ τὸ μὲν ἀξίωμά φασιν εἶναι λεκτὸν αὐτοτελὲς ἀποφαντὸν ὅσον
ἐφ' ἑαυτῷ, (3) ὑγιὲς δὲ συνημμένον τὸ μὴ ἀρχόμενον ἀπὸ ἀληθοῦς καὶ   5
λῆγον ἐπὶ ψεῦδος. τὸ γὰρ συνημμένον ἤτοι ἄρχεται ἀπὸ ἀληθοῦς καὶ λήγει
ἐπὶ ἀληθές, οἷον "εἰ ἡμέρα ἔστι, φῶς ἔστιν", ἢ ἄρχεται ἀπὸ ψεύδους καὶ
λήγει ἐπὶ ψεῦδος, οἷον "εἰ πέταται ἡ γῆ, πτερωτή ἐστιν ἡ γῆ", ἢ ἄρχεται
ἀπὸ ἀληθοῦς καὶ λήγει ἐπὶ ψεῦδος, οἷον "εἰ ἔστιν ἡ γῆ, πέταται ἡ γῆ", ἢ
ἄρχεται ἀπὸ ψεύδους καὶ λήγει ἐπὶ ἀληθές, οἷον "εἰ πέταται ἡ γῆ, ἔστιν ἡ   10
γῆ". τούτων δὲ μόνον τὸ ἀπὸ ἀληθοῦς ἀρχόμενον καὶ λῆγον ἐπὶ ψεῦδος
μοχθηρὸν εἶναί φασιν, τὰ δ' ἄλλα ὑγιῆ. (4) προκαθηγούμενον δὲ λέγουσι τὸ
ἐν συνημμένῳ ἀρχομένῳ ἀπὸ ἀληθοῦς καὶ λήγοντι ἐπὶ ἀληθὲς ἡγούμενον.
(5) ἐκκαλυπτικὸν δέ ἐστι τοῦ λήγοντος, ἐπεὶ τὸ "γάλα ἔχει αὕτη" τοῦ
"κεκύηκεν αὕτη" δηλωτικὸν εἶναι δοκεῖ ἐν τούτῳ τῷ συνημμένῳ "εἰ γάλα   15
ἔχει αὕτη, κεκύηκεν αὕτη".

Context: attack on signs; cf. **42**.

    2–4   For the definition, see Burnyeat [484], 222–3.

    4–5   Cf. **34A**.

    5–12   For the attribution of this Philonian criterion (cf. **B 2**) to the Stoics, see also
S.E., *M.* 8.245–7, 449; D.L. 7.81.

    14–16   The example is already in Plato, *Menexenus* 237c and Aristotle, *An. pr.*
II.27.

D Gellius 16.8.10–11 (*FDS* 967, part)

item quod illi συμπεπλεγμένον, nos uel "coniunctum" uel "copulatum"
dicimus, quod est huiuscemodi: "P. Scipio, Pauli filius, et bis consul fuit et
triumphauit et censura functus est et collega in censura L. Mummii fuit." in
omni autem coniuncto si unum est mendacium, etiamsi cetera uera sunt,
totum esse mendacium dicitur.   5

Context: some introductory information on dialectic, reflecting Stoic logic.

E Gellius 16.8.12–14 (*FDS* 976)

(1) est item aliud, quod Graeci διεζευγμένον ἀξίωμα, nos "disiunctum"
dicimus. id huiuscemodi est: "aut malum est uoluptas aut bonum aut neque
bonum neque malum est." (2) omnia autem, quae disiunguntur, pugnantia
esse inter sese oportet, eorumque opposita, quae ἀντικείμενα Graeci dicunt, ea
quoque ipsa inter se aduersa esse. (3) ex omnibus, quae disiunguntur, unum   5
esse uerum debet, falsa cetera. (4) quod si aut nihil omnium uerum, aut omnia
pluraue quam unum uera erunt, aut quae disiuncta sunt non pugnabunt, aut
quae opposita eorum sunt contraria inter sese non erunt, tunc id disiunctum
mendacium est et appellatur παραδιεζευγμένον, (5) sicuti hoc est, in quo,
quae opposita, non sunt contraria: "aut curris aut ambulas aut stas." nam ipsa   10

quidem inter se adversa sunt, sed opposita eorum non pugnant; "non ambulare" enim et "non stare" et "non currere" contraria inter sese non sunt, quoniam "contraria" ea dicuntur, quae simul vera esse non queunt; possis enim simul eodemque tempore neque ambulare neque stare neque currere.

Context: as **D**.

For other evidence on the παραδιεζευγμένον, see Frede [407], 98–100.

36 Arguments

A Diogenes Laertius 7.76–81

(1) λόγος δέ ἐστιν, ὡς οἱ περὶ τὸν Κρῖνίν φασι, τὸ συνεστηκὸς ἐκ λήμματος ἢ λημμάτων καὶ προσλήψεως καὶ ἐπιφορᾶς, οἷον ὁ τοιοῦτος, "εἰ ἡμέρα ἔστι, φῶς ἔστι· ἡμέρα δὲ ἔστι· φῶς ἄρα ἔστι." λῆμμα μὲν γάρ ἐστι τὸ "εἰ ἡμέρα ἔστι, φῶς ἔστι"· πρόσληψις τὸ "ἡμέρα δὲ ἔστιν"· ἐπιφορὰ δὲ τὸ "φῶς ἄρα ἔστι". (2) τρόπος δέ ἐστιν οἱονεὶ σχῆμα λόγου, οἷον ὁ τοιοῦτος, "εἰ τὸ πρῶτον, τὸ δεύτερον· ἀλλὰ μὴν τὸ πρῶτον· τὸ ἄρα δεύτερον." (3) λογότροπος δέ ἐστι τὸ ἐξ ἀμφοτέρων σύνθετον, οἷον "εἰ ζῇ Πλάτων, ἀναπνεῖ Πλάτων· ἀλλὰ μὴν τὸ πρῶτον· τὸ ἄρα δεύτερον." παρεισήχθη δὲ ὁ λογότροπος ὑπὲρ τοῦ ἐν ταῖς μακροτέραις συντάξεσι τῶν λόγων μηκέτι τὴν πρόσληψιν μακρὰν οὖσαν καὶ τὴν ἐπιφορὰν λέγειν, ἀλλὰ συντόμως ἐπενεγκεῖν, "τὸ δὲ πρῶτον· τὸ ἄρα δεύτερον." (4) τῶν δὲ λόγων οἱ μέν εἰσιν ἀπέραντοι, οἱˋ δὲ περαντικοί. ἀπέραντοι μὲν ὦν τὸ ἀντικείμενον τῆς ἐπιφορᾶς οὐ μάχεται τῇ διὰ τῶν λημμάτων συμπλοκῇ, οἷον οἱ τοιοῦτοι, "εἰ ἡμέρα ἔστι, φῶς ἔστι· ἡμέρα δὲ ἔστι· περιπατεῖ ἄρα Δίων." (5) τῶν δὲ περαντικῶν λόγων οἱ μὲν ὁμωνύμως τῷ γένει λέγονται περαντικοί· οἱ δὲ συλλογιστικοί. συλλογιστικοὶ μὲν οὖν εἰσιν οἱ ἤτοι ἀναπόδεικτοι ὄντες ἢ ἀναγόμενοι ἐπὶ τοὺς ἀναποδείκτους κατά τι τῶν θεμάτων ἤ τινα, οἷον οἱ τοιοῦτοι, "εἰ περιπατεῖ Δίων, ⟨κινεῖται Δίων· ἀλλὰ μὴν περιπατεῖ Δίων·⟩ κινεῖται ἄρα Δίων." (6) περαντικοὶ δέ εἰσιν εἰδικῶς οἱ συνάγοντες μὴ συλλογιστικῶς, οἷον οἱ τοιοῦτοι, "ψεῦδός ἐστι τὸ ἡμέρα ἔστι καὶ νὺξ ἔστι· ἡμέρα δὲ ἔστιν· οὐκ ἄρα νὺξ ἔστιν." (7) ἀσυλλόγιστοι δ' εἰσὶν οἱ παρακείμενοι μὲν πιθανῶς τοῖς συλλογιστικοῖς, οὐ συνάγοντες δέ, οἷον "εἰ ἵππος ἐστὶ Δίων, ζῷόν ἐστι Δίων· ἀλλὰ μὴν ἵππος οὐκ ἔστι Δίων· οὐκ ἄρα ζῷόν ἐστι Δίων." (8) ἔτι τῶν λόγων οἱ μὲν ἀληθεῖς εἰσιν, οἱ δὲ ψευδεῖς. ἀληθεῖς μὲν οὖν εἰσι λόγοι οἱ δι' ἀληθῶν συνάγοντες, οἷον "εἰ ἡ ἀρετὴ ὠφελεῖ, ἡ κακία βλάπτει· ⟨ἀλλὰ μὴν ὠφελεῖ ἡ ἀρετή· ἡ κακία ἄρα βλάπτει⟩." (9) ψευδεῖς δέ εἰσιν οἱ τῶν λημμάτων ἔχοντές τι ψεῦδος ἢ ἀπέραντοι ὄντες, οἷον "εἰ ἡμέρα ἔστι, φῶς ἔστιν· ἡμέρα δὲ ἔστι· ζῇ ἄρα Δίων." (10) καὶ δυνατοὶ δ' εἰσὶ λόγοι καὶ ἀδύνατοι καὶ ἀναγκαῖοι καὶ οὐκ ἀναγκαῖοι· (11) εἰσὶ δὲ καὶ ἀναπόδεικτοί τινες, τῷ μὴ χρῄζειν ἀποδείξεως, ἄλλοι μὲν παρ' ἄλλοις, παρὰ δὲ τῷ Χρυσίππῳ πέντε, δι' ὧν πᾶς λόγος πλέκεται· οἵτινες λαμβάνονται ἐπὶ τῶν περαντικῶν καὶ ἐπὶ τῶν συλλο-

Stoic logic and semantics

γισμῶν καὶ ἐπὶ τῶν τροπικῶν. (12) πρῶτος δέ ἐστιν ἀναπόδεικτος ἐν ᾧ πᾶς
λόγος συντάσσεται ἐκ συνημμένου καὶ τοῦ ἡγουμένου, ἀφ' οὗ ἄρχεται τὸ
συνημμένον, καὶ τὸ λῆγον ἐπιφέρει, οἷον "εἰ τὸ πρῶτον, τὸ δεύτερον· ἀλλὰ   35
μὴν τὸ πρῶτον· τὸ ἄρα δεύτερον." (13) δεύτερος δ' ἐστὶν ἀναπόδεικτος ὁ
διὰ συνημμένου καὶ τοῦ ἀντικειμένου τοῦ λήγοντος τὸ ἀντικείμενον τοῦ
ἡγουμένου ἔχων συμπέρασμα, οἷον "εἰ ἡμέρα ἔστι, φῶς ἔστιν· ἀλλὰ μὴν
φῶς οὐκ ἔστιν· οὐκ ἄρα ἡμέρα ἔστιν." ἡ γὰρ πρόσληψις γίνεται ἐκ τοῦ
ἀντικειμένου τῷ λήγοντι καὶ ἡ ἐπιφορὰ ἐκ τοῦ ἀντικειμένου τῷ ἡγουμένῳ.   40
(14) τρίτος δέ ἐστιν ἀναπόδεικτος ὁ δι' ἀποφατικῆς συμπλοκῆς καὶ ἑνὸς
τῶν ἐν τῇ συμπλοκῇ ἐπιφέρων τὸ ἀντικείμενον τοῦ λοιποῦ, οἷον "οὐχὶ
τέθνηκε Πλάτων καὶ ζῇ Πλάτων· ἀλλὰ μὴν τέθνηκε Πλάτων· οὐκ ἄρα ζῇ
Πλάτων." (15) τέταρτος δέ ἐστιν ἀναπόδεικτος ὁ διὰ διεζευγμένου καὶ
ἑνὸς τῶν ἐν τῷ διεζευγμένῳ τὸ ἀντικείμενον τοῦ λοιποῦ ἔχων συμπέρ-   45
ασμα, οἷον "ἤτοι τὸ πρῶτον ἢ τὸ δεύτερον· ἀλλὰ μὴν τὸ πρῶτον· οὐκ ἄρα
τὸ δεύτερον." (16) πέμπτος δέ ἐστιν ἀναπόδεικτος ἐν ᾧ πᾶς λόγος
συντάσσεται ἐκ διεζευγμένου καὶ ⟨τοῦ⟩ ἑνὸς τῶν ἐν τῷ διεζευγμένῳ
ἀντικειμένου καὶ ἐπιφέρει τὸ λοιπόν, οἷον "ἤτοι ἡμέρα ἔστιν ἢ νὺξ ἔστιν·
οὐχὶ δὲ νὺξ ἔστιν· ἡμέρα ἄρα ἔστιν."   50

2 ἢ λημμάτων secl. Beier   καὶ προσλήψεως secl. Egli   18 suppl. Arnim   26–7 suppl.
Arnim   48 suppl. Shorey

Context: shortly after **38D**.

1–2   λῆμμα normally just means 'premise' (cf. **B 1–2**), and Crinis' narrower
usage, if accurately reported, is exceptional. But emendation does not help: Beier's
excision (see apparatus) wrongly restricts Stoic arguments to precisely two premises,
and Egli's would sanction the heretical one-premise argument (see **C 7, D**).
30–50   Cf. especially S.E., *M*. 8.223–6.

B Sextus Empiricus, *PH* 2.135–43

(1) ἔστιν οὖν, ὥς φασίν, ἡ ἀπόδειξις λόγος δι' ὁμολογουμένων λημμάτων
κατὰ συναγωγὴν ἐπιφορὰν ἐκκαλύπτων ἄδηλον. σαφέστερον δὲ ὃ λέγουσιν
ἔσται διὰ τούτων. (2) λόγος ἐστὶ σύστημα ἐκ λημμάτων καὶ ἐπιφορᾶς·
τούτου δὲ λήμματα μὲν εἶναι λέγεται τὰ πρὸς κατασκευὴν τοῦ συμπεράσματος συμφώνως λαμβανόμενα ἀξιώματα, ἐπιφορὰ δ' ἢ συμπέρασμα τὸ   5
ἐκ τῶν λημμάτων κατασκευαζόμενον ἀξίωμα. οἷον ἐν [τούτῳ] τῷ "εἰ
ἡμέρα ἔστι, φῶς ἔστιν· ἀλλὰ μὴν ἡμέρα ἔστιν· φῶς ἄρα ἔστιν" τὸ μὲν "φῶς
ἄρα ἔστιν" συμπέρασμά ἐστι, τὰ δὲ λοιπὰ λήμματα. (3) τῶν δὲ λόγων οἱ
μέν εἰσι συνακτικοὶ οἱ δὲ ἀσύνακτοι, συνακτικοὶ μέν, ὅταν τὸ συνημμένον
τὸ ἀρχόμενον μὲν ἀπὸ τοῦ διὰ τῶν τοῦ λόγου λημμάτων συμπεπλεγμένου,   10
λῆγον δὲ εἰς τὴν ἐπιφορὰν αὐτοῦ, ὑγιὲς ᾖ, οἷον ὁ προειρημένος λόγος
συνακτικός ἐστιν, ἐπεὶ τῇ διὰ τῶν λημμάτων αὐτοῦ συμπλοκῇ ταύτῃ
"ἡμέρα ἔστι καὶ εἰ ἡμέρα ἔστι, φῶς ἔστιν" ἀκολουθεῖ τὸ "φῶς ἔστιν" ἐν
τούτῳ τῷ συνημμένῳ "εἰ ἡμέρα ἔστι, καὶ εἰ ἡμέρα ἔστι, φῶς ἔστιν, ⟨φῶς

214

ἔστιν⟩." ἀσύνακτοι δὲ οἱ μὴ οὕτως ἔχοντες. (4) τῶν δὲ συνακτικῶν οἱ μέν   15
εἰσιν ἀληθεῖς οἱ δὲ οὐκ ἀληθεῖς, ἀληθεῖς μέν, ὅταν μὴ μόνον τὸ συνημμένον
ἐκ τῆς τῶν λημμάτων συμπλοκῆς καὶ τῆς ἐπιφορᾶς, ὡς προειρήκαμεν,
ὑγιὲς ᾖ, ἀλλὰ καὶ τὸ συμπέρασμα καὶ τὸ διὰ τῶν λημμάτων αὐτοῦ
συμπεπλεγμένον ἀληθὲς ὑπάρχῃ, ὅ ἐστιν ἡγούμενον ἐν τῷ συνημμένῳ.
ἀληθὲς δὲ συμπεπλεγμένον ἐστὶ τὸ πάντα ἔχον ἀληθῆ, ὡς τὸ "ἡμέρα ἔστι,   20
καὶ εἰ ἡμέρα ἔστι, φῶς ἔστιν". (5) οὐκ ἀληθεῖς δὲ οἱ μὴ οὕτως ἔχοντες. ὁ
γὰρ τοιοῦτος λόγος "εἰ νὺξ ἔστι, σκότος ἔστιν· ἀλλὰ μὴν νὺξ ἔστιν· σκότος
ἄρα ἔστιν" συνακτικὸς μέν ἐστιν, ἐπεὶ τὸ συνημμένον τοῦτο ὑγιές ἐστιν "εἰ
νὺξ ἔστι, καὶ εἰ νὺξ ἔστι, σκότος ⟨ἔστι, σκότος⟩ [ἄρα] ἔστιν", οὐ μέντοι
ἀληθής. τὸ γὰρ ἡγούμενον συμπεπλεγμένον ψεῦδός ἐστι, τὸ "νὺξ ἔστι, καὶ   25
εἰ νὺξ ἔστι, σκότος ἔστι", ψεῦδος ἔχον ἐν ἑαυτῷ τὸ "νὺξ ἔστιν"· ψεῦδος γάρ
ἐστι συμπεπλεγμένον τὸ ἔχον ἐν ἑαυτῷ ψεῦδος. (6) ἔνθεν καὶ ἀληθῆ λόγον
εἶναί φασι τὸν δι' ἀληθῶν λημμάτων ἀληθὲς συνάγοντα συμπέρασμα. (7)
πάλιν δὲ τῶν ἀληθῶν λόγων οἱ μέν εἰσιν ἀποδεικτικοί, οἱ δ' οὐκ
ἀποδεικτικοί, καὶ ἀποδεικτικοὶ μὲν οἱ διὰ προδήλων ἄδηλόν τι συνάγον-   30
τες, οὐκ ἀποδεικτικοὶ δὲ οἱ μὴ τοιοῦτοι. οἷον ὁ μὲν τοιοῦτος λόγος "εἰ
ἡμέρα ἔστι, φῶς ἔστιν· ἀλλὰ μὴν ἡμέρα ἔστιν· φως ἄρα ἔστιν" οὐκ ἔστιν
ἀποδεικτικός· τὸ γὰρ φῶς εἶναι, ὅπερ ἐστὶν αὐτοῦ συμπέρασμα, πρόδηλόν
ἐστιν. ὁ δὲ τοιοῦτος "εἰ ἱδρῶτες ῥέουσι διὰ τῆς ἐπιφανείας, εἰσὶ νοητοὶ
πόροι· ἀλλὰ μὴν ἱδρῶτες ῥέουσι διὰ τῆς ἐπιφανείας· εἰσὶν ἄρα νοητοὶ   35
πόροι" ἀποδεικτικός ἐστι, τὸ συμπέρασμα ἔχων ἄδηλον, τὸ "εἰσὶν ἄρα
νοητοὶ πόροι". (8) τῶν δὲ ἄδηλόν τι συναγόντων οἱ μὲν ἐφοδευτικῶς μόνον
ἄγουσιν ἡμᾶς διὰ τῶν λημμάτων ἐπὶ τὸ συμπέρασμα, οἱ δὲ ἐφοδευτικῶς
ἅμα καὶ ἐκκαλυπτικῶς. (9) οἷον ἐφοδευτικῶς μὲν οἱ ἐκ πίστεως καὶ
μνήμης ἠρτῆσθαι δοκοῦντες, οἷός ἐστιν ὁ τοιοῦτος "εἴ τίς σοι ⟨θεῶν⟩ εἶπεν   40
ὅτι πλουτήσει οὗτος, πλουτήσει οὗτος· οὑτοσὶ δὲ ὁ θεός (δείκνυμι δὲ καθ'
ὑπόθεσιν τὸν Δία) εἶπέ σοι ὅτι πλουτήσει οὗτος· πλουτήσει ἄρα οὗτος"·
συγκατατιθέμεθα γὰρ τῷ συμπεράσματι οὐχ οὕτως διὰ τὴν τῶν
λημμάτων ἀνάγκην ὡς πιστεύοντες τῇ τοῦ θεοῦ ἀποφάσει. (10) οἱ δὲ οὐ
μόνον ἐφοδευτικῶς ἀλλὰ καὶ ἐκκαλυπτικῶς ἄγουσιν ἡμᾶς ἐπὶ τὸ   45
συμπέρασμα, ὡς ὁ τοιοῦτος "εἰ ῥέουσι διὰ τῆς ἐπιφανείας ἱδρῶτες, εἰσὶ
νοητοὶ πόροι. ἀλλὰ μὴν τὸ πρῶτον· τὸ δεύτερον ἄρα"· τὸ γὰρ ῥεῖν τοὺς
ἱδρῶτας ἐκκαλυπτικόν ἐστι τοῦ πόρους εἶναι, διὰ τὸ προειλῆφθαι ὅτι διὰ
ναστοῦ σώματος ὑγρὸν οὐ δύναται φέρεσθαι. (11) ἡ οὖν ἀπόδειξις καὶ
λόγος εἶναι ὀφείλει καὶ συνακτικὸς καὶ ἀληθὴς καὶ ἄδηλον ἔχων   50
συμπέρασμα καὶ ἐκκαλυπτόμενον ὑπὸ τῆς δυνάμεως τῶν λημμάτων, καὶ
διὰ τοῦτο εἶναι λέγεται ἀπόδειξις λόγος δι' ὁμολογουμένων λημμάτων
κατὰ συναγωγὴν ἐπιφορὰν ἐκκαλύπτων ἄδηλον.

5 δ' ἤ Sedley: δέ codd.   14–15, 24 suppl. et del. Mates   51 καὶ–λημμάτων secl. Brunschwig

Context: critique of the notion of demonstration.

It is argued by Ebert [412] that this passage, along with the parallel *M.* 8.300–15 and

411–23, represents the Dialectical school, not, as usually assumed, the Stoics. It would nevertheless be good evidence for the Stoics, who (cf. *M.* 8.411) adopted at least the essentials of the same theory.
For analysis, see the outstanding studies of Brunschwig [444] and Barnes [445]. On most points we have been persuaded by Barnes.

3 This, despite **A** 1–2, is what became the standard Stoic definition of argument; cf. e.g. D.L. 7.45.

30 Barnes [445], 180 argues that since the premises must be 'pre-evident' there cannot be sequences of proofs, in which the naturally non-evident conclusion of one proof might become a premise of the next. But even if he is right in denying that a 'revealed' proposition might be held to become 'pre-evident' in the required sense, the series of proofs could be expressed as a single complex syllogism analysable by the third or fourth θέμα, in which case no 'revealed' proposition would feature as a premise – e.g. 'If *p*, *q*; if *q*, *r*; but *p*; therefore *r*', where *q* is an ἄδηλον.

C Sextus Empiricus, *M.* 8.429–34, 440–3

(1) τοίνυν φασὶ τετραχῶς γίγνεσθαι τὸν ἀπέραντον λόγον, ἤτοι κατὰ διάρτησιν ἢ κατὰ παρολκὴν ἢ κατὰ τὸ ἐν μοχθηρῷ ἠρωτῆσθαι σχήματι ἢ κατὰ ἔλλειψιν. (2) ἀλλὰ κατὰ διάρτησιν μέν, ὅταν μηδεμίαν ἔχῃ κοινωνίαν καὶ συνάρτησιν τὰ λήμματα πρὸς ἄλληλά τε καὶ πρὸς τὴν ἐπιφοράν, οἷον ἐπὶ τοῦ τοιούτου λόγου "εἰ ἡμέρα ἔστι, φῶς ἔστιν· ἀλλὰ μὴν πυροὶ ἐν 5 ἀγορᾷ πωλοῦνται· φῶς ἄρα ἔστιν." ὁρῶμεν γὰρ ὡς ἐπὶ τούτου οὔτε τὸ "εἰ ἡμέρα ἔστιν" ἔχει τινὰ σύμπνοιαν καὶ συμπλοκὴν πρὸς τὸ "πυροὶ ἐν ἀγορᾷ πωλοῦνται", οὔτε ἑκάτερον αὐτῶν πρὸς τὸ "φῶς ἄρα ἔστιν", ἀλλ' ἕκαστον ἀπὸ τῶν ἄλλων διήρτηται. (3) κατὰ δὲ παρολκὴν ἀπέραντος γίνεται ὁ λόγος, ὅταν ἔξωθέν τι καὶ περισσῶς παραλαμβάνηται τοῖς λήμμασι, 10 καθάπερ ἐπὶ τοῦ οὕτως ἔχοντος "εἰ ἡμέρα ἔστι, φῶς ἔστιν· ἀλλὰ μὴν ἡμέρα ἔστιν, ἀλλὰ καὶ ἡ ἀρετὴ ὠφελεῖ· φῶς ἄρα ἔστιν." τὸ γὰρ τὴν ἀρετὴν ὠφελεῖν περισσῶς συμπαρείληπται τοῖς ἄλλοις λήμμασιν, εἴγε δυνατόν ἐστιν ἐξαιρεθέντος αὐτοῦ διὰ τῶν περιλειπομένων, τοῦ τε "εἰ ἡμέρα ἔστι, φῶς ἔστιν" καὶ τοῦ "ἀλλὰ μὴν ἡμέρα ἔστιν", συνάγεσθαι τὴν ἐπιφορὰν τὸ 15 "φῶς ἄρα ἔστιν". (4) διὰ δὲ τὸ ἐν μοχθηρῷ ἠρωτῆσθαι σχήματι ἀπέραντος γίνεται ⟨ὁ⟩ λόγος, ὅταν ἔν τινι τῶν παρὰ τὰ ὑγιῆ σχήματα θεωρουμένων ἐρωτηθῇ σχήματι· οἷον ὄντος ὑγιοῦς σχήματος τοῦ τοιούτου "εἰ τὸ πρῶτον, τὸ δεύτερον, τὸ δέ γε πρῶτον, τὸ ἄρα δεύτερον", ὄντος δὲ καὶ τοῦ "εἰ τὸ πρῶτον, τὸ δεύτερον, οὐχὶ δέ γε τὸ δεύτερον, οὐκ ἄρα τὸ πρῶτον", 20 φαμὲν τὸν ἐν τοιούτῳ σχήματι ἐρωτηθέντα "εἰ τὸ πρῶτον, τὸ δεύτερον, οὐχὶ δέ γε τὸ πρῶτον, οὐκ ἄρα τὸ δεύτερον" ἀπέραντον εἶναι, οὐχ ὅτι ἀδύνατόν ἐστιν ἐν τῷ τοιούτῳ σχήματι λόγον συνερωτᾶσθαι δι' ἀληθῶν ἀληθὲς συνάγοντα (δύναται γάρ, οἷον ὁ τοιοῦτος "εἰ τὰ τρία τέσσαρά ἐστιν, τὰ ἓξ ὀκτώ ἐστιν· οὐχὶ δέ γε τὰ τρία τέσσαρά ἐστιν, οὐκ ἄρα τὰ ἓξ ὀκτώ 25 ἐστιν"), τῷ δὲ δύνασθαί τινας λόγους ἐν αὐτῷ τάττεσθαι μοχθηρούς, καθάπερ καὶ τὸν τοιοῦτον "εἰ ἡμέρα ἔστι, φῶς ἔστιν· ἀλλὰ μὴν οὐκ ἔστιν

ἡμέρα· οὐκ ἄρα ἔστι φῶς." (5) κατ᾽ ἔλλειψιν δὲ ἀπέραντος γίνεται ὁ λόγος,
ὅταν ἐλλείπῃ τι τῶν συνακτικῶν λημμάτων. οἷον "ἤτοι κακόν ἐστιν ὁ
πλοῦτος ἢ ἀγαθόν ἐστιν ὁ πλοῦτος· οὐχὶ δέ γε κακόν ἐστιν ὁ πλοῦτος·   30
ἀγαθὸν ἄρα ἐστὶν ὁ πλοῦτος." ἐλλείπει γὰρ ἐν τῷ διεζευγμένῳ τὸ
ἀδιάφορον εἶναι τὸν πλοῦτον, ὥστε τὴν ὑγιῆ συνερώτησιν τοιαύτην μᾶλλον
ὑπάρχειν "ἤτοι ἀγαθόν ἐστιν ὁ πλοῦτος ἢ κακόν ἐστιν ἢ ἀδιάφορον· οὔτε δὲ
ἀγαθόν ἐστιν ὁ πλοῦτος οὔτε κακόν· ἀδιάφορον ἄρα ἐστίν" . . . (6) τοίνυν
ὑποτυγχάνοντες οἱ ἀπὸ τῆς σκέψεως ἐροῦσιν ὡς, εἴπερ ἀπέραντός ἐστιν ὁ   35
λόγος κατὰ παρολκήν, ἐφ᾽ οὗ ἀρθέντος τινὸς λήμματος ἐκ τῶν περιλειπομένων συνάγεται ἡ ἐπιφορά, ῥητέον ἀπέραντον εἶναι καὶ τὸν ἐν τῷ πρώτῳ
τρόπῳ ἐρωτώμενον, ἔχοντα δὲ οὕτως "εἰ ἡμέρα ἔστι, φῶς ἔστιν· ἀλλὰ μὴν
ἡμέρα ἔστιν· φῶς ἄρα ἔστιν." παρέλκει γὰρ ἐν αὐτῷ πρὸς τὴν τοῦ
συμπεράσματος κατασκευὴν τὸ τροπικὸν τὸ "εἰ ἡμέρα ἔστι, ⟨φῶς ἔστι⟩",   40
καὶ δύναται ἐκ τοῦ "ἡμέρα ἔστι" μόνου συνάγεσθαι τὸ "φῶς ἄρα ἔστιν".
τοῦτο δὲ πρόδηλον μὲν ἦν καὶ αὐτόθεν, ἔστι δὲ καὶ αὐτὸ ἐκ τῆς ὡς πρὸς
ἐκείνους ἀκολουθίας παραμυθεῖσθαι. ἤτοι γὰρ ἀκολουθεῖν φήσουσι τῷ
ἡμέραν εἶναι τὸ φῶς εἶναι, ἢ μὴ ἀκολουθεῖν. καὶ εἰ μὲν ἀκολουθεῖ, αὐτόθεν
ὁμολογηθέντος ἀληθοῦς εἶναι τοῦ "ἡμέρα ἔστι" συνάγεται καὶ τὸ "φῶς   45
ἔστι", κατ᾽ ἀνάγκην ἑπόμενον αὐτῷ· ὅπερ ἦν συμπέρασμα. εἰ δὲ οὐκ
ἀκολουθεῖ, οὐδ᾽ ἐπὶ τοῦ συνημμένου ἀκολουθήσει, καὶ διὰ τοῦτο ἔσται
ψεῦδος τὸ συνημμένον, μὴ ἀκολουθοῦντος ἐν αὐτῷ τοῦ λήγοντος τῷ
ἡγουμένῳ. ὥστε δυεῖν θάτερον ὅσον ἐπὶ τῇ προειρημένῃ τεχνολογίᾳ, ἢ
ἀπέραντον εὑρίσκεσθαι τὸν ἐν τῷ πρώτῳ τρόπῳ ἠρωτημένον παρέλκοντος   50
ἐν αὐτῷ τοῦ τροπικοῦ, ἢ ψευδῆ πάντως διὰ τὸ ψεῦδος ἐν αὐτῷ εἶναι τὸ
τροπικόν. (7) τὸ μὲν γὰρ λέγειν μὴ ἀρέσκειν τῷ Χρυσίππῳ μονολημμάτους εἶναι λόγους, ὃ τάχα τινὲς ἐροῦσι πρὸς τὴν τοιαύτην ἔνστασιν, τελέως
ληρῶδες. οὔτε γὰρ ταῖς Χρυσίππου φωναῖς ὡς πυθοχρήστοις παραγγέλ-
μασιν ἀνάγκη πείθεσθαι, οὔτε μαρτυρίᾳ προσέχειν ἀνδρῶν ἔστιν εἰς   55
οἰκείαν ἀπόρρησιν ἐκ μάρτυρος τοῦ τὸ ἐναντίον λέγοντος· Ἀντίπατρος
γάρ, τῶν ἐν τῇ Στωικῇ αἱρέσει ἐπιφανεστάτων ἀνδρῶν, ἔφη δύνασθαι καὶ
μονολημμάτους λόγους συνίστασθαι.

20 τὸ δεύτερον, οὐκ ἄρα τὸ πρῶτον Mutschmann: τὸ πρῶτον, οὐκ ἄρα τὸ δεύτερον codd.   40 add.
Kochalsky   56 ἀπόρρησιν ed. Genevensis: ἀπόρησιν vel ἀπορύησιν codd.

Context: attack on the notion of demonstration. Stoic demonstration is a species of
valid argument (cf. **B**), but by their own criteria of invalidity, it is argued, their basic
argument forms come out invalid. Cf. also *PH* 2.146ff.
    9–16, 34–52   For analysis, see especially Barnes [445].
    56–8   Cf. **D**.

D Apuleius, *De int.* 184,16–23 (*FDS* 1050, part)

. . . in qua definitione . . . concessis aliquibus pluraliter dictum est, quia ex una acceptione
non fit collectio, licet Antipatro Stoico contra omnium sententiam videatur

Stoic logic and semantics

plena conclusio esse "vides, vivis igitur", cum sit illo modo plena "si vides, vivis; atqui vides; vivis igitur."

Context: discussion of Aristotle's definition of the syllogism at *An. pr.* 1.1, 24b18–20. For further evidence on Antipater's view, see **C 7**, and Hülser [321], *FDS* 1050–7. For his logical heterodoxy, cf. **H 2**.

E Sextus Empiricus, *PH* 1.69

κατὰ δὲ τὸν Χρύσιππον τὸν μάλιστα πολεμοῦντα τοῖς ἀλόγοις ζῴοις καὶ τῆς ἀοιδίμου διαλεκτικῆς μετέχει. φησὶ γοῦν αὐτὸν ὁ προειρημένος ἀνὴρ ἐπιβάλλειν τῷ πέμπτῳ διὰ πλειόνων ἀναποδείκτῳ, ὅταν ἐπὶ τρίοδον ἐλθὼν καὶ τὰς δύο ὁδοὺς ἰχνεύσας δι' ὧν οὐ διῆλθε τὸ θηρίον, τὴν τρίτην μηδ' ἰχνεύσας εὐθέως ὁρμήσῃ δι' αὐτῆς. δυνάμει γὰρ τοῦτο αὐτὸν λογίζεσθαί   5
φησιν ὁ ἀρχαῖος "ἤτοι τῇδε ἢ τῇδε ἢ τῇδε διῆλθε τὸ θηρίον· οὔτε δὲ τῇδε οὔτε τῇδε· τῇδε ἄρα."

Context: the first Sceptic mode, based on differences between different animals' impressions (see **72B**). Sextus here resists the challenge that humans and irrational animals are not comparable.

1 **πολεμοῦντα**   Not corrupt, as commonly held. The Stoics are seen by Sextus (cf. ibid. 65) as leading proponents of the challenge under discussion (see above); yet even they, despite this antipathy to irrational animals, allow them some degree of rationality.

3 **διὰ πλειόνων**   Here 'with multiple disjuncts' (cf. **37I** 4), rather than 'with multiple premises' (cf. **F** 1–2, **H** 1).

F Origen, *Cels.* 7.15 (*FDS* 1181, part)

ὅταν δὲ δύο συνημμένα λήγῃ εἰς τὰ ἀλλήλοις ἀντικείμενα τῷ καλουμένῳ "διὰ δύο τροπικῶν" θεωρήματι, ἀναιρεῖται τὸ ἐν ἀμφοτέροις τοῖς συνημμένοις ἡγούμενον, ὅπερ ἐν τούτοις ἐστὶ τὸ προλέγειν τοὺς προφήτας τὸν μέγαν θεὸν δουλεύειν ἢ νοσήσειν ἢ τεθνήξεσθαι. συνάγεται οὖν τὸ "οὐκ ἄρα προεῖπον οἱ προφῆται τὸν μέγαν θεὸν δουλεύσειν ἢ νοσήσειν ἢ τεθνήξεσθαι", καὶ ὑπάγεταί γε ὁ λόγος τρόπῳ τοιούτῳ· εἰ τὸ πρῶτον, καὶ τὸ   5
δεύτερον· εἰ τὸ πρῶτον, οὐ τὸ δεύτερον· οὐκ ἄρα τὸ πρῶτον. φέρουσι δὲ καὶ ἐπὶ ὕλης τὸν τρόπον τοῦτον οἱ ἀπὸ τῆς Στοας, λέγοντες τὸ "εἰ ἐπίστασαι ὅτι τέθνηκας, ⟨τέθνηκας· εἰ ἐπίστασαι ὅτι τέθνηκας,⟩ οὐ τέθνηκας." ἀκολουθεῖ τὸ "οὐκ ἄρα ἐπίστασαι ὅτι τέθνηκας".

8 suppl. Valesius

Context: criticism of Celsus for implicitly not excluding the possibility that the prophets could have predicted God's suffering evils.

G Sextus Empiricus, *M.* 8.229–37

(1) οὐχ ἁπλοῖ δέ εἰσιν οἱ ἐκ τῶν ἁπλῶν πεπλεγμένοι καὶ ἔτι χρείαν ἔχοντες τῆς εἰς ἐκείνους ἀναλύσεως, ἵνα γνωσθῶσιν, ὅτι καὶ αὐτοὶ συνάγουσιν. (2)

τούτων δὲ τῶν οὐχ ἁπλῶν οἱ μὲν ἐξ ὁμογενῶν εἰσὶ συνεστῶτες, οἱ δὲ ἐξ
ἀνομογενῶν, καὶ ἐξ ὁμογενῶν μὲν ὥσπερ οἱ ἐκ δυεῖν πρώτων ἀναποδείκτων πεπλεγμένοι ἢ ἐκ δυεῖν δευτέρων, ἐξ ἀνομογενῶν δὲ ὥσπερ οἱ ἐκ   5
πρώτου ⟨καὶ τρίτου⟩ ἀναποδείκτου συνεστῶτες ἢ ἐκ δευτέρου καὶ τρίτου,
καὶ κοινῶς οἱ τούτοις παραπλήσιοι. (3) ἐξ ὁμογενῶν μὲν οὖν συνέστηκεν
οἷον ὁ τοιοῦτος "εἰ ἡμέρα ἔστι, ⟨εἰ ἡμέρα ἔστι⟩ φῶς ἔστιν· ἀλλὰ μὴν ἡμέρα
ἔστιν· φῶς ἄρα ἔστιν." πέπλεκται γὰρ ἐκ πρώτων δυεῖν ἀναποδείκτων, ὡς
ἀναλύσαντες αὐτὸν εἰσόμεθα. (4) γνωστέον γὰρ ὅτι θεώρημα διαλεκτικὸν   10
ἔστιν εἰς τὰς τῶν συλλογισμῶν ἀναλύσεις παραδιδόμενον τοιοῦτον "ὅταν
τά τινος συμπεράσματος συνακτικὰ λήμματα ἔχωμεν, δυνάμει κἀκεῖνο ἐν
τούτοις ἔχομεν τὸ συμπέρασμα, κἂν κατ᾽ ἐκφορὰν μὴ λέγηται." (5) ἐπεὶ
οὖν δύο ἔχομεν λήμματα, τό τε συνημμένον τὸ "εἰ ἡμέρα ἔστιν, ⟨εἰ ἡμέρα
ἔστι φῶς ἔστιν⟩", ὅπερ ἄρχεται μὲν ἀπὸ ἁπλοῦ ἀξιώματος τοῦ "ἡμέρα   15
ἔστιν", λήγει δὲ εἰς οὐχ ἁπλοῦν συνημμένον τὸ "εἰ ἡμέρα ἔστιν, φῶς
ἔστιν", καὶ ἔτι τὸ ἡγούμενον ἐν αὐτῷ τὸ "ἡμέρα ἔστιν", ἐκ τούτων
συναχθήσεται ἡμῖν πρώτῳ ἀναποδείκτῳ τὸ λῆγον ἐν ἐκείνῳ τῷ συνημμένῳ τὸ "εἰ ἄρα ἡμέρα ἔστιν, φῶς ἔστιν". τοῦτ᾽ οὖν δυνάμει μὲν ἔχομεν ἐν
τῷ λόγῳ συναγόμενον, κατὰ δὲ τὴν ἐκφορὰν παραλελειμμένον, ⟨ὃ⟩   20
τάξαντες μετὰ τῆς τοῦ ἐκκειμένου λόγου προσλήψεως τῆς "ἡμέρα ἔστιν",
ἔξομεν συναγόμενον τὸ "φῶς ἔστιν" πρώτῳ ἀναποδείκτῳ, ὅπερ ἦν
ἐπιφορὰ τοῦ ἐκκειμένου λόγου. ὥστε δύο γίγνεσθαι πρώτους ἀναποδείκτους, ἕνα μὲν τὸν τοιοῦτον "εἰ ἡμέρα ἔστι⟨ν, εἰ ἡμέρα ἔστι⟩ φῶς ἔστιν·
⟨ἀλλὰ μὴν ἡμέρα ἔστιν· εἰ ἄρα ἡμέρα ἔστιν φῶς ἔστιν⟩", ἕτερον δὲ τὸν   25
τοιοῦτον "εἰ ἡμέρα ἔστι, φῶς ἔστιν· ἀλλὰ μὴν ἡμέρα ἔστιν· φῶς ἄρα
ἔστιν." (6) τοιόσδε μὲν οὖν ἐστιν ὁ χαρακτὴρ τῶν ἐξ ὁμογενῶν τὴν πλοκὴν
ἐχόντων λόγων· ἐξ ἀνομογενῶν δὲ λοιπόν ἐστι καθάπερ ὁ παρὰ τῷ
Αἰνησιδήμῳ περὶ σημείου ἐρωτηθείς, ἔχων δὲ οὕτως· "εἰ τὰ φαινόμενα
πᾶσι τοῖς ὁμοίως διακειμένοις παραπλησίως φαίνεται καὶ τὰ σημεῖά ἐστι   30
φαινόμενα, τὰ σημεῖα πᾶσι τοῖς ὁμοίως διακειμένοις παραπλησίως
φαίνεται· τὰ δέ γε σημεῖα οὐ πᾶσι τοῖς ὁμοίως διακειμένοις παραπλησίως
φαίνεται· τὰ δὲ φαινόμενα πᾶσι τοῖς ὁμοίως διακειμένοις παραπλησίως
φαίνεται· οὐκ ἄρα φαινόμενά ἐστι τὰ σημεῖα." (7) συνέστηκε γὰρ ὁ
τοιοῦτος λόγος ἐκ δευτέρου τε ἀναποδείκτου καὶ τρίτου, καθὼς πάρεστι   35
μαθεῖν ἐκ τῆς ἀναλύσεως, ἥτις σαφεστέρα μᾶλλον γενήσεται ἐπὶ τοῦ
τρόπου ποιησαμένων ἡμῶν τὴν διδασκαλίαν, ἔχοντος οὕτως· "εἰ τὸ
πρῶτον καὶ τὸ δεύτερον, τὸ τρίτον· οὐχὶ δὲ τὸ τρίτον, ἀλλὰ καὶ τὸ πρῶτον·
οὐκ ἄρα τὸ δεύτερον." ἐπεὶ γὰρ ἔχομεν συνημμένον ἐν ᾧ ἡγεῖται
συμπεπλεγμένον τὸ πρῶτον καὶ τὸ δεύτερον, λήγει δὲ τὸ τρίτον, ἔχομεν δὲ   40
καὶ τὸ ἀντικείμενον τοῦ λήγοντος τὸ "οὐ τὸ τρίτον", συναχθήσεται ἡμῖν
καὶ τὸ ἀντικείμενον τοῦ ἡγουμένου, τὸ "οὐκ ἄρα τὸ πρῶτον καὶ τὸ
δεύτερον", δευτέρῳ ἀναποδείκτῳ. ἀλλὰ δὴ τοῦτο αὐτὸ κατὰ μὲν τὴν
δύναμιν ἔγκειται τῷ λόγῳ, ἐπεὶ ἔχομεν τὰ συνακτικὰ αὐτοῦ λήμματα,
κατὰ δὲ τὴν προφορὰν παρεῖται. ὅπερ τάξαντες μετὰ τοῦ λειπομένου   45

Stoic logic and semantics

λήμματος, τοῦ πρώτου, ἕξομεν συναγόμενον τὸ συμπέρασμα τὸ "οὐκ ἄρα
τὸ δεύτερον" τρίτῳ ἀναποδείκτῳ. ὥστε δύο εἶναι ἀναποδείκτους, ἕνα μὲν
τοιοῦτον "εἰ τὸ πρῶτον καὶ τὸ δεύτερον, τὸ τρίτον· οὐχὶ δέ γε τὸ τρίτον·
οὐκ ἄρα τὸ πρῶτον καὶ τὸ δεύτερον", ὅς ἐστι δεύτερος ἀναπόδεικτος,
ἕτερον δὲ τρίτον τὸν οὕτως ἔχοντα "οὐχὶ τὸ πρῶτον καὶ τὸ δεύτερον· ἀλλὰ   50
μὴν τὸ πρῶτον· οὐκ ἄρα τὸ δεύτερον." ἐπὶ μὲν οὖν τοῦ τρόπου ἡ ἀνάλυσίς
ἐστι τοιαύτη, ἀναλογεῖ δὲ καὶ ἐπὶ τοῦ λόγου.

omnia supplementa secundum Kochalsky

Context: defence of Aenesidemus' argument against evident signs, as syllogistically
valid on Stoic principles.

1   The subject, carried over from ibid. 228, is still strictly ἀναπόδεικτοι. Here,
and possibly at *PH* 2.157, Sextus differs from all other sources (cf. **A**) in appearing to
use this term to cover *all* valid syllogisms. (For discussion see Frede [407], 128–31.)
But in both contexts he also seems to assume the normal restriction of the term to
elementary syllogisms, and the apparently broader usage may be due to nothing more
than carelessness of expression.

10–13   This 'dialectical theorem' resembles the 'synthetic theorem' which
Alexander (*In Ar. An. pr.* 274) ascribes to Aristotle and (ibid. 284,10ff.) equates in
function with the second, third and fourth Stoic θέματα.

H Galen, *Plac.* 2.3.18–19

(1) νυνὶ δὲ πῶς μὲν οἱ διὰ δύο τροπικῶν ⟨ἢ⟩ τριῶν ἀναλύονται συλλογισμοὶ
καὶ πῶς οἱ ἀδιαφόρως περαίνοντες ἤ τινες ἄλλοι τοιοῦτοι τῷ πρώτῳ καὶ
δευτέρῳ θέματι προσχρώμενοι, πολλοῖς ἔστι συντυχεῖν ἀκριβῶς ἠσκημέ-
νοις, ὥσπερ ἀμέλει καὶ ἐπ᾽ ἄλλοις ὅσους διὰ τοῦ τρίτου θέματος ἢ
τετάρτου συλλογισμοὺς ἀναλύουσι. (2) καίτοι τούτων τοὺς πλείστους   5
ἔνεστιν ἑτέρως ἀναλύειν συντομώτερον, ὡς Ἀντίπατρος ἔγραψε, πρὸς τῷ
καὶ περιεργίαν εἶναι οὐ μικρὰν ἀχρήστου πράγματος ἅπασαν τὴν τῶν
τοιούτων συλλογισμῶν πλοκήν, ὡς αὐτὸς ὁ Χρύσιππος ἔργῳ μαρτυρεῖ
μηδαμόθι τῶν ἑαυτοῦ συγγραμμάτων εἰς ἀπόδειξιν δόγματος ἐκείνων
δεηθεὶς τῶν συλλογισμῶν.   10

1 ⟨ἢ⟩ Ricci   τριῶν M Ald.: om. C   4 ἐπ᾽ ἄλλοις codd.: ἐν ἄλλοις Müller: ἄλλοις ἐφ᾽ De
Lacy   ὅσους R(corr.): ὅσοις cett.

Context: criticism of Chrysippus' argument at **34J**. The Stoics are accused of
incompetence at scientific demonstration, and of being too preoccupied with useless
areas of logic.

1   For syllogisms 'with two hypothetical premises', cf. **F** 1–2.
2   For these 'tautologically valid' syllogisms, see Frede [407], 184–5, and *FDS*
1169–77.
2–5   For the first θέμα, see **I**, and for the third, **J**. The suggestions for the second
and fourth adopted in vol 1, 219–20 are based on those of Frede [407], 172–96, whose
discussion should also be consulted for their use in reduction of the kinds of syllogism
mentioned in 1–2.

I Apuleius, *De int.* 191,5–21 (*FDS* 1161, part)

est et altera probatio communis omnium etiam indemonstrabilium, quae dicitur per impossibile appellaturque a Stoicis prima constitutio vel primum expositum. quod sic definiunt: "si ex duobus tertium quid colligitur, alterum eorum cum contrario illationis colligit contrarium reliquo." veteres autem sic definierunt: "omnis conclusionis si sublata sit illatio, assumpta alterutra propositione tolli   5
reliquam." quae res inventa est adversus eos qui, concessis acceptionibus, id quod ex illis colligitur impudenter recusant. per hoc enim compelluntur ad impossibilia, dum ex eo quod negant contrarium aliquid invenietur ei quod ante concesserant. porro contraria simul esse vera impossibile est. ergo per impossibile compelluntur ad conclusionem. nec frustra constituerunt dialectici eum modum verum esse, cuius adversum illationis cum alterutra acceptione tollit   10
reliquam.

Context: the reducibility of arguments to the indemonstrables.
    For the Aristotelian *per impossibile* proof, see G. Patzig, *Aristotle's theory of the syllogism* (1959; Engl. transl. 1969), §29.
    4 **veteres** These will be, as often, the Peripatetics.

J Alexander, *In Ar. An. pr.* 278,11–14 (*FDS* 1167, part)

τοῦ δέ γε τρίτου καλουμένου θέματος ἡ περιοχὴ καὶ αὐτοῦ ἔχει ὧδε "ὅταν
ἐκ δυεῖν τρίτον τι συνάγηται, ἑνὸς δὲ αὐτῶν ἔξωθεν ληφθῇ συλλογιστικά,
ἐκ τοῦ λοιποῦ καὶ ἐκ τῶν ἔξωθεν τοῦ ἑτέρου συλλογιστικῶν τὸ αὐτὸ
συναχθήσεται."

Context: commentary on Aristotle, *An. pr.* 1.25, 42a8, comparing the Stoic third θέμα to the synthetic theorem, which Alexander (ibid. 274) ascribes to Aristotle.
    For another version, see Simplicius, *In Ar. De caelo* 236,33–237,9 = *FDS* 1168.

37 Fallacy

A Sextus Empiricus, *PH* 2.229–35

(1) οὐκ ἄτοπον δὲ ἴσως καὶ τῷ περὶ τῶν σοφισμάτων ἐπιστῆσαι λόγῳ διὰ
βραχέων, ἐπεὶ καὶ εἰς τὴν τούτων διάλυσιν ἀναγκαίαν εἶναι λέγουσι τὴν
διαλεκτικὴν οἱ σεμνύνοντες αὐτήν. εἰ γὰρ τῶν τε ἀληθῶν καὶ ψευδῶν
λόγων, φασίν, ἐστὶν αὕτη διαγνωστική, ψευδεῖς δὲ λόγοι καὶ τὰ
σοφίσματα, καὶ τούτων ἂν εἴη διακριτικὴ λυμαινομένων τὴν ἀλήθειαν   5
φαινομέναις πιθανότησιν. ὅθεν ὡς βοηθοῦντες οἱ διαλεκτικοὶ σαλεύοντι τῷ
βίῳ καὶ τὴν ἔννοιαν καὶ τὰς διαφορὰς καὶ τὰς ἐπιλύσεις δὴ τῶν
σοφισμάτων μετὰ σπουδῆς ἡμᾶς πειρῶνται διδάσκειν, (2) λέγοντες
σόφισμα εἶναι λόγον πιθανὸν καὶ δεδολιευμένον ὥστε προσδέξασθαι τὴν
ἐπιφορὰν ἤτοι ψευδῆ ἢ ὡμοιωμένην ψευδεῖ ἢ ἄδηλον ἢ ἄλλως ἀπρόσδεκτον   10
(3) οἷον ψευδῆ μὲν ὡς ἐπὶ ⟨τούτου⟩ τοῦ σοφίσματος ἔχει "οὐδεὶς δίδωσι
κατηγόρημα πιεῖν· κατηγόρημα δέ ἐστι τὸ ἀψίνθιον πιεῖν· οὐδεὶς ἄρα

Stoic logic and semantics

δίδωσιν ἀψίνθιον πιεῖν", (4) ἔτι δὲ ὅμοιον ψευδεῖ ὡς ἐπὶ τούτου "ὃ μήτε
ἐνεδέχετο μήτε ἐνδέχεται, τοῦτο οὐκ ἔστιν ἄτοπον· οὔτε δὲ ἐνεδέχετο οὔτε
ἐνδέχεται τὸ ὁ ἰατρός, καθὸ ἰατρός ἐστι, φονεύει· ⟨οὐκ ἄρα ἄτοπόν ἐστι τὸ   15
ὁ ἰατρός, καθὸ ἰατρός ἐστι, φονεύει⟩." (5) ἔτι δὲ ἄδηλον οὕτως "οὐχὶ καὶ
ἠρώτηκά τί σε πρῶτον, καὶ οὐχὶ οἱ ἀστέρες ἄρτιοί εἰσιν· ἠρώτηκα δέ τί σε
πρῶτον· οἱ ἄρα ἀστέρες ἄρτιοί εἰσιν." (6) ἔτι δὲ ἀπρόσδεκτον ἄλλως, ὡς οἱ
λεγόμενοι σολοικίζοντες λόγοι, οἷον "ὃ βλέπεις, ἔστιν· βλέπεις δὲ
φρενιτικόν· ἔστιν ἄρα φρενιτικόν." "ὃ ὁρᾷς, ἔστιν· ὁρᾷς δὲ φλεγμαίνοντα   20
τόπον· ἔστιν ἄρα φλεγμαίνοντα τόπον." (7) εἶτα μέντοι καὶ τὰς ἐπιλύσεις
αὐτῶν [ὁρᾶν ἤτοι] παριστᾶν ἐπιχειροῦσι, λέγοντες ἐπὶ μὲν τοῦ πρώτου
σοφίσματος, ὅτι ἄλλο διὰ τῶν λημμάτων συγκεχώρηται καὶ ἄλλο
ἐπενήνεκται. συγκεχώρηται γὰρ τὸ μὴ πίνεσθαι κατηγόρημα, καὶ εἶναι
κατηγόρημα τὸ ἀψίνθιον πίνειν, οὐκ αὐτὸ τὸ ἀψίνθιον. διὸ δέον ἐπιφέρειν   25
"οὐδεὶς ἄρα πίνει τὸ ἀψίνθιον πίνειν", ὅπερ ἐστὶν ἀληθές, ἐπενήνεκται
"οὐδεὶς ἄρα ἀψίνθιον πίνει", ὅπερ ἐστὶ ψεῦδος, οὐ συναγόμενον ἐκ τῶν
συγκεχωρημένων λημμάτων. (8) ἐπὶ δὲ τοῦ δευτέρου, ὅτι δοκεῖ μὲν ἐπὶ
ψεῦδος ἀπάγειν ὡς ποιεῖν τοὺς ἀνεπιστάτους ὀκνεῖν αὐτῷ συγκατατίθεσθαι, συνάγει δὲ ἀληθές, τὸ "οὐκ ἄρα ἄτοπόν ἐστι τὸ ὁ ἰατρός, καθὸ ἰατρός   30
ἐστι, φονεύει". οὐδὲν γὰρ ἀξίωμα ἄτοπόν ἐστιν, ἀξίωμα δέ ἐστι τὸ "ὁ
ἰατρός, καθὸ ἰατρός ἐστι, φονεύει". διὸ οὐδὲ τοῦτο ἄτοπον. (9) ἡ δὲ ἐπὶ τὸ
ἄδηλον ἀπαγωγή, φασίν, ὅτι ἐκ τοῦ γένους τῶν μεταπιπτόντων ἐστίν.
μηδενὸς γὰρ προηρωτημένου κατὰ τὴν ὑπόθεσιν τὸ ἀποφατικὸν τῆς
συμπλοκῆς ἀληθὲς γίνεται, ψευδοῦς τῆς συμπλοκῆς οὔσης παρὰ τὸ   35
ἐμπεπλέχθαι ψεῦδος τὸ "ἠρώτηκά τί σε πρῶτον" ἐν αὐτῇ. μετὰ δὲ τὸ
ἐρωτηθῆναι τὸ ἀποφατικὸν τῆς συμπλοκῆς, τῆς προσλήψεως ἀληθοῦς
γενομένης "ἠρώτηκα δέ τί σε πρῶτον", διὰ τὸ ἠρωτῆσθαι πρὸ τῆς
προσλήψεως τὸ ἀποφατικὸν τῆς συμπλοκῆς ἡ τοῦ ἀποφατικοῦ τῆς
συμπλοκῆς πρότασις γίνεται ψευδὴς τοῦ ἐν τῷ συμπεπλεγμένῳ ψεύδους   40
γενομένου ἀληθοῦς· ὡς μηδέποτε δύνασθαι συναχθῆναι τὸ συμπέρασμα μὴ
συνυπάρχοντος τοῦ ἀποφατικοῦ τῆς συμπλοκῆς τῇ προσλήψει. (10) τοὺς
δὲ τελευταίους, φασὶν ἔνιοι, τοὺς σολοικίζοντας λόγους, ἀτόπως ἐπάγεσ-
θαι παρὰ τὴν συνήθειαν.

15-16 suppl. Bekker   22 ὁρᾶν ἤτοι om. T

Context: criticism of doctrinaire treatments of fallacy.
    The idea that this text may represent the Dialectical school we owe to Ebert [412].
Our suggestion in vol. 1, 230 that the school excluded ambiguity from its analysis of
sophisms on doctrinal grounds may be thought to conflict with *PH* 2.256–9. But that
section, on ambiguities, is quite separate from the preceding one on sophisms, and
need not represent the same opponents.
    9 πιθανόν   Cf. **M**.
    13–14 **μήτε ἐνεδέχετο μήτε ἐνδέχεται**   This unusual expression looks Diodor-
ean: cf. **35B 3**.
    40 ψευδής is strictly incorrect. One would expect ἄδηλος or ἀπρόσδεκτος.

222

B Diogenes Laertius 7.192–8 (with omissions)

λογικοῦ τόπου περὶ τὰς λέξεις καὶ τὸν κατ' αὐτὰς λόγον σύνταξις πρώτη· Περὶ τῶν ἐνικῶν
καὶ πληθυντικῶν ἐκφορῶν ς', Περὶ λέξεων πρὸς Σωσιγένην καὶ 'Αλέξανδρον ε', (1) περὶ
τῆς κατὰ τὰς λέξεις ἀνωμαλίας πρὸς Δίωνα δ', Περὶ τῶν πρὸς τὰς φωνὰς
σωριτῶν λόγων γ', Περὶ σολοικισμῶν ά, Περὶ σολοικιζόντων λόγων πρὸς
Διονύσιον α', Λόγοι παρὰ τὰς συνηθείας α', Λέξεις πρὸς Διονύσιον α'   5
. . . (2) σύνταξις τρίτη· Πρὸς τοὺς μὴ διαιρουμένους β', Περὶ ἀμφιβολιῶν
πρὸς 'Απολλᾶν δ', Περὶ τῶν τροπικῶν ἀμφιβολιῶν α', Περὶ συνημμένης
τροπικῆς ἀμφιβολίας β', Πρὸς τὸ περὶ ἀμφιβολιῶν Πανθοίδου β', Περὶ
τῆς εἰς τὰς ἀμφιβολίας εἰσαγωγῆς ε', 'Επιτομὴ τῶν πρὸς 'Επικράτην
ἀμφιβολιῶν α', Συνημμένα πρὸς τὴν εἰσαγωγὴν τὴν εἰς τὰς ἀμφιβολίας β'.   10
(3) λογικοῦ τόπου πρὸς τοὺς λόγους καὶ τοὺς τρόπους . . . σύνταξις πέμπτη· περὶ τῆς εἰς
τὸν ψευδόμενον εἰσαγωγῆς πρὸς 'Αριστοκρέοντα α', Λόγοι ψευδόμενοι
πρὸς εἰσαγωγὴν α', Περὶ τοῦ ψευδομένου πρὸς 'Αριστοκρέοντα ς'. σύνταξις
ἕκτη· Πρὸς τοὺς νομίζοντας καὶ ψευδῆ καὶ ἀληθῆ εἶναι α', Πρὸς τοὺς διὰ
τομῆς διαλύοντας τὸν ψευδόμενον λόγον πρὸς 'Αριστοκρέοντα β',   15
'Αποδείξεις πρὸς τὸ μὴ δεῖν τέμνειν τὰ ἀόριστα α', Πρὸς τὰ ἀντειρημένα
τοῖς κατὰ τῆς τομῆς τῶν ἀορίστων πρὸς Πασύλον γ', Λύσις κατὰ τοὺς
ἀρχαίους πρὸς Διοσκουρίδην α', Περὶ τῆς τοῦ ψευδομένου λύσεως πρὸς
'Αριστοκρέοντα γ', Λύσις τῶν 'Ηδύλου ὑποθετικῶν πρὸς 'Αριστοκρέοντα
καὶ 'Απολλᾶν α'. σύνταξις ἑβδόμη· Πρὸς τοὺς φάσκοντας τὰ λήμματα ἔχειν   20
ψευδῆ τὸν ψευδόμενον λόγον α', (4) Περὶ ἀποφάσκοντος πρὸς τὸν
'Αριστοκρέοντα β', Λόγοι ἀποφάσκοντες πρὸς γυμνασίαν α', Περὶ τοῦ
παρὰ μικρὸν λόγου πρὸς Στησαγόραν β', Περὶ τῶν εἰς τὰς ὑπολήψεις
λόγων καὶ ἡσυχαζόντων πρὸς 'Ονήτορα β', Περὶ τοῦ ἐγκεκαλυμμένου
πρὸς 'Αριστόβουλον β', Περὶ τοῦ διαλεληθότος πρὸς 'Αθηνάδην α'. (5)   25
σύνταξις ὀγδόη· Περὶ τοῦ οὔτιδος πρὸς Μενεκράτην η', Περὶ τῶν ἐξ ἀορίστου
καὶ ὡρισμένου λόγων πρὸς Πασύλον β', Περὶ οὔτιδος λόγου πρὸς
'Επικράτην α'. (6) σύνταξις ἐνάτη· Περὶ τῶν σοφισμάτων πρὸς 'Ηρακλείδην
καὶ Πόλλιν β', Περὶ τῶν ἀπόρων Διαλεκτικῶν λόγων πρὸς Διοσκουρίδην
ε', Πρὸς τὸ 'Αρκεσιλάου μεθόδιον πρὸς Σφαῖρον α'.   30

10 τὴν² Hübner: τῶν codd.

25 On the Elusive Argument, cf. Sedley [11], 94–5.

C Diogenes Laertius 7.44 (= 31A 8)

ὧν εἶναι ψευδομένους λόγους καὶ ἀληθεύοντας καὶ ἀποφάσκοντας σωρίτας
τε καὶ τοὺς ὁμοίους τούτοις, ἐλλιπεῖς καὶ ἀπόρους καὶ περαίνοντας, καὶ
ἐγκεκαλυμμένους κερατίνας τε καὶ οὔτιδας καὶ θερίζοντας.

1 What is the difference between Lying Arguments and Truth-telling Arguments? The former is usually taken as the name for arguments beginning 'If someone says that he is lying, and says so truly . . .' (cf. **H 5–6**). In fact, though, the evidence

Stoic logic and semantics

(*FDS* 1210–18) suggests that 'Lying Argument' is strictly used for arguments beginning 'If someone says that he is lying, and says so *falsely* . . .'. It thus seems a fair guess that the ' . . . says so truly' version is the Truth-telling Argument. If so, the two versions appear to have no philosophically interesting difference, and no doubt discussions of the 'Lying Argument' in fact applied to both.

D Diogenes Laertius 7.82.

(1) καὶ ἄποροι δέ τινές εἰσι λόγοι ἐγκεκαλυμμένοι καὶ διαλεληθότες καὶ σωρῖται καὶ κερατίδες καὶ οὔτιδες. ἔστι δὲ ἐγκεκαλυμμένος, οἷον ὁ τοιοῦτος ⟨. . .⟩ (2) ⟨ἔστι δὲ σωρίτης οἷον ὁ τοιοῦτος⟩ "οὐχὶ τὰ μὲν δύο ὀλίγα ἐστίν, οὐχὶ δὲ καὶ τὰ τρία, οὐχὶ δὲ καὶ ταῦτα μέν, οὐχὶ δὲ καὶ τὰ τέσσαρα καὶ οὕτω μέχρι τῶν δέκα· τὰ δύο ὀλίγα ἐστί· καὶ τὰ δέκα ἄρα." 5

3 suppl. Sedley   5 δέκα¹ codd.: μυρίων Egli   δέκα ἄρα codd.: μύρια ἄρα ⟨ὀλίγα ἐστίν⟩ Egli

Context: shortly after **36A**.

3–5 For a comparable Stoic use of negated conjunctions in Soritical arguments, cf. **62J**, with note.

5 No need to emend 'ten' to 'ten thousand'. Estimates of the borderline between few and many vary alarmingly, but in **H 3** it is imagined as coming somewhere in the vicinity of ten. Ten is certainly many for children in a family or courses in a meal.

E Galen, *Med. exp.* 16.1–17.3

This work survives only in Arabic. The translation in vol. 1 is that of R. Walzer, with a few improvements by A. Bruce-Watt as reported by J. Barnes [450], 33–4.

F Sextus Empiricus, *M.* 7.416

ἐπὶ γὰρ τοῦ σωρίτου τῆς ἐσχάτης καταληπτικῆς φαντασίας τῇ πρώτῃ ἀκαταλήπτῳ παρακειμένης καὶ δυσδιορίστου σχεδὸν ὑπαρχούσης, φασὶν οἱ περὶ τὸν Χρύσιππον ὅτι ἐφ' ὧν μὲν φαντασιῶν ὀλίγη τις οὕτως ἐστὶ διαφορά, στήσεται ὁ σοφὸς καὶ ἡσυχάσει, ἐφ' ὧν δὲ πλείων προσπίπτει, ἐπὶ τούτων συγκαταθήσεται τῇ ἑτέρᾳ ὡς ἀληθεῖ. 5

Context: attack on the Stoic 'cognitive impression' (see **40**).

The difficult argument appears to go as follows. Let '50 are few' be the last cognitive impression, and (this appears to have fallen out of the text here, but is made explicit at ibid. 419) '51 are few' the first non-cognitive impression. By applying the Stoic principle cited in the text, the sage may assent to '50 are few', as being far removed from the non-cognitive '10,000 are few.' But he cannot then reasonably withhold assent from '51 are few', which is not significantly different and is still far removed from '10,000 is few'. And once he has assented to one non-cognitive impression, he cannot avoid assenting to *any* non-cognitive impression, including '10,000 are few'. For, by analogy with their 'All wrong actions are equal' (**590**), the Stoics should hold that 'All non-cognitive impressions are equal.' (Note that the slide to '10,000 are few' is not, as commonly assumed, itself achieved by a Sorites.)

224

The argument is a curious one, and may rest on a misunderstanding. The Stoic principle cited in the text is far more plausibly interpreted as *dis*allowing assent to the last cognitive impression, '50 are few.'
For the ἡσυχάζειν principle, cf. PH 2.253, and H 3. The latter's greater precision in placing ἡσυχάζειν *before* the marginal cases begin deserves credence because of the passage's overall superiority in detail and accuracy. For ἡσυχάζειν as a dialectical tactic against a *non*-soritical sophism, see S.

G Chrysippus, Quaest. log. III, 9.7–12 (SVF 2.298, part)

καὶ ἕως τίνος δεῖ ταῦ|θ' ὑπακούε[ι]ν παρέξει ἐπίστα|σιν κατὰ τὸν παρὰ μικρὸν | λόγον. οἷον ἐ[πὶ] τοῦ [εἰ] δεῖ πε|ρὶ τῆς ἀποκρίσεως τεμεῖν· πι|θανὸν δὲ μη[δὲ] τοῦτο ὑπά[ρ]χειν.

Context: a series of logical perplexities, listed without definitive solutions.
The above text slightly modifies the earlier reading of D.N. Sedley, reported by Barnes [450], n. 68, the improvement being owed to palaeographical advice from Catherine Atherton. The condition of the papyrus is poor, and even the modified version should be treated with caution.
    1 ἐπίστα|σιν 'Puzzlement' – a central notion in the book.
    1–2 παρὰ μικρὸν | λόγον The Sorites; cf. B 22–3.
    2 τεμεῖν Comparison with B 3 shows that τομή was a device, favoured by some, for the solution of puzzles. Our suggestion in vol. 1, 229 that it involves the analysis of a single proposition into constituent propositions is purely conjectural. Barnes' 'make a cut-off point' is tempting, but might be hard to square with B 3.
    2–3 If the final sentence is assumed to have been restored correctly, it *may* mean 'But it is plausible that not even this is the case.'

H Cicero, Acad. 2.92–6

(1) sed quoniam tantum in ea arte ponitis, videte ne contra vos tota nata sit; quae primo progressa festive tradit elementa loquendi et ambiguorum intellegentiam concludendique rationem, tum paucis additis venit ad soritas, lubricum sane et periculosum locum, quod tu modo dicebas esse vitiosum interrogandi genus. quid ergo istius vitii num nostra culpa est? (2) rerum   5
natura nullam nobis dedit cognitionem finium, ut ulla in re statuere possimus quatenus, nec hoc in acervo tritici solum, unde nomen est, sed nulla omnino in re minutatim interrogati, dives pauper clarus obscurus sit, multa pauca magna parva longa brevia lata angusta, quanto aut addito aut dempto certum respondeamus non habemus. (3) "at vitiosi sunt soritae." frangite igitur eos si   10
potestis, ne molesti sint; erunt enim nisi cavetis. "cautum est" inquit; "placet enim Chrysippo, cum gradatim interrogetur verbi causa tria pauca sint anne multa, aliquanto prius quam ad multa perveniat quiescere" (id est quod ab his dicitur ἡσυχάζειν). "per me vel stertas licet" inquit Carneades "non modo quiescas. sed quid proficit? sequitur enim qui te ex somno excitet et eodem   15
modo interroget: "quo in numero conticuisti, si ad eum numerum unum

addidero, multane erunt?" progrediere rursus quoad videbitur. quid plura;
hoc enim fateris, neque ultimum te paucorum neque primum multorum
respondere posse. cuius generis error ita manat, ut non videam quo non possit
accedere. "nihil me laedit" inquit; "ego enim ut agitator callidus priusquam ad   20
finem veniam equos sustinebo, eoque magis si locus is quo ferentur equi
praeceps erit. sic me" inquit "ante sustineo nec diutius captiose interroganti
respondeo." si habes quod liqueat neque respondes, superbe; si non habes, ne
tu quidem percipis. si quia obscura, concedo; sed negas te usque ad obscura
progredi; ⟨in⟩ inlustribus igitur rebus insistis. si id tantum modo ut taceas,   25
nihil adsequeris; quid enim ad illum qui te captare vult, utrum tacentem
inretiat te an loquentem? sin autem usque ad novem verbi gratia sine
dubitatione respondes pauca esse, in decumo insistis, etiam a certis et
inlustrioribus cohibes adsensum; hoc idem me in obscuris facere non sinis. (4)
nihil igitur te contra soritas ars ista adiuvat, quae nec augendi nec minuendi   30
quid aut primum sit aut postremum docet. quid quod eadem illa ars quasi
Penelopae telam retexens tollit ad extremum superiora: utrum ea vestra an
nostra culpa est? (5) nempe fundamentum dialecticae est, quidquid enuntietur
(id autem appellant ἀξίωμα, quod est quasi effatum) aut verum esse aut
falsum. quid igitur haec vera an falsa sunt: "si te mentiri dicis idque verum   35
dicis, mentiris ⟨an⟩ verum dicis?" haec scilicet inexplicabilia esse dicitis; quod
est odiosius quam illa quae nos non conprehensa et non percepta dicimus – sed
hoc omitto, illud quaero: si ista explicari non possunt nec eorum ullum
iudicium invenitur, ut respondere possitis verane an falsa sint, ubi est illa
definitio, effatum esse id quod aut verum aut falsum sit? (6) rebus sumptis   40
adiungam ex iis ⟨eiusdem generis conclusionibus quarum una sit recta, ceteras
ex his⟩ sequendas esse, alias inprobandas quae sint in genere contrario. quo
modo igitur hoc conclusum esse iudicas: "si dicis nunc lucere et verum dicis,
⟨lucet; dicis autem nunc lucere et verum dicis;⟩ lucet igitur"? probatis certe
genus et rectissime conclusum dicitis, itaque in docendo eum primum   45
concludendi modum traditis. aut quidquid igitur eodem modo concluditur
probabitis, aut ars ista nulla est. vide ergo hanc conclusionem probaturusne sis:
"si dicis te mentiri verumque dicis, mentiris; dicis autem te mentiri verumque
dicis; mentiris igitur." qui potes hanc non probare, cum probaveris eiusdem
generis superiorem? haec Chrysippea sunt, ne ab ipso quidem dissoluta.   50

41–2 suppl. Sedley   44 suppl. Manutius

Context: Cicero's speech on behalf of the New Academy, here attacking Antiochus'
faith in Stoic dialectic. The material probably derives from Clitomachus (on whom
see vol. 1, 448) and can be taken as authentically Carneadean.

11–13   Here, as in the simile at 20–3, the policy is: (a) stop *some way* before the
true–false borderline. At 24–5 it is: (b) stop before the unclear cases. This latter Cicero
at 25–9 interprets as: (c) stop *some way* before the unclear cases. He appears to be
justified, for only thus can (a) and (b) come out as equivalent. That stopping before the
borderline requires stopping *somewhere* before the unclear cases is obvious, since any

unclear case could be beyond the borderline. But if (b) were interpreted as 'Stop at the last clear case', that might sometimes involve stopping at a point adjacent to the true–false borderline, contrary to (a).

(c) may itself appear problematic. There could surely be no possible risk in going on to assent to any remaining *clear* cases (cf. 27–9). Chrysippus must be envisaging a second Sorites in which we slide unwittingly, not from true to false, but from clear to unclear cases. There *are* a last clear case and a first unclear case (**F**), but the unclear case may be lent a spurious air of clarity when considered in conjunction with the adjacent and barely distinguishable clear case. A Sorites pushes us nearer and nearer to the borderline between clear and unclear, and therefore, Chrysippus might say, the only safe precaution is to stop at a case which appears clear when considered independently of the Sorites context (that may indeed be the point made in the final words of **F**). That the stopping point is arbitrarily chosen does not matter. Similarly the question 'How near to a precipice is it safe to drive?' may in theory admit of a scientifically exact answer, but the obscurity or complexity of that answer renders prudent the simpler advice, 'Stay at least five yards away from it.'

35–6   For the form of the argument, see on **C**.

50   Cf. 36, *inexplicabilia*. It is probably a mistake, then, to look for any definitive Chrysippean solution to the Lying Argument. One is sometimes claimed at *Quaest. log.* III, 10.12–18 (*SVF* 2, pp. 106–7), but there is insufficient context there to justify the claim, and the aporetic nature of the work as a whole (see 'Context' note on **G**) is against it.

I Plutarch, *Comm. not.* 1059D–E

ἐμοὶ δοκεῖ μετὰ πλείστης ἐπιμελείας καὶ δεινότητος οὗτος ὁ ἀνὴρ
ἀνατρέπειν καὶ καταβάλλειν τὴν συνήθειαν, ὡς ἔνια γοῦν καὐτοὶ μαρτυρ-
οῦσιν οἱ τὸν ἄνδρα σεμνύνοντες ὅταν αὐτῷ περὶ τοῦ ψευδομένου μάχωνται.
τὸ γὰρ ἀορίστων συμπεπλεγμένον τι δι' ἀντικειμένων μὴ φάναι ψεῦδος
εὐπόρως εἶναι λόγους δὲ πάλιν αὖ φάναι τινὰς ἀληθῆ τὰ λήμματα καὶ τὰς   5
ἀγωγὰς ὑγιεῖς ἔχοντας, ἔτι καὶ τὰ ἀντικείμενα τῶν συμπερασμάτων ἔχειν
ἀληθῆ, ποίαν ἔννοιαν ἀποδείξεως ἢ τίνα πίστεως οὐκ ἀνατρέπει πρόληψιν;
τὸν μέν γε πολύποδά φασι τὰς πλεκτάνας· αὐτοῦ περιβιβρώσκειν ὥρᾳ
χειμῶνος, ἡ δὲ Χρυσίππου διαλεκτικὴ τὰ κυριώτατα μέρη καὶ τὰς ἀρχὰς
αὐτῆς ἀναιροῦσα καὶ περικόπτουσα τίνα τῶν ἄλλων ἐννοιῶν ἀπολέλοιπεν   10
ἀνύποπτον;

2 καὐτοὶ Cherniss: καίτοι codd.: καὶ αὐτοὶ Wyttenbach   4 ἀορίστων scripsimus: ὦ ἄριστε codd.: ἀορίστως Wyttenbach

Context: opening moves of an attack on Chrysippus for violating the 'common conceptions'.

2–3   These internal Stoic critics are unidentified, but one might think of Antipater (cf. **36C 7, D, H; 38A 4**).

4 ἀορίστων   Cf. Cicero, *Fat.* 15, *negationes infinitarum coniunctionum*.

5–7   The inference in question will presumably be that at **H** 48–9.

Stoic logic and semantics

J Epictetus, *Diss.* 1.7.1, 10–21

περὶ τῆς χρείας τῶν μεταπιπτόντων καὶ ὑποθετικῶν καὶ τῶν ὁμοίων

(1) ἡ περὶ τοὺς μεταπίπτοντας καὶ ὑποθετικούς, ἔτι δὲ τῷ ἡρωτῆσθαι περαίνοντας καὶ πάντας ἁπλῶς τοὺς τοιούτους λόγους πραγματεία λανθάνει τοὺς πολλοὺς περὶ καθήκοντος οὖσα. (2) [=31R] (3) δεῖ δὲ μαθεῖν πῶς τί τισιν ἀκόλουθον γίνεται, καὶ πότε μὲν ἓν ἑνὶ ἀκολουθεῖ πότε δὲ 5 πλείοσιν κοινῇ. μή ποτε οὖν καὶ τοῦτο ἀνάγκη προσλαβεῖν τὸν μέλλοντα ἐν λόγῳ συνετῶς ἀναστραφήσεσθαι καὶ αὐτόν τε ἀποδείξειν ἕκαστα ἀποδόντα καὶ τοῖς ἀποδεικνύουσι παρακολουθήσειν μηδ' ὑπὸ τῶν σοφιζομένων διαπλανηθήσεσθαι ὡς ἀποδεικνυόντων; οὐκοῦν ἐλήλυθεν ἡμῖν περὶ τῶν συναγόντων λόγων καὶ τρόπων πραγματεία καὶ γυμνασία καὶ 10 ἀναγκαία πέφηνεν. (4) ἀλλὰ δὴ ἔστιν ἐφ' ὧν δεδώκαμεν ὑγιῶς τὰ λήμματα καὶ συμβαίνει τουτὶ ἐξ αὐτῶν· ψεῦδος δὲ ὂν οὐδὲν ἧττον συμβαίνει. τί οὖν μοι καθήκει ποιεῖν; προσδέχεσθαι τὸ ψεῦδος; καὶ πῶς οἷόν τε; ἀλλὰ λέγειν ὅτι "οὐχ ὑγιῶς παρεχώρησα τὰ ὡμολογημένα"; καὶ μὴν οὐδὲ τοῦτο δίδοται. ἀλλ' ὅτι "οὐ συμβαίνει διὰ τῶν παρακεχωρημένων"; ἀλλ' οὐδὲ 15 τοῦτο δίδοται. τί οὖν ἐπὶ τούτων ποιητέον; ἢ μή ποτε ὡς οὐκ ἀρκεῖ τὸ δανείσασθαι πρὸς τὸ ἔτι ὀφείλειν, ἀλλὰ δεῖ προσεῖναι καὶ τὸ ἐπιμένειν ἐπὶ τοῦ δανείου καὶ μὴ διαλελύσθαι αὐτό, οὕτως οὐκ ἀρκεῖ πρὸς τὸ δεῖν παραχωρεῖν τὸ ἐπιφερόμενον, τὸ δεδωκέναι τὰ λήμματα, δεῖ δ' ἐπιμένειν ἐπὶ τῆς παραχωρήσεως αὐτῶν. καὶ δὴ μενόντων μὲν αὐτῶν εἰς τέλος ὁποῖα 20 παρεχωρήθη πᾶσα ἀνάγκη ἡμᾶς ἐπὶ τῆς παραχωρήσεως ἐπιμένειν καὶ τὸ ἀκόλουθον αὐτοῖς προσδέχεσθαι, ⟨μὴ μενόντων δέ, οὐκέτι.⟩ οὐδὲ γὰρ ἡμῖν ἔτι οὐδὲ καθ' ἡμᾶς συμβαίνει τοῦτο τὸ ἐπιφερόμενον, ἐπειδὴ τῆς συγχωρήσεως τῶν λημμάτων ἀπέστημεν. δεῖ οὖν καὶ τὰ τοιαῦτα τῶν λημμάτων ἱστορῆσαι καὶ τὴν τοιαύτην μεταβολήν τε καὶ μετάπτωσιν 25 αὐτῶν, καθ' ἣν ἐν αὐτῇ τῇ ἐρωτήσει ἢ τῇ ἀποκρίσει ἢ τῷ συλλελογίσθαι ἤ τινι ἄλλῳ τοιούτῳ λαμβάνοντα τὰς μεταπτώσεις ἀφορμὴν παρέχει τοῖς ἀνοήτοις τοῦ ταράσσεσθαι μὴ βλέπουσι τὸ ἀκόλουθον. τίνος ἕνεκα; ἵν' ἐν τῷ τόπῳ τούτῳ μὴ παρὰ τὸ καθῆκον μηδ' εἰκῇ μηδὲ συγκεχυμένως ἀναστρεφώμεθα. 30

2 τῷ Parisinus gr. 1959: om. cett.   22 supplevimus

2–3 For μεταπίπτοντες and τῷ ἡρωτῆσθαι περαίνοντες, cf. **A 5, 9, K**. **ὑποθετικούς** Hypotheses are not propositions (D.L. 7.66), but can function as premises in arguments. This raises issues about the status both of the hypothetical arguments (D.L. 7.196) and of the hypotheses themselves (Epictetus, *Diss.* 1.7.22–9).

K Simplicius, *In Ar. Phys.* 1299,36–1300,10 (*FDS* 1025)

ἐκ δὴ τούτων τῶν λόγων, φησὶν ὁ Ἀλέξανδρος, δυνατὸν ὁρμώμενον δεικνύναι τὰ παρὰ τοῖς Στωικοῖς ἀξιώματα, ἃ μεταπίπτοντά τινες λέγουσιν ἀπεριγράφως, μὴ ὄντα τοιαῦτα. ἔστι δὲ ταῦτα τοιαῦτα· "εἰ ζῇ Δίων,

ζήσεται Δίων." τοῦτο γὰρ εἰ καὶ ἀληθές ἐστι νῦν ἀρχόμενον ἀπὸ ἀληθοῦς
τοῦ "ζῇ Δίων" καὶ λῆγον εἰς ἀληθὲς τὸ "ζήσεται", ἀλλ' ἔσται ποτέ, ὅτε   5
τῆς προσλήψεως ἀληθοῦς οὔσης τῆς "ἀλλὰ μὴν ζῇ Δίων" μεταπεσεῖται τὸ
συνημμένον εἰς ψεῦδος τῷ ἔσεσθαί ποτε, ὅτε ἀληθοῦς ὄντος ἔτι τοῦ "ζῇ
Δίων", οὐκ ἔσται ἀληθὲς τὸ "καὶ ζήσεται", οὗ μὴ ὄντος ἀληθοῦς τὸ ὅλον
συνημμένον γίνοιτο ἂν ψεῦδος μεταπῖπτον· οὐ γὰρ ἀεί, ὅτε τὸ "ζῇ"
ἀληθές, καὶ τὸ "ζήσεται", ἐπεὶ οὕτως ἀθάνατος ἂν εἴη ὁ Δίων. οὐ μὴν   10
ἔσται ὁρίσαντας εἰπεῖν, πότε οὐκ ἀληθὲς ἔσται ζῶντος αὐτοῦ τὸ
"ζήσεται". διὸ καὶ ἐν ἀπεριγράφῳ καὶ ἀορίστῳ χρόνῳ λέγουσι γίνεσθαι
τὴν τῶν τοιούτων ἀξιωμάτων μετάπτωσιν.

Context: discussion of Aristotle's analysis of the instant of change. It disposes of the
Stoic example cited: there is no last instant at which Dion is alive.

2   Unusually, we have talk here of changing propositions, not arguments (contrast
A 9, J). But of course changing arguments are so called by courtesy of propositions
within them which change their truth value. Besides, Alexander's mention of the
'additional premise' at 6 shows that he does in fact have arguments in mind.

4–9   The conditional is treated as subject to the Philonian criterion of soundness;
cf. 35.

L Lucian, Vit. auct. 22 (SVF 2.287, part)

ΧΡΥΣΙΠΠΟΣ καὶ ἄλλα γάρ σε διδάξομαι θαυμασιώτερα – τὸν θερίζοντα καὶ τὸν
κυριεύοντα καὶ ἐπὶ πᾶσι τὴν Ἠλέκτραν καὶ τὸν ἐγκεκαλυμμένον . . . Ἠλέκτραν μὲν
ἐκείνην . . . ἢ τὰ αὐτὰ οἶδέ τε ἅμα καὶ οὐκ οἶδεν· παρεστῶτος γὰρ αὐτῇ τοῦ Ὀρέστου ἔτι
ἀγνώστος, οἶδε μὲν Ὀρέστην, ὅτι ἀδελφὸς αὐτῆς, ὅτι δὲ οὗτος Ὀρέστης ἀγνοεῖ. τὸν δ'
αὖ ἐγκεκαλυμμένον καὶ πάνυ θαυμαστὸν ἀκούσῃ λόγον. ἀπόκριναι γάρ   5
μοι, τὸν πατέρα οἶσθα τὸν σεαυτοῦ;
ΩΝΗΤΗΣ ναί.
ΧΡΥΣ. τί οὖν; ἢν σοι παραστήσας τινὰ ἐγκεκαλυμμένον ἔρωμαι "τοῦτον
οἶσθα;" τί φήσεις;
ΩΝ. δηλαδὴ ἀγνοεῖν.   10
ΧΡΥΣ. ἀλλὰ μὴν αὐτὸς οὗτος ἦν ὁ πατὴρ ὁ σός, ὥστε εἰ τοῦτον ἀγνοεῖς,
δῆλος εἶ τὸν πατέρα τὸν σὸν ἀγνοῶν.

Context: Chrysippus, up for auction, is displaying his philosophical skills.
For the ἐγκεκαλυμμένος, cf. Sedley [11], 95–6. The Electra is apparently just a
variant of it.

M Diogenes Laertius 7.75

πιθανὸν δέ ἐστιν ἀξίωμα τὸ ἄγον εἰς συγκατάθεσιν, οἷον "εἴ τίς τι ἔτεκεν,
ἐκείνη ἐκείνου μήτηρ ἐστί". ψεῦδος δὲ τοῦτο· οὐ γὰρ ἡ ὄρνις ᾠοῦ ἐστι
μήτηρ.

Context: immediately following 35A.
In Stoicism, πιθανός is often 'specious', of fallacies (as here), but also 'convincing'
or 'cogent', of presumed truths. See further, 39G; 42I; 69D 5.

Stoic logic and semantics

N Gellius 11.12.1–3 (*SVF* 2.152; Diodorus fr. 7 Giannantoni, part)

(1) Chrysippus ait omne uerbum ambiguum natura esse, quoniam ex eodem duo uel plura accipi possunt. (2) Diodorus autem, cui Crono cognomentum fuit, "nullum" inquit "uerbum est ambiguum, nec quisquam ambiguum dicit aut sentit, nec aliud dici uideri debet, quam quod se dicere sentit is qui dicit. at cum ego" inquit "aliud sensi, tu aliud accepisti, obscure magis dictum uideri   5 potest quam ambigue; ambigui enim uerbi natura illa esse debuit, ut, qui id diceret, duo uel plura diceret. nemo autem duo uel plura dicit, qui se sensit unum dicere."

O Ammonius, *In Ar. De int.* 38,17–20 (Diodorus fr. 7 Giannantoni, part)

. . . ὡς οὐκ ἀποδεξόμεθα τὸν Διαλεκτικὸν Διόδωρον πᾶσαν οἰόμενον φωνὴν σημαντικὴν εἶναι καὶ πρὸς πίστιν τούτου καλέσαντα τῶν ἑαυτοῦ τινα οἰκετῶν "'Ἀλλαμὴν" καὶ ἄλλον ἄλλῳ συνδέσμῳ.

Context: comment on Aristotle's theory of signification.

That 'every utterance is capable of signifying' depends in turn on Diodorus' equation of meaning with speaker's meaning (**N**), so that the slave example (cf. Plato, *Crat.* 384d) ultimately supports this latter thesis. (Although the example illustrates the randomness of names, the name is not chosen *entirely* at random. Diodorus was a master logician, and ἀλλὰ μήν was a standard connective for introducing an additional premise, e.g. **36A**.)

P Diogenes Laertius 7.62

ἀμφιβολία δέ ἐστι λέξις δύο ἢ καὶ πλείονα πράγματα σημαίνουσα λεκτικῶς καὶ κυρίως καὶ κατὰ τὸ αὐτὸ ἔθος, ὥσθ' ἅμα τὰ πλείονα ἐκδέξασθαι κατὰ ταύτην τὴν λέξιν.

Context: survey of Stoic dialectic (see on **33A**).

Q Galen, *Soph.* 4 (*SVF* 2.153, part)

(1) τὰς δὲ διαφορὰς τῶν λεγομένων ἀμφιβολιῶν αὐτὰς ληπτέον· εἰσί γε πρὸς τῶν χαριεστέρων λεγόμεναι τὸν ἀριθμὸν η'. (2) μία μέν, ἣν κοινὴν ὀνομάζουσι τοῦ τε ⟨δι⟩ῃρημένου καὶ τοῦ ⟨ἀ⟩διαιρέτου, οἵα ἐστὶν ἡ "ΑΥΛΗΤΡΙΣ ΠΕΣΟΥΣΑ"· κοινὴ γὰρ αὕτη τοῦ τε αὐλητρὶς ὀνόματος καὶ τοῦ ⟨δι⟩ῃρημένου. (3) δευτέρα δὲ παρὰ τὴν ἐν τοῖς ἁπλοῖς ⟨ὁμωνυμίαν⟩,   5 οἷον "ἀνδρεῖος", ἢ γὰρ χιτὼν ἢ ἄνθρωπος· (4) τρίτον δὲ παρὰ τὴν ἐν τοῖς συνθέτοις ὁμωνυμίαν, οἷον "ἄνθρωπός ἐστιν"· ἀμφίβολος γὰρ ὁ λόγος, εἴτε τὴν οὐσίαν εἴτε τὴν πτῶσιν εἶναι σημαίνει. (5) τέταρτον δέ ἐστι παρὰ τὴν ἔλλειψιν, ὡς "τίνος σὺ εἶ;" καὶ γὰρ ἐλλείπει τὸ διὰ μέσου, οἷον δεσπότου ἢ πατρός. (6) πέμπτον δὲ παρὰ τὸν πλεονασμόν, ὥσπερ ἡ   10 τοιαύτη "ἀπηγόρευσεν αὐτῷ. μὴ πλεῖν"· τὸ γὰρ "μὴ" προσκείμενον ἀμφίδοξον ποιεῖ τὸ πᾶν, εἴτε τὸ πλεῖν ἀπηγόρευσεν εἴτε τὸ μὴ πλεῖν. (7)

ἕκτην φασὶν εἶναι τὴν μὴ διασαφοῦσαν τί μετὰ τίνος ἄσημον μόριον
τέτακται, ὡς ἐν τῷ "ΚΑΙΝΥΚΕΝΗΠΑΡΕΛΑΣΣΕΝ"· τὸ γὰρ ⟨η⟩ στοιχεῖον
ἂν γένοιτο ⟨ἢ πρῶτον ἢ τελευταῖον ἢ⟩ διαζευκτικόν. (8) ἑβδόμη δέ ἐστιν ἡ   15
μὴ δηλοῦσα τί μετὰ τίνος τέτακται σημαντικὸν μόριον, ὡς ἐν τῷ
"πεντήκοντ' ἀνδρῶν ἑκατὸν λίπε δῖος 'Αχιλλεύς". (9) ὀγδόη ⟨δ' ἡ⟩ μὴ
δηλοῦσα τί ἐπὶ τί ἀναφέρεται, ὡς ἐν τῷ "Δίων ⟨ἐστὶ καὶ⟩ Θέων" εὖροις
ἄν· ἄδηλον γάρ ἐστιν, εἴτε ἐπὶ τὴν ἀμφοτέρων ὕπαρξιν ἀναφέρεται εἴτε ἐπὶ
τοιοῦτον οἷον ὁ Δίων Θέων ἐστὶν ἢ πάλιν.   20

3 ⟨δι⟩ηρημένου Ebbesen: εἰρημένου cod.   ⟨ἀ⟩διαιρέτου Ebbesen   5 ⟨δι⟩ηρημένου Kalbfleisch:
εἰρημένου cod.   ⟨ὁμωνυμίαν⟩ Arnim   9 ὡς "τίνος συ εἶ;" Sedley: ὅ ἐστιν ὡς συὶ cod.: ⟨ὡς⟩ σός
ἐστιν [ὡς] υἱός Gabler   14 Il. 23.382 rest. Arnim: καὶ νῦν καὶ μὴ παρέλασε cod.   14–15
supplementa secundum Gabler   17 secundum Ar. Soph. el. 166a37–8 rest. ed. Charteriana: πεντήκοντ'
ἀνδρῶν ρ' λείπεται cod.   18–19 Δίων–ἂν Sedley: Δίων Θέων εὖρω cod.: Δίων Θέων ἐστί ed.
Charteriana

Context: Galen's defence of his own classification of linguistic fallacies against the Stoic
one.

For detailed commentary, cf. Edlow [453] and Ebbesen [454]. The latter usefully
compares Theon, Prog. 81,30–83,13 (in Spengel, Rhetores Graeci II), which seems to
derive ultimately from the same classification.

The text is in poor shape. Some deficiencies may be attributable to Galen's
memory, especially the two verse examples at 14 and 17. There is little doubt what the
original hexameters were, but note that the MS reading at 14 just about scans, and
although it gives poor sense, the unemended analytic comment is appropriate to it
(because the MS μή in 14 could be read as μ' ἤ). Again, the MS reading in 17, although
not verse, conveys the gist (perhaps read λείπει or λείπονται for λείπεται) of a line
already differently misquoted in chapter 1 of the work. So the emendations which we
accept at 14–15 and 17 can be taken as an attempt to restore, not necessarily Galen's
text, but the Stoic original on which it is based.

8 πτῶσιν   The genus of which 'noun' is a species – see vol. 1, 201. For οὐσίαν, the
material entity, see especially 28. The same example, the double signification of homo,
is used by Augustine, De magistro 8 (22) 45–52, p. 181. The ambiguity 'in complex
expressions' is not ambiguity due to the construction itself (that is left for types 4–8),
but still homonymy of a single word. How then does it differ from the preceding
type? Probably 'equivocation in simple expressions', as in ἀνδρεῖος, covers that kind
which exists in simple expressions taken in isolation but is eliminated by the context;
whereas 'equivocation in complex expressions' is a kind which may persist even
within a broader linguistic context.

9   Gabler's more ingenious restoration (see apparatus) tries to identify the
ambiguity with the sophism discussed by Aristotle at Soph. el. 179b39–180a7. But (a)
it leaves τὸ διὰ μέσου with no obvious sense or function. And (b) it is based on the
dubious expectation that a sophism rather than a routine example will be used to
illustrate the type of ambiguity in question: against this, cf. the pedestrian example at
7, where the sophism of R was available if wanted.

13–15   The example, whether on the MS or on the emended reading, does not
suggest much difference from the species of equivocation illustrated at 2–5. But it does
contrast usefully with that at 15–17, the difference indicated being that between

construal of phonetic elements and construal of semantic elements. Apparently in this context conjunctions, like ἤ, are not considered 'semantic' – cf. **O**.

17–20   Our emendation to the example is designed to fit the analysis which follows. What point does τί ἐπὶ τί ἀναφέρεται make? If this is meant to be interestingly different from the preceding type of ambiguity, one would expect the point to be that it is unclear which noun is the subject and which (if any) the complement. But if so, the use of ἀναφέρεται in 19 must be admitted to be untechnical and careless.

R   Diogenes Laertius 7.187

"εἴ τι λαλεῖς, τοῦτο διὰ τοῦ στόματός σου διέρχεται· ἄμαξαν δὲ λαλεῖς· ἄμαξα ἄρα διὰ τοῦ στόματός σου διέρχεται."

Context: sophisms used by Chrysippus.
Cf. **33O** for virtually the same sophism.

S   Simplicius, *In Ar. Cat.* 24,9–21 (*FDS* 1257)

καὶ λέγουσιν καλῶς, ὅτι ἀπὸ τῶν πραγμάτων γίνεται δῆλα τὸ ὁμώνυμα, ὅταν τοῦ αὐτοῦ ὀνόματος ῥηθέντος ἐγὼ μὲν ἄλλην ἔννοιαν, σὺ δὲ ἄλλην περὶ τοῦ ὀνόματος προβαλλώμεθα, ὥσπερ τοῦ κύων ὀνόματος ῥηθέντος ἐγὼ μὲν τὸν χερσαῖον, σὺ δὲ τὸν θαλάττιον ἐννοήσειας. διὸ καὶ ἐν τοῖς παρ' ὁμωνυμίαν συλλογισμοῖς ἡσυχάζειν οἱ διαλεκτικοὶ παρακελεύονται, ἕως ἂν ἐπ' ἄλλο σημαινόμενον ὁ ἐρωτῶν μεταγάγῃ τὸ   5
ὄνομα· οἷον, εἴ τις ἐρωτᾷ εἰ ὁ χιτὼν ἀνδρεῖος, εἰ τύχοι ἀνδρεῖος ὤν, συγχωρησόμεθα· κἂν ἐρωτήσῃ εἰ ὁ ἀνδρεῖος εὔψυχος, καὶ τοῦτο συγχωρησόμεθα, ἀληθὲς γάρ· εἰ δὲ συναγάγῃ ὅτι ὁ χιτὼν ἄρα εὔψυχος, ἐνταῦθα τὴν ὁμωνυμίαν τοῦ ἀνδρείου διαστείλασθαι καὶ δεῖξαι [τὴν ἀνδρείαν ἤγουν τὴν εὐψυχίαν] ὅτι ἄλλως μὲν ἐπὶ τοῦ χιτῶνος, ἄλλως δὲ ἐπὶ τοῦ τὴν ἀνδρείαν   10
ἔχοντος λέγεται. ὥστε τὰ πράγματα κυρίως, οὐχὶ τὰ ὀνόματα ποιεῖ τὴν ὁμωνυμίαν.

5 μεταγάγῃ J: ἐπαγάγῃ Κν

Context: commentary on *Cat.* 1a1, the definition of ὁμώνυμα. The puzzle addressed is why Aristotle's discussion focuses on the homonymous things themselves, not on the linguistic aspects of homonymy.

    4 οἱ διαλεκτικοί   Here, as often, the term will refer primarily to Stoic logicians: the tactic of ἡσυχάζειν (4) is the hallmark of Chrysippus (cf. **F**, **H**).

38 Modality

A   Epictetus, *Diss.* 2.19.1–5 (Diodorus fr. 24 Giannantoni, part)

(1) ὁ κυριεύων λόγος ἀπὸ τοιούτων τινῶν ἀφορμῶν ἠρωτῆσθαι φαίνεται· (2) κοινῆς γὰρ οὔσης μάχης τοῖς τρισὶ τούτοις πρὸς ἄλληλα, τῷ [τὸ] "πᾶν παρεληλυθὸς ἀληθὲς ἀναγκαῖον εἶναι" καὶ τῷ "δυνατῷ ἀδύνατον μὴ ἀκολουθεῖν" καὶ τῷ "δυνατὸν εἶναι, ὃ οὔτ' ἔστιν ἀληθὲς οὔτ' ἔσται", (3) συνιδὼν τὴν μάχην ταύτην ὁ Διόδωρος τῇ τῶν πρώτων δυεῖν πιθανότητι   5
συνεχρήσατο πρὸς παράστασιν τοῦ "μηδὲν εἶναι δυνατόν, ὃ οὔτ' ἔστιν

ἀληθὲς οὔτ᾽ ἔσται". (4) λοιπὸν ὁ μέν τις ταῦτα τηρήσει τῶν δυεῖν, ὅτι ἔστι
τέ τι δυνατόν, ὃ οὔτ᾽ ἔστιν ἀληθὲς οὔτ᾽ ἔσται, καὶ δυνατῷ ἀδύνατον οὐκ
ἀκολουθεῖ· οὐ πᾶν δὲ παρεληλυθὸς ἀληθὲς ἀναγκαῖόν ἐστιν, καθάπερ οἱ
περὶ Κλεάνθην φέρεσθαι δοκοῦσιν, οἷς ἐπὶ πολὺ συνηγόρησεν Ἀντίπα-   10
τρος. (5) οἱ δὲ τἆλλα δύο, ὅτι δυνατόν τ᾽ ἐστίν, ὃ οὔτ᾽ ἔστιν ἀληθὲς οὔτ᾽
ἔσται, καὶ πᾶν παρεληλυθὸς ἀληθὲς ἀναγκαῖόν ἐστιν, δυνατῷ δ᾽ ἀδύνατον
ἀκολουθεῖ. (6) τὰ τρία δ᾽ ἐκεῖνα τηρῆσαι ἀμήχανον διὰ τὸ κοινὴν εἶναι
αὐτῶν μάχην. ἂν οὖν τίς μου πύθηται· "σὺ δὲ ποῖα αὐτῶν τηρεῖς;"
ἀποκρινοῦμαι πρὸς αὐτὸν ὅτι οὐκ οἶδα· παρείληφα δ᾽ ἱστορίαν τοιαύτην,   15
ὅτι Διόδωρος μὲν ἐκεῖνα ἐτήρει, οἱ δὲ περὶ Πανθοίδην οἶμαι καὶ Κλεάνθην
τὰ ἄλλα, οἱ δὲ περὶ Χρύσιππον τὰ ἄλλα.

On the Master Argument the best philosophical studies are perhaps those of Prior
[456] and Denyer [463], and an invaluable survey of modern scholarship can be found
in Giannantoni [462].

To Denyer we owe the following two points. First, any successful reconstruction
must so interpret and use Proposition 1 that it will come out true when restated in
terms of Diodorus' own eventual definition of 'necessary' as 'what, being true, will
not be false' (C). Second, the inference from 'It neither is nor will be the case that p' to
'It has been false that it would be the case that p' is debatable. On a continuum theory
of time, like that of the Stoics (see **50A**), it could be argued that now might be the first
time at which 'not-p' is the case and that, if so, there was *no* preceding instant at which
'It will be the case that p' was false. Diodorus (**11i** 18–21) could himself avoid this by
his thesis of time minima. The Stoics, on the other hand, unless they just missed the
relevance of the objection, may have rejected it on the ground that 'It has been false
that it would be the case that p', even if of indeterminate truth value at the outset, has
become true by the stage in the argument at which it is appealed to. For such 'changing'
arguments, cf. **37**, especially **J–K**.

Beyond this, in formulating the brief reconstruction in vol. 1 we have been
motivated above all by the consideration that the argument, which was a favourite
subject of learned conversation even at dinner (Plutarch, *Qu. conv.* 615A, *De san. tu.*
133B–C; Epictetus, *Diss.* 2.19.8), cannot have been unduly complex in structure.

4 ἀκολουθεῖν   Cf. on **35B** 4–5.
10   For Cleanthes, who wrote a work on this argument (ibid. 2.19.9), cf. 16–17
and E 25.
16   For Panthoides the Dialectician, see also **37B 2**, and D.L. 5.68.

B Alexander, *In Ar. An. pr.* 183,34–184,10 (Diodorus fr. 27 Giannantoni,
part)

(1) δύναται λέγειν καὶ περὶ τῶν δυνατῶν, τοῦ τε, ὃ Διοδώρειον λέγεται, ὃ ἢ
ἔστιν ἢ ἔσται· τὸ γὰρ ἢ ὂν ἢ ἐσόμενον πάντως δυνατὸν μόνον ἐκεῖνος
ἐτίθετο. τὸ γὰρ ἐμὲ ἐν Κορίνθῳ γενέσθαι δυνατὸν κατ᾽ αὐτόν, εἰ εἴην ἐν
Κορίνθῳ, ἢ εἰ πάντως μέλλοιμι ἔσεσθαι· εἰ δὲ μὴ γενοίμην, οὐδὲ δυνατὸν
ἦν· καὶ τὸ τὸ παιδίον γενέσθαι γραμματικὸν δυνατόν, εἰ πάντως ἔσοιτο. οὗ   5
εἰς κατασκευὴν καὶ ὁ κυριεύων ἠρώτηται λόγος [ὁ] ὑπὸ τοῦ Διοδώρου. (2)

ὁμοίως καὶ περὶ τοῦ κατὰ Φίλωνα· ἦν δὲ τοῦτο τὸ κατὰ ψιλὴν λεγόμενον
τὴν ἐπιτηδειότητα τοῦ ὑποκειμένου, κἂν ὑπό τινος ἔξωθεν ἀναγκαίου ᾖ
γενέσθαι κεκωλυμένον, οὕτως τὸ ἄχυρον τὸ ἐν τῇ ἀτόμῳ ἢ τὸ ἐν τῷ βυθῷ
δυνατὸν ἔλεγε καυθῆναι ὂν ἐκεῖ, καίτοι κωλυόμενον ὑπὸ τῶν περιεχόντων   I
αὐτὸ ἐξ ἀνάγκης.

1 ὃ ἦ Wallies: ἦ ὃ codd.   8 ἀναγκαίου Wallies: -ον codd.

Context: commentary on Aristotle, *An. pr.* 1.14, 34a12ff., with Aristotle's position
represented as midway between those of Diodorus and Philo.
   9   The strange 'chaff' example recurs at ibid. 184, 12–18.

C   Boethius, *In Ar. De int.* 234,22–6 (Diodorus fr. 28 Giannantoni, part)

Diodorus possibile esse determinat, quod aut est aut erit; inpossibile, quod
cum falsum sit non erit verum; necessarium, quod cum verum sit non erit
falsum; non necessarium, quod aut iam est aut erit falsum.

Context: commentary on *De interpretatione* 9, comparing the modal theories of Philo,
Diodorus and the Stoics.
   2–3   It is generally assumed that *non . . . verum* and *non . . . falsum* are equivalent
to, respectively, 'false' and 'true'. But perhaps the more cautious wording suggests
that allowance is being made for the possibility of a proposition's losing its truth value
altogether (cf. the Stoic notion of 'being destroyed' in **F**).

D   Diogenes Laertius 7.75

ἔτι τε τὰ μέν ἐστι δυνατά, τὰ δ᾽ ἀδύνατα· καὶ τὰ μὲν ἀναγκαῖα, τὰ δ᾽ οὐκ
ἀναγκαῖα. δυνατὸν μὲν τὸ ἐπιδεκτικὸν τοῦ ἀληθὲς εἶναι, τῶν ἐκτὸς μὴ
ἐναντιουμένων εἰς τὸ ἀληθὲς εἶναι, οἷον "ζῇ Διοκλῆς"· ἀδύνατον δὲ ὃ μή
ἐστιν ἐπιδεκτικὸν τοῦ ἀληθὲς εἶναι, ⟨ἢ ἐπιδεκτικὸν μέν ἐστι τὰ δ᾽ ἐκτὸς
αὐτῷ ἐναντιοῦται πρὸς τὸ ἀληθὲς εἶναι⟩, οἷον "ἡ γῆ ἵπταται". ἀναγκαῖον   5
δέ ἐστιν ὅπερ ἀληθὲς ὂν οὐκ ἔστιν ἐπιδεκτικὸν τοῦ ψεῦδος εἶναι, ἢ
ἐπιδεκτικὸν μέν ἐστι, τὰ δ᾽ ἐκτὸς αὐτῷ ἐναντιοῦται πρὸς τὸ ψεῦδος εἶναι,
οἷον "ἡ ἀρετὴ ὠφελεῖ". οὐκ ἀναγκαῖον δέ ἐστιν ὃ καὶ ἀληθές ἐστιν καὶ
ψεῦδος οἷόν τε εἶναι, τῶν ἐκτὸς μηδὲν ἐναντιουμένων, οἷον τὸ "περιπατεῖ
Δίων".   I

4–5 add. Frede

Context: immediately following **37M**.
   We follow Frede [407], 107–17, both in his textual supplement and in his
interpretation of the genitive absolutes as adding *further* conditions for a proposition's
having the modal property in question (see vol. 1, translation). This, as he shows, is
required if the four definitions are to come out as properly interdefinable.

E   Cicero, *Fat.* 12–15

(1) vigila, Chrysippe, ne tuam causam, in qua tibi cum Diodoro, valente

dialectico, magna luctatio est, deseras. si enim est verum, quod ita conectitur: "si quis oriente Canicula natus est, is in mari non morietur", illud quoque verum est: "si Fabius oriente Canicula natus est, Fabius in mari non morietur." pugnant igitur haec inter se, Fabium oriente Canicula natum esse, et Fabium in   5 mari moriturum; et quoniam certum in Fabio ponitur, natum esse eum Canicula oriente, haec quoque pugnant, et esse Fabium, et in mari esse moriturum. ergo haec quoque coniunctio est ex repugnantibus, "et est Fabius, et in mari Fabius morietur", quod, ut propositum est, ne fieri quidem potest. ergo illud, "morietur in mari Fabius", ex eo genere est, quod fieri non potest.   10 omne ergo, quod falsum dicitur in futuro, id fieri non potest. (2) at hoc, Chrysippe, minime vis, maximeque tibi de hoc ipso cum Diodoro certamen est. ille enim id solum fieri posse dicit, quod aut sit verum aut futurum sit verum, et quicquid futurum sit, id dicit fieri necesse esse, et quicquid non sit futurum, id negat fieri posse. (3) tu et quae non sint futura, posse fieri dicis, ut   15 frangi hanc gemmam, etiamsi id numquam futurum sit, neque necesse fuisse Cypselum regnare Corinthi, quamquam id millensimo ante anno Apollinis oraculo editum esset. (4) at si ista comprobabis divine praedicta, et quae falsa in futuris dicentur, in iis habebis, ut ea fieri non possint, ut si dicatur Africanum Carthagine potiturum, et, si vere dicatur de futuro, idque ita futurum sit, dicas   20 esse necessarium; quae est tota Diodori vobis inimica sententia. (5) etenim si illud vere conectitur, "si oriente Canicula natus es, in mari non moriere", primumque quod est in conexo, "natus es oriente Canicula", necessarium est (omnia enim vera in praeteritis necessaria sunt, ut Chrysippo placet dissentienti a magistro Cleanthe, quia sunt inmutabilia nec in falsum e vero   25 praeterita possunt convertere), si igitur quod primum in conexo est, necessarium est, fit etiam quod consequitur necessarium. quamquam hoc Chrysippo non videtur valere in omnibus; sed tamen, si naturalis est causa, cur in mari Fabius non moriatur, in mari Fabius mori non potest. (6) hoc loco Chrysippus aestuans falli sperat Chaldaeos ceterosque divinos, neque eos   30 usuros esse coniunctionibus, ut ita sua percepta pronuntient, "si quis natus est oriente Canicula, is in mari non morietur", sed potius ita dicant, "non et natus est quis oriente Canicula, et is in mari morietur." o licentiam iocularem! ne ipse incidat in Diodorum, docet Chaldaeos, quo pacto eos exponere percepta oporteat.   35

19–20 *ut si–potiturum* secl. Christ

2–11   The argument is garbled here, but the same point is better argued at 21–7. For 'Fabius exists' to entail 'Fabius was born at the rising of the Dogstar' (as it must if Cicero's point is to be correct) would presuppose a variety of essentialism which cannot easily be attributed to the Stoics or to any other Hellenistic school.

11–15   Cf. **A**.

29–33   For the use of the negated conjunction, cf. Frede [407], 85–6; Sorabji [459], 266–70; Sedley [243], 253–5 and [440].

31, 34   *percepta* = 'theorems', cf. vol. 1, 264.

Stoic logic and semantics

F Alexander, *In Ar. An. pr.* 177,25–178,1 (*SVF* 2.202a, part)

Χρύσιππος δὲ λέγων μηδὲν κωλύειν καὶ δυνατῷ ἀδύνατον ἕπεσθαι πρὸς
μὲν τὴν ὑπ' Ἀριστοτέλους εἰρημένην δεῖξιν οὐδὲν λέγει, πειρᾶται δὲ διὰ
παραδειγμάτων τινῶν οὐχ ὑγιῶς συγκειμένων δεικνύναι τοῦτο μὴ οὕτως
ἔχον. φησὶ γὰρ ἐν τῷ συνημμένῳ τῷ "εἰ τέθνηκε Δίων, τέθνηκεν οὗτος"
δεικνυμένου τοῦ Δίωνος ἀληθεῖ ὄντι τὸ μὲν ἡγούμενον ⟨τὸ⟩ "τέθνηκε   5
Δίων" δυνατὸν εἶναι τῷ δύνασθαί ποτε ἀληθὲς γενέσθαι τὸ τεθνηκέναι
Δίωνα, τὸ δὲ "τέθνηκεν οὗτος" ἀδύνατον· ἀποθανόντος γὰρ Δίωνος
φθείρεσθαι τὸ ἀξίωμα τὸ "οὗτος τέθνηκε" μηκέτ' ὄντος τοῦ τὴν δεῖξιν
ἀναδεχομένου· ἐπὶ γὰρ ζῶντος καὶ κατὰ ζῶντος ἡ δεῖξις. εἰ οὖν μή⟨τε⟩
τεθνεῶτος αὐτοῦ ἔτι τὸ "οὗτος" οἷόν τε, μήτε πάλιν [ἢ] ὑφίσταται ὁ Δίων   10
ὡς δύνασθαι ἐπ' αὐτοῦ ῥηθῆναι τὸ "τέθνηκεν οὗτος", ἀδύνατον τὸ
"τέθνηκεν οὗτος".

5 suppl. Ald.   9 suppl. Wallies   10 ἢ del. Wallies   11 ὡς Wallies: ᾧ codd.

Context: comment on Aristotle, *An. pr.* I.14, 34a10ff.: the impossible does not follow
from the possible. See also *FDS* 994–7, and context note on **52F**.

G Cicero, *Fat.* 20–1

concludit enim Chrysippus hoc modo: "si est motus sine causa, non omnis
enuntiatio, quod ἀξίωμα dialectici appellant, aut vera aut falsa erit; causas
enim efficientis quod non habebit, id nec verum nec falsum erit; omnis autem
enuntiatio aut vera aut falsa est; motus ergo sine causa nullus est. quod si ita est,
omnia, quae fiunt, causis fiunt antegressis; id si ita est, fato omnia fiunt;   5
efficitur igitur fato fieri quaecumque fiant."

Context: comparison of Chrysippus and Epicurus on determinism (continued at **20E**).

H Alexander, *Fat.* 176,14–24 (*FDS* 1009, part)

τὸ δὲ λέγειν μὴ ἀναιρεῖσθαι πάντων γινομένων καθ' εἱμαρμένην τὸ δυνατόν
τε καὶ ἐνδεχόμενον τῷ δυνατὸν μὲν εἶναι γενέσθαι τοῦτο ὃ ὑπ' οὐδενὸς
κωλύεται γενέσθαι, κἂν μὴ γένηται, τῶν δὲ καθ' εἱμαρμένην γινομένων οὐ
κεκωλῦσθαι τὰ ἀντικείμενα γενέσθαι, διὸ καίτοι μὴ γινόμενα ὅμως ἐστὶ
δυνατά, καὶ τοῦ μὴ κεκωλῦσθαι γενέσθαι αὐτὰ ἀπόδειξιν φέρειν τὸ ἡμῖν τὰ   5
κωλύοντα αὐτὰ [ἂν] ἄγνωστα εἶναι, πάντως μέν τινα ὄντα (ἃ γάρ ἐστιν
αἴτια τοῦ γίνεσθαι τὰ ἀντικείμενα αὐτοῖς καθ' εἱμαρμένην, ταῦτα καὶ τοῦ
μὴ γίνεσθαι τούτοις αἴτια, εἴ γε ὥς φασιν ἀδύνατον τῶν αὐτῶν
περιεστώτων γίνεσθαι τὰ ἀντικείμενα· ἀλλ' ὅτι μὴ ἡμῖν ἐστι γνώριμά τινα
ἅ ἐστι, διὰ τοῦτο ἀκώλυτον αὐτῶν τὸ μὴ γίνεσθαι λέγουσιν), τὸ δὴ ταῦτα   10
λέγειν πῶς οὐ παιζόντων ἐστὶν ἐν οὐ παιδιᾶς λόγοις δεομένοις;

4 κεκωλῦσθαι Usener: κεκώλυται codd.   6 ἂν V¹: del. V²: om. A¹²   10 μὴ del. Bruns

236

38 Modality

Context: argument against opponents (unnamed but clearly Stoics) who defend universal necessitation as compatible with human experience.

For commentary, cf. Sharples [333], 134–7.

2–3 This definition of 'possible' is probably just a loose or incomplete statement of the Stoic one at **D**. The vagueness suits Alexander's purpose, since it enables him to argue that *anything* that does not come about should on the Stoic definition be impossible, because somehow 'prevented' (6–9). Against this, a reasonable reading of **D** would allow us to take 'prevented' in a suitably restricted way which would exclude as a case of prevention the mere absence of a causal chain leading to the actualization of a possibility.

5–10 All that is with certainty attributed to the Stoics here is an appeal to our ignorance as proof that certain counterfactuals are not prevented. The inferences πάντως (6)–ἀντικείμενα (9) may be Alexander's own. And although he would have us believe that their not being prevented was claimed to *consist* in our ignorance of the preventing factors, the Stoics in question may either just have claimed that there genuinely were no such factors, and by way of proof challenged anyone to find them, or restricted 'prevented' to *evident* obstacles in order to prevent all relevant factors, however tenuous or negative (cf. previous note), from counting as obstacles. The latter explanation is (as Nicholas Denyer points out to us) supported by Simplicius, *In Ar. Cat.* 196,2–4, where what seems to be the Stoic definition of 'possible' is set out as intrinsic fitness μηδένος φανεροῦ κωλύματος ἐνισταμένου.

I Ammonius, *In Ar. De int.* 131,20–32 (*FDS* 1252, part)

τοσαύτην οὖν δύναμιν ἔχοντος τοῦ θεωρήματος πρὸς πάντα ἡμῶν τὸν βίον ἀναγκαῖον ἡγοῦμαι τῶν πάντα ἀναγκάζειν πειρωμένων λόγων τοὺς δοκοῦντας παρέχειν τινὰ τοῖς ἀκούουσιν ἀπορίαν ἐκθέσθαί τε καὶ διαλῦσαι. δύο δὲ τούτων ὄντων, τοῦ μὲν λογικωτέρου τοῦ δὲ πραγματειωδεστέρου, ὁ μὲν λογικώτερος προάγεται ὡς ἐπί τινος ἡμῶν ἐνεργείας, οἷον τῆς κατὰ τὸ θερίζειν, τὸν τρόπον τοῦτον· εἰ θεριεῖς, φησίν, 5 οὐχὶ τάχα μὲν θεριεῖς τάχα δὲ οὐ θεριεῖς, ἀλλὰ πάντως θεριεῖς, καὶ εἰ μὴ θεριεῖς, ὡσαύτως οὐχὶ τάχα μὲν θεριεῖς τάχα δὲ οὐ θεριεῖς, ἀλλὰ πάντως οὐ θεριεῖς· ἀλλὰ μὴν ἐξ ἀνάγκης ἤτοι θεριεῖς ἢ οὐ θεριεῖς· ἀνήρηται ἄρα τὸ τάχα, εἴπερ μήτε κατὰ τὴν ἀντίθεσιν τοῦ θεριεῖν πρὸς τὸ μὴ θεριεῖν ἔχει χώραν, ἐξ ἀνάγκης τοῦ ἑτέρου τούτων ἐκβαίνοντος, μήτε κατὰ τὸ 10 ἑπόμενον ὁποτερᾳοῦν τῶν ὑποθέσεων· τὸ δὲ τάχα ἦν τὸ εἰσφέρον τὸ ἐνδεχόμενον· οἴχεται ἄρα τὸ ἐνδεχόμενον.

Context: commentary on *De interpretatione* 9.

For Stoic interest in the Mowing Argument, cf. D.L. 7.25; **37C, L** 1. The last of these associates it with the Master Argument, whose origin in the Dialectical school of Diodorus it probably shared (**31M**).

1 **θεωρήματος** Aristotle's controversial qualification of the Law of the Excluded Middle in *De int.* 9. Ammonius himself interprets Aristotle not as rejecting the law for statements about future contingents, but as denying them 'definite' truth or falsity.

4 **τοῦ δέ** The reference is to an argument for determinism based on divine foreknowledge, set out at ibid. 132,8–135,11.

EPISTEMOLOGY: STOICS AND ACADEMICS

39 Impressions

A Diogenes Laertius 7.49–51 (*SVF* 2.52, 55, 61)

(1) ἀρέσκει τοῖς Στωικοῖς τὸν περὶ φαντασίας καὶ αἰσθήσεως προτάττειν λόγον, καθότι τὸ κριτήριον, ᾧ ἡ ἀλήθεια τῶν πραγμάτων γινώσκεται, κατὰ γένος φαντασία ἐστί, καὶ καθότι ὁ περὶ συγκαταθέσεως καὶ ὁ περὶ καταλήψεως καὶ νοήσεως λόγος, προάγων τῶν ἄλλων, οὐκ ἄνευ φαντασίας συνίσταται. (2) προηγεῖται γὰρ ἡ φαντασία, εἶθ᾽ ἡ διάνοια ἐκλαλητικὴ   5
ὑπάρχουσα, ὃ πάσχει ὑπὸ τῆς φαντασίας, τοῦτο ἐκφέρει λόγῳ. (3)
διαφέρει δὲ φαντασία καὶ φάντασμα· φάντασμα μὲν γάρ ἐστι δόκησις
διανοίας οἵα γίνεται κατὰ τοὺς ὕπνους, φαντασία δέ ἐστι τύπωσις ἐν ψυχῇ,
τουτέστιν ἀλλοίωσις, ὡς ὁ Χρύσιππος ἐν τῷ β᾽ Περὶ ψυχῆς ὑφίσταται. οὐ
γὰρ δεκτέον τὴν τύπωσιν οἱονεὶ τύπον σφραγιστῆρος, ἐπεὶ ἀνένδεκτόν ἐστι   10
πολλοὺς τύπους κατὰ τὸ αὐτὸ περὶ τὸ αὐτὸ γίνεσθαι. νοεῖται δὲ φαντασία ἡ ἀπὸ
ὑπάρχοντος κατὰ τὸ ὑπάρχον ἐναπομεμαγμένη καὶ ἐναποτετυπωμένη καὶ ἐναπεσφραγισ-
μένη, οἵα οὐκ ἂν γένοιτο ἀπὸ μὴ ὑπάρχοντος. (4) τῶν δὲ φαντασιῶν κατ᾽ αὐτοὺς αἱ
μέν εἰσιν αἰσθητικαί, αἱ δ᾽ οὔ· αἰσθητικαὶ μὲν αἱ δι᾽ αἰσθητηρίου ἢ
αἰσθητηρίων λαμβανόμεναι, οὐκ αἰσθητικαὶ δ᾽ αἱ διὰ τῆς διανοίας   15
καθάπερ τῶν ἀσωμάτων καὶ τῶν ἄλλων τῶν λόγῳ λαμβανομένων. (5) τῶν
δ᾽ αἰσθητικῶν ⟨αἱ μὲν⟩ ἀπὸ ὑπαρχόντων μετ᾽ εἴξεως καὶ συγκαταθέσεως
γίνονται. εἰσὶ δὲ τῶν φαντασιῶν καὶ ἐμφάσεις αἱ ὡσανεὶ ἀπὸ ὑπαρχόντων
γινόμεναι. (6) ἔτι τῶν φαντασιῶν αἱ μέν εἰσι λογικαί, αἱ δὲ ἄλογοι· λογικαὶ
μὲν αἱ τῶν λογικῶν ζῴων, ἄλογοι δὲ αἱ τῶν ἀλόγων. αἱ μὲν οὖν λογικαὶ   20
νοήσεις εἰσίν, αἱ δ᾽ ἄλογοι οὐ τετυχήκασιν ὀνόματος. (7) καὶ αἱ μέν εἰσι
τεχνικαί, αἱ δὲ ἄτεχνοι· ἄλλως γοῦν θεωρεῖται ὑπὸ τεχνίτου εἰκὼν καὶ
ἄλλως ὑπὸ ἀτέχνου.

9 τῷ β΄ A.A.Long: τω ιβ BFP: τῷ δευτέρῳ H.S.Long   16 καθάπερ BP: καθάπερ καὶ ἐπὶ F   καὶ
BP: καὶ ἐπὶ F   τῶν post ἄλλων om. Suda, secl. Egli   λαμβανομένων ⟨τινὲς⟩ Egli   17 ⟨αἱ μὲν⟩
Arnim

Context: opening section of Diocles of Magnesia's synopsis of Stoic dialectic; see note
on **33A**.

3 **συγκαταθέσεως**   The noun is probably a Stoic coinage. For pre-Stoic uses of
the verb, cf. Plato, *Gorg.* 501c (with δόξα as object); Aristotle, *Top.* III.1, 116a11;
Epicurus, *SV* 29.

5–6   = **33D**

7 **φάντασμα**   This pejorative use of the term was canonized by Plato, e.g. *Rep.*,
2.382a, *Phd.* 81d, and especially, *Soph.* 266b. So too the Epicurean doxography in **16B**
12, which contrasts with Epicurus' normally unloaded use of the word, e.g. **19A**.

9–11   Explained fully by Sextus, *M.* 7.228–31, as Chrysippus' amendment of
Cleanthes; see Rist [303], 136. Our translations of κατὰ τὸ αὐτό as κατὰ τὸν αὐτὸν
χρόνον, and περὶ τὸ αὐτό as 'the same subject' (i.e. the recipient of the impressions),
are justified by Sextus loc. cit.

11–13   See **40E 3**.

13–16   For the two sources of φαντασία, cf. Aristotle, *De an.* III.10, 433b29; III.11, 434a6; *De motu* 8, 702a19. For the apprehension of incorporeals, see **27E**.

17 **εἴξεως**   Similarly coupled with συγκατάθεσις at **53S**; cf. note on **53O**.

18 **ἐμφάσεις**   The Stoic use of this term (contrast the Academic, e.g. **69D 2**) is exemplified in *SVF* 2.673 by the face of the man in the moon.

19 **ἄλογοι**   Non-rational, as distinct from irrational, which characterizes disobedience to reason. These senses are distinguished in *SVF* 3.375.

21 **νοήσεις**   See the excellent discussion by Frede [468], 68–71. Aristotle treats φαντασία as νόησίς τις in *De an.* III.10, 433a10.

22 **τεχνικαί**   See **40I 2, N 4**.

B   Aetius 4.12.1–5 (*SVF* 2.54, part)

(1) Χρύσιππος διαφέρειν ἀλλήλων φησὶ τέτταρα ταῦτα. (2) φαντασία μὲν οὖν ἐστι πάθος ἐν τῇ ψυχῇ γιγνόμενον, ἐνδεικνύμενον αὐτό τε καὶ τὸ πεποιηκός· οἷον ἐπειδὰν δι᾽ ὄψεως θεωρῶμεν τὸ λευκόν, ἔστι πάθος τὸ ἐγγεγενημένον διὰ τῆς ὁράσεως ἐν τῇ ψυχῇ. καὶ ⟨κατὰ⟩ τοῦτο τὸ πάθος εἰπεῖν ἔχομεν, ὅτι ὑπόκειται λευκὸν κινοῦν ἡμᾶς· ὁμοίως καὶ διὰ τῆς ἁφῆς   5
καὶ τῆς ὀσφρήσεως. (3) εἴρηται δὲ ἡ φαντασία ἀπὸ τοῦ φωτός· καθάπερ γὰρ τὸ φῶς αὐτὸ δείκνυσι καὶ τὰ ἄλλα τὰ ἐν αὐτῷ περιεχόμενα, καὶ ἡ φαντασία δείκνυσιν ἑαυτὴν καὶ τὸ πεποιηκὸς αὐτήν. (4) φανταστὸν δὲ τὸ ποιοῦν τὴν φαντασίαν· οἷον τὸ λευκὸν καὶ τὸ ψυχρὸν καὶ πᾶν ὅ τι ἂν δύνηται κινεῖν τὴν ψυχήν, τοῦτ᾽ ἔστι φανταστόν. (5) φανταστικὸν δέ ἐστι   10
διάκενος ἑλκυσμός, πάθος ἐν τῇ ψυχῇ ἀπ᾽ οὐδενὸς φανταστοῦ γινόμενον καθάπερ ἐπὶ τοῦ σκιαμαχοῦντος καὶ κενοῖς ἐπιφέροντος τὰς χεῖρας· τῇ γὰρ φαντασίᾳ ὑπόκειταί τι φανταστόν, τῷ δὲ φανταστικῷ οὐδέν. (6) φάντασμα δέ ἐστιν, ἐφ᾽ ὃ ἑλκόμεθα κατὰ τὸν φανταστικὸν διάκενον ἑλκυσμόν· ταῦτα δὲ γίνεται ἐπὶ τῶν μελαγχολώντων καὶ μεμηνότων· ὁ γοῦν τραγικὸς Ὀρέστης   15
ὅταν λέγῃ . . .

2 αὐτό τε GC: ἐν αὐτῷ Nemesii 172 aliqui codd.   3 τι λευκόν Reiske   4 ⟨κατὰ⟩ Wyttenbach
7 αὐτό] αὐτὸ ABC   12 κενοῖς Reiske: κενὰς codd.

1–4   Cf. **70A 5–6**, which supports the choice of αὐτό as the reading in line 2.
6 **ἀπὸ τοῦ φωτός**   So already Aristotle, *De an.* III. 3, 429a3.
10 **φανταστικόν**   A further mark of the influence of Plato, *Soph.*; cf. 266d, 268c.
15–16   The omitted quotation is Euripides, *Or.* 255–9, Orestes being a favourite example of delusion; cf. **G 9; 16F; 40E 5**.

C   Cicero, *Acad.* 2.21

(1) atqui qualia sunt haec quae sensibus percipi dicimus talia secuntur ea quae non sensibus ipsis percipi dicuntur sed quodam modo sensibus, ut haec: "illud est album, hoc dulce, canorum illud, hoc bene olens, hoc asperum": animo iam haec tenemus conprehensa non sensibus. (2) "ille" deinceps "equus est, ille canis." (3) cetera series deinde sequitur maiora nectens, ut haec quae quasi   5
expletam rerum conprehensionem amplectuntur: "si homo est, animal est

mortale rationis particeps." (4) quo e genere nobis notitiae rerum inprimuntur sine quibus nec intellegi quicquam nec quaeri ⟨nec⟩ disputari potest.

8 ⟨nec⟩ Plasberg: *disputari*⟨*ve*⟩ A²B²: ⟨*aut*⟩ *disp.* V²

Context: an early stage in Lucullus' defence of Stoic epistemology on Antiochus' behalf.

Since the Stoics regarded all perception as taking place in the ἡγεμονικόν (cf. 53M), the distinction between *sensibus* and *animo* is potentially misleading. The general accuracy of the report, however, is assured by its closeness to Chrysippus in 53G. What the distinction amounts to is broadly analogous to Locke's distinction between 'simple' and 'complex' ideas, whereby the former have their source in the sensible qualities of things and the latter are constructed by the mind out of the simple ideas by which it is affected via the senses. For a close parallel to **C**, cf. S.E., *M.* 7.344–5; and for its bearing on the relation between 'simple' (pre-rational) concepts and rational impressions, see Frede [468], 68–9.

7   *quo e genere* must refer back to *talia*, 1, and not, as *quo* could imply, to *cetera series*, 5.

D Diogenes Laertius 7.53 (*SVF* 2.87, part)

(1) κατὰ περίπτωσιν μὲν οὖν ἐνοήθη τὰ αἰσθητά· (2) καθ' ὁμοιότητα δὲ τὰ ἀπό τινος παρακειμένου, ὡς Σωκράτης ἀπὸ τῆς εἰκόνος· (3) κατ' ἀναλογίαν δὲ αὐξητικῶς μέν, ⟨ὡς⟩ ὁ Τιτυὸς καὶ Κύκλωψ· μειωτικῶς δέ, ὡς ὁ Πυγμαῖος. καὶ τὸ κέντρον δὲ τῆς γῆς κατ' ἀναλογίαν ἐνοήθη ἀπὸ τῶν μικροτέρων σφαιρῶν. (4) κατὰ μετάθεσιν δέ, οἷον ὀφθαλμοὶ ἐπὶ τοῦ   5 στήθους· (5) κατὰ σύνθεσιν δὲ ἐνοήθη Ἱπποκένταυρος· (6) καὶ κατ' ἐναντίωσιν θάνατος. (7) νοεῖται δὲ καὶ κατὰ μετάβασίν τινα, ὡς τὰ λεκτὰ καὶ ὁ τόπος. (8) φυσικῶς δὲ νοεῖται δίκαιόν τι καὶ ἀγαθόν. (9) καὶ κατὰ στέρησιν, οἷον ἄχειρ.

1 οὖν om. F   3 ⟨ὡς⟩ Hübner   8 δίκαιον codd.: καὶ ὄν Suda

Context: see on **33A**.

For concept formation by methods *1–3* and *5*, see S.E., *M.* 8.56–60, and the similar doctrine attested for Epicurus, **12F**. For *1–4* in Stoicism, see **60D** 1. For *7*, see vol. 1, 165. For *8*, see **60C**.

E Aetius 4.11.1–4 (*SVF* 2.83)

(1) οἱ Στωικοί φασιν· ὅταν γεννηθῇ ὁ ἄνθρωπος, ἔχει τὸ ἡγεμονικὸν μέρος τῆς ψυχῆς ὥσπερ χάρτην εὔεργον εἰς ἀπογραφήν· εἰς τοῦτο μίαν ἑκάστην τῶν ἐννοιῶν ἐναπογράφεται. (2) πρῶτος δὲ ὁ τῆς ἀναγραφῆς τρόπος ὁ διὰ τῶν αἰσθήσεων. αἰσθόμενοι γάρ τινος οἷον λευκοῦ ἀπελθόντος αὐτοῦ μνήμην ἔχουσιν· ὅταν δὲ ὁμοειδεῖς πολλαὶ μνῆμαι γένωνται, τότε φαμὲν   5 ἔχειν ἐμπειρίαν· ἐμπειρία γάρ ἐστι τὸ τῶν ὁμοειδῶν φαντασιῶν πλῆθος. (3) τῶν δὲ ἐννοιῶν αἱ μὲν φυσικῶς γίνονται κατὰ τοὺς εἰρημένους τρόπους καὶ ἀνεπιτεχνήτως, αἱ δὲ ἤδη δι' ἡμετέρας διδασκαλίας καὶ ἐπιμελείας·

αὗται μὲν οὖν ἔννοιαι καλοῦνται μόνον, ἐκεῖναι δὲ καὶ προλήψεις. (4) ὁ δὲ
λόγος, καθ᾽ ὃν προσαγορευόμεθα λογικοὶ ἐκ τῶν προλήψεων συμπληροῦσ-   10
θαι λέγεται κατὰ τὴν πρώτην ἑβδομάδα.

2 εὔεργον Diels: ἐνεργὸν (-ῶν) codd.   4 αἰσθόμενοι Diels: αἰσθανόμενοι codd.   5 φαμὲν GAB:
φασὶν C   6 φαντασιῶν G: om. (A)BC: ἐννοιῶν Reiske   7 ante τῶν lacunam stat. Sandbach
φυσικῶς G: φυσικαὶ (A)BC   9 μόνον vulgo: μόναι codd.

Context: doxography of the origins of sensation and thought.
The striking similarities between this passage and Aristotle, *An. Pst.* II.19, 99b35–
100a9 are noted by Sandbach [304], 51–2, concerned though he is to minimize
Aristotle's influence on Stoicism; cf. also Aristotle, *Metaph.* A.1, 980a27–981a7.

3–4   The empiricist implications are fully developed in S.E., *M.* 8.56, 60 (*SVF*
2.88).

5–6   Cf. Aristotle, *Metaph.* A.1, 980b29–30, αἱ γὰρ πολλαὶ μνῆμαι τοῦ αὐτοῦ
πράγματος μιᾶς ἐμπειρίας ἀποτελοῦσιν. Chrysippus defined memory as θησαυρισ-
μὸς φαντασιῶν, *SVF* 1.64.

7–9   For this passage, and the difference between ἔννοια and πρόληψις, cf.
Sandbach [470]. However, we cannot accept his (p. 26) and others' belief that κατὰ
τοὺς εἰρημένους τρόπους, 7, shows 'that something has fallen out after the preceding
sentence' along the lines of **D**. The processes outlined in **E 2** are quite sufficient to
explain the plural τρόπους, while much of **D** does not fit the scope of ἔννοιαι.
(Sandbach [304], 80 n. 118, has now retracted his belief in the text's defectiveness.)

9–11   Cf. **53V** and **33H** 3, where fourteen is given as the age for rational maturity.
The counting by sevens was traditional; cf. Aristotle, *Pol.* VII, 1333b34, 1336b40.
Sandbach, loc. cit., suggests that Aetius has confused 'the beginning of the growth of
reason in the first seven years of life with its completion round the age of fourteen'.

F Plutarch, *Comm. not.* 1084F–1085A (*SVF* 2.847, part)

φαντασία γάρ τις ἡ ἔννοιά ἐστι, φαντασία δὲ τύπωσις ἐν ψυχῇ· . . . τὰς
ἐννοίας ⟨ἐν⟩αποκειμένας τινὰς ὁριζόμενοι νοήσεις, μνήμας δὲ μονίμους
καὶ σχετικὰς τυπώσεις.

2 ⟨ἐν⟩αποκειμένας Pohlenz

Context: the alleged incompatibility of the soul's volatile material with the
requirements of stable impressions.

2 **νοήσεις**   See λογικαὶ φαντασίαι, **A 6**.

G Sextus Empiricus, *M.* 7.242–6 (*SVF* 2.65, part)

(1) τούτων γὰρ αἱ μέν εἰσι πιθαναί, αἱ δὲ ἀπίθανοι, αἱ δὲ πιθαναὶ ἅμα καὶ
ἀπίθανοι, αἱ δὲ οὔτε πιθαναὶ οὔτε ἀπίθανοι. (2) πιθαναὶ μὲν οὖν εἰσιν αἱ
λεῖον κίνημα περὶ ψυχὴν ἐργαζόμεναι, ὥσπερ νῦν τὸ "ἡμέραν εἶναι" καὶ τὸ
"ἐμὲ διαλέγεσθαι" καὶ πᾶν ὃ τῆς ὁμοίας ἔχεται περιφανείας, (3) ἀπίθανοι
δὲ αἱ μὴ τοιαῦται ἀλλ᾽ ἀποστρέφουσαι ἡμᾶς τῆς συγκαταθέσεως, οἷον "εἰ   5
ἡμέρα ἐστίν, οὐκ ἔστιν ἥλιος ὑπὲρ γῆς· εἰ σκότος ἐστίν, ἡμέρα ἐστίν." (4)

πιθαναὶ δὲ καὶ ἀπίθανοι καθεστᾶσιν αἱ κατὰ τὴν πρός τι σχέσιν ὀτὲ μὲν
τοῖαι γινόμεναι ὀτὲ δὲ τοῖαι, οἷον αἱ τῶν ἀπόρων λόγων, (5) οὔτε δὲ πιθαναὶ
οὔτε ἀπίθανοι καθάπερ αἱ τῶν τοιούτων πραγμάτων "ἄρτιοί εἰσιν οἱ
ἀστέρες· περισσοί εἰσιν οἱ ἀστέρες." (6) τῶν δὲ πιθανῶν ἢ ἀπιθάνων   10
φαντασιῶν αἱ μέν εἰσιν ἀληθεῖς, αἱ δὲ ψευδεῖς, αἱ δὲ ἀληθεῖς καὶ ψευδεῖς, αἱ
δὲ οὔτε ἀληθεῖς οὔτε ψευδεῖς. (7) ἀληθεῖς μὲν οὖν εἰσιν ὧν ἔστιν ἀληθῆ
κατηγορίαν ποιήσασθαι, ὡς τοῦ "ἡμέρα ἐστίν" ἐπὶ τοῦ παρόντος ἢ τοῦ
"φῶς ἐστι", (8) ψευδεῖς δὲ ὧν ἔστι ψευδῆ κατηγορίαν ποιήσασθαι, ὡς τοῦ
κεκλάσθαι τὴν κατὰ βυθοῦ κώπην ἢ μύουραν εἶναι τὴν στοάν, (9) ἀληθεῖς   15
δὲ καὶ ψευδεῖς, ὁποία προσέπιπτεν 'Ορέστῃ κατὰ μανίαν ἀπὸ τῆς
'Ηλέκτρας (καθὸ μὲν γὰρ ὡς ἀπὸ ὑπάρχοντός τινος προσέπιπτεν, ἦν
ἀληθής, ὑπῆρχε γὰρ 'Ηλέκτρα, καθὸ δ' ὡς ἀπὸ 'Ερινύος, ψευδής, οὐκ ἦν
γὰρ 'Ερινύς), καὶ πάλιν εἴ τις ἀπὸ Δίωνος ζῶντος κατὰ τοὺς ὕπνους ὡς
ἀπὸ παρεστῶτος ὀνειροπολεῖται ψευδῆ καὶ διάκενον ἑλκυσμόν. (10) οὔτε   20
δὲ ἀληθεῖς οὔτε ψευδεῖς εἰσιν αἱ γενικαί.

10 ἢ ἀπιθάνων del. Arnim   16, 17 προσέπιπτεν Bekker: προύπιπτεν codd.   21 εἰσιν ς: ἦσαν cett.

Context: exposition of Stoic accounts of φαντασία. After indicating the Stoics'
difficulties in defining φαντασία, Sextus continues, 7.241: τῶν δὲ φαντασιῶν πολλαὶ
μὲν καὶ ἄλλαι εἰσὶ διαφοραί, ἀπαρκέσουσι δὲ αἱ λεχθησόμεναι.

Other differentiae that he might have mentioned will include those of **39A 4–7**, a
scheme wholly different in its content and sequence of simple disjunctions from the
elaborate division of **G**, which continues at **40E** with a division of true impressions
into καταληπτικαί and οὐ καταληπτικαί.

10   According to the transmitted text, true impressions are a subdivision of
πιθανῶν ἢ ἀπιθάνων. Since the examples of ἀπίθανοι in **3** are both of patent
falsehoods while the examples in **7–9** are all of πιθαναί, and since the inclusion of both
disjuncts would violate the proper procedure for definition by diairesis (on which see
32), there are grounds for deleting ἢ ἀπιθάνων, as von Arnim proposed, followed by
the Loeb and Teubner editions. However, the retention of ἢ ἀπιθάνων is prima facie
justified by the subsequent inclusion in the same division (**40E 2**) of true and non-
cognitive impressions which often are unconvincing (fail to gain assent). This
problem therefore raises a larger question concerning the coherence of the whole
division in terms of πιθανόν, of which Diogenes Laertius (**A** and **40C**) has no trace.
Clearly the Stoics thought that a cognitive impression is normally convincing (for the
exceptional case of its not being believed, cf. **40K 2**); but there are good reasons for
doubting whether this property was one that they wished to emphasize, since it never
appears in their accounts of the attributes of a cognitive impression. Indeed, Stoic
interest in πιθαναὶ φαντασίαι concentrates on their speciousness; cf. *SVF* 3.228, 229a,
and **31B 2**. Such considerations suggest that the diairesis in **G** and **40E** may involve
conflation of a Stoic classification of φαντασίαι πιθαναὶ ἢ ἀπίθανοι with a separate
one of ἀληθεῖς and ψευδεῖς. Such a conflation could well account for the intrusive ἢ
ἀπιθάνων, 10, as a clumsy attempt to tie the two divisions together. The importance
of the πιθανὴ φαντασία from Carneades onwards (see **69D–E**) may have infected
reports of the Stoics on which Sextus drew, reflecting modifications within the Stoa

and Academic contributions. This would be all the more likely if Antiochus is Sextus' source here, as certainly elsewhere (cf. *M*. 7.161, 201, and notes on **16E, 18A**). For these reasons, we divide the material between **G** and **40E**.

40 The criteria of truth

A Diogenes Laertius 7.54 (*SVF* 2.105, Posidonius fr. 42)

(1) κριτήριον δὲ τῆς ἀληθείας φασὶ τυγχάνειν τὴν καταληπτικὴν φαντασίαν, τουτέστι τὴν ἀπὸ ὑπάρχοντος, καθά φησι Χρύσιππος ἐν τῇ δευτέρᾳ τῶν Φυσικῶν καὶ 'Αντίπατρος καὶ 'Απολλόδωρος. (2) ὁ μὲν γὰρ Βόηθος κριτήρια πλείονα ἀπολείπει, νοῦν καὶ αἴσθησιν καὶ ὄρεξιν καὶ ἐπιστήμην· (3) ὁ δὲ Χρύσιππος διαφερόμενος πρὸς αὐτὸν ἐν τῷ πρώτῳ Περὶ λόγου 5 κριτήριά φησιν αἴσθησιν καὶ πρόληψιν· ἔστι δ' ἡ πρόληψις ἔννοια φυσικὴ τῶν καθόλου. (4) ἄλλοι δέ τινες τῶν ἀρχαιοτέρων Στωικῶν τὸν ὀρθὸν λόγον κριτήριον ἀπολείπουσιν, ὡς ὁ Ποσειδώνιος ἐν τῷ Περὶ κριτηρίου φησί.

2 δευτέρᾳ Arnim: δυωδεκάτῃ codd.   4 πλείονα BP: πολλὰ F   5 αὐτὸν Arnim: αὐτὸν codd.

Context: immediately following **39D**.

1 **καταληπτικήν** For the sense of the term, cf. Sandbach [474], 14–15.

2 **ἀπὸ ὑπάρχοντος** A truncated version of the standard formula, cf. **C** 4–5, **E** 4–7; **39A** 11–13.

3–4 Boethus' list resembles the faculties cited as criteria of many philosophers by Sextus Empiricus (e.g. *M*. 7. 141–49), probably deriving from classifications made by Antiochus. Cf. Long [477].

5–6 αὐτόν seems to be the right reading, since Chrysippus was too senior to disagree with Boethus. On αἴσθησιν καὶ πρόληψιν, cf. Striker [9], 90–102. Although Chrysippus did pronounce, here and at **48C 5**, on the criteria of truth, this was not in works with overtly epistemological themes, and the striking lack of attributions to him of epistemological works or doctrines (see Index of philosophers vol. 1, s.v. Chrysippus) leads us to wonder whether he made any innovations in this area of Stoicism, beyond its integration within the broader spectrum of dialectic (see vol. 1, 190).

7–9 The assumption that this is a bona fide piece of doxography (e.g. Pohlenz [298] 1, 62) will not survive a comparison with S.E., *M*. 7.89–140, a passage almost certainly of Posidonian origin (cf. especially 7.93, 115–21) and perhaps even from his work cited here. There the attribution of λόγος or ὀρθὸς λόγος as a criterion to various philosophers is offered not as straight doxography but as speculative interpretation of their methodology or isolated pronouncements; cf. especially 7.122ff. on Empedocles.

B Cicero, *Acad*. 1.40–1 (*SVF* 1.55, 61, 60, part)

(1) plurima autem in illa tertia philosophiae parte mutavit. in qua primum de sensibus ipsis quaedam dixit nova, quos iunctos esse censuit e quadam quasi

Epistemology: Stoics and Academics

impulsione oblata extrinsecus . . . sed ad haec quae visa sunt et quasi accepta sensibus assensionem adiungit animorum, quam esse vult in nobis positam et voluntariam. (2) visis non omnibus adiungebat fidem sed is solum quae 5 propriam quandam haberent declarationem earum rerum quae viderentur; id autem visum cum ipsum per se cerneretur, comprehendibile . . . (3) sed cum acceptum iam et approbatum esset, comprehensionem appellabat, similem is rebus quae manu prenderentur.

Context: Varro's 'Antiochean' account of Zeno's divergences from Platonism. For what follows B, see **41B**.

1 **tertia . . . parte** I.e. logic.

7 **comprehendibile** Cicero offers this as a translation of καταληπτόν. With its passive sense, καταληπτόν should mean 'capable of being grasped', cf. its use at **68T**, and this suits *cerneretur*, 7. For suggestions about why καταληπτός replaces the usual term καταληπτικός, cf. Sandbach [474], 20–1 n. 13.

C Diogenes Laertius 7.46 (*SVF* 2.53, part)

τὴν δὲ φαντασίαν εἶναι τύπωσιν ἐν ψυχῇ, τοῦ ὀνόματος οἰκείως μετενηνεγμένου ἀπὸ τῶν τύπων τῶν ἐν τῷ κηρῷ ὑπὸ τοῦ δακτυλίου γινομένων. (1) τῆς δὲ φαντασίας τὴν μὲν καταληπτικήν, τὴν δὲ ἀκατάληπτον· (2) καταληπτικὴν μέν, ἥν κριτήριον εἶναι τῶν πραγμάτων φασί, τὴν γινομένην ἀπὸ ὑπάρχοντος κατ' αὐτὸ τὸ ὑπάρχον ἐναπεσφραγισμένην καὶ ἐναπομεμαγμένην· (3) ἀκατάληπτον δὲ ἤ 5 τὴν μὴ ἀπὸ ὑπάρχοντος, ἤ ἀπὸ ὑπάρχοντος μέν, μὴ κατ' αὐτὸ δὲ τὸ ὑπάρχον· τὴν μὴ τρανῆ μηδὲ ἔκτυπον.

2 τῶν F: om. BP   γινομένων BP: γενομένων F   4 φασί P: om. BF

Context: immediately preceding **31B**

1–2 See **39A** 8–11.

3–5 This formulation of the cognitive impression recalls its early Zenonian form (cf. **D** 4), omitting the clause οἵα οὐκ ἂν γένοιτο ἀπὸ μὴ ὑπάρχοντος, which Diogenes does include in **39A** 13. Also, in the more elaborate analysis of **E** 5–6, ἐναπεσφραγισμένην καὶ ἐναπομεμαγμένην is distinguished as a third attribute over and above being merely κατ' αὐτὸ τὸ ὑπάρχον.

7 For ἔκτυπον, cf. ἐκτύπως, the opposite of συγκεχυμένως, **69D** 4.

D Cicero, *Acad.* 2.77–8

(1) quaesivit de Zenone fortasse quid futurum esset si nec percipere quicquam posset sapiens nec opinari sapientis esset. (2) ille credo nihil opinaturum, quoniam esset quod percipi posset. (3) quid ergo id esset? visum credo. (4) quale igitur visum? tum illum ita definisse: ex eo quod esset sicut esset inpressum et signatum et effictum. (5) post requisitum etiamne si eius modi 5 esset visum verum quale vel falsum. (6) hic Zenonem vidisse acute nullum esse visum quod percipi posset, si id tale esset ab eo quod est cuius modi ab eo quod non est posset esse. (7) recte consensit Arcesilas ad definitionem additum,

neque enim falsum percipi posse neque verum si esset tale quale vel falsum; (8)
incubuit autem in eas disputationes ut doceret nullum tale esse visum a vero ut   10
non eiusdem modi etiam a falso possit esse. (9) haec est una contentio quae
adhuc permanserit.

Context: following **68O** and continued at **69H**.

In judging the historicity of Zeno's arguments with Arcesilaus, note Cicero's
qualifications, *fortasse*, 1, *credo*, 2–3. On the evidence of Diogenes Laertius, it could
appear that the Stoic who principally defended the epistemology against Arcesilaus
was Aristo; cf. 7.162–3 and Long [622]. No doubt, however, attaches to the revision
of the definition of the cognitive impression, 6–8, which Arcesilaus prompted; cf. **E**
23–6. For some novel suggestions about Arcesilaus' part in prompting the Stoics to
refine Zeno's epistemology, cf. Ioppolo [620], 325ff.

E Sextus Empiricus, *M.* 7.247–52 (*SVF* 2.65, part)

(1) τῶν δὲ ἀληθῶν αἱ μέν εἰσι καταληπτικαὶ αἱ δὲ οὔ, (2) οὐ καταληπτικαὶ
μὲν αἱ προσπίπτουσαί τισι κατὰ πάθος· μυρίοι γὰρ φρενιτίζοντες καὶ
μελαγχολῶντες ἀληθῆ μὲν ἕλκουσι φαντασίαν, οὐ καταληπτικὴν δὲ ἀλλ᾽
ἔξωθεν καὶ ἐκ τύχης οὕτω συμπεσοῦσαν, ὅθεν οὐδὲ διαβεβαιοῦνται περὶ
αὐτῆς πολλάκις, οὐδὲ συγκατατίθενται αὐτῇ. (3) καταληπτικὴ δέ ἐστιν ἡ   5
ἀπὸ ὑπάρχοντος καὶ κατ᾽ αὐτὸ τὸ ὑπάρχον ἐναπομεμαγμένη καὶ ἐναπεσ-
φραγισμένη, ὁποία οὐκ ἂν γένοιτο ἀπὸ μὴ ὑπάρχοντος· ἄκρως γὰρ
ποιούμενοι ἀντιληπτικὴν εἶναι τῶν ὑποκειμένων τήνδε τὴν φαντασίαν καὶ
πάντα τεχνικῶς τὰ περὶ αὐτοῖς ἰδιώματα ἀναμεμαγμένην, ἕκαστον
τούτων φασὶν ἔχειν συμβεβηκός. (4) ὧν πρῶτον μὲν τὸ ἀπὸ ὑπάρχοντος   10
γίνεσθαι· πολλαὶ γὰρ τῶν φαντασιῶν προσπίπτουσιν ἀπὸ μὴ ὑπάρχοντος
ὥσπερ ἐπὶ τῶν μεμηνότων, αἵτινες οὐκ ἂν εἶεν καταληπτικαί. (5) δεύτερον
δὲ τὸ καὶ ἀπὸ ὑπάρχοντος εἶναι καὶ κατ᾽ αὐτο τὸ ὑπάρχον· ἔνιαι γὰρ πάλιν
ἀπὸ ὑπάρχοντος μέν εἰσιν, οὐκ αὐτὸ δὲ τὸ ὑπάρχον ἰνδάλλονται, ὡς ἐπὶ τοῦ
μεμηνότος Ὀρέστου μικρῷ πρότερον ἐδείκνυμεν. εἷλκε μὲν γὰρ φαντασίαν ἀπὸ   15
ὑπάρχοντος, τῆς Ἠλέκτρας, οὐ κατ᾽ αὐτὸ δὲ τὸ ὑπάρχον· μίαν γὰρ τῶν Ἐρινύων
ὑπελάμβανεν αὐτὴν εἶναι ... (6) οὐ μὴν ἀλλὰ καὶ ἐναπομεμαγμένην καὶ
ἐναπεσφραγισμένην τυγχάνειν, ἵνα πάντα τεχνικῶς τὰ ἰδιώματα τῶν
φανταστῶν ἀναμάττηται. ὡς γὰρ οἱ γλυφεῖς πᾶσι τοῖς μέρεσι συμβάλλουσι τῶν
τελουμένων, καὶ ὃν τρόπον αἱ διὰ τῶν δακτυλίων σφραγῖδες ἀεὶ πάντας ἐπ᾽   20
ἀκριβὲς τοὺς χαρακτῆρας ἐναπομάττονται τῷ κηρῷ, οὕτω καὶ οἱ
κατάληψιν ποιούμενοι τῶν ὑποκειμένων πᾶσιν ὀφείλουσιν αὐτῶν τοῖς
ἰδιώμασιν ἐπιβάλλειν. (7) τὸ δὲ "οἷα οὐκ ἂν γένοιτο ἀπὸ μὴ ὑπάρχοντος"
προσέθεσαν, ἐπεὶ οὐχ ὥσπερ οἱ ἀπὸ τῆς Στοᾶς ἀδύνατον ὑπειλήφασι κατὰ
πάντα ἀπαράλλακτόν τινα εὑρεθήσεσθαι, οὕτω καὶ οἱ ἀπὸ τῆς Ἀκαδη-   25
μίας. ἐκεῖνοι μὲν γάρ φασιν ὅτι ὁ ἔχων τὴν καταληπτικὴν φαντασίαν
τεχνικῶς προσβάλλει τῇ ὑπούσῃ τῶν πραγμάτων διαφορᾷ, ἐπείπερ καὶ
εἶχέ τι τοιοῦτον ἰδίωμα ἡ τοιαύτη φαντασία παρὰ ἄλλας φαντασίας

καθάπερ οἱ κεράσται παρὰ τοὺς ἄλλους ὄφεις· οἱ δὲ ἀπὸ τῆς ᾽Ακαδημίας τοὐναντίον φασὶ δύνασθαι τῇ καταληπτικῇ φαντασίᾳ ἀπαράλλακτον εὑρεθήσεσθαι ψεῦδος.   30

8 ποιούμενοι codd.: πιστούμενοι Kayser   9 αὐτοῖς Bekker: αὐτοὺς codd.   10 ὧν Bekker: ὃ codd.: del. Kochalsky   16 οὐ κατ᾽ Bekker: οὐκ codd.   19 φανταστῶν Apelt: φαντασιῶν codd.

Context: continuing 39G.

The fullness of this account is impressive, by comparison with C. Notice, however, that while the two accounts agree on the two primary conditions which fail to make a φαντασία kataleptic (C 6–7 and E 4–5), these ἀκατάληπτοι φαντασίαι, as C calls them, are not the same as the οὐ καταληπτικαί with which E starts. The latter unlike the former are all a subdivision of *true* impressions, with their failure to be kataleptic explained by their being experiences of abnormal people, 1–5. The focus on abnormal people continues as the first two attributes of the cognitive impression are laid out, 4–5. Impressions which are either ἀπὸ μὴ ὑπάρχοντος or, though they arise from what is, fail to represent the object, are false; and the examples of Orestes and Heracles make the presumption that normal people do not typically have such impressions. Then, at 6, the condition is specified which marks off cognitive impressions from impressions which may be true but fall short of being cognitive – the stamping and sealing of the object's properties on the impression. Here the focus is clearly on people quite generally, since there can be nothing pathological about having impressions from time to time that fail to meet this condition. On 7, cf. Frede [468], 81. We agree with him that this clause should not refer to some attribute of cognitive impressions over and above the previous ones, but that it spells out the distinctiveness those attributes confer on such impressions.

9 ἰδιώματα   These need not be confined to ἰδίως ποιά; cf. vol. 1, 194, for ἴδιον used of the distinguishing characteristic of a species or kind. For the interpretation of πάντα, see note on 41B 8.

F Diogenes Laertius 7.177 (*SVF* 1.625) and Athenaeus 354E (*SVF* 1.624, part)

... (1) Σφαῖρος ὁ Βοσποριανός, ὃς προκοπὴν ἱκανὴν περιποιησάμενος λόγων εἰς ᾽Αλεξάνδρειαν ἀπῄει πρὸς Πτολεμαῖον τὸν Φιλοπάτορα. λόγου δέ ποτε γενομένου περὶ τοῦ δοξάσειν τὸν σοφὸν καὶ τοῦ Σφαίρου εἰπόντος ὡς οὐ δοξάσει, βουλόμενος ὁ βασιλεὺς ἐλέγξαι αὐτόν, κηρίνας ῥόας ἐκέλευσε παρατεθῆναι· (2) τοῦ δὲ Σφαίρου ἀπατηθέντος ἀνεβόησεν ὁ βασιλεὺς   5 ψευδεῖ συγκατατεθεῖσθαι αὐτὸν φαντασίᾳ. πρὸς ὃν ὁ Σφαῖρος εὐστόχως ἀπεκρίνατο, εἰπὼν οὕτως συγκατατεθεῖσθαι, οὐχ ὅτι ῥόαι εἰσίν, ἀλλ᾽ ὅτι εὔλογόν ἐστι ῥόας αὐτὰς εἶναι· (3) διαφέρειν δὲ τὴν καταληπτικὴν φαντασίαν τοῦ εὐλόγου ... τὴν μὲν γὰρ ἀδιάψευστον εἶναι, τὸ δ᾽ εὔλογον ⟨κἂν⟩ ἄλλως ἀποβαίνειν.   10

2 ἀπῄει F: ἀπῆρε BP   10 ⟨κἂν⟩ Wilamowitz

Context: life of Sphaerus.

9–10   We have supplemented Diogenes' account by adding Athenaeus' explanation of the difference between καταληπτικός and εὔλογος. On the latter, cf. D.L. 7.76, εὔλογον δέ ἐστιν ἀξίωμα τὸ πλείονας ἀφορμὰς ἔχον εἰς τὸ ἀληθὲς εἶναι, οἷον "βιώσομαι αὔριον", and 59B 1; 69B.

40 The criteria of truth

G Plutarch, *Comm. not.* 1059B–C (*SVF* 2.33)

(1) εἶτά τις εἶπεν αὐτῶν ὡς οὐκ ἀπὸ τύχης ἀλλ᾽ ἐκ προνοίας θεῶν νομίζοι
μετ᾽ Ἀρκεσίλαον καὶ πρὸ Καρνεάδου γεγονέναι Χρύσιππον, ὧν ὁ μὲν
ὑπῆρξε τῆς εἰς τὴν συνήθειαν ὕβρεως καὶ παρανομίας ὁ δ᾽ ἤνθησε μάλιστα
τῶν Ἀκαδημαικῶν. (2) Χρύσιππος γοῦν ἐν μέσῳ γενόμενος ταῖς πρὸς
Ἀρκεσίλαον ἀντιγραφαῖς καὶ τὴν Καρνεάδου δεινότητα ἐνέφραξε, πολλὰ   5
μὲν τῇ αἰσθήσει καταλιπὼν ὥσπερ εἰς πολιορκίαν βοηθήματα, τὸν δὲ περὶ
τὰς προλήψεις καὶ τὰς ἐννοίας τάραχον ἀφελὼν παντάπασι καὶ διαρθρώσας ἑκάστην καὶ θέμενος εἰς τὸ οἰκεῖον· ὥστε καὶ τοὺς αὖθις ἐκκρούειν τὰ
πράγματα καὶ παραβιάζεσθαι βουλομένους μηδὲν περαίνειν ἀλλ᾽ ἐλέγχεσθαι [βουλομέ-
νους] κακουργοῦντας καὶ σοφιζομένους.   10

2 ὧν Leonicus, Basil.: οἷον codd.   7–8 διαρθρώσας Wyttenbach: διορθώσας codd.   9–10
βουλομένους² del. Reiske

Context: Stoics' resentment of the older (sceptical) Academics' sophistry; cf. 8–10.

3 **συνήθειαν** For this use of the term, cf. 31O 5.

4–5 Chrysippus wrote a book against Arcesilaus' μεθόδιον, 37B 6; for his
comments on argument designed to induce ἐποχή, cf. 31P.

6–8 This is not the claim that Chrysippus removed confusion surrounding the
ideas of ἔννοια and πρόληψις (thus e.g. Sandbach [470], 22), but merely that he
clarified individual concepts by 'articulating' them, i.e. by framing their definitions.
Cf. 32H 5–8, and for the association of 'articulation' with definition, see 32I with
note.

H Sextus Empiricus, *M.* 7.402–10

(1) τούτων δὲ τὰ μὲν ἄλλα λέγουσιν οἱ περὶ τὸν Καρνεάδην συγχωρήσειν
τοῖς ἀπὸ τῆς Στοᾶς, τὸ δὲ "οἷα οὐκ ἂν γένοιτο ἀπὸ μὴ ὑπάρχοντος"
ἀσυγχώρητον εἶναι. γίνονται γὰρ καὶ ἀπὸ μὴ ὑπαρχόντων φαντασίαι ὡς
ἀπὸ ὑπαρχόντων. (2) καὶ τεκμήριον τῆς ἀπαραλλαξίας τὸ ἐπ᾽ ἴσης ταύτας
ἐναργεῖς καὶ πληκτικὰς εὑρίσκεσθαι, τοῦ δὲ ἐπ᾽ ἴσης πληκτικὰς καὶ   5
ἐναργεῖς εἶναι τὸ τὰς ἀκολούθους πράξεις ἐπιζεύγνυσθαι. ὥσπερ γὰρ ἐν
τοῖς ὕπαρ ὁ μὲν διψῶν ἀρυόμενος ποτὸν ἥδεται, ὁ δὲ θηρίον ἢ ἄλλο τι τῶν
δειμαλέων φεύγων βοᾷ καὶ κέκραγεν, οὕτω καὶ κατὰ τοὺς ὕπνους ἥ μὲν
διάχυσίς ἐστι τοῖς διψῶσι καὶ ἀπὸ κρήνης πίνειν δοκοῦσιν, ἀνάλογον δὲ
φόβος τοῖς δειματουμένοις . . . καὶ ὃν τρόπον ἐν καταστάσει τοῖς τρανό-   10
τατα φαινομένοις πιστεύομεν καὶ συγκατατιθέμεθα, οἷον Δίωνι μὲν ὡς
Δίωνι, Θέωνι δὲ ὡς Θέωνι προσφερόμενοι, οὕτω καὶ ἐν μανίᾳ τὸ
παραπλήσιον πάσχουσί τινες. ὁ γοῦν Ἡρακλῆς μανείς, καὶ λαβὼν
φαντασίαν ἀπὸ τῶν ἰδίων παίδων ὡς Εὐρυσθέως, τὴν ἀκόλουθον πρᾶξιν
ταύτῃ φαντασίᾳ συνῆψεν. ἀκόλουθον δὲ ἦν τὸ τοὺς τοῦ ἐχθροῦ παῖδας   15
ἀνελεῖν, ὅπερ καὶ ἐποίησεν. (3) εἰ οὖν καταληπτικαί τινές εἰσι φαντασίαι
παρόσον ἐπάγονται ἡμᾶς εἰς συγκατάθεσιν καὶ εἰς τὸ τὴν ἀκόλουθον
αὐταῖς πρᾶξιν συνάπτειν, ἐπεὶ καὶ ψευδεῖς τοιαῦται πεφήνασι, λεκτέον
ἀπαραλλάκτους εἶναι ταῖς καταληπτικαῖς φαντασίαις τὰς ἀκαταλήπτους.

247

Epistemology: Stoics and Academics

καὶ μὴν ὃν τρόπον ἀπὸ τῶν τόξων ἐλάμβανε φαντασίαν ὁ ἥρως, οὕτω καὶ ἀπὸ τῶν ἰδίων   20
παίδων ὅτι Εὐρυσθέως εἰσὶ παῖδες. μία γὰρ καὶ ἡ αὐτὴ προυπέκειτο καὶ ὡσαύτως ἔχοντι
φαντασία. ἀλλ' ἦν ἡ μὲν ἀπὸ τῶν τόξων ἀληθής, ἡ δὲ ἀπὸ τῶν παίδων ψευδής. ἐπ' ἴσης οὖν
κινουσῶν ἀμφοτέρων ὁμολογητέον ἀπαράλλακτον εἶναι τὴν ἑτέραν τῇ ἑτέρᾳ· καὶ εἰ ἡ ἀπὸ
τῶν τόξων λέγεται καταληπτική, ὅτι ⟨ἡ⟩ ἀκόλουθος αὐτῇ πρᾶξις ἐπεζεύχθη τοῖς τόξοις
αὐτοῦ ὡς τόξοις χρησαμένου, λεγέσθω καὶ ἡ ἀπὸ τῶν παίδων μὴ διαφέρειν ταύτης,   25
παρόσον καὶ ταύτῃ τὸ ἀκόλουθον ἐπεζεύχθη ἔργον, τουτέστι τὸ τοὺς τοῦ ἐχθροῦ παῖδας
δεῖν ἀναιρεῖν. ἀλλὰ γὰρ αὕτη μὲν ἡ ἀπαραλλαξία τῶν τε καταληπτικῶν καὶ τῶν
ἀκαταλήπτων φαντασιῶν κατὰ τὸ ἐναργὲς καὶ ἔντονον ἰδίωμα παρίσταται. (4) οὐδὲν δὲ
ἧττον δείκνυται τοῖς ἀπὸ τῆς Ἀκαδημίας καὶ ἡ κατὰ χαρακτῆρα καὶ [ἡ]
κατὰ τύπον. καλοῦσι δὲ ἐπὶ τὰ φαινόμενα τοὺς Στωικούς. ἐπὶ γὰρ τῶν   30
ὁμοίων μὲν κατὰ μορφήν, διαφερόντων δὲ κατὰ τὸ ὑποκείμενον, ἀμήχανόν
ἐστι διορίζειν τὴν καταληπτικὴν φαντασίαν ἀπὸ τῆς ψευδοῦς καὶ
ἀκαταλήπτου· οἷον δυεῖν ᾠῶν ἄκρως ἀλλήλοις ὁμοίων ⟨εἰ⟩ ἐναλλὰξ τῷ
Στωικῷ δίδωμι πρὸς διάκρισιν, [εἰ] ἐπιβαλὼν ὁ σοφὸς ἰσχύσει λέγειν
ἀδιαπτώτως πότερον ἕν ἐστι τὸ δεικνύμενον ᾠὸν ἢ ἄλλο καὶ ἄλλο; ὁ δ'   35
αὐτὸς λόγος ἐστὶ καὶ ἐπὶ διδύμων· λήψεται γὰρ ψευδῆ φαντασίαν ὁ
σπουδαῖος καὶ ⟨ὅμ⟩ως ἀπὸ ὑπάρχοντος καὶ κατ' αὐτὸ τὸ ὑπάρχον
ἐναπομεμαγμένην καὶ ἐναπεσφραγισμένην ἔχων τὴν φαντασίαν, ἐὰν ἀπὸ
Κάστορος ὡς ἀπὸ Πολυδεύκους φαντασιωθῇ. ἐντεῦθεν γοῦν καὶ ὁ ἐγκεκαλυμμένος συνέστη λόγος.   40

5 τοῦ Hervetus: τὸ codd.   10 ἐν ⟨ὑγιεῖ⟩ Mutschmann   20 τόξων ⟨ὡς τόξων⟩ Heintz   23
κινουσῶν N: κλινουσῶν cett.   24 ⟨ἡ⟩ Heintz   29 ἡ del. Bekker   30 ἐπὶ Bekker: ἐπεὶ
codd.   33–4 ⟨εἰ⟩ ... [εἰ] Heintz   34 σοφὸς ⟨οὐκ⟩ Heintz   37 καὶ ⟨ὅμ⟩ως A.A.Long: καὶ ὡς
codd.: καίπερ Bekker: ὡς secl. Kayser

Context: report of Carneades' criticism of the cognitive impression.

1 τὰ μὲν ἄλλα I.e. E 4–6.

5–6 πληκτικὰς καὶ ἐναργεῖς Carneades is picking on the Stoics' own
terminology; cf. K 17–18.

13–19 Carneades can be seen to draw first on the Stoics' analysis of a πιθανὸν
ἀξίωμα (cf. 37M) and secondly to exploit the Stoics' concept of a καθῆκον; cf. 59B
where this concept is analysed in terms of ἀκόλουθον and εὔλογον: assenting and then
acting consequentially are no grounds for supposing that the agent has securely
grasped something true.

39–40 For this argument, see 37B–D.

I Cicero, Acad. 2.57

hic pugnes licet, non repugnabo, (1) quin etiam concedam illum ipsum sapientem,
de quo omnis hic sermo est, cum ei res similes occurrant quas non habeat
dinotatas, retenturam adsensum nec umquam ulli viso adsensurum nisi quod
tale fuerit quale falsum esse non possit. (2) sed et ad ceteras res habet quandam
artem qua vera a falsis possit distinguere, et ad similitudines istas usus   5

adhibendus est: ut mater geminos internoscit consuetudine oculorum, sic tu internosces si adsueveris.

4 *et ad* V²: *et* V¹: *ad* A²B [A¹]

Context: Lucullus' defence of Stoic–Antiochean epistemology against New Academic criticism.

J Cicero, *Acad.* 2.83–5

(1) quattuor sunt capita quae concludant nihil esse quod nosci percipi conprehendi possit, de quo haec tota quaestio est. e quibus primum est esse aliquod visum falsum, (2) secundum non posse id percipi, (3) tertium inter quae visa nihil intersit fieri non posse ut eorum alia percipi possint alia non possint, (4) quartum nullum esse visum verum a sensu profectum cui non 5 adpositum sit visum aliud quod ab eo nihil intersit quodque percipi non possit. (5) horum quattuor capitum secundum et tertium omnes concedunt; primum Epicurus non dat, vos, quibuscum res est, id quoque conceditis; omnis pugna de quarto est. (6) qui igitur P. Servilium Geminum videbat, si Quintum se videre putabat, incidebat in eius modi visum quod percipi non posset, quia 10 nulla nota verum distinguebatur a falso; qua distinctione sublata quam haberet in C. Cotta, qui bis cum Gemino consul fuit, agnoscendo eius modi notam quae falsa esse non possit? (7) negas tantam similitudinem in rerum natura esse; . . . ne sit sane: videri certe potest; fallet igitur sensus. et si una fefellerit similitudo, dubia omnia reddiderit; sublato enim iudicio illo quo oportet 15 agnosci, etiam si ipse erit quem videris qui tibi videbitur, tamen non ea nota iudicabis qua dicis oportere ut non possit esse eiusdem modi falsa . . . (8) omnia dicis sui generis esse, nihil esse idem quod sit aliud. Stoicumst id quidem nec admodum credibile, nullum esse pilum omnibus rebus talem qualis sit pilus alius, nullum granum. (9) haec refelli possunt, sed pugnare nolo; ad id 20 enim quod agitur nihil interest omnibusne partibus visa re nihil differat an internosci non possit etiam si differat.

18   *Stoicum est id* Lb: *stoicum sedem* A¹V¹B¹: *stoicum sed est* A²V²B²

Context: Cicero's account of the Academic strategy for undermining cognition.

8   For Epicurus' position, see **16**.

18–20   For an excellent discussion of the bearing of this thesis (the identity of indiscernibles) on Stoic epistemology, cf. Frede [468], 77.

K Sextus Empiricus, *M.* 7.253–60

(1) ἀλλὰ γὰρ οἱ μὲν ἀρχαιότεροι τῶν Στωικῶν κριτήριόν φασιν εἶναι τῆς ἀληθείας τὴν καταληπτικὴν ταύτην φαντασίαν, οἱ δὲ νεώτεροι προσετίθεσαν καὶ τὸ μηδὲν ἔχουσαν ἔνστημα. ἔσθ' ὅτε γὰρ καταληπτικὴ μὲν προσπίπτει φαντασία, ἄπιστος δὲ διὰ τὴν ἔξωθεν περίστασιν. (2) οἷον ὅτε Ἀδμήτῳ ὁ Ἡρακλῆς τὴν Ἄλκηστιν γῆθεν ἀναγαγὼν παρέστησε, τότε ὁ 5

Epistemology: Stoics and Academics

Ἄδμητος ἔσπασε μὲν καταληπτικὴν φαντασίαν ἀπὸ τῆς Ἀλκήστιδος,
ἠπίστει δ᾽ αὐτῇ· καὶ ὅτε ἀπὸ Τροίας ὁ Μενέλαος ἀνακομισθεὶς ἑώρα τὴν ἀληθῆ Ἑλένην
παρὰ τῷ Πρωτεῖ, [καὶ] καταλιπὼν ἐπὶ τῆς νεὼς τὸ ἐκείνης εἴδωλον, περὶ οὗ δεκαετῆς
συνέστη πόλεμος, ἀπὸ ὑπάρχοντος μὲν καὶ κατ᾽ αὐτὸ τὸ ὑπάρχον καὶ ἐναπομεμαγμένην καὶ
ἐναπεσφραγισμένην ἐλάμβανε φαντασίαν, οὐκ εἶκε δὲ αὐτῇ, ὥσθ᾽ ἡ μὲν καταληπτικὴ   10
φαντασία κριτήριόν ἐστι μηδὲν ἔχουσα ἔνστημα, αὗται δὲ καταληπτικαὶ μὲν ἦσαν, εἶχον δὲ
ἐνστάσεις· ὅ τε γὰρ Ἄδμητος ἐλογίζετο ὅτι τέθνηκεν ἡ Ἄλκηστις καὶ ὅτι ὁ
ἀποθανὼν οὐκέτι ἀνίσταται, ἀλλὰ δαιμόνιά τινά ποτε ἐπιφοιτᾷ· ὅ τε
Μενέλαος συνεώρα ὅτι ἀπολέλοιπεν ἐν τῇ νηὶ φυλαττομένην τὴν Ἑλένην, καὶ οὐκ ἀπίθανον
μέν ἐστιν Ἑλένην μὴ εἶναι τὴν ἐπὶ τῆς Φάρου εὑρεθεῖσαν, φάντασμα δέ τι καὶ δαιμόνιον. (3)   15
ἐνθένδε οὐχ ἁπλῶς κριτήριον γίνεται τῆς ἀληθείας ἡ καταληπτικὴ
φαντασία, ἀλλ᾽ ὅταν μηδὲν ἔνστημα ἔχῃ. αὕτη γὰρ ἐναργὴς οὖσα καὶ
πληκτικὴ μόνον οὐχὶ τῶν τριχῶν, φασί, λαμβάνεται, κατασπῶσα ἡμᾶς εἰς
συγκατάθεσιν, καὶ ἄλλου μηδενὸς δεομένη εἰς τὸ τοιαύτη προσπίπτειν ἢ
εἰς τὸ τὴν πρὸς τὰς ἄλλας διαφορὰν ὑποβάλλειν. (4) διὸ δὴ καὶ πᾶς   20
ἄνθρωπος, ὅταν τι σπουδάζῃ μετὰ ἀκριβείας καταλαμβάνεσθαι, τὴν
τοιαύτην φαντασίαν ἐξ ἑαυτοῦ μεταδιώκειν φαίνεται, οἷον ἐπὶ τῶν
ὁρατῶν, ὅταν ἀμυδρὰν λαμβάνῃ τοῦ ὑποκειμένου φαντασίαν. ἐντείνει γὰρ
τὴν ὄψιν καὶ σύνεγγυς ἔρχεται τοῦ ὁρωμένου ὡς τέλεον μὴ πλανᾶσθαι,
παρατρίβει τε τοὺς ὀφθαλμοὺς καὶ καθόλου πάντα ποιεῖ, μέχρις ἂν τρανὴν   25
καὶ πληκτικὴν σπάσῃ τοῦ κρινομένου φαντασίαν, ὡς ἐν ταύτῃ κειμένην
θεωρῶν τὴν τῆς καταλήψεως πίστιν. (5) καὶ γὰρ ἄλλως τοὐναντίον
ἀδύνατόν ἐστι λέγειν, καὶ ἀνάγκη τὸν ἀφιστάμενον τοῦ ἀξιοῦν ὅτι
φαντασία κριτήριόν ἐστι, καθ᾽ ἑτέρας φαντασίας ὑπόστασιν τοῦτο
πάσχοντα βεβαιοῦν τὸ φαντασίαν εἶναι κριτήριον, (6) τῆς φύσεως οἱονεὶ   30
φέγγος ἡμῖν πρὸς ἐπίγνωσιν τῆς ἀληθείας τὴν αἰσθητικὴν δύναμιν
ἀναδούσης καὶ τὴν δι᾽ αὐτῆς γινομένην φαντασίαν. ἄτοπον οὖν ἐστι
τοσαύτην δύναμιν ἀθετεῖν καὶ τὸ ὥσπερ φῶς αὐτῶν ἀφαιρεῖσθαι. (7) ὃν
γὰρ τρόπον ὁ χρώματα μὲν ἀπολείπων καὶ τὰς ἐν τούτοις διαφοράς, τὴν δὲ
ὅρασιν ἀναιρῶν ὡς ἀνύπαρκτον ἢ ἄπιστον, καὶ φωνὰς μὲν εἶναι λέγων,   35
ἀκοὴν δὲ μὴ ὑπάρχειν ἀξιῶν, σφόδρα ἐστὶν ἄτοπος (δι᾽ ὧν γὰρ ἐνοήσαμεν
χρώματα καὶ φωνάς, ἐκείνων ἀπόντων οὐδὲ χρῆσθαι δυνατοὶ χρώμασιν ἢ
φωναῖς), οὕτω καὶ ὁ τὰ πράγματα μὲν ὁμολογῶν, τὴν δὲ φαντασίαν τῆς
αἰσθήσεως, δι᾽ ἧς τῶν πραγμάτων ἀντιλαμβάνεται, διαβάλλων τελέως
ἐστὶν ἐμβρόντητος, καὶ τοῖς ἀψύχοις ἴσον αὐτὸν ποιῶν.   40

---

8 καὶ del. Bekker   10 εἶκε ... αὐτῇ Lachelier: εἶχε ... αὐτὴν codd.   19 προσπίπτειν N:
προπίπτειν cett.   25 τε Mutschmann: γὰρ codd.   28 καὶ ἀνάγκη Hirzel: κατ᾽ ἀνάγκην codd.

Context: following **E**.

2 **νεώτεροι** These Stoics, on the evidence of **H**, were answering Carneades'
objections. Thus they probably included Antipater; and their rejoinder to the
Academics was also repeated by Antiochus; compare **K** 17–20, 27–40 with **N 5, O 3**.

L Sextus Empiricus, *M.* 7.424

ἵνα γε μὴν αἰσθητικὴ γένηται φαντασία κατ᾽ αὐτούς, οἷον ὁρατική, δεῖ
πέντε συνδραμεῖν, τό τε αἰσθητήριον καὶ τὸ αἰσθητὸν καὶ τὸν τόπον καὶ τὸ
πῶς καὶ τὴν διάνοιαν, ὡς ἐὰν τῶν ἄλλων παρόντων ἓν μόνον ἀπῇ, καθάπερ
διάνοια παρὰ φύσιν ἔχουσα, οὐ σωθήσεται, φασίν, ἡ ἀντίληψις. ἔνθεν καὶ
τὴν καταληπτικὴν φαντασίαν ἔλεγόν τινες μὴ κοινῶς εἶναι κριτήριον, ἀλλ᾽   5
ὅταν μηδὲν ἔχῃ κατὰ ⟨τοῦτον⟩ τὸν τρόπον ἔνστημα.

3 πῶς codd.: φῶς Heintz   4 σωθήσεται] συνθήσεται N   5 εἶναι om. ς   6 ⟨τοῦτον⟩
A.A.Long   τρόπον codd.: τόπον Mutschmann

Context: a few sections after (Academic-inspired?) criticism of the cognitive
impression by means of the Sorites (including **37F**).
  2 **συνδραμεῖν** Cf. the συνδρομή of factors required by Carneades for the
ἀπερίσπαστος φαντασία, **69E** 1–3.
  6 **ἔνστημα** See **K**.

M Cicero, *Acad.* 2.22

quod si essent falsae notitiae (ἐννοίας enim notitias appellare tu videbare) – (1) si igitur
essent eae falsae aut eius modi visis inpressae qualia visa a falsis discerni non
possent, quo tandem his modo uteremur? (2) quo modo autem quid cuique rei
consentaneum esset quid repugnaret videremus? (3) memoriae quidem certe,
quae non modo philosophiam sed omnis vitae usum omnesque artes una   5
maxime continet, nihil omnino loci relinquitur. quae potest enim esse
memoria falsorum? aut quid quisquam meminit quod non animo conprehen-
dit et tenet?

Context: following **39C** and preceding **42B**.
  For ἔννοιαι and memory, cf. **N** 1; **39E–F**.

N Cicero, *Acad.* 2.30–1

(1) mens enim ipsa, quae sensuum fons est atque etiam ipsa sensus est,
naturalem vim habet quam intendit ad ea quibus movetur. itaque alia visa sic
arripit ut iis statim utatur, alia quasi recondit, e quibus memoria oritur; cetera
autem similitudinibus construit, ex quibus efficiuntur notitiae rerum, quas
Graeci tum ἐννοίας tum προλήψεις vocant; (2) eo cum accessit ratio   5
argumentique conclusio rerumque innumerabilium multitudo, tum et
perceptio eorum omnium apparet et eadem ratio perfecta is gradibus ad
sapientiam pervenit. (3) ad rerum igitur scientiam vitaeque constantiam
aptissima cum sit mens hominis, amplectitur maxime cognitionem et istam
κατάληψιν . . . cum ipsam per se amat (nihil enim est ei veritatis luce dulcius) tum   10
etiam propter usum. (4) quocirca et sensibus utitur et artes efficit quasi sensus
alteros et usque eo philosophiam ipsam corroborat ut virtutem efficiat, ex qua
re una vita omnis apta sit. (5) ergo i qui negant quicquam posse conprendi haec

ipsa eripiunt vel instrumenta vel ornamenta vitae, vel potius etiam totam
vitam evertunt funditus ipsumque animal orbant animo, ut difficile sit de   15
temeritate eorum perinde ut causa postulat dicere.

Context: Lucullus' recourse to natural teleology in defence of Stoic–Antiochean
epistemology.

1 **mens . . . ipsa sensus est**   We take *sensus* as a plural, since the senses are not
something independent of the mind, nor would it be Stoic doctrine to describe the
mind as *a* sense over and above the standard five; cf. note on **39C**.

10   Cf. Cicero, *Fin.* 3.17, καταλήψεις . . . *propter se asciscendas arbitramur.*

12–13 **ex qua–omnis**   Virtue is περὶ ὅλον τὸν βίον τέχνη, **61G 2**.

13–16   Similarly **K 5–7**.

O Cicero, *Acad.* 2.37–8

(1) nam cum vim quae esset in sensibus explicabamus, simul illud aperiebatur,
comprehendi multa et percipi sensibus, quod fieri sine adsensione non potest.
(2) deinde cum inter inanimum et animal hoc maxime intersit quod animal
agit aliquid (nihil enim agens ne cogitari quidem potest quale sit), aut ei sensus
adimendus est aut ea quae est in nostra potestate sita reddenda adsensio. (3) at   5
vero animus quodam modo eripitur iis quos neque sentire neque adsentiri
volunt; ut enim necesse est lancem in libram ponderibus inpositis deprimi, sic
animum perspicuis cedere. nam quo modo non potest animal ullum non
adpetere id quod accommodatum ad naturam adpareat (Graeci id οἰκεῖον
appellant), sic non potest obiectam rem perspicuam non adprobare.   10

7 *libram*| *liberam* V¹: *libra* A²B²

Context: account of assent, in defence of Stoic–Antiochean epistemology.

1   The reference is to **N** and the sentences preceding it.

3–5   On this attribution of assent to animals in general, cf. vol. 1, 322.

5   *in nostra potestate* = ἐφ' ἡμῖν. Stoicism sees no conflict between assent's being
both 'in our power', as here, and necessitated (7–10); see **62G**.

7–8   The analogy with the balance is particularly appropriate for illustrating the
criterion of truth; cf. **31S** 1–2.

P Diogenes Laertius 7.52

ἡ δὲ κατάληψις γίνεται κατ' αὐτοὺς αἰσθήσει μὲν λευκῶν καὶ μελάνων καὶ
τραχέων καὶ λείων, λόγῳ δὲ τῶν δι' ἀποδείξεως συναγομένων, ὥσπερ τὸ
θεοὺς εἶναι, καὶ προνοεῖν τούτους.

Context: immediately following **Q**.
For αἰσθήσει . . . λόγῳ, see **39A 4**, and for the examples of sensible qualities, **39C**
1.

Q Diogenes Laertius 7.52 (*SVF* 2.71)

αἴσθησις δὲ λέγεται κατὰ τοὺς Στωικοὺς τό τ᾽ ἀφ᾽ ἡγεμονικοῦ πνεῦμα ἐπὶ τὰς αἰσθήσεις διῆκον καὶ ἡ δι᾽ αὐτῶν κατάληψις καὶ ἡ περὶ τὰ αἰσθητήρια κατασκευή, καθ᾽ ἥν τινες πηροὶ γίνονται. καὶ ἡ ἐνέργεια δὲ αἴσθησις καλεῖται.

Context: immediately following 39A.
1–2 τό τ᾽-διῆκον   See 53H 1–2 with notes.

R Plutarch, *Comm. not.* 1060A

βούλομαι ἀπολαῦσαι τῆς ἀμύνης ἐλεγχομένους εἰς ταὐτὸν τοὺς ἄνδρας ἐπιδών, τὸ παρὰ τὰς ἐννοίας καὶ τὰς προλήψεις τὰς κοινὰς φιλοσοφεῖν, ἀφ᾽ ὧν μάλιστα τὴν αἵρεσιν ὡς σπερμάτων ἀνα⟨βλαστεῖν⟩ δοκοῦσι καὶ μόνην ὁμολογεῖν τῇ φύσει λέγουσιν.

2 τὸ Reiske: τῷ codd.   3 ὡς σπερμάτων ἀνα⟨βλαστεῖν⟩ Cherniss: ὥσπερ ἐπὶ τῶν ἀνα⟨. . . .⟩ codd.

Context: a few sections after G.
4   This recalls the Stoics' definition of the ethical end; cf. 63A.

S Epictetus, *Diss.* 1.22.1–3, 9–10

(1) ⟨αἱ⟩ προλήψεις κοιναὶ πᾶσιν ἀνθρώποις εἰσὶ καὶ πρόληψις προλήψει οὐ μάχεται. τίς γὰρ ἡμῶν οὐ τίθησιν, ὅτι τὸ ἀγαθὸν συμφέρον ἐστὶ [ἐστι] καὶ αἱρετὸν καὶ ἐκ πάσης αὐτὸ περιστάσεως δεῖ μετιέναι καὶ διώκειν; τίς δ᾽ ἡμῶν οὐ τίθησιν, ὅτι τὸ δίκαιόν ἐστι καὶ πρέπον; πότ᾽ οὖν ἡ μάχη γίνεται; περὶ τὴν ἐφαρμογὴν τῶν προλήψεων ταῖς ἐπὶ μέρους οὐσίαις, ὅταν ὁ μὲν εἴπῃ   5
"καλῶς ἐποίησεν, ἀνδρεῖός ἐστιν," ⟨ὁ δ᾽⟩ "οὔ, ἀλλ᾽ ἀπονενοημένος." ἔνθεν ἡ μάχη γίνεται τοῖς ἀνθρώποις πρὸς ἀλλήλους . . . (2) τί οὖν ἐστι τὸ παιδεύεσθαι; μανθάνειν τὰς φυσικὰς προλήψεις ἐφαρμόζειν ταῖς ἐπὶ μέρους οὐσίαις καταλλήλως τῇ φύσει καὶ λοιπὸν διελεῖν, ὅτι τῶν ὄντων τὰ μέν ἐστιν ἐφ᾽ ἡμῖν, τὰ δὲ οὐκ ἐφ᾽ ἡμῖν.   10

2 ἐστι² del. s   6 ὁ δ᾽ add. s

Context: discourse περὶ τῶν προλήψεων.
8 ἐφαρμόζειν.   On this fundamental theme in Epictetus, cf. Bonhöffer [311], 192.

T Sextus Empiricus, *M.* 8.337–332a

καίτοι τινὲς εἰώθασιν ἡμῖν, καὶ μάλιστα οἱ ἀπὸ τῆς Ἐπικούρου αἱρέσεως, ἀγροικότερον ἐνίστασθαι, λέγοντες "ἤτοι νοεῖτε, τί ἐστιν ἡ ἀπόδειξις, ἢ οὐ νοεῖτε. καὶ εἰ μὲν νοεῖτε καὶ ἔχετε ἔννοιαν αὐτῆς, ἔστιν ἀπόδειξις· εἰ δὲ οὐ νοεῖτε, πῶς ζητεῖτε τὸ μηδ᾽ ἀρχὴν νοούμενον ὑμῖν;" ταῦτα γὰρ λέγοντες ὑφ᾽ ἑαυτῶν σχεδὸν περιτρέπονται, ἐπείπερ (1) τὸ μὲν παντὸς τοῦ ζητουμένου πρόληψιν καὶ ἔννοιαν δεῖν προηγεῖσθαι ὁμόλογόν ἐστιν.   5
πῶς γάρ τις καὶ ζητῆσαι δύναται μηδεμίαν ἔννοιαν ἔχων τοῦ ζητουμένου πράγματος; οὔτε γὰρ ἐπιτυχὼν εἴσεται, ὅτι ἐπέτυχεν, οὔτε ἀστοχήσας, ὅτι ἠστόχησεν.

(2) ὥστε τοῦτο μὲν δίδομεν, καὶ τοσοῦτόν γε ἀπέχομεν τοῦ λέγειν ἔννοιαν
μὴ ἔχειν παντὸς τοῦ ζητουμένου πράγματος, ὡς καὶ ἀνάπαλιν πολλάς γ'
ἐννοίας αὐτοῦ καὶ προλήψεις ἔχειν ἀξιοῦν, καὶ χάριν τοῦ μὴ δύνασθαι   10
ταύτας διακρίνειν καὶ τὴν ἐξ αὐτῶν κυριωτάτην ἀνευρεῖν εἰς ἐποχὴν καὶ
ἀρρεψίαν περιίστασθαι.

Context: beginning of a refutation of the existence of proof.

Although Sextus' argument is specifically directed against the Epicureans, his
objections in fact apply equally to the Stoics, who took over the concept of προληψις
from Epicurus; cf. **23E 3**.

41 Knowledge and opinion

A Cicero, *Acad.* 2.145 (*SVF* 1.66)

at scire negatis quemquam rem ullam nisi sapientem. (1) et hoc quidem Zeno gestu
conficiebat. (2) nam cum extensis digitis adversam manum ostenderat,
"visum" inquiebat "huius modi est"; (3) dein cum paulum digitos
contraxerat, "adsensus huius modi"; (4) tum cum plane conpresserat
pugnumque fecerat, conprensionem illam esse dicebat, qua ex similitudine   5
etiam nomen ei rei, quod ante non fuerat, κατάληψιν imposuit; (5) cum
autem laevam manum admoverat et illum pugnum arte vehementerque
conpresserat, scientiam talem esse dicebat, cuius compotem nisi sapientem esse
neminem.

4 *contraxerat* dett. Vict.: *contexerat* A: *constrinxerat* N: *conxerat* B

Context: the Stoic distinction between κατάληψις and ἐπιστήμη.

For discussion of the four epistemological states (sections 2–5), cf. Sandbach [474],
11–12; Long [3], 126–9; Görler [479]. The modern tendency is to interpret them as
picking out levels of cognition, not chronologically successive stages. However,
Ioppolo [620], 329ff., argues that the latter was Zeno's doctrine, and was then
modified to the former position by Chrysippus, in response to criticism by Arcesilaus.

1 **gestu**   Note also Zeno's use of the hand to illustrate the difference between
dialectic and rhetoric, **31E**.

B Cicero, *Acad.* 1.41–2 (*SVF* 1.60 part)

(1) quod autem erat sensu comprensum id ipsum sensum appellabat, et si ita
erat comprensum ut convelli ratione non posset scientiam, sin aliter
inscientiam nominabat; ex qua existeret etiam opinio, quae esset imbecilla et
cum falso incognitoque communis. (2) sed inter scientiam et inscientiam
comprehensionem illam quam dixi collocabat, eamque neque in rectis neque   5
in pravis numerabat, sed soli credendum esse dicebat. (3) e quo sensibus etiam
fidem tribuebat, quod ut supra dixi comprehensio facta sensibus et vera esse illi
et fidelis videbatur, non quod omnia quae essent in re comprehenderet, sed
quia nihil quod cadere in eam posset relinqueret, quodque natura quasi

normam scientiae et principium sui dedisset unde postea notiones rerum in   10
animis imprimerentur; e quibus non principia solum sed latiores quaedam ad
rationem inveniendam viae reperiuntur. (4) errorem autem et temeritatem et
ignorantiam et opinationem et suspicionem et uno nomine omnia quae essent
aliena firmae et constantis assensionis a virtute sapientiaque removebat.

3 *existeret* ρω: *-erat* π: *extiterat* Γ: *existebat* Plasberg   6 *soli*] *solum ei* Christ   12 *reperiuntur* codd.:
aperiuntur Manutius: *aperirentur* Davies

Context: immediately following **40B**.

  2 **scientiam**   See also **C** 4–5, **H** 1–2; **31B** 7–8.

  3–4 **ex qua–communis**   Cicero's Latin is too compressed to elucidate the precise
relationship Zeno is supposed to have posited between *inscientia* (ἄγνοια) and *opinio*
(δόξα). The interpretation suggested in vol. 1, 257 ff., is close to that of Arthur [469],
77; but he seems not to recognize that *opinio* as used here could include an ignorant
person's weak assent to cognitive impressions; cf. Long [3], 129, which is also
misleading, however, in its attempt to restrict weak assent to such cases. See also
Ioppolo [620], 321–3.

  5–6   Reading *solum ei* for *soli*, Rackham in the Loeb edition translates: 'he
reckoned it neither as a right nor as a wrong impression, but said that it was only
"credible"'. But *neque in rectis neque in pravis* must refer to right and wrong mental
dispositions, i.e. *scientia/inscientia*, and *soli* makes excellent sense: κατάληψις, a mode
of cognition which straddles scientific knowledge and ignorance, is to be trusted 'on
its own' – i.e. all by itself – because it embraces everything necessary to a criterion of
truth; for this use of *solus*, cf. Cicero, *Top.* 59, *sapientia efficit sapientis sola per se*.

  8 **non–comprehenderet**   According to **40E 6**, by contrast, a cognitive
impression has to represent *all* the impressor's ἰδιώματα. Hence there is a prima facie
conflict between the two passages. Note, however, that Cicero, 9, insists that
cognition does apprehend everything *quod cadere in eam posset*, and it is reasonable to
interpret this as meaning that e.g., a visual cognitive impression does apprehend all the
visual properties of the sense object, though not of course any of its other properties.
40E 6 may not be intending to assert anything stronger than that.

  11–12   Cf. **39C**; **40N**.

C Sextus Empiricus, *M.* 7.150–7

οἱ δὲ περὶ τὸν Ἀρκεσίλαον προηγουμένως μὲν οὐδὲν ὥρισαν κριτήριον, οἱ δὲ καὶ ὡρικέναι
δοκοῦντες τοῦτο κατὰ ἀντιπαρεξαγωγὴν τὴν ὡς πρὸς τοὺς Στωικοὺς ἀπέδοσαν. (1) τρία
γὰρ εἶναί φασιν ἐκεῖνοι τὰ συζυγοῦντα ἀλλήλοις, ἐπιστήμην καὶ δόξαν καὶ
τὴν ἐν μεθορίῳ τούτων τεταγμένην κατάληψιν, (2) ὧν ἐπιστήμην μὲν εἶναι
τὴν ἀσφαλῆ καὶ βεβαίαν καὶ ἀμετάθετον ὑπὸ λόγου κατάληψιν, (3) δόξαν   5
δὲ τὴν ἀσθενῆ καὶ ψευδῆ συγκατάθεσιν, (4) κατάληψιν δὲ τὴν μεταξὺ
τούτων, ἥτις ἐστὶ καταληπτικῆς φαντασίας συγκατάθεσις· καταληπτικὴ
δὲ φαντασία κατὰ τούτους ἐτύγχανεν ἡ ἀληθὴς καὶ τοιαύτη οἵα οὐκ ἂν
γένοιτο ψευδής. (5) ὧν τὴν ⟨μὲν⟩ ἐπιστήμην ἐν μόνοις ὑφίστασθαι λέγουσι
τοῖς σοφοῖς, τὴν δὲ δόξαν ἐν μόνοις τοῖς φαύλοις, τὴν δὲ κατάληψιν κοινὴν   10
ἀμφοτέρων εἶναι, καὶ ταύτην κριτήριον ἀληθείας καθεστάναι. (6) ταῦτα δὴ

λεγόντων τῶν ἀπὸ τῆς Στοᾶς ὁ 'Αρκεσίλαος ἀντικαθίστατο, δεικνὺς ὅτι
οὐδέν ἐστι μεταξὺ ἐπιστήμης καὶ δόξης κριτήριον ἡ κατάληψις. (7) αὕτη
γὰρ ἥν φασι κατάληψιν καὶ καταληπτικῇ φαντασίᾳ συγκατάθεσιν, ἤτοι ἐν
σοφῷ ἢ ἐν φαύλῳ γίνεται. ἀλλ' ἐάν τε ἐν σοφῷ γένηται, ἐπιστήμη ἐστίν,   15
ἐάν τε ἐν φαύλῳ, δόξα, καὶ οὐδὲν ἄλλο παρὰ ταῦτα ἢ μόνον ὄνομα
μετείληπται. (8) εἴπερ τε ἡ κατάληψις καταληπτικῆς φαντασίας συγκατά-
θεσίς ἐστιν, ἀνύπαρκτός ἐστι, πρῶτον μὲν ὅτι ἡ συγκατάθεσις οὐ πρὸς
φαντασίαν γίνεται ἀλλὰ πρὸς λόγον (τῶν γὰρ ἀξιωμάτων εἰσὶν αἱ
συγκαταθέσεις), δεύτερον ὅτι οὐδεμία τοιαύτη ἀληθὴς φαντασία εὑρίσκε-   20
ται οἵα οὐκ ἂν γένοιτο ψευδής, ὡς διὰ πολλῶν καὶ ποικίλων παρίσταται.
(9) μὴ οὔσης δὲ καταληπτικῆς φαντασίας οὐδὲ κατάληψις γενήσεται· ἣν
γὰρ καταληπτικῇ φαντασίᾳ συγκατάθεσις. μὴ οὔσης δὲ καταλήψεως
πάντ' ἔσται ἀκατάληπτα. πάντων δὲ ὄντων ἀκαταλήπτων ἀκολουθήσει
καὶ κατὰ τοὺς Στωικοὺς ἐπέχειν τὸν σοφόν. (10) σκοπῶμεν δὲ οὑτωσί.   25
πάντων ὄντων ἀκαταλήπτων διὰ τὴν ἀνυπαρξίαν τοῦ Στωικοῦ κριτηρίου,
εἰ συγκαταθήσεται ὁ σοφός, δοξάσει ὁ σοφός· μηδενὸς γὰρ ὄντος
καταληπτοῦ εἰ συγκατατίθεταί τινι, τῷ ἀκαταλήπτῳ συγκαταθήσεται, ἡ
δὲ τῷ ἀκαταλήπτῳ συγκατάθεσις δόξα ἐστίν. ὥστε εἰ τῶν συγκατατιθεμένων ἐστὶν ὁ σοφός, τῶν δοξαστῶν ἔσται ὁ σοφός. οὐχὶ δέ γε τῶν   30
δοξαστῶν ἐστιν ὁ σοφός (τοῦτο γὰρ ἀφροσύνης ἥν κατ' αὐτούς, καὶ τῶν
ἁμαρτημάτων αἴτιον)· οὐκ ἄρα τῶν συγκατατιθεμένων ἐστὶν ὁ σοφός. εἰ δὲ
τοῦτο, περὶ πάντων αὐτὸν δεήσει ἀσυγκαταθετεῖν. τὸ δὲ ἀσυγκαταθετεῖν
οὐδὲν ἕτερόν ἐστιν ἢ τὸ ἐπέχειν· ἐφέξει ἄρα περὶ πάντων ὁ σοφός.

14 καταληπτικῇ φαντασίᾳ συγκατάθεσιν Bekker: καταληπτικῆς φαντασίας συγκαταθέσεις N:
καταληπτικὴν φαντασίαν συγκατάθεσιν cett.   23 ἂν post γὰρ N: om. cett.: αὕτη Mutschmann   23 καταληπτικῇ φαντασίᾳ Fabricius: -ικὴ -ία codd.   25 οὕτωσί Bekker: οὕτως. εἰ codd.

Context: doxography of the Academics on the criterion of truth.
  5–6 Cf. **B** 3–4.
  19–20 τῶν—συγκαταθέσεις This is the Stoics' own position; cf. **33I**.
  29 δόξα. Cf. **E** 7.
  30–2 Cf. **40D** 1–2.
  33 περὶ—ἀσυγκαταθετεῖν The hallmark of the Academic sceptic himself; cf. **68**.

D Anon. Stoic. (P. Herc. 1020), col. 4, col. 1 (*SVF* 2. 131, part)

(1) ... ὅ[τ]ι τὴν [ἀ]προπτωσί[αν] | τιμῶμ[ε]ν καὶ τὴν [ἀνει]|καιότ[η]τα,
πρὸς δὲ | τὰς ἐναντίας δι[α]βε|βλήμεθα ὀρθῶ[ς]. ἐσ|τι δ' ἡ μ[ὲ]ν ἀπροπτω-
|σία διάθε[σ]ις ἀσυνκα|τάθετος πρὸ καταλή[ψ]εως, συνκαταθετι|κὴν κατὰ
νερ....αι | φαντασίᾳ κατα[λ]η|πτῶι, ἰσχύουσα τ' ἐν | φαντασίαις καὶ ἄνει|κτον
παρεχο[μ]έν[η] | ταῖς μὴ καταλη|πτικαῖς. δεῖ γὰρ | τὸν ἀπρόπτωτον | ἀ-   5
[ν]έλ[κ]υστόν τε εἶναι ὑπὸ φαντασίας | ἀκαταλήπτου καὶ | ἰσχύειν ἐν ταῖς
φαν|τασίαις, ὥστε μὴ ἕλ|κεσθαι ἀπὸ φαντα|σιῶν ἀκαταλήπτων | καὶ | κρατεῖν
τῶν | συγκαταθέσεων ... (2) [τῶι] δὲ μὴ [δ]οξάζειν | τὸ[ν σο]φὸ[ν πλείω]
ἀκο|λου[θε]ῖν [φαμε]ν τοιαῦτ[α· πρ]ῶ[το]ν μὲν τὸ | μὴ δοκε[ῖν] αὐ[τ]ῷ

41 Knowledge and opinion

μηδέν· ἡ γὰρ δόκη[σί]ς ἐσ[[τιν δό]ξ[α ἀ]κατάλ[ηπ]τ[ος . . . (3) τούτοις δὲ   10
ὡς π[λέον] | ἀκολ[ο]υθεῖ καὶ τὸ τοὺς | σοφο[ὺ]ς ἀνεξαπατή|τους εἶναι καὶ
ἀναμαρ|τήτους κατ᾽ ἀξ[ίαν] τε ζῆν | καὶ πάντα πράττειν εὖ· διὸ καὶ περὶ
τὰς συν[[κ]ατάθεσεις ὅπως γίνον|ται μὴ ἄλλως, ἀλλὰ με|τὰ καταλήψεως
πλεί|ω γέγονεν ἐ[π]ιστρο|φή.

(For lines 1–10 we print Arnim's text in SVF, with his restorations. Tiziano Dorandi kindly examined the
papyrus for us and confirmed the correctness of these readings.)

11 π[λέον] Gigante   12 κατ᾽ ἀξ[ίαν] τε ζῆν Capasso: καταξ[. . .]τεζην pap.

The context and nature of the book which contained these fragments are unknown.

1 [ἀ]προπτωσί[αν], [ἀνει]καιότ[η]τα   Cf. 31B 2–4.

12 κατ᾽ ἀξ[ίαν] τε ζῆν   This restoration by Capasso [481], 465–6, is based upon a
new autopsy of the papyrus. It is of unusual importance because Arnim in SVF 2.131
prints κατ᾽ ᾽Αρι[στ]οτέλην, a reading he was persuaded to adopt by Crönert [482],
549–50, n. 2. In his first publication of the text, working purely from the apographs,
Arnim [480] had printed καὶ διξ̣ τε [ζ]ην. Eleven years later, Crönert examined the
papyrus, and wrote: 'κατ᾽ ᾽Αριστοτέλην zu verbessern sind (αρι ̣ οτελην der Pap.),
vgl. Politik Z. 1319a3 ἀναμάρτητοι ὄντες οἱ ἐπιεικεῖς.' As Capasso observes,
Crönert's supposed parallel is not at all to the point, once its context is examined; and
the papyrus, independently examined for us by Dr Dorandi, accords with Capasso's
reading. Aristotle's name has no place in this text.

Capasso's restoration seems virtually certain, but we question whether he is right to
take ἀξία as a technical reference to the Stoic concept of value. κατ᾽ ἀξίαν ζῆν seems
too condensed to refer to anything as complex as the doctrine of **58D**, to which he
refers. We take the expression to mean 'live worthily', i.e. live as they should.

E Plutarch, St. rep. 1056E–F (SVF 2.993, part)

ἄνευ δὲ τούτων, εἰ μὲν αἱ φαντασίαι μὴ γίνονται καθ᾽ εἱμαρμένην ⟨οὐδ᾽ αἰτίαν εἶναι δεῖ τὴν
εἱμαρμένην⟩ τῶν συγκαταθέσεων· εἰ δ᾽ ὅτι ποιεῖ φαντασίας ἀγωγοὺς ἐπὶ τὴν συγκατάθεσιν, καθ᾽ εἱμαρμένην αἱ συγκαταθέσεις γίνεσθαι λέγονται, πῶς οὐ μάχεται πρὸς ἑαυτὴν
πολλάκις ἐν τοῖς μεγίστοις διαφόρους ποιοῦσα φαντασίας καὶ περισπώσας
ἐπὶ τἀναντία τὴν διάνοιαν, ὅτε τοὺς προστιθεμένους τῇ ἑτέρᾳ καὶ μὴ   5
ἐπέχοντας ἁμαρτάνειν λέγουσιν, ἂν μὲν ἀδήλοις εἴκωσι, προπίπτοντας, ἂν
δὲ ψευδέσι, διαψευδομένους, ἂν δὲ κοινῶς ἀκαταλήπτοις, δοξάζοντας;

1–2 suppl. Cherniss   6 προπίπτοντας Salmasius: προσπίπτοντας codd.

Context: criticism of the Stoic doctrine of fate.

7 κοινῶς ἀκαταλήπτοις   As Görler [479], 88, has shown, κοινῶς (cf. communis,
B 4), indicates that ἀκαταλήπτοις embraces the two previous objects of assent,
ἀδήλοις which may be true or false, and ψευδέσι. He rightly criticizes Long [3], 129 n.
1, for restricting to what is false the scope of assent to ἀκατάληπτα.

F Plutarch, St. rep. 1057A–B (SVF 3.177, part)

αὖθις δέ φησι Χρύσιππος καὶ τὸν θεὸν ψευδεῖς ἐμποιεῖν φαντασίας καὶ τὸν
σοφόν, οὐ συγκατατιθεμένων οὐδ᾽ εἰκόντων δεομένους ἡμῶν, ἀλλὰ

πραττόντων μόνον καὶ ὁρμώντων ἐπὶ τὸ φαινόμενον· ἡμᾶς δὲ φαύλους
ὄντας ὑπ' ἀσθενείας συγκατατίθεσθαι ταῖς τοιαύταις φαντασίαις.

Context: a few lines after **E** and immediately after **53S**.
For the wise man's virtuous use of falsehoods, cf. Long [426], 99–101.

G Stobaeus 2.111,18–112,8 (*SVF* 3.548, part)

(1) ψεῦδος δ' ὑπολαμβάνειν οὐδέποτέ φασι τὸν σοφόν, οὐδὲ τὸ παράπαν
ἀκαταλήπτῳ τινὶ συγκατατίθεσθαι, διὰ τὸ μηδὲ δοξάζειν αὐτὸν μηδ'
ἀγνοεῖν μηδέν. (2) τὴν γὰρ ἄγνοιαν μεταπτωτὴν εἶναι συγκατάθεσιν καὶ
ἀσθενῆ. (3) μηδὲν δ' ὑπολαμβάνειν ἀσθενῶς, ἀλλὰ μᾶλλον ἀσφαλῶς καὶ
βεβαίως, διὸ καὶ μηδὲ δοξάζειν τὸν σοφόν. (4) διττὰς γὰρ εἶναι δόξας, τὴν   5
μὲν ἀκαταλήπτῳ συγκατάθεσιν, τὴν δὲ ὑπόληψιν ἀσθενῆ· ταύτας ⟨δ'⟩
ἀλλοτρίους εἶναι τῆς τοῦ σοφοῦ διαθέσεως· (5) δι' ὃ καὶ τὸ προπίπτειν πρὸ
καταλήψεως ⟨καὶ⟩ συγκατατίθεσθαι κατὰ τὸν προπετῆ φαῦλον εἶναι καὶ
μὴ πίπτειν εἰς τὸν εὐφυῆ καὶ τέλειον ἄνδρα καὶ σπουδαῖον.

3 μεταπτωτὴν codd.: -ικὴν Usener   6 ἀκαταλήπτῳ Wachsmuth: -ων codd.   ⟨δ'⟩ Heeren   8
⟨καὶ⟩ Salmasius   φαῦλον Wachsmuth: μᾶλλον codd.

Context: doxography of Stoic ethics.
6 **ὑπόληψιν ἀσθενῆ** Görler [479], 88–9, argues that this species of δόξα is
equivalent to Plutarch's 'yielding to ἄδηλα' (**E** 6) and hence that it is a form of
assenting to ἀκατάληπτα. But this buys consistency between these testimonies at the
cost of misrepresenting Stobaeus. As we point out in vol. 1, 257ff., some of the
evidence, e.g. **B 1**, appears to envisage 'opinion' as a term which covers all epistemic
conditions of the non-wise man (cf. Ioppolo [620], 321ff.), and in any case there is no
reason to confine the scope of 'weakness' so narrowly. ἀσθένεια is just the right term
to describe κατάληψις which is not ἀσφαλής, and hence lacks an essential attribute of
ἐπιστήμη, **H** 1–2.

H Stobaeus 2.73,16–74,3 (*SVF* 3.112, part)

(1) εἶναι δὲ τὴν ἐπιστήμην κατάληψιν ἀσφαλῆ καὶ ἀμετάπτωτον ὑπὸ
λόγου· (2) ἑτέραν δὲ ἐπιστήμην σύστημα ἐξ ἐπιστημῶν τοιούτων, οἷον ἡ
τῶν κατὰ μέρος λογικὴ ἐν τῷ σπουδαίῳ ὑπάρχουσα· (3) ἄλλην δὲ σύστημα
ἐξ ἐπιστημῶν τεχνικῶν ἐξ αὐτοῦ ἔχον τὸ βέβαιον, ὡς ἔχουσιν αἱ ἀρεταί· (4)
ἄλλην δὲ ἕξιν φαντασιῶν δεκτικὴν ἀμετάπτωτον ὑπὸ λόγου, ἥν τινά φασιν   5
ἐν τόνῳ καὶ δυνάμει κεῖσθαι.

2 ἑτέραν codd.: ἑτέρως Wachsmuth   ἐξ ἐπιστημῶν codd.: καταλήψεων Wachsmuth   3
ὑπάρχουσα Heeren: -αν codd.   ἄλλην codd.: ἄλλως Wachsmuth   4 αὐτοῦ Meineke: αὐτοῦ P:
αὐτῶν F   ἔχουσιν Canter: ἔχουσαν codd.   5 ἄλλην codd.: ἄλλως Wachsmuth   6 τόνῳ F: τῷ
νῷ P

Context: doxography of Stoic ethics.
A series of unnecessary emendations by Wachsmuth has obscured the clear
movement of this text. Stobaeus reports four different senses of ἐπιστήμη, starting

with the most particular (a specific instance of utterly secure cognition) and concluding with the most general (the persistent ἕξις of a knower).

2–3 ἡ–λογική Sc. κατάληψις, from 1.

3–4 For the virtues as τέχναι and ἐπιστῆμαι, cf. 60K; 61D; and for βέβαιον as an attribute of virtuous actions, 59I.

I Stobaeus 2.68,18–23 (*SVF* 3.663)

ἔτι δὲ λέγουσι πάντα φαῦλον μαίνεσθαι, ἄγνοιαν ἔχοντα αὐτοῦ καὶ τῶν καθ' αὑτόν, ὅπερ ἐστὶ μανία. τὴν δ' ἄγνοιαν εἶναι ἐναντίαν κακίαν τῇ σωφροσύνῃ· ταύτην δὲ πρός τί πως ἔχουσαν ἀκαταστάτους καὶ πτοιώδεις παρεχομένην τὰς ὁρμὰς μανίαν εἶναι· διὸ καὶ ὑπογράφουσι τὴν μανίαν οὕτως· ἄγνοιαν πτοιώδη.   5

1 ἔτι Canter: ἐπεί codd.   αὐτοῦ Heeren: αὑτοῦ codd.   2 αὑτόν Canter: αὑτό codd.   3 σωφροσύνῃ codd.: φρονήσει Usener   3, 5 πτοιώδεις . . . πτοιώδη Canter: ποιώδεις . . . ποιώδη codd.

Context: doxography of Stoic ethics.

3   Usener's widely accepted emendation is inappropriate. The vice opposite to every virtue is a form of ἄγνοια, Stobaeus 2.59,10–60,5; and the opposite to σωφροσύνη is wanted here because ὁρμαί are the field of this virtue; cf. Stobaeus 2.60,12. For πρός τί πως ἔχουσαν, cf. **29C–F**. Surprisingly, the interrelation of the vices is here analysed in line not with Chrysippus' doctrine on the interrelation of the virtues, but with that of Aristo (**29E; 61B–C**).

42 Scientific methodology

A Olympiodorus, *In Plat. Gorg.* 12.1

(1) Κλεάνθης τοίνυν λέγει ὅτι "τέχνη ἐστὶν ἕξις ὁδῷ πάντα ἀνύουσα." (2) ἀτελὴς δ' ἐστὶν οὗτος ὁ ὅρος, καὶ γὰρ ἡ φύσις ἕξις τίς ἐστιν ὁδῷ πάντα ποιοῦσα· (3) ὅθεν ὁ Χρύσιππος προσθεὶς τὸ "μετὰ φαντασιῶν" εἶπεν ὅτι "τέχνη ἐστὶν ἕξις ὁδῷ προιοῦσα μετὰ φαντασιῶν" . . . (4) Ζήνων δέ φησιν ὅτι "τέχνη ἐστὶ σύστημα ἐκ καταλήψεων συγγεγυμνασμένων πρός τι   5 τέλος εὔχρηστον τῶν ἐν τῷ βίῳ."

5 συγγεγυμνασμένον codd., sed cf. *SVF* 1.73.

Context: commentary on *Gorg.* 462b. Olympiodorus is comparing these definitions of τέχνη, which rhetoric may be held to fulfil, with Plato's, which it does not.

The second and third definitions are reported and endorsed earlier (2.2), without explicit attribution to the Stoics.

1 ὁδῷ   See note on **46A** 1.

2–3   Nature is sometimes defined as a certain sort of ἕξις (**43A** 4), sometimes as πῦρ τεχνικὸν ὁδῷ βαδίζον εἰς γένεσιν (D.L. 7.156; cf. the definition of 'god' at **46A** 1). The present description conflates these accounts. It presumably echoes Chrysippus' own criticism of Cleanthes' definition.

5–6   This definition of τέχνη, widely invoked in rhetorical handbooks and

259

Epistemology: Stoics and Academics

elsewhere, was apparently taken over by Zeno from the Dialectical school, to which it is attributed by Syrianus, *In Herm.* 2.6,1, 9,18 Rabe; Marcellinus, *In Herm. Stas.* 53,30· Walz, *Rhetores Graeci* IV (οἱ Διαλεκτικοὶ φιλόσοφοι); *Prolegomena in Herm. Stas.* 295,21–4 Rabe, *Rhetores Graeci* XIV.

B Cicero, *Acad.* 2.22

(1) ars vero quae potest esse nisi quae non ex una aut duabus sed ex multis animi perceptionibus constat? quam si subtraxeris, qui distingues artificem ab inscio: non enim fortuito hunc artificem dicemus esse illum negabimus, sed cum alterum percepta et conprehensa tenere videmus alterum non item. (2) cumque artium aliud eius modi genus sit ut tantum modo animo rem cernat, aliud ut moliatur aliquid et faciat, quo modo aut geometres cernere ea potest quae aut nulla sunt aut internosci a falsis non possunt, aut is qui fidibus utitur explere numeros et conficere versus . . ?

Context: the indispensability of κατάληψις.

C Cicero, *Div.* 1.34

(1) iis igitur adsentior, qui duo genera divinationum esse dixerunt, unum quod particeps esset artis, alterum quod arte careret. est enim ars in iis qui novas res coniectura persequuntur, veteres observatione didicerunt. (2) carent autem arte ii qui non ratione aut coniectura observatis ac notatis signis, sed concitatione quadam animi aut soluto liberoque motu futura praesentiunt, quod et somniantibus saepe contingit et non numquam vaticinantibus per furorem.

Context: interim conclusion of the long catalogue of historical examples of scientific divination launched at ibid. 11.

D Cicero, *Div.* 1.82–3 (*SVF* 2.1192)

(1) quam quidem esse re vera hac Stoicorum ratione concluditur: (2) "si sunt di, neque ante declarant hominibus quae futura sint, aut non diligunt homines, aut quid eventurum sit ignorant, aut existumant nihil interesse hominum scire quid sit futurum, aut non censent esse suae maiestatis praesignificare hominibus quae sunt futura, aut ea ne ipsi quidem di significare possunt. at neque non diligunt nos (sunt enim benefici generique hominum amici) neque ignorant ea quae ab ipsis constituta et designata sunt; neque nostra nihil interest scire ea quae eventura sint (erimus enim cautiores, si sciemus), neque hoc alienum ducunt maiestate sua (nihil est enim beneficentia praestantius) neque non possunt futura praenoscere. non igitur sunt di nec significant futura. sunt autem di; significant ergo. (3) et non, si significant, nullas vias dant nobis ad significationis scientiam (frustra enim significarent); nec, si dant vias,

non est divinatio; est igitur divinatio." (4) hac ratione et Chrysippus et Diogenes et Antipater utitur.

11 *non si* Ascensiana 1521: *si non* codd.

For the logical form of the argument, cf. **36G 6–7**. For Cicero's reply to it, see *Div.* 2.101–6.

5–7 For divine benevolence, see **54**.

E Cicero, *Div.* 1.117–18 (*SVF* 2.1210)

haec si tenemus, quae mihi quidem non videntur posse convelli, profecto hominibus a dis futura significari necesse est. sed distinguendum videtur, quonam modo. nam non placet Stoicis singulis iecorum fissis aut avium cantibus interesse deum; neque enim decorum est nec dis dignum nec fieri ullo pacto potest; sed ita a principio inchoatum esse mundum, ut certis rebus certa 5 signa praecurrerent, alia in extis, alia in avibus, alia in fulgoribus, alia in ostentis, alia in stellis, alia in somniantium visis, alia in furentium vocibus. ea quibus bene percepta sunt, ii non saepe falluntur; male coniecta maleque interpretata falsa sunt non rerum vitio, sed interpretum inscientia.

Context: how does divination come to be possible?

F Cicero, *Acad.* 2.36

quid autem tam absurde dici potest quam cum ita locuntur: "est hoc quidem illius rei signum aut argumentum, et ea re id sequor, sed fieri potest ut id quod significatur aut falsum sit aut nihil sit omnino."

Context: attack on the Philonian Academy's professed reliance on the merely πιθανόν (see vol. 1, 449).

3 **aut falsum** ... **aut nihil** The disjunction caters for the alternatives of viewing sign and significate as propositions and as things, on which see especially Burnyeat [484], 211–14.

G Philodemus, *Sign.* 1.2–4.13

(1) καὶ μὴν δι' οὐθὲν | ἕτερον κοινόν ἐστιν ἢ διότι | καὶ ὄντος τοῦ ἀδήλου καὶ μὴ ὄν|τος ὑπάρχειν τοῦτο δύναται. | τόν γέ τοι νομίζοντα [ὡ]ς χρηστὸς | ὅδε τίς ἐστιν ἄνθρωπος ἕνεκα | τοῦ πλουτεῖν μοχθη[ρ]ῶι φαμεν | καὶ κοινῶι χρῆσθαι σημείω[ι δι]|ὰ τὸ πολλοὺς μὲν πλο[υ]τοῦντας | ἀτόπ-ους εὑρίσκεσθαι [π]ολλο[ὺς] | δὲ χρηστούς· ὥσ[τ]ε τὸ ἴδιον εἴ[περ] | ἀναγ- 5 καστικὸν ἀδυνατεῖν ἀλ|[λ]ως ὑπάρχειν ἢ σὺν τῶι ὃ λέγο|[μ]εν αὐτοῦ κατ' ἀνάγκην εἶνα[ι, | τ]ἀφανές, οὗ σ[η]μεῖόν ἐ[σ]τι, μη[.]ε|[.]ο̣δεμη[. . . .] ἄδηλον. ὃ γ[ίνε]τα]ι τῶι κα[τ]' ἀ[να]σκε]υὴν τρόπωι | [τ]ῆς σημ[ειώσεως]. (2) ἔ[τι δὲ] πρ[ὸς | τ]ὰ μοναχὰ [τὰ ἐν τοῖς παρ' ἡμῖν | φ]αινόμενα τό[ποις οὐκ ἀνα|γ]κάζειν ὁ διὰ τῆς ὁ[μοιότη]τος | ἔοικεν τρόπος, ε[ἰ λίθων] πολλῶν 10

| καὶ παντ[οδ]απῶν [ὄντ]ων ἐν ἔσ|τι τούτων εἶδος ἐπι[σ]πώμε|νον τὸν
σίδηρον, ἣν καλοῦσιν | μα[γ]νῆτιν λίθον, οἱ δ' Ἡρακλε|[ῶτιν], μόνον δὲ
καὶ τὸ ἤλεκτρον | [ἑλκυσ]τικόν ἐστι τῶν ἀχύρων, | [καὶ] τετράγωνος
ἀριθμὸς εἷς | μόνος ὁ τέτταρ' ἐπὶ τέτταρα | τὴν περίμετρον ἴσην ἔχει
τῶι | ἐμβαδῶι. πόθεν οὖν ἔχομεν | εἰπεῖν ὡς οὐκ ἔστιν τι γένος   15
| ἀνθρώπων ὃ μόνον οὐκ ἀπο|θνήσκει διαιρούμενον τὴν | καρδίαν, ὥστε
μὴ κατ' ἀνάγ|[κην] εἶναι λαβε[ῖν ἐκ τοῦ] τοὺς | παρ' ἡμῖν ἀνθρώπους
διαιρουμέ|νους τὴν καρδίαν ἀποθνήσκειν | τὸ καὶ πάντας; καὶ σπάνια δ'
ἐ|στὶν παρ' ἡμῖν ἔνια, καθάπερ ὁ γε|νόμενος ἡμίπηχυς ἄνθρωπος | ἐν
Ἀλεξανδρείαι κεφαλὴν δὲ | κολοσσικ[ὴ]ν ἔχων ἐφ' ἧς ἐσφυροκό|πουν, ὃν   20
[ἐ]πεδείκνυον οἱ ταρει|χευταί, [κ]αὶ ὁ γαμηθεὶς ὡς παρ|θένος [ἐν]
Ἐπιδαύρωι κἄπειτα | γενόμ[εν]ος ἀνήρ, καὶ ὁ γενόμε|νος ἐν [Κρή]τηι
πηχῶν ὀκτὼι καὶ | τεττ[αρά]κοντα τοῖς ἐκ τῶν εὑ|ρεθέν[των] ὀστῶν
σημειουμέ|νοις ἔτ[ι δ' οὗ]ς ἐν Ἀκώρει πυγμαί|ους δ[εικνύ]ουσιν, ἀμέλει δ'
ἀν|α[λ]όγο[υς τοῖς οὖς] Ἀντώνιος νῦν | ἐξ Ὑρία[ς ἐκο]μίσ[ατο . . . (3)   25
ὅταν | δὲ κατ[αξ]ιῶμεν· ἐπεὶ οἱ παρ' ἡ|μῖν ἄν[θρω]ποι θνητοί εἰσι,
καὶ | τοὺς π[άντας, τ]ὸ διὰ τῆς ὁμοι|ότ[η]τρ[ς ἑλόμενοι] κατὰ πάντα
| τοὺ[ς ἐν τοῖς ἀ]δήλοις ὁμοίους | ὑπο[τιθέμ]εθα τοῖς παρ' ἡμῖν, ὥσ|τε κ[αὶ
κατ]ὰ τὸ θνητοὺς ὑπάρ|χειν, [τού]του χωρίς. εἰ μὲν γὰρ | κατὰ [πάν]τα,
καὶ κατ' αὐτὸ τοῦ|τό γ' ὀ[ρθ]ότατα σημειωσόμε|θα. τ[οιοῦ]τος γὰρ ὁ   30
τρόπος ἔσται | δή[π]ουθε]ν, "ἔ[πε]ὶ οἱ παρ' ἡμῖν | ἄνθ[ρωπο]ι θνητ[οί εἰσιν,
κα[ὶ εἴ] | που κατ' ἄλλους τόπους εἰσὶν ἄν|θρωποι τοῖς παρ' ἡμῖν
ὡμοιωμέ|νοι κατά τε τἆλλα καὶ κατὰ τὸ θνη|τοὶ εἶναι, θνητοὶ ἂν εἴησαν."
τ[όδε] | γὰρ κατελίπετ' ἐν [[τεν]] τῶι σημεί|ωι. τ[ίνι δ]ὲ διοίσει τοῦ
σημεί|ου ἀφ' [οὗ πόλ]λ' αὐτοὶ σημειούμε|θα, εἴ γε ἑκάτερα θ[ν]ητὰ   35
ὑποτι|θέμεθα καὶ τοιοῦ[τ]ό τι λέγομεν, | "ἐπεὶ οἱ παρ' ἡμῖν [θν]ητοί εἰσιν
ἄν|θρωποι, κ̣αὶ εἴ πού [εἰσ]ιν θνητοὶ ἄ[ν]|θρω[ποι, θν]ητοί [εἰσι]ν"; εἰ δ'
οὐχὶ καὶ | κατὰ [τὸ θνητ]ο[ὺς ὑπ]άρχειν ὁμο[ί]|ους [ἐκείνο]υς ὑ[πο]τιθέμε-
θα | [π]ε[ρὶ ὧν σ]ημει[ούμ]εθα, ἀλλὰ τα[ύ]τηι [δι]α[λ]λάττον[τας] καὶ
διαφορ[ὰ]ς | [παρέχ]οντα[ς . .]σπερ[. . . . . .].|ε[. . . .]θα δῆ[λον ὡ]ς οὐκ   40
[ἔχει | τ]ὴ[ν ἀ]ν[ά]γκην ἡ [ση]μείωσις· [οὐ]κ ἄ[ρ'] ἀν[αγ]καῖον ἔ[σται]
τοὺ[ς ἐν ἀ|δήλοις ἀ]νθρώπ[ους] ε[ἶ]ναι θν[η]τούς, οὐδὲ τοὺς ἄλ[λου]ς, τοὺς
κα[τὰ | μὲ]ν τἆλλ' ὁμοίου[ς] κατὰ δὲ τὸ | [θνητοὺς ὑ]πά[ρχειν διαλλ]άτ-
τον|τας, κα[ὶ] κατὰ το[ῦτ' ἐ]οικέναι τοῖς | παρ' ἡμῖν. (4) καθό[λο]υ τ' εἰ
κατα[[ξ]ιοῖ, "[ἐπε]ὶ οἱ παρ' ἡμ[ῖν ἄν[θρ]ωποι | [θν]ητοί εἰσιν, καὶ ε[ἴ πού   45
εἰσιν ἄ]νθρω[[πο]ι θνητοὺς ε[ἶναι"· εἰ τοῦτο] | μὲν ἴσον αὐ[τῶι τούτωι,
"ἐπεὶ οἱ πα]ρ' ἡμῖν ἄνθρωποι ἦι] ἄν[θ]ρωποι | καὶ καθὸ ἄνθ[ρωποί] εἰσι
θνητοί | εἰσιν, καὶ τοὺς π[αντ]αχῆ θνητοὺς | ὑπάρχειν", ὀρθ[ῶς ἀ]ξιώσει
τοῦ|το· εἰ δὲ ἄλλω[ς συ]μβεβηκότος | τούτου τοῖς π[αρ'] ἡμῖν ἀνθρώ|ποις,
τοῦ θνητ[οὺς] εἶναι, ἀξιώ|σει, "ἐπεὶ οἱ πα[ρ' ἡμῖ]ν εἰσι θνη|τοί, καὶ τοὺς   50
πανταχῆι θνητοὺς | εἶνα[ι]", ματαίως ἀξιώσει. μὰ Δία | γὰρ οὐδ' ὅτι οἱ
παρ' ἡμῖν εἰσιν ὀλι|γοχρόνιοι [κ]αὶ τ[οὺς] Ἀκροθωίτας | ἐροῦμεν ὀλιγο-
[χρο]νίους εἶναι. δει|κτέον τοίνυν [καὶ τ]οὺς ἀνθρώπους | ἧι καὶ καθό εἰ|σιν

ἄ]νθρωπ[ο]ι θνη|τοὺς ὑπάρ[χ]ε[ι]ν, εἰ μέλλο[μ]εν | ἀναγκαστ[ι]κ[ὸν τ]ὸ
προ[κεί]με|νον συστῆσ[αι· δυνάμ]ενο[ι δὲ κα]|τ᾿ ἀ[ν]ασκευὴν τοῦτο δει[κ-   55
νύ]ε⟨ι⟩ν, | τὸν κατὰ τ[ὴν] ὁμοιότητ[α] πα|ρήσομεν τρ[όπον].

8 κα[τ]᾿ ἀ[νασκε]υὴν Sedley secundum pap.   27 ἐλόμενοι] Sedley: ὑγιές ⟨ἐστιν⟩ εἰ] De Lacy   29
|τού]του scripsimus: [οὐ τού|του Fränkel: [ἡ τού|του T. Gomperz   34-5 τ[όδε|-πόλ]λ᾿ rest. Sedley
secundum pap.
    For fuller apparatus, see De Lacy [152].

Context: catalogue of Stoic objections to the Epicurean Similarity Method, recorded
by Philodemus from the lectures of his teacher Zeno of Sidon. Zeno's replies to the
objections excerpted here run from 14.2 to 17.28.
    1 κοινόν   I.e. 'common to truth and falsity' (cf. Cicero, Acad. 2.33–4), rather than
'common to two or more significates', the more usual meaning of κοινὸν σημεῖον.
See Sedley [243], 243–4.
    9–25   For a comparable Pyrrhonist objection to induction; cf. 72C 9.
    24 ἀμέλει δ᾿   This signals what must for chronological reasons (cf. next note) be
Philodemus' own addition to the Stoic list of examples.
    25 ἐξ Ὑρία|ς   A south Italian town where Antony won an engagement in 40
B.C. (Appian, BC 5.58). Most scholars prefer to read the sequence of letters as
representing ἐκ Συρίας (for the controversy, see De Lacy [152], 163–4), which would
suggest a reference to Antony's return from Syria in 54 B.C. But such an orthography
would be quite uncharacteristic of Philodemean papyri. There is therefore perhaps
some support in these lines for dating the De signis to 40 B.C. or soon after.
    34 ἐν τῶι σημεί|ωι   The reference is not to the 'Since . . .' clause, but to the
'if . . .' clause at 32–3 (if the restoration εἰ is correct), recalling the official Stoic
definition of a sign as the true antecedent in a certain kind of conditional (35C 1).

H   Philodemus, Sign. 6.1–14

πότερον τὸ ἀπ[α]ράλλακτον | εἰς τὴν [σ]ημείωσιν παραληψό|μεθα ἢ τὸ
ὅμοιον ἢ τὸ πόσην ἔ|χον προσεμφέρεια[ν]; τὸ μὲν οὖν ἀ|παράλλακτον
λέγ[ε]ιν γελοῖον· | τί γὰρ μᾶλλον ἔσται τὸ φανε|ρὸν τἀφανοῦς σημεῖον ἢ
ἀντιστρ[ό]||φως; οὐκ ἔσται τε ἔτι τὸ μὲν φα|νερὸν τὸ δὲ ἄδηλον,
ἀπαρα[λ]||λαξίας ὑπαρχούσης. εἰ δὲ τ[ὸ] ὅ|μοιον, πόθεν ἔξομεν εἰπ[εῖν]   5
ὡς | οὐχὶ καθ᾿ ἣν ἔχει διαφορὰν [καὶ πα]||ραλλάτ[τ]ει τοῦ φαινομένου
[ἀφ᾿ | ο]ὖ ποιού[μ]εθα τὴν σημε[ί]ωσιν;

3 ἢ T. Gomperz: ὃ pap.
    For fuller apparatus, see De Lacy [152].

Context: as G.

I   Cicero, Acad. 2.99–100

etenim is quoque qui a vobis sapiens inducitur multa sequitur probabilia non
conprehensa neque percepta neque adsensa sed similia veri, quae nisi probet
omnis vita tollatur. quid enim, conscendens navem sapiens num conprehen-

sum animo habet atque perceptum se ex sententia navigaturum? qui potest? sed si iam ex hoc loco proficiscatur Puteolos stadia triginta probo navigio 5 bono gubernatore hac tranquillitate, probabile videatur se illuc venturum esse salvum.

Context: defence of the φαντασία πιθανὴ καὶ ἀπερίσπαστος (cf. **69E** 1–2) as an adequate basis for the conduct of life.

J Philodemus, *Sign.* 7.26–38

(1) ἔτι δὲ λε|γόν[τω]ν ὡς καὶ τὰ τερατώδη | πρός [τιν' ὅ]μοια κατ' αὑτοὺς, εἰ | μὴ τ[ὰ π]αρ' ἡμῖν ὅμοια τούτοις | οὐχ [ὑπά]ρχειν ἀποκόψομεν, (2) τῶι | τε κ[ατ' ἀ]νασκευὴν ἀποκό[ψ]ειν | φησ[ίν, (3) οὐ] μὴν ἀλλ' ἐπαρκε[ῖν] ἡ|μῖν [τό τε] πεπεῖσθαι περὶ τ[ο]ύ|τω[ν καὶ π]ερὶ τῶν ἐκ τῆς πε[ί]ρας | κατ[ὰ τὴν] εὐλογίαν, ὃν τρόπον | ὅτι [γενη]σόμεθα πλέοντες | θέρ[ους] ἐν 5 ἀσφαλεῖ [

3 ἐπαρκε[ῖν] Sedley: ἐπαρκέ[σει] T. Gomperz

Context: as **G**.
For a defence of our reconstruction, see Sedley [243], 248ff.
  1 **αὐτούς** It is unclear whether the Stoics or the Epicureans are meant.
  3 **τῶι–φησ[ίν** This first part of Dionysius' reply is little more than a joke: the Epicurean remark quoted in 2 sounds like an appeal to the Stoic Elimination Method.
  4 **τ[ο]ύτω[ν** Probably inferences based on similarity.

PHYSICS

43 The scope of physics

A Diogenes Laertius 7.148–9 (*SVF* 2.1022 and 2.1132)

(1) οὐσίαν δὲ θεοῦ Ζήνων μέν φησι τὸν ὅλον κόσμον καὶ τὸν οὐρανόν, ὁμοίως δὲ καὶ Χρύσιππος ἐν τῷ πρώτῳ Περὶ θεῶν καὶ Ποσειδώνιος ἐν πρώτῳ Περὶ θεῶν . . .(2) φύσιν δὲ ποτὲ μὲν ἀποφαίνονται τὴν συνέχουσαν τὸν κόσμον, ποτὲ δὲ τὴν φύουσαν τὰ ἐπὶ γῆς. ἔστι δὲ φύσις ἕξις ἐξ αὑτῆς κινουμένη κατὰ σπερματικοὺς λόγους ἀποτελοῦσά τε καὶ συνέχουσα τὰ ἐξ 5 αὑτῆς ἐν ὡρισμένοις χρόνοις καὶ τοιαῦτα δρῶσα ἀφ' οἵων ἀπεκρίθη. ταύτην δὲ καὶ τοῦ συμφέροντος στοχάζεσθαι καὶ ἡδονῆς, ὡς δῆλον ἐκ τῆς τοῦ ἀνθρώπου δημιουργίας.

Context: doxography of Stoic physics.
  1 **οὐσίαν** The term does not refer here to the passive ἀρχή, as in **44B–C**, but simply helps to state the thesis (cf. **54B**) that the entire world *is* god; cf. **44F** 1–4 for this sense of κόσμος.
  4–5 For this use of ἕξις, cf. συνέχειν, **47F, G, I 2**, and for σπερματικὸς λόγος, see **46A** 2, **B** 4.
  7 **ἡδονῆς** We know no other evidence that confirms or fully explains this

striking claim. For Stoic views on pleasure, see vol. 1, 421, and **57A 3**; there pleasure is described as an ἐπιγέννημα, which arises only when nature has 'adopted the proper requirements for a creature's constitution'. That thesis is consistent with what is said here; cf. Görler [558], 398. But that nature 'aims . . . at pleasure' is not what we expect to hear from philosophers who strenuously resisted the Epicurean claim that all creatures naturally pursue pleasure. Perhaps ἡδονή can be interpreted as a very general term for gratification or contentment: nature intends that creatures should be pleased with their constitution as well as finding it useful to them. It does not follow from this statement that creatures are designed to make pleasurable feelings one of their primary objectives.

B Diogenes Laertius 7.132

τὸν δὲ φυσικὸν λόγον διαιροῦσιν εἴς τε τὸν περὶ σωμάτων τόπον καὶ περὶ ἀρχῶν καὶ στοιχείων καὶ θεῶν καὶ περάτων καὶ τόπου καὶ κενοῦ. καὶ οὕτω μὲν εἰδικῶς, γενικῶς δ' εἰς τρεῖς τόπους, τόν τε περὶ κόσμου καὶ τὸν περὶ τῶν στοιχείων καὶ τρίτον τὸν αἰτιολογικόν.

2 καὶ τόπου καὶ κενοῦ codd.: τοῦ κόσμου καὶ τόπου κενοῦ Suda   3 τόπους F: τούτους BP

Context: opening section of Diogenes' doxography of Stoic physics.
1 **σωμάτων**   For the priority of bodies to ἀρχαί, see vol. 1, 268. Diogenes gives a detailed account of body in 7.135 (including **50E**), treating it after ἀρχαί and along with mathematical concepts which fall under the last topic of his 'specific' division.
3–4   We omit D.L. 7.132–3 in which the first and third topics of the 'generic' division are subdivided.

44 Principles

A Sextus Empiricus, *M*. 9.332 (*SVF* 2.524, part)

καὶ δὴ οἱ μὲν ἀπὸ τῆς Στοᾶς φιλόσοφοι διαφέρειν ὑπολαμβάνουσι τὸ ὅλον καὶ τὸ πᾶν· ὅλον μὲν γὰρ εἶναι λέγουσι τὸν κόσμον, πᾶν δὲ τὸ σὺν τῷ κόσμῳ ἔξωθεν κενόν, καὶ διὰ τοῦτο τὸ μὲν ὅλον πεπερασμένον εἶναι (πεπέρασται γὰρ ὁ κόσμος), τὸ δὲ πᾶν ἄπειρον (τοιοῦτον γὰρ τὸ ἐκτὸς τοῦ κόσμου κενόν).   5

Context: doxography of 'whole' and 'all'.
For the same doctrine, cf. *SVF* 2.522–3. On the void external to the world, see **49**.

B Diogenes Laertius 7.134 (*SVF* 2.300, part, and 2.299)

(1) δοκεῖ δ' αὐτοῖς ἀρχὰς εἶναι τῶν ὅλων δύο, τὸ ποιοῦν καὶ τὸ πάσχον. (2) τὸ μὲν οὖν πάσχον εἶναι τὴν ἄποιον οὐσίαν τὴν ὕλην, τὸ δὲ ποιοῦν τὸν ἐν αὐτῇ λόγον τὸν θεόν· τοῦτον γὰρ ἀίδιον ὄντα διὰ πάσης αὐτῆς δημιουργεῖν ἕκαστα. . . . (3) διαφέρειν δέ φασιν ἀρχὰς καὶ στοιχεῖα· τὰς μὲν γὰρ εἶναι ἀγενήτους ⟨καὶ⟩ ἀφθάρτους, τὰ δὲ στοιχεῖα κατὰ τὴν ἐκπύρωσιν   5

Stoic physics

φθείρεσθαι. ἀλλὰ καὶ σώματα εἶναι τὰς ἀρχὰς καὶ ἀμόρφους, τὰ δὲ μεμορφῶσθαι.

5 καὶ Suda: om. codd.   6 σώματα codd.: ἀσωμάτους Suda

Context: shortly after **43B**.

2 **ἄποιον** Our translation, 'unqualified', is supported by ἀσχημάτιστος, **C** 2, and by **D** 5–6. Todd [493], 140–1, prefers 'inert' or 'not acting'; but this makes the term a trivial repetition of πάσχον, and fails to register the cardinal point that what qualifies matter is god. See also **28q** 8–10 and **55E**.

4 **στοιχεῖα** See **46–7**.

6 **σώματα** Our reasons for preferring this reading are given in vol. 1, 273–4; and cf. **45G** 2. Defenders of ἀσωμάτους include Todd [493], 139–43, and, implicitly, Sandbach [296], 73–4. **ἀρχάς** Hahm [488], 29ff., suggests that these were discussed 'probably after the account of cosmogony', because Diogenes' Stoic authorities for **B** 1 include Χρύσιππος ἐν τῇ πρώτῃ τῶν Φυσικῶν πρὸς τῷ τέλει. This is hardly decisive evidence for his suggestion; and even if it were true, the conceptual priority of the ἀρχαί would not be affected.

C Sextus Empiricus, *M.* 9.75–6 (*SVF* 2.311)

(1) ἡ τοίνυν τῶν ὄντων οὐσία, φασίν, ἀκίνητος οὖσα ἐξ αὑτῆς καὶ ἀσχημάτιστος ὑπό τινος αἰτίας ὀφείλει κινεῖσθαί τε καὶ σχηματίζεσθαι· (2) καὶ διὰ τοῦτο, ὡς χαλκούργημα περικαλλὲς θεασάμενοι ποθοῦμεν μαθεῖν τὸν τεχνίτην ἅτε καθ' αὑτὴν τῆς ὕλης ἀκινήτου καθεστώσης, οὕτω καὶ τὴν τῶν ὅλων ὕλην θεωροῦντες κινουμένην καὶ ἐν μορφῇ τε καὶ 5 διακοσμήσει τυγχάνουσαν εὐλόγως ἂν σκεπτοίμεθα τὸ κινοῦν αὐτὴν καὶ πολυειδῶς μορφοῦν αἴτιον. (3) τοῦτο δὲ οὐκ ἄλλο τι πιθανόν ἐστιν εἶναι ἢ δύναμίν τινα δι' αὐτῆς πεφοιτηκυῖαν, καθάπερ ἡμῖν ψυχὴ πεφοίτηκεν. (4) αὕτη οὖν ἡ δύναμις ἤτοι αὐτοκίνητός ἐστιν ἢ ὑπὸ ἄλλης κινεῖται δυνάμεως. (5) καὶ εἰ μὲν ὑφ' ἑτέρας κινεῖται, τὴν ἑτέραν ἀδύνατον ἔσται κινεῖσθαι μὴ 10 ὑπ' ἄλλης κινουμένην, ὅπερ ἄτοπον. ἔστι τις ἄρα καθ' ἑαυτὴν αὐτοκίνητος δύναμις, ἥτις ἂν εἴη θεία καὶ ἀΐδιος. (6) ἢ γὰρ ἐξ αἰῶνος κινήσεται ἢ ἀπό τινος χρόνου. (7) ἀλλ' ἀπό τινος χρόνου μὲν οὐ κινήσεται· οὐ γὰρ ἔσται τις αἰτία τοῦ ἀπό τινος αὐτὴν χρόνου κινεῖσθαι. ἀΐδιος τοίνυν ἐστὶν ἡ κινοῦσα τὴν ὕλην δύναμις καὶ τεταγμένως αὐτὴν εἰς γενέσεις καὶ μεταβολὰς 15 ἄγουσα. ὥστε θεὸς ἂν εἴη αὕτη.

Context: doxography of god.

Though not explicitly attributed to the Stoics, this argument can be credited to them on the evidence of its content and context. In its reliance on analogy between artefacts and the world-order, it resembles **54C** 6, an argument by Cleanthes, who is named a little later by Sextus (*M.* 9.88) as the author of another argument. But it is equally possible that **C** derives from Chrysippus; cf. Dragona–Monachou [528], 128.

9 **αὐτοκίνητος** This, or an equivalent term, is a standard attribute of cosmic nature, or the active principle. Cf. **43A** 4–5; *SVF* 2.1133. The inference from self-movement to divinity has illustrious precedents. In Plato, *Phdr.* 245c–e, Socrates

266

argues that something which has self-movement as its nature is everlasting, thereby inferring the immortality of soul. In *Phys.* VIII, Aristotle rejects an infinite series of movers, and concludes, by an analysis of what self-movement involves, that there must be a prime unmoved mover.

D Calcidius 292 (*SVF* 1.88, part)

(1) Zeno hanc ipsam essentiam finitam esse dicit unamque eam communem omnium quae sunt esse substantiam, (2) dividuam quoque et usque quaque mutabilem. (3) partes quippe eius verti sed non interire, ita ut de existentibus consumantur in nihilum. sed ut innumerabilium diversarum etiam cerearum figurarum, sic neque formam neque figuram nec ullam omnino qualitatem   5
propriam fore censet fundamenti rerum omnium silvae, coniunctam tamen esse semper et inseparabiliter cohaerere alicui qualitate. (4) cumque tam sine ortu sit quam sine interitu, quia neque de non existente substitit nec consumetur in nihilum, non deesse ei spiritum ac vigorem ex aeternitate, qui moveat eam rationabiliter totam interdum, non numquam pro portione.   10

Context: doxography of 'matter', in discussion of Plato, *Tim.* 47e–48e.
  1 **essentiam**   This term is Calcidius' translation of οὐσία. At **E** 3–4 he identifies *essentia* with 'prime matter'; see **28q** where πρώτη ὕλη is described as everlasting and invariant in magnitude as distinct from its parts – the ὕλη of particular things. The identification of the passive ἀρχή with substance and prime matter is standard Stoicism (so correctly Hahm [488], 40, and not Lapidge [492], 243, who takes 'prime matter' to include both ἀρχαί).
  3 **mutabilem**   Cf. **50B** 2–3.
  7–10   How does the everlastingness of substance support the inference that it 'never lacks breath and vitality'? We are probably to supply from 6–7 its constant connexion with 'some quality or other' (i.e. its constant connexion with the divine active ἀρχή).

E Calcidius 293

(1) ergo corpus universum iuxta Stoicos determinatum est et unum et totum et essentia. (2) totum quidem, quia nihil ei partium deest; unum autem, quia inseparabiles eius partes sunt et invicem sibi cohaerent; essentia vero, quia princeps silva est omnium corporum per quam ire dicunt rationem solidam atque universam, perinde ut semen per membra genitalia. (3) quam quidem   5
rationem ipsum fore opificem volunt, cohaerens vero corpus et sine qualitate, patibile totum et commutabile silvam sive essentiam. (4) quae vertatur quidem nec intereat tamen neque tota neque partium excidio, ideo quia philosophorum omnium commune dogma est neque quid fieri ex nihilo nec in nihilum interire. licet enim cuncta corpora casu aliquo diffluant, silva tamen   10
semper est et opifex deus, ratio scilicet, in qua sit fixum quo quidque tempore tam nascatur quam occidat. (5) proptereaque de existentibus genituram fieri et

Stoic physics

in existens desinere quod finiatur immortalibus perseverantibus, a quo fit et item ex quo fit quod gignitur.

Context: immediately following **D**.

1 **corpus universum** The phrase seems to be an unusual expression for the passive ἀρχή. The language is confusing (see Waszink [494] ad loc.), but it can hardly refer to 'the whole', **A**, which includes the active ἀρχή; cf. **D** 1–2. **determinatum** Cf. **50B** 1.

5 **ut semen** This image for the creativity of the active ἀρχή is standard; cf. **28q** 4, *SVF* 1.107, and see **46A–B** for its cosmogonical application.

9 **commune dogma** The appeal to a philosophical consensus could reflect an early Stoic appeal to a κοινὴ ἔννοια. Cf. **40R**; **48C** 5.

12–14 These lines recall Empedocles (31 B 8;11–12 DK), an authority the early Stoics acknowledged; cf. *SVF* 2, p. 137, 7–11.

F Diogenes Laertius 7.137–8 (*SVF* 2.526)

λέγουσι δὲ κόσμον τριχῶς· αὐτόν τε τὸν θεὸν τὸν ἐκ τῆς ἁπάσης οὐσίας ἰδίως ποιόν, ὃς δὴ ἄφθαρτός ἐστι καὶ ἀγένητος, δημιουργὸς ὢν τῆς διακοσμήσεως, κατὰ χρόνων ποιὰς περιόδους ἀναλίσκων εἰς ἑαυτὸν τὴν ἅπασαν οὐσίαν καὶ πάλιν ἐξ ἑαυτοῦ γεννῶν· καὶ αὐτὴν δὲ τὴν διακόσμησιν [τῶν ἀστέρων] κόσμον εἶναι λέγουσι· καὶ τρίτον τὸ συνεστηκὸς ἐξ ἀμφοῖν.   5
καὶ ἔστι κόσμος ὁ ἰδίως ποιὸς τῆς τῶν ὅλων οὐσίας ἤ, ὥς φησι Ποσειδώνιος ἐν τῇ Μετεωρολογικῇ στοιχειώσει, σύστημα ἐξ οὐρανοῦ καὶ γῆς καὶ τῶν ἐν τούτοις φύσεων, ἢ σύστημα ἐκ θεῶν καὶ ἀνθρώπων καὶ τῶν ἕνεκα τούτων γεγονότων.

3 χρόνων codd.: χρόνου Suda   5 τῶν ἀστέρων del. Arnim   8 θεῶν codd.: στοιχείων Suda

Context: doxography of Stoic physics.

1–2 **τὸν—ποιόν** For the expression, cf. Arius Didymus (*SVF* 2.528, p. 169, 17, 21): τὸ ἐκ πάσης τῆς οὐσίας ποιόν. The account of κόσμος in line 6 appears to be identical. As the ἰδίως ποιός of all substance, god is identical to 'designing fire' (**46A**, **D**) and fieriness is the one quality always connected with substance through its connexion with god.

5 τῶν ἀστέρων should be deleted, as an intrusion from ἐξ οὐρανοῦ, 7, interpolated here to explain διακόσμησιν and ἀμφοῖν. In fact διακόσμησιν refers to the present world-order as a whole, and ἀμφοῖν to the combination of κόσμος in this sense and κόσμος in the first sense = god.

g Plotinus 2.4.1 (*SVF* 2.320, part)

καὶ δὴ καὶ τολμῶσι καὶ μέχρι θεῶν αὐτὴν [*sc.* ὕλην] ἄγειν· καὶ τέλος δὴ καὶ αὐτὸν αὐτῶν τὸν θεὸν ὕλην ταύτην πως ἔχουσαν εἶναι.

1 αὐτῶν vel αὐτῷ codd.: del. Vitringa, Arnim

Context: discussion of ὕλη, with an attack on the Stoics for confining existing things to bodies.

This description of god appears to be a Plotinian distortion of the Stoic ἀρχαί and the Stoic genus 'disposed', πῶς ἔχον; cf. **29**, and see Rist [303], 259; Graeser [316], 36. Although the Stoics identified the *world* with 'their god' (αὐτῶν τὸν θεόν), 2, they did not describe god as 'a disposition of matter' but as the principle which causes matter to have its dispositions.

h Plato, *Soph.* 247d8–e4

ΞΕΝΟΣ. λέγω δὴ τὸ καὶ ὁποιανοῦν [τινα] κεκτημένον δύναμιν εἴτ᾽ εἰς τὸ ποιεῖν ἕτερον ὁτιοῦν πεφυκὸς εἴτ᾽ εἰς τὸ παθεῖν καὶ σμικρότατον ὑπὸ τοῦ φαυλοτάτου, κἂν εἰ μόνον εἰς ἅπαξ, πᾶν τοῦτο ὄντως εἶναι· τίθεμαι γὰρ ὅρον [ὁρίζειν] τὰ ὄντα ὡς ἔστιν οὐκ ἄλλο τι πλὴν δύναμις.

1 τινα om. B   3 ὁρίζειν del. Ast

Context: the Eleatic stranger advances the 'capacity to act or be acted upon' as an exhaustive mark of existing things, in response to the claim of the 'Giants' that nothing intangible exists. See Long [3], 153; and cf. Aristotle, *Top.* vi.9, 139a4–8; vii.7, 146a21–32.

45 Body

A Cicero, *Acad.* 1.39 (*SVF* 1.90)

discrepabat [*sc.* Zeno] etiam ab iisdem [*sc.* Academicis et Peripateticis] quod nullo modo arbitrabatur quidquam effici posse ab ea [*sc.* natura] quae expers esset corporis – cuius generis Xenocrates et superiores etiam ·animum esse dixerant – nec vero aut quod efficeret aliquid aut quod efficeretur posse esse non corpus.   5

Context: the speaker is Varro, who expounds Antiochus' interpretation of Zeno's deviations from the Academic–Peripatetic tradition.

B Sextus Empiricus, *M.* 8.263 (*SVF* 2.363)

τὸ γὰρ ἀσώματον κατ᾽ αὐτοὺς οὔτε ποιεῖν τι πέφυκεν οὔτε πάσχειν.

Context: refutation of the Stoic theory of *lekta* (cf. **33**).

C Nemesius 78,7–79,2 (*SVF* 1.518, part)

(1) ἔτι φησίν· οὐδὲν ἀσώματον συμπάσχει σώματι, οὐδὲ ἀσωμάτῳ σῶμα, ἀλλὰ σῶμα σώματι· (2) συμπάσχει δὲ ἡ ψυχὴ τῷ σώματι νοσοῦντι καὶ τεμνομένῳ, καὶ τὸ σῶμα τῇ ψυχῇ· αἰσχυνομένης γοῦν ἐρυθρὸν γίνεται καὶ φοβουμένης ὠχρόν· (3) σῶμα ἄρα ἡ ψυχή.

Context: survey and criticism of Stoic psychology.

Nemesius is reporting a second argument by Cleanthes for the soul's corporeality. In the first argument, 76,14–77,3, Cleanthes reaches this conclusion by arguing that children resemble their parents in respect of soul as well as body, and that resemblance

Stoic physics

and difference pertain to bodies but not to incorporeals; cf. **53C**. For detailed discussion, see Hahm [488], 16–17.

3–4 Cf. Aristotle, *De an.* I.1, 403a18–19: ἅμα γὰρ τούτοις [*sc.* τοῖς τῆς ψυχῆς πάθεσι] πάσχει τι τὸ σῶμα.

D Nemesius 81,6–10 (*SVF* 2.790, part)

(1) Χρύσιππος δέ φησιν ὅτι ὁ θάνατός ἐστι χωρισμὸς ψυχῆς ἀπὸ σώματος· (2) οὐδὲν δὲ ἀσώματον ἀπὸ σώματος χωρίζεται· (3) οὐδὲ γὰρ ἐφάπτεται σώματος ἀσώματον· (4) ἡ δὲ ψυχὴ καὶ ἐφάπτεται καὶ χωρίζεται τοῦ σώματος· (5) σῶμα ἄρα ἡ ψυχή.

Context: shortly after **C**.

For the antecedents of this argument, cf. Hahm [488], 15–16. As was also the case with Stoic utilization of **44h**, it exploits a Platonic point (death is the separation of the soul from the body, cf. *Phd.* 64c, 67c–d), to yield an un-Platonic conclusion. For the notion of contact as the relation between body and soul, see **53B 5–9**.

E Diogenes Laertius 7.135 (*SVF* 3 Apollodorus 6, part)

σῶμα δ' ἐστίν, ὥς φησιν Ἀπολλόδωρος ἐν τῇ Φυσικῇ, τὸ τριχῇ διαστατόν, εἰς μῆκος, εἰς πλάτος, εἰς βάθος· τοῦτο δὲ καὶ στερεὸν σῶμα καλεῖται.

Context: immediately following **44B**.

2 στερεόν The term means solid as in 'solid geometry', and implies nothing about physical mass.

F Galen, *Qual. inc.* 19.483, 13–16 (*SVF* 2.381, part)

διὰ τί δὲ μόνον . . . τοῦ σώματος τούτον ὅρον εἶναί φασιν τὸ τριχῇ διαστατὸν μετὰ ἀντιτυπίας, οὐχὶ δὲ καὶ χρόαν καὶ χυλὸν καὶ χυμὸν καὶ τῶν λοιπῶν συμβεβηκότων ἕκαστον οὕτως ὁρίζονται;

Context: part of an argument against the Stoics for not extending this definition to include qualities such as colour and flavour.

The same definition is ascribed to Epicurus at S.E., *M.* 1.21, though it does not occur in his extant writings. See also *M.* 11.226, *PH* 3.39, and Mueller [652], 75–7.

G Aristocles (Eusebius, *Pr. ev.* 15.14.1 = *SVF* 1.98, part)

στοιχεῖον εἶναί φησι [*sc.* Ζήνων] τῶν ὄντων τὸ πῦρ, καθάπερ Ἡράκλειτος, τούτου δ' ἀρχὰς ὕλην καὶ θεόν, ὡς Πλάτων. ἀλλ' οὗτος ἄμφω σώματά φησιν εἶναι, καὶ τὸ ποιοῦν καὶ τὸ πάσχον, ἐκείνου τὸ πρῶτον ποιοῦν αἴτιον ἀσώματον εἶναι λέγοντος.

1 φησι vel φασι codd.

Context: an excerpt from Zeno's doctrine of ἀρχαί, taken from book 7 of Aristocles, *On philosophy*.

Aristocles is no doubt characteristic of his time (see note on **1F**) in assimilating Plato to the Stoic scheme of ἀρχαί (cf. D.L. 3.69); but a reading of the *Timaeus* as making matter and god the two ἀρχαί had already been current by Zeno's day, as Theophrastus (ap. Simpl., *In Ar. Phys.* 26,11–13, Diels, *Dox.*, 484–5) shows. And in other respects Aristocles' evidence (called 'suspiciously schematic' by Hahm [488], 50 n. 19) may be unimpeachable; cf. also Sandbach [304], 36.

It was probably in fact the doctrines of Xenocrates that initiated this (to us) 'stoicizing' reading of Plato. They thus, either directly or via that reading of Plato, may in turn have influenced Zeno's choice of ἀρχαί, given his Platonic background (though he was too young to have studied with Xenocrates himself for ten years, D.L. 7.2). Xenocrates' own terms for his ἀρχαί were ἕν and ἀέναον ('the ever-flowing'), but the former was also called Zeus and Nous, and the latter could be identified by doxographers with ὕλη; cf. Aetius 1.3.23, 1.7.30, and Sandbach [304], 35–6, who points out that the second Aetius passage 'ascribes to Xenocrates a belief in two gods, the One, which he also called Zeus and mind, his primary god . . . and another, which was the soul of the universe. The continuation of the passage is mutilated, but contains the phrase . . . ἐνδιήκειν τοῖς ὑλικοῖς στοιχείοις . . . and ends with . . . ταῦτα χορηγήσας [*sc.* Xenocrates] τοῖς Στωικοῖς τὰ πρότερα μεταπέφρακεν παρὰ Πλάτωνος.' Sandbach could have also mentioned Calcidius 294: *haec Stoici de silva deque initiis rerum partim a Platone usurpantes partim commenti.*

1 **στοιχεῖον** For this use of the term, cf. **47A 3–4**. Although the Stoics regularly spoke of god as fire when referring to god's activity in the world, god is not called fire in the texts which specify him as one of the two ἀρχαί. Aristocles is probably correct, and philosophically sound, in treating fire, the foundational stuff, as something which has god and matter as its ἀρχαί. Cf. Sandbach [296], 73–4.

2 **ἄμφω σώματα** See note on **43B**.

H Alexander, *Mixt.* 224,32–225,3 (*SVF* 2.310, part)

αἰτιάσαιτο δ' ἄν τις εὐλόγως αὐτῶν ἐνταῦθα τοῦ λόγου γενόμενος καὶ τὸ δύο ἀρχὰς τῶν πάντων λέγοντας εἶναι ὕλην τε καὶ θεόν, ὧν τὸν μὲν ποιοῦντα εἶναι τὴν δὲ πάσχουσαν, μεμίχθαι τῇ ὕλῃ λέγειν τὸν θεόν, διὰ πάσης αὐτῆς διήκοντα καὶ σχηματίζοντα αὐτήν, καὶ μορφοῦντα καὶ κοσμοποιοῦντα τούτῳ τῷ τρόπῳ. 5

2 ποιοῦντα Bruns: ποιοῦν codd.   3 λέγειν Apelt: λέγει codd.

Context: part of an argument attacking the Stoics for making god and matter bodies such that god completely pervades matter.

Alexander's polemic does not cast doubt on the accuracy of his report here; cf. **44C 3**; **46A 2**; **47O**.

46 God, fire, cosmic cycle

A Aetius 1.7.33 (*SVF* 2.1027, part)

(1) οἱ Στωικοὶ νοερὸν θεὸν ἀποφαίνονται, πῦρ τεχνικὸν ὁδῷ βαδίζον ἐπὶ γενέσει κόσμου, ἐμπεριειληφός ⟨τε⟩ πάντας τοὺς σπερματικοὺς λόγους

Stoic physics

καθ᾿ οὓς ἅπαντα καθ᾿ εἱμαρμένην γίνεται, (2) καὶ πνεῦμα μὲν ἐνδιῆκον δι᾿
ὅλου τοῦ κόσμου, τὰς δὲ προσηγορίας μεταλαμβάνον κατὰ τὰς τῆς ὕλης,
δι᾿ ἧς κεχώρηκε, παραλλάξεις.   5

2 γενέσει vel γένεσιν codd.   ἐμπεριειληφός ⟨τε⟩ Dübner: ἐμπεριειληφὸς vel ἐμπεριειληφότος
codd.   3 ἅπαντα vel ἕκαστα codd.   ἐνδιῆκον vel διῆκον codd.   4–5 κατὰ τὰς ... παραλλάξεις Galen, Athenagoras: δι᾿ ὅλης ... παραλλάξεις (vel παραλλὰξ vel παραλλάξαν) codd.; cf. Diels, Dox.
Graec., pp. 5, 51

Context: doxography of god.

1–2 πῦρ–γενέσει   Cf. D.L. 7.156, said of φύσις (cf. also **42A 2**), and Cicero, *ND*
2.57, who attributes the notion of nature as 'designer' to Zeno. Intelligence is
regularly attributed to the world (e.g. *SVF* 2.633), which one Stoic usage of
κόσμος is identical to god; cf. **44F** and **47C**.

1 ὁδῷ βαδίζον   The metaphorical use of ὁδός = 'method' or 'system' goes back
to Plato. Zeno's liking for it reappears in his account of τέχνη (*SVF* 1.72) as ἕξις
ὁδοποιητική (ὁδῷ ποιητική, Festa); cf. **42A**.

2 σπερματικοὺς λόγους   A Stoic technical term (cf. **B 4**) whose significance is
not restricted to cosmogony; cf. *SVF* 1.497, 2.780, 3.141. For its cosmic usage, see
Origen, *Cels.* 4.48 (*SVF* 2.1074), which employs a Stoic allegory of the two ἀρχαί,
god as Zeus = male, and matter as Hera = female: τοὺς σπερματικοὺς λόγους τοῦ
θεοῦ ἡ ὕλη παραδεξαμένη ἔχει ἐν ἑαυτῇ εἰς κατακόσμησιν τῶν ὅλων. Cf. Hahm
[488], 75–6.

4 προσηγορίας   Perhaps a deliberate reminiscence of Heraclitus 22 в 67 DK,
where god undergoes alteration just as fire is named according to the scent of different
spices. For different manifestations of πνεῦμα, cf. **47L, N**.

B Diogenes Laertius 7.135–6 (*SVF* 1.102, part)

(1) ἕν τ᾿ εἶναι θεὸν καὶ νοῦν καὶ εἱμαρμένην καὶ Δία, πολλαῖς τ᾿ ἑτέραις
ὀνομασίαις προσονομάζεσθαι. (2) κατ᾿ ἀρχὰς μὲν οὖν καθ᾿ αὑτὸν ὄντα
τρέπειν τὴν πᾶσαν οὐσίαν δι᾿ ἀέρος εἰς ὕδωρ. καὶ ὥσπερ ἐν τῇ γονῇ τὸ
σπέρμα περιέχεται, οὕτω καὶ τοῦτον σπερματικὸν λόγον ὄντα τοῦ κόσμου,
τοιόνδε ὑπολείπεσθαι ἐν τῷ ὑγρῷ, εὐεργὸν αὑτῷ ποιοῦντα τὴν ὕλην πρὸς   5
τὴν τῶν ἑξῆς γένεσιν. (3) εἶτ᾿ ἀπογεννᾶν πρῶτον τὰ τέσσαρα στοιχεῖα,
πῦρ, ὕδωρ, ἀέρα, γῆν.

Context: shortly after **45E**.

3 τρέπειν recalls τροπή in Heraclitus, 22 в 31 DK; cf. Long [353], 139–41.
Mention of air and water is confusing at this pre-cosmic stage. Air seems to be a phase
in the subsidence of the conflagration, culminating in a pre-cosmic liquid state.

3 γονῇ   The term almost certainly means seminal fluid here, as regularly in
Aristotle; so Hahm [488], 60ff. In allegorical terms (cf. note on **A 2**), Zeus has
intercourse with Hera (air), and 'through her' produces seminal fluid in which he is
present as the fiery sperm. Lapidge [491], 166, takes γονή as 'womb', but this very rare
use of the word hardly gives the right correspondence with τὸ ὑγρόν.

C Diogenes Laertius 7.142 (*SVF* 1.102, part)

(1) γίνεσθαι δὲ τὸν κόσμον ὅταν ἐκ πυρὸς ἡ οὐσία τραπῇ δι' ἀέρος εἰς ὑγρόν· εἶτα τὸ παχυμερὲς αὐτοῦ συστὰν ἀποτελεσθῇ γῆ, τὸ δὲ λεπτομερὲς ἐξαραιωθῇ, καὶ τοῦτ' ἐπὶ πλέον λεπτυνθὲν πῦρ ἀπογεννήσῃ. (2) εἶτα κατὰ μίξιν ἐκ τούτων φυτά τε καὶ ζῷα καὶ τὰ ἄλλα γένη.

2 ὑγρόν FP: ὑγρότητα B

This account of how the elements arise has a complex background; cf. Heraclitus 22 B 31 DK; Plato, *Tim.* 49b–c; and Hahm [488], 57ff. For parallel Stoic texts, see *SVF* 1.497, 2.579. For an excellent discussion of change in density as the principle of elemental change, see Hahm [495].

2   Although many editors accept ὑγρότητα, the expression τὸ παχυμερὲς αὐτοῦ points clearly to ὑγρόν as the right reading. Reading ὑγρότητα, we have no suitable noun for αὐτοῦ to refer to.

D Stobaeus 1.213,15–21 (*SVF* 1.120, part)

(1) Ζήνων τὸν ἥλιόν φησι καὶ τὴν σελήνην καὶ τῶν ἄλλων ἄστρων ἕκαστον εἶναι νοερὸν καὶ φρόνιμον, πύρινον ⟨δὲ⟩ πυρὸς τεχνικοῦ. (2) δύο γὰρ γένη πυρός, τὸ μὲν ἄτεχνον καὶ μεταβάλλον εἰς ἑαυτὸ τὴν τροφήν, τὸ δὲ τεχνικόν, αὐξητικόν τε καὶ τηρητικόν, οἷον ἐν τοῖς φυτοῖς ἐστι καὶ ζῴοις, ὃ δὴ φύσις ἐστὶ καὶ ψυχή. (3) τοιούτου δὴ πυρὸς εἶναι τὴν τῶν ἄστρων   5 οὐσίαν.

2 πύρινον ⟨δὲ⟩ πυρὸς Diels; cf. Stob. 1.219, 13: πύρινον πῦρ ὡς vel πῦρ ὡς codd.

Context: doxography of astronomy.

On the two kinds of fire, cf. *SVF* 1.504, 2.422, 682. The doctrine and its philosophical antecedents are well discussed by Lapidge [492], 268–72, but it need not exclude, as he seems to think, the essential unity of all fire.

In crediting the heavenly bodies with intelligence, the Stoics agreed with Plato and Aristotle against Epicurus, and they opted for this region as the location of the world's 'commanding-faculty'; cf. **470**, and Rist [303], 259ff.

E Plutarch, *St. rep.* 1052c–d (*SVF* 2.604, part)

(1) ἐν δὲ τῷ πρώτῳ Περὶ προνοίας τὸν Δία φησὶν αὔξεσθαι μέχρι ἂν εἰς αὐτὸν ἅπαντα καταναλώσῃ· "ἐπεὶ γὰρ ὁ θάνατος μέν ἐστι ψυχῆς χωρισμὸς ἀπὸ τοῦ σώματος, ἡ δὲ τοῦ κόσμου ψυχὴ οὐ χωρίζεται μὲν αὔξεται δὲ συνεχῶς μέχρι ἂν εἰς αὐτὴν ἐξαναλώσῃ τὴν ὕλην, οὐ ῥητέον ἀποθνήσκειν τὸν κόσμον." ... (2) σαφῶς γὰρ αὐτὸς ἐν τῷ αὐτῷ γέγραφεν· "αὐτάρκης δ'   5 εἶναι λέγεται μόνος ὁ κόσμος διὰ τὸ μόνος ἐν αὑτῷ πάντ' ἔχειν ὧν δεῖται, καὶ τρέφεται ἐξ αὑτοῦ καὶ αὔξεται, τῶν ἄλλων μορίων εἰς ἄλληλα καταλλαττομένων."

8 καταλλαττομένων Meziriac: κατατατττομένων vel alia codd.

Context: Plutarch seeks to show that Chrysippus is inconsistent in attributing growth

273

Stoic physics

to Zeus here, when he elsewhere – in book 3 of his *On gods*, cited at 1052B – denies that Zeus and the world require τροφή.

F Plutarch, *St. rep.* 1053B (*SVF* 2.605, part)

(1) καὶ μὴν ὅταν ἐκπύρωσις γένηται διόλου, ⟨τὸν κόσμον διόλου⟩ ζῆν καὶ ζῷον εἶναί φησι, σβεννύμενον δ' αὖθις καὶ παχυνόμενον εἰς ὕδωρ καὶ γῆν καὶ τὸ σωματοειδὲς τρέπεσθαι. (2) λέγει δ' ἐν τῷ πρώτῳ Περὶ προνοίας· "διόλου μὲν γὰρ ὢν ὁ κόσμος πυρώδης εὐθὺς καὶ ψυχή ἐστιν ἑαυτοῦ καὶ ἡγεμονικόν· ὅτε δέ, μεταβαλὼν εἴς τε τὸ ὑγρὸν καὶ τὴν ἐναπολειφθεῖσαν   5 ψυχήν, τρόπον τινὰ εἰς σῶμα καὶ ψυχὴν μετέβαλεν ὥστε συνεστάναι ἐκ τούτων, ἄλλον τινὰ ἔσχε λόγον."

1 suppl. Cherniss   2 ζῷον ⟨ἔμψυχον τὸν κόσμον⟩ Pohlenz

Context: supposed inconsistencies in Chrysippus' views about the relationship of heating and cooling to animation.

1–3 appears to be Plutarch's paraphrase of Chrysippus' own words in 4–7. Chrysippus is careful to say that the world's transformation into moisture and the residual soul is a change into body and soul τρόπον τινά. Plutarch, omitting this qualification, gives the misleading impression that the change is from a purely psychic into a purely corporeal state; cf. **B 2, H**.

G Aristocles (Eusebius, *Pr. ev.* 15.14.2 = *SVF* 1.98, part)

(1) ἔπειτα δὲ καὶ κατά τινας εἱμαρμένους χρόνους ἐκπυροῦσθαι τὸν σύμπαντα κόσμον, εἶτ' αὖθις πάλιν διακοσμεῖσθαι. (2) τὸ μέντοι πρῶτον πῦρ εἶναι καθαπερεί τι σπέρμα, τῶν ἁπάντων ἔχον τοὺς λόγους καὶ τὰς αἰτίας τῶν γεγονότων καὶ τῶν γιγνομένων καὶ τῶν ἐσομένων· τὴν δὲ τούτων ἐπιπλοκὴν καὶ ἀκολουθίαν εἱμαρμένην καὶ ἐπιστήμην καὶ   5 ἀλήθειαν καὶ νόμον εἶναι τῶν ὄντων ἀδιάδραστόν τινα καὶ ἄφυκτον. (3) ταύτῃ δὲ πάντα διοικεῖσθαι τὰ κατὰ τὸν κόσμον ὑπέρευ, καθάπερ ἐν εὐνομωτάτῃ τινὶ πολιτείᾳ.

Context: immediately following **45G**.

5–6 Cf. **55M 3** for a similar set of terms explaining εἱμαρμένη.

7–8 The conception of the world as a commonwealth or city is standard doctrine; cf. *SVF* 2.528, 645, 3.327, 333.

H Origen, *Cels.* 4.14 (*SVF* 2.1052, part)

ἀλλὰ καὶ ὁ τῶν Στωικῶν θεός, ἅτε σῶμα τυγχάνων, ὁτὲ μὲν ἡγεμονικὸν ἔχει τὴν ὅλην οὐσίαν, ὅταν ἡ ἐκπύρωσις ᾖ· ὁτὲ δὲ ἐπὶ μέρους γίνεται αὐτῆς, ὅταν ᾖ διακόσμησις.

Context: Origen is contrasting his belief in the unchangeability of God with Epicurean and Stoic views.

I Alexander Lycopolis 19,2–4

τὸν Ζήνωνος τοῦ Κιτιέως . . . λόγον, ὃς "τὸ πᾶν ἐκπυρωθήσεται" λέγων·
"πᾶν τὸ καῖον ἔχον ⟨ὅτι⟩ καύσῃ ὅλον καύσει· καὶ ὁ ἥλιος πῦρ ἐστιν καὶ ὃ
ἔχει οὐ καύσει;" ἐξ οὗ συνήγετο, ὡς ᾤετο, "τὸ πᾶν ἐκπυρωθήσεσθαι".

2 ⟨ὅτι⟩ Brinkmann

Context: refutation of the Manichean conception of evil, to which Zeno's doctrine of
the conflagration is likened. Alexander proceeds to remark that the conflagration is
implausible because there is no evidence that the sun has so far destroyed anything.

Mansfeld has restored this important evidence, missed by Arnim, to general
circulation; cf. [498] and [496], 148–52. He suggests that the passage 'must come from
Zeno's work *On the whole*, i.e. the Universe (Περὶ τοῦ ὅλου) in which he treated the
genesis and destruction of the universe'. For relevant Aristotelian material, cf.
Mansfeld [496], 149ff.

2 ἔχον ⟨ὅτι⟩ καύσῃ Not 'having what it burns' (Mansfeld), but 'having
something to burn', since καύσῃ is subjunctive.

3 If the argument is complete, the second premise must be taken to presuppose
that 'what the sun has' is τὸ πᾶν. Why should Zeno regard this as plausible? Cleanthes
regarded the sun as the world's commanding-faculty (**470**), deducing this from its
being 'the largest heavenly body and its contributing most to the direction of the
universe' (*SVF* 1.499); cf. **L**. Hence it must have been supposed that 'all the world' is
available to the sun to burn.

J Diogenes Laertius 7.141 (*SVF* 2.589, part)

ἀρέσκει δ' αὐτοῖς καὶ φθαρτὸν εἶναι τὸν κόσμον, ἅτε γενητὸν τῷ λόγῳ τῶν
δι' αἰσθήσεως νοουμένων, οὗ τε τὰ μέρη φθαρτά ἐστι, καὶ τὸ ὅλον· τὰ δὲ
μέρη τοῦ κόσμου φθαρτά· εἰς ἄλληλα γὰρ μεταβάλλει· φθαρτὸς ἄρα ὁ
κόσμος.

Context: a few lines before **C**.

In denying that the present world-order is everlasting, the Stoics differed radically
from Plato and the Peripatetics. The grounds given here for its perishability
correspond to the third of four considerations cited by Theophrastus according to
Philo, *Aet. mundi* 117–31; the others are the earth's irregularity, the sea's recession, and
the extinction of certain animal species. Theophrastus does not name any philosophers
in this passage, but Zeller [500] gave good reasons for attributing the arguments to
Zeno and for making Aristotle their target; cf. the confirmatory discussion by Graeser
[340], 187–206, and reservations by Mansfeld [496], 144 n. 43.

K Eusebius, *Pr. ev.* 15.18.2 (*SVF* 2.596, part)

οὐ γὰρ ἐπὶ τῆς τοῦ κόσμου κατὰ περιόδους τὰς μεγίστας γινομένης φθορᾶς
κυρίως παραλαμβάνουσι τὴν φθορὰν οἱ τὴν εἰς πῦρ ἀνάλυσιν τῶν ὅλων
δογματίζοντες, ἣν δὴ καλοῦσιν ἐκπύρωσιν, ἀλλ' ἀντὶ τῆς κατὰ φύσιν
μεταβολῆς χρῶνται τῇ προσηγορίᾳ τῆς φθορᾶς.

Context: doxography of Stoic cosmology.

Stoic physics

L Plutarch, *Comm. not.* 1075D (*SVF* 1.510)

ἔτι τοίνυν ἐπαγωνιζόμενος ὁ Κλεάνθης τῇ ἐκπυρώσει λέγει τὴν σελήνην
καὶ τὰ λοιπὰ ἄστρα τὸν ἥλιον ⟨ὡς ἡγεμονικὸν⟩ ἐξομοιῶσαι πάντα ἑαυτῷ
καὶ μεταβαλεῖν εἰς ἑαυτόν.

2 suppl. Cherniss: ⟨τότε συσπεύδοντ'⟩ Sandbach (alii alia): vac. codd.   ἐξομοιῶσαι codd.: -σειν
Zeller, Arnim

Context: attack on the Stoics for introducing perishable gods, i.e. the heavenly bodies
destroyed at the conflagration.

2   Cherniss' ingenious supplement for the 11-letter space in the MSS supplies a
reason for the sun's assimilation of the other heavenly bodies in line with Cleanthes'
doctrine; cf. **47O**, and more generally, **F** and **H** of this section. Other scholars have
filled the space with an expression which anticipates Plutarch's subsequent criticism.

M Philo, *Aet. mundi* 90 (*SVF* 1.511)

ὅτι τὸν κόσμον ἐκπυρωθέντα γενέσθαι μὲν ἄνθρακι παραπλήσιον ἀμήχανον, ὡς
δέδεικται, γεώδους πολλῆς ἂν ὑπολειφθείσης οὐσίας, ᾗ δεήσει τὸ πῦρ ἐλλοχᾶν, ἴσως δ' οὐδ'
ἐκπυρώσεως τότε κρατούσης, εἴ γε μένει τὸ στοιχείων βαρύτατον καὶ δυσαναλωτότατον
ἔτι, γῆ μὴ διαλυθεῖσα, μεταβάλλειν δὲ ἢ εἰς φλόγα ἢ εἰς αὐγὴν ἀναγκαῖον, εἰς
μὲν φλόγα, ὡς ᾤετο Κλεάνθης, εἰς δ' αὐγήν, ὡς ὁ Χρύσιππος.   5

3 εἴ γε edd.: εἴτε codd.

Context: criticism of the doctrine of conflagration.

N Plutarch, *Comm. not.* 1067A (*SVF* 2.606)

ὅταν ἐκπυρώσωσι τὸν κόσμον οὗτοι, κακὸν μὲν οὐδὲ ὁτιοῦν ἀπολείπεται,
τὸ δὲ ὅλον φρόνιμόν ἐστι τηνικαῦτα καὶ σοφόν.

Context: an argument to show that the world's complete prudence during the
conflagration is incompatible with the Stoic definition of φρόνησις as ἀγαθῶν καὶ
κακῶν ἐπιστήμη; cf. **61H** 1.

The absence of all evil from the universe during the conflagration is likely to be a
genuine Stoic inference from the doctrine that Zeus and his providence are then
coextensive with everything, **28O** 4. But the notion, found in later antiquity, that the
purpose of the conflagration is to purge evil from the world, e.g. *SVF* 2.598, seems to
be a mainly Christian interpretation – although Seneca comes close to it, *NQ* 3.28.7.

O Seneca, *Ep.* 9.16 (*SVF* 2.1065)

qualis tamen futura est vita sapientis, si sine amicis relinquatur in custodiam
coniectus vel in aliqua gente aliena destitutus vel in navigatione longa retentus
aut in desertum litus eiectus? qualis est Iovis, cum resoluto mundo et dis in
unum confusis paulisper cessante natura adquiescit sibi cogitationibus suis
traditus. tale quiddam sapiens facit: in se reconditur, secum est.   5

Context: the wise man's contentment at all times.

P Philo, *Aet. mundi* 76–7

Βοηθὸς γοῦν ὁ Σιδώνιος καὶ Παναίτιος . . . τὰς ἐκπυρώσεις καὶ παλιγγε-
νεσίας καταλιπόντες πρὸς θειότερον δόγμα τὸ τῆς ἀφθαρσίας τοῦ κόσμου
παντὸς ηὐτομόλησαν. λέγεται δὲ καὶ Διογένης ἡνίκα νέος ἦν συνεπι-
γραψάμενος τῷ δόγματι τῆς ἐκπυρώσεως ὀψὲ τῆς ἡλικίας ἐνδοιάσας
ἐπισχεῖν.   5

2 θειότερον codd.: ὁσιώτερον Cumont

Context: see on **M**.

Panaetius' rejection of the conflagration, and defence of the world's eternity, are
the most widely reported of all his doctrines; cf. van Straaten [323], 64–9.
Unfortunately no evidence survives concerning his reasons for deviating from the
earlier Stoic position.

47 Elements, breath, tenor, tension

A Stobaeus 1.129,2–130,13 (*SVF* 2.413, part)

(1) Χρυσίππου. περὶ δὲ τῶν ἐκ τῆς οὐσίας στοιχείων τοιαῦτά τινα
ἀποφαίνεται, τῷ τῆς αἱρέσεως ἡγεμόνι Ζήνωνι κατακολουθῶν, (2)
τέτταρα λέγων εἶναι στοιχεῖα ⟨πῦρ, ἀέρα, ὕδωρ, γῆν, ἐξ ὧν συνίστασθαι
πάντα ⟨καὶ ζῷα⟩ καὶ φυτὰ καὶ τὸν ὅλον κόσμον καὶ τὰ ἐν αὐτῷ
περιεχόμενα) καὶ εἰς ταῦτα διαλύεσθαι. (3) τὸ δὲ κατ' ἐξοχὴν στοιχεῖον   5
λέγεσθαι διὰ τὸ ἐξ αὐτοῦ πρώτου τὰ λοιπὰ συνίστασθαι κατὰ μεταβολὴν
καὶ εἰς αὐτὸ ἔσχατον πάντα χεόμενα διαλύεσθαι, τοῦτο δὲ μὴ ἐπιδέχεσθαι
τὴν εἰς ἄλλο χύσιν ἢ ἀνάλυσιν· . . . (4) κατὰ μὲν τὸν λόγον τοῦτον
αὐτοτελῶς λεγομένου τοῦ πυρὸς στοιχείου· οὐ μετ' ἄλλου γάρ· κατὰ δὲ τὸν
πρότερον καὶ μετ' ἄλλων συστατικὸν εἶναι, πρώτης μὲν γιγνομένης τῆς ἐκ   10
πυρὸς κατὰ σύστασιν εἰς ἀέρα μεταβολῆς, δευτέρας δ' ἀπὸ τούτου εἰς
ὕδωρ, τρίτης δ' ἔτι μᾶλλον κατὰ τὸ ἀνάλογον συνισταμένου τοῦ ὕδατος εἰς
γῆν. πάλιν δ' ἀπὸ ταύτης διαλυομένης καὶ διαχεομένης πρώτη μὲν
γίγνεται χύσις εἰς ὕδωρ, δευτέρα δ' ἐξ ὕδατος εἰς ἀέρα, τρίτη δὲ καὶ
ἐσχάτη εἰς πῦρ. (5) λέγεσθαι πῦρ τὸ πυρῶδες πᾶν καὶ ἀέρα τὸ ἀερῶδες καὶ   15
ὁμοίως τὰ λοιπά. (6) τριχῶς δὴ λεγομένου κατὰ Χρύσιππον τοῦ στοιχείου,
(7) καθ' ἕνα μὲν τρόπον τοῦ πυρός, διὰ τὸ ἐξ αὐτοῦ τὰ λοιπὰ συνίστασθαι
κατὰ μεταβολὴν καὶ εἰς αὐτὸ λαμβάνειν τὴν ἀνάλυσιν, (8) καθ' ἕτερον δέ,
καθὸ λέγεται τὰ τέσσαρα στοιχεῖα, πῦρ, ἀήρ, ὕδωρ, γῆ (ἐπεὶ διὰ τούτων
τινὸς ἢ τινῶν ἢ καὶ πάντων τὰ λοιπὰ συνέστηκε, διὰ μὲν τῶν τεττάρων, ὡς   20
τὰ ζῷα καὶ τὰ ἐπὶ γῆς πάντα συγκρίματα, διὰ δυοῖν δέ, ὡς ἡ σελήνη διὰ
πυρὸς καὶ ἀέρος συνέστηκε, δι' ἑνὸς δὲ ὡς ὁ ἥλιος, διὰ πυρὸς γὰρ μόνου, ὁ
γὰρ ἥλιος πῦρ ἐστιν εἰλικρινές), (9) κατὰ τρίτον λόγον λέγεται στοιχεῖον

Stoic physics

εἶναι ὃ πρῶτον συνέστηκεν οὕτως, ὥστε γένεσιν διδόναι ἀφ' αὑτοῦ ὁδῷ
μέχρι τέλους καὶ ἐξ ἐκείνου τὴν ἀνάλυσιν δέχεσθαι εἰς ἑαυτὸ τῇ ὁμοίᾳ ὁδῷ.　25

3–4 add. Diels　5 δὲ ⟨πῦρ καὶ⟩ Diels: ⟨πῦρ⟩ Heeren　7 δὲ ⟨καὶ⟩ P　9 οὐ μετ' ἄλλου γάρ huc transpos. Heeren: post πρότερον, 10, codd.　15 λέγεσθαι ⟨δὲ⟩ Heeren　16 δὴ Wachsmuth: δὲ codd.

Context: doxography of ἀρχαί and στοιχεῖα.

5　The addition of πῦρ is not only unnecessary; it also distorts the structure of the
passage. Chrysippus is explaining different senses of the term στοιχεῖον. It would be
premature to mention fire at this point, where an account is being offered which will
help to explain why fire, 8–9, can be identified with the element κατ' ἐξοχήν, an
expression probably picked up by αὐτοτελῶς, 9.

6–9　The reference is to the initial generation of the elements air, water and earth,
and their dissolution at the conflagration; cf. **46G**.

8　The omitted passage is a redundant one, rightly excised by Wachsmuth.

9–15　Cf. **46C**.

16–25　The three senses of στοιχεῖον correspond to the previous discussion as
follows: the first (17–18) to 9–15; the second (18–23) to 1–5; the third (23–5) to 5–9.

B Diogenes Laertius 7.136–7 (*SVF* 2.580)

ἔστι δὲ στοιχεῖον ἐξ οὗ πρώτου γίνεται τὰ γινόμενα καὶ εἰς ὃ ἔσχατον ἀναλύεται. τὰ δὴ
τέτταρα στοιχεῖα εἶναι ὁμοῦ τὴν ἄποιον οὐσίαν τὴν ὕλην· (1) εἶναι δὲ τὸ μὲν πῦρ τὸ
θερμόν, τὸ δ' ὕδωρ τὸ ὑγρόν, τόν τ' ἀέρα τὸ ψυχρόν, καὶ τὴν γῆν τὸ ξηρόν.
οὐ μὴν ἀλλὰ καὶ ἔτι ἐν τῷ ἀέρι εἶναι τὸ αὐτὸ μέρος. (2) ἀνωτάτω μὲν οὖν εἶναι τὸ
πῦρ, ὃ δὴ αἰθέρα καλεῖσθαι, ἐν ᾧ πρώτην τὴν τῶν ἀπλανῶν σφαῖραν　5
γεννᾶσθαι, εἶτα τὴν τῶν πλανωμένων· μεθ' ἣν τὸν ἀέρα, εἶτα τὸ ὕδωρ,
ὑποστάθμην δὲ πάντων τὴν γῆν, μέσην ἁπάντων οὖσαν.

2 τὴν ἄποιον FP(corr.): τινὰ ποιὸν BP　4 ἔτι om. F

Context: two lines after **46B**.

1　This corresponds to the first part of Aristotle's account of what most early
philosophers took as the ἀρχή and στοιχεῖον of reality, *Metaph. A.* 2, 983b6–11.

2　ἄποιον　This seems a nonsensical account of the four elements; cf. Lapidge
[492], 265. Elsewhere ὕλη is said to underlie them; and cf. Sextus, *M.* 10.312, who says
that they are generated by the alteration of ἄποιος ὕλη.

2–4　The allocation of these qualities to the elements goes back to the Sicilian
doctor Philistion, contemporary with Plato; cf. Anon. Lond. 20.25, and discussion by
Hahm [488], 98ff., [495]; Longrigg [503], 227–8.

C Cicero, *ND* 2.23–5, 28–30

(1) sic enim res se habet, ut omnia quae alantur et quae crescant contineant in se
vim caloris, sine qua neque ali possent nec crescere. nam omne quod est
calidum et igneum cietur et agitur motu suo; quod autem alitur et crescit
motu quodam utitur certo et aequabili; qui quam diu remanet in nobis tam diu
sensus et vita remanet, refrigerato autem et extincto calore occidimus ipsi et　5

extinguimur. (2) quod quidem Cleanthes his etiam argumentis docet, quanta vis insit caloris in omni corpore: negat enim esse ullum cibum tam gravem quin is nocte et die concoquatur; cuius etiam in reliquiis inest calor iis quas natura respuerit. iam vero venae et arteriae micare non desinunt quasi quodam igneo motu, animadversumque saepe est cum cor animantis alicuius evolsum   10 ita mobiliter palpitaret ut imitaretur igneam celeritatem. omne igitur quod vivit, sive animal sive terra editum, id vivit propter inclusum in eo calorem. ex quo intellegi debet eam caloris naturam vim habere in se vitalem per omnem mundum pertinentem. (3) atque id facilius cernemus toto genere hoc igneo quod tranat omnia subtilius explicato. omnes igitur partes mundi (tangam   15 autem maximas) calore fultae sustinentur. quod primum in terrena natura perspici potest . . . (4) ex quo concluditur, cum omnes mundi partes sustineantur calore, mundum etiam ipsum simili parique natura in tanta diuturnitate servari, eoque magis quod intellegi debet calidum illud atque igneum ita in omni fusum esse natura, ut in eo insit procreandi vis et causa   20 gignendi, a quo et animantia omnia et ea quorum stirpes terra continentur et nasci sit necesse et augescere. (5) natura est igitur quae contineat mundum omnem eumque tueatur, et ea quidem non sine sensu atque ratione. omnem enim naturam necesse est, quae non solitaria sit neque simplex sed cum alio iuncta atque conexa, habere aliquem in se principatum, ut in homine mentem,   25 in belua quiddam simile mentis unde oriantur rerum adpetitus; in arborum autem et earum rerum quae gignuntur e terra radicibus inesse principatus putatur. principatum autem id dico quod Graeci ἡγεμονικόν vocant, quo nihil in quoque genere nec potest nec debet esse praestantius. ita necesse est illud etiam in quo sit totius naturae principatus esse omnium optumum omniumque rerum potestate   30 dominatuque dignissimum. (6) videmus autem in partibus mundi (nihil est enim in omni mundo quod non pars universi sit) inesse sensum atque rationem. in ea parte igitur, in qua mundi inest principatus, haec inesse necessest, et acriora quidem atque maiora. quocirca sapientem esse mundum necesse est, naturamque eam quae res omnes conplexa teneat perfectione   35 rationis excellere, eoque deum esse mundum omnemque vim mundi natura divina contineri. atque etiam mundi ille fervor purior perlucidior mobiliorque multo ob easque causas aptior ad sensus commovendos quam hic noster calor, quo haec quae nota nobis sunt retinentur et vigent.

Context: survey of Stoic arguments concerning the existence and nature of god. In its transmitted form, the whole passage probably contains elements subsequent to Cleanthes, but its gist should be attributed to him and not to Posidonius, as Reinhardt [372], 60–177, maintained; cf. Solmsen [352].

17   The omitted lines cite evidence for the presence of heat in earth, air and water.
39   *animantem esse mundum* is the final conclusion of this argument, *ND* 2.32.

Stoic physics

D Nemesius 164,15–18 (*SVF* 2.418)

λέγουσι δὲ οἱ Στωικοὶ τῶν στοιχείων τὰ μὲν εἶναι δραστικά, τὰ δὲ παθητικά· δραστικὰ μὲν ἀέρα καὶ πῦρ, παθητικὰ δὲ γῆν καὶ ὕδωρ.

Context: doxography of the elements.

E Galen, *Nat. fac.* 106,13–17 (*SVF* 2.406)

καίτοι τούτοις μέν, ὡς ἂν καὶ αὐτῶν τῶν στοιχείων τὴν εἰς ἄλληλα μεταβολὴν χύσεσί τέ τισι καὶ πλήσεσιν ἀναφέρουσιν, εὔλογον ἦν ἀρχὰς δραστικὰς ποιήσασθαι τὸ θερμὸν καὶ τὸ ψυχρόν, Ἀριστοτέλει δ' οὐχ οὕτως.

Context: Galen is discussing the views of philosophers and doctors who 'make the hot and the cold active, and the dry and the moist passive.' He observes that the Stoics were better justified than Aristotle in adopting this theory of change since they accounted for elemental change by rarefaction and condensation (i.e. processes caused by heat and cold respectively), whereas Aristotle explained it by the four qualities. See **46C**, **55F**, and Hahm [495], 48–9.

F Galen, *Plen.* 7.525,7–14 (*SVF* 2.439) and 527,13–16 (*SVF* 2.440, part)

ποιεῖν δ' εἰς ἑαυτὸ λέγειν ὁτιοῦν ἢ ἐνεργεῖν εἰς ἑαυτὸ παρὰ τὴν ἔννοιάν ἐστιν· οὕτως οὖν καὶ συνέχειν ἑαυτό. καὶ γὰρ οἱ μάλιστα εἰσηγησάμενοι τὴν συνεκτικὴν δύναμιν, ὡς οἱ Στωικοί, τὸ μὲν συνέχον ἕτερον ποιοῦσι, τὸ συνεχόμενον δὲ ἄλλο· τὴν μὲν γὰρ πνευματικὴν οὐσίαν τὸ συνέχον, τὴν δὲ ὑλικὴν τὸ συνεχόμε- νον· ὅθεν ἀέρα μὲν καὶ πῦρ συνέχειν φασί, γῆν δὲ καὶ ὕδωρ συνέχεσ- 5 θαι . . . οὐδὲ γὰρ οὐδ' οἱ πολλοὶ τῶν Ἡροφιλείων οὐδ' οἱ νεώτεροι Στωικοὶ λέγουσί τινα ἀπόδειξιν τοῦ τὸ μὲν πνεῦμα καὶ τὸ πῦρ συνέχειν ἑαυτό τε καὶ τὰ ἄλλα, τὸ δὲ ὕδωρ καὶ τὴν γῆν ἑτέρου δεῖσθαι τοῦ συνέξοντος.

Context: Galen has been developing a thesis concerning the structure of bodily mass (πλῆθος). He distinguishes between πλῆθος qua δύναμις, 'the capacity of something to support bodily mass', and πλῆθος qua ἔγχυμα, 'the filling or contents of a body'. At the beginning of this extract, he insists on the necessity of making this distinction: 'something cannot activate or sustain itself'. He then cites the Stoic distinction between συνέχον and συνεχόμενον in support of his thesis.

6 We omit a long attack on the 'self-styled present-day followers of Herophilus' for their alleged failure to clarify the nature of the συνεκτικὴ δύναμις, which they defend. Galen accuses them of an infinite regress – 'they insist that everything needs something to sustain it'. He then, 6–8, groups them with recent Stoics, and attacks them both for holding that 'breath and fire sustain both themselves and the rest'. If he is claiming that Chrysippus refrained from attributing self-sustainment to air and fire, he is probably mistaken; cf. **G**.

G Plutarch, *Comm. not.* 1085C–D (*SVF* 2.444, part)

γῆν μὲν γάρ φασι καὶ ὕδωρ οὔθ' αὐτὰ συνέχειν οὔθ' ἕτερα, πνευματικῆς δὲ

μετοχῇ καὶ πυρώδους δυνάμεως τὴν ἑνότητα διαφυλάττειν· ἀέρα δὲ καὶ
πῦρ αὐτῶν τ᾽ εἶναι δι᾽ εὐτονίαν ἑκτικά, καὶ τοῖς δυσὶν ἐκείνοις ἐγκεκρα-
μένα τόνον παρέχειν καὶ τὸ μόνιμον καὶ οὐσιῶδες.

1 φασι Arnim: τιθέασι Pohlenz: ἴσασι codd.　　2 μετοχῇ Wyttenbach: μετοχῆς codd.　　3 ἑκτικά
Arnim: συνεκτικά Pohlenz: ἐκτατικά codd.

Context: Plutarch tries to maintain that these doctrines are inconsistent with the Stoic
claim that earth and water are elements; cf. **I 1**.

　　2 **ἑνότητα**　Cf. **J 6**.
　　3 **δι᾽ εὐτονίαν**　Cf. **48C 12**.

H　Galen, *Plac.* 5.3.8 (*SVF* 2.841, part)

τοῦτ᾽ οὖν τὸ πνεῦμα δύο μὲν κέκτηται μόριά τε καὶ στοιχεῖα καὶ
καταστάσεις, δι᾽ ὅλων ἀλλήλοις κεκραμ[μ]ένα, τὸ ψυχρὸν καὶ θερμόν,
εἴπερ δ᾽ ἑτέροις ὀνόμασι καὶ ἀπὸ τῶν οὐσιῶν ἐθέλοι τις αὐτὰ προσαγορεύειν, ἀέρα τε καὶ πῦρ· οὐ μὴν ἀλλὰ καὶ ἰκμάδα τινὰ προσείληφεν ἀπὸ τῶν
σωμάτων ἐν οἷς διαιτᾶται.　　　　　　　　　　　　　　　　　　　5

1-2 καὶ καταστάσεις secl. Müller

Context: Galen tries to argue that Chrysippus is committed, against his will, to
referring the health of the commanding-faculty to the proportion (συμμετρία) of the
constituents of its πνεῦμα; cf. note on **53V** for Galen's earlier attack on the same point.

I　Alexander, *Mixt.* 224,14–27 (*SVF* 2.442)

(1) πρὸς δὲ τούτοις, εἰ τὸ πνεῦμα γεγονὸς ἐκ πυρός τε καὶ ἀέρος διὰ πάντων
πεφοίτηκε τῶν σωμάτων ⟨τῷ⟩ πᾶσιν αὐτοῖς κεκρᾶσθαι καὶ ἑκάστῳ
αὐτῶν ἐκ τούτου ἠρτῆσθαι τὸ εἶναι, πῶς ἂν ἔτι ἁπλοῦν τι εἴη σῶμα; πῶς δ᾽
ἄν, εἰ ὕστερον τὸ ἔκ τινων συγκείμενον τῶν ἁπλῶν, τὸ πῦρ ἂν καὶ ὁ ἀὴρ εἴη, ἐξ ὧν
μιγνυμένων τὸ πνεῦμα γίνεται, οὗ χωρὶς ἀδύνατον εἶναί τι σῶμα; εἰ γὰρ ἐξ ἐκείνων μὲν ἡ　　5
γένεσις τῷ πνεύματι, ἀδύνατον δὲ ἐκείνων εἶναί τι χωρὶς πνεύματος, οὔτ᾽ ἂν ἐκείνων τι εἴη
πρὸ τῆς τοῦ πνεύματος γενέσεως, οὔτ᾽ ἂν τὸ πνεῦμα γίνοιτο, οὐκ ὄντων, ἐξ ὧν ἡ γένεσις
αὐτῷ. πῶς δ᾽ ἄν τις ἐν τῷ ψυχρῷ ἐνεργείᾳ τι θερμὸν εἶναι λέγοι; (2) τίς δὲ καὶ ἡ εἰς τὸ
ἐναντίον ἅμα κίνησις αὐτοῦ, καθ᾽ ἣν συνέχειν τὰ ἐν οἷς ἂν ᾖ, ὃν ὥς φασι
πνεῦμα κινούμενον ἅμα ἐξ αὐτοῦ τε καὶ εἰς αὐτό; καὶ κατὰ τί εἶδος　　10
κινήσεως γίνεται; κατ᾽ οὐδὲν γὰρ οἷόν τ᾽ ἐστὶ νοῆσαί τι ἅμα εἰς τὰ ἐναντία κινούμενον
καθ᾽ αὑτό.

2 ⟨τῷ⟩ Ideler　　9 αὐτοῦ Apelt: αὐτοῖς; οὐ codd.　　συνέχειν codd.: συνέχει Ideler　　ὃν Apelt: ὧν
codd.　　10 πνεῦμα codd.: πνεύματος Ideler　　κινούμενον Apelt: κινουμένου codd.　　αὐτοῦ . . . αὐτό Todd: αὐτοῦ . . . αὐτό codd.　　τί Apelt: τι codd.

Context: objections to the Stoic doctrine of πνεῦμα.

　　1–8　Alexander tries to make difficulty by arguing that if the composite πνεῦμα is
the cause of *every* body's existence, there could be no elements (simple bodies),
including fire and air whose mixture constitutes πνεῦμα, and so no πνεῦμα either.
The most promising rejoinder is the one suggested by Hahm [495]. Ancient critics,

Stoic physics

wilfully or not, tend to confuse the Stoics' account of the formation of the elements, which is explained by rarefaction and condensation of prime matter (see E; 46C), with the qualities that πνεῦμα generates in water and earth, where the latter are treated as the matter of particular objects. Alexander is probably working from a passage in which the dependence of every body on πνεῦμα refers only to particular compound bodies and does not include the elements earth and water; Nemesius' criticism in J can be explained similarly. The Stoic position, as set out in F and G, makes water and earth the pre-existing material with which πνεῦμα blends, and which it causes to take on perceptible properties; cf. M.

J Nemesius 70,6–71,4

(1) εἰ τοίνυν σῶμά ἐστιν ἡ ψυχὴ οἱονδήποτε, εἰ καὶ λεπτομερέστατον, τί πάλιν ἐστὶ τὸ συνέχον ἐκείνην; (2) ἐδείχθη γὰρ πᾶν σῶμα δεῖσθαι τοῦ συνέχοντος, καὶ οὕτως εἰς ἄπειρον, ἕως ἂν καταντήσωμεν εἰς ἀσώματον. (3) εἰ δὲ λέγοιεν, καθάπερ οἱ Στωικοί, τονικήν τινα εἶναι κίνησιν περὶ τὰ σώματα, εἰς τὸ ἔσω ἅμα καὶ εἰς τὸ ἔξω κινουμένην, καὶ τὴν μὲν εἰς τὸ ἔξω   5
μεγεθῶν καὶ ποιοτήτων ἀποτελεστικὴν εἶναι, τὴν δὲ εἰς τὸ ἔσω ἑνώσεως καὶ οὐσίας, ἐρωτητέον αὐτούς, ἐπειδὴ πᾶσα κίνησις ἀπό τινός ἐστι δυνάμεως, τίς ἡ δύναμις αὕτη καὶ ἐν τίνι οὐσίωται;

Context: doxography of soul.

2–3 The 'proof' is that all bodies are naturally unstable and infinitely divisible, and therefore need soul as their unifying principle; cf. Nemesius 70,2–6.

4–8 This is the most precise surviving testimony concerning the internal effects of πνεῦμα within a compound body; cf. G, M 2.

K Galen, *Musc. mot.* 4.402,12–403,10 (*SVF* 2.450, part)

(1) ἔστω τις ὑψηλὸς ὄρνις ἐν ταὐτῷ τόπῳ φαινόμενος μένειν. πότερον ἀκίνητον εἶναι τοῦτον λεκτέον, ὥσπερ εἰ καὶ κρεμάμενος ἄνωθεν ἔτυχεν, ἢ κινεῖσθαι τὴν ἐπὶ τὰ ἄνω κίνησιν εἰς τοσοῦτον εἰς ὅσον ἤγαγεν αὐτὸν κάτω τὸ τοῦ σώματος βάρος; ἐμοὶ μὲν τοῦτο ἀληθέστερον εἶναι δοκεῖ. στερήσας γοῦν αὐτὸν τῆς ψυχῆς ἢ τοῦ τῶν μυῶν τόνου, ταχέως ἐπὶ τὴν γῆν ὄψει   5
καταφερόμενον· ᾧ δῆλον ὅτι τὴν σύμφυτον τῷ τοῦ σώματος βάρει κάτω ῥοπὴν εἰς ἴσον ἀντεσήκου τῇ κατὰ τὸν τῆς ψυχῆς τόνον ἄνω φορᾷ. (2) πότερον οὖν ἐν ταῖς τοιαύταις ἁπάσαις καταστάσεσι ποτὲ μὲν κάτω ποτὲ δὲ ἄνω τὸ σῶμα φέρεται τἀναντία πάσχον ἐν μέρει, διὰ δὲ τὸ ταχείας τε καὶ ὀξυρρόπους γίνεσθαι τὰς μεταβολὰς καὶ κατὰ βραχυτάτων διαστημάτων   10
φέρεσθαι τὰς κινήσεις ἐν ταὐτῷ φαίνεται τόπῳ μένειν, ἢ ὄντως ἕνα διὰ παντὸς τοῦ χρόνου κατέχει τόπον, οὐ τοῦ παρόντος καιροῦ διελθεῖν.

Context: is muscular activity to be explained by τονικὴ κίνησις? At 4.402, 1–12, Galen illustrates his problem by the example of a swimmer who remains in the same place if his own movement against the current exactly counterbalances the current's strength.

For further discussion, cf. Sambursky [490], 32–3.

L Alexander, *Mixt.* 223,25–36 (*SVF* 2.441, part)

(1) τούτου δ᾽ οὕτως ἔχοντος, πῶς ἂν ἔτι ἀληθὲς εἴη τὸ πᾶν ἡνῶσθαί τε καὶ
συνέχεσθαι, πνεύματός τινος διὰ παντὸς διήκοντος αὐτοῦ; (2) ἔπειτα δ᾽
εὔλογον μὲν ἦν ὁμοίαν τὴν ὑπὸ τοῦ πνεύματος συνοχὴν γινομένην ἐν πᾶσιν
εἶναι τοῖς σώμασιν· οὐχ οὕτως δ᾽ ἔχει. τῶν γὰρ σωμάτων τὰ μέν ἐστι
συνεχῆ, τὰ δὲ διωρισμένα. διὸ εὐλογώτερον ἕκαστον αὐτῶν ὑπὸ τοῦ   5
οἰκείου εἴδους συνέχεσθαί τε καὶ ἡνῶσθαι λέγειν πρὸς ἑαυτό, καθό ἐστιν
αὐτῶν ἑκάστῳ τὸ εἶναι, τὴν ⟨δὲ⟩ συμπάθειαν αὐτῶν σῴζεσθαι τὴν πρὸς
ἄλληλα διά τε τὴν τῆς ὕλης κοινωνίαν καὶ τὴν τοῦ περικειμένου θείου
σώματος αὐτοῖς φύσιν, ἢ τῷ διὰ τοῦ πνεύματος δεσμῷ. (3) τίς γὰρ καὶ ὁ
τόνος τοῦ πνεύματος, ὑφ᾽ οὗ συνδούμενα τήν τε συνέχειαν ἔχει τὴν πρὸς τὰ   10
οἰκεῖα μέρη καὶ συνῆπται τοῖς παρακειμένοις;

7 ⟨δὲ⟩ Bruns   9 αὐτοῖς A.A. Long: αὐτῷ codd.   9 τῷ vel τὸ codd.   δεσμῷ. τίς Arnim:
δεσμώτης codd.

Context: problems posed by the Stoic concept of πνεῦμα, discussed shortly before
those of **I**.

1–2   Alexander concludes that the unifying power of πνεῦμα throughout the
world is excluded by the fact, as he claims, that some bodies, e.g. water, can never be
mixed with it. The Stoics disagreed; cf. *SVF* 2.721 on fish breathing the air which is
blended with water when the elements are originally formed.

2–9   Here Alexander seeks to turn against the Stoics their acknowledgement of
some bodies which are not unified; cf. **28M**. For his own account of unity and
interaction, cf. Todd [332] ad loc.

9 αὐτοῖς   The only possible antecedent for αὐτῷ, the MSS reading, seems to be
ἕκαστον αὐτῶν. That is very harsh in view of the second αὐτῶν in line 7, and
erroneous copying of singular and plural occurs elsewhere, e.g. 224,24, where Apelt's
αὐτοῦ must be read in place of αὐτοῖς.

M Plutarch, *St. rep.* 1053F–1054B (*SVF* 2.449)

(1) πάλιν ἐν τοῖς Περὶ ἕξεων οὐδὲν ἄλλο τὰς ἕξεις πλὴν ἀέρας εἶναί φησιν·
"ὑπὸ τούτων γὰρ συνέχεται τὸ σώματα· καὶ τοῦ ποιὸν ἕκαστον εἶναι τῶν
ἕξει συνεχομένων αἴτιος ὁ συνέχων ἀήρ ἐστιν, ὃν σκληρότητα μὲν ἐν
σιδήρῳ πυκνότητα δ᾽ ἐν λίθῳ λευκότητα δ᾽ ἐν ἀργύρῳ καλοῦσι" ... (2)
καίτοι πανταχοῦ τὴν ὕλην ἀργὸν ἐξ ἑαυτῆς καὶ ἀκίνητον ὑποκεῖσθαι ταῖς   5
ποιότησιν ἀποφαίνουσι, τὰς δὲ ποιότητας πνεύματα οὔσας καὶ τόνους
ἀερώδεις, οἷς ἂν ἐγγένωνται μέρεσι τῆς ὕλης, εἰδοποιεῖν ἕκαστα καὶ
σχηματίζειν.

6 οὔσας vel οὓς δὲ codd.   7 οἷς vel οἷος codd.

Context: the self-contradictory nature of Chrysippus' conception of air. He takes air to
be naturally soft and dark, and yet makes it responsible for such qualities as the
whiteness of silver and the hardness of iron.

5–8   Plutarch, following these lines, claims that the thesis about ὕλη and

Stoic physics

ποιότητες is incompatible with the natural qualities of air. If air is soft and dark, it should make inert matter soft and dark; if, on the other hand, air acquires different characteristics by being blended with each body, it is functioning more like matter than an active principle. Hahm [495], 48, convincingly suggests that Chrysippus is not referring here to prime matter (see 44) but to perceptible qualities generated in the water and earth which constitute the matter of compound bodies; cf. notes on I.

N Galen, *Intr.* 14.726,7–11 (*SVF* 2.716, part)

τοῦ δὲ ἐμφύτου πνεύματος διττὸν εἶδος, τὸ μὲν φυσικόν, τὸ δὲ ψυχικόν·
εἰσὶ δὲ οἳ καὶ τρίτον εἰσάγουσι, τὸ ἑκτικόν· ἑκτικὸν μὲν οὖν ἐστι πνεῦμα τὸ
συνέχον τοὺς λίθους, φυσικὸν δὲ τὸ τρέφον τὰ ζῷα καὶ τὰ φυτά, ψυχικὸν δὲ
τὸ ἐπὶ τῶν ἐμψύχων αἰσθητικά τε ποιοῦν τὰ ζῷα καὶ κινούμενα πᾶσαν
κίνησιν.   5

Context: the constitutive principles of living beings. At 14.697, 7, Galen identifies those who introduce the third πνεῦμα as Stoics. On **N–O** and their bearing on the Stoics' theory of the differences between plants, animals and humans, cf. Long [520], 43ff.

O Diogenes Laertius 7.138–9 (including *SVF* 2.634)

(1) τὸν δὴ κόσμον διοικεῖσθαι κατὰ νοῦν καὶ πρόνοιαν, καθά φησι Χρύσιππός τ᾽
ἐν τῷ πέμπτῳ Περὶ προνοίας καὶ Ποσειδώνιος ἐν τῷ τρισκαιδεκάτῳ Περὶ θεῶν, εἰς ἅπαν
αὐτοῦ μέρος διήκοντος τοῦ νοῦ, καθάπερ ἐφ᾽ ἡμῶν τῆς ψυχῆς· (2) ἀλλ᾽ ἤδη
δι᾽ ὧν μὲν μᾶλλον, δι᾽ ὧν δὲ ἧττον. δι᾽ ὧν μὲν γὰρ ὡς ἕξις κεχώρηκεν, ὡς
διὰ τῶν ὀστῶν καὶ τῶν νεύρων· δι᾽ ὧν δὲ ὡς νοῦς, ὡς διὰ τοῦ ἡγεμονικοῦ.   5
(3) οὕτω δὴ καὶ τὸν ὅλον κόσμον ζῷον ὄντα καὶ ἔμψυχον καὶ λογικόν, ἔχειν
ἡγεμονικὸν μὲν τὸν αἰθέρα, καθά φησιν Ἀντίπατρος ὁ Τύριος ἐν τῷ ὀγδόῳ
Περὶ κόσμου. (4) Χρύσιππος δ᾽ ἐν τῷ πρώτῳ Περὶ προνοίας καὶ
Ποσειδώνιος ἐν τῷ Περὶ θεῶν τὸν οὐρανόν φασι τὸ ἡγεμονικὸν τοῦ
κόσμου, Κλεάνθης δὲ τὸν ἥλιον. ὁ μέντοι Χρύσιππος διαφορώτερον πάλιν   10
τὸ καθαρώτατον τοῦ αἰθέρος ἐν ταὐτῷ· ὃ καὶ πρῶτον θεὸν ⟨ὄν⟩ λέγουσιν
αἰσθητικῶς ὥσπερ κεχωρηκέναι διὰ τῶν ἐν ἀέρι καὶ διὰ τῶν ζώων
ἁπάντων καὶ φυτῶν, διὰ δὲ τῆς γῆς αὐτῆς καθ᾽ ἕξιν.

1 διοικεῖσθαι B: μὲν οἰκεῖσθαι F: οἰκεῖσθαι P   2 τῷ πέμπτῳ F(corr.): τοῖς ε̄ BP   τῷ ιγ´ F: τοῖς ιγ´ BP: τρίτῳ d   4 κεχώρηκεν BP: ἐχώρησε F   10 μέντοι BP: δὲ F   11 καθαρώτατον BP: -τερον FP(corr.)   ⟨ὄν⟩ A.A. Long: lac. indic. Arnim

Context: one line after **44F**. On the theology of the whole extract, cf. **C**; **44F**; **46A**; **54A–B**.

P Philo, *Leg. alleg.* 2.22–3 (*SVF* 2.458, part)

(1) ὁ γυμνὸς καὶ ἀνένδετος σώματι νοῦς – περὶ γὰρ τοῦ μήπω ἐνδεδεμένου ἐστὶν ὁ
λόγος – πολλὰς ἔχει δυνάμεις, ἑκτικὴν φυσικὴν ψυχικὴν λογικὴν διανοη-
τικήν, ἄλλας μυρίας κατά τε εἴδη καὶ γένη. (2) ἡ μὲν ἕξις κοινὴ καὶ τῶν ἀψύχων

ἐστὶ λίθων καὶ ξύλων, ἧς μετέχει καὶ τὰ ἐν ἡμῖν ἐοικότα λίθοις ὀστέα. (3) ἡ
δὲ φύσις διατείνει καὶ ἐπὶ τὰ φυτά· καὶ ἐν ἡμῖν δέ ἐστιν ἐοικότα φυτοῖς, 5
ὄνυχές τε καὶ τρίχες· ἔστι δὲ ἡ φύσις ἕξις ἤδη κινουμένη. (4) ψυχὴ δέ ἐστι
φύσις προσειληφυῖα φαντασίαν καὶ ὁρμήν· αὕτη κοινὴ καὶ τῶν ἀλόγων
ἐστίν· ἔχει δὲ καὶ ὁ ἡμέτερος νοῦς ἀναλογοῦν τι ἀλόγου ψυχή. πάλιν ἡ διανοητικὴ δύναμις
ἰδία τοῦ νοῦ ἐστι, καὶ ἡ λογικὴ κοινὴ μὲν τάχα καὶ τῶν θειοτέρων φύσεων, ἰδία δὲ ὡς ἐν
θνητοῖς ἀνθρώπου· αὕτη δὲ διττή, ἡ μὲν καθ᾽ ἣν λογικοί ἐσμεν νοῦ μετέχοντες, ἡ δὲ καθ᾽ ἣν 10
διαλεγόμεθα.

2 φυσικὴν A.A. Long: φυτικὴν codd.   ψυχικὴν codd.: φυσικὴν Arm.   λογικὴν om. Arm.   9 ἡ
λογικὴ secl. Colson

Context: Philo interprets the nakedness of Adam and Eve (Genesis 2.25) as a reference
to the faculties of the unembodied soul.

2   The reading φυτικὴν is almost certainly a scribal error derived from line 5.
Some reference to φύσις is essential both doctrinally and to the structure of the
passage. Philo conflates the mind's faculties, one of which is λόγος (cf. 53K), with the
various faculties of πνεῦμα or divine νοῦς; cf. N, O 1–2, Q 1.

2–3, 8–11 λογική, διανοητική   Both terms seem to be Philonian amplifications
of the Stoic triad, ἕξις, φύσις, ψυχή. The Stoics, moreover, use λόγος and διάνοια
indifferently to refer to the faculty of reason; cf. Bonhöffer [311], 113 ff. Colson may
be right to delete ἡ λογική, 9.
   6 ψυχή   Cf. 53A 4, P–Q.
   8 ἀναλογοῦν–ψυχῇ. Cf. C 25–6.

Q Philo, Quod deus sit immutabilis 35–6 (SVF 2.458, part)

(1) τῶν γὰρ σωμάτων τὰ μὲν ἐνεδήσατο ἕξει, τὰ δὲ φύσει, τὰ δὲ ψυχῇ, τὰ δὲ
λογικῇ ψυχῇ. (2) λίθων μὲν οὖν καὶ ξύλων, ἃ δὴ τῆς συμφυίας ἀπέσπασται,
δεσμὸν κραταιότατον ἕξιν εἰργάζετο· ἡ δέ ἐστι πνεῦμα ἀναστρέφον ἐφ᾽
ἑαυτό· ἄρχεται μὲν γὰρ ἀπὸ τῶν μέσων ἐπὶ τὰ πέρατα τείνεσθαι, ψαῦσαν
δὲ ἄκρας ἐπιφανείας ἀνακάμπτει πάλιν, ἄχρις ἂν ἐπὶ τὸν αὐτὸν ἀφίκηται 5
τόπον, ἀφ᾽ οὗ τὸ πρῶτον ὡρμήθη· (3) ἕξεως ὁ συνεχὴς οὗτος δίαυλος
ἄφθαρτος.

Context: interpretation of God's creative organization (Genesis 6.6).
   1–2 Cf. N, O 2, P.
   2–6 Cf. R 3.
   7 ἄφθαρτος   The sense is presumably that the stone or log cannot exist without
the incessant movement of its ἕξις.

R Philo, Quaestiones et solutiones in Genesin 2.4 (SVF 2.802)

Context: explanation of Genesis 6.14.
   The only complete version of this work is a medieval Armenian translation from
the Greek. Our version in vol. 1 is based upon Aucher's Latin translation (printed in
SVF), and supplemented by comparisons with the more recent translations by

Stoic physics

Marcus in the Loeb edition of Philo, vol. x, and Mercier in vol. 34A of *Les Oeuvres de Philon d'Alexandrie*, ed. Arnaldez, Pouilloux, Mondévert.

S Simplicius, *In Ar. Cat.* 237,25–238,20 (*SVF* 2.393, part)

(1) ἄξιον δὲ καὶ τὴν τῶν Στωικῶν συνήθειαν περὶ τὰ ὀνόματα ταῦτα
καταμαθεῖν. δοκοῦσι γὰρ οὗτοί τισιν ἀνάπαλιν τῷ Ἀριστοτέλει τὴν
διάθεσιν τῆς ἕξεως μονιμωτέραν ἡγεῖσθαι· (2) τὸ δὲ ἀφορμὴν μὲν ἔχει τῆς
τοιαύτης ὑπονοίας, οὐ μέντοι κατὰ τὸ μονιμώτερον ἢ μὴ παρὰ τοῖς
Στωικοῖς ἡ τούτων εἴληπται διαφορά, ἀλλὰ κατ᾽ ἄλλας διαθέσεις· καὶ γὰρ   5
τὰς μὲν ἕξεις ἐπιτείνεσθαί φασιν δύνασθαι καὶ ἀνίεσθαι, τὰς δὲ διαθέσεις
ἀνεπιτάτους εἶναι καὶ ἀνανέτους. διὸ καὶ τὴν εὐθύτητα τῆς ῥάβδου, κἂν
εὐμετάβολος ᾖ δυναμένη κάμπτεσθαι, διάθεσιν εἶναί φασιν· μὴ γὰρ ἂν
ἀνεθῆναι ἢ ἐπιταθῆναι τὴν εὐθύτητα μηδὲ ἔχειν τὸ μᾶλλον ἢ ἧττον, διόπερ
εἶναι διάθεσιν. οὕτωσὶ δὲ καὶ τὰς ἀρετὰς διαθέσεις εἶναι, οὐ κατὰ τὸ   10
μόνιμον ἰδίωμα, ἀλλὰ κατὰ τὸ ἀνεπίτατον καὶ ἀνεπίδεκτον τοῦ μᾶλλον·
τὰς δὲ τέχνας καίτοι δυσκινήτους οὔσας [ἢ] μὴ εἶναι διαθέσεις. (3) καὶ
ἐοίκασιν τὴν μὲν ἕξιν ἐν τῷ πλάτει τοῦ εἴδους θεωρεῖν, τὴν δὲ διάθεσιν ἐν
τῷ τέλει τοῦ εἴδους καὶ ἐν τῷ μάλιστα, εἴτε κινοῖτο καὶ μεταβάλλοι, ὡς τὸ
εὐθὺ τῆς ῥάβδου, εἴτε καὶ μή. (4) μᾶλλον δὲ ἐχρῆν ἐκεῖνο ἐπιστῆσαι, μὴ ἡ   15
παρὰ τοῖς Στωικοῖς σχέσις ἡ αὐτή ἐστιν τῇ παρὰ Ἀριστοτέλει διαθέσει,
κατὰ τὸ εὐανάλυτον καὶ δυσανάλυτον διισταμένη πρὸς τὴν ἕξιν. ἀλλ᾽ οὐδὲ
οὕτως συμφωνοῦσιν. ὁ μὲν γὰρ Ἀριστοτέλης τὴν ἀβέβαιον ὑγίειαν
διάθεσιν εἶναί φησιν, οἱ δὲ ἀπὸ τῆς Στοᾶς τὴν ὑγίειαν, ὅπως ἂν ἔχῃ, οὐ
συγχωροῦσιν σχέσιν εἶναι· φέρειν γὰρ τὸ τῆς ἕξεως ἰδίωμα· τὰς μὲν γὰρ   20
σχέσεις ταῖς ἐπικτήτοις καταστάσεσιν χαρακτηρίζεσθαι, τὰς δὲ ἕξεις ταῖς
ἐξ ἑαυτῶν ἐνεργείαις. (5) ὅθεν οὐδὲ χρόνου μήκει ἢ ἰσχύι εἰδοποιοῦνται αἱ
ἕξεις κατ᾽ αὐτούς, ἰδιότητι δέ τινι καὶ χαρακτῆρι, καὶ ὥσπερ τὰ
ἐρριζωμένα μᾶλλον καὶ ἧττον ἐρρίζωται, ἓν δὲ ἔχει τὸ κοινὸν ἰδίωμα τὸ
ἀντέχεσθαι τῆς γῆς, οὕτω καὶ ἡ ἕξις ἐπὶ τῶν δυσκινήτων καὶ εὐκινήτων ἡ   25
αὐτὴ θεωρεῖται· ὅλως γὰρ τῷ γένει πολλὰ ποιὰ ὄντα ἐκλελυμένον ἐκεῖνο τὸ
ἰδίωμα ἔχει καθ᾽ ὃ εἰδοποιεῖται, ὡς ὁ αὐστηρὸς οἶνος καὶ ἀμύγδαλα πικρὰ
καὶ Μολοττικὸς κύων καὶ Μελιταῖος, οἷς πᾶσιν μέτεστι μὲν ὁ γενικὸς
χαρακτήρ, ἐπὶ βραχὺ δὲ καὶ ἀνειμένως, καὶ ὅσον ἐπ᾽ αὐτοῖς τοῖς ἐν τῇ ἕξει
λόγοις ἐπιμένει ἐπὶ μιᾶς καταστάσεως αὕτη, τὸ δὲ εὐκίνητον πολλάκις ἐξ   30
ἄλλης αἰτίας ἔχει.

12 καίτοι Arnim: ἤτοι codd.   ἢ del. Arnim

Context: commentary on Aristotle, *Cat.* 8, 8b26: ἐν μὲν οὖν εἶδος ποιότητος ἕξις καὶ
διάθεσις λεγέσθωσαν. διαφέρει δὲ ἕξις διαθέσεως τῷ μονιμώτερον καὶ πολυχρο-
νιώτερον εἶναι. Cf. 2–3.

10 ἀρετάς For the place of virtue in the Stoic genera (or so-called categories), cf.
29B, E.

12 Since some virtues are τέχναι (cf. **61D 1**), the transmitted text could be

286

justified accordingly. But Arnim's suspicions were well founded. Simplicius is probably referring to the μέσαι τέχναι which, he says (*SVF* 2, p. 130, 29ff.), the Stoics acknowledged to admit of varying intensification. Moreover, τέχναι are regularly referred to as ἕξεις (cf. **42A**), and those called ἐπιτηδεύματα (cf. **26H**), e.g. prophecy, are specifically classed as ἕξεις and not διαθέσεις (*SVF* 3.104–5).

16 σχέσις   Cf. **28 N 2–3**.

22–3   Cf. **28H**.

T Plutarch, *Prim. frig.* 948D–E, 949B (*SVF* 2.430, part)

(1) ἐπεὶ τὸ πῦρ θερμὸν ἅμα καὶ λαμπρόν ἐστι, δεῖ τὴν ἀντικειμένην τῷ πυρὶ φύσιν ψυχράν τ᾽ εἶναι καὶ σκοτεινήν· ἀντίκειται γὰρ ὡς τῷ λαμπρῷ τὸ ζοφερὸν οὕτω τῷ θερμῷ τὸ ψυχρόν· ἔστι γὰρ ὡς ὄψεως τὸ σκοτεινὸν οὕτω τὸ ψυχρὸν ἀφῆς συγχυτικόν, ἡ δὲ θερμότης διαχεῖ τὴν αἴσθησιν τοῦ ἁπτομένου καθάπερ ἡ λαμπρότης τοῦ ὁρῶντος. τὸ ἄρα πρώτως σκοτεινὸν   5
ἐν τῇ φύσει πρώτως καὶ ψυχρόν ἐστιν. ὅτι δ᾽ ἀὴρ τὸ πρώτως σκοτεινόν ἐστιν, οὐδὲ τοὺς ποιητὰς λέληθεν· ... (2) καὶ μὴν ἁπάντων γε τῶν γινομένων ὑπὸ ψυχρότητος ἐν τοῖς σώμασι σφοδρότατον καὶ βιαιότατον ἡ πῆξις οὖσα πάθος μέν ἐστιν ὕδατος ἔργον δ᾽ ἀέρος· αὐτὸ μὲν γὰρ καθ᾽ ἑαυτὸ τὸ ὕδωρ εὐδιάχυτον καὶ ἀπαγὲς καὶ ἀσύστατόν ἐστιν, ἐντείνεται δὲ   10
καὶ συνάγεται τῷ ἀέρι σφιγγόμενον ὑπὸ ψυχρότητος.

Context: Stoic doctrine of τὸ πρώτως ψυχρόν.

48 Mixture

A Diogenes Laertius 7.151 (*SVF* 2.479)

καὶ τὰς κράσεις δὲ δι᾽ ὅλου γίνεσθαι, καθά φησιν ὁ Χρύσιππος ἐν τῇ τρίτῃ τῶν Φυσικῶν, καὶ μὴ κατὰ περιγραφὴν καὶ παράθεσιν· καὶ γὰρ εἰς πέλαγος ὀλίγος οἶνος βληθεὶς ἐπὶ ποσὸν ἀντιπαρεκταθήσεται, εἶτα συμφθαρήσεται.

1 δι᾽ ὅλου A.A. Long: διόλου codd.: δι᾽ ὅλων Todd [332], 31 n. 45

Context: immediately following **50B**, discussion of the infinite divisibility of substance.

1 **δι᾽ ὅλου**   For this, rather than δι᾽ ὅλων, as the correct reading, cf. **C** 48, 51; **46A** 3–4; **49A** 2. The plural is used when the context is concerned with many bodies or substances, e.g. **C** 9, 41.

3 **ἐπὶ ποσόν**   This phrase, preceding εἶτα, should mean 'for a while', rather than 'to a certain extent', Todd [332], 31 n. 47. Cherniss [326], 810 n., suggests ἐπὶ τοσοῦτον, comparing **C** 45.

4 **συμφθαρήσεται**   This verb describes the effects not of κρᾶσις but of σύγχυσις; cf. **C** 3. The appropriate word would be συγκραθήσεται, and our translation in vol. 1 is modified accordingly.

Stoic physics

B Plutarch, *Comm. not.* 1078E (*SVF* 2.480)

καὶ ταῦτα προσδέχεται Χρύσιππος εὐθὺς ἐν τῷ πρώτῳ τῶν Φυσικῶν ζητημάτων οὐδὲν ἀπέχειν φάμενος οἴνου σταλαγμὸν ἕνα κεράσαι τὴν θάλατταν· καὶ ἵνα δὴ μὴ τοῦτο θαυμάζωμεν, εἰς ὅλον φησὶ τὸν κόσμον διατενεῖν τῇ κράσει τὸν σταλαγμόν.

Context: a few lines after **E**. ταῦτα refers to Chrysippus' acceptance of Plutarch's own illustration of the 'absurdity' of κρᾶσις δι' ὅλου: that a single measure or drop of liquid, once fallen into the Aegean or Cretan sea, would be blended through and through with the whole of the Mediterranean sea and the Atlantic ocean.

Chrysippus' admission that οἴνου σταλαγμὸν ἕνα κεράσαι τὴν θάλατταν has been regularly interpreted as a direct rejoinder to Aristotle, *GC* 1.10, 328a24–8: πολλὰ μὲν ὀλίγοις καὶ μεγάλα μικροῖς συντιθέμενα οὐ ποιεῖ μίξιν, ἀλλ' αὔξησιν τοῦ κρατοῦντος· μεταβάλλει γὰρ θάτερον εἰς τὸ κρατοῦν, οἷον σταλαγμὸς οἴνου μυρίοις χοεῦσιν ὕδατος οὐ μίγνυται· λύεται γὰρ τὸ εἶδος καὶ μεταβάλλει εἰς τὸ πᾶν ὕδωρ. Sandbach [304], 33–4, has recently argued that any influence from Aristotle 'can be confidently denied': Chrysippus' doctrine in **B**, Sandbach maintains, is shown by Plutarch's context to be his acceptance of Arcesilaus' polemical jest in **E**, substituting for the 'putrefied leg' the through-and-through blending with the sea of εἰς . . . τις κύαθος ἢ μία σταγών (*Comm. not.* 1078D), 'a substitution which may well have been made by Lacydes or some other Academic'. Further, he argues, Chrysippus did not need Aristotle's account in *GC* above as the stimulus to his own very different suggestion of the effects for mixture of two ingredients with radically different volumes. 'The most familiar form of κρᾶσις is that of wine and water, an everyday event in Greece.'

Neither of these points seems to us compelling. Sandbach is quite right to draw attention to the non-Aristotelian dialectical context of **E**. But that context does not show that Chrysippus' 'wine and sea' example reached him from Academic critics. Arcesilaus' joke about the putrefied leg could just as well be a more vivid way of illustrating the supposed absurdity of a doctrine already discussed in terms of the mixing of two liquids of different volumes. In any case, the principal reason for regarding 'through-and-through blending' as a rejoinder to Aristotle is not the identity of the 'wine and water' example but the fact (see vol. 1, 292) that Stoic theorizing about mixture has too many Aristotelian features to make its totally independent formulation seem plausible.

For a subtle defence of the Stoic theory against Plutarch's criticism in *Comm. not.* 1078A, cf. White [505].

C Alexander, *Mixt.* 216,14–218,6 (*SVF* 2.473)

(1) ἔστι δὲ ἡ Χρυσίππου δόξα περὶ κράσεως ἥδε· ἡνῶσθαι μὲν ὑποτίθεται τὴν σύμπασαν οὐσίαν, πνεύματός τινος διὰ πάσης αὐτῆς διήκοντος, ὑφ' οὗ συνέχεταί τε καὶ συμμένει καὶ σύμπαθές ἐστιν αὑτῷ τὸ πᾶν· (2) τῶν δὲ μιγνυμένων ἐν αὐτῇ σωμάτων τὰς μὲν παραθέσει μίξεις γίνεσθαι λέγει, δύο τινῶν ἢ καὶ πλειόνων οὐσιῶν εἰς ταὐτὸν συντεθειμένων καὶ παρατιθε-   5
μένων ἀλλήλαις, ὥς φησιν, καθ' ἁρμήν, σωζούσης ἑκάστης αὐτῶν ἐν τῇ

τοιαύτῃ παραθέσει κατὰ τὴν περιγραφὴν τὴν οἰκείαν οὐσίαν τε καὶ
ποιότητα, ὡς ἐπὶ κυάμων φέρε εἰπεῖν καὶ πυρῶν ἐν τῇ παρ' ἀλλήλους θέσει
γίνεσθαι· (3) τὰς δέ τινας συγχύσει δι' ὅλων τῶν τε οὐσιῶν αὐτῶν καὶ τῶν
ἐν αὐταῖς ποιοτήτων συμφθειρομένων ἀλλήλαις, ὡς γίνεσθαί φησιν ἐπὶ   10
τῶν ἰατρικῶν φαρμάκων κατὰ σύμφθαρσιν τῶν μιγνυμένων, ἄλλου τινὸς
ἐξ αὐτῶν γεννωμένου σώματος· (4) τὰς δέ τινας γίνεσθαι μίξεις λέγει δι'
ὅλων τινῶν οὐσιῶν τε καὶ τῶν τούτων ποιοτήτων ἀντιπαρεκτεινομένων
ἀλλήλαις μετὰ τοῦ τὰς ἐξ ἀρχῆς οὐσίας τε καὶ ποιότητας σώζειν ἐν τῇ
μίξει τῇ τοιᾷδε, ἥντινα τῶν μίξεων κρᾶσιν ἰδίως εἶναι λέγει. τὴν γάρ δύο ἢ καὶ   15
πλειόνων τινῶν σωμάτων ὅλων δι' ὅλων ἀντιπαρέκτασιν ἀλλήλοις οὕτως, ὡς σώζειν
ἕκαστον αὐτῶν ἐν τῇ μίξει τῇ τοιαύτῃ τήν τε οἰκείαν οὐσίαν καὶ τὰς ἐν αὐτῇ ποιότητας,
λέγει κρᾶσιν εἶναι μόνην τῶν μίξεων. εἶναι γὰρ ἴδιον τῶν κεκραμένων τὸ
δύνασθαι χωρίζεσθαι πάλιν ἀπ' ἀλλήλων, ὃ μόνως γίνεται τῷ σώζειν ἐν τῇ
μίξει τὰ κεκραμένα τὰς αὐτῶν φύσεις. (5) τὸ δὲ ταύτας τὰς διαφορὰς εἶναι   20
τῆς μίξεως πειρᾶται πιστοῦσθαι διὰ τῶν κοινῶν ἐννοιῶν, μάλιστα δὲ
κριτήρια τῆς ἀληθείας φησὶν ἡμᾶς παρὰ τῆς φύσεως λαβεῖν ταύτας· (6)
ἄλλην γοῦν φαντασίαν ἔχειν ἡμᾶς τῶν καθ' ἁρμὴν συγκειμένων, καὶ ἄλλην
τῶν συγκεχυμένων τε καὶ συνεφθαρμένων, καὶ ἄλλην τῶν κεκραμένων τε
καὶ ἀλλήλοις δι' ὅλων ἀντιπαρεκτεινομένων οὕτως ὡς σώζειν ἕκαστον   25
αὐτῶν τὴν οἰκείαν φύσιν. ἣν διαφορὰν φαντασιῶν οὐκ ἂν εἴχομεν, εἰ πάντα
τὰ ὁπωσοῦν μιγνύμενα παρέκειτο ἀλλήλοις καθ' ἁρμήν. (7) τὴν δὲ
τοιαύτην ἀντιπαρέκτασιν τῶν κιρναμένων ὑπολαμβάνει γίνεσθαι
χωρούντων δι' ἀλλήλων τῶν κιρναμένων σωμάτων, ὡς μηδὲν μόριον ἐν
αὐτοῖς εἶναι μὴ μετέχον πάντων τῶν ἐν τῷ τοιούτῳ κεκραμένῳ μίγματι.   30
οὐκέτι γὰρ ἄν, εἰ μὴ τοῦτο εἴη, κρᾶσιν, ἀλλὰ παράθεσιν τὸ γινόμενον εἶναι.
(8) τοῦ δὲ τοῦτο οἴεσθαι γίνεσθαι πίστεις φέρουσιν οἱ προιστάμενοι τῆσδε
τῆς δόξης τό τε πολλὰ τῶν σωμάτων σώζειν τὰς ἑαυτῶν ποιότητας ἐπί τ'
ἐλαττόνων ἐναργῶν ὄγκων καὶ ἐπὶ μειζόνων ὄντα (ὡς ὁρᾶν ἔστιν ἐπὶ τοῦ
λιβανωτοῦ, ὃς ἐν τῷ θυμιᾶσθαι λεπτυνόμενος ἐπὶ πλεῖστον τὴν αὐτοῦ   35
φυλάσσει ποιότητα), ἔτι τε τὸ πολλὰ εἶναι, ἃ καθ' ἑαυτὰ μὴ οἷά τε ὄντα ἐπί
τι ἐλθεῖν μέγεθος ὑπ' ἄλλων βοηθούμενα ἐπ' αὐτὸ πρόεισι. τὸν γοῦν χρυσὸν
ὑπό τινων μιγνυμένων φαρμάκων ἐπὶ πλεῖστον χεῖσθαί τε καὶ λεπτύνεσ-
θαι, ἐφ' ὅσον καθ' αὑτὸν ἐλαυνόμενος οὐκ ἐδύνατο ... (9) ὧν οὕτως
ἐχόντων οὐδέν φασι θαυμαστὸν τὸ καὶ σώματά τινα βοηθούμενα ὑπ'   40
ἀλλήλων οὕτως ἀλλήλοις ἐνοῦσθαι δι' ὅλων, ὡς αὐτὰ σωζόμενα μετὰ τῶν
οἰκείων ποιοτήτων ἀντιπαρεκτείνεσθαι ἀλλήλοις δι' ὅλων ὅλα, κἂν ᾖ τινα
ἐλάττω τὸν ὄγκον καὶ μὴ δυνάμενα καθ' αὑτὰ ἐπὶ τοσοῦτον χεῖσθαί τε καὶ
σώζειν τὰς οἰκείας ποιότητας. οὕτω γὰρ καὶ τὸν κύαθον τοῦ οἴνου
κιρνᾶσθαι τῷ ὕδατι τῷ πολλῷ βοηθούμενον ὑπ' αὐτοῦ εἰς τὴν ἐπὶ τοσοῦτον   45
ἔκτασιν. (10) τοῦ δὲ τοῦθ' οὕτως ἔχειν ὡς ἐναργέσι χρῶνται μαρτυρίοις τῷ
τε τὴν ψυχὴν ἰδίαν ὑπόστασιν ἔχουσαν, ὥσπερ καὶ τὸ δεχόμενον αὐτὴν
σῶμα, δι' ὅλου τοῦ σώματος διήκειν ἐν τῇ μίξει τῇ πρὸς αὐτὸ σώζουσαν
τὴν οἰκείαν οὐσίαν (οὐδὲν γὰρ ψυχῆς ἄμοιρον τοῦ τὴν ψυχὴν ἔχοντος

Stoic physics

σώματος), ὁμοίως δὲ ἔχειν καὶ τὴν τῶν φυτῶν φύσιν, ἀλλὰ καὶ τὴν ἕξιν ἐν   50
τοῖς συνεχομένοις ὑπὸ τῆς ἕξεως. (11) ἀλλὰ καὶ τὸ πῦρ ὅλον δι᾽ ὅλου χωρεῖν
τοῦ σιδήρου λέγουσι, σώζοντος αὐτῶν ἑκατέρου τὴν οἰκείαν οὐσίαν. (12)
καὶ τῶν στοιχείων δέ φασι τῶν τεσσάρων τὰ δύο, τό τε πῦρ καὶ τὸν ἀέρα,
λεπτομερῆ τε καὶ κοῦφα καὶ εὔτονα ὄντα, διὰ τῶν δύο, γῆς τε καὶ ὕδατος,
παχυμερῶν καὶ βαρέων καὶ ἀτόνων ὄντων διαπεφοιτηκέναι ὅλα δι᾽ ὅλων,   55
σώζοντα τὴν οἰκείαν φύσιν καὶ συνέχειαν αὐτά τε καὶ ἐκεῖνα.

4 παραθέσει μίξεις Ideler: παραθέσεις μίξει codd.   6 ἁρμήν Bruns: ὁρμὴν codd.   8–9 θέσει
γίνεσθαι codd.: θέσει γίνεται Bruns: θέσει· γίνεσθαι Apelt, Todd   συγχύσει Ideler: συγχύσεις
ABCSRa: συγχύσεως P   22 λαβεῖν ταύτας Bruns: λαβόντας codd.   23, 27 ἁρμὴν Bruns: ὁρμὴν
codd.   27 ἀλλήλοις Apelt: ἀλλήλους codd.   51 τῆς Ra: om. cett.

Context: account of those who say ἡνῶσθαι τὴν ὕλην.
For the relation of this evidence to other sources, cf. Todd [332], 30–65. For reasons
given in vol. 1, 293, it may be doubted whether he is right to claim, 51, 56ff., that
'mutual co-extension' (ἀντιπαρεκτείνεσθαι ἀλλήλοις, C 25, etc.) is an inaccurate
description of the Stoic thesis of κρᾶσις δι᾽ ὅλου.
21 κοινῶν ἐννοιῶν   Cf. 40R and vol. 1, 252.
39   We omit a passage giving further examples.
46–50 Cf. vol. 1, 320–1.
53–6   Cf. 47F–I.

D   Stobaeus 1.155,5–11 (SVF 2.471, part)

ὅτι δ᾽ ἐπὶ τοιούτων κράσεων διαμένουσιν αἱ ποιότητες τῶν συγκραθέντων,
πρόδηλον ἐκ τοῦ πολλάκις ἐξ ἐπιμηχανήσεως ἀποχωρίζεσθαι ταῦτα ἀπ᾽
ἀλλήλων. ἐὰν γοῦν σπόγγον ἠλαιωμένον καθῇ τις εἰς οἶνον ὕδατι
κεκραμένον, ἀποχωρίσει τὸ ὕδωρ τοῦ οἴνου ἀναδραμόντος τοῦ ὕδατος εἰς
τὸν σπόγγον.   5

3 ἠλαιωμένον Meineke: ἐλαιούμενον codd.

Context: doxography of mixture. The full passage in Stobaeus corresponds closely to
the gist of C, but it reserves the term κρᾶσις for the ἀντιπαρέκτασις of moist bodies,
using μίξις as a term to include such cases as fire pervading iron, 1.154,14–155,5. By
using μίξις as a generic term, Alexander in C may have simplified his source, but
nothing of interest seems to lie behind the Stobaeus terminology; and the activity of
πνεῦμα, a dry body, is regularly presented as an instance of κρᾶσις.

E   Plutarch, Comm. not. 1078B–D (including SVF 2.465, part)

(1) ἀλλ᾽ ἀνάγκη γιγνομένης ὥσπερ ἀξιοῦσι τῆς ἀνακράσεως ἐν ἀλλήλοις τὰ
μιγνύμενα γίγνεσθαι καὶ ταὐτὸν ὁμοῦ τῷ ἐνυπάρχειν περιέχεσθαι καὶ τῷ
δέχεσθαι περιέχειν θάτερον· καὶ μηδέτερον αὐτῶν αὖ πάλιν δυνατὸν εἶναι
συμβαίνει, ἀμφότερα τῆς κράσεως δι᾽ ἀλλήλων διιέναι καὶ μηδὲν
ἐπιλείπεσθαι μηδενὸς μόριον ἀλλὰ ⟨πᾶν⟩ παντὸς ἀναπίμπλασθαι βιαζο-   5
μένης. (2) ἐνταῦθα δήπου καὶ τὸ θρυλούμενον ἐν ταῖς διατριβαῖς

'Αρκεσιλάου σκέλος ἥκει ταῖς ἀπορίαις ἐπεμβαῖνον αὐτῶν μετὰ γέλωτος.
εἰ γάρ εἰσιν αἱ κράσεις δι' ὅλων, τί κωλύει, τοῦ σκέλους ἀποκοπέντος καὶ
κατασαπέντος καὶ ῥιφέντος εἰς τὴν θάλατταν καὶ διαχυθέντος, οὐ τὸν
'Αντιγόνου μόνον στόλον διεκπλεῖν, ὡς ἔλεγεν 'Αρκεσίλαος, ἀλλὰ τὰς   10
Ξέρξου χιλίας καὶ διακοσίας καὶ τὰς 'Ελληνικὰς ὁμοῦ τριακοσίας τριήρεις
ἐν τῷ σκέλει ναυμαχούσας;

1 ἀνάγκη Wyttenbach: ἀνάγκης codd.   2 γίγνεσθαι vel μίγνυσθαι codd.   3 μηδέτερον Arnim: μὴ
δ' ἕτερον codd.   4 συμβαίνειν δ' ἀμφότερα Wyttenbach: συμβαίνει δ' ἀμφότερα Arnim: συμβαίνειν,
ἀμφότερα Pohlenz   5 ⟨πᾶν⟩ Madvig   6 δήπου Bernardakis: δεῖ τοῦ vel δὴ codd.

Context: attack on the Stoics for making 'one body the place for another body, and
body pass through body', 1077E; cf. F. Plutarch goes on to supply the transition to
Chrysippus' rejoinder (see notes on B) by arguing that a single ladleful of the putrefied
leg should, in consistency with Chrysippus' doctrine, extend throughout the whole
Mediterranean.
10 Antigonus Gonatas is meant, ruler of Macedon and effectively of Greece
during Arcesilaus' headship of the Academy.

F Themistius, In Ar. Phys. 104,9–19 (including SVF 2.468)

(1) ἀλλ' ὅρα μὴ περαιτέρω τοῦ δέοντος τὸν τόπον ἀποσεμνύνωμεν· σκέψαι
γὰρ καὶ τοὺς ἐναντίους λόγους οἳ πρὸς τῷ μηδὲν αὐτῷ προστιθέναι καὶ
καθάπαξ αὐτὸν ἀναιροῦσιν. εἰ γὰρ ἐπιχειρήσεις ... τί ἐστιν ὁ τόπος
ἀποδιδόναι, εἰς τὸ μὴ εἶναι αὐτὸν ὁμολογεῖν περιαχθήσῃ· πρῶτον γὰρ εἰς
τί γένος ἀνάξεις τὸν τόπον; ἢ δῆλον ὅτι εἰς σῶμα; καὶ γὰρ ὁ τόπος ἐπὶ τρία   5
διέστηκεν. (2) ἀλλ' οὕτω τὸ πάντων ἀτοπώτατον ἀπαντήσεται· σῶμα γὰρ
διὰ σώματος χωρήσει δι' ὅλου καὶ δύο σώματα τὸν αὐτὸν ἐφέξει τόπον· εἰ
γὰρ καὶ ὁ τόπος σῶμα καὶ τὸ γενόμενον ἐν αὐτῷ σῶμα καὶ ἴσα τοῖς
διαστήμασιν ἄμφω, τὸ σῶμα ἔσται ἐν ἴσῳ ἑτέρῳ σώματι. τοῦτο δὲ
Χρυσίππῳ μὲν καὶ τοῖς ἀπὸ Ζήνωνος δόγμασίν ἐστιν, οἱ παλαιοὶ δὲ   10
ἀπάγουσιν ὡς εἰς ἀδύνατον ἐναργῶς.

Context: commentary on Aristotle's definition of τόπος, Phys. IV. I.
Themistius refutes the suggestion that place can be defined as a body by showing
that this leads to there being two bodies in the same place. It is only this last point that
he ascribes to the Stoics. For the same argument, cf. Philoponus, In Ar. Phys. 505,10–
15; for discussion of the Peripatetic criticism of the Stoics, see Todd [332], 73–88.

49 Place and void

A Stobaeus 1.161,8–26 (SVF 2.503)

(1) Χρυσίππου. τόπον δ' εἶναι ὁ Χρύσιππος ἀπεφαίνετο τὸ κατεχόμενον δι'
ὅλου ὑπὸ ὄντος, ἢ τὸ οἷον ⟨τε⟩ κατέχεσθαι ὑπὸ ὄντος καὶ δι' ὅλου
κατεχόμενον εἴτε ὑπό τινος ⟨εἴτε⟩ ὑπό τινων. ἐὰν δὲ τοῦ οἷου τε κατέχεσθαι ὑπὸ

Stoic physics

ὄντος τὶ μὲν κατέχηται, τὶ δὲ μή, τὸ ὅλον ⟨οὔτε⟩ κενὸν ἔσεσθαι οὔτε τόπον, ἔτερον δέ τι οὐκ
ὠνομασμένον· τὸ μὲν γὰρ κενὸν τοῖς κενοῖς ἀγγείοις λέγεσθαι παραπλησίως, τὸν δὲ τόπον   5
τοῖς πλήρεσι· χώραν δὲ πότερον τὸ μεῖζον οἷόν τε κατέχεσθαι ὑπὸ ὄντος καὶ οἷον μεῖζον
ἀγγεῖον σώματος, ἢ τὸ χωροῦν μεῖζον σῶμα; (2) τὸ μὲν οὖν κενὸν ἄπειρον εἶναι
λέγεσθαι· τὸ γὰρ ἐκτὸς τοῦ κόσμου τοιοῦτ᾽ εἶναι· τὸν δὲ τόπον
πεπερασμένον διὰ τὸ μηδὲν σῶμα ἄπειρον εἶναι. καθάπερ δὲ τὸ σωματικὸν
πεπερασμένον εἶναι, οὕτως τὸ ἀσώματον ἄπειρον, ὅ τε γὰρ χρόνος ἄπειρος   10
καὶ τὸ κενόν. ὥσπερ γὰρ τὸ μηδὲν οὐδέν ἐστι πέρας, οὕτως οὐδὲ τοῦ
μηδενός, οἷόν ἐστι τὸ κενόν. κατὰ γὰρ τὴν αὐτοῦ ὑπόστασιν ἄπειρόν ἐστι·
περατοῦται δ᾽ αὖ τοῦτο ἐκπληρούμενον· τοῦ δὲ πληροῦντος ἀρθέντος οὐκ
ἔστιν αὐτοῦ νοῆσαι πέρας.

2 ⟨τε⟩ Diels   3 ⟨εἴτε⟩ Heeren   4 ⟨οὔτε⟩ Canter   ἔσεσθαι ... τόπον Usener: ἔσται ... τόπος codd.   δέ τι Canter: δέ τε codd.   5 ἀγγείοις Canter: αἰτίοις codd.   7 ἀγγεῖον Canter:
αἴτιον codd.   11 οὐδὲ Usener: δὲ FP: καὶ Vat. et Aug.   12 αὐτοῦ Diels: αὐτοῦ codd.

Context: doxography of place and void.

1–3   Chrysippus' first account of τόπος seems to differ only verbally from the one
Sextus attributes to the Stoics in **B** 3–4 where ἐξισαζούμενον τῷ κατέχοντι αὐτόν
should be interpreted as specifying the 'through-and-through' occupancy expressed
here by δι᾽ ὅλου. Chrysippus' second account, in starting from τὸ οἷόν τε κατέχεσθαι,
which is also an attribute of void (cf. **B** 1–2), makes it clear that void is *potentially*
place. The unoriginality of these Stoic formulations can be inferred from comparison
with Aristotle, *Cael.* 1.9, 279a14–15: ἐν ἅπαντι γὰρ τόπῳ δυνατὸν ὑπάρξαι σῶμα·
κενὸν δ᾽ εἶναί φασιν ἐν ᾧ μὴ ἐνυπάρχει σῶμα, δυνατὸν δ᾽ ἐστὶ γενέσθαι.
3–5   This conception of χώρα (cf. **B** 5–7) seems to be original. For Epicurus'
different usage and etymology of χώρα, cf. **5**.
5–7 ἀγγεῖον   Cf. Aristotle, *Phys.* IV.2, 209b28–30, etc.
9–12   Void is compared to 'nothing' in its lack of limit, but Hahm [488], 103, is
incorrect to say that 'the Stoics and Aristotle agreed that there is nothing outside the
cosmos'. For the Stoics, the void is 'something' (τι); cf. **27D**; **43B**.

B Sextus Empiricus, *M.* 10.3–4 (*SVF* 2.505, part)

(1) καὶ οἱ Στωικοὶ δὲ κενὸν μὲν εἶναί φασι τὸ οἷόν τε ὑπὸ ὄντος κατέχεσθαι
μὴ κατεχόμενον δέ, ἢ διάστημα ἔρημον σώματος, ἢ διάστημα ἀκαθεκτού-
μενον ὑπὸ σώματος. (2) τόπον δὲ τὸν ὑπὸ ὄντος κατεχόμενον καὶ
ἐξισαζόμενον τῷ κατέχοντι αὐτόν, νῦν ὂν καλοῦντες τὸ σῶμα, καθὼς καὶ
ἐκ τῆς μεταλήψεως τῶν ὀνομάτων ἐστὶ συμφανές. (3) χώραν δέ φασιν εἶναι   5
διάστημα κατὰ μέν τι κατεχόμενον ὑπὸ σώματος, κατὰ δέ τι ἀκαθεκτού-
μενον. ἔνιοι δὲ χώραν ἔλεξαν ὑπάρχειν τὸν τοῦ μείζονος σώματος τόπον.

3–4 τὸν ... αὐτόν codd.: fort. τὸ ... αὐτό A.A. Long

Context: doxography of place, room and void.

5–7   Cf. **A** 3–7.

292

C Cleomedes 8,10–14 (*SVF* 2.541)

ἀναγκαῖον τοίνυν εἶναί τινα ὑπόστασιν κενοῦ. ἔστι δὲ ἁπλουστάτη αὐτοῦ ἡ
ἐπίνοια, ἀσωμάτου τε καὶ ἀναφοῦς ὄντος, καὶ οὔτε σχῆμα ἔχοντος οὔτε
σχηματιζομένου, καὶ οὔτε τι πάσχοντος οὔτε ποιοῦντος, ἁπλῶς δὲ σῶμα
δέχεσθαι οἵου τε ὄντος.

2–3 καὶ ante οὔτε om. ML

Context: conclusion of an argument to show the absurdity of claiming that nothing
exists outside the κόσμος.

D Galen, *Diff. puls.* 8.674,13–14 (*SVF* 2.424, part)

οὐ γὰρ εἶναι τοιαύτην οὐδεμίαν [*sc.* κενὴν χώραν] ἐν κόσμῳ νομίζουσιν,
ἀλλ᾽ ἡνῶσθαι τὴν ὅλην οὐσίαν ἑαυτῇ.

Context: Galen is considering in what sense if any the pulse might be called κενός. The
Pneumatic doctors' views, as reported here, seem good evidence for Stoicism,
reasoning from the world's internal unity to the absence of void therein; cf. **48C 1**.

E Galen, *Qual. inc.* 19.464,10–14 (*SVF* 2.502)

ὅτι δὲ κοινόν ἐστι τοῦτο [δῆλον] (λέγω δὲ τὸ τριχῇ διαστατόν) σώματός τε
καὶ κενοῦ καὶ τόπου, Στωικοὺς μὲν ὁμολογεῖν ἀναγκαῖον, ἅτε κενὸ⸍
ἀπολιπόντας ἐν τῇ τῶν ὄντων πραγμάτων φύσει, κἂν ἐν τῷ κόσμῳ τοῦθ᾽
ὑπάρχειν μὴ λέγωσι.

1 δῆλον del. Kalbfleisch

Context: Galen has just observed that resistance (ἀντίτυπον) must be added to three-
dimensionality if σῶμα is to be distinguished from place and void; cf. **45F** from the
same work.

3 Note Galen's non-Stoic use of ὄντων, in contrast with the use of ὄν in **A** and **B**.
For the Stoics, place and void are τινά but not ὄντα; cf. **27**.

F Simplicius, *In Ar. De caelo* 284,28–285,2 (*SVF* 2.535)

(1) οἱ δὲ ἀπὸ τῆς Στοᾶς ἔξω τοῦ οὐρανοῦ κενὸν εἶναι βουλόμενοι διὰ
τοιαύτης αὐτὸ κατασκευάζουσιν ὑποθέσεως. (2) ἔστω, φασίν, ἐν τῷ
ἐσχάτῳ τῆς ἀπλανοῦς ἐστῶτά τινα ἐκτείνειν πρὸς τὸ ἄνω τὴν χεῖρα· (3) καὶ
εἰ μὲν ἐκτείνει, λαμβάνουσιν, ὅτι ἔστι τι ἐκτὸς τοῦ οὐρανοῦ, εἰς ὃ ἐξέτεινεν,
εἰ δὲ μὴ δύναιτο ἐκτεῖναι, ἔσται τι καὶ οὕτως ἐκτὸς τὸ κωλῦσαν τὴν τῆς   5
χειρὸς ἔκτασιν. (4) κἂν πρὸς τῷ πέρατι πάλιν ἐκείνου στὰς ἐκτείνῃ, ὁμοία
ἡ ἐρώτησις· (5) εἶναι γὰρ δειχθήσεται κἀκείνου τι ἐκτὸς ὄν.

Context: Simplicius' commentary on Aristotle, *Cael.* 1.9, 279a11, which denies that
place, void or time exist outside the world.
     The thought experiment is also reported, without attribution to the Stoics, by

Stoic physics

Alexander (*SVF* 2.536), on whom Simplicius certainly drew for his refutations at 285, 2–9 and 285,27–286,2. Lucretius records a similar argument to prove the world's infinity, **10B 3**. The source for Stoics and Epicureans is likely to have been either Eudemus, who credits the experiment to the Pythagorean Archytas (47 A 24 DK) as a proof of the existence of infinite body and place, or Archytas himself. Alexander, as reported by Simplicius at 285,27ff., argues, on Aristotelian lines, that the Stoics are not entitled to posit an infinite void: their definition of [infinite] void as 'capable of receiving body' (cf. **B 1**), would require the existence of an infinite body, an impossibility which they themselves admit. But the Stoics are not disturbed by this objection. Given their theory of modality (see **38E 3**), and their not being bound by the Aristotelian notion that every potentiality presupposes a corresponding actuality, they can perfectly well reply that the non-existence of an infinite body has no bearing on the limits of the void's capacity.

G Cleomedes 6,11–17 (*SVF* 2.537)

εἰ δὲ καὶ εἰς πῦρ ἀναλύεται ἡ πᾶσα οὐσία, ὡς τοῖς χαριεστάτοις τῶν φυσικῶν δοκεῖ, ἀνάγκη πλέον ἢ μυριοπλασίονα τόπον αὐτὴν καταλαμβάνειν, ὥσπερ καὶ τὰ εἰς ἀτμὸν ἐκθυμιώμενα τῶν στερεῶν σωμάτων. ὁ τοίνυν ἐν τῇ ἐκπυρώσει ὑπὸ τῆς οὐσίας ἐκχεομένης καταλαμβανόμενος τόπος νῦν κενός ἐστιν, οὐδενός γε σώματος αὐτὸν πεπληρωκότος.   5

4 ἐκχεομένης vel χεομένης codd.

Context: part of a series of arguments to prove the existence of void.
For the terminology describing the ἐκπύρωσις, cf. **46K**; **47A**.

H Cleomedes 10,24–12,5 (*SVF* 2.540)

(1) λέγεται κἀκεῖνο ὑπ᾽ αὐτῶν, ὡς εἰ ἦν ἔξω τοῦ κόσμου κενόν, χεομένη δι᾽ αὐτοῦ ἡ οὐσία ἐπ᾽ ἄπειρον διεσκεδάσθη ἂν καὶ διεσκορπίσθη. (2) ἀλλὰ φήσομεν, ὡς μηδὲ τοῦτο δύναται παθεῖν· ἕξιν γὰρ ἔχει τὴν συνέχουσαν αὐτὴν καὶ συντηροῦσαν. (3) καὶ τὸ μὲν περιέχον αὐτὴν κενὸν οὐδὲν ποιεῖ· αὐτὴ δ᾽ ὑπερβαλλούσῃ δυνάμει χρωμένη συντηρεῖ ἑαυτήν, συστελλομένη   5 τε καὶ πάλιν χεομένη ἐν αὐτῷ κατὰ τὰς φυσικὰς αὐτῆς μεταβολάς, ἄλλοτε μὲν εἰς πῦρ χεομένη, ἄλλοτε δὲ καὶ ἐπὶ κοσμογονίαν ὁρμῶσα.

5 αὐτὴ Ziegler: αὕτη codd.   7 ἐπὶ vel ἐπὶ τὴν codd.

Context: continuing an attack on the Peripatetic denial of void.
3 ἕξιν Cf. **47F–G, I, L–M, O**.

I Plutarch, *St. rep.* 1054E (*SVF* 2.550, part)

οὐ γὰρ ὑπάρχειν ἐν τῷ κενῷ διαφορὰν ᾗ τὰ σώματα δευρὶ μᾶλλον ἢ δευρὶ προσάγεται, τὴν δὲ τοῦ κόσμου σύνταξιν αἰτίαν εἶναι τῆς κινήσεως ἐπὶ τὸ κέντρον καὶ τὸ μέσον αὐτοῦ νευόντων καὶ φερομένων πανταχόθεν.

3 φερομένων ⟨πάντων τῶν μερῶν⟩ Pohlenz, Cherniss

49 Place and void

Context: Plutarch cites Chrysippus' views on the void with the object of showing that they contradict Chrysippus' supposed belief that bodies naturally move to the centre οὐ τῆς οὐσίας ἀλλὰ τῆς περιεχούσης τὴν οὐσίαν χώρας. I.e. Chrysippus is alleged to have both posited and denied that an infinite void can have a centre. For detailed discussion, cf. Hahm [488], 122–6, and the references given by Cherniss [326] ad loc.

Even if Chrysippus equivocated over the possibility of an infinite void's having a centre, his primary interest was to defend the Zenonian view (cf. J) that the world's stability is due to the natural tendency of all bodies to move towards its (the world's) centre, Cf. Furley [168], 20–1, and see **29D** – the sequel to this passage.

J Stobaeus 1.166,4–22 (*SVF* 1.99)

(1) Ζήνωνος. τῶν δ' ἐν τῷ κόσμῳ πάντων τῶν κατ' ἰδίαν ἕξιν συνεστώτων τὰ μέρη τὴν φορὰν ἔχειν εἰς τὸ τοῦ ὅλου μέσον, ὁμοίως δὲ καὶ αὐτοῦ τοῦ κόσμου· (2) διόπερ ὀρθῶς λέγεσθαι πάντα τὰ μέρη τοῦ κόσμου ἐπὶ τὸ μέσον τοῦ κόσμου τὴν φορὰν ἔχειν, μάλιστα δὲ τὰ βάρος ἔχοντα· (3) ταὐτὸν δ' αἴτιον εἶναι καὶ τῆς τοῦ κόσμου μονῆς ἐν ἀπείρῳ κενῷ, καὶ τῆς γῆς   5 παραπλησίως ἐν τῷ κόσμῳ περὶ τὸ τούτου κέντρον καθιδρυμένης ἰσοκρατῶς. (4) οὐ πάντως δὲ σῶμα βάρος ἔχειν, ἀλλ' ἀβαρῆ εἶναι ἀέρα καὶ πῦρ· τείνεσθαι δὲ καὶ ταῦτά πως ἐπὶ τὸ τῆς ὅλης σφαίρας τοῦ κόσμου μέσον, τὴν δὲ σύστασιν πρὸς τὴν περιφέρειαν αὐτοῦ ποιεῖσθαι· φύσει γὰρ ἀνώφοιτα ταῦτ' εἶναι διὰ τὸ μηδενὸς μετέχειν βάρους. (5) παραπλησίως δὲ   10 τούτοις οὐδ' αὐτόν φασι τὸν κόσμον βάρος ἔχειν διὰ τὸ τὴν ὅλην αὐτοῦ σύστασιν ἔκ τε τῶν βάρος ἐχόντων στοιχείων εἶναι καὶ ἐκ τῶν ἀβαρῶν. (6) τὴν δ' ὅλην γῆν καθ' ἑαυτὴν μὲν ἔχειν ἀρέσκει βάρος· παρὰ δὲ τὴν θέσιν διὰ τὸ τὴν μέσην ἔχειν χώραν (πρὸς δὲ τὸ μέσον εἶναι τὴν φορὰν τοῖς τοιούτοις σώμασιν) ἐπὶ τοῦ τόπου τούτου μένειν.   15

5 τῆς γῆς Heeren: τῇ γῇ codd.   8 τείνεσθαι Diels: γίνεσθαι codd.: κινεῖσθαι Meineke   10 ἀνώφοιτα Canter: ἀνώφυτα vel ἀνώτατα codd.

Context: doxography of motion. For a very full discussion, cf. Hahm [488], 107–22, 249–59.

1–3   The argument of the whole passage starts from a thesis concerning what are elsewhere called 'unified things', **28M 2**, i.e. natural substances such as minerals, plants and animals. The parts, of which these are here said to consist, are the four elements. The gravity that is an attribute of each such unified thing, in virtue of its constituent elements, is also an attribute of the world at large.

7–8   Furley [168], 20, takes the weightlessness of air and fire to be something distinct from 'positive lightness', treating the absence of the latter as the reason why these elements do not fly off into the infinite void. He is criticized on this point by Hahm [488], 132 n. 52, who cogently observes that the weightlessness of these elements needs to be regarded as an absolute, centrifugal property in order to explain their location at the world's periphery and the fact that they counterbalance the heavy elements in such a way that the world as a whole, 10–12, does not have weight. The centripetal tendency of air and fire, 8–9, should be regarded not as an intrinsic property countervailing their weightlessness, but as a necessary consequence of their indissoluble blending with earth and water.

295

50 Continuum

A Stobaeus 1.142,2–6 (*SVF* 2.482, part)

Χρύσιππος ἔφασκε τὰ σώματα εἰς ἄπειρον τέμνεσθαι καὶ τὰ τοῖς σώμασι προσεοικότα, οἷον ἐπιφάνειαν, γραμμήν, τόπον, κενόν, χρόνον· εἰς ἄπειρόν τε τούτων τεμνομένων οὔτε σῶμα ἐξ ἀπείρων σωμάτων συνέστηκεν οὔτ᾽ ἐπιφάνεια οὔτε γραμμὴ οὔτε τόπος.

4 τόπος ⟨οὔτε κενὸν οὔτε χρόνος⟩ Heeren

B Diogenes Laertius 7.150–1 (*SVF* 2.482, part)

σῶμα δέ ἐστι κατ᾽ αὐτοὺς ἡ οὐσία, καὶ πεπερασμένη καθά φησιν Ἀντίπατρος ἐν δευτέρῳ Περὶ οὐσίας καὶ Ἀπολλόδωρος ἐν τῇ Φυσικῇ. καὶ παθητὴ δέ ἐστιν, ὡς ὁ αὐτός φησιν. εἰ γὰρ ἦν ἄτρεπτος, οὐκ ἂν τὰ γινόμενα ἐξ αὐτῆς ἐγίνετο. ἔνθεν κἀκεῖνος· (1) ἥ τε τομὴ εἰς ἄπειρόν ἐστιν· (2) ἣν ἄπειρόν φησιν ὁ Χρύσιππος (οὐ γάρ ἐστί τι ἄπειρον, εἰς ὃ γίνεται ἡ τομή, ἀλλ᾽ ἀκατάληκτός ἐστι). (3) καὶ τὰς κράσεις δὲ δι᾽   5
ὅλου γίνεσθαι.

3 κἀκεῖνος BP: κἀκείνως F: κἀκ⟨ολουθ⟩εῖν ὡς Arnim   4 ἣν ἄπειρον, ⟨οὐκ εἰς ἄπειρον⟩ Arnim

Context: the Stoic view of substance (cf. **28**, **44–5**). The text continues as **48A**.

Despite the suspect text immediately preceding the translated portion, the general connexion of thought appears to be that the creative versatility of substance depends on its total fusion with the active principle, and hence implies its infinite divisibility.

2 ὁ αὐτός Apollodorus.

3 ἔνθεν κἀκεῖνος This, if sound, would introduce in the next six words a direct quotation from Antipater. But we are not confident enough of the reading to supply quotation marks.

C Plutarch, *Comm. not.* 1078E–1081A

ΔΙΑΔΟΥΜΕΝΟΣ ... (1) καὶ μὴν παρὰ τὴν ἔννοιαν μήτ᾽ ἄκρον ἐν τῇ φύσει τῶν σωμάτων μήτε πρῶτον μήτ᾽ ἔσχατον ⟨εἶναι⟩ μηδὲν εἰς ὃ λήγει τὸ μέγεθος τοῦ σώματος ἀλλ᾽ ἀεί ⟨τι⟩ τοῦ ληφθέντος ἐπέκεινα φαινόμενον εἰς ἄπειρον καὶ ἀόριστον ἐμβάλλειν τὸ ὑποκείμενον. οὔτε γὰρ μεῖζον οὔτ᾽ ἔλαττον ἔσται νοεῖν ἕτερον ἑτέρου μέγεθος, εἰ τὸ προιέναι τοῖς μέρεσιν ἐπ᾽   5
ἄπειρον ἀμφοτέροις ὡσ⟨αύτως⟩ συμβέβηκεν, ἀλλ᾽ ἀνισότητος αἴρεται φύσις· ἀνίσων γὰρ νοουμένων, τὸ μὲν προαπολείπεται τοῖς ἐσχάτοις μέρεσι τὸ δὲ παραλλάττει καὶ περίεστι. μὴ οὔσης δ᾽ ἀνισότητος, ἕπεται μὴ ἀνωμαλίαν εἶναι μηδὲ τραχύτητα σώματος· ἀνωμαλία μὲν γάρ ἐστι μιᾶς ἐπιφανείας ἀνισότης πρὸς ἑαυτήν, τραχύτης δ᾽ ἀνωμαλία μετὰ σκληρότητος, ὧν οὐδὲν ἀπολείπουσιν οἱ σῶμα μηδὲν εἰς ἔσχατον μέρος περαίνοντες ἀλλὰ   10
πάντα πλήθει μερῶν ἐπ᾽ ἄπειρον ἐξάγοντες. (2) καίτοι πῶς οὐκ ἐναργές ἐστι τὸν ἄνθρωπον ἐκ πλειόνων συνεστηκέναι μορίων ἢ τὸν δάκτυλον τοῦ ἀνθρώπου, καὶ πάλιν τὸν κόσμον ἢ τὸν ἄνθρωπον; ταῦτα γὰρ ἐπίστανται καὶ διανοοῦνται πάντες, ἂν μὴ Στωικοὶ γένωνται· γενόμενοι δὲ Στωικοὶ

τἀναντία λέγουσι καὶ δοξάζουσιν ὡς οὐκ ἔστιν ἐκ πλειόνων μορίων ὁ   15
ἄνθρωπος ἢ ὁ δάκτυλος οὐδὲ ὁ κόσμος ἢ ὁ ἄνθρωπος. ἐπ' ἄπειρον γὰρ ἡ
τομὴ βράττει τὰ σώματα, τῶν δ' ἀπείρων οὐδέν ἐστι πλέον οὐδ' ἔλαττον
οὐδὲ ὅλως ὑπερβάλλει πλῆθος ἢ παύσεται τὰ μέρη τοῦ ὑπολειπομένου μεριζόμενα καὶ
παρέχοντα πλῆθος ἐξ αὐτῶν.
ΕΤΑΙΡΟΣ. τί οὖν; οὐκ ἀμύνονται ταύτας τὰς ἀπορίας;   20
ΔΙΑΔΟΥΜ. εὐμηχάνως κομιδῇ καὶ ἀνδρείως. (3) λέγει γὰρ ὁ Χρύσιππος ἐρωτωμέ-
νους ἡμᾶς εἴ τινα ἔχομεν μέρη καὶ πόσα καὶ ἐκ τίνων συγκείμενα μερῶν
καὶ πόσων διαστολῇ χρήσεσθαι, τὸ μὲν ὁλοσχερὲς τιθέντας ὡς ἐκ κεφαλῆς
καὶ θώρακος καὶ σκελῶν συγκείμεθα· τοῦτο γὰρ ἦν πᾶν τὸ ζητούμενον καὶ
ἀπορούμενον· ἐὰν δ' ἐπὶ τὰ ἔσχατα μέρη τὸ ἐρωτᾶν προάγωσιν, οὐδέν φησι   25
τῶν τοιούτων ἐστὶν ὑποληπτέον, ἀλλὰ ῥητέον οὔτ' ἐκ τίνων συνεστάναι
καὶ ὁμοίως οὔτ' ἐξ ὁπόσων, οὔτ' ⟨ἐξ⟩ ἀπείρων οὔτ' ἐκ πεπερασμένων. καί
μοι δοκῶ ταῖς ἐκείνου κεχρῆσθαι λέξεσιν αὐταῖς, ὅπως συνίδῃς ὃν τρόπον
διεφύλαττε τὰς κοινὰς ἐννοίας, κελεύων ἡμᾶς νοεῖν τῶν σωμάτων ἕκαστον
οὔτ' ἔκ τινων οὔτ' ἐξ ὁποσωνοῦν μερῶν, οὔτ' ἐξ ἀπείρων οὔτ' ἐκ   30
πεπερασμένων συγκείμενον. εἰ μὲν γάρ, ὡς ἀγαθοῦ καὶ κακοῦ τὸ
ἀδιάφορον, οὕτως πεπερασμένου τι καὶ ἀπείρου μέσον ἐστίν, εἰπόντα τί
τοῦτ' ἐστὶν ἔδει λῦσαι τὴν ἀπορίαν· εἰ δέ, ὡς τὸ μὴ ἴσον εὐθὺς ἄνισον καὶ τὸ
μὴ φθαρτὸν ἄφθαρτον, οὕτως τὸ μὴ πεπερασμένον ἄπειρον νοοῦμεν,
ὅμοιόν ἐστιν, οἶμαι, [τῷ] τὸ σῶμα εἶναι μήτ' ἐκ πεπερασμένων μήτ' ἐξ   35
ἀπείρων τῷ λόγον εἶναι μήτ' ἐξ ἀληθῶν λημμάτων μήτ' ἐκ ψευδῶν μήτ' ἐξ
⟨ἀληθῶν καὶ ψευδῶν⟩. (4) ἐπὶ δὲ τούτοις ἐπινεανιευόμενός φησι τῆς
πυραμίδος ἐκ τριγώνων συνισταμένης τὰς πλευρὰς κατὰ τὴν συναφὴν
ἐκκεκλιμένας ἀνίσους μὲν εἶναι μὴ ὑπερέχειν δὲ ᾗ μείζονές εἰσιν. οὕτως
ἐτήρει τὰς ἐννοίας. εἰ γὰρ ἔστι τι μεῖζον καὶ μὴ ὑπερέχον, ἔσται τι   40
μικρότερον καὶ μὴ ἐλλεῖπον, ὥστε καὶ ἄνισον μήθ' ὑπερέχον μήτ'
ἐλλεῖπον, τουτέστιν ἴσον τὸ ἄνισον καὶ οὐ μεῖζον τὸ μεῖζον οὐδὲ
μικρότερον τὸ μικρότερον. (5) ἔτι τοίνυν ὅρα τίνα τρόπον ἀπήντησε
Δημοκρίτῳ, διαποροῦντι φυσικῶς καὶ ἐμψύχως εἰ κῶνος τέμνοιτο παρὰ
τὴν βάσιν ἐπιπέδῳ, τί χρὴ διανοεῖσθαι τὰς τῶν τμημάτων ἐπιφανείας,   45
ἴσας ἢ ἀνίσους γινομένας· ἄνισοι μὲν γὰρ οὖσαι τὸν κῶνον ἀνώμαλον
παρέξουσι, πολλὰς ἀποχαράξεις λαμβάνοντα βαθμοειδεῖς καὶ τραχύτη-
τας· ἴσων δ' οὐσῶν ἴσα τμήματα ἔσται καὶ φανεῖται τὸ τοῦ κυλίνδρου
πεπονθὼς ὁ κῶνος, ἐξ ἴσων συγκείμενος καὶ οὐκ ἀνίσων κύκλων, ὅπερ
ἐστὶν ἀτοπώτατον. ἐνταῦθα δὴ τὸν Δημόκριτον ἀποφαίνων ἀγνοοῦντα τὰς   50
μὲν ἐπιφανείας φησὶ μήτ' ἴσας εἶναι μήτ' ἀνίσους, ἄνισα δὲ τὰ σώματα τῷ
μήτ' ἴσας εἶναι μήτ' ἀνίσους τὰς ἐπιφανείας. τὸ μὲν δὴ νομοθετεῖν τῶν
ἐπιφανειῶν μήτ' ἴσων ⟨μήτ' ἀνίσων⟩ οὐσῶν τὰ σώματα συμβαίνειν ἄνισα εἶναι θαυμαστὴν
ἐξουσίαν αὐτῷ τοῦ γράφειν ὅ τι ἂν εἴη διδόντος ἐστί. τοὐναντίον γὰρ ὁ λόγος μετὰ τῆς
ἐναργείας νοεῖν δίδωσι τῶν ἀνίσων σωμάτων ἀνίσους εἶναι τὰς ἐπιφανείας καὶ μείζονα τὴν   55
τοῦ μείζονος, εἴ γε μὴ μέλλει τὴν ὑπεροχήν, ᾗ μείζόν ἐστιν, ἐστερημένην ἐπιφανείας ἕξειν.
εἰ γὰρ οὐχ ὑπερβάλλουσι τὰς τῶν ἐλαττόνων ἐπιφανείας αἱ τῶν μειζόνων ἀλλὰ

Stoic physics

προαπολείπουσιν, ἔσται σώματος πέρας ἔχοντος μέρος ἄνευ πέρατος καὶ ἀπεράτωτον. εἰ
γὰρ λέγει ὅτι βιαζόμενος οὕτω ⟨ταύτας νοεῖσθαι σώζει τὸν κῶνον, ἐλέγχεται φάσκων·⟩
"ἃς γὰρ ὑφορᾶται περὶ τὸν κῶνον ἀναχαράξεις ἢ τῶν σωμάτων ἀνισότης δήπουθεν οὐχ ἡ   60
τῶν ἐπιφανειῶν ἀπεργάζεται." γελοῖον οὖν τὸ τὰς ἐπιφανείας ὑπεξαιρούμενον ἐν τοῖς
σώμασιν ἐλεγχομένην ἀπολιπεῖν ἀνωμαλίαν. ἀλλ᾽ ἂν μένωμεν ἐπὶ τῆς ὑποθέσεως, τί
μᾶλλόν ἐστι παρὰ τὴν ἔννοιαν ἢ τὰ τοιαῦτα πλάττειν; εἰ γὰρ ἐπιφάνειαν ἐπιφανείᾳ θήσομεν
μήτ᾽ ἴσην εἶναι μήτ᾽ ἄνισον, καὶ τὸ μέγεθος ἔσται μεγέθει φάναι καὶ ἀριθμὸν ἀριθμῷ μήτ᾽
ἴσον εἶναι μήτ᾽ ἄνισον, καὶ ταῦτ᾽ ἴσου καὶ ἀνίσου μέσον, ὃ μηδέτερόν ἐστιν, οὐκ ἔχοντας   65
εἰπεῖν οὐδὲ νοῆσαι δυναμένους . . .

   καὶ μὴν τὸ μηδενὸς ἅπτεσθαι μηδὲν παρὰ τὴν ἔννοιάν ἐστιν. οὐχ ἧττον δὲ τοῦτο,
ἅπτεσθαι μὲν ἀλλήλων τὰ σώματα μηδενὶ δὲ ἅπτεσθαι. τοῦτο δ᾽ ἀνάγκη προσδέχεσθαι τοῖς
μὴ ἀπολείπουσιν ἐλάχιστα μέρη σώματος ἀλλ᾽ ἀεί τι τοῦ δοκοῦντος ἅπτεσθαι πρότερον
λαμβάνουσι καὶ μηδέποτε τοῦ προάγειν ἐπέκεινα παυομένοις. (6) ὃ γοῦν αὐτοὶ   70
μάλιστα προφέρουσι τοῖς τῶν ἀμερῶν προϊσταμένοις, τοῦτ᾽ ἐστὶ τὸ μήθ᾽
ὅλοις ὅλων ἁφὴν εἶναι μήτε μέρεσι μερῶν· τὸ μὲν γὰρ οὐχ ἁφὴν ἀλλὰ
κρᾶσιν ποιεῖν, τὸ δ᾽ οὐκ εἶναι δυνατόν, μέρη τῶν ἀμερῶν οὐκ ἐχόντων. (7)
πῶς οὖν οὐκ αὐτοὶ τούτῳ περιπίπτουσι, μηδὲν μέρος ἔσχατον μηδὲ
πρῶτον ἀπολείποντες; ὅτι νὴ Δία ψαύειν κατὰ πέρας τὰ σώματ᾽ ἀλλήλων,   75
οὐ κατὰ μέρος λέγουσιν. (8) τὸ δὲ πέρας σῶμα οὔκ ἐστιν. ἅψεται τοίνυν
σῶμα σώματος ἀσωμάτῳ καὶ οὐχ ἅψεται πάλιν, ἀσωμάτου μεταξὺ ὄντος.
εἰ δ᾽ ἅψεται, καὶ ποιήσει τι καὶ πείσεται τῷ ἀσωμάτῳ τὸ σῶμα· ποιεῖν γάρ τι
καὶ πάσχειν ὑπ᾽ ἀλλήλων τῷ ἅπτεσθαι τὰ σώματα πέφυκεν. εἰ δὲ ἁφὴν ἴσχει τῷ ἀσωμάτῳ
τὸ σῶμα, καὶ συναφὴν ἕξει καὶ κρᾶσιν καὶ συμφυίαν. ἔστιν ἄρ᾽ ἐν ταῖς συναφαῖς καὶ   80
κράσεσιν ἢ μένειν ἀναγκαῖον ἢ μὴ μένειν ἀλλ᾽ ἐφθάρθαι τὰ πέρατα τῶν σωμάτων. ἑκάτερον
δὲ παρὰ τὴν ἔννοιάν ἐστι· φθορὰς μὲν γὰρ ἀσωμάτων καὶ γενέσεις οὐδ᾽ αὐτοὶ καταλείπουσι,
κρᾶσις δὲ καὶ συναφὴ σωμάτων ἰδίοις χρωμένων πέρασιν οὐκ ἂν γένοιτο.

2 add. Pohlenz: ⟨μέρος εἶναι⟩ Arnim   3 add. Dübner   6 add. Pohlenz   13 ταῦτα Wyttenbach:
αὐτὰ codd.   17 βράττει Chერniss: πράττει codd.: προάγει Wyttenbach   27 οὔτ᾽ ⟨ἐξ⟩ Rasmus:
αὔτε codd.   35 del. Rasmus   37 suppl. Sedley: spatium in codd.: ⟨ἀδυνάτων μήτ᾽ ἐκ δυνατῶν⟩
Pohlenz: ⟨ἁπλῶν μήτ᾽ ἐξ οὐχ ἁπλῶν⟩ Chერniss   39 ἐκκεκλιμένας codd.: ἐγκεκλιμένας Bernardakis   53 suppl. Wyttenbach   59 suppl. Chერniss: spatium in codd.: ⟨τὴν ἐνάργειαν ἐλέγχεται, αὐτὸν
ἐλέγχει φάσκων⟩ Pohlenz   75 νὴ Δία ψαύειν Wyttenbach: μὴ διαψαύειν codd.   ἀλλήλων
Chერniss: ὅλα ὅλων codd.   79 τῷ[1] Giesen: καὶ codd.   80 ἐστιν ἄρ᾽ Pohlenz: ἔτι γὰρ codd.

Context: following the critique of Stoic theory of mixture at **48B**.
   1 **ἄκρον** Cf. the Epicurean usage at **9A** 10, **9B** 749, **9C** 599.
   37   Our conjecture to fill the lacuna left in the codd. makes the comparison
between the two classes less exact, but is required in logic because, for an argument,
'having its premises true' and 'having its premises false' are not straight contradictories
(cf. **36B 5**): it could have some premises true and some false.
   37–43   In vol. 1 we follow the same general interpretation as Hahm [508], 217–
19, which is in fact facilitated by our retention of the MSS reading in 39 in preference
to the standard emendation ἐγκεκλιμένας. If, as in the cone, we are to envisage the
production of the two adjacent planes by physically cutting the pyramid parallel to

298

the base, there is no need to read Chrysippus as analysing the pyramid into parallel three-dimensional plates or laminae (Sambursky [490], 94; Hahm, loc cit.).

43–50   For the vexed history of interpretation of Democritus' puzzle, see Cherniss [326], 820.

50–2   The first interpretation of Chrysippus' solution considered in vol. 1, 302 is that of Cherniss [326], 820–2. The second, which we favour, owes most to Sambursky [490], 93–5, and White [511]. For another reading, which relies on a different interpretation of Democritus' cone puzzle, see Hahm [508].

60–1   This is taken by Pohlenz and Cherniss in their editions to be a quotation from Chrysippus, referring to Democritus. Against, see Hahm [508], 214–17.

73 κρᾶσιν   See 48.

D   Proclus, *In Eucl. El. I* 89,15–21 (*SVF* 2.488)

ὅτι δὲ οὐ δεῖ νομίζειν κατ' ἐπίνοιαν ψιλὴν ὑφεστάναι τὰ τοιαῦτα πέρατα, λέγω τῶν σωμάτων, ὥσπερ οἱ ἀπὸ τῆς Στοᾶς ὑπέλαβον, ἀλλ' εἶναί τινας φύσεις ἐν τοῖς οὖσι τοιάσδε καὶ λόγους αὐτῶν προεστάναι δημιουργικούς, ἀναμνησθείημεν ἂν εἰς τὸν ὅλον κόσμον ἀποβλέψαντες . . .

Context: commentary on Euclid's first definition, arguing that mathematical limits, among which the point is primary, are integral to the physical world.

Cf. **51F**, where Proclus attributes to the Stoics, less plausibly, a similar view about time.

E   Diogenes Laertius 7.135

ἐπιφάνεια δ' ἐστὶ σώματος πέρας ἢ τὸ μῆκος καὶ πλάτος ἔχον βάθος δ' οὔ· ταύτην δὲ Ποσειδώνιος ἐν πέμπτῳ Περὶ μετεώρων καὶ κατ' ἐπίνοιαν καὶ καθ' ὑπόστασιν ἀπολείπει. γραμμὴ δ' ἐστὶν ἐπιφανείας πέρας ἢ μῆκος ἀπλατὲς ἢ τὸ μῆκος μόνον ἔχον. στιγμὴ δ' ἐστὶ γραμμῆς πέρας, ἥτις ἐστὶ σημεῖον ἐλάχιστον.   5

Context: immediately following **45E**.

Cf. Mansfeld [344], 160, 166, who interprets Posidonius' thesis as the highly unorthodox one that a surface is a body, and links it with the doctrine that limits are bodies, reported without specific attribution by ps.-Galen, *Hist. phil.* 23 (Diels, *Dox.* 613,1–2). But Posidonius' view is just the standard Stoic view cited in **D**, and the ps.-Galen reference could be to the Epicureans (cf. **9A–C**). In having 'subsistence', limits differ from those other mental constructs, universals, which do not *even* subsist: **27C**.

F   Sextus Empiricus, *M.* 10.121–6, 139–42

(1) πρὸς τούτοις· πᾶσα κίνησις τριῶν τινῶν ἔχεται, καθάπερ σωμάτων τε καὶ τόπων καὶ χρόνων, σωμάτων μὲν τῶν κινουμένων, τόπων δὲ τῶν ἐν οἷς ἡ κίνησις γίνεται, χρόνων δὲ τῶν καθ' οὓς ἡ κίνησις γίνεται. ἤτοι οὖν πάντων τούτων εἰς ἀπείρους τεμνομένων τόπους καὶ χρόνους καὶ εἰς ἄπειρα σώματα γίνεται ἡ κίνησις, ἢ πάντων εἰς ἀμερὲς καὶ ἐλάχιστον   5

Stoic physics

καταληγόντων, ἢ τινῶν μὲν εἰς ἄπειρον τεμνομένων, τινῶν δὲ εἰς ἀμερὲς καὶ ἐλάχιστον καταληγόντων. ἐάν τε δὲ πάντα εἰς ἄπειρον τέμνηται, ἐάν τε πάντα εἰς ἀμερὲς καταλήγῃ, ⟨ἐάν τε τινὰ μὲν εἰς ἄπειρον τέμνηται, τινὰ δὲ εἰς ἀμερὲς καταλήγῃ,⟩ ἄπορος ὁ περὶ τῆς κινήσεως εὑρεθήσεται λόγος. (2) τάξει δὲ ἀπὸ τῆς πρώτης στάσεως ποιώμεθα τὴν ἐπιχείρησιν, καθ' ἣν πάντα εἰς ἄπειρον τέμνεται. καὶ δὴ οἱ προεστῶτες αὐτῆς φασι τὸ κινούμενον σῶμα ὑφ' ἕνα καὶ τὸν αὐτὸν χρόνον ἄθρουν μεριστὸν ἀνύειν διάστημα, καὶ οὐ τὸ πρῶτον τοῦ διαστήματος μέρος πρῶτον ἐπιλαμβάνειν τῷ πρώτῳ αὐτοῦ μέρει καὶ τὸ δεύτερον τῇ τάξει δεύτερον, ἀλλ' ὑφ' ἓν τὸ ὅλον μεριστὸν διάστημα καὶ ἀθρόως διέρχεσθαι. (3) ὅπερ ἐστὶν ἄτοπον καὶ ποικίλως τοῖς φαινομένοις μαχόμενον. εἰ γοῦν ἐπὶ τῶν αἰσθητῶν τούτων σωμάτων νοήσωμέν τινα κατὰ σταδιαίου τροχάζοντα διαστήματος, πάντως ὑποπεσεῖται ὅτι ὀφείλει ὁ τοιοῦτος τὸ πρῶτον ἡμιστάδιον ἀνύειν πρῶτον καὶ τὸ δεύτερον τῇ τάξει δεύτερον· τὸ γὰρ ὑφ' ἓν ἀξιοῦν τὸ ὅλον ἀνύειν τοῦ σταδίου διάστημα τελέως ἄτοπον. καὶ εἰ τέμοιμεν τὸ ἕτερον ἡμιστάδιον εἰς δύο τεταρτημόρια, πάντως πρῶτον διελεύσεται τὸ πρῶτον τεταρτημόριον· καὶ εἰ εἰς πλείονα τέμοιμεν, ὡσαύτως. κἂν κατὰ πεφωτισμένου δὲ τροχάζῃ τοῦ σταδίου, φαίνεται ὡς οὐχ ὑφ' ἓν σκιάσει τὸ στάδιον, ἀλλὰ τὸ μέν τι πρῶτον μέρος, τὸ δὲ δεύτερον, τὸ δὲ τρίτον. καὶ εἰ παραθέοι δὲ τῷ τοίχῳ μεμιλτωμένῃ τῇ χειρὶ τούτου ἐφαπτόμενος, οὐχ ὑφ' ἕνα καὶ τὸν αὐτὸν χρόνον τὸν ὅλον τοῦ σταδίου τοῖχον μιλτώσει, ἀλλὰ κατὰ τάξιν καὶ κατὰ τὸ πρότερον πρότερον. ὅπερ οὖν ὁ λόγος ἐπὶ τῶν αἰσθητῶν ἔδειξε πραγμάτων, τουτὶ καὶ ἐπὶ τῶν νοητῶν προσδεκτέον ἐστὶν ἡμῖν ... (4) ὥστε τὸ μὲν κατ' ἄθρουν διάστημα γίνεσθαι τὴν κίνησιν οὕτως ἐστὶν ἄπορον τοῖς προειρημένοις ἀνδράσιν· πολλῷ δὲ τούτου ἀπορώτερον τὸ μὴ κατ' ἄθρουν γίνεσθαι μεριστὸν διάστημα, ἀλλὰ κατὰ τὸ πρότερον πρότερον καὶ κατὰ τὸ δεύτερον δεύτερον. εἰ γὰρ οὕτω γίνεται ἡ κίνησις, πάντων εἰς ἄπειρον τεμνομένων τῶν τε σωμάτων καὶ τόπων καὶ χρόνων, οὐκ ἔσται τις ἀρχὴ κινήσεως. ἵνα γάρ τι κινηθῇ πηχυαῖον διάστημα, ὀφείλει τὸ πρῶτον ἡμίπηχυ διέρχεσθαι πρῶτον καὶ τὸ δεύτερον τῇ τάξει δεύτερον. ἀλλ' ἵνα καὶ τὸ πρῶτον ἀνύσῃ ἡμίπηχυ διάστημα, ὀφείλει τὸ πρῶτον τεταρτημόριον τοῦ πηχυαίου διαστήματος διελθεῖν, εἶτα τότε τὸ δεύτερον. ἀλλὰ κἂν εἰς πέντε διαιρεθῇ, ⟨τὸ πρῶτον πεμπτημόριον⟩, κἂν εἰς ἕξ, τὸ πρῶτον ἑκτημόριον. παντὸς οὖν τοῦ πρώτου μέρους ἄλλο πρῶτον ἔχοντος μέρος διὰ τὴν εἰς ἄπειρον τομήν, ἀνάγκη μηδέποτε ἀρχὴν γίνεσθαι κινήσεως διὰ τὸ ἀνέκλειπτα εἶναι τὰ μέρη τοῦ διαστήματος καὶ τὰ τοῦ σώματος, καὶ τὸ ἐκ τούτων λαμβανόμενον ἔχειν ἄλλα μέρη. (5) πρὸς μὲν οὖν τοὺς εἰς ἄπειρον τέμνεσθαι λέγοντας τά τε σώματα καὶ τοὺς τόπους καὶ τοὺς χρόνους (οὗτοι δέ εἰσιν οἱ ἀπὸ τῆς Στοᾶς) ταῦθ' ἥρμοζε λέγειν.

8–9 add. Bekker   38 add. Bekker

Context: 'Does motion exist?' Cf. PH 3.76–81.

The 'divisible leaps' interpretation discussed in vol. 1 is proposed by Sorabji [22],

53, who compares Damascius ap. Simpl. *In Ar. Phys.* 796,32–797,13. For an interesting but mathematically anachronistic reading, see White [511].

G Proclus, *In Eucl. El.* I 395,13–21 (*SVF* 2.365)

τὰ δ' οὖν τοιαῦτα τῶν θεωρημάτων, ὥς φησιν ὁ Γεμῖνος, ἀπείκαζεν ὁ Χρύσιππος ταῖς ἰδέαις. ὡς γὰρ ἐκεῖναι τῶν ἀπείρων ἐν πέρασιν ὡρισμένοις τὴν γένεσιν περιλαμβάνουσιν, οὕτως καὶ ἐν τούτοις τῶν ἀπείρων ἐν ὡρισμένοις τόποις ἡ περίληψις γίνεται. καὶ διὰ τὸν ὅρον τοῦτον ἡ ἰσότης ἀναφαίνεται. τὸ γὰρ ὕψος τῶν παραλλήλων τὸ αὐτὸ μένον ἀπείρων νοουμένων ἐπὶ τῆς 5 αὐτῆς βάσεως παραλληλογράμμων πάντα ἴσα ἀλλήλοις ἀποφαίνει.

2 ἰδέαις vel ἰδίαις codd.

Context: commentary on Euclid, Prop. 35 theorem 25.

Mansfeld [344], 158ff. takes the comparison with Ideas to make a point about the unreality of mathematical objects. But what is compared to Ideas is the theorems themselves, not their objects, and the comparison is about universality, not metaphysical status.

51 Time

A Simplicius, *In Ar. Cat.* 350,14–16 (*SVF* 2.510, part)

ὁ μὲν Ἀριστοτέλης ἀριθμὸν κινήσεως εἶναί φησι τὸν χρόνον, τῶν δὲ Στωικῶν Ζήνων μὲν πάσης ἁπλῶς κινήσεως διάστημα τὸν χρόνον εἶπεν, Χρύσιππος δὲ διάστημα τῆς τοῦ κόσμου κινήσεως.

Context: commentary on Aristotle, *Cat.* 9, 11b10, περὶ τοῦ ποτὲ καὶ ποῦ.

B Stobaeus I.106,5–23 (*SVF* 2.509)

(1) Χρυσίππου. ὁ δὲ Χρύσιππος χρόνον εἶναι κινήσεως διάστημα, καθ' ὃ ποτὲ λέγεται μέτρον τάχους τε καὶ βραδύτητος· ἢ τὸ παρακολουθοῦν διάστημα τῇ τοῦ κόσμου κινήσει. (2) καὶ κατὰ μὲν τὸν χρόνον κινεῖσθαί τε ἕκαστα καὶ εἶναι, εἰ μὴ ἄρα διττὸς λέγεται ὁ χρόνος, καθάπερ ἥ τε γῆ καὶ ἡ θάλαττα καὶ τὸ κενόν, τά τε ὅλα καὶ τὰ μέρη τὰ αὐτῶν. ὥσπερ δὲ τὸ κενὸν πᾶν 5 ἄπειρον εἶναι πάντῃ καὶ τὸν χρόνον πάντα ἄπειρον εἶναι ἐφ' ἑκάτερα· καὶ γὰρ τὸν παρεληλυθότα καὶ τὸν μέλλοντα ἄπειρον εἶναι. (3) ἐμφανέστατα δὲ τοῦτο λέγει, ὅτι οὐθεὶς ὅλως ἐνίσταται χρόνος. ἐπεὶ γὰρ εἰς ἄπειρον ἡ τομὴ τῶν συνεχόντων ἐστί, κατὰ τὴν διαίρεσιν ταύτην καὶ πᾶς χρόνος εἰς ἄπειρον ἔχει τὴν τομήν· ὥστε μηθένα κατ' ἀπαρτισμὸν 10 ἐνεστάναι χρόνον, ἀλλὰ κατὰ πλάτος λέγεσθαι. (4) μόνον δ' ὑπάρχειν φησὶ τὸν ἐνεστῶτα, τὸν δὲ παρῳχημένον καὶ τὸν μέλλοντα ὑφεστάναι μέν, ὑπάρχειν δὲ οὐδαμῶς, †εἰσὶν ὡς καὶ κατηγορήματα ὑπάρχειν λέγεται

Stoic physics

μόνα τὰ συμβεβηκότα, οἷον τὸ περιπατεῖν ὑπάρχει μοι ὅτε περιπατῶ, ὅτε
δὲ κατακέκλιμαι ἢ κάθημαι οὐχ ὑπάρχει.　　　　　　　　　　　　　　　15

1 ὃ Heeren: ὃν codd.　　11 φησὶ Canter: φασὶ codd.　　13 εἰσὶν codd.: εἰ μὴ Canter: φησιν
Arnim　　14 μόνα codd.: μόνον Usener

Context: doxography of time, immediately following E.

11–13　For the difference between ὑπάρχειν and ὑφεστάναι, cf. vol. 1, 164, and
Long [426], 89–93; Sandbach [304], 79–80 n. 117. Sorabji [22], 22ff., translates
ὑπάρχειν by 'exist', but acknowledges that existence should strictly not pertain to any
time, since time is an incorporeal. For this reason we prefer the translation 'belong',
which brings out Chrysippus' parallelism with the conditions under which predicates
belong to subjects; cf. Lloyd [392], 232–4. As the time signified by *is* (cf. the question
'what time is it?'), the present is really here – belongs to the world as it is – as distinct
from what has been or will be.

13 εἰσίν　No satisfactory emendation of this corruption has been proposed.
Canter's εἰ μή, though often accepted, gives entirely the wrong sense since it makes
ὡς–ὑπάρχει, 13–15, refer to the past and the future, whereas the ὑπάρχειν of
predicates must correspond to that of the present. Since the sense seems complete
without supplying a replacement for εἰσίν (cf. Arnim's conjecture), οὐδαμῶς εἶναι is
worth considering: 'cannot belong in any way'.

C Plutarch, *Comm. not.* 1081C–1082A.

(1) παρὰ τὴν ἔννοιάν ἐστι χρόνον εἶναι μέλλοντα καὶ παρῳχημένον,
ἐνεστῶτα δὲ μὴ εἶναι χρόνον, ἀλλὰ τὸ μὲν ἄρτι καὶ τὸ πρῴην ὑφεστάναι, τὸ
δὲ νῦν ὅλως μηδὲν εἶναι. (2) καὶ μὴν τοῦτο συμβαίνει τοῖς Στωικοῖς
ἐλάχιστον χρόνον μὴ ἀπολείπουσι μηδὲ τὸ νῦν ἀμερὲς εἶναι βουλομένοις,
ἀλλὰ ὅ τι ἄν τις ὡς ἐνεστὼς οἴηται λαβὼν διανοεῖσθαι, τούτου τὸ μὲν　　5
μέλλον τὸ δὲ παρῳχημένον εἶναι φάσκουσιν. (3) ὥστε μηδὲν κατὰ τὸ νῦν
ὑπομένειν μηδὲ λείπεσθαι μόριον χρόνου παρόντος, ἂν ὅς λέγεται παρεῖναι
τούτου τὰ μὲν εἰς τὰ μέλλοντα τὰ δ' εἰς τὰ παρῳχημένα διανέμηται . . . (4)
οἱ δ' ἄλλοι πάντες ἄνθρωποι καὶ τὸ "ἄρτι" καὶ τὸ "μετὰ μικρόν" ὡς ἕτερα
τοῦ "νῦν" μόρια, καὶ τὸ μὲν μετὰ τὸ νῦν τὸ δὲ πρὸ τοῦ νῦν τίθενται καὶ　　10
νοοῦσι καὶ νομίζουσι. τούτων ⟨δ'⟩ Ἀρχέδημος μὲν ἀρχήν τινα καὶ
συμβολὴν εἶναι λέγων τοῦ παρῳχημένου καὶ τοῦ ἐπιφερομένου τὸ "νῦν"
λέληθεν αὐτὸν ὡς ἔοικε τὸν πάντα χρόνον ἀναιρῶν. εἰ γὰρ τὸ νῦν οὐ χρόνος
ἐστὶν ἀλλὰ πέρας χρόνου πᾶν δὲ μόριον χρόνου τοιοῦτον οἷον τὸ νῦν ἐστιν,
οὐδὲν φαίνεται μέρος ἔχων ὁ σύμπας χρόνος ἀλλ' εἰς πέρατα διόλου καὶ　　15
συμβολὰς καὶ ἀρμὰς ἀναλυόμενος. (5) Χρύσιππος δὲ βουλόμενος φιλοτεχ-
νεῖν περὶ τὴν διαίρεσιν ἐν μὲν τῷ Περὶ τοῦ κενοῦ καὶ ἄλλοις τισὶ τὸ μὲν
παρῳχημένον τοῦ χρόνου καὶ τὸ μέλλον οὐχ ὑπάρχειν ἀλλὰ ὑφεστηκέναι
φησί, μόνον δ' ὑπάρχειν τὸ ἐνεστηκός, ἐν δὲ τῷ τρίτῳ καὶ τετάρτῳ καὶ
πέμπτῳ Περὶ τῶν μερῶν τίθησι τοῦ ἐνεστηκότος χρόνου τὸ μὲν μέλλον　　20
εἶναι τὸ δὲ παρεληλυθός. (6) ὥστε συμβαίνει τὸ ὑπάρχον αὐτῷ τοῦ χρόνου
διαιρεῖν εἰς τὰ μὴ ὑπάρχοντα τοῦ ὑπάρχοντος, μᾶλλον δὲ ὅλως τοῦ χρόνου

302

51 Time

μηδὲν ἀπολείπειν ὑπάρχον, εἰ τὸ ἐνεστηκὸς οὐδὲν ἔχει μέρος ὃ μὴ μέλλον
ἐστὶν ἢ παρῳχημένον.

7 ὅς Leonicus: ὡς codd.   11 ⟨δ'⟩ Sandbach   ἁρμήν Arnim: ἀρχήν codd.   13 οὐ Leonicus,
Basiliensis: ὁ codd.   16 ἁρμὰς Arnim: ὁρμὰς codd.   22 τοῦ ὑπάρχοντος del.
Rasmus: τοῦ ὑπάρχοντος ⟨καὶ τὰ ὑπάρχοντα τοῦ ὑπάρχοντος⟩ Sandbach: τό θ' ὑπάρχον Bury, Cherniss

Context: criticism of the Stoic conception of time.

1–8   These lines seek to exploit difficulties in the Stoics' claim (see **B 3, E 3**) that
no time is exactly present. We omit a section (1081D–E) which develops this further.
With 16–21, cf. **B 4, E 3**.

11–16   Sandbach [304], 50–1, does not mention Archedemus in his attempt to
undermine the dependence on Aristotle of Stoic views of time. Cf. Aristotle, *Physics*
IV.13, 222a10–12: τὸ δὲ νῦν ἐστιν συνέχεια χρόνου . . . συνέχει γὰρ τὸν χρόνον τὸν
παρεληλυθότα καὶ ἐσόμενον, καὶ πέρας χρόνου ἐστίν.

16–21   Sorabji [22], 22, noting that Chrysippus wrote about time in different
books, suggests that 'perhaps he first declared that only the present existed, but then,
when he came to write on *parts*, realized that some revision was called for'. We do not
think that Chrysippus' theories, as we interpret them in vol. 1, suggest he was much
concerned with the ontological status of time – the issue that Sorabji thinks underlies
his remarks on the relation of past, present and future.

22 τοῦ ὑπάρχοντος   These words have frequently been judged corrupt or
lacunose, but they seem defensible. For Plutarch's argument τὸ ὑπάρχον τοῦ χρόνου,
21, is 'the present'. If this consists of two parts, future and past, which 'do not belong',
then these are 'non-belonging parts of what belongs' (τὰ μὴ ὑπάρχοντα τοῦ
ὑπάρχοντος), and it is quite reasonable of Plutarch to say that 'the belonging part' of
time is divided into these: cf. 1081D, τοῦ ὑπάρχοντος τὸ μὲν μέλλον ἐστὶ τὸ δὲ
παρῳχημένον.

D Stobaeus 1.105,8–16 (*SVF* 3 Apollodorus 8)

Ἀπολλόδωρος δ' ἐν τῇ Φυσικῇ τέχνῃ οὕτως ὁρίζεται τὸν χρόνον· χρόνος δ' ἐστὶ τῆς
τοῦ κόσμου κινήσεως διάστημα· οὕτως δ' ἐστὶν ἄπειρος ὡς ὁ πᾶς ἀριθμὸς
ἄπειρος λέγεται εἶναι· τὸ μὲν γάρ ἐστιν αὐτοῦ παρεληλυθός, τὸ δὲ
ἐνεστηκός, τὸ δὲ μέλλον. ἐνεστάναι δὲ τὸν πάντα χρόνον ὡς τὸν ἐνιαυτὸν
ἐνεστηκέναι λέγομεν κατὰ μείζονα περιγραφήν· καὶ ὑπάρχειν ὁ πᾶς χρόνος   5
λέγεται, οὐδενὸς αὐτοῦ τῶν μερῶν ὑπάρχοντος ἀπαρτιζόντως.

6 ἀπαρτιζόντως Heeren: ἀπαρτίζοντος codd.

Context: shortly before **B**.

E Stobaeus 1.105,17–106,4 (Posidonius fr. 98)

(1) Ποσειδωνίου. τὰ μέν ἐστι κατὰ πᾶν ἄπειρα, ὡς ὁ σύμπας χρόνος· τὰ δὲ
κατά τι, ὡς ὁ παρεληλυθὼς χρόνος καὶ ὁ μέλλων· κατὰ γὰρ τὸν παρόντα
μόνον ἑκάτερος πεπέρανται. (2) τὸν δὲ χρόνον οὕτως ὁρίζεται· διάστημα
κινήσεως ἢ μέτρον τάχους τε καὶ βραδυτῆτος. (3) καί †πως ἔχει† τὸν
ἐπινοούμενον κατὰ τὸ πότε τοῦ χρόνου τὸν μὲν εἶναι παρεληλυθότα, τὸν δὲ   5

303

Stoic physics

μέλλοντα, τὸν δὲ παρόντα, ὃς ἔκ τινος μέρους τοῦ παρεληλυθότος καὶ τοῦ
μέλλοντος περὶ τὸν διορισμὸν αὐτὸν συνέστηκε· τὸν δὲ διορισμὸν
σημειώδη εἶναι. (4) τὸ δὲ νῦν καὶ τὰ ὅμοια ἐν πλάτει [χρόνου] καὶ οὐχὶ κατ᾽
ἀπαρτισμὸν νοεῖσθαι. (5) λέγεσθαι δὲ τὸ νῦν καὶ κατὰ τὸν ἐλάχιστον πρὸς
αἴσθησιν χρόνον περὶ τὸν διορισμὸν τοῦ μέλλοντος καὶ παρεληλυθότος   10
συνιστάμενον.

3 ἑκάτερος πεπέρανται Diels: ἑκατέροις πεπέρασται codd.   4–5 καί πως ἔχει τὸν codd.: ὅπως ἔχει
τὸ Heeren qui interpunxit post ἐπινοούμενον   5 κατὰ ⟨δὲ⟩ Heeren: ⟨καὶ⟩ κατὰ Diels, Kidd   8
χρόνου del. Heeren: χρόνου Usener, Kidd   9 κατὰ del. Wachsmuth, Kidd   10 ⟨τὸν⟩ περὶ Usener

Context: immediately following D.

With 1–3, cf. B 5–7; with 3–4, cf. A, B 1–3; with 4–8, cf. C 3–8, 16–21; with 8–9,
cf. B 10–11.

4–5   We see no obvious way to mend the corruption here. The common
expedient of reading τὸ ἐπινοούμενον and connecting the words with διάστημα–
βραδυτῆτος does not seem at all plausible. Good sense can be given to the general
thrust of the passage by taking τὸν ἐπινοούμενον with what follows: 'the time which
is thought of in terms of when', and supposing that πως ἔχει conceals some verb
meaning 'he supposes'.

9–10 **κατὰ–χρόνον**   This recalls Epicurus, τὸ ἐλάχιστον τὸ ἐν τῇ αἰσθήσει, 9A
7, which refers to the minimum extension of anything perceptible. Goldschmidt
[302], 36, takes this to be the interpretation of Chrysippus' 'broad' sense of present
time, B 10–11.

F   Proclus, In Plat. Tim. 271D (SVF 2.521)

(1) ἔτι δὲ κἀκεῖνο ληπτέον ἀπὸ τῶν προειρημένων, ὅτι πολλοῦ δεῖ τοιοῦτον
ὑπονοῆσαι τὸν χρόνον ὁ Πλάτων οἷον οἱ ἀπὸ τῆς Στοᾶς ὑπέλαβον ἢ τῶν ἐκ
τοῦ Περιπάτου πολλοί, (2) οἱ μὲν κατ᾽ ἐπίνοιαν ψιλὴν αὐτὸν συνιστάντες
ἀμενηνὸν καὶ ἔγγιστα τοῦ μὴ ὄντος (ἐν γὰρ ἦν τῶν παρ᾽ αὐτοῖς ἀσωμάτων
ὁ χρόνος, ἃ δὴ καταπεφρόνηται παρ᾽ αὐτοῖς ὡς ἀδρανῆ καὶ οὐκ ὄντα καὶ ἐν   5
ἐπινοίαις ὑφιστάμενα ψιλαῖς), (3) οἱ δὲ συμβεβηκὸς τῆς κινήσεως
λέγοντες.

Context: commentary on Plato, Tim. 39d–e. Proclus takes Platonic time to be an
independently existing number.

5–6 **ἐν ἐπινοίαις ... ψιλαῖς**   Nothing in the reported statements of Stoic
philosophers justifies Proclus' reduction of time to a mere thought. He may have been
influenced by such stronger doxographical formulations as S.E., M. 10.277:
ἀσώματόν τι καθ᾽ αὐτὸ νοούμενον ὑπεστήσαντο τὸν χρόνον (=7C 39).

G   Plutarch, Comm. not. 1084C–D (SVF 2.665)

καὶ μὴ δυσχεραινέτωσαν ἐπὶ ταῦτ᾽ ἀγόμενοι τῷ κατὰ μικρὸν λόγῳ,
Χρυσίππου μνημονεύοντες ἐν τῷ πρώτῳ τῶν Φυσικῶν ζητημάτων οὕτω

προσάγοντος· "οὐχ ἡ μὲν νὺξ σῶμ᾽ ἐστίν, ἡ δ᾽ ἑσπέρα καὶ ὁ ὄρθρος καὶ τὸ
μέσον τῆς νυκτὸς σώματ᾽ οὔκ ἐστιν· οὐδὲ ἡ μὲν ἡμέρα σῶμ᾽ ἐστὶν οὐχὶ δὲ
καὶ ἡ νουμηνία σῶμα καὶ ἡ δεκάτη καὶ πεντεκαιδεκάτη καὶ ἡ τριακὰς καὶ ὁ   5
μὴν σῶμ᾽ ἐστὶ καὶ τὸ θέρος καὶ τὸ φθινόπωρον καὶ ὁ ἐνιαυτός."

6 σῶμ᾽ ἐστί fortasse delendum

Context: criticism of Stoic materialism.
1 κατὰ μικρόν   For this argument, cf. 37G and vol. 1, 229.

H Sextus Empiricus, M. 8.254–5 (SVF 2.221, part)

(1) ἔτι, φασί, τὸ σημεῖον παρὸν παρόντος εἶναι δεῖ σημεῖον. (2) ἔνιοι γὰρ
ἐξαπατώμενοι καὶ παρὸν παρῳχημένου θέλουσιν εἶναι σημεῖον, ὡς ἐπὶ τοῦ
"εἰ οὐλὴν ἔχει οὗτος, ἕλκος ἔσχηκεν οὗτος". τὸ μὲν γὰρ "οὐλὴν ἔχει" παρόν
ἐστι, φαίνεται γάρ, τὸ δὲ ἕλκος ἐσχηκέναι παρῳχημένον, οὐκέτι γὰρ ἔστιν
ἕλκος, καὶ παρὸν μέλλοντος, ὡς τὸ περιεχόμενον τῷ τοιούτῳ συνημμένῳ   5
"εἰ καρδίαν τέτρωται οὗτος, ἀποθανεῖται οὗτος"· τὸ μὲν γὰρ τραῦμα τῆς
καρδίας εἶναί φασιν ἤδη, τὸν δὲ θάνατον μέλλειν. (3) ἀγνοοῦσι δὴ οἱ τὰ
τοιαῦτα λέγοντες ὅτι ἄλλ᾽ ἐστὶ τὰ παρῳχημένα καὶ τὰ μέλλοντα, τὸ μέντοι
σημεῖον καὶ σημειωτὸν κἀν τούτοις παρὸν παρόντος ἐστίν. (4) ἔν τε γὰρ τῷ
προτέρῳ τῷ "εἰ οὐλὴν ἔχει οὗτος, ἕλκος ἔσχηκεν οὗτος" τὸ μὲν ἕλκος γέγονεν ἤδη   10
καὶ παρῴχηκεν, τὸ δὲ ἕλκος ἐσχηκέναι τοῦτον, ἀξίωμα καθεστηκός,
ἐνέστηκεν, περὶ γεγονότος τινὸς λεγόμενον· ἔν τε τῷ "εἰ καρδίαν τέτρωται
οὗτος, ἀποθανεῖται οὗτος" ὁ μὲν θάνατος μέλλει, τὸ δὲ ἀποθανεῖσθαι
τοῦτον ἀξίωμα ἐνέστηκεν, περὶ μέλλοντος λεγόμενον, παρὸ καὶ νῦν ἐστιν
ἀληθές.   15

3 τὸ Kochalsky: εἰ codd.

Context: account of the Stoic theory of signs. Sextus does not refer to the Stoics by
name here, but that he is reporting their doctrines can be inferred from M. 8.244,
where he begins to discuss the views of those who take τὸ σημεῖον to be νοητόν as
distinct from αἰσθητόν. In M. 8.177 he has identified these as Stoics and Epicureans
respectively. What occurs between M. 8.244 and our extract is an account of
conditional propositions which enlarges upon 35C, where the Stoics are named.

52 Everlasting recurrence

A Philo, Aet. mundi 52, 54

εἰ γὰρ ἀγένητος ὁ χρόνος, ἐξ ἀνάγκης καὶ ὁ κόσμος ἀγένητος ... (1) ὥστ᾽ εὐθυβόλως
ἀποδεδόσθαι πρὸς τῶν εἰωθότων τὰ πράγματα ὁρίζεσθαι χρόνον
διάστημα τῆς τοῦ κόσμου κινήσεως. ἐπεὶ δὲ τοῦθ᾽ ὑγιές ἐστι, γίνεται ὁ
κόσμος ἰσῆλιξ τοῦ χρόνου καὶ αἴτιος ... (2) τάχα τις εὑρεσιλογῶν
Στωικὸς ἐρεῖ τὸν χρόνον ἀποδεδόσθαι διάστημα τῆς τοῦ κόσμου κινήσεως   5

305

Stoic physics

οὐχὶ τοῦ νυνὶ διακεκοσμημένου μόνον ἀλλὰ καὶ τοῦ κατὰ τὴν ἐκπύρωσιν
ὑπονοουμένου.

Context: proof of the world's eternity. Philo, drawing on Plato, Tim. 37e, urges that
time (which is without beginning and end) and the world must have the same
duration.

1–3 Chrysippus' definition of time, 51A, is invoked here.

4–7 According to Plutarch, De E apud Delphos 389C, the Delphic priests' rituals
could be interpreted, in reference to the seasons of the year, as treating winter as three
months or διακόσμησις, and the rest of the year as nine months or ἐκπύρωσις. Stoic
allegory is pervasive in the whole passage, which strengthens the likelihood that the
conflagration was thought to be in time, though probably not of a duration as precise
as three times the length of each world-order.

B Lactantius, Div. inst. 7.23 (SVF 2.623)

melius Chrysippus quem Cicero ait fulcire porticum Stoicorum, qui in libris quos de
providentia scripsit, cum de innovatione mundi loqueretur haec intulit: τούτου δ᾽
οὕτως ἔχοντος, δῆλον ὡς οὐδὲν ἀδύνατον καὶ ἡμᾶς μετὰ τὸ τελευτῆσαι
πάλιν περιόδων τινῶν εἰλημμένων χρόνου εἰς ὃ νῦν ἐσμεν καταστήσεσθαι
σχῆμα.   5

Context: Lactantius, discussing the resurrection, finds Chrysippus' account of rebirth
preferable to the Pythagorean doctrine of transmigration of souls.

C Nemesius 309,5–311,2 (SVF 2.625)

(1) οἱ δὲ Στωικοί φασιν ἀποκαθισταμένους τοὺς πλάνητας εἰς τὸ αὐτὸ
σημεῖον, κατά τε μῆκος καὶ πλάτος, ἔνθα τὴν ἀρχὴν ἕκαστος ἦν ὅτε τὸ
πρῶτον ὁ κόσμος συνέστη, ἐν ῥηταῖς χρόνων περιόδοις ἐκπύρωσιν καὶ
φθορὰν τῶν ὄντων ἀπεργάζεσθαι. (2) καὶ πάλιν ἐξ ὑπαρχῆς εἰς τὸ αὐτὸ τὸν
κόσμον ἀποκαθίστασθαι· καὶ τῶν ἀστέρων ὁμοίως πάλιν φερομένων,   5
ἕκαστον ἐν τῇ προτέρᾳ περιόδῳ γινόμενον ἀπαραλλάκτως ἀποτελεῖσθαι.
ἔσεσθαι γὰρ πάλιν Σωκράτη καὶ Πλάτωνα καὶ ἕκαστον τῶν ἀνθρώπων
σὺν τοῖς αὐτοῖς καὶ φίλοις καὶ πολίταις· καὶ τὰ αὐτὰ πείσεσθαι καὶ τοῖς
αὐτοῖς συντεύξεσθαι καὶ τὰ αὐτὰ μεταχειριεῖσθαι, καὶ πᾶσαν πόλιν καὶ
κώμην καὶ ἀγρὸν ὁμοίως ἀποκαθίστασθαι. (3) γίνεσθαι δὲ τὴν ἀποκατάσ-   10
τασιν τοῦ παντὸς οὐχ ἅπαξ ἀλλὰ πολλάκις· μᾶλλον δὲ εἰς ἄπειρον καὶ
ἀτελευτήτως τὰ αὐτὰ ἀποκαθίστασθαι. (4) τοὺς δὲ θεοὺς τοὺς μὴ
ὑποκειμένους τῇ φθορᾷ, ταύτῃ παρακολουθήσαντας μιᾷ περιόδῳ, γινώσκειν ἐκ ταύτης πάντα τὰ μέλλοντα ἔσεσθαι ἐν ταῖς ἑξῆς περιόδοις. οὐδὲν
γὰρ ξένον ἔσεσθαι παρὰ τὰ γενόμενα πρότερον, ἀλλὰ πάντα ὡσαύτως   15
ἀπαραλλάκτως ἄχρι καὶ τῶν ἐλαχίστων.

Context: Nemesius contrasts Stoic views on fate with the position of Plato and Judaeo-
Christian theology.

1–4   The astrology refers to the end of the 'great' or 'greatest' year (cf. **D 4**), an event already referred to by Plato, *Tim.* 39d, and connected by him with a return of the planets to their original positions relative to one another. Plato himself does not speak, and probably did not know, of the doctrine that the planets will all then be in one sign of the zodiac. The notion was probably first disseminated to the Greeks by the Babylonian Berosus, early in the third century B.C. (cf. Long [485], 166–7), of whom Seneca, *NQ* 3.29.1 writes: *arsura enim terrena contendit, quandoque omnia sidera quae nunc diversos agunt cursus in Cancrum convenerint, sic sub eodem posita vestigia ut recta linea exire per orbes omnium possit; inundationem futuram, cum eadem siderum turba in Capricornum convenerit.* Hence early Stoics will have had precedents for the doctrine that Nemesius reports, though a cosmic flood has no recorded place in their thinking. For further details, cf. Mansfeld [496], 146–7 n. 51; Long [497], 18–19.

6   **ἀπαραλλάκτως**   This and related words seem to begin their life in Stoic/Academic debates concerning the possibility of two particulars existing which are indistinguishable from one another by their intrinsic properties; cf. **40E; 70A 8.** Since the Stoics denied that the same ἰδίως ποιόν can occur in two distinct particulars (see **28P**), for them the occurrence of something ἀπαράλλακτον should imply the recurrence of the same particular. (This implication, however, appears to be abandoned in the revisionary doctrine of **G 1**.)

12–13 **τοὺς–φθορᾳ** I.e. Zeus or god the active principle, as distinct from the perishable elements that the Stoics identified with other deities; cf. Plutarch, *Comm. not.* 1075A–E, and note on **70B** 14–15.

D Eusebius, *Pr. ev.* 15.19.1–2 (*SVF* 2.599, part)

(1) ἐπὶ τοσοῦτον δὲ προελθὼν ὁ κοινὸς λόγος καὶ ⟨ἡ⟩ κοινὴ φύσις μείζων καὶ πλείων γενομένη, τέλος ἀναξηράνασα πάντα καὶ εἰς ἑαυτὴν ἀναλαβοῦσα ἐν τῇ πάσῃ οὐσίᾳ γίνεται, (2) ἐπανελθοῦσα εἰς τὸν πρῶτον ῥηθέντα λόγον καὶ εἰς τὴν ἀνάστασιν ἐκείνην τὴν ποιοῦσαν ἐνιαυτὸν τὸν μέγιστον, καθ' ὃν ἀπ' αὐτῆς μόνης εἰς αὐτὴν πάλιν γίνεται ἡ ἀποκατάστασις. (3)   5
ἐπανελθοῦσα δὲ διὰ τάξιν, ἀφ' οἵας διακοσμεῖν ὡσαύτως ἤρξατο, κατὰ λόγον πάλιν τὴν αὐτὴν διεξαγωγὴν ποιεῖται, τῶν τοιούτων περιόδων ἐξ ἀιδίου γινομένων ἀκαταπαύστως. οὔτε γὰρ τῆς αἰτίας ἀρχὴν κἀπόπαυσιν οἷόν τε γίνεσθαι οὔτε τοῦ διοικοῦντος αὐτά.

1 ⟨ἡ⟩ Diels

Context: report of Stoic views on everlasting recurrence, placed shortly after **46K**.

1–3   Cf. **46E–H.** We translate καί, 1, by 'or' not 'and', to indicate that κοινὸς λόγος and κοινὴ φύσις are two descriptions of the same thing – god the active principle of the universe. For this use of κοινός, cf. **60A** 2, 5.

3 **ῥηθέντα** The term seems to mean 'so-called', but πρῶτος λόγος is not a Stoic expression; perhaps it is Eusebius', or his source's, way of referring to σπερματικὸς λόγος.

4 **ἀνάστασιν** This is the standard term in Christian writers for the resurrection; cf. Long [497], 35 n. 72. **ἐνιαυτὸν τὸν μέγιστον** Diogenes of Babylon computed its length at 365 × 18,000 solar years (*SVF* 3 Diogenes 28). For the background to such computations, cf. van der Waerden [515].

Stoic physics

E Simplicius, *In Ar. Phys.* 886,12–16 (*SVF* 2.627, part)

λέγοντες γὰρ ἐκεῖνοι τὸν αὐτὸν ἐμὲ πάλιν γίνεσθαι ἐν τῇ παλιγγενεσίᾳ ζητοῦσιν εἰκότως πότερον εἷς εἰμι τῷ ἀριθμῷ ὁ νῦν καὶ τότε, διὰ τὸ τῇ οὐσίᾳ εἶναι ὁ αὐτός, ἢ τῇ κατατάξει τῇ εἰς ἄλλην καὶ ἄλλην κοσμοποιίαν διαφοροῦμαι.

Context: commentary on Aristotle, *Physics* v. 4, 228a3–6. Aristotle is raising a question about the identity of the change that Socrates would undergo if he were subject to the specifically (τῷ εἴδει) same change at different times: if a later occurrence can be numerically identical to an earlier one, he argues, the change itself would be μία; if not, the change would be ἡ αὐτὴ μέν, μία δ' οὔ.

F Alexander, *In Ar. An. pr.* 180,33–6 and 181,25–31 (*SVF* 2.624, part)

(1) ἀρέσκει γὰρ αὐτοῖς τὸ μετὰ τὴν ἐκπύρωσιν πάλιν πάντα ταὐτὰ ἐν τῷ κόσμῳ γίνεσθαι κατ' ἀριθμόν, ὡς καὶ τὸν ἰδίως ποιὸν πάλιν τὸν αὐτὸν τῷ πρόσθεν εἶναί τε καὶ γίνεσθαι ἐν ἐκείνῳ τῷ κόσμῳ, ὡς ἐν τοῖς Περὶ κόσμου Χρύσιππος λέγει . . . (2) καὶ λέγουσι δὲ καὶ τοῖς ἰδίως ποιοῖς τοῖς ὕστερον γινομένοις πρὸς τοὺς πρόσθεν παραλλαγὰς μόνον γίνεσθαι κατά τινα τῶν 5
ἔξωθεν συμβεβηκότων, οἷαι παραλλαγαὶ καὶ ἐπὶ τοῦ αὐτοῦ μένοντός τε καὶ ζῶντος Δίωνος οὐκ ἀλλάσσουσιν αὐτόν. (3) οὐ γὰρ ἄλλος γίνεται εἰ πρότερον ἔχων ἐπὶ τῆς ὄψεως φακοὺς ὕστερον μηκέτ' ἔχοι· τοιαύτας δέ φασι τὰς ἐν τοῖς ἰδίως ποιοῖς τοῖς ἐν ἄλλῳ κόσμῳ παρὰ τοὺς ἐν ἄλλῳ γίνεσθαι. 10

Context: about 3 pages after **38F**. Alexander is continuing his refutation of Chrysippus' claim that 'nothing prevents something impossible following even from something possible'. According to Chrysippus, the proposition 'this one is dead' is impossible with reference to Dion, when Dion is dead, but it follows from the proposition 'Dion is dead'. Alexander replies that 'this one is dead' will not be impossible for Chrysippus, if it means 'this man's soul and body have been separated' (Chrysippus' definition of death, cf. **45D**); for in the Stoic doctrine of recurrence, the recurrence of Dion just is the recombination of the soul and body of 'this man'.

5–6 **παραλλαγαί** See note on C 16, where no discernibility however slight is admitted, in agreement with Origen, *Cels.* 4.12 (*SVF* 2.628): ταυτότητας καὶ ἀπαραλλάκτους τοῖς ἰδίως ποιοῖς καὶ τοῖς συμβεβηκόσιν αὐτοῖς ⟨κόσμους⟩.

G Origen, *Cels.* 4.68 and 5.20 (*SVF* 2.626, part)

(1) πειρώμενοι μέντοι θεραπεύειν πως τὰς ἀπεμφάσεις οἱ ἀπὸ τῆς Στοᾶς οὐκ οἶδ' ὅπως ἀπαραλλάκτους φασὶν ἔσεσθαι κατὰ περίοδον τοῖς ἀπὸ τῶν προτέρων περιόδων πάντας, ἵνα μὴ Σωκράτης πάλιν γένηται, ἀλλ' ἀπαράλλακτός τις τῷ Σωκράτει, γαμήσων ἀπαράλλακτον τῇ Ξανθίππῃ, καὶ κατηγορηθησόμενος ὑπὸ ἀπαραλλάκτων Ἀνύτῳ καὶ Μελήτῳ. οὐκ 5
οἶδα δὲ πῶς ὁ μὲν κόσμος ἀεὶ ὁ αὐτός ἐστι καὶ οὐκ ἀπαράλλακτος ἕτερος

308

ἑτέρῳ· τὰ δ' ἐν αὐτῷ οὐ τὰ αὐτά, ἀλλ' ἀπαράλλακτα . . . (2) ὅσοι δ' αὐτῶν ἠδέσθησαν τὸ δόγμα, ὀλίγην εἰρήκασι παραλλαγὴν καὶ σφόδρα βραχεῖαν γίνεσθαι κατὰ περίοδον τοῖς ἐπὶ τῆς πρὸ αὐτῆς περιόδου.

4 τῇ Ξανθίππῃ Delarue: τὴν Ξανθίππην codd.: τινα Ξανθίππῃ Gundermann, Arnim

Context: Origen contrasts Celsus' doctrine of a fixed and everlasting cycle of mortals with the Stoic theory which also includes immortals.

3–5   Barnes [513], 10, assimilates this account of what recurs to that of **F 2**, but we take **G** to deny numerical identity, which is postulated in **F 1**.

H Marcus Aurelius 2.14

(1) κἂν τρισχίλια ἔτη βιώσεσθαι μέλλῃς καὶ τοσαυτάκις μύρια, ὅμως μέμνησο ὅτι οὐδεὶς ἄλλον ἀποβάλλει βίον ἢ τοῦτον ὃν ζῇ, οὐδὲ ἄλλον ζῇ ἢ ὃν ἀποβάλλει. εἰς ταὐτὸν οὖν καθίσταται τὸ μήκιστον τῷ βραχυτάτῳ. τὸ γὰρ παρὸν πᾶσιν ἴσον, καὶ τὸ ἀπολλύμενον οὖν ἴσον· καὶ τὸ ἀποβαλλόμενον οὕτως ἀκαριαῖον ἀναφαίνεται. οὔτε γὰρ τὸ παρῳχηκὸς οὔτε τὸ μέλλον   5
ἀποβάλλοι ἄν τις. ὃ γὰρ οὐκ ἔχει, πῶς ἄν τις τοῦτο αὐτοῦ ἀφέλοιτο; (2) τούτων οὖν τῶν δύο ἀεὶ μεμνῆσθαι· ἑνὸς μέν, ὅτι πάντα ἐξ ἀιδίου ὁμοειδῆ καὶ ἀνακυκλούμενα καὶ οὐδὲν διαφέρει πότερον ἐν ἑκατὸν ἔτεσιν ἢ ἐν διακοσίοις ἢ ἐν τῷ ἀπείρῳ χρόνῳ τὰ αὐτά τις ὄψεται· ἑτέρου δέ, ὅτι καὶ ὁ πολυχρονιώτατος καὶ ὁ τάχιστα τεθνηξόμενος τὸ ἴσον ἀποβάλλει. τὸ γὰρ   10
παρόν ἐστι μόνον οὗ στερίσκεσθαι μέλλει, εἴπερ γε ἔχει καὶ τοῦτο μόνον, καὶ ὃ μὴ ἔχει τις οὐκ ἀποβάλλει.

7 ἀεὶ Farquharson: δεῖ P: ἂν AD

On this passage, and on Marcus Aurelius 11.1–2, with which it should be compared, cf. Long [497], 30–1.

i Simplicius, In Ar. Phys. 732,26–733,1

ὁ δὲ αὐτὸς χρόνος πότερον γίνεται ὥσπερ ἔνιοί φασιν ἢ οὔ, ἀπορήσειεν ἄν τις. πλεοναχῶς δὴ λεγομένου τοῦ ταὐτοῦ τῷ μὲν εἴδει φαίνεται γίνεσθαι τὸ αὐτὸ οἷον θέρος καὶ χειμὼν καὶ αἱ λοιπαὶ ὧραί τε καὶ περίοδοι, ὁμοίως δὲ καὶ αἱ κινήσεις αἱ αὐταὶ γίνονται τῷ εἴδει, τροπὰς γὰρ καὶ ἰσημερίας καὶ τὰς λοιπὰς πορείας ὁ ἥλιος ἀποτελεῖ. εἰ δέ τις πιστεύσειε τοῖς Πυθαγορείοις, ὥστε πάλιν τὰ αὐτὰ ἀριθμῷ, κἀγὼ μυθολογήσω τὸ ῥαβδίον ἔχων ὑμῖν   5
καθημένοις οὕτω, καὶ τὰ ἄλλα πάντα ὁμοίως ἕξει, καὶ τὸν χρόνον εὔλογόν ἐστι τὸν αὐτὸν εἶναι. μιᾶς γὰρ καὶ τῆς αὐτῆς κινήσεως, ὁμοίως δὲ καὶ πολλῶν τῶν αὐτῶν τὸ πρότερον καὶ ὕστερον ἓν καὶ ταὐτόν, καὶ ὁ τούτων δὴ ἀριθμός· πάντα ἄρα τὰ αὐτά, ὥστε καὶ ὁ χρόνος.

Context: quotation from the Aristotelian Eudemus.

6   Sorabji [22], 183–4, is probably right to take Eudemus to be drawing his own inference that the time will be the same, and using that inference as a reductio ad absurdum of the Pythagorean theory. Our suggestion is that the inference suited Chrysippus very well.

53 Soul

A Origen, *Princ.* 3.1.2–3 (*SVF* 2.988, part)

(1) τῶν κινουμένων τὰ μέν τινα ἐν ἑαυτοῖς ἔχει τὴν τῆς κινήσεως αἰτίαν, ἕτερα δὲ ἔξωθεν μόνον κινεῖται. (2) ἔξωθεν μὲν οὖν μόνον κινεῖται τὰ φορητά, οἷον ξύλα καὶ λίθοι καὶ πᾶσα ἡ ὑπὸ ἕξεως·μόνης συνεχομένη ὕλη . . . (3) ἐν ἑαυτοῖς δὲ ἔχει τὴν αἰτίαν τοῦ κινεῖσθαι ζῷα καὶ φυτὰ καὶ ἁπαξαπλῶς ὅσα ὑπὸ φύσεως ἢ ψυχῆς συνέχεται, ἐξ ὧν φασιν εἶναι καὶ τὰ   5 μέταλλα. πρὸς δὲ τούτοις καὶ τὸ πῦρ αὐτοκίνητόν ἐστι, τάχα δὲ καὶ αἱ πηγαί. (4) τῶν δὲ ἐν ἑαυτοῖς τὴν αἰτίαν τοῦ κινεῖσθαι ἐχόντων τὰ μέν φασιν ἐξ ἑαυτῶν κινεῖσθαι, τὰ δὲ ἀφ᾽ ἑαυτῶν· ἐξ ἑαυτῶν μὲν τὰ ἄψυχα, ἀφ᾽ ἑαυτῶν δὲ τὰ ἔμψυχα. καὶ ἀφ᾽ ἑαυτῶν κινεῖται τὰ ἔμψυχα φαντασίας ἐγγινομένης ὁρμὴν προκαλουμένης . . . (5) τὸ μέντοι λογικὸν ζῷον καὶ λόγον ἔχει πρὸς τῇ   10 φανταστικῇ φύσει τὸν κρίνοντα τὰς φαντασίας, καὶ τινὰς μὲν ἀποδοκιμάζοντα, τινὰς δὲ παραδεχόμενον, ἵνα ἄγηται τὸ ζῷον κατ᾽ αὐτάς.

2 μὲν om. Arnim silenter   9 καὶ ἀφ᾽ ἑαυτῶν codd.: ἀφ᾽ ἑαυτῶν γὰρ Arnim silenter

Context: the freedom of the will. For similar uses of Stoicism by Origen, cf. *SVF* 2.989–90, and **47O–Q** for the threefold system of classification by means of ἕξις, φύσις, ψυχή. For detailed discussion, see Inwood [547], 21–6.

7–9 **ἐξ ἑαυτῶν, ἀφ᾽ ἑαυτῶν** In Simplicius' report of these peculiarly Stoic terms, *SVF* 2.499, the second is related, as in Origen, to ἀφ᾽ ὁρμῆς ποιεῖν, but the former is illustrated by a knife's power to cut, ἐκ τῆς οἰκείας κατασκευῆς (κατὰ γὰρ τὸ σχῆμα καὶ τὸ εἶδος ἡ ποίησις ἐπιτελεῖται). Simplicius applies a third term δι᾽ ἑαυτοῦ to the movement of plants; but Origen, in another report, says that δι᾽ αὐτῶν (*SVF* 2, p. 289, 4) is the term that *he thinks* describes the movement of rational animals. Inwood [547], 23–4, gives good reason for thinking that Simplicius' account, in its divergences from Origen, is contaminated with Aristotelian and Neoplatonic adaptations. But some uncertainty persists concerning Stoic application of the term δι᾽ (ἑ)αυτῶν; the preposition διά, at this date, does not seem as strong a word for conveying personal agency as ἀπό.

10–12 **λόγον . . . παραδεχόμενον** Origen may be taken to subsume the faculty of assent under his account of λόγος; cf. **S**.

B Hierocles, 1.5–33, 4.38–53

(1) τὸ τοίνον σπέρμ[α] καταπεσὸν εἰς ὑστέρα[ν] ἔ[ν] τε και|ρῶι τῶι προσήκοντι καὶ ἅμ[α ὑπ᾽] ἐ[ρ]ρωμένου τοῦ ἀγγείου σ[υλ]ληφθὲ[ν] | οὐκέτι ἤρεμεῖ, καθά[πε]ρ τέως, ἀλλ᾽ ἀνακινηθὲν ἄρ|χ[ε]ται τῶν ἰδίων [ἔ]|ργων, περί τε [τοῦ] κυοφοροῦντος σώμα[τος] ἐπι|σπώμενον τὴν ὕλην δια[πλάτ]-τει τὸ ἔμβρυον κατά [τι]νας ἀ|παρα[β]άτους τάξεις, ἔωσ[πε]ρ οὗ πρὸς   5 τ[έ]λος ἀφίκη[ται] καὶ πρὸς ἀπό|τεξιν εὐτρεπὲς ἀπεργάσηιται τὸ δημιούργημα. | (2) τοῦτον μέντοι πάντα τὸν χρόνον (λέγω δὲ τὸν ἀπὸ συλλήψεως [μέχρι ἀπο]τέξε[ω]ς) διαμένει φύσι[ς], τοῦτ᾽ [ἔστι] πν[εῦ]|μα,

53 Soul

μεταβε[βλη]κὸ[ς] ἐκ [σπ]έρματ[ο]ς καὶ ὁδῶι κ[ειν]ού|μενον ἀπ᾽ ἀρχῆς εἰς
[τέ]λος· [ἤ]δη δὲ κατὰ [μὲν] τὰ πρῶτ[α τοῦ χρόνο]υ | παχύτερόν πώς ἐστι   10
πν[εῦ]μα ἡ φύσις καὶ μακ[ρὰ]ν ἀ|φεστηκυῖα ψυχῆς, κα[τ]όπιν δὲ τούτων
κάπ[ειδ]ὰν | σχεδὸν ἥκηι τῆς ἀποτ[έ]ξεως, ἀπο[λ]επτύνε[ται] . . .| διὸ δὴ
καὶ θύραζε χω[ρήσ]α[σ]α ἱκανοῦται τῶι [περι]έχοντι, | ὥστε οἷον στομω-
θε[ῖσα] πρὸς αὐτοῦ μεταβαλεῖν . . . | εἰς ψυχήν. (3) καθάπε[ρ] γὰρ τὸ ἐν
τοῖς λίθοις π[ν]εῦ|μα ταχέως ὑπὸ πλ[η]γῆς ἐκπυροῦται διὰ τὴν πρὸς   15
ταύ|την τὴν μεταβολὴν ἑτοιμότητα, τὸν αὐτὸν τρόπον | καὶ φύσις ἐμβρύου
πέπον[ος] ἤδη γεγονό[τος] οὐ | βραδύνε[ι τ]ὸ μεταβά[λλ]ειν εἰς ψυχὴν
ἐμ[πεσ]οῦ|σα τῶι [περιέ]χοντι. ταύτηι [δὲ] π[ά]ν τὸ ἐκπεσ[ὸν] ὑ|στέρας
εὐθέως ἐστὶ ζ[ῶιο]ν . . .| (4) [τοῦ]ντεῦθεν ἐ[νθ]υ[μητέο]ν [ἐστὶν ὅτι πᾶν]
ζῶιον | [τοῦ] μὴ ζώ[ι]ου δυο[ῖν] ἔ[χει διαφοράν, αἰσθή]σει | τε καὶ   20
ὁρμῆι . . . | (5) ἐπεὶ το[ίνυν ἐξ ἀμφ]οτέρ[ων ἐστὶ τὸ] ζῶιον . . . σύνθετον,
ἐκ σώ[μ]α|τος [καὶ] ψυχῆς, ἄμφω δ᾽ ἐστὶ θ[ικ]τὰ καὶ πρόσβλητα καὶ
τ.ρ | ἐρεί[σει δ]ὴ ὑπόπτωτα, ἔτ[ι δὲ] δι᾽ ὅλων κέκραται, καὶ [θά]|τερ[ον]
μέν ἐστιν αὐτῶν δύναμ[ις αἰ]σθητική, τὸ δ᾽ αὐτ[ὸ] | τοῦτο καὶ τρόπον, ὃν
[ὑ]πεδείξ[αμεν, κ]εινεῖται, δῆλον ὅτι δ[ι]|ανεκῶς αἰσθάνοιτ᾽ ἂν [τὸ ζῶιον]   25
ἑαυτοῦ. (6) τεινομένη γὰρ ἔ[ξω ἡ ψυχ[ὴ μετ᾽] ἀφέσεως [προσβάλ]λει πᾶσι
τοῦ σώματος τοῖς | μέρεσιν, ἐ[πε]ιδὴ καὶ κέκραται πᾶσι, προσβάλλου|σα
δὲ ἀν[τι]προσ[βάλλ]εται. (7) ἀντιβατικὸν γὰρ καὶ τὸ σῶμα, | [κ]αθάπ[ερ]
καὶ [ἡ] ψυχή· καὶ τὸ πάθος συνερειστικ[ὸν] | ὁμοῦ καὶ ἀντερειστικὸν
ἀποτελεῖται. (8) κ[αὶ ἀπὸ τῶν ἀκροτά]|των μερῶν εἴσω νε[ῦο]ν ἐπὶ τὴν   30
ἡγεμονίαν τ.....|θους σ.. ἀναφέρ[εται], ὡς ἀντίληψιν γίνεσθαι ⟨τῶν⟩
| μερῶν [ἁ]πά[ν]των τῶν [τε τ]οῦ σώματος καὶ τῶν τῆς ψυχῆς. (9) τοῦ|τ[ο]
δέ ἐστιν [ἴ]σον τῶι τ[ὸ ζῶιον αἰ]σθά[ν]εσθαι ἑαυτοῦ.

For the text and its supplementation, cf. Arnim [572] ad loc.

Context: the beginning of Hierocles' treatise, Ἠθικὴ στοιχείωσις. In the previous
sentence, the first of the whole work, he announces his intention of beginning with an
account of the genesis of ensouled creatures, and their primary attributes. For extracts
from the passage that follows B, cf. 57C. For further details and bibliography, see
Long [520], 46–7; Inwood [575].

5 κατά–τάξεις   The terminology refers to the inviolable laws of nature; cf. 52D
6, and the descriptions of εἱμαρμένη, 55J–K.
8 φύσις   Cf. Chrysippus, cited by Plutarch, St. rep. 1052F: τὸ βρέφος ἐν τῇ
γαστρὶ φύσει τρέφεσθαι νομίζει καθάπερ φυτόν; and see Long [520], 43–4.
9–10   Cf. the similar description of god's activity in cosmogony, 46A.
10–12   This too has Chrysippus' authority; cf. Plutarch (note on 8 above): τὴν
ψυχὴν ἀραιότερον πνεῦμα τῆς φύσεως καὶ λεπτομερέστερον. After ἀπολεπτύνεται
we omit a line which is too defective to be intelligible.
13–14   Cf. Chrysippus in C 1–2 and ap. Plutarch (n. 8 above): ψυχόμενον [sc. τὸ
βρέφος] ὑπὸ τοῦ ἀέρος καὶ στομούμενον τὸ πνεῦμα μεταβάλλειν καὶ γίγνεσθαι
ζῶον. Hence he claimed justification for ψῦξις as the etymology of ψυχή, Plutarch
loc. cit.

Stoic physics

21ff. The context of these lines, which occur after an interval of several pages, is the soul's corporeal nature and its through-and-through blending (see **48**) with the body.

24 **δύναμις αἰσθητική** A way of referring to the soul, which suggests that δύναμιν (not Arnim's φύσιν) should fill the lacuna in D.L. 7.156, τὴν δὲ ψυχὴν αἰσθητικὴν ⟨ ... ⟩.

26 **τεινομένη** Cf. **47J, Q, R**.

30–1 **ἐπὶ-ἀναφέρεται** Arnim did not offer any supplement for the missing letters. Since Hierocles appears to have used ἡγεμονίαν in place of the standard ἡγεμονικόν, he may have thought it needed some expansion. We suggest, if the traces are compatible, ἡγεμονίαν τ[οῦ στή]θους 'the rulership of the chest' (cf. [φάσκειν] Χρύσιππον δ᾽ ἐν τῷ στή[θ]ει τὸ ἡγεμονικὸν [ε]ἶναι, *SVF* 3, p. 217, 20–1), and more tentatively [συν]αναφέρ[εται].

C Plutarch, *St. rep.* 1053C–D (*SVF* 2.806)

γίγνεσθαι μὲν γάρ φησι τὴν ψυχὴν ὅταν τὸ βρέφος ἀποτεχθῇ καθάπερ στομώσει τῇ περιψύξει τοῦ πνεύματος μεταβαλόντος, ἀποδείξει δὲ χρῆται τοῦ γεγονέναι τὴν ψυχὴν καὶ μεταγενεστέραν εἶναι μάλιστα τῷ καὶ τὸν τρόπον καὶ τὸ ἦθος ἐξομοιοῦσθαι τὰ τέκνα τοῖς γονεῦσι.

Context: alleged inconsistencies in Chrysippus' statements about the soul's origin.

1–2 Cf. **B** 13–14.

2–4 The 'proof' of the soul's posteriority to the body is at best implicit, and absent from other Stoic accounts of hereditary resemblances, *SVF* 1.518 and Cicero, *Tusc.* 1.79. Chrysippus' point is perhaps that the temperamental and character resemblances between parents and children cannot be referred to a pre-natal state, when the body already existed, since they presuppose a parental environment for the child. But if this is his point, it patently fails to show that *all* the soul's properties are subsequent to the generation of the body.

D Galen, *Foet.* 4.698,2–9 (*SVF* 2.761, part)

(1) οὗ τὴν πρώτην εὐθέως ὑπόθεσιν ἄγνωστον μὲν αἰσθήσει, λόγῳ δ᾽ ἀνεύρετον ὑποτίθενται τὴν καρδίαν ἁπάντων πρώτην γίγνεσθαι λέγοντες· (2) δευτέραν δ᾽ ἐπὶ τῇδε τἆλλα μόρια διαπλάττειν ἐκείνην, ὡς ἀπολυμένου τοῦ διαπλάσαντος αὐτήν, ὅστις ποτ᾽ ἐστί, καὶ μηκέτ᾽ ὄντος· (3) εἶτ᾽ ἐφεξῆς ὡς ἀκόλουθον ἐπιφέροντες ὅτι καὶ τὸ βουλευόμενον ἡμῶν μέρος τῆς ψυχῆς 5 ἐν ταύτῃ καθέστηκεν.

Galen's reference to the Stoics is secured by his attributing the first two points to Chrysippus 'and many other Stoics and Peripatetics' at *Foet.* 4,674, and by his constant criticism of the third point; cf. **65H**. Here he refers to them obliquely as 'people totally unversed in anatomical research, who go in for rash assertions'.

E Galen, *In Hipp. Ep. VI* 270,26–8 (*SVF* 2.782)

ὅσοι γὰρ οἴονται τὴν ψυχὴν εἶναι πνεῦμα διασώζεσθαι λέγουσιν αὐτὴν ἔκ

τε τῆς ἀναθυμιάσεως τοῦ αἵματος καὶ τοῦ κατὰ τὴν εἰσπνοὴν ἑλκομένου
διὰ τῆς τραχείας ἀρτηρίας εἴσω τοῦ σώματος ⟨ἀέρος⟩.

3 ⟨ἀέρος⟩ Arnim

Context: interpretation of Hippocrates' views on the soul.

2 ἀναθυμιάσεως   This term (together with πνεῦμα, 1) establishes the Stoic
provenance of Galen's generalized statement; cf. SVF 1.141, 519–20. In their use of it
the Stoics claimed to have the authority of Heraclitus; cf. Long [353], 150–2.

F Sextus Empiricus, M. 7.234

ἄλλοι δὲ ἀπὸ τῆς αὐτῆς ὁρμώμενοι δυνάμεως γλαφυρώτερον ἀπελογήσαντο. φασὶ γὰρ
ψυχὴν λέγεσθαι διχῶς, τό τε συνέχον τὴν ὅλην σύγκρισιν καὶ κατ᾽ ἰδίαν τὸ
ἡγεμονικόν. ὅταν γὰρ εἴπωμεν συνεστάναι τὸν ἄνθρωπον ἐκ ψυχῆς καὶ
σώματος, ἢ τὸν θάνατον εἶναι χωρισμὸν ψυχῆς ἀπὸ σώματος, ἰδίως
καλοῦμεν τὸ ἡγεμονικόν.   5

Context: critical survey of Stoic differences of opinion concerning φαντασία.

2 διχῶς   For the significance of the two senses of soul, in relation to the Stoic
distinction between soul and body, cf. Long [520], 44–5.

4   For the account of death, cf. **45D** 1.

5 ἡγεμονικόν   This term for the soul's 'commanding-faculty' may be Zeno's
invention, though it may also have been coined or used independently by the
Peripatetic Strato; he differed from the Stoics in locating the ἡγεμονικόν in the head,
but his insistence that all αἴσθησις takes place there, including bodily pains and
pleasures, and not in the affected regions (ps.-Plutarch fragment, pp. 43–7 Sandbach)
corresponds to the Stoic position (cf. **M**).

G Calcidius 220 (SVF 2.879, part)

(1) item Chrysippus "una et eadem" inquit "certe re spiramus et vivimus. (2)
spiramus autem naturali spiritu. (3) ergo etiam vivimus eodem spiritu. (4)
vivimus autem anima. (5) naturalis igitur spiritus anima esse invenitur." "haec
igitur" inquit "octo in partes divisa invenitur; constat enim e principali et quinque sensibus,
etiam vocali substantia et serendi procreandique potentia. (6) porro partes animae velut   5
ex capite fontis cordis sede manantes per universum corpus porriguntur,
omniaque membra usque quaque vitali spiritu complent reguntque et
moderantur innumerabilibus diversisque virtutibus, nutriendo, adolendo,
movendo motibus localibus, instruendo sensibus, compellendo ad operan-
dum, (7) totaque anima sensus, qui sunt eius officia, velut ramos ex principali   10
parte illa tamquam trabe pandit futuros eorum quae sentiunt nuntios, ipsa de
his quae nuntiaverint iudicat ut rex. (8) ea porro quae sentiuntur composita
sunt utpote corpora singulique item sensus unum quiddam sentiunt, hic
colores, sonos alius, ast ille sucorum sapores discernit, hic vapores odoraminum, ille
asperum levigationemque tactu, atque haec omnia ad praesens; neque tamen   15

Stoic physics

praeteritorum meminit sensus ullus nec suspicatur futura. (9) intimae vero deliberationis et considerationis proprium cuiusque sensus intellegere passionem et ex his quae nuntiant colligere quid sit illud, et praesens quidem accipere, absentis autem meminisse, futurum item providere." definit idem intimam mentis deliberationem sic: "intimus est motus animae vis rationabilis." 20

3 *igitur* vel *ergo* codd.   19 *absentis* vel *absens* codd.

Context: doxography of soul. Immediately following this extract, Calcidius describes the commanding-faculty of non-rational animals, and then cites Chrysippus' comparison of a rational commanding-faculty to a spider, located at the centre of its web, the threads of which, gripped by the spider's feet, correspond to the starting-points of the senses. (The image is also anachronistically attributed to Heraclitus, 22 B 67a DK.)

3 **naturalis spiritus**   Cf. the much fuller account Chrysippus gave in his Περὶ ψυχῆς, *SVF* 2.885: ἡ γὰρ ψυχὴ πνεῦμά ἐστι σύμφυτον ἡμῖν συνεχὲς παντὶ τῷ σώματι διῆκον, ἔστ᾽ ἂν ἡ τῆς ζωῆς εὔπνοια παρῇ ἐν τῷ σώματι. A medical origin for the term σύμφυτον πνεῦμα has been suspected, but Aristotle is its only known user before Stoicism; cf. Sandbach [304], 46–8.

12–15   These lines recall the Aristotelian doctrine of the 'special sensibles' of each sense; cf. also for Epicureanism, **16C**, with note. According to Aetius (*SVF* 2.852), a Stoic account of κοινὴ αἴσθησις (to cater for the Aristotelian concept?) was ἐντὸς ἁφή, καθ᾽ ἣν καὶ ἡμῶν αὐτῶν ἀντιλαμβανόμεθα; cf. Lloyd [524], 194–5.

15 **ad praesens**   Absence of a developed sense of time is something that differentiates animals from humans, Cicero, *Off.* 1.11; cf. also **T 2**.

16–17 **intimae deliberationis**   Cf. Epicurus' account of δόξα as a secondary internal process, **15A 12**. For Stoic accounts of the mind's organization of empirical data, cf. **39C–E**.

H Aetius 4.21.1–4 (*SVF* 2.836, part)

(1) οἱ Στωικοί φασιν εἶναι τῆς ψυχῆς ἀνώτατον μέρος τὸ ἡγεμονικόν, τὸ ποιοῦν τὰς φαντασίας καὶ συγκαταθέσεις καὶ αἰσθήσεις καὶ ὁρμάς· καὶ τοῦτο λογισμὸν καλοῦσιν. (2) ἀπὸ δὲ τοῦ ἡγεμονικοῦ ἑπτὰ μέρη ἐστὶ τῆς ψυχῆς ἐκπεφυκότα καὶ ἐκτεινόμενα εἰς τὸ σῶμα καθάπερ αἱ ἀπὸ τοῦ πολύποδος πλεκτάναι. (3) τῶν δὲ ἑπτὰ μερῶν τῆς ψυχῆς πέντε μέν εἰσι τὰ 5 αἰσθητήρια, ὅρασις ὄσφρησις ἀκοὴ γεῦσις καὶ ἁφή. ὧν ἡ μὲν ὅρασις ἐστι πνεῦμα διατεῖνον ἀπὸ ἡγεμονικοῦ μέχρις ὀφθαλμῶν, ἀκοὴ δὲ πνεῦμα διατεῖνον ἀπὸ τοῦ ἡγεμονικοῦ μέχρις ὤτων . . . (4) τῶν δὲ λοιπῶν τὸ μὲν λέγεται σπέρμα, ὅπερ καὶ αὐτὸ πνεῦμά ἐστι διατεῖνον ἀπὸ τοῦ ἡγεμονικοῦ μέχρι τῶν παραστατῶν. (5) τὸ δὲ "φωναεν" ὑπὸ τοῦ Ζήνωνος εἰρημένον, ὃ καὶ 10 φωνὴν καλοῦσιν, ἔστι πνεῦμα διατεῖνον ἀπὸ τοῦ ἡγεμονικοῦ μέχρι φάρυγγος καὶ γλώττης καὶ τῶν οἰκείων ὀργάνων. αὐτὸ δὲ τὸ ἡγεμονικὸν ὥσπερ ἐν κόσμῳ κατοικεῖ ἐν τῇ ἡμετέρᾳ σφαιροειδεῖ κεφαλῇ.

2 καί¹ A: καὶ τὰς BC   13 κόσμῳ ⟨ἥλιος⟩ Diels

Context: doxography of Stoic psychology.

314

2 **αἰσθήσεις** Not normally listed as a specific faculty of the ἡγεμονικόν; cf. **K 2,** **P.** Placed here between συγκαταθέσεις and ὁρμάς, αἰσθήσεις should be interpreted in the strong cognitive sense explained in **40Q.**
4 **ἐκπεφυκότα** The term is used by Alexander, *De an.* 94,30, for the veins' 'outgrowth' from the heart. His discussion throughout *De an.* 94–100 illustrates the dissemination of Stoic psychology.
13 **κεφαλῇ** Not Chrysippus' doctrine (cf. **65H**) but that of some unnamed Stoics; cf. *SVF* 3 Diogenes 33.

I Nemesius 212,6–9 (Panaetius fr. 86)

Παναίτιος δὲ ὁ φιλόσοφος τὸ μὲν φωνητικὸν τῆς καθ᾽ ὁρμὴν κινήσεως μέρος εἶναι βούλεται, λέγων ὀρθότατα· τὸ δὲ σπερματικὸν οὐ τῆς ψυχῆς μέρος ἀλλὰ τῆς φύσεως.

Nemesius says this after reporting Zeno's doctrines of an eight-part soul. Panaetius probably subsumed the vocal faculty under ὁρμή in order to avoid any suggestion that it is only an instrumental part of the soul; cf. Rist [303], 180–1; Long [520], 48. His allocation of reproduction to φύσις looks like an Aristotelian move in the opposite direction, downgrading this faculty to the level of involuntary nutrition; cf. Nemesius 249–50 = Panaetius fr. 86a.

J Cicero, *Off.* 1.132 (Panaetius fr. 88)

motus autem animorum duplices sunt: alteri cogitationis, alteri appetitus. cogitatio in vero exquirendo maxime versatur, appetitus impellit ad agendum. curandum est igitur ut cogitatione ad res quam optimas utamur, appetitum rationi oboedientem praebeamus.

Context: discussion of *decorum*.

Together with Cicero, *Off.* 1.101 (Panaetius fr. 87), this passage is regularly treated as evidence for Panaetius' psychology; it is also frequently interpreted (cf. Rist [303], 182–4) as a deviation from Chrysippus' rational monism in favour of Aristotelian bipartition of the soul (e.g. *EN* 1.13, 1102b16–1103a3) into rationality and the irrational appetitive faculty which can obey or disobey reason. What recalls Aristotle, however, is not so much the notion of 'making impulse obedient to reason' – Chrysippus himself explains ἄλογος or 'excessive impulse' as 'disobedient to reason', **65J** – as the implied division between theoretical and practical activity; and this too is standard Stoicism; cf. D.L. 7.130, γεγονέναι . . . ὑπὸ τῆς φύσεως ἐπίτηδες τὸ λογικὸν ζῷον πρὸς θεωρίαν καὶ πρᾶξιν; also **61D 2.**

K Iamblichus, *De anima* (Stobaeus 1.368,12–20; *SVF* 2.826, part)

(1) πῶς οὖν διακρίνονται; κατὰ μὲν τοὺς Στωικοὺς ἔνιαι μὲν διαφορότητι ⟨τῶν⟩ ὑποκειμένων σωμάτων· πνεύματα γὰρ ἀπὸ τοῦ ἡγεμονικοῦ φασιν οὗτοι διατείνειν ἄλλα καὶ ἄλλα, τὰ μὲν εἰς ὀφθαλμούς, τὰ δὲ εἰς ὦτα, τὰ δὲ εἰς ἄλλα αἰσθητήρια. (2) ἔνιαι δὲ ἰδιότητι ποιότητος περὶ τὸ αὐτὸ

315

Stoic physics

ὑποκείμενον· ὥσπερ γὰρ τὸ μῆλον ἐν τῷ αὐτῷ σώματι τὴν γλυκύτητα ἔχει 5
καὶ τὴν εὐωδίαν, οὕτω καὶ τὸ ἡγεμονικὸν ἐν ταὐτῷ φαντασίαν, συγκατάθεσιν, ὁρμήν, λόγον συνείληφε.

2 ⟨τῶν⟩ Heeren   3 καὶ codd.: κατ᾽ Meineke, Wachsmuth

Context: doxography of soul; cf. **28F** for an earlier extract, which discusses the
ontology of lines 4–7. For detailed discussion, cf. Inwood [547], 30–41, who amply
vindicates the reliability of Iamblichus' evidence.

1 **διακρίνονται** Supply αἱ δυνάμεις τῆς ψυχῆς.

6–7 On the puzzling inclusion of λόγος in the list of faculties, cf. Long [520], 49–
50, and contrast λογισμός (**H** 3) as the name of the entire ἡγεμονικόν.

L Seneca, *Ep.* 113.23 (*SVF* 2.836, part)

inter Cleanthen et discipulum eius Chrysippum non convenit quid sit
ambulatio. Cleanthes ait spiritum esse a principali usque in pedes permissum,
Chrysippus ipsum principale.

Context: exposition of the doctrine that the virtues are 'living beings' (cf. **61E**). Seneca
has been elucidating 'assent': 'I walk', he says, 'immediately following my saying that
I should walk and *approving* this judgement of mine' (*Ep.* 113.18). But Seneca is out of
line with Chrysippean psychology in treating the 'impulse to walk' as prior, in the
causal sequence, to assent, and thus as something to be approved or disapproved; cf.
Inwood [547], 176, 282 n. 193. In Chrysippus' doctrine, the impulse is a component of
the assent, a decision issuing in action; see **33I**. His disagreement with Cleanthes is
difficult to elucidate, but probably relates to a wish to avoid any suggestion that
purposive bodily movements are even locally separable from the mind's activity. In
Cleanthes' account, walking is a mind-directed pneumatic movement *in* the legs;
Chrysippus' claim – walking simply is the mind at work – implies that the legs'
movements are not the outcome of an anterior decision, but are actually identical with
the mind's assent and impulse to walk. For further discussion, cf. Rist [303], 33–4;
Inwood [547], 50–1.

M Aetius 4.23.1 (*SVF* 2.854)

οἱ Στωικοὶ τὰ μὲν πάθη ἐν τοῖς πεπονθόσι τόποις, τὰς δὲ αἰσθήσεις ἐν τῷ
ἡγεμονικῷ.

Context: doxography περὶ παθῶν σωματικῶν εἰ συναλγεῖ τούτοις ἡ ψυχή.

The terms πάθη and αἰσθήσεις are not used here in any technical Stoic sense. As the
context explains, πάθος refers to bodily states or changes (e.g. damage to a finger) and
αἴσθησις to the corresponding sensations. The Stoic doctrine agrees with that of
Strato, whose view, as described by ps.-Plutarch (cf. note on **F** 5), uses αἴσθησις in the
same sense as here, a usage which fits the otherwise misleading attribution to the Stoics
of the proposition that all αἰσθήσεις are true, *SVF* 2.78 (cf. **40Q**). For a full account of
the Stoic concept of διάδοσις – the transmission of a bodily affection to the
ἡγεμονικόν which feels the affection – see Plotinus, *Enn.* 4.7.7; and for συμπάθεια of
body and soul, cf. **B** 4–8; **45C**.

N Diogenes Laertius 7.157 (*SVF* 2.867)

ὁρᾶν δὲ τοῦ μεταξὺ τῆς ὁράσεως καὶ τοῦ ὑποκειμένου φωτὸς ἐντεινομένου κωνοειδῶς, καθά φησι Χρύσιππος ἐν δευτέρῳ τῶν Φυσικῶν καὶ Ἀπολλόδωρος. γίνεσθαι μὲν τὸ κωνοειδὲς τοῦ ἀέρος πρὸς τῇ ὄψει, τὴν δὲ βάσιν πρὸς τῷ ὁρωμένῳ. ὡς διὰ βακτηρίας οὖν τοῦ ταθέντος ἀέρος τὸ βλεπόμενον ἀναγγέλλεσθαι.   5

3 μὲν BP: μέντοι FP(corr.)

Context: doxography of Stoic psychology.

  1 **ὁράσεως** The soul's visual faculty is meant, consisting of πνεῦμα stretching from the ἡγεμονικόν to the eye; cf. **H** 6–7. By its contact with the illuminated air outside, it makes this into a cone-shaped visual medium, the technical name for which is συνέντασις; cf. *SVF* 2.863–6.

  4 **βακτηρίας** Explained by Alexander, *SVF* 2.864, as a way of signifying the 'contact' the imprinted air establishes between the visual object and the percipient.

  5 **ἀναγγέλλεσθαι** For the senses as reporters to the mind; cf. **G** 7; **70A** 7.

O Nemesius 291,1–8 (*SVF* 2.991, part)

ἑκάστῳ γὰρ τῶν γενομένων δεδόσθαι τι καθ' εἱμαρμένην, ὡς τῷ ὕδατι τὸ ψύχειν, καὶ ἑκάστῳ τῶν φυτῶν τὸ τοιόνδε καρπὸν φέρειν, καὶ τῷ λίθῳ τὸ κατωφερές, καὶ τῷ πυρὶ τὸ ἀνωφερές, οὕτω καὶ τῷ ζῴῳ τὸ συγκατατίθεσθαι καὶ ὁρμᾶν· ὅταν δὲ ταύτῃ τῇ ὁρμῇ μηδὲν ἀντιπέσῃ τῶν ἔξωθεν καὶ καθ' εἱμαρμένην, τότε τὸ περιπατεῖν τέλεον ἐφ' ἡμῖν εἶναι, καὶ πάντως περιπατήσομεν.   5

Context: Stoic reconciliation of human autonomy and fate (cf. 4–5), attributed to Chrysippus, Philopator, and 'many other distinguished men'.

  Animals in general are similarly credited with assent by Alexander, *Fat.* 182,16–183,24 (including **62G 6**), and by the Antiochean Stoic Lucullus at **40O 3**. Texts which seem to restrict assent to rational animals include **A 5**, **P 1**; **62K**. For discussion, cf. Long [520], 50; Sharples [333], 144–5; and especially Inwood [547], 70–91, who argues that Nemesius and Alexander misrepresent Stoicism by amalgamating what the Stoics called εἴκειν, 'an automatic response' to impressions (cf. **S** and **39A 5**), with assent; the Stoics, Inwood maintains, may have attributed the former, but not the latter, to animals and young children. This is a promising suggestion. But however the evidence is interpreted, it seems best to hold on to the notion that rational assent has a rudimentary non-rational counterpart in animal behaviour.

P Philo, *Leg. alleg.* 1.30 (*SVF* 2.844)

(1) τὸ γὰρ ζῷον τοῦ μὴ ζῴου δυσὶ προὔχει, φαντασίᾳ καὶ ὁρμῇ. (2) ἡ μὲν οὖν φαντασία συνίσταται κατὰ τὴν τοῦ ἐκτὸς πρόσοδον τυποῦντος νοῦν δι' αἰσθήσεως. (3) ἡ δὲ ὁρμή, τὸ ἀδελφὸν τῆς φαντασίας, κατὰ τὴν τοῦ νοῦ τονικὴν δύναμιν, ἣν τείνας δι' αἰσθήσεως ἅπτεται τοῦ ὑποκειμένου καὶ πρὸς αὐτὸ χωρεῖ γλιχόμενος ἐφικέσθαι καὶ συλλαβεῖν αὐτό.   5

Context: how mental faculties are related to each other. Philo's terminology, though

Stoic physics

always eclectic, is so distinctively Stoic here (cf. τονικήν, 4) that the passage can be
treated as good evidence for orthodox Stoicism; cf. Inwood [547], 31.

4 αἰσθήσεως The term refers here to the activity of the senses (cf. the last usage
cited in **40Q**) and not to cognition of perceptible objects.

Q Stobaeus 2.86,17–87,6 (*SVF* 3.169, part)

(1) τὸ δὲ κινοῦν τὴν ὁρμὴν οὐδὲν ἕτερον εἶναι λέγουσιν ἀλλ' ἢ φαντασίαν
ὁρμητικὴν τοῦ καθήκοντος αὐτόθεν. (2) τὴν δὲ ὁρμὴν εἶναι φορὰν ψυχῆς
ἐπί τι κατὰ τὸ γένος. (3) ταύτης δ' ἐν εἴδει θεωρεῖσθαι τήν τε ἐν τοῖς
λογικοῖς γιγνομένην ὁρμὴν καὶ τὴν ἐν τοῖς ἀλόγοις ζῴοις· οὐ κατωνομασ-
μέναι δ' εἰσίν. ἡ γὰρ ὄρεξις οὐκ ἔστι λογικὴ ὁρμή, ἀλλὰ λογικῆς ὁρμῆς   5
εἶδος. (4) τὴν δὲ λογικὴν ὁρμὴν δεόντως ἄν τις ἀφορίζοιτο λέγων εἶναι
φορὰν διανοίας ἐπί τι τῶν ἐν τῷ πράττειν· ταύτῃ δ' ἀντιτίθεσθαι ἀφορμήν.

1 ἀλλ' ἢ Meurer: ἀλλὰ codd.   3 ἐν εἴδει Hirzel: ἔνι ἀεὶ F: ἄγι ἀεὶ (om. ταύτης) P   4
κατωνομασμένα codd.: corr. Heeren   6 ἄν τις ἀφορίζοιτο Salmasius: ἀνταφορίζοιτο codd.   7
ἀντίθεσθαι codd.: corr. Heeren

Context: doxography of Stoic ὁρμή. The passage and its sequel are discussed in
illuminating detail by Inwood [547], 55–6, 224–42.

1–2   See note on **59E**. Inwood [547], 224, takes αὐτόθεν with καθήκοντος, but it
seems better to regard it as modifying ὁρμητικήν: the impression 'then and there' has
the power to activate a proper function, i.e. its mere appearance is sufficient to warrant
assent and impulse.

4–5   The ὁρμή of rational animals differs from that of the non-rational, but the
same term ὁρμή applies to them both. ὄρεξις is not the generic name for 'rational
impulse', but a specific type of such impulse; cf. note on **56C**, and Inwood [547],
227ff.

R Plutarch, *St. rep.* 1037F (*SVF* 3.175, part)

καὶ μὴν ἡ ὁρμὴ κατά γ' αὐτὸν τοῦ ἀνθρώπου λόγος ἐστὶ προστακτικὸς
αὐτῷ τοῦ ποιεῖν, ὡς ἐν τῷ Περὶ νόμου γέγραφεν. οὐκοῦν καὶ ἡ ἀφορμὴ
λόγος ἀπαγορευτικός.

Context: supposed inconsistencies in Chrysippus' accounts of law.

As an imperative (προστακτικός, cf. D.L. 7.67), ὁρμή manifests itself in a type of
lekton; cf. note on **33I**, and see the very full treatment by Inwood [547], 46–7, 61–6,
92–5, 160.

S Plutarch, *St. rep.* 1057A (*SVF* 3.177, part)

καὶ μὴν ἔν γε τοῖς πρὸς τοὺς Ἀκαδημαικοὺς ἀγῶσιν ὁ πλεῖστος λόγος
αὐτῷ τε Χρυσίππῳ καὶ Ἀντιπάτρῳ περὶ τίνος γέγονε; περὶ τοῦ μήτε
πράττειν μήθ' ὁρμᾶν ἀσυγκαταθέτως, ἀλλὰ πλάσματα λέγειν καὶ κενὰς

318

ὑποθέσεις τοὺς ἀξιοῦντας οἰκείας φαντασίας γενομένης εὐθὺς ὁρμᾶν μὴ
εἴξαντας μηδὲ συγκαταθεμένους.　　　　　　　　　　　　　　　　　5

1 λόγος X³g: om. cett.　　2 περὶ τίνος X³g: τίνος vel τόνος cett.: πόνος Stephanus: ὁ πλεῖστος
[λόγος] . . . πόνος περὶ τίνος Pohlenz

Context: alleged inconsistencies in the Stoic doctrine of fate. This extract is
immediately followed by 41F.
　　For the Stoics' arguments with the Academics on this issue, cf. vol. 1, 455–7. The
Stoic challenge here is a direct rejoinder to Arcesilaus in 69A 5.

T Sextus Empiricus, M. 8.275–6 (SVF 2.223, part)

(1) φασὶν ὅτι ἄνθρωπος οὐχὶ τῷ προφορικῷ λόγῳ διαφέρει τῶν ἀλόγων
ζῴων (καὶ γὰρ κόρακες καὶ ψιττακοὶ καὶ κίτται ἐνάρθρους προφέρονται
φωνάς), ἀλλὰ τῷ ἐνδιαθέτῳ. (2) οὐδὲ τῇ ἁπλῇ μόνον φαντασίᾳ (ἐφαντα-
σιοῦτο γὰρ κἀκεῖνα), ἀλλὰ τῇ μεταβατικῇ καὶ συνθετικῇ. (3) διόπερ
ἀκολουθίας ἔννοιαν ἔχων εὐθὺς καὶ σημείου νόησιν λαμβάνει διὰ τὴν　　5
ἀκολουθίαν· καὶ γὰρ αὐτὸ τὸ σημεῖόν ἐστι τοιοῦτον "εἰ τόδε, τόδε". (4)
ἕπεται ἄρα τῇ φύσει καὶ κατασκευῇ τἀνθρώπου τὸ καὶ σημεῖον ὑπάρχειν.

Context: arguments for and against the existence of signs. Sextus' δογματικοί, 1, are
primarily, if not exclusively, Stoics. This identification is established by the
immediately preceding context, which discusses the Stoic doctrine of signs; cf. note on
51H.
　　Burnyeat [484], 206–8, shows that the argument crucially depends on the claim
that human nature, 7, is providentially structured (S.E., M. 8.285–6), a point which
assures its Stoic provenance; cf. 63E. However, we do not share his view ([206], n. 33)
that ἁπλῇ μόνον φαντασίᾳ, 3, means φαντασίᾳ simpliciter. Followed as it is by
συνθετικῇ, 4, ἁπλῇ must mean 'simple' as distinct from 'complex'; cf. S.E., M. 7.135,
228–9. For further discussion, cf. Long [426], 87ff.; and 95–6, on ἀκολουθία, lines 5–
6.

U Galen, Plac. 2.5.9–13 (SVF 3 Diogenes 29, part)

(1) τὸν αὐτὸν δὴ τοῦτον λόγον Διογένης οὐ κατὰ τὴν αὐτὴν ἐρωτᾷ λέξιν, ἀλλ'ὧδε· "ὅθεν
ἐκπέμπεται ἡ φωνή, καὶ ἡ ἔναρθρος, οὐκοῦν καὶ ἡ σημαίνουσα ἔναρθρος
φωνὴ ἐκεῖθεν. (2) τοῦτο δὲ λόγος. (3) καὶ λόγος ἄρα ἐκεῖθεν ἐκπέμπεται
ὅθεν καὶ ἡ φωνή. (4) ἡ δὲ φωνὴ οὐκ ἐκ τῶν κατὰ τὴν κεφαλὴν τόπων
ἐκπέμπεται ἀλλὰ φανερῶς ἐκ τῶν κάτωθεν μᾶλλον. ἐκφανὴς γοῦν ἐστι διὰ　　5
τῆς ἀρτηρίας διεξιοῦσα. (5) καὶ ὁ λόγος ἄρα οὐκ ἐκ τῆς κεφαλῆς
ἐκπέμπεται, ἀλλὰ κάτωθεν μᾶλλον. (6) ἀλλὰ μήν γε κἀκεῖνο ἀληθές, τὸ τὸν
λόγον ἐκ τῆς διανοίας ἐκπέμπεσθαι. ἔνιοι γοῦν καὶ ὁριζόμενοι αὐτόν φασιν
εἶναι φωνὴν σημαίνουσαν ἀπὸ διανοίας ἐκπεμπομένην. (7) καὶ ἄλλως δὲ
πιθανὸν ὑπὸ τῶν ἐννοιῶν ἐνσεσημασμένον τῶν ἐν τῇ διανοίᾳ καὶ οἷον　　10
ἐκτετυπωμένον ἐκπέμπεσθαι τὸν λόγον, καὶ παρεκτείνεσθαι τῷ χρόνῳ
κατά τε τὸ διανενοῆσθαι καὶ τὴν κατὰ τὸ λέγειν ἐνέργειαν. (8) καὶ ἡ διάνοια

Stoic physics

ἄρα οὐκ ἔστιν ἐν τῇ κεφαλῇ ἀλλ᾽ ἐν τοῖς κατωτέρω τόποις, μάλιστά πως περὶ τὴν καρδίαν."

5 ἐκφανὴς codd.: ἐμφανὴς Ald.

Context: various Stoic arguments for locating the mind in the heart; cf. **65H**. For the linguistic concepts invoked here, cf. **33A, C**.

V Galen, *Plac.* 5.2.49 and 5.3.1 (*SVF* 2.841, part)

"ἔστι δέ ⟨γε⟩ τῆς ψυχῆς μέρη δι᾽ ὧν ὁ ἐν αὐτῇ λόγος συνέστηκε καὶ ἡ ἐν αὐτῷ διάθεσις. καὶ ἔστι καλὴ ἢ αἰσχρὰ ψυχὴ κατὰ τὸ ἡγεμονικὸν μόριον ἔχον ⟨οὕτως⟩ ἢ οὕτως κατὰ τοὺς οἰκείους μερισμούς." . . . ἀνα-μιμνῄσκων ἴσως ἡμᾶς τῶν ἐν τοῖς Περὶ τοῦ λόγου γεγραμμένων ὧν σὺ διῆλθες, ὡς ἔστιν ἐννοιῶν τέ τινων καὶ προλήψεων ἄθροισμα.   5

1 ⟨γε⟩ Müller; cf. 5.3.1   3 ⟨οὕτως⟩ Ricci, Cornarius

Context: Galen is objecting to Chrysippus' explanation of mental health/ill-health by reference to proportion/disproportion of the 'parts' of the ἡγεμονικόν; cf. **47H**. Since the latter, says Galen, is supposed to be a single part of the soul, Chrysippus is compelled to treat its 'activities' as if they were parts, and fails anywhere to specify the nature of its οἰκεῖοι μερισμοί, 3. The answer Galen offers Chrysippus from his own writings in 4–5 is polemical. Chrysippus would probably have said that the μερισμοί of the ἡγεμονικόν are the four faculties specified in **K 2**; i.e. the soul's health depends upon a concordant relationship between these faculties, such that a person makes correct use of impressions, avoids excessive impulses, knows when to give or withhold assent, and, in general, acts in rational agreement with nature; cf. **31B**; **62K**; **63C, E**; **65J**.

5   Cf. **39E–F**.

W Eusebius, *Pr. ev.* 15.20.6 (*SVF* 2.809)

(1) τὴν δὲ ψυχὴν γενητήν τε καὶ φθαρτὴν λέγουσιν. οὐκ εὐθὺς δὲ τοῦ σώματος ἀπαλλαγεῖσαν φθείρεσθαι, ἀλλ᾽ ἐπιμένειν τινὰς χρόνους καθ᾽ ἑαυτήν, τὴν μὲν τῶν σπουδαίων μέχρι τῆς εἰς πῦρ ἀναλύσεως τῶν πάντων, τὴν δὲ τῶν ἀφρόνων πρὸς ποσούς τινας χρόνους. (2) τὸ δὲ διαμένειν τὰς ψυχὰς οὕτως λέγουσιν, ὅτι διαμένομεν ἡμεῖς ψυχαὶ γενόμενοι τοῦ   5 σώματος χωρισθέντες καὶ εἰς ἐλάττω μεταβαλόντες οὐσίαν τὴν τῆς ψυχῆς, τὰς δὲ τῶν [ἀφρόνων καὶ] ἀλόγων ζῴων ψυχὰς συναπόλλυσθαι τοῖς σώμασι.

6 χωρισθέντος codd.: corr. Diels   6 εἰς DE: οὐκ CFG   μεταβαλόντος codd.: corr. Diels   7 ἀφρόνων καὶ del. A.A. Long

Context: doxography of Stoic psychology.
    For further evidence and discussion, cf. Hoven [525]; Rist [302], 256–61.

7 **ἀφρόνων** The repetition of this word, cf. 4, not only risks ambiguity (so Hoven [525], 49 n. 5), but is utterly out of place. ἄφρων is not an attribute of non-

rational animals. The words ἀφρόνων καί, even if Eusebius wrote them, should be deleted from the text when it is treated as testimony for Stoicism.

X Diogenes Laertius 7.143 (*SVF* 2.633, part)

ἔμψυχον [sc. τὸν κόσμον] δέ, ὡς δῆλον ἐκ τῆς ἡμετέρας ψυχῆς ἐκεῖθεν οὔσης ἀποσπάσματος.

Context: doxography of Stoic cosmology.

2 ἀποσπάσματος   The biological resonance of the term is influenced by its usage in early Stoicism, where σπέρμα is described as ψυχῆς ἀπόσπασμα, *SVF* 1.128; cf. Rist [302], 264–5.

Y Cicero, *ND* 2.58 (*SVF* 1.172, part)

atque ut ceterae naturae suis seminibus quaeque gignuntur augescunt continentur, sic natura mundi omnis motus habet voluntarios, conatusque et adpetitiones, quas ὁρμάς Graeci vocant, et his consentaneas actiones sic adhibet ut nosmet ipsi qui animis movemur et sensibus.

Context: defence of Stoic theology; cf. **54B, G–H**.

54 Theology

A Diogenes Laertius 7.147 (*SVF* 2.1021)

θεὸν δ᾽ εἶναι ζῷον ἀθάνατον, λογικὸν ἢ νοερόν, τέλειον ἐν εὐδαιμονίᾳ, κακοῦ παντὸς ἀνεπίδεκτον, προνοητικὸν κόσμου τε καὶ τῶν ἐν κόσμῳ· μὴ εἶναι μέντοι ἀνθρωπόμορφον. εἶναι δὲ τὸν μὲν δημιουργὸν τῶν ὅλων καὶ ὥσπερ πατέρα πάντων κοινῶς τε καὶ τὸ μέρος αὐτοῦ τὸ διῆκον διὰ πάντων, ὃ πολλαῖς προσηγορίαις προσονομάζεται κατὰ τὰς δυνάμεις. Δία   5 μὲν γάρ φασι δι᾽ ὃν τὰ πάντα, Ζῆνα δὲ καλοῦσι παρ᾽ ὅσον τοῦ ζῆν αἴτιός ἐστιν ἢ διὰ τοῦ ζῆν κεχώρηκεν, ᾿Αθηνᾶν δὲ κατὰ τὴν εἰς αἰθέρα διάτασιν τοῦ ἡγεμονικοῦ αὐτοῦ, ῞Ηραν δὲ κατὰ τὴν εἰς ἀέρα, καὶ ῞Ηφαιστον κατὰ τὴν εἰς τὸ τεχνικὸν πῦρ, καὶ Ποσειδῶνα κατὰ τὴν εἰς τὸ ὑγρόν, καὶ Δήμητραν κατὰ τὴν εἰς γῆν· ὁμοίως δὲ καὶ τὰς ἄλλας προσηγορίας ἐχόμενοί τινος οἰκειότητος ἀπέδοσαν.   10

1 ἢ νοερόν, τέλειον Sedley: τέλειον ἢ νοερὸν BP: τέλειον om. F

Context: outline of Stoic cosmology.

1   For god's immortality, cf. note on **70C** 14–15.
5–10   For Stoic allegorical interpretations of divine names, cf. *SVF* 2.1061–1100; **B** 11ff.; Philodemus, *Piet.* cols. 1–10 in Henrichs [529].

B Cicero, *ND* 1.39–41 (*SVF* 2.1077)

iam vero Chrysippus, qui Stoicorum somniorum vaferrumus habetur interpres, magnam turbam congregat ignotorum deorum, atque ita ignotorum ut eos ne coniectura quidem

Stoic physics

informare possimus, cum mens nostra quidvis videatur cogitatione posse depingere. ait enim vim divinam in ratione esse positam et in universae naturae animo atque mente, ipsumque mundum deum dicit esse et eius animi fusionem universam, 5 tum eius ipsius principatum qui in mente et ratione versetur, communemque rerum naturam universam atque omnia continentem, tum fatalem vim et necessitatem rerum futurarum, ignem praeterea et eum quem ante dixi aethera, tum ea quae natura fluerent atque manarent, ut et aquam et terram et aera, solem lunam sidera universitatemque rerum qua omnia continerentur, 10 atque etiam homines eos qui inmortalitatem essent consecuti. idemque disputat aethera esse eum quem homines Iovem appellarent, quique aer per maria manaret eum esse Neptunum, terramque eam esse quae Ceres diceretur, similique ratione persequitur vocabula reliquorum deorum. idemque etiam legis perpetuae et aeternae vim, quae quasi dux vitae et magistra officiorum sit, Iovem dicit esse, eandemque fatalem necessitatem appellat sempiter- 15 nam rerum futurarum veritatem; quorum nihil tale est ut in eo vis divina inesse videatur. et haec quidem in primo libro de natura deorum; in secundo autem volt Orphei Musaei Hesiodi Homerique fabellas accommodare ad ea quae ipse primo libro de deis inmortalibus dixerit, ut etiam veterrimi poetae, qui haec ne suspicati quidem sint, Stoici fuisse videantur.

7 *vim* Davies: *umbram* codd.: *veritatem* Creuzer

Context: hostile historical sketch of the theological doctrines of other Greek philosophers, by the Epicurean spokesman Velleius. Cf. the preceding accounts of Zeno, Aristo, Cleanthes and Persaeus, ibid. 1.36–8. The entire passage 1.25–41 seems to share much of its material with Philodemus, *Piet*. 3–17 (for a direct comparison, see Diels, *Dox*. 529–50; for a more up-to-date text, see Henrichs [529]).

8–9   The deification of aether was explained at *ND* 1.37 as central to Cleanthes' theology.

8–14   This deification of elemental masses provides the material for some of Carneades' anti-Stoic Sorites arguments: cf. **70E**, and Couissin [625].

C Cicero, *ND* 2.12–15

(1) itaque inter omnis omnium gentium summa constat; omnibus enim innatum est et in animo quasi insculptum esse deos. quales sint varium est, esse nemo negat. (2) Cleanthes quidem noster quattuor de causis dixit in animis hominum informatas deorum esse notiones. (3) primam posuit eam de qua modo dixi, quae orta esset ex praesensione rerum futurarum; (4) alteram 5 quam cepimus ex magnitudine commodorum, quae percipiuntur caeli temperatione fecunditate terrarum aliarumque commoditatum complurium copia; (5) tertiam quae terreret animos fulminibus tempestatibus nimbis nivibus grandinibus vastitate pestilentia terrae motibus et saepe fremitibus lapideisque imbribus et guttis imbrium quasi cruentis, tum labibus aut repentinis terrarum hiatibus tum praeter naturam 10 hominum pecudumque portentis, tum facibus visis caelestibus tum stellis is quas Graeci κομήτας nostri cincinnatas vocant, quae nuper bello Octaviano magnarum fuerunt calamitatum praenuntiae, tum sole geminato, quod ut e patre audivi Tuditano et Aquilio

consulibus evenerat, quo quidem anno P. Africanus sol alter extinctus est, quibus exterriti
homines vim quandam esse caelestem et divinam suspicati sunt; (6) quartam   15
causam esse eamque vel maximam aequabilitatem motus, conversionem
caeli, solis lunae siderumque omnium distinctionem utilitatem pulchritudinem ordinem, quarum rerum aspectus ipse satis indicaret non esse ea fortuita:
ut, si quis in domum aliquam aut in gymnasium aut in forum venerit, cum
videat omnium rerum rationem modum disciplinam, non possit ea sine causa   20
fieri iudicare, sed esse aliquem intellegat qui praesit et cui pareatur, multo
magis in tantis motionibus tantisque vicissitudinibus, tam multarum rerum
atque tantarum ordinibus, in quibus nihil umquam inmensa et infinita vetustas
mentita sit, statuat necesse est ab aliqua mente tantos naturae motus gubernari.

Context: Balbus' defence of Stoic theology, here resuming his earlier appeal (*ND* 2.4–
5) to mankind's unanimity as to the existence of god.
   For a condensed, and somewhat different, version, see *ND* 3.16. Cleanthes' first and
fourth explanations seem to be modelled closely on Aristotle, *De philosophia* fr. 12
Ross. His third has aroused some puzzlement, since it appears to appeal to a false
conception of god as angry or malevolent. Note, however, that the standard Stoic
response to the inadequacy of primitive theological notions is not rejection but
allegorical reinterpretation. Hence the thunderbolt, a prime example of these divine
terrors, is retained by Cleanthes (**I 2**), but as a symbol of the creativity of fire. Likewise
he may well have argued that fear of the supernatural is a primitive forerunner of a
very proper wonder at the divine.
   1–2 Cf. S.E., *M.* 9.60–5. If the existence of god is uncontroversial, why do the
Stoics expend so much effort on proving it (cf. *ND* 3.8–9)? Partly because even the
obvious may need defence if attacked by sceptics (cf. Cicero, *Acad.* 2.17). Partly
because the existence of the specifically Stoic god, who is identical with the world, is
not uncontroversial. Cf. Schofield [471].

D Sextus Empiricus, *M.* 9.133–6

(1) Ζήνων δὲ καὶ τοιοῦτον ἠρώτα λόγον· "τοὺς θεοὺς εὐλόγως ἄν τις
τιμῴη· ⟨τοὺς δὲ μὴ ὄντας οὐκ ἄν τις εὐλόγως τιμῴη·⟩ εἰσὶν ἄρα θεοί." (2)
ᾧ λόγῳ τινὲς παραβάλλοντές φασι· "τοὺς σοφοὺς ἄν τις εὐλόγως τιμῴη·
τοὺς δὲ μὴ ὄντας οὐκ ἄν τις εὐλόγως τιμῴη· εἰσὶν ἄρα σοφοί." ὅπερ οὐκ
ἤρεσκε τοῖς ἀπὸ τῆς Στοᾶς, μέχρι τοῦ νῦν ἀνευρέτου ὄντος τοῦ κατ' αὐτοὺς   5
[τοῦ] σοφοῦ. (3) ἀπαντῶν δὲ πρὸς τὴν παραβολὴν Διογένης ὁ Βαβυλώνιος
τὸ δεύτερόν φησι λῆμμα τοῦ Ζήνωνος λόγου τοιοῦτον εἶναι τῇ δυνάμει·
"τοὺς δὲ μὴ πεφυκότας εἶναι οὐκ ἄν τις εὐλόγως τιμῴη·" τοιούτου γὰρ
λαμβανομένου δῆλον ὡς πεφύκασιν εἶναι θεοί· εἰ δὲ τοῦτο, καὶ εἰσὶν ἤδη· εἰ
γὰρ ἅπαξ ποτὲ ἦσαν, καὶ νῦν εἰσίν, ὥσπερ εἰ ἄτομοι ἦσαν, καὶ νῦν εἰσίν·   10
ἄφθαρτα γὰρ καὶ ἀγένητα τὰ τοιαῦτά ἐστι κατὰ τὴν ἔννοιαν τῶν
σωμάτων. διὸ καὶ κατὰ ἀκόλουθον ἐπιφορὰν συνάξει ὁ λόγος. οἱ δέ γε
σοφοὶ οὐκ ἐπεὶ πεφύκασιν εἶναι, ἤδη καὶ εἰσίν. (4) ἄλλοι δέ φασι τὸ πρῶτον
λῆμμα τοῦ Ζήνωνος, τὸ "τοὺς θεοὺς εὐλόγως ἄν τις τιμῴη," ἀμφίβολον

Stoic physics

εἶναι· ἐν μὲν γὰρ σημαίνει "τοὺς θεοὺς εὐλόγως ἄν τις τιμῴη", ἕτερον δὲ   15
"τιμητικῶς ἔχοι". λαμβάνεσθαι δὲ τὸ πρῶτον, ὅπερ ψεῦδος ἔσται ἐπὶ τῶν
σοφῶν.

2 suppl. Fabricius

Context: review of doctrinaire, especially Stoic, theological arguments.
See Schofield [345] on this argument and the anonymous παραβολή.
12 Why this comment? Diogenes interprets 'existent' as 'such as to exist' in the
additional premise. This compels him to reinterpret the conclusion along the same
lines, as he does at 8–12, in order to give 'exist' a consistent sense throughout. The
point of the addition is to remark that validity is thus restored.

E Cicero, *ND* 2.16 (*SVF* 2.1012, part)

Chrysippus quidem, quamquam est acerrimo ingenio, tamen ea dicit ut ab ipsa natura didicisse,
non ut ipse repperisse videatur. (1) "si enim" inquit "est aliquid in rerum natura
quod hominis mens quod ratio quod vis quod potestas humana efficere non
possit, est certe id quod illud efficit homine melius; atqui res caelestes
omnesque eae quarum est ordo sempiternus ab homine confici non possunt;   5
est igitur id quo illa conficiuntur homine melius. id autem quid potius dixeris
quam deum? (2) etenim si di non sunt, quid esse potest in rerum natura
homine melius? in eo enim solo est ratio, qua nihil potest esse praestantius. esse
autem hominem qui nihil in omni mundo melius esse quam se putet
desipientis adrogantiae est; ergo est aliquid melius. est igitur profecto deus."   10

Context: immediately following **C**.
Cf. *ND* 3.18, 25; Lactantius, *De ira dei* 10.36–7.

F Sextus Empiricus, *M.* 9.104, 108–10

(1) καὶ πάλιν ὁ Ζήνων φησίν· "[εἰ] τὸ λογικὸν τοῦ μὴ λογικοῦ κρεῖττόν
ἐστιν· οὐδὲν δέ γε κόσμου κρεῖττόν ἐστιν· λογικὸν ἄρα ὁ κόσμος. καὶ
ὡσαύτως ἐπὶ τοῦ νοεροῦ καὶ ἐμψυχίας μετέχοντος. τὸ γὰρ νοερὸν τοῦ μὴ
νοεροῦ καὶ ⟨τὸ⟩ ἔμψυχον τοῦ μὴ ἐμψύχου κρεῖττόν ἐστιν· οὐδὲν δέ γε
κόσμου κρεῖττον· νοερὸς ἄρα καὶ ἔμψυχός ἐστιν ὁ κόσμος." ... (2) ἀλλ' ὅ   5
γε 'Αλεξῖνος τῷ Ζήνωνι παρέβαλε τρόπῳ τῷδε· "τὸ ποιητικὸν τοῦ μὴ
ποιητικοῦ καὶ τὸ γραμματικὸν τοῦ μὴ γραμματικοῦ κρεῖττόν ἐστι, καὶ τὸ
κατὰ τὰς ἄλλας τέχνας θεωρούμενον κρεῖττόν ἐστι τοῦ μὴ τοιούτου· οὐδὲ
ἓν δὲ κόσμου κρεῖττόν ἐστιν· ποιητικὸν ἄρα καὶ γραμματικόν ἐστιν ὁ
κόσμος." (3) πρὸς ἣν ἀπαντῶντες παραβολὴν οἱ Στωικοί φασιν, ὅτι Ζήνων   10
τὸ καθάπαξ κρεῖττον εἴληφεν, τουτέστι τὸ λογικὸν τοῦ μὴ λογικοῦ καὶ τὸ
νοερὸν τοῦ μὴ νοεροῦ καὶ τὸ ἔμψυχον τοῦ μὴ ἐμψύχου, ὁ δὲ 'Αλεξῖνος
οὐκέτι· οὐ γὰρ ἐν τῷ καθάπαξ τὸ ποιητικὸν τοῦ μὴ ποιητικοῦ καὶ τὸ
γραμματικὸν τοῦ μὴ γραμματικοῦ κρεῖττον. ὥστε μεγάλην ἐν τοῖς λόγοις
θεωρεῖσθαι διαφοράν· ἰδοὺ γὰρ 'Αρχίλοχος ποιητικὸς ὢν οὐκ ἔστι   15

324

Σωκράτους τοῦ μὴ ποιητικοῦ κρείττων, καὶ Ἀρίσταρχος γραμματικὸς ὢν οὐκ ἔστι Πλάτωνος τοῦ μὴ γραμματικοῦ κρείττων.

1 del. Bekker   4 add. Bekker

Context: as **D**.
On Alexinus' παραβολή, and the Stoic response, see Schofield [345].
5 The omitted passage compares Zeno's argument to Plato, *Tim.* 29d–30b.

G Cicero, *ND* 2.22

(1) idemque hoc modo: "nullius sensu carentis pars aliqua potest esse sentiens; mundi autem partes sentientes sunt; non igitur caret sensu mundus." (2) pergit idem et urguet angustius: "nihil" inquit "quod animi quodque rationis est expers, id generare ex se potest animantem compotemque rationis; mundus autem generat animantis compotesque rationis; animans est igitur mundus   5 composque rationis." (3) idemque similitudine, ut saepe solet, rationem conclusit hoc modo: "si ex oliva modulate canentes tibiae nascerentur, num dubitares quin inesset in oliva tibicini quaedam scientia? quid si platani fidiculas ferrent numerose sonantes, idem scilicet censeres in platanis inesse musicam. cur igitur mundus non animans sapiensque iudicetur, cum ex se   10 procreet animantis atque sapientis?"

Context: part of Balbus' defence of Stoic theology, following a version of Zeno's argument in **F 1**.
   Zeno argues from the capacities of individual animals to those of the world by appeal to the qualitative similarity alleged to exist, first between part and whole, and second between product and cause. **53X**, and the treatment of a similar Zenonian argument at Sextus, *M.* 9.101–3, suggest that these two principles were not kept entirely distinct. Cf. Schofield [345], 44–8.

H Cicero, *ND* 2.37–9

(1) neque enim est quicquam aliud praeter mundum cui nihil absit quodque undique aptum atque perfectum expletumque sit omnibus suis numeris et partibus. scite enim Chrysippus, ut clipei causa involucrum, vaginam autem gladii, sic praeter mundum cetera omnia aliorum causa esse generata, ut eas fruges atque fructus quos terra gignit animantium causa, animantes autem   5 hominum, ut equum vehendi causa, arandi bovem, venandi et custodiendi canem; ipse autem homo ortus est ad mundum contemplandum et imitandum – nullo modo perfectus sed est quaedam particula perfecti. sed mundus quoniam omnia conplexus est neque est quicquam quod non insit in eo, perfectus undique est. (2) qui igitur potest ei deesse id quod est optimum?   10 nihil autem est mente et ratione melius; ergo haec mundo deesse non possunt. (3) bene igitur idem Chrysippus, qui similitudines adiungens omnia in perfectis et maturis docet esse meliora, ut in equo quam in eculeo, in cane

325

quam in catulo, in viro quam in puero. item quod in omni mundo optimum
sit id in perfecto aliquo atque absoluto esse debere; est autem nihil mundo   15
perfectius, nihil virtute melius; igitur mundi est propria virtus.
(4) nec vero
hominis natura perfecta est, et efficitur tamen in homine virtus; quanto igitur
in mundo facilius; est ergo in eo virtus. sapiens est igitur et propterea deus.

Context: Balbus' defence of Stoic theology.
2 **omnibus suis numeris**   See on **59K**.
7–8   Cf. **63E**.
17 **efficitur tamen in homine virtus**   Contrast **D 2**, and cf. **61K, N 2**.

I Cleanthes, *Hymn.* (Stobaeus 1.25,3–27,4 = *SVF* 1.537)

(1) κύδιστ' ἀθανάτων, πολυώνυμε παγκρατὲς αἰεί,
Ζεῦ φύσεως ἀρχηγέ, νόμου μέτα πάντα κυβερνῶν,
χαῖρε· σὲ γὰρ καὶ πᾶσι θέμις θνητοῖσι προσαυδᾶν.
ἐκ σοῦ γὰρ γενόμεσθα θεοῦ μίμημα λαχόντες
μοῦνοι, ὅσα ζώει τε καὶ ἕρπει θνήτ' ἐπὶ γαῖαν·   5
τῷ σε καθυμνήσω καὶ σὸν κράτος αἰὲν ἀείσω.
(2) σοὶ δὴ πᾶς ὅδε κόσμος ἑλισσόμενος περὶ γαῖαν
πείθεται ᾗ κεν ἄγῃς, καὶ ἑκὼν ὑπὸ σεῖο κρατεῖται·
τοῖον ἔχεις ὑποεργὸν ἀνικήτοις ἐνὶ χερσὶν
ἀμφήκη πυρόεντ' αἰειζώοντα κεραυνόν·   10
τοῦ γὰρ ὑπὸ πληγῆς φύσεως πάντ' ἔργα βέβηκεν,
ᾧ σὺ κατευθύνεις κοινὸν λόγον, ὃς διὰ πάντων
φοιτᾷ μιγνύμενος μεγάλῳ μικροῖς τε φάεσσιν
†ὡς τόσσος γεγαὼς ὕπατος βασιλεὺς διὰ παντός.†
(3) οὐδέ τι γίγνεται ἔργον ἐπὶ χθονὶ σοῦ δίχα, δαῖμον,   15
οὔτε κατ' αἰθέριον θεῖον πόλον, οὔτ' ἐνὶ πόντῳ,
πλὴν ὁπόσα ῥέζουσι κακοὶ σφετέραισιν ἀνοίαις.
ἀλλὰ σὺ καὶ τὰ περισσὰ ἐπίστασαι ἄρτια θεῖναι,
καὶ κοσμεῖν τἄκοσμα, καὶ οὐ φίλα σοὶ φίλα ἐστίν.
ὧδε γὰρ εἰς ἓν πάντα συνήρμοκας ἐσθλὰ κακοῖσιν,   20
ὥσθ' ἕνα γίγνεσθαι πάντων λόγον αἰὲν ἐόντα·
ὃν φεύγοντες ἐῶσιν ὅσοι θνητῶν κακοί εἰσιν,
δύσμοροι, οἵ τ' ἀγαθῶν μὲν ἀεὶ κτῆσιν ποθέοντες
οὔτ' ἐσορῶσι θεοῦ κοινὸν νόμον οὔτε κλύουσιν,
ᾧ κεν πειθόμενοι σὺν νῷ βίον ἐσθλὸν ἔχοιεν·   25
αὐτοὶ δ' αὖθ' ὁρμῶσιν ἄνοι κακὸν ἄλλος ἐπ' ἄλλο,
οἳ μὲν ὑπὲρ δόξης σπουδὴν δυσέριστον ἔχοντες,
οἳ δ' ἐπὶ κερδοσύνας τετραμμένοι οὐδενὶ κόσμῳ,
ἄλλοι δ' εἰς ἄνεσιν καὶ σώματος ἡδέα ἔργα
⟨. . . . .⟩ ἐπ' ἄλλοτε δ' ἄλλα φέρονται,   30
σπεύδοντες μάλα πάμπαν ἐναντία τῶνδε γενέσθαι.

(4) ἀλλὰ Ζεῦ πάνδωρε κελαινεφὲς ἀργικέραυνε,
ἀνθρώπους ῥύου ⟨μὲν⟩ ἀπειροσύνης ἀπὸ λυγρῆς,
ἣν σύ, πάτερ, σκέδασον ψυχῆς ἄπο, δὸς δὲ κυρῆσαι
γνώμης, ᾗ πίσυνος σὺ δίκης μέτα πάντα κυβερνᾷς,   35
ὄφρ' ἂν τιμηθέντες ἀμειβώμεσθά σε τιμῇ,
ὑμνοῦντες τὰ σὰ ἔργα διηνεκές, ὡς ἐπέοικε
θνητὸν ἐόντ', ἐπεὶ οὔτε βροτοῖς γέρας ἄλλο τι μεῖζον
οὔτε θεοῖς, ἢ κοινὸν ἀεὶ νόμον ἐν δίκῃ ὑμνεῖν.

4 γενόμεσθα θεοῦ Pearson (ap. Powell [354]): γένος ἐσμὲν ἤχου cod.: γενόμεσθα λόγου Meincke: γενόμεσθα σέθεν Zuntz [359]   26 ἄνοι κακὸν Wachsmuth: ἄνευ κακοῦ cod.: ἄνευ νόου Wilamowitz   30 vacat cod.: ἀλλὰ κακοῖς ἐπέκυρσαν Arnim: ὧδ' ἀνόητ' ἔρδουσιν Pearson   32 ἀργικέραυνε Meincke: ἀρχικέραυνε cod.

For textual issues, see especially Pearson [322], Powell [354], and Zuntz [355].

Readers familiar with Heraclitus will recognize numerous echoes of Cleanthes' favourite Presocratic. For the significance of these, cf. Long [353].

4   Pearson's solution to this well-known crux, adopted above, has strong support from Musonius, fr. 17 Hense, ἄνθρωπος μίμημα μὲν θεοῦ μόνον τῶν ἐπιγείων ἐστί. If the reference to 'god' is thought less likely in a context where Zeus is addressed in the second person, Zuntz's σέθεν is available as an alternative. But note θεοῦ in 24. Man resembles god in his rationality and capacity for virtue: cf. 61J.

J   Cicero, *ND* 2.75–6

(1) dico igitur providentia deorum mundum et omnes mundi partes et initio constitutas esse et omni tempore administrari. eamque disputationem tris in partes nostri fere dividunt. (2) quarum prima pars est quae ducitur ab ea ratione quae docet esse deos; quo concesso confitendum est eorum consilio mundum administrari. (3) secunda est autem quae docet omnes res subiectas   5
esse naturae sentienti ab eaque omnia pulcherrume geri; quo᾽ constituto sequitur ab animantibus principiis eam esse generatam. (4) tertius est locus qui ducitur ex admiratione rerum caelestium atque terrestrium. (5) primum igitur aut negandum est esse deos, quod et Democritus simulacra et Epicurus imagines inducens quodam pacto negat, aut qui deos esse concedant is   10
fatendum est eos aliquid agere idque praeclarum; nihil est autem praeclarius mundi administratione; deorum igitur consilio administratur.

Context: Balbus' defence of Stoic theology, here introducing the proofs of providence.

Cicero's sources for this section are disputed. In favour of a largely Chrysippean origin, see Dragona-Monachou [528], 133–4.

2–8   The three parts listed correspond to, respectively, ibid. 2.76–80, 81–90 (including **L**), and 90–153 (including **M** and **N**).

9   **Epicurus**   See 23.

K   Plutarch, *Comm. not.* 1075E (*SVF* 2.1126)

καὶ μὴν αὐτοί γε πρὸς τὸν Ἐπίκουρον οὐδὲν ἀπολείπουσι τῶν πραγμάτων

Stoic physics

"ἰοὺ ἰού, φεῦ φεῦ" βοῶντες, ὡς συγχέοντα τὴν τῶν θεῶν πρόληψιν ἀναιρουμένης τῆς προνοίας· οὐ γὰρ ἀθάνατον καὶ μακάριον μόνον ἀλλὰ καὶ φιλάνθρωπον καὶ κηδεμονικὸν καὶ ὠφέλιμον προλαμβάνεσθαι καὶ νοεῖσθαι τὸν θεόν.   5

Context: opening of new anti-Stoic argument, criticizing the inconsistency of claiming that god is provident yet making the benefits he confers not 'goods' but 'indifferents'.
   Cf. id., St. rep. 1051D–F, where this Stoic thesis is associated specifically with Chrysippus and Antipater.

L   Cicero, ND 2.88

quod si in Scythiam aut in Britanniam sphaeram aliquis tulerit hanc quam nuper familiaris noster effecit Posidonius, cuius singulae conversiones idem efficiunt in sole et in luna et in quinque stellis errantibus quod efficitur in caelo singulis diebus et noctibus, quis in illa barbaria dubitet quin ea sphaera sit perfecta ratione? hi autem dubitant de mundo, ex quo et oriuntur et fiunt   5
omnia, casune ipse sit effectus aut necessitate aliqua an ratione ac mente divina; et Archimedem arbitrantur plus valuisse in imitandis sphaerae conversionibus quam naturam in efficiendis; praesertim cum multis partibus sint illa perfecta quam haec simulata sollertius.

Context: see J and note.
   Astronomical mechanisms like those of Archimedes were possibly the most advanced creations of antiquity. See Price [50] on one such relic, the Antikythera mechanism, which is contemporary with that of Posidonius.
   5 hi   Those who deny providence, especially the Epicureans (cf. M).

M   Cicero, ND 2.93

sic ego non mirer esse quemquam qui sibi persuadeat corpora quaedam solida atque individua vi et gravitate ferri mundumque effici ornatissimum et pulcherrimum ex eorum corporum concursione fortuita? hoc qui existimat fieri potuisse non intellego cur non idem putet, si innumerabiles unius et viginti formae litterarum vel aureae vel qualeslibet aliquo coiciantur, posse ex   5
is in terram excussis annales Enni ut deinceps legi possint effici; quod nescio an ne in uno quidem versu possit tantum valere fortuna.

Context: see J and note.
   1–3   The reference is to the Epicurean account of cosmogony. Cf. 13C, D, H 2.

N   Cicero, ND 2.133

sin quaeret quispiam cuiusnam causa tantarum rerum molitio facta sit. arborumne et herbarum, quae quamquam sine sensu sunt tamen a natura sustinentur? at id quidem absurdum est. an bestiarum? nihilo probabilius deos

328

mutarum et nihil intellegentium causa tantum laborasse. quorum igitur causa
quis dixerit effectum esse mundum? eorum scilicet animantium quae ratione   5
utuntur; hi sunt di et homines; quibus profecto nihil est melius, ratio est enim
quae praestet omnibus. ita fit credibile deorum et hominum causa factum esse
mundum quaeque in eo mundo sint omnia.

Context: see **J** and note.

O Plutarch, *St. rep.* 1044D (*SVF* 2.1163)

ἐν μὲν οὖν τῷ πέμπτῳ Περὶ φύσεως, εἰπὼν ὅτι οἱ κόρεις εὐχρήστως
ἐξυπνίζουσιν ἡμᾶς καὶ οἱ μύες ἐπιστρέφουσιν ἡμᾶς μὴ ἀμελῶς ἕκαστα
τιθέναι, φιλοκαλεῖν δὲ τὴν φύσιν τῇ ποικιλίᾳ χαίρουσαν εἰκός ἐστι, ταῦτα
κατὰ λέξιν εἴρηκε· "γένοιτο δ᾽ ἂν μάλιστα τούτου ἔμφασις ἐπὶ τῆς κέρκου
τοῦ ταώ. ἐνταῦθα γὰρ ἐπιφαίνει τὸ ζῷον γεγονέναι ἕνεκα τῆς κέρκου καὶ   5
οὐκ ἀνάπαλιν, τῷ ⟨δ᾽⟩ ἄρρενι γενομένῳ οὕτως ἡ θῆλυς συνηκολούθηκεν."

6 ἡ θῆλυς συνηκολούθηκεν Pohlenz: ἢ θηλυδοῦν (vel θηλυγοῦν) ἠκολούθηκεν (vel -θησαν) codd.

Context: criticism of Chrysippus for censuring those who keep ornamental peacocks
yet holding the bird's beauty to be the gift of providence.

6 **συνηκολούθηκεν** Even if the prefix is correctly restored, the term is probably
equivalent to Chrysippus' technical term παρακολούθησις (**Q** 28). The peacock exists
for his beauty, the peahen as a necessary concomitant, not intrinsically valuable, but
indispensable to his reproduction.

P Porphyry, *Abst.* 3.20.1–3 (including *SVF* 2.1152)

(1) ἀλλ᾽ ἐκεῖνο νὴ Δία τοῦ Χρυσίππου πιθανὸν [ἢ] ὡς ἡμᾶς αὐτῶν καὶ
ἀλλήλων οἱ θεοὶ χάριν ἐποιήσαντο, ἡμῶν δὲ τὰ ζῷα· συμπολεμεῖν μὲν
ἵππους καὶ συνθηρεύειν κύνας, ἀνδρείας δὲ γυμνάσια παρδάλεις καὶ
ἄρκτους καὶ λέοντας. ἡ δὲ ὗς – ἐνταῦθα γάρ ἐστι τῶν χαρίτων τὸ ἥδιστον –
οὐ δι᾽ ἄλλο τι πλὴν θύεσθαι ἐγεγόνει, καὶ τῇ σαρκὶ τὴν ψυχὴν ὁ θεὸς οἷον   5
ἅλας ἐνέμιξεν, εὐοψίαν ἡμῖν μηχανώμενος. ὅπως δὲ ζωμοῦ καὶ παραδειπνίων
ἀφθονίαν ἔχωμεν, ὄστρεά τε παντοδαπὰ καὶ πορφύρας καὶ ἀκαλήφας καὶ γένη πτηνῶν
ποικίλα παρεσκεύασεν, οὐκ ἀλλαχόθεν, ἀλλ᾽ ὡς αὐτοῦ μέγα μέρος ἐνταῦθα τρέψας, εἰς
γλυκυθυμίας τὰς τιτθὰς ὑπερβαλλόμενος καὶ καταπυκνώσας ταῖς ἡδοναῖς καὶ ἀπολαύσεσι
τὸν περίγειον τόπον. (2) ὅτῳ δὴ ταῦτα δοκεῖ τι τοῦ πιθανοῦ καὶ θεῷ πρέποντος   10
μετέχειν, σκοπείτω τί πρὸς ἐκεῖνον ἐρεῖ τὸν λόγον ὃν Καρνεάδης ἔλεγεν·
ἕκαστον τῶν φύσει γεγονότων, ὅταν τοῦ πρὸς ὃ πέφυκε καὶ γέγονε
τυγχάνῃ τέλους, ὠφελεῖται. (κοινότερον δὲ τῆς ὠφελείας, ἣν εὐχρηστίαν
οὗτοι λέγουσιν, ἀκουστέον.) ἡ δὲ ὗς φύσει γέγονε πρὸς τὸ σφαγῆναι καὶ
καταβρωθῆναι· καὶ τοῦτο πάσχουσα τυγχάνει τοῦ πρὸς ὃ πέφυκε, καὶ   15
ὠφελεῖται.

1 ἢ del. Bernardakis: ἦν Dübner

Stoic physics

Context: response to Peripatetic and Stoic positions which conflict with Porphyry's vegetarianism.
Cf. the very similar Cicero, ND 2.160–1.
12–14   Carneades makes it clear that he is borrowing a Stoic premise – his regular method. But we have not found any close Stoic parallel for the premise in question.
13 εὐχρηστίαν   For this Stoic term for non-moral 'advantage', as contrasted with ὠφελεία in its narrow moral sense, cf. SVF 3.123, 674.

Q Gellius 7.1.1–13 (SVF 2.1169–70)

(1) ⟨quibus non videtur mundus dei et hominum causa institutus neque res humanae providentia gubernari, gravi se argumento uti putant cum ita dicunt: "si esset providentia, nulla essent mala." nihil enim minus aiunt providentiae congruere, quam in eo mundo, quem propter⟩ homines fecisse dicatur, tantam vim esse aerumnarum et malorum. adversus ea Chrysippus 5
cum in libro Περὶ προνοίας quarto dissereret: "nihil est prorsus istis" inquit "insubidius, qui opinantur bona esse potuisse si non essent ibidem mala. nam cum bona malis contraria sint, utraque necessum est opposita inter sese et quasi mutuo adverso quaeque fulta nisu consistere; nullum adeo contrarium est sine contrario altero. quo enim pacto iustitiae sensus esse posset, nisi essent iniuriae? 10
aut quid aliud iustitia est quam iniustitiae privatio? quid item fortitudo intellegi posset nisi ex ignaviae adpositione? quid continentia nisi ex intemperantiae? quo item modo prudentia esset, nisi foret contra inprudentia? proinde" inquit "homines stulti cur non hoc etiam desiderant, ut veritas sit et non sit mendacium? namque itidem sunt bona et mala, felicitas et infortunitas, 15
dolor et voluptas; alterum enim ex altero, sicuti Plato ait, verticibus inter se contrariis deligatum est; si tuleris unum, abstuleris utrumque." (2) idem Chrysippus in eodem libro tractat consideratque dignumque esse id quaeri putat, εἰ αἱ τῶν ἀνθρώπων νόσοι κατὰ φύσιν γίνονται, id est, ⟨si⟩ natura ipsa rerum vel providentia, quae compagem hanc mundi et genus hominum fecit, 20
morbos quoque et debilitates et aegritudines corporum, quas patiuntur homines, fecerit. existimat autem non fuisse hoc principale naturae consilium, ut faceret homines morbis obnoxios; numquam enim hoc convenisse naturae auctori parentique omnium rerum bonarum. "sed cum multa" inquit "atque magna gigneret pareretque aptissima et utilissima, alia quoque simul adgnata 25
sunt incommoda his ipsis quae faciebat cohaerentia"; eaque per naturam, sed per sequellas quasdam necessarias facta dicit, quod ipse appellat κατὰ παρακολούθησιν. "sicut" inquit "cum corpora hominum natura fingeret, ratio subtilior et utilitas ipsa operis postulavit ut tenuissimis minutisque ossiculis caput compingeret, sed hanc utilitatem rei maioris alia quaedam 30
incommoditas extrinsecus consecuta est ut fieret caput tenuiter munitum et ictibus offensionibusque parvis fragile; proinde morbi quoque et aegritudines partae sunt dum salus paritur. (3) sicut hercle" inquit "dum virtus hominibus

per consilium naturae gignitur, vitia ibidem per adfinitatem contrariam nata
sunt." 35

1–4 e Lactantio, *epit. Div. inst.* 24.5 supplenda   26 post *eaque* ⟨*non*⟩ vel ⟨*neque*⟩ vulgo

1–5   These opponents are likely to be Academics (cf. **R**) and Epicureans (cf. **13F**
6–7).

R Lactantius, *De ira dei* 13.9–10 (*SVF* 2.1172)

sed Academici contra Stoicos disserentes solent quaerere cur, si omnia deus
hominum causa fecerit, etiam multa contraria et inimica et pestifera nobis
reperiantur tam in mari quam in terra. quod Stoici veritatem non perspicientes
ineptissime reppulerunt. aiunt enim multa esse in gignentibus et in numero
animalium quorum adhuc lateat utilitas, sed eam processu temporum   5
inventu⟨i⟩ri, sicut iam multa prioribus saeculis incognita necessitas et usus
invenerit.

6 *inventu*⟨*i*⟩*ri* (cf. id. *Div. inst.* 1.6.13) Brandt: *inventuri* codd.: *inveniri* edd. ceteri

Context: defence of the Stoic theory of providence, with Lactantius' modification that
evils were created along with goods in order to confront human wisdom with choices,
rather than for the reason quoted here.

S Plutarch, *St. rep.* 1051B–C (*SVF* 2.1178, part)

(1) ἔτι περὶ τοῦ μηδὲν ἐγκλητὸν εἶναι μηδὲ μεμπτὸν κόσμῳ, κατὰ τὴν
ἀρίστην φύσιν ἁπάντων περαινομένων, πολλάκις γεγραφώς, (2) ἔστιν ὅπου
πάλιν ἐγκλητάς τινας ἀμελείας οὐ περὶ μικρὰ καὶ φαῦλα καταλείπει. ἐν
γοῦν τῷ τρίτῳ Περὶ οὐσίας μνησθεὶς ὅτι συμβαίνει τινὰ τοῖς καλοῖς
κἀγαθοῖς τοιαῦτα, "πότερον" φησίν "ἀμελουμένων τινῶν, καθάπερ ἐν   5
οἰκίαις μείζοσι παραπίπτει τινὰ πίτυρα καὶ ποσοὶ πυροί τινες τῶν ὅλων εὖ
οἰκονομουμένων, ἢ διὰ τὸ καθίστασθαι ἐπὶ τῶν τοιούτων δαιμόνια φαῦλα ἐν
οἷς τῷ ὄντι γίγνονται καὶ ἐγκλητέαι ἀμέλειαι;" (3) φησὶ δὲ πολὺ καὶ τὸ τῆς
ἀνάγκης μεμῖχθαι.

It may be doubted whether any real contradiction is involved. The suggestions at 5–8
are in interrogative form, and Chrysippus may not have entertained them seriously
(although some Stoics did accept the first, to judge from Cicero, *ND* 3.86, 90). There
may possibly have been evil spirits in Chrysippus' world (cf. *SVF* 2.1101, 1104), but if
so they were surely part of its providential structure. The assertion about necessity at
8–9 certainly is meant seriously, but if good men's sufferings are necessary they are
indispensable 'concomitants' of nature's irreproachable plan (cf. **Q 2**), and therefore
not 'blameworthy cases of negligence' (3).

T Plutarch, *St. rep.* 1050B–D (*SVF* 2.937, part)

καίτοι ὁ μὲν Ἐπίκουρος ἀμωσγέπως στρέφεται καὶ φιλοτεχνεῖ, τῆς ἀιδίου κινήσεως

μηχανώμενος ἐλευθερῶσαι καὶ ἀπολῦσαι τὸ ἑκούσιον ὑπὲρ τοῦ μὴ καταλιπεῖν ἀνέγκλητον
τὴν κακίαν· ⟨ὁ δὲ Χρύσιππος⟩ ἀναπεπταμένην παρρησίαν αὐτῇ δίδωσιν ὡς
οὐ μόνον ἐξ ἀνάγκης οὐδὲ καθ' εἱμαρμένην ἀλλὰ καὶ κατὰ λόγον θεοῦ καὶ
κατὰ φύσιν πεποιημένῃ τὴν ἀρίστην. ἔτι δὲ καὶ ταῦθ' ὁρᾶται κατὰ λέξιν   5
οὕτως ἔχοντα· "τῆς γὰρ κοινῆς φύσεως εἰς πάντα διατεινούσης δεήσει πᾶν
τὸ ὁπωσοῦν γιγνόμενον ἐν τῷ ὅλῳ καὶ τῶν μορίων ὁτῳοῦν κατ' ἐκείνην
γενέσθαι καὶ τὸν ἐκείνης λόγον κατὰ τὸ ἑξῆς ἀκωλύτως διὰ τὸ μήτ' ἔξωθεν
εἶναι τὸ ἐνστησόμενον τῇ οἰκονομίᾳ μήτε τῶν μερῶν μηδὲν ἔχειν ὅπως
κινηθήσεται ἢ σχήσει ἄλλως ⟨ἢ⟩ κατὰ τὴν κοινὴν φύσιν." τίνες οὖν αἱ τῶν   10
μερῶν σχέσεις εἰσὶ καὶ κινήσεις; δῆλον μὲν ὅτι σχέσεις αἱ κακίαι καὶ τὰ
νοσήματα, φιλαργυρίαι φιληδονίαι φιλοδοξίαι δειλίαι ἀδικίαι, κινήσεις δὲ
μοιχεῖαι κλοπαὶ προδοσίαι ἀνδροφονίαι πατροκτονίαι. τούτων οἴεται
Χρύσιππος οὔτε μικρὸν οὔτε μέγα παρὰ τὸν τοῦ Διὸς λόγον εἶναι καὶ νόμον
καὶ δίκην καὶ πρόνοιαν.   15

7 ὅλῳ Wyttenbach: λόγῳ codd.

Context: criticism of Chrysippus for his alleged self-contradiction in holding the view
quoted yet stating elsewhere that god is responsible for nothing shameful.
   1–3   The Epicurean 'swerve' doctrine: see **20**.
   10–11   For this standard division of qualities into states and processes, cf. **28N 2–
3**.

U Calcidius 144 (*SVF* 2.933)

(1) itaque non nulli putant praesumi differentiam providentiae fatique, cum
reapse una sit. quippe providentiam dei fore voluntatem, voluntatem porro
eius seriem esse causarum. et ex eo quidem, quia uoluntas, providentia est.
porro quia eadem series causarum est, fatum cognominatạm. ex quo fieri ut
quae secundum fatum sunt etiam ex providentia sint, eodemque modo quae   5
secundum providentiam ex fato, ut putat Chrysippus. (2) alii uero, quae
quidem ex providentiae auctoritate fataliter quoque provenire, nec tamen
quae fataliter ex providentia, ut Cleanthes.

Context: discussion of the view, attributed to Plato on the strength of *Tim.* 41d8–e3,
that providence preceded fate.
   3 **providentia est**   The interjection of direct speech is harsh. Emending to
providentiam or *providentiam esse* would restore the grammar, but we are not convinced
that it would be justified.

55 Causation and fate

A Stobaeus 1.138,14–139,4 (*SVF* 1.89 and 2.336)

(1) Ζήνωνος. αἴτιον δ' ὁ Ζήνων φησὶν εἶναι δι' ὅ, οὗ δὲ αἴτιον συμβεβηκός·
καὶ τὸ μὲν αἴτιον σῶμα, οὗ δὲ αἴτιον κατηγόρημα. (2) ἀδύνατον δ' εἶναι τὸ

μὲν αἴτιον παρεῖναι, οὗ δέ ἐστιν αἴτιον μὴ ὑπάρχειν. (3) τὸ δὲ λεγόμενον
τοιαύτην ἔχει δύναμιν· αἴτιόν ἐστι δι' ὃ γίνεταί τι, οἷον διὰ τὴν φρόνησιν
γίνεται τὸ φρονεῖν καὶ διὰ τὴν ψυχὴν γίνεται τὸ ζῆν καὶ διὰ τὴν   5
σωφροσύνην γίνεται τὸ σωφρονεῖν. ἀδύνατον γὰρ εἶναι σωφροσύνης περί
τινα οὔσης μὴ σωφρονεῖν, ἢ ψυχῆς μὴ ζῆν, ἢ φρονήσεως μὴ φρονεῖν. (4)
Χρυσίππου. Χρύσιππος αἴτιον εἶναι λέγει δι' ὅ· καὶ τὸ μὲν αἴτιον ὂν καὶ
σῶμα, ⟨οὗ δὲ αἴτιον μήτε ὂν μήτε σῶμα·⟩ καὶ αἴτιον μὲν ὅτι, οὐ δὲ αἴτιον
διὰ τί. (5) αἰτίαν δ' εἶναι λόγον αἰτίου, ἢ λόγον τὸν περὶ τοῦ αἰτίου ὡς   10
αἰτίου.

9 add. Wachsmuth coll. 139, 7–8   μὲν L: om. FP   10 διὰ τί scripsimus: διατί codd.: διά τι Heeren

Context: doxography of cause.
 1 συμβεβηκός   An actualized κατηγόρημα, cf. 51B 4.

B Sextus Empiricus, M. 9.211 (SVF 2.341)

εἴγε Στωικοὶ μὲν πᾶν αἴτιον σῶμά φασι σώματι ἀσωμάτου τινὸς αἴτιον
γίνεσθαι, οἷον σῶμα μὲν τὸ σμιλίον, σώματι δὲ τῇ σαρκί, ἀσωμάτου δὲ τοῦ
τέμνεσθαι κατηγορήματος· καὶ πάλιν σῶμα μὲν τὸ πῦρ, σώματι δὲ τῷ
ξύλῳ, ἀσωμάτου δὲ τοῦ καίεσθαι κατηγορήματος.

Context: classification of views on the nature of cause.

C Clement, Strom. 8.9.26.3–4

τὸ γίνεσθαι οὖν καὶ τὸ τέμνεσθαι, τὰ οὗ ἐστιν αἴτιον, ἐνέργειαι οὖσαι
ἀσώματοί εἰσιν. εἰς ὃν λόγον κατηγορημάτων ἢ, ὥς τινες, λεκτῶν (λεκτὰ
γὰρ τὰ κατηγορήματα καλοῦσιν Κλεάνθης καὶ 'Αρχέδημος) τὰ αἴτια· ἢ,
ὅπερ καὶ μᾶλλον, τὰ μὲν κατηγορημάτων αἴτια λεχθήσεται, οἷον τοῦ
τέμνεται, οὗ πτῶσις τὸ τέμνεσθαι, τὰ δ' ἀξιωμάτων, ὡς τοῦ ναῦς γίνεται,   5
οὗ πάλιν ἡ πτῶσίς ἐστι τὸ ναῦν γίνεσθαι.

1 οὗ codd.: ὧν Stählin   αἴτιον Wedel: αἴτια codd.   2 εἰς codd.: καθ' Arnim: δι' Stählin   4 τοῦ
Arnim: τὸ codd.   5 τέμνεται Hervet: τέμνεσθαι codd.   γίνεται Hervet: γίνεσθαι codd.   6 ἡ
del. Arnim, Wilamowitz

Context: exposition of causal theory. Here Clement is reporting the view that effects
are incorporeal. He is not speaking as a Stoic, but there seems every indication that he
is using Stoic causal theory.
    Clement contrasts the view that effects are predicates with the view that they are
προσηγορίαι (cf. S.E., PH 3.14 for the same opposition). The latter, which he
attributes to Aristotle, is not of course the thesis that effects are linguistic items. The
debate is as to whether effects are properly things, expressible with common nouns
and adjectives, or predicates which come to be true of things.
    3 Κλεάνθης   As Frede has observed ([534], 233), this is the earliest attribution of
the doctrine of incorporeal λεκτά, and it is not unlikely that it was in the context of
causation that the doctrine was first developed.

Stoic physics

5-6 πτῶσις 'Substantival form.' See vol. 1, 201. We see no reason to share Frede's doubts ([418], 67-8) that this is a Stoic usage, although we do recognize a departure from Stoic orthodoxy in 33O, which follows almost directly after this text (see vol. 1, 201, vol. 2 ad loc.).

D Clement, *Strom.* 8.9.30.1-3 (*SVF* 2.349)

(1) ἀλλήλων οὐκ ἔστι τὰ αἴτια, ἀλλήλοις δὲ αἴτια. ἡ γὰρ σπληνικὴ διάθεσις προυποκειμένη οὐ πυρετοῦ αἴτιος, ἀλλὰ τοῦ γίνεσθαι τὸν πυρετόν· καὶ ὁ πυρετὸς προυποκείμενος οὐ σπληνός, ἀλλὰ τοῦ αὔξεσθαι τὴν διάθεσιν. (2) οὕτως καὶ αἱ ἀρεταὶ ἀλλήλαις αἴτιαι τοῦ μὴ χωρίζεσθαι διὰ τὴν ἀντακολουθίαν, καὶ οἱ ἐπὶ τῆς ψαλίδος λίθοι ἀλλήλοις εἰσὶν αἴτιοι τοῦ 5 μένειν κατηγορήματος, ἀλλήλων δὲ οὐκ εἰσὶν αἴτιοι· καὶ ὁ διδάσκαλος δὲ καὶ ὁ μανθάνων ἀλλήλοις εἰσὶν αἴτιοι τοῦ προκόπτειν κατηγορήματος. (3) λέγεται δὲ ἀλλήλοις αἴτια ποτὲ μὲν τῶν αὐτῶν, ὡς ὁ ἔμπορος καὶ ὁ κάπηλος ἀλλήλοις εἰσὶν αἴτιοι τοῦ κερδαίνειν, ποτὲ δὲ ἄλλου καὶ ἄλλου, καθάπερ ἡ μάχαιρα καὶ ἡ σάρξ· ἡ μὲν γὰρ τῇ σαρκὶ τοῦ τέμνεσθαι, ἡ σὰρξ 10 δὲ τῇ μαχαίρᾳ τοῦ τέμνειν.

4 τοῦ Sylburg: τῷ codd.

Context: as **C**.
5 ἀντακολουθίαν See vol. 1, 383-4.

E Seneca, *Ep.* 65.2

dicunt, ut scis, Stoici nostri duo esse in rerum natura ex quibus omnia fiant, causam et materiam. materia iacet iners, res ad omnia parata, cessatura si nemo moveat; causa autem, id est ratio, materiam format et quocumque vult versat, ex illa varia opera producit. esse ergo debet unde fiat aliquid, deinde a quo fiat: hoc causa est, illud materia.   5

Context: a discourse on the primary cause, comparing the Stoic account favourably with those of Plato and Aristotle.
3 **ratio** Identified with god at ibid. 23; cf. **44**.

F Galen, *Caus. cont.* 1.1-2.4

(1) Stoycos philosophos novi primos contentivam causam que et coniuncta dicitur nominare. volunt enim ex quatuor quidem elementis facta esse vocata ab Aristotile quidem omiomera corpora, primogenita autem a Platone, ex hiis autem alia corpora componi. elementorum autem quedam quidem materialia nuncupant, quedam autem activa et virtuosa, et contineri dicunt a virtuosis 5 materialia, et esse ignem quidem et aerem activa, terram vero et aquam materialia, et pertransire tota per tota in concrecionibus, scilicet virtuosa per materialia, ut aerem et ignem per aquam et terram, et esse aerem quidem frigidum, ignem uero calidum, et congregari et impilari substantiam ab aerea

natura, extendi vero et effundi et multum accipere locum ab ignea et esse 10
leptomerea quidem elementa activa, grossiparcia vero reliqua. spiritum autem
vocant leptomeream substantiam omnem, et eius opus esse continere alia
corpora physica et ea que animalium. nomino autem physica, quorum
generatio non ab hominibus sed a natura fit: talia autem sunt es et ferrum et
aurum et ligna et particularum que in animalibus prime et omiomere vocate, 15
scilicet nervus et vena et arteria et cartillago et os et quecumque alie tales. sicut
autem homines ligna per collam et colligationem et clavos et lutum et gipsum
et calcem couniunt ad invicem, sic videmus et naturam per colligationem
⟨et⟩ cartillaginem et carnem unientem et applicantem ad invicem omnes
particulas animalis. et vocare licet ei quicumque voluerit coniunctas causas 20
compositarum particularum eas que †naturam operantur simplicium que sunt
in eis, sicut in exterioribus quecumque non natura sed ars humana compaginat
scilicet lutum et gipsum et calcem et quecumque alia talia hiis utilitatibus
famulantur. vocantur autem a Stoycis non hec coniuncte cause entium, sed
suptilipartis substantia materialis. (2) Athineum igitur Attaleum, qui spiritua- 25
lem nominatam heresim in medicativa primo cepit, coniunctam vocare
causam egritudinum decens est ceu a Stoicorum heresi deductum (conversatus
enim fuit cum Posidonio), alios vero medicos, quicumque dogmata colunt
alia, coniunctam causam singule egritudinum non congruit querere, sicut
neque omiomerorum corporum que secundum naturam habent: ergo neque 30
differentias causarum sicut Athineus dicebat tres esse primas et generalissimas
contingit dicere eos. (3) differentie vero, quas dicebat Athineus esse tres, sunt
hee: prima quidem coniunctarum, secunda vero antecedentium, tercia autem
in procatarticarum materia continetur. vocant autem ita omnia quecumque
extra corpus existentia nocent ei operantia egritudinem; de genere autem 35
operantium intus existencia antecedentes cause vocantur; alterationes autem
innati spiritus que fiunt ab hiis et etiam ab extrinsecis humectato et siccato et
infrigidato et calefacto corpore coniunctas egritudinum ait esse causas,
pertransit enim spiritus iste per omiomera corpora sibi ipsi coalterans ea.
multociens igitur confestim a procatarticis causis fieri dicunt coniunctas. 40

This work survives only in Arabic and Latin translations, of which the latter, by
Niccolo di Deoprepio da Reggio di Calabria (fourteenth century), is given above.
Our translation, however, is an adaptation of that from the Arabic by M.C. Lyons,
whose advice on some points of detail we also gratefully acknowledge.

   12   We take 'all the substance with fine parts' – perhaps τὴν λεπτομερῆ οὐσίαν
πᾶσαν – to refer back to the combination of the two active elements. The Arabic does
mean '*any* substance with fine parts', but that would give a quite unparalleled usage of
πνεῦμα, and we suspect the translator of missing the precise sense intended by Galen.
Possibly the definite article had fallen out of his copy.

   32ff.   For this technical medical use of αἴτια προηγούμενα, cf. also Galen, *Meth.*
med. 10.65–7, *Praes. puls.* 9.386, *Syn. puls.* 458, *Caus. puls.* 9.2–3, and the attribution of
it to Athenaeus at *Def. med.* 19.392. However, the more general application to any

Stoic physics

temporally antecedent cause, which we ascribe to the Stoics in vol. 1, is also frequent in Galen, even in these very same works, eg. *Praes. puls.* 9.267, *Caus. puls.* 9.156.

G Aetius 1.11.5 (*SVF* 2.340)

οἱ Στωικοὶ πάντα τὰ αἴτια σωματικά· πνεύματα γάρ.

Context: doxography of cause. This sentence occupies the same position in the ps.-Plutarch version as **A** does in the Stobaeus version.

H Galen, *Syn. puls.* 9.458,8–14 (*SVF* 2.356)

μεμνῆσθαι μέντοι χρὴ πρὸ πάντων ὅπως ἔφαμεν ὀνομάζειν ἐνίοτε συνεκτικὸν αἴτιον, ὅτι μὴ κυρίως, ἀλλὰ καταχρώμενοι τῇ προσηγορίᾳ. τὸ μὲν γὰρ κυρίως λεγόμενον αἴτιον συνεκτικὸν οὔτ᾽ ὠνόμασέ τις ἄλλος πρὸ τῶν Στωικῶν οὔτ᾽ εἶναι συνεχώρησε· τὰ δὲ καὶ πρὸ ἡμῶν οἷον συνεκτικὰ λεγόμενα γενέσεώς τινος, οὐχ ὑπάρξεως αἴτια.   5

Context: the three basic kinds of cause (as listed in **F** 3) of pulses.

I Clement, *Strom.* 8.9.33.1–9 (*SVF* 2.351)

(1) τῶν μὲν οὖν προκαταρκτικῶν αἱρομένων μένει τὸ ἀποτέλεσμα, (2) συνεκτικὸν δέ ἐστιν αἴτιον, οὗ παρόντος μένει τὸ ἀποτέλεσμα καὶ αἱρομένου αἴρεται. τὸ δὲ συνεκτικὸν συνωνύμως καὶ αὐτοτελὲς καλοῦσιν, ἐπειδὴ αὐτάρκως δι᾽ αὐτοῦ ποιητικόν ἐστι τοῦ ἀποτελέσματος. (3) εἰ δὲ ⟨τοῦτο⟩ τὸ αἴτιον αὐτοτελοῦς ἐνεργείας ἐστὶ δηλωτικόν, τὸ συνεργὸν   5
ὑπηρεσίαν σημαίνει καὶ τὴν σὺν ἑτέρῳ λειτουργίαν. εἰ μὲν οὖν μηδὲν παρέχεται, οὐδὲ συνεργὸν λεχθήσεται, εἰ δὲ παρέχεται, τούτου πάντως γίνεται αἴτιον οὗ καὶ παρέχεται, τουτέστιν τοῦ δι᾽ αὐτοῦ γινομένου. ἔστιν οὖν συνεργὸν οὗ παρόντος ἐγίνετο τὸ ἀποτέλεσμα, προδήλως μὲν οὖν παρόντος ⟨προδήλου⟩, ἀδήλως δὲ ἀδήλου. (4) καὶ τὸ συναίτιον δὲ ἐκ τοῦ   10
γένους ἐστὶ τῶν αἰτίων, καθάπερ ὁ συστρατιώτης στρατιώτης καὶ ὁ συνέφηβος ἔφηβος. τὸ μὲν οὖν συνεργὸν αἴτιον τῷ συνεκτικῷ πρὸς τὴν ἐπίτασιν βοηθεῖ τοῦ ὑπ᾽ αὐτοῦ γινομένου, τὸ δὲ συναίτιον οὐκ ἐπὶ τῆς αὐτῆς ἐστιν ἐννοίας· δύναται γὰρ συναίτιον ὑπάρχειν, κἂν μὴ συνεκτικὸν αἴτιον ᾖ τι. νοεῖται γὰρ σὺν ἑτέρῳ τὸ συναίτιον οὐδ᾽ αὐτῷ δυναμένῳ κατ᾽   15
ἰδίαν ποιῆσαι τὸ ἀποτέλεσμα, αἴτιον ὂν σὺν αἰτίῳ. (5) διαφέρει δὲ τοῦ συναιτίου τὸ συνεργὸν ἐν τῷ τὸ συναίτιον ⟨μεθ᾽ ἑτέρου⟩ κατ᾽ ἰδίαν μὴ ποιοῦντος τὸ ἀποτέλεσμα παρέχειν, τὸ δὲ συνεργόν, ἐν τῷ κατ᾽ ἰδίαν μὴ ποιεῖν, ἑτέρῳ δὲ προσερχόμενον, τῷ κατ᾽ ἰδίαν ποιοῦντι συνεργεῖ⟨ν⟩ αὐτῷ πρὸς τὸ σφοδρότατον γίνεσθαι τὸ ἀποτέλεσμα. μάλιστα δὲ τὸ ἐκ   20
προκαταρκτικοῦ συνεργὸν γεγονέναι τὴν τοῦ αἰτίου διατείνειν δύναμιν παρίστησιν.

5 ⟨τοῦτο⟩ τὸ Sedley· τὸ ⟨αὐτοτελὲς⟩ Stählin   9–10 προδήλως . . . ἀδήλως Pohlenz, Arnim: προδήλῳ . . . ἀδήλῳ codd.   10 ⟨προδήλου⟩ Pohlenz   17 ⟨μεθ᾽ ἑτέρου⟩ Stählin   18 ἐν τῷ del. Stählin   19 συνεργεῖ⟨ν⟩ Stählin   20 σφοδρότατον codd.: -ότερον Arnim

336

Context: classification of causes. Cf. **C**.

1 **προκαταρκτικῶν** Defined earlier (ibid. 8.9.25.2) as τὰ πρώτως ἀφορμὴν παρεχόμενα εἰς τὸ γίγνεσθαί τι.

J Aetius 1.28.4 (*SVF* 2.917)

οἱ Στωικοὶ εἱρμὸν αἰτιῶν, τουτέστι τάξιν καὶ ἐπισύνδεσιν ἀπαράβατον.

1 ἐπισύνδεσιν vel ἐπίδεσιν codd.

Context: doxography of views on fate.

K Gellius 7.2.3 (*SVF* 2.1000, part)

in libro enim Περὶ προνοίας quarto εἱμαρμένην esse dicit φυσικήν τινα σύνταξιν τῶν ὅλων ἐξ ἀιδίου τῶν ἑτέρων τοῖς ἑτέροις ἐπακολουθούντων καὶ μεταπολουμένων ἀπαραβάτου οὔσης τῆς τοιαύτης ἐπιπλοκῆς.

3 μεταπολουμένων Kumanudes: ΜΕΑΠΟΑΥΜΕΝΩΝ codd.: μὴ ἀπολυομένων Usener

Context: how Chrysippus reconciled fate with human responsibility (cf. **62D**).

L Cicero, *Div.* 1.125–6 (*SVF* 2.921)

(1) fatum autem id appello, quod Graeci εἱμαρμένην, id est ordinem seriemque causarum, cum causae causa nexa rem ex se gignat. (2) ea est ex omni aeternitate fluens veritas sempiterna. quod cum ita sit, nihil est factum quod non futurum fuerit, eodemque modo nihil est futurum cuius non causas id ipsum efficientes natura contineat. (3) ex quo intellegitur ut fatum sit non id 5 quod superstitiose, sed id quod physice dicitur, causa aeterna rerum, cur et ea quae praeterierunt facta sint, et quae instant fiant, et quae sequuntur futura sint.

Context: appeal to fate as providing the theoretical basis for divination. Cf. **42**.
2–5 Cf. **13H** 26–8.

M Stobaeus 1.79,1–12 (*SVF* 2.913, part)

(1) Χρύσιππος δύναμιν πνευματικὴν τὴν οὐσίαν τῆς εἱμαρμένης, τάξει τοῦ παντὸς διοικητικήν. τοῦτο μὲν οὖν ἐν τῷ δευτέρῳ Περὶ κόσμου, (2) ἐν δὲ τῷ δευτέρῳ Περὶ ὡρῶν καὶ ἐν τοῖς Περὶ τῆς εἱμαρμένης καὶ ἐν ἄλλοις σποράδην πολυτρόπως ἀποφαίνεται λέγων· εἱμαρμένη ἐστὶν ὁ τοῦ κόσμου λόγος, ἢ λόγος τῶν ἐν τῷ κόσμῳ προνοίᾳ διοικουμένων, ἢ λόγος καθ' ὃν τὰ 5 μὲν γεγονότα γέγονε, τὰ δὲ γινόμενα γίνεται, τὰ δὲ γενησόμενα γενήσεται. (3) μεταλαμβάνει δ' ἀντὶ τοῦ λόγου τὴν ἀλήθειαν, τὴν αἰτίαν, τὴν φύσιν, τὴν ἀνάγκην, προστιθεὶς καὶ ἑτέρας ὀνομασίας, ὡς ἐπὶ τῆς αὐτῆς οὐσίας τασσομένας καθ' ἑτέρας καὶ ἑτέρας ἐπιβολάς.

3 ὡρῶν F: ὁρῶν Heeren   9 ἐπιβολάς Wachsmuth: ἐπιβουλάς codd.

Stoic physics

Context: doxography of views on fate (sharing its source with that from which **J** is excerpted).

N Alexander, *Fat.* 191,30–192,28 (*SVF* 2.945)

(1) φασὶν δὴ τὸν κόσμον τόνδε, ἕνα ὄντα καὶ πάντα τὰ ὄντα ἐν αὐτῷ περιέχοντα καὶ ὑπὸ φύσεως διοικούμενον ζωτικῆς τε καὶ λογικῆς καὶ νοερᾶς, ἔχειν τὴν τῶν ὄντων διοίκησιν ἀΐδιον κατὰ εἱρμόν τινα καὶ τάξιν προιοῦσαν, τῶν πρώτων τοῖς μετὰ ταῦτα γινομένοις αἰτίων γινομένων, καὶ τούτῳ τῷ τρόπῳ συνδεομένων ἀλλήλοις ἁπάντων, καὶ μήτε οὕτως   5
τινὸς ἐν αὐτῷ γινομένου ὡς μὴ πάντως ἐπακολουθεῖν αὐτῷ καὶ συνῆφθαι
ὡς αἰτίῳ ἕτερόν τι, μήτ᾽ αὖ τῶν ἐπιγινομένων τινὸς ἀπολελύσθαι
δυναμένου τῶν προγεγονότων ὡς μή τινι ἐξ αὐτῶν ἀκολουθεῖν ὥσπερ
συνδεόμενον· ἀλλὰ παντί τε τῷ. γενομένῳ ἕτερόν τι ἐπακολουθεῖν,
ἠρτημένον ⟨ἐξ⟩ αὐτοῦ ἐξ ἀνάγκης ὡς αἰτίου, καὶ πᾶν τὸ γινόμενον ἔχειν τι   10
πρὸ αὐτοῦ, ᾧ ὡς αἰτίῳ συνήρτηται. (2) μηδὲν γὰρ ἀναιτίως μήτε εἶναι μήτε
γίνεσθαι τῶν ἐν τῷ κόσμῳ διὰ τὸ μηδὲν εἶναι τῶν ἐν αὐτῷ ἀπολελυμένον τε
καὶ κεχωρισμένον τῶν προγεγονότων ἁπάντων. διασπᾶσθαι γὰρ καὶ
διαιρεῖσθαι καὶ μηκέτι τὸν κόσμον ἕνα μένειν, αἰεὶ κατὰ μίαν τάξιν τε καὶ
οἰκονομίαν διοικούμενον, εἰ ἀναίτιός τις εἰσάγοιτο κίνησις· ἣν εἰσάγεσθαι,   15
εἰ μὴ πάντα τὰ ὄντα τε καὶ γινόμενα ἔχοι τινὰ αἴτια προγεγονότα οἷς ἐξ
ἀνάγκης ἕπεται· ὅμοιόν τε εἶναί φασιν καὶ ὁμοίως ἀδύνατον τὸ ἀναιτίως
τῷ γίνεσθαί τι ἐκ μὴ ὄντος. τοιαύτην δὲ οὖσαν τὴν τοῦ παντὸς διοίκησιν ἐξ
ἀπείρου εἰς ἄπειρον ἐναργῶς τε καὶ ἀκαταστρόφως γίνεσθαι. (3) οὔσης δέ
τινος διαφορᾶς ἐν τοῖς αἰτίοις, ἣν ἐκτιθέντες σμῆνος [γὰρ] αἰτίων   20
καταλέγουσιν, τὰ μὲν προκαταρκτικά, τὰ δὲ συναίτια, τὰ δὲ ἑκτικά, τὰ δὲ
συνεκτικά, τὰ δὲ ἄλλο τι (οὐδὲν γὰρ δεῖ τὸν λόγον μηκύνειν, πάντα τὰ
λεγόμενα παρατιθέμεν⟨ον, ἀλλ⟩ὰ τὸ βούλημα αὐτῶν δεῖξαι τοῦ περὶ τῆς
εἱμαρμένης δόγματος)· ὄντων δὴ πλειόνων αἰτίων, ἐπ᾽ ἴσης ἐπὶ πάντων
αὐτῶν ἀληθές φασιν εἶναι τὸ ἀδύνατον εἶναι τῶν αὐτῶν ἁπάντων   25
περιεστηκότων περί τε τὸ αἴτιον καὶ ᾧ ἐστιν αἴτιον, ὁτὲ μὲν δὴ μὴ οὑτωσί
πως συμβαίνειν, ὁτὲ δὲ οὕτως. ἔσεσθαι γάρ, εἰ οὕτως γίνοιτο, ἀναίτιόν
τινα κίνησιν. (4) τὴν δὲ εἱμαρμένην αὐτὴν καὶ τὴν φύσιν καὶ τὸν λόγον καθ᾽
ὃν διοικεῖται τὸ πᾶν, θεὸν εἶναί φασιν, οὖσαν ἐν τοῖς οὖσίν τε καὶ γινομένοις
ἅπασιν καὶ οὕτως χρωμένην ἁπάντων τῶν ὄντων τῇ οἰκείᾳ φύσει πρὸς τὴν   30
τοῦ παντὸς οἰκονομίαν.

10 add. Orelli   19 ἐναργῶς codd.: ἐνεργῶς Usener, Arnim   20 del. Arnim   21 ἑκτικά vel ἀκτικά vel ἀρκτικά vel ἐκτικά codd.   23 suppl. Arnim   24 δὴ vel δ᾽ ἤδη codd.

Context: critique of the Stoic defence of determinism.

11 ἀναιτίως Cf. Plutarch, *St. rep.* 1045C: in defending strict determinism, Chrysippus found himself resisting certain philosophers who had posited an ἐπελευστική τις κίνησις in the commanding-faculty, to solve the 'Buridan's ass' problem of how a person, faced with having to take one of two 'indiscernibles' (e.g.

338

two identical-looking coins, see note on **58B**), succeeds in deciding between them. These philosophers had introduced a 'supervenient mental motion' because, as they claimed, 'no cause directs us to one rather than the other'. Chrysippus, in his rejoinder, insisted that the person's impulse, in such circumstances, *is* caused, even though the cause eludes the person's consciousness. What might be mistakenly regarded as genuinely spontaneous events, e.g. the fall of a dice, are, he argued, entirely determined by causal factors, which are features either of the dice itself or of its external conditions. Chrysippus' opponents in this passage are often regarded as Epicureans, and their 'supervenient mental motion' identified with the swerve of atoms (cf. **20**). But both suppositions are dubious. Plutarch's language does not recall Epicureanism, nor is the problem these philosophers address one which is known to have interested the Epicureans. The Academics are more promising candidates. Criticism of Stoic determinism, and facing the Stoics with problems over apparent 'indiscernibles', were well-known Academic preoccupations. If this is so, the position Chrysippus opposes will not have been an official school doctrine, but a problem and solution canvassed by Academics in order to discomfit the Stoics.

21 **ἐκτικά** A unique occurrence of this term in lists of causes, if the reading is sound. For the problem, see Rieth [551], 67 ff., Sharples [333], 153–4.

28–31 For these equivalences, cf. **54B**.

O Cicero, *Div.* 1.127 (*SVF* 2.944)

praeterea, cum fato omnia fiant (id quod alio loco ostendetur), si quis mortalis possit esse qui conligationem causarum omnium perspiciat animo, nihil eum profecto fallat. qui enim teneat causas rerum futurarum, idem necesse est omnia teneat quae futura sint. quod cum nemo facere nisi deus possit, relinquendum est homini ut signis quibusdam consequentia declarantibus 5 futura praesentiat. non enim illa quae futura sunt, subito exsistunt, sed est quasi rudentis explicatio sic traductio temporis nihil novi efficientis et primum quidque replicantis.

Context: shortly after **L**.

P Diogenianus (Eusebius, *Pr. ev.* 4.3.1 = *SVF* 2.939, part)

φέρει δὲ καὶ ἄλλην ἀπόδειξιν ἐν τῷ προειρημένῳ βιβλίῳ τοιαύτην τινά· μὴ γὰρ ἂν τὰς τῶν μάντεων προρρήσεις ἀληθεῖς εἶναί φησιν, εἰ μὴ πάντα ὑπὸ τῆς εἱμαρμένης περιείχοντο.

Context: attack on Chrysippus' doctrine of fate. Chrysippus is accused of circularity: fate is here proved from divination, but belief in divination already presupposes the fate doctrine (cf. **O**).

Q Cicero, *Fat.* 7–8

(1) ad Chrysippi laqueos revertamur, cui quidem primum de ipsa contagione rerum respondeamus, reliqua postea persequemur. inter locorum naturas

quantum intersit videmus; alios esse salubris, alios pestilentis; in aliis esse pituitosos et quasi redundantis, in aliis exsiccatos atque aridos; multaque sunt alia quae inter locum et locum plurimum differant. Athenis tenue caelum, ex 5 quo etiam acutiores putantur Attici; crassum Thebis, itaque pingues Thebani et valentes. (2) tamen neque illud tenue caelum efficiet, ut aut Zenonem quis aut Arcesilam aut Theophrastum audiat; neque crassum, ut Nemea potius quam Isthmo victoriam petat. diiunge longius: quid enim loci natura adferre potest, ut in porticu Pompei potius quam in Campo ambulemus? tecum quam cum alio? Idibus potius quam 10 Kalendis? ut igitur ad quasdam res natura loci pertinet aliquid, ad quasdam autem nihil, sic astrorum adfectio valeat, si vis, ad quasdam res, ad omnis certe non valebit. (3) at enim, quoniam in naturis hominum dissimilitudines sunt, ut alios dulcia, alios subamara delectent, alii libidinosi, alii iracundi aut crudeles aut superbi sint, alii ⟨a⟩ talibus vitiis abhorreant; quoniam igitur, inquit, tantum natura a 15 natura distat, quid mirum est has dissimilitudines ex differentibus causis esse factas?

Context: attack on the doctrine of fate, here replying to arguments of Chrysippus recorded in the lost part of the work. What school is represented by the speaker is a matter of controversy (see the introduction to Yon's edition).

R Plutarch, *St. rep.* 1056b–c (*SVF* 2.997, part)

(1) ὁ δὲ λέγων ὅτι Χρύσιππος οὐκ αὐτοτελῆ τούτων αἰτίαν ἀλλὰ προκαταρτικὴν μόνον ἐποιεῖτο τὴν εἱμαρμένην, ἐκεῖ πάλιν αὐτὸν ἀποδεί-ξει μαχόμενον πρὸς αὐτόν, ὅπου τὸν μὲν "Ὅμηρον ὑπερφυῶς ἐπαινεῖ περὶ τοῦ Διὸς λέγοντα "τῷ ἔχεθ᾽ ὅττι κεν ὔμμι κακὸν πέμπῃσιν ἑκάσ-τῳ", . . . αὐτὸς δὲ πολλὰ τούτοις ὁμολογούμενα γράφει, τέλος δέ φησι 5 μηδὲν ἴσχεσθαι μηδὲ κινεῖσθαι μηδὲ τοὐλάχιστον ἄλλως ἢ κατὰ τὸν τοῦ Διὸς λόγον, ὃν τῇ εἱμαρμένῃ τὸν αὐτὸν εἶναι. (2) ἔτι τοίνυν τὸ μὲν προκαταρκτικὸν αἴτιον ἀσθενέστερόν ἐστι τοῦ αὐτοτελοῦς, καὶ οὐκ ἐξικνεῖται κρατούμενον ὑπ᾽ ἄλλων ἐνισταμένων· τὴν δ᾽ εἱμαρμένην αἰτίαν ἀνίκητον καὶ ἀκώλυτον καὶ ἄτρεπτον ἀποφαίνων. 10

9 ἐνισταμένων vel ἐξανισταμένων codd.

Context: critique of Chrysippus' thesis that φαντασίαι do not themselves compel assent. If this is so, argues Plutarch, fate will not compel assent either.

For this Chrysippean idea that fate operates on us by means of φαντασίαι only, which constitute preliminary, not complete, causes, cf. **62C**.

S Cicero, *Fat.* 28–30

(1) nec nos impediet illa "ignava ratio" quae dicitur (appellatur enim quidam a philosophis ἀργὸς λόγος); cui si pareamus, nihil omnino agamus in vita. sic enim interrogant: "si fatum tibi est ex hoc morbo convalescere, sive tu medicum adhibueris sive non adhibueris, convalesces; item, si fatum tibi est ex

hoc morbo non convalescere, sive tu medicum adhibueris sive non adhibueris, 5
non convalesces; et alterutrum fatum est; medicum ergo adhibere nihil
attinet." . . . (2) haec ratio a Chrysippo reprehenditur. quaedam enim sunt,
inquit, in rebus simplicia, quaedam copulata. simplex est "morietur illo die
Socrates"; huic, sive quid fecerit sive non fecerit, finitus est moriendi dies. at si
ita fatum sit "nascetur Oedipus Laio", non poterit dici "sive fuerit Laius cum 10
muliere sive non fuerit"; copulata enim res est et confatalis. sic enim appellat
quia ita fatum sit et concubiturum cum uxore Laium et ex ea Oedipum
procreaturum. ut, si esset dictum "luctabitur Olympiis Milon", et referret
aliquis "ergo sive habuerit adversarium sive non habuerit, luctabitur", erraret.
est enim copulatum "luctabitur", quia sine adversario nulla luctatio est. (3) 15
omnes igitur istius generis captiones eodem modo refelluntur. "sive tu
adhibueris medicum sive non adhibueris, convalesces" captiosum; tam enim
est fatale medicum adhibere quam convalescere. haec, ut dixi, confatalia ille
appellat.

Context: see 70G.

2 ἀργὸς λόγος   For the form of the title, cf. vol. 1, 229. The argument's origin is
unknown, but there is an obvious temptation to guess that it is from the same stable as
the κυριεύων λόγος and the θερίζων λόγος (31M; 38A–B, 1), namely the Dialectical
school.

11 confatalis   = συνειμαρμένος. See the parallel passage at 62F.

ETHICS

56 The division of ethical topics

A Diogenes Laertius 7.84 (*SVF* 3.1)

τὸ δ' ἠθικὸν μέρος τῆς φιλοσοφίας διαιροῦσιν εἴς τε τὸν περὶ ὁρμῆς καὶ εἰς
τὸν περὶ ἀγαθῶν καὶ κακῶν τόπον καὶ εἰς τὸν περὶ παθῶν καὶ περὶ ἀρετῆς
καὶ περὶ τέλους περί τε τῆς πρώτης ἀξίας καὶ τῶν πράξεων καὶ περὶ τῶν
καθηκόντων προτροπῶν τε καὶ ἀποτροπῶν. οὕτω δ' ὑποδιαιροῦσιν οἱ περὶ
Χρύσιππον καὶ Ἀρχέδημον καὶ Ζήνωνα τὸν Ταρσέα καὶ Ἀπολλόδωρον 5
καὶ Διογένην καὶ Ἀντίπατρον καὶ Ποσειδώνιον· ὁ μὲν γὰρ Κιτιεὺς Ζήνων
καὶ ὁ Κλεάνθης, ὡς ἂν ἀρχαιότεροι, ἀφελέστερον περὶ τῶν πραγμάτων
διέλαβον. οὗτοι δὲ διεῖλον καὶ τὸν λογικὸν καὶ τὸν φυσικόν.

Context: the beginning of Diogenes' doxography of Stoic ethics.

B Seneca, *Ep.* 89.14

ergo cum tripertita sit philosophia, moralem eius partem primum incipiamus
disponere. quam in tria rursus dividi placuit . . . primum enim est ut quanti
quidque sit iudices, secundum ut impetum ad illa capias ordinatum

Stoic ethics

temperatumque, tertium ut inter impetum tuum actionemque conveniat, ut
in omnibus istis tibi ipse consentias.   5

2 *quanti* Muret: *quantum* codd.

Context: the divisions of philosophy.
Panaetius may well be responsible for the tripartite division of ethics. His name is
absent from **A**, which includes Posidonius; and Cicero, *Off.* 2.18, probably based on
Panaetius, specifies three spheres of action for every virtue, which closely correspond
to the arrangement laid out in **B–C**.

C Epictetus, *Diss.* 3.2.1–5

(1) τρεῖς εἰσι τόποι, περὶ οὓς ἀσκηθῆναι δεῖ τὸν ἐσόμενον καλὸν καὶ
ἀγαθόν· (2) ὁ περὶ τὰς ὀρέξεις καὶ τὰς ἐκκλίσεις, ἵνα μήτ᾽ ὀρεγόμενος
ἀποτυγχάνῃ μήτ᾽ ἐκκλίνων περιπίπτῃ· (3) ὁ περὶ τὰς ὁρμὰς καὶ ἀφορμὰς
καὶ ἁπλῶς ὁ περὶ τὸ καθῆκον, ἵνα τάξει, ἵνα εὐλογίστως, ἵνα μὴ ἀμελῶς·
(4) τρίτος ἐστὶν ὁ περὶ τὴν ἀνεξαπατησίαν καὶ ἀνεικαιότητα καὶ ὅλως ὁ   5
περὶ τὰς συγκαταθέσεις. (5) τούτων κυριώτατος καὶ μάλιστα ἐπείγων
ἐστὶν ὁ περὶ τὰ πάθη· πάθος γὰρ ἄλλως οὐ γίνεται εἰ μὴ ὀρέξεως
ἀποτυγχανούσης ἢ ἐκκλίσεως περιπιπτούσης. οὗτός ἐστιν ὁ ταραχάς,
θορύβους, ἀτυχίας, ὁ δυστυχίας ἐπιφέρων, ὁ πένθη, οἰμωγάς, φθόνους, ὁ
φθονερούς, ὁ ζηλοτύπους ποιῶν, δι᾽ ὧν οὐδ᾽ ἀκοῦσαι λόγου δυνάμεθα. (6)   1
δεύτερός ἐστιν ὁ περὶ τὸ καθῆκον· οὐ δεῖ γάρ με εἶναι ἀπαθῆ ὡς ἀνδριάντα,
ἀλλὰ τὰς σχέσεις τηροῦντα τὰς φυσικὰς καὶ ἐπιθέτους ὡς εὐσεβῆ, ὡς υἱόν,
ὡς ἀδελφόν, ὡς πατέρα, ὡς πολίτην. (7) τρίτος ἐστὶν ὁ ἤδη τοῖς
προκόπτουσιν ἐπιβάλλων, ὁ περὶ τὴν αὐτῶν τούτων ἀσφάλειαν, ἵνα μηδ᾽ ἐν
ὕπνοις λάθῃ τις ἀνεξέταστος παρελθοῦσα φαντασία μηδ᾽ ἐν οἰνώσει μηδὲ   1
μελαγχολῶντος.

Context: the opening of a discourse on the subjects that must be studied for moral
progress.
    For detailed discussion, cf. Bonhöffer [311], 19–28. Epictetus refers to one or more
of these topics in 1.17.22; 2.17.15–16, 32–3; 4.1.69; 4.4.13; 4.10.13.
    2 ὀρέξεις Epictetus treats ὄρεξις as a distinct psychological faculty whereas in
Chrysippean Stoicism it refers to a species of ὁρμή; cf. **53Q** 4–5. In Epictetus, as his
first two 'topics' indicate, the object of ὄρεξις is the good or the apparent good (cf.
60F), that of ὁρμή the performance of καθήκοντα; cf. Inwood [547], 115–26.
    5 ἀνεικαιότητα Cf. **31B** 3; **41D** 1. The presence of this 'dialectical' virtue shows
that Epictetus' topics, though all ethical in their orientation, draw upon some material
which earlier Stoics (cf. **26**) would have assigned to another 'part' of philosophy.
    7 ὁ περὶ τὰ πάθη I.e. the first topic.
    11–13 Cf. **59Q**; **66F** 2.
    15–16 Intoxication and depression are singled out because they are the standard
instances of conditions which could destroy virtue; cf. **61I** 2. Zeno (*SVF* 1.234)
claimed that everyone could assess their progress from the moral purity or impurity of
their dreams, a tougher index of a sound character than even Plato required; cf. *Rep.* 9,
572b.

57 Impulse and appropriateness

A Diogenes Laertius 7.85–6 (*SVF* 3.178)

(1) τὴν δὲ πρώτην ὁρμήν φασι τὸ ζῷον ἴσχειν ἐπὶ τὸ τηρεῖν ἑαυτό,
οἰκειούσης αὐτὸ τῆς φύσεως ἀπ' ἀρχῆς, καθά φησιν ὁ Χρύσιππος ἐν τῷ
πρώτῳ Περὶ τελῶν, (2) πρῶτον οἰκεῖον λέγων εἶναι παντὶ ζῴῳ τὴν αὐτοῦ
σύστασιν καὶ τὴν ταύτης συνείδησιν· οὔτε γὰρ ἀλλοτριῶσαι εἰκὸς ἦν αὐτὸ
τὸ ζῷον, οὔτε ποιήσασαν αὐτὸ μήτ' ἀλλοτριῶσαι μήτ' [οὐκ] οἰκειῶσαι.   5
ἀπολείπεται τοίνυν λέγειν συστησαμένην αὐτὸ οἰκειῶσαι πρὸς ἑαυτό·
οὕτω γὰρ τά τε βλάπτοντα διωθεῖται καὶ τὰ οἰκεῖα προσίεται. (3) ὃ δὲ
λέγουσί τινες, πρὸς ἡδονὴν γίγνεσθαι τὴν πρώτην ὁρμὴν τοῖς ζῴοις,
ψεῦδος ἀποφαίνουσιν. ἐπιγέννημα γάρ φασιν, εἰ ἄρα ἔστιν, ἡδονὴν εἶναι
ὅταν αὐτὴ καθ' αὑτὴν ἡ φύσις ἐπιζητήσασα τὰ ἐναρμόζοντα τῇ συστάσει   10
ἀπολάβῃ, ὃν τρόπον ἀφιλαρύνεται τὰ ζῷα καὶ θάλλει τὰ φυτά. (4) οὐδέν τε,
φασί, διήλλαξεν ἡ φύσις ἐπὶ τῶν φυτῶν καὶ ἐπὶ τῶν ζῴων, ὅτε χωρὶς ὁρμῆς
καὶ αἰσθήσεως κἀκεῖνα οἰκονομεῖ καὶ ἐφ' ἡμῶν τινα φυτοειδῶς γίνεται. ἐκ
περιττοῦ δὲ τῆς ὁρμῆς τοῖς ζῴοις ἐπιγενομένης, ᾗ συγχρώμενα πορεύεται
πρὸς τὰ οἰκεῖα, τούτοις μὲν τὸ κατὰ φύσιν τὸ κατὰ τὴν ὁρμὴν διοικεῖσθαι·   15
(5) τοῦ δὲ λόγου τοῖς λογικοῖς κατὰ τελειοτέραν προστασίαν δεδομένου, τὸ
κατὰ λόγον ζῆν ὀρθῶς γίνεσθαι ⟨τού⟩τοις κατὰ φύσιν· τεχνίτης γὰρ οὗτος
ἐπιγίνεται τῆς ὁρμῆς.

2 αὐτὸ BP: αὐτῷ F   4 συνείδησιν] συναίσθησιν Pohlenz   αὐτὸ ⟨αὐτῷ⟩ Arnim   5 ποιήσασαν
Reiske: ποιῆσαι ἂν codd.   οὐκ del. Zeller   οἰκειῶσαι Stephanus: οἰκείως codd.   10 αὐτὴ P:
αὐτὴν BF   12 ὅτε BFP Suda: ὅτι d   15 τὸ BF: τῷ P   17 ⟨τού⟩τοις Kayser

Context: immediately following **56A**. With 1–9, cf. Cicero, *Fin.* 3.16.

3 **πρῶτον οἰκεῖον**   For the interpretation of the term, cf. Pembroke [564], 141 n.
8.

5   Zeller's deletion of οὐκ needs to be reasserted, in view of recent support for the
MSS reading; cf. Kerferd [567], 185 n. 1. If οὐκ is retained, οὐκ οἰκειῶσαι becomes
virtually synonymous with ἀλλοτριῶσαι, and this destroys the argument since
οἰκείωσις must be established as the only reasonable alternative to ἀλλοτρίωσις,
which has been eliminated.

9 **ἐπιγέννημα**   This account of pleasure (cf. **43A** 7) is often thought to betray the
influence of Aristotle, *EN* x.3, 1174b31ff., τελειοῖ δὲ τὴν ἐνέργειαν ἡ ἡδονὴ . . . ὡς
ἐπιγινόμενόν τι τέλος, οἷον τοῖς ἀκμαίοις ἡ ὥρα; cf. Long [549], 80, and Sandbach
[304], 27–8, who is unconvinced. With ἐπιγέννημα, cf. ἐπακολούθημα in *SVF*
3.405, and see note on **65A** 8–9.

11–18   For a detailed analysis of this argument, cf. Long [555], 96–101.

12 **ὅτε**   This, though much the better attested reading, is regularly rejected in
favour of ὅτι; it also makes much better sense. Before birth animal life is plantlike (cf.
53B 2 with notes), and the focus of this sentence is on the continuity between all forms
of life. Also κἀκεῖνα, 13, should refer to ζῴων and not to φυτῶν, as it would if ὅτι is
adopted.

Stoic ethics

16 **προστασίαν** In translating this by 'management' we follow Striker [570], 155 n. 12, retracting 'prescription' in Long [555].

17 **ὀρθῶς** We take the adverb with τὸ κατὰ λόγον ζῆν, treating it as a variant of the familiar ὀρθὸς λόγος (58M 6; 61G 5). Striker, loc. cit., thinks it modifies γίνεσθαι and thus states the correctness of the inference. This does not seem convincing as Greek, nor suitable to the context as continued at 63C. As the craftsman of impulse, reason shapes a way of living correctly. (Note the description of the virtues – dispositions of reason – as τέχναι, 61D 1.)

B Seneca, *Ep.* 121.6–15

(1) nemo aegre molitur artus suos, nemo in usu sui haesitat. hoc edita protinus faciunt; cum hac scientia prodeunt . . . (2) adeo autem non adigit illa ad hoc doloris timor ut in naturalem motum etiam dolore prohibente nitantur. sic infans qui stare meditatur et ferre se adsuescit, simul temptare vires suas coepit, cadit et cum fletu totiens resurgit donec se per dolorem ad id quod natura   5
poscit exercuit . . . nullum tormentum sentit supina testudo, inquieta est tamen desiderio naturalis status nec ante desinit niti, quatere se, quam in pedes constitit. ergo omnibus constitutionis suae sensus est et inde membrorum tam expedita tractatio . . . (3) unicuique aetati sua constitutio est, alia infanti, alia puero, ⟨alia adulescenti⟩, alia seni: omnes ei constitutioni conciliantur in qua   10
sunt. infans sine dentibus est: huic constitutioni suae conciliatur. enati sunt dentes: huic constitutioni conciliatur.

1 *haesitat* Madvig: *haesit. ad* codd.   10 suppl. Gertz

Context: animals' awareness of their own constitution.

2–9   A rejoinder to the objection that animals move their bodily parts *apte*, under the constraint of fear of pain if they move otherwise. Cf. the rejection of pleasure as the object of the primary impulse in **A 3**. In the next sections, omitted here, Seneca explains that a baby's recognition that it has a constitution does not imply any knowledge of what its constitution is.

C Hierocles, 1.34–9, 51–7; 2.1–9

(1) βραχέα δὲ δοκεῖ γε περὶ [τῆς] αἰσ[θ]ῆσ[ε]ω[ς] εἰ|πεῖν· φέρει γὰρ εἰς γνῶσι[ν τοῦ πρώ]το[υ ο]ἰκείου, | [ὃ]ν δὴ λόγον ἀρχὴν ἀρίσ[την] ἔφαμεν ἔ[σ]ε|[σθαι τῆς] ἠθικῆς στοιχειώ[σεως]. (2) οὐκ ἀγνοητέον [ὅ]τι | τὸ [ζ]ῷιον εὐθὺς ἅμα [τῶι γ]εν[έσ]θαι [αἰ]σθά[ν]εται [ἑα]υ|τοῦ . . . τὰ ζῷια πρῶτον μὲν μερῶν τῶν ἰδίων αἰ[σ]θάνεται . . . καὶ [ὅ]τι ἔχε[ι] καὶ πρὸς ἣν   5
ἔ[χ]ει | [χ]ρείαν, ἡμεῖς τε αὐτο[ὶ ὀ]φθαλμῶν [καὶ ὤτων] καὶ [τῶν] ἄλ[λων]. τ]ῆι|δε γοῦν κἀπειδὰν μὲν ἰδεῖν [ἐ]θέλωμέν τι, τοὺς ὀφ[θαλμοὺς ἐ]ν|τείνο-μεν ὡς ἐπὶ τὸ ὁρατὸν οὐχὶ δὲ τὰ [ὦ]τα . . . διὸ πρώτη πίστις το[ῦ] αἰ|σθάνεσθαι τὸ ζῷιον ἅπαν ἑαυτοῦ ἡ τῶν μερῶν καὶ τῶν ἔργων, ὑπὲρ | ὧν ἐδόθη τὰ μέρη, συναίσθησις· (3) δευτέρα δὲ ὅτι οὐδὲ | τῶν πρὸς ἄμυναν   10
παρασκευασθέντων αὐτοῖς ἀναισθήτως δία|κειται. καὶ γὰρ ταῦροι μὲν εἰς

μαχὴν καθιστάμενοι ταύροις | ἑτέροις ἢ καί τισιν ἑτερογενέσι ζώιοις τὰ κέρατα πρ[ο]ίσχον|ται καθάπερ ὅπλα συμφυᾶ πρὸς τὴν ἀντίταξιν. οὕτω δ᾿ ἔχει | καὶ τῶν λοιπῶν ἕκαστον πρὸς τὸ οἰκεῖον καί, ἵν᾿ οὕτως εἴπω, συμ|φυὲς ὅπλον.   15

For the text, cf. Arnim [572] ad loc.

Context: one line after **53B 4**. Having specified αἴσθησις and ὁρμή as the distinguishing features of animals, Hierocles says he has no need of the latter for his present purpose, but will deal briefly with the former.

4   We omit 12 lines after ἑαυτοῦ in which Hierocles criticizes unnamed people who claim that the only function of αἴσθησις is for perceiving external things. For a very full discussion, cf. Inwood [575], 167–78. He identifies Hierocles' opponents with Academic and Peripatetic philosophers like Antiochus who took over Stoic οἰκείωσις but treated it as an automatic process not involving any cognitive faculty.

8   After ὦτα the point is developed with further examples which we omit.

D   Hierocles 9.3–10, 11.14–18

(1) ὅτι [δὲ] ἡ μὲν πρὸς ἑαυτὸ εὐνοητ[ική, στερ||κτ[ι]κ[ὴ δὲ ἡ συγ]γεν-
[ι]κ[ή]· . . . καθάπερ [οὖν] στε[ρ]κτικῶς μὲν κ[ατὰ τοῦτο οἱ]|κε[ι]ούμεθα
τοῖς τέκνοις, αἱρετικ[ῶς] δὲ [τοῖς ἐκ|τὸ]ς χρήμασιν, οὔ[τ]ω καὶ [τὸ ζῷον]
ἑαυτῷ[ι. . . . . .]ι. . . .ως, τοῖς δὲ πρὸς τ[ὴν χ]ρῆσιν τὴν συστη[ματικὴν
φέ]|ρουσ[ι]ν [ἐκ]λεκτικ[ῶς . . . (2) [ἔσ]μεν ζῷον, ἀλλὰ [συνα]γελαστικὸν   5
καὶ | [δε]όμενον ἑ[τερο[ῦ]· διὰ τοῦτο καὶ κατὰ π[όλει]ς οἰκοῦμεν· οὐ|[δεὶ]ς
γὰρ ἄνθρωπος [ὃ]ς οὐχὶ πόλεως ἔστι μέρος· ἔπειτα | [καὶ ῥαι]δίως
συντιθ[έ]μεθα φιλίας· ἐκ γὰρ τοῦ συνεστια||[θῆ]ναι ἢ τ[οῦ συγκαθί]σαι ἐν
θεάτρωι . . .

For the text, cf. Arnim [572] ad loc.

Context: this part of the papyrus is extremely fragmentary. Column 9 has τέλος as the last word of its heading.

1   The feminine noun to be supplied with the adjectives must be οἰκείωσις.
3 **τοῖς ἐκ|τό]ς**   That these words preceded χρήμασιν is confirmed by τὰ ἐκτὸς χ[. . . in 9.5.
4   The gap might be filled by μὲν τηρητικῶς or κηδεμονικῶς, cf. Anon. *In Plat. Theaet.*, 7.41–8.1.
5–9   Section 2 comes more than 100 lines later than section 1; no legible context survives. Following the break after θεάτρῳ, 9, Hierocles used the word θαυμασιώτα-τον, perhaps in reference to the fraternizing of soldiers in opposing armies; so Arnim [572] ad loc.

E   Plutarch, *St. rep.* 1038B (*SVF* 3.179, 2.724)

(1) πῶς οὖν ἀποκναίει πάλιν ἐν παντὶ βιβλίῳ φυσικῷ νὴ Δία καὶ ἠθικῷ γράφων ὡς οἰκειούμεθα πρὸς αὑτοὺς εὐθὺς γενόμενοι καὶ τὰ μέρη καὶ τὰ

345

Stoic ethics

ἔκγονα τὰ ἑαυτῶν; (2) ἐν δὲ τῷ πρώτῳ Περὶ δικαιοσύνης καὶ τὰ θηρία φησὶ
συμμέτρως τῇ χρείᾳ τῶν ἐκγόνων ᾠκειῶσθαι πρὸς αὐτά, πλὴν τῶν
ἰχθύων· αὐτὰ γὰρ τὰ κυήματα τρέφεται δι' αὐτῶν. ἀλλ' οὔτ' αἴσθησίς ἐστιν οἷς   5
μηδὲν αἰσθητὸν οὔτ' οἰκείωσις οἷς μηδὲν οἰκεῖον· ἡ γὰρ οἰκείωσις αἴσθησις ἔοικε τοῦ
οἰκείου καὶ ἀντίληψις εἶναι.

1 νὴ Δία Reiske: ἰδίω vel ἰδία codd.

Context: Plutarch finds a contradiction between Chrysippus' claim that nothing is
οἰκεῖον to the φαῦλος and his doctrine reported here.

3–5   For animals' love of their offspring, and fish abandoning their eggs, cf.
Cicero, ND 2.129.

6–7   The likelihood that this is orthodox Stoicism is supported by Porphyry, Abst
3.19.2, οἰκειώσεως πάσης καὶ ἀλλοτριώσεως ἀρχὴ τὸ αἰσθάνεσθαι; cf. Inwood
[575], 172–3.

F Cicero, Fin. 3.62–8

(1) pertinere autem ad rem arbitrantur intellegi natura fieri ut liberi a
parentibus amentur. a quo initio profectam communem humani generis
societatem persequimur. quod primum intellegi debet figura membrisque
corporum, quae ipsa declarant procreandi a natura habitam esse rationem.
neque vero haec inter se congruere possent, ut natura et procreari vellet et   5
diligi procreatos non curaret. atque etiam in bestiis vis naturae perspici potest;
quarum in fetu et in educatione laborem cum cernimus, naturae ipsius vocem
videmur audire. quare ⟨ut⟩ perspicuum est natura nos a dolore abhorrere, sic
apparet a natura ipsa, ut eos, quos genuerimus, amemus, inpelli. (2) ex hoc
nascitur ut etiam communis hominum inter homines naturalis sit commenda-   10
tio, ut oporteat hominem ab homine ob id ipsum, quod homo sit, non
alienum videri. ut enim in membris alia sunt tamquam sibi nata, ut oculi, ut
aures, alia etiam ceterorum membrorum usum adiuvant, ut crura, ut manus,
sic inmanes quaedam bestiae sibi solum natae sunt, at . . . formicae, apes,
ciconiae aliorum etiam causa quaedam faciunt. multo haec coniunctius   15
homines. itaque natura sumus apti ad coetus, concilia, civitates. (3) mundum
autem censent regi numine deorum, eumque esse quasi communem urbem et
civitatem hominum et deorum, et unum quemque nostrum eius mundi esse
partem; ex quo illud natura consequi, ut communem utilitatem nostrae
anteponamus . . . ex quo fit, ut laudandus is sit, qui mortem oppetat pro re   20
publica, quod deceat cariorem nobis esse patriam quam nosmet ipsos . . . (4)
inpellimur autem natura, ut prodesse velimus quam plurimis in primisque
docendo rationibusque prudentiae tradendis. itaque non facile est invenire qui
quod sciat ipse non tradat alteri; ita non solum ad discendum propensi sumus,
verum etiam ad docendum . . . (5) et quo modo hominum inter homines iuris   25
esse vincula putant, sic homini nihil iuris esse cum bestiis. praeclare enim
Chrysippus, cetera nata esse hominum causa et deorum, eos autem

346

communitatis et societatis suae, ut bestiis homines uti ad utilitatem suam possint sine iniuria. (6) quoniamque ea natura esset hominis, ut ei cum genere humano quasi civile ius intercederet, qui id conservaret, eum iustum, qui 30 migraret, iniustum fore. (7) sed quem ad modum, theatrum cum commune sit, recte tamen dici potest eius esse eum locum, quem quisque occuparit, sic in urbe mundove communi non adversatur ius, quo minus suum quidque cuiusque sit. (8) cum autem ad tuendos conservandosque homines hominem natum esse videamus, consentaneum est huic naturae, ut sapiens velit gerere et 35 administrare rem publicam atque, ut e natura vivat, uxorem adiungere et velle ex ea liberos.

8 ⟨ut⟩ Manutius   13 alia Marsus: aliqua ARN: aliaque BE: reliqua V   15–16 coniunctius homines Madvig: coniunctio est hominis codd.   29 ei Lambinus: et ABEN: om. RV

Context: transition from the treatment of 'proper functions' concerning oneself to those concerning other people. Cf. Stobaeus 2.94,7–20, and for a comparable passage in the account of Antiochean ethics, see Cicero, Fin. 5.65–8.

The naturalness of community life is a fundamental step in the grounding of Stoic ethics. For supporting material, cf. 59Q; 63K; 66E, F; Marcus Aurelius 4.4 (deriving the civic character of the world from the community of rational beings; cf. 46G 3); 7.55 (τὸ κοινωνικόν as the 'leading' element in the human constitution). These passages support and illuminate Cicero's claims in 19–20 concerning the preferability of the common advantage to our own, though strictly, as he points out in Off. 3, these should coincide; cf. Epictetus in 59Q 3 and Marcus Aurelius 5.22. For the crucial concept of being a pars mundi, 18–19, cf. 63C 3. Cicero does not develop its theological implications in Fin. 3, though at the end of the book he refers to the Chrysippean doctrine (60A) that ethics should be founded on the government of the world.

G Hierocles (Stobaeus 4.671,7–673,11)

(1) ὅλως γὰρ ἕκαστος ἡμῶν οἷον κύκλοις πολλοῖς περιγέγραπται, τοῖς μὲν σμικροτέροις, τοῖς δὲ μείζοσι, καὶ τοῖς μὲν περιέχουσι, τοῖς δὲ περιεχομέ-νοις, κατὰ τὰς διαφόρους καὶ ἀνίσους πρὸς ἀλλήλους σχέσεις. (2) πρῶτος μὲν γάρ ἐστι κύκλος καὶ προσεχέστατος, ὃν αὐτός τις καθάπερ περὶ κέντρον τὴν ἑαυτοῦ γέγραπται διάνοιαν· ἐν ᾧ κύκλῳ τό τε σῶμα 5 περιέχεται καὶ τὰ τοῦ σώματος ἕνεκα παρειλημμένα. σχεδὸν γὰρ ὁ βραχύτατος καὶ μικροῦ δεῖν αὐτοῦ προσαπτόμενος τοῦ κέντρου κύκλος οὗτος. (3) δεύτερος δ' ἀπὸ τούτου καὶ πλέον μὲν ἀφεστὼς τοῦ κέντρου, περιέχων δὲ τὸν πρῶτον, ἐν ᾧ τετάχαται γονεῖς ἀδελφοὶ γυνὴ παῖδες. ὁ δ' ἀπὸ τούτων τρίτος, ἐν ᾧ θεῖοι καὶ τηθίδες, πάπποι τε καὶ τῆθαι, καὶ 10 ἀδελφῶν παῖδες, ἔτι δ' ἀνεψιοί. μεθ' ὃν ὁ τοὺς ἄλλους περιέχων συγγενεῖς. τούτῳ δ' ἐφεξῆς ὁ τῶν δημοτῶν καὶ μετ' αὐτὸν ὁ τῶν φυλετῶν, εἶθ' ὁ πολιτῶν, καὶ λοιπὸν οὕτως ὁ μὲν ἀστυγειτόνων, ὁ δὲ ὁμοεθνῶν. (4) ὁ δ' ἐξωτάτω καὶ μέγιστος περιέχων τε πάντας τοὺς κύκλους ὁ τοῦ παντὸς ἀνθρώπων γένους. (5) τούτων οὖν τεθεωρημένων, κατὰ τὸν ἐντεταμένον 15

347

Stoic ethics

ἐστὶ περὶ τὴν δέουσαν ἑκάστων χρῆσιν τὸ ἐπισυνάγειν πως τοὺς κύκλους
ὡς ἐπὶ τὸ κέντρον καὶ τῇ σπουδῇ μεταφέρειν ἀεὶ τοὺς ἐκ τῶν περιεχόντων
εἰς τοὺς περιεχομένους ... (6) πρόσκειται δ' ὅτι καὶ τούτοις μὲν ὁμοίως
τιμητέον τοὺς ἐκ τοῦ τρίτου κύκλου, τούτοις δ' αὖ πάλιν τοὺς συγγενεῖς.
ἀφαιρήσεται μὲν γάρ τι τῆς εὐνοίας τὸ καθ' αἷμα διάστημα πλέον ὄν· ἡμῖν   2c
δ' ὅμως σπουδαστέα περὶ τὴν ἐξομοίωσίν ἐστιν. ἥκοι μὲν γὰρ ἂν εἰς τὸ
μέτριον, εἰ διὰ τῆς ἡμετέρας αὐτῶν ἐνστάσεως ἐπιτεμνόμεθα τὸ μῆκος τῆς
πρὸς ἕκαστον τὸ πρόσωπον σχέσεως. τὸ μὲν οὖν συνέχον καὶ πραγματικώ-
τερον εἴρηται· (7) χρὴ δ' ἐπιμετρεῖν καὶ κατὰ τὴν τῶν προσηγοριῶν
χρῆσιν, τοὺς μὲν ἀνεψιοὺς καὶ θείους καὶ τηθίδας ἀδελφοὺς ἀποκαλοῦντας   2ς
πατέρας τε καὶ μητέρας, τῶν δὲ συγγενῶν τοὺς μὲν θείους, τοὺς δὲ ἀδελφιδοῦς, τοὺς
δὲ ἀνεψιούς, ὡς ἂν καὶ τὰ τῆς ἡλικίας παρείκῃ ἕνεκα τῆς ἐν τοῖς ὀνόμασιν ἐκτενείας. οὗτος
γὰρ τῆς προσρήσεως ὁ τρόπος ἅμα μὲν ἂν σημεῖον οὐκ ἀμαυρὸν εἴη τῆς
οὔσης ἡμῖν σπουδῆς περὶ ἑκάστους, ἅμα δ' ἂν ἐποτρύνοι καὶ προσεντείνοι
πρὸς τὴν ὑποδεδειγμένην οἷον συνολκὴν τῶν κύκλων.   3c

1 ὅλως MA: ὅλος S   8 τούτου Trincavelli: τούτων codd.   15 τὸν ἐντεταμένον S: τὸ ἐντεταγμένον
MA   24 ἐπιμετρεῖν Bentley: ἐπὶ μετρίαν SM: ἐπὶ μετρίαιν A

Context: one of seven chapters on ethical subjects excerpted from Hierocles. Entitled
'how to treat one's relatives', it probably formed part of a book which included
similarly titled chapters on the gods, native land, and parents. For Hierocles as the
Stoic philosopher named by Aulus Gellius 9.5.8, cf. Praechter [573], 106–7, and for his
identity with the Hierocles of **C–D**, see Arnim [572], vii–xi.

1 The image of concentric circles is used by Seneca, *Ep.* 12.6, to represent the
temporal stages of a person's life.

15–16 **κατὰ τὸν ἐντεταμένον ἐστί** A similar expression, κατὰ τὸν φιλοίκειον
... ἐστί, begins the sentence which follows περιεχομένους, 18. Inwood [575], 181,
renders 'serious man'; but this translation fails to capture the probably technical sense
of ἐντείνομαι. We prefer 'a well-tempered man', a sense which the verb can denote
even without the addition of the adverb εὖ; cf. the Stoic use of εὐτονία, **65T** 3.

22 **ἐνστάσεως** Cf. Epictetus, *Diss.* 3.14.7, 3.22.19.

H Anon., *In Plat. Theaet.*, 5.18–6.31

(1) ὠκειώμε|θα γὰρ τοῖς ὁμοειδέσι· | (2) μᾶλλον μέντοι ὠι|κείωται το[ῖς
ἑα]υτοῦ πολίται[ς· ἐπιτείνε]|ται γὰρ καὶ ἀ[νίετ]α[ι] ἡ | οἰκείωσις· (3) ὅ[σοι
το]ίνυν | ἀπὸ τῆς οἰκε[ι]ώσεως | εἰσάγουσι τὴν δι[κ]αι[ο]|σύνην, εἰ μὲν
λέγου|σιν ἴσην αὐτοῦ τε πρὸς | αὐτὸν καὶ πρὸς [τὸν ἔ]||[σ]χατον Μυσῶν,
τεθέν|τος μὲν τούτου σώζε|ται ἡ δικαιοσ[ύ]νη, οὐ | συγχωρεῖται [δ]ὲ [εἶ]|ναι   5·
ἴσην· παρὰ γὰ[ρ τὴν] ἐνάργειάν ἐστιν [κ]α[ὶ] | τὴν συναίσθησιν. (4) ἡ | μὲν
γὰρ πρὸς ἑαυτὸν | οἰκείωσις φυσική ἐστιν | καὶ ἄλογος, ἡ δὲ πρὸς | τοὺς
πλησίον φυσικὴ | μὲν καὶ αὐτή, οὐ μέν|τοι ἄνευ λόγου. (5) ἐὰν γοῦν | κα-
ταγνῶμεν πονη|ρίαν τινῶν, οὐ μόνον | ψέγομεν αὐτούς, ἀλλὰ | καὶ ἀλλο-
τριούμεθα | πρὸς αὐτούς, αὐτοὶ δὲ | ἁμαρτάνοντες οὐ|κ ἀποδέχονται   10
μὲν | τὰ [.] . . . ὁμενα, οὐ δύναν|τ[αι δ]ὲ μεισῆσαι αὐτούς. (6) | οὐκ ἔστιν

348

τοίνυν ἴση | ἡ ο[ἴ]κε[ἴ]ωσις πρὸς ἑ|αυτὸν [καὶ π]ρὸς ὅντιν|οῦν, ὅπου μηδὲ
πρὸς | τὰ [ἑ]αυτῶν μέρη ἐπ᾽ ἴ]ση[ς] ὠκε[ι]ώμεθα. οὐ γὰρ | ὁμοίως ἔχομεν
πρὸς | ὀφ[θα]λμ[ὸ]ν κα[ὶ] δάκτυ|λον, ἵνα μὴ λέγω πρὸς | ὄνυχας [κ]αὶ
τρίχας, ἐπεὶ | οὐδὲ πρὸς τὴν ἀποβο|λὴν αὐτῶν ὁμοίως | ἠλλοτριώμ[εθ]α,   15
ἀλλὰ μᾶλλον κ[αὶ ἧτ]τον. | (7) εἰ δὲ καὶ α[ὐτ]οὶ φήσου|σι ἐπιτεί[ν]εσθα[ι]
τὴν | οἰκείω[σιν, ἔσ]ται μὲν | φιλανθρ[ωπί]α, ἐλέγξου|σι δὲ τ[ούτους α]ἴ
περιστάσεις [ναυαγῶ]ν, ὅ|που ἀνάν[κη μό]νον | σώζεσθαι τὸν ἕτε|ρον
αὐτῶν· (8) κἂν μὴ γέ|νωνται δὲ περιστά|σεις, ἀλλ᾽ αὐτοί γε οὕ]τως
διάκ[εινται] ὡς ἐ|λεγχθησόμενοι. ὅθεν | καὶ ἐρω[τ]ῶσιν οἱ ἐξ Ἀ|καδη-   20
με[ίας ο]ὕ[τ]ω[ς].

11 τὰ [μ]αχόμενα Diels

Context: commentary on Plato, Tht. 143d.
  2 Variation of intensification is the mark of a ἕξις as distinct from a διάθεσις; cf.
47S.
  3 εἰ μέν As interpreted in vol. I, 353, these words introduce the first horn of a
dilemma, the second horn of which begins at εἰ δὲ καί, 16.
  4 τὸν ἔ||[σ]χατον Μυσῶν An allusion to Plato, Tht. 209b.
  11 If ψεγόμενα is compatible with the traces of missing letters, it would suit the
context better than Diels᾽ μαχόμενα.
  18 ναυαγῶ]ν Diels᾽ virtually certain supplement has important implications for
the origin of this controversy, as Pembroke [564], 127–9, observes. Reference to the
Academics, 20–1, points to Carneades᾽ arguments, adducing shipwreck, against
justice (Cicero, Rep. 3.30), which were subsequently answered by Panaetius᾽ pupil
Hecato (Cicero, Off. 3.90). For further discussion, cf. Inwood [575], 182–3.

58 Value and indifference

A Diogenes Laertius 7.101–3

(1) τῶν δ᾽ ὄντων φασὶ τὰ μὲν ἀγαθὰ εἶναι, τὰ δὲ κακά, τὰ δ᾽ οὐδέτερα. (2) ἀ-
γαθὰ μὲν οὖν τάς τ᾽ ἀρετάς, φρόνησιν, δικαιοσύνην, ἀνδρείαν, σωφροσύνην
καὶ τὰ λοιπά· (3) κακὰ δὲ τὰ ἐναντία, ἀφροσύνην, ἀδικίαν καὶ τὰ λοιπά. (4)
οὐδέτερα δὲ ὅσα μήτ᾽ ὠφελεῖ μήτε βλάπτει, οἷον ζωή, ὑγίεια, ἡδονή,
κάλλος, ἰσχύς, πλοῦτος, δόξα, εὐγένεια· καὶ τὰ τούτοις ἐναντία, θάνατος,   5
νόσος, πόνος, αἶσχος, ἀσθένεια, πενία, ἀδοξία, δυσγένεια καὶ τὰ παραπλήσια . . . μὴ γὰρ εἶναι ταῦτ᾽ ἀγαθά, ἀλλ᾽ ἀδιάφορα κατ᾽ εἶδος προηγμένα.
(5) ὡς γὰρ ἴδιον θερμοῦ τὸ θερμαίνειν, οὐ τὸ ψύχειν, οὕτω καὶ ἀγαθοῦ τὸ
ὠφελεῖν, οὐ τὸ βλάπτειν· οὐ μᾶλλον δ᾽ ὠφελεῖ ἢ βλάπτει ὁ πλοῦτος καὶ ἡ
ὑγίεια· οὐκ ἄρ᾽ ἀγαθὸν οὔτε πλοῦτος οὔθ᾽ ὑγίεια. (6) ἔτι τέ φασιν, ᾧ ἔστιν   10
εὖ καὶ κακῶς χρῆσθαι, τοῦτ᾽ οὐκ ἔστιν ἀγαθόν· πλούτῳ δὲ καὶ ὑγιείᾳ ἔστιν
εὖ καὶ κακῶς χρῆσθαι· οὐκ ἄρ᾽ ἀγαθὸν πλοῦτος καὶ ὑγίεια.

5 δόξα BFP: εὐδοξία fr

Context: doxography of Stoic ethics, concluding the treatment of ἀγαθά and

349

Stoic ethics

beginning that of ἀδιάφορα. Editions of Diogenes regularly but incorrectly print the first sentence as the last of the preceding section. Stobaeus' doxography of Stoic ethics, 2.57, 19–20, begins with this 'division' of existing things; cf. Long [561], 55–6. The doctrine is largely a Stoicized version of Plato; cf. *Meno* 87e–88a, *Euthyd.* 280e for health, strength, beauty and wealth as things that benefit us when used correctly (ὀρθὴ χρῆσις) and harm us when used incorrectly, and *Gorg.* 467e for the division of ὄντα into ἀγαθόν, κακόν and μεταξὺ τούτων, where the 'intermediates' (e.g. sitting, walking) are items 'which sometimes participate in the good, sometimes in the bad, and sometimes in neither'. At *Meno* 88c Socrates argues that virtue, in order to be necessarily ὠφέλιμος, must be a kind of φρόνησις. Aristotle, *Top.* vi.9, 147a34, shows that it was a commonplace to describe τὸ ποιητικὸν ἀγαθοῦ as ὠφέλιμον.

9 οὐ μᾶλλον   See note on 1A 7–10.

B   Diogenes Laertius 7.104–5 (*SVF* 3.119)

(1) διχῶς δὲ λέγεσθαι ἀδιάφορα· ἅπαξ μὲν τὰ μήτε πρὸς εὐδαιμονίαν μήτε πρὸς κακοδαιμονίαν συνεργοῦντα, ὡς ἔχει πλοῦτος, δόξα, ὑγίεια, ἰσχὺς καὶ τὰ ὅμοια· ἐνδέχεται γὰρ καὶ χωρὶς τούτων εὐδαιμονεῖν, τῆς ποιᾶς αὐτῶν χρήσεως εὐδαιμονικῆς οὔσης ἢ κακοδαιμονικῆς. (2) ἄλλως δὲ λέγεται ἀδιάφορα τὰ μήθ᾽ ὁρμῆς μήτ᾽ ἀφορμῆς κινητικά, ὡς ἔχει τὸ   5 ἀρτίας ἔχειν ἐπὶ τῆς κεφαλῆς τρίχας ἢ περιττάς, ἢ ἐκτεῖναι τὸν δάκτυλον ἢ συστεῖλαι, (3) τῶν προτέρων ἀδιαφόρων οὐκέθ᾽ οὕτω λεγομένων· ὁρμῆς γάρ ἐστιν ἐκεῖνα καὶ ἀφορμῆς κινητικά. διὸ τὰ μὲν αὐτῶν ἐκλέγεται ⟨τὰ δὲ ἀπεκλέγεται⟩, τῶν [δ᾽] ἑτέρων ἐπίσης ἐχόντων πρὸς αἵρεσιν καὶ φυγήν.

8–9 suppl. Arnim   9 δ᾽ del. Ménage

Context: a few lines after **A**.

For essentially the same account, cf. Stobaeus 2.79,4–17. A third sense of 'indifference' is mentioned by Sextus, *M.* 11.59–61: πρὸς ὃ ὁρμὴ μὲν καὶ ἀφορμὴ γίνεται, οὐ μᾶλλον δὲ πρὸς τόδε ἢ τόδε, e.g. selecting one of two coins which are indistinguishable in their properties. See further, note on **55N** 11.

C   Stobaeus 2.79,18–80,13; 82,20–1

(1) καὶ τὰ μὲν εἶναι κατὰ φύσιν, τὰ δὲ παρὰ φύσιν, τὰ δὲ οὔτε παρὰ φύσιν οὔτε κατὰ φύσιν. (2) κατὰ φύσιν μὲν οὖν τὰ τοιαῦτα· ὑγίειαν, ἰσχύν, αἰσθητηρίων ἀρτιότητα, καὶ τὰ παραπλήσια τούτοις· παρὰ φύσιν δὲ τὰ τοιαῦτα· νόσον, ἀσθένειαν, πήρωσιν καὶ τὰ τοιαῦτα· οὔτε δὲ κατὰ φύσιν οὔτε παρὰ φύσιν· ψυχῆς κατάστασιν καὶ σώματος, καθ᾽ ἃς ἡ μέν ἐστι φαντασιῶν ψευδῶν δεκτική, τὸ δὲ   5 τραυμάτων καὶ πηρώσεων δεκτικόν, καὶ τὰ τούτοις ὅμοια. (3) ποιεῖσθαι δὲ λέγουσι τὸν περὶ τούτων λόγον ⟨ἀπὸ⟩ τῶν πρώτων κατὰ φύσιν καὶ παρὰ φύσιν. τὸ γὰρ διαφέρον καὶ τὸ ἀδιάφορον τῶν πρός τι λεγομένων εἶναι. διότι κἄν φασι, λέγωμεν ἀδιάφορα τὰ σωματικὰ καὶ τὰ ἐκτός, πρὸς τὸ εὐσχημόνως ζῆν (ἐν ᾧπέρ ἐστι τὸ εὐδαιμόνως) ἀδιάφορά φαμεν αὐτὰ εἶναι, οὐ μὰ Δία   10

350

πρὸς τὸ κατὰ φύσιν ἔχειν οὐδὲ πρὸς ὁρμὴν καὶ ἀφορμήν . . . (4) πάντα δὲ
⟨τὰ⟩ κατὰ φύσιν ληπτὰ εἶναι καὶ παντὰ τὰ ⟨παρὰ⟩ φύσιν ἀληπτά.

5 καθ᾽ ἃς codd.: καθ᾽ ὃ schol. Luc.: καθ᾽ ἣν Heeren   6 τραυμάτων Wachsmuth: τρωμάτων codd.:
τρωτὸν schol. Luc. Meineke   7 ⟨ἀπὸ⟩ Wachsmuth   10 ᾧπέρ ἐστι Meineke: ᾧ πάρεστι
codd.   12 ⟨τὰ⟩ Meineke   ⟨παρὰ⟩ schol. Luc.: om. codd.

Context: doxography of τὰ ἀδιάφορα.
5–6 These examples are strikingly different from those in **B** 6–7. What the
present ones seem to illustrate are mental and bodily conditions which are neither part
of nature's providential plan nor contrary to it since they are unavoidable properties of
the way soul and body are structured; cf. **54Q** 2.
7 **πρώτων κατὰ φύσιν** Cf. **59D** 1–2. They are exemplified at Stobaeus 2.82,12–
15, by κίνησις ἢ σχέσις κατὰ τοὺς σπερματικοὺς λόγους γινομένη, οἷον ὑγίεια καὶ
αἴσθησις . . . καὶ ἰσχύς; cf. his much fuller list outside the Stoic doxography at
2.47,20–48,3.
12 **ληπτά** Cf. sumenda, **59D** 11. Stobaeus 2.83,1–6, distinguishes between καθ᾽
αὐτὰ ληπτά, e.g. health, and δι᾽ ἕτερα or ποιητικά, e.g. wealth. ληπτόν in turn is
importantly distinguished from αἱρετόν in virtue of the fact that the latter is τὸ ὁρμῆς
αὐτοτελῶς [αὐτοτελοῦς codd.] κινητικόν, whereas τὰ κατὰ φύσιν are simply ὁρμῆς
κινητικά (SVF 3.121, 131). For the interpretation of the distinction, cf. Long [434],
81–6; Inwood [547], 125, 208.

D Stobaeus 2.83,10–84,2 (SVF 3.124)

(1) πάντα δὲ τὰ κατὰ φύσιν ἀξίαν ἔχειν καὶ πάντα τὰ παρὰ φύσιν ἀπαξίαν.
(2) τὴν δὲ ἀξίαν λέγεσθαι τριχῶς, τήν τε δόσιν καὶ τιμὴν καθ᾽ αὐτό, καὶ τὴν
ἀμοιβὴν τοῦ δοκιμαστοῦ· καὶ τὴν τρίτην, ἣν ὁ Ἀντίπατρος ἐκλεκτικὴν
προσαγορεύει, καθ᾽ ἣν διδόντων τῶν πραγμάτων τάδε τινὰ μᾶλλον ἀντὶ
τῶνδε αἱρούμεθα, οἷον ὑγίειαν ἀντὶ νόσου καὶ ζωὴν ἀντὶ θανάτου καὶ   5
πλοῦτον ἀντὶ πενίας. (3) κατὰ τὸ ἀνάλογον δὲ καὶ τὴν ἀπαξίαν τριχῶς φασι
λέγεσθαι.

2 τε F: δὲ P   2 τιμὴν Meineke: τὴν codd.   3 ἣν F: καὶ P

Context: continuation of the doxography of τὰ ἀδιάφορα.
For other accounts of three senses of ἀξία, cf. Stobaeus, 2.84,4–17 (Diogenes of
Babylon) and D.L. 7.105, with discussion by Görler [581], 446–51. The present one
does not purport to specify different kinds of valuable items but different senses of the
value instantiated in things in accordance with nature. There seems to be no reason
why the same thing, e.g. health, should not have value in all three senses. If our
commentary in vol. 1, 357–9, is on the right lines, health is something valuable per se.
To credit it with 'selective value' is to make the additional point that, other things
being equal, one always has reason to opt for health rather than sickness; cf. **59D** 1.
3 **ἐκλεκτικήν** Cf. **64C** 13.
5 **αἱρούμεθα** This verb is misleading since in strict Stoic usage its object is
restricted to ἀγαθόν; cf. **33J**.

Stoic ethics

E Stobaeus, 2.84,18–85,11 (*SVF* 3.128)

(1) τῶν δ' ἀξίαν ἐχόντων τὰ μὲν ἔχειν πολλὴν ἀξίαν, τὰ δὲ βραχεῖαν. ὁμοίως δὲ καὶ τῶν ἀπαξίαν ἐχόντων ἃ μὲν ἔχειν πολλὴν ἀπαξίαν, ἃ δὲ βραχεῖαν. (2) τὰ μὲν πολλὴν ἔχοντα ἀξίαν προηγμένα λέγεσθαι, τὰ δὲ πολλὴν ἀπαξίαν ἀποπροηγμένα, Ζήνωνος ταύτας τὰς ὀνομασίας θεμένου πρώτου τοῖς πράγμασι. (3) προηγμένον δ' εἶναι λέγουσιν, ὃ ἀδιάφορον 5 ⟨ὂν⟩ ἐκλεγόμεθα κατὰ προηγούμενον λόγον. τὸν δ' ὅμοιον λόγον ἐπὶ τῷ ἀποπροηγμένῳ εἶναι, καὶ τὰ παραδείγματα κατὰ τὴν ἀναλογίαν ταὐτά. (4) οὐδὲν δὲ τῶν ἀγαθῶν εἶναι προηγμένον διὰ τὸ τὴν μεγίστην ἀξίαν αὐτὰ ἔχειν. τὸ δὲ προηγμένον, τὴν δευτέραν χώραν καὶ ἀξίαν ἔχον, συνεγγίζειν πως τῇ τῶν ἀγαθῶν φύσει· οὐδὲ γὰρ ἐν αὐλῇ τῶν προηγμένων εἶναι τὸν 10 βασιλέα, ἀλλὰ τοὺς μετ' αὐτὸν τεταγμένους.

3 μὲν ⟨οὖν⟩ Heeren   6 ⟨ὂν⟩ Heeren   λόγον Mullach: ἀνάλογον codd.: ἄρα λόγον Heeren   6–7 τῷ ἀποπροηγμένῳ Wachsmuth: τὸ ἀποπροηγμένον (vel -ος) codd.   9 προηγμένον] προηγούμενον codd.   10 ἐν αὐλῇ τῶν Canter: ἂν αὐλητῶν codd.   προηγμένων Madvig: προαγόμενον codd.

Context: one paragraph after **D**.

1–5 Cf. Cicero, *Fin.* 3.50–1, and Stobaeus 2.80,14–21, where ἀδιάφορα are divided into those with more value/disvalue and those with less. Diogenes 7.105 incorrectly calls '[all] indifferent things with value' προηγμένα. For subdivisions of προηγμένα, cf. **m**; Stobaeus 2.80,22–81,6; 81,19–82,4; Cicero, *Fin.* 3.56.

5–11 Similarly Cicero, *Fin.* 3.51–2. 'Preferred' is defined in *Fin* 3.53 as *quod sit indifferens cum aestimatione mediocri.*

F Sextus Empiricus, *M.* 11.64–7 (*SVF* 1.361)

(1) μὴ εἶναι δὲ προηγμένον ἀδιάφορον τὴν ὑγείαν καὶ πᾶν τὸ κατ' αὐτὴν παραπλήσιον ἔφησεν Ἀρίστων ὁ Χῖος. (2) ἴσον γάρ ἐστι τὸ προηγμένον αὐτὴν λέγειν ἀδιάφορον τῷ ἀγαθὸν ἀξιοῦν, καὶ σχεδὸν ὀνόματι μόνον διαφέρον. (3) καθόλου γὰρ τὰ μεταξὺ ἀρετῆς καὶ κακίας ἀδιάφορα μὴ ἔχειν μηδεμίαν παραλλαγήν, μηδὲ τινὰ μὲν εἶναι φύσει προηγμένα, τινὰ δὲ 5 ἀποπροηγμένα, ἀλλὰ παρὰ τὰς διαφόρους τῶν καιρῶν περιστάσεις μήτε τὰ λεγόμενα προῆχθαι πάντως γίνεσθαι προηγμένα, μήτε τὰ λεγόμενα ἀποπροῆχθαι κατ' ἀνάγκην ὑπάρχειν ἀποπροηγμένα. (4) ἐὰν γοῦν δέη τοὺς μὲν ὑγιαίνοντας ὑπηρετεῖν τῷ τυράννῳ καὶ διὰ τοῦτο ἀναιρεῖσθαι, τοὺς δὲ νοσοῦντας ἀπολυομένους τῆς ὑπηρεσίας συναπολύεσθαι καὶ τῆς ἀναιρέ- 10 σεως, ἕλοιτ' ἂν μᾶλλον ὁ σοφὸς τὸ νοσεῖν κατὰ τοῦτον τὸν καιρὸν ἢ [ὅτι] τὸ ὑγιαίνειν. (5) καὶ ταύτῃ οὔτε ἡ ὑγεία προηγμένον ἐστὶ πάντως οὔτε ἡ νόσος ἀποπροηγμένον. ὥσπερ οὖν ἐν ταῖς ὀνοματογραφίαις ἄλλοτ' ἄλλα προτάττομεν στοιχεῖα, πρὸς τὰς διαφόρους περιστάσεις ἀρτιζόμενοι, καὶ τὸ μὲν δέλτα ὅτε τὸ τοῦ Δίωνος ὄνομα γράφομεν, τὸ δὲ ἰῶτα ὅτε τὸ τοῦ Ἴωνος, τὸ δὲ ὦ ὅτε 15 τὸ τοῦ Ὠρίωνος, οὐ τῇ φύσει ἑτέρων παρὰ τὰ ἕτερα γράμματα προκρινομένων, τῶν δὲ καιρῶν τοῦτο ποιεῖν ἀναγκαζόντων, οὕτως κἂν τοῖς μεταξὺ

352

ἀρετῆς καὶ κακίας πράγμασιν οὐ φυσική τις γίνεται ἑτέρων παρ' ἕτερα πρόκρισις, κατὰ περίστασιν δὲ μᾶλλον.

11 ὅτι del. Arnim

Context: immediately following an account of the orthodox Stoic doctrine of ἀδιάφορον.
This was Aristo's most famous doctrine; cf. SVF 1.362–9.
5 παραλλαγήν   Cf. H 3. Aristo's thesis amounts to the claim that things intermediate between virtue and vice are completely indiscernible from one another in terms of value; cf. note on 52C 6.

G   Diogenes Laertius 7.160 (SVF 1.351 part)

'Αρίστων ὁ Χῖος . . . τέλος ἔφησεν εἶναι τὸ ἀδιαφόρως ἔχοντα ζῆν πρὸς τὰ μεταξὺ ἀρετῆς καὶ κακίας μηδ' ἡντινοῦν ἐν αὐτοῖς παραλλαγὴν ἀπολείποντα, ἀλλ' ἐπίσης ἐπὶ πάντων ἔχοντα· εἶναι γὰρ ὅμοιον τὸν σοφὸν τῷ ἀγαθῷ ὑποκριτῇ, ὃς ἄν τε Θερσίτου ἄν τε 'Αγαμέμνονος πρόσωπον ἀναλάβῃ, ἑκάτερον ὑποκρίνεται προσηκόντως.   5

1 τὰ fr: τι codd.

Context: opening of Diogenes' life of Aristo.
1–3   Cf. the account of Pyrrho's position in 1F 3, and 2F.

H   Plutarch, St. rep. 1048A (SVF 3.137)

ἐν δὲ τῷ πρώτῳ Περὶ ἀγαθῶν τρόπον τινὰ συγχωρεῖ καὶ δίδωσι τοῖς βουλομένοις τὰ προηγμένα καλεῖν ἀγαθὰ καὶ κακὰ τἀναντία ταύταις ταῖς λέξεσιν· "εἴ τις βούλεται κατὰ τὰς τοιαύτας παραλλαγὰς τὸ μὲν ἀγαθὸν αὐτῶν λέγειν τὸ δὲ κακόν, ἐπὶ ταῦτα φερόμενος τὰ πράγματα καὶ μὴ ἄλλως ἀποπλανώμενος, ⟨ἀποδεκτέον ὡς⟩ ἐν μὲν τοῖς σημαινομένοις οὐ   5
διαπίπτοντος αὐτοῦ τὰ δ' ἄλλα στοχαζομένου τῆς κατὰ τὰς ὀνομασίας συνηθείας."

4 ἐπὶ ταῦτα codd.: ἐπ' αὐτὰ Reiske: ἐπὶ ταῦτὰ φερόμενος [τὰ] Rüstow   5 suppl. Sandbach: ⟨ἀποδεχόμεθ' ὡς⟩ Arnim: ⟨οὐ καταγνωστέον⟩ Pohlenz

Context: alleged inconsistency in Chrysippus' doctrine of προηγμένα.
3–7   By παραλλαγάς are meant the differences between 'indifferents', signified by προηγμένα and ἀποπροηγμένα, which Aristo denied; cf. F 5, G 2. Cherniss [326], ad loc., clarifies the main points of the text well, but introduces an unnecessary complication by taking ταῦτα τὰ πράγματα, 4, to refer to the senses of the terms προηγμένον and ἀποπροηγμένον. The antecedent of ταῦτα must be αὐτῶν, i.e. the actual differences between 'indifferents' designated by προηγμένα and ἀποπροηγμένα.

I   Cicero, Fin. 3.50 (SVF 1.365)

deinceps explicatur differentia rerum, quam si non ullam esse diceremus, confunderetur omnis vita, ut ab Aristone, neque ullum sapientiae munus aut opus inveniretur, cum inter res eas quae ad vitam degendam pertinerent nihil omnino interesset, neque ullum dilectum adhiberi oporteret.

Context: transition from exposition of 'goods' to that of 'indifferents'. This criticism of Aristo is frequently stated in Cicero (cf. **2G–H**; *Leg.* 1.38) and attributed to Chrysippus at *Fin.* 4.68.

J Epictetus, *Diss.* 2.6.9. (*SVF* 3.191)

διὰ τοῦτο καλῶς ὁ Χρύσιππος λέγει ὅτι "μέχρις ἂν ἄδηλά μοι ᾖ τὰ ἑξῆς, ἀεὶ τῶν εὐφυεστέρων ἔχομαι πρὸς τὸ τυγχάνειν τῶν κατὰ φύσιν· αὐτὸς γὰρ μ' ὁ θεὸς ἐποίησεν τούτων ἐκλεκτικόν. εἰ δέ γε ᾔδειν ὅτι νοσεῖν μοι καθείμαρται νῦν, καὶ ὥρμων ἂν ἐπ' αὐτό. καὶ γὰρ ὁ πούς, εἰ φρένας εἶχεν, ὥρμα ἂν ἐπὶ τὸ πηλοῦσθαι."   5

3 τούτων vel τοιούτων codd.

Context: illustration of the maxim, 'You will never be disturbed if you are always mindful of what is yours and what is not'; cf. **62K**.

The passage is excellently discussed by Sandbach [296], 36, who observes that the foot stands to the whole man as the individual stands to the world as a whole: 'Man is part of the world [cf. **63C**] and should co-operate to serve the world's purposes against his own advantage. But this is not against his own good. His good is achieved by rational decision, and reason demands that he should co-operate.'

3 ἐκλεκτικόν Cf. **B** 8, **D** 3, **K**.

K Stobaeus 2.76,9–15

(1) Διογένης δέ· "εὐλογιστεῖν ἐν τῇ τῶν κατὰ φύσιν ἐκλογῇ καὶ ἀπεκλογῇ" ... (2) Ἀντίπατρος δέ· "ζῆν ἐκλεγομένους μὲν τὰ κατὰ φύσιν, ἀπεκλεγομένους δὲ τὰ παρὰ φύσιν διηνεκῶς." πολλάκις δὲ καὶ οὕτως ἀπεδίδου· "πᾶν τὸ καθ' αὑτὸν ποιεῖν διηνεκῶς καὶ ἀπαραβάτως πρὸς τὸ τυγχάνειν τῶν προηγουμένων κατὰ φύσιν."   5

1 εὐλογιστεῖν Davies: εὐλογιστίαν codd.   2–3 ἐκλεγομένους ... ἀπεκλεγομένους cod. Aug.: -όμενος ... -όμενος FP   4 καθ' αὑτὸν Meineke: κατὰ αὑτὸν codd.

Context: Stoic philosophers' different formulations of the τέλος.

5 προηγουμένων It has been recently argued by Görler [581], 456–62, that this term is meant to include not only certain kinds of *AN* things but even ἀγαθά. As far as we can see, this novel interpretation of Antipater is not justified by the evidence he cites, nor does it seem compatible with Antipater's controversy with Carneades; see **64**.

l Diogenes Laertius 7.165 (*SVF* 1.411, part)

Ἡριλλος ... εἶπε ... διαφέρειν δὲ τέλος καὶ ὑποτελίδα· τῆς μὲν γὰρ καὶ τοὺς μὴ σοφοὺς στοχάζεσθαι, τοῦ δὲ μόνον τὸν σοφόν. τὰ δὲ μεταξὺ ἀρετῆς καὶ κακίας ἀδιάφορα εἶναι.

Context: life of Herillus.

Herillus specified ἐπιστήμη as the τέλος; cf. *SVF* 1.411, 413–117, 419–21. In Cicero, our principal informant, he is regularly associated with Aristo, and is criticized like Aristo for his unpracticality in acknowledging no difference between [morally indifferent] things. He is the only Stoic credited with the term ὑποτελίς, and may have invented it. In Stobaeus 2.47, 12–48, 5 (where Herillus is not named) ὑποτελίς is used as a generic term for the object of a living creature's first impulse. Stobaeus is drawing here upon the *Carneadea divisio* (cf. **64G**), but it is implausible that his use of ὑποτελίς should be independent of Herillus'. On the evidence of Cicero, *Fin.* 4.40, Herillus was open to the charge of having posited two quite independent ultimate ends. No doubt there is distortion of his true position here. Perhaps Herillus argued that the continuity orthodox Stoics posited between the first impulse, aimed at self-preservation, and the *summum bonum* was quite illusory. For a very full discussion, which interprets the evidence somewhat differently, cf. Ioppolo [349].

m Diogenes Laertius 7.107 (*SVF* 3.135)

ἔτι τῶν προηγμένων τὰ μὲν δι' αὐτὰ προῆκται, τὰ δὲ δι' ἔτερα, τὰ δὲ καὶ δι' αὐτὰ καὶ δι' ἔτερα. δι' αὐτὰ μὲν εὐφυΐα, προκοπὴ καὶ τὰ ὅμοια· δι' ἔτερα δὲ πλοῦτος, εὐγένεια καὶ τὰ ὅμοια· δι' αὐτὰ δὲ καὶ δι' ἔτερα ἰσχύς, εὐαισθησία, ἀρτιότης. δι' αὐτὰ μέν, ὅτι κατὰ φύσιν ἐστί· δι' ἔτερα δέ, ὅτι περιποιεῖ χρείας οὐκ ὀλίγας. ὁμοίως δ' ἔχει καὶ τὸ ἀποπροηγμένον κατὰ τὸν ἐναντίον λόγον. 5

1 προῆκται BP: προήχθη F

Context: report of the Stoic theory of ἀδιάφορα.

A distinction is drawn here between those valuable indifferents which are preferred because they are κατὰ φύσιν, and those such as wealth which are preferred for their utility. This distinction, though perfectly intelligible, is potentially misleading. It should not be interpreted as marking off wealth from the class of *AN* items; cf. the citation of Diogenes of Babylon at Stobaeus 2.84,4–6, which shows that utility is referred to φύσις. The 'natural' value of wealth is attested by Stobaeus 2.82,20–83,7 in a context which distinguishes it from health as above (cf. note on **C** 12, and **59D** 7). In summary accounts προηγμένα are treated as a monolithic class (cf. Cicero, *Fin.* 3.53; *Acad.* 1.36–7), but Stobaeus 2.83,1–7 notes that health activates impulse in a different way from wealth.

59 Proper functions

A Plutarch, *Comm. not.* 1069E (*SVF* 3.491)

"πόθεν οὖν", φησίν, "ἄρξωμαι; καὶ τίνα λάβω τοῦ καθήκοντος ἀρχὴν καὶ ὕλην τῆς ἀρετῆς, ἀφεὶς τὴν φύσιν καὶ τὸ κατὰ φύσιν;"

1 ἄρξωμαι Rasmus: ἄρξομαι codd.   2 κατὰ Meziriac: παρὰ codd.

Context: Chrysippus' alleged inconsistency in making ἀδιάφορα the foundation of ethics; cf. Cicero, *Fin.* 4.48.

2 **ὕλην** Cf. **64C** 13; **66G 3**; and for discussion, see Tsekourakis [556], 30–7. Plutarch interprets τὸ κατὰ φύσιν as if it referred restrictedly to τὰ κατὰ φύσιν. On the evidence of **60A** this probably distorts Chrysippus' point.

Stoic ethics

B Stobaeus 2.85,13–86,4 (*SVF* 3.494)

(1) ὁρίζεται δὴ τὸ καθῆκον· "τὸ ἀκόλουθον ἐν ζωῇ, ὃ πραχθὲν εὔλογον ἀπολογίαν ἔχει"· παρὰ τὸ καθῆκον δὲ τὸ ἐναντίως. (2) τοῦτο διατείνει καὶ εἰς τὰ ἄλογα τῶν ζῴων, ἐνεργεῖ γάρ τι κἀκεῖνα ἀκολούθως τῇ ἑαυτῶν φύσει· (3) ἐπὶ τῶν λογικῶν ζῴων οὕτως ἀποδίδοται· "τὸ ἀκόλουθον ἐν βίῳ." (4) τῶν δὲ καθηκόντων τὰ μὲν εἶναί φασι τέλεια, ἃ δὴ καὶ   5
κατορθώματα λέγεσθαι. κατορθώματα δ' εἶναι τὰ κατ' ἀρετὴν ἐνεργή-
ματα, οἷον τὸ φρονεῖν, τὸ δικαιοπραγεῖν. οὐκ εἶναι δὲ κατορθώματα τὰ μὴ
οὕτως ἔχοντα, ἃ δὴ οὐδὲ τέλεια καθήκοντα προσαγορεύουσιν, ἀλλὰ μέσα,
οἷον τὸ γαμεῖν, τὸ πρεσβεύειν, τὸ διαλέγεσθαι, τὰ τούτοις ὅμοια.

1 δὴ codd.: δέ Heeren   πραχθὲν Ménage: παραχθὲν codd.   6–7 τὰ ... ἐνεργήματα Davies:
τὸ ... ἐνέργημα codd.

Context: beginning of doxography of ὁ περὶ τοῦ καθήκοντος τόπος, described as
ἀκόλουθος τῷ λόγῳ τῷ περὶ τῶν προηγμένων.
1–4 Cf. F 2–5; D.L. 7.107.
1 **εὔλογον** See notes on **40F, 69B**. In a very full discussion, Tsekourakis [556],
25–30, convincingly takes 'with a good reason', not 'probable', to be the sense of the
term here.

C Diogenes Laertius 7.107 (*SVF* 3.493, part)

(1) ὅπερ καὶ ἐπὶ τὰ φυτὰ καὶ ζῷα διατείνει· ὁρᾶσθαι γὰρ κἀπὶ τούτων
καθήκοντα. (2) κατωνομάσθαι δὲ οὕτως ὑπὸ πρώτου Ζήνωνος τὸ καθῆκον,
ἀπὸ τοῦ κατά τινας ἥκειν τῆς προσονομασίας εἰλημμένης. (3) ἐνέργημα δ'
αὐτὸ εἶναι ταῖς κατὰ φύσιν κατασκευαῖς οἰκεῖον.

Context: in the preceding sentence Diogenes states the gist of **B 1–3**.
2–3 Zeno wrote a book Περὶ τοῦ καθήκοντος (D.L. 7.4), and was no doubt the
first philosopher to use the term technically. (In some Stoic texts ἐπιβάλλει/
ἐπιβάλλοντα are used very similarly; cf. Chrysippus in Plutarch, *Comm. not.* 1064E–F,
and Dyroff [545], 137–9.) The etymology advanced here has never been satisfactorily
explained (for various attempts, cf. Bonhöffer [312], 208; Dyroff [545], 134). Its key
feature is presumably κατά, so basic a preposition in Stoic ethics, with τινας
(unnecessary to the etymology) implying accordance with 'people's natures'; cf. line
4.

D Cicero, *Fin.* 3.17,20–2

(1) satis esse autem argumenti videtur quam ob rem illa quae prima sunt
adscita natura diligamus, quod est nemo quin, cum utrumvis liceat, aptas
malit et integras omnis partis corporis quam, eodem usu, inminutas aut
detortas habere ... (2) progrediamur igitur, quoniam, inquit, ab his principiis
naturae discessimus, quibus congruere debent quae sequuntur. sequitur autem   5
haec prima divisio: aestimabile esse dicunt – sic enim, ut opinor, appellemus –
id quod aut ipsum secundum naturam sit aut tale quid efficiat, ut selectione

356

dignum propterea sit, quod aliquod pondus habeat dignum aestimatione, quam illi ἀξίαν vocant, contraque inaestimabile quod sit superiori contrarium. (3) initiis igitur ita constitutis, ut ea quae secundum naturam sunt ipsa propter   10
se sumenda sint contrariaque item reicienda, primum est officium – id enim appello καθῆκον – ut se conservet in naturae statu, deinceps ut ea teneat quae secundum naturam sint pellatque contraria. qua inventa selectione et item reiectione sequitur deinceps cum officio selectio, deinde ea perpetua, tum ad extremum constans consentaneaque naturae, (4) in qua primum inesse incipit   15
et intellegi quid sit quod vere bonum possit dici. prima est enim conciliatio hominis ad ea quae sunt secundum naturam. simul autem cepit intellegentiam vel notionem potius, quam appellant ἔννοιαν illi, viditque rerum agendarum ordinem et, ut ita dicam, concordiam, multo eam pluris aestimavit quam omnia illa quae prima dilexerat, atque ita cognitione et ratione collegit, ut   20
statueret in eo collocatum summum illud hominis per se laudandum et expetendum bonum; (5) quod cum positum sit in eo quod ὁμολογίαν Stoici, nos appellemus convenientiam, si placet – cum igitur in eo sit id bonum quo omnia referenda sint, [omnia] honeste facta ipsumque honestum, quod solum in bonis ducitur, quamquam post oritur, tamen id solum vi sua et dignitate   25
expetendum est; eorum autem quae sunt prima naturae propter se nihil est expetendum. (6) cum vero illa quae officia esse dixi proficiscantur ab initiis naturae, necesse est ea ad haec referri, ut recte dici possit omnia officia eo referri, ut adipiscamur principia naturae, nec tamen ut hoc sit bonorum ultimum, propterea quod non inest in primis naturae conciliationibus honesta   30
actio; consequens enim est et post oritur, ut dixi. est tamen ea secundum naturam multoque nos ad se expetendam magis hortatur quam superiora omnia.

6 appellemus Bentley: *appellamus* codd.   9 *illi . . . vocant* Pearce: *ille . . . vocat* codd.   24 *omnia* del. Madvig

Context: exposition of οἰκείωσις and the objects of the first impulse; cf. **57A**, and *SVF* 3.181. The sections omitted after *habere*, 4, deal first with the intrinsic desirability of καταλήψεις and *artes*, and then digress from the main point.

6 **divisio** I.e. between what has value and what has disvalue; cf. **58D 1, I**. For ἄξια, see also **60C 5**.

10–11 **propter se sumenda** This does not contradict the later thesis, 26–7, that no *PAN* thing is *propter se expetendum*. 'Takeable', not 'desirable', is a property of *AN* things; cf. vol. 1, 358.

14 **cum officio selectio** This expression has always been found difficult, owing to its apparent redundancy after *primum officium*, 11. It presumably refers to selection (cf. **58D 2, E 3**) as a deliberate act – a development in moral awareness quite distinct from the infant's behaviour, and in line with the doctrine of an evolving constitution, **57B 3**.

19–27 White [569] argues that the understanding of the good, as described here, should be completely distinguished from any notion of 'self-realization' or 'perfection of human nature'. These conceptions, he argues, which belong to Antiochean ethics

357

Stoic ethics

(cf. **64K**), have no place in early Stoicism. Though unable to argue the point at length here, we venture to disagree. The Stoics, to be sure, differ from Antiochus in treating the *summum bonum* as quite incommensurable with all other valuables; in his philosophy it consists in the totalization of everything worth having, including the objects of the first impulses; cf **64K 4**. But that radical difference does not serve to make White's point. Notice that in this text *honesta actio* is described as a *consequens* of nature's first affiliations (30–1), as *secundum naturam* and *expetendam* (31–2), both of which attributes applied to the 'earlier objects', and as the highest *human* good (21). Outside this passage, cf. especially **57B 3, F; 60H 4; 61L** (Cleanthes); D.L. 7.94.

25 **vi sua**   Cf. **60D 6**.

E Diogenes Laertius, 7.108–9 (*SVF* 3,495, 496)

(1) τῶν γὰρ καθ᾽ ὁρμὴν ἐνεργουμένων τὰ μὲν καθήκοντα εἶναι, τὰ δὲ παρὰ τὸ καθῆκον, ⟨τὰ δ᾽ οὔτε καθήκοντα οὔτε παρὰ τὸ καθῆκον⟩. (2) καθήκοντα μὲν οὖν εἶναι ὅσα λόγος αἱρεῖ ποιεῖν, ὡς ἔχει τὸ γονεῖς τιμᾶν, ἀδελφούς, πατρίδα, συμπεριφέρεσθαι φίλοις· παρὰ τὸ καθῆκον δέ, ὅσα μὴ 5 αἱρεῖ λόγος, ὡς ἔχει τὰ τοιαῦτα, γονέων ἀμελεῖν, ἀδελφῶν ἀφροντιστεῖν, φίλοις μὴ συνδιατίθεσθαι, πατρίδα ὑπερορᾶν καὶ τὰ παραπλήσια· οὔτε δὲ καθήκοντα οὔτε παρὰ τὸ καθῆκον ὅσα οὔθ᾽ αἱρεῖ λόγος πράττειν οὔτ᾽ ἀπαγορεύει, οἷον κάρφος ἀνελέσθαι, γραφεῖον κρατεῖν ἢ στλεγγίδα καὶ τὰ ὅμοια τούτοις. (3) καὶ τὰ μὲν εἶναι καθήκοντα ἄνευ περιστάσεως, τὰ δὲ 10 περιστατικά. καὶ ἄνευ περιστάσεως τάδε, ὑγιείας ἐπιμελεῖσθαι καὶ αἰσθητηρίων καὶ τὰ ὅμοια· κατὰ περίστασιν δὲ τὸ πηροῦν ἑαυτὸν καὶ τὴν κτῆσιν διαρριπτεῖν. ἀνὰ λόγον δὲ καὶ τῶν παρὰ τὸ καθῆκον. (4) ἔτι τῶν καθηκόντων τὰ μὲν ἀεὶ καθήκει, τὰ δὲ οὐκ ἀεί. καὶ ἀεὶ μὲν καθήκει τὸ κατ᾽ ἀρετὴν ζῆν, οὐκ ἀεὶ δὲ τὸ ἐρωτᾶν καὶ ἀποκρίνεσθαι καὶ περιπατεῖν καὶ τὰ 15 ὅμοια. ὁ δ᾽ αὐτὸς λόγος καὶ ἐπὶ τῶν παρὰ τὸ καθῆκον.

2 suppl. Casaubon   7 λόγος P: λόγῳ BF   8 ἀπαγορεύει P: -ειν BF

Context: immediately following **C**.

Stobaeus (**53Q**) says that impulse is activated by φαντασία ὁρμητικὴ τοῦ καθήκοντος αὐτόθεν. This is consistent with 1–2 if Stobaeus' statement refers to the causes of action generally, while allowing for moral error in the fact that what is actually καθῆκον may fail to coincide with the agent's φαντασία ὁρμητική; cf. Epictetus, *Diss.* 1.18.2, ἀμήχανον . . . ἄλλο μὲν κρίνειν καθῆκον, ἐπ᾽ ἄλλο δὲ ὁρμᾶν, with moral error attributed to ignorance of the good.

F Cicero, *Fin.* 3.58–9

(1) sed cum quod honestum sit id solum bonum esse dicamus, consentaneum tamen est fungi officio, cum id officium nec in bonis ponamus nec in malis. est enim aliquid in his rebus probabile, et quidem ita ut eius ratio reddi possit, ergo ut etiam probabiliter acti ratio reddi possit. est autem officium quod ita factum est ut eius facti probabilis ratio reddi possit. ex quo intellegitur officium medium quiddam esse, quod neque in bonis 5 ponatur neque in contrariis. quoniamque in iis rebus quae neque in virtutibus sunt neque in

358

vitiis, est tamen quiddam, quod usui possit esse, tollendum id non est. est autem eius generis actio quoque quaedam, et quidem talis ut ratio postulet agere aliquid et facere eorum. quod autem ratione actum est, id officium appellamus. est igitur officium eius generis quod nec in bonis ponatur nec in contrariis. (2) atque perspicuum etiam illud est, in istis rebus   10 mediis aliquid agere sapientem. iudicat igitur, cum agit, officium illud esse. quod quoniam numquam fallitur in iudicando, erit in mediis rebus officium. (3) quod efficitur hac etiam conclusione rationis: quoniam enim videmus esse quiddam quod recte factum appellemus, id autem est perfectum officium, erit [autem] etiam inchoatum, (4) ut, si iuste depositum reddere in recte factis sit,   15 in officiis ponatur depositum reddere; illo enim addito "iuste" fit recte factum, per se autem hoc ipsum reddere in officio ponitur. (5) quoniamque non dubium est quin in iis quae media dicimus sit aliud sumendum, aliud reiciendum, quicquid ita fit aut dicitur omne officio continetur. (6) ex quo intellegitur, quoniam se ipsi omnes natura diligant, tam insipientem quam   20 sapientem sumpturum quae secundum naturam sint reiecturumque contraria. (7) ita est quoddam commune officium sapientis et insipientis, ex quo efficitur versari in iis quae media dicamus.

5 *quiddam* Madvig: *quoddam* codd.   6 *iis*] *his* codd.   9 *est* Madvig: *sit* codd.   15 *autem* del. Lambinus   16 *fit* Lambinus: *facit* codd.   19 *omne* Gruter: *omni* codd.

Context: transition from treatment of *praeposita* to account of *officia*. What follows F is continued, after the omission of one sentence, at **66G**.

This is a difficult passage, largely because Cicero fails to make it explicit that the wise man's proper functions are always 'perfect', and are thus 'intermediate' or shared by fools as well only in an equivocal sense, i.e. when the action is considered independently of the agent's moral character. In 2–11 two arguments are advanced to show that the existence of 'morally neutral' *officia* is consistent with the thesis that *honestum* is the only good. The first argument, 2–6, takes part of the definition of καθῆκον in **B** 1–2, ὃ πραχθὲν εὔλογον ἀπολογίαν ἔχει, and maintains that this is satisfied by something in the sphere of 'indifferent' things, and specifically by *officium*. Thus the morally neutral status of *officium* is inferred by establishing coincidence between its *definiens* and a characteristic of indifferent things. The second argument, 7–10, drawing on the formulation of καθῆκον in **E** 3, ὅσα λόγος αἱρεῖ ποιεῖν, is exactly similar. In 10–12 the morally neutral status of *officia* is inferred from the observation that the wise man performs certain actions in the intermediate domain. Since he judges such an action to be an *officium*, and his judgement is infallible, the intermediate domain contains *officia*. This argument, however, ignores the fact that everything done by the wise man is actually a perfect *officium*.

G Sextus Empiricus, *M*.11.200–1 (*SVF* 3.516, part)

ἀλλὰ πρὸς τοῦθ' ὑπαντῶντές φασι πάντα μὲν κοινὰ εἶναι καὶ πάντων τὰ ἔργα, διορίζεσθαι δὲ τῷ ἀπὸ τεχνικῆς [διαιρέσεως καὶ] διαθέσεως ἢ ἀπὸ ἀτέχνου γίνεσθαι. (1) οὐ γὰρ τὸ ἐπιμελεῖσθαι γονέων καὶ ἄλλως τιμᾶν γονεῖς τοῦ σπουδαίου ἐστὶν ἔργον, ἀλλὰ σπουδαίου τὸ ἀπὸ φρονήσεως τοῦτο ποιεῖν· (2) καὶ ὡς τὸ μὲν ὑγιάζειν

κοινόν ἐστι τοῦ τε ἰατροῦ καὶ ἰδιώτου, τὸ δὲ ἰατρικῶς ὑγιάζειν τοῦ   5
τεχνίτου ἴδιον, ὧδε καὶ τὸ μὲν τιμᾶν τοὺς γονεῖς κοινὸν τοῦ τε σπουδαίου
καὶ μὴ σπουδαίου, τὸ δὲ ἀπὸ φρονήσεως τιμᾶν τοὺς γονεῖς ἴδιον τοῦ σοφοῦ,
(3) ὥστε καὶ τέχνην αὐτὸν ἔχειν περὶ τὸν βίον, ἧς ἴδιόν ἐστιν ἔργον τὸ
ἕκαστον τῶν πραττομένων ἀπὸ ἀρίστης διαθέσεως πράττειν.

1 τοῦθ' ὑπαντῶντες Fabricius: τοὺς ὑπαντῶντας codd.   2 διαιρέσεως καὶ del. Bekker

Context: Stoic reply to the objection that φρόνησις cannot be a τέχνη περὶ τὸν βίον
[cf. **61G 2**] since its supposed work – e.g. honouring parents or returning a deposit –
is common to the wise and the unwise.

H Philo, *Cher.* 14–15 (*SVF* 3.513)

(1) τὸ δέον πολλάκις δεόντως οὐκ ἐνεργεῖται καὶ τὸ μὴ καθῆκον ἔστιν ὅτε
δρᾶται καθηκόντως· (2) οἷον ἡ μὲν τῆς παρακαταθήκης ἀπόδοσις ὅταν μὴ
ἀπὸ γνώμης ὑγιοῦς γίγνηται ἀλλ' ἢ ἐπὶ βλάβῃ τοῦ λαμβάνοντος ἢ ἐπ' ἐνέδρᾳ
τῆς περὶ μείζονα πίστιν ἀρνήσεως, καθῆκον ἔργον οὐ δεόντως ἐπιτελεῖται· (3) τὸ
δὲ τῷ κάμνοντι μὴ ἀληθεῦσαι τὸν ἰατρὸν κενοῦν ἢ τέμνειν ἢ καίειν   5
διεγνωκότα ἐπ' ὠφελείᾳ τοῦ νοσοῦντος, ἵνα μὴ προλαβὼν τὰ δεινὰ φύγῃ τὴν
θεραπείαν ἢ ἐξασθενήσας ἀπείπῃ πρὸς αὐτήν, ἢ πρὸς τοὺς πολεμίους τὸν σοφὸν ψεύσασθαι
ἐπὶ τῇ τῆς πατρίδος σωτηρίᾳ, δείσαντα μὴ ἐκ τοῦ ἀληθεῦσαι ῥωσθῇ τὰ τῶν ἀντιπάλων, οὐ
καθῆκον ἔργον δεόντως ἐνεργεῖται.

Context: interpretation of the Book of Numbers 5.18. Philo takes 'the priest's placing
the woman ἐναντίον κυρίου and uncovering her head' to refer to God's judgement of
a person's unseen motive.
     4–8 For the examples, cf. S.E., *M.* 7.43–5, in discussion of the difference between
'truth' and 'the true' (**33P**).

I Stobaeus 5.906,18–907,5 (*SVF* 3.510)

Χρυσίππου· ὁ δ' ἐπ' ἄκρον, φησί, προκόπτων ἅπαντα πάντως ἀποδίδωσι
τὰ καθήκοντα καὶ οὐδὲν παραλείπει. τὸν δὲ τούτου βίον οὐκ εἶναί πω φησὶν
εὐδαίμονα, ἀλλ' ἐπιγίνεσθαι αὐτῷ τὴν εὐδαιμονίαν, ὅταν αἱ μέσαι πράξεις
αὗται προσλάβωσι τὸ βέβαιον καὶ ἑκτικὸν καὶ ἰδίαν πῆξιν τινὰ λάβωσιν.

Context: collection of statements on happiness by philosophers.
     For the progressive's distance from happiness, cf. **61T–U**, and for προκοπή in
general, see Luschnat [605]. Seneca (*Ep.* 75.8–18) reports a doctrine which
distinguishes three grades of progress: (a) those at the stage described in the present
text, whom he describes as adjacent to but not yet in possession of wisdom, free of
passions and vices, equipped with moral knowledge in a still untested way, beyond the
possibility of lapsing but not yet confident of this; (b) those who are free of the greatest
mental troubles and passions, but still capable of lapsing; (c) those who are beyond
many great vices but not beyond all.

J Diogenes Laertius 7.88 (*SVF* 3 Archedemus 20, part)

Ἀρχέδημος δὲ [sc. τέλος φησὶ] τὸ πάντα τὰ καθήκοντα ἐπιτελοῦντα ζῆν.

Context: Stoic formulations of the τέλος.

In view of the technical expression τέλεια καθήκοντα (**B** 8, **K** 2) it seems justifiable to interpret ἐπιτελοῦντα accordingly – 'perfecting' – and not give it the weaker sense, 'performing'.

K Stobaeus 2.93,14–18 (*SVF* 3.500)

κατόρθωμα δ᾽ εἶναι λέγουσι καθῆκον πάντας ἀπέχον τοὺς ἀριθμούς, ἢ καθάπερ προείπομεν, τέλειον καθῆκον· ἁμάρτημά τε τὸ παρὰ τὸν ὀρθὸν λόγον πραττόμενον, ἢ ἐν ᾧ παραλέλειπταί τι καθῆκον ὑπὸ λογικοῦ ζῴου.

1 ἀπέχον codd.: ἐπέχον Canter (sed cf. D.L. 7.100)   2 ἁμάρτημά τε Heeren: ἁμαρτήματα codd.

Context: doxography of unrelated Stoic ethical concepts.

1 **πάντας ἀπέχον τοὺς ἀριθμούς** A standard Stoic image for the completeness or perfect harmony of virtue and virtuous actions; cf. D.L. 7.100, καλὸν δὲ λέγουσι τὸ τέλειον ἀγαθὸν παρὰ τὸ πάντας ἀπέχειν τοὺς ἐπιζητουμένους ἀριθμοὺς ὑπὸ τῆς φύσεως ἢ τὸ τελέως σύμμετρον, and see **61F**; **64H 3**. For ἀπέχειν = 'have in full', cf. LSJ s.v. IV. Perfect harmony is achieved by the conjunction of all the cardinal virtues; cf. D.L. loc. cit., εἴδη δ᾽ εἶναι τοῦ καλοῦ τέτταρα. For other instances of the expression, cf. **54H** 2; Cicero, *Off.* 3.14; Seneca, *Ep.* 71.16; Marcus Aurelius 6.26, where the numerical image is applied to 'completing' proper functions (μέμνησο ὅτι πᾶν καθῆκον ἐξ ἀριθμῶν τινων συμπληροῦται); and see note on **O**. The origins of the expression, which has never been properly studied, are to be sought in musical harmony; cf. Aristo's description of the four cardinal vices as 'the whole tetrachord' (*SVF* 1.370). 'Part' seems to be sometimes used as a variant for 'number' (cf. **L** 2; Stobaeus 2.63,5).

L Cicero, *Fin.* 3.32 (*SVF* 3.504)

(1) quicquid enim a sapientia proficiscitur, id continuo debet expletum esse omnibus suis partibus; in eo enim positum est id quod dicimus esse expetendum. (2) nam ut peccatum est patriam prodere, parentes violare, fana depeculari, quae sunt in effectu, sic timere, sic maerere, sic in libidine esse peccatum est etiam sine effectu. (3) verum ut haec non in posteris et in consequentibus, sed in primis continuo peccata sunt, sic ea quae proficiscuntur a virtute, susceptione prima, non perfectione, recta sunt iudicanda.   5

Context: the difference between wisdom and other types of expertise. Wisdom is like acting or dancing, not navigation or medicine, in having its own performance as its end; cf. **64H**. Yet it is also unique in being complete at any moment and wholly self-contained.

Stoic ethics

M Stobaeus 2.96,18–97,14 (*SVF* 3.501,502)

(1) ἔτι δὲ τῶν ἐνεργημάτων φασὶ τὰ μὲν εἶναι κατορθώματα, τὰ δὲ ἁμαρτήματα, τὰ δ' οὐδέτερα· (2) κατορθώματα μὲν τὰ τοιαῦτα· φρονεῖν, σωφρονεῖν, δικαιοπραγεῖν, χαίρειν, εὐεργετεῖν, εὐφραίνεσθαι, φρονίμως περιπατεῖν, πάνθ' ὅσα κατὰ τὸν ὀρθὸν λόγον πράττεται· (3) ἁμαρτήματα δ' εἶναι τό τε ἀφραίνειν καὶ τὸ ἀκολασταίνειν καὶ τὸ ἀδικεῖν καὶ τὸ λυπεῖσθαι 5 καὶ τὸ φοβεῖσθαι καὶ τὸ κλέπτειν καὶ καθόλου ὅσα παρὰ τὸν ὀρθὸν λόγον πράττεται· (4) οὔτε δὲ κατορθώματα οὔτε ἁμαρτήματα τὰ τοιαῦτα· λέγειν, ἐρωτᾶν, ἀποκρίνεσθαι, περιπατεῖν, ἀποδημεῖν καὶ τὰ τούτοις παραπλήσια. πάντα δὲ τὰ κατορθώματα δικαιοπραγήματα εἶναι καὶ εὐνομήματα καὶ εὐτακτήματα καὶ εὐεπιτηδεύματα καὶ εὐτυχήματα καὶ εὐδαιμονήματα καὶ εὐκαιρήματα 10 καὶ εὐσχημονήματα· οὐκ ἔτι μέντοιγε φρονιμεύματα, ἀλλὰ μόνα τὰ ἀπὸ φρονήσεως· καὶ ὁμοίως ἐπὶ τῶν ἄλλων ἀρετῶν, εἰ καὶ μὴ ὠνόμασται, οἷον σωφρονήματα μὲν τὰ ἀπὸ σωφροσύνης, δικαιώματα δὲ τὰ ἀπὸ δικαιοσύνης. τὰ δὲ ἁμαρτήματα ἐκ τῶν ἀντικειμένων ἀδικοπραγήματα καὶ ἀνομήματα καὶ ἀτακτήματα.

9 εὐνομήματα Dindorf: εὐνοήματα codd. 10 εὐεπιτηδεύματα Heeren: ἐπιτηδεύματα vel ἐπιτεύματα codd. 12 ὁμοίως Heeren: ὁμοιώσεως codd: 12 σωφρονήματα Canter: σωφρονηεύματα vel σωφρονικεύματα codd.

Context: doxography of unrelated Stoic ethical concepts.

2 **οὐδέτερα** Cf. Rist [303], 99–101.
4 **ὀρθὸν λόγον**. Cf. 61G 5; 63C 9.
9–14 Chrysippus, in Plutarch, *St. rep.* 1041A, argues as follows: (1) Every κατόρθωμα is both a εὐνόμημα and a δικαιοπράγημα. (2) Anything done in accordance with moderation, prudence or courage is a κατόρθωμα. (3) Therefore it is also a δικαιοπράγημα. In conjunction with the present passage, this shows that predicating δικαιοπράγημα of κατόρθωμα is not the familiar thesis of the unity of the virtues; cf. **61C–F**. What all the terms listed in 9–11 share is their utterly general applicability to any κατόρθωμα. Given the fact that the Stoics described κατόρθωμα as a νόμου πρόσταγμα, *SVF* 3.520, we can infer that δικαιοπραγήματα, 9, is not a reference to specifically just acts, but to the 'rightness' which informs all κατορθώματα; cf. Dyroff [545], 130–1. Lines 11–13 now fall into place. To be properly described as a 'prudent' act, a κατόρθωμα must be initiated by prudence, and to be properly called a δικαίωμα, it must issue from the virtue of justice. But these and all other virtuous acts can be properly called δικαιοπραγήματα. The whole passage seems to tie in well with our interpretation of Chrysippus' position on the inseparability of the virtues, vol. 1, 384.

N Stobaeus 2.99,3–8

ἀρέσκει γὰρ τῷ Ζήνωνι καὶ τοῖς ἀπ' αὐτοῦ Στωικοῖς φιλοσόφοις δύο γένη τῶν ἀνθρώπων εἶναι, τὸ μὲν τῶν σπουδαίων, τὸ δὲ τῶν φαύλων· καὶ τὸ μὲν τῶν σπουδαίων διὰ παντὸς τοῦ βίου χρῆσθαι ταῖς ἀρεταῖς, τὸ δὲ τῶν φαύλων ταῖς κακίαις· ὅθεν τὸ μὲν ἀεὶ κατορθοῦν ἐν ἅπασιν οἷς προστίθε-ται, τὸ δὲ ἁμαρτάνειν.　　　　5

1 ἀπ' Heeren: ὑπ' codd.

59 Proper functions

Context: characterization of the virtuous and inferior types of men. This doctrine differentiates Stoics from contemporary Peripatetics, who recognized a μέσος βίος or ἕξις, to which they assigned προκοπή (**61I** 1). Stoics confined μέσος, in its reference to humans, to children, who are excluded from virtue or vice by their undeveloped rationality; cf. D.L. 7.110, and *SVF* 3.535, 537–8.

O Stobaeus 2.113,18–23 (*SVF* 3.529, part)

(1) πάντων τε τῶν ἁμαρτημάτων ἴσων ὄντων καὶ τῶν κατορθωμάτων, καὶ τοὺς ἄφρονας ἐπίσης πάντας ἄφρονας εἶναι, τὴν αὐτὴν καὶ ἴσην ἔχοντας διάθεσιν. (2) ἴσων δὲ ὄντων τῶν ἁμαρτημάτων, εἶναί τινας ἐν αὐτοῖς διαφοράς, καθ' ὅσον τὰ μὲν αὐτῶν ἀπὸ σκληρᾶς καὶ δυσιάτου διαθέσεως γίνεται, τὰ δ' οὔ.

Context: characterization of virtuous men.
Cf. *SVF* 3.524–43, and for the absence of degrees of virtue and vice, see **61I**. The differentiation of ἁμαρτήματα, 3–5, is necessary to account for progress and the teachability of virtue. For another Stoic way of expressing difference of type between wrong acts, cf. Cicero, *Fin.* 4.56: *peccata autem partim esse tolerabilia, partim nullo modo, propterea quod alia peccata plures, alia pauciores quasi numeros officii praeterirent*, with discussion of 'numbers' in note on **K**.

P Cicero, *Off.* 1.15,152

quae quattuor quamquam inter se colligata atque implicata sunt, tamen ex singulis certa officiorum genera nascuntur, velut ex ea parte, quae prima discripta est, in qua sapientiam et prudentiam ponimus, inest indagatio atque inventio veri, eiusque virtutis hoc munus est proprium . . . sed ab iis partibus, quae sunt honestatis, quem ad modum officia ducerentur, satis expositum videtur.

2 *discripta* Heine: *descripta* codd.

Context: the beginning and the end of Cicero's account of *officia*, which drew heavily on Panaetius' lost work, Περὶ τοῦ καθήκοντος; cf. Cicero, *Ad Att.* 16.11.4.
1 For Panaetius' account of the unity of the virtues, cf. **63G**; and for the common foundation of virtue and proper functions, see **A**.
3–4 Panaetius seems to have differed from earlier Stoics in stressing the heuristic function of φρόνησις rather than its practical application; cf. **61H** 1.
4–5 Analysis of proper functions by reference to virtues may have been helped by the elaborate classifications of 'subordinate virtues', **61H** 6–7. E.g. the characterization of how a courageous man should act, Cicero, *Off.* 1.66, recalls the subordinate virtues of courage set out in **61H** 16–17.

Q Epictetus, *Diss.* 2.10.1–12

(1) πῶς ἀπὸ τῶν ὀνομάτων τὰ καθήκοντα ἔστιν εὑρίσκειν; (2) σκέψαι τίς εἶ. τὸ πρῶτον ἄνθρωπος, τοῦτο δ' ἔστιν οὐδὲν ἔχων κυριώτερον προαιρέσεως,

363

Stoic ethics

ἀλλὰ ταύτῃ τὰ ἄλλα ὑποτεταγμένα, αὐτὴν δ᾽ ἀδούλευτον καὶ ἀνυπότακ-
τον. σκόπει οὖν, τίνων κεχώρισαι κατὰ λόγον. κεχώρισαι θηρίων, κεχώρισαι προβάτων.
(3) ἐπὶ τούτοις πολίτης εἶ τοῦ κόσμου καὶ μέρος αὐτοῦ, οὐχ ἓν τῶν   5
ὑπηρετικῶν, ἀλλὰ τῶν προηγουμένων· παρακολουθητικὸς γὰρ εἶ τῇ θείᾳ
διοικήσει καὶ τοῦ ἑξῆς ἐπιλογιστικός. τίς οὖν ἐπαγγελία πολίτου; μηδὲν
ἔχειν ἰδίᾳ συμφέρον, περὶ μηδενὸς βουλεύεσθαι ὡς ἀπόλυτον, ἀλλ᾽ ὥσπερ ἄν,
εἰ ἡ χεὶρ ἢ ὁ ποὺς λογισμὸν εἶχον καὶ παρηκολούθουν τῇ φυσικῇ κατασκευῇ, οὐδέποτ᾽ ἂν
ἄλλως ὥρμησαν ἢ ὠρέχθησαν ἢ ἐπανενεγκόντες ἐπὶ τὸ ὅλον . . . (4) μετὰ τοῦτο   10
μέμνησο ὅτι υἱός εἶ . . . μετὰ τοῦτο ἴσθι ὅτι καὶ ἀδελφὸς εἶ . . . μετὰ ταῦτα
εἰ βουλευτὴς πόλεώς τινος, ὅτι βουλευτής· ⟨εἰ⟩ νέος, ὅτι νέος· εἰ
πρεσβύτης, ὅτι πρεσβύτης· εἰ πατήρ, ὅτι πατήρ. ἀεὶ γὰρ ἕκαστον τῶν
τοιούτων ὀνομάτων εἰς ἐπιλογισμὸν ἐρχόμενον ὑπογράφει τὰ οἰκεῖα ἔργα.

2 **προαιρέσεως** This common term in Epictetus for 'moral purpose' is not
attested with this sense in earlier Stoicism.
4–7 Cf. **63E**.
10 **ἐπὶ τὸ ὅλον**. In the section omitted after these words, Epictetus expands this
point by repeating the gist of **58J**.
10–14 Cf. **66F 2**.

60 Good and bad

A Plutarch, *St. rep.* 1035C–D (*SVF* 3.68)

"οὐ γὰρ ἔστιν εὑρεῖν τῆς δικαιοσύνης ἄλλην ἀρχὴν οὐδ᾽ ἄλλην γένεσιν ἢ τὴν ἐκ τοῦ Διὸς καὶ
τὴν ἐκ τῆς κοινῆς φύσεως· ἐντεῦθεν γὰρ δεῖ πᾶν τὸ τοιοῦτον τὴν ἀρχὴν ἔχειν, εἰ μέλλομέν τι
ἐρεῖν περὶ ἀγαθῶν καὶ κακῶν." (1) πάλιν ἐν ταῖς Φυσικαῖς θέσεσιν "οὐ γὰρ ἔστιν
ἄλλως οὐδ᾽ οἰκειότερον ἐπελθεῖν ἐπὶ τὸν τῶν ἀγαθῶν καὶ κακῶν λόγον οὐδ᾽
ἐπὶ τὰς ἀρετὰς οὐδ᾽ ἐπ᾽ εὐδαιμονίαν, ἀλλ᾽ ⟨ἢ⟩ ἀπὸ τῆς κοινῆς φύσεως καὶ   5
ἀπὸ τῆς τοῦ κόσμου διοικήσεως." (2) προελθὼν δ᾽ αὖθις· "δεῖ γὰρ τούτοις
συνάψαι τὸν περὶ ἀγαθῶν καὶ κακῶν λόγον, οὐκ οὔσης ἄλλης ἀρχῆς αὐτῶν
ἀμείνονος οὐδ᾽ ἀναφορᾶς, οὐδ᾽ ἄλλου τινὸς ἕνεκεν τῆς φυσικῆς θεωρίας
παραληπτῆς οὔσης ἢ πρὸς τὴν περὶ ἀγαθῶν ἢ κακῶν διάστασιν."

2 μέλλομέν τι Basil.: μέλλομεν (vel μέλλοιμεν vel μέλλωμεν) ἔρωτι codd.   5 ⟨ἢ⟩ Leonicus

Context: Chrysippus' alleged inconsistency in making theology the final topic of
physics (cf. **26C**) while introducing all his ethical inquiries with Zeus, fate and
providence. The passage quoted in 1–3 is taken from book 3 of his *On gods.*
For the identity of Zeus, universal nature and fate, cf. **46B**; **54A–B**. For the thesis
that everything is determined by universal nature, cf. **54T**. For universal nature in
specifications of the τέλος, cf. **63C**. For the place of κακά in the divine administration,
cf. **54Q–T**.

364

B Plutarch, *St. rep.* 1041E (*SVF* 3.69)

τὸν περὶ ἀγαθῶν καὶ κακῶν λόγον, ὃν αὐτὸς εἰσάγει καὶ δοκιμάζει, συμφωνότατον εἶναί φησι τῷ βίῳ καὶ μάλιστα τῶν ἐμφύτων ἅπτεσθαι προλήψεων. ταυτὶ γὰρ ἐν τῷ τρίτῳ τῶν Προτρεπτικῶν εἴρηκεν, ἐν δὲ τῷ πρώτῳ τοῦτον τὸν λόγον φησὶν ἀπὸ τῶν ἄλλων ἁπάντων ἀφέλκειν τὸν ἄνθρωπον ὡς οὐδὲν ὄντων πρὸς ἡμᾶς οὐδὲ συνεργούντων πρὸς εὐδαιμονίαν οὐδέν.   5

Context: demonstration of the inconsistency between Chrysippus' statement in 1–3, and that in 4–5. Plutarch cites **66A** a few lines later, in confirmation of his claim.

2–3 ἐμφύτων ... προλήψεων   For πρόληψις in general, cf. **39–40**. That their content included ordinary evaluations of *AN* and *CN* things (see vol. 1, 357) is confirmed by 4–5, and cf. Plutarch, *St. rep.* 1047E, where Chrysippus ascribes madness to those who set no value on wealth, health etc. At *Comm. not.* 1070C Plutarch is probably drawing on Stoic doctrine when he contrasts the 'internal' origin of value concepts (ταῦτα δ' ἐκ τῶν ἀγαθῶν [generally emended to ἀρχῶν] τῶν ἐν ἡμῖν σύμφυτον ἔχει τὴν γένεσιν) with the external source of impressions of hot, cold etc. For reasons suggested in vol. 1, 375, οἰκείωσις seems the best candidate for the generative power 'in us'.

C Diogenes Laertius 7.53 (=**39D** 8)

φυσικῶς δὲ νοεῖται δίκαιόν τι καὶ ἀγαθόν.

For the context on concept formation, of which this sentence forms a part, see **39D** and discussion by Sandbach [470], 33–4.

D Cicero, *Fin.* 3.33–4 (*SVF* 3.72)

(1) cumque rerum notiones in animis fiant, si aut usu aliquid cognitum sit aut coniunctione aut similitudine aut collatione rationis, hoc quarto quod extremum posui boni notitia facta est. (2) cum enim ab iis rebus quae sunt secundum naturam ascendit animus collatione rationis, tum ad notionem boni pervenit. (3) hoc autem ipsum bonum non accessione neque crescendo aut   5 cum ceteris comparando, sed propria vi sua et sentimus et appellamus bonum. (4) ut enim mel, etsi dulcissimum est, suo tamen proprio genere saporis, non comparatione cum aliis dulce esse sentitur, sic bonum hoc de quo agimus est illud quidem plurimi aestimandum, sed ea aestimatio genere valet, non magnitudine. (5) nam cum aestimatio, quae ἀξία dicitur, neque in bonis   10 numerata sit nec rursus in malis, quantumcumque eo addideris, in suo genere manebit. alia est igitur propria aestimatio virtutis, quae genere, non crescendo valet.

3 *boni* Lambinus: *bonum* codd.

Context: the nature of the good. This text should be read in conjunction with **59D**.

1–3 Cf. **39D**, which includes **C**; and for the exact repetition of the fourfold scheme, see **16F**.

4 ascendit The image of 'ascent' is probably a deliberate reminiscence of Plato, *Rep.* 7, 515e, on climbing out of the cave to view the sun (the Form of the good).

5–10 Two claims are made concerning the *ipsum bonum*: (a) it is analogous to *AN* things, with which it shares the property of having value, just as honey shares the property of sweetness with other things; thus those *AN* things can be used as steps towards conceptualizing it. (b) Its value is incommensurable with that of anything else, just as honey has to be experienced in order for its particular brand of sweetness to be grasped; thus the value of the good is not arrived at by adding or increasing or comparing the value of other valuable things. Since analogy functions by magnification or diminution (**39D**), the denials in 5–6 reveal the limits of the process. Analogy puts us in a position to form a concept of something supremely valuable. But the character of the thing which answers to that concept can only be perceived by direct acquaintance.

E Seneca, *Ep.* 120.3–5, 8–11

(1) nunc ergo ad id revertor de quo desideras dici, quomodo ad nos prima boni honestique notitia pervenerit. (2) hoc nos natura docere non potuit: semina nobis scientiae dedit, scientiam non dedit. quidam aiunt nos in notitiam incidisse, quod est incredibile, virtutis alicui speciem casu occucurrisse. (3) nobis videtur observatio collegisse et rerum saepe factarum inter se conlatio; 5 per analogian nostri intellectum et honestum et bonum iudicant . . . noveramus corporis sanitatem: ex hac cogitavimus esse aliquam et animi. noveramus vires corporis: ex his collegimus esse et animi robur. (4) aliqua benigna facta, aliqua humana, aliqua fortia nos obstupefecerant: haec coepimus tamquam perfecta mirari. suberant illis multa vitia quae species conspicui alicuius facti 10 fulgorque celabat: haec dissimulavimus. natura iubet augere laudanda, nemo non gloriam ultra verum tulit: ex his ergo speciem ingentis boni traximus . . . (5) mala interdum speciem honesti obtulere et optimum ex contrario enituit. sunt enim, ut scis, virtutibus vitia confinia, et perditis quoque ac turpibus recti similitudo est: sic mentitur prodigus liberalem, cum plurimum 15 intersit utrum quis dare sciat an servare nesciat . . . (6) haec nos similitudo coegit adtendere et distinguere specie quidem vicina, re autem plurimum inter se dissidentia. dum observamus eos quos insignes egregium opus fecerat, coepimus adnotare quis rem aliquam generoso animo fecisset et magno impetu, sed semel. hunc vidimus in bello fortem, in foro timidum, animose 20 paupertatem ferentem, humiliter infamiam: factum laudavimus, contempsimus virum. (7) alium vidimus adversus amicos benignum, adversus inimicos temperatum, et publica et privata sancte ac religiose administrantem; non deesse ei in iis quae toleranda erant patientiam, in iis quae agenda prudentiam. vidimus ubi tribuendum esset plena manu dantem, ubi laborandum, pertinacem et obnixum et lassitudinem corporis 25 animo sublevantem. praeterea idem erat semper et in omnia actu par sibi, iam non consilio bonus, sed more eo perductus ut non tantum recte facere posset, sed nisi recte facere non posset. intelleximus in illo perfectam esse virtutem. (8)

hanc in partes divisimus: oportebat cupiditates refrenari, metus conprimi,
facienda provideri, reddenda distribui: conprehendimus temperantiam, 30
fortitudinem, prudentiam, iustitiam et suum cuique dedimus officium. ex quo
ergo virtutem intelleximus? ostendit illam nobis ordo eius et decor et
constantia et omnium inter se actionum concordia et magnitudo super omnia
efferens sese. hinc intellecta est illa beata vita secundo defluens cursu, arbitrii
sui tota. 35

2–3   Cf. **61L**, and Cicero, *Fin.* 5.59, [*natura*] *virtutem ipsam inchoavit, nihil amplius.*
13   In the omitted passage Seneca refers to the fortitude of Fabricius and Horatius
Cocles as examples of the kind of behaviour that provides an *imago* of virtue.
18–28   Illustrations of the heuristic powers of observation and comparison, 5,
which are Seneca's analysis of 'analogy'.
28 **perfectam . . . virtutem**   Seneca speaks in the factual mode; cf. **D 6**. The
earliest Stoics, for whom the wise man was as 'rare as the Phoenix', could not have
supposed that virtue has to be actually observed in order to be grasped as a concept.
But it became commonplace to instance Socrates and Diogenes the Cynic as Stoic
sages. The character of such men, we can take Seneca to be saying, has provided us
with the means of distinguishing the fundamental features of virtue as a whole, 32–4,
from spurious instances of isolated virtues.
32–3 **ordo . . . concordia**   Cf. **59D** 18–19, *rerum agendarum ordinem . . . et
concordiam.*
34 **beata . . . cursu**   An allusion to Zeno's definition of happiness; **63A** 4–5.

F Epictetus, *Diss.* 3.3.2–4

(1) πέφυκεν δὲ πᾶσα ψυχὴ ὥσπερ τῷ ἀληθεῖ ἐπινεύειν, πρὸς τὸ ψεῦδος
ἀνανεύειν, πρὸς τὸ ἄδηλον ἐπέχειν, οὕτως πρὸς μὲν τὸ ἀγαθὸν ὀρεκτικῶς
κινεῖσθαι, πρὸς δὲ τὸ κακὸν ἐκκλιτικῶς, πρὸς δὲ τὸ μήτε κακὸν μήτ'
ἀγαθὸν οὐδετέρως . . . (2) τὸ ἀγαθὸν φανὲν εὐθὺς ἐκίνησεν ἐφ' αὑτό, τὸ
κακὸν ἀφ' αὑτοῦ. οὐδέποτε δ' ἀγαθοῦ φαντασίαν ἐναργῆ ἀποδοκιμάσει   5
ψυχή, οὐ μᾶλλον ἢ τὸ Καίσαρος νόμισμα. ἔνθεν ἐξήρτηται πᾶσα κίνησις
καὶ ἀνθρώπου καὶ θεοῦ.

Context: opening of a discourse on the good.
In Epictetus' psychology, ὄρεξις is always motivated by the good or the apparent
good; cf. note on **56C** 1. In the absence of a 'clear impression' of the good, people are
motivated by false judgements of value; mistaking things which fall outside their
moral purpose for good, they experience frustration and disappointment.
5–6   Cf. **40O 3**.

G Sextus Empiricus, *M.* 11.22–6 (*SVF* 3.75)

(1) οἱ μὲν οὖν Στωικοὶ τῶν κοινῶν ὡς εἰπεῖν ἐννοιῶν ἐχόμενοι ὁρίζονται
τἀγαθὸν τρόπῳ τῷδε "ἀγαθόν ἐστιν ὠφέλεια ἢ οὐχ ἕτερον ὠφελείας",
ὠφέλειαν μὲν λέγοντες τὴν ἀρετὴν καὶ τὴν σπουδαίαν πρᾶξιν, οὐχ ἕτερον

Stoic ethics

δὲ ὠφελείας τὸν σπουδαῖον ἄνθρωπον καὶ τὸν φίλον. (2) ἡ μὲν γὰρ ἀρετή
πως ἔχον ἡγεμονικὸν καθεστηκυῖα καὶ ἡ σπουδαία πρᾶξις ἐνέργειά τις   5
οὖσα κατ᾽ ἀρετήν, ἄντικρύς ἐστιν ὠφέλεια· ὁ δὲ σπουδαῖος ἄνθρωπος καὶ ὁ
φίλος, πάλιν τῶν ἀγαθῶν ὄντες καὶ αὐτοί, οὔτε ὠφέλεια λεχθεῖεν ἂν
ὑπάρχειν οὔθ᾽ ἕτεροι ὠφελείας δι᾽ αἰτίαν τοιαύτην. (3) τὰ γὰρ μέρη,
Στωικῶν φασι παῖδες, οὔτε τὰ αὐτὰ τοῖς ὅλοις ἐστὶν οὔτε ἑτεροῖα τῶν
ὅλων, οἷον ἡ χεὶρ οὔτε ἡ αὐτή ἐστιν ὅλῳ ἀνθρώπῳ, οὐ γὰρ ὅλος ἄνθρωπός   10
ἐστιν ἡ χείρ, οὔτε ἑτέρα τοῦ ὅλου, σὺν γὰρ τῇ [ὅλῃ] χειρὶ ὅλος ὁ ἄνθρωπος
νοεῖται ἄνθρωπος. (4) ἐπεὶ οὖν καὶ τοῦ σπουδαίου ἀνθρώπου καὶ τοῦ φίλου
μέρος ἐστὶν ἡ ἀρετή, τὰ δὲ μέρη οὔτε ταὐτὰ τοῖς ὅλοις ἐστὶν οὔτε ἕτερα τῶν
ὅλων, εἴρηται ὁ σπουδαῖος ἄνθρωπος καὶ ὁ φίλος οὐχ ἕτερος ὠφελείας. (5)
ὥστε πᾶν ἀγαθὸν τῷ ὅρῳ ἐμπεριειλῆφθαι, ἐάν τε ἐξ εὐθείας ὠφέλεια   15
τυγχάνῃ ἐάν τε μὴ ᾖ ἕτερον ὠφελείας. ἔνθεν καὶ κατ᾽ ἀκολουθίαν τριχῶς εἰπόντες
ἀγαθὸν προσαγορεύεσθαι, ἕκαστον τῶν σημαινομένων κατ᾽ ἰδίαν πάλιν ἐπιβολὴν
ὑπογράφουσιν. λέγεται γὰρ ἀγαθόν, φασί, καθ᾽ ἕνα μὲν τρόπον τὸ ὑφ᾽ οὗ ἢ ἀφ᾽ οὗ ἔστιν
ὠφελεῖσθαι, ὃ δὴ ἀρχικώτατον ὑπῆρχε καὶ ἀρετή· ἀπὸ γὰρ ταύτης ὥσπερ τινὸς πηγῆς
πᾶσα πέφυκεν ἀνίσχειν ὠφέλεια. καθ᾽ ἕτερον δὲ τὸ καθ᾽ ὃ συμβαίνει ὠφελεῖσθαι· οὕτως οὐ   20
μόνον αἱ ἀρεταὶ λεχθήσονται ἀγαθὰ ἀλλὰ καὶ αἱ κατ᾽ αὐτὰς πράξεις, εἴπερ καὶ κατὰ ταύτας
συμβαίνει ὠφελεῖσθαι. κατὰ δὲ τὸν τρίτον καὶ τελευταῖον τρόπον λέγεται ἀγαθὸν τὸ οἷόν τε
ὠφελεῖν, ἐμπεριλαμβανούσης τῆς ἀποδόσεως ταύτης τάς τε ἀρετὰς καὶ τὰς ἐναρέτους
πράξεις καὶ τοὺς φίλους καὶ τοὺς σπουδαίους ἀνθρώπους θεούς τε καὶ σπουδαίους
δαίμονας.   25

11 ὅλῃ del. Arnim   13 ἐστὶν² Fabricius: ἔσται codd.   23 ἐμπεριλαμβανούσης Bekker: ἐκ- codd.

Context: doxography of good, bad and indifferent.
These elaborate distinctions provide the Stoics with the logical apparatus for
accommodating different kinds of good things, while retaining a univocal sense of
ἀγαθόν, cf. especially 15–16, 22–5. The whole passage is consistent with the account
of ὠφελεῖν as κινεῖν ἢ ἴσχειν κατ᾽ ἀρετήν, D.L. 7.104. For parallel evidence, cf. SVF
3.74, 76; Sextus, PH 3.169–71, with discussion by Tsekourakis [556], 70–1.

9 Στωικῶν ... παῖδες   Probably meaning 'later Stoics', since the doctrine in
question is explicitly attributed only to them, cf. 28D 9.

20–2   This use of 'good' in reference to the beneficial results of virtuous actions
seems to be similar to what is elsewhere called ὠφέλημα and distinguished from
ἀγαθόν; cf. 33J.

H   Seneca, Ep. 124.13–14

"dixisti" inquit "aliquod bonum esse arboris, aliquod herbae; potest ergo aliquod esse et
infantis." (1) verum bonum nec in arboribus nec in mutis animalibus: hoc quod
in illis bonum est precario bonum dicitur. "quod est?" inquis. "hoc quod
secundum cuiusque naturam est. (2) bonum quidem cadere in mutum animal
nullo modo potest; felicioris meliorisque naturae est. nisi ubi rationi locus est,   5
bonum non est. (3) quattuor hae naturae sunt, arboris, animalis, hominis, dei:

60 *Good and bad*

haec duo, quae rationalia sunt, eandem naturam habent, illo diversa sunt quod
alterum inmortale, alterum mortale est. ex his ergo unius bonum natura
perficit, dei scilicet, alterius cura, hominis. (4) cetera tantum in sua natura
perfecta sunt, non vere perfecta, a quibus abest ratio. hoc enim demum   10
perfectum est quod secundum universam naturam perfectum, universa autem
natura rationalis est: cetera possunt in suo genere esse perfecta."

7 *illo* Schweighaüser: *illa* codd.

Context: cognition of the good.

4–6   Cf. section 9 of the letter: *est aliquod inrationale animal, est aliquod nondum
rationale* [i.e. child], *est rationale sed inperfectum* [i.e. ordinary adult human]; *in nullo
horum bonum, ratio illud secum adfert.*

I Clement, *Paid.* 1.8.63.1–2 (*SVF* 2.1116, part)

(1) ὁ δὲ φιλῶν τι ὠφελεῖν αὐτὸ βούλεται, τὸ δὲ ὠφελοῦν τοῦ μὴ ὠφελοῦντος
πάντως ἄν που κρεῖττον εἴη· τοῦ δὲ ἀγαθοῦ κρεῖττον οὐδὲ ἕν· ὠφελεῖ ἄρα
τὸ ἀγαθόν. (2) ἀγαθὸς δὲ ὁ θεὸς ὡμολογεῖται· ὠφελεῖ ἄρα ὁ θεός. (3) τὸ δὲ
ἀγαθὸν ᾗ ἀγαθόν ἐστιν οὐδὲν ἄλλο ποιεῖ ἢ ὅτι ὠφελεῖ· πάντα ἄρα ὠφελεῖ ὁ
θεός. (4) καὶ οὐ δήπου ὠφελεῖ μέν τι τὸν ἄνθρωπον, οὐχὶ δὲ κήδεται αὐτοῦ,   5
οὐδὲ κήδεται μέν, οὐχὶ δὲ καὶ ἐπιμελεῖται αὐτοῦ· κρεῖττον μὲν γὰρ τὸ κατὰ
γνώμην ὠφελοῦν τοῦ μὴ ὠφελοῦντος κατὰ γνώμην· τοῦ δὲ θεοῦ κρεῖττον
οὐδέν· καὶ οὐκ ἄλλο τι ἐστὶ τὸ κατὰ γνώμην ὠφελεῖν, εἰ μὴ ἐπιμελεῖσθαι
τοῦ ἀνθρώπου· κήδεται ἄρα καὶ ἐπιμελεῖται τοῦ ἀνθρώπου ὁ θεός.

9 τοῦ ἀνθρώπου secl. Arnim

Context: elaboration of an argument showing god and λόγος to be φιλάνθρωποι.
Though not attributed to the Stoics, the syllogistic form of the argument strongly
recalls early Stoic proofs of the world's divine nature; cf. **54E–H**.
   For beneficence as a Stoic attribute of god, cf. **54K**.

J Stobaeus 2.73,1–15 (*SVF* 3.111)

(1) ἔτι δὲ τῶν ἀγαθῶν τὰ μὲν εἶναι ἐν κινήσει, τὰ δὲ ἐν σχέσει. ἐν κινήσει
μὲν τὰ τοιαῦτα, χαράν, εὐφροσύνην, σώφρονα ὁμιλίαν· ἐν σχέσει δὲ τὰ
τοιαῦτα, εὔτακτον ἡσυχίαν, μονὴν ἀτάραχον, προσοχὴν ἔπανδρον. (2) τῶν
δὲ ἐν σχέσει τὰ μὲν καὶ ἐν ἕξει εἶναι, οἷον τὰς ἀρετάς· τὰ δ' ἐν σχέσει μόνον,
ὡς τὰ ῥηθέντα. (3) ἐν ἕξει δὲ οὐ μόνας εἶναι τὰς ἀρετάς, ἀλλὰ καὶ τὰς ἄλλας   5
τέχνας τὰς ἐν τῷ σπουδαίῳ ἀνδρὶ ἀλλοιωθείσας ὑπὸ τῆς ἀρετῆς καὶ
γενομένας ἀμεταπτώτους· οἱονεὶ γὰρ ἀρετὰς γίγνεσθαι. (4) φασὶ δὲ καὶ
τῶν ἐν ἕξει ἀγαθῶν εἶναι καὶ τὰ ἐπιτηδεύματα καλούμενα, οἷον
φιλομουσίαν, φιλογραμματίαν, φιλογεωμετρίαν καὶ τὰ παραπλήσια. εἶναι

369

Stoic ethics

γὰρ ὁδόν τινα ἐκλεκτικὴν τῶν ἐν ταύταις ταῖς τέχναις οἰκείων πρὸς ἀρετήν, ἀναφέρουσαν   10
αὐτὰ ἐπὶ τὸ τοῦ βίου τέλος.

4 τά ... τά Rieth: τὰς ... τας codd.   5–6 τὰς ἄλλας τέχνας P: τὰς ἀλλὰ καὶ τὰς τέχνας F: τὰς τέχνας
Wachsmuth   10 ἐκλεκτικὴν Meurer: ἐκλεκτὴν codd.

Context: doxography of goods.

1   For this division, cf. the two aspects of ὠφελεῖν cited in note on **G**, and Rieth [551], 29–31.

2   For χαρά and εὐφροσύνη, see also **K** 2–3, **M** 3; **21R** 8–9. They are also classified as goods which do not belong to all φρόνιμοι, nor to [any of] them all the time, Stobaeus 2.69,3–4.

9–11   Cf. **26H** 5–7.

K   Stobaeus 2.58,5–15 (*SVF* 3.95, part)

(1) τῶν δὲ ἀγαθῶν τὰ μὲν εἶναι ἀρετάς, τὰ δ᾽ οὔ. φρόνησιν μὲν οὖν καὶ
σωφροσύνην ⟨καὶ δικαιοσύνην⟩ καὶ ἀνδρείαν ἀρετάς· χαρὰν δὲ καὶ
εὐφροσύνην καὶ θάρρος καὶ βούλησιν καὶ τὰ παραπλήσια οὐκ εἶναι ἀρετάς.
(2) τῶν δὲ ἀρετῶν τὰς μὲν ἐπιστήμας τινῶν καὶ τέχνας, τὰς δ᾽ οὔ. φρόνησιν
μὲν οὖν καὶ σωφροσύνην καὶ δικαιοσύνην καὶ ἀνδρείαν ἐπιστήμας εἶναι   5
τινῶν καὶ τέχνας· μεγαλοψυχίαν δὲ καὶ ῥώμην καὶ ἰσχὺν ψυχῆς οὔτ᾽
ἐπιστήμας τινῶν εἶναι οὔτε τέχνας. (3) ἀνάλογον δὲ καὶ τῶν κακῶν τὰ μὲν
εἶναι κακίας, τὰ δ᾽ οὔ.

2 ⟨καὶ δικαιοσύνην⟩ Meineke   ἀνδρείαν ⟨καὶ μεγαλοψυχίαν καὶ ῥώμην καὶ ἰσχὺν ψυχῆς⟩
Wachsmuth

Context: Stobaeus' first division of goods.

2–3   χαρά and βούλησις, along with εὐλάβεια, are the three εὐπάθειαι (**65F**), a term absent from Stobaeus' doxography.

6   **μεγαλοψυχίαν**   In **61H 7** this is classified as subordinate to ἀνδρεία, and at Stobaeus 2.61,15 it is defined by reference to ἐπιστήμη (cf. D.L. 7.93), so it seems a wrong example to illustrate virtues which are neither ἐπιστῆμαι nor τέχναι.

L   Stobaeus 2.70,21–71,6 (*SVF* 3.104, part)

τῶν δὲ περὶ ψυχὴν ἀγαθῶν τὰ μὲν εἶναι διαθέσεις, τὰ δὲ ἕξεις μὲν διαθέσεις
δ᾽ οὔ, τὰ δ᾽ οὔτε ἕξεις οὔτε διαθέσεις. διαθέσεις μὲν τὰς ἀρετὰς πάσας,
ἕξεις δὲ μόνον καὶ οὐ διαθέσεις τὰ ἐπιτηδεύματα ὡς τὴν μαντικὴν καὶ τὰ
παραπλήσια· οὔτε δὲ ἕξεις οὔτε διαθέσεις τὰς κατ᾽ ἀρετὰς ἐνεργείας, οἷον
φρονίμευμα καὶ τὴν τῆς σωφροσύνης κτῆσιν καὶ τὰ παραπλήσια.   5

3 ὡς τὴν Heeren: καὶ τὴν codd.   4 ἀρετὰς Meineke; αὐτὰς codd.

Context: 2 pages before **J**.

5   **φρονίμευμα**   Cf. **59M** 11.

370

M Stobaeus 2.71,15–72,6 (*SVF* 3.106, part)

τῶν τε ἀγαθῶν τὰ μὲν εἶναι τελικά, τὰ δὲ ποιητικά, τὰ δὲ ἀμφοτέρως
ἔχοντα. ὁ μὲν οὖν φρόνιμος ἄνθρωπος καὶ ὁ φίλος ποιητικὰ μόνον ἐστὶν
ἀγαθά· χαρὰ δὲ καὶ εὐφροσύνη καὶ θάρρος καὶ φρονίμη περιπάτησις
τελικὰ μόνον ἐστὶν ἀγαθά· αἱ δ' ἀρεταὶ πᾶσαι καὶ ποιητικά ἐστιν ἀγαθὰ
καὶ τελικά, καὶ γὰρ ἀπογεννῶσι τὴν εὐδαιμονίαν καὶ συμπληροῦσι, μέρη   5
αὐτῆς γινόμεναι. ἀνάλογον δὲ καὶ τῶν κακῶν . . .

6 γινόμεναι Usener: γινόμενα codd.

Context: a few lines after **L**.

For this division, see also D.L. 7.96 and Cicero, *Fin.* 3.55. It closely recalls the
tripartite classification of goods in Plato, *Rep.* 2, 357b–d: (a) desirable not for their
consequences but for their own sake; (b) desirable both for their consequences and for
their own sake; (c) desirable not for their own sake but for their consequences. Stoic
τελικά correspond to (a) and ποιητικά to (c). Plato's prime example of (b) is φρονεῖν,
with χαίρειν one of his examples of (a) and exercise of (c), all of which are taken over
in **M**. Cf. also the bipartite division into δι' αὐτὰ and ποιητικά, Stobaeus 2.72,14–18.

N Cicero, *Fin.* 3.27

sed consectaria me Stoicorum brevia et acuta delectant. concluduntur igitur eorum argumenta
sic: (1) quod est bonum, omne laudabile est; quod autem laudabile est, omne
est honestum; bonum igitur quod est, honestum est. satisne hoc conclusum
videtur? certe; quod enim efficiebatur ex iis duobus quae erant sumpta, in eo
vides esse conclusum. (2) duorum autem e quibus effecta conclusio est, contra   5
superius dici solet non omne bonum esse laudabile. nam quod laudabile sit
honestum esse conceditur. (3) illud autem perabsurdum, bonum esse aliquid
quod non expetendum sit, aut expetendum quod non placens, aut si id, non
etiam diligendum; ergo et probandum; ita etiam laudabile; id autem
honestum. ita fit ut quod bonum sit, id etiam honestum sit.   10

4 iis Baiter: *his* codd.   5 *vides* ed. princ.: *vide* codd.

Context: proof that *honestum* is the only good. The syllogism is criticized at *Fin.* 4.48.

The whole passage, minus the elementary lesson in logic, is ultimately derived
from Chrysippus; cf. Plutarch, *St. rep.* 1039C. For discussion of this and similar Stoic
arguments, cf. Irwin [594].

O Diogenes Laertius 7.101 (*SVF* 3.92)

δοκεῖ δὲ πάντα τὰ ἀγαθὰ ἴσα εἶναι καὶ πᾶν ἀγαθὸν ἐπ' ἄκρον εἶναι αἱρετὸν
καὶ μήτ' ἄνεσιν μήτ' ἐπίτασιν ἐπιδέχεσθαι.

Context: one sentence before **58A**.

2   The defining characteristic of a διάθεσις; cf. **47S**.

Stoic ethics

P Stobaeus 2.101,21–102,3 (*SVF* 3.626)

τὰ δ' ἀγαθὰ πάντα κοινὰ εἶναι τῶν σπουδαίων, τῶν δὲ φαύλων τὰ κακά. δι'
ὃ καὶ τὸν ὠφελοῦντά τινα καὶ αὐτὸν ὠφελεῖσθαι, τὸν δὲ βλάπτοντα καὶ
ἑαυτὸν βλάπτειν. πάντας δὲ τοὺς σπουδαίους ὠφελεῖν ἀλλήλους, οὔτε φίλους
ὄντας ἀλλήλων πάντως οὔτε εὔνους ⟨οὔτε⟩ εὐδοκίμους οὔτε ἀποδεχομένους παρὰ τὸ μήτε
καταλαμβάνεσθαι μήτ' ἐν ταὐτῷ κατοικεῖν τόπῳ, εὐνοητικῶς μέντοι γε πρὸς ἀλλήλους   5
διακεῖσθαι καὶ φιλικῶς καὶ δοκιμαστικῶς καὶ ἀποδεκτικῶς· τοὺς δὲ ἄφρονας ἐν τοῖς
ἐναντίοις τούτων ὑπάρχειν.

4 ⟨οὔτε⟩ Heeren

Context: see note on **59N**.

1–2 Similarly Stobaeus 2.93,19–94,1, where the thesis concerning virtuous men
is followed by the definition of ὁμόνοια as ἐπιστήμη κοινῶν ἀγαθῶν; this is a feature
of all virtuous men διὰ τὸ συμφωνεῖν ἐν τοῖς κατὰ τὸν βίον.

Q Cleanthes (Clement, *Protr.* 6.72.7; *SVF* 1.557)

τἀγαθὸν ἐρωτᾷς μ' οἷον ἔστ'; ἄκουε δή·
τεταγμένον, δίκαιον, ὅσιον, εὐσεβές,
κρατοῦν ἑαυτοῦ, χρήσιμον, καλόν, δέον,
αὐστηρόν, αὐθέκαστον, αἰεὶ συμφέρον,
ἄφοβον, ἄλυπον, λυσιτελές, ἀνώδυνον,   5
ὠφέλιμον, εὐάρεστον, ἀσφαλές, φίλον,
ἔντιμον ⟨ . . . ⟩ ὁμολογούμενον,
εὐκλεές, ἄτυφον, ἐπιμελές, πρᾷον, σφοδρόν,
χρονιζόμενον, ἄμεμπτον, αἰεὶ διαμένον.

7 ἔντιμον ⟨εὐχάριστον⟩ Arnim

Context: the verses are quoted as Cleanthes' 'revelation' concerning the nature of god.
Most of the attributes are too familiar to require comment. The following are more
distinctive: 4 αὐστηρόν, cf. *SVF* 3.637–9, Aristotle, *EE* VII.5, 1240a2; 5 ἄφοβον,
ἄλυπον – free from two of the cardinal passions, cf. **R** 6; 7 ὁμολογούμενον – recalling
the definition of the τέλος, cf. **63A** 1; 8 ἄτυφον, cf. notes on **1D**; **2B** 4.

R Plutarch, *St. rep.* 1042E–F (*SVF* 3.85)

(1) τἀγαθὰ πρὸς τὰ κακὰ τὴν πᾶσαν ἔχειν διαφορὰν ὁμολογεῖ Χρύσιππος.
καὶ ἀναγκαῖόν ἐστιν εἰ τὰ μὲν ἐσχάτως ποιεῖ κακοδαίμονας εὐθὺς οἷς ἂν
παρῇ τὰ δ' ἐπ' ἄκρον εὐδαίμονας. (2) αἰσθητὰ δ' εἶναι τἀγαθὰ καὶ τὰ κακὰ
φησιν, ἐν τῷ προτέρῳ Περὶ τέλους ταῦτα γράφων· "ὅτι μὲν γὰρ αἰσθητά ἐστι
τἀγαθὰ καὶ τὰ κακὰ καὶ τούτοις ἐκποιεῖ λέγειν· οὐ γὰρ μόνον τὰ πάθη ἐστὶν   5
αἰσθητὰ σὺν τοῖς εἴδεσιν, οἷον λύπη καὶ φόβος καὶ τὰ παραπλήσια, ἀλλὰ
καὶ κλοπῆς καὶ μοιχείας καὶ τῶν ὁμοίων ἔστιν αἰσθέσθαι καὶ καθόλου
ἀφροσύνης καὶ δειλίας καὶ ἄλλων οὐκ ὀλίγων κακιῶν οὐδὲ μόνον χαρᾶς καὶ

εὐεργεσιῶν καὶ ἄλλων πολλῶν κατορθώσεων ἀλλὰ καὶ φρονήσεως καὶ
ἀνδρείας καὶ τῶν λοιπῶν ἀρετῶν." 10

7 καθόλου Reiske: γὰρ ὅλον codd.

Context: Plutarch finds these doctrines absurdly inconsistent with the Stoic thesis that
a man may change from vice to virtue without perceiving the change; cf. **61U**.

6 **σὺν τοῖς εἴδεσιν** For the translation, 'people's appearance', cf. Burnyeat [484],
228–9, who aptly refers to D.L. 7.173 where Cleanthes is reported to have vindicated
a Zenonian doctrine that moral character is καταληπτὸν ἐξ εἴδους; and cf. **45C** for
Cleanthes' use of the visible signs of shame and fear – blushing and pallor – in his
argument for the soul's corporeality.

S Seneca, *Ep.* 117.2–3

(1) placet nostris quod bonum est corpus esse, quia quod bonum est facit,
quidquid facit corpus est. quod bonum est prodest; faciat autem aliquid
oportet ut prosit; si facit, corpus est. (2) sapientiam bonum esse dicunt;
sequitur ut necesse sit illam corporalem quoque dicere. at sapere non putant
eiusdem condicionis esse. incorporale est et accidens alteri, id est sapientiae; itaque nec facit 5
quicquam nec prodest. "quid ergo?" inquit "non dicimus: bonum est sapere?" dicimus
referentes ad id ex quo pendet, id est ad ipsam sapientiam.

Context: exposition of the corporeality of wisdom.
1–3 Cf. **45A–B**.
4–7 Cf. **33E** and note on **33J**.

61 Virtue and vice

A Diogenes Laertius 7.89 (*SVF* 3.39)

(1) τήν τ' ἀρετὴν διάθεσιν εἶναι ὁμολογουμένην· καὶ αὐτὴν δι' αὐτὴν εἶναι
αἱρετήν, οὐ διά τινα φόβον ἢ ἐλπίδα ἤ τι τῶν ἔξωθεν· (2) ἐν αὐτῇ τ' εἶναι
τὴν εὐδαιμονίαν, ἅτ' οὔσῃ ψυχῇ πεποιημένῃ πρὸς τὴν ὁμολογίαν παντὸς
τοῦ βίου.

Context: immediately following **63C**.
3 The identification of virtue with a soul of this kind seems to be a purely verbal
difference from the more familiar account of it as a διάθεσις of the soul or the soul's
commanding-faculty; cf. **B 8**. In Stobaeus 2.64,18–23 the corporeality of the virtues is
inferred from the fact that they are identical to the soul's commanding part καθ'
ὑπόστασιν.

B Plutarch, *Virt. mor.* 440E–441D

(1) Μενέδημος μὲν ὁ ἐξ Ἐρετρίας ἀνῄρει τῶν ἀρετῶν καὶ τὸ πλῆθος καὶ τὰς
διαφοράς, ὡς μιᾶς οὔσης καὶ χρωμένης πολλοῖς ὀνόμασι· τὸ γὰρ αὐτὸ

Stoic ethics

σωφροσύνην καὶ ἀνδρείαν καὶ δικαιοσύνην λέγεσθαι, καθάπερ βροτὸν καὶ
ἄνθρωπον. (2) Ἀρίστων δ᾽ ὁ Χῖος τῇ μὲν οὐσίᾳ μίαν καὶ αὐτὸς ἀρετὴν
ἐποίει καὶ ὑγίειαν ὠνόμαζε· (3) τῷ δὲ πρός τί πως διαφόρους καὶ πλείονας,   5
ὡς εἴ τις ἐθέλοι τὴν ὅρασιν ἡμῶν λευκῶν μὲν ἀντιλαμβανομένην λευκοθέαν
καλεῖν, μελάνων δὲ μελανοθέαν ἤ τι τοιοῦτον ἕτερον. καὶ γὰρ ἡ ἀρετὴ ποιητέα
μὲν ἐπισκοποῦσα καὶ μὴ ποιητέα κέκληται φρόνησις, ἐπιθυμίαν δὲ κοσμοῦσα καὶ τὸ
μέτριον καὶ τὸ εὔκαιρον ἐν ἡδοναῖς ὁρίζουσα σωφροσύνη, κοινωνήμασι δὲ καὶ συμβολαίοις
ὁμιλοῦσα τοῖς πρὸς ἑτέρους δικαιοσύνη· (4) καθάπερ τὸ μαχαίριον ἓν μέν ἐστιν   10
ἄλλοτε δ᾽ ἄλλο διαιρεῖ, καὶ τὸ πῦρ ἐνεργεῖ περὶ ὕλας διαφόρους μιᾷ φύσει
χρώμενον. (5) ἔοικε δὲ καὶ Ζήνων εἰς τοῦτό πως ὑποφέρεσθαι ὁ Κιτιεύς,
ὁριζόμενος τὴν φρόνησιν ἐν μὲν ἀπονεμητέοις δικαιοσύνην ἐν δ᾽ αἱρετέοις
σωφροσύνην ἐν δ᾽ ὑπομενετέοις ἀνδρείαν· (6) ἀπολογούμενοι δ᾽ ἀξιοῦσιν ἐν
τούτοις τὴν ἐπιστήμην φρόνησιν ὑπὸ τοῦ Ζήνωνος ὠνομάσθαι. (7)   15
Χρύσιππος δέ, κατὰ τὸ ποιὸν ἀρετὴν ἰδίᾳ ποιότητι συνίστασθαι νομίζων,
ἔλαθεν αὐτὸν κατὰ τὸν Πλάτωνα "σμῆνος ἀρετῶν" οὐ σύνηθες οὐδὲ
γνώριμον ἐγείρας· ὡς γὰρ παρὰ τὸν ἀνδρεῖον ἀνδρείαν καὶ παρὰ τὸν πρᾶον
πραότητα καὶ δικαιοσύνην παρὰ τὸν δίκαιον, οὕτω παρὰ τὸν χαρίεντα
χαριεντότητα καὶ παρὰ τὸν ἐσθλὸν ἐσθλότητα καὶ παρὰ τὸν μέγαν μεγαλότητα   20
καὶ παρὰ τὸν καλὸν καλότητα ἑτέρας τε τοιαύτας ἐπιδεξιότητας εὐαπαντησίας εὐτραπε-
λίας ἀρετὰς τιθέμενος πολλῶν καὶ ἀτόπων ὀνομάτων οὐδὲν δεομένην
ἐμπέπληκε φιλοσοφίαν. (8) κοινῶς δ᾽ ἅπαντες οὗτοι τὴν ἀρετὴν τοῦ
ἡγεμονικοῦ τῆς ψυχῆς διάθεσίν τινα καὶ δύναμιν γεγενημένην ὑπὸ λόγου,
μᾶλλον δὲ λόγον οὖσαν αὐτὴν ὁμολογούμενον καὶ βέβαιον καὶ ἀμετάπτω-   25
τον ὑποτίθενται· (9) καὶ νομίζουσιν οὐκ εἶναι τὸ παθητικὸν καὶ ἄλογον
διαφορᾷ τινι καὶ φύσει ψυχῆς τοῦ λογικοῦ διακεκριμένον, ἀλλὰ τὸ αὐτὸ
τῆς ψυχῆς μέρος, ὃ δὴ καλοῦσι διάνοιαν καὶ ἡγεμονικόν, δι᾽ ὅλου
τρεπόμενον καὶ μεταβάλλον ἔν τε τοῖς πάθεσι καὶ ταῖς καθ᾽ ἕξιν ἢ διάθεσιν
μεταβολαῖς κακίαν τε γίνεσθαι καὶ ἀρετήν, καὶ μηδὲν ἔχειν ἄλογον ἐν   30
ἑαυτῷ, (10) λέγεσθαι δ᾽ ἄλογον, ὅταν τῷ πλεονάζοντι τῆς ὁρμῆς ἰσχυρῷ
γενομένῳ καὶ κρατήσαντι πρός τι τῶν ἀτόπων παρὰ τὸν αἱροῦντα λόγον
ἐκφέρηται· (11) καὶ γὰρ τὸ πάθος εἶναι λόγον πονηρὸν καὶ ἀκόλαστον ἐκ
φαύλης καὶ διημαρτημένης κρίσεως σφοδρότητα καὶ ῥώμην προσλα-
βούσης.   35

16 τὸ codd.: τὸν Pohlenz   20 χαριεντότητα . . . ἐσθλότητα etc. vel -ότητας codd.   27 ψυχῆς del.
Hartman

Context: the unitary conception of virtue held by those philosophers who, mistakenly
in Plutarch's opinion, have defended a unitary conception of the soul.
  1 Menedemus' position recalls that of the Megarians, D.L. 7.161.
  5 ὑγίειαν   Cf. Plato, Rep. 4, 444d.
  12–14   The position attributed to Zeno closely resembles Aristotle's account of
Socrates' doctrine on the relationship between virtue, knowledge and φρόνησις; cf.
EN VI.13, 1144b17–30.
  14–15   Evidence that the task of Zeno's successors in this matter was, as so often,

to impose some formal coherence on his pronouncements. The 'defence' (ἀπολογού-μενοι) probably concerns the awkward double role of φρόνησις as both genus and one species of virtue; cf. **C 2**.

16 **τὸ ποιόν**   The MSS reading should be retained: τὸ ποιόν refers to the genus of 'the qualified' (cf. **28**) in contrast with that of 'relative disposition' (cf. **29**), as proposed (though perhaps not explicitly, see vol. 1, 179) by Aristo, 5–10.

17   The Platonic reference is to *Meno* 72a.

20–3   χαριεντότης and the succeeding virtue terms are Chrysippean innovations. He presumably took his own theory to require names for each virtue which would unambiguously denote the quality corresponding to each virtue adjective. Available nouns such as χάρις, μέγεθος, κάλλος may have seemed too general for this purpose. He could have avoided the 'swarm of virtues' only by either treating some virtue adjectives as synonyms or leaving the corresponding virtues nameless (cf. Aristotle's procedure in *EN* ii.7).

25–6 **βέβαιον καὶ ἀμετάπτωτον**   The terms connote properties of ἐπιστήμη and the wise man's character; cf. especially **41H**, **59I**, and see also *SVF* 3.542.

27 **διαφορᾷ–ψυχῆς**   We take διαφορᾷ τινι καὶ φύσει as a hendiadys. ψυχῆς, though often deleted, is essential to the argument. The Stoics acknowledge that passion and irrationality are different from rationality, but do not locate their difference in different parts of the soul. Cf. **65G**.

31 **πλεονάζοντι**   The technical term for an 'excessive' impulse; cf. **65A, J**.

32 **αἱροῦντα λόγον**   Cf. **59E 2**, where ὁ αἱρῶν λόγος is a definiens of καθῆκον and may be taken to stand to it as ὀρθὸς λόγος stands to a κατόρθωμα. Thus the account of irrationality here should be taken to refer to a mind which is temporarily under the direction of passion, and not to the character of all who lack the wise man's perfect reason.

C Plutarch, *St. rep.* 1034C–E

(1) ἀρετὰς ὁ Ζήνων ἀπολείπει πλείονας κατὰ διαφοράς, ὥσπερ ὁ Πλάτων, οἷον φρόνησιν ἀνδρείαν σωφροσύνην δικαιοσύνην, ὡς ἀχωρίστους μὲν οὔσας ἑτέρας δὲ καὶ διαφερούσας ἀλλήλων. (2) πάλιν δὲ ὁριζόμενος αὐτῶν ἑκάστην τὴν μὲν ἀνδρείαν φησὶν εἶναι φρόνησιν ⟨ἐν ὑπομενετέοις τὴν δὲ σωφροσύνην φρόνησιν ἐν αἱρετέοις τὴν δ' ἰδίως λεγομένην φρόνησιν   5 φρόνησιν⟩ ἐν ἐνεργητέοις τὴν δὲ δικαιοσύνην φρόνησιν ἐν ἀπονεμητέοις, ὡς μίαν οὖσαν ἀρετὴν ταῖς δὲ πρὸς τὰ πράγματα σχέσεσι κατὰ τὰς ἐνεργείας διαφέρειν δοκοῦσαν. (3) οὐ μόνον δὲ ὁ Ζήνων περὶ ταῦτα φαίνεται αὐτῷ μαχόμενος, ἀλλὰ καὶ Χρύσιππος 'Αρίστωνι μὲν ἐγκαλῶν ὅτι μιᾶς ἀρετῆς σχέσεις ἔλεγε τὰς ἄλλας εἶναι (4) Ζήνωνι δὲ συνηγορῶν   10 οὕτως ὁριζομένῳ τῶν ἀρετῶν ἑκάστην. (5) ὁ δὲ Κλεάνθης ἐν Ὑπομνήμασι φυσικοῖς εἰπὼν ὅτι πληγὴ πυρὸς ὁ τόνος ἐστί, κἂν ἱκανὸς ἐν τῇ ψυχῇ γένηται πρὸς τὸ ἐπιτελεῖν τὰ ἐπιβάλλοντα, ἰσχὺς καλεῖται καὶ κράτος ἐπιφέρει κατὰ λέξιν "ἡ δ' ἰσχὺς αὕτη καὶ τὸ κράτος, ὅταν μὲν ἐν τοῖς φανεῖσιν ἐμμενετέοις ἐγγένηται, ἐγκράτειά ἐστιν, ὅταν δ' ἐν τοῖς   15

Stoic ethics

ὑπομενετέοις, ἀνδρεία· περὶ τὰς ἀξίας δὲ δικαιοσύνη· περὶ δὲ τὰς αἱρέσεις καὶ ἐκκλίσεις σωφροσύνη."

1 κατὰ διαφοράς vel καὶ διαφόρους codd.   4 6 suppl. Pohlenz   14 ἐν vel ἐπὶ codd.   15 φανεῖσιν Hirzel: ἐπιφανέσιν codd.   15 ἐν codd.: ἐπὶ Herwerden

Context: alleged Stoic self-contradictions.

12 **τόνος** Cleanthes' physicalist account of virtue (for τόνος, cf. **47J–M**) has left clear traces in later Stoic terminology. See **65T** for ἀτονία as a mark of moral weakness; and for εὐτονία as well as ἀτονία, cf. also SVF 3.270, 473. As a term that evokes the stringing and harmonics of a lyre (cf. vol. 1, 288 n. 1), τόνος fits the Stoics' favoured image of the 'concordance' that exists between the specific virtues. Cf. notes on **57G** and **59K**.

D Stobaeus 2.63,6–24 (SVF 3.280, part)

(1) πάσας δὲ τὰς ἀρετὰς ὅσαι ἐπιστῆμαί εἰσι καὶ τέχναι κοινά τε θεωρήματα ἔχειν καὶ τέλος, ὡς εἴρηται, τὸ αὐτό· διὸ καὶ ἀχωρίστους εἶναι· τὸν γὰρ μίαν ἔχοντα πάσας ἔχειν, καὶ τὸν κατὰ μίαν πράττοντα κατὰ πάσας πράττειν. διαφέρειν δ᾽ ἀλλήλων τοῖς κεφαλαίοις. (2) φρονήσεως μὲν γὰρ εἶναι κεφάλαια τὸ μὲν θεωρεῖν καὶ πράττειν, ὃ ποιητέον, προηγου- 5
μένως, κατὰ δὲ τὸν δεύτερον λόγον τὸ θεωρεῖν καὶ ἃ δεῖ ἀπονέμειν ⟨καὶ ἃ δεῖ αἱρεῖσθαι καὶ ἃ δεῖ ὑπομένειν⟩, χάριν τοῦ ἀδιαπτώτως πράττειν ὃ ποιητέον. (3) τῆς δὲ σωφροσύνης ἴδιον κεφάλαιόν ἐστι τὸ παρέχεσθαι τὰς ὁρμὰς εὐσταθεῖς καὶ θεωρεῖν αὐτὰς προηγουμένως, κατὰ δὲ τὸν δεύτερον λόγον τὰ ὑπὸ τὰς ἄλλας ἀρετάς, ἕνεκα τοῦ ἀδιαπτώτως ἐν ταῖς ὁρμαῖς 10
ἀναστρέφεσθαι· (4) καὶ ὁμοίως τὴν ἀνδρείαν προηγουμένως μὲν πᾶν ὃ δεῖ ὑπομένειν, κατὰ δὲ τὸν δεύτερον λόγον τὰ ὑπὸ τὰς ἄλλας· (5) καὶ τὴν δικαιοσύνην προηγουμένως μὲν τὸ κατ᾽ ἀξίαν ἑκάστῳ σκοπεῖν, κατὰ δὲ τὸν δεύτερον λόγον καὶ τὰ λοιπά. (6) πάσας γὰρ τὰς ἀρετὰς τὰ πασῶν βλέπειν καὶ τὰ ὑποτεταγμένα ἀλλήλαις. 15

6–7 suppl. Usener   10 τὰ Heeren: τὰς codd.   15 ἀλλήλαις Usener: -λοις codd.

Context: doxography of the Stoic virtues.

1 **ἐπιστῆμαί . . . καὶ τέχναι** Cf. **60K 2**.

2 **τέλος** The 'end' of the virtues is reported by Stobaeus 2.62,7–8, as τὸ ἀκολούθως τῇ φύσει ζῆν; see also **63B, C, G**.

14–15 **τὰ πασῶν βλέπειν** What we call (vol. 1, 384) the 'primary' and 'secondary' perspectives of each virtue is illuminated by Cicero, Off. 2.18. There three spheres of action (cf. 'common theorems', 1–2) are specified for every virtue; cf. note on **56B**.

E Seneca, Ep. 113. 24

"non sunt" inquit "virtutes multa animalia, et tamen animalia sunt. nam quemadmodum aliquis et poeta est et orator, et tamen unus, sic virtutes istae animalia sunt sed multa non sunt. idem est animus et temperans et iustus et prudens et fortis, ad singulas virtutes quodam modo se habens."

3 *temperans* A.A. Long: *animus* codd.: *animus* ⟨*temperans*⟩ Hense

Context: concluding discussion of the Stoic thesis (cf. Stobaeus 2.65,1–4) that the virtues are living beings. The thesis is grounded in the conception of the *animus* as *animal*, and virtue as *animus quodam modo se habens* = **29B**.

1 **inquit** The subject is Seneca's imaginary Stoic interlocutor, who has been defending the thesis about the virtues' being *animalia* against Seneca's objections. Cf. *Ep.* 113.9: '*non sunt*', *inquit*, '*multa, quia ex uno religata sunt et partes unius ac membra sunt.*'

F Plutarch, *St. rep.* 1046E–F (*SVF* 3.299,243)

(1) τὰς ἀρετάς φασιν ἀντακολουθεῖν ἀλλήλαις; οὐ μόνον τῷ τὸν μίαν ἔχοντα πάσας ἔχειν ἀλλὰ καὶ τῷ τὸν κατὰ μίαν ὁτιοῦν ἐνεργοῦντα κατὰ πάσας ἐνεργεῖν· οὔτε γὰρ ἄνδρα φασὶ τέλειον εἶναι τὸν μὴ πάσας ἔχοντα τὰς ἀρετὰς οὔτε πρᾶξιν τελείαν ἥτις οὐ κατὰ πάσας πράττεται τὰς ἀρετάς. (2) ἀλλὰ μὴν ἐν τῷ ἕκτῳ τῶν Ἠθικῶν ζητημάτων ὁ Χρύσιππος οὐκ ἀεί 5 φησιν ἀνδρίζεσθαι τὸν ἀστεῖον οὐδὲ δειλαίνειν τὸν φαῦλον, ὡς δέον ἐν φαντασίαις ἐπιφερομένων τινῶν τὸν μὲν ἐμμένειν τοῖς κρίμασι τὸν δ' ἀφίστασθαι, πιθανὸν δέ φησι μηδ' ἀκολασταίνειν ἀεὶ τὸν φαῦλον.

1 φασιν vel φησιν codd.   1–2 τὸν μίαν ἔχοντα g: τὴν μίαν ἔχοντι (vel ἔχοντα) cett.   6 δέον ἐν codd.: δεινῶν ἐν Madvig: alii alia

Context: an alleged Stoic self-contradiction.

G Stobaeus 2.66,14–67,4 (*SVF* 3.560)

(1) λέγουσι δὲ καὶ πάντ' εὖ ποιεῖν τὸν σοφόν. ἃ ποιεῖ, δηλον⟨ότι⟩· ὃν τρόπον γὰρ λέγομεν πάντ' εὖ ποιεῖν τὸν αὐλητὴν ἢ κιθαρῳδόν, συνυπακ-ουομένου τοῦ ὅτι τὰ μὲν κατὰ τὴν αὔλησιν, τὰ δὲ κατὰ τὴν κιθαρῳδίαν, τὸν αὐτὸν τρόπον πάντ' εὖ ποιεῖν τὸν φρόνιμον, καθ' ὅσα ποιεῖ καὶ οὐ μὰ Δία καὶ ἃ μὴ ποιεῖ. (2) τῷ γὰρ κατὰ λόγον ὀρθὸν ἐπιτελεῖν πάντα καὶ †οἷον κατ' 5 ἀρετήν, περὶ ὅλον οὖσαν τὸν βίον τέχνην, ἀκόλουθον ᾠήθησαν τὸ περὶ τοῦ πάντ' εὖ ποιεῖν τὸν σοφὸν δόγμα. (3) κατὰ τὸ ἀνάλογον δὲ καὶ τὸν φαῦλον πάντα ὅσα ποιεῖ κακῶς ποιεῖν κατὰ πάσας τὰς κακίας.

1 δηλον⟨ότι⟩ Mullach: δῆλον codd.   4 καθ' Sedley: καὶ codd.   καὶ οὐ codd.: ναὶ [οὐ] Hense   5 οἷον corruptelam notavimus

Context: characterization of the Stoic sage.

H Stobaeus 2.59,4–60,2; 60,9–24 (*SVF* 3.262, 264, part)

(1) φρόνησιν δ' εἶναι ἐπιστήμην ὧν ποιητέον καὶ οὐ ποιητέον καὶ οὐδετέρων, ἢ ἐπιστήμην ἀγαθῶν καὶ κακῶν καὶ οὐδετέρων φύσει

377

Stoic ethics

πολιτικοῦ ζῴου ... (2) σωφροσύνην δ᾽ εἶναι ἐπιστήμην αἱρετῶν καὶ φευκτῶν καὶ οὐδετέρων· (3) δικαιοσύνην δὲ ἐπιστήμην ἀπονεμητικὴν τῆς ἀξίας ἑκάστῳ· (4) ἀνδρείαν δὲ ἐπιστήμην δεινῶν καὶ οὐ δεινῶν καὶ 5 οὐδετέρων· (5) ἀφροσύνην δὲ ⟨ἄγνοιαν⟩ ἀγαθῶν καὶ κακῶν καὶ οὐδετέρων, ἢ ἄγνοιαν ὧν ποιητέον καὶ οὐ ποιητέον καὶ οὐδετέρων ... (6) τῶν δ᾽ ἀρετῶν τὰς μὲν εἶναι πρώτας, τὰς δὲ ταῖς πρώταις ὑποτεταγμένας· πρώτας δὲ τέτταρας εἶναι, φρόνησιν, σωφροσύνην, ἀνδρείαν, δικαιοσύνην.

καὶ τὴν μὲν φρόνησιν περὶ τὰ καθήκοντα γίνεσθαι· τὴν δὲ σωφροσύνην περὶ τὰς ὁρμὰς τοῦ 10 ἀνθρώπου· τὴν δὲ ἀνδρείαν περὶ τὰς ὑπομονάς· τὴν δὲ δικαιοσύνην περὶ τὰς ἀπονεμήσεις. τῶν δὲ ὑποτεταγμένων ταῖς ἀρεταῖς ταύταις τὰς μὲν τῇ φρονήσει ὑποτετάχθαι, τὰς δὲ τῇ σωφροσύνῃ, τὰς δὲ τῇ ἀνδρείᾳ, τὰς δὲ τῇ δικαιοσύνῃ. (7) τῇ μὲν οὖν φρονήσει ὑποτάττεσθαι εὐβουλίαν, εὐλογιστίαν, ἀγχίνοιαν, νουνέχειαν, εὐμηχα- νίαν· (8) τῇ δὲ σωφροσύνῃ εὐταξίαν, κοσμιότητα, αἰδημοσύνην, ἐγκρά- 15 τειαν· (9) τῇ δὲ ἀνδρείᾳ καρτερίαν, θαρραλεότητα, μεγαλοψυχίαν, εὐψυχίαν, φιλοπονίαν· (10) τῇ δὲ δικαιοσύνῃ εὐσέβειαν, χρηστότητα, εὐκοινωνησίαν, εὐσυναλλαξίαν.

3 δ᾽ εἶναι Heeren: δὲ καὶ codd.   6 ⟨ἄγνοιαν⟩ Heeren

Context: a few lines after 60K.

2–3 φύσει–ζῴου Cf. 57D 2, F 2; 63K 5–6; 67R. For man as so specified, cf. Aristotle, Pol. 1.2, 1253a2–3.

5–6 For alternative Stoic definitions of courage, cf. 32H.

13–18 In the passage that follows this extract these subordinate virtues are all defined in terms of ἐπιστήμη.

I Diogenes Laertius 7.127

(1) ἀρέσκει δ᾽ αὐτοῖς μηδὲν μεταξὺ εἶναι ἀρετῆς καὶ κακίας, τῶν Περιπατητικῶν μεταξὺ ἀρετῆς καὶ κακίας εἶναι λεγόντων τὴν προκοπήν· ὡς γὰρ δεῖν φασιν ἢ ὀρθὸν εἶναι ξύλον ἢ στρεβλόν, οὕτως ἢ δίκαιον ἢ ἄδικον, οὔτε δὲ δικαιότερον οὔτ᾽ ἀδικώτερον, καὶ ἐπὶ τῶν ἄλλων ὁμοίως. (2) καὶ μὴν τὴν ἀρετὴν Χρύσιππος μὲν ἀποβλητήν, Κλεάνθης δὲ 5 ἀναπόβλητον· ὁ μὲν ἀποβλητὴν διὰ μέθην καὶ μελαγχολίαν, ὁ δὲ ἀναπόβλητον διὰ βεβαίους καταλήψεις· (3) καὶ αὐτὴν δι᾽ ⟨αὑτὴν⟩ αἱρετὴν εἶναι. αἰσχυνόμεθα γοῦν ἐφ᾽ οἷς κακῶς πράττομεν, ὡς ἂν μόνον τὸ καλὸν εἰδότες ἀγαθόν. αὐτάρκη τ᾽ εἶναι αὐτὴν πρὸς εὐδαιμονίαν, καθά φησι Ζήνων καὶ Χρύσιππος ἐν τῷ πρώτῳ Περὶ ἀρετῶν καὶ Ἑκάτων ἐν τῷ δευτέρῳ Περὶ ἀγαθῶν. 10

7 δι᾽ P: δὲ BF   ⟨αὑτὴν⟩ Arnim

Context: doxography of the Stoic virtues.

7 βεβαίους καταλήψεις This expression alludes to Stoic accounts of ἐπιστῆμαι (cf. 41H). Cleanthes, then, is arguing that qua ἐπιστῆμαι (cf. 60K 2) the cardinal virtues are necessarily secure.

8–9 This appears to offer empirical support for the sole goodness of τὸ καλόν.

378

But shame at behaving badly provides no ground for so strong a claim. The sentence has the look of being garbled or heavily condensed. Cf. **60N**.
10   After a quotation from Hecato the passage continues at **64o**.

J Plutarch, *Comm. not.* 1076A (*SVF* 3.246)

τὸ τρίτον τοίνυν τῆς περὶ θεῶν ἐννοίας ἐστὶ μηδενὶ τοσοῦτον τοὺς θεοὺς τῶν ἀνθρώπων διαφέρειν ὅσον εὐδαιμονίᾳ καὶ ἀρετῇ διαφέρουσιν. ἀλλὰ κατὰ Χρύσιππον οὐδὲ τοῦτο περίεστιν αὐτοῖς· ἀρετῇ τε γὰρ οὐχ ὑπερέχειν τὸν Δία τοῦ Δίωνος ὠφελεῖσθαί θ᾽ ὁμοίως ὑπ᾽ ἀλλήλων τὸν Δία καὶ τὸν Δίωνα, σοφοὺς ὄντας, ὅταν ἅτερος θατέρου τυγχάνῃ κινουμένου.   5

4 ἅτερος Herwerden: ἕτερος codd.

Context: polemic against Stoic theology.

This doctrine, though shocking to conventional Greek piety (cf. 1–2), is entirely consistent with the Stoics' thinking on goods (cf. **60P**), and their psychology (cf. **53X**; **62K 3**).

K Diogenes Laertius 7.91 (*SVF* 3.223)

διδακτήν τ᾽ εἶναι . . . τὴν ἀρετήν . . . ὅτι δὲ διδακτή ἐστι, δῆλον ἐκ τοῦ γίνεσθαι ἀγαθοὺς ἐκ φαύλων.

Context: doxography of Stoic virtue. The first sentence is ascribed to Chrysippus, Cleanthes, Posidonius and Hecato.

L Stobaeus 2.65,8 (*SVF* 1.566, part)

πάντας γὰρ ἀνθρώπους ἀφορμὰς ἔχειν ἐκ φύσεως πρὸς ἀρετήν . . . κατὰ τὸν Κλεάνθην.

Context: the absence of anything in between virtue and vice (cf. **I** 1). Cleanthes is quoted in support of that thesis, which, as amplified, takes the vicious or φαῦλοι to be imperfect (ἀτελεῖς) and the virtuous to be perfected (τελειωθέντες).
1   ἀφορμάς Cf. **63C** 2–3.

M Alexander, *Fat.* 196,24–197,3 (*SVF* 2.984, part)

(1) "εἰ", φασίν, "ταῦτά ἐστιν ἐφ᾽ ἡμῖν, ὧν καὶ τὰ ἀντικείμενα δυνάμεθα, καὶ ἐπὶ τοῖς τοιούτοις οἵ τε ἔπαινοι καὶ οἱ ψόγοι, προτροπαί τε καὶ ἀποτροπαί, κολάσεις τε καὶ τιμαί, οὐκ ἔσται τὸ φρονίμοις εἶναι καὶ τὰς ἀρετὰς ἔχειν ἐπὶ τοῖς ἔχουσιν, ὅτι μηκέτ᾽ εἰσὶν τῶν ἀντικειμένων κακιῶν ταῖς ἀρεταῖς δεκτικοί, ὁμοίως δὲ οὐδὲ αἱ κακίαι ἐπὶ τοῖς κακοῖς· οὐδὲ γὰρ   5
ἐπὶ τούτοις τὸ μηκέτ᾽ εἶναι κακοῖς. (2) ἀλλὰ μὴν ἄτοπον τὸ μὴ λέγειν τὰς

ἀρετὰς καὶ τὰς κακίας ἐφ' ἡμῖν μηδὲ τοὺς ἐπαίνους καὶ τοὺς ψόγους ἐπὶ τούτων γίνεσθαι· (3) οὐκ ἄρα τὸ ἐφ' ἡμῖν τοιοῦτον."

Context: a problem raised by the unnamed determinists who are Alexander's target, and who, with qualifications (cf. Long [541]), can be identified with Stoics. The passage has the appearance of being an authentic (Stoic) argument, but some think it may be distorted, or even formulated, by Alexander; cf. Sharples [333] ad loc. For further discussion, see Long [535], 183–5; Stough [539], 208–13.

4, 6 **μηκέτ'** We have reverted to 'no longer' as our translation, instead of 'not now', as proposed by Long loc. cit.

N Alexander, *Fat.* 199,14–22 (*SVF* 3.658, part)

(1) εἰ γὰρ ἡ μὲν ἀρετή τε καὶ κακία μόναι κατ' αὐτοὺς ἡ μὲν ἀγαθόν, ἡ δὲ κακόν, καὶ οὐδὲν τῶν ἄλλων ζῴων οὐδετέρου τούτων ἐστὶν ἐπιδεκτικόν, (2) τῶν δὲ ἀνθρώπων οἱ πλεῖστοι κακοί, μᾶλλον δὲ ἀγαθὸς μὲν εἷς ἢ δεύτερος ὑπ' αὐτῶν γεγονέναι μυθεύεται, ὥσπερ τι παράδοξον ζῷον καὶ παρὰ φύσιν σπανιώτερον τοῦ φοίνικος τοῦ παρ' Αἰθίοψιν, (3) οἱ δὲ πάντες   5 κακοὶ καὶ ἐπίσης ἀλλήλοις τοιοῦτοι, ὡς μηδὲν διαφέρειν ἄλλον ἄλλου, μαίνεσθαι δὲ ὁμοίως πάντας ὅσοι μὴ σοφοί, (4) πῶς οὐκ ἂν ἀθλιώτατον ζῷον ἁπάντων ὁ ἄνθρωπος εἴη, ἔχων τήν τε κακίαν καὶ τὸ μαίνεσθαι σύμφυτα αὐτῷ καὶ συγκεκληρωμένα;

Context: the inconsistency of these doctrines with the thesis that man's welfare is nature's goal.

4–5 For this paradox, cf. Plutarch, *Comm. not.* 1076B, where the wise man is alleged to have never existed, and *St. rep.* 1048E, where Chrysippus is said to disclaim virtue for himself and all his acquaintances and teachers.

O Cicero, *Tusc.* 4.29, 34–5

(1) vitiositas autem est habitus aut adfectio in tota vita inconstans et a se ipsa dissentiens . . . (2) ex qua concitantur perturbationes, quae sunt, ut paulo ante diximus, turbidi animorum concitatique motus, aversi a ratione et inimicissimi mentis vitaeque tranquillae. (3) important enim aegritudines anxias atque acerbas animosque adfligunt et debilitant metu; iidem inflammant adpetitione   5 nimia, quam tum cupiditatem, tum libidinem dicimus, impotentiam quandam animi a temperantia et moderatione plurimum dissidentem . . . (4) eorum igitur malorum in una virtute posita sanatio est.

2 *concitantur* Manutius: *cogitantur* codd.

Context: an account, based on Stoicism, of the diseases of the soul; cf. **65R**.
   Cicero at *Tusc.* 4.30 distinguishes *vitia*, as persistent *adfectiones* (i.e. διαθέσεις), from intermittent *perturbationes*. *vitiositas* is his translation of κακία; cf. 4.34.

P Marcus Aurelius 8.14

ᾧ ἂν ἐντυγχάνῃς, εὐθὺς σαυτῷ πρόλεγε· οὗτος τίνα δόγματα ἔχει περὶ
ἀγαθῶν καὶ κακῶν; εἰ γὰρ περὶ ἡδονῆς καὶ πόνου καὶ τῶν ποιητικῶν
ἑκατέρου καὶ περὶ δόξης, ἀδοξίας, θανάτου, ζωῆς, τοιάδε τινὰ δόγματα
ἔχει, οὐδὲν θαυμαστὸν ἢ ξένον μοι δόξει, ἐὰν τάδε τινὰ ποιῇ, καὶ
μεμνήσομαι ὅτι ἀναγκάζεται οὕτως ποιεῖν.   5

Cf. Epictetus, *Diss.* 1.18.3–4, especially πεπλάνηνται περὶ ἀγαθῶν καὶ κακῶν; and
for ἀναγκάζεται, 5, see **62D 3**.

Q Plutarch, *St. rep.* 1039E (*SVF* 3.761, part)

καὶ προελθὼν δέ φησιν ὅτι καὶ τοῖς φαύλοις καθήκει μένειν ἐν τῷ ζῆν· εἶτα
κατὰ λέξιν· "πρῶτον γὰρ ἡ ἀρετὴ ψιλῶς οὐδέν ἐστι πρὸς τὸ ζῆν ἡμᾶς, οὕτως
δ' οὐδὲ ἡ κακία οὐδέν ἐστι πρὸς τὸ δεῖν ἡμᾶς ἀπιέναι."

Context: Chrysippus' alleged self-contradiction in also approving Antisthenes' saying,
'one should get intelligence or a hangman's rope'. Prior to this extract, Chrysippus is
reported to have criticized Plato, *Clitopho* 408a – life is no advantage to someone who
has not learned how to live.

For the irrelevance of virtue or vice, on their own, to reasons for living or dying, cf.
66G.

R Plutarch, *St. rep.* 1050E–F, 1051A–B (*SVF* 2.1181, part; 1182)

ἐπιτείνει δὲ τὴν ὑπεναντίωσιν (1) ἐν τῷ δευτέρῳ Περὶ φύσεως γράφων τάδε· "ἡ
δὲ κακία πρὸς τὰ δεινὰ συμπτώματα ἴδιόν τιν' ἔχει λόγον· (2) γίγνεται μὲν
γὰρ καὶ αὐτή πως κατὰ τὸν τῆς φύσεως λόγον καί, ἵνα οὕτως εἴπω, οὐκ
ἀχρήστως γίγνεται πρὸς τὰ ὅλα· (3) οὐδὲ γὰρ ἂν τἀγαθὸν ἦν." ... (4)
πάλιν ἐν τῷ πρώτῳ Περὶ δικαιοσύνης, εἰπὼν περὶ τῶν θεῶν ὡς   5
ἐνισταμένων ἐνίοις ἀδικήμασι, (5) "κακίαν δέ", φησι, "καθόλου ἆραι οὔτε
δυνατόν ἐστιν οὔτ' ἔχει καλῶς ἀρθῆναι."

2 λόγον codd.: ὅρον Rasmus; cf. *Comm. not.* 1065A   4 οὐδὲ—ἦν *Comm. not.* 1065B: οὔτε γὰρ τἀγαθὰ ἦν
codd.   6 ἐνισταμένων ἐνίοις vel ἐνισταμένοις ἐνίων codd.

Context: Chrysippus' statements on κακία; cf. *Comm. not.* 1065A, where the same
passage is quoted with slight verbal differences.

For Chrysippus' general position, cf. **60A**, and for the accommodation of vice to
divine providence, see **54T**. For the necessary coexistence of opposites, cf. **54Q 1**.

S Plutarch, *Prof.* 75C (*SVF* 3.539, part)

(1) οὕτως ἐν τῷ φιλοσοφεῖν οὔτε τινὰ προκοπὴν οὔτε προκοπῆς αἴσθησιν
ὑποληπτέον, εἰ μηθὲν ἡ ψυχὴ μεθίησι μηδ' ἀποκαθαίρεται τῆς ἀβελτερίας,
ἀλλ' ἄχρι τοῦ λαβεῖν τὸ ἄκρον ἀγαθὸν καὶ τέλειον ἀκράτῳ τῷ κακῷ
χρῆται. (2) καὶ γὰρ ἀκαρεῖ χρόνου καὶ ὥρας ἐκ τῆς ὡς ἔνι μάλιστα

Stoic ethics

φαυλότητος εἰς οὐκ ἔχουσαν ὑπερβολὴν ἀρετῆς διάθεσιν μεταβαλὼν ὁ   5
σοφός, ἧς οὐδ᾽ ἐν χρόνῳ πολλῷ μέρος ἀφεῖλε κακίας, ἅμα πᾶσαν ἐξαίφνης
ἀποπέφευγε.

1 ὑποληπτέον vel ἀπολειπτέον codd.   5 μεταβαλὼν vel μεταβάλοι ἂν codd.

Context: Plutarch's rejection of this Stoic thesis.
    1 οὕτως   By analogy with technical and medical treatment.
    4 ἀκαρεῖ χρόνου   Cf. 63I 2.

T Plutarch, Comm. not. 1063A–B (SVF 3.539, part)

"ναί", φασίν, "ἀλλὰ ὥσπερ ὁ πῆχυν ἀπέχων ἐν θαλάττῃ τῆς ἐπιφανείας
οὐδὲν ἧττον πνίγεται τοῦ καταδεδυκότος ὀργυιὰς πεντακοσίας, οὕτως
οὐδὲ οἱ πελάζοντες ἀρετῇ τῶν μακρὰν ὄντων ἧττόν εἰσιν ἐν κακίᾳ· καὶ
καθάπερ οἱ τυφλοὶ τυφλοί εἰσιν κἂν ὀλίγον ὕστερον ἀναβλέπειν μέλλωσιν,
οὕτως οἱ προκόπτοντες ἄχρι οὗ τὴν ἀρετὴν ἀναλάβωσιν, ἀνόητοι καὶ   5
μοχθηροὶ διαμένουσιν."

Context: attack on the Stoic doctrine of progress.

U Plutarch, Comm. not. 1062B

τοῦτο δ᾽ οὐκ ἂν μάλιστα θαυμάσαις αὐτῶν ἀλλὰ ὅτι τῆς ἀρετῆς καὶ τῆς
εὐδαιμονίας παραγιγνομένης πολλάκις οὐδ᾽ αἰσθάνεσθαι τὸν κτησάμενον
οἴονται διαλεληθέναι δὲ αὐτὸν ὅτι μικρῷ πρόσθεν ἀθλιώτατος ὢν καὶ
ἀφρονέστατος νῦν ὁμοῦ φρόνιμος καὶ μακάριος γέγονεν.

3 αὐτὸν Wyttenbach: αὑτὸν codd.

Context: shortly after 63I, to which τοῦτο, 1, refers.
    3 διαλεληθέναι   A famous paradox; cf. Plutarch, Prof. 75D; SVF 3.540–1; and
Sedley [11], 94–5.

62 Moral responsibility

A Hippolytus, Haer. 1.21 (SVF 2.975)

καὶ αὐτοὶ δὲ τὸ καθ᾽ εἱμαρμένην εἶναι πάντα διεβεβαιώσαντο παραδείγματι χρησάμενοι τοιούτῳ, ὅτι ὥσπερ ὀχήματος ἐὰν ᾖ ἐξηρτημένος κύων,
ἐὰν μὲν βούληται ἕπεσθαι, καὶ ἕλκεται καὶ ἕπεται, ποιῶν καὶ τὸ
αὐτεξούσιον μετὰ τῆς ἀνάγκης [οἷον τῆς εἱμαρμένης]· ἐὰν δὲ μὴ βούληται
ἕπεσθαι, πάντως ἀναγκασθήσεται· τὸ αὐτὸ δήπου καὶ ἐπὶ τῶν ἀνθρώπων·   5
καὶ μὴ βουλόμενοι γὰρ ἀκολουθεῖν ἀναγκασθήσονται πάντως εἰς τὸ
πεπρωμένον εἰσελθεῖν.

4 secl. Röper

Context: summary of Stoic cosmology.

B Cleanthes (Epictetus, *Ench.* 53; *SVF* 1.527)

ἄγου δέ μ᾽, ὦ Ζεῦ, καὶ σύ γ᾽ ἡ Πεπρωμένη,
ὅποι ποθ᾽ ὑμῖν εἰμι διατεταγμένος·
ὡς ἕψομαί γ᾽ ἄοκνος· ἢν δέ γε μὴ θέλω,
κακὸς γενόμενος, οὐδὲν ἧττον ἕψομαι.

Context: the close of the *Enchiridion*. The lines are cited along with others from Euripides and Plato, the dominant theme being the merits of complying with fate and the divine will.

C Cicero, *Fat.* 39–43 (*SVF* 2.974)

(1) ac mihi quidem videtur, cum duae sententiae fuissent veterum philosophorum, una eorum qui censerent omnia ita fato fieri ut id fatum vim necessitatis adferret, in qua sententia Democritus, Heraclitus, Empedocles, Aristoteles fuit, (2) altera eorum quibus viderentur sine ullo fato esse animorum motus voluntarii, (3) Chrysippus tamquam arbiter honorarius 5 medium ferire voluisse, sed adplicat se ad eos potius qui necessitate motus animorum liberatos volunt; dum autem verbis utitur suis, delabitur in eas difficultates, ut necessitatem fati confirmet invitus. (4) atque hoc, si placet, quale sit, videamus in adsensionibus, quas prima oratione tractavi. eas enim veteres illi quibus omnia fato fieri videbantur, vi effici et necessitate dicebant. 10 qui autem ab iis dissentiebant, fato adsensiones liberabant negabantque fato adsensionibus adhibito necessitatem ab his posse removeri; iique ita disserebant: "si omnia fato fiunt, omnia fiunt causa antecedente; et, si adpetitus, illa etiam quae adpetitum secuntur, ergo etiam adsensiones; at, si causa adpetitus non est sita in nobis, ne ipse quidem adpetitus est in nostra potestate; quod si ita 15 est, ne illa quidem quae adpetitu efficiuntur sunt sita in nobis; non sunt igitur neque adsensiones neque actiones in nostra potestate. ex quo efficitur ut nec laudationes iustae sint nec vituperationes nec honores nec supplicia." quod cum vitiosum sit, probabiliter concludi putant non omnia fato fieri quaecumque fiant. (5) Chrysippus autem, cum et necessitatem inprobaret et 20 nihil vellet sine praepositis causis evenire, causarum genera distinguit, ut et necessitatem effugiat et retineat fatum. "causarum enim" inquit "aliae sunt perfectae et principales, aliae adiuvantes et proximae. quam ob rem, cum dicimus omnia fato fieri causis antecedentibus, non hoc intellegi volumus, causis perfectis et principalibus, sed causis adiuvantibus [antecedentibus] et 25 proximis." (6) itaque illi rationi quam paulo ante conclusi sic occurrit: si omnia fato fiant, sequi illud quidem, ut omnia causis fiant antepositis, verum non principalibus causis et perfectis, sed adiuvantibus et proximis. quae si ipsae non sunt in nostra potestate, non sequitur ut ne adpetitus quidem sit in nostra potestate. at hoc sequeretur, si omnia perfectis et principalibus causis fieri 30 diceremus, ut, cum eae causae non essent in nostra potestate, ne ille quidem

esset in nostra potestate. (7) quam ob rem, qui ita fatum introducunt ut necessitatem adiungant, in eos valebit illa conclusio; qui autem causas antecedentis non dicent perfectas neque principalis, in eos nihil valebit. (8) quod enim dicantur adsensiones fieri causis antepositis, id quale sit, facile a se 3̣5̣ explicari putat. nam quamquam adsensio non possit fieri nisi commota viso, tamen, cum id visum proximam causam habeat, non principalem, hanc habet rationem, ut Chrysippus vult, quam dudum diximus; non ut illa quidem fieri possit nulla vi extrinsecus excitata (necesse est enim adsensionem viso commoveri), sed revertitur ad cylindrum et ad turbinem suum, quae moveri 4̣0̣ incipere nisi pulsa non possunt. id autem cum accidit, suapte natura, quod superest, et cylindrum volvi et versari turbinem putat. (9) "ut igitur" inquit "qui protrusit cylindrum, dedit ei principium motionis, volubilitatem autem non dedit, sic visum obiectum imprimet illud quidem et quasi signabit in animo suam speciem, sed adsensio nostra erit in potestate, eaque, quem ad 4̣5̣ modum in cylindro dictum est, extrinsecus pulsa, quod reliquum est, suapte vi et natura movebitur. (10) quod si aliqua res efficeretur sine causa antecedente, falsum esset omnia fato fieri; sin omnibus quaecumque fiunt veri simile est causam antecedere, quid adferri poterit cur non omnia fato fieri fatendum sit? modo intellegatur quae sit causarum distinctio ac dissimilitudo." 5̣0̣

7 *animorum* Davies: *animos* codd.   25 del. Davies

Context: qualified defence of Chrysippus' position.

4 Aristoteles A puzzling characterization of Aristotle, perhaps by inference from his approval of divination, noted by Cicero at *Div.* 1.53, 81. Aristotle's celebrated Sea Battle discussion at *De int.* 9 was evidently not cited in the Hellenistic debate (despite Epicurus' similar treatment of the issue at **20H–I**), or he could hardly have failed to find his way into the libertarian group, mentioned next.

13–20 This is a general, rather than a specifically anti-Stoic, argument, since it does not reflect the Stoics' own account of the relation of impulse to assent: cf. note on **33I**.

23 adiuvantes et proximae See vol. 1, 342, where we argue, in agreement with Frede (|534|, 240–1), that this represents συνεργὰ καὶ προκαταρκτικά.

D Gellius 7.2.6–13 (*SVF* 2.1000, part)

(1) contra ea Chrysippus tenuiter multa et argute disserit; sed omnium fere, quae super ea re scripsit, huiuscemodi sententia est. "quamquam ita sit" inquit "ut ratione quadam necessaria et principali coacta atque conexa sint fato omnia, ingenia tamen ipsa mentium nostrarum proinde sunt fato obnoxia, ut proprietas eorum est ipsa et qualitas. (2) nam si sunt per naturam primitus 5 salubriter utiliterque ficta, omnem illam uim quae de fato extrinsecus ingruit inoffensius tractabiliusque transmittunt. sin vero sunt aspera et inscita et rudia nullisque artium bonarum adminiculis fulta, etiamsi parvo sive nullo fatalis incommodi conflictu urgeantur, sua tamen scaevitate et voluntario impetu in

assidua delicta et in errores se ruunt. (3) idque ipsum ut ea ratione fiat, naturalis   10
illa et necessaria rerum consequentia efficit, quae fatum vocatur. est enim
genere ipso quasi fatale et consequens, ut mala ingenia peccatis et erroribus
non vacent." (4) huius deinde fere rei exemplo non hercle nimis alieno neque
inlepido utitur. "sicut" inquit "lapidem cylindrum si per spatia terrae prona
atque derupta iacias, causam quidem ei et initium praecipitantiae feceris, mox   15
tamen ille praeceps volvitur, non quia tu id iam facis, sed quoniam ita sese
modus eius et formae volubilitas habet: sic ordo et ratio et necessitas fati genera
ipsa et principia causarum movet, impetus vero consiliorum mentiumque
nostrarum actionesque ipsas voluntas cuiusque propria et animorum ingenia
moderantur." (5) infert deinde verba haec his quae dixi congruentia: διὸ καὶ   20
ὑπὸ τῶν Πυθαγορείων εἴρηται· "γνώσει δ᾽ ἀνθρώπους αὐθαίρετα πήματ᾽
ἔχοντας" ὡς τῶν βλαβῶν ἑκάστοις παρ᾽ αὐτοὺς γινομένων καὶ καθ᾽ ὁρμὴν
αὐτῶν ἁμαρτανόντων τε καὶ βλαπτομένων καὶ κατὰ τὴν αὐτῶν διάνοιαν
καὶ ⟨διά⟩θεσιν. (6) propterea negat oportere ferri audirique homines aut
nequam aut ignavos et nocentes et audaces, qui, cum in culpa et in maleficio   25
revicti sunt, perfugiunt ad fati necessitatem tamquam in aliquod fani asylum
et, quae pessime fecerunt, ea non suae temeritati, sed fato esse attribuenda
dicunt.

13 *fere rei* Herz: *fieri* VP: *rei* recentiores   22 αὐτοὺς V: αὐτοῖς recentiores   24 ⟨διά⟩θεσιν Sedley

Context: as **55K**.
5 **proprietas** . . . **et qualitas**   Perhaps an attempt to render ἰδία ποιότης (see **28**).

E Diogenes Laertius 7.23

δοῦλον ἐπὶ κλοπῇ, φασίν, ἐμαστίγου· τοῦ δ᾽ εἰπόντος, "εἵμαρτό μοι
κλέψαι", ἔφη, "καὶ δαρῆναι."

Context: life of Zeno.

F Diogenianus (Eusebius, *Pr. ev.* 6.8.25–9: *SVF* 2.998)

(1) ἐν μὲν οὖν τῷ πρώτῳ Περὶ εἱμαρμένης βιβλίῳ τοιαύταις τισὶν
ἀποδείξεσι κέχρηται, ἐν δὲ τῷ δευτέρῳ λύειν πειρᾶται τὰ ἀκολουθεῖν
δοκοῦντα ἄτοπα τῷ λόγῳ τῷ πάντα κατηναγκάσθαι λέγοντι, ἅπερ καὶ
ἡμεῖς κατ᾽ ἀρχὰς ἐτίθεμεν· οἷον τὸ ἀναιρεῖσθαι δι᾽ αὐτοῦ τὴν ἐξ ἡμῶν
αὐτῶν προθυμίαν περὶ ψόγους τε καὶ ἐπαίνους καὶ προτροπὰς καὶ πάνθ᾽   5
ὅσα παρὰ τὴν ἡμετέραν αἰτίαν γιγνόμενα φαίνεται. (2) φησὶν οὖν ἐν τῷ
δευτέρῳ βιβλίῳ τὸ μὲν ἐξ ἡμῶν πολλὰ γίνεσθαι δῆλον εἶναι, οὐδὲν δὲ ἧττον
συγκαθειμάρθαι καὶ ταῦτα τῇ τῶν ὅλων διοικήσει. (3) κέχρηταί τε
παραδείγμασι τοιούτοις τισί· τὸ γὰρ μὴ ἀπολεῖσθαι, φησί, θοἰμάτιον οὐχ
ἁπλῶς καθείμαρτο, ἀλλὰ μετὰ τοῦ φυλάττεσθαι, καὶ τὸ ἐκ τῶν πολεμίων   10
σωθήσεσθαι τόνδε τινὰ μετὰ τοῦ φεύγειν αὐτὸν τοὺς πολεμίους, καὶ τὸ

Stoic ethics

γενέσθαι παῖδας μετὰ τοῦ βούλεσθαι κοινωνεῖν γυναικί. (4) ὥσπερ γάρ,
φησίν, εἰ λέγοντός τινος 'Ηγήσαρχον τὸν πύκτην ἐξελεύσεσθαι τοῦ
ἀγῶνος πάντως ἄπληκτον ἀτόπως ἄν τις ἠξίου καθιέντα τὰς χεῖρας τὸν
'Ηγήσαρχον μάχεσθαι, ἐπεὶ ἄπληκτον αὐτὸν καθείμαρτο ἀπελθεῖν, τοῦ   15
τὴν ἀπόφασιν ποιησαμένου διὰ τὴν περιττοτέραν τἀνθρώπου πρὸς τὸ μὴ
πλήττεσθαι φυλακὴν τοῦτο εἰπόντος, οὕτω καὶ ἐπὶ τῶν ἄλλων ἔχει. (5)
πολλὰ γὰρ μὴ δύνασθαι γενέσθαι χωρὶς τοῦ καὶ ἡμᾶς βούλεσθαι καὶ
ἐκτενεστάτην γε περὶ αὐτὰ προθυμίαν τε καὶ σπουδὴν εἰσφέρεσθαι, ἐπειδὴ
μετὰ τούτου, φησίν, αὐτὰ γενέσθαι καθείμαρτο.   20

Context: attack on Chrysippus' doctrine of fate (cf. 55P).

1 τοιαύταις The reference is to Chrysippus' allegorical etymologies of
εἱμαρμένη, πεπρωμένη, etc., which Diogenianus has somewhat implausibly (ibid.
6.8.8–24) interpreted as attempted *proofs* of determinism.

G Alexander, *Fat.* 181,13–182,20 (*SVF* 2.979)

(1) ἀναιροῦντες γὰρ τὸ ἐξουσίαν ἔχειν τὸν ἄνθρωπον τῆς αἱρέσεώς τε καὶ
πράξεως τῶν ἀντικειμένων λέγουσιν ἐφ' ἡμῖν εἶναι τὸ γινόμενον [καὶ] δι'
ἡμῶν. (2) ἐπεὶ γάρ, φασίν, τῶν ὄντων τε καὶ γινομένων αἱ φύσεις ἕτεραί τε
καὶ διάφοροι (οὐ γὰρ αἱ αὐταὶ τῶν ἐμψύχων τε καὶ τῶν ἀψύχων, ἀλλ' οὐδὲ
τῶν ἐμψύχων ἁπάντων αἱ αὐταὶ πάλιν· αἱ γὰρ κατ' εἶδος τῶν ὄντων   5
διαφοραὶ τὰς τῶν φύσεων αὐτῶν διαφορὰς δεικνύουσιν), γίνεται δὲ τὰ ὑφ'
ἑκάστου γινόμενα κατὰ τὴν οἰκείαν φύσιν, τὰ μὲν ὑπὸ λίθου κατὰ τὴν
λίθου, τὰ δ' ὑπὸ πυρὸς κατὰ τὴν πυρὸς καὶ τὰ ὑπὸ ζῴου κατὰ τὴν (ὑπὸ)
ζῴου, οὐδὲν μὲν τῶν κατὰ τὴν οἰκείαν φύσιν ὑφ' ἑκάστου γινομένων
δύνασθαί φασιν ἄλλως ἔχειν, ἀλλ' ἕκαστον τῶν γινομένων ὑπ' αὐτῶν   10
γίνεσθαι κατηναγκασμένως, (3) κατ' ἀνάγκην οὐ τὴν ἐκ βίας, ἀλλ' ἐκ τοῦ
μὴ δύνασθαι τὸ δὴ πεφυκὸς οὕτως (ὄντων τῶν περιεστώτων τοιούτων ⟨ἃ⟩
ἀδύνατον αὐτῷ μὴ περιεστάναι τότε) ἄλλως πως καὶ μὴ οὕτως κινηθῆναι.
(4) μήτε γὰρ τὸν λίθον, εἰ ἀπὸ ὕψους ἀφεθείη τινός, δύνασθαι μὴ φέρεσθαι
κάτω μηδενὸς ἐμποδίζοντος· τῷ ⟨γὰρ⟩ βαρύτητα μὲν ἔχειν αὐτὸν ἐν   15
αὐτῷ, ταύτην δ' εἶναι τῆς τοιαύτης κινήσεως κατὰ φύσιν ⟨αἰτίαν⟩, ὅταν
καὶ τὰ ἔξωθεν αἴτια τὰ πρὸς τὴν κατὰ φύσιν κίνησιν τῷ λίθῳ συντελοῦντα
παρῇ, ἐξ ἀνάγκης τὸν λίθον ὡς πέφυκε φέρεσθαι· πάντως δ' αὐτῷ καὶ ἐξ
ἀνάγκης παρεῖναι ταῦτα τὰ αἴτια δι' ἃ κινεῖται τότε, οὐ μόνον μὴ
δυναμένῳ μὴ κινεῖσθαι τούτων [μὴ] παρόντων, ἀλλὰ καὶ ἐξ ἀνάγκης   20
κινεῖσθαι τότε, καὶ γίνεσθαι τὴν τοιαύτην κίνησιν ὑπὸ τῆς εἱμαρμένης διὰ
τοῦ λίθου· (5) ὁ δ' αὐτὸς καὶ ἐπὶ τῶν ἄλλων λόγος. ὡς δὲ ἐπὶ τῶν ἀψύχων
ἔχει, οὕτως δὴ καὶ ἐπὶ τῶν ζῴων ἔχειν φασίν. εἶναι γάρ τινα καὶ τοῖς ζῴοις
κίνησιν κατὰ φύσιν, ταύτην δ' εἶναι τὴν καθ' ὁρμήν· πᾶν γὰρ ζῷον ὡς ζῷον
κινούμενον κινεῖσθαι ⟨τὴν⟩ καθ' ὁρμὴν κίνησιν ὑπὸ τῆς εἱμαρμένης διὰ   25
ζῴου γινομένην. (6) οὕτως δὲ τούτων ἐχόντων, καὶ γινομένων ὑπὸ τῆς εἱμαρμένης
κινήσεών τε καὶ ἐνεργειῶν ἐν τῷ κόσμῳ τῶν μὲν διὰ γῆς, ἂν οὕτω τύχῃ, τῶν δὲ δι' ἀέρος,

τῶν δὲ διὰ πυρός, τῶν δὲ δι᾽ ἄλλου τινός, γινομένων δέ τινων καὶ διὰ ζώων (τοιαῦται δὲ αἱ
καθ᾽ ὁρμὴν κινήσεις), τὰς διὰ τῶν ζώων ὑπὸ τῆς εἱμαρμένης γινομένας ἐπὶ τοῖς
ζώοις εἶναι λέγουσιν, ὁμοίως δὲ ὡς πρὸς τὸ ἀναγκαῖον τοῖς ἄλλοις   30
γινομένας ἅπασιν, τῷ δεῖν καὶ τούτοις ἐξ ἀνάγκης τὰ ἔξωθεν αἴτια
παρεῖναι τότε, ὥστε αὐτὰ τὴν ἐξ ἑαυτῶν τε καὶ καθ᾽ ὁρμὴν κίνησιν ἐξ
ἀνάγκης οὕτω πως ἐνεργεῖν, ὅτι δὲ αὗται μὲν δι᾽ ὁρμῆς τε καὶ
συγκαταθέσεως, ἐκείνων δὲ αἱ μὲν διὰ βαρύτητα γίνονται, αἱ δὲ διὰ
θερμότητα, αἱ δὲ κατ᾽ ἄλλην τινά ⟨αἰτίαν⟩, ταύτην μὲν ἐπὶ τοῖς ζώοις   35
λέγοντες, οὐκέτι δὲ ἐκείνων ἑκάστην, τὴν μὲν ἐπὶ τῷ λίθῳ, τὴν δὲ ἐπὶ τῷ
πυρί. (7) καὶ τοιαύτη μὲν αὐτῶν ἡ περὶ τοῦ ἐφ᾽ ἡμῖν δόξα ὡς δι᾽ ὀλίγων
εἰπεῖν.

12 δὴ Gercke: μὴ codd.   ⟨ἃ⟩ Arnim: ⟨ὡς⟩ Lond.   15 add. Arnim   16 add. B²   20
δυναμένῳ H ut vid., Gercke: -μενον a¹²: -μένων V: -μένου B²   μὴ² om a¹ Lond., secl. Orelli
31 τούτοις Donini: τοῖς codd.: τὰ Arnim   35 ⟨αἰτίαν⟩ Rodier

Context: critique of Stoic determinism. Cf. 53O, and SVF 2.991.

H Alexander, Fat. 185,7–11 (SVF 2.982)

τὸ δ᾽ ἐποχουμένους τῷ "εἰ δὴ τῶν αὐτῶν περιεστώτων ὁτὲ μὲν οὕτως ὁτὲ
δὲ ἄλλως ἐνεργήσει τις, ἀναίτιον κίνησιν εἰσάγεσθαι" διὰ τοῦτο λέγειν μὴ
δύνασθαι οὗ πράξει τις πρᾶξαι τὸ ἀντικείμενον, μήποτε καὶ αὐτὸ τῶν
ὁμοίως τοῖς προειρημένοις παρορωμένων.

1 ἐποχουμένους Bruns: -μένων codd.

Context: as G.
2 ἀναίτιον κίνησιν εἰσάγεσθαι Cf. 55N 2.
4 τοῖς προειρημένοις The reference is to Alexander's criticism of the Stoic
argument in G, which, he has alleged, fails to take account of the special causal
character of human agency as a capacity for either of a pair of opposed actions.

I Alexander, Fat. 205,24–206,2 (SVF 2.1002)

(1) λαβόντες γὰρ τὸ ἕκαστον τῶν συνεστώτων φύσει καθ᾽ εἱμαρμένην εἶναι
τοιοῦτον, ὁποῖόν ἐστι, ὡς ταὐτοῦ ὄντος τοῦ τε φύσει καὶ τοῦ καθ᾽
εἱμαρμένην, (2) προστιθέασιν τὸ "οὐκοῦν κατὰ τὴν εἱμαρμένην καὶ
αἰσθήσεται τὰ ζῷα καὶ ὁρμήσει, καὶ τὰ μὲν τῶν ζώων ἐνεργήσει μόνον τὰ
δὲ πράξει τὰ λογικά, καὶ τὰ μὲν ἁμαρτήσεται τὰ δὲ κατορθώσει. ταῦτα   5
γὰρ τούτοις κατὰ φύσιν. (3) μενόντων δὲ καὶ ἁμαρτημάτων καὶ
κατορθωμάτων καὶ τῶν τοιούτων φύσεων καὶ ποιοτήτων μὴ ἀναιρουμένων, καὶ ἔπαινοι μένου⟨σι⟩ καὶ ψόγοι καὶ κολάσεις καὶ τιμαί. ταῦτα
γὰρ οὕτως ἔχει ἀκολουθίας τε καὶ τάξεως."

7–8 ἀναιρουμένων Arnim: ἀγνοουμένων codd.   8 ἔπαινοι μένου⟨σι⟩ Arnim: ἔπαινοι codd., sed ex
ἐπαινουμένου corr. V¹

Stoic ethics

Context: as **G**. This argument in effect extends to moral concepts themselves the point defended in **G** with respect to movement in accordance with impulse.

J Alexander, *Fat.* 207,5–21 (*SVF* 2.1003)

(1) λέγουσιν γὰρ "οὐ γὰρ ἔστι μὲν τοιαύτη ἡ εἱμαρμένη, οὐκ ἔστι δὲ πεπρωμένη, ⟨οὐδὲ ἔστι μὲν πεπρωμένη⟩ οὐκ ἔστι δὲ αἶσα, οὐδὲ ἔστι μὲν αἶσα, οὐκ ἔστι δὲ νέμεσις, οὐδὲ ἔστι μὲν νέμεσις, οὐκ ἔστι δὲ νόμος, οὐδ' ἔστι μὲν νόμος, οὐδ' ἔστιν δὲ λόγος ὀρθὸς προστακτικὸς μὲν ὧν ποιητέον, ἀπαγορευτικὸς δὲ ὧν οὐ ποιητέον. (2) ἀλλὰ ἀπαγορεύεται μὲν τὰ   5
ἁμαρτανόμενα, προστάττεται δὲ τὰ κατορθώματα. οὐκ ἄρα ἔστι μὲν τοιαύτη ἡ εἱμαρμένη, οὐκ ἔστι δὲ ἁμαρτήματα καὶ κατορθώματα. (3) ἀλλ' εἰ ἔστιν ἁμαρτήματα καὶ κατορθώματα, ἔστιν ἀρετὴ καὶ κακία, εἰ δὲ ταῦτα, ἔστι καλὸν καὶ αἰσχρόν. ἀλλὰ τὸ μὲν καλὸν ἐπαινετόν, τὸ δὲ αἰσχρὸν ψεκτόν. οὐκ ἄρα ἐστὶ μὲν τοιαύτη ἡ εἱμαρμένη, οὐκ ἔστι δὲ   10
ἐπαινετὸν καὶ ψεκτόν. (4) ἀλλὰ τὰ μὲν ἐπαινετὰ τιμῆς ἄξια, τὰ δὲ ψεκτὰ κολάσεως. οὐκ ἄρα ἔστι μὲν τοιαύτη ἡ εἱμαρμένη, οὐκ ἔστι δὲ τιμὴ καὶ κόλασις, (5) ἀλλ' ἔστιν μὲν τιμὴ γέρως ἀξίωσις, ἡ δὲ κόλασις ἐπανόρθωσις. οὐκ ἄρα ἔστι μὲν τοιαύτη ἡ εἱμαρμένη, οὐκ ἔστι ⟨δὲ⟩ γέρως ἀξίωσις καὶ ἐπανόρθωσις. (6) εἰ δὲ ταῦτα, ἅπερ εἴρηται μένει πάντα, πάντων   15
γινομένων καθ' εἱμαρμένην κατορθώματά τε καὶ ἁμαρτήματα καὶ τιμαὶ καὶ κολάσεις καὶ γέρως ἀξιώσεις καὶ ἔπαινοι καὶ ψόγοι."

2 suppl. Orelli   15 ἅπερ–πάντα Hackforth: ἀπείρηται μὲν εἶναι codd.

Context: as **G**. Cf. the similar argument at ibid. 210,15–28.

The negated conjunctions, standardly preferred to conditionals in Stoic formulations of Sorites arguments, probably indicate that the implications are not strict συνάρτησις entailments (see **35**) but appeals to similarity (vol. 1, 229–30; Sedley [440]): there is little significant difference between εἱμαρμένη and πεπρωμένη, or between πεπρωμένη and αἶσα, or between . . . etc. The conditionals, on the other hand (8–9), can be held to supply strict entailments.

K Epictetus, *Diss.* 1.1.7–12

(1) ὥσπερ οὖν ἦν ἄξιον, τὸ κράτιστον ἁπάντων καὶ κυριεῦον οἱ θεοὶ μόνον ἐφ' ἡμῖν ἐποίησαν, τὴν χρῆσιν τὴν ὀρθὴν ταῖς φαντασίαις, (2) τὰ δ' ἄλλα οὐκ ἐφ' ἡμῖν. ἆρά γε ὅτι οὐκ ἤθελον; ἐγὼ μὲν δοκῶ ὅτι, εἰ ἠδύναντο, κἀκεῖνα ἂν ἡμῖν ἐπέτρεψαν· ἀλλὰ πάντως οὐκ ἠδύναντο. ἐπὶ γῆς γὰρ ὄντας καὶ σώματι συνδεδεμένους τοιούτῳ καὶ κοινωνοῖς τοιούτοις πῶς οἷόν τ' ἦν   5
εἰς ταῦτα ὑπὸ τῶν ἐκτὸς μὴ ἐμποδίζεσθαι; (3) ἀλλὰ τί λέγει ὁ Ζεύς; "'Ἐπίκτητε, εἰ οἷόν τε ἦν, καὶ τὸ σωμάτιον ἄν σου καὶ τὸ κτησίδιον ἐποίησα ἐλεύθερον καὶ ἀπαραπόδιστον. νῦν δέ, μή σε λανθανέτω, τοῦτο οὐκ ἔστιν σόν, ἀλλὰ πηλὸς κομψῶς πεφυραμένος. ἐπεὶ δὲ τοῦτο οὐκ ἠδυνάμην, ἔδωκα μέν σοι μέρος τι ἡμέτερον, τὴν δύναμιν ταύτην τὴν   10
ὁρμητικήν τε καὶ ἀφορμητικὴν καὶ ὀρεκτικήν τε καὶ ἐκκλιτικὴν καὶ ἁπλῶς

388

τὴν χρηστικὴν ταῖς φαντασίαις, ἧς ἐπιμελούμενος καὶ ἐν ᾗ τὰ σαυτοῦ τιθέμενος οὐδέποτε κωλυθήσῃ, οὐδέποτ' ἐμποδισθήσῃ, οὐ στενάξεις, οὐ μέμψῃ, οὐ κολακεύσεις οὐδένα."

Context: on what is, and what is not, ἐφ' ἡμῖν.

63 The end and happiness

A Stobaeus 2.77,16–27 (SVF 3.16)

(1) τέλος δέ φασιν εἶναι τὸ εὐδαιμονεῖν, οὗ ἕνεκα πάντα πράττεται, αὐτὸ δὲ πράττεται μὲν οὐδενὸς δὲ ἕνεκα· τοῦτο δὲ ὑπάρχειν ἐν τῷ κατ' ἀρετὴν ζῆν, ἐν τῷ ὁμολογουμένως ζῆν, ἔτι, ταὐτοῦ ὄντος, ἐν τῷ κατὰ φύσιν ζῆν. (2) τὴν δὲ εὐδαιμονίαν ὁ Ζήνων ὡρίσατο τὸν τρόπον τοῦτον· εὐδαιμονία δ' ἐστὶν εὔροια βίου. κέχρηται δὲ καὶ Κλεάνθης τῷ ὅρῳ τούτῳ ἐν τοῖς ἑαυτοῦ συγγράμμασι καὶ ὁ Χρύσιππος καὶ οἱ ἀπὸ τούτων πάντες, τὴν εὐδαιμονίαν εἶναι λέγοντες οὐχ ἑτέραν τοῦ εὐδαίμονος βίου, (3) καίτοι γε λέγοντες τὴν μὲν εὐδαιμονίαν σκοπὸν ἐκκεῖσθαι, τέλος δ' εἶναι τὸ τυχεῖν τῆς εὐδαιμονίας, ὅπερ ταὐτὸν εἶναι τῷ εὐδαιμονεῖν.

3 ταὐτοῦ Heeren: τοῦ codd.   6 τὴν P: καὶ F

Context: doxography of the Stoic τέλος.

1–2 For further Stoic formulations, cf. SVF 3.2–3.

5 **εὔροια βίου** Probably Zeno's metaphor for happiness, though he will have had such precedents as Aeschylus, Per. 601, ὅταν δ' ὁ δαίμων εὐροῇ, a condition sanctioning confidence in stability of fortune. For Cleanthes' and Chrysippus' use of this formula, cf. S.E., M. 11.30.

8 **σκοπὸν . . . τέλος** This distinction seems to originate with the Stoics; for the synonymous use of the terms, cf. Aristotle, Pol. VIII.13, 1331b28–33. Its point is clarified by Stobaeus 2.77,1–5 (cf. 2.47,7–11), according to which the σκοπός is the bodily objective at which one aims, while the τέλος is the corresponding incorporeal predicate; see vol. 1, 400, and cf. Stobaeus 2.76,19–21, λέγουσι δὲ καὶ τὸν σκοπὸν τέλος, οἷον τὸν ὁμολογούμενον βίον ἀναφορικῶς λέγοντες ἐπὶ τὸ παρακείμενον κατηγόρημα, which should be compared with 33J 2–3.

B Stobaeus 2.75,11–76,8

(1) τὸ δὲ τέλος ὁ μὲν Ζήνων οὕτως ἀπέδωκε· "τὸ ὁμολογουμένως ζῆν." τοῦτο δ' ἐστὶ καθ' ἕνα λόγον καὶ σύμφωνον ζῆν, ὡς τῶν μαχομένως ζώντων κακοδαιμονούντων. (2) οἱ δὲ μετὰ τοῦτον προσδιαρθροῦντες οὕτως ἐξέφερον "ὁμολογουμένως τῇ φύσει ζῆν" ὑπολαβόντες ἔλαττον εἶναι ⟨ἢ⟩ κατηγόρημα τὸ ὑπὸ τοῦ Ζήνωνος ῥηθέν. (3) Κλεάνθης γὰρ πρῶτος διαδεξάμενος αὐτοῦ τὴν αἵρεσιν προσέθηκε "τῇ φύσει" καὶ οὕτως ἀπέδωκε· "τέλος ἐστὶ τὸ ὁμολογουμένως τῇ φύσει ζῆν." (4) ὅπερ ὁ

389

Stoic ethics

Χρύσιππος σαφέστερον βουλόμενος ποιῆσαι, ἐξήνεγκε τὸν τρόπον τοῦτον·
"ζῆν κατ᾽ ἐμπειρίαν τῶν φύσει συμβαινόντων."

2-3 μαχομένως ζώντων schol Luc.: μαχομένων ζώων codd.   5 ⟨ἢ⟩ Sedley; cf. 33q 14

Context: doxography of the Stoic τέλος; see 58K for what follows B.

2 This explanation of ὁμολογουμένως has the ring of Zeno's etymologies (cf.
59C 2): ὁμο-(= σύμφωνον), -λογουμ-(= λόγον), -εν-(= ἕνα), -ως (= καθ᾽). His
concept of the best life as one of internal 'harmony' cannot fail to recall Plato, e.g. Rep.
4, 443d; and cf. note on 59K.

6 προσέθηκε This conflicts with C 1, which attributes the full formulation to
Zeno. Rist [342], 167–72, resolves the inconsistency with the suggestion that Zeno
used both formulations, adopting the full one 'when he came across an account of
nature' [probably Polemo's, cf. Cicero, Fin. 4.45] 'which enabled him to develop his
own particular version of the consistent life'.

9 Regularly attributed to Chrysippus; cf. C 2; 64I 4–5.

C Diogenes Laertius 7.87–9

(1) διόπερ πρῶτος ὁ Ζήνων ἐν τῷ Περὶ ἀνθρώπου φύσεως τέλος εἶπε τὸ
ὁμολογουμένως τῇ φύσει ζῆν, ὅπερ ἐστὶ κατ᾽ ἀρετὴν ζῆν· ἄγει γὰρ πρὸς
ταύτην ἡμᾶς ἡ φύσις. ὁμοίως δὲ καὶ Κλεάνθης ἐν τῷ Περὶ ἡδονῆς καὶ
Ποσειδώνιος καὶ Ἑκάτων ἐν τοῖς Περὶ τελῶν. (2) πάλιν δ᾽ ἴσον ἐστὶ τὸ
κατ᾽ ἀρετὴν ζῆν τῷ κατ᾽ ἐμπειρίαν τῶν φύσει συμβαινόντων ζῆν, ὥς φησι   5
Χρύσιππος ἐν τῷ πρώτῳ Περὶ τελῶν· μέρη γάρ εἰσιν αἱ ἡμέτεραι φύσεις
τῆς τοῦ ὅλου. (3) διόπερ τέλος γίνεται τὸ ἀκολούθως τῇ φύσει ζῆν, ὅπερ
ἐστὶ κατά τε τὴν αὐτοῦ καὶ κατὰ τὴν τῶν ὅλων, οὐδὲν ἐνεργοῦντας ὧν
ἀπαγορεύειν εἴωθεν ὁ νόμος ὁ κοινός, ὅσπερ ἐστὶν ὁ ὀρθὸς λόγος, διὰ
πάντων ἐρχόμενος, ὁ αὐτὸς ὢν τῷ Διί, καθηγεμόνι τούτῳ τῆς τῶν ὄντων   10
διοικήσεως ὄντι· (4) εἶναι δ᾽ αὐτὸ τοῦτο τὴν τοῦ εὐδαίμονος ἀρετὴν καὶ
εὔροιαν βίου, ὅταν πάντα πράττηται κατὰ τὴν συμφωνίαν τοῦ παρ᾽
ἑκάστῳ δαίμονος πρὸς τὴν τοῦ τῶν ὅλων διοικητοῦ βούλησιν . . . (5) φύσιν
δὲ Χρύσιππος μὲν ἐξακούει, ᾗ ἀκολούθως δεῖ ζῆν, τήν τε κοινὴν καὶ ἰδίως
τὴν ἀνθρωπίνην· ὁ δὲ Κλεάνθης τὴν κοινὴν μόνην ἐκδέχεται φύσιν, ᾗ   15
ἀκολουθεῖν δεῖ, οὐκέτι δὲ καὶ τὴν ἐπὶ μέρους.

8 κατά τε τὴν αὐτοῦ dw: κατά γε τὴν αὐτοῦ FP: κατ᾽ ἀρετὴν αὐτοῦ B   9 ὅσπερ Hübner: ὅπερ
codd.   10 ὢν Ménage: ἐν codd.   ὄντων BP: πάντων F   13 τῶν ὅλων d: ὅλου BFP.

Context: immediately following 57A.

2–3 ἄγει . . . φύσις Cf. 61L.

4 τελῶν The plural suggests that such books considered and rejected other
possible ends by way of establishing the Stoic doctrine; cf. note on 64G.

6 μέρη For this fundamental notion, cf. Marcus Aurelius 5.24: μέμνησο τῆς
συμπάσης οὐσίας, ἧς ὀλίγιστον μετέχεις . . . καὶ τῆς εἱμαρμένης, ἧς πόστον εἰ
μέρος; and for discussion, see Long [535], 179–80.

8–9 οὐδὲν . . . κοινός There are strong reasons to interpret this phrase by
reference to καθήκοντα; cf. 59A, C 3–4, E 2; 67S 1; and see Long [557], 192–3.

390

63 *The end and happiness*

13 **δαίμονος** Is this a reference to the individual's *ἡγεμονικόν*? That suits the context, and such a use of *δαίμων* is common in later Stoicism. We are doubtful that (as Rist [303], 262–6, argues) it need imply the Platonizing psychology of Posidonius, and so be excluded for Chrysippus; he too regarded persons as composites of soul and body. Rist interprets the present passage by reference to D.L. 7.151, which refers to daemons who have *συμπάθεια* with men and oversee their affairs. But they do not seem appropriate to the present context.

The lines omitted after *βούλησιν* report formulations of the *τέλος* by Diogenes of Babylon (see **58K**) and Archedemus (see **59J**).

D Seneca, *Ep.* 76.9–10 (*SVF* 3,200a)

(1) in homine quid est optimum? ratio: hac antecedit animalia, deos sequitur. ratio ergo perfecta proprium bonum est, cetera illi cum animalibus satisque communia sunt . . . (2) quid est in homine propium? ratio: haec recta et consummata felicitatem hominis implevit. ergo si omnis res, cum bonum suum perfecit, laudabilis est et ad finem naturae suae pervenit, homini autem suum bonum ratio est, si hanc perfecit laudabilis est et finem naturae suae tetigit. (3) haec ratio perfecta virtus vocatur eademque honestum est.

Context: a proof that *honestum* is the only good; cf. **60H**.

The argument depends on the assumption that the *proprium bonum* of any creature is the fulfilment of its peculiar function; cf. Aristotle, *EN* 1.6, 1097b34, *ζητεῖται δὲ τὸ ἴδιον* [*sc.* *ἔργον τοῦ ἀνθρώπου*].

E Epictetus, *Diss.* 1.6.12–22

(1) πολλὰ μὲν ἐπὶ μόνων, ὧν ἐξαιρέτως χρείαν εἶχε τὸ λογικὸν ζῷον, πολλὰ δὲ κοινὰ εὑρήσεις ἡμῖν καὶ πρὸς τὰ ἄλογα. (2) ἆρ᾽ οὖν καὶ παρακολουθεῖ τοῖς γινομένοις ἐκεῖνα; οὐδαμῶς. ἄλλο γάρ ἐστι χρῆσίς καὶ ἄλλο παρακολούθησις. ἐκείνων χρείαν εἶχεν ὁ θεὸς χρωμένων ταῖς φαντασίαις, ἡμῶν δὲ παρακολουθούντων τῇ χρήσει. (3) διὰ τοῦτο ἐκείνοις μὲν ἀρκεῖ τὸ 5 ἐσθίειν καὶ πίνειν καὶ τὸ ἀναπαύεσθαι καὶ ὀχεύειν καὶ τἆλλ᾽ ὅσα ἐπιτελεῖ αὐτῶν ἕκαστον, ἡμῖν δ᾽, οἷς καὶ τὴν παρακολουθητικὴν δύναμιν ἔδωκεν, οὐκέτι ταῦτ᾽ ἀπαρκεῖ, ἀλλ᾽ ἂν μὴ κατὰ τρόπον καὶ τεταγμένως καὶ ἀκολούθως τῇ ἑκάστου φύσει καὶ κατασκευῇ πράττωμεν, οὐκέτι τοῦ τέλους τευξόμεθα τοῦ ἑαυτῶν. (4) ὧν γὰρ αἱ κατασκευαὶ διάφοροι, τούτων 10 καὶ τὰ ἔργα καὶ τὰ τέλη . . . (5) τὸν δ᾽ ἄνθρωπον θεατὴν εἰσήγαγεν αὐτοῦ τε καὶ τῶν ἔργων τῶν αὐτοῦ, καὶ οὐ μόνον θεατήν, ἀλλὰ καὶ ἐξηγητὴν αὐτῶν. (6) διὰ τοῦτο αἰσχρόν ἐστιν τῷ ἀνθρώπῳ ἄρχεσθαι καὶ καταλήγειν ὅπου καὶ τὰ ἄλογα, ἀλλὰ μᾶλλον ἔνθεν μὲν ἄρχεσθαι, καταλήγειν δ᾽ ἐφ᾽ ὃ κατέληξεν ἐφ᾽ ἡμῶν καὶ ἡ φύσις. κατέληξεν δ᾽ ἐπὶ θεωρίαν καὶ 15 παρακολούθησιν καὶ σύμφωνον διεξαγωγὴν τῇ φύσει. ὁρᾶτε οὖν, μὴ ἀθέατοι τούτων ἀποθάνητε.

7 αὐτῶν s: τῶν αὐτῶν S: τῶν αὐτῶν Kronenberg

391

Stoic ethics

Context: divine providence as revealed in each creature's constitution.

2 **παρακολουθεῖ** The term signifies both 'following intellectually' (understanding) and 'following willingly' (conforming). Much of Epictetus' thought in the extract is summed up in his favourite expression, χρῆσις ὀρθὴ ταῖς φαντασίαις (**62K** 1).

F Seneca, *Ep.* 92.3

(1) quid est beata vita? securitas et perpetua tranquillitas. hanc dabit animi magnitudo, dabit constantia bene iudicati tenax. (2) ad haec quomodo pervenitur? si veritas tota perspecta est; si servatus est in rebus agendis ordo, modus, decor, innoxia voluntas ac benigna, intenta rationi nec umquam ab illa recedens, amabilis simul mirabilisque. (3) denique ut breviter tibi formulam 5 scribam, talis animus esse sapientis viri debet qualis deum deceat.

Context: the dependence of happiness on the perfection of reason.

G Stobaeus 2.63,25–64,12 (Panaetius fr. 109, part)

(1) ὅμοιον γὰρ ἔλεγεν εἶναι ὁ Παναίτιος τὸ συμβαῖνον ἐπὶ τῶν ἀρετῶν, ὡς εἰ πολλοῖς τοξόταις εἷς σκοπὸς εἴη κείμενος, ἔχοι δ' οὗτος ἐν αὐτῷ γραμμὰς διαφόρους τοῖς χρώμασιν· (2) εἶθ' ἕκαστος μὲν στοχάζοιτο τοῦ τυχεῖν τοῦ σκοποῦ, ἤδη δ' ὁ μὲν διὰ τοῦ πατάξαι εἰς τὴν λευκὴν εἰ τύχοι γραμμήν, ὁ δὲ διὰ τοῦ εἰς τὴν μέλαιναν, ἄλλος ⟨δὲ⟩ διὰ τοῦ εἰς ἄλλο τι 5 χρῶμα γραμμῆς. (3) καθάπερ γὰρ τούτους ὡς μὲν ἀνωτάτω τέλος ποιεῖσθαι τὸ τυχεῖν τοῦ σκοποῦ, ἤδη δ' ἄλλον κατ' ἄλλον τρόπον προτίθεσθαι τὴν τεῦξιν, τὸν αὐτὸν τρόπον καὶ τὰς ἀρετὰς πάσας ποιεῖσθαι μὲν τέλος τὸ εὐδαιμονεῖν, ὅ ἐστι κείμενον ἐν τῷ ζῆν ὁμολογουμένως τῇ φύσει, τούτου δ' ἄλλην κατ' ἄλλον τυγχάνειν. 10

2 αὐτῷ Meineke: αὐτῶ codd.   4 τοῦ πατάξαι Usener: τὸ ὑποτάξαι codd.   5 ⟨δὲ⟩ Heeren
τοῦ² Usener: τὸ codd.   10 ἄλλην Heine: ἄλλον codd.   ἄλλον Canter: ἄλλαν P: ἄλλην F

Context: immediately following **61D**. In company with that passage (see note ad loc.), Panaetius' image illustrates the different perspectives and common end of the specific virtues.

6–7 **τέλος ... σκοποῦ** Cf. **A** 3; and for the virtues' τέλος, see note on **61D** 2.

H Plutarch, *St. rep.* 1042A (*SVF* 3.55)

οὐσίαν κακοδαιμονίας ἀποφαίνει τὴν κακίαν, ἐν παντὶ βιβλίῳ φυσικῷ καὶ ἠθικῷ γράφων καὶ διατεινόμενος ὅτι τὸ κατὰ κακίαν ζῆν τῷ κακοδαιμόνως ζῆν ταὐτόν ἐστιν.

Context: a series of alleged self-contradictions by Chrysippus in his ethical writings.

I Plutarch, *Comm. not.* 1061F (*SVF* 3.54, part)

οὐ μόνον οὖν ταῦτα λέγουσιν οἱ ἄνδρες ἀλλὰ κἀκεῖνα πρὸς τούτοις, ὅτι ἀγαθὸν ὁ χρόνος οὐκ αὔξει προσγιγνόμενος ἀλλά, κἂν ἀκαρές τις ὥρας γένηται φρόνιμος, οὐδὲν πρὸς εὐδαιμονίαν ἀπολειφθήσεται τοῦ τὸν αἰῶνα χρωμένου τῇ ἀρετῇ καὶ μακαρίως ἐν αὐτῇ καταβιοῦντος.

3 οὐδὲν Rasmus: οὐδενὶ codd.

Context: the alleged inconsistency of this statement with the further doctrine that to get happiness or virtue only for a moment is useless.

Plutarch's criticism here, and at *St. rep.* 1046C–E, confronts two Stoic theses which are mutually consistent in fact. (1) [=I] The duration of happiness makes no difference to the amount of happiness someone enjoys at any moment; (2) it is not worthwhile to be happy only for a moment. The point of stating (2) was perhaps to meet objections to (1). If happiness, as an all-or-nothing affair, is complete at any moment, why should momentary happiness not be worth striving for? Answer: happiness is constituted solely by virtue, and it is not worthwhile to acquire virtue of only momentary duration. In *St. rep.* 1046C–E and *Comm. not.* 1062A, it is the utility of momentary virtue which the Stoics explicitly reject.

J Clement, *Strom.* 2.21.129.4–5 (Panaetius fr. 96; Posidonius fr. 186, part)

(1) πρὸς τούτοις ἔτι Παναίτιος τὸ ζῆν κατὰ τὰς δεδομένας ἡμῖν ἐκ φύσεως ἀφορμὰς τέλος ἀπεφήνατο· (2) ἐπὶ πᾶσί τε ὁ Ποσειδώνιος τὸ ζῆν θεωροῦντα τὴν τῶν ὅλων ἀλήθειαν καὶ τάξιν καὶ συγκατασκευάζοντα αὐτὴν κατὰ τὸ δυνατόν, κατὰ μηδὲν ἀγόμενον ὑπὸ τοῦ ἀλόγου μέρους τῆς ψυχῆς. (3) τινὲς δὲ τῶν νεωτέρων Στωικῶν οὕτως ἀπέδοσαν, τέλος εἶναι   5 τὸ ζῆν ἀκολούθως τῇ τοῦ ἀνθρώπου κατασκευῇ.

4 αὐτὴν codd.: αὐτὸν Sylburg

Context: doxography of the Stoic τέλος.

2 ἀφορμάς   Used here just as in 61L.

2–5   The first part of Posidonius' formulation emphasizes the cosmic dimension, absent from Panaetius'. The second part recalls Aristotle's connexion between a moral life that promotes θεωρία of god, and ἥκιστα αἰσθάνεσθαι τοῦ ἀλόγου μέρους τῆς ψυχῆς, *EE* VIII.3, 1249b17–23.

5–6   Cf. E 3–4.

K Marcus Aurelius 5.16

οἷα ἂν πολλάκις φαντασθῇς, τοιαύτη σοι ἔσται ἡ διάνοια· βάπτεται γὰρ ὑπὸ τῶν φαντασιῶν ἡ ψυχή. βάπτε οὖν αὐτὴν τῇ συνεχείᾳ τῶν τοιούτων φαντασιῶν· οἷον . . . ὅτι (1) οὗπερ ἕνεκεν ἕκαστον κατεσκεύασται, ⟨πρὸς τοῦτο κατεσκεύασται·⟩ (2) πρὸς ὃ δὲ κατεσκεύασται, πρὸς τοῦτο φέρεται· (3) πρὸς ὃ φέρεται δέ, ἐν τούτῳ τὸ τέλος αὐτοῦ· (4) ὅπου δὲ τὸ τέλος, ἐκεῖ καὶ τὸ συμφέρον καὶ τὸ ἀγαθὸν   5 ἑκάστου· (5) τὸ ἄρα ἀγαθὸν τοῦ λογικοῦ ζῴου κοινωνία. (6) ὅτι γὰρ πρὸς

κοινωνίαν γεγόναμεν, πάλαι δέδεικται· (7) ἢ οὐκ ἦν ἐναργὲς ὅτι τὰ χείρω
τῶν κρειττόνων ἕνεκεν, τὰ δὲ κρείττω ἀλλήλων; (8) κρείττω δὲ τῶν μὲν
ἀψύχων τὰ ἔμψυχα, τῶν δὲ ἐμψύχων τὰ λογικά.

The conclusion, stated at 5, depends on 1–4, 'the good of something is that for the sake
of which it is made', and 6–8, 'community is that for the sake of which rational beings
are made'. For the latter in earlier Stoicism, cf. **57D, F**.

7–9   Cf. **54P–R**.

L Cicero, *Tusc.* 5.40–1

(1) sed mihi videntur etiam beatissimi. quid enim deest ad beate vivendum ei
qui confidit suis bonis? aut, qui diffidit, beatus esse qui potest? at diffidat
necesse est, qui bona dividit tripertito. qui enim poterit aut corporis firmitate
aut fortunae stabilitate confidere? atqui nisi stabili et fixo et permanente bono
beatus esse nemo potest . . . (2) nam qui timebit ne quid ex is deperdat, beatus   5
esse non poterit. volumus enim eum, qui beatus sit, tutum esse, inexpugnabi-
lem, saeptum atque munitum, non ut parvo metu praeditus sit, sed ut nullo.

Context: the speaker defends the sufficiency of virtue for supreme happiness (the Stoic
position) against the Academic–Peripatetic view of Antiochus (cf. **64K**) that bodily
and external goods (cf. *tripertito*, 3) are also necessary for this.

M Cicero, *Tusc.* 5.81–2

(1) sapientis est enim proprium nihil quod paenitere possit facere, nihil
invitum, splendide, constanter, graviter, honeste omnia, nihil ita exspectare
quasi certo futurum, nihil, cum acciderit, admirari, ut inopinatum ac novum
accidisse videatur, omnia ad suum arbitrium referre, suis stare iudiciis. (2) quo
quid sit beatius, mihi certe in mentem venire non potest. (3) Stoicorum   5
quidem facilis conclusio est; qui cum finem bonorum esse senserint congruere
naturae cumque ea convenienter vivere, cum id sit in sapientis situm non
officio solum verum etiam potestate, (4) sequatur necesse est ut, cuius in
potestate summum bonum, in eiusdem vita beata sit. (5) ita fit semper vita
beata sapientis.   10

7 *sapientis* Lambinus: *sapiente* codd.

Context: wisdom and happiness will not be affected by fear of pain.

8–9 **in potestate**   This is what makes the Stoics' conclusion 'easy', 6.

64 The end: Academic criticism and Stoic defence

A Cicero, *Fin.* 3.31 (*SVF* 3.15)

relinquitur ut summum bonum sit vivere scientiam adhibentem earum rerum

quae natura eveniant, seligentem quae secundum naturam et quae contra
naturam sint reicientem, id est convenienter congruenterque naturae vivere.

3 *sint* Madvig: *sunt* codd.

Context: Cato's conclusion concerning the *summum bonum*, which he reaches by
elimination of all opinions which locate it in anything other than virtue, or which
maintain the wise man's complete indifference to everything he encounters. For the
criticism this invited, cf. **L**.

B Alexander, *Mantissa* 164,3–9

(1) οὐδὲ γὰρ ἄλλη τις τέχνη ἐκλέγεταί τι αὐτοῦ χάριν τοῦ ἐκλέξασθαι
μόνου, ἀλλὰ πάντων ἡ ἐκλογὴ πρὸς τὸ τέλος ἔχει τὴν ἀναφοράν. ἐν γὰρ τῇ
χρήσει τῶν ἐκλεγομένων, οὐκ ἐν τῇ ἐκλογῇ τῶν ὑποκειμένων τὸ τέλος, (2)
καὶ καθόλου πῶς οὐκ ἄτοπον τὸ τὴν ἀρετὴν ἐπὶ τοῦτο λέγειν εἶναι μόνον,
ἐπὶ τὸ ἐκλέγεσθαι; εἰ γὰρ ἀδιάφορος ἡ κτῆσις τῶν ἐκλεγομένων καὶ μὴ   5
συντείνουσα πρὸς τὸ τέλος, κενὴ ἂν εἴη καὶ ματαία ἡ ἐκλογή.

Context: part of a lengthy refutation of the Stoic thesis that virtue is sufficient for
happiness. Alexander has used a Sorites, in order to argue that the necessity of selecting
AN things, which the Stoics admit, requires them for consistency to accept that such
selection is πρὸς τὸ τέλος. Section 2 is his justification for this claim; cf. **C 5**, **E**.

C Plutarch, *Comm. not.* 1070F–1071E

(1) παρὰ τὴν ἔννοιάν ἐστι δύο τέλη καὶ σκοποὺς προκεῖσθαι τοῦ βίου καὶ μὴ
πάντων ὅσα πράττομεν ἐφ' ἕν τι γίγνεσθαι τὴν ἀναφοράν, (2) ἔτι δὲ μᾶλλόν
ἐστι παρὰ τὴν ἔννοιαν ἄλλο μὲν εἶναι τέλος ἐπ' ἄλλο δὲ τῶν πραττομένων
ἕκαστον ἀναφέρεσθαι. (3) τούτων δ' αὐτοὺς ὑπομένειν ἀνάγκη θάτερον. (4)
εἰ γὰρ αὐτὰ μὲν ⟨τὰ⟩ πρῶτα κατὰ φύσιν ⟨ἀγ⟩αθὰ μή ἐστιν ἡ δ'   5
εὐλόγιστος ἐκλογὴ καὶ λῆψις αὐτῶν καὶ τὸ πάντα τὰ παρὰ ἑαυτὸν ποιεῖν
ἕκαστον ἕνεκα τοῦ τυγχάνειν τῶν πρώτων κατὰ φύσιν, ἐπ' ἐκεῖνο δεῖ
πάντα ἔχειν τὰ πραττόμενα τὴν ἀναφοράν, τὸ τυγχάνειν τῶν πρώτων κατὰ
φύσιν. (5) εἴπερ δ' ἄρ' οἴονται μὴ στοχαζομένους μηδ' ἐφιεμένους τοῦ
τυχεῖν ἐκείνων τὸ τέλος ἔχειν, ⟨ἐπ'⟩ ἄλλο οὗ ἕνεκα δεῖ ἀναφέρεσθαι τὴν   10
τούτων ἐκλογὴν καὶ μὴ τοῦτο· (6) τέλος μὲν γὰρ τὸ ἐκλέγεσθαι καὶ
λαμβάνειν ἐκεῖνα φρονίμως, ἐκεῖνα δ' αὐτὰ καὶ τὸ τυγχάνειν αὐτῶν οὐ
τέλος ἀλλὰ ὥσπερ ὕλη τις ὑπόκειται τὴν ἐκλεκτικὴν ἀξίαν ἔχουσα ... σκόπει δὲ ὅτι ταὐτὸ πάσχουσι τοῖς τὴν σκιὰν ὑπεράλλεσθαι τὴν ἑαυτῶν ἐφιεμένοις· οὐ γὰρ
ἀπολείπουσιν ἀλλὰ συμμεταφέρουσι τὴν ἀτοπίαν τῷ λόγῳ, πορρωτάτω τῶν ἐννοιῶν   15
ἀφισταμένην. (7) ὡς γὰρ εἰ τοξεύοντα φαίη τις οὐχὶ πάντα ποιεῖν τὰ παρὰ
αὐτὸν ἕνεκα τοῦ βαλεῖν τὸν σκοπὸν ἀλλὰ ἕνεκα τοῦ πάντα ποιῆσαι τὰ παρ'
αὐτόν, αἰνίγμασιν ὅμοια καὶ τεράστια δόξειεν ἂν περαίνειν· (8) οὕτως οἱ
τριπέμπελοι βιαζόμενοι μὴ τὸ τυγχάνειν τῶν κατὰ φύσιν τοῦ στοχάζεσθαι
τῶν κατὰ φύσιν εἶναι τέλος ἀλλὰ τὸ λαμβάνειν καὶ ἐκλέγεσθαι μηδὲ τὴν   20

395

Stoic ethics

ἔφεσιν τῆς ὑγιείας καὶ δίωξιν εἰς τὸ ὑγιαίνειν ἑκάστῳ τελευτᾶν ἀλλὰ
τοὐναντίον τὸ ὑγιαίνειν ἐπὶ τὴν ἔφεσιν αὐτοῦ καὶ δίωξιν ἀναφέρεσθαι ... (9) τί γὰρ διαφέρει τοῦ λέγοντος γεγονέναι τὴν ὑγίειαν τῶν
φαρμάκων ἕνεκα, μὴ τὰ φάρμακα τῆς ὑγιείας, ὁ τὴν ἐκλογὴν τὴν περὶ τὰ
φάρμακα καὶ σύνθεσιν καὶ χρῆσιν αὐτῶν αἱρετωτέραν ποιῶν τῆς ὑγιείας,   2
μᾶλλον δὲ τὴν μὲν οὐδὲ ὅλως αἱρετὸν ἡγούμενος, ἐν δὲ τῇ περὶ ἐκεῖνα
πραγματείᾳ τὸ τέλος τιθέμενος καὶ τὴν ἔφεσιν ἀποφαίνων ⟨τέλος⟩ τῆς
τεύξεως, οὐ τῆς ἐφέσεως τὴν τεῦξιν; (10) "τῇ γὰρ ἐφέσει νὴ Δία τὸ
εὐλογίστως καὶ τὸ φρονίμως πρόσεστι." (11) πάνυ μὲν οὖν, φήσομεν, ἂν ὡς
πρὸς τέλος ὁρᾷ τὴν τεῦξιν ὧν διώκει καὶ τὴν κτῆσιν· εἰ δὲ μή, τὸ   3⟨
εὐλόγιστον αὐτῆς ἀφαιρεῖται, πάντα ποιούσης ἕνεκα τοῦ τυχεῖν, οὗ τυχεῖν
οὐ σεμνὸν οὐδὲ μακάριόν ἐστιν.

5 ⟨τὰ⟩ Wyttenbach   ⟨ἀγ⟩αθὰ Wyttenbach   7 δεῖ E: δὲ B   9 δ' ἄρ' Wyttenbach: γὰρ
codd.   10 ⟨ἐπ'⟩ Rasmus   οὗ ἕνεκα δεῖ Cherniss: ἕνεκα οὗ δεῖ E: οὗ δεῖ ἕνεκα B   11 τοῦτο
scripsimus: ταῦτα codd.: ταὐτό Cherniss   16–17 παρὰ αὐτὸν Reiske: περὶ αὐτὸν codd.   20 καὶ
Pohlenz: τὸ codd.   27 ⟨τέλος⟩ Meziriac   30 ὁρᾷ Meziriac: ὁρᾶν codd.

Context: attack on Stoic formulations of the τέλος.

1 τέλη καὶ σκοπούς   The terms are used synonymously here, and not as at 63A 3.

4 θάτερον   I.e. either of the alternatives mentioned in 1–2. Since Antipater's
second formula (58K 2) is explicitly cited as evidence that the Stoics do not set up two
ends (cf. F), Plutarch probably intended to attack Diogenes' 'selection' formula in the
first horn of his dilemma, and Antipater's 'goal-directed' formula in the second horn.
Thus 4 might be taken as the development of 2, and 5 of 1. But by conflating the two
formulae, as in 6–7, Plutarch has obscured the proper development of his dilemma; cf.
Long [591], 69, 81–2; Soreth [592], 58–63; Striker [593], 190–1.

5 ⟨τὰ⟩ πρῶτα κατὰ φύσιν   If this expression has its normal Stoic sense (cf. vol.
1, 357), Plutarch seriously distorts the formulae of Diogenes and Antipater reported in
58K (cf. also Posidonius in I 2). Diogenes does not restrict the AN things which are to
be selected to the objects of the primary impulse, and Antipater uses the word
προηγούμενα, which means 'leading' or 'predominating' in worth. Sandbach [296],
56, rightly suspects Carneades (cf. G 2–4) of introducing the term πρῶτα for
polemical purposes, with Posidonius and Plutarch following suit.

9–11   Sense can be made of this very difficult sentence along the lines proposed by
Cherniss [326] ad loc. and by reading τοῦτο in 11, taking 'this' to refer to τὸ
τυγχάνειν τῶν πρώτων κατὰ φύσιν, 8–9. I.e., if 'this' is not the point of selecting AN
things, the selection of them must be for the sake of something else, a second τέλος; cf.
lines 29–30, and Cicero, Fin. 4.46.

11–13   Purporting to state the Stoics' own position; cf. A. For ἐκλεκτικὴ ἀξία,
Antipater's expression, see 58D 2.

16   For the archer analogy, cf. F.

28–9   Purporting to state the Stoics' defence of Diogenes' 'selection' formula; cf. J.

D Plutarch, Comm. not. 1072E–F (SVF 3 Antipater 59, part)

(1) ἤδη τοίνυν ἀποκαλύψας ὅρα τὸ συμβαῖνον αὐτοῖς, ὅτι τέλος ἐστὶ τὸ

396

64 The end: Academic criticism and Stoic defence

εὐλογιστεῖν ἐν ταῖς ἐκλογαῖς τῶν ἀξίαν ἐχόντων πρὸς τὸ εὐλογιστεῖν·
ἄλλην γὰρ οὐσίαν τἀγαθοῦ καὶ τῆς εὐδαιμονίας οὔτ᾽ ἔχειν φασὶν οὔτε νοεῖν
οἱ ἄνδρες ἢ τὴν πολυτίμητον εὐλογιστίαν ταύτην περὶ τὰς ἐκλογὰς τῶν
ἀξίαν ἐχόντων. (2) ἀλλὰ τοῦτο μέν εἰσιν οἱ πρὸς ᾿Αντίπατρον οἰόμενοι   5
λέγεσθαι μὴ πρὸς τὴν αἵρεσιν· ἐκεῖνον γὰρ ὑπὸ Καρνεάδου πιεζόμενον εἰς
ταύτας καταδύεσθαι τὰς εὑρησιλογίας.

7 καταδύεσθαι Wyttenbach: καταλύεσθαι codd.

Context: resuming the criticism of **C** 11; cf. 1072C, ἐκλογὴ δ᾽ οὐκ ἔστιν εὐλόγιστος ἡ
μὴ πρός τι γενομένη τέλος, and **B**.

5–7   This is puzzling since εὑρησιλογίας should refer to 1–2, a tendentious
statement of the 'selection' formula (**58K**) expressed in Diogenes' language, not
Antipater's. According to the view taken in vol. 1, 407–9, the 'selection' formula was
not advanced as a Stoic rejoinder to Carneades; rather, it was this formulation of the
τέλος that provoked his attack, prompting Antipater to offer the 'goal-directed'
formula in its place, which is the better candidate for εὑρησιλογίας; cf. **I 2–3**. But, as
noted on **C**, Plutarch fails to distinguish clearly between the two formulae.

E   Cicero, *Fin.* 5.16

(1) quod quoniam in quo sit magna dissensio est, Carneadea nobis adhibenda
divisio est, qua noster Antiochus libenter uti solet. ille igitur vidit, non modo
quot fuissent adhuc philosophorum de summo bono, sed quot omnino esse
possent sententiae. (2) negabat igitur ullam esse artem quae ipsa a se
proficisceretur; etenim semper illud extra est quod arte comprehenditur. nihil   5
opus est exemplis hoc facere longius. est enim perspicuum nullam artem ipsam
in se versari, sed esse aliud artem ipsam, aliud quod propositum sit arti. (3)
quoniam igitur, ut medicina valitudinis, navigationis gubernatio, sic vivendi
ars est prudentia, necesse est eam quoque ab aliqua re esse constitutam et
profectam.   10

Context: the beginning of Piso's exposition of Antiochean ethics.
1 **quo** I.e. *quid sit et bonorum extremum et malorum.*
2 **divisio** See **G.**
8   Stock examples of a τέχνη and its τέλος; cf. Aristotle, *EN* I.1, 1094a8–9.

F   Cicero, *Fin.* 3.22 (*SVF* 3.18)

(1) sed ex hoc primum error tollendus est ne quis sequi existimet, ut duo sint
ultima bonorum. (2) etenim, si cui propositum sit conliniare hastam aliquo aut
sagittam, sicut nos ultimum in bonis dicimus, sic illi facere omnia quae possit
ut conliniet. (3) huic in eius modi similitudine omnia sint facienda, ut
conliniet. (4) et tamen, ut omnia faciat quo propositum adsequatur, sit hoc   5

Stoic ethics

quasi ultimum quale nos summum in vita bonum dicimus, illud autem, ut feriat, quasi seligendum, non expetendum.

2 *etenim* Schiche: *ut enim* codd.   3–4 *sic* . . . *conliniet* secl. Madvig, Schiche   5 *sit* Ernesti: *sed* codd.

Context: immediately following **59D**.

The Latin is obscure, but less corrupt than has often been supposed (cf. Soreth [592], 52–4). *sic*, 3, must answer the previous *sicut*, and *etenim*, 2, is preferable to the otiose *ut enim*. With *sic illi* understand *ultimum sit* from *sicut–dicimus*. In 4–5, *huic–conliniet*, the point of the analogy is stated: the archer must indeed try his best *to aim straight* (i.e. hit the target), since that is his *propositum*, 2–3. But his *ultimum*, as distinct from his *propositum*, is *ut omnia faciat, quo propositum adsequatur*, 5, reading *sit* for *sed*, and taking *hoc* as a reference to *ut omnia faciat quo propositum adsequatur*. The actual attainment of his *propositum*, 'hitting the target' (*illud* . . . *ut feriat*, 6–7), is *seligendum* (ληπτόν), not *expetendum* (αἱρετόν); cf. **58C 4**; **59D 5**.

The archer analogy illustrates Antipater's second formulation of the τέλος (**58K 2**). It employs the notion that virtue, the expertise of life, is a στοχαστικὴ τέχνη, the τέλος of which is reported by Alexander (*SVF* 3.19) as τὸ πάντα τὰ παρ' αὑτὰς ποιεῖν πρὸς τὸ τοῦ προκειμένου τυγχάνειν. Alexander also shows, loc. cit., that upholders of this notion distinguished such τέχναι from other crafts by the fact that the former require certain external conditions to be met, in addition to the display of expertise, if the objective is to be attained. There were earlier precedents for this notion; cf. Aristotle, *Top.* 1.3, 101b7, where the orator and doctor exemplify τέχναι which do not require consistent success from their practitioners, but ἐκ τῶν ἐνδεχομένων ποιεῖν ἃ προαιρούμεθα. Antipater thus opts for a formulation of the τέλος as an art of life which, though it specifies an objective outside its own performance (cf. Carneades in **F**), treats the τέλος itself not as the attainment of this objective (the getting of *AN* things) but τὸ ἀποπληρῶσαι τὰ τῆς τέχνης (Alexander, loc. cit.). For an illuminating discussion of what can be said for and against his strategy, cf. Striker [593].

G Cicero, *Fin.* 5.17–21

(1) constitit autem fere inter omnes id in quo prudentia versaretur et quod assequi vellet, aptum et accommodatum naturae esse oportere et tale, ut ipsum per se invitaret et alliceret appetitum animi, quem ὁρμήν Graeci vocant. quid autem sit, quod ita moveat itaque a natura in primo ortu appetatur, non constat, deque eo est inter philosophos, cum summum bonum exquiritur, omnis dissensio. totius enim quaestionis   5
eius quae habetur de finibus bonorum et malorum, cum quaeritur in his quid sit extremum et ultimum, fons reperiendus est in quo sint prima invitamenta naturae; quo invento omnis ab eo quasi capite de summo bono et malo disputatio ducitur. (2) voluptatis alii primum appetitum putant et primam depulsionem doloris. vacuitatem doloris alii censent primum ascitam et primum declinatum dolorem. ab iis alii, quae   10
prima secundum naturam nominant, proficiscuntur, in quibus numerant incolumitatem conservationemque omnium partium, valitudinem, sensus integros, doloris vacuitatem, viris, pulchritudinem, cetera generis eiusdem, quorum similia sunt prima in animis quasi virtutum igniculi et semina. (3) ex

398

his tribus cum unum aliquid sit, quo primum natura moveatur vel ad   15
appetendum vel ad repellendum, nec quicquam omnino praeter haec tria
possit esse, necesse est omnino officium aut fugiendi aut sequendi ad eorum
aliquid referri, ut illa prudentia, quam artem vitae esse diximus, in earum
trium rerum aliqua versetur, a qua totius vitae ducat exordium. (4) ex eo
autem quod statuerit esse quo primum natura moveatur, existet recti etiam   20
ratio atque honesti, quae cum uno aliquo ex tribus illis congruere possit, ut aut
id honestum sit facere omnia [aut] voluptatis causa, etiam si eam non
consequare, aut non dolendi, etiam si id assequi nequeas, aut eorum quae
secundum naturam sunt adipiscendi, etiam si nihil consequare. ita fit ut, quanta
differentia est in principiis naturalibus, tanta sit in finibus bonorum malorumque dissimilitudo.   25
alii rursum isdem a principiis omne officium referent aut ad voluptatem aut ad
non dolendum aut ad prima illa secundum naturam optinenda. (5) expositis
iam igitur sex de summo bono sententiis trium proximarum hi principes:
voluptatis Aristippus, non dolendi Hieronymus, fruendi rebus iis quas primas
secundum naturam esse diximus Carneades non ille quidem auctor, sed   30
defensor disserendi causa fuit. (6) superiores tres erant quae esse possent,
quarum est una sola defensa, eaque vehementer. nam voluptatis causa facere
omnia cum, etiamsi nihil consequamur, tamen ipsum illud consilium ita
faciendi per se expetendum et honestum et solum bonum sit, nemo dixit. ne
vitationem quidem doloris ipsam per se quisquam in rebus expetendis putavit,   35
nisi etiam evitare posset. at vero facere omnia, ut adipiscamur quae secundum
naturam sint etiam si ea non assequamur, id esse et honestum et solum per se
expetendum et solum bonum Stoici dicunt. sex igitur hae sunt simplices de summo
bonorum malorumque sententiae, duae sine patrono, quattuor defensae. iunctae autem et
duplices expositiones summi boni tres omnino fuerunt, nec vero plures, si penitus rerum   40
naturam videas, esse potuerunt. nam aut voluptas adiungi potest ad honestatem, ut Calliphonti
Dinomachoque placuit, aut doloris vacuitas, ut Diodoro, aut prima naturae, ut antiquis, quos
eosdem Academicos et Peripateticos nominavimus.

10 ascitam Madvig: as(s)citum vel assertum codd.   iis Lambinus: his codd.   15 aliquid Wesenberg:
aliquod codd.   primum dett.: prima vel primo cett.   22 aut secl. Madvig   36 nisi Ursinus: ne si
codd.   37 sint vel sunt codd.

Context: immediately following **E**.
        On Carneades' division, and its interest for Antiochus, cf. Glucker [42], 52–62. The
origin of such a classification of ends goes back as far as Chrysippus (cf. Cicero, *Acad.*
2.138), perhaps expounded in his Περὶ τελῶν (**63C** 4–6).
        30–1   For other opinions defended by Carneades for dialectical purposes, cf. **68M**;
69H, **L**.
        38–9   The addition of *iunctae* to *simplices* accords with Chrysippus' classification
(Cicero, loc. cit.), which posits *honestas*, *voluptas*, *utrumque*.
        40 **nec ... plures**   Indicating that these composite ends could not, practically
speaking, include the mere pursuit of 'rectitude plus pleasure' etc. irrespective of their
attainment.
        42–3 **antiquis–Peripateticos**   The trademark of Antiochus.

Stoic ethics

H Cicero, *Fin.* 3.24-5 (*SVF* 3.11, part)

(1) nec enim gubernationi aut medicinae similem sapientiam esse arbitramur, sed actioni illi potius, quam modo dixi, et saltationi, ut in ipsa insit, non foris petatur extremum, id est artis effectio. (2) et tamen est etiam aliqua cum his ipsis artibus sapientiae dissimilitudo, propterea quod in illis quae recte facta sunt non continent tamen omnes partes e quibus constant; (3) quae autem nos aut recta aut recte facta dicamus, si placet, illi autem appellant κατορθώματα, omnes numeros virtutis continent. sola enim sapientia in se tota conversa est, quod idem in ceteris artibus non fit.

Context: shortly after **59D**.

1 For the rejected analogies, see **E 3**.

2 **quam modo dixi** Cato has just used acting and dancing, to make the point that these *artes*, like the *ars vivendi*, require determinate activities (*certus* contrasted with *quivis*) of their practitioners.

7 **omnes numeros** See note on **59K**.

I Galen, *Plac.* 5.6.10-14 (Posidonius fr. 187, part)

(1) οὐκ ἀρκεσθεὶς δὲ τούτοις ὁ Ποσειδώνιος ἐναργέστερόν τε καὶ σφοδρότερον καθάπτεται τῶν περὶ τὸν Χρύσιππον ὡς οὐκ ὀρθῶς ἐξηγουμένων τὸ τέλος. (2) ἔχει δὲ ἡ ῥῆσις ὧδε· "ἃ δὴ παρέντες ἔνιοι τὸ ὁμολογουμένως ζῆν συστέλλουσιν εἰς τὸ πᾶν τὸ ἐνδεχόμενον ποιεῖν ἕνεκα τῶν πρώτων κατὰ φύσιν, ὅμοιον αὐτῷ ποιοῦντες τῷ σκοπὸν ἐκτίθεσθαι τὴν ἡδονὴν ἢ τὴν ἀοχλησίαν ἢ ἄλλο τι τοιοῦτον. ἔστι δὲ μάχην ἐμφαῖνον κατ᾽ αὐτὴν τὴν ἐκφοράν, καλὸν δὲ καὶ εὐδαιμονικὸν οὐδέν· παρέπεται γὰρ κατὰ τὸ ἀναγκαῖον τῷ τέλει, τέλος δὲ οὐκ ἔστιν. (3) ἀλλὰ καὶ τούτου διαληφθέντος ὀρθῶς, ἔξεστι μὲν αὐτῷ χρῆσθαι πρὸς τὸ διακόπτειν τὰς ἀπορίας ἃς οἱ σοφισταὶ προτείνουσι, (4) μὴ μέντοι γε τῷ κατ᾽ ἐμπειρίαν τῶν κατὰ τὴν ὅλην φύσιν συμβαινόντων ζῆν, ὅπερ ἰσοδυναμεῖ τῷ ὁμολογουμένως εἰπεῖν ζῆν ἡνίκα μὴ τοῦτο μικροπρεπῶς συντείνειν εἰς τὸ τῶν ἀδιαφόρων τυγχάνειν." (5) ἤρκει μὲν οὖν ἴσως καὶ τοῦτο πρὸς ἔνδειξιν τῆς ἀτοπίας ὧν ὁ Χρύσιππος εἴρηκε περὶ τοῦ τέλους ἐξηγούμενος ὅπως ἄν τις τυγχάνοι τοῦ ὁμολογουμένως τῇ φύσει ζῆν· ἄμεινον μὴν ἡγοῦμαι καὶ τὰ τούτοις ἐξῆς ὑπὸ τοῦ Ποσειδωνίου γεγραμμένα παραθέσθαι τόνδε τὸν τρόπον ἔχοντα· (6) "ταύτην τε δὴ τὴν ἀτοπίαν διέλυσεν ἡ αἰτία τῶν παθῶν ὁραθεῖσα καὶ τὰς ἀρχὰς ἔδειξε τῆς ἐν τοῖς ὀρεκτοῖς καὶ φευκτοῖς διαστροφῆς καὶ τοὺς τρόπους τῆς ἀσκήσεως διεῖλε καὶ τὰ διαπορούμενα περὶ τῆς ἐκ πάθους ὁρμῆς ἐξέφηνεν."

5 αὐτῷ HL: αὐτὸ M   7 καλὸν H(corr.): μᾶλλον L   10 τῷ Bake: τὸ codd.   11-12 ἰσοδυναμεῖν ... εἶπε Hirzel   12 ζῆν ἡνίκα H: ζήνωνι· καὶ L: ζῆν ἡνίκ᾽ ἅ⟨ν⟩ A.A. Long   συντείνειν codd.: συντείνει Cornarius   13 ἀδιαφόρων Wyttenbach: διαφορῶν codd.: διαφόρων Bake   17 τε H: δὲ L   αἰτία H: ἀτοπία L   18 ὀρεκτοῖς Ald.: ὁρατοις codd.

Context: Galen is using Posidonius, to attack Chrysippus' monistic psychology, which

400

excludes the Platonic distinction between rational and irrational parts of the soul. The Posidonian position, approved by Galen, is that correct doctrines on the τέλος and the virtues depend upon understanding the πάθη, which arise when the irrational part of the soul is in command (*Plac.* 5.6.1–5). As Galen understands him, Posidonius interpreted ὁμολογουμένως τῇ φύσει ζῆν to mean, 'as Plato has taught us, following the lead of the better part' (*Plac.* 5.6.6–9); i.e., living κατὰ λόγον and not κατὰ πάθος. It is this interpretation of the τέλος which οἱ περὶ τὸν Χρύσιππον, 2, have neglected.

4–5   A version of Antipater's second formulation of the τέλος (**58K** 2). Posidonius' direct allusion to this is confirmed by his comparisons with ἡδονή and ἀοχλησία, 6, which, along with τὰ πρῶτα κατὰ φύσιν, comprise Carneades' division of the possible σκοποί (**G** 2; cf. note on **C** 5).

7 **παρέπεται**   The subject must be the τέλος, as formulated by Antipater.

8 **τούτου**   Some take this to refer to Posidonius' own account of the end (**63 J** 2); cf. Edelstein [373], 314. This might seem appropriate in view of the general context and the attack on Chrysippeans in 6–13, who must include Antipater. But better sense is produced by reading it as 'Antipater's formulation', understood in the light of lines 7–8. ἀλλὰ καί, 8, is a concession, and contrasts with μὴ μέντοι γε, 10, which introduces an unequivocal rejection of Chrysippus' formula (cf. **63D 4**) as a means of combating the difficulties raised by the 'sophists' (i.e. Carneades). This reading gives point to Posidonius' qualified acceptance of Antipater's formula as a 'necessary adjunct' of the τέλος; and Antipater best fits **3**.

10–13   An interpretation of these very difficult lines is needed which will show why Chrysippus' formula, κατ' ἐμπειρίαν–ζῆν, is incapable of meeting the problems raised by 'the sophists' and why it is 'absurd', 14. The point, we suggest, is this: Antipater's formula has at least the dialectical merit of incorporating Carneades' requirement that action should be consistently aimed at getting *AN* things (see **F, G** 6). But Chrysippus is evasive in his attitude towards them, holding that they are not to be pursued in all circumstances; cf. **58J**, 'I should pursue sickness if I know I am fated to fall ill'. For Chrysippus, the overriding requirement is acting in agreement with *universal* nature (cf. **63C 3–4**), a point Posidonius emphasizes by adding ὅλην in 11 to Chrysippus' formula. So it is impossible to act consistently with *human* nature, since there will be times when aiming at getting *AN* things (what human nature dictates) would be acting out of tune with universal nature. Posidonius, then, argues that all problems disappear once the τέλος is perceived as reason's consistent control of the passions, 17–20. Reason will decide what should be pursued and avoided, in such a way that no emotional conflict will arise (no clash between human and universal nature) in the attitude towards *AN* things. So construed, the clause beginning ὅπερ, 11, is Posidonius' own gloss, and so ἰσοδυναμεῖ should not be changed to ἰσοδυναμεῖν. συντείνειν, infinitive, can stand as dependent on εἰπεῖν, a usage of the infinitive in temporal and adverbial clauses for which Kühner/Gerth 2.551 give many examples from classical Attic prose. ἡνίκα μή seems to have quasi-conditional force, 'when' = 'in all cases if'. Sense and grammar would be improved by reading ἡνίκ' ⟨ἄν⟩ (so **65M** 43); for ἐπεί with infinitive and ἄν, cf. Thucydides 2.93.3. συντείνειν is equivalent in sense to πᾶν τὸ ἐνδεχόμενον ποιεῖν ἕνεκα, 4; cf. Rieth [590], 38 n. 1. This adds further support to the view that 8–13 contrast the dialectical effectiveness of Chrysippus' and Antipater's formulae.

Stoic ethics

J Seneca, *Ep.* 92.11–13

(1) "quid ergo?" inquit "si virtutem nihil inpeditura sit bona valetudo et quies et dolorum vacatio, non petes illas?" (2) quidni petam? non quia bona sunt, sed quia secundum naturam sunt, et quia bono a me iudicio sumentur. (3) quid erit tunc in illis bonum? hoc unum, bene eligi. nam cum vestem qualem decet sumo, cum ambulo ut oportet, cum ceno quemadmodum debeo, non cena aut ambulatio aut vestis bona sunt, sed meum in iis propositum servantis in quaque re rationi convenientem modum. . . . (4) itaque non est bonum per se munda vestis sed mundae vestis electio, quia non in re bonum est sed in electione quali; actiones nostrae honestae sunt, non ipsa quae aguntur . . . (5) sumpturum quidem me, si detur electio, et sanitatem et vires, bonum autem futurum iudicium de illis meum, non ipsa.

4 *eligi* vel *elegi* codd.

Context: developing the thesis that virtue is the only good; cf. **m** and **63F**.
    4 **bene eligi** Cf. **D** 3–5.

K Cicero, *Fin.* 4.26–7, 29–30, 32, 39

(1) quaero igitur, quo modo hae tantae commendationes a natura profectae subito a sapientia relictae sint. quodsi non hominis summum bonum quaereremus, sed cuiusdam animantis, is autem esset nihil nisi animus . . . , tamen illi animo non esset hic vester finis. (2) desideraret enim valitudinem, vacuitatem doloris, appeteret etiam conservationem sui earumque rerum custodiam finemque sibi constitueret secundum naturam vivere, quod est, ut dixi, habere ea quae secundum naturam sint, vel omnia vel plurima et maxima . . . (3) sin dicit obscurari quaedam nec apparere, quia valde parva sint, nos quoque concedimus; quod dicit Epicurus etiam de voluptate, quae minimae sint voluptates, eas obscurari saepe et obrui. sed non sunt in eo genere tantae commoditates corporis tamque productae temporibus tamque multae . . . habent enim accessionem dignam, in qua elaboretur, ut mihi in hoc Stoici iocari videantur interdum, cum ita dicant, si ad illam vitam quae cum virtute degatur ampulla aut strigilis accedat, sumpturum sapientem eam vitam potius quo haec adiecta sint, nec beatiorem tamen ob eam causam fore . . . (4) atqui si, ut convenire debet inter nos, est quaedam appetitio naturalis ea quae secundum naturam sunt appetens, eorum omnium est aliquae summa facienda . . . (5) itaque non discedit ab eorum curatione quibus praeposita vitam omnem debet gubernare, ut mirari satis istorum inconstantiam non possim. naturalem enim appetitionem . . . itemque officium, ipsam etiam virtutem volunt esse earum rerum quae secundum naturam sunt. cum autem ad summum bonum volunt pervenire, transiliunt omnia et duo nobis opera

pro uno relinquunt, ut alia sumamus, alia expetamus, potius quam uno fine utrumque concluderent.

19 *istorum* Wesenberg: *eorum* codd.   20 *possim* Madvig: *possum* vel *possimus* codd.   21 post *virtutem* addunt dett. *tuentem*   23 *expetamus* Baiter: *ea petamus* codd.

Context: representative excerpts from the Antiochean criticism of Stoic ethics.

1–8   Antiochus accepts the Stoics' account of self-preservation as the object of the primary impulse (**57A**), but claims that in this allegedly 'ancient doctrine' (cf. Cicero, *Fin.* 4.24), the end must, for consistency, require preservation of the whole person (body as well as soul). Hence these lines are advanced as a reductio ad absurdum.

8–9   Taking up the Stoic point at *Fin.* 3.45, which was advanced against the Peripatetic postulation of multiple 'goods', defended by Antiochus; see also **m**.

22 **duo . . . opera**   For the Stoics' answer to this charge, cf. **F**.

L   Cicero, *Fin.* 4.78

quid enim est tam repugnans quam eundem dicere, quod honestum sit, solum id bonum esse, qui dicat appetitionem rerum ad vivendum accommodatarum ⟨a⟩ natura profectam? ita cum ea volunt retinere quae superiori sententiae conveniunt in Aristonem incidunt; cum id fugiunt, re eadem defendunt quae Peripatetici, verba tenent mordicus.   5

3 ⟨*a*⟩ Manutius

Context: concluding the Antiochean criticism of Stoic ethics.

For Aristo, see **2F–H**; **58F, G, I**. Antiochus constantly accuses the Stoics of being Peripatetics (and Platonists) in everything but terminology; cf. Cicero, *Acad.* 1.37; *Fin.* 4.19–23.

m   Seneca, *Ep.* 92.5 (*SVF* 3 Antipater 53)

quidam tamen augeri summum bonum iudicant, quia parum sit fortuitis repugnantibus. Antipater quoque inter magnos sectae huius auctores aliquid se tribuere dicit externis, sed exiguum admodum. vides autem quale sit die non esse contentum nisi aliquis igniculus adluxerit: quod potest in hac claritate solis habere scintilla momentum?

3 *die non* Erasmus: *zenon* BQ*ψ*: *et te non* D: *te non θ*: *sole te non* Arnim

Context: virtue is the only good.

The 'light' image is used by Cato in Cicero, *Fin.* 3.45, to show how the value of bodily advantages is completely eclipsed by that of virtue. Piso, speaking for Antiochus at *Fin.* 5.72, accepts this too, while also insisting against the Stoics that they are *parva ad beate vivendum momenta*. What is here attributed to Antipater looks like the latter thesis, and his arguments with Carneades certainly gained him the dubious reputation of having made concessions to the Academic; cf. Cicero, *Fin.* 3.57. Antipater devoted three books to defending the thesis that 'according to Plato virtue is the only good', which was taken to show that he too regarded virtue as sufficient for happiness (*SVF* 3 Antipater 56). Yet Antiochus also accepted the latter, while denying the former; cf. Cicero, *Fin.* 5.81. Given the state of the evidence, it is impossible to know whether Antipater's apparent concessions were substantial or only dialectical and verbal. We incline to the second alternative.

n Diogenes Laertius 7.103 (Posidonius fr. 171, part)

Ποσειδώνιος μέντοι καὶ ταῦτά φησι [sc. πλοῦτος καὶ ὑγίεια] τῶν ἀγαθῶν εἶναι.

Context: immediately following **58A**.
This bald statement (absurdly exaggerated in Posidonius fr. 172) is completely contradicted by Seneca, *Ep.* 87.31, 35, where Posidonius is credited with arguments to prove that wealth and health are not goods. Cf. Kidd [578], 162–3.

o Diogenes Laertius 7.128 (Posidonius fr. 173, part, Panaetius fr. 110)

ὁ μέντοι Παναίτιος καὶ Ποσειδώνιος οὐκ αὐτάρκη λέγουσι τὴν ἀρετήν, ἀλλὰ χρείαν εἶναί φασι καὶ ὑγιείας καὶ χορηγίας καὶ ἰσχύος.

Context: shortly after **61I**. For the likelihood that this is misrepresentation, cf. Kidd [578], 159–60.

65 The passions

A Stobaeus 2.88,8–90,6 (*SVF* 3.378,389, part)

(1) πάθος δ᾽ εἶναί φασιν ὁρμὴν πλεονάζουσαν καὶ ἀπειθῆ τῷ αἱροῦντι λόγῳ ἢ κίνησιν ψυχῆς ⟨ἄλογον⟩ παρὰ φύσιν (εἶναι δὲ πάθη πάντα τοῦ ἡγεμονικοῦ τῆς ψυχῆς), (2) διὸ καὶ πᾶσαν πτοίαν πάθος εἶναι, ⟨καὶ⟩ πάλιν ⟨πᾶν⟩ πάθος πτοίαν. (3) τοῦ δὲ πάθους τοιούτου ὄντος ὑποληπτέον, τὰ μὲν πρῶτα εἶναι καὶ ἀρχηγά, τὰ δ᾽ εἰς ταῦτα τὴν ἀναφορὰν ἔχειν. πρῶτα δ᾽   5
εἶναι τῷ γένει ταῦτα τὰ τέσσαρα, ἐπιθυμίαν, φόβον, λύπην, ἡδονήν. (4) ἐπιθυμίαν μὲν οὖν καὶ φόβον προηγεῖσθαι, τὴν μὲν πρὸς τὸ φαινόμενον ἀγαθόν, τὸν δὲ πρὸς τὸ φαινόμενον κακόν. ἐπιγίγνεσθαι δὲ τούτοις ἡδονὴν καὶ λύπην, ἡδονὴν μὲν ὅταν τυγχάνωμεν ὧν ἐπεθυμοῦμεν ἢ ἐκφύγωμεν ἃ ἐφοβούμεθα· λύπην δέ, ὅταν ἀποτυγχάνωμεν ὧν ἐπεθυμοῦμεν ἢ περι-   10
πέσωμεν οἷς ἐφοβούμεθα. (5) [=**65C**] (6) τὸ δὲ "ἄλογον" καὶ τὸ "παρὰ φύσιν" οὐ κοινῶς, ἀλλὰ τὸ μὲν "ἄλογον" ἴσον τῷ ἀπειθὲς τῷ λόγῳ. πᾶν γὰρ πάθος βιαστικόν ἐστι, ὡς πολλάκις ὁρῶντας τοὺς ἐν τοῖς πάθεσιν ὄντας ὅτι συμφέρει τόδε οὐ ποιεῖν, ὑπὸ τῆς σφοδρότητος ἐκφερομένους, καθάπερ ὑπό τινος ἀπειθοῦς ἵππου, ἀνάγεσθαι πρὸς τὸ ποιεῖν αὐτό . . . (7)   15
καὶ τὸ "παρὰ φύσιν" δ᾽ εἴληπται ἐν τῇ τοῦ πάθους ὑπογραφῇ, ὡς συμβαίνοντος παρὰ τὸν ὀρθὸν καὶ κατὰ φύσιν λόγον. πάντες δ᾽ οἱ ἐν τοῖς πάθεσιν ὄντες ἀποστρέφονται τὸν λόγον, οὐ παραπλησίως δὲ τοῖς ἐξηπατημένοις ἐν ὁτῳοῦν, ἀλλ᾽ ἰδιαζόντως. (8) οἱ μὲν γὰρ ἠπατημένοι, λόγου χάριν περὶ ⟨τοῦ⟩ τὰς ἀτόμους ἀρχὰς εἶναι, διδαχθέντες ὅτι οὐκ   20
εἰσιν, ἀφίστανται τῆς κρίσεως· οἱ δ᾽ ἐν τοῖς πάθεσιν ὄντες, κἂν μάθωσι,

65 The passions

κἂν μεταδιδαχθῶσιν ὅτι οὐ δεῖ λυπεῖσθαι ἢ φοβεῖσθαι, ἢ ὅλως ἐν τοῖς
πάθεσιν εἶναι τῆς ψυχῆς, ὅμως οὐκ ἀφίστανται τούτων, ἀλλ᾽ ἄγονται ὑπὸ
τῶν παθῶν εἰς τὸ ὑπὸ τῆς τούτων κρατεῖσθαι τυραννίδος.

1 ἀπειθῆ F: ἀπαθῆ P   2 ⟨ἄλογον⟩ Wachsmuth   2–3 τοῦ ἡγεμονικοῦ Wachsmuth: τῷ γένει ἢ
codd.   3 ⟨καὶ⟩ Heeren   4 ⟨πᾶν⟩ Meineke   9, 10 ἐπεθυμοῦμεν Meurer: ἐπιθ- codd.   12
ἴσον Usener: ὅσον codd.   ἀπειθὲς Usener: ἀπειθῶς codd.   13 ὡς Meineke: καὶ codd.   14 τόδε
οὐ Canter: τόδε, οὐ Salmasius: τὸ δὲ εὖ codd.   20 ⟨τοῦ⟩ Wachsmuth

Context: following 331.
1–2   The same two accounts of πάθος are attributed to Zeno at D.L. 7.110; cf.
also Cicero, Tusc. 4.11. For αἱροῦντι λόγῳ, cf. 59E 2, from which it is inferable that
πάθη are παρὰ τὸ καθῆκον.
3 **ἡγεμονικοῦ**   Wachsmuth's emendation seems certain; cf. G 7–8.   **πτοίαν**
Zeno's metaphor, cf. SVF 1.206.
5–6 **πρῶτα ... τέσσαρα**   For the Platonic/Aristotelian background of this
distinctively Stoic classification, cf. Pohlenz [298] 2, 80–2; Forschner [544], 123–34.
8–9 **ἡδονήν**   It is widely agreed that this πάθος pleasure is not identical to the
ἡδονή called ἐπιγέννημα in 57A 3 and which must be the pleasure referred to in 58A 4
as a 'preferred indifferent', or as simply 'indifferent' (SVF 3.70), or as 'neither natural
nor valuable' (SVF 3.155). We are not persuaded by Gosling/Taylor [19], 426–7, who
assimilate all ἡδονή to the former type and make it depend in all cases upon the mind's
assent.
11 **ἄλογον**   More fully explained in J 4.
15 **ἵππου**   An allusion to Plato, Phdr. 246a6ff., which may suggest the influence
of Posidonius on this sentence; cf. Kidd [383].

B   Andronicus, De passionibus 1 (SVF 3.391, part)

(1) λύπη μὲν οὖν ἐστιν ἄλογος συστολή· ἢ δόξα πρόσφατος κακοῦ
παρουσίας, ἐφ᾽ ᾧ οἴονται δεῖν συστέλλεσθαι. (2) φόβος δὲ ἄλογος ἔκκλισις·
ἢ φυγὴ ἀπὸ προσδοκωμένου δεινοῦ. (3) ἐπιθυμία δὲ ἄλογος ὄρεξις· ἢ
δίωξις προσδοκωμένου ἀγαθοῦ. (4) ἡδονὴ δὲ ἄλογος ἔπαρσις· ἢ δόξα
πρόσφατος ἀγαθοῦ παρουσίας, ἐφ᾽ ᾧ οἴονται δεῖν ἐπαίρεσθαι.   5

Context: definitions of the πάθη.
For further evidence to the same effect, cf. Stobaeus 2.90,7–18; Cicero, Tusc. 3.24–
5; SVF 3.386–8, 392–3. Stobaeus, loc. cit., expresses Andronicus' ἐφ᾽ ᾧ οἴονται δεῖν,
2, by ἐφ᾽ ᾧ καθήκει; cf. note on A 1–2.
3 **δεινοῦ**   A literary variant for the standard κακοῦ; cf. Plato, Prot. 358d6;
Aristotle, EN III.6, 1115a9.

C   Stobaeus 2.88,22–89,3 (SVF 3.378, part; =65A 5)

ἐπὶ πάντων δὲ τῶν τῆς ψυχῆς παθῶν, ἐπεὶ δόξας αὐτὰ λέγουσιν εἶναι,
παραλαμβάνεσθαι τὴν δόξαν ἀντὶ τῆς ἀσθενοῦς ὑπολήψεως, τὸ δὲ
πρόσφατον ἀντὶ τοῦ κινητικοῦ συστολῆς ἀλόγου ⟨ἢ⟩ ἐπάρσεως.

3 ⟨ἢ⟩ Salmasius

Stoic ethics

Context: see **A 5**.

2 ἀσθενοῦς ὑπολήψεως   Cf. **41G** with note. 'Weakness' contrasts with the βεβαιότης of the wise man's judgements, and focuses upon the 'changeability' (cf. **G 3**) of the passions.

3 πρόσφατον   Applied only to pleasure and distress (cf. **B**, except at Stobaeus 2.90, 13). See also Cicero, *Tusc.* 3.75, and, for discussion of the term, Inwood [547], 146–55.

D Galen, *Plac.* 4.2.1–6 (*SVF* 3.463, part)

ὥσπερ δ' ἐν τούτοις ἐπελάθετό τε ἅμα τῶν ἑαυτῷ γεγραμμένων οὐκ ἠξίωσέ τε πρὸς τὸ τῶν παλαιῶν ἀντειπεῖν δόγμα, κατὰ τὸν αὐτὸν τρόπον (1) ἐν τοῖς ὁρισμοῖς τῶν γενικῶν παθῶν οὓς πρώτους ἐξέθετο, τελέως ἀποχωρεῖ τῆς γνώμης αὐτῶν, τὴν λύπην ὁριζόμενος δόξαν πρόσφατον κακοῦ παρουσίας, τὸν δὲ φόβον προσδοκίαν κακοῦ, τὴν δ' ἡδονὴν δόξαν πρόσφατον ἀγαθοῦ παρουσίας. (2) ἄντικρυς γὰρ   5
ἐν τούτοις τοῦ λογιστικοῦ τῆς ψυχῆς μόνου μέμνηται παραλείπων τό τ' ἐπιθυμητικὸν καὶ τὸ θυμοειδές· καὶ γὰρ τὴν δόξαν καὶ τὴν προσδοκίαν ἐν τῷ λογιστικῷ μόνῳ συνίστασθαι νομίζει ... ἐν μέντοι δὴ τούτοις τοῖς ὅροις ὁρμὰς καὶ δόξας καὶ κρίσεις ὑπάρχειν οἴεται τὰ πάθη, (3) κατὰ δέ τινας τῶν ἐφεξῆς Ἐπικούρῳ καὶ Ζήνωνι μᾶλλον ἢ τοῖς ἑαυτοῦ δόγμασιν ἀκόλουθα γράφει. (4) τήν τε γὰρ   10
λύπην ὁριζόμενος, "μείωσιν εἶναι", φησιν, "ἐπὶ φευκτῷ δοκοῦντι ὑπάρχειν τήν θ' ἡδονὴν ἔπαρσιν ἐφ' αἱρετῷ δοκοῦντι ὑπάρχειν." (5) καὶ γὰρ αἱ μειώσεις καὶ αἱ ἐπάρσεις καὶ αἱ συστολαὶ καὶ αἱ διαχύσεις – καὶ γὰρ τούτων ἐνίοτε μέμνηται – τῆς ἀλόγου δυνάμεώς ἐστι παθήματα ταῖς δόξαις ἐπιγιγνόμενα.   15

12 θ' Müller: δ' H

Context: Chrysippus' doctrine that the πάθη are κρίσεις (8–9) is set against statements in his 'writings' (1, i.e. Περὶ ψυχῆς) that love belongs to the ἐπιθυμητικὴ δύναμις and anger to the θυμοειδής. Galen's quotations (4.1.5–17) seem to show that Chrysippus used this Platonic terminology; but his purpose in doing so was probably to argue that Plato should have located these faculties together with τὸ λογιστικόν in the heart (4.1.6); cf. **H**. No surviving quotation from Chrysippus proves him to have ever supported Plato's psychology in the manner alleged by Galen.

2 γενικῶν   Cf. **A 3**.

8   In the omitted lines Galen cites the definition of ἐπιθυμία as ἄλογος ὄρεξις (cf. **B 3**) as a 'verbal' acknowledgement of the soul's ἄλογος δύναμις.

9–13   For Epicurean use of the term διάχυσις, cf. Usener [133] s.v.; and for Zeno, cf. **K 1**.

11 μείωσιν   The more familar term is ἔκκλισις, **B 2**.

E Stobaeus 2.90,19–91,9 (*SVF* 3.394, part)

(1) ὑπὸ μὲν οὖν τὴν ἐπιθυμίαν ὑπάγεται τὰ τοιαῦτα· ὀργὴ καὶ τὰ εἴδη αὐτῆς (θυμὸς καὶ χόλος καὶ μῆνις καὶ κότος καὶ πικρίαι καὶ τὰ τοιαῦτα), ἔρωτες σφοδροὶ καὶ

406

πόθοι καὶ ἵμεροι καὶ φιληδονίαι καὶ φιλοπλουτίαι καὶ φιλοδοξίαι καὶ τὰ
ὅμοια· (2) ὑπὸ δὲ τὴν ἡδονὴν ἐπιχαιρεκακίαι καὶ ἀσμενισμοὶ καὶ γοητεῖαι
καὶ τὰ ὅμοια· (3) ὑπὸ δὲ τὸν φόβον ὄκνοι καὶ ἀγωνίαι καὶ ἔκπληξις καὶ   5
αἰσχύναι καὶ θόρυβοι καὶ δεισιδαιμονίαι καὶ δέος καὶ δείματα· (4) ὑπὸ δὲ
τὴν λύπην φθόνος, ζῆλος, ζηλοτυπία, ἔλεος, πένθος, ἄχθος, ἄχος, ἀνία,
ὀδύνη, ἄση.

2 κότος Canter: σκότος P: om. F

Context: a few lines after **A**.
For similar classifications, cf. D.L. 7.111–14; Cicero, *Tusc.* 4.16.

7 ἔλεος   Included as a blameworthy passion on the dubious ground that
susceptibility to pity (distress at another's misfortunes) implies susceptibility to envy
(distress at another's prosperity); cf. Plutarch, *St. rep.* 1046C; Cicero, *Tusc.* 3.21.

F Diogenes Laertius 7.116 (*SVF* 3.431)

(1) εἶναι δὲ καὶ εὐπαθείας φασὶ τρεῖς, χαράν, εὐλάβειαν, βούλησιν. (2) καὶ
τὴν μὲν χαρὰν ἐναντίαν φασὶν εἶναι τῇ ἡδονῇ, οὖσαν εὔλογον ἔπαρσιν· τὴν
δ᾽ εὐλάβειαν τῷ φόβῳ, οὖσαν εὔλογον ἔκκλισιν. φοβηθήσεσθαι μὲν γὰρ τὸν
σοφὸν οὐδαμῶς, εὐλαβηθήσεσθαι δέ. (3) τῇ δ᾽ ἐπιθυμίᾳ ἐναντίαν φασὶν
εἶναι τὴν βούλησιν, οὖσαν εὔλογον ὄρεξιν. (4) καθάπερ οὖν ὑπὸ τὰ πρῶτα   5
πάθη πίπτει τινά, τὸν αὐτὸν τρόπον καὶ ὑπὸ τὰς πρώτας εὐπαθείας· καὶ
ὑπὸ μὲν τὴν βούλησιν εὔνοιαν, εὐμένειαν, ἀσπασμόν, ἀγάπησιν· ὑπὸ δὲ τὴν
εὐλάβειαν αἰδῶ, ἁγνείαν· ὑπὸ δὲ τὴν χαρὰν τέρψιν, εὐφροσύνην, εὐθυμίαν.

2, 4 φασὶν om. F   εὐλαβηθήσεσθαι F: εὐλαβήσεσθαι BP   6 πίπτει FP: -ειν B

Context: doxography of πάθη.

The term εὐπάθεια is not attributed to Chrysippus by name, and it is absent from
the accounts of Stoic ethics in Stobaeus and Cicero, *Fin.* 3. Plutarch, however, says the
Stoics are correct to give this name, and not ἀπάθειαι, to χαραί, βουλήσεις, and
εὐλάβειαι, *Virt. mor.* 449B. Cicero too, at *Tusc.* 4.12–14, gives a full account of the
doctrine. If Chrysippus did not authorize it in its transmitted form, he certainly
foreshadowed its account of εὐλάβεια (*SVF* 3.175). See further *SVF* 3.432–42. Since
ὁρμή is a necessary condition of any action, and the wise man's ὁρμή is *always*
φρονίμη (Stobaeus 2.69,1), one of the εὐπάθειαι should always characterize his
impulse. If, however, we can interpret the concept from Stobaeus' statements about
χαρά and εὐφροσύνη (2.69,3–4), εὐπάθειαι are not universal or permanent attributes
of all wise men. In D.L. 7.94 χαρά and εὐφροσύνη are described as ἐπιγεννήματα of
virtue. The absence of a εὐπάθεια corresponding to λυπή is due to the wise man's
never being affected by the 'presence' of κακόν; cf. Cicero, *Tusc.* 4.14. For further
discussion, see Inwood [547], 173–5.

5 εὔλογον ὄρεξιν   Is this the same as what Chrysippus calls ὁρμὴ λογικὴ ἐπί τι
ὅσον χρὴ ἥδον (*SVF* 3.463)? The use of ἥδομαι here implies that the technical
distinction between χαρά and ἡδονή is compatible with regarding the former as a
species of pleasure in ordinary language use.

Stoic ethics

G Plutarch, *Virt. mor.* 446F–447A (*SVF* 3.459, part)

(1) ἔνιοι δέ φασιν οὐχ ἕτερον εἶναι τοῦ λόγου τὸ πάθος οὐδὲ δυεῖν διαφορὰν καὶ στάσιν, ἀλλ᾽ ἑνὸς λόγου τροπὴν ἐπ᾽ ἀμφότερα, λανθάνουσαν ἡμᾶς ὀξύτητι καὶ τάχει μεταβολῆς, (2) οὐ συνορῶντας ὅτι ταὐτόν ἐστι τῆς ψυχῆς ᾧ πέφυκεν ἐπιθυμεῖν καὶ μετανοεῖν, ὀργίζεσθαι καὶ δεδιέναι, φέρεσθαι πρὸς τὸ αἰσχρὸν ὑφ᾽ ἡδονῆς καὶ φερομένης πάλιν αὐτῆς 5 ἐπιλαμβάνεσθαι· (3) καὶ γὰρ ἐπιθυμίαν καὶ ὀργὴν καὶ φόβον καὶ τὰ τοιαῦτα πάντα δόξας εἶναι καὶ κρίσεις πονηράς, οὐ περὶ ἕν τι γινομένας τῆς ψυχῆς μέρος, ἀλλ᾽ ὅλου τοῦ ἡγεμονικοῦ ῥοπὰς καὶ εἴξεις καὶ συγκαταθέσεις καὶ ὁρμὰς καὶ ὅλως ἐνεργείας τινὰς οὔσας ἐν ὀλίγῳ μεταπτωτάς, ὥσπερ αἱ τῶν παίδων ἐπιδρομαὶ τὸ ῥαγδαῖον καὶ τὸ σφοδρὸν ἐπισφαλὲς 10 ὑπ᾽ ἀσθενείας καὶ ἀβέβαιον ἔχουσι.

4 ᾧ vel ὃ codd.   5 φερομένης codd.: φερομένη Arnim   αὐτῆς Pohlenz: ἑαυτῆς G: αὐτῆς cett.

Context: a few pages after **61B** and continuing the same subject.
2 **τροπήν** Cf. **61B** 29.
6–11 Cf. Cicero, *Acad.* 1.39, reporting Zeno, especially *perturbationes voluntarias esse putabat*.

H Galen, *Plac.* 3.1.25 (*SVF* 2.886, part)

"κοινῇ δέ μοι δοκοῦσιν οἱ πολλοὶ φέρεσθαι ἐπὶ τοῦτο ὡσανεὶ συναισθανό-μενοι περὶ τὸν θώρακα αὐτοῖς τῶν κατὰ τὴν διάνοιαν παθῶν γιγνομένων καὶ μάλιστα καθ᾽ ὃν ἡ καρδία τέτακται τόπον, οἷον μάλιστα ἐπὶ τῶν λυπῶν καὶ τῶν φόβων καὶ ἐπὶ τῆς ὀργῆς καὶ μάλιστα τοῦ θυμοῦ."

1 κοινῇ vel κοινοὶ codd.   πολλοί Ricci: λοιποὶ codd.   2 αὑτοῖς Einarson: αὐτοῖς codd.

Context: quotation from book 1 of Chrysippus, *On soul*.

I Galen, *Plac.* 5.6.34–7 (Posidonius frr. 33, 166, part)

(1) καὶ γὰρ καὶ τοῦτο δείκνυσιν ἐν τοῖς ἑξῆς ὁ Ποσειδώνιος – οὐ τοῖς φαινομένοις μόνοις ἀλλὰ καὶ Ζήνωνι καὶ Κλεάνθει διαφέρεται. (2) τὴν μὲν οὖν τοῦ Κλεάνθους γνώμην ὑπὲρ τοῦ παθητικοῦ τῆς ψυχῆς ἐκ τῶνδε φαίνεσθαί φησι τῶν ἐπῶν·

> τί ποτ᾽ ἔσθ᾽ ὃ βούλει, θυμέ; τοῦτό μοι φράσον.   5
> ἐγώ, λογισμέ; πᾶν ὃ βούλομαι ποιεῖν.
> ⟨ἦ⟩ βασιλικόν γε· πλὴν ὅμως εἶπον πάλιν.
> ὡς ἂν ἐπιθυμῶ, ταῦθ᾽ ὅπως γενήσεται.

(3) ταυτὶ τὰ ἀμοιβαῖα Κλεάνθους φησὶν εἶναι Ποσειδώνιος ἐναργῶς ἐνδεικνύμενα τὴν περὶ τοῦ παθητικοῦ τῆς ψυχῆς γνώμην αὐτοῦ, εἴ γε δὴ 10 πεποίηκε τὸν λογισμὸν τῷ θυμῷ διαλεγόμενον ὡς ἕτερον ἑτέρῳ. (4) ὁ δὲ Χρύσιππος οὔθ᾽ ἕτερον εἶναι νομίζει τὸ παθητικὸν τῆς ψυχῆς τοῦ

λογιστικοῦ καὶ τῶν ἀλόγων ζῴων ἀφαιρεῖται τὰ πάθη φανερῶς ἐπιθυμίᾳ
τε καὶ θυμῷ διοικουμένων, ὡς καὶ ὁ Ποσειδώνιος ὑπὲρ αὐτῶν ἐπὶ πλέον
διεξέρχεται.　　15

3 οὖν om. H　τοῦ om. L　5 ὃ H(corr.): ὅτε H: ὅτι Ald.　6 ἐγώ codd.: λέγω Powell　7 ⟨ἢ⟩
Powell　8 ὡς codd.: ὧν Cornarius: ὅσ᾽ Wyttenbach　10 ἐνδεικνύμενα Bake: -ος codd.　14 ὁ
om. H

Context: Posidonius' account of the abatement of passions.
2 **φαινομένοις** The 'facts' as explained in **P**.

J Galen, *Plac.* 4.2.10–18 (*SVF* 3.462, part)

(1) "δεῖ δὲ πρῶτον ἐντεθυμῆσθαι ὅτι τὸ λογικὸν ζῷον ἀκολουθητικὸν φύσει
ἐστὶ τῷ λόγῳ καὶ κατὰ τὸν λόγον ὡς ἂν ἡγεμόνα πρακτικόν. (2) πολλάκις
μέντοι καὶ ἄλλως φέρεται ἐπί τινα καὶ ἀπό τινων ἀπειθῶς τῷ λόγῳ
ὠθούμενον ἐπὶ πλεῖον, (3) καθ᾽ ἣν φορὰν ἀμφότεροι ἔχουσιν οἱ ὅροι, τῆς
παρὰ φύσιν κινήσεως ἀλόγως οὕτως γινομένης καὶ τοῦ ἐν ταῖς ὁρμαῖς　5
πλεονασμοῦ. (4) τὸ γὰρ ἄλογον τουτὶ ληπτέον ἀπειθὲς λόγῳ καὶ
ἀπεστραμμένον τὸν λόγον, καθ᾽ ἣν φορὰν καὶ ἐν τῷ ἔθει τινάς φαμεν
ὠθεῖσθαι καὶ ἀλόγως φέρεσθαι ἄνευ λόγου ⟨καὶ⟩ κρίσεως· ⟨οὐ γὰρ⟩ ὡς εἰ
διημαρτημένως φέρεται καὶ παριδών τι κατὰ τὸν λόγον, ταῦτ᾽ ἐπισημαι-
νόμεθα, ἀλλὰ μάλιστα καθ᾽ ἣν ὑπογράφει φοράν, οὐ πεφυκότος τοῦ　10
λογικοῦ ζῴου κινεῖσθαι οὕτως κατὰ τὴν ψυχήν, ἀλλὰ κατὰ τὸν λόγον." ἡ
μὲν οὖν ἑτέρα τῶν τοῦ Χρυσίππου ῥήσεων ἐξηγουμένη τὸν πρότερον τῶν ὅρων τοῦ πάθους
ἐνταυθοῖ τελευτᾷ. τὴν δ᾽ ὑπόλοιπον ἐν ᾗ τὸν ἕτερον ὅρον ἐξηγεῖται γεγραμμένην ἐφεξῆς
τῇδε κατὰ τὸ πρῶτον σύγγραμμα Περὶ παθῶν ἤδη σοι παραθήσομαι· (5) "κατὰ τοῦτο
δὲ καὶ ὁ πλεονασμὸς τῆς ὁρμῆς εἴρηται, διὰ τὸ τὴν καθ᾽ αὐτοὺς καὶ　15
φυσικὴν τῶν ὁρμῶν συμμετρίαν ὑπερβαίνειν. (6) γένοιτο δ᾽ ἂν τὸ
λεγόμενον διὰ τούτων γνωριμώτερον, οἷον ἐπὶ τοῦ πορεύεσθαι καθ᾽ ὁρμὴν
οὐ πλεονάζει ἡ τῶν σκελῶν κίνησις ἀλλὰ συναπαρτίζει τι τῇ ὁρμῇ ὥστε
καὶ στῆναι, ὅταν ἐθέλῃ, καὶ μεταβάλλειν. (7) ἐπὶ δὲ τῶν τρεχόντων καθ᾽
ὁρμὴν οὐκέτι τοιοῦτον γίνεται, ἀλλὰ πλεονάζει παρὰ τὴν ὁρμὴν ἡ τῶν　20
σκελῶν κίνησις ὥστε ἐκφέρεσθαι καὶ μὴ μεταβάλλειν εὐπειθῶς οὕτως
εὐθὺς ἐναρξαμένων. (8) αἷς οἶμαί τι παραπλήσιον καὶ ἐπὶ τῶν ὁρμῶν
γίνεσθαι διὰ τὸ τὴν κατὰ λόγον ὑπερβαίνειν συμμετρίαν, ὥσθ᾽ ὅταν ὁρμᾷ
μὴ εὐπειθῶς ἔχειν πρὸς αὐτόν, (9) ἐπὶ μὲν τοῦ δρόμου τοῦ πλεονασμοῦ
λεγομένου παρὰ τὴν ὁρμήν, ἐπὶ δὲ τῆς ὁρμῆς παρὰ τὸν λόγον. συμμετρία　25
γάρ ἐστι φυσικῆς ὁρμῆς ἡ κατὰ τὸν λόγον καὶ ἕως τοσούτου ⟨οὗ⟩ [καὶ ἕως]
αὐτὸς ἀξιοῖ. διὸ δὴ καὶ τῆς ὑπερβάσεως κατὰ τοῦτο καὶ οὕτως γινομένης πλεονάζουσά
τε ὁρμὴ λέγεται εἶναι καὶ παρὰ φύσιν καὶ ἄλογος κίνησις ψυχῆς."

8 ⟨καὶ⟩ Petersen ⟨οὐ γὰρ⟩ De Lacy　10 ὑπογράφει codd.: ὑπογράφομεν Müller　18 τῇ ὁρμῇ
Müller: τῆς ὁρμῆς codd.　26 οὗ suppl., καὶ ἕως del. A.A. Long et C. Murgia: καὶ del. Müller

Context: a few lines after **D**. Galen takes Chrysippus to be implying that the soul

409

Stoic ethics

contains an irrational faculty analogous to a runner's weight (cf. *Plac.* 4.2.32). With 1–
4, cf. **A 1, 6–7**.

3 **φέρεται–τινων** Referring to the standard account of action caused by impulse
or repulsion; cf. **53P–Q**.

10 **ὑπογράφει** If the text is sound, it is best to take the subject as 'the expressions'
ὠθεῖσθαι–κρίσεως, 8.

16 **συμμετρίαν** Cf. Epictetus, *Diss.* 4.1.84 on having an ὄρεξις which is
σύμμετρος.

K Galen, *Plac.* 4.3.2–5 (Posidonius fr. 34, part)

(1) καὶ γὰρ Ζήνωνι κατά γε τοῦτο καὶ ἑαυτῷ καὶ πολλοῖς ἄλλοις μάχεται
τῶν Στωικῶν, οἳ οὐ τὰς κρίσεις αὐτὰς τῆς ψυχῆς ἀλλὰ καὶ τὰς ἐπὶ ταύταις
ἀλόγους συστολὰς καὶ ταπεινώσεις καὶ δήξεις ἐπάρσεις τε καὶ διαχύσεις
ὑπολαμβάνουσιν εἶναι τὰ τῆς ψυχῆς πάθη. (2) Ποσειδώνιος μέν γε τελέως
ἀπεχώρησεν ἀμφοτέρων τῶν δοξῶν· οὔτε γὰρ κρίσεις οὔτε ἐπιγιγνόμενα   5
κρίσεσιν, ἀλλ' ὑπὸ τῆς θυμοειδοῦς τε καὶ ἐπιθυμητικῆς δυνάμεως ἡγεῖται
γίγνεσθαι τὰ πάθη κατὰ πᾶν ἀκολουθήσας τῷ παλαιῷ λόγῳ. (3) καὶ
πυνθάνεταί γε τῶν περὶ τὸν Χρύσιππον οὐκ ὀλιγάκις ἐν τῇ Περὶ παθῶν
ἑαυτοῦ πραγματείᾳ, "τίς ἡ τῆς πλεοναζούσης ὁρμῆς ἐστιν αἰτία; ὁ μὲν γὰρ
λόγος οὐκ ἂν δύναιτό γε πλεονάζειν παρὰ τὰ ἑαυτοῦ πράγματά τε καὶ   10
μέτρα. πρόδηλον οὖν ὡς ἑτέρα τις ἄλογός ἐστι δύναμις αἰτία τοῦ
πλεονάζεσθαι τὴν ὁρμὴν ὑπὲρ τὰ μέτρα τοῦ λόγου, καθάπερ τοῦ
πλεονάζεσθαι τὸν δρόμον ὑπὲρ τὰ μέτρα τῆς προαιρέσεως ἄλογος ἡ αἰτία,
τὸ βάρος τοῦ σώματος."

8 τῶν Kidd: τοὺς codd.

Context: shortly after **J**.

1 **Ζήνωνι** Pohlenz [335], 188–93, found support here for his view that Zeno and
Cleanthes (cf. **I**) regarded the πάθη as quite independent of λόγος, i.e. ἄλογοι
κινήσεις in an unqualified sense of ἄλογος which Chrysippus modified. The recent
tendency has been to minimize the differences between the two Stoics. Cf. Rist [303],
28–33; Lloyd [596], 239–41.

9 **L and N** bear on Posidonius' question.

13 **δρόμον** Taking up Chrysippus' analogy in **J 6–9**.

L Galen, *Plac.* 4.5.21–6 (*SVF* 3.480, part)

(1) "οὐ γὰρ ἐν τῷ κρίνειν ἀγαθὰ ἕκαστα τούτων λέγεται ἀρρωστήματα
ταῦτα, ἀλλὰ καὶ κατὰ τὸ ἐπὶ πλέον ἐκπεπτωκέναι πρὸς ταῦτα τοῦ κατὰ
φύσιν." . . . (2) ὡς εἰ καὶ οὕτως ἔλεγεν, ἀρρωστήματα γίνεσθαι κατὰ τὴν ψυχὴν
οὐχ ἁπλῶς τῷ ψευδῶς ὑπειληφέναι περί τινων ὡς ἀγαθῶν ἢ κακῶν, ἀλλὰ τῷ μέγιστα
νομίζειν αὐτά· μηδέπω γὰρ ἀρρώστημα τὴν περὶ τῶν χρημάτων εἶναι δόξαν   5
ὡς ἀγαθῶν, ἀλλ' ἐπειδάν τις αὐτὰ μέγιστον ἀγαθὸν εἶναι νομίζῃ καὶ μηδὲ
ζῆν ἄξιον ὑπολαμβάνῃ τῷ στερηθέντι χρημάτων· ἐν τούτῳ γὰρ συνίστασ-

410

65 The passions

θαι τήν τε φιλοχρηματίαν καὶ τὴν φιλαργυρίαν ἀρρωστήματα οὔσας. ἀλλὰ
τῷ ταῦτα φάσκοντι Ποσειδώνιος ἀντιλέγων ὡδέ πώς φησι· "τοιούτων δ' ὑπὸ τοῦ
Χρυσίππου λεγομένων . . ."   10

7 ὑπολαμβάνῃ Kühn: -οι codd.

Context: the alleged inconsistency of Chrysippus' statement in 1–3 with his thesis that
the πάθη are κρίσεις.
3–8   These lines seem to report a Chrysippean position (cf. 9–10) though
expressed as only a possible interpretation of his words (cf. ἴσως ἄν τις φήσειε, two
lines before ὡς εἰ . . .).
8 ἀρρωστήματα   Cf. S 2–3, and Seneca, Ep. 75.11–12, distinguishing adfectus
from morbus.

M Galen, Plac. 5.5.8–26 (Posidonius fr. 169, part)
(1) τριῶν οὖν τούτων ἡμῖν οἰκειώσεων ὑπαρχουσῶν φύσει καθ' ἕκαστον
τῶν μορίων τῆς ψυχῆς εἶδος, πρὸς μὲν τὴν ἡδονὴν διὰ τὸ ἐπιθυμητικόν,
πρὸς δὲ τὴν νίκην διὰ τὸ θυμοειδές, πρὸς δὲ τὸ καλὸν διὰ τὸ λογιστικόν, (2)
Ἐπίκουρος μὲν τὴν τοῦ χειρίστου μορίου τῆς ψυχῆς οἰκείωσιν ἐθεάσατο
μόνην, ὁ δὲ Χρύσιππος τὴν τοῦ βελτίστου, φάμενος ἡμᾶς οἰκειοῦσθαι πρὸς   5
μόνον τὸ καλόν, ὅπερ εἶναι δηλονότι καὶ ἀγαθόν. (3) ἐάσας οὖν τὰς δύο ὁ
Χρύσιππος εἰκότως ἀπορεῖ περὶ τῆς κατὰ τὴν κακίαν γενέσεως οὔτ' αἰτίαν
ἔχων εἰπεῖν αὐτῆς οὔτε τρόπους τῆς συστάσεως οὔθ' ὅπως ἁμαρτάνει τὰ παιδία
δυνάμενος ἐξευρεῖν, ἅπερ εὐλόγως οἶμαι πάντα καὶ ὁ Ποσειδώνιος αὐτοῦ
καταμέμφεται καὶ ἐλέγχει. (4) εἰ γὰρ δὴ πρὸς τὸ καλὸν εὐθὺς ἐξ ἀρχῆς   10
ᾠκείωται τὰ παιδία, τὴν κακίαν οὐκ ἔνδοθεν οὐδ' ἐξ ἑαυτῶν ἀλλ' ἔξωθεν
μόνον ἐχρῆν αὐτοῖς ἐγγίγνεσθαι. ἀλλὰ μὴν ὁρᾶταί γε, κἂν χρηστοῖς ἔθεσιν
ἐντρέφηται καὶ προσηκόντως παιδεύηται, πάντως ἐξαμαρτάνοντά τι, καὶ
τοῦτ' αὐτὸ καὶ ὁ Χρύσιππος ὁμολογεῖ. (5) καίτοι γ' ἐνῆν αὐτῷ ὑπεριδόντι
τῶν ἐναργῶς φαινομένων αὐτὸ μόνον ὁμολογῆσαι τὸ ταῖς ἰδίαις ὑποθέσε-   15
σιν ἀκόλουθον, εἰ καλῶς ἀχθείη τὰ παιδία, πάντως αὐτὰ φάσκοντι σοφοὺς
ἄνδρας γενήσεσθαι τοῦ χρόνου προιόντος. (6) ἀλλ' οὐκ ἐτόλμησε τοῦτό γε
καταψεύσασθαι τῶν φαινομένων, ἀλλὰ κἂν ὑπὸ φιλοσόφῳ τρέφηται μόνῳ
καὶ μηδὲν μήτε θεάσηται μήτ' ἀκούσῃ πώποτε παράδειγμα κακίας, ὅμως
οὐκ ἐξ ἀνάγκης αὐτὰ φιλοσοφήσειν . . . (7) ἐπειδὰν γὰρ λέγῃ τὰς περὶ   20
ἀγαθῶν καὶ κακῶν ἐγγίνεσθαι τοῖς φαύλοις διαστροφὰς διά τε τὴν
πιθανότητα τῶν φαντασιῶν καὶ τὴν κατήχησιν, ἐρωτητέον αὐτὸν τὴν
αἰτίαν δι' ἣν ἡδονὴ μὲν ὡς ἀγαθὸν ἀλγηδὼν δ' ὡς κακὸν πιθανὴν
προβάλλουσι φαντασίαν. οὕτως δὲ καὶ διὰ τί τὴν μὲν νίκην τὴν ἐν
Ὀλυμπίασιν καὶ τὴν τῶν ἀνδριάντων ἀνάθεσιν ἐπαινούμενά τε καὶ   25
μακαριζόμενα πρὸς τῶν πολλῶν ἀκούοντες ὡς ἀγαθά, περὶ δὲ τῆς ἥττης τε
καὶ τῆς ἀτιμίας ὡς κακῶν, ἑτοίμως πειθόμεθα; (8) καὶ γὰρ καὶ ταῦθ' ὁ
Ποσειδώνιος μέμφεται καὶ δεικνύναι πειρᾶται πασῶν τῶν ψευδῶν ὑπολήψεων τὰς
αἰτίας ἐν μὲν τῷ θεωρητικῷ διὰ τῆς παθητικῆς ὁλκῆς, προηγεῖσθαι δ' αὐτῆς τὰς ψευδεῖς

411

Stoic ethics

δόξας ἀσθενήσαντος περὶ τὴν κρίσιν τοῦ λογιστικοῦ· γεννᾶσθαι γὰρ τῷ ζῴῳ τὴν   30
ὁρμὴν ἐνίοτε μὲν ἐπὶ τῇ τοῦ λογιστικοῦ κρίσει, πολλάκις δ' ἐπὶ τῇ κινήσει
τοῦ παθητικοῦ. (9) συνάπτει δ' εἰκότως τοῖς λόγοις τούτοις ὁ Ποσειδώνιος
τὰ κατὰ τὸν φυσιογνώμονα φαινόμενα· καὶ γὰρ τῶν ζῴων καὶ τῶν
ἀνθρώπων ὅσα μὲν εὐρύστερνά τε καὶ θερμότερα θυμικώτερα πάνθ'
ὑπάρχει⟨ν⟩ φύσει, ὅσα δὲ πλατυίσχιά τε καὶ ψυχρότερα δειλότερα. (10)   35
καὶ κατὰ τὰς χώρας δὲ οὐ σμικρῷ τινι διενηνοχέναι τοῖς ἤθεσι τοὺς
ἀνθρώπους εἰς δειλίαν καὶ τόλμαν ἢ τὸ φιλήδονόν τε καὶ φιλόπονον, ὡς τῶν
παθητικῶν κινήσεων τῆς ψυχῆς ἑπομένων ἀεὶ τῇ διαθέσει τοῦ σώματος,
ἣν ἐκ τῆς κατὰ τὸ περιέχον κράσεως οὐ κατ' ὀλίγον ἀλλοιοῦσθαι. καὶ γὰρ
δὴ καὶ τὸ αἷμα διαφέρειν ἐν τοῖς ζῴοις φησὶ θερμότητι καὶ ψυχρότητι καὶ   40
πάχει καὶ λεπτότητι καὶ ἄλλαις [φησὶ] διαφοραῖς οὐκ ὀλίγαις, ὑπὲρ ὧν
Ἀριστοτέλης ἐπὶ πλεῖστον διῆλθεν. ἡμεῖς δὲ κατὰ τὸν οἰκεῖον καιρὸν ἐπὶ
προήκοντι τῷ λόγῳ μνημονεύσομεν αὐτῶν, ἡνίκα ἂν καὶ αὐτὰς τὰς Ἱπποκράτους τε καὶ
Πλάτωνος ῥήσεις περὶ τούτων παραγράφωμεν. (11) ἐν δὲ τῷ παρόντι πρὸς τοὺς
περὶ τὸν Χρύσιππον ὁ λόγος ἐνέστηκέ μοι μήτ' ἄλλο τι γιγνώσκοντας τῶν   45
κατὰ τὰ πάθη μήθ' ὡς αἱ τοῦ σώματος κράσεις οἰκείας ἑαυταῖς ἐργάζονται
τὰς παθητικὰς κινήσεις· οὕτως γὰρ ὁ Ποσειδώνιος ὀνομάζειν εἴωθεν.

5 οἰκειοῦσθαι Bas.: οἰκειῶσθαι H: ὠκειῶσθαι L   7 ἀπορεῖ περὶ Diels: ἀπορεῖν ἐρεῖ codd.   καὶ
ἐλέγχει H: τε καὶ λέγει L   12 γε H: τε L   14 καὶ om. L   γ' ἐνῆν H: γέγονεν L   19 ἀκούσῃ
Kühn: ἀκούσειε H: ἀκούσῃ μήτε L   ὅμως H: ὅπως L   20 τὰς H: τίς L   21 ἀγαθῶν καὶ κακῶν
H: ἀγαθοῦ καὶ κακοῦ L   27 κακῶν Müller: κακὰ codd.   29 θεωρηματικῶ L   θεωρητικῶ L
⟨σκέμματι γινομένων διὰ τῆς ἀμαθίας, ἐν δὲ τῷ πρακτικῷ⟩ Edelstein/Kidd: θεωρητικῷ ⟨γίγνεσθαι δι'
ἀμαθίας, ἐν δὲ τῷ πρακτικῷ⟩ De Lacy   αὐτῆς H: αὐταῖς L   30 ἀσθενήσαντος L: -τας H   33
τὸν φυσιογνώμονα H: τὴν φυσιογνωμονίαν L   35 ὑπάρχει⟨ν⟩ Kühn: -ει codd.   41 φησι del.
Müller   43 αὐτὰς Kühn: ταύτας codd.   44 παραγράφωμεν Ald.: περιγράφωμεν codd.   46
κράσεις H: κρίσεις L

Context: exposition of the soul's tripartite nature, and criticism of Chrysippus' denial
of this.

1–3   For Galen's dependence on Posidonius here, cf. *Plac.* 4.7.35 and N.

20–2 τὰς ... διαστροφὰς ... κατήχησιν The standard Chrysippean doctrine; cf. *SVF* 3.228–36, especially 229, which answers Posidonius' question in 22–4,
and Long [531], 336–7.

28–30   The text of these important lines is so obscure that we omit them from
vol. 1. Posidonius wishes to show why Chrysippus' account of the external source of
false value judgements is inadequate. His own answer, as sketched in K 3 (cf. N, P 1),
is to invoke the 'pull' of the irrational faculties of soul – hence παθητικὴ ὁλκή. 29–30
recalls his formulation of the τέλος. Cf. 63J, 64I; and Galen, *Plac.* 5.6.4–5, especially
τὸ δὴ τῶν παθῶν αἴτιον ... κατὰ μηδὲν ἄγεσθαι ὑπὸ τοῦ ἀλόγου ... τῆς ψυχῆς.
Since Posidonius wants completely to reject the view that the passions have any
rational foundation, or result from false judgements (cf. K 2), it is hard to make any
sense of 29–30, 'false opinions precede the pull of passion', even with the lacuna and
supplements (see ap. crit.) suggested after θεωρητικῷ. Nor can we conjecture what
that term signifies here.

42   Posidonius had the reputation of 'Aristotelizing' (Strabo 2.3.8); cf. Kidd [379],
210–11.

N Galen, *Plac.* 5.6.18–19 (Posidonius fr. 161, part)

"καὶ τὰς ἀρχὰς δὲ τῆς ἐν τοῖς αἱρετοῖς τε καὶ φευκτοῖς διαστροφῆς ἐδίδαξεν ἡ αἰτία τῶν παθῶν εὑρεθεῖσα." τὰ γὰρ οἰκεῖα ταῖς ἀλόγοις δυνάμεσι τῆς ψυχῆς ἐξαπατώμενοί τινες ὡς ἁπλῶς οἰκεῖα δοξάζουσιν οὐκ εἰδότες ὡς τὸ μὲν ἥδεσθαί τε καὶ τὸ κρατεῖν τῶν πέλας τοῦ ζωώδους τῆς ψυχῆς ἐστιν ὀρεκτά, σοφία δὲ καὶ πᾶν ὅσον ἀγαθόν τε καὶ καλὸν ἅμα τοῦ λογικοῦ τε καὶ θείου. 5

Context: a few lines after **64I**.

O Galen, *Plac.* 4.7.12–17 (*SVF* 3.466, part)

ὅτι δ' ἐν τῷ χρόνῳ μαλάττεται τὰ πάθη, κἂν αἱ δόξαι μένωσι τοῦ κακόν τι αὐτοῖς γεγονέναι, καὶ ὁ Χρύσιππος ἐν τῷ δευτέρῳ Περὶ παθῶν μαρτυρεῖ γράφων ὧδε· (1) "ζητῆσαι δ' ἄν τις καὶ περὶ τῆς ἀνέσεως τῆς λύπης, πῶς γίνεται, πότερον δόξης τινὸς μετακινουμένης ἢ πασῶν διαμενουσῶν, καὶ διὰ τί τοῦτ' ἔσται." εἶτ' ἐπιφέρων φησί, (2) "δοκεῖ δέ μοι ἡ μὲν τοιαύτη δόξα διαμένειν, ὅτι κακὸν 5 αὐτὸ ὃ δὴ πάρεστιν, ἐγχρονιζομένης δ' ἀνίεσθαι ἡ συστολὴ καὶ ὡς οἶμαι ἡ ἐπὶ τὴν συστολὴν ὁρμή. (3) τυχὸν δὲ καὶ ταύτης διαμενούσης οὐχ ὑπακούσεται τὰ ἑξῆς, διὰ ποιὰν ἄλλην ἐπιγινομένην διάθεσιν ἀσυλλόγιστον τούτων γινομένων. (4) οὕτω γὰρ καὶ κλαίοντες παύονται καὶ μὴ βουλόμενοι κλαίειν κλαίουσιν, ὅταν μὴ ὁμοίας τὰς φαντασίας τὰ 10 ὑποκείμενα ποιῇ καὶ ἐνιστῆταί τι ἢ μηθέν. ὃν τρόπον γὰρ ἡ θρήνων παῦσις γίνεται καὶ κλαυθμοί, τοιαῦτα εὔλογον καὶ ἐπ' ἐκείνων συντυγχάνειν ἐν ταῖς ἀρχαῖς μᾶλλον τῶν πραγμάτων κινούντων, καθάπερ ἐπὶ τῶν τὸν γέλωτα κινούντων γίνεσθαι ἔφην, καὶ τὰ ὅμοια τούτοις."

8–9 ἀσυλλόγιστον Müller: δισυλλόγιστον vel sim. codd.: δυσσυλλόγιστον Pohlenz   10 μὴ secl. Ricci

Context: Posidonius' refutations of Chrysippus.

5–11   Obscure text and train of thought. In 5–7 Chrysippus appears to take up his first alternative in 3–4, δόξης τινὸς μετακινουμένης, identifying the 'impulse to the contraction' with an opinion that alters. In 7–9, where ταύτης should refer to ἡ ἐπὶ τὴν συστολὴν ὁρμή, he takes up the second alternative in 4, πασῶν [δοξῶν] διαμενουσῶν. τὰ ἑξῆς, 8, then, should refer to the contraction itself, which 'will not correspond' (οὐχ ὑπακούσεται) with the impulse (cf. *Plac.* 4.7.36, where Posidonius denies this possibility). Thus, if the passionate mental state were represented as 'here is something very bad, therefore I should contract (feel depressed)', the depression fails to occur owing to a different διάθεσις which does not draw the inference necessary to produce the passion. Some such thought seems required by 8–9, where Müller's ἀσυλλόγιστον (cf. **P** 7, and **36A** 21 for its technical sense) fits the change of emotional state exemplified in 9–11. Galen (4.7.19) claims that Chrysippus confessed to finding the cause of the abatement of passion δυσλόγιστον, but this, we suggest, is a polemical misrepresentation of whatever -λογιστος word Chrysippus used in 8.

10 μή   Omitted in the repetition of these lines at 4.7.37; but what explains the change of emotional state must be the occurrence of impressions *not* similar to those which prompted the passion.

Stoic ethics

P Galen, *Plac.* 4.7.24–41 (Posidonius fr. 165, part)

(1) αὐτός τε δείκνυσιν ὡς ὑπὸ θυμοῦ καὶ ἐπιθυμίας γίγνεται τὰ πάθη καὶ διὰ τίνα τὴν αἰτίαν ἐν τῷ χρόνῳ καθίσταται, κἂν αἱ δόξαι τε καὶ αἱ κρίσεις ἔτι μένωσι τοῦ κακὸν ὑπάρχειν αὐτοῖς ἢ γεγονέναι . . . (2) ὡς γὰρ ἐφίεται τὸ παθητικὸν τῆς ψυχῆς οἰκείων τινῶν ὀρεκτῶν, οὕτως καὶ τυγχάνον αὐτῶν ἐμπίπλαται κἂν τούτῳ τὴν ἑαυτοῦ κίνησιν καθίστησιν, ἥτις ἐκράτει   5
τῆς ὁρμῆς τοῦ ζῴου καὶ καθ' ἑαυτὴν ἦγεν ἐφ' ὅ τι παρήγετο. (3) οὔκουν ἀσυλλόγιστοι τῆς παύλης τῶν παθῶν εἰσιν αἱ αἰτίαι, καθάπερ ὁ Χρύσιππος ἔλεγεν . . . (4) διὰ τοῦτο τοίνυν καὶ τὰ ἔθη φαίνεται πλεῖστον δυνάμενα καὶ ὅλως ὁ χρόνος εἰς τὰς παθητικὰς κινήσεις. ἐν μὲν γὰρ τοῖς ἔθεσιν οἰκειοῦται κατὰ βραχὺ τὸ τῆς ψυχῆς ἄλογον οἷς ἂν ἐντρέφηται.   10

4 ὀρεκτῶν Μ: ὀρεκτικῶν Η   τυγχάνον De Lacy: τυγχανόντων καὶ τυγχανόντων codd.   5 ἑαυτοῦ Müller: ἑαυτῶν codd.   9 ὅλως Pohlenz: ὅλος codd.

Context: Posidonius' response to Chrysippus in **O**.

Q Galen, *Plac.* 5.6.22–6 (including Posidonius fr. 162)

(1) τῷ μὲν γὰρ ἀλόγῳ διὰ τῶν ἀλόγων ἥ τε ὠφέλεια καὶ ἡ βλάβη, τῷ λογικῷ δὲ δι' ἐπιστήμης τε καὶ ἀμαθίας. (2) καὶ ταῦτ' οὖν ἐκ τῆς τῶν παθῶν αἰτίας γνωσθείσης ὠφελεῖσθαί φησιν ἡμᾶς ὁ Ποσειδώνιος καὶ προσέτι "τὰ διαπορούμενα", φησί, "περὶ τῆς ἐκ πάθους ὁρμῆς ἐξέφηνεν." εἶτ' αὐτὸς ἅττα ποτ' αὐτά ἐστιν ἐπιφέρων ἐξηγεῖται τόνδε τὸν τρόπον· (3) "οἶμαι γὰρ   5
ὅτι πάλαι βλέπετε πῶς διὰ λόγου μὲν πεισθέντες κακὸν ἑαυτοῖς παρεῖναι ἢ ἐπιφέρεσθαι οὔτε φοβοῦνται οὔτε λυποῦνται, φαντασίας δ' ἐκείνων αὐτῶν λαμβάνοντες. (4) πῶς γὰρ ἄν τις λόγῳ κινήσειε τὸ ἄλογον, ἐὰν μή τινα ἀναζωγράφησιν προσβάληται αἰσθητῇ παραπλησίαν; οὕτως γοῦν ἐκ διηγήσεώς τινες εἰς ἐπιθυμίαν ἐκπίπτουσιν καὶ ἐναργῶς ἐγκελευσαμένου   10
φεύγειν τὸν ἐπιφερόμενον λέοντα οὐκ ἰδόντες φοβοῦνται."

4 ἐκ πάθους Η: ἐμφανοῦς L   5 αὐτά om. L   8 λαμβάνοντες L: -ονται Η   λόγῳ Η: λόγος L

Context: a few lines after **N**.
For discussion, cf. Kidd [379], 205–6.

R Galen, *Plac.* 5.2.3–7 (Posidonius fr. 163, part)

(1) Χρύσιππος μὲν γὰρ ἀνάλογον ἔχειν αὐτήν φησι τοῖς ἐπιτηδείοις σώμασιν εἰς πυρετοὺς ἐμπίπτειν ἢ διαρροίας ἤ τι τοιοῦτον ἕτερον ἐπὶ μικρᾷ καὶ τυχούσῃ προφάσει. (2) καὶ μέμφεταί γε ὁ Ποσειδώνιος αὐτοῦ τὴν εἰκόνα· χρῆναι γάρ φησιν οὐ τούτοις ἀλλὰ τοῖς ἁπλῶς ὑγιαίνουσι σώμασιν εἰκάσαι τὴν τῶν φαύλων ψυχήν· (3) εἴτε γὰρ ἐπὶ μεγάλοις αἰτίοις   5
εἴτ' ἐπὶ μικροῖς πυρέττοιεν οὐδὲν διαφέρειν ὡς πρὸς τὸ πάσχειν τε αὐτὰ καὶ εἰς πάθος ἄγεσθαι καθ' ὁτιοῦν, ἀλλὰ τῷ τὰ μὲν εὐέμπτωτα εἶναι τὰ δὲ δύσπτωτα διαφέρειν ἀλλήλων. (4) οὔκουν ὀρθῶς εἰκάζεσθαί φησιν ὑπὸ τοῦ

Χρυσίππου τὴν μὲν ὑγίειαν τῆς ψυχῆς τῇ τοῦ σώματος ὑγιείᾳ, τὴν δὲ νόσον
τῇ ῥᾳδίως εἰς νόσημα ἐμπιπτούσῃ καταστάσει τοῦ σώματος· ἀπαθῆ μὲν   10
γὰρ γίγνεσθαι ψυχὴν τὴν τοῦ σοφοῦ δηλονότι, σῶμα δ' οὐδὲν ὑπάρχειν
ἀπαθές· (5) ἀλλὰ δικαιότερον εἶναι προσεικάζειν τὰς τῶν φαύλων ψυχὰς
"ἤτοι τῇ σωματικῇ ὑγιείᾳ ἐχούσῃ τὸ εὐέμπτωτον εἰς νόσον" – οὕτω γὰρ
ὠνόμασεν ὁ Ποσειδώνιος – "ἢ αὐτῇ τῇ νόσῳ", εἶναι γὰρ ἤτοι νοσώδη τινὰ
ἕξιν ἢ ἤδη νοσοῦσαν. (6) συμφέρεται μέντοι τῷ Χρυσίππῳ καὶ αὐτὸς ὡς   15
νοσεῖν τε λέγειν τὴν ψυχὴν ἅπαντας τοὺς φαύλους ἐοικέναι τε τὴν νόσον
αὐτῶν ταῖς εἰρημέναις τοῦ σώματος καταστάσεσι. (7) λέγει γοῦν ὧδε κατὰ
λέξιν· "διὸ καὶ ἡ νόσος τῆς ψυχῆς ἔοικεν οὐχ ὡς ὁ Χρύσιππος ὑπείληφε τῇ
νοσώδει καχεξίᾳ τοῦ σώματος, καθ' ἣν ὑποφέρεται ῥεμβώδεσιν οὐχὶ
περιοδικοῖς οἷά τ' ἐμπίπτειν πυρετοῖς, ἀλλὰ μᾶλλον ἔοικεν ἡ ψυχικὴ νόσος   20
ἤτοι σωματικῇ ὑγιείᾳ ἐχούσῃ τὸ εὐέμπτωτον εἰς τὴν νόσον ἢ αὐτῇ τῇ
νόσῳ. ἔστι γὰρ ἡ μὲν σωματικὴ νόσος ἕξις ἤδη νοσοῦσα, ἡ δὲ ὑπὸ τοῦ
Χρυσίππου λεγομένη νόσος εὐεμπτωσίᾳ μᾶλλον ἔοικεν εἰς πυρετούς."

19 ῥεμβώδεσιν Cornarius: ῥομβώδεσιν codd.

Context: the difference between Chrysippus' and Posidonius' accounts of the souls of
the φαῦλοι.
For the ethical application of such medical analogies, cf. **610**; and for the details of
R, see Kidd [383].

S Stobaeus 2.93,1-13 (SVF 3.421)

(1) εὐεμπτωσίαν δ' εἶναι εὐκαταφορίαν εἰς πάθος, εἴς τι τῶν παρὰ φύσιν
ἔργων, οἷον ἐπιλυπίαν, ὀργιλότητα, φθονερίαν, ἀκροχολίαν καὶ τὰ ὅμοια.
γίγνεσθαι δὲ εὐεμπτωσίας καὶ εἰς ἄλλα ἔργα τῶν παρὰ φύσιν, οἷον εἰς
κλοπὰς καὶ μοιχείας καὶ ὕβρεις, καθ' ἃς κλέπται τε καὶ ὑβρισταὶ καὶ
μοιχοὶ λέγονται. (2) νόσημα δ' εἶναι δόξαν ἐπιθυμίας ἐρρυηκυῖαν εἰς ἕξιν   5
καὶ ἐνεσκιρωμένην, καθ' ἣν ὑπολαμβάνουσι τὰ μὴ αἱρετὰ σφόδρα αἱρετὰ
εἶναι, οἷον φιλογυνίαν, φιλοινίαν, φιλαργυρίαν· εἶναι δέ τινα καὶ ἐναντία
⟨τούτοις⟩ τοῖς νοσήμασι κατὰ προσκοπὴν γινόμενα, οἷον μισογυνίαν,
μισοινίαν, μισανθρωπίαν. (3) τὰ δὲ νοσήματα μετ' ἀσθενείας συμβαίνοντα
ἀρρωστήματα καλεῖσθαι.   10

8 ⟨τούτοις⟩ Heeren   προσκοπὴν F: προκοπὴν P

Context: conclusion of doxography of πάθη.
1 **εὐεμπτωσίαν** Cf. **R** 7, 21-3, and Kidd [383].
5-11 Cf. **L**, and for the terminology and examples, Cicero, Tusc. 4.23-9.

T Galen, Plac. 4.6.2-3 (SVF 3.473, part)

ὅσα γὰρ οὐκ ὀρθῶς πράττουσιν ἄνθρωποι, τὰ μὲν εἰς μοχθηρὰν κρίσιν
ἀναφέρει, τὰ δ' εἰς ἀτονίαν καὶ ἀσθένειαν τῆς ψυχῆς, ὥσπερ γε καὶ ὧν

Stoic ethics

κατορθοῦσιν ἡ ὀρθὴ κρίσις ἐξηγεῖται μετὰ τῆς κατὰ τὴν ψυχὴν εὐτονίας
... ἀφίστασθαί τέ φησιν ἔστιν ὅτε τῶν ὀρθῶς ἐγνωσμένων ἡμῖν ἐνδόντος
τοῦ τόνου τῆς ψυχῆς καὶ μὴ παραμείναντος ἕως παντὸς μηδ' ἐξυπηρετή-   5
σαντος τοῖς τοῦ λόγου προστάγμασιν.

5 μηδ' Müller: μήτ' codd.

Context: Galen takes Chrysippus' uses of the terms ἀτονία and ἀσθένεια τῆς ψυχῆς to
indicate his admitting a faculty other than the rational as the cause of the πάθη.

3 **εὐτονίας**   This defines the soul's excellence (εὐψυχία) at fulfilling its own
functions (SVF 3.270). Changes in πνεῦμα (i.e. psychic tension) are specified as the
causes of the πάθη in D.L. 7.158; cf. Lloyd [596], 242–4, and note on **61C**.

6 **προστάγμασιν**   The term recalls the accounts of ὁρμή (**53R**) and κατορθώματα (**62J** 6; SVF 3.520).

U Epictetus, *Ench.* 5

ταράσσει τοὺς ἀνθρώπους οὐ τὰ πράγματα, ἀλλὰ τὰ περὶ τῶν πραγμάτων
δόγματα· οἷον ὁ θάνατος οὐδὲν δεινόν, ἐπεὶ καὶ Σωκράτει ἂν ἐφαίνετο,
ἀλλὰ τὸ δόγμα τὸ περὶ τοῦ θανάτου, διότι δεινόν, ἐκεῖνο τὸ δεινόν ἐστιν.
ὅταν οὖν ἐμποδιζώμεθα ἢ ταρασσώμεθα ἢ λυπώμεθα, μηδέποτε ἄλλον
αἰτιώμεθα, ἀλλ' ἑαυτούς, τοῦτ' ἔστι τὰ ἑαυτῶν δόγματα.   5

A favourite theme in Epictetus; cf. Lloyd [596], 244–5; Long [385], 991–2.

V Epictetus, *Diss.* 1.12.20–1

(1) σὺ δ' ἀταλαίπωρος εἶ καὶ δυσάρεστος κἂν μὲν μόνος ᾖς, ἐρημίαν καλεῖς
τοῦτο, ἂν δὲ μετὰ ἀνθρώπων, ἐπιβούλους λέγεις καὶ λῃστάς, μέμφῃ δὲ καὶ
γονεῖς τοὺς σεαυτοῦ καὶ τέκνα καὶ ἀδελφοὺς καὶ γείτονας. (2) ἔδει δὲ μόνον
μένοντα ἡσυχίαν καλεῖν αὐτὸ καὶ ἐλευθερίαν καὶ ὅμοιον τοῖς θεοῖς
ἡγεῖσθαι αὐτόν, μετὰ πολλῶν δ' ὄντα μὴ ὄχλον καλεῖν μηδὲ θόρυβον μηδ'   5
ἀηδίαν, ἀλλ' ἑορτὴν καὶ πανήγυριν καὶ οὕτως πάντα εὐαρέστως δέχεσθαι.

Context: a discourse on contentment.
   For discussion of 'redescription', as therapy for the passions, cf. the references cited
on **U**.

W Stobaeus 2.115,5–17 (SVF 3.564,632)

(1) λέγουσι δὲ μήτε παρὰ τὴν ὄρεξιν μήτε παρὰ τὴν ὁρμὴν μήτε παρὰ τὴν
ἐπιβολὴν γίνεσθαί τι περὶ τὸν σπουδαῖον, διὰ τὸ μεθ' ὑπεξαιρέσεως πάντα
ποιεῖν τὰ τοιαῦτα καὶ μηδὲν αὐτῷ τῶν ἐναντιουμένων ἀπρόληπτον
προσπίπτειν. (2) εἶναι δὲ καὶ πρᾶον, τῆς πραότητος οὔσης ἕξεως καθ' ἣν
πράως ἔχουσι πρὸς τὸ ποιεῖν τὰ ἐπιβάλλοντα ἐν πᾶσι καὶ μὴ ἐκφέρεσθαι   5
εἰς ὀργὴν ἐν μηδενί. (3) καὶ ἡσύχιον δὲ καὶ κόσμιον εἶναι, τῆς κοσμιότητος
οὔσης ἐπιστήμης κινήσεων πρεπουσῶν, ἡσυχιότητος δὲ εὐταξίας περὶ τὰς

416

κατὰ φύσιν κινήσεις καὶ μονὰς ψυχῆς καὶ σώματος, (4) τῶν ἐναντίων τούτοις ἐπὶ πάντων φαύλων γιγνομένων.

1 μήτε Wachsmuth: μηδέ codd.   2 ἐπιβολὴν Meurer: ἐπιβουλὴν codd.   8 μονὰς Canter: μόνας codd.   9 ἐπὶ Meineke: περὶ codd.   πάντων F: πάντα P

Context: doxography of the wise man.

2 ὑπεξαιρέσεως For the importance of this concept, cf. Inwood [547], 119–26, 165–75, who interprets 'excessive impulse' (see A 1, J) in terms of its lack of 'reservation'. This is strongly supported by other instances of the word. Cf. Epictetus fr. 27, Ench. 2; Marcus Aurelius 4.1, 5.20, 6.50.

X Seneca, De ira 2.3.1–2.4

(1) nihil ex his quae animum fortuito inpellunt adfectus vocari debet: ista, ut ita dicam, patitur magis animus quam facit. ergo adfectus est non ad oblatas rerum species moveri, sed permittere se illis et hunc fortuitum motum prosequi. nam si quis pallorem et lacrimas procidentis et irritationem umoris obsceni altumve suspirium et oculos subito acriores aut quid his simile 5 indicium adfectus animique signum putat, fallitur nec intellegit corporis hos esse pulsus ... (2) ira non moveri tantum debet sed excurrere; est enim impetus; numquam autem impetus sine adsensu mentis est, neque enim fieri potest ut de ultione et poena agatur animo nesciente.

Context: the voluntariness of anger.

Seneca (and Epictetus in **Y**) are sharply distinguishing between involuntary emotional reactions and passions, properly so called, which are subsequent to the former and depend on the mind's assent. The first, in modern scholarship, are sometimes called προπάθειαι, a rare word of seemingly medical origin; cf. Plutarch, San. praec. 127C, 128D. There is no evidence that the early Stoics themselves used this term; but the likelihood that they acknowledged the concept, in the manner of **X** and **Y**, is well argued by Abel [601]. Two particularly relevant texts are Seneca, De ira 3.16.7, ut dicit Zenon in sapientis quoque animo etiam cum vulnus sanatum est cicatrix manet. sentiet itaque suspiciones quasdam et umbras adfectuum, ipsis quidem carebit; and SVF 3.574, ἔλεγεν [sc. Χρύσιππος] ἀλγεῖν μὲν τὸν σοφόν, μὴ βασανίζεσθαι δέ· μὴ γὰρ ἐνδιδόναι τῇ ψυχῇ. καὶ δεῖσθαι μέν, μὴ προσδέχεσθαι δέ.

8 Cf. 33I; 53S.

Y Gellius 19.1.17–18 (Epictetus fr. 9)

(1) propterea cum sonus aliquis formidabilis aut caelo aut ex ruina aut repentinus nescio cuius periculi nuntius vel quid aliud est eiusmodi factum, sapientis quoque animum paulisper moveri et contrahi et pallescere necessum est non opinione alicuius mali praecepta, sed quibusdam motibus rapidis et inconsultis officium mentis atque rationis praevertentibus. (2) mox tamen ille sapiens ibidem τὰς 5 τοιαύτας φαντασίας, id est visa istaec animi sui terrifica, non adprobat, hoc est οὐ

417

συγκατατίθεται οὐδὲ προσεπιδοξάζει, sed abicit respuitque, nec ei metuendum esse in his quicquam videtur.

4 *praecepta* Fγ: *percepta* F(corr.)δ   5 *rationis* γ: *orationis* Fδ

Context: a Latin version of an extract from book 5 (now lost) of Epictetus' *Discourses*, supposedly reported to Gellius by a Stoic philosopher, to explain the Stoics' position on 'necessary and natural fear'. In the preceding lines Epictetus explains the difference between the involuntary nature of φαντασίαι and the voluntary nature of assent to them.

7 **προσεπιδοξάζει** Explained a few lines later by *sua adsensione adprobabat*, which is the response of the fool in contrast with the wise man's lack of assent. The word is not found elsewhere. For the doctrine, see note on **X**.

66 Ethics in action

A Plutarch, *St. rep.* 1041F (*SVF* 3.545)

ἐν τῷ τρίτῳ Περὶ δικαιοσύνης ταῦτ' εἴρηκε· "διὸ καὶ διὰ τὴν ὑπερβολὴν τοῦ τε μεγέθους καὶ τοῦ κάλλους πλάσμασι δοκοῦμεν ὅμοια λέγειν καὶ οὐ κατὰ τὸν ἄνθρωπον καὶ τὴν ἀνθρωπίνην φύσιν."

Context: the alleged inconsistency between this statement and **60B**.

The context does not show what Chrysippus had previously said, to explain his διό. It was perhaps along the lines of Cicero, *Leg.* 1.28: *nihil est . . . praestabilius quam plane intellegi nos ad iustitiam esse natos*. On justice, see also **57F 5–6, H; 60A** 1–2, **C; 61C 2, D 5, H 3**.

B Plutarch, *St. rep.* 1034B (*SVF* 3.698)

Χρύσιππος δὲ πάλιν ἐν τῷ Περὶ ῥητορικῆς γράφων οὕτως ῥητορεύσειν καὶ πολιτεύσεσθαι τὸν σοφὸν ὡς καὶ τοῦ πλούτου ὄντος ἀγαθοῦ καὶ τῆς δόξης καὶ τῆς ὑγιείας ὁμολογεῖ τοὺς λόγους αὐτῶν ἀνεξόδους εἶναι καὶ ἀπολιτεύτους.

Context: the internal contradictions of Stoic political theory.

This passage is explained by Luschnat [605], 187, as an acknowledgement of what he calls man's 'empirical' as distinct from his Logos-nature. Such a supposed bifurcation in the Stoic concept of human nature is one that we resist strongly. Chrysippus is making the point that a wise man, i.e. someone who *knows* the indifference of wealth etc., will utter conventional value judgements in his efforts to influence public affairs. The passage is about the psychology of effective persuasion, and should be related to the notion that the wise man will resort to fiction where necessary; cf. **41F**.

C Seneca, *Ep.* 116.5 (Panaetius fr. 114, part)

eleganter mihi videtur Panaetius respondisse adulescentulo cuidam quaerenti an sapiens amaturus esset. "de sapiente" inquit "videbimus; mihi et tibi, qui

adhuc a sapiente longe absumus, non est committendum ut incidamus in rem
commotam, inpotentem, alteri emancupatam, vilem sibi."

Context: is it better to indulge emotions to a moderate degree (as the Peripatetics
claim) or to follow the Stoics in extirpating them?
    Sexual love is defined as 'an impulse to form friendships because of the manifest
beauty of handsome young people'; as such it is attributed to the wise man by reliable
sources (cf. *SVF* 3.650–3). Though the latter is denied by D.L. 7.113, ἔρως is included
by him at 7.130 in the context of virtue. See also **67D**.
    For the concept of 'progress', which is implied here in the notion of distance from
wisdom, see note on **59I**.

D Cicero, *Off.* 1.46

quoniam autem vivitur non cum perfectis hominibus pleneque sapientibus,
sed cum iis in quibus praeclare agitur si sunt simulacra virtutis, etiam hoc
intellegendum puto, neminem omnino esse neglegendum in quo aliqua
significatio virtutis appareat.

1 *pleneque* vel *planeque* codd.

Context: discussion of generosity (*beneficentia*).
    2 **simulacra virtutis** Cf. *Off.* 3.13, and *Fin.* 5.43 (Antiochean ethics).

E Cicero, *Off.* 1.107, 110–11, 114–17 (including Panaetius fr. 97)

(1) intellegendum etiam est duabus quasi nos a natura indutos esse personis;
quarum una communis est, ex eo quod omnes participes sumus rationis
praestantiaeque eius qua antecellimus bestiis; a qua omne honestum
decorumque trahitur et ex qua ratio inveniendi officii exquiritur. (2) altera   5
autem quae proprie singulis est tributa. ut enim in corporibus magnae
dissimilitudines sunt, alios videmus velocitate ad cursum, alios viribus ad luctandum
valere, itemque in formis aliis dignitatem inesse, aliis venustatem, sic in animis existunt
maiores etiam varietates ... (3) admodum autem tenenda sunt sua cuique,
non vitiosa, sed tamen propria, quo facilius decorum illud quod quaerimus
retineatur. sic enim est faciendum ut contra universam naturam nihil   10
contendamus, ea tamen conservata propriam nostram sequamur, ut etiamsi
sint alia graviora atque meliora, tamen nos studia nostra nostrae naturae regula
metiamur. neque enim attinet naturae repugnare nec quicquam sequi quod
assequi non queas ... (4) omnino si quicquam est decorum, nihil est profecto
magis quam aequabilitas ⟨cum⟩ universae vitae, tum singularum actionum,   15
quam conservare non possis si aliorum naturam imitans omittas tuam ... (5)
suum quisque igitur noscat ingenium acremque se et bonorum et vitiorum
suorum iudicem praebeat ... (6) ad quas igitur res aptissimi erimus, in iis
potissimum elaborabimus. sin aliquando necessitas nos ad ea detruserit quae
nostri ingenii non erunt, omnis adhibenda erit cura, meditatio, diligentia, ut   20

ea, si non decore, ut quam minime indecore facere possimus . . . (7) ac duabus iis personis quas supra dixi tertia adiungitur, quam casus aliqui aut tempus imponit; quarta etiam, quam nobismet ipsi iudicio nostro accommodamus. nam regna, imperia, nobilitas, honores, divitiae, opes eaque quae sunt his contraria, in casu sita, temporibus gubernantur. ipsi autem gerere quam   2 personam velimus a nostra voluntate proficiscitur. itaque se alii ad philosophiam, alii ad ius civile, alii ad eloquentiam applicant, ipsarumque virtutum in alia alius mavult excellere . . . (8) in primis autem constituendum est quos nos et quales esse velimus et in quo genere vitae, quae deliberatio est omnium difficillima.   3(

15 ⟨cum⟩ Lambinus

Context: the great superiority of human nature to that of other creatures.

4 decorumque   This notion (Greek πρέπον), cardinal to the present extract, has already been under discussion since *Off.* 1.93, where Cicero began his treatment of the virtue moderation. It appears to have been a particular feature of Panaetius' ethics. Cicero insists both on its factual inseparability from *honestum* and on its theoretical independence. *decorum* is to virtue what charm and beauty are to health. We may think of it as the aesthetic aspect of morality, or as that feature of morality which displays itself outwardly and engages admiration (cf. *Off.* 1.95, 98). In much of Cicero's later discussion of moderation it means good manners, gentlemanly etiquette, good taste – matters which the ancients found it natural to regard as part of the ethical domain. Panaetius' theoretical grounds for doing so are his claim that *decorum* is 'what accords with man's superiority in the area where his nature differs from that of other creatures' (*Off.* 1.96). For further discussion, see Philippson [367]; Brunt [604].

8   What we omit here and elsewhere in this extract are mainly Cicero's historical examples.   8–13 Cf. Panaetius' formulation of the τέλος (**63J** 1), and vol. 1, 401.
28–30 Cf. Plato, *Rep.* 1, 352d, οὐ γὰρ περὶ τοῦ ἐπιτυχόντος ὁ λόγος, ἀλλὰ περὶ τοῦ ὅντινα τρόπον χρὴ ζῆν. Bernard Williams (*Ethics and the limits of philosophy*, Cambridge, Mass., 1986) argues that Socrates' question is the best place for moral philosophy to start.

F   Epictetus, *Diss.* 4.12.15–19

(1) πρῶτον μὲν οὖν ταῦτα ἔχειν [*sc.* δεῖ] πρόχειρα καὶ μηδὲν δίχα τούτων ποιεῖν, ἀλλὰ τετάσθαι τὴν ψυχὴν ἐπὶ τοῦτον τὸν σκοπόν, μηδὲν τῶν ἔξω διώκειν, μηδὲν τῶν ἀλλοτρίων, ἀλλ' ὡς διέταξεν ὁ δυνάμενος, τὰ προαιρετικὰ ἐξ ἅπαντος, τὰ δ' ἄλλα ὡς ἂν δίδωται. (2) ἐπὶ τούτοις δὲ μεμνῆσθαι τίνες ἐσμὲν καὶ τί ἡμῖν ὄνομα, καὶ πρὸς τὰς δυνάμεις τῶν   5 σχέσεων πειρᾶσθαι τὰ καθήκοντα ἀπευθύνειν· τίς καιρὸς ᾠδῆς, τίς καιρὸς παιδιᾶς, τίνων παρόντων· τί ἔσται ἀπὸ τοῦ πράγματος . . . πότε σκῶψαι καὶ τίνας ποτὲ καταγελάσαι, καὶ ἐπὶ τίνι ποτὲ συμπεριενεχθῆναι καὶ τίνι, καὶ λοιπὸν ἐν τῇ συμπεριφορᾷ πῶς τηρῆσαι τὸ αὑτοῦ . . . (3) τί οὖν; δυνατὸν ἀναμάρτητον ἤδη εἶναι; ἀμήχανον, ἀλλ' ἐκεῖνο δυνατὸν πρὸς τὸ μὴ   1(

ἁμαρτάνειν τετάσθαι διηνεκῶς. ἀγαπητὸν γὰρ εἰ μηδέποτ᾽ ἀνιέντες ταύτην τὴν προσοχὴν ὀλίγων γε ἁμαρτημάτων ἐκτὸς ἐσόμεθα.

1 δεῖ add. ς, sed cf. Diss. 4.12.7, τίσιν οὖν δεῖ με προσέχειν;

Context: a discourse on moral vigilance (προσοχή).
2 τετάσθαι   Cf. ἀτονία/εὐτονία, 65T.
2–4 μηδὲν δίδωται   Cf. 58J; 62K.
4–9   Cf. 59Q.

G Cicero, Fin. 3.60–1 (SVF 3.763)

(1) in quo enim plura sunt quae secundum naturam sunt, huius officium est in vita manere; in quo autem aut sunt plura contraria aut fore videntur, huius officium est de vita excedere. (2) ex quo apparet et sapientis esse aliquando officium excedere e vita, cum beatus sit, et stulti manere in vita, cum sit miser. (3) nam bonum illud et malum (quod saepe iam dictum est) postea   5
consequitur; prima autem illa naturae sive secunda sive contraria sub iudicium sapientis et dilectum cadunt, estque illa subiecta quasi materia sapientiae. (4) itaque et manendi in vita et migrandi ratio omnis iis rebus quas supra dixi metienda. nam neque virtute retinetur ⟨ille⟩ in vita, nec iis qui sine virtute sunt mors est oppetenda. (5) et saepe officium est sapientis desciscere a vita   10
cum sit beatissimus, si id opportune facere possit . . . (6) quam ob rem cum vitiorum ista vis non sit ut causam afferant mortis voluntariae, perspicuum est etiam stultorum, qui idem miseri sint, officium esse manere in vita, si sint in maiore parte rerum earum quas secundum naturam esse dicimus.

9 ⟨ille⟩ Schiche

Context: immediately following 59F.
For further material on justified suicide, cf. SVF 3.758–68.
7 materia sapientiae   Cf. 59A.

H Diogenes Laertius 7.130 (SVF 3.757)

εὐλόγως τέ φασιν ἐξάξειν ἑαυτὸν τοῦ βίου τὸν σοφὸν καὶ ὑπὲρ πατρίδος καὶ ὑπὲρ φίλων, κἂν ἐν σκληροτέρᾳ γένηται ἀλγηδόνι ἢ πηρώσεσιν ἢ νόσοις ἀνιάτοις.

Context: features of the wise man.

I Seneca, Ep. 94.2, 31, 50–1

(1) Ariston Stoicus e contrario hanc partem levem existimat et quae non descendat in pectus usque, anilia habentem praecepta; plurimum ait proficere ipsa decreta philosophiae constitutionemque summi boni: "quam qui bene intellexit ac didicit quid in quaque re faciendum sit sibi ipse praecipit" . . . "si quis"

inquit "non habet recta decreta, quid illum admonitiones iuvabunt vitiosis   5
obligatum?" (2) hoc scilicet, ut illis liberetur; non enim extincta in illo indoles
naturalis est, sed obscurata et oppressa. sic quoque temptat resurgere et contra
prava nititur, nacta vero praesidium et adiuta praeceptis evalescit, si tamen
illam diutina pestis non infecit nec enecuit; hanc enim ne disciplina quidem
philosophiae toto impetu suo conisa restituet. quid enim interest inter decreta   10
philosophiae et praecepta nisi quod illa generalia praecepta sunt, haec
specialia? utraque res praecipit, sed altera in totum, particulatim altera . . . (3)
inbecillioribus quidem ingeniis necessarium est aliquem praeire: "hoc vitabis,
hoc facies." praeterea si expectat tempus quo per se sciat quid optimum factu
sit, interim errabit et errando inpedietur quominus ad illud perveniat quo   15
possit se esse contentus; regi ergo debet dum incipit posse se regere.

2 *anilia* Bücheler: *anilla* vel *at illa(m)* codd.

Context: discussion of the educational value of specific precepts. In *Ep.* 94 Seneca
marshals arguments for and against the thesis that *praecepta* are educationally useless,
and that only *decreta* are necessary. In *Ep.* 95 (cf. J) he opposes the thesis that *praecepta*
are sufficient to produce right actions and happiness.

  1 For Aristo's position, cf. Ioppolo [346], 123–33; and for the distinction between
praecepta and *decreta*, see Kidd [582].

J Seneca, *Ep.* 95.10–12, 61, 63–4

(1) philosophia autem et contemplativa est et activa; spectat simul agitque
. . . sequitur ergo ut, cum contemplativa sit, habeat decreta sua. quid quod
facienda quoque nemo rite obibit nisi is cui ratio erit tradita qua in quaque re
omnis officiorum numeros exsequi possit? quos non servabit qui in rem
praecepta acceperit, non in omne. inbecilla sunt per se et, ut ita dicam, sine radice quae   5
partibus dentur. decreta sunt quae muniant, quae securitatem nostram tranquilli-
tatemque tueantur, quae totam vitam totamque rerum naturam simul
contineant. hoc interest inter decreta philosophiae et praecepta quod inter
elementa et membra: haec ex illis dependent, illa et horum causae sunt et
omnium . . . (2) quaedam admonitionem in philosophia desiderant, quaedam   10
probationem . . . si probationes ⟨necessariae sunt⟩, necessaria sunt et decreta
quae veritatem argumentis colligunt . . . denique cum monemus aliquem ut
amicum eodem habeat loco quo se, ut ex inimico cogitet fieri posse amicum,
in illo amorem incitet, in hoc odium moderetur, adicimus "iustum est,
honestum." iustum autem honestumque decretorum nostrorum continet   15
ratio; ergo haec necessaria est, sine qua nec illa sunt. sed utrumque iungamus;
namque et sine radice inutiles rami sunt et ipsae radices iis quae genuere
adiuvantur.

11 ⟨*necessariae sunt*⟩ Schweighäuser

Context: see on I.
  4 officiorum numeros Cf. note on **59K**.

67 Political theory

A Plutarch, *Alex. fort.* 329A–B (*SVF* 1.262, part)

(1) καὶ μὴν ἡ πολὺ θαυμαζομένη πολιτεία τοῦ τὴν Στωικῶν αἵρεσιν καταβαλομένου Ζήνωνος εἰς ἓν τοῦτο συντείνει κεφάλαιον, ἵνα μὴ κατὰ πόλεις μηδὲ κατὰ δήμους οἰκῶμεν, ἰδίοις ἕκαστοι διωρισμένοι δικαίοις, ἀλλὰ πάντας ἀνθρώπους ἡγώμεθα δημότας καὶ πολίτας, εἷς δὲ βίος ᾖ καὶ κόσμος, ὥσπερ ἀγέλης συννόμου νόμῳ κοινῷ συντρεφομένης. (2) τοῦτο 5
Ζήνων μὲν ἔγραψεν ὥσπερ ὄναρ ἢ εἴδωλον εὐνομίας φιλοσόφου καὶ πολιτείας ἀνατυπωσάμενος, Ἀλέξανδρος δὲ τῷ λόγῳ τὸ ἔργον παρέσχεν.

Context: why Alexander the Great should be regarded as a philosopher. The subsequent lines were a principal source of the now discredited idea of Alexander's cosmopolitan mission.

B Diogenes Laertius 7.32–3

(1) ἔνιοι μέντοι, ἐξ ὧν εἰσιν οἱ περὶ Κάσσιον τὸν σκεπτικόν, ἐν πολλοῖς κατηγοροῦντες τοῦ Ζήνωνος, (2) πρῶτον μὲν τὴν ἐγκύκλιον παιδείαν ἄχρηστον ἀποφαίνειν λέγουσιν ἐν ἀρχῇ τῆς Πολιτείας, (3) δεύτερον ἐχθροὺς καὶ πολεμίους καὶ δούλους καὶ ἀλλοτρίους λέγειν αὐτὸν ἀλλήλων εἶναι πάντας τοὺς μὴ σπουδαίους, καὶ γονεῖς τέκνων καὶ ἀδελφοὺς 5
ἀδελφῶν, ⟨καὶ⟩ οἰκείους οἰκείων. (4) πάλιν ἐν τῇ Πολιτείᾳ παριστάντα πολίτας καὶ φίλους καὶ οἰκείους καὶ ἐλευθέρους τοὺς σπουδαίους μόνον . . . κοινάς τε τὰς γυναῖκας δογματίζειν ὁμοίως ἐν τῇ Πολιτείᾳ καὶ κατὰ τοὺς διακοσίους ⟨στίχους⟩ μήθ᾽ ἱερὰ μήτε δικαστήρια μήτε γυμνάσια ἐν ταῖς πόλεσιν οἰκοδομεῖσθαι. (5) περί τε νομίσματος οὕτως 10
γράφειν, "νόμισμα δ᾽ οὔτ᾽ ἀλλαγῆς ἕνεκεν οἴεσθαι δεῖν κατασκευάζειν οὔτ᾽ ἀποδημίας ἕνεκεν." καὶ ἐσθῆτι δὲ τῇ αὐτῇ κελεύει χρῆσθαι ἄνδρας καὶ γυναῖκας καὶ μηδὲν μόριον ἀποκεκρύφθαι.

3 λέγουσιν Reiske: λέγοντα codd.   4 πολεμίους Hübner: -ικούς codd.   6 ⟨καὶ⟩ Hübner   9
⟨στίχους⟩ Ménage   10 ἐν F: ἐπὶ BP

Context: report of Zeno's critics.

2 ἐγκύκλιον παιδείαν   See note on **26H**. Zeno's extreme attitude, rejected by Chrysippus (cf. *SVF* 3.738), was probably, like much else in his *Republic*, inspired by the Cynic Diogenes; cf. D.L. 6.72–3. The authenticity of the *Republic* attributed to Diogenes is made virtually certain by the fragments of Philodemus, Περὶ τῶν Στωικῶν, in which references to the work by Cleanthes, Chrysippus and Antipater are cited; cf. Dorandi [334]; Diogenes fr. 126 Giannantoni [36].

8 κοινάς . . . γυναῖκας   So too Chrysippus in his Περὶ πολιτείας, D.L. 7.131.

9–10   Even the much more conventional Panaetius disapproved of theatres, colonnades and new temples; cf. fr. 122 van Straaten [323].

11–12   A probably direct contradiction of Plato, *Rep.* 2, 371b, ἡμῖν καὶ νόμισμα σύμβολον τῆς ἀλλαγῆς ἕνεκα.

Stoic ethics

C Plutarch, *St. rep.* 1034B (*SVF* 1.264, part)

ἔτι δόγμα Ζήνωνος ἔστιν ἱερὰ θεῶν μὴ οἰκοδομεῖν· ἱερὸν γὰρ μὴ πολλοῦ ἄξιον καὶ ἅγιον οὐκ ἔστιν, οἰκοδόμων δ᾽ ἔργον καὶ βαναύσων οὐδέν ἐστι πολλοῦ ἄξιον.

Context: immediately following **66B**.

D Athenaeus 561C (*SVF* 1.263, part)

Ποντιανὸς δὲ Ζήνωνα ἔφη τὸν Κιτιέα ὑπολαμβάνειν τὸν Ἔρωτα θεὸν εἶναι φιλίας καὶ ἐλευθερίας, ἔτι δὲ καὶ ὁμονοίας παρασκευαστικόν, ἄλλου δὲ οὐδενός. διὸ καὶ ἐν τῇ Πολιτείᾳ ἔφη τὸν Ἔρωτα θεὸν εἶναι συνεργὸν ὑπάρχοντα πρὸς τὴν τῆς πόλεως σωτηρίαν.

2 φιλίας–ὁμονοίας A: φιλίας καὶ ὁμονοίας, καὶ ἐλευθερίας C

Context: miscellaneous remarks on ἔρως and κάλλος.

1 **Ποντιανός** He figures in Athenaeus as a philosopher, possibly fictional, from Nicomedia. **Ἔρωτα** The proper object of sexual desire, according to Zeno, is friendship, not intercourse; cf. D.L. 7.130, and note on **66C**.
2 **ὁμονοίας** Cf. note on **60P**.

E Clement, *Strom.* 5.9.58.2 (*SVF* 1.43)

οἱ Στωικοὶ λέγουσι Ζήνωνι τῷ πρώτῳ γεγράφθαι τινά, ἃ μὴ ῥᾳδίως ἐπιτρέπουσι τοῖς μαθηταῖς ἀναγιγνώσκειν μὴ οὐχὶ πεῖραν δεδωκόσι πρότερον, εἰ γνησίως φιλοσοφοῖεν.

Context: esoteric doctrines and writings of Greek philosophers.

For later Stoic embarrassment over Zeno's *Republic*, cf. Philodemus, Περὶ τῶν Στωικῶν, edited by Dorandi [334]. Philodemus reports a whole spectrum of reactions to the work, ranging from those who regarded it as irreproachable to Stoics who even disclaimed Zeno's foundation of the school. It is commonly supposed, on the basis of his concern with bourgeois respectability plus the evidence of Cicero, *Off.* 1.128, that Panaetius principally authorized the hostile reaction. Athenodorus, the Stoic in charge of the Pergamene library in the first century B.C., is said to have been caught expunging certain of the disapproved passages, D.L. 7.34.

1 **πρώτῳ** To distinguish the founder from Zeno of Tarsus (see Index of philosophers, vol. 1).
3 Cf. Plato, *Rep.* 5, 473d φιλοσοφήσωσι γνησίως τε καὶ ἱκανῶς.

F Plutarch, *St. rep.* 1044F–1045A (*SVF* 3.753, part)

καὶ μὴν ἐν τῷ ⟨ . . . ⟩ τῶν Προτρεπτικῶν, εἰπὼν ὅτι καὶ τὸ μητράσιν ἢ ἀδελφαῖς συγγενέσθαι καὶ τὸ φαγεῖν τι καὶ προελθεῖν ἀπὸ λεχοῦς ἢ θανάτου πρὸς ἱερὸν ἀλόγως διαβέβληται, καὶ πρὸς τὰ θηρία φησὶ δεῖν

424

ἀποβλέπειν, καὶ τοῖς ὑπ' ἐκείνων γινομένοις τεκμαίρεσθαι τὸ μηδὲν
ἄτοπον μηδὲ παρὰ φύσιν εἶναι τῶν τοιούτων.   5

1 lacunam ind. Xylander   2 λεχοῦς Emperius: λέχους codd.
Context: inconsistencies in Chrysippus' political theory.

G Sextus Empiricus, *PH* 3.247–8

(1) "καὶ ἐὰν τῶν ζώντων ἀποκοπῇ τι μέρος πρὸς τροφὴν χρήσιμον, μήτε
κατορύττειν αὐτὸ μήτε ἄλλως ῥίπτειν, ἀναλίσκειν δὲ αὐτό, ὅπως ἐκ τῶν
ἡμετέρων ἕτερον μέρος γένηται." (2) ἐν δὲ τοῖς περὶ τοῦ καθήκοντος περὶ
τῆς τῶν γονέων ταφῆς ῥητῶς φησιν "ἀπογενομένων δὲ τῶν γονέων ταφαῖς
χρηστέον ταῖς ἁπλουστάταις, ὡς ἂν τοῦ σώματος, καθάπερ ὀνύχων ἢ   5
ὀδόντων ἢ τριχῶν, οὐδὲν ὄντος πρὸς ἡμᾶς, καὶ οὐδὲ ἐπιστροφῆς ἢ
πολυωρίας προσδεομένων ἡμῶν τοιαύτης τινός. διὸ καὶ χρησίμων μὲν
ὄντων τῶν κρεῶν τροφῇ χρήσονται αὐτοῖς, καθάπερ καὶ τῶν ἰδίων μερῶν,
οἷον ποδὸς ἀποκοπέντος, ἐπέβαλλε χρῆσθαι αὐτῷ καὶ τοῖς παραπλησίοις·
ἀχρείων δὲ ὄντων ἢ κατορύξαντες ἐάσουσιν, ἢ κατακαύσαντες τὴν τέφραν ἀφήσουσιν, ἢ   10
μακρότερον ῥίψαντες οὐδεμίαν αὐτῶν ἐπιστροφὴν ποιήσονται καθάπερ ὄνυχος ἢ τριχῶν."

9 ἐπέβαλλε Bekker: ἐπέβαλε codd.

Context: demonstration by quotation that philosophers' theories are too unpractical to
warrant their claims to propound an art of life.

H Plutarch, *De exilio* 600E (*SVF* 1.371, part)

φύσει γὰρ οὐκ ἔστι πατρίς, ὥσπερ οὐδ' οἶκος οὐδ' ἀγρὸς οὐδὲ χαλκεῖον, ὡς
'Αρίστων ἔλεγεν, οὐδ' ἰατρεῖον· ἀλλὰ γίνεται μᾶλλον δ' ὀνομάζεται καὶ
καλεῖται τούτων ἕκαστον ἀεὶ πρὸς τὸν οἰκοῦντα καὶ χρώμενον.

Context: quotations to illustrate the thesis that exile is not an evil.

I Stobaeus 2.103,14–17 (*SVF* 1.587, part)

ἱκανῶς δὲ καὶ Κλεάνθης περὶ τὸ σπουδαῖον εἶναι τὴν πόλιν λόγον ἠρώτησε τοιοῦτον· πόλις
μὲν ⟨εἰ⟩ ἔστιν οἰκητήριον κατασκεύασμα, εἰς ὃ καταφεύγοντας ἔστι δίκην
δοῦναι καὶ λαβεῖν, οὐκ ἀστεῖον δὴ πόλις ἐστίν; ἀλλὰ μὴν τοιοῦτόν ἐστιν ἡ
πόλις οἰκητήριον· ἀστεῖον ἄρ' ἔστιν ἡ πόλις.

2 ⟨εἰ⟩ Heeren

Context: doxography of Stoic political theory.

3 ἀστεῖον   A pun which seeks to make a conceptual link between city and moral
refinement. Cf. D.L. 6.72 (the Cynic Diogenes).

J Dio Chrysostom 36.20 (*SVF* 3.329)

τὴν πόλιν φασὶν εἶναι πλῆθος ἀνθρώπων ἐν ταὐτῷ κατοικούντων ὑπὸ
νόμου διοικούμενον.

Context: elucidation of the meaning of ἄνθρωπος.

Stoic ethics

That Dio's φασίν refers to Stoics is proved by section 29 of his oration, where he gives this definition in an abbreviated form, and precedes it with the words τῶν ἡμετέρων τὸν κόσμον ἀποφαινομένων πόλιν.

K Seneca, *De otio* 4.1

duas res publicas animo complectamur, alteram magnam et vere publicam qua di atque homines continentur, in qua non ad hunc angulum respicimus aut ad illum sed terminos civitatis nostrae cum sole metimur, alteram cui nos adscripsit condicio nascendi.

Context: the contemplative life, practised at leisure, is a service to the world community.

L Arius Didymus (Eusebius, *Pr. ev.* 15.15.3–5; *SVF* 2.528, part)

καὶ τὸ μὲν ἐκ τῆς πάσης οὐσίας ποιὸν κόσμον ἀίδιον εἶναι καὶ θεόν· λέγεσθαι δὲ κόσμον σύστημα ἐξ οὐρανοῦ καὶ ἀέρος καὶ γῆς καὶ θαλάττης καὶ τῶν ἐν αὐτοῖς φύσεων (1) λέγεσθαι δὲ κόσμον καὶ τὸ οἰκητήριον θεῶν καὶ ἀνθρώπων ⟨καὶ τὸ ἐκ θεῶν καὶ ἀνθρώπων⟩ καὶ τῶν ἕνεκα τούτων γενομένων σύστημα· (2) ὃν γὰρ τρόπον πόλις λέγεται διχῶς, τό τε οἰκητήριον καὶ τὸ ἐκ τῶν ἐνοικούντων   5
σὺν τοῖς πολίταις σύστημα, οὕτως καὶ ὁ κόσμος οἱονεὶ πόλις ἐστὶν ἐκ θεῶν καὶ ἀνθρώπων συνεστῶσα, τῶν μὲν θεῶν τὴν ἡγεμονίαν ἐχόντων, τῶν δὲ ἀνθρώπων ὑποτεταγμένων. (3) κοινωνίαν δ' ὑπάρχειν πρὸς ἀλλήλους διὰ τὸ λόγου μετέχειν, ὅς ἐστι φύσει νόμος· τὰ δ' ἄλλα πάντα γεγονέναι τούτων ἕνεκα.   10

3–4 ⟨καὶ-ἀνθρώπων⟩ Arnim   4 σύστημα Arnim: συνεστῶτα codd.

Context: doxography of Stoic cosmology.

1–2 See notes on **44F**.
6 **οἱονεὶ πόλις** Cf. **46G 3**.
8–10 Cf. **54N**; **63K 5–8**.

M Diogenes Laertius 7.121–2

(1) μόνον τ' ἐλεύθερον [sc. τὸν σοφόν], τοὺς δὲ φαύλους δούλους· εἶναι γὰρ τὴν ἐλευθερίαν ἐξουσίαν αὐτοπραγίας, τὴν δὲ δουλείαν στέρησιν αὐτοπραγίας. εἶναι δὲ καὶ ἄλλην δουλείαν τὴν ἐν ὑποτάξει καὶ τρίτην τὴν ἐν κτήσει τε καὶ ὑποτάξει, ᾗ ἀντιτίθεται ἡ δεσποτεία, φαύλη οὖσα καὶ αὕτη. (2) οὐ μόνον δ' ἐλευθέρους εἶναι τοὺς σοφούς, ἀλλὰ καὶ βασιλέας, τῆς βασιλείας   5
οὔσης ἀρχῆς ἀνυπευθύνου, ἥτις περὶ μόνους ἂν τοὺς σοφοὺς συσταίη, καθά φησι Χρύσιππος ἐν τῷ Περὶ τοῦ κυρίως κεχρῆσθαι Ζήνωνα τοῖς ὀνόμασιν· ἐγνωκέναι γάρ φησι δεῖν τὸν ἄρχοντα περὶ ἀγαθῶν καὶ κακῶν, μηδένα δὲ τῶν φαύλων ἐπίστασθαι ταῦτα. (3) ὁμοίως δὲ καὶ ἀρχικοὺς δικαστικούς τε καὶ ῥητορικοὺς μόνους εἶναι, τῶν δὲ φαύλων οὐδένα.   10

4 ἀντιτίθεται BP: ἀντιτίθεται καὶ F   6 συσταίη Ménage e Suda: σταίη codd.

426

Context: characteristics of the wise man.

1 Cf. **B 4**.

2 **ἐξουσίαν αὐτοπραγίας** Said to be got by the wise man 'from the divine law' (SVF 3.544), which shows that 'self-mastery' or 'moral freedom' is the intended sense. The thought here and in 4–6 is Platonic; cf. especially *Rep*. 9, 577d–580c.

2–4 The second sense of slavery seems to signify a 'subordinate' position in society, as distinct from being 'owned' as well as subordinate – the third sense. Cf. **Q**, and Chrysippus' further account of 'slave' as *perpetuus mercenarius* (Seneca, *Ben*. 3.22.1). For a convincing argument that the early Stoics rejected any natural basis to slavery, see Griffin [384], 459–60.

N Philo, *Quod omnis probus liber sit* 97 (SVF 1.218)

ἐπὶ δὴ τοιαύταις ἀποφάσεσι καὶ γνώμαις ἆρ᾽ οὐκ ἄξιον τὸ Ζηνώνειον ἐπιφωνῆσαι, ὅτι ''θᾶττον ἂν ἀσκὸν βαπτίσαι τις πλήρη πνεύματος ἢ βιάσαιτο τῶν σπουδαίων ὁντινοῦν ἄκοντα δρᾶσαί τι τῶν ἀβουλήτων''; ἀνένδοτος γὰρ ψυχὴ καὶ ἀήττητος, ἣν ὁ ὀρθὸς λόγος δόγμασι παγίοις ἐνεύρωσε.

1 δή M: om. cett.   2 τις G: om. cett.   βιάσαιτο vel βιάσαι codd.   2–3 τῶν σπουδαίων MG: τὴν τοῦ σπουδαίου A: τὸν σπουδαῖον cett.

Context: Zeno's saying is quoted for its resemblance to a letter sent by the gymnosophist Calanus to Alexander, in which Calanus remarks that no ruler will compel Indian philosophers to act against their will.

3–4 Cf. **59I**; **61G 2**; **63L 2**.

O Plutarch, *De audiendis poetis* 33D (SVF 1.219)

καὶ ὁ Ζήνων ἐπανορθούμενος τὸ τοῦ Σοφοκλέους·

    ὅστις δὲ πρὸς τύραννον ἐμπορεύεται,
    κείνου 'στὶ δοῦλος, κἂν ἐλεύθερος μόλῃ

μετέγραφεν

    οὐκ ἔστι δοῦλος, ἢν ἐλεύθερος μόλῃ,   5

τῷ ἐλευθέρῳ νῦν συνεκφαίνων τὸν ἀδεᾶ καὶ μεγαλόφρονα καὶ ἀταπείνωτον.

Context: approval of Stoics for rewriting verses in a morally improving way.

The Sophoclean lines (= fr. 873 Pearson) are frequently quoted, with or without the tragedian's name. D.L. 2.82 refers the 'correction' to Aristippus. Even if he originated the change, Zeno may still have adopted it.

P Diogenes Laertius 7.124 (SVF 3.631)

λέγουσι δὲ καὶ τὴν φιλίαν ἐν μόνοις τοῖς σπουδαίοις εἶναι, διὰ τὴν ὁμοιότητα· φασὶ δ᾽ αὐτὴν κοινωνίαν τινὰ εἶναι τῶν κατὰ τὸν βίον, χρωμένων ἡμῶν τοῖς φίλοις ὡς ἑαυτοῖς. δι᾽ αὐτόν θ᾽ αἱρετὸν τὸν φίλον

Stoic ethics

ἀποφαίνονται καὶ τὴν πολυφιλίαν ἀγαθόν. ἔν τε τοῖς φαύλοις μὴ εἶναι
φιλίαν μηδενί τε τῶν φαύλων φίλον εἶναι.					5

2 αὐτὴν BP: αὐτοῖς FP(corr.)

Context: characteristics of the wise man.
On friendship, see **60G**, **M**, and, for 'goods being common to the virtuous', **60P**.
3 **δι' αὐτόν θ' αἱρετόν**   For Epicureanism, cf. **22F** 1.

Q Athenaeus 267B (*SVF* 3.353)

διαφέρειν δέ φησι Χρύσιππος δοῦλον οἰκέτου γράφων ἐν δευτέρῳ Περὶ
ὁμονοίας διὰ τὸ τοὺς ἀπελευθέρους μὲν δούλους ἔτι εἶναι, οἰκέτας δὲ τοὺς
μὴ τῆς κτήσεως ἀφειμένους. "ὁ γὰρ οἰκέτης" φησί "δοῦλός ἐστι κτήσει
κατατεταγμένος."

Context: discussion of slavery.
For Chrysippus' distinction, see note on **M** 2–4.

R Marcian 1 (*SVF* 3.314)

... Chrysippus sic incipit libro quem fecit Περὶ νόμου: "ὁ νόμος πάντων
ἐστὶ βασιλεὺς θείων τε καὶ ἀνθρωπίνων πραγμάτων· δεῖ δὲ αὐτὸν
προστάτην τε εἶναι τῶν καλῶν καὶ τῶν αἰσχρῶν καὶ ἄρχοντα καὶ ἡγεμόνα,
καὶ κατὰ τοῦτο κανόνα τε εἶναι δικαίων καὶ ἀδίκων καὶ τῶν φύσει
πολιτικῶν ζῴων προστακτικὸν μὲν ὧν ποιητέον, ἀπαγορευτικὸν δὲ ὧν οὐ		5
ποιητέον."

Note the weight and formality of the language. The opening words recall Pindar's
famous phrase (fr. 152.1 Bowra).
4–5 **φύσει πολιτικῶν ζῴων**   Cf. note on **61H** 2–3.

S Cicero, *Rep.* 3.33 (*SVF* 3.325)

(1) est quidem vera lex recta ratio, naturae congruens, diffusa in omnis,
constans, sempiterna, quae vocet ad officium iubendo, vetando a fraude
deterreat, (2) quae tamen neque probos frustra iubet aut vetat, nec improbos
iubendo aut vetando movet. (3) huic legi nec obrogari fas est, neque derogari
aliquid ex hac licet, neque tota abrogari potest, nec vero aut per senatum aut		5
per populum solvi hac lege possumus, neque est quaerendus explanator aut
interpres Sextus Aelius, (4) nec erit alia lex Romae, alia Athenis, alia nunc, alia
posthac, sed et omnes gentes et omni tempore una lex et sempiterna et
inmutabilis continebit, (5) unusque erit communis quasi magister et imperator
omnium deus: ille legis huius inventor, disceptator, lator; (6) cui qui non		10
parebit, ipse se fugiet, ac naturam hominis aspernatus hoc ipso luet maximas
poenas, etiamsi cetera supplicia quae putantur effugerit.

The original context of this passage (quoted by Lactantius, *Inst. div.* 6.8.6–9) is lost.
1 **recta ratio**   Cf. **63C** 9.
3–4   Cf. **54I** 3.

67 *Political theory*

T Cicero, *Rep.* 1.34 (Panaetius fr. 119)

... quod memineram persaepe te cum Panaetio disserere solitum coram Polybio, duobus Graecis vel peritissimis rerum civilium, multaque colligere ac docere, optimum longe statum civitatis esse eum quem maiores nostri nobis reliquissent.

The original context is lost.

For Polybius' admiration for the Roman constitution, cf. his *History* 3.2.6, 6.11–18. Given his general interest in different constitutions (sometimes regarded as dependent on Panaetius), lines 3–4 probably state a position supported by him and Panaetius as well as by Scipio.

U Diogenes Laertius 7.131 (*SVF* 3.700)

πολιτείαν δ' ἀρίστην τὴν μικτὴν ἔκ τε δημοκρατίας καὶ βασιλείας καὶ ἀριστοκρατίας.

Context: doxography of Stoic political theory.

This sentence is inconsequentially added after a passage reporting the views of Zeno and Chrysippus on community of wives. It chimes so little with their known political theory and so well with the position of Polybius (cf. his *History* 6.10.6–7, 6.18.7) that we incline to regard 'the mixed constitution' as the system approved by later Stoics, especially Panaetius.

V Cicero, *Off.* 2.73 (Panaetius fr. 118)

hanc enim ob causam maxime, ut sua tenerentur, res publicae civitatesque constitutae sunt. nam, etsi duce natura congregabantur homines, tamen spe custodiae rerum suarum urbium praesidia quaerebant.

Context: the statesman's duty to preserve people's property and to prevent the state from interfering with private ownership.

This interesting defence of capitalism is likely to have a philosophical source, for which Panaetius would be the best candidate; cf. Reesor [608], 28–9. Earlier Stoics will hardly have agreed that capitalism is the state's primary function and justification. However, there is no reason to think that Zeno, even in his *Republic*, was hostile to private property; and the compatibility of private ownership with a communal world is stated in an image (**57F 7**) probably derived from Chrysippus. Wealth, though indifferent for happiness, is something 'preferred' (**58m**).

W Stobaeus 2.109,10–110,4 (*SVF* 3.686, part)

(1) τρεῖς δὲ προηγουμένους εἶναι βίους, τόν τε βασιλικὸν καὶ τὸν πολιτικὸν καὶ τρίτον τὸν ἐπιστημονικόν· (2) ὁμοίως δὲ καὶ χρηματισμοὺς τρεῖς προηγουμένους, τόν τε ἀπὸ τῆς βασιλείας, καθ' ἣν ἢ αὐτὸς βασιλεύσει ἢ μοναρχικῶν χρημάτων εὐπορήσει· (3) δεύτερον δὲ τὸν ἀπὸ τῆς πολιτείας, πολιτεύσεσθαι γὰρ κατὰ τὸν προηγούμενον λόγον· καὶ γὰρ γαμήσειν καὶ 5 παιδοποιήσεσθαι, ἀκολουθεῖν ⟨γὰρ⟩ ταῦτα τῇ τοῦ λογικοῦ ζῴου καὶ

429

κοινωνικοῦ καὶ φιλαλλήλου ⟨φύσει⟩. χρηματιεῖσθαι οὖν καὶ ἀπὸ τῆς
πολιτείας καὶ ἀπὸ τῶν φίλων, τῶν ἐν ὑπεροχαῖς ὄντων. (4) περὶ δὲ τοῦ
σοφιστεύσειν καὶ ἀπὸ σοφιστείας εὐπορήσειν χρημάτων διέστησαν οἱ ἀπὸ
τῆς αἱρέσεως κατὰ τὸ σημαινόμενον. τὸ μὲν γὰρ χρηματιεῖσθαι ἀπὸ τῶν 10
κατὰ τὴν παιδείαν καὶ μισθοὺς ποτε λήψεσθαι παρὰ τῶν φιλομαθούντων
διωμολογήσαντο· περὶ δὲ τὸ σημαινόμενον ἐγένετό τις ἐν αὐτοῖς
ἀμφισβήτησις, τῶν μὲν αὐτὸ τοῦτο λεγόντων σοφιστεύειν, τὸ ἐπὶ μισθῷ
μεταδιδόναι τῶν τῆς φιλοσοφίας δογμάτων, τῶν δ' ὑποτοπησάντων ἐν τῷ
σοφιστεύειν περιέχεσθαί τι φαῦλον, οἱονεὶ λόγους καπηλεύειν. 15

1 προηγουμένους Heeren: προηγορουμένους codd.   3 ἢ Heine: καὶ codd.   4 μοναρχικῶν Heeren:
-ικοῖς codd.   5 πολιτεύσεσθαι Meineke: πολιτεύεσθαι codd.   6 ⟨γὰρ⟩ Heeren   7 ⟨φύσει⟩
Heeren   9 σοφιστεύσειν Usener: σοφιστεύειν codd.

Context: characterization of the wise man.

For further material on the three preferable lives, cf. *SVF* 3.690–704.

4 δεύτερον In his books *Περὶ βίων* (*SVF* 3.693) Chrysippus specified the second
livelihood only as ἀπὸ φίλων (cf. 8), and not also as ἀπὸ τῆς πολιτείας. Perhaps this
reflects his belief that a political career is not possible for a Stoic in some communities
(*SVF* 3.695–6), and that it is extremely difficult to combine political popularity and
moral integrity (*SVF* 3.694).

5–7. Cf. **57F 8. φιλαλλήλου** Cf. **22S** 2.

15 λόγους καπηλεύειν A clear reminiscence of Socrates' characterization of the
sophists' profession (Plato, *Prot.* 313c–314a).

X Plutarch, *St. rep.* 1033C–D (*SVF* 3.702)

αὐτὸς γοῦν Χρύσιππος ἐν τῷ τετάρτῳ Περὶ βίων οὐδὲν οἴεται τὸν σχολαστικὸν βίον τοῦ
ἡδονικοῦ διαφέρειν· αὐτὰς δὲ παραθήσομαι τὰς λέξεις· "ὅσοι δ' ὑπολαμβάνουσι
φιλοσόφοις ἐπιβάλλειν μάλιστα τὸν σχολαστικὸν βίον ἀπ' ἀρχῆς τί μοι
δοκοῦσι διαμαρτάνειν, ὑπονοοῦντες διαγωγῆς τινος ἔνεκεν δεῖν τοῦτο
ποιεῖν ἢ ἄλλου τινὸς τούτῳ παραπλησίου, καὶ τὸν ὅλον βίον οὕτω πως 5
διελκύσαι· τοῦτο δ' ἐστίν, ἂν σαφῶς θεωρηθῇ, ἡδέως· οὐ γὰρ δεῖ λανθάνειν
τὴν ὑπόνοιαν αὐτῶν, πολλῶν μὲν σαφῶς τοῦτο λεγόντων οὐκ ὀλίγων δ'
ἀδηλότερον."

Context: Chrysippus' inconsistency in stating this while spending his life as a scholar.

7 πολλῶν is a reference to the Epicureans, and οὐκ ὀλίγων are generally identified
with the Peripatetics; cf. Cherniss [326] ad loc.

Y Seneca, *Ep.* 90.5–7 (Posidonius fr. 284, part)

(1) illo ergo saeculo quod aureum perhibent penes sapientes fuisse regnum
Posidonius iudicat. hi continebant manus et infirmiorem a validioribus
tuebantur, suadebant dissuadebantque et utilia atque inutilia monstrabant;
horum prudentia ne quid deesset suis providebat, fortitudo pericula arcebat,
beneficentia augebat ornabatque subiectos . . . (2) sed postquam subrepenti- 5

bus vitiis in tyrannidem regna conversa sunt, opus esse legibus coepit, quas et ipsas inter initia tulere sapientes . . . (3) hactenus Posidonio adsentior: artes quidem a philosophia inventas quibus in cotidiano vita utitur non concesserim, nec illi fabricae adseram gloriam. "illa" inquit "sparsos et aut casis tectos aut aliqua rupe suffossa aut exesae arboris trunco docuit tecta moliri."   10

2 *iudicat* vel *indicat* codd.   *infirmiorem* B: *-iores* cett.   8 *in cotidiano vita utitur* vel *cotidiana vita utimur* codd.   9 *sparsos et aut casis* Summers: *sparsos e causis* vel sim. codd.

Context: critique of Posidonius' account of the origin of culture.

1–5   The largely unoriginal nature of Posidonius' account is indicated by its close similarity to Epicurean theories; cf. **22L–N** and Cole [273], 18–19, 35–6. He seems to have drawn upon a long-standing 'pattern of prehistory' (Cole's phrase), to which his special contribution was the identification of the πρῶτος εὑρετής with philosophers. Even this notion, as applied to technology, is an exaggeration, rather than a complete modification, of the pattern; cf. **22L** 1107, 1143–4, **M 3, N 1–2**.

The Academics

68 Methodology

A Cicero, *Acad.* 1.43–6

(1) tum Varro "tuae sunt nunc partes", inquit, "qui ab antiquorum ratione desciscis et ea quae ab Arcesila novata sunt probas, docere quod et qua de causa discidium factum sit, ut videamus satisne ista sit iusta defectio." (2) tum ego "cum Zenone", inquam, "ut accepimus Arcesilas sibi omne certamen instituit, non pertinacia aut studio vincendi ut quidem mihi videtur, sed earum 5
rerum obscuritate quae ad confessionem ignorationis adduxerant Socratem, et iam ante Socratem Democritum Anaxagoram Empedoclem omnes paene veteres, qui nihil cognosci nihil percipi nihil sciri posse dixerunt, angustos sensus, imbecillos animos, brevia curricula vitae, et (ut Democritus) in profundo veritatem esse demersam, opinionibus et institutis omnia teneri, 10
nihil veritati relinqui, deinceps omnia tenebris circumfusa esse dixerunt. (3) itaque Arcesilas negabat esse quicquam quod sciri posset, ne illud quidem ipsum quod Socrates sibi reliquisset, ut nihil scire se sciret; sic omnia latere censebat in occulto, neque esse quicquam quod cerni aut intellegi posset. (4) quibus de causis nihil oportere neque profiteri neque affirmare quemquam 1
neque assensione approbare, cohibereque semper et ab omni lapsu continere temeritatem, quae tum esset insignis cum aut falsa aut incognita res approbaretur, neque hoc quicquam esse turpius quam cognitioni et perceptioni assensionem approbationemque praecurrere. (5) huic rationi quod erat consentaneum faciebat, ut contra omnium sententias disserens de sua 2
plerosque deduceret, ut cum in eadem re paria contrariis in partibus momenta rationum invenirentur, facilius ab utraque parte assensio sustineretur. (6) hanc Academiam novam appellant, quae mihi vetus videtur, si quidem Platonem ex illa vetere numeramus, cuius in libris nihil affirmatur et in utramque partem multa disseruntur, de omnibus quaeritur, nihil certi dicitur. sed tamen illa 2
quam exposuisti vetus, haec nova nominetur: quae usque ad Carneadem perducta, qui quartus ab Arcesila fuit, in eadem Arcesilae ratione permansit."

7 *iam ante* Davies: *veluti amantes* codd.   13 *ut–sciret* om. *Δv*   20 *disserens de sua* Γ: *dies iam Δ: dicens in eam* Madvig   26 *exposuisti* Durand: *exposui* codd.

Context: a few lines after **41B**, Varro's account of Zeno's epistemology.

432

1 **antiquorum ratione** The position of the Old Academy, as interpreted by Antiochus.

4 **cum Zenone** Cf. **G**, **40D**. But the elderly Zeno was not Arcesilaus' only Stoic opponent in epistemology. For the neglected importance of Aristo in this connexion, cf. Long [622], 441–3.

7 The cognitive pessimism of Anaxagoras and Empedocles, unlike that of Democritus, is a historical distortion, to say the least. In the case of Empedocles it appears to be founded on 31 b 2 DK. Its attribution to Anaxagoras seems to go back to Aristotle's odd interpretation of his remarks about the primal mixture of everything; cf. *Metaph.* Γ.4, 1007b25, and 5, 1009a27, where Anaxagoras is mentioned alongside Democritus (as in the doxographical tradition at 59 A 96 DK). For the Academics' interest in collecting illustrious precursors, cf. **H 3** and Cicero, *Acad.* 2.14.

9 For Democritus' famous assertion, which is quoted again at **R 1**, cf. 68 b 117 DK. See also vol. 1, 17.

20 **de sua** Understand *sententia*. This reading, though commonly rejected in favour of Madvig's *in eam* (for the nonsensical *dies iam*), makes excellent sense. What is *consentaneum* with Arcesilaus' recommendation of suspension of judgement about everything is his 'drawing people away from their own opinion', and he achieves this by 'arguing against everyone's opinion'. Madvig's emendation does not show why this methodology should result in people's 'accepting Arcesilaus' *ratio*' (the presumed sense of *in eam deduceret*), nor how this would be consistent with his scepticism.

B Cicero, *Acad.* 1.13

"relictam a te veterem Academiam", inquit [*sc.* Varro], "tractari autem novam." "quid ergo", inquam, . . . "Antiocho id magis licuerit nostro familiari remigrare in domum veterem e nova, quam nobis in novam e vetere? certe enim recentissima quaeque sunt correcta et emendata maxime; quamquam Antiochi magister Philo, magnus vir ut tu existimas ipse, negat in 5 libris, quod coram etiam ex ipso audiebamus, duas Academias esse, erroremque eorum qui ita putarent coarguit." "est", inquit, "ut dicis; sed ignorare te non arbitror quae contra ⟨ea⟩ Philonis Antiochus scripserit."

1 *Academiam* Bentley: *iam* codd.   5 *negat* Davies: *negaret* codd.   8 ⟨*ea*⟩ Reid

Context: Varro's interest in Cicero's recent change of philosophical allegiance, from the 'Old' Academy of Antiochus to the 'New' Academy of Philo.

3 **in domum veterem e nova** An allusion to Antiochus' secession from Philo; cf. vol. 1, 449.

4 **recentissima–maxime** Well explained by Glucker [42], 105, as an ironical rejoinder to Antiochus (who had represented Stoicism as a *correctio veteris Academiae*, Cicero, *Acad.* 1.43), implying the superiority of the New Academy of Philo.

8 Referring to Antiochus' *Sosus* (Cicero, *Acad.* 2.12).

C Cicero, *Acad.* 2.16

(1) Arcesilas Zenoni ut putatur obtrectans nihil novi reperienti sed emendanti

superiores inmutatione verborum, dum huius definitiones labefactare volt, conatus est clarissimis rebus tenebras obducere. (2) cuius primo non admodum probata ratio (quamquam floruit cum acumine ingeni tum admirabili quodam lepore dicendi), proxime a Lacyde solo retenta est, post autem confecta a 5 Carneade.

Context: the New Academy's perversion of the history of philosophy.

1–2 What is attributed here to Arcesilaus sounds suspiciously like Antiochus' own account of the relation of Stoicism to the Academic tradition; cf. note on **B** 4.

3 **clarissimis rebus** A reference to Arcesilaus' rejection of the φαντασία καταληπτική; cf. **40D**.

D Diogenes Laertius 4.28

οὗτός ἐστιν ὁ τῆς μέσης Ἀκαδημείας κατάρξας, πρῶτος ἐπισχὼν τὰς ἀποφάσεις διὰ τὰς ἐναντιότητας τῶν λόγων. πρῶτος δὲ καὶ εἰς ἑκάτερον ἐπεχείρησε, καὶ πρῶτος τὸν λόγον ἐκίνησε τὸν ὑπὸ Πλάτωνος παραδεδομένον καὶ ἐποίησε δι᾽ ἐρωτήσεως καὶ ἀποκρίσεως ἐριστικώτερον.

Context: the opening of Diogenes' life of Arcesilaus.
For its anachronisms and inaccuracies, cf. Long [622], 444–7.

1 **μέσης** The earliest reference to the Middle Academy is in the Herculaneum papyrus *Academicorum index* (probably composed by Philodemus), 21.37, where it is said to have been 'stabilized' by Lacydes.

1–2 **πρῶτος–λόγων** Cf. note on **1A** 6.

2–3 **πρῶτος–ἐπεχείρησε** In fact, argument pro and contra the same thesis has a history which goes back to Protagoras, as D.L. 9.51 acknowledges.

E Diogenes Laertius 4.32–3

(1) Κράτητος δὲ ἐκλιπόντος κατέσχε τὴν σχολήν, ἐκχωρήσαντος αὐτῷ Σωκρατίδου τινός. διὰ δὲ τὸ περὶ πάντων ἐπέχειν οὐδὲ βιβλίον, φασί τινες, συνέγραψεν· οἱ δέ, ὅτι ἐφωράθη τινὰ κατορθῶν, ἅ φασιν οἱ μὲν ἐκδοῦναι, οἱ δὲ κατακαῦσαι. ἐῴκει δὴ θαυμάζειν καὶ τὸν Πλάτωνα καὶ τὰ βιβλία ἐκέκτητο αὐτοῦ. (2) ἀλλὰ καὶ τὸν Πύρρωνα κατά τινας ἐζηλώκει, καὶ τῆς 5 διαλεκτικῆς εἴχετο καὶ τῶν Ἐρετρικῶν ἥπτετο λόγων, ὅθεν καὶ ἐλέγετο ἐπ᾽ αὐτοῦ ὑπ᾽ Ἀρίστωνος "πρόσθε Πλάτων, ὄπιθεν Πύρρων, μέσσος Διόδωρος." καὶ ὁ Τίμων ἐπ᾽ αὐτοῦ φησιν οὕτως "τῇ γὰρ ἔχων Μενέδημον ὑπὸ στέρνοισι μόλυβδον | θεύσεται ἢ Πύρρωνα τὸ πᾶν κρέας ἢ Διόδωρον." καὶ διαλιπὼν αὐτὸν ποιεῖ λέγοντα "νήξομαι εἰς Πύρρωνα καὶ εἰς σκολιὸν 10 Διόδωρον."

7 ὄπιθεν S.E., *PH* 1.234: ὄπι(σ)θε δὲ codd.   8 γὰρ codd.: μὲν Numenius ap. Euseb., *Praep. ev.* 14.5.13   Μενέδημον BF: -ον P, Numenius   9 θεύσεται Numenius: θήσεται codd.   ἢ ⟨'s⟩ Πύρρωνα Meineke   κρέας codd.: κέρας Lloyd-Jones, cf. Hom., *Il.* 24.81

Context: life of Arcesilaus.

1–2 *Acad. index* col. 18 expands the point about Socratides, and indicates that his

68 Methodology

seniority was the reason for his being the first choice to succeed Crates; cf. Glucker [42], 234 n. 25; Long [622], 434–5.

3–4   This puzzling sentence is illuminated by *Acad. index* 18.34–6, according to which Arcesilaus edited and revised some memoirs left by Crantor.

5 ἐκέκτητο   This probably means that Arcesilaus was in possession of Plato's own library and manuscripts.

6 διαλεκτικῆς   In this context, an allusion to the school of Diodorus. Ἐρετρικῶν refers to that of Menedemus.

7–8   Aristo's famous verse is a parody of the Homeric description of the Chimaera, πρόσθε λέων, ὄπιθεν δὲ δράκων, μέσση δὲ χίμαιρα, *Il.* 6.181. Its significance is well explained by Glucker [42], 35–6: 'What Aristo must have meant is that the *teachings* of Arcesilaus [not his philosophical education] presented such a chimaeric spectacle to him. They were officially expounded as Platonic; they appeared to Aristo to be identical with those of Pyrrho; while their central core consisted of [Diodorus'] dialectical arguments. . . .'

8–9   Our interpretation of these very obscure lines is based on Long [69], 80. (For other views, cf. Caizzi [64], 188–90.) μόλυβδον (cf. *Il.* 24.80) should refer to the lead weight of a fishing line, and Arcesilaus himself was probably (cf. 10), as Plato was certainly (Timon fr. 804), represented as a large fish. Menedemus' dialectic, we conjecture, is such attractive bait for Arcesilaus that he has devoured it, and is now in pursuit of further philosophical nutriment. For another account of Arcesilaus by Timon, see **3E**.

F Numenius (Eusebius, *Pr. ev.* 14.6.4–6)

(1) οὕτως μὲν δὴ ἔνθεν καταρτυθείς, πλὴν τῆς προσρήσεως, ἐνέμεινε Πυρρωνείως τῇ πάντων ἀναιρέσει. Μνασέας γοῦν καὶ Φιλόμηλος καὶ Τίμων οἱ σκεπτικοὶ σκεπτικὸν αὐτὸν προσονομάζουσιν, ὥσπερ καὶ αὐτοὶ ἦσαν, ἀναιροῦντα καὶ αὐτὸν τὸ ἀληθὲς καὶ τὸ ψεῦδος καὶ τὸ πιθανόν. (2) λεχθεὶς οὖν ἂν αἰτίᾳ τῶν Πυρρωνείων Πυρρώνειος, αἰδοῖ τοῦ ἐραστοῦ   5 ὑπέμεινε λέγεσθαι Ἀκαδημαικὸς ἔτι. ἦν μὲν τοίνυν Πυρρώνειος, πλὴν τοῦ ὀνόματος· Ἀκαδημαικὸς δ᾽ οὐκ ἦν, πλὴν τοῦ λέγεσθαι. οὐ γὰρ πείθομαι τοῦ Κνιδίου Δι⟨και⟩οκλέους φάσκοντος ἐν ταῖς ἐπιγραφομέναις Διατρι- βαῖς Ἀρκεσίλαον φόβῳ τῶν Θεοδωρείων τε καὶ Βίωνος τοῦ σοφιστοῦ ἐπεξιόντων τοῖς φιλοσοφοῦσι καὶ οὐδὲν ὀκνούντων ἀπὸ παντὸς ἐλέγχειν,   10 αὐτὸν ἐξευλαβηθέντα ἵνα μὴ πράγματα ἔχῃ, μηδὲν μὲν δόγμα ὑπειπεῖν φαινόμενον, ὥσπερ δὲ τὸ μέλαν τὰς σηπίας προβάλλεσθαι πρὸ ἑαυτοῦ τὴν ἐποχήν. τοῦτ᾽ οὖν ἐγὼ οὐ πείθομαι.

1 οὕτως Kiessling: οὗτος codd.   2 Πυρρωνείως Wilamowitz: Πύρρωνι ὡς codd.   5 ἂν αἰτίᾳ Heinichen: ἀναίτια vel sim. codd.   8 Δικαιοκλέους Wilamowitz: Διοκλέους codd.   10 ἐπε- ξιόντων Wilamowitz: ἐπεισιόντων codd.   11 ὑπειπεῖν ID: ἀπειπεῖν ON

Context: Arcesilaus' educational background, incorporating Theophrastus, Crantor, Diodorus and Pyrrho.

2–3   Philomelus is completely unknown. Mnaseas may be the Methodist doctor of that name, who lived at the time of Nero, and is referred to by Galen (14.684

435

Kühn). If so, later Pyrrhonists may have counted him as a 'Sceptic' (cf. S.E., *PH* 1.236–41), and he in turn would be regarding Arcesilaus similarly to Sextus in **I 1**. 4 **τὸ πιθανόν** Confirmed by Sextus in **I 2**. Carneades' and later Academics' adoption of the πιθανόν (cf. **69D–F, I**) as a practical criterion will have encouraged subsequent writers to stress Arcesilaus' difference in this respect, a difference which is doubtless genuine, even though Arcesilaus may not have expressed himself exactly as stated here. 5 **ἐραστοῦ** Crantor is meant; cf. Numenius at Eusebius, *Praep. ev.* 14.6.2; D.L. 4.22, 29. 8 **Δι⟨και⟩οκλέους** For this emendation of the MSS *Διοκλέους*, cf. Wilamowitz [31], 313 n. 23. Dicaeocles of Cnidus is referred to by Athenaeus (508) as a writer of *Diatribes*. He is a much more likely source for Numenius than the historian of philosophy Diocles of Magnesia, as suggested by Weische [616], 21. 9 For Theodorus and Bion, cf. vol. 1, Index of philosophers; and for the extant testimonia, see Giannantoni [36] 1, 301–15 (Theodorus), and Kindstrand [39]. Bion is also described as a 'sophist' at D.L. 4.47, which may help to identify the sophistic critics of Arcesilaus in **H 10**. For his hostility to the Academy, cf. D.L. 4.51, and for his personal connexions with Arcesilaus, see Kindstrand [39], 154.

G Numenius (Eusebius, *Pr. ev.* 14.6.12–13)

τὸν δ' οὖν Ζήνωνα ὁ 'Αρκεσίλαος ἀντίτεχνον καὶ ἀξιόνικον ὑπάρχοντα
θεωρῶν τοὺς παρ' ἐκείνου ἀποφερομένους λόγους καθῄρει καὶ οὐδὲν
ὤκνει . . . τὸ δὲ δόγμα τοῦτο αὐτοῦ πρώτου εὑρομένου καυτὸ καὶ τὸ ὄνομα
βλέπων εὐδοκιμοῦν ἐν ταῖς 'Αθήναις, τὴν καταληπτικὴν φαντασίαν, πάσῃ
μηχανῇ ἐχρῆτο ἐπ' αὐτήν.   5

Context: shortly after **F**.

3–5 For Zeno's innovation, cf. **40B**, and for Arcesilaus' opposition to it, **A 2** and note on **C 3**.

H Plutarch, *Col.* 1120C, 1121E–1122A

(1) γενόμενος δ' οὖν ὁ Κωλώτης ἀπὸ τῶν παλαιῶν τρέπεται πρὸς τοὺς καθ'
ἑαυτὸν φιλοσόφους, οὐδενὸς τιθεὶς ὄνομα . . . βούλεται δὲ προτέρους μέν,
ὡς ὑπονοῶ, τοὺς Κυρηναικοὺς ἐλέγχειν, δευτέρους δὲ τοὺς περὶ 'Αρκεσί-
λαον 'Ακαδημαικούς. οὗτοι γὰρ ἦσαν οἱ περὶ πάντων ἐπέχοντες . . . (2)
τοῦ δὲ 'Αρκεσιλάου τὸν 'Επικούρειον οὐ μετρίως ἔοικεν ἡ δόξα   5
παραλυπεῖν ἐν τοῖς τότε χρόνοις μάλιστα τῶν φιλοσόφων ἀγαπηθέντος.
μηδὲν γὰρ αὐτὸν ἴδιον λέγοντά φησιν ὑπόληψιν ἐμποιεῖν καὶ δόξαν
ἀνθρώποις ἀγραμμάτοις . . . (3) ὁ δ' 'Αρκεσίλαος τοσοῦτον ἀπέδει τοῦ
καινοτομίας τινὰ δόξαν ἀγαπᾶν καὶ ὑποποιεῖσθαί ⟨τι⟩ τῶν παλαιῶν ὥστε
ἐγκαλεῖν τοὺς τότε σοφιστὰς ὅτι προστρίβεται Σωκράτει καὶ Πλάτωνι   10
καὶ Παρμενίδῃ καὶ 'Ηρακλείτῳ τὰ περὶ τῆς ἐποχῆς δόγματα καὶ τῆς
ἀκαταληψίας οὐδὲν δεομένοις, ἀλλ' οἷον ἀναγωγὴν καὶ βεβαίωσιν αὐτῶν
εἰς ἄνδρας ἐνδόξους ποιούμενος. ὑπὲρ μὲν οὖν τούτου Κωλώτῃ χάρις καὶ

παντὶ τῷ τὸν Ἀκαδημαικὸν λόγον ἄνωθεν ἥκειν εἰς Ἀρκεσίλαον
ἀποφαίνοντι.   15

5 Ἐπικούρειον Crönert: ἐπίκουρον codd.   7 post ἐμποιεῖν ⟨καινοτομίας⟩ Reiske   9 ⟨τι⟩ Reiske

Context: 1–4, transition from the Epicurean Colotes' attack on Democritus,
Empedocles, Parmenides, Socrates, Plato and Stilpo to his anonymous critique of
contemporary philosophers whom he charges with making life impossible; 5–15, the
beginning of Colotes' attack on Academic scepticism, following his refutation of the
Cyrenaics.

5 Ἐπικούρειον   Crönert's emendation, though by no means certain, seems
highly probable. There is no independent evidence of controversy between Epicurus
himself and Arcesilaus; and the subject of φησι, 7, must be Colotes.

5–6   For Arcesilaus' contemporary renown, cf. Strabo 1.15, who cites Eratosthenes' judgement of him and the Stoic Aristo as the leading philosophers of his time.

10 σοφιστάς   See note on F 9. For Arcesilaus' appeals to philosophical precedent,
cf. A 2 with note, and Sedley [59], 15–16.

I Sextus Empiricus, *PH* 1.232–4

(1) ὁ μέντοι Ἀρκεσίλαος, ὃν τῆς μέσης Ἀκαδημίας ἐλέγομεν εἶναι
προστάτην καὶ ἀρχηγόν, πάνυ μοι δοκεῖ τοῖς Πυρρωνείοις κοινωνεῖν
λόγοις, ὡς μίαν εἶναι σχεδὸν τὴν κατ' αὐτὸν ἀγωγὴν καὶ τὴν ἡμετέραν. (2)
οὔτε γὰρ περὶ ὑπάρξεως ἢ ἀνυπαρξίας τινὸς ἀποφαινόμενος εὑρίσκεται,
οὔτε κατὰ πίστιν ἢ ἀπιστίαν προκρίνει τι ἕτερον ἑτέρου, ἀλλὰ περὶ πάντων   5
ἐπέχει. (3) καὶ τέλος μὲν εἶναι τὴν ἐποχήν, ᾗ συνεισέρχεσθαι τὴν ἀταραξίαν
ἡμεῖς ἐφάσκομεν. λέγει δὲ καὶ ἀγαθὰ μὲν εἶναι τὰς κατὰ μέρος ἐποχάς,
κακὰ δὲ τὰς κατὰ μέρος συγκαταθέσεις. (4) ἐκτὸς εἰ μὴ λέγοι τις ὅτι ἡμεῖς
μὲν κατὰ τὸ φαινόμενον ἡμῖν ταῦτα λέγομεν καὶ οὐ διαβεβαιωτικῶς,
ἐκεῖνος δὲ ὡς πρὸς τὴν φύσιν, ὥστε καὶ ἀγαθὸν μὲν εἶναι αὐτὸν λέγειν τὴν   10
ἐποχήν, κακὸν δὲ τὴν συγκατάθεσιν. (5) εἰ δὲ δεῖ καὶ τοῖς περὶ αὐτοῦ
λεγομένοις πιστεύειν, φασὶν ὅτι κατὰ μὲν τὸ πρόχειρον Πυρρώνειος
ἐφαίνετο εἶναι, κατὰ δὲ τὴν ἀλήθειαν δογματικὸς ἦν· καὶ ἐπεὶ τῶν ἑταίρων
ἀπόπειραν ἐλάμβανε διὰ τῆς ἀπορητικῆς, εἰ εὐφυῶς ἔχουσι πρὸς τὴν
ἀνάληψιν τῶν Πλατωνικῶν δογμάτων, δόξαι αὐτὸν ἀπορητικὸν εἶναι, τοῖς   15
μέντοι γε εὐφυέσι τῶν ἑταίρων τὰ Πλάτωνος παρεγχειρεῖν.

8 ἐκτὸς Mutschmann: ἤτοι πλὴν LEAB: ἐξὸν M: πλὴν Bury   10 αὐτὸν Mutschmann: αὐτὴν codd.

Context: survey of schools that are thought to resemble Pyrrhonist scepticism.

5 πίστιν ἢ ἀπιστίαν   See note on F 4.

6–11   The bald way in which Sextus formulates these 'doctrines' of Arcesilaus'
should be presumed to ignore qualifications and defences against dogmatizing which
the Academic would have made himself. For the position which we conjecture to be
the basis of Sextus' remarks see vol. 1, 447, and Sedley [59], 13–15. For what the later
Pyrrhonist says about suspension of judgement, and his difference from the
Academics, cf. 71A, C.

11–16   This tradition, which Sextus himself views with suspicion, probably
underlies Dicaeocles' charges in F 11–13. For a similar story told about Carneades, cf.

The Academics

Numenius in Eusebius, *Praep. ev.* 14.8.12–14. Notice that what is said to be concealed in **Q** is not Platonic *doctrine*, but the Academics' own opinion; cf. Glucker [42], 303–4. Sextus continues by relating what he has just said to Aristo's verse (**E** 7).

J Cicero, *Fin.* 2.2

is [*sc.* Socrates] enim percontando atque interrogando elicere solebat eorum opiniones quibuscum disserebat, ut ad ea quae ii respondissent, si quid videretur, diceret. qui mos cum a posterioribus non esset retentus, Arcesilas eum revocavit instituitque ut ii qui se audire vellent non de se quaererent, sed ipsi dicerent quid sentirent. quod cum dixissent, ille contra. sed eum qui   5 audiebant, quoad poterant, defendebant sententiam suam.

1 *percontando* A(corr.): *percun(c)tando* cett.

Context: Cicero's approval of the Socratic method of discourse.

5 **quid sentirent** Arcesilaus' instruction should be interpreted as the Socratic requirement that the interlocutor give an *honest* statement of his own opinion, and be prepared to engage in a serious dialectical examination of that opinion; cf. for instance Plato, *Gorg.* 500b, *Rep.* 1, 346a, and Long [622], 446–8.

6 In what follows our extract, Cicero goes on to observe that in the contemporary Academy the pupil merely puts up a thesis for discussion, and then listens to a formal refutation of it.

K Cicero, *Fin.* 5.10

disserendique ab isdem [*sc.* Peripateticis] non dialectice solum, sed etiam oratorie praecepta sunt tradita; ab Aristoteleque principe de singulis rebus in utramque partem dicendi exercitatio est instituta, ut non contra omnia semper, sicut Arcesilas, diceret, et tamen ut in omnibus rebus quicquid ex utraque parte dici posset expromeret.

Context: survey of the Peripatetic school.

This characterization of Aristotle is a Ciceronian commonplace; cf. **L** and *Tusc.* 2.9. It appears to be based on such passages as *Top.* 1.2, 101a34–6 and *Metaph.* B.1, 995b2–4.

L Cicero, *De or.* 3.80

sin aliquis extiterit aliquando qui Aristotelio more de omnibus rebus in utramque sententiam possit dicere et in omni causa duas contrarias orationes praeceptis illius cognitis explicare, aut hoc Arcesilae modo et Carneadi contra omne quod propositum sit disserat quique ad eam rationem exercitationem- que adiungat hunc rhetoricum usum moremque [exercitationemque] dicendi,   5 is sit verus, is perfectus, is solus orator.

4–5 *exercitationemque* huc transtul. Kumaniecki ex linea 5   5 *rhetoricum* del. Schütz   *moremque* del. Lambinus

Context: the best orator needs both training in public speaking and expertise in philosophical techniques of argument.

M Lactantius, *Div. inst.* 5.14.3–5 and *Epit.* 50.8

is [*sc.* Carneades] cum legatus ab Atheniensibus Romam missus esset, disputavit de iustitia copiose audiente Galba et Catone Censorio maximis tunc oratoribus. sed idem disputationem suam postridie contraria disputatione subvertit et iustitiam quam pridie laudaverit sustulit, non quidem philosophi gravitate, cuius firma et stabilis debet esse sententia, sed quasi oratorio exercitii 5 genere in utramque partem disserendi . . . Carneades autem ut Aristotelem refelleret ac Platonem iustitiae patronos, prima illa disputatione collegit ea omnia quae pro iustitia dicebantur, ut posset illam, sicut fecit, evertere . . . non quia vituperandam esse iustitiam sentiebat, sed ut illos defensores eius ostenderet nihil certi, nihil firmi de iustitia disputare.   10

Context: excerpt and paraphrase of a now lost section of Cicero's *De republica* (inserted by modern editors as 3.9–11).

   The Athenian embassy to Rome took place in 156–5 B.C. Carneades was accompanied by the Stoic Diogenes of Babylon and the Peripatetic Critolaus. For further details of his arguments for and against justice, see Long [3], 104–6.

N Cicero, *Acad.* 2.28–9

(1) sed Antipatro hoc idem postulanti, cum diceret ei qui adfirmaret nihil posse percipi [consentaneum esse] unum tamen illud dicere percipi posse consentaneum esse, ut alia non possent, Carneades acutius resistebat; nam tantum abesse dicebat ut id consentaneum esset, ut maxime etiam repugnaret. qui enim negaret quicquam esse quod perciperetur, eum nihil excipere; ita necesse 5 esse ne id ipsum quidem quod exceptum non esset conprendi et percipi ullo modo posse. (2) Antiochus ad istum locum pressius videbatur accedere. quoniam enim id haberent Academici decretum (sentitis enim iam hoc me δόγμα dicere) nihil posse percipi, non debere eos in suo decreto sicut in ceteris rebus fluctuari, praesertim cum in eo summa consisteret: hanc enim esse 10 regulam totius philosophiae, constitutionem veri falsi cogniti incogniti. quam rationem quoniam susciperent docereque vellent quae visa accipi oporteret quae repudiari, certe hoc ipsum, ex quo omne veri falsique iudicium esset, percipere eos debuisse.

2 *consentaneum esse* del. Manutius   12 *visa* Halm: *vis* codd.

Context: Lucullus' defence of Antiochus' epistemology against the New Academy.
   6–7 **ne id ipsum–posse** Cf. Arcesilaus in **A 3**.
   12–13 **docereque–repudiari**. Cf. **70B**.

O Cicero, *Acad.* 2.76–7

Arcesilan vero non obtrectandi causa cum Zenone pugnavisse sed verum invenire voluisse sic intellegitur; nemo umquam superiorum non modo expresserat sed ne dixerat quidem posse hominem nihil opinari, nec solum posse sed ita necesse esse sapienti. visa est Arcesilae cum vera sententia tum honesta et digna sapienti. 5

Context: rejoinder to the criticism of Arcesilaus stated in **C**; cf. **A 2**.
2 **sic intellegitur** From 4–5 combined with Arcesilaus' scrutiny of Zeno's position (**40D**).
3–5 The necessity and moral worth of the wise man's freedom from opinion, though not explained here, should be seen as a deduction from (a) the impossibility of cognition, and (b) the supreme moral badness of assenting in advance of cognition (**A 4**). With *honesta* and *neque . . . quicquam . . . turpius* (**A** 18), cf. Plato, *Soph.* 230b–e on the value of cathartic dialectic which rids the soul of the conceit of untested opinions, especially 230d8–e3, τὸν ἀνέλεγκτον αὖ νομιστέον . . . ἀπαίδευτόν τε καὶ αἰσχρὸν γεγονέναι ταῦτα ἃ καθαρώτατον καὶ κάλλιστον ἔπρεπε τὸν ὄντως ἐσόμενον εὐδαίμονα εἶναι.

P Augustine, *Acad.* 2.11

nam et Academicis placuit nec homini scientiam posse contingere earum dumtaxat rerum quae ad philosophiam pertinent – nam cetera curare se Carneades negabat – et tamen hominem posse esse sapientem sapientisque totum munus, ut abs te quoque, Licenti, illo sermone dissertum est, in conquisitione veri explicari. 5

Context: beginning of Augustine's account of the New Academy.
1–2 Cf. Epiphanius, *Adv. haeres.* 3.29, ᾿Αρκεσίλαος ἔφασκε τῷ θεῷ ἐφικτὸν εἶναι μόνῳ [Diels: μόνον codd.] τὸ ἀληθές, ἀνθρώπῳ δὲ οὔ. Καρνεάδης τὰ αὐτὰ τῷ ᾿Αρκεσιλάῳ ἐδόξασεν.
4 Licentius, in his exposition (*Acad.* 1.11–12), had argued that the quest for truth is sufficient for happiness, even though truth cannot be found.

Q Cicero, *Acad.* 2.60

restat illud quod dicunt veri inveniundi causa contra omnia dici oportere et pro omnibus. volo igitur videre quid invenerint. "non solemus" inquit "ostendere." quae sunt tandem ista mysteria, aut cur celatis quasi turpe aliquid sententiam vestram? "ut qui audient" inquit "ratione potius quam auctoritate ducantur." 5

Context: concluding section of Antiochus' criticism of the New Academy, as reported by Lucullus.
1 **veri inveniundi causa** Cf. **O** 1–2, **S** 1. Reference to the latter passage strongly suggests Philo as the Academic authority for this heuristic goal. Note the absence of any reference to suspension of judgement.
3–4 **celatis . . . sententiam** Cf. note on **I** 11–16 and Tarrant [629], 35–7.

R Cicero, *Acad.* 2.32

(1) nec vero satis constituere possum quod sit eorum consilium aut quid velint.

interdum enim cum adhibemus ad eos orationem eius modi, "si ea quae disputentur vera sint tum omnia fore incerta," respondent: "quid ergo istud ad nos? num nostra culpa est? naturam accusa, quae in profundo veritatem, ut ait Democritus, penitus abstruserit." (2) alii autem elegantius, qui etiam   5 queruntur quod eos insimulemus omnia incerta dicere, quantumque intersit inter incertum et id quod percipi non possit docere conantur eaque distinguere. (3) cum his igitur agamus qui haec distingunt, illos qui omnia sic incerta dicunt ut stellarum numerus par an impar sit quasi desperatos aliquos relinquamus. volunt enim . . . probabile aliquid esse et quasi veri simile, eaque   10 se uti regula et in agenda vita et in quaerendo ac disserendo.

Context: immediately following **40N**.

We are inclined to identify the hard-line Academics of 2–5 with philosophers like Aenesidemus (cf. **71C**), who refused to risk compromising their scepticism along the lines taken by Philo. As for the *alii*, 5–11, these are best treated as Philo and his followers, who extended Carneades' *probabile* from a purely practical criterion (cf. **69D–E**) to a heuristic and dialectical instrument (10–11); note the way these two functions are distinguished by Sextus in his criticism of the Academics (*M.* 7.435–7). At Cicero, *Acad.* 2.34, Lucullus refers to a group of Academics who want to distinguish between *perspicua* and *percepta*. These are certainly Philonians (cf. Tarrant [629], 53–7), and they are plainly presented in Cicero's text as identical to the *alii* of 5–11.

5 **Democritus** Cf. **A 9**.

S Cicero, *Acad.* 2.7–8

(1) neque nostrae disputationes quicquam aliud agunt nisi ut in utramque partem dicendo et audiendo eliciant et tamquam exprimant aliquid quod aut verum sit aut ad id quam proxime accedat. (2) nec inter nos et eos qui se scire arbitrantur quicquam interest nisi quod illi non dubitant quin ea vera sint quae defendunt, nos probabilia multa habemus, quae sequi facile, adfirmare vix   5 possumus. hoc autem liberiores et solutiores sumus, quod integra nobis est iudicandi potestas nec ut omnia quae praescripta a quibusdam et quasi imperata sint defendamus necessitate ulla cogimur.

7 *a quibusdam* Canter, Reid: *et quibus* codd.: secl. cett. edd.

Context: Cicero's defence of the New Academy.

For regarding this passage as the manifesto of Philo's Academy, cf. Tarrant [629], 4, 25–6.

T Sextus Empiricus, *PH* 1.235

οἱ δὲ περὶ Φίλωνά φασιν ὅσον μὲν ἐπὶ τῷ Στωικῷ κριτηρίῳ, τουτέστι τῇ καταληπτικῇ φαντασίᾳ, ἀκατάληπτα εἶναι τὰ πράγματα, ὅσον δὲ ἐπὶ τῇ φύσει τῶν πραγμάτων αὐτῶν, καταληπτά. ἀλλὰ καὶ ὁ Ἀντίοχος τὴν Στοὰν μετήγαγεν εἰς τὴν Ἀκαδημίαν, ὡς καὶ εἰρῆσθαι ἐπ' αὐτῷ ὅτι ἐν

The Academics

Ἀκαδημίᾳ φιλοσοφεῖ τὰ Στωικά· ἐπεδείκνυε γὰρ ὅτι παρὰ Πλάτωνι 5
κεῖται τὰ τῶν Στωικῶν δόγματα.

Context: shortly after **I**.

1–3 What Philo meant by leaving things 'cognitive', so far as their nature is concerned, is a question on which certainty is unattainable. For Platonic precedents on which he might have drawn, including that of god's superior cognition (as attested for his New Academic predecessors by Epiphanius, note to **P** 1–2), cf. Sedley [630], 72–3. We are intrigued, but not persuaded, by the novel proposal by Tarrant [629], 53–9, to attribute a non-Stoic sense of cognition to Philo, which would suffice to get at the nature of things.

3–6 Cf. what is said of Antiochus at Cicero, *Acad.* 1.43 (note to **B** 4).

U Cicero, *Acad.* 2.17–18

(1) iam Clitomacho Philo vester operam multos annos dedit; Philone autem vivo patrocinium Academiae non defuit. (2) sed quod nos facere nunc ingredimur, ut contra Academicos disseramus, id quidam e philosophis et i quidem non mediocres faciundum omnino non putabant. nec vero esse ullam rationem disputare cum is qui nihil probarent, Antipatrumque Stoicum qui 5 multus in eo fuisset reprehendebant. nec definiri aiebant necesse esse quid esset cognitio aut perceptio aut, si verbum e verbo volumus, conprehensio (quam κατάληψιν illi vocant), eosque qui persuadere vellent esse aliquid quod conprehendi et percipi posset inscienter facere dicebant, propterea quod nihil esset clarius ἐναργείᾳ . . . nec ea quae tam clara essent definienda cense- 10 bant . . .(3) Philo autem dum nova quaedam commovet, quod ea sustinere vix poterat quae contra Academicorum pertinaciam dicebantur, et aperte mentitur . . . et, ut docuit Antiochus, in id ipsum se induit quod timebat. cum enim ita negaret quicquam esse quod conprehendi posset . . . iudicium tollit incogniti et cogniti. ex quo efficitur nihil posse conprehendi, ita inprudens eo 15 quo minime volt revolvitur.

Context: a little after **C**.

3–11 Our guess at the identity of these philosophers is the Peripatetic school under Critolaus, contemporary with Antipater. For Peripatetic interest in the criterial role of τὸ ἐναργές, cf. S.E., *M.* 7.218 (Theophrastus), and for their rejection of the absolute certainty invoked by the Stoic criterion of truth, see Cicero, *Acad.* 2.143. The Epicureans (suggested by Schofield [471], 288) seem less likely, since they certainly did argue against scepticism (**16**).

15 **nihil posse conprehendi** Contrary to his claim in **T** 2–3.

V Galen, *Opt. doctr.* 1

(1) τὴν εἰς ἑκάτερα ἐπιχείρησιν ἀρίστην εἶναι διδασκαλίαν ὁ Φαβωρῖνός φησιν. ὀνομάζουσι δ' οὕτως οἱ Ἀκαδημαικοὶ καθ' ἣν τοῖς ἀντικειμένοις συναγορεύουσιν. οἱ μὲν οὖν παλαιότεροι τελευτᾶν αὐτὴν εἰς ἐποχὴν

442

ὑπολαμβάνουσιν, ἐποχὴν καλοῦντες τὴν ὡς ἂν εἴποι τις ἀοριστίαν, ὅπερ
ἐστὶ περὶ μηδενὸς πράγματος ὁρίσασθαι μηδ' ἀποφήνασθαι βεβαίως. (2) οἱ   5
νεώτεροι δ' - οὐ γὰρ μόνος ὁ Φαβωρῖνος - ἐνίοτε μὲν εἰς τοσοῦτον
προάγουσι τὴν ἐποχὴν ὡς μηδὲ τὸν ἥλιον ὁμολογεῖν εἶναι καταληπτόν,
ἐνίοτε δ' εἰς τοσοῦτον τὴν κρίσιν ὡς καὶ τοῖς μαθηταῖς ἐπιτρέπειν αὐτὴν
ἄνευ τοῦ διδαχθῆναι πρότερον ἐπιστημονικὸν κριτήριον . . . καὶ μέντοι
κἂν τῷ μετὰ ταῦτα γραφέντι βιβλίῳ τῷ Ἀλκιβιάδῃ τοὺς Ἀκαδημαικοὺς   10
ἐπαινεῖ συναγορεύοντας μὲν ἑκατέρῳ τῶν ἀντικειμένων ἀλλήλοις λόγων,
ἐπιτρέποντας δὲ τοῖς μαθηταῖς αἱρεῖσθαι τοὺς ἀληθεστέρους. (3) ἀλλ' ἐν
τούτῳ μὲν εἴρηκε πιθανὸν ἑαυτῷ φαίνεσθαι μηδὲν εἶναι καταληπτόν, ἐν δὲ
τῷ Πλουτάρχῳ συγχωρεῖν ἔοικεν εἶναί τι βεβαίως γνωστόν.

Context: the opening of the treatise.
3–4 Cf. **1G** for early Pyrrhonian precedent.
9 For Galen's views on the criterion of truth, cf. Long [477].

69 Living without opinions

A Plutarch, *Col.* 1122A–F

(1) τὴν δὲ περὶ πάντων ἐποχὴν οὐδ' οἱ πολλὰ πραγματευσάμενοι καὶ
κατατείναντες εἰς τοῦτο συγγράμματα καὶ λόγους ἐκίνησαν· ἀλλ' ἐκ τῆς
Στοᾶς αὐτῇ τελευτῶντες ὥσπερ Γοργόνα τὴν ἀπραξίαν ἐπάγοντες
ἀπηγόρευσαν, ὡς πάντα πειρῶσι καὶ στρέφουσιν αὐτοῖς οὐχ ὑπήκουσεν ἡ
ὁρμὴ γενέσθαι συγκατάθεσις οὐδὲ τῆς ῥοπῆς ἀρχὴν ἐδέξατο τὴν αἴσθησιν,   5
ἀλλ' ἐξ ἑαυτῆς ἀγωγὸς ἐπὶ τὰς πράξεις ἐφάνη, μὴ δεομένη τοῦ
προστίθεσθαι . . . λέγεται δὲ τοῖς συνεπομένοις καὶ ἀκούουσιν, ὅτι (2)
τριῶν περὶ τὴν ψυχὴν κινημάτων ὄντων, φανταστικοῦ καὶ ὁρμητικοῦ καὶ
συγκαταθετικοῦ, τὸ μὲν φανταστικὸν οὐδὲ βουλομένοις ἀνελεῖν ἔστιν, ἀλλ'
ἀνάγκη προεντυγχάνοντας τοῖς πράγμασι τυποῦσθαι καὶ πάσχειν ὑπ'   10
αὐτῶν, (3) τὸ δ' ὁρμητικὸν ἐγειρόμενον ὑπὸ τοῦ φανταστικοῦ πρὸς τὰ
οἰκεῖα πρακτικῶς κινεῖ τὸν ἄνθρωπον, οἷον ῥοπῆς ἐν τῷ ἡγεμονικῷ καὶ
νεύσεως γινομένης. οὐδὲ τοῦτ' οὖν ἀναιροῦσιν οἱ περὶ πάντων ἐπέχοντες,
ἀλλὰ χρῶνται τῇ ὁρμῇ φυσικῶς ἀγούσῃ πρὸς τὸ φαινόμενον οἰκεῖον. (4) τί
οὖν φεύγουσι μόνον; ᾧ μόνῳ ψεῦδος ἐμφύεται καὶ ἀπάτη, τὸ δοξάζειν καὶ   15
προπίπτειν τὴν συγκατάθεσιν, εἴξιν οὖσαν ὑπ' ἀσθενείας τῷ φαινομένῳ,
χρήσιμον δ' οὐδὲν ἔχουσαν. (5) ἡ γὰρ πρᾶξις δυοῖν δεῖται, φαντασίας τοῦ
οἰκείου καὶ πρὸς τὸ φανὲν οἰκεῖον ὁρμῆς, ὧν οὐδέτερον τῇ ἐποχῇ μάχεται.
δόξης γάρ, οὐχ ὁρμῆς οὐδὲ φαντασίας ὁ λόγος ἀφίστησιν. ὅταν οὖν φανῇ τὸ
[ἡδὺ] οἰκεῖον, οὐθὲν δεῖ πρὸς τὴν ἐπ' αὐτὸ κίνησιν καὶ φορὰν δόξης, ἀλλ'   20
ἦλθεν εὐθὺς ἡ ὁρμή, κίνησις οὖσα καὶ φορὰ τῆς ψυχῆς . . . (6) "ἀλλὰ πῶς
οὐκ εἰς ὄρος ἄπεισι τρέχων ὁ ἐπέχων ἀλλ' εἰς βαλανεῖον, οὐδὲ πρὸς τὸν
τοῖχον ἀλλὰ πρὸς τὰς θύρας ἀναστὰς βαδίζει, βουλόμενος εἰς ἀγορὰν
προελθεῖν;" τοῦτ' ἐρωτᾷς ἀκριβῆ τὰ αἰσθητήρια λέγων εἶναι καὶ τὰς

The Academics

φαντασίας ἀληθεῖς· ὅτι φαίνεται δήπουθεν αὐτῷ βαλανεῖον οὐ τὸ ὄρος   2ξ
ἀλλὰ τὸ βαλανεῖον, καὶ θύρα οὐχ ὁ τοῖχος ἀλλ' ἡ θύρα, καὶ τῶν ἄλλων
ὁμοίως ἕκαστον. (7) ὁ γὰρ τῆς ἐποχῆς λόγος οὐ παρατρέπει τὴν αἴσθησιν,
οὐδὲ τοῖς ἀλόγοις πάθεσιν αὐτοῖς καὶ κινήμασιν ἀλλοίωσιν ἐμποιεῖ
διαταράττουσαν τὸ φανταστικόν, ἀλλὰ τὰς δόξας μόνον ἀναιρεῖ χρῆται δὲ
τοῖς ἄλλοις ὡς πέφυκεν.   3ς

3 αὐτῇ Pohlenz: αὐτῆς codd.   5 αἴσθησιν codd.: πρόσθεσιν Pohlenz   12 κινεῖ Stephanus: κινεῖν
codd.   16 προπίπτειν Salmasius: προσ- codd.   20 ἡδὺ del. Einarson/De Lacy   28 αὐτοῖς codd.:
αὐτῆς Reiske

Context: immediately after **68H**.
Reasons for regarding Arcesilaus as the author of the argument in 7–21 are briefly
noted in vol. 1, 456. (See further Westman [139], 294–5, 302–3.) They are compatible
with Plutarch's report, 1–3, that the controversy was protracted, as is equally clear
from Antiochus' continuing insistence on assent as a precondition of impulse and
action; cf. **40O** and Cicero, *Acad.* 2.24–5. It is likely that some of the language of
Plutarch's report is derived from this later time. For further study of the argument, cf.
Striker [467], 65 n. 29, 67–9.
    3 **Γοργόνα** Cf. Epictetus, *Diss.* 1.5.1–3. ἀπραξία by this date is a technical term
for the impossibility of action, imputed to sceptics by their critics.
    5 **ῥοπῆς** Cf. *lancem* **40O** 7.
    7 **προστίθεσθαι** A synonym for συγκατατίθεσθαι; cf. S.E., *M.* 7.225.
    8–9   The three movements refer to the three specific Stoic faculties of soul; cf.
53H 1, **K** 2, and vol. 1, 321–2.
    14 **φυσικῶς** The crucial role this notion plays in Arcesilaus' argument is
recognized by Striker (see above); cf. also ὡς πέφυκεν, 30, and Plutarch's rejoinder to
the Epicureans in the section we omit after ψυχῆς, 21. Arcesilaus is best interpreted
not as intruding a non-Stoic concept, but as exploiting the *natural* causal connexion
Stoics could be taken to posit between an impression of what is appropriate and action
in pursuit thereof (cf. **40O** 3, **60F** 2; and note the combination φυσικῶς καὶ οἰκείως,
34J 4). He could argue that such passages make assent a superfluous link in a causal
chain, rather than the precondition of every impulse, as the Stoics want to maintain.
    20 **[ἡδύ]** The word is clearly out of place, and looks like an Epicurean gloss on
οἰκεῖον.
    21   In the omitted lines Plutarch argues that suspension of judgement is
compatible with the Epicureans' theory of action, given their doctrine concerning the
natural attractiveness of pleasure (cf. **21A** 1–3). He then quotes an objection to
Arcesilaus by Colotes, which is very similar to Aristotle's insistence on the
impossibility of acting if one really rejected the principle of non-contradiction
(*Metaph.* Γ.4, 1008b12–16; cf. Long [57], 96–7). Plutarch's rejoinder, 24–30, is
offered on behalf of Arcesilaus. There seems to be no evidence, here or elsewhere, to
show that Arcesilaus himself engaged in argument with the Epicureans.

B Sextus Empiricus, *M.* 7.158

(1) ἀλλ' ἐπεὶ μετὰ τοῦτο ἔδει καὶ περὶ τῆς τοῦ βίου διεξαγωγῆς ζητεῖν, ἥτις
οὐ χωρὶς κριτηρίου πέφυκεν ἀποδίδοσθαι, ἀφ' οὗ καὶ ἡ εὐδαιμονία,

τουτέστι τὸ τοῦ βίου τέλος, ἠρτημένην ἔχει τὴν πίστιν, φησὶν ὁ
Ἀρκεσίλαος, ὅτι ὁ περὶ πάντων ἐπέχων κανονιεῖ τὰς αἱρέσεις καὶ φυγὰς
καὶ κοινῶς τὰς πράξεις τῷ εὐλόγῳ, κατὰ τοῦτό τε προερχόμενος τὸ   5
κριτήριον κατορθώσει· (2) τὴν μὲν γὰρ εὐδαιμονίαν περιγίνεσθαι διὰ τῆς
φρονήσεως, τὴν δὲ φρόνησιν κεῖσθαι ἐν τοῖς κατορθώμασιν, τὸ δὲ
κατόρθωμα εἶναι ὅπερ πραχθὲν εὔλογον ἔχει τὴν ἀπολογίαν. (3) ὁ
προσέχων οὖν τῷ εὐλόγῳ κατορθώσει καὶ εὐδαιμονήσει.

4 ὁ Hervetus: οὐ codd.   7 κεῖσθαι N: κινεῖσθαι cett.

Context: immediately following 41C.

5 τῷ εὐλόγῳ For the Stoic definition of a εὔλογον ἀξίωμα, cf. note to 40F; and
for further Stoic background to this concept, and to those which follow, see vol. 1,
457. The most interesting attempt to credit Arcesilaus with substantive ethical
doctrines (although we ourselves resist it) is that of Ioppolo [621].

C Diogenes Laertius 7.171

εἰπόντος δέ τινος Ἀρκεσίλαον μὴ ποιεῖν τὰ δέοντα, "παῦσαι", ἔφη [sc.
Κλεάνθης], "καὶ μὴ ψέγε· εἰ γὰρ καὶ λόγῳ τὸ καθῆκον ἀναιρεῖ, τοῖς γοῦν
ἔργοις αὐτὸ τιθεῖ." καὶ ὁ Ἀρκεσίλαος, "οὐ κολακεύομαι", φησί. πρὸς ὃν ὁ
Κλεάνθης, "ναί", ἔφη, "σὲ κολακεύω φάμενος ἄλλα μὲν λέγειν, ἕτερα δὲ
ποιεῖν."   5

4 ναί FP: καί B

Context: life of Cleanthes.
4 The imputation of inconsistency is very barbed flattery; cf. 68A 5.

D Sextus Empiricus, M. 7.166–75

(1) ταῦτα μὲν ἀντιπαρεξάγων τοῖς ἄλλοις φιλοσόφοις ὁ Καρνεάδης εἰς τὴν
ἀνυπαρξίαν τοῦ κριτηρίου διεξήρχετο· ἀπαιτούμενος δὲ καὶ αὐτός τι
κριτήριον πρός τε τὴν τοῦ βίου διεξαγωγὴν καὶ πρὸς τὴν τῆς εὐδαιμονίας
περίκτησιν, δυνάμει ἐπαναγκάζεται καὶ καθ' αὑτὸν περὶ τούτου διατάτ-
τεσθαι, προσλαμβάνων τήν τε πιθανὴν φαντασίαν καὶ τὴν πιθανὴν ἅμα καὶ   5
ἀπερίσπαστον καὶ διεξωδευμένην. (2) τίς δέ ἐστιν ἡ τούτων διαφορά,
συντόμως ὑποδεικτέον. ἡ τοίνυν φαντασία τινὸς φαντασία ἐστίν, οἷον τοῦ
τε ἀφ' οὗ γίνεται καὶ τοῦ ἐν ᾧ γίνεται, καὶ ⟨τοῦ⟩ ἀφ' οὗ μὲν γίνεται ὡς τοῦ
ἐκτὸς ὑποκειμένου αἰσθητοῦ, τοῦ ἐν ᾧ δὲ γίνεται καθάπερ ἀνθρώπου.
τοιαύτη δὲ οὖσα δύο ἂν ἔχοι σχέσεις, μίαν μὲν ὡς πρὸς τὸ φανταστόν,   10
δευτέραν δὲ ὡς πρὸς τὸν φαντασιούμενον. κατὰ μὲν οὖν τὴν πρὸς τὸ
φανταστὸν σχέσιν ἢ ἀληθὴς γίνεται ἢ ψευδής, καὶ ἀληθὴς μὲν ὅταν
σύμφωνος ᾖ τῷ φανταστῷ, ψευδὴς δὲ ὅταν διάφωνος. κατὰ δὲ τὴν πρὸς τὸν
φαντασιούμενον σχέσιν ἡ μέν ἐστι φαινομένη ἀληθὴς ἡ δὲ οὐ φαινομένη
ἀληθής, ὧν ἡ μὲν φαινομένη ἀληθὴς ἔμφασις καλεῖται παρὰ τοῖς   15
Ἀκαδημαικοῖς καὶ πιθανότης καὶ πιθανὴ φαντασία, ἡ δ' οὐ φαινομένη

445

ἀληθὴς ἀπέμφασίς τε προσαγορεύεται καὶ ἀπειθὴς καὶ ἀπίθανος φαν-
τασία· οὔτε γὰρ τὸ αὐτόθεν φαινόμενον ψευδὲς οὔτε τὸ ἀληθὲς μέν, μὴ
φαινόμενον δὲ ἡμῖν πείθειν ἡμᾶς πέφυκεν. (3) τούτων δὲ τῶν φαντασιῶν ἡ
μὲν φανερῶς ψευδὴς καὶ μὴ φαινομένη ἀληθὴς παραγράψιμός ἐστι καὶ οὐ   20
κριτήριον, [ἐάν τε ⟨ . . . ⟩ ἀπὸ ὑπάρχοντος μέν, διαφώνως δὲ τῷ ὑπάρχοντι καὶ μὴ κατ᾽
αὐτὸ τὸ ὑπάρχον, ὁποία ἦν ἡ ἀπὸ Ἠλέκτρας προσπεσοῦσα τῷ Ὀρέστῃ, μίαν τῶν Ἐρινύων
αὐτὴν δοξάζοντι καὶ κεκραγότι· "μέθες· μί᾽ οὖσα τῶν ἐμῶν Ἐρινύων."] (4) τῆς δὲ
φαινομένης ἀληθοῦς ἡ μέν τίς ἐστιν ἀμυδρά, ὡς ἡ ἐπὶ τῶν παρὰ μικρότητα
τοῦ θεωρουμένου ἢ παρὰ ἱκανὸν διάστημα ἢ καὶ παρὰ ἀσθένειαν τῆς ὄψεως   25
συγκεχυμένως καὶ οὐκ ἐκτύπως τι λαμβανόντων, ἡ δέ τις ἦν σὺν τῷ
φαίνεσθαι ἀληθὴς ἔτι καὶ σφοδρὸν ἔχουσα τὸ φαίνεσθαι αὐτὴν ἀληθῆ. ὧν
πάλιν ἡ μὲν ἀμυδρὰ καὶ ἔκλυτος φαντασία οὐκ ἂν εἴη κριτήριον· τῷ γὰρ
μήτε αὐτὴν μήτε τὸ ποιῆσαν αὐτὴν τρανῶς ἐνδείκνυσθαι οὐ πέφυκεν ἡμᾶς
πείθειν οὐδ᾽ εἰς συγκατάθεσιν ἐπισπᾶσθαι. ἡ δὲ φαινομένη ἀληθὴς καὶ   30
ἱκανῶς ἐμφαινομένη κριτήριόν ἐστι τῆς ἀληθείας κατὰ τοὺς περὶ τὸν
Καρνεάδην. (5) κριτήριον δὲ οὖσα πλάτος εἶχεν ἱκανόν, καὶ ἐπιτεινομένη
αὐτὴ ἄλλην ἄλλης ἐν εἴδει πιθανωτέραν τε καὶ πληκτικωτέραν ἴσχει
φαντασίαν. τὸ δὲ πιθανὸν ὡς πρὸς τὸ παρὸν λέγεται τριχῶς, καθ᾽ ἕνα μὲν
τρόπον τὸ ἀληθές τε ὂν καὶ φαινόμενον ἀληθές, καθ᾽ ἕτερον δὲ τὸ ψευδὲς   35
μὲν καθεστὼς φαινόμενον δὲ ἀληθές, κατὰ δὲ τρίτον τὸ ἀληθὲς ⟨φαινόμε-
νον ὅπερ ἐστὶ⟩ κοινὸν ἀμφοτέρων. ὅθεν τὸ κριτήριον ἔσται μὲν ἡ
φαινομένη ἀληθὴς φαντασία, ἣν καὶ πιθανὴν προσηγόρευον οἱ ἀπὸ τῆς
Ἀκαδημίας, ἐμπίπτει δὲ ἔσθ᾽ ὅτε καὶ ψευδής, ὥστε ἀνάγκην ἔχειν καὶ τῇ
κοινῇ ποτε τοῦ ἀληθοῦς καὶ ψευδοῦς φαντασίᾳ χρῆσθαι. οὐ μέντοι διὰ τὴν   40
σπάνιον ταύτης παρέμπτωσιν, λέγω δὲ τῆς μιμουμένης τὸ ἀληθές,
ἀπιστητέον ἐστὶ τῇ ὡς ⟨ἐπὶ⟩ τὸ πολὺ ἀληθευούσῃ· τῷ γὰρ ὡς ἐπὶ τὸ πολὺ
τάς τε κρίσεις καὶ τὰς πράξεις κανονίζεσθαι συμβέβηκεν.

4 ἐπαναγκάζεται Bekker: ἀπ- codd.   6 διεξοδευμένην N: διεξοδευμένην cett.   8 ⟨τοῦ⟩
Heintz   11, 13 τὸν LEABR: τὸ NV   21–4 ἐάν τε . . . Ἐρινύων secl. Heintz   21 τε ⟨ἀπὸ μὴ
ὑπάρχοντος γίγνεται ἐάν τε⟩ Bekker   26 λαμβανόντων Bekker: λαμβανούσης codd.   32–3
ἐπιτεινομένη αὐτὴ ἄλλην A.A. Long: ἐπιτεινομένης αὐτῆς ἄλλη codd.   36–7 suppl. A.A. Long: del.
ἀληθές Bekker, Mutschmann   42 ⟨ἐπὶ⟩ Kayser

Context: immediately following **70A**.
For Carneades' use of Stoic concepts here and in **E**, see vol. 1, 459, where our
commentary has benefited from the opportunity to read an unpublished paper by
Myles Burnyeat. The gist of Carneades' analysis of 'convincing' impressions is
presented more summarily by Cicero at *Acad.* 2.99–101 (cf. **42I**), on the basis of book
1 of Clitomachus' *On suspension of judgement.* Sextus criticizes it at *M.* 7.435–8.

2 **καὶ αὐτός** In addition to Arcesilaus, **B 1**.
15 **ἔμφασις** This use of the term, with the coinage of ἀπέμφασις as its opposite,
is an Academic initiative. By itself ἔμφασις simply means 'appearance', and can be
used as a synonym for φαντασία; cf. S.E., *M.* 10.300. In Stoicism (cf. **39A** 18) it even
stands for φαντασίαι which are 'mere appearances' and have no corresponding object.
21–4 The garbled intrusion of Stoicism, with its anticipation of the Orestes

example (see **39G 9**; **40E 6**), is quite out of place here. It should probably be explained as a marginal note, based on the later passages, which was unthinkingly incorporated into the text under the influence of the Menelaus example in **E 2**.

32–3 ἐπιτεινομένη–ἄλλην   Cf. **E 24**. Our emendation is an attempt to restore grammar and sense. As transmitted, the text presents a genitive absolute which refers to the subject of ἴσχει, and ἄλλη yields the surely impossible thought that 'one [impression which appears true] *has* a more convincing . . . impression than another'. Note Bury's unacceptably free translation of the unemended text in the Loeb edition: 'and when extended one presentation reveals itself as more probable . . . than another'.

36–7   To make sense, either the word ἀληθές must be deleted, or something must be supplied after it. We prefer the second alternative. Our supplement, τὸ ἀληθὲς ⟨φαινόμενον ὅπερ ἐστὶ⟩, fits the language and thought of 35–40, allows the retention of ἀληθές, and exhibits the logic of the passage more clearly than the first alternative. It is easier to explain the accidental omission of the words we supply than to account for the incorrect intrusion of ἀληθές.

E Sextus Empiricus, *M.* 7.176–84

(1) τὸ μὲν οὖν πρῶτον καὶ κοινὸν κριτήριον κατὰ τοὺς περὶ τὸν Καρνεάδην
ἐστὶ τοιοῦτον· ἐπεὶ δὲ οὐδέποτε φαντασία μονοειδὴς ὑφίσταται ἀλλ᾽
ἀλύσεως τρόπον ἄλλη ἐξ ἄλλης ἤρτηται, δεύτερον προσγενήσεται
κριτήριον ἡ πιθανὴ ἅμα καὶ ἀπερίσπαστος φαντασία. οἷον ὁ ἀνθρώπου
σπῶν φαντασίαν ἐξ ἀνάγκης καὶ τῶν περὶ αὐτὸν λαμβάνει φαντασίαν καὶ   5
τῶν ἐκτός, τῶν μὲν περὶ αὐτὸν ⟨ὡς⟩ χρόας μεγέθους σχήματος κινήσεως
λαλιᾶς ἐσθῆτος ὑποδέσεως, τῶν δὲ ἐκτὸς ὡς ἀέρος φωτὸς ἡμέρας οὐρανοῦ
γῆς φίλων, τῶν ἄλλων ἁπάντων. ὅταν οὖν μηδεμία τούτων τῶν φαντασιῶν
περιέλκῃ ἡμᾶς τῷ φαίνεσθαι ψευδής, ἀλλὰ πᾶσαι συμφώνως φαίνωνται
ἀληθεῖς, μᾶλλον πιστεύομεν. ὅτι γὰρ οὗτός ἐστι Σωκράτης, πιστεύομεν ἐκ   10
τοῦ πάντα αὐτῷ προσεῖναι τὰ εἰωθότα, χρῶμα μέγεθος σχῆμα διάλεξιν
τρίβωνα, τὸ ἐνθάδε εἶναι ὅπου οὐθείς ἐστιν αὐτῷ ἀπαράλλακτος. καὶ ὃν
τρόπον τινὲς τῶν ἰατρῶν τὸν κατ᾽ ἀλήθειαν πυρέσσοντα οὐκ ἐξ ἑνὸς λαμβάνουσι
συμπτώματος, καθάπερ σφυγμοῦ σφοδρότητος ἢ δαψιλοῦς θερμασίας, ἀλλ᾽ ἐκ συνδρομῆς,
οἷον θερμασίας ἅμα καὶ σφυγμοῦ καὶ ἑλκώδους ἁφῆς καὶ ἐρυθήματος καὶ δίψους καὶ τῶν   15
ἀνάλογον, οὕτω καὶ ὁ Ἀκαδημαϊκὸς τῇ συνδρομῇ τῶν φαντασιῶν ποιεῖται τὴν κρίσιν τῆς
ἀληθείας, μηδεμιᾶς τε τῶν ἐν τῇ συνδρομῇ φαντασιῶν περισπώσης αὐτὸν ὡς ψευδοῦς λέγει
ἀληθὲς εἶναι τὸ προσπῖπτον. καὶ ὅτι ἡ ἀπερίσπαστός ἐστι συνδρομὴ τοῦ πίστιν ἐμποιεῖν,
φανερὸν ἀπὸ Μενελάου· (2) καταλιπὼν γὰρ ἐν τῇ νηὶ τὸ εἴδωλον τῆς Ἑλένης,
ὅπερ ἀπὸ Τροίας ἐπήγετο ὡς Ἑλένην, καὶ ἐπιβὰς τῆς Φάρου νήσου ὁρᾷ   20
τὴν ἀληθῆ Ἑλένην, σπῶν τε ἀπ᾽ αὐτῆς ἀληθῆ φαντασίαν ὅμως οὐ πιστεύει
τῇ τοιαύτῃ φαντασίᾳ διὰ τὸ ὑπ᾽ ἄλλης περισπᾶσθαι, καθ᾽ ἣν ᾔδει
ἀπολελοιπὼς ἐν τῇ νηὶ τὴν Ἑλένην. τοιαύτη γοῦν ἐστι καὶ ἡ ἀπερίσπαστος
φαντασία· ἥτις καὶ αὐτὴ πλάτος ἔχειν ἔοικε διὰ τὸ ἄλλην ἄλλης μᾶλλον
ἀπερίσπαστον εὑρίσκεσθαι. (3) τῆς δὲ ἀπερισπάστου φαντασίας πιστο-   25
τέρα μᾶλλόν ἐστι καὶ τελειοτάτην ποιοῦσα τὴν κρίσιν, ἢ σὺν τῷ

447

The Academics

ἀπερίσπαστος εἶναι ἔτι καὶ διεξωδευμένη καθέστηκεν. τίς δέ ἐστι καὶ ὁ
ταύτης χαρακτήρ, παρακειμένως ὑποδεικτέον. ἐπὶ μὲν γὰρ τῆς ἀπερισπάστου ψιλὸν ζητεῖται τὸ μηδεμίαν τῶν ἐν τῇ συνδρομῇ φαντασιῶν ὡς
ψευδῆ ἡμᾶς περισπᾶν, πάσας δὲ εἶναι ἀληθεῖς τε [καὶ] φαινομένας καὶ μὴ   30
ἀπιθάνους· ἐπὶ δὲ τῆς κατὰ τὴν περιωδευμένην συνδρομῆς ἑκάστην τῶν ἐν
τῇ συνδρομῇ ἐπιστατικῶς δοκιμάζομεν, ὁποῖόν τι γίνεται καὶ ἐν ταῖς
ἐκκλησίαις, ὅταν ὁ δῆμος ἕκαστον τῶν μελλόντων ἄρχειν ἢ δικάζειν
ἐξετάζῃ εἰ ἄξιός ἐστι τοῦ πιστευθῆναι τὴν ἀρχὴν ⟨ἢ⟩ τὴν κρίσιν. (4) οἷον
ὄντων κατὰ τὸν τῆς κρίσεως τόπον τοῦ τε κρίνοντος καὶ τοῦ κρινομένου καὶ τοῦ δι'   35
οὗ ἡ κρίσις, ἀποστήματός τε καὶ διαστήματος, τόπου χρόνου τρόπου διαθέσεως ἐνεργείας,
ἕκαστον τῶν τοιούτων ὁποῖόν ἐστι φυλοκρινοῦμεν, τὸ μὲν κρῖνον, μὴ ἡ
ὄψις ἤμβλυται (τοιαύτη γὰρ οὖσα ἄθετός ἐστι πρὸς τὴν κρίσιν), τὸ δὲ κρινόμενον,
μὴ μικρὸν ἄγαν καθέστηκε, τὸ δὲ δι' οὗ ἡ κρίσις, μὴ ὁ ἀὴρ ζοφερὸς
ὑπάρχει, τὸ δὲ ἀπόστημα, μὴ μέγα λίαν ὑπόκειται, τὸ δὲ διάστημα, μὴ   40
συγκέχυται, τὸν δὲ τόπον, μὴ ἀχανής ἐστι, τὸν δὲ χρόνον, μὴ ταχύς ἐστι, τὴν
δὲ διάθεσιν, μὴ μανιώδης θεωρεῖται, τὴν δὲ ἐνέργειαν, μὴ ἀπρόσδεκτός
ἐστιν. (5) ταῦτα γὰρ πάντα καθ' ἓν γίνεται κριτήριον, ἥ τε πιθανὴ
φαντασία καὶ ἡ πιθανὴ ἅμα καὶ ἀπερίσπαστος, πρὸς δὲ τούτοις ἡ πιθανὴ
ἅμα καὶ ἀπερίσπαστος καὶ διεξωδευμένη. παρ' ἣν αἰτίαν ὃν τρόπον ἐν τῷ   45
βίῳ, ὅταν μὲν περὶ μικροῦ πράγματος ζητῶμεν, ἕνα μάρτυρα ἀνακρίνομεν,
ὅταν δὲ περὶ μείζονος, πλείονας, ὅταν δ' ἔτι μᾶλλον περὶ ἀναγκαιοτέρου,
καὶ ἕκαστον τῶν μαρτυρούντων ἐξετάζομεν ἐκ τῆς τῶν ἄλλων ἀνθομο-
λογήσεως, οὕτως, φασὶν οἱ περὶ τὸν Καρνεάδην, ἐν μὲν τοῖς τυχοῦσι
πράγμασι τῇ πιθανῇ μόνον φαντασίᾳ κριτηρίῳ χρώμεθα, ἐν δὲ τοῖς   50
διαφέρουσι τῇ ἀπερισπάστῳ, ἐν δὲ τοῖς πρὸς εὐδαιμονίαν συντείνουσι τῇ
περιωδευμένῃ.

6 ⟨ὡς⟩ Bekker   11 διάλεξιν Bekker: διάληψιν codd.   18 προσπίπτον N: προπίπτον cett.   26
τελειοτάτην Bekker: τελειοτάτη ἡ codd.   30 καὶ del. Heintz   31 συνδρομῆς Heintz: συνδρομὴν
codd.   34 ⟨ἢ⟩ ed. Genevensis

Context: immediately following D.

12–19 We omit this section from our translation because of a doubt about the
historicity of the medical analogy so far as Carneades is concerned; it reads like Sextus'
own comment. However, the term συνδρομή also occurs in lines 29, 31.

19–25 For the Menelaus example, see also **40K 2**.

F Cicero, *Acad.* 2.59

(1) illud vero perabsurdum quod dicitis, probabilia vos sequi si nulla re
impediamini. primum qui potestis non impediri, cum a veris falsa non distent?
deinde quod iudicium est veri, cum sit commune falsi? (2) ex his illa necessario
nata est ἐποχή id est adsensionis retentio, in qua melius sibi constitit Arcesilas, si
vera sunt quae de Carneade non nulli existimant. si enim percipi nihil potest,   5
quod utrique visum est, tollendus adsensus est; quid enim est tam futtile quam

448

quicquam adprobare non cognitum? (3) Carneadem autem etiam heri audiebamus solitum esse ⟨eo⟩ delabi interdum ut diceret opinaturum id est peccaturum esse sapientem.

8 ⟨*eo*⟩ Ernesti

Context: Lucullus' account of Antiochus' criticism of the New Academy, which is concluded in **68Q** and its immediate continuation.

1–2 **nulla re impediamini** A reference to Carneades' ἀπερίσπαστος requirement (**E**); cf. Cicero, *Acad.* 2.33.

3 **commune** Picking up and attacking Carneades. Cf. **D** 37–44; Cicero, *Acad.* 2.34.

7 **heri** In Catulus' speech in the lost *Academica priora* I. See introductory note on **K**.

9 **peccaturum esse sapientem** Attacking Carneades by citing Arcesilaus' position on the wise man. Cf. **G**; **68A 4**, **O**.

G Cicero, *Acad.* 2.66–7

(1) non sum sapiens; itaque visis cedo nec possum resistere. sapientis autem hanc censet Arcesilas vim esse maximam Zenoni adsentiens, cavere ne capiatur, ne fallatur videre . . . (2) haec primum conclusio quam habeat vim considera: "si ulli rei sapiens adsentietur umquam, aliquando etiam opinabitur; numquam autem opinabitur; nulli igitur rei adsentietur." hanc conclusionem Arcesilas probabat; confirmabat enim et primum et secundum. Carneades non numquam secundum illud dabat, adsentiri aliquando; ita sequebatur etiam opinari, quod tu non vis, et recte ut mihi videris.   5

7–8 *ita sequebatur* Manutius: *id adsequebatur* vel sim. codd.

Context: Cicero's defence of the New Academy.

H Cicero, *Acad.* 2.78

haec est una contentio quae adhuc permanserit. nam illud, nulli rei adsensurum esse sapientem, nihil ad hanc controversiam pertinebat. licebat enim "nihil percipere et tamen opinari"; quod a Carneade dicitur probatum: equidem Clitomacho plus quam Philoni aut Metrodoro credens hoc magis ab eo disputatum quam probatum puto.   5

Cf. introductory note on **K**.

I Cicero, *Acad.* 2.102–4

explicavi paulo ante Clitomacho auctore quo modo ista Carneades diceret; accipe quem ad modum eadem dicantur a Clitomacho in eo libro quem ad C. Lucilium scripsit poetam, cum scripsisset isdem de rebus ad L. Censorinum eum qui consul cum M'. Manilio fuit. scripsit igitur his fere verbis (sunt enim mihi nota propterea quod earum ipsarum rerum de quibus agimus

prima institutio et quasi disciplina illo libro continetur) – sed scriptum est ita: (1) Academicis 5
placere esse rerum eius modi dissimilitudines ut aliae probabiles videantur aliae
contra. id autem non esse satis cur alia posse percipi dicas alia non posse,
propterea quod multa falsa probabilia sint, nihil autem falsi perceptum et
cognitum possit esse. itaque ait vehementer errare eos qui dicant ab Academia
sensus eripi, a quibus numquam dictum sit aut colorem aut saporem aut 10
sonum nullum esse, illud sit disputatum, non inesse in iis propriam quae
nusquam alibi esset veri et certi notam. (2) quae cum exposuisset, adiungit
dupliciter dici adsensus sustinere sapientem, uno modo cum hoc intellegatur,
omnino eum rei nulli adsentiri, altero cum se a respondendo ut aut adprobet
quid aut inprobet sustineat, ut neque neget aliquid neque aiat. id cum ita sit, 15
alterum placere ut numquam adsentiatur, alterum tenere ut sequens
probabilitatem, ubicumque haec aut occurrat aut deficiat, aut "etiam" aut
"non" respondere possit. (3) etenim cum placeat eum qui de omnibus rebus
contineat se ab adsentiendo moveri tamen et agere aliquid, relinquit eius modi
visa quibus ad actionem excitemur, item ea quae interrogati in utramque 20
partem respondere possimus sequentes tantum modo quod ita visum sit, dum
sine adsensu; neque tamen omnia eius modi visa adprobari sed ea quae nulla re
impedirentur.

18 *etenim cum* Reid: *nec ut* codd.: *nam cum* Lambinus   19 *relinquit* Davies: *reliquit* codd.

Context: Cicero's defence of the New Academy.
    1   Cicero's cross-reference is to *Acad.* 2.98.   **ista**   Lucullus' charge, on behalf of
Antiochus, that the New Academy, in suspending judgement, undermines ordinary
sense experience (**400** 2–3). Cicero is doubtless correct in maintaining, 9–10, that
Clitomachus defended the school against a similar charge; but that charge cannot, for
chronological reasons, have been mounted by Antiochus; cf. Glucker [42], 412–13.
    3   The date of this consulship is 149 B.C.
    12–18   The general sense of the Latin is easier to make out than some of the
linguistic details. *alterum placere*, 16, must refer to *uno modo*, 13: assenting to nothing at
all. Since *alterum tenere*, 16, is compatible with responding 'yes' or 'no', *tenere* must
mean 'retains' the kind of assent which is withheld in the second sense of 'suspending
judgement', *altero*, 14. By responding 'yes' or 'no', the Academic does indicate a
qualified form of affirmation or negation; contrast *adprobari*, 22, with its withholding
in 14–15. Hence his suspension of judgement does not have the unqualified
consequence *ut neque neget aliquid neque aiat*, 15. These words should probably be
interpreted as a misleadingly strong way of saying *ut neque 'etiam' respondeat neque
'non'*.

J   Cicero, *Acad.* 2.108

ego enim etsi maximam actionem puto repugnare visis obsistere opinionibus
adsensus lubricos sustinere, credoque Clitomacho ita scribenti, Herculi
quendam laborem exanclatum a Carneade, quod ut feram et inmanem
beluam sic ex animis nostris adsensionem id est opinationem et temeritatem

extraxisset, tamen, ut ea pars defensionis relinquatur, quid impediet actionem eius 5
qui probabilia sequitur nulla re impediente?

Context: Cicero's defence of the New Academy against the charge that suspension of
judgement is incompatible with action.

1 **maximam actionem** The behaviour of the wise man, from whom Cicero
distances himself in **G** 1.

5–6 **impediet . . . impediente** Cicero extends the Carneadean notion of
'undivertedness' from the ἀπερίσπαστος φαντασία to the action which such
impressions can guide.

K Cicero, *Acad.* 2.148

tum Catulus "egone?" inquit; "ad patris revolvor sententiam, quam quidem ille
Carneadeam esse dicebat, ut percipi nihil putem posse, adsensurum autem non
percepto, id est opinaturum, sapientem existumem, sed ita ut intellegat se
opinari sciatque nihil esse quod conprehendi et percipi possit. †per epochen illam
omnium rerum comprobans, illi alteri sententiae, nihil esse quod percipi possit, vehementer 5
adsentior."

4 *per* codd.: *quare* Manutius: *parum* ed. anon. ap. Reid: *nec* †urnebus   5 *comprobans*: codd.: *non probans*
Madvig: *improbans* Davies

Context: conclusion of the debate between the New Academy and the supporters of
Antiochus.

As Glucker has argued ([42], 417–18), Catulus' speech in the lost *Academica priora* 1
was probably based on a speech by the loyal Philonian Heraclitus in Antiochus' *Sosus*,
representing the standard position of the Philonian Academy prior to Philo's
idiosyncratic new thesis (**68T**) of 89 B.C. (vol. 1, 449). Thus Catulus, here and as
referred to at **F 3**, represents the Philonian Academy of the early first century, to
which Antiochus himself had previously adhered. Cicero's dismissal of Catulus'
position as not the proper Academic one (directly after our passage) indicates not
Catulus' heterodoxy (as suggested by Frede [61], 268), but Cicero's own preference
for Clitomachus' over Philo's interpretation of Carneades.

2–3 That the wise man will hold opinions is the position of Philo and Metrodorus
(**H**), no doubt based on a simplistic understanding of Carneades' argument at **G 2**
without adequate attention to its dialectical character (see vol. 1, 456).

3–4 **intellegat . . . sciatque** Probably not terms for κατάληψις, but used
untechnically, as by Aenesidemus at **71C** 8 (on which see vol. 1, 472–3).

4 **per** The favoured emendation *quare* makes Catulus say that he both approves
of *suspension of assent* about all things and vehemently *assents* to the view that nothing
is cognitive. So blatant a contradiction seems unlikely unless we take Catulus to be
exploiting Clitomachus' distinction between two kinds of assent (**I 2–3**), as suggested
by Reid [328], 348. But there is no hint in the text that any such equivocation is
intended, and, if it were, it would be incredible that Catulus should use *vehementer
adsentior* to express the *weaker* kind of assent, as this interpretation would require. We
therefore find *parum* a less implausible emendation. But the corruption may well run
deeper.

The Academics

L Cicero, *Acad.* 2.139

cuius [*sc.* Calliphontis] quidem sententiam Carneades ita studiose defensitabat ut eam probare etiam videretur; quamquam Clitomachus adfirmabat numquam se intellegere potuisse quid Carneadi probaretur.

Context: Cicero's treatment of ethics, in defence of the New Academy. For Callipho's position (*honestas cum voluptate*), cf. Cicero, *Fin.* 2.19, 5.21.

70 Contributions to philosophical debates

A Sextus Empiricus, *M.* 7.159–65

(1) ὁ δὲ Καρνεάδης οὐ μόνον τοῖς Στωικοῖς ἀλλὰ καὶ πᾶσι τοῖς πρὸ αὐτοῦ ἀντιδιετάσσετο περὶ τοῦ κριτηρίου. (2) καὶ δὴ πρῶτος μὲν αὐτῷ καὶ κοινὸς πρὸς πάντας ἐστὶ λόγος καθ' ὃν παρίσταται ὅτι οὐδέν ἐστιν ἁπλῶς ἀληθείας κριτήριον, οὐ λόγος, οὐκ αἴσθησις, οὐ φαντασία, οὐκ ἄλλο τι τῶν ὄντων· πάντα γὰρ ταῦτα συλλήβδην διαψεύδεται ἡμᾶς. (3) δεύτερον δὲ 5 καθ' ὃ δείκνυσιν ὅτι καὶ εἰ ἔστι τὸ κριτήριον τοῦτο, οὐ χωρὶς τοῦ ἀπὸ τῆς ἐναργείας πάθους ὑφίσταται. (4) ἐπεὶ γὰρ αἰσθητικῇ δυνάμει διαφέρει τὸ ζῷον τῶν ἀψύχων, πάντως διὰ ταύτης ἑαυτοῦ τε καὶ τῶν ἐκτὸς ἀντιληπτικὸν γενήσεται. ἡ δέ γε αἴσθησις ἀκίνητος μὲν οὖσα καὶ ἀπαθὴς καὶ ἄτρεπτος οὔτε αἴσθησίς ἐστιν οὔτε ἀντιληπτική τινος, τραπεῖσα δὲ καί 10 πως παθοῦσα κατὰ τὴν τῶν ἐναργῶν ὑπόπτωσιν, τότε ἐνδεικνύει τὰ πράγματα. (5) ἐν ἄρα τῷ ἀπὸ τῆς ἐναργείας πάθει τῆς ψυχῆς ζητητέον ἐστὶ τὸ κριτήριον. τοῦτο δὲ τὸ πάθος αὐτοῦ ἐνδεικτικὸν ὀφείλει τυγχάνειν καὶ τοῦ ἐμποιήσαντος αὐτὸ φαινομένου, ὅπερ πάθος ἐστὶν οὐχ ἕτερον τῆς φαντασίας. ὅθεν καὶ φαντασίαν ῥητέον εἶναι πάθος τι περὶ τὸ ζῷον ἑαυτοῦ 15 τε καὶ τοῦ ἑτέρου παραστατικόν. (6) οἷον προσβλέψαντές τινι, φησὶν ὁ Ἀντίοχος, διατιθέμεθά πως τὴν ὄψιν, καὶ οὐχ οὕτως αὐτὴν διακειμένην ἴσχομεν ὡς πρὶν τοῦ βλέψαι διακειμένην εἴχομεν· κατὰ μέντοι τὴν τοιαύτην ἀλλοίωσιν δυεῖν ἀντιλαμβανόμεθα, ἑνὸς μὲν αὐτῆς τῆς ἀλλοιώσεως, τουτέστι τῆς φαντασίας, δευτέρου δὲ τοῦ τὴν ἀλλοίωσιν ἐμποιήσαν- 20 τος, τουτέστι τοῦ ὁρατοῦ. καὶ ἐπὶ τῶν ἄλλων αἰσθήσεων τὸ παραπλήσιον. ὥσπερ οὖν τὸ φῶς ἑαυτό τε δείκνυσι καὶ πάντα τὰ ἐν αὐτῷ, οὕτω καὶ ἡ φαντασία, ἀρχηγὸς οὖσα τῆς περὶ τὸ ζῷον εἰδήσεως, φωτὸς δίκην ἑαυτήν τε ἐμφανίζειν ὀφείλει καὶ τοῦ ποιήσαντος αὐτὴν ἐναργοῦς ἐνδεικτικὴ καθεστάναι. (7) ἀλλ' ἐπεὶ οὐ τὸ κατ' ἀλήθειαν ἀεί ποτε ἐνδείκνυται, 25 πολλάκις δὲ διαψεύδεται καὶ διαφωνεῖ τοῖς ἀναπέμψασιν αὐτὴν πράγμασιν ὡς οἱ μοχθηροὶ τῶν ἀγγέλων, κατ' ἀνάγκην ἠκολούθησε τὸ μὴ πᾶσαν φαντασίαν δύνασθαι κριτήριον ἀπολείπειν ἀληθείας, ἀλλὰ μόνην, εἰ καὶ ἄρα, τὴν ἀληθῆ. (8) πάλιν οὖν ἐπεὶ οὐδεμία ἐστὶν ἀληθὴς τοιαύτη οἷα οὐκ ἂν γένοιτο ψευδής, ἀλλὰ πάσῃ τῇ δοκούσῃ ἀληθεῖ καθεστάναι εὑρίσκεταί 30 τις ἀπαράλλακτος ψευδής, γενήσεται τὸ κριτήριον ἐν κοινῇ φαντασίᾳ, τοῦ τε ἀληθοῦς καὶ ψεύδους. ἡ δὲ κοινὴ τούτων φαντασία οὐκ ἔστι

κaταληπτική, μὴ οὖσα δὲ καταληπτικὴ οὐδὲ κριτήριον ἔσται. (9)
μηδεμιᾶς δὲ οὔσης φαντασίας κριτικῆς οὐδὲ λόγος ἂν εἴη κριτήριον· ἀπὸ
φαντασίας γὰρ οὗτος ἀνάγεται. καὶ εἰκότως· πρῶτον μὲν γὰρ δεῖ φανῆναι   35
αὐτῷ τὸ κρινόμενον, φανῆναι δὲ οὐδὲν δύναται χωρὶς τῆς ἀλόγου
αἰσθήσεως. (10) οὔτε οὖν ἡ ἄλογος αἴσθησις οὔτε ὁ λόγος ἦν κριτήριον.

Context: following **69B** in Sextus' history of doctrines on the criterion of truth. This
part of the history is probably derived by him from Antiochus' *Canonica*.

    36–7   Carneades' talk of αἴσθησις as ἄλογος is primarily Epicurean (cf. **16B**). As a
Stoic criterion, αἴσθησις is sensory *cognition*, and hence a form of judgement
(especially **40Q**). The Stoic equivalent of Epicurean αἴσθησις is φαντασία αἰσθητική
(**39A 4**).

B Cicero, *Acad.* 2.40–2

(1) sed prius potestis totius eorum rationis quasi fundamenta cognoscere. (2)
conponunt igitur primum artem quandam de his quae visa dicimus,
eorumque et vim et genera definiunt, in his quale sit id quod percipi et
conprendi possit, totidem verbis quot Stoici. (3) deinde illa exponunt duo,
quae quasi contineant omnem hanc quaestionem: quae ita videantur ut etiam   5
alia eodem modo videri possint nec in is quicquam intersit, non posse eorum
alia percipi alia non percipi; nihil interesse autem non modo si omni ex parte
eiusdem modi sint sed etiam si discerni non possint. (4) quibus positis unius
argumenti conclusione tota ab his causa conprenditur. conposita autem ea
conclusio sic est: eorum quae videntur alia vera sunt alia falsa; et quod falsum   10
est id percipi non potest; quod autem verum visum est, id omne tale est ut
eiusdem modi falsum etiam possit videri; et quae visa sint eius modi ut in is
nihil intersit, non posse accidere ut eorum alia percipi possint alia non possint;
nullum igitur est visum quod percipi possit. (5) quae autem sumunt ut
concludant id quod volunt, ex his duo sibi putant concedi (neque enim   15
quisquam repugnat); ea sunt haec: quae visa falsa sint ea percipi non posse; et
alterum: inter quae visa nihil intersit, ex is non posse alia talia esse ut percipi
possint alia ut non possint. (6) reliqua vero multa et varia oratione defendunt,
quae sunt item duo: unum, quae videantur eorum alia vera esse alia falsa;
alterum, omne visum quod sit a vero tale esse quale etiam a falso possit esse.   20
haec duo proposita non praetervolant sed ita dilatant ut non mediocrem curam adhibeant et
diligentiam. dividunt enim in partes et eas quidem magnas, primum in sensus, deinde in ea quae
ducuntur a sensibus et ab omni consuetudine, quam obscurari volunt; tum perveniunt ad eam
partem ut ne ratione quidem et coniectura ulla res percipi possit. haec autem universa concidunt
etiam minutius. ut enim de sensibus hesterno sermone vidistis item faciunt de reliquis, in   25
singulisque rebus, quas in minima dispertiunt, volunt efficere iis omnibus quae visa sint veris
adiuncta esse falsa quae a veris nihil differant; ea cum talia sint non posse conprendi.

23 *ducuntur*] *dicuntur* A¹V¹B¹

Context: criticism of the New Academy. Their highly methodical approach, it is
argued, is hardly the mark of people in a state of sceptical doubt.

The Academics

C Sextus Empiricus, M. 9.139–41

(1) εἴγ' ἄρ' εἰσὶ θεοί, ζῷά εἰσιν. εἰ δὲ ζῷά εἰσιν, αἰσθάνονται· πᾶν γὰρ ζῷον αἰσθήσεως μετοχῇ νοεῖται ζῷον. (2) εἰ δὲ αἰσθάνονται, καὶ πικράζονται καὶ γλυκάζονται· οὐ γὰρ δι' ἄλλης μέν τινος αἰσθήσεως ἀντιλαμβάνονται τῶν αἰσθητῶν, οὐχὶ δὲ καὶ διὰ τῆς γεύσεως. (3) ὅθεν καὶ τὸ περικόπτειν ταύτην ἤ τινα αἴσθησιν ἄλλην ἁπλῶς τοῦ θεοῦ παντελῶς ἐστιν ἀπίθανον· 5 περιττοτέρας γὰρ αἰσθήσεις ἔχων ὁ ἄνθρωπος ἀμείνων αὐτοῦ γενήσεται, δέον μᾶλλον, ὡς ἔλεγεν ὁ Καρνεάδης, σὺν ταῖς πᾶσιν ὑπαρχούσαις πέντε ταύταις αἰσθήσεσι καὶ ἄλλας αὐτῷ περισσοτέρας προσμαρτυρεῖν, ἵν' ἔχῃ πλειόνων ἀντιλαμβάνεσθαι πραγμάτων, ἀλλὰ μὴ τῶν πέντε ἀφαιρεῖν. (4) ῥητέον οὖν γεῦσίν τινα ἔχειν τὸν θεόν, καὶ διὰ ταύτης ἀντιλαμβάνεσθαι 10 τῶν γευστῶν. ἀλλ' εἰ διὰ γεύσεως ἀντιλαμβάνεται, ⟨γλυκάζεται⟩ καὶ πικράζεται. γλυκαζόμενος δὲ καὶ πικραζόμενος εὐαρεστήσει τισὶ καὶ δυσαρεστήσει. δυσαρεστῶν δέ τισι καὶ ὀχλήσεως ἔσται δεκτικὸς καὶ τῆς ἐπὶ τὸ χεῖρον μεταβολῆς. εἰ δὲ τοῦτο, φθαρτός ἐστιν. (5) ὥστε εἴπερ εἰσὶ θεοί, φθαρτοί εἰσιν. οὐκ ἄρα θεοὶ εἰσίν. 15

1 εἴγ' ἄρ' Sedley: εἰ γὰρ codd.   7 πᾶσιν Bekker: πάσαις codd.   11 ⟨γλυκάζεται⟩ Fabricius

Context: attempt to produce equipollence between arguments for and against the existence of god.

1 ζῷά εἰσιν   This expresses the conclusion of an argument at *M*. 9.138, which mimics the Stoic syllogism at **54F**: an animal is better than a non-animal; but nothing is better than god; therefore god is an animal. Of course, with or without this formal defence, the Stoics do hold the conclusion to be true (cf. **54A**).

14–15   This argument, like many of the other anti-theistic arguments reported by Sextus at *M*. 9.137–81, and those of Carneades at Cicero, *ND* 3.29–34, takes imperishability to be an inalienable feature of god. Yet in Stoic theology, the principal target of these arguments, imperishability receives little emphasis, no doubt because although Zeus does endure through the cosmic conflagration (**28O 4**), lesser gods, such as sun, moon, aether etc., are destroyed in it (Plutarch, *St. rep.* 1052A). On the other hand, Antipater, Carneades' chief Stoic antagonist in his own day, did contrive to stress the gods' imperishability (Plutarch, *St. rep.* 1051E–F). We may perhaps take this as a sign of a new theological emphasis generated in the course of their confrontation. God's imperishability is cardinal to most non-Stoic theologies, including the Epicurean (**23**). (**54A, K**, which may at first sight appear also to make the gods imperishable, in fact call them only 'deathless', ἀθάνατος; and since θάνατος is defined as the separation of soul from body, which is not the mode of the gods' destruction, *all* gods are technically ἀθάνατοι, though only Zeus is also ἄφθαρτος: Plutarch, *Comm. not.* 1075C, cf. id. *St. rep.* 1052C.)

15   As editors note, a premise has fallen out or been suppressed before the conclusion, e.g. οὐχὶ δέ γε φθαρτοί εἰσιν (Heintz).

D Cicero, *ND* 3.43–4

(1) ". . . Iovem et Neptunum deum numeras; ergo etiam Orcus frater eorum

454

deus, et illi qui fluere apud inferos dicuntur, Acheron Cocytus Pyriphle-
gethon, tum Charon tum Cerberus di putandi. at id quidem repudiandum; ne
Orcus quidem igitur; quid dicitis ergo de fratribus?" (2) haec Carneades
aiebat, non ut deos tolleret (quid enim philosopho minus conveniens?), sed ut 5
Stoicos nihil de dis explicare convinceret.

Context: critique of Stoic theology. The present argument is an informal Sorites, cf. **E**
with notes.

  5 **non ut deos tolleret**   This is strictly speaking correct, since atheism would be
as un-sceptical a stance as theism. Cotta is also no doubt right about the anti-Stoic
context of the argument. But to judge from his parenthesis he probably means to be
understood as making Carneades himself some sort of theist. And that is symptomatic
of the Philonian Academy's reading of Carneades' dialectical arguments as doctrinally
motivated (see vol. 1, 448–9). Cf. the Philonian interpretation of Carneades' purpose
at Cicero, *ND* 1.4–5.

E   Sextus Empiricus, *M.* 9.182–4

τοιοῦτον μὲν δὴ καὶ τὸ τῶν λόγων τούτων εἶδός ἐστιν· (1) ἠρώτηνται δὲ ὑπὸ τοῦ
Καρνεάδου καὶ σωριτικῶς τινες, οὓς ὁ γνώριμος αὐτοῦ Κλειτόμαχος ὡς
σπουδαιοτάτους καὶ ἀνυτικωτάτους ἀνέγραψεν, ἔχοντας τὸν τρόπον
τοῦτον. (2) "εἰ Ζεὺς θεός ἐστι, καὶ ὁ Ποσειδῶν θεός ἐστιν·

> τρεῖς γάρ τ' ἐκ Κρόνου ἦμεν ἀδελφεοί, οὓς τέκετο 'Ρέα,   5
> Ζεὺς καὶ ἐγώ, τρίτατος δ' Ἅιδης ἐνέροισιν ἀνάσσων.
> τριχθὰ δὲ πάντα δέδασται, ἕκαστος δ' ἔμμορε τιμῆς.

ὥστε εἰ ὁ Ζεὺς θεός ἐστι, καὶ ὁ Ποσειδῶν ἀδελφὸς ὢν τούτου θεὸς γενήσεται. εἰ
δὲ ὁ Ποσειδῶν θεός ἐστι, καὶ ὁ Ἀχελῷος ἔσται θεός· εἰ δὲ ὁ Ἀχελῷος, καὶ
ὁ Νεῖλος· εἰ ὁ Νεῖλος, καὶ πᾶς ποταμός· εἰ πᾶς ποταμός, καὶ οἱ ῥύακες ἂν   10
εἶεν θεοί· εἰ οἱ ῥύακες, καὶ αἱ χαράδραι. οὐχὶ δὲ οἱ ῥύακες· οὐδὲ ὁ Ζεὺς ἄρα
θεός ἐστιν. εἰ δέ γε ἦσαν θεοί, καὶ ὁ Ζεὺς ἦν ἂν θεός. οὐκ ἄρα θεοί εἰσίν." (3)
καὶ μὴν "εἰ ὁ ἥλιος θεός ἐστιν, καὶ ἡμέρα ἂν εἴη θεός· οὐ γὰρ ἄλλο τι ἦν
ἡμέρα ἢ ἥλιος ὑπὲρ γῆς. εἰ δ' ἡμέρα ἐστὶ θεός, καὶ ὁ μὴν ἔσται θεός·
σύστημα γάρ ἐστιν ἐξ ἡμερῶν. εἰ δὲ ὁ μὴν θεός ἐστι, καὶ ὁ ἐνιαυτὸς ἂν εἴη   15
θεός· σύστημα γάρ ἐστιν ἐκ μηνῶν ὁ ἐνιαυτός. οὐχὶ δέ γε τοῦτο· τοίνυν
οὐδὲ τὸ ἐξ ἀρχῆς." σὺν τῷ ἄτοπον εἶναι, φασί, τὴν μὲν ἡμέραν θεὸν εἶναι λέγειν, τὴν δὲ
ἕω καὶ τὴν μεσημβρίαν καὶ τὴν δείλην μηκέτι.

11 ῥύακες οὐδὲ ⟨αἱ χαράδραι· οὐδὲ⟩ ὁ Ζεὺς Bekker dubitanter

Context: as **C**. For comment, see especially Burnyeat [451]; also Couissin [625].
   13–17   While a Sorites normally has no need to justify its inference from '*a* is *F*' to
'*b* is *F*', the obvious similarity of *a* to *b* being sufficient ground (see vol. 1, 229–30), the
present one is unusual in offering a precise metaphysical ground for each step, namely
that *a* consists of *b*. The metaphysics is presumably borrowed from Carneades' Stoic
opponents. Cf. *SVF* 2.693, and **51G**.

F Cicero, *Div.* 2.9–10

(1) etenim me movet illud quod in primis Carneades quaerere solebat, quarumnam rerum divinatio esset. earumne quae sensibus perciperentur? at eas quidem cernimus, audimus, gustamus, olfacimus, tangimus. num quid ergo in his rebus est, quod provisione aut permotione mentis magis quam natura ipsa sentiamus? aut num nescio qui ille divinus, si oculis captus sit, ut Tiresias fuit, 5 possit quae alba sint, quae nigra dicere aut, si surdus sit, varietates vocum aut modos noscere? ad nullam igitur earum rerum quae sensu accipiuntur divinatio adhibetur. (2) atqui ne in iis quidem rebus quae arte tractantur divinatione opus est. etenim ad aegros non vates aut hariolos, sed medicos solemus adducere. nec vero qui fidibus aut tibiis uti volunt ab haruspicibus accipiunt earum tractationem, sed a musicis. 1o eadem in litteris ratio est reliquisque rebus quarum est disciplina.

Context: the opening of Cicero's critique of divination.

The argument tries to render divination redundant by showing that all its possible objects are already pre-empted by other capacities or skills. It is as Platonic an argument as any recorded for Carneades, being closely modelled on the treatment of justice at *Rep.* 1, 332d–333e.

G Cicero, *Fat.* 26–33 (continuing **20E**)

(1) quod cum ita sit, quid est cur non omnis pronuntiatio aut vera aut falsa sit, nisi concesserimus fato fieri quaecumque fiant? (2) "quia futura vera" inquit "non possunt esse ea quae causas cur futura sint non habent; habeant igitur causas necesse est ea quae vera sunt; ita, cum evenerint, fato evenerint." (3) confectum negotium, si quidem concedendum tibi est aut fato omnia fieri, aut 5 quicquam fieri posse sine causa. (4) an aliter haec enuntiatio vera esse non potest, "capiet Numantiam Scipio", nisi ex aeternitate causa causam serens hoc erit effectura? an hoc falsum potuisset esse, si esset sescentis saeculis ante dictum? (5) et si tum non esset vera haec enuntiatio, "capiet Numantiam Scipio", ne illa quidem eversa vera est haec enuntiatio, "cepit Numantiam 1o Scipio". potest igitur quicquam factum esse quod non verum fuerit futurum esse? nam ut praeterita ea vera dicimus quorum superiore tempore vera fuerit instantia, sic futura quorum consequenti tempore vera erit instantia, ea vera dicemus. (6) nec, si omne enuntiatum aut verum aut falsum est, sequitur ilico esse causas inmutabilis, easque aeternas, quae prohibeant quicquam secus 1 cadere atque casurum sit. fortuitae sunt causae quae efficiant ut vere dicantur quae ita dicentur, "veniet in senatum Cato", non inclusae in rerum natura atque mundo. (7) et tamen tam est inmutabile venturum, cum est verum, quam venisse; nec ob eam causam fatum aut necessitas extimescenda est. (8) etenim erit confiteri necesse: si haec enuntiatio, "veniet in Tusculanum 2o Hortensius", vera non est, sequitur ut falsa sit. (quorum isti neutrum volunt, quod fieri non potest.) (9) [=**55S**] (10) Carneades genus hoc totum non probabat et nimis inconsiderate concludi hanc rationem putabat. itaque

premebat alio modo, nec ullam adhibebat calumniam; cuius erat haec conclusio: "si omnia antecedentibus causis fiunt, omnia naturali conligatione 25 conserte contexteque fiunt; quod si ita est, omnia necessitas efficit; id si verum est, nihil est in nostra potestate; est autem aliquid in nostra potestate; at si omnia fato fiunt, omnia causis antecedentibus fiunt; non igitur fato fiunt, quaecumque fiunt." (11) hoc artius adstringi ratio non potest. nam si quis velit idem referre atque ita dicere, "si omne futurum ex aeternitate verum est, ut ita 30 certe eveniat quem ad modum sit futurum, omnia necesse est conligatione naturali conserte contexteque fieri", nihil dicat. multum enim differt utrum causa naturalis ex aeternitate futura vera efficiat, an etiam sine aeternitate naturali futura quae sint ea vera esse possint intellegi. (12) itaque dicebat Carneades ne Apollinem quidem futura posse dicere, nisi ea quorum causas 35 natura ita contineret ut ea fieri necesse esset. (13) quid enim spectans deus ipse diceret Marcellum eum qui ter consul fuit in mari esse periturum? erat hoc quidem verum ex aeternitate, sed causas id efficientis non habebat. (14) ita ne praeterita quidem ea quorum nulla signa tamquam vestigia exstarent Apollini nota esse censebat; quo minus futura? causis enim efficientibus quamque rem 40 cognitis posse denique sciri quid futurum esset. (15) ergo nec de Oedipode potuisse Apollinem praedicere nullis in rerum natura causis praepositis cur ab eo patrem interfici necesse esset, nec quicquam eius modi.

10 *cepit* Ramus: *capiet* codd.

For discussion, cf. Long [3], 101–4. For a possible earlier Academic criticism of Stoic determinism, see note on **55N** 11.

The Pyrrhonist revival

71 Why to suspend judgement

A Diogenes Laertius 9.106–7

(1) καὶ Αἰνεσίδημος ἐν τῷ πρώτῳ Πυρρωνείων λόγων οὐδέν φησιν ὁρίζειν τὸν Πύρρωνα δογματικῶς διὰ τὴν ἀντιλογίαν, τοῖς δὲ φαινομένοις ἀκολουθεῖν. ταὐτὰ δὲ λέγει κἀν τῷ Κατὰ σοφίας κἀν τῷ Περὶ ζητήσεως. ἀλλὰ καὶ Ζεῦξις ὁ Αἰνεσιδήμου γνώριμος ἐν τῷ Περὶ διττῶν λόγων καὶ Ἀντίοχος ὁ Λαοδικεὺς καὶ Ἀπελλᾶς ἐν τῷ Ἀγρίππᾳ τιθέασι τὰ φαινόμενα μόνα. (2) ἔστιν οὖν   5
κριτήριον κατὰ τοὺς Σκεπτικοὺς τὸ φαινόμενον, ὡς καὶ Αἰνεσίδημός φησιν· οὕτω δὲ καὶ Ἐπίκουρος. Δημόκριτος δὲ μηδὲν εἶναι τῶν φαινομένων, τὰ δὲ μὴ εἶναι... (3) τέλος δὲ οἱ Σκεπτικοί φασι τὴν ἐποχήν, ᾗ σκιᾶς τρόπον ἐπακολου^θεῖ ἡ ἀταραξία, ὥς φασιν οἵ τε περὶ τὸν Τίμωνα καὶ Αἰνεσίδη-
μον.   10

Context: summary of Pyrrhonism – from the life of Pyrrho, but principally representing later Pyrrhonist teaching.

5–7 For τὸ φαινόμενον as 'criterion' (with appropriate qualifications) see S.E., *PH* 1.21–4.

6 **Σκεπτικούς** This title is unlikely to date back to Aenesidemus, despite its occurrence in non-verbatim quotations here and at S.E., *PH* 1.210. Cf. Janáček [644]; Sedley [59], 27–8, n. 61; and, in partial disagreement, Tarrant [629], 22–9.

7–8 A fairly shallow assimilation of the Pyrrhonist and Epicurean (cf. **17**) criteria, possibly reflecting Aenesidemus' respect for Epicurus (cf. **72M** 7–9, with note, and the surprising gesture towards hedonism at **1F 5**). The next sentence appears to mean 'Democritus says that it [the criterion] is none of the things that appear, and that they [the things that appear] do not exist'. Diogenes' source for this passage perhaps wanted to downgrade Democritus' credentials as a sceptic (contrast D.L. 9.76) in favour of Epicurus'.

8–9 The shadow simile is also at S.E., *PH* 1.29 (and cf. **72A** 1–2), but with the difference that there ἀταραξία is itself the τέλος. For a suggested explanation of this shift of emphasis, cf. Sedley [59], 21–2.

B Diogenes Laertius 9.78

ἔστιν οὖν ὁ Πυρρώνειος λόγος μνήμη τις τῶν φαινομένων ἢ τῶν ὁπωσοῦν νοουμένων, καθ' ἣν πάντα πᾶσι συμβάλλεται καὶ συγκρινόμενα πολλὴν

458

ἀνωμαλίαν καὶ ταραχὴν ἔχοντα εὑρίσκεται, καθά φησιν Αἰνεσίδημος ἐν τῇ εἰς τὰ Πυρρώνεια ὑποτυπώσει.

3 ἀνωμαλίαν Kühn: ἀνωφελείαν codd.

Context: as **A**.

C Photius, *Bibl.* 169b18–170b3

(1) ἀνεγνώσθη Αἰνησιδήμου Πυρρωνίων λόγοι η'. ἡ μὲν ὅλη πρόθεσις τοῦ βιβλίου βεβαιῶσαι ὅτι οὐδὲν βέβαιον εἰς κατάληψιν, οὔτε δι' αἰσθήσεως, ἀλλ' οὔτε μὴν διὰ νοήσεως. (2) διὸ οὔτε τοὺς Πυρρωνίους οὔτε τοὺς ἄλλους εἰδέναι τὴν ἐν τοῖς οὖσιν ἀλήθειαν, ἀλλὰ τοὺς μὲν κατὰ ἄλλην αἵρεσιν φιλοσοφοῦντας ἀγνοεῖν τε τἆλλα καὶ ἑαυτοὺς μάτην κατατρίβειν καὶ 5 δαπανᾶν συνεχέσιν ἀνίαις, καὶ αὐτὸ δὲ τοῦτο ἀγνοεῖν, ὅτι οὐδὲν αὐτοῖς τῶν δοξάντων εἰς κατάληψιν ἐληλυθέναι κατείληπται. (3) ὁ δὲ κατὰ Πύρρωνα φιλοσοφῶν τά τε ἄλλα εὐδαιμονεῖ, καὶ σοφός ἐστι τοῦ μάλιστα εἰδέναι ὅτι οὐδὲν αὐτῷ βεβαίως κατείληπται· ἃ δὲ καὶ εἰδείη, οὐδὲν μᾶλλον αὐτῶν τῇ καταφάσει ἢ τῇ ἀποφάσει γενναῖός ἐστι συγκατατίθεσθαι. (4) ἡ μὲν ὅλη 10 τοῦ βιβλίου διάληψις ὃ βούλεται, εἴρηται. γράφει δὲ τοὺς λόγους Αἰνησίδημος προσφωνῶν αὐτοὺς τῶν ἐξ Ἀκαδημίας τινὶ συναιρεσιώτῃ Λευκίῳ Τοβέρωνι, γένος μὲν Ῥωμαίῳ, δόξῃ δὲ λαμπρῷ ἐκ προγόνων καὶ πολιτικὰς ἀρχὰς οὐ τὰς τυχούσας μετιόντι. (5) ἐν μὲν οὖν τῷ πρώτῳ λόγῳ διαφορὰν τῶν τε Πυρρωνίων καὶ τῶν Ἀκαδημαικῶν εἰσάγων μικροῦ 15 γλώσσῃ αὐτῇ ταῦτά φησιν, ὡς οἱ μὲν ἀπὸ τῆς Ἀκαδημίας δογματικοί τέ εἰσι καὶ τὰ μὲν τίθενται ἀδιστάκτως, τὰ δὲ αἴρουσιν ἀναμφιβόλως, (6) οἱ δ' ἀπὸ Πύρρωνος ἀπορητικοί τέ εἰσι καὶ παντὸς ἀπολελυμένοι δόγματος, καὶ οὐδεὶς αὐτῶν τὸ παράπαν οὔτε ἀκατάληπτα πάντα εἴρηκεν οὔτε καταληπτά, ἀλλ' οὐδὲν μᾶλλον τοιάδε ἢ τοιάδε, ἤ τότε μὲν τοῖα τότε δὲ οὐ 20 τοῖα, ἢ ᾧ μὲν τοιαῦτα ᾧ δὲ οὐ τοιαῦτα ᾧ δ' οὐδ' ὅλως ὄντα· οὐδὲ μὴν ἐφικτὰ πάντα κοινῶς ἢ τινα τούτων ἢ οὐκ ἐφικτά, ἀλλ' οὐδὲν μᾶλλον ἐφικτὰ ἢ οὐκ ἐφικτά, ἢ τότε μὲν ἐφικτὰ τότε δ' οὐκέτι, ἢ τῷ μὲν ἐφικτὰ τῷ δ' οὔ. (7) καὶ μὴν οὐδ' ἀληθινὸν οὐδὲ ψεῦδος, οὐδὲ πιθανὸν οὐδ' ἀπίθανον, οὐδ' ὂν οὐδὲ μὴ ὄν, ἀλλὰ τὸ αὐτὸ ὡς εἰπεῖν οὐ μᾶλλον ἀληθὲς ἢ ψεῦδος, ἢ 25 πιθανὸν ἢ ἀπίθανον, ἢ ὂν ἢ οὐκ ὄν, ἢ τότε μὲν τοῖον τότε δὲ τοῖον, ἢ ᾧ μὲν τοιονδὶ ᾧ δὲ καὶ οὐ τοιονδί. (8) καθόλου γὰρ οὐδὲν ὁ Πυρρώνιος ὁρίζει, ἀλλ' οὐδὲ αὐτὸ τοῦτο, ὅτι οὐδὲν διορίζεται· ἀλλ' οὐκ ἔχοντες, φησίν, ὅπως τὸ νοούμενον ἐκλαλήσωμεν, οὕτω φράζομεν. (9) οἱ δ' ἀπὸ τῆς Ἀκαδημίας, φησί, μάλιστα τῆς νῦν, καὶ Στωικαῖς συμφέρονται ἐνίοτε δόξαις, καὶ εἰ 30 χρὴ τἀληθὲς εἰπεῖν, Στωικοὶ φαίνονται μαχόμενοι Στωικοῖς. δεύτερον περὶ πολλῶν δογματίζουσιν. ἀρετήν τε γὰρ καὶ ἀφροσύνην εἰσάγουσι, καὶ ἀγαθὸν καὶ κακὸν ὑποτίθενται, καὶ ἀλήθειαν καὶ ψεῦδος, καὶ δὴ καὶ πιθανὸν καὶ ἀπίθανον καὶ ὂν καὶ μὴ ὄν, ἄλλα τε πολλὰ βεβαίως ὁρίζουσι, διαμφισβητεῖν δέ φασι περὶ μόνης τῆς καταληπτικῆς φαντασίας. (10) διὸ 35

459

The Pyrrhonist revival

οἱ μὲν ἀπὸ Πύρρωνος ἐν τῷ μηδὲν ὁρίζειν ἀνεπίληπτοι τὸ παράπαν
διαμένουσιν, οἱ δ' ἐξ 'Ακαδημίας, φησίν, ὁμοίας τὰς εὐθύνας τοῖς ἄλλοις
φιλοσόφοις ὑπέχουσι. (11) τὸ δὲ μέγιστον, οἱ μὲν περὶ παντὸς τοῦ
προτεθέντος διαποροῦντες τό τε σύστοιχον διατηροῦσι καὶ ἑαυτοῖς οὐ
μάχονται, οἱ δὲ μαχόμενοι ἑαυτοῖς οὐ συνίσασι· τὸ γὰρ ἅμα τιθέναι τι καὶ   40
αἴρειν ἀναμφιβόλως, ἅμα τε φάναι κοινῶς ⟨μὴ⟩ ὑπάρχειν καταληπτά,
μάχην ὁμολογουμένην εἰσάγει, ἐπεὶ πῶς οἷόν τε γινώσκοντα τόδε μὲν εἶναι
ἀληθὲς τόδε δὲ ψεῦδος ἔτι διαπορεῖν καὶ διστάσαι, καὶ οὐ σαφῶς τὸ μὲν
ἑλέσθαι τὸ δὲ περιστῆναι; (12) εἰ μὲν γὰρ ἀγνοεῖται ὅτι τόδε ἐστὶν ἀγαθὸν ἢ
κακόν, ἢ τόδε μὲν ἀληθὲς τόδε δὲ ψεῦδος, καὶ τόδε μὲν ὂν τόδε δὲ μὴ ὄν,   45
πάντως ὁμολογητέον ἕκαστον ἀκατάληπτον εἶναι· εἰ δ' ἐναργῶς κατ'
αἴσθησιν ἢ κατὰ νόησιν καταλαμβάνεται, καταληπτὸν ἕκαστον φατέον.
(13) ταῦτα μὲν ἀρχόμενος τῶν λόγων καὶ τοιαῦθ' ἕτερα τὴν διαφορὰν τῶν
Πυρρωνίων καὶ 'Ακαδημαικῶν ὑποδεικνύς, ἀναγράφει ὁ Αἰνησίδημος ὁ ἐξ
Αἰγῶν· ἐφεξῆς δὲ κατὰ τὸν αὐτὸν λόγον πρῶτον καὶ τὴν ὅλην ἀγωγὴν ὡς   50
τύπῳ καὶ κεφαλαιωδῶς τῶν Πυρρωνίων παραδίδωσι λόγων.

28 φησίν Bekker: φασί codd.   41 ⟨μὴ⟩ ὑπάρχειν καταληπτά Sandbach: ὑπάρχειν καὶ μὴ ὑπάρχειν
καταληπτά A³mg.: ὑπάρχειν ⟨ἀ⟩κατάληπτα Hirzel: ⟨μὲν⟩ ὑπάρχειν καταληπτά, ⟨ἰδίως δ' ἕκαστα
ἀκατάληπτα⟩ Glucker: ὑπάρχειν καταληπτά ⟨τὰ πράγματα καὶ πάντως ἀκατάληπτα⟩ Tarrant
exempli causa

Context: a work written by Photius to supply his brother with summaries of books he
had not been able to read. Our excerpt continues at 72L. Cf. Janáček [636], who
vindicates the basic authenticity of Photius' report.

27   Cf. 1G for οὐδὲν ὁρίζειν as the sense of οὐ μᾶλλον according to Timon.

32–5   This description puts it beyond doubt that the reference is to the Philonian
Academy (despite the inclusion of 29–46 by Luck [631], as fr. 54 of Antiochus). Philo
certainly had his own set of doctrines, especially in ethics (cf. Stobaeus 2.39,19ff.), but,
unlike Antiochus, never gave up his opposition to the φαντασία καταληπτική (cf.
68T–U).

40–2   The supplement ⟨μὴ⟩ (suggested privately by Prof. Sandbach) makes
μαχή refer to the conflict between the two ἅμα clauses. Tarrant ([628], 89–92 and
[629], 59–61; see ap. crit.) prefers to emend in such a way as to locate the conflict
within each ἅμα clause. But that seems to be ruled out by the closely parallel language
of 17, where no conflict is intended.

D Anon., *In Plat. Theaet.* 60.48–61.46

(1) ἐπεὶ ὁ | Θεαίτητος ἐπερωτηθεὶς περὶ ἐπιστήμης, | τί ἐστιν, εἶπεν
"καὶ | ὣς γε νυνὶ φαίνεται", | ἀποδέχεται Σωκρά|της ὅτι οὐκ ὀκνεῖ
λέγε[ι]ν ὃ φαίνεται αὐ|τῶι καὶ νομίζει εἶ|ναι τὴν ἐπιστήμην. | οὐ γὰρ
ἐκεῖνό φησιν | τὸ Πυρρώνειον, ὅτι | οὐδὲν καθοριστικῶς | ἄν τ[ι]ς δογμα-
τίζοι, | ἀλλά φησιν φαίνεσ|θαι αὐτῶι. (2) κατὰ γὰρ τὸν | ἄνδρα οὔτε ὁ   5
λόγος | κριτήριον οὔτε ἀληθὴς φαντασία οὔτε | πιθανὴ οὔτε κατα|ληπ-
τικὴ οὔτε ἄλλο | τι τ[οιο]ῦτον, ἀλλ' ὅτι | νῦν αὐτῶι φαίνε[τ]αι. | (3) εἰ δὲ
τοιοῦτόν ἐστιν | ἢ οὐκ ἔστιν, οὐκ ἀπο|φαίνεται, διὰ τὸ οἴε|σθαι ἰσοκρατεῖς

460

εἶ|ναι τοὺς εἰς τὰ ἐναν|τία λόγους, καὶ ἐξομα|λίζειν τὰς φαντασίας, καὶ
μηδεμίαν ἐν | αὐταῖς ἀπολείπειν | διαφορὰν κατὰ τὸ ἀ|ληθὲς ἢ ψεῦδος,   10
πι|θανὸν ἢ ἀπίθανον, | ἐναργὲς ἢ ἀμυδρόν, | καταληπτὸν ἢ ἀκα|τάληπτον,
ἀλλὰ πά|σας εἶναι ὁμοίας, (4) οὐ|δὲ τοῦτο δογματί|ζοντος, ὡς ἕπεται, | τὸ
διεξάγειν κατὰ | τὴν ἀεὶ προσπίπτου|σαν φαντασίαν, οὐ|χ ὡς ἀληθῆ, ἀλλ'
ὅτι | νῦν αὐτῶι φαίνε|ται.

Context: commentary on *Tht.* 151e4-5, where Socrates praises Theaetetus' willing-
ness to stick his neck out and state his current belief. The commentator explains that
Theaetetus' expression 'as it now appears [i.e. to me]' involves the epistemic use of
'appear' to express beliefs (νομίζει, 3), by contrast with the non-epistemic use of the
term in Pyrrhonism (cf. vol. 1, 471). The text thus lends support to Burnyeat's
interpretation of Pyrrhonist appearance as non-epistemic ([645]; [60], 230 n. 14). The
commentary was long dated to the second century A.D., but Tarrant [633] has now
made an impressive case for the first century B.C.

72 How to suspend judgement

A Sextus Empiricus, *PH* 1.31-9

(ιγ´ Περὶ τῶν ὁλοσχερῶν τρόπων τῆς ἐποχῆς.) ἐπεὶ δὲ τὴν ἀταραξίαν ἀκολουθεῖν
ἐφάσκομεν τῇ περὶ πάντων ἐποχῇ, ἀκόλουθον ἂν εἴη λέγειν ὅπως ἡμῖν ἡ ἐποχὴ περιγίνεται.
(1) γίνεται τοίνυν αὕτη, ὡς ἂν ὁλοσχερέστερον εἴποι τις, διὰ τῆς
ἀντιθέσεως τῶν πραγμάτων. ἀντιτίθεμεν δὲ ἢ φαινόμενα φαινομένοις ἢ
νοούμενα νοουμένοις ἢ ἐναλλάξ, (2) οἷον φαινόμενα μὲν φαινομένοις, ὅταν   5
λέγωμεν "ὁ αὐτὸς πύργος πόρρωθεν μὲν φαίνεται στρογγύλος, ἐγγύθεν δὲ
τετράγωνος", (3) νοούμενα δὲ νοουμένοις, ὅταν πρὸς τὸν κατασκευάζοντα
ὅτι ἔστι πρόνοια ἐκ τῆς τάξεως τῶν οὐρανίων, ἀντιτιθῶμεν τὸ τοὺς μὲν
ἀγαθοὺς δυσπραγεῖν πολλάκις τοὺς δὲ κακοὺς εὐπραγεῖν, καὶ διὰ τούτου
συνάγωμεν τὸ μὴ εἶναι πρόνοιαν· (4) νοούμενα δὲ φαινομένοις, ὡς ὁ   10
Ἀναξαγόρας τῷ ⟨κατασκευάζοντι⟩ λευκὴν εἶναι τὴν χιόνα ἀντετίθει, ὅτι
ἡ χιὼν ὕδωρ ἐστὶ πεπηγός, τὸ δὲ ὕδωρ ἐστὶ μέλαν, καὶ ἡ χιὼν ἄρα μέλαινά
ἐστιν. (5) καθ' ἑτέραν δὲ ἐπίνοιαν ἀντιτίθεμεν ὁτὲ μὲν παρόντα παροῦσιν,
ὡς τὰ προειρημένα· ὁτὲ δὲ παρόντα παρεληλυθόσιν ἢ μέλλουσιν, οἷον ὅταν
τις ἡμᾶς ἐρωτήσῃ λόγον ὃν λῦσαι οὐ δυνάμεθα, φαμὲν πρὸς αὐτὸν ὅτι,   15
ὥσπερ πρὸ τοῦ γενέσθαι τὸν εἰσηγησάμενον τὴν αἵρεσιν ἣν μετέρχῃ,
οὐδέπω ὁ κατ' αὐτὴν λόγος ὑγιὴς ὢν ἐφαίνετο, ὑπέκειτο μέντοι ὡς πρὸς
τὴν φύσιν, οὕτως ἐνδέχεται καὶ τὸν ἀντικείμενον τῷ ὑπὸ σοῦ ἐρωτηθέντι
νῦν λόγῳ ὑποκεῖσθαι μὲν ὡς πρὸς τὴν φύσιν, μηδέπω δ' ἡμῖν φαίνεσθαι,
ὥστε οὐδέπω χρὴ συγκατατίθεσθαι ἡμᾶς τῷ δοκοῦντι νῦν ἰσχυρῷ εἶναι   20
λόγῳ. (6) ὑπὲρ δὲ τοῦ τὰς ἀντιθέσεις ταύτας ἀκριβέστερον ἡμῖν ὑποπεσεῖν,
καὶ τοὺς τρόπους ὑποθήσομαι δι' ὧν ἡ ἐποχὴ συνάγεται, οὔτε περὶ τοῦ
πλήθους οὔτε περὶ τῆς δυνάμεως αὐτῶν διαβεβαιούμενος· ἐνδέχεται γὰρ

αὐτοὺς καὶ σαθροὺς εἶναι καὶ πλείους τῶν λεχθησομένων. (7) (ιδ᾽ Περὶ τῶν
δέκα τρόπων.) παραδίδονται τοίνυν συνήθως παρὰ τοῖς ἀρχαιοτέροις   2⟨
Σκεπτικοῖς τρόποι, δι᾽ ὧν ἡ ἐποχὴ συνάγεσθαι δοκεῖ, δέκα τὸν ἀριθμόν,
οὓς καὶ λόγους καὶ τύπους συνωνύμως καλοῦσιν. εἰσὶ δὲ οὗτοι, (8) πρῶτος
ὁ παρὰ τὴν τῶν ζῴων ἐξαλλαγήν, δεύτερος ὁ παρὰ τὴν τῶν ἀνθρώπων
διαφοράν, τρίτος ὁ παρὰ τὰς διαφόρους τῶν αἰσθητηρίων κατασκευάς,
τέταρτος ὁ παρὰ τὰς περιστάσεις, πέμπτος ὁ παρὰ τὰς θέσεις καὶ τὰ   3ς
διαστήματα καὶ τοὺς τόπους, ἕκτος ὁ παρὰ τὰς ἐπιμιξίας, ἕβδομος ὁ παρὰ
τὰς ποσότητας καὶ σκευασίας τῶν ὑποκειμένων, ὄγδοος ὁ ἀπὸ τοῦ πρός τι,
ἔννατος ὁ παρὰ τὰς συνεχεῖς ἢ σπανίους ἐγκυρήσεις, δέκατος ὁ παρὰ τὰς
ἀγωγὰς καὶ τὰ ἔθη καὶ τοὺς νόμους καὶ τὰς μυθικὰς πίστεις καὶ τὰς
δογματικὰς ὑπολήψεις. χρώμεθα δὲ τῇ τάξει ταύτῃ θετικῶς. (9) τούτων δὲ   3ς
ἐπαναβεβηκότες εἰσὶ τρόποι τρεῖς, ὁ ἀπὸ τοῦ κρίνοντος, ὁ ἀπὸ τοῦ
κρινομένου, ὁ ἐξ ἀμφοῖν· τῷ μὲν γὰρ ἀπὸ τοῦ κρίνοντος ὑποτάσσονται οἱ
πρῶτοι τέσσαρες (τὸ γὰρ κρῖνον ἢ ζῷόν ἐστιν ἢ ἄνθρωπος ἢ αἴσθησις καὶ
ἔν τινι περιστάσει), εἰς δὲ τὸν ἀπὸ τοῦ κρινομένου ⟨ἀνάγονται⟩ ὁ ἕβδομος
καὶ ὁ δέκατος, εἰς δὲ τὸν ἐξ ἀμφοῖν σύνθετον ὁ πέμπτος καὶ ὁ ἕκτος καὶ ὁ   4⟨
ὄγδοος καὶ ὁ ἔννατος. (10) πάλιν δὲ οἱ τρεῖς οὗτοι ἀνάγονται εἰς τὸν πρός τι,
ὡς εἶναι γενικώτατον μὲν τὸν πρός τι, εἰδικοὺς δὲ τοὺς τρεῖς, ὑποβεβηκό-
τας δὲ τοὺς δέκα. ταῦτα μὲν περὶ τῆς ποσότητος αὐτῶν κατὰ τὸ πιθανὸν
λέγομεν· περὶ δὲ τῆς δυνάμεως τάδε.

11 ⟨κατασκευάζοντι⟩: *construenti* T   39 ⟨ἀνάγονται⟩ Pappenheim

Context: following Sextus' account of the Pyrrhonist τέλος at *PH* 1.25–30.

We will not attempt comparison of Sextus' version of the modes with those of
Diogenes Laertius (9.79–88) and Philo (*Ebr.* 169–202), a task usefully performed by
Annas/Barnes [641]. We choose Sextus' version (**A–K**) as the fullest and most
philosophically worthwhile, even though we recognize that not every word of it goes
back to Aenesidemus himself.

B Sextus Empiricus, *PH* 1.40–61

(1) πρῶτον ἐλέγομεν εἶναι λόγον καθ᾽ ὃν παρὰ τὴν διαφορὰν τῶν ζῴων οὐχ
αἱ αὐταὶ ἀπὸ τῶν αὐτῶν ὑποπίπτουσι φαντασίαι. τοῦτο δὲ ἐπιλογιζόμεθα
ἔκ τε τῆς περὶ τὰς γενέσεις αὐτῶν διαφορᾶς καὶ ἐκ τῆς περὶ τὰς συστάσεις
τῶν σωμάτων παραλλαγῆς. (2) περὶ μὲν οὖν τὰς γενέσεις, ὅτι τῶν ζῴων τὰ
μὲν χωρὶς μίξεως γίνεται τὰ δ᾽ ἐκ συμπλοκῆς. καὶ τῶν μὲν χωρὶς μίξεως   5
γινομένων τὰ μὲν ἐκ πυρὸς γίνεται ὡς τὰ ἐν ταῖς καμίνοις φαινόμενα
ζωύφια, τὰ δ᾽ ἐξ ὕδατος φθειρομένου ὡς κώνωπες, τὰ δ᾽ ἐξ οἴνου τρεπομένου ὡς
σκνῖπες, τὰ δ᾽ ἐκ γῆς ⟨ὡς ___ ⟩, τὰ δ᾽ ἐξ ἰλύος ὡς βάτραχοι, τὰ δ᾽ ἐκ βορβόρου ὡς σκώληκες,
τὰ δ᾽ ἐξ ὄνων ὡς κάνθαροι, τὰ δ᾽ ἐκ λαχάνων ὡς κάμπαι, τὰ δ᾽ ἐκ καρπῶν ὡς οἱ ἐκ τῶν
ἐρινεῶν ψῆνες, τὰ δ᾽ ἐκ ζῴων σηπομένων ὡς μέλισσαι ταύρων καὶ σφῆκες ἵππων· τῶν δ᾽   1C
ἐκ συμπλοκῆς τὰ μὲν ἐξ ὁμοιογενῶν ὡς τὰ πλεῖστα, τὰ δ᾽ ἐξ ἀνομοιογενῶν
ὡς ἡμίονοι. πάλιν κοινῇ τῶν ζῴων τὰ μὲν ζῳοτοκεῖται ὡς ἄνθρωποι, τὰ δ᾽ ᾠοτοκεῖται

ὡς ὄρνιθες, τὰ δὲ σαρκοτοκεῖται ὡς ἄρκτοι. εἰκὸς οὖν τὰς περὶ τὰς γενέσεις
ἀνομοιότητας καὶ διαφορὰς μεγάλας ποιεῖν ἀντιπαθείας, τὸ ἀσύγκρατον
καὶ ἀσυνάρμοστον καὶ μαχόμενον ἐκεῖθεν φερομένας. (3) ἀλλὰ καὶ ἡ   15
διαφορὰ τῶν κυριωτάτων μερῶν τοῦ σώματος, καὶ μάλιστα τῶν πρὸς τὸ
ἐπικρίνειν καὶ πρὸς τὸ αἰσθάνεσθαι πεφυκότων, μεγίστην δύναται ποιεῖν
μάχην τῶν φαντασιῶν παρὰ τὴν τῶν ζῴων παραλλαγήν. οἱ γοῦν
ἰκτεριῶντες ὠχρά φασιν εἶναι τὰ ἡμῖν φαινόμενα λευκά, καὶ οἱ ὑπόσφαγμα
ἔχοντες αἱμωπά. ἐπεὶ οὖν καὶ τῶν ζῴων τὰ μὲν ὠχροὺς ἔχει τοὺς   20
ὀφθαλμοὺς τὰ δ᾽ ὑφαίμους τὰ δὲ λευκανθίζοντας τὰ δ᾽ ἄλλην χροιὰν
ἔχοντας, εἰκός, οἶμαι, διάφορον αὐτοῖς τὴν τῶν χρωμάτων ἀντίληψιν
γίγνεσθαι . . . (4) ὁ δὲ αὐτὸς καὶ περὶ τῶν ἄλλων αἰσθήσεων λόγος· πῶς
γὰρ ἂν λεχθείη ὁμοίως κινεῖσθαι κατὰ τὴν ἁφὴν τά τε ὀστρακόδερμα καὶ
τὰ σαρκοφανῆ καὶ τὰ ἠκανθωμένα καὶ τὰ ἐπτερωμένα ἢ λελεπιδωμένα;   25
πῶς δὲ ὁμοίως ἀντιλαμβάνεσθαι κατὰ τὴν ἀκοὴν τά τε στενώτατον ἔχοντα
τὸν πόρον τὸν ἀκουστικὸν καὶ τὰ εὐρυτάτῳ τούτῳ κεχρημένα, ἢ τὰ
τετριχωμένα τὰ ὦτα καὶ τὰ ψιλὰ ταῦτα ἔχοντα, ὅπου γε καὶ ἡμεῖς ἄλλως
μὲν κινούμεθα κατὰ τὴν ἀκοὴν παραβύσαντες τὰ ὦτα, ἄλλως δὲ ἦν ἁπλῶς
αὐτοῖς χρώμεθα; . . . (5) ὥσπερ γὰρ ἡ αὐτὴ τροφὴ ἀναδιδομένη ὅπου μὲν   30
γίνεται φλὲψ ὅπου δὲ ἀρτηρία ὅπου δὲ ὀστέον ὅπου δὲ νεῦρον καὶ τῶν
ἄλλων ἕκαστον, παρὰ τὴν διαφορὰν τῶν ὑποδεχομένων αὐτὴν μερῶν
διάφορον ἐπιδεικνυμένη δύναμιν, καὶ ὥσπερ τὸ ὕδωρ ἓν καὶ μονοειδὲς ἀναδιδόμενον
εἰς τὰ δένδρα ὅπου μὲν γίνεται φλοιὸς ὅπου δὲ κλάδος ὅπου δὲ καρπὸς καὶ ἤδη σῦκον καὶ
ῥοιὰ καὶ τῶν ἄλλων ἕκαστον, καὶ καθάπερ τὸ τοῦ μουσουργοῦ πνεῦμα ἓν καὶ τὸ αὐτὸ   35
ἐμπνεόμενον τῷ αὐλῷ ὅπου μὲν γίνεται ὀξὺ ὅπου δὲ βαρύ, καὶ ἡ αὐτὴ ἐπέρεισις τῆς χειρὸς
ἐπὶ τῆς λύρας ὅπου μὲν βαρὺν φθόγγον ποιεῖ ὅπου δὲ ὀξύν, οὕτως εἰκὸς καὶ τὰ ἐκτὸς
ὑποκείμενα διάφορα θεωρεῖσθαι παρὰ τὴν διάφορον κατασκευὴν τῶν τὰς
φαντασίας ὑπομενόντων ζῴων. (6) ἐναργέστερον δὲ τὸ τοιοῦτον ἔστι
μαθεῖν ἀπὸ τῶν αἱρετῶν τε καὶ φευκτῶν τοῖς ζῴοις. μύρον γοῦν ἀνθρώποις   40
μὲν ἥδιστον φαίνεται, κανθάροις δὲ καὶ μελίσσαις δυσανάσχετον· καὶ τὸ
ἔλαιον τοὺς μὲν ἀνθρώπους ὠφελεῖ, σφῆκας δὲ καὶ μελίσσας ἀναιρεῖ
καταρραινόμενον· καὶ τὸ θαλάττιον ὕδωρ ἀνθρώποις μὲν ἀηδές ἐστι
πινόμενον καὶ φαρμακῶδες, ἰχθύσι δὲ ἥδιστον καὶ πότιμον. σύες τε ἥδιον
βορβόρῳ λούονται δυσωδεστάτῳ ἢ ὕδατι διειδεῖ καὶ καθαρῷ . . . ἀλλ᾽ ἵνα μὴ   45
μᾶλλον τοῦ δέοντος ἐνδιατρίβειν δοκῶμεν, εἰ τὰ αὐτὰ τοῖς μέν ἐστιν ἀηδῆ τοῖς δὲ
ἡδέα, τὸ δὲ ἡδὺ καὶ ἀηδὲς ἐν φαντασίᾳ κεῖται, διάφοροι γίνονται τοῖς ζῴοις
ἀπὸ τῶν ὑποκειμένων φαντασίαι. (7) εἰ δὲ τὰ αὐτὰ πράγματα ἀνόμοια
φαίνεται παρὰ τὴν τῶν ζῴων ἐξαλλαγήν, ὁποῖον μὲν ἡμῖν θεωρεῖται τὸ
ὑποκείμενον ἕξομεν λέγειν, ὁποῖον δὲ ἔστι πρὸς τὴν φύσιν ἐφέξομεν. οὐδὲ   50
γὰρ ἐπικρίνειν αὐτοὶ δυνησόμεθα τὰς φαντασίας τάς τε ἡμετέρας καὶ τὰς
τῶν ἄλλων ζῴων, μέρος καὶ αὐτοὶ τῆς διαφωνίας ὄντες καὶ διὰ τοῦτο τοῦ
ἐπικρινοῦντος δεησόμενοι μᾶλλον ἢ αὐτοὶ κρίνειν δυνάμενοι. (8) καὶ ἄλλως
οὔτε ἀναποδείκτως δυνάμεθα προκρίνειν τὰς ἡμετέρας φαντασίας τῶν
παρὰ τοῖς ἀλόγοις ζῴοις γινομένων οὔτε μετ᾽ ἀποδείξεως. πρὸς γὰρ τῷ μὴ   55

The Pyrrhonist revival

εἶναι ἀπόδειξιν ἴσως, ὡς ὑπομνήσομεν, αὐτὴ ἡ λεγομένη ἀπόδειξις ἤτοι φαινομένη ἡμῖν ἔσται ἢ οὐ φαινομένη. καὶ εἰ μὲν μὴ φαινομένη, οὐδὲ μετὰ πεποιθήσεως αὐτὴν προοισόμεθα· εἰ δὲ φαινομένη ἡμῖν, ἐπειδὴ περὶ τῶν φαινομένων τοῖς ζῴοις ζητεῖται καὶ ἡ ἀπόδειξις ἡμῖν φαίνεται ζῴοις οὖσι, καὶ αὐτὴ ζητηθήσεται εἰ ἔστιν ἀληθὴς καθό ἐστι φαινομένη. ἄτοπον δὲ τὸ   6c
ζητούμενον διὰ τοῦ ζητουμένου κατασκευάζειν ἐπιχειρεῖν, ἐπεὶ ἔσται τὸ αὐτὸ πιστὸν καὶ
ἄπιστον, ὅπερ ἀμήχανον, πιστὸν μὲν ᾗ βούλεται ἀποδεικνύειν, ἄπιστον δὲ ᾗ ἀποδείκνυται.
οὐχ ἔξομεν ἄρα ἀπόδειξιν δι' ἧς προκρινοῦμεν τὰς ἑαυτῶν φαντασίας τῶν παρὰ τοῖς
ἀλόγοις καλουμένοις ζῴοις γινομένων. (9) εἰ οὖν διάφοροι γίνονται αἱ φαντασίαι
παρὰ τὴν τῶν ζῴων ἐξαλλαγήν, ἃς ἐπικρῖναι ἀμήχανόν ἐστιν, ἐπέχειν   6ς
ἀνάγκη περὶ τῶν ἐκτὸς ὑποκειμένων.

8 ⟨ὡς μῦς⟩ Fabricius: alii alia   9 ὄνων ⟨κοπροῦ⟩ dubitanter Annas/Barnes

18–19   For amplification of this popular fiction that people with jaundice see things yellow, see **G 3**.

30–9   This argument (cf. **D** 20–4) is criticized as flawed and out of place by Annas/Barnes [641], 42, but we find it both clear and apposite. It generalizes the previous examples into the point that sensory input is *processed* by the receiving organs, and that this may well involve modifications as radical and varied as those resulting from the processing of food by different organisms or bodily parts, wind by different musical instruments, etc.

39–45   A group of examples with a particularly rich history; see Annas/Barnes [641], 43–4. Those at 44–5 are from Heraclitus (22 B 61 and 13 DK).

C Sextus Empiricus, *PH* 1.79–91

(1) καὶ ὁ μὲν πρῶτος τῆς ἐποχῆς τρόπος τοιοῦτός ἐστι, δεύτερον δὲ ἐλέγομεν εἶναι τὸν ἀπὸ τῆς διαφορᾶς τῶν ἀνθρώπων· ἵνα γὰρ καθ' ὑπόθεσιν καὶ συγχωρήσῃ τις πιστοτέρους εἶναι τῶν ἀλόγων ζῴων τοὺς ἀνθρώπους, εὑρήσομεν καὶ ὅσον ἐπὶ τῇ ἡμετέρᾳ διαφορᾷ τὴν ἐποχὴν εἰσαγομένην. (2) δύο τοίνυν εἶναι λεγομένων ἐξ ὧν σύγκειται ὁ ἄνθρωπος,   5
ψυχῆς καὶ σώματος, κατ' ἄμφω ταῦτα διαφέρομεν ἀλλήλων, οἷον κατὰ σῶμα ταῖς τε μορφαῖς καὶ ταῖς ἰδιοσυγκρισίαις. διαφέρει μὲν γὰρ κατὰ μορφὴν σῶμα Σκύθου Ἰνδοῦ σώματος, τὴν δὲ παραλλαγὴν ποιεῖ, καθάπερ φασίν, ἡ διάφορος τῶν χυμῶν ἐπικράτεια. παρὰ δὲ τὴν διάφορον τῶν χυμῶν ἐπικράτειαν διάφοροι γίνονται καὶ αἱ φαντασίαι, καθάπερ καὶ ἐν τῷ   ιc
πρώτῳ λόγῳ παρεστήσαμεν. ταῦτά τοι καὶ ἐν τῇ αἱρέσει καὶ φυγῇ τῶν ἐκτὸς
διαφορὰ πολλή κατ' αὐτούς ἐστιν· ἄλλοις γὰρ χαίρουσιν Ἰνδοὶ καὶ ἄλλοις οἱ καθ' ἡμᾶς, τὸ
δὲ διαφόροις χαίρειν τοῦ παρηλλαγμένας ἀπὸ τῶν ὑποκειμένων φαντασίας λαμβάνειν ἐστὶ
μηνυτικόν. (3) κατὰ δὲ ἰδιοσυγκρισίας διαφέρομεν ὡς ἐνίους κρέα βόεια
πετραίων ἰχθυδίων ῥᾶον πέττειν καὶ ὑπὸ Λεσβίου οἰναρίου εἰς χολέραν   ις
περιτρέπεσθαι. ἦν δέ, φασίν, γραῦς Ἀττικὴ τριάκοντα ὁλκὰς κωνείου
ἀκινδύνως προσφερομένη, Λῦσις δὲ καὶ μηκωνείου τέσσαρας ὁλκὰς
ἀλύπως ἐλάμβανεν. καὶ Δημοφῶν μὲν ὁ Ἀλεξάνδρου τραπεζοποιὸς ἐν
ἡλίῳ γινόμενος ἢ ἐν βαλανείῳ ἐρρίγου, ἐν σκιᾷ δὲ ἐθάλπετο ... (4)

72 *How to suspend judgement*

τοσαύτης οὖν παραλλαγῆς οὔσης ἐν τοῖς ἀνθρώποις κατὰ τὰ σώματα, ἵνα   20
ὀλίγα ἀπὸ πολλῶν τῶν παρὰ τοῖς δογματικοῖς κειμένων ἀρκεσθῶμεν
εἰπόντες, εἰκός ἐστι καὶ κατ᾽ αὐτὴν τὴν ψυχὴν διαφέρειν ἀλλήλων τοὺς
ἀνθρώπους· τύπος γάρ τίς ἐστι τὸ σῶμα τῆς ψυχῆς, ὡς καὶ ἡ
φυσιογνωμονικὴ σοφία δείκνυσιν. (5) τὸ δὲ μέγιστον δεῖγμα τῆς κατὰ τὴν
διάνοιαν τῶν ἀνθρώπων πολλῆς καὶ ἀπείρου διαφορᾶς ἡ διαφωνία τῶν   25
παρὰ τοῖς δογματικοῖς λεγομένων περί τε τῶν ἄλλων καὶ περὶ τοῦ τίνα μὲν
αἱρεῖσθαι προσήκει τίνα δὲ ἐκκλίνειν . . . (6) ἐπεὶ οὖν ἡ αἵρεσις καὶ ἡ φυγὴ
ἐν ἡδονῇ καὶ ἀηδισμῷ ἐστιν, ἡ δὲ ἡδονὴ καὶ ὁ ἀηδισμὸς ἐν αἰσθήσει κεῖται
καὶ φαντασίᾳ, ὅταν τὰ αὐτὰ οἱ μὲν αἱρῶνται οἱ δὲ φεύγωσιν, ἀκόλουθον
ἡμᾶς ἐπιλογίζεσθαι ὅτι οὐδὲ ὁμοίως ὑπὸ τῶν αὐτῶν κινοῦνται, ἐπεὶ   30
ὁμοίως ἂν τὰ αὐτὰ ἡροῦντο ἢ ἐξέκλινον. (7) εἰ δὲ τὰ ⟨αὐτὰ⟩ διαφόρως κινεῖ
παρὰ τὴν διαφορὰν τῶν ἀνθρώπων, εἰσάγοιτ᾽ ἂν εἰκότως καὶ κατὰ τοῦτο ἡ
ἐποχή, ὅ τι μὲν ἕκαστον φαίνεται τῶν ὑποκειμένων ὡς πρὸς ἑκάστην
διαφορὰν ἴσως λέγειν ἡμῶν δυναμένων, τί δὲ ἔστι κατὰ δύναμιν ὡς πρὸς
τὴν φύσιν οὐχ οἵων τε ὄντων ἀποφήνασθαι. (8) ἤτοι γὰρ πᾶσι τοῖς   35
ἀνθρώποις πιστεύσομεν ἢ τισίν. ἀλλ᾽ εἰ μὲν πᾶσιν, καὶ ἀδυνάτοις
ἐπιχειρήσομεν καὶ τὰ ἀντικείμενα παραδεξόμεθα· εἰ δὲ τισίν, εἰπάτωσαν
ἡμῖν τίσι χρὴ συγκατατίθεσθαι· ὁ μὲν γὰρ Πλατωνικὸς λέξει ὅτι
Πλάτωνι, ὁ Ἐπικούρειος δὲ Ἐπικούρῳ, καὶ οἱ ἄλλοι ἀναλόγως, καὶ οὕτως
ἀνεπικρίτως στασιάζοντες αὖθις ἡμᾶς εἰς τὴν ἐποχὴν περιστήσουσιν. (9) ὁ   40
δὲ λέγων ὅτι τοῖς πλείστοις δεῖ συγκατατίθεσθαι παιδαριῶδές τι
προσίεται, οὐδενὸς δυναμένου πάντας τοὺς ἀνθρώπους ἐπελθεῖν καὶ
διαλογίσασθαι τί τοῖς πλείστοις ἀρέσκει, ἐνδεχομένου τοῦ ἔν τισιν ἔθνεσιν,
ἃ ἡμεῖς οὐκ ἴσμεν, τὰ μὲν παρ᾽ ἡμῖν σπάνια τοῖς πλείοσι προσεῖναι τὰ δὲ   45
ἡμῶν τοῖς πολλοῖς συμβαίνοντα σπάνια ὑπάρχειν, ὡς τοὺς πολλοὺς μὲν ὑπὸ
φαλαγγίων δακνομένους μὴ ἀλγεῖν, τινὰς δὲ σπανίως ἀλγεῖν, καὶ ἐπὶ τῶν ἄλλων τῶν
ἔμπροσθεν εἰρημένων ἰδιοσυγκρισιῶν τὸ ἀνάλογον. ἀναγκαῖον οὖν καὶ διὰ τὴν τῶν
ἀνθρώπων διαφορὰν εἰσάγεσθαι τὴν ἐποχήν . . . (10) ἐπεὶ δὲ φίλαυτοί τινες ὄντες οἱ
δογματικοί φασι δεῖν τῶν ἄλλων ἀνθρώπων ἑαυτοὺς προκρίνειν ἐν τῇ
κρίσει τῶν πραγμάτων, ἐπιστάμεθα μὲν ὅτι ἄτοπός ἐστιν ἡ ἀξίωσις αὐτῶν   50
(μέρος γάρ εἰσι καὶ αὐτοὶ τῆς διαφωνίας· καὶ ἐὰν αὑτοὺς προκρίνοντες
οὕτω κρίνωσι τὰ φαινόμενα, πρὶν ἄρξασθαι τῆς κρίσεως τὸ ζητούμενον
συναρπάζουσιν, ἑαυτοῖς τὴν κρίσιν ἐπιτρέποντες), ὅμως δ᾽ οὖν ἵνα καὶ ἐπὶ
ἑνὸς ἀνθρώπου τὸν λόγον ἱστάντες, οἷον τοῦ παρ᾽ αὐτοῖς ὀνειροπολουμένου
σοφοῦ, ἐπὶ τὴν ἐποχὴν καταντῶμεν, τὸν τρίτον τῇ τάξει τρόπον   55
προχειριζόμεθα.

31 add. Bekker   39 Ἐπικούρειος Stephanus secundum T: Ἐπίκουρος codd.   52 τὸ ζητούμενον
Mutschmann secundum T: τὰ φαινόμενα codd.

7–9 Cf. **55Q**.

21 **δογματικοῖς** Referring principally to medical writers, whose theories of
'humours' are heavily exploited in this mode.

40–8 For comparable objections to induction from a Stoic source, see **42G–H**.

465

The Pyrrhonist revival

D Sextus Empiricus, *PH* 1.91–8

(1) τοῦτον δ' ἐλέγομεν τὸν ἀπὸ τῆς διαφορᾶς τῶν αἰσθήσεων. ὅτι δὲ διαφέρονται αἱ αἰσθήσεις πρὸς ἀλλήλας, πρόδηλον. (2) αἱ γοῦν γραφαὶ τῇ μὲν ὄψει δοκοῦσιν εἰσοχὰς καὶ ἐξοχὰς ἔχειν, οὐ μὴν καὶ τῇ ἁφῇ. καὶ τὸ μέλι τῇ μὲν γλώττῃ ἡδὺ φαίνεται ἐπί τινων, τοῖς δ' ὀφθαλμοῖς ἀηδές· ἀδύνατον οὖν ἐστιν εἰπεῖν πότερον ἡδύ ἐστιν εἰλικρινῶς ἢ ἀηδές. καὶ ἐπὶ τοῦ μύρου   5
ὁμοίως· τὴν μὲν γὰρ ὄσφρησιν εὐφραίνει, τὴν δὲ γεῦσιν ἀηδίζει. τό τε εὐφόρβιον ἐπεὶ τοῖς μὲν ὀφθαλμοῖς λυπηρόν ἐστι τῷ δὲ ἄλλῳ σώματι παντὶ ἄλυπον, οὐχ ἕξομεν εἰπεῖν πότερον ἄλυπόν ἐστιν εἰλικρινῶς τοῖς σώμασιν ὅσον ἐπὶ τῇ ἑαυτοῦ φύσει ἢ λυπηρόν. τό τε ὄμβριον ὕδωρ ὀφθαλμοῖς μέν ἐστιν ὠφέλιμον, ἀρτηρίαν δὲ καὶ πνεύμονα τραχύνει, καθάπερ καὶ τὸ ἔλαιον, καίτοι τὴν ἐπιφάνειαν παρηγορεῖ. καὶ ἡ θαλαττία νάρκη   10
τοῖς μὲν ἄκροις προστεθεῖσα ναρκᾶν ποιεῖ, τῷ δ' ἄλλῳ σώματι ἀλύπως παρατίθεται. (3) διόπερ ὁποῖον μὲν ἔστι πρὸς τὴν φύσιν ἕκαστον τούτων οὐχ ἕξομεν λέγειν, ὁποῖον δὲ φαίνεται ἑκάστοτε δυνατὸν εἰπεῖν. (4) καὶ ἄλλα δὲ πλείω τούτων ἔνεστι λέγειν· ἀλλ' ἵνα μὴ διατρίβωμεν, διὰ τὴν πρόθεσιν [τοῦ τρόπου] τῆς συγγραφῆς ἐκεῖνο λεκτέον. ἕκαστον τῶν φαινομένων ἡμῖν αἰσθητῶν ποικίλον ὑποπίπτειν   15
δοκεῖ, οἷον τὸ μῆλον λεῖον εὐῶδες γλυκὺ ξανθόν. ἄδηλον οὖν πότερόν ποτε ταύτας μόνας ὄντως ἔχει τὰς ποιότητας, ἢ μονόποιον μέν ἐστιν, παρὰ δὲ τὴν διάφορον κατασκευὴν τῶν αἰσθητηρίων διάφορον φαίνεται, ἢ καὶ πλείονας μὲν τῶν φαινομένων ἔχει ποιότητας, ἡμῖν δ' οὐχ ὑποπίπτουσί τινες αὐτῶν. (5) μονόποιον μὲν γὰρ εἶναι τοῦτο ἐνδέχεται λογίζεσθαι ἐκ   20
τῶν ἔμπροσθεν ἡμῖν εἰρημένων περὶ τῆς εἰς τὰ σώματα ἀναδιδομένης τροφῆς καὶ τοῦ ὕδατος τοῦ εἰς τὰ δένδρα ἀναδιδομένου καὶ τοῦ πνεύματος τοῦ ἐν αὐλοῖς καὶ σύριγξι καὶ τοῖς παραπλησίοις ὀργάνοις· δύναται γὰρ καὶ τὸ μῆλον μονοειδὲς μὲν εἶναι, διάφορον δὲ θεωρεῖσθαι παρὰ τὴν διαφορὰν τῶν αἰσθητηρίων περὶ ἃ γίνεται αὐτοῦ ἡ ἀντίληψις. (6) πλείονας δὲ τῶν φαινομένων ἡμῖν ποιοτήτων ἔχειν τὸ μῆλον ποιότητας   25
δύνασθαι οὕτως ἐπιλογιζόμεθα. ἐννοήσωμέν τινα ἐκ γενετῆς ἁφὴν μὲν ἔχοντα καὶ ὄσφρησιν καὶ γεῦσιν, μήτε δὲ ἀκούοντα μήτε ὁρῶντα. οὗτος τοίνυν ὑπολήψεται μήτε ὁρατόν τι εἶναι τὴν ἀρχὴν μήτε ἀκουστόν, ἀλλὰ μόνα ἐκεῖνα τὰ τρία γένη τῶν ποιοτήτων ὑπάρχειν ὧν ἀντιλαμβάνεσθαι δύναται. καὶ ἡμᾶς οὖν ἐνδέχεται τὰς πέντε μόνας αἰσθήσεις ἔχοντας μόνον   30
ἀντιλαμβάνεσθαι, ἐκ τῶν περὶ τὸ μῆλον ποιοτήτων, ὧν ἐσμεν ἀντιληπτικοί· ὑποκεῖσθαι δὲ ἄλλας οἷόν τέ ἐστι ποιότητας, ὑποπιπτούσας ἑτέροις αἰσθητηρίοις, ὧν ἡμεῖς οὐ μετεσχήκαμεν, διὸ οὐδὲ ἀντιλαμβανόμεθα τῶν κατ' αὐτὰ αἰσθητῶν. (7) ἀλλ' ἡ φύσις συνεμετρήσατο, φήσει τις, τὰς αἰσθήσεις πρὸς τὰ αἰσθητά. ποία φύσις, διαφωνίας τοσαύτης ἀνεπικρίτου   35
παρὰ τοῖς δογματικοῖς οὔσης περὶ τῆς ὑπάρξεως τῆς κατ' αὐτήν; ὁ γὰρ ἐπικρίνων αὐτὸ τοῦτο εἰ ἔστι φύσις, εἰ μὲν ἰδιώτης εἴη, ἄπιστος ἔσται κατ' αὐτούς, φιλόσοφος δὲ ὢν μέρος ἔσται τῆς διαφωνίας καὶ κρινόμενος αὐτὸς ἀλλ' οὐ κριτής.

14 secl. Mutschmann   34 αὐτὰ Annas/Barnes: αὐτὰς codd.

2–3 Cf. **F 4**; **1H 1**.
16ff. For the apple example, cf. **53K 2**, and Annas/Barnes [641], 71ff.

E Sextus Empiricus, *PH* 1.100–13

(1) ἵνα δὲ καὶ ἐπὶ μιᾶς ἑκάστης αἰσθήσεως ἱστάντες τὸν λόγον, ἢ καὶ ἀφιστάμενοι τῶν αἰσθήσεων, ἔχωμεν καταλήγειν εἰς τὴν ἐποχήν, παραλαμβάνομεν καὶ τὸν τέταρτον τρόπον αὐτῆς. ἔστι δ' οὗτος ὁ παρὰ τὰς περιστάσεις καλούμενος, περιστάσεις λεγόντων ἡμῶν τὰς διαθέσεις. θεωρεῖσθαι δ' αὐτόν φαμεν ἐν τῷ κατὰ φύσιν ἢ παρὰ φύσιν ⟨ἔχειν⟩, ἐν τῷ   5
ἐγρηγορέναι ἢ καθεύδειν, παρὰ τὰς ἡλικίας, παρὰ τὸ κινεῖσθαι ἢ ἠρεμεῖν,
παρὰ τὸ μισεῖν ἢ φιλεῖν, παρὰ τὸ ἐνδεεῖς εἶναι ἢ κεκορεσμένους, παρὰ τὸ
μεθύειν ἢ νήφειν, παρὰ τὰς προδιαθέσεις, παρὰ τὸ θαρρεῖν ἢ δεδιέναι, [ἢ]
παρὰ τὸ λυπεῖσθαι ἢ χαίρειν. (2) οἷον παρὰ μὲν τὸ κατὰ φύσιν ἢ παρὰ φύσιν
ἔχειν ἀνόμοια ὑποπίπτει τὰ πράγματα, ἐπεὶ οἱ μὲν φρενιτίζοντες καὶ οἱ   10
θεοφορούμενοι δαιμόνων ἀκούειν δοκοῦσιν, ἡμεῖς δὲ οὔ . . . καὶ τὸ αὐτὸ
μέλι ἐμοὶ μὲν φαίνεται γλυκύ, τοῖς δὲ ἰκτερικοῖς πικρόν. (3) εἰ δέ τις λέγει
ὅτι χυμῶν τινων παραπλοκὴ ἀνοικείους φαντασίας ἐκ τῶν ὑποκειμένων
ποιεῖ τοῖς παρὰ φύσιν ἔχουσιν, λεκτέον ὅτι ἐπεὶ καὶ οἱ ὑγιαίνοντες χυμοὺς
ἔχουσιν ἀνακεκραμένους, δύνανται οὗτοι τὰ ἐκτὸς ὑποκείμενα, τοιαῦτα   15
ὄντα τῇ φύσει ὁποῖα φαίνεται τοῖς παρὰ φύσιν ἔχειν λεγομένοις, ἑτεροῖα
φαίνεσθαι ποιεῖν τοῖς ὑγιαίνουσιν. τὸ γὰρ ἐκείνοις μὲν τοῖς χυμοῖς
μεταβλητικὴν τῶν ὑποκειμένων διδόναι δύναμιν, τούτοις δὲ μή, πλασματικόν ἐστιν, ἐπεὶ καὶ ὥσπερ οἱ ὑγιαίνοντες κατὰ φύσιν μὲν τὴν τῶν
ὑγιαινόντων ἔχουσι, παρὰ φύσιν δὲ τὴν τῶν νοσούντων, οὕτω καὶ οἱ   20
νοσοῦντες παρὰ φύσιν μὲν ἔχουσι τὴν τῶν ὑγιαινόντων, κατὰ φύσιν δὲ τὴν
τῶν νοσούντων, ὥστε κἀκείνοις πρός τι κατὰ φύσιν ἔχουσι πιστευτέον. (4)
παρὰ δὲ τὸ ὑπνοῦν ἢ ἐγρηγορέναι διάφοροι γίνονται φαντασίαι, ἐπεὶ ὡς καθ' ὕπνους
φανταζόμεθα, οὐ φανταζόμεθα ἐγρηγορότες, οὐδὲ ὡς φανταζόμεθα ἐγρηγορότες, καὶ κατὰ
τοὺς ὕπνους φανταζόμεθα, ὥστε εἶναι αὐτοῖς ἢ μὴ εἶναι γίνεται οὐχ ἁπλῶς ἀλλὰ πρός τι·   25
πρὸς γὰρ τὸ καθ' ὕπνους ἢ πρὸς ἐγρήγορσιν. εἰκότως οὖν καθ' ὕπνους ὁρῶμεν ταῦτα ἅ ἐστιν
ἀνύπαρκτα ἐν τῷ ἐγρηγορέναι, οὐκ ἐν τῷ καθάπαξ ἀνύπαρκτα ὄντα· ἔστι γὰρ καθ' ὕπνους,
ὥσπερ τὰ ὕπαρ ἔστιν κἂν μὴ ᾖ καθ' ὕπνους. παρὰ δὲ τὰς ἡλικίας, ὅτι ὁ αὐτὸς ἀὴρ
τοῖς μὲν γέρουσι ψυχρὸς εἶναι δοκεῖ τοῖς δὲ ἀκμάζουσιν εὔκρατος, καὶ τὸ
αὐτὸ χρῶμα τοῖς μὲν πρεσβυτέροις ἀμαυρὸν φαίνεται τοῖς δὲ ἀκμάζουσι   30
κατακορές, καὶ φωνὴ ὁμοίως ἡ αὐτὴ τοῖς μὲν ἀμαυρὰ δοκεῖ τυγχάνειν τοῖς δ'
ἐξάκουστος. καὶ παρὰ τὰς αἱρέσεις δὲ καὶ φυγὰς ἀνομοίως κινοῦνται οἱ ταῖς ἡλικίαις
διαφέροντες· παισὶ μὲν γάρ, εἰ τύχοι, σφαῖραι καὶ τροχοὶ διὰ σπουδῆς εἰσιν, οἱ ἀκμάζοντες
δὲ ἄλλα αἱροῦνται, καὶ ἄλλα οἱ γέροντες. ἐξ ὧν συνάγεται ὅτι διάφοροι γίνονται φαντασίαι
ὑπὸ τῶν αὐτῶν ὑποκειμένων καὶ παρὰ τὰς διαφόρους ἡλικίας. παρὰ δὲ τὸ κινεῖσθαι ἢ   35
ἠρεμεῖν ἀνόμοια φαίνεται τὰ πράγματα, ἐπεὶ ἅπερ ἑστῶτες ὁρῶμεν
ἀτρεμοῦντα, ταῦτα παραπλέοντες κινεῖσθαι δοκοῦμεν . . . παρὰ δὲ τὸ
μεθύειν ἢ νήφειν, ὅτι ἅπερ νήφοντες αἰσχρὰ εἶναι δοκοῦμεν, ταῦτα ἡμῖν
μεθύουσιν οὐκ αἰσχρὰ φαίνεται. παρὰ δὲ τὰς προδιαθέσεις, ὅτι ὁ αὐτὸς
οἶνος τοῖς μὲν φοίνικας ἢ ἰσχάδας προφαγοῦσιν ὀξώδης φαίνεται, τοῖς δὲ   40
κάρυα ἢ ἐρεβίνθους προσενεγκαμένοις ἡδὺς εἶναι δοκεῖ . . . (5) τοσαύτης

467

The Pyrrhonist revival

οὖν οὔσης ἀνωμαλίας καὶ παρὰ τὰς διαθέσεις, καὶ ἄλλοτε ἄλλως ἐν ταῖς
διαθέσεσι τῶν ἀνθρώπων γινομένων, ὁποῖον μὲν ἕκαστον τῶν ὑποκειμένων ἑκάστῳ φαίνεται ῥᾴδιον ἴσως εἰπεῖν, ὁποῖον δὲ ἔστιν οὐκέτι, ἐπεὶ
καὶ ἀνεπίκριτός ἐστιν ἡ ἀνωμαλία. ὁ γὰρ ἐπικρίνων ταύτην ἤτοι ἔν τισι   4⁵
τῶν προειρημένων διαθέσεών ἐστιν ἢ ἐν οὐδεμιᾷ τὸ παράπαν ἐστὶ
διαθέσει. τὸ μὲν οὖν λέγειν ὅτι ἐν οὐδεμιᾷ διαθέσει τὸ σύνολόν ἐστιν, οἷον
οὔτε ὑγιαίνει οὔτε νοσεῖ, οὔτε κινεῖται οὔτε ἠρεμεῖ, οὔτε ἔν τινι ἡλικίᾳ
ἐστίν, ἀπήλλακται δὲ καὶ τῶν ἄλλων διαθέσεων, τελέως ἀπεμφαίνει. εἰ δὲ
ἔν τινι διαθέσει ὢν κρινεῖ τὰς φαντασίας, μέρος ἔσται τῆς διαφωνίας, καὶ   5⁰
ἄλλως οὐκ εἰλικρινὴς τῶν ἐκτὸς ὑποκειμένων ἔσται κριτὴς διὰ τὸ
τεθολῶσθαι ταῖς διαθέσεσιν ἐν αἷς ἔστιν.

5 add. Mutschmann   30 χρῶμα Bekker: βρῶμα codd.

Cf. Annas/Barnes [641], 85 for the interesting suggestion, on the strength of Sextus'
exegesis of Protagorean relativism in very similar terms at *M.* 7.60–4, that the
material in mode 4 was first collected by Protagoras. However, since *M.* 7.60–4 is
itself probably derived from Aenesidemus (cf. the thoroughly Aenesidemean
reworking of Gorgias at *M.* 7.65–87, and the extensive reliance throughout *M.* 7.46–
262 on handbooks by Aenesidemus' contemporaries Antiochus and Posidonius), we
find it more plausible that Aenesidemus had simply borrowed material from his own
mode 4 to aid an exegesis of Protagoras based ultimately, like most of the ancient
Protagorean doxography, on Plato (especially *Tht.* 157e–160a).

F Sextus Empiricus, *PH* 1.118–20

(1) πέμπτος ἐστὶ λόγος ὁ παρὰ τὰς θέσεις καὶ τὰ διαστήματα καὶ τοὺς
τόπους· καὶ γὰρ παρὰ τούτων ἕκαστον τὰ αὐτὰ πράγματα διάφορα
φαίνεται. (2) οἷον ἡ αὐτὴ στοὰ ἀπὸ μὲν τῆς ἑτέρας ἀρχῆς ὁρωμένη μείουρος
φαίνεται, ἀπὸ δὲ τοῦ μέσου σύμμετρος πάντοθεν, καὶ τὸ αὐτὸ πλοῖον
πόρρωθεν μὲν μικρὸν φαίνεται καὶ ἑστώς, ἐγγύθεν δὲ μέγα καὶ κινούμενον,   5
καὶ ὁ αὐτὸς πύργος πόρρωθεν μὲν φαίνεται στρογγύλος, ἐγγύθεν δὲ
τετράγωνος. ταῦτα μὲν παρὰ τὰ διαστήματα, (3) παρὰ δὲ τοὺς τόπους ὅτι
τὸ λυχνιαῖον φῶς ἐν ἡλίῳ μὲν ἀμαυρὸν φαίνεται ἐν σκότῳ δὲ λαμπρόν, καὶ
ἡ αὐτὴ κώπη ἔναλος μὲν κεκλασμένη ἔξαλος δὲ εὐθεῖα . . . (4) παρὰ δὲ τὰς
θέσεις ὅτι ἡ αὐτὴ εἰκὼν ἐξυπτιαζομένη μὲν λεία φαίνεται, ποσῶς δὲ   1⁰
ἐπινευομένη εἰσοχὰς καὶ ἐξοχὰς ἔχειν δοκεῖ. καὶ οἱ τράχηλοι δὲ τῶν
περιστερῶν παρὰ τὰς διαφόρους ἐπικλίσεις διάφοροι φαίνονται κατὰ
χρῶμα.

These are standard ancient examples of optical illusion. Cf. **16G** for the tower (6–7).

G Sextus Empiricus, *PH* 1.124–8

(1) ἕκτος ἐστὶ τρόπος ὁ παρὰ τὰς ἐπιμιγάς, καθ' ὃν συνάγομεν ὅτι, ἐπεὶ
μηδὲν τῶν ὑποκειμένων καθ' ἑαυτὸ ἡμῖν ὑποπίπτει ἀλλὰ σύν τινι, ὁποῖον

468

μέν ἐστι τὸ μῖγμα ἔκ τε τοῦ ἐκτὸς καὶ τοῦ ᾧ συνθεωρεῖται τάχα δυνατὸν
εἰπεῖν, ὁποῖον δέ ἐστι τὸ ἐκτὸς ὑποκείμενον εἰλικρινῶς οὐκ ἂν ἔχοιμεν
λέγειν. (2) ὅτι δὲ οὐδὲν τῶν ἐκτὸς καθ' αὑτὸ ὑποπίπτει ἀλλὰ πάντως σύν   5
τινι, καὶ ὅτι παρὰ τοῦτο ἀλλοῖον θεωρεῖται, πρόδηλον, οἶμαι. τὸ γοῦν
ἡμέτερον χρῶμα ἀλλοῖον μὲν ὁρᾶται ἐν ἀλεεινῷ ἀέρι, ἀλλοῖον δὲ ἐν τῷ
ψυχρῷ, καὶ οὐκ ἂν ἔχοιμεν εἰπεῖν ὁποῖον ἔστι τῇ φύσει τὸ χρῶμα ἡμῶν,
ἀλλ' ὁποῖον σὺν ἑκάστῳ τούτων θεωρεῖται. καὶ ἡ αὐτὴ φωνὴ ἀλλοία μὲν
φαίνεται σὺν λεπτῷ ἀέρι, ἀλλοία δὲ σὺν παχυμερεῖ, καὶ τὰ ἀρώματα ἐν   10
βαλανείῳ καὶ ἡλίῳ πληκτικώτερα μᾶλλόν ἐστιν ἢ ἐν ἀέρι καταψύχρῳ, καὶ
τὸ σῶμα ὑπὸ ὕδατος μὲν περιεχόμενον κοῦφόν ἐστιν, ὑπὸ δὲ ἀέρος βαρύ.
(3) ἵνα δὲ καὶ τῆς ἔξωθεν ἐπιμιξίας ἀποστῶμεν, οἱ ὀφθαλμοὶ ἡμῶν ἔχουσιν
ἐν ἑαυτοῖς καὶ χιτῶνας καὶ ὑγρά. τὰ οὖν ὁρατὰ ἐπεὶ μὴ ἄνευ τούτων
θεωρεῖται, οὐ καταληφθήσεται πρὸς ἀκρίβειαν· τοῦ γὰρ μίγματος   15
ἀντιλαμβανόμεθα. καὶ διὰ τοῦτο οἱ μὲν ἰκτερικοὶ πάντα ὠχρὰ ὁρῶσιν, οἱ δ'
ὑπόσφαγμα ἔχοντες ὕφαιμα. καὶ ἐπεὶ ἡ φωνὴ ἡ αὐτὴ ἀλλοία μὲν φαίνεται ἐν
ἀναπεπταμένοις τόποις, ἀλλοία δὲ ἐν στενοῖς καὶ ἑλικοειδέσι, καὶ ἀλλοία μὲν ἐν καθαρῷ
ἀέρι, ἀλλοία δὲ ἐν τεθολωμένῳ, εἰκός ἐστι μὴ ἀντιλαμβάνεσθαι ἡμᾶς εἰλικρινῶς τῆς φωνῆς·
τὰ γὰρ ὦτα σκολιόπορά ἐστι καὶ στενόπορα καὶ ἀτμώδεσιν ἀποφορήσεσιν, αἵ δὴ ἀπὸ τῶν   20
περὶ τὴν κεφαλὴν φέρεσθαι λέγονται τόπων, τεθολωμένα. ἀλλὰ καὶ ἐν τοῖς μυξωτῆρσι καὶ
ἐν τοῖς τῆς γεύσεως τόποις ὑλῶν ὑποκειμένων, μετ' ἐκείνων ἀντιλαμβανόμεθα τῶν
γευστῶν καὶ τῶν ὀσφρητῶν ἀλλ' οὐκ εἰλικρινῶς. ὥστε διὰ τὰς ἐπιμιξίας αἱ αἰσθήσεις οὐκ
ἀντιλαμβάνονται ὁποῖα πρὸς ἀκρίβειαν τὰ ἐκτὸς ὑποκείμενά ἐστιν. (4) ἀλλ' οὐδὲ ἡ
διάνοια, μάλιστα μὲν ἐπεὶ αἱ ὁδηγοὶ αὐτῆς αἰσθήσεις σφάλλονται· ἴσως δὲ   25
καὶ αὐτὴ ἐπιμιξίαν τινὰ ἰδίαν ποιεῖται πρὸς τὰ ὑπὸ τῶν αἰσθήσεων
ἀναγγελλόμενα· περὶ γὰρ ἕκαστον τῶν τόπων ἐν οἷς τὸ ἡγεμονικὸν εἶναι
δοκοῦσιν οἱ δογματικοί, χυμούς τινας ὑποκειμένους θεωροῦμεν, εἴτε περὶ
ἐγκέφαλον εἴτε περὶ καρδίαν εἴτε περὶ ὁτιδήποτε οὖν μέρος τοῦ ζῴου
τοῦτο τίθεσθαι βούλοιτό τις. (5) καὶ κατὰ τοῦτον οὖν τὸν τρόπον ὁρῶμεν,   30
ὅτι περὶ τῆς φύσεως τῶν ἐκτὸς ὑποκειμένων οὐδὲν εἰπεῖν ἔχοντες ἐπέχειν
ἀναγκαζόμεθα.

H Sextus Empiricus, PH 1.129–32

(1) ἕβδομον τρόπον ἐλέγομεν εἶναι τὸν παρὰ τὰς ποσότητας καὶ σκευασίας
τῶν ὑποκειμένων, σκευασίας λέγοντες κοινῶς τὰς συνθέσεις. ὅτι δὲ καὶ
κατὰ τοῦτον τὸν τρόπον ἐπέχειν ἀναγκαζόμεθα περὶ τῆς φύσεως τῶν
πραγμάτων, δῆλον. (2) οἷον γοῦν τὰ ξέσματα τοῦ κέρατος τῆς αἰγὸς
φαίνεται μὲν λευκὰ ἁπλῶς καὶ ἄνευ συνθέσεως θεωρούμενα, συντιθέμενα   5
δὲ ἐν τῇ τοῦ κέρατος ὑπάρξει μέλανα θεωρεῖται. καὶ τοῦ ἀργύρου [τὰ μέρη] τὰ
ῥινήματα κατ' ἰδίαν μὲν ὄντα μέλανα φαίνεται, σὺν δὲ τῷ ὅλῳ ὡς λευκὰ ὑποπίπτει. καὶ τῆς
Ταιναρείας λίθου τὰ μὲν μέρη λευκὰ ὁρᾶται ὅταν λεανθῇ, σὺν δὲ τῇ ὁλοσχερεῖ ξανθὰ
φαίνεται. καὶ αἱ ἀπ' ἀλλήλων ἐσκεδασμέναι ψάμμοι τραχεῖαι φαίνονται, ὡς
σωρὸς δὲ συντεθεῖσαι ἁπαλῶς κινοῦσι τὴν αἴσθησιν. καὶ ὁ ἑλλέβορος λεπτὸς μὲν   10

469

καὶ χνοώδης προσφερόμενος πνιγμὸν ἐπιφέρει, κριμνώδης δὲ ὢν οὐκέτι. (3) καὶ ὁ οἶνος σύμμετρος μὲν πινόμενος ῥώννυσιν ἡμᾶς, πλείων δὲ λαμβανόμενος παραλύει τὸ σῶμα. καὶ ἡ τροφὴ παραπλησίως παρὰ τὴν ποσότητα διάφορον ἐπιδείκνυται δύναμιν· πολλάκις γοῦν διὰ τὸ πολλὴ προσενεχθῆναι καθαίρει τὸ σῶμα διά τε ἀπεψιῶν καὶ χολερικῶν παθῶν. (4) ἕξομεν οὖν   1 5
κἀνταῦθα λέγειν ὁποῖόν ἐστι τοῦ κέρατος τὸ λεπτὸν καὶ ὁποῖον τὸ ἐκ πολλῶν λεπτομερῶν συγκείμενον, καὶ ὁποῖος μέν ἐστιν ὁ μικρομερὴς ἄργυρος ὁποῖος δὲ ὁ ἐκ πολλῶν μικρομερῶν συγκείμενος, καὶ ὁποία μὲν ἡ ἀκαριαία Ταιναρεία λίθος ὁποία δὲ ἡ ἐκ πολλῶν μικρῶν συγκειμένη, καὶ ἐπὶ τῶν ψάμμων καὶ τοῦ ἐλλεβόρου καὶ τοῦ οἴνου καὶ τῆς τροφῆς τὸ πρός τι, τὴν μέντοι φύσιν τῶν πραγμάτων   2 0
καθ᾽ ἑαυτὴν οὐκέτι διὰ τὴν παρὰ τὰς συνθέσεις τῶν φαντασιῶν ἀνωμαλίαν.

6 secl. Mutschmann

16–17 **ἐστι . . . ἐστιν** See the useful remarks of Annas/Barnes [641], 123–4. As they note, it is striking and odd that Sextus should not restrict himself to φαίνεται here. This might be used in support of Frede's view ([646], cf. [61]) that the Pyrrhonist is willing to assent to everyday, non-technical truth claims. On the other hand, the warning at I 2 may be adequate explanation.

I Sextus Empiricus, *PH* 1.135–40

(1) ὄγδοός ἐστι τρόπος ὁ ἀπὸ τοῦ πρός τι, καθ᾽ ὃν συνάγομεν ὅτι, ἐπεὶ πάντα ἐστὶ πρός τι, περὶ τοῦ τίνα ἐστὶν ἀπολύτως καὶ ὡς πρὸς τὴν φύσιν ἐφέξομεν. (2) ἐκεῖνο δὲ χρὴ γινώσκειν ὅτι ἐνταῦθα, ὥσπερ καὶ ἐν ἄλλοις, τῷ "ἔστι" καταχρώμεθα ἀντὶ τοῦ "φαίνεται", δυνάμει τοῦτο λέγοντες "πρός τι πάντα φαίνεται." (3) τοῦτο δὲ διχῶς λέγεται, ἅπαξ μὲν ὡς πρὸς   5
τὸ κρῖνον (τὸ γὰρ ἐκτὸς ὑποκείμενον καὶ κρινόμενον πρὸς τὸ κρῖνον φαίνεται), καθ᾽ ἕτερον δὲ τρόπον πρὸς τὰ συνθεωρούμενα, ὡς τὸ δεξιὸν πρὸς τὸ ἀριστερόν. (4) ὅτι δὲ πάντα ἐστὶ πρός τι, ἐπελογισάμεθα μὲν καὶ ἔμπροσθεν, οἷον κατὰ τὸ κρῖνον, ὅτι πρὸς τόδε τὸ ζῷον καὶ τόνδε τὸν ἄνθρωπον καὶ τήνδε τὴν αἴσθησιν ἕκαστον φαίνεται καὶ πρὸς τοιάνδε   1 0
περίστασιν, κατὰ δὲ τὰ συνθεωρούμενα, ὅτι πρὸς τήνδε τὴν ἐπιμιξίαν καὶ τόνδε τὸν τόπον καὶ τὴν σύνθεσιν τήνδε καὶ τὴν ποσότητα καὶ τὴν θέσιν ἕκαστον φαίνεται. (5) καὶ ἰδίᾳ δὲ ἐνδέχεται συνάγειν ὅτι πάντα ἐστὶ πρός τι, τόνδε τὸν τρόπον· πότερον διαφέρει τῶν πρός τι τὰ κατὰ διαφορὰν ἢ οὔ; εἰ μὲν οὐ διαφέρει, καὶ αὐτὰ πρός τι ἐστίν· εἰ δὲ διαφέρει, ἐπεὶ πᾶν τὸ   1 5
διαφέρον πρός τι ἐστίν (λέγεται γὰρ πρὸς ἐκεῖνο οὗ διαφέρει), πρός τι ἐστὶ τὰ κατὰ διαφοράν. (6) τῶν τε ὄντων τὰ μέν ἐστιν ἀνωτάτω γένη κατὰ τοὺς δογματικούς, τὰ δ᾽ ἔσχατα εἴδη, τὰ δὲ γένη καὶ εἴδη· πάντα δὲ ταῦτά ἐστι πρός τι· πάντα ἄρα ἐστὶ πρός τι. ἔτι τῶν ὄντων τὰ μέν ἐστι πρόδηλα, τὰ δὲ ἄδηλα, ὡς αὐτοί φασιν, καὶ σημαίνοντα μὲν τὰ φαινόμενα, σημαινόμενα δὲ ὑπὸ τῶν φαινομένων τὰ   2 0
ἄδηλα· ὄψις γὰρ κατ᾽ αὐτοὺς τῶν ἀδήλων τὰ φαινόμενα. τὸ δὲ σημαῖνον καὶ τὸ σημαινόμενόν ἐστι πρός τι· πρός τι ἄρα ἐστὶ πάντα. πρὸς τούτοις τῶν ὄντων τὰ μέν ἐστι

ὅμοια τὰ δὲ ἀνόμοια καὶ τὰ μὲν ἴσα τὰ δὲ ἄνισα· ταῦτα δέ ἐστι πρός τι· πάντα ἄρα ἐστὶ πρός τι. (7) καὶ ὁ λέγων δὲ μὴ πάντα εἶναι πρός τι βεβαιοῖ τὸ πάντα εἶναι πρός τι· καὶ αὐτὸ γὰρ τὸ πάντα εἶναι πρός τι πρὸς ἡμᾶς εἶναι δείκνυσι, καὶ οὐ 25 καθόλου, δι᾽ ὧν ἡμῖν ἐναντιοῦται. (8) πλὴν ἀλλ᾽ οὕτω παριστάντων ἡμῶν ὅτι πάντα ἐστὶ πρός τι, δῆλόν ἐστι λοιπόν ὅτι ὁποῖον ἔστιν ἕκαστον τῶν ὑποκειμένων κατὰ τὴν ἑαυτοῦ φύσιν καὶ εἰλικρινῶς λέγειν οὐ δυνησόμεθα, ἀλλ᾽ ὁποῖον φαίνεται ἐν τῷ πρός τι. ἀκολουθεῖ τὸ περὶ τῆς φύσεως τῶν πραγμάτων δεῖν ἡμᾶς ἐπέχειν. 30

12 τόπον Pappenheim: τρόπον codd.

This mode is usefully discussed by Striker [640], and Annas/Barnes [641], 128–45 (cf. their important remarks on the difference between relativism and scepticism at 96–8). We ourselves, however, disagree with Striker's interpretation (alluded to in vol. 1, 485–6), and our analysis in vol. 1 tries to represent the arguments as less sophistical than Annas/Barnes take them to be. Annas/Barnes argue that this version of the mode derives from the later five modes of Agrippa (*PH* 1.164–9), and was grafted into its present place by Sextus. But we think it at least as likely that Agrippa himself borrowed from the Aenesidemean modes.

J Sextus Empiricus, *PH* 1.141–4

(1) περὶ δὲ τοῦ κατὰ τὰς συνεχεῖς ἢ σπανίους συγκυρήσεις τρόπου, ὃν ἔννατον ἐλέγομεν εἶναι τῇ τάξει, τοιαῦτά τινα διέξιμεν. (2) ὁ ἥλιος πολλῷ δήπου ἐκπληκτικώτερός ἐστιν ἀστέρος κομήτου· ἀλλ᾽ ἐπεὶ τὸν μὲν ἥλιον συνεχῶς ὁρῶμεν, τὸν δὲ κομήτην ἀστέρα σπανίως, ἐπὶ μὲν τῷ ἀστέρι ἐκπλησσόμεθα ὥστε καὶ διοσημείαν αὐτὸν εἶναι δοκεῖν, ἐπὶ δὲ τῷ ἡλίῳ 5 οὐδαμῶς. ἐὰν μέντοι γε ἐννοήσωμεν τὸν ἥλιον σπανίως μὲν φαινόμενον, σπανίως δὲ δυόμενον, καὶ πάντα μὲν ἀθρόως φωτίζοντα, πάντα δὲ ἐξαίφνης ἐπισκιάζεσθαι ποιοῦντα, πολλὴν ἔκπληξιν ἐν τῷ πράγματι θεωρήσομεν. καὶ ὁ σεισμὸς δὲ οὐχ ὁμοίως θορυβεῖ τούς τε πρῶτον αὐτοῦ πειρωμένους καὶ τοὺς ἐν ἔθει τούτου γεγενημένους. πόσην δὲ ἔκπληξιν ἀνθρώπῳ φέρει θάλασσα πρῶτον 10 ὀφθεῖσα. ἀλλὰ καὶ κάλλος σώματος ἀνθρωπίνου πρῶτον καὶ ἐξαίφνης θεωρούμενον συγκινεῖ μᾶλλον ἡμᾶς ἢ εἰ ἐν ἔθει τοῦ ὁρᾶσθαι γένοιτο. (3) καὶ τὰ μὲν σπάνια τίμια εἶναι δοκεῖ, τὰ δὲ σύντροφα ἡμῖν καὶ εὔπορα οὐδαμῶς. ἐὰν γοῦν ἐννοήσωμεν τὸ ὕδωρ σπανίζον, πόσῳ ἂν τῶν τιμίων εἶναι δοκούντων ἁπάντων τιμιώτερον ἡμῖν φανείη. ἢ ἐὰν ἐνθυμηθῶμεν τὸν χρυσὸν ἁπλῶς 15 ἐπὶ τῆς γῆς ἐρριμμένον πολὺν παραπλησίως τοῖς λίθοις, τίνι δόξομεν ἔσεσθαι τοῦτον τίμιον ἢ κατάκλειστον οὕτως; (4) ἐπεὶ οὖν τὰ αὐτὰ πράγματα παρὰ τὰς συνεχεῖς ἢ σπανίους περιπτώσεις ὁτὲ μὲν ἐκπληκτικὰ ἢ τίμια, ὁτὲ δὲ οὐ τοιαῦτα εἶναι δοκεῖ, ἐπιλογιζόμεθα ὅτι ὁποῖον μὲν φαίνεται τούτων ἕκαστον μετὰ συνεχοῦς περιπτώσεως ἢ σπανίας ἴσως 20 δυνησόμεθα λέγειν, ψιλῶς δὲ ὁποῖον ἔστιν ἕκαστον τῶν ἐκτὸς ὑποκειμένων οὐκ ἐσμὲν δυνατοὶ φάσκειν. καὶ διὰ τοῦτον οὖν τὸν τρόπον περὶ αὐτῶν ἐπέχομεν.

The Pyrrhonist revival

K Sextus Empiricus, *PH* 1.145–63

(1) δέκατός ἐστι τρόπος, ὃς καὶ μάλιστα συνέχει πρὸς τὰ ἠθικά, ὁ παρὰ τὰς ἀγωγὰς καὶ τὰ ἔθη καὶ τοὺς νόμους καὶ τὰς μυθικὰς πίστεις καὶ τὰς δογματικὰς ὑπολήψεις. (2) ἀγωγὴ μὲν οὖν ἐστιν αἵρεσις βίου ἤ τινος πράγματος περὶ ἕνα ἢ πολλοὺς γινομένη, οἷον περὶ Διογένην ἢ τοὺς Λάκωνας· (3) νόμος δέ ἐστιν ἔγγραφος συνθήκη παρὰ τοῖς πολιτευομένοις, 5 ἣν ὁ παραβαίνων κολάζεται, ἔθος δὲ ἢ συνήθεια (οὐ διαφέρει γάρ) πολλῶν ἀνθρώπων κοινὴ πράγματός τινος παραδοχή, ἣν ὁ παραβὰς οὐ πάντως κολάζεται, οἷον νόμος ἐστὶ τὸ μὴ μοιχεύειν, ἔθος δὲ ἡμῖν τὸ μὴ δημοσίᾳ γυναικὶ μίγνυσθαι. (4) μυθικὴ δὲ πίστις ἐστὶ πραγμάτων ἀγενήτων τε καὶ πεπλασμένων παραδοχή, οἷά ἐστιν ἄλλα τε καὶ τὰ περὶ τοῦ Κρόνου 10 μυθευόμενα· ταῦτα γὰρ πολλοὺς εἰς πίστιν ἄγει. (5) δογματικὴ δέ ἐστιν ὑπόληψις παραδοχὴ πράγματος δι' ἀναλογισμοῦ ἤ τινος ἀποδείξεως κρατύνεσθαι δοκοῦσα, οἷον ὅτι ἄτομα ἔστι τῶν ὄντων στοιχεῖα ἢ ὁμοιομερῆ ⟨ἢ⟩ ἐλάχιστα ἤ τινα ἄλλα. (6) ἀντιτίθεμεν δὲ τούτων ἕκαστον ὁτὲ μὲν ἑαυτῷ, ὁτὲ δὲ τῶν ἄλλων ἑκάστῳ. (7) οἷον ἔθος μὲν ἔθει οὕτως· 15 τινὲς τῶν Αἰθιόπων στίζουσι τὰ βρέφη, ἡμεῖς δ' οὔ· καὶ Πέρσαι μὲν ἀνθοβαφεῖ ἐσθῆτι καὶ ποδήρει χρῆσθαι νομίζουσιν εὐπρεπὲς εἶναι, ἡμεῖς δὲ ἀπρεπές· καὶ οἱ μὲν Ἰνδοὶ ταῖς γυναιξὶ δημοσίᾳ μίγνυνται, οἱ δὲ πλεῖστοι τῶν ἄλλων αἰσχρὸν τοῦτο εἶναι ἡγοῦνται. (8) νόμον δὲ νόμῳ οὕτως· παρὰ μὲν τοῖς Ῥωμαίοις ὁ τῆς πατρῴας ἀποστὰς οὐσίας οὐκ ἀποδίδωσι τὰ 20 τοῦ πατρὸς χρέα, παρὰ δὲ τοῖς Ῥοδίοις πάντως ἀποδίδωσιν· καὶ ἐν μὲν Ταύροις τῆς Σκυθίας νόμος ἦν τοὺς ξένους τῇ Ἀρτέμιδι καλλιερεῖσθαι, παρὰ δὲ ἡμῖν ἄνθρωπον ἀπείρηται πρὸς ἱερῷ φονεύεσθαι. (9) ἀγωγὴν δὲ ἀγωγῇ, ὅταν τὴν Διογένους ἀγωγὴν ἀντιτιθῶμεν τῇ τοῦ Ἀριστίππου ἢ τὴν τῶν Λακώνων τῇ τῶν Ἰταλῶν. (10) μυθικὴν δὲ πίστιν πίστει μυθικῇ, ὅταν 25 ὅπου μὲν ⟨λέγωμεν⟩ τὸν Δία μυθεύεσθαι πατέρα ἀνδρῶν τε θεῶν τε, ὅπου δὲ τὸν Ὠκεανόν, λέγοντες "'Ὠκεανόν τε θεῶν γένεσιν καὶ μητέρα Τηθύν". (11) δογματικὰς δὲ ὑπολήψεις ἀλλήλαις ἀντιτίθεμεν, ὅταν λέγωμεν τοὺς μὲν ἓν εἶναι στοιχεῖον ἀποφαίνεσθαι, τοὺς δὲ ἄπειρα, καὶ τοὺς μὲν θνητὴν τὴν ψυχήν, τοὺς δὲ ἀθάνατον, καὶ τοὺς μὲν προνοίᾳ θεῶν διοικεῖσθαι τὰ 30 καθ' ἡμᾶς, τοὺς δὲ ἀπρονοήτως. (12) τὸ ἔθος δὲ τοῖς ἄλλοις ἀντιτίθεμεν, οἷον νόμῳ μέν, ὅταν λέγωμεν παρὰ μὲν Πέρσαις ἔθος εἶναι ἀρρενομιξίαις χρῆσθαι, παρὰ δὲ Ῥωμαίοις ἀπαγορεύεσθαι νόμῳ τοῦτο πράτ-τειν ... (13) ἀγωγῇ δὲ ἔθος ἀντιτίθεται, ὅταν οἱ μὲν πολλοὶ ἄνθρωποι ἀναχωροῦντες μιγνύωνται ταῖς ἑαυτῶν γυναιξίν, ὁ δὲ Κράτης τῇ 35 Ἱππαρχίᾳ δημοσίᾳ· καὶ ὁ μὲν Διογένης ἀπὸ ἐξωμίδος περιῄει, ἡμεῖς δὲ ὡς εἰώθαμεν. (14) μυθικῇ δὲ πίστει, [ὡς] ὅταν λέγωσιν οἱ μῦθοι ὅτι ὁ Κρόνος κατῆσθιεν αὐτοῦ τὰ τέκνα, ἔθους ὄντος ἡμῖν προνοεῖσθαι παίδων· καὶ παρ' ἡμῖν μὲν συνήθεια ὡς ἀγαθοὺς καὶ ἀπαθεῖς κακῶν σέβειν τοὺς θεούς, τιτρωσκόμε-νοι δὲ καὶ φθονοῦντες ἀλλήλοις ὑπὸ τῶν ποιητῶν εἰσάγονται. (15) 40 δογματικῇ δὲ ὑπολήψει, ὅταν ἡμῖν μὲν ἔθος ᾖ παρὰ θεῶν αἰτεῖν τὰ ἀγαθά, ὁ

472

δὲ Ἐπίκουρος λέγῃ μὴ ἐπιστρέφεσθαι ἡμῶν τὸ θεῖον ... (16) πολλὰ μὲν
οὖν καὶ ἄλλα ἐνῆν καθ᾽ ἑκάστην τῶν προειρημένων ἀντιθέσεων λαμβάνειν
παραδείγματα· ὡς ἐν συντόμῳ δὲ λόγῳ ταῦτα ἀρκέσει. πλὴν τοσαύτης
ἀνωμαλίας πραγμάτων καὶ διὰ τούτου τοῦ τρόπου δεικνυμένης, ὁποῖον   45
μὲν ἔστι τὸ ὑποκείμενον κατὰ τὴν φύσιν οὐχ ἕξομεν λέγειν, ὁποῖον δὲ
φαίνεται πρὸς τήνδε τὴν ἀγωγὴν ἢ πρὸς τόνδε τὸν νόμον ἢ πρὸς τόδε τὸ
ἔθος καὶ τῶν ἄλλων ἕκαστον. καὶ διὰ τοῦτον οὖν περὶ τῆς φύσεως τῶν
ἐκτὸς ὑποκειμένων πραγμάτων ἐπέχειν ἡμᾶς ἀνάγκη. (17) οὕτω μὲν οὖν
διὰ τῶν δέκα τρόπων καταλήγομεν εἰς τὴν ἐποχήν.   50

14 ⟨ἢ⟩: aut T   26 ⟨λέγωμεν⟩: dicimus T   37 ὡς om. T

13–14   The doctrines are respectively those of Epicurus (and Democritus), of
Anaxagoras, and of Diodorus (11i 3).

L Photius, *Bibl.* 170b3–35

(1) ἓν δὲ τῷ β΄ κατὰ μέρος ἤδη ἀρχόμενος ἐπεξιέναι τὰ ἐν κεφαλαίῳ
εἰρημένα, περί τε ἀληθῶν καὶ αἰτίων διαλαμβάνει καὶ παθῶν καὶ
κινήσεως, γενέσεώς τε καὶ φθορᾶς καὶ τῶν τούτοις ἐναντίων, κατὰ πάντων
αὐτῶν τὸ ἄπορόν τε καὶ ἀκατάληπτον πυκνοῖς, ὡς οἴεται, ἐπιλογισμοῖς
ὑποδεικνύς. (2) καὶ ὁ γ΄ δὲ αὐτῷ λόγος περὶ κινήσεως καὶ αἰσθήσεως καὶ   5
τῶν κατ᾽ αὐτὰς ἰδιωμάτων, τὰς ὁμοίας περιεργαζόμενος ἐναντιολογίας,
εἰς τὸ ἀνέφικτον καὶ ἀκατάληπτον ὑποφέρει καὶ αὐτά. (3) ἐν δὲ τῷ δ΄
σημεῖα μὲν ὥσπερ τὰ φανερὰ φαμὲν τῶν ἀφανῶν, οὐδ᾽ ὅλως εἶναί φησιν,
ἠπατῆσθαι δὲ κενῇ προσπαθείᾳ τοὺς οἰομένους· ἐγείρει δὲ τὰς ἐξ ἔθους
ἐφεξῆς ἀπορίας περί τε ὅλης τῆς φύσεως καὶ κόσμου καὶ θεῶν, οὐδὲν   10
⟨τού⟩των εἰς κατάληψιν πεσεῖν ἐντεινόμενος. (4) προβάλλεται αὐτῷ καὶ ὁ
ε΄ λόγος τὰς κατὰ τῶν αἰτίων ἀπορητικὰς λαβάς, μηδὲν μὲν μηδενὸς αἴτιον
ἐνδιδοὺς εἶναι, ἠπατῆσθαι δὲ τοὺς αἰτιολογοῦντας φάσκων, καὶ τρόπους
ἀριθμῶν καθ᾽ οὓς οἴεται αὐτοὺς αἰτιολογεῖν ὑπαχθέντας εἰς τὴν τοιαύτην
περιενεχθῆναι πλάνην. (5) καὶ ὁ ς΄ δὲ τὰ ἀγαθὰ καὶ κακά, καὶ μὴν καὶ τὰ   15
αἱρετὰ καὶ φευκτά, ἔτι δὲ προηγούμενά τε καὶ ἀποπροηγούμενα, εἰς τὰς
αὐτὰς ἐρεσχελίας ἄγει τό γε ἐπ᾽ αὐτῷ καὶ ταῦτα τῆς καταλήψεως ἡμῶν
καὶ γνώσεως ἀποκλείων. (6) τὸν μέντοι ζ΄ κατὰ τῶν ἀρετῶν ὁπλίζει, διὰ
κενῆς λέγων τοὺς φιλοσοφοῦντας περὶ αὐτῶν ἀναπλάσαι δόξας, καὶ
ἑαυτοὺς ἀποβουκολεῖν ὡς εἰς τὴν τούτων εἴησαν πρᾶξίν τε καὶ θεωρίαν   20
ἀφιγμένοι. (7) ὁ δ᾽ ἐπὶ πᾶσι καὶ η΄ κατὰ τοῦ τέλους ἐνίσταται, μήτε τὴν
εὐδαιμονίαν μήτε τὴν ἡδονὴν μήτε τὴν φρόνησιν μήτ᾽ ἄλλο τι τέλος
ἐπιχωρῶν εἶναι, ὅπερ ἄν τις τῶν κατὰ φιλοσοφίαν αἱρέσεων δοξάσειεν,
ἀλλ᾽ ἁπλῶς οὐκ εἶναι τέλος τὸ πᾶσιν ὑμνούμενον.

11 suppl. Sedley

Context: see on **71C**.

473

The Pyrrhonist revival

M Sextus Empiricus, *PH* 1.180–5

ὥσπερ δὲ τοὺς τρόπους ⟨τῆς⟩ ἐποχῆς παραδίδομεν, οὕτω καὶ τρόπους ἐκτίθενταί τινες, καθ' οὓς ἐν ταῖς κατὰ μέρος αἰτιολογίαις διαποροῦντες ἐφιστῶμεν τοὺς δογματικοὺς διὰ τὸ μάλιστα ἐπὶ ταύταις αὐτοὺς μέγα φρονεῖν. (1) καὶ δὴ Αἰνησίδημος ὀκτὼ τρόπους παραδίδωσι καθ' οὓς οἴεται πᾶσαν δογματικὴν αἰτιολογίαν ὡς μοχθηρὰν ἐλέγχων ἀποφήνασθαι, (2) ὧν πρῶτον μὲν εἶναί φησι καθ' ὃν [τρόπον] τὸ   5
τῆς αἰτιολογίας γένος ἐν ἀφανέσιν ἀναστρεφόμενον οὐχ ὁμολογουμένην ἔχει τὴν ἐκ τῶν φαινομένων ἐπιμαρτύρησιν· (3) δεύτερον δὲ καθ' ὃν πολλάκις εὐεπιφορίας οὔσης δαψιλοῦς ὥστε πολυτρόπως αἰτιολογῆσαι τὸ ζητούμενον, καθ' ἕνα μόνον τρόπον τοῦτό τινες αἰτιολογοῦσιν· (4) τρίτον καθ' ὃν τῶν τεταγμένως γινομένων αἰτίας ἀποδιδόασιν οὐδεμίαν τάξιν   10
ἐπιφαινούσας· (5) τέταρτον καθ' ὃν τὰ φαινόμενα λαβόντες ὡς γίνεται, καὶ τὰ μὴ φαινόμενα νομίζουσιν ὡς γίνεται κατειληφέναι, τάχα μὲν ὁμοίως τοῖς φαινομένοις τῶν ἀφανῶν ἐπιτελουμένων, τάχα δ' οὐχ ὁμοίως ἀλλ' ἰδιαζόντως· (6) πέμπτον καθ' ὃν πάντες ὡς ἔπος εἰπεῖν κατὰ τὰς ἰδίας τῶν στοιχείων ὑποθέσεις ἀλλ' οὐ κατά τινας κοινὰς καὶ ὁμολογουμένας   1
ἐφόδους αἰτιολογοῦσιν· (7) ἕκτον καθ' ὃν πολλάκις τὰ μὲν φωρατὰ ταῖς ἰδίαις ὑποθέσεσι παραλαμβάνουσιν, τὰ δὲ ἀντιπίπτοντα καὶ τὴν ἴσην ἔχοντα πιθανότητα παραπέμπουσιν· (8) ἕβδομον καθ' ὃν πολλάκις ἀποδιδόασιν αἰτίας οὐ μόνον τοῖς φαινομένοις ἀλλὰ καὶ ταῖς ἰδίαις ὑποθέσεσι μαχομένας· (9) ὄγδοον καθ' ὃν πολλάκις ὄντων ἀπόρων ὁμοίως   2
τῶν τε φαίνεσθαι δοκούντων καὶ τῶν ἐπιζητουμένων, ἐκ τῶν ὁμοίως ἀπόρων περὶ τῶν ὁμοίως ἀπόρων ποιοῦνται τὰς διδασκαλίας. (10) οὐκ ἀδύνατον δέ φησι καὶ κατά τινας ἐπιμίκτους τρόπους, ἠρτημένους ἐκ τῶν προειρημένων, διαπίπτειν ἐνίους ἐν ταῖς αἰτιολογίαις.

Context: following discussion of the modes of ἐποχή (including **A–K**). For comment, see especially Barnes [637].
    7–9   Probably Epicurean-inspired criticism (cf. **18C 4**), especially in view of the Epicurean term ἐπιμαρτύρησιν at 7. See also note on **71A** 7–8.

N Sextus Empiricus, *M.* 9.237–40

(1) καὶ μὴν εἰ ἔστι τι αἴτιον, ἤτοι αὐτοτελῶς καὶ ἰδίᾳ μόνον προσχρώμενον δυνάμει τινός ἐστιν αἴτιον, ἢ συνεργοῦ πρὸς τοῦτο δεῖται τῆς πασχούσης ὕλης, ὥστε τὸ ἀποτέλεσμα κατὰ κοινὴν ἀμφοτέρων νοεῖσθαι σύνοδον. (2) καὶ εἰ μὲν αὐτοτελῶς καὶ ἰδίᾳ προσχρώμενον δυνάμει ποιεῖν τι πέφυκεν, ὤφειλε διὰ παντός ἑαυτὸ ἔχον καὶ τὴν ἰδίαν δύναμιν πάντοτε ποιεῖν τὸ   5
ἀποτέλεσμα καὶ μὴ ἐφ' ὧν μὲν ποιεῖν ἐφ' ὧν δὲ ἀπρακτεῖν. (3) εἰ δέ, ὡς φασί τινες τῶν δογματικῶν, οὐ τῶν ἀπολελυμένων καὶ ἀφεστηκότων ἐστίν, ἀλλὰ τῶν πρός τι διὰ τὸ καὶ αὐτὸ πρὸς τῷ πάσχοντι θεωρεῖσθαι καὶ τὸ πάσχον πρὸς αὐτῷ, χεῖρόν τι ἀνακύψει. (4) εἰ γὰρ τὸ ἕτερον πρὸς τῷ ἑτέρῳ νοεῖται, ὧν τὸ μὲν ποιοῦν τὸ δὲ πάσχον, ἔσται μία μὲν ἔννοια, δυεῖν   1
δ' ὀνομάτων τεύξεται, τοῦ τε ποιοῦντος καὶ πάσχοντος· καὶ διὰ τοῦτο οὐ

474

μᾶλλον ἐν αὐτῷ ἢ ἐν τῷ λεγομένῳ πάσχειν ἐγκείσεται ἡ δραστήριος δύναμις. ὡς γὰρ αὐτὸ οὐδὲν δύναται ποιεῖν χωρὶς τοῦ λεγομένου πάσχειν, οὕτως οὐδὲ τὸ λεγόμενον πάσχειν δύναται χωρὶς τῆς ἐκείνου παρουσίας πάσχειν. (5) ὥσθ' ἕπεται τὸ μὴ μᾶλλον ἐν αὐτῷ ἢ ἐν τῷ πάσχοντι 15 ὑποκεῖσθαι τὴν δραστήριον τοῦ ἀποτελέσματος δύναμιν.

10 ὧν Hervetus: οὗ codd.

Context: critique of the notion of cause. Sextus indicates a borrowing from Aenesidemus, starting at M. 9.218, and probably, though not demonstrably, continuing to and beyond the excerpted passage.

4–6 This equation of true causes with sufficient conditions is Stoic in origin (55A 2–3), relying on the Stoic notion of αἴτιον αὐτοτελές (55I 2). It quickly came to serve non-Stoics as a weapon against other kinds of cause, especially προκαταρκτικά. That is how it was already being used in the middle of the third century B.C. by the doctor Erasistratus (Celsus, Med. pr. 54; Galen, De causis procatarcticis, passim), as well as by later Pyrrhonists.

Bibliography

GENERAL

The following are comprehensive studies of two or more of the Hellenistic schools:

[1] E. Zeller, *Die Philosophie der Griechen in ihrer geschichtlichen Entwicklung*, vol. III.1 (first publ. 1852; ed. 5, rev. E. Wellmann, Leipzig, 1923). English translation, with some abridgement, by O. Reichel, under the title, *Stoics, Epicureans and Sceptics* (London, 1880)
[2] R.D. Hicks, *Stoic and Epicurean* (London, 1910)
[3] A.A. Long, *Hellenistic philosophy* (London/New York, 1974; ed. 2, London/Berkeley/ Los Angeles, 1986)
[4] G. Reale, *Storia della filosofia antica* III–V (Milan, 1976–80)

Specific aspects of Hellenistic philosophy are studied in four important anthologies:

[5] M. Schofield, M. Burnyeat, J. Barnes (edd.), *Doubt and dogmatism: studies in Hellenistic epistemology* (Oxford, 1980)
[6] J. Barnes, J. Brunschwig, M. Burnyeat, M. Schofield (edd.), *Science and speculation: studies in Hellenistic theory and practice* (Cambridge/Paris, 1982)
[7] M. Schofield and G. Striker (edd.), *The norms of nature: studies in Hellenistic ethics* (Cambridge/Paris, 1986)
[8] H. Flashar and O. Gigon (edd.), *Aspects de la philosophie hellénistique*. Fondation Hardt, *Entretiens sur l'antiquité classique* XXXII (Vandoeuvres–Geneva, 1986)

The criterion of truth is the subject of a valuable monograph by

[9] G. Striker, "Κριτήριον τῆς ἀληθείας", *Nachrichten der Akademie der Wissenschaften in Göttingen*, Phil.-hist. Kl., 1974, 2, 47–110

For studies of dialectical strategies and their background, see

[10] M.F. Burnyeat, 'Protagoras and self-refutation in later Greek philosophy', *Philosophical Review* 85 (1976), 44–69
[11] D. Sedley, 'Diodorus Cronus and Hellenistic philosophy', *Proceedings of the Cambridge Philological Society* N.S. 23 (1977), 74–120

The influence of Plato and his immediate successors on some central concepts of the Hellenistic schools is studied by

[12] H.-J. Krämer, *Platonismus und hellenistische Philosophie* (Berlin, 1971)

The history of Aristotelianism from the first century B.C. to the second century A.D. is the subject of an enormous but uncompleted work by P. Moraux, *Der Aristotelismus bei den Griechen von Andronikos bis Alexander von Aphrodisias*

[13] vol. I *Die Renaissance des Aristotelismus im I. Jh. v. Chr.* (Berlin, 1973)

476

[14] vol. 2 *Der Aristotelismus im I. und II. Jh. N. Chr.* (Berlin, 1984)

There has been no sourcebook comparable in scope to the present work; cf. however

[15] J. Adam, *Texts to illustrate a course of elementary lectures on Greek philosophy after Aristotle* (London, 1902)
[16] C.J. De Vogel, *Greek philosophy III. The Hellenistic–Roman period* (Leiden, 1959)

The following studies include detailed treatments of many aspects of Hellenistic philosophy:

[17] H.C. Baldry, *The unity of mankind in Greek thought* (Cambridge, 1965)
[18] J.C. Fraisse, *Philia. La notion d'amitié dans la philosophie antique* (Paris, 1974)
[19] J.C.B. Gosling, C.C.W. Taylor, *The Greeks on pleasure* (Oxford, 1982)
[20] A. Dihle, *The theory of will in classical antiquity* (Berkeley/Los Angeles, 1982)
[21] R.R.K. Sorabji, *Necessity, cause and blame: perspectives on Aristotle's theory* (London, 1980)
[22] R.R.K. Sorabji, *Time, creation and the continuum* (London, 1983)
[23] J. Moreau, *L'Ame du monde de Platon aux stoïciens* (Paris, 1939)
[24] S. Sambursky, *The physical world of the Greeks* (London, 1956)
[25] G.E.R. Lloyd, *Greek science after Aristotle* (London, 1973)
[26] P. Natorp, *Forschungen zur Geschichte des Erkenntnisproblems im Alterthum* (Stuttgart, 1884; repr. Hildesheim, 1965)
[27] M.F. Burnyeat, 'Idealism and Greek philosophy: what Descartes saw and Berkeley missed', *Philosophical Review* 91 (1982), 3–40
[28] P.M. Huby and G.C. Neale (edd.), *The criterion of truth. Studies in honour of George Kerferd on his seventieth birthday* (Liverpool, 1987)
[29] F. Solmsen, *Kleine Schriften*, 3 vols. (Hildesheim, 1968–82)

The historiography of Hellenistic philosophy is discussed in a monumental, if somewhat dated, work:

[30] R. Hirzel, *Untersuchungen zu Ciceros philosophischen Schriften*, 3 vols. (Leipzig, 1877–83)

and in

[31] U. von Wilamowitz-Moellendorff, *Antigonus von Karystos* (Berlin, 1881)
[32] J. Mejer, *Diogenes Laertius and his Hellenistic background* (Wiesbaden, 1978)

On Cicero, see also

[33] K. Bringmann, *Untersuchungen zum späten Cicero* (Göttingen, 1971)
[34] O. Gigon, 'Cicero und die griechische Philosophie', in *Aufstieg und Niedergang der römischen Welt* I.4 (Berlin, 1972), 226–61
[35] W. Görler, *Untersuchungen zu Ciceros Philosophie* (Heidelberg, 1974)

The work of the important 'Socratic' forerunners of the Hellenistic philosophers is most conveniently available in

[36] G. Giannantoni, *Socraticorum reliquiae*, 4 vols. (Naples, 1983–5)

See also, for individual Socratic schools,

[37] K. Döring, *Die Megariker. Kommentierte Sammlung der Testimonien* (Amsterdam, 1972)
[38] D.R. Dudley, *A history of Cynicism* (London, 1937)
[39] J.F. Kindstrand, *Bion of Borysthenes. A collection of the fragments with introduction and commentary* (Uppsala, 1976)

and for their influence on Hellenistic philosophy, Sedley [11] and

[40] G. Giannantoni (ed.), *Scuole socratiche minori e filosofia ellenistica* (Bologna, 1977)

477

Bibliography

On the organization and fortunes, in the Hellenistic period, of the Platonic and Aristotelian schools, see the outstanding studies

[41] J.P. Lynch, *Aristotle's school* (Berkeley/Los Angeles, 1972)
[42] J. Glucker, *Antiochus and the late Academy* (Göttingen, 1978)

Social, political and other aspects of Hellenistic civilization can be studied in Frischer [108], and in

[43] P.M. Frazer, *Ptolemaic Alexandria*, 3 vols. (Oxford, 1972)
[44] R. Pfeiffer, *A history of classical scholarship*, vol. 1 (Oxford, 1968)
[45] F.W. Walbank, *The Hellenistic world* (London, 1981)
[46] E.S. Gruen, *The Hellenistic world and the coming of Rome*, 2 vols. (Berkeley/Los Angeles, 1984)

On Hellenistic science, see especially Lloyd [25], and

[47] G.E.R. Lloyd, 'Observational error in later Greek science', in [6], 128–64
[48] G. Giannantoni, M. Vegetti (edd.), *La scienza ellenistica* (Naples, 1984)
[49] D.E. Hahm, 'Early Hellenistic theories of vision and the perception of colour', in P.K. Machamer, R.G. Turnbull (edd.), *Studies in perception: interrelations in the history of philosophy and science* (Columbus, 1978), 60–95
and, for a fascinating glimpse of the level of technological sophistication reached in the applied mechanics of the period,

[50] D. de Solla Price, *Gears from the Greeks* (New York, 1975)

General studies of ancient scepticism

The most detailed and reliable of the comprehensive studies is

[51] M. Dal Pra, *Lo scetticismo greco*, 2 vols. (first publ. 1950; ed. 2, Rome/Bari, 1975)

Still valuable is the classic work by

[52] V. Brochard, *Les Sceptiques grecs* (first publ. 1887; ed. 2, Paris, 1923)

Other useful surveys include

[53] C.L. Stough, *Greek skepticism* (Berkeley/Los Angeles, 1969)
[54] J.-P. Dumont, *Le Scepticisme et le phénomène* (Paris, 1972)

For more specialized aspects, see

[55] G. Striker, 'Über den Unterschied zwischen den Pyrrhoneern und den Akademikern', *Phronesis* 26 (1981), 153–71
[56] F. Decleva Caizzi, 'Pirroniani ed accademici nel III secolo a. C.', in [8], 147–83
[57] A.A. Long, 'Aristotle and the history of Greek scepticism', in D.J. O'Meara (ed.), *Studies in Aristotle* (Washington, D.C., 1981), 79–106
[58] M.F. Burnyeat (ed.), *The skeptical tradition* (Berkeley/Los Angeles, 1983)
[59] D. Sedley, 'The motivation of Greek skepticism' in [58], 9–30
[60] M.F. Burnyeat, 'The sceptic in his place and time', in R. Rorty, J.B. Schneewind, Q. Skinner (edd.), *Philosophy in history* (Cambridge, 1984), 225–54
[61] M. Frede, 'The sceptic's two kinds of assent and the question of the possibility of knowledge', in Rorty et al. (see previous entry), 255–78
[62] G. Giannantoni (ed.), *Lo scetticismo antico*, 2 vols. (Rome, 1981)
This last, which includes a comprehensive bibliography, is reviewed by

[63] M.R. Stopper, 'Schizzi pirroniani', *Phronesis* 28 (1983), 265–97

1–3 EARLY PYRRHONISM

Texts and commentaries

For Pyrrho the authoritative collection of testimonia, with Italian translation and extensive commentary, is

[64] F. Decleva Caizzi, *Pirrone testimonianze* (Naples, 1981)

She discusses the methodology of selecting this material in

[65] 'Prolegomeni ad una raccolta delle fonti relative a Pirrone di Elide' in [62], 95–128

For Timon of Phlius the best text, with brief annotation, is

[66] H. Lloyd-Jones and P. Parsons, *Supplementum Hellenisticum* (Berlin, 1981), 368–95

Useful material on Timon is also to be found in the older editions of

[67] C. Wachsmuth, *Corpusculum poesis epicae ludibundae*, vol. ii: *De Timone Phliasio ceterisque sillographis commentatio* (Leipzig, 1885)

[68] H. Diels, *Poetarum philosophorum fragmenta* (Berlin, 1901)

See also, for a general study of Timon's work,

[69] A.A. Long, 'Timon of Phlius: Pyrrhonist and satirist', *Proceedings of the Cambridge Philological Society* N.S. 24 (1978), 68–91

Detailed interpretations

Older studies of the historical Pyrrho tend to suffer from a failure to distinguish his position from that of later Pyrrhonism. Much of value may still be found in Brochard [52]. Later studies, all written prior to the recent Italian focus on Pyrrho, include Dal Pra [51], Stough [53], Dumont [54], and

[70] L. Robin, *Pyrrhon et le scepticisme grec* (Paris, 1944)

[71] K. von Fritz, 'Pyrrhon', in Pauly-Wissowa, *Real-Encyclopädie der klassischen Altertumswissenschaft* XXIV (1963), cols. 89–106

[72] M. Conche, *Pyrrhon ou l'apparence* (Villers-sur-Mer, 1973)

The differences between Pyrrho's scepticism and that of Arcesilaus were the subject of an important study by

[73] V. Couissin, 'L'origine et l'évolution de l'ἐποχή', *Revue des Etudes Grecques* 42 (1929), 373–97

Pyrrho's philosophy and its historical background occupy a large part of the proceedings of a Rome conference [62], which includes a major study by

[74] G. Reale, 'Ipotesi per una rilettura della filosofia di Pirrone di Elide', 245–336.

This, along with other articles in the collection, is reviewed by M.R. Stopper [63], who is critical of the attempt to find antecedents to Pyrrho's scepticism among the philosophers who reject the principle of non-contradiction, according to Aristotle in *Metaphysics* Γ, as proposed by

[75] E. Berti, 'La critica allo scetticismo nel iv libro della "*Metafisica*"' in [62], 63–79 and also considered by A.A. Long [57].

On Pyrrho's ethics, see

Bibliography

[76] M. Pohlenz, 'Das Lebensziel der Skeptiker', *Hermes* 39 (1904), 15–29

[77] M.F. Burnyeat, 'Tranquillity without a stop: Timon frag. 68', *Classical Quarterly* N.S. 30 (1980), 86–93

[78] G.A. Ferrari, 'L'immagine dell'equilibrio' in [62], 337–70

On Timon's contributions to philosophical debates, see

[79] F. Decleva Caizzi, 'Timone di Fliunte: i frammenti 74, 75, 76 Diels', in F. Angeli (ed.), *La storia della filosofia come sapere critico: studi offerti a Mario Dal Pra* (Milan, 1984), 92–105

Background studies

On the origins of the 'no more' formula, see

[80] P. De Lacy, 'οὐ μᾶλλον and the antecedents of ancient scepticism', *Phronesis* 3 (1958), 59–71

[81] A. Graeser, 'Demokrit und die skeptische Formel', *Hermes* 96 (1970), 300–17

On Pyrrho and Democritus more specifically, see

[82] F. Decleva Caizzi, 'Pirrone e Democrito – gli atomi: un "mito"?', *Elenchos* 5 (1984), 3–21

On the Cynic background, see Long [69], 71–7, Kindstrand [39], and

[83] A. Brancacci, 'La filosofia di Pirrone e le sue relazioni con il cinismo', in [62], 213–42

[84] F. Decleva Caizzi, 'Τῦφος: contributo alla storia di un concetto', *Sandalion* 3 (1980), 53–66

On Pyrrho's possible indebtedness to Indian thought, see

[85] A.M. Frenkian, 'Der griechische Skeptizismus und die indische Philosophie', *Biblioteca Classica Orientalis* 4 (1958), 211–50

[86] E. Flintoff, 'Pyrrho and India', *Phronesis* 25 (1980), 88–108

For Pyrrho's and Timon's background, see also Hirzel [30] and

[87] H. Krüger, 'Der Ausgang der antiken Skepsis', *Archiv für Geschichte der Philosophie* 36 (1925), 100–16

[88] G.A. Ferrari, 'Due fonti sullo scetticismo antico: Diog. La. IX 66–108; Eus. *Praep. ev.* XIV 18, 1–20', *Studi Italiani di Filologia Classica* 40 (1968), 200–24

On the relation of Pyrrho to philosophical successions, see Glucker [42], and Giannantoni's introductory paper in his [62], 13–34.

4–25 EPICUREANISM

General

[89] C. Bailey, *The Greek atomists and Epicurus* (Oxford, 1928)

[90] E. Bignone, *L'Aristotele perduto e la formazione filosofica di Epicuro*, 2 vols. (Florence, 1936). This massive work contains many valuable insights in spite of the author's excessive interest in establishing the influence of Aristotle's lost works.

[91] N.W. de Witt, *Epicurus and his philosophy* (Minneapolis, 1954); chiefly useful for its study of the organization of the Epicurean school

[92] W. Schmid, *Epikur*, in *Reallexikon für Antike und Christentum* v (1961), 681–819
[93] B. Farrington, *The faith of Epicurus* (London, 1967); a Marxist interpretation
[94] H. Steckel, 'Epikuros', in Pauly-Wissowa, *Real-Encyclopädie*, suppl. xi (Stuttgart, 1968), cols. 579–652
[95] J.M. Rist, *Epicurus: an introduction* (Cambridge, 1972)
[96] D. Pesce, *Saggio su Epicuro* (Rome/Bari, 1974)
[97] D. Pesce, *Introduzione a Epicuro* (Rome/Bari, 1980)

Three major anthologies of work on Epicurus are
[98] Association Guillaume Budé, *Actes du VIIIᵉ congrès* (Paris, 1969)
[99] J. Bollack, A. Laks (edd.), *Etudes sur l'épicurisme antique*, in *Cahiers de Philologie* 1 (1976)
[100] *ΣΥΖΗΤΗΣΙΣ. Studi sull'epicureismo greco e latino offerti a Marcello Gigante*, 2 vols. (Naples, 1983); vol. 2 contains an excellent bibliographical survey

For an earlier critical bibliography, see
[101] H. Mette, 'Epikuros 1963–1978', *Lustrum* 21 (1978), 45–116

The articles of two eminent scholars are collected in
[102] C. Diano, *Scritti epicurei* (Florence, 1974)
[103] R. Philippson, *Studien zu Epikur und den Epikureern*, ed. C.J. Classen (Hildesheim, 1983)

Various historical aspects of Epicureanism are dealt with in
[104] D. Sedley, 'Epicurus and his professional rivals', in [99], 119–59
[105] D. Sedley, 'Epicurus and the mathematicians of Cyzicus', *Cronache Ercolanesi* 6 (1976), 23–54
[106] M. Gigante, *Scetticismo e epicureismo* (Naples, 1981)
[107] D. Fowler, review of [106], in *Oxford Studies in Ancient Philosophy* 2 (1984), 237–67
[108] B. Frischer, *The sculpted word: Epicureanism and philosophical recruitment in ancient Greece* (Berkeley/Los Angeles, 1982)
[109] D. Clay, 'Epicurus in the archives of Athens', *Hesperia* suppl. 19 (1982), 17–26
[110] P.M. Huby, 'Epicurus' attitude to Democritus', *Phronesis* 23 (1978), 80–6
[111] G. Arrighetti, 'Un passo dell' opera "Sulla natura" di Epicuro, Democrito, e Colote', *Cronache Ercolanesi* 9 (1979), 5–10

For the location of the Epicurean Garden, as represented in vol. 1, 4, see
[112] G.W. Dontas, 'Εἰκονιστικὰ Β', *Archaiologikon Deltion* 26 (1971), 16–33

For prominent Epicureans at Rome, see
[113] A.D. Momigliano, review of *Science and politics in the ancient world* by B. Farrington, *Journal of Roman Studies* 31 (1941), 149–57, repr. in his *Secondo contributo alla storia degli studi classici* (Rome, 1960)
[114] P. Grimal, 'Les éléments philosophiques dans l'idée de monarchie à Rome à la fin de la République', in [8], 233–81

Texts, commentaries and translations

The fundamental collection of Epicurean material is still
[115] H. Usener, *Epicurea* (Leipzig, 1887)

Bibliography

Other valuable editions of the primary texts are

[116] P. von der Mühll, *Epicurus. Epistulae tres et ratae sententiae* (Leipzig, 1923)
[117] C. Bailey, *Epicurus. The extant remains* (Oxford, 1926)
[118] C. Diano, *Epicuri ethica et epistulae* (Florence, 1946, repr. 1974); also contains many fragments

The only comprehensive edition of Epicurus' own surviving work, including the papyrus fragments omitted by Usener [115], is

[119] G. Arrighetti, *Epicuro opere* (first publ. Turin, 1960; ed. 2, 1973)

There is also an Italian translation, with commentary, of all the surviving works and important testimonia,

[120] M. Isnardi Parente, *Opere di Epicuro* (Turin, 1974)
and another important annotated Italian translation is
[121] E. Bignone, *Epicuro, opere, frammenti, testimonianze* (Bari, 1920)

Four editions by the idiosyncratic Lille school are

[122] J. Bollack, M. Bollack, H. Wismann, *La Lettre d'Epicure* (Paris, 1971): the *Letter to Herodotus*
[123] J. Bollack, *La Pensée du plaisir. Epicure: textes moraux, commentaires* (Paris, 1975): the *Letter to Menoeceus*, and other ethical writings
[124] J. Bollack, A. Laks, *Epicure à Pythoclès* (*Cahiers de Philologie* 3, Lille, 1978)
[125] A. Laks, 'Edition critique et commentée de la "vie d'Epicure" dans Diogène Laerce (x, 1–34)', in [99], 1–118

Editions of papyrus fragments of Epicurus, *On nature*

[126] D. Sedley, 'Epicurus, *On nature* book XXVIII', *Cronache Ercolanesi* 3 (1973), 5–83
[127] C. Millot, 'Epicure de la nature livre XV', *Cronache Ercolanesi* 7 (1977), 9–39
[128] G. Leone, 'Epicuro, *Della natura*, libro XIV', *Cronache Ercolanesi* 14 (1984), 17–107

For differing views on the structure of Epicurus' major work, *On nature*, see

[129] G. Arrighetti, 'L'opera "Sulla natura" di Epicuro', *Cronache Ercolanesi* 1 (1971), 41–56
[130] G. Arrighetti, 'L'opera "Sulla natura" e le lettere di Epicuro a Erodoto e Pitocle', *Cronache Ercolanesi* 5 (1975), 39–51
[131] D. Sedley, 'The structure of Epicurus' *On nature*', *Cronache Ercolanesi* 4 (1974), 89–92
[132] D. Sedley, 'The character of Epicurus' *On nature*', *Atti del XVII congresso internazionale di papirologia* (Naples, 1984), 381–7

A magnificent tool of research, which indexes much of the papyrological material and the secondary sources, is

[133] H. Usener, *Glossarium Epicureum*, ed. by M. Gigante, W. Schmid (Rome, 1977)

Other early Epicureans

[134] F. Longo Auricchio, 'La scuola di Epicuro', *Cronache Ercolanesi* 8 (1978), 21–37
[135] A. Koerte, *Metrodori Epicurei fragmenta. Jahrbücher für Classische Philologie*, suppl. 17 (1980)
[136] A. Vogliano, 'Frammento di un nuovo "gnomologium epicureum"', *Studi Italiani di Filologia Classica* 13 (1936), 268–81

Epicureanism

[137] K. Krohn, *Der Epikureer Hermarchos* (Berlin, 1871)

[138] W. Crönert, *Kolotes und Menedemos* (Leipzig, 1906), a study which also includes valuable papyrological material on early Hellenistic philosophers in general

[139] R. Westman, *Plutarch gegen Kolotes*, in *Acta Philosophica Fennica* 7 (Helsinki, 1955)

[140] A. Angeli, 'I frammenti di Idomeneo di Lampsaco', *Cronache Ercolanesi* 11 (1981), 41–101

[141] G. Indelli, *Polistrato sul disprezzo irrazionale delle opinioni popolari* (Naples, 1978)
For our own view on Polystratus' target, see

[142] D. Sedley, review of [141] in *Classical Review* N.S. 33 (1983), 335–6

Epicureans of 2nd and 1st centuries B.C.

[143] V. de Falco, *L'Epicureo Demetrio Lacone* (Naples, 1923)

[144] C. Romeo, 'Demetrio Lacone sulla grandezza del sole (PHerc. 1013)', *Cronache Ercolanesi* 9 (1979), 11–35

[145] E. Puglia', 'Nuove letture nei PHerc. 1012 e 1786 (Demetrii Laconis opera incerta)', *Cronache Ercolanesi* 10 (1980), 25–53

[146] A. Angeli, M. Colaizzo, 'I frammenti di Zenone sidonio', *Cronache Ercolanesi* 11 (1981), 47–133

The recent spate of work on Philodemus has produced a range of editions and studies too extensive to cover fully here, but see especially the seminal contributions and bibliography in

[147] M. Gigante, *Ricerche filodemee* (ed. 2, Naples, 1983)

For works by Philodemus of primary relevance to this sourcebook, see Philippson [240], Henrichs [529], Sedley [243], and

[148] T. Gomperz, *Philodem, über Frömmigkeit* (Leipzig, 1866)

[149] W. Scott, *Fragmenta Herculanensia* (Oxford, 1885), in which several important papyrus texts are edited

[150] A. Olivieri, *Philodemi Περὶ παρρησίας libellus* (Leipzig, 1914)

[151] H. Diels, *Philodemos über die Götter (bks. 1,3)*, *Abh. Preuss. Akad. Wiss.* 1915–16 (Berlin, 1916–17)

[152] P. and E. De Lacy, *Philodemus, On methods of inference* (ed. 2, Naples, 1978)

For an accessible survey of Philodemus' work on literary themes, see

[153] A.A. Long, in *Cambridge history of classical literature*, vol. 1 *Greek literature* (Cambridge, 1985), 628–30, 842–3

Lucretius

The standard text and commentary on the whole of *De rerum natura* is still the monumental, if somewhat dated, work by

[154] C. Bailey, *Titi Lucreti Cari De rerum natura libri sex*, 3 vols. (Oxford, 1947)
Note that this supersedes Bailey's Oxford Classical Text (ed. 2, 1922). For a more recent text, with excellent translation and valuable annotation, see

[155] W.H.D. Rouse, *Lucretius De rerum natura*, revised with new text, introduction, notes, and index by M.F. Smith. Loeb Classical Library (Cambridge, Mass./London, 1975)

Bibliography

The following are also valuable

[156] H.A.J. Munro, commentary only (ed. 4, London, 1900)
[157] A. Ernout, L. Robin, commentary only, 3 vols. (Paris, 1925–8)
[158] J. Martin, critical text only (Leipzig, 1934)
[159] R. Heinze, text and commentary on book 3 (Leipzig, 1897)
[160] E.J. Kenney, text and commentary on book 3 (Cambridge, 1971)

For studies of Lucretius' treatment of Epicureanism, see Konstan [253], and
[161] P. Boyancé, *Lucrèce et l'épicurisme* (Paris, 1963)
[162] D. Clay, *Lucretius and Epicurus* (Ithaca/London, 1983)
and the anthology of articles
[163] O. Gigon (ed.), *Lucrèce*. Fondation Hardt, *Entretiens sur l'antiquité classique* XXIV (Vandoeuvres–Geneva, 1978)

Other valuable studies include
[164] G. Giussani, *Studi lucreziani* (Turin, 1896)
[165] G. Müller, *Die Darstellung der Kinetik bei Lukrez* (Berlin, 1959)
[166] K. Sallmann, 'Studien zum philosophischen Naturbegriff der Römer mit besonderer Berüchsichtigung des Lukrez', *Archiv für Begriffsgeschichte* 7 (1962), 140–284
[167] D. West, 'Lucretius' methods of argument', *Classical Quarterly* N.S. 25 (1975), 94–116
[168] D.J. Furley, 'Lucretius and the Stoics', *Bulletin of the Institute of Classical Studies* 13 (1966), 13–33
whose scepticism about Lucretius' interest in the Stoics is contested by
[169] J. Schmidt, *Lukrez und die Stoiker. Quellen und Untersuchungen zu De rerum natura* (Marburg, 1975)

Diogenes of Oenoanda

The standard text of fragments discovered prior to 1970 is
[170] C.W. Chilton, *Diogenes Oenoandensis* (Leipzig, 1967)
For commentary and translation of these, see
[171] C.W. Chilton, *Diogenes of Oenoanda. The fragments* (London/New York/Toronto, 1971)
For another edition of the same material, see
[172] A. Grilli, *Diogenis Oenoandensis fragmenta* (Milan, 1960)

The new fragments are published as follows:
[173] M.F. Smith, 'Fragments of Diogenes of Oenoanda discovered and rediscovered', *American Journal of Archaeology* 74 (1970), 51–62 (new frr. 1–4)
[174] M.F. Smith, 'New fragments of Diogenes of Oenoanda', *American Journal of Archaeology* 75 (1971), 357–89 (new frr. 5–16)
[175] M.F. Smith, 'Two new fragments of Diogenes of Oenoanda', *Journal of Hellenic Studies* 92 (1972), 147–55 (new frr. 17–18)
[176] M.F. Smith, 'New readings in the text of Diogenes of Oenoanda', *Classical Quarterly* N.S. 22 (1972), 159–62 (new frr. 1, 2, 7)
[177] D. Clay, 'Sailing to Lampsacus: Diogenes of Oenoanda, New Fragment 7', *Greek, Roman and Byzantine Studies* 14 (1973), 49–59
[178] M.F. Smith, *Thirteen new fragments of Diogenes of Oenoanda*, in *Denkschrift Akad. Wien* 117 (1974) (new frr. 19–31)

484

[179] M.F. Smith, 'Seven new fragments of Diogenes of Oenoanda', *Hermathena* 118 (1974), 110–29 (new frr. 32–8)

[180] M.F. Smith, 'More new fragments of Diogenes of Oenoanda', in [99], 279–318 (new frr. 39–51)

[181] A. Laks, C. Millot, 'Réexamen de quelques fragments de Diogène d'Oenoanda sur l'âme, la connaissance et la fortune', in [99], 321–57

[182] A. Barigazzi, 'Sui nuovi frammenti di Diogene d'Enoanda', *Prometheus* 3 (1977), 1–20, 97–111

[183] G. Arrighetti', 'Il nuovo Diogene di Enoanda', *Atene e Roma* N.S. 23 (1978), 161–72

[184] M.F. Smith, 'Diogenes of Oenoanda, New Fragment 24', *American Journal of Philology* 99 (1978) 329–31

[185] M.F. Smith, 'Fifty-five new fragments of Diogenes of Oenoanda', *Anatolian Studies* 28 (1978), 39–92 (new frr. 52–106)

[186] M.F. Smith, 'Eight new fragments of Diogenes of Oenoanda', *Anatolian Studies* 29 (1979), 69–89 (new frr. 107–14)

[187] M.F. Smith, 'Diogenes of Oenoanda, new fragments 115–121', *Prometheus* 8 (1982), 193–212

[188] R. Westman, 'Zu einigen new fragments des Diogenes von Oinoanda', in [100], 374–84

[189] M.F. Smith, 'Diogenes of Oenoanda, new fragments 122–124', *Anatolian Studies* 34 (1984), 43–57

For details of other work on Diogenes of Oenoanda, see

[190] M.F. Smith's bibliography in [100], 683–95

4–15 Epicurean physics

4–5 *First principles*

See Clay [162], Asmis [225], and

[191] D. Clay, 'Epicurus' last will and testament', *Archiv für Geschichte der Philosophie* 55 (1973), 252–80

[192] J. Brunschwig, 'L'argument d'Epicure sur l'immutabilité du tout', in *Permanence de la philosophie, mélanges offerts à Joseph Moreau* (Neuchâtel, 1977), 127–50

[193] F. Solmsen, 'Epicurus on void, matter and genesis', *Phronesis* 22 (1977), 263–81, repr. in [29] III, 333–51

5–6. 11 *Void and motion*

On the concept of void, see Solmsen [193], and

[194] F. Adorno, 'Epicuro: Epistola a Erodoto 39,7–40,3', *Elenchos* 1 (1980), 245–75

[195] B. Inwood, 'The origin of Epicurus' concept of void', *Classical Philology* 76 (1981), 273–85

[196] D. Sedley, 'Two conceptions of vacuum', *Phronesis* 27 (1982), 175–93

On the relationship of motion to void, see Müller [165], Inwood [195], and

[197] D.J. Furley, 'Aristotle and the atomists on motion in a void', in P.K. Machamer, R.G. Turnbull (edd.), *Motion and time, space and matter: interrelations in the history and philosophy of science* (Columbus, 1976), 83–100

[198] J. Mau, 'Raum und Bewegung: zu Epikurs Brief zu Herodot 60', *Hermes* 82 (1954), 13–24

Bibliography

7 *Secondary attributes, time, etc.*
The Lucretius text, **7A**, has been much discussed by editors, and in a helpful note by
[199] K. Wellesley, 'Lucretius 1.469–70', *Classical Review* N.S. 13 (1963), 16–17
On the Epicurean treatment of time, cf. Sorabji [22], and
[200] D. Puliga, 'χρόνος e θάνατος in Epicuro', *Elenchos* 4 (1983), 235–60
and the Epicurean papyrus text discussed in
[201] R. Cantarella, G. Arrighetti, 'Il libro "Sul tempo" (Pap. Herc. 1413) dell' opera di
Epicuro "Sulla natura" ', *Cronache Ercolanesi* 2 (1972), 5–46
[202] M. Isnardi Parente, 'χρόνος ἐπινοούμενος e χρόνος οὐ νοούμενος in Epicuro Pap. Herc.
1413', *Parola del Passato* 167 (1976), 168–75

8 *Atoms*
See Leone [128] for Epicurus' critique of Plato's theory of the elements; and for some
useful cautionary remarks about an Epicurean 'molecular' theory, see
[203] R.B. Todd, review of Long [3], *Phoenix* 29 (1975), 295–9

9 *Minimal parts*
Epicurus' theory has been most illuminatingly discussed by
[204] D.J. Furley, *Two studies in the Greek atomists* (Princeton, 1967)

Other contributions include Krämer [12], Sorabji [22], Sedley [105], Mueller [652], and
[205] J. Mau, *Zum Problem des Infinitesimalen bei den antiken Atomisten* (Berlin, 1954)
[206] D. Konstan, 'Problems in Epicurean physics', *Isis* 70 (1979), 394–418, repr. in J.P.
Anton, A. Preus (edd.), *Essays in ancient Greek philosophy* II (Albany, 1983), 431–64
[207] D. Konstan, 'Ancient atomism and its heritage: minimal parts', *Ancient Philosophy* 2
(1982), 60–75
and the unorthodox view of
[208] G. Vlastos, 'Minimal parts in Epicurean atomism', *Isis* 56 (1965), 121–47

For Diodorus Cronus' theory of minimal parts, cf. Sedley [11], Giannantoni [36], and
[209] N. Denyer, 'The atomism of Diodorus Cronus', *Prudentia* 13 (1981), 33–45

10 *Infinity*
[210] D.J. Furley, 'Aristotle and the atomists on infinity', in I. Düring (ed.), *Naturphilosophie
bei Aristoteles und Theophrast* (Heidelberg, 1969), 85–96
[211] D.J. Furley, 'The Greek theory of the infinite universe', *Journal of the History of Ideas* 42
(1981), 571–85
[212] H.B. Gottschalk, 'Lucretius 1.983', *Classical Philology* 70 (1975), 42–4
[213] I. Avotins, 'On some Epicurean and Lucretian arguments for the infinity of the
universe', *Classical Quarterly* N.S. 33 (1983), 421–7
[214] D. Konstan, 'Epicurus on "up" and "down" (*Letter to Herodotus* 60)', *Phronesis* 17 (1972),
269–78

13 *Anti-teleology*
For Epicurus' doctrines concerning nature, chance and teleology, see Schrijvers [247],
and
[215] F. Solmsen, 'Epicurus and cosmological heresies', *American Journal of Philology* 72 (1951),
1–23, repr. in his [29] I, 461–83

Epicureanism

[216] F. Solmsen, 'Epicurus on the growth and decline of the cosmos', *American Journal of Philology* 74 (1953), 34–51, repr. in his [29] I, 484–501

[217] P. De Lacy, 'Limit and variation in the Epicurean philosophy', *Phoenix* 23 (1969), 104–13

[218] J. Moreau, 'Le mécanisme épicurien et l'ordre de la nature', *Les Etudes Philosophiques* 30 (1975), 467–86

[219] A.A. Long, 'Chance and natural law in Epicureanism', *Phronesis* 22 (1977), 63–88

14 Soul

The fullest modern discussion is

[220] G.B. Kerferd, 'Epicurus' doctrine of the soul', *Phronesis* 16 (1971), 80–96

15 Sensation etc.

For the mechanisms of sense-perception, sleep and dreaming, see Asmis [225], Hahm [49], and

[221] P.H. Schrijvers, 'La pensée d'Epicure et de Lucrèce sur le sommeil', in [99], 229–59

[222] D. Clay, 'An Epicurean interpretation of dreams', *American Journal of Philology* 101 (1980), 342–65

[223] I. Avotins, 'Alexander of Aphrodisias on vision in the atomists', *Classical Quarterly* N.S. 30 (1980), 429–54

[224] E. Asmis, 'Lucretius' explanation of moving dream figures at 4.768–76', *American Journal of Philology* 102 (1981), 138–45

16–19 Epicurean epistemology

The most comprehensive and scholarly treatment of this topic is

[225] E. Asmis, *Epicurus' scientific method* (Ithaca/London, 1984)
For earlier accounts, cf. especially Bailey [89], and
[226] F. Merbach, *De Epicuri canonica* (Leipzig, 1909)

16 Sensation

The thesis that all impressions are true is interestingly discussed by

[227] G. Striker, 'Epicurus on the truth of sense impressions', *Archiv für Geschichte der Philosophie* 59 (1977), 125–42
although our own interpretation owes more to
[228] C.C.W. Taylor, '"All perceptions are true"', in [5], 105–24
Epicurus' reaction to scepticism is examined by Gigante [106], Fowler [107], and
[229] M.F. Burnyeat, 'The upside-down back-to-front sceptic of Lucretius IV 472', *Philologus* 122 (1978), 197–206
Further aspects are treated in
[230] F. Solmsen, 'Αἴσθησις in Aristotelian and Epicurean thought', in his [29] I, 612–33

[231] W. Detel, 'Αἴσθησις und λογισμός: zwei Probleme der epikureischen Methodologie', *Archiv für Geschichte der Philosophie* 57 (1975), 21–35

[232] A.A. Long, 'Aisthesis, prolepsis, and linguistic theory in Epicurus', *Bulletin of the Institute of Classical Studies* 18 (1971), 114–33

[233] E.N. Lee, 'The sense of an object: Epicurus on seeing and hearing', in P.K. Machamer, R.G. Turnbull (edd.), *Studies in perception* (Columbus, 1978), 27–59

Bibliography

[234] D.K. Glidden, 'Epicurus on self-perception', *American Philosophical Quarterly* 16 (1979), 297–306

[235] D.K. Glidden, '*Sensus* and sense perception in the *De rerum natura*', *California Studies in Classical Antiquity* 12 (1981), 155–81

[236] D. Sedley, 'Epicurus on the common sensibles', in [28]

17 The criteria of truth

On the Epicurean criteria, especially 'preconception', see Long [232], Sedley [126], Striker [9], and

[237] A. Manuwald, *Die Prolepsislehre Epikurs* (Bonn, 1972)

[238] V. Goldschmidt, 'Remarques sur l'origine épicurienne de la prénotion', in [411], 155–69

[239] D.K. Glidden, 'Epicurean prolepsis', in *Oxford Studies in Ancient Philosophy* 3 (1985), 175–218

18 Scientific methodology

See Striker [9], De Lacy [152], Asmis [225], and

[240] R. Philippson, *De Philodemi libro qui est Περὶ σημείων καὶ σημειώσεων* (Berlin, 1881)

[241] D.J. Furley, 'Knowledge of atoms and void in Epicureanism', in J.P. Anton, G.L. Kustas (edd.), *Essays in ancient Greek philosophy* 1 (Albany, 1971), 607–19

[242] A. Wasserstein, 'Epicurean science', *Hermes* 106 (1978), 484–94

[243] D. Sedley, 'On signs', in [6], 239–72

For Epicurus' idiosyncratic doctrine on the size of the sun, see Sedley [105], Romeo [144]

19 Language

Epicurus' theory of the origin of language has been much discussed. See especially Giussani [164], Cole [273], Sedley [126], Glidden [234], and

[244] G. Vlastos, 'On the prehistory in Diodorus', *American Journal of Philology* 67 (1946), 51–9

[245] H. Dahlmann, *De philosophorum graecorum sententiis ad loquellae originem pertinentibus capita duo* (Leipzig, 1928)

[246] C.W. Chilton, 'The Epicurean theory of the origin of language', *American Journal of Philology* 83 (1962), 139–67

[247] P.H. Schrijvers, 'La pensée de Lucrèce sur l'origine du langage', *Mnemosyne* 27 (1974), 337–64

[248] J. Brunschwig, 'Epicure et le problème du langage privé', *Revue des Sciences Humaines* 43 (1977), 157–77

On the relation of language to epistemology, see Long [232], Manuwald [237], Sedley [126], Asmis [225], and

[249] P.H. De Lacy, 'The Epicurean analysis of language', *American Journal of Philology* 60 (1939), 85–92

[250] D.K. Glidden, 'Epicurean semantics', in [100], 185–226

20–5 Epicurean ethics

For general treatments, see Bailey [89], Rist [95], Long [3], Pesce [97]. Ethics and moral psychology are treated in more detail by

[251] M. Guyau, *La Morale d'Epicure et ses rapports avec les doctrines contemporaines* (ed. 5, Paris, 1910)

Epicureanism

[252] H. Steckel, *Epikurs Prinzip der Einheit von Schmerzlosigkeit und Lust* (Göttingen, 1960)

[253] D. Konstan, *Some aspects of Epicurean psychology* (Leiden, 1973) and with enormous learning in Diano [102], of which we cite separately

[254] C. Diano, 'Note epicuree', *Studi Italiani di Filologia Classica* 12 (1935), 61–86, 237–89

20 Free will

Important studies include Guyau [251] and Bailey [89], but new precision was injected into the discussion by Furley's study in [204]. In his wake, recent contributions have included Long [3] and

[255] I. Avotins, 'The question of *mens* in Lucretius 2.289', *Classical Quarterly* N.S. 29 (1979), 95–100

[256] M. Isnardi Parente, 'Stoici, epicurei e il "motus sine causa" ', *Rivista Critica di Storia della Filosofia* 35 (1980), 23–31

[257] K. Kleve, '*Id facit exiguum clinamen*', *Symbolae Osloenses* 55 (1980), 27–30

[258] D. Fowler, 'Lucretius on the *clinamen* and "free will" (II 251–93)', in [100], 329–52

[259] T.J. Saunders, 'Free will and the atomic swerve in Lucretius', *Symbolae Osloenses* 59 (1984), 37–59

Our own view is more fully developed in

[260] D. Sedley, 'Epicurus' refutation of determinism', in [100], 11–51

For an excellent critique of current scholarship on the matter, together with a novel interpretation, cf.

[261] W.G. Englert, *Epicurus on the swerve and voluntary action* (Atlanta, Georgia, 1987)

For a useful assessment of Epicurus' historical importance on this issue, cf.

[262] P.M. Huby, 'The first discovery of the freewill problem', *Philosophy* 42 (1967), 353–62

21, 25 Pleasure, tranquillity

On pleasure and the foundations of Epicurean ethics, cf. Gosling/Taylor [19], and

[263] J. Brunschwig, 'The cradle argument in Epicureanism and Stoicism', in [7], 113–44

[264] J.M. Rist, 'Pleasure: 360–300 B.C.', *Phoenix* 28 (1974), 167–79

[265] P. Merlan, *Studies in Epicurus and Aristotle* (Wiesbaden, 1960), chapter 1

[266] G. Giannantoni, 'Il piacere cinetico nell' etica epicurea', *Elenchos* 5 (1984), 25–44

[267] M. Hossenfelder, 'Epicurus: hedonist malgré lui', in [7], 245–63

On tranquillity, and the value of philosophy, cf.

[268] D. Clay, 'Epicurus' Κυρία Δόξα XVII', *Greek, Roman and Byzantine Studies* 13 (1972), 59–66

[269] A. Grilli, 'ΔΙΑΘΕΣΙΣ in Epicuro', in [100], 93–109

[270] M. Nussbaum, 'Therapeutic arguments: Epicurus and Aristotle', in [7], 31–74

[271] M. Gigante, 'Philosophia medicans in Filodemo', *Cronache Ercolanesi* 5 (1975), 53–61

22 Society

On friendship and society, cf.

[272] R. Philippson, 'Die Rechtsphilosophie der Epikureer', *Archiv für Geschichte der Philosophie* 23 (1910), 289–337, 433–46 = [103], 27–89

[273] T. Cole, *Democritus and the origins of Greek anthropology* (Cleveland, 1967)

[274] J. Bollack, 'Les maximes de l'amitié', in [98], 221–36

Bibliography

[275] R. Müller, *Die epikureische Gesellschaftstheorie* (Berlin, 1972)

[276] V. Goldschmidt, *La doctrine d'Epicure et le droit* (Paris, 1977)

[277] J.M. Rist, 'Epicurus on friendship', *Classical Philology* 75 (1980), 121–9

[278] D.J. Furley, 'Lucretius the Epicurean. On the history of man', in [163], 1–37

[279] N. Denyer, 'The origins of justice', in [100], 133–52

[280] A.A. Long, 'Pleasure and social utility – the virtues of being Epicurean', in [8], 283–324

[281] P. Mitsis, 'Friendship and altruism in Epicureanism', *Oxford Studies in Ancient Philosophy* 5 (1987)

23 God

Epicurean theology has generated more than its fair share of scholarly literature. The following is a small selection. An outline of the view which we advance was first offered by a Kantian

[282] F.A. Lange, *Geschichte des Materialismus* (ed. 2, Iserlohn, 1873) I, 76–7

and a version of it is adopted by Bollack [123]. A fascinating portrayal of the place of theology in Epicurus' system, in a brilliant book marred only by excessive reliance on extravagantly restored papyrus texts, is

[283] A.J. Festugière, *Epicurus and his gods* (Engl. transl., Oxford, 1955; 2nd French ed., with revisions, Paris, 1968)

Two major recent contributions are

[284] K. Kleve, *Gnosis theon*, in *Symbolae Osloenses* suppl. 19 (Oslo, 1963)

[285] D. Lemke, *Die Theologie Epikurs* (Munich, 1973)

Other important studies include chapter 2 of Merlan [265], Diels [151], Henrichs [529], and

[286] W. Scott, 'The physical constitution of the Epicurean gods', *Journal of Philology* 12 (1883), 212–47

[287] W. Schmid, 'Götter und Menschen in Theologie Epikurs', *Rheinisches Museum* 94 (1951), 97–156

[288] G. Pfligersdorffer, 'Cicero über Epikurs Lehre vom Wesen der Götter (nat. deor. I 49)', *Wiener Studien* 70 (1957), 235–53

[289] J. Brunschwig, review of Kleve [284], *Revue des Etudes Grecques* 77 (1964), 352–6

[290] K. Kleve, 'On the beauty of god. A discussion between Epicureans, Stoics and sceptics', *Symbolae Osloenses* 53 (1978), 69–83

[291] D.D. Obbink, 'P. Oxy. 215 and Epicurean religious *theoria*', *Atti del XVII congresso internazionale di papirologia* (Naples, 1984), 607–19

There is also much useful comparative material in Pease [329]

24 Death

Aspects of the Epicurean treatment of death are discussed in Sorabji [22], Puliga [200], and

[292] M. Gigante, 'La chiusa del *De morte* di Filodemo', in [147]

[293] J. Fallot, *Il piacere e la morte nella filosofia di Epicuro* (Turin, 1977)

[294] D.J. Furley, 'Nothing to us?', in [7], 75–91

For a critique of Lucretius' argument in **24E**, cf.

[295] T. Nagel, *Mortal questions* (Cambridge, 1979), chapter 1

26–67 STOICISM

General

The most comprehensive short introduction is

[296] F.H. Sandbach, *The Stoics* (London, 1975)

On Stoicism at Rome, much of value may still be learned from

[297] E.V. Arnold, *Roman Stoicism* (Cambridge, 1911)

The most thorough general study, with valuable testimonia in the second volume, is

[298] M. Pohlenz, *Die Stoa. Geschichte einer geistigen Bewegung* (ed. 2, Göttingen, 1959; later editions do not alter the main text)

More philosophically stimulating are

[299] E. Bréhier, *Chrysippe et l'ancien stoicisme* (ed. 2, Paris, 1951)

[300] J. Christensen, *An essay on the unity of Stoic philosophy* (Copenhagen, 1962)

[301] L. Edelstein, *The meaning of Stoicism* (Cambridge, Mass., 1966)

More specialized are

[302] V. Goldschmidt, *Le système stoicien et l'idée de temps* (ed. 4, Paris, 1979)

[303] J.M. Rist, *Stoic philosophy* (Cambridge, 1969)

An important monograph which calls in question the influence of Aristotle is

[304] F.H. Sandbach, *Aristotle and the Stoics.* (*Proceedings of the Cambridge Philological Society,* suppl. 10, 1985)

Four anthologies of articles on various aspects of Stoicism are

[305] Association Guillaume Budé, *Actes du VIIe congrès* (Paris, 1964)

[306] A.A. Long (ed.), *Problems in Stoicism* (London, 1971)

[307] J.M. Rist (ed.), *The Stoics* (Berkeley/Los Angeles, 1978)

[308] R. Epp (ed.), *Spindel Conference 1984: recovering the Stoics.* (*Southern Journal of Philosophy,* xxiii suppl., 1985)

See in particular the survey articles

[309] R. Epp, 'Stoicism bibliography', in [308] 125–82: a list of over 1,100 publications

[310] J.M. Rist, 'Stoicism: some reflections on the state of the art', in [308], 1–11

Two fundamental studies, more comprehensive than their titles suggest, are

[311] A. Bonhöffer, *Epictet und die Stoa* (Stuttgart, 1890)

[312] A. Bonhöffer, *Die Ethik des Stoikers Epictet* (Stuttgart, 1894)

Various historical aspects of Stoicism are treated in [305], especially in

[313] P. Boyancé, 'Le stoicisme à Rome', in [305], 218–55

and also in

[314] J.-M. André, *La Philosophie à Rome* (Paris, 1977)

[315] A.A. Long, 'Stoa and sceptical Academy: origins and growth of a tradition', *Liverpool Classical Monthly* 5 (1980), 161–74

[316] A. Graeser, *Plotinus and the Stoics* (Leiden, 1972)

[317] M. Spanneut, *Le Stoicisme des pères de l'Eglise: de Clément de Rome à Clément d'Alexandrie* (Paris, 1957)

Bibliography

[318] M. Spanneut, *Permanence du stoicisme, de Zénon à Malraux* (Gembloux, 1973)
[319] G. Verbeke, *The presence of Stoicism in medieval thought* (Washington, D.C., 1983)

Texts, commentaries and translations

The basic collection of material on Stoicism from Zeno to Stoic philosophers of the mid-second century B.C. is still
[320] H. von Arnim, *Stoicorum veterum fragmenta*. 3 vols. (Leipzig, 1903–5); vol. 4, indexes by M. Adler (Leipzig, 1924). Standardly abbreviated as *SVF*.

However, for all material relating to grammar and semantics, epistemology and logic, Arnim's selection has been eclipsed by the monumental collection, with German translation, by
[321] K. Hülser, *Die Fragmente zur Dialektik der Stoiker* (forthcoming)
An antiquated but still valuable study is
[322] A.C. Pearson, *The fragments of Zeno and Cleanthes* (London, 1891)

For Panaetius, the standard edition is
[323] M. van Straaten, *Panaetii Rhodii fragmenta* (ed. 3, Leiden, 1962)

For Posidonius, a collection based entirely on named fragments is
[324] L. Edelstein, I.G. Kidd, *Posidonius. Vol. 1, the fragments* (Cambridge, 1972); vol. 2, a commentary by I.G. Kidd, will appear shortly
A further collection, which includes some unnamed fragments, and commentary is
[325] W. Theiler, *Poseidonios, die Fragmente*, 2 vols. (Berlin, 1982)

For editions of Cicero, Seneca, Epictetus and Marcus Aurelius, see vol. 1 Index of sources. A number of further editions, most with commentary and some also with translation, have valuable notes on fragments of Chrysippus and other Stoics:
[326] H. Cherniss, *Plutarch, Moralia XIII*, part II. Loeb Classical Library (Cambridge, Mass./ London, 1976).
[327] P. De Lacy, *Galen On the doctrines of Hippocrates and Plato* (*Corpus medicorum Graecorum* v.4.1.2), 3 vols. (Berlin, 1978–84); the third volume, containing the notes, appeared too late for us to consult
[328] J.S. Reid (ed.), *Cicero. Academica* (London, 1885)
[329] A.S. Pease (ed.), *Cicero. De natura deorum.*, 2 vols. (Cambridge, Mass., 1955–8)
[330] A.S.L. Farquharson (ed.), *Marcus Aurelius. Meditations*, 2 vols. (Oxford, 1944)
[331] M. Billerbeck, *Epiktet von Kynismus* (Leiden, 1978)
[332] R.B. Todd, *Alexander of Aphrodisias on Stoic physics* (Leiden, 1976)
[333] R.W. Sharples, *Alexander of Aphrodisias On fate* (London, 1983)
[334] T. Dorandi, 'Filodemo, *Gli stoici* (PHerc. 155 e 339)', *Cronache Ercolanesi* 12 (1982), 91– 133

Studies of individual Stoic philosophers

Much of the recent research has focused, with the exception of Posidonius and Roman Stoicism, on concepts and arguments which it is easier to credit to Chrysippus or to early Stoicism in general than to other individual Stoics. There are, however, a good many studies which isolate, or seek to isolate, the contributions of Zeno, Cleanthes, and others.

We list these separately here – with cross-references, as appropriate, in the bibliographies of topics.

Zeno

[335] M. Pohlenz, 'Zenon und Chrysipp', *Nachricht. der Akad. der Wiss. in Göttingen*, phil.-hist. Kl. 1 2.9 (1938), 173–210

[336] M. Pohlenz, 'Grundfragen der stoischen Philosophie', *Abh. der Göttingen Gesell.*, phil-hist. Kl. 3.26 (1940), 1–122

[337] K. von Fritz, 'Zenon von Kition', in Pauly-Wissowa, *Real-Encyclopädie der klassischen Altertumswissenschaft*, suppl. 10A

[338] H.C. Baldry, 'Zeno's ideal state', *Journal of Hellenic Studies* 79 (1959), 3–15

[339] L. Stroux, *Vergleich und Metaphor in der Lehre des Zenon von Kition* (Berlin, 1965)

[340] A. Graeser, *Zenon von Kition. Positionen und Probleme* (Berlin, 1975)

[341] H.A.K. Hunt, *A physical interpretation of the universe. The doctrines of Zeno the Stoic* (Melbourne, 1976)

[342] J.M. Rist, 'Zeno and Stoic consistency', *Phronesis* 22 (1977), 161–74, repr. in J.P. Anton, A. Preus (edd.), *Essays in ancient Greek philosophy* II (Albany, 1983), 465–77

[343] J.M. Rist, 'Zeno and the origins of Stoic logic', in [411], 387–400

[344] J. Mansfeld, 'Zeno of Citium: critical observations on a recent study', *Mnemosyne* 31 (1978), 134–78 (review of [340])

[345] M. Schofield, 'The syllogisms of Zeno of Citium', *Phronesis* 28 (1983), 31–58

Aristo

His interesting and unorthodox contributions have been excellently studied by

[346] A.M. Ioppolo, *Aristone di Chio e lo stoicismo antico* (Rome, 1980)

which prompted two review articles,

[347] M. Schofield, 'Ariston of Chios and the unity of virtue', *Ancient Philosophy* 4 (1984), 83–96

[348] N. White, 'Nature and regularity in Stoic ethics: a discussion of Anna Maria Ioppolo, *Aristone di Chio e lo stoicismo antico*', *Oxford Studies in Ancient Philosophy* 5 (1985), 289–306

Herillus

[349] A. M. Ioppolo, 'Lo stoicismo di Erillo', *Phronesis* 32 (1985), 58–78

Cleanthes

In general, see Pearson [322], and

[350] G. Verbeke, *Kleanthes van Assos* (Brussels, 1949)

[351] J.D. Meerwaldt, 'Cleanthea' I and II, *Mnemosyne* 4 (1951), 40–69; 5 (1952), 1–12

On his contributions to physics, see

[352] F. Solmsen, 'Cleanthes or Posidonius? The basis of Stoic physics', in his [29] I, 436–60

[353] A.A. Long, 'Heraclitus and Stoicism', *Philosophia* 5/6 (1975/6), 133–56

His *Hymn to Zeus* has generated an extensive literature, including editions by Pearson [322], and

[354] J.U. Powell, *Collectanea Alexandrina* (Oxford, 1925), 227–9

[355] G. Zuntz, 'Zum Kleanthes-Hymnus', *Harvard Studies in Classical Philology* 63 (1958), 289–308

and discussions by Meerwaldt [351], Long [353], and

Bibliography

[356] E. Neustadt, 'Der Zeushymnus des Kleanthes', *Hermes* 66 (1931), 387–401
[357] A.J. Festugière, *La révélation d'Hermès Trismégiste* II (Paris, 1949), 310–32
[358] M. Marcovich, 'Zum Zeushymnus des Kleanthes', *Hermes* 94 (1966), 245–50
[359] G. Zuntz, 'Vers 4 des Kleanthes-Hymnus', *Rheinisches Museum* 122 (1979), 97–8
[360] A.W. James, 'The Zeus hymns of Cleanthes and Aratus', *Antichthon* 6 (1972), 28–38
[361] M. Dragona-Monachou, "Ο "ὕμνος στὸ Δία" καὶ τὰ Χρυσᾶ ἔπη. Ἡ ποιητικὴ θεολογία τοῦ Κλεάνθη καὶ ἡ 'Ορφικο-Πυθαγορικὴ παραδοσή', *Philosophia* 1 (1971), 339–78 (includes summary in English)

Chrysippus
See especially Pohlenz [335], [336], Bréhier [299], Cherniss [326], and
[362] J.B. Gould, *The philosophy of Chrysippus* (Leiden, 1970)
[363] D. Babut, *Plutarque et le stoicisme* (Paris, 1969)

Diogenes of Babylon and Antipater of Tarsus
Most of the literature concerns their contributions to the doctrine of the ethical end (64), see [590]–[593]

Panaetius
In addition to van Straaten's collection of fragments [323], there are general studies by
[364] A. Schmekel, *Die Philosophie der mittleren Stoa in ihrem geschichtlichen Zusammenhange dargestellt* (Berlin, 1892)
[365] B.N. Tatakis, *Panétius de Rhodes: le fondateur du moyen Stoicisme* (Paris, 1931)
[366] M. van Straaten, *Panétius, sa vie, ses écrits et sa doctrine* (Amsterdam, 1946)
See also
[367] R. Philippson, 'Das Sittlichschöne bei Panaitios', *Philologus* 85 (1930), 357–413
[368] A. Grilli, 'Studi paneziani', *Studi Italiani di Filologia Classica* 29 (1957), 31–97
[369] F.A. Steinmetz, *Die Freundschaftslehre des Panaitios nach einer Analyse von Ciceros Laelius De amicitia* (Wiesbaden, 1967)
[370] A. Dyck, 'The plan of Panaetius' Περὶ τοῦ καθήκοντος', *American Journal of Philology* 100 (1979), 408–16
[371] A. Dyck, 'On Panaetius' conception of μεγαλοψυχία', *Museum Helveticum* 38 (1981), 153–61

Posidonius
For collections of the fragments, see [324], [325].

The older German studies were based on an over-generous conception of Posidonius' presence in texts where he is not named. In spite of these shortcomings one such study is still important,
[372] K. Reinhardt, *Kosmos und Sympathie: neue Untersuchungen über Poseidonios* (Munich, 1926)

A much more critical approach was developed by
[373] L. Edelstein, 'The philosophical system of Posidonius', *American Journal of Philology* 57 (1936), 286–325
and see also
[374] J. F. Dobson, 'The Posidonius myth', *Classical Quarterly* 12 (1918), 179–95

The best comprehensive studies, for the present, are

|375| A.D. Nock, 'Posidonius', *Journal of Roman Studies* 49 (1959), 1–16
|376| M. Laffranque, *Poseidonios d'Apamée* (Paris, 1964)

For study of details, see Pohlenz |336| and

|377| G. Nebel, 'Zur Ethik des Poseidonios', *Hermes* 74 (1939), 34–57
|378| B.L.Hijmans, 'Posidonius' ethics', *Acta Classica* 2 (1959), 27–42
|379| I.G. Kidd, 'Posidonius on emotions', in |306|, 200–15
|380| A. Dihle, 'Posidonius' system of moral philosophy', *Journal of Hellenic Studies* 93 (1973), 50–7
|381| I.G. Kidd, 'Posidonius and logic', in |411|, 273–84
|382| I.G. Kidd, 'Philosophy and science in Posidonius', *Antike und Abendland* 24 (1978), 7–15
|383| I.G. Kidd, '*Euemptosia* – proneness to disease', in |546|, 107–13

Stoics of the Roman imperial age
The Stoicism of Seneca, Epictetus and Marcus Aurelius cannot be covered adequately here. However, see especially Bonhöffer |311|, |312|, Arnold |297|, Sandbach |296|, and

|384| M.T. Griffin, *Seneca, a philosopher in politics* (Oxford, 1976)
|385| A.A. Long, 'Epictetus, Marcus Aurelius', in T.J. Luce (ed.), *Ancient writers* II (New York, 1982), 985–1002
|386| J. Xenakis, *Epictetus, philosopher–therapist* (The Hague, 1969)
|387| M. Dragona-Monachou, '*Prohairesis* in Aristotle and Epictetus', *Philosophia* 8/9 (1978), 265–310
|388| P.A. Brunt, 'Marcus Aurelius in his *Meditations*', *JRS* 64 (1974), 1–20
|389| J.M. Rist, 'Are you a Stoic? The case of Marcus Aurelius', in B.F. Meyer, E.P. Sanders (edd.), *Jewish and Christian self-definition* III (Philadelphia, 1982), 23–45

For Hierocles, see |572|–|575|.

26 The philosophical curriculum

See Kidd |381|, |382|, Kerferd |478|, Long |429|, and
|390| A. Dihle, 'Philosophie–Fachwissenschaft–Allgemeinbildung', in |8|, 185–231

27–30 Stoic ontology

Two pioneering studies on the concept of 'incorporeals' and 'something' are Goldschmidt |302| and
|391| E. Bréhier, *La Théorie des incorporels dans l'ancien Stoicisme* (Paris, 1910)

For various aspects of Stoic metaphysics, see Rieth |551| and
|392| A.C. Lloyd, 'Activity and description in Aristotle and the Stoa', *Proceedings of the British Academy* 56 (1970), 227–40

On existence and subsistence, cf. Long |426|, 88–90, and
|393| V. Goldschmidt, '*ὑπάρχειν* et *ὑφεστάναι* dans la philosophie stoicienne', *Revue des Etudes Grecques* 85 (1972), 331–44

What are called in this work the 'four genera', traditionally called the 'four categories', are discussed by

Bibliography

[394] P.H. de Lacy, 'The Stoic categories as methodological principles', *Transactions and Proceedings of the American Philological Society* 76 (1945), 246–63

[395] M.E. Reesor, 'The Stoic concept of quality', *American Journal of Philology* 75 (1954), 40–58

[396] M.E. Reesor, 'The Stoic categories', *American Journal of Philology* 78 (1957), 63–82

[397] M.E. Reesor, '*Poion* and *poiotes* in Stoic philosophy', *Phronesis* 17 (1972), 279–85

[398] J.M. Rist, 'Categories and their uses', in [303], 152–72 and [306], 38–57

and suggestions about their connexion with parts of speech are made by

[399] A.C. Lloyd, 'Grammar and metaphysics in the Stoa', in [306], 58–74

For an attempt to discover an alternative system of Stoic categories in Simplicius, see

[400] A. Graeser, 'The Stoic categories', in [411], 199–222

Our interpretation of the theory of universals is also developed in

[401] D. Sedley, 'The Stoic theory of universals', in [308], 87–92

For a full discussion of material treated in **28**, see

[402] D. Sedley, 'The Stoic criterion of identity', *Phronesis* 27 (1982), 255–75

and for parallel Aristotelian treatment of one of the central issues, cf.

[403] G.E.M. Anscombe, 'The principle of individuation', *Proceedings of the Aristotelian Society*, suppl. 27 (1953), 83–96, repr. in J. Barnes, M. Schofield, R. Sorabji (edd.), *Articles on Aristotle* III (London, 1979)

31–8 Stoic logic and semantics

For the texts and German translation, see Hülser [321]. Landmarks in the modern rediscovery and reappraisal of Stoic logic include the pioneering

[404] B. Mates, *Stoic logic* (Berkeley/Los Angeles, 1953)

[405] W. and M. Kneale, *The development of logic* (Oxford, 1962), 113–76

[406] M. Mignucci, *Il significato della logica stoica* (ed. 2, Bologna, 1967)

and the most authoritative analysis of the formal logic,

[407] M. Frede, *Die stoische Logik* (Göttingen, 1974)

A valuable introduction to the subject is

[408] I. Mueller, 'An introduction to Stoic logic', in [307], 1–26

See also

[409] W.H. Hay, 'Stoic use of logic', *Archiv für Geschichte der Philosophie* 51 (1969), 145–57

Recent work is surveyed by

[410] V. Celluprica, 'La logica stoica in alcune recenti interpretazioni', *Elenchos* 3 (1980), 123–50

For a rich collection of papers on all aspects of the subject, see

[411] J. Brunschwig (ed.), *Les Stoiciens et leur logique* (Paris, 1978)

One topic that still awaits full investigation is the growth of Stoic logic out of that of the Dialectical school. Some of our ideas on this are developed in Sedley [11], but we are also heavily indebted to a monograph which discerns evidence for the Dialectical school in some texts which scholars have previously taken to represent the Stoics themselves,

[412] T. Ebert, *Dialektiker und frühe Stoiker bei Sextus Empiricus* (forthcoming)

On contributions by individual Stoics, see Rist [343], Schofield [345], Kidd [381].

Stoic grammatical theory falls largely outside the scope of our collection. For evidence and discussions, see Lloyd [399], and

[413] R.T. Schmidt, *Die Grammatik der Stoiker*, German transl. of the 1839 Latin edition by K. Hülser, with new introduction and bibliography by U. Egli (Wiesbaden, 1979)

[414] H. Steinthal, *Geschichte der Sprachwissenschaft bei den Griechen und Römern*, 2 vols. (ed. 2, Berlin, 1890–1)

[415] K. Barwick, *Probleme der Stoischen Sprachlehre und Rhetorik* (Berlin, 1957)

[416] J. Pinborg, 'Historiography of linguistics: classical antiquity: Greece', in *Current Trends in Linguistics* 13 (The Hague, 1975), 69–126

[417] M. Frede, 'Some remarks on the origin of traditional grammar', in R. Butts, J. Hintikka (edd.), *Logic, methodology, and philosophy of science* (Dordrecht, 1976), 609–37

[418] M. Frede, 'Principles of Stoic grammar', in [307], 27–76

[419] D.L. Blank, *Ancient philosophy and grammar: the Syntax of Apollonius Dyscolus* (Chico, California, 1982)

[420] P. Hadot, 'La notion de "cas" dans la logique stoicienne', *Actes du XXXme congrès des sociétés de philosophie de langue française* (Geneva, 1966), 109–12

31–2 Dialectic and rhetoric

For the general philosophical significance of dialectic, see

[421] A.A. Long, 'Dialectic and the Stoic sage', in [307], 101–24

[422] K. Hülser, 'Expression and content in Stoic linguistic theory', in R. Baüerle, U. Egli, A. von Stechow (edd.), *Semantics from different points of view* (Heidelberg, 1979), 287–306

On the Stoics' contributions to rhetoric, see Barwick [415], and

[423] G. Kennedy, *The art of persuasion in Greece* (Princeton, 1963)

32 Definition and division

See Rieth [551], 45–54, and cf. an interesting related study,

[424] D.E. Hahm, 'The diaeretic method and the purpose of Arius' doxography', in [546], 15–37

33 Sayables (lekta)

The theory of the *lekton* has been extensively discussed in recent years. In addition to Mates [404], Kneale [405], Watson [464], Hadot [420], see

[425] C.H. Kahn, 'Stoic logic and Stoic logos', *Archiv für Geschichte der Philosophie* 51 (1969), 158–72

[426] A.A. Long, 'Language and thought in Stoicism', in [306], 75–113

[427] G. Nuchelmans, *Theories of the proposition. Ancient and medieval conceptions of the bearers of truth and falsity* (Amsterdam, 1973)

[428] J.D.G. Evans, 'The Old Stoa on the truth-value of oaths', *Proceedings of the Cambridge Philological Society* n.s. 20 (1974), 43–7

[429] A.A. Long, 'The Stoic distinction between truth and the true', in [411], 297–316

[430] A. Graeser, 'The Stoic theory of meaning', in [307], 77–100

[431] U. Egli, 'Stoic syntax and semantics', in [411], 135–54

[432] G.B. Kerferd, 'The problem of *synkatathesis* and *katalepsis*', in [411], 251–72

Bibliography

[433] W. Detel, R. Hülser, G. Krüger, W. Lorenz, 'λεκτὰ ἐλλιπῆ in der stoischen Sprachphilosophie', *Archiv für Geschichte der Philosophie* 62 (1980), 276–88

There has been much interest in the thesis that the object of a practical impulse is a predicate (**33H**). See Kerferd [603], Inwood [547], chapter 3, and

[434] A.A. Long, 'The early Stoic concept of moral choice', in *Images of man in ancient and medieval thought. Studies presented to G. Verbeke* (Louvain, 1976), 77–92

34 Simple propositions
Following on the seminal discussion of this topic in Frede [407], see now also

[435] P. Pachet, 'La deixis selon Zénon et Chrysippe', *Phronesis* 20 (1975), 241–6
[436] A.C. Lloyd, 'Definite propositions and the concept of reference', in [411], 285–96
[437] R. Goulet, 'La classification stoicienne des propositions simples', in [411], 171–98

35 Non-simple propositions
For various aspects of this topic, see Frede [407], Verbeke [483], Burnyeat [484], Sedley [243], and

[438] J.B. Gould, 'Chrysippus: on the criteria for the truth of a conditional proposition', *Phronesis* 12 (1967), 152–61
[439] J. Brunschwig, 'Le modèle conjonctif', in [411], 58–86
[440] D. Sedley, 'The negated conjunction in Stoicism', *Elenchos* 5 (1984), 311–16

36 Arguments
See Frede [407], Schofield [345], Burnyeat [484], and

[441] I. Mueller, 'Stoic and Peripatetic logic', *Archiv für Geschichte der Philosophie* 51 (1969), 173–87
[442] M. Frede, 'Stoic vs. Aristotelian syllogistic', *Archiv für Geschichte der Philosophie* 56 (1974), 1–32
[443] J. Gould, 'Deduction in Stoic logic', in J. Corcoran (ed.), *Ancient logic and its modern interpretations* (Boston, 1974), 151–68
[444] J. Brunschwig, 'Proof defined', in [5], 125–60
[445] J. Barnes, 'Proof destroyed', in [5], 161–81
[446] M. Nasti di Vincentis, 'Logica scettica e implicazione stoica', in [62], 501–32
[447] M. Nasti di Vincentis, 'Stopper on Nasti's contention and Stoic logic', *Phronesis* 29 (1984), 313–24 (a reply to [63])

For the suggestion of a Peripatetic background to the Stoic indemonstrables, see

[448] J. Barnes, 'Theophrastus and hypothetical syllogistic', in W.W. Fortenbaugh, P.M. Huby, A.A. Long (edd.), *Theophrastus of Eresus. On his life and work* (New Brunswick/Oxford, 1985), 125–42

37 Fallacy
On the origins and history of various Stoic logical paradoxes, cf. Sedley [11].

The Sorites has aroused much recent discussion, cf. Couissin [625], and

[449] G. Sillitti, 'Alcune considerazioni sull' aporia del sorite', in [40], 75–92
and the outstanding studies by
[450] J. Barnes, 'Medicine, experience and logic', in [6], 24–68
[451] M.F. Burnyeat, 'Gods and heaps', in M. Schofield, M. Nussbaum (edd.), *Language and*

logos: studies in ancient Greek philosophy presented to G.E.L. Owen (Cambridge, 1982), 315–38

For a history of the Lying Argument, see

[452] A. Rüstow, *Der Lügner, Theorie, Geschichte, und Auflösung* (Leipzig, 1910)

Stoic treatments of ambiguity are covered in

[453] R.B. Edlow, *Galen on language and ambiguity* (Leiden, 1977)
[454] S. Ebbesen, *Commentators and commentaries on Aristotle's Sophistici elenchi*, 3 vols. (Leiden, 1981)

38 Modality

The most comprehensive treatment is

[455] P.-M. Schuhl, *Le Dominateur et les possibles* (Paris, 1960)
For more sophisticated discussions, especially in relation to the Master Argument, see Kneale [405], and

[456] A.N. Prior, 'Diodoran modalities', *Philosophical Quarterly* 5 (1955), 205–13; 8 (1958), 226–30
[457] M. Mignucci, 'Sur la logique modale des stoïciens', in [411], 317–46
[458] P.L. Donini, 'Crisippo e la nozione del possibile', *Rivista di Filologia* 101 (1973), 333–51
[459] R. Sorabji, 'Causation, laws, and necessity', in [5], 250–82 (a version of which also appears as chapter 4 of his [21])
[460] V. Celluprica, 'L' argomento dominatore di Diodoro Crono e il concetto di possibile di Crisippo', in [40], 55–74
[461] V. Celluprica, 'Necessità megarica e fatalità stoica', *Elenchos* 3 (1982), 361–85
[462] G. Giannantoni, 'Il κυριεύων λόγος di Diodoro Crono', *Elenchos* 2 (1981), 239–72
[463] N.C. Denyer, 'Time and modality in Diodorus Cronus', *Theoria* 47 (1981), 31–53

39–42 Epistemology: Stoics and Academics

The most wide-ranging study of Stoic concepts, though one which deals only briefly with the 'cognitive impression', is

[464] G. Watson, *The Stoic theory of knowledge* (Belfast, 1966)

For general study of the controversy between Stoics and Academics, see Dal Pra [51], Stough [53], Long [315].

Two outstanding contributions, which first clearly established the nature of the dialectical encounter between Stoics and Academics, are Couissin [73], and

[465] P. Couissin, 'Le stoïcisme de la nouvelle Académie', *Revue d'Histoire de la Philosophie et d'Histoire Générale de la Civilization* 36 (1929), 241–76; English transl. in [58], 31–63

Of older studies, valuable material is still to be found in Credaro [614], and

[466] H. Hartmann, *Gewissheit und Wahrheit: der Streit zwischen Stoa und akademischer Skepsis* (Halle, 1927)
For an innovative study of the history of Academic arguments against Stoics, see
[467] G. Striker, 'Sceptical strategies', in [5], 54–83

Bibliography

39 Impressions

There is a masterly article on this subject, and on Stoic and Academic epistemology more generally, by

[468] M. Frede, 'Stoics and skeptics on clear and distinct impressions', in [58], 65–93

See also

[469] E.P. Arthur, 'Stoic analysis of the mind's reactions to presentations', *Hermes* 111 (1983), 69–78

On 'common conceptions' and 'preconceptions', see the basic study by

[470] F. H. Sandbach, '*Ennoia* and *prolepsis*' in [306], 22–37 (first publ. in *Classical Quarterly* 24 (1930), 45–51)

and also Watson [464], 22–37, Long [429], 304–9, and

[471] M. Schofield, 'Preconception, argument and god', in [5], 283–308

[472] R.B. Todd, 'The Stoic common notions', *Symbolae Osloenses* 48 (1973), 47–75

For the use to which the Stoic theory of impressions was put in aesthetics, cf.

[473] C. Imbert, 'Stoic logic and Alexandrian poetics', in [5], 182–216

40 The criteria of truth

Stoicism is covered in Striker [9]; see also Rist [303], chapter 8, Graeser [340], 39–68, and

[474] F.H. Sandbach, '*Phantasia kataleptike*', in [306], 9–21

[475] J. Annas, 'Truth and knowledge', in [5], 84–104

[476] H. von Staden, 'The Stoic theory of perception and its "Platonic" critics', in P.K. Machamer, R.G. Turnbull (edd.), *Studies in perception* (Columbus, 1978), 96–136

For some later developments, see Long [651], and

[477] A.A. Long, 'Ptolemy *On the criterion*: an epistemology for the practising scientist', in [28]

41 Knowledge and opinion

For various aspects, see Long [3], 126–31, [429], [426], 99–104; Annas [475]; Arthur [469]; and

[478] G.B. Kerferd. 'What does the wise man know?', in [307], 125–36

[479] W. Görler, ''Ασθενὴς συγκατάθεσις, zur stoischen Erkenntnistheorie', *Würzburger Jahrbücher für die Altertumswissenschaft* N.F. 3 (1977), 83–92

On the text of **41D**, see

[480] H. von Arnim, 'Über einen stoischen Papyrus der Herculanensischen Bibliothek', *Hermes* 25 (1890), 473–95

[481] M. Capasso, 'Il saggio infallibile (PHerc. 1020 col. 1)', in *La regione sotterrata dal Vesuvio* (Naples, 1982), 455–69, which corrects the unfounded reference to Aristotle proposed by

[482] W. Crönert, 'Die ΛΟΓΙΚΑ ΖΗΤΗΜΑΤΑ des Chrysippos', *Hermes* 36 (1901), 548–79

42 Scientific methodology

For issues relating to the Stoic use of signs, see Long [426], Brunschwig [444], De Lacy [152], Glidden [653], Ebert [412], Sedley [243], and

[483] G. Verbeke, 'La philosophie du signe chez les stoiciens', in [411], 401–24
and for a seminal study of the theory and its background,
[484] M.F. Burnyeat, 'The origins of non-deductive inference', in [6], 193–238

For two contrasting views on the extent of Stoic interest in astrology, see
[485] A.A. Long, 'Astrology: arguments pro and contra', in [6], 165–92
[486] A.M. Ioppolo, 'L'astrologia nello stoicismo antico', in [48], 73–91

In defence of the Stoic theory of divination, cf.
[487] N. Denyer, 'The case against divination: an examination of Cicero's *De divinatione*',
Proceedings of the Cambridge Philological Society N.S. 31 (1985), 1–10

43–55 Stoic physics
The most comprehensive study is
[488] D.E. Hahm, *The origins of Stoic cosmology* (Columbus, 1977)
See also
[489] L. Bloos, *Probleme der stoischen Physik* (Hamburg, 1973)
For an important pioneering work, which suggests interesting analogies between Stoic
and modern physics, see
[490] S. Sambursky, *Physics of the Stoics* (London, 1959)

A useful introduction to the subject is
[491] M. Lapidge, 'Stoic cosmology', in [307], 161–86

For Heraclitus' influence, see Long [353]; for Plato's, Moreau [23]; and for that of
Platonism, Krämer [12], 108–30

44–5 Principles and body
The most thorough study of the evidence is
[492] M. Lapidge, '*Archai* and *stoicheia*: a problem in Stoic cosmology', *Phronesis* 18 (1973),
240–78
See also Sandbach [296], 71–5, Graeser [340], 89–118, Hunt [341], 17–25, and
[493] R.B. Todd, 'Monism and immanence: foundations of Stoic physics', in [307], 137–60

Valuable testimonia are contained in
[494] J.H. Waszink, *Calcidius in Timaeum (Corpus Platonicum medii aevi*, London/Leiden, 1962)

46 God, fire, cosmic cycle
For cosmogony, see Lapidge [491], and
[495] D.E. Hahm, 'The Stoic theory of change', in [308], 39–56

For the dialectical background to the cosmic cycle, cf. Hahm [488], and the excellent
study by
[496] J. Mansfeld, 'Providence and the destruction of the universe in early Stoic thought', in
M.J. Vermaseren (ed.), *Studies in Hellenistic religions* (Leiden, 1979), 129–88
but we dissent from Mansfeld's view that the conflagration is the best state for the world:
see

Bibliography

|497| A.A. Long, 'The Stoics on world-conflagration and everlasting recurrence' in |308|, 13–38

On the evidence for Zeno from Alexander Lycopolis, see
|498| P.W. van der Horst, J. Mansfeld, *An Alexandrian Platonist against dualism* (Leiden, 1974)

For god as nature, see
|499| F. Solmsen, 'Nature as craftsman in Greek thought', in |29|, 1, 332–55

On the Stoic concept of the world-soul, see Moreau |23|. On Zeno's arguments against the eternity of the world, see Graeser |340|, 187–206, who follows up the early work of
|500| E. Zeller, 'Der Streit Theophrasts gegen Zenon über die Ewigkeit der Welt', *Hermes* 11 (1876), 422–9

47 *Elements, breath, tenor, tension*
For the history of the concept of breath, see Solmsen |523|, and
|501| G. Verbeke, *L'Evolution de la doctrine du pneuma du stoicisme à S. Augustin* (Paris, 1945)
|502| F. Solmsen, 'The vital heat, the inborn pneuma and the aether', in |29|, 1, 605–11
On the elements, and their transformations, there are studies by Hahm |495|, and
|503| J. Longrigg, 'Elementary physics in the Lyceum and Stoa', *Isis* 66 (1975), 211–29

On the role of Cleanthes in developing Stoic physics, cf. Solmsen |352|, and Long |353|. For the concept of tensional movement, see Sambursky |490|, 21–48

48 *Mixture*
For the main evidence, and commentary on it, see Todd |332|, and for further discussion
|504| J. Mansfeld, 'Zeno and Aristotle on mixture', *Mnemosyne* 36 (1983), 306–10
|505| M.J. White, 'Can unequal quantities of stuffs be totally blended?', *History of Philosophy Quarterly* (forthcoming)

49 *Place and void*
The principal discussion is Hahm |488|, 103–25. See also Sambursky |490|, 108–15, and Furley |168|, 20–3

50 *Continuum*
Many issues concerning the continuum, as discussed by the Stoics and their adversaries, are illuminated by Sorabji |22| and Mueller |652|. There is some challenging speculation in
|506| J. Mansfeld, 'Intuitionism and formalism: Zeno's definition of geometry in a fragment of L. Calvenus Taurus', *Phronesis* 28 (1983), 59–74
although his central contention has now been refuted by
|507| H. Tarrant, 'Zeno on knowledge or on geometry? The evidence of anon. *In Theaetetum*', *Phronesis* 29 (1984), 96–9

For further interpretations, partly different from our own, see Sambursky |490|, Mansfeld |344|, 158ff., and
|508| D.E. Hahm, 'Chrysippus' solution to the Democritean dilemma of the cone', *Isis* 63 (1972), 205–20

|509| R.B. Todd, 'Chrysippus on infinite divisibility', *Apeiron* 7 (1973), 121–34

|510| J.-P. Dumont, 'Mos geometricus, mos physicus', in |411|, 121–34

|511| M.J. White, 'Zeno's arrow, divisible infinitesimals, and Chrysippus', *Phronesis* 27 (1982), 239–54

51–2 *Time and everlasting recurrence*

Major discussions of the evidence on Stoic theories of time include Goldschmidt |302|, and Sorabji |22|, 17–32; see also Lloyd |392|, Rist |303|, chapter 15, and

|512| M.J. White, 'Time and determinism in the Hellenistic philosophical schools', *Archiv für Geschichte der Philosophie* 65 (1983), 40–62

On everlasting recurrence, see Mansfeld |496|, and Long |497|, who defends the logical coherence of the doctrine against the interpretation offered by

|513| J. Barnes, 'La doctrine du retour éternel', in |411|, 3–20

See also

|514| M.J. White, 'Cosmic cycles, time, and determinism', in his *Agency and integrality: philosophical themes in the ancient discussions of determinism and responsibility* (Basel, 1985), 173–214

On calculations of the duration of the 'great year', see

|515| B.L. van der Waerden, 'Das grosse Jahr und die ewige Wiederkehr', *Hermes* 80 (1952), 129–57

For modern discussions of closed or circular time, see

|516| A.N. Prior, *Past, present and future* (Oxford, 1967)

|517| W. Newton-Smith, *The structure of time* (London, 1980)

On everlasting recurrence in Nietzsche, see

|518| A. Nehamas, 'The eternal recurrence', *Philosophical Review* 89 (1980), 331–56

53 *Soul*

Stoic psychology, apart from epistemology and ethics, has only recently become a major subject of discussion. Of the older literature, the best work is that of Bonhöffer |311|, which refers to an invaluable range of material, though the discussion of this is not always reliable as history or philosophy.

An important advance in the understanding of elementary animal psychology and moral motivation was achieved with the publication of the papyrus fragments of Hierocles by von Arnim |572|. On these see the study by Pembroke |564|, and also Inwood |575|.

Two attempts to give a comprehensive account of the Stoic concept of mind are

|519| R. Philippson, 'Zur Psychologie der Stoa', *Rheinisches Museum* 86 (1937), 140–79

|520| A.A. Long, 'Soul and body in Stoicism', *Phronesis* 27 (1982), 34–57

One subject which has been discussed with considerable success is the unification of all mental faculties and the psychology of action to which this gave rise. This is an important theme in Inwood |547|, and also treated in

Bibliography

|521| B. Inwood, 'The Stoics on the grammar of action', in |308|, 75–86
Other related studies include chapters 2, 3, 12, 14 of Rist |303|, Long |434|, and
|522| A.J. Voelke, *L'Idée de volonté dans le stoicisme* (Paris, 1973)
|523| F. Solmsen, 'Greek philosophy and the discovery of the nerves', *Museum Helveticum* 18 (1961), 150–97, repr. in |29| I, 536–82

For suggestions about the Stoics' contribution to a debate on self-consciousness, see
|524| A.C. Lloyd, 'Nosce teipsum and conscientia', *Archiv für Geschichte der Philosophie* 46 (1964), 188–200

The soul's survival is the subject of
|525| R. Hoven, *Stoicisme et stoiciens face au problème de l'au-delà* (Paris, 1971)

On the doctrine of the world-soul, see Moreau |23|.

For the mechanics of vision, there are Hahm |49|, and
|526| H.-G. Ingenkamp, 'Zur stoischen Lehre vom Sehen', *Rheinisches Museum* 114 (1971), 240–6
|527| R.B. Todd, '*Sunentasis* and the Stoic theory of perception', *Grazer Beiträge* 2 (1974), 251–61

54 Theology
The nearest to a comprehensive study of Stoic theology, and one which takes the story well beyond the period covered in this work, is
|528| M. Dragona-Monachou, *The Stoic arguments for the existence and the providence of the gods* (Athens, 1976)

A vast amount of primary evidence is collected by Pease |329|. See also the important text, probably by Philodemus, edited in
|529| A. Henrichs, 'Die Kritik der stoischen Theologie im PHerc. 1428', *Cronache Ercolanesi* 4 (1974), 5–32

The historical background is explored by Moreau |23| and Hahm |488|. On dialectical aspects of Stoic theology, see the excellent studies by Schofield |345|, |471|. Cf. also
|530| P. Boyancé, 'Les preuves stoiciennes de l'existence des dieux d'après Cicéron', *Hermes* 90 (1962), 46–71

On the relation of Stoic theology to Academic counterarguments, see Couissin |625| and Burnyeat |451|.

For Cleanthes' *Hymn to Zeus*, see |322|, and |354|–|361|.

On providence in relation to the destruction of the world, see the differing views of Mansfeld |496| and Long |497|.

For Stoic theodicy, see
|531| A.A. Long, 'The Stoic concept of evil', *Philosophical Quarterly* 18 (1968), 329–42
|532| G.B. Kerferd, 'The origin of evil in Stoic thought', *Bulletin of the John Rylands Library* 60 (1978), 482–94.

|533| M. Dragona-Monachou, 'Providence and fate in Stoicism and prae-Neoplatonism: Calcidius as an authority on Cleanthes' theodicy (*SVF* 2.933)', *Philosophia* 3 (1973), 262–306

55 Causation and fate
The Stoic view of causation is explained in the seminal study by
|534| M. Frede, 'The original notion of cause', in |5|, 217–49
and also touched on in Barnes |637|

The large literature on Stoic 'fate' includes |455|–|463|, Sorabji |21|, |459|, Isnardi Parente |256|, White |512|, |514| ch. 4, and
|535| A.A. Long, 'Freedom and determinism in the Stoic theory of human action', in |306|, 173–99
|536| J.B. Gould, 'The Stoic conception of fate', *Journal of the History of Ideas* 35 (1974), 17–32, repr. in J.P. Anton, A. Preus (edd.), *Essays in ancient Greek philosophy* II (Albany, 1983), 478–94
|537| P.L. Donini, 'Fato e volontà umana in Crisippo', *Atti dell' Accademia delle Scienze di Torino* 109 (1975), 187–230
|538| M.E. Reesor, 'Necessity and fate in Stoic philosophy', in |307|, 187–202
|539| C. Stough, 'Stoic determinism and moral responsibility', in |307|, 203–31
|540| R.W. Sharples, 'Necessity in the Stoic doctrine of fate', *Symbolae Osloenses* 16 (1981), 81–97

On Alexander's important critique of the Stoic theory, see especially the edition by R.W. Sharples |333|, which incorporates the results of his earlier writings on the same work. Other contributions include
|541| A.A. Long, 'Stoic determinism and Alexander of Aphrodisias *De fato* (I–xiv)', *Archiv für Geschichte der Philosophie* 52 (1970), 247–68
|542| P.L. Donini, 'Stoici e megarici nel *de fato* di Alessandro di Afrodisia', in |40|, 173–94
|543| D. Frede, 'The dramatization of determinism: Alexander of Aphrodisias *De Fato*', *Phronesis* 27 (1982), 276–98

56–67 Stoic ethics
The most comprehensive study, which digests much of the recent work, is
|544| M. Forschner, *Die stoische Ethik: über die Zusammenhang von Natur-Sprach-u. Moralphilosophie im altstoischen System* (Stuttgart, 1981)
An older book, which still contains much of value, is
|545| A. Dyroff, *Die Ethik der alten Stoa* (Berlin, 1897)

For introductory accounts, see Pohlenz |298|, Long |3|, Sandbach |296|.

Books which give detailed discussions of many of the topics we handle here include Bonhöffer |312|, Rist |303|, Schofield/Striker |7|, and
|546| W.W. Fortenbaugh (ed.), *On Stoic and Peripatetic ethics. The work of Arius Didymus* (New Brunswick/London, 1983)

On moral psychology there is an outstanding monograph by
|547| B. Inwood, *Ethics and human action in early Stoicism* (Oxford, 1985)

Bibliography

The doxography of Stoic ethics is studied in a work which contains a mass of valuable information, even if the author's thesis of a unitary doxographical source is dubious:

[548] M. Giusta, *I dossografi di etica*, 2 vols. (Turin, 1964–7)

Aristotelian influence on Stoic ethics is perceived by Rist [303], chapter 1, and

[549] A.A. Long, 'Aristotle's legacy to Stoic ethics', *Bulletin of the Institute of Classical Studies* 15 (1968), 72–85, and contested by Sandbach [304]. See also

[550] E. Grumach, *Physis und Agathon in der alten Stoa* (Berlin, 1932; repr. Berlin/Zürich/ Dublin, 1966)

Other studies which cover many aspects of Stoic ethics are White [348], Irwin [594], and

[551] O. Rieth, *Grundbegriffe der stoischen Ethik* (Berlin, 1933)
[552] G. Rodier, 'La cohérence de la morale stoïcienne', in *Etudes de philosophie grecque* (Paris, 1926; repr. 1957)
[553] H. Reiner, 'Der Streit um die stoische Ethik', *Zeitschrift für philosophische Forschung* 21 (1967), 261–81, published in revised form in
[554] H. Reiner, 'Die ethische Weisheit der Stoiker heute', *Gymnasium* 76 (1969), 330–7
[555] A.A. Long, 'The logical basis of Stoic ethics', *Proceedings of the Aristotelian Society* 71 (1970/1), 85–104
[556] D. Tsekourakis, *Studies in the terminology of early Stoic ethics* (Wiesbaden, 1974)
[557] A.A. Long, 'Greek ethics after MacIntyre and the Stoic community of reason', *Ancient Philosophy* 3 (1983), 184–99
[558] W. Görler, 'Pflicht und "Lust" in der Ethik der alten Stoa', *Actes du VIIᵐᵉ congrès de la F.I.E.C.* II (Budapest, 1983), 397–413
[559] N.P. White, 'The role of physics in Stoic ethics', in [308], 57–74
[560] M. Forschner, 'Das Gute und die Güter. Zur Aktualität der stoischen Ethik', in [8], 325– 59

56 The division of ethical topics

See Dyroff [545], Giusta [548], Hahm [424], and

[561] A.A. Long, 'Arius Didymus and the exposition of Stoic ethics', in [546], 41–66
[562] N.P. White, 'Comments' on A.A. Long [561], in [546] 67–74
[563] P. Hadot, 'Une clé des pensées de Marc Aurèle: les trois *topoi* philosophiques selon Epictète', *Etudes Philosophiques* 33 (1978), 65–83

57 Impulse and appropriateness

The significance of these concepts was first adequately appreciated by Pohlenz [336], and further light has been shed on them in a brilliant study,

[564] S.G. Pembroke, 'Oikeiosis' in [306], 114–49
See also Brunschwig [263], Long [555], [557], and
[565] R. Philippson, 'Das "erste Naturgemässe"', *Philologus* 87 (1932), 445–66
[566] C.O. Brink, 'οἰκείωσις and οἰκειότης: Theophrastus and Zeno on nature in moral theory', *Phronesis* 1 (1956), 123–45
[567] G.B. Kerferd, 'The search for personal identity in Stoic thought', *Bulletin of the John Rylands Library* 55 (1972), 177–96
[568] A. Graeser, 'Zirkel oder Deduktion? Zur Begründung der stoischen Ethik', *Kant Studien* 63 (1972), 213–24, in part a rejoinder to Long [555]

[569] N.P. White, 'The basis of Stoic ethics', *Harvard Studies in Classical Philology* 83 (1979), 143–78

[570] G. Striker, 'The role of *oikeiosis* in Stoic ethics', *Oxford Studies in Ancient Philosophy* 1 (1983), 145–67

[571] T. Engberg-Pedersen, 'Discovering the good: *oikeiosis* and *kathekonta* in Stoic ethics', in [7], 145–83

For the text of Hierocles, see

[572] H. von Arnim, *Hierocles. Ethische Elementarlehre*, Berliner Klassikertexte Heft 4 (Berlin, 1906)

Hierocles' work as a Stoic philosopher is studied by

[573] K. Praechter, *Hierokles der Stoiker* (Leipzig, 1901)

[574] R. Philippson, 'Hierokles der Stoiker', *Rheinisches Museum* 83 (1933), 97–114

[575] B. Inwood, 'Hierocles: theory and argument in the second century A.D', *Oxford Studies in Ancient Philosophy* 2 (1984), 151–84

For appropriation (*oikeiosis*) in Antiochus and later Peripatetic ethics, see

[576] H. Görgemanns, '*Oikeiosis* in Arius Didymus', in [546], 165–89, with comments by

[577] B. Inwood, in [546], 190–202

For appropriation (*oikeiosis*) in the anonymous commentary on Plato's *Theaetetus*, see Tarrant [633], 186, Inwood [575], 168n.

58 Value and indifference

The material studied in this and the previous section spills over into other sections, especially **59, 60** and **64**. For introductory treatments of it all, see Long [3], 184–205, Sandbach [296], 28–48. Specialized reading on the ancient controversies stimulated by the concept of indifferent 'things in accordance with nature' is given in the bibliography to **64**. The best scholarly starting-point is an article by

[578] I.G. Kidd, 'Stoic intermediates and the end for man', in [306], 150–72, first published in *Classical Quarterly* N.S. 5 (1955), 181–94

See also Dyroff [545], 100–25, Grumach [550], Rieth [551], 95–108, Reiner [553], [554], and

[579] M.E. Reesor, 'The "indifferents" in the Old and Middle Stoa', *Transactions and Proceedings of the American Philological Association* 82 (1951), 102–10

[580] G.B. Kerferd, 'Cicero and Stoic ethics', in J.R.C. Martyn (ed.), *Cicero and Virgil: studies in honour of Harold Hunt* (Amsterdam, 1972), 60–74

[581] W. Görler, 'Zum virtus-Fragment des Lucilius (1326–1338 Marx) und zur Geschichte der stoischen Güterlehre', *Hermes* 112 (1984), 445–68

For the unorthodox positions of Aristo and Herillus, see Ioppolo [346], [349].

59 Proper functions

On the interpretation of this concept scholarly opinions have varied widely, and in our view there is still no study which can be regarded as definitive. The most detailed modern treatment, with ample discussion of alternative interpretations, is Tsekourakis [556], 1–60. See also Kidd [578], Long [549], [557], Rist [303], chapter 6, Engberg-Pedersen [571], and

Bibliography

[582] I.G. Kidd, 'Moral actions and rules in Stoic ethics' in [307], 247–58, and also, among earlier studies,

[583] G. Nebel, 'Der Begriff des *KAΘHKON* in der alten Stoa', *Hermes* 70 (1935), 439–60

[584] W. Wiersma, 'Telos und Kathekon in der alten Stoa', *Mnemosyne* 5 (1937), 219–28

60 Good and bad

The terminology the Stoics used for elucidating their concept of 'good' is studied most thoroughly by Tsekourakis [556], 61–84. See also Rieth [551], 29–35, Görler [581], and Reiner [553], [554], whose articles are discussed by

[585] A. Graeser, 'Zur Funktion des Begriffes "Gut" in der stoischen Ethik', *Zeitschrift für Philosophische Forschung* 26 (1972), 417–25
to whom Reiner in turn responded in

[586] A. Reiner, 'Zum Begriff des Guten (Agathon) in der stoischen Ethik', *Zeitschrift für Philosophische Forschung* 28 (1974), 228–34
See also

[587] M.E. Reesor, 'On the Stoic goods in Stobaeus, *Eclogae* 2', in [546], 75–84
with comments by

[588] D. Sedley in [546], 85–6

For three views on the relationship between Stoic and Aristotelian goods, see Long [549], Irwin [594], and

[589] A.M. Ioppolo, 'La dottrina stoica dei beni esterni e i suoi rapporti con l'etica aristotelica', *Rivista Critica di Storia della Filosofia* 29 (1974), 363–85

61 Virtue and vice

The concept of virtue, though discussed in all extended accounts of Stoic ethics, has received surprisingly little detailed treatment. For the unity of the virtues, see Ioppolo [346], and Schofield [347]. For vice, in its relation to the Stoic concept of evil, see Long [531] and Kerferd [532].

62 Moral responsibility

See Voelke [522], and studies collected under '55 Causation and fate', [535]–[540].

63–4 The end

For a pioneering treatment of the material in both these sections, cf.

[590] O. Rieth, 'Über des Telos der Stoiker', *Hermes* 69 (1934), 13–45

Our own view on the debate between Antipater and Carneades stems from

[591] A.A. Long, 'Carneades and the Stoic telos', *Phronesis* 12 (1967), 59–90
but the issue is controversial, and readers should also consult

[592] M. Soreth, 'Die zweite Telosformel des Antipater von Tarsos', *Archiv für Geschichte der Philosophie* 50 (1968), 48–72

[593] G. Striker, 'Antipater, or the art of living', in [7], 185–204

See also Long [549], Rist [342], Reiner [553], [554], Görler [581], and

[594] T.H. Irwin, 'Stoic and Aristotelian conceptions of happiness', in [7], 205–44

For the technical distinction between ends and targets, see

[595] R. Alpers-Goelz, *Der Begriff 'Skopos' in der Stoa und seine Vorgeschichte* (Hildesheim, 1976)

65 The passions

The philosophical interest of the Stoic doctrine is particularly well brought out by Inwood [547], chapter 5, and by

[596] A.C. Lloyd, 'Emotion and decision in Stoic psychology', in [307], 233–46

[597] M. Frede, 'The Stoic doctrine of the affections of the soul', in [7], 93–110

Good feelings (*eupatheiai*) and the wise man's emotional disposition are discussed by Long [549], Rist [607], and Görler [558]. For the more specific problems associated with pleasure, see Rist [303], chapter 3, Gosling/Taylor [19], 415–27, and

[598] R.P. Haynes, 'The theory of pleasure in the old Stoa', *American Journal of Philology* 83 (1962), 412–19

See also Gould [362], 181–96, and

[599] I.M. Ioppolo, 'La dottrina delle passioni in Crisippo', *Rivista Critica di Storia della Filosofia* 27 (1972), 251–68

[600] M. Daraki-Mallet, 'Les fonctions psychologiques du logos', in [411], 87–120

[601] K. Abel, 'Das Propatheia-theorem: ein Beitrag zur stoischen Affektenlehre', *Hermes* 111 (1983), 78–97

[602] C.J. Gill, 'Did Chrysippus understand Medea?', *Phronesis* 28 (1983), 136–49

The representation of the passions as illnesses is well discussed in

[603] G.B. Kerferd, 'Two problems concerning impulses', in [546], 87–98

On the Platonizing views of Posidonius, see Kidd [379], [383].

66 Ethics in action

For a general appraisal, see Long [557], and especially the interesting study by

[604] P.A. Brunt, 'Aspects of the social thought of Dio Chrysostom and of the Stoics', *Proceedings of the Cambridge Philological Society* N.S. 19 (1973), 9–34

For the concept of progress, see

[605] O. Luschnat, 'Das Problem der ethischen Fortschritts in der alten Stoa', *Philologus* 102 (1958), 178–214

Studies of the middle Stoa's work on applied ethics include Hijmans [378], Kidd [582], and, on Panaetius,

[606] P.H. De Lacy, 'The four Stoic personae', *Illinois Classical Studies* 2 (1977), 163–72

For a sympathetic view of the wise man's conduct, see

[607] J.M. Rist, 'The Stoic concept of detachment', in [307], 259–72

The best treatment of the Stoics' attitude to suicide is Rist [303], chapter 13.

67 Political theory

The surviving fragments of Zeno's controversial *Republic* are well studied by Baldry [338]. See also Dorandi [334].

Bibliography

For Stoic political theory more generally, see

[608] M.E. Reesor, *The political theory of the old and middle Stoa* (New York, 1951)
[609] F.E. Devine, 'Stoicism on the best regime', *Journal of the History of Ideas* 31 (1970), 323–36

and for a judicious treatment of Stoic cosmopolitanism, Baldry [17]

On Stoicism and natural law, see

[610] G. Watson, 'The natural law and Stoicism', in [306], 216–38
[611] J. Finnis, *Natural law and natural rights* (Oxford, 1980)

For the influence of Stoicism on political life, see Grimal [114], and

[612] I. Hadot, 'Tradition stoïcienne et idées politiques au temps des Gracques', *Revue des Etudes Latines* 48 (1970), 133–79

The continuity of Platonist and Stoic political thought is stressed by

[613] M. Isnardi Parente, 'La politica della Stoa antica', *Sandalion* 3 (1980), 67–98

68–70 THE ACADEMICS

The epistemological debates between the Academics and the Stoics are covered in Couissin [73], [465], Sedley [402], Hartmann [466], Striker [467], Frede [468], and von Staden [476], and their ethical debates in Reiner [553], [554], Long [591], Soreth [592], and Striker [593]. General treatments of the character of Academic scepticism will be found in Brochard [52], Dal Pra [51], Striker [55], Glucker [42], and

[614] L. Credaro, *Lo scetticismo degli accademici* (Rome, 1889; repr. Milan, 1985)
[615] O. Gigon, 'Zur Geschichte der sogenannten Neuen Akademie', *Museum Helveticum* 1 (1944), 47–64

For Cicero's place in and contribution to the history of Academic scepticism, see

[616] A. Weische, *Cicero und die Neue Akademie. Untersuchungen zur Entstehung und Geschichte der antiken Skeptizismus* (Münster, 1961)
[617] W. Burkert, 'Cicero als Platoniker und Skeptiker. Zum Platonverständnis der "Neuen Akademie"', *Gymnasium* 72 (1965), 175–200

Testimonia for the New Academy from Arcesilaus to Clitomachus are collected in two articles which came to our notice only when our book was already in proof:

[618] H.J. Mette, 'Zwei Akademiker heute: Krantor und Arkesilaos', *Lustrum* 26 (1984), 7–94
[619] H.J. Mette, 'Weitere Akademiker heute: von Lakydes bis zu Kleitomachos', *Lustrum* 27 (1985), 39–148

On Arcesilaus' philosophical background and the perspective in which his criticism of the Stoics should be viewed, there is a fine study by

[620] A.M. Ioppolo, 'Doxa ed epoché in Arcesilao', *Elenchos* 5 (1984), 317–63

See also Couissin [73], [465], Krämer [12], and

[621] A.M. Ioppolo, 'Il concetto di eulogon nella filosofia di Arcesilao', in [62], 143–61
[622] A.A. Long, 'Diogenes Laertius' Life of Arcesilaus', *Elenchos* 7 (1986), 429–49

For discussion and criticism of the interpretation of Arcesilaus as a crypto-dogmatist, see Glucker [42], 296–306, and

[623] C. Lévy, 'Scepticisme et dogmatisme dans l'Académie: "l'ésotérisme de Arcésilas"', *Revue des Etudes Latines* 56 (1978), 335–48

For Carneades the only collection of testimonia, prior to Mette [619], was the seriously incomplete

[624] B. Wisniewski, *Karneades, Fragmente* (Wroclaw/Warsaw/Krakow, 1970)

On aspects of his philosophy, see Long [3], 94–106, [591], Soreth [592], Burnyeat [451], and

[625] P. Couissin, 'Les sorites de Carnéade contre le polythéisme', *Revue des Etudes Grecques* 54 (1941), 43–57

[626] S. Pieri, *Carneade* (Padua, 1978)

[627] A.M. Ioppolo, 'Carneade e il terzo libro delle *Tusculanae*', *Elenchos* 1 (1980), 76–91

The work of Philo of Larissa is extensively covered by Glucker [42], and the highly original studies of

[628] H. Tarrant, 'Agreement and the self-evident in Philo of Larissa', *Dionysius* 5 (1981), 66–97

[629] H. Tarrant, *Scepticism or Platonism? The philosophy of the Fourth Academy* (Cambridge, 1985)

On the grounds for his rift with Antiochus, cf.

[630] D. Sedley, 'The end of the Academy', *Phronesis* 26 (1981), 67–75

The testimonia for Antiochus himself are collected and discussed by

[631] G. Luck, *Der Akademiker Antiochus* (Bern/Stuttgart, 1953)

See also Glucker [42], and

[632] J. Dillon, *The Middle Platonists* (London, 1977)

An important text from the sceptical Academy is discussed in Tarrant [629], and

[633] H. Tarrant, 'The date of anon. *In Theaetetum*', *Classical Quarterly* N.S. 33 (1983), 161–87

71–2 THE PYRRHONIST REVIVAL

Much of the modern scholarship on later Pyrrhonism is to be found under 'General studies of ancient Pyrrhonism' ([51]–[63] above).

On Aenesidemus, there is important material in Dal Pra [51] and Tarrant [629]. See also Natorp [26], and

[634] P. Natorp, 'Untersuchungen über die Skepsis im Alterthum: Aenesidem', *Rheinisches Museum* 38 (1883), 28–91

[635] K. Janáček, 'Aenesidemos und Sextus Empiricus', *Eirene* 17 (1980), 5–16

On the status of the primary text on Aenesidemus in Photius, see also

[636] K. Janáček, 'Zur Interpretation des Photius Abschnittes über Aenesidemos', *Eirene* 14 (1976), 93–100

Aenesidemus' critique of causation is illuminatingly studied in

[637] J. Barnes, 'Ancient scepticism and causation', in [58], 149–203

Bibliography

For the problem of Aenesidemus' alleged Heracliteanism, see

[638] J.M. Rist, 'The Heracliteanism of Aenesidemus', *Phoenix* 24 (1970), 309–19
[639] U. Burkhard, *Die angebliche Heraklit-Nachfolge des Skeptikers Aenesidem* (Bonn, 1973)

Little has been written on the ten modes, but the situation has now radically improved with

[640] G. Striker, 'The ten tropes of Aenesidemus', in [58], 95–115
and the first-rate translation and philosophical commentary by
[641] J. Annas, J. Barnes, *The modes of Scepticism* (Cambridge, 1985)

There is some useful comparative material in the earlier studies of

[642] E. Pappenheim, *Die Tropen der griechischen Skeptiker* (Berlin, 1885)
[643] A.E. Chatzilysandros, *Geschichte der skeptischen Tropen* (Munich, 1970)

Important light is shed on the history of the school's title in

[644] K. Janáček, 'Das Wort *Skeptikos* in Philons Schriften', *Listy Filologicke* 101 (1979), 65–8
although there is an important qualification to his findings in Tarrant [629], 22–9

Most of the best recent philosophical discussion of later Pyrrhonism focuses on Sextus Empiricus, whose work falls outside the immediate scope of our book but bears directly on the interpretation of Aenesidemus. See especially the important debate on sceptic 'appearances' involving Burnyeat [60], Frede [61], and

[645] M.F. Burnyeat, 'Can the Sceptic live his Scepticism?' in [5], 20–53, and [58], 117–48
[646] M. Frede, 'Des Skeptikers Meinungen', *Neue Heft für Philosophie* 15/16 (1979), 102–29
[647] J. Barnes, 'The beliefs of a Pyrrhonist', *Proceedings of the Cambridge Philological Society* n.s. 28 (1982), 1–29, and *Elenchos* 4 (1983), 5–43
[648] C. Stough, 'Sextus Empiricus on non-assertion', *Phronesis* 29 (1984), 137–64

Other studies include Burnyeat [10], and

[649] W. Heintz, *Studien zu Sextus Empiricus* (Halle, 1932)
[650] R.M. Chisholm, 'Sextus Empiricus and modern empiricism', *Philosophy of Science* 8 (1941), 371–84
[651] A.A. Long, 'Sextus Empiricus on the criterion of truth', *Bulletin of the Institute of Classical Studies* 25 (1978), 35–49
[652] I. Mueller, 'Geometry and scepticism', in [6], 69–95
[653] D. Glidden, 'Skeptic semiotics', *Phronesis* 28 (1983) 213–55
[654] J. Annas, 'Doing without objective values: ancient and modern strategies', in [7], 3–29

Help on some important Pyrrhonist terminology can be found in

[655] K. Janáček, *Sextus Empiricus' Sceptical methods* (Prague, 1972)

Lightning Source UK Ltd.
Milton Keynes UK
UKOW041859060613

211890UK00001B/66/A